MARKETING

Dedication

From Philip Kotler
To my wife Nancy, my daughters Amy, Melissa and Jessica,
and my sons-in-law Joel, Steve and Dan—with love

From Linden Brown
To my wife Marie-Noelle, my son Christopher,
and my daughter Veronique

From Stewart Adam
To my wife Maureen, my son Michael, and
my daughters Melissa and Vanessa

From Sue Burton
To my parents Ted and Anne—with love and gratitude

From Gary Armstrong
To my family—Kathy, KC, Keri, Mandy and Matt

7TH EDITION

MARKETING

PHILIP
KOTLER
LINDEN
BROWN
STEWART
ADAM
SUZAN
BURTON
GARY
ARMSTRONG

PEARSON

Prentice
Hall

Pearson Education Australia
Unit 4, Level 3
14 Aquatic Drive
Frenchs Forest NSW 2086

www.pearsoned.com.au

Senior Acquisitions Editor: Sonia Wilson
Acquisitions Editor: Paul Burgess
Senior Project Editor: Rebecca Pomponio
Editorial Coordinator: Roisin Fitzgerald
Copy Editor: Jennifer Coombs
Proofreader: Kathryn Lamberton
Copyright and Pictures Editor: Liz de Rome
Cover and internal design by DiZign
Typeset by Midland Typesetters, Australia

Printed in China (SWTC)

5 11 10 09 08

National Library of Australia
Cataloguing-in-Publication Data

Marketing.

    Includes index.
    For tertiary students.
    ISBN 9780733975776.

    ISBN 0 7339 7577 1.

    1. Marketing – Textbooks. I. Kotler, Philip.

    658.8

An imprint of Pearson Education Australia
(a division of Pearson Australia Group Pty Ltd)

About the authors

As a team, the authors, Philip Kotler, Linden Brown, Stewart Adam, Suzan Burton and Gary Armstrong, provide a blend of skills and experience uniquely suited to writing the seventh edition of this widely acclaimed marketing text. Together they make the complex world of marketing practical, approachable and enjoyable.

PHILIP KOTLER is SC Johnson & Son Distinguished Professor of International Marketing at the Kellogg Graduate School of Management, Northwestern University. Professor Kotler is one of the world's leading authorities on marketing. He received his master's degree at the University of Chicago and his Ph.D. at MIT, both in economics. Dr Kotler is author of *Marketing Management: Analysis Planning, Implementation and Control* (Prentice Hall), now in its eleventh edition and the most widely used marketing textbook in graduate schools of business. He has authored several other successful books and he has written over ninety articles for leading journals. He is the only three-time winner of the coveted *Alpha Kappa Psi* award for the best annual article in the *Journal of Marketing*. Dr Kotler's numerous major honours include the Paul D. Converse Award given by the American Marketing Association to honour 'outstanding contributions to science in marketing' and Stuart Henderson Britt Award as Marketer of the Year. In 1985, he was named the first recipient of two major awards: the Distinguished Marketing Educator of the Year Award given by the American Marketing Association and the Philip Kotler Award for Excellence in Health Care Marketing presented by the Academy for Health Care Services Marketing. In 1989, he received the Charles Coolidge Parlin Award which each year honours an outstanding leader in the field of marketing ■

Philip Kotler

Sydney 1996–2005. He has been Visiting Professor at INSEAD, France in 1999 and at Cranfield University, England 2000–2002. He is one of Australia's leading consultants and academics. His Ph.D. in marketing at the University of New South Wales followed a first degree in accounting and economics. He has lectured marketing at a number of universities including the Melbourne Graduate School of Management and the University of New South Wales. His books, *Competitive Marketing Strategy*, published in 1990 and 1997, and *International Marketing: An Asia-Pacific Perspective*, co-authored with Richard Fletcher and published in 1999, 2002 and 2005, focus on marketing in an Australasian context. He also co-authored with Malcolm McDonald, *Competitive Marketing Strategy for Europe*. He is co-author of *Principles of Marketing* with Philip Kotler, Stewart Adam and Gary Armstrong. This is in its third edition and published in 2006. As a marketing practitioner Dr Brown has initiated and developed a number of businesses in the transport, printing and food marketing areas. His current research, teaching and consulting work is in the area of strategic market analysis, value based pricing and the development of marketing strategies that drive marketing profitability. Dr Brown is founder and Chairman of Interstrat which provides marketing consultancy and marketing development programs worldwide to multinational companies ■

Linden Brown

LINDEN BROWN has been Adjunct Professor of Marketing and head of the Market Strategy and Technology Group within the School of Marketing, University of Technology,

STEWART ADAM is Associate Professor in Electronic Marketing and Associate Head of the Bowater School of Management and Marketing in the Faculty of Business and Law,

Stewart Adam

Deakin University, Melbourne, Australia. He is co-author with Professors Philip Kotler (*Northwestern University*), Linden Brown (*University of Technology, Sydney*), and Gary Armstrong (*University of North Carolina*) of the third, fourth, fifth, sixth, and now seventh editions of *Marketing* as well as the first, second and third editions of *Principles of Marketing*. Dr Adam is lead author with Dr Eugene Clark, Dean and Professor of Law, Charlotte Law School, North Carolina, of the second edition of *eMarketing @ Internet: Connecting People and Business*.

Dr Adam has a psychology and sociology undergraduate degree from the University of New South Wales, a graduate diploma in financial management from the University of New England, a research Master of Commerce degree and a PhD in marketing from Deakin University. He is an Associate Fellow of the Australian Institute of Management (AFAIM). For many years, he has been involved in the development of flexible learning materials, and online delivery methodologies. This follows on from his on-and-off-campus teaching experience with universities in New South Wales and Victoria, for which he and his teams have received various teaching awards. He has spent over 30 years almost equally divided between marketing practice and facilitating learning in marketing and management. His marketing practitioner experience includes account management with advertising agencies in Europe and Australia. Additionally, Stewart has worked as product manager, marketing manager, consultant and general manager in both the manufacturing and services sectors, and has consulted to a number of marketing organisations. His other publications and interests may be viewed at <www.stewartadam.com> ∎

Suzan Burton

SUZAN BURTON is an Associate Professor and the Associate Dean of Teaching and Learning at Macquarie Graduate School of Management, Macquarie University, Sydney. She is an Adjunct Professor at the University of Sydney, and has had previous appointments as an adjunct faculty member on MBA programs at the Australian Graduate School of Management and Melbourne Business School. She has undergraduate and postgraduate degrees in health, and an MBA and PhD from the University of New South Wales. Dr Burton has extensive consulting experience in the public and private sectors in the design and implementation of marketing strategy, particularly in the area of customer feedback and information systems. Her research interests include customer satisfaction and retention, and Internet marketing. She is co-editor, with Peter Steane of the recent book, *Surviving Your Thesis*, and the author of over 50 journal articles and conference papers. Dr Burton has received teaching awards from Macquarie University (the Macquarie University Award for Teaching Excellence) and from the Australian and New Zealand Marketing Academy Conference (ANZMAC). Her research has been recognised by best paper awards by the Australia and New Zealand Marketing Academy Conference and Western Decision Sciences (twice) ∎

GARY ARMSTRONG is Crist W. Blackwell Distinguished Professor of Undergraduate Education in the Kenan-Flagler Business School at the University of North Carolina at Chapel Hill. He holds undergraduate and masters degrees in business from Wayne State University in Detroit and received his Ph.D. in marketing from Northwestern University. Dr. Armstrong has contributed numerous articles to leading business journals. As a consultant and researcher, he has worked with many companies on marketing research, sales management, and marketing strategy. But Professor Armstrong's first love is teaching. His Blackwell Distinguished Professorship is the only permanent endowed professorship for distinguished undergraduate teaching at the University of North Carolina at Chapel Hill. He has been very active in the teaching and administration of Kenan-Flagler's undergraduate program. His administrative posts include Chair of the Marketing Faculty, Associate Director of the Undergraduate Business Program, Director of the Business Honours Program, and others. He works closely with business student groups and has received several campus-wide and Business School teaching awards. He is the only repeat recipient of the school's highly regarded Award for Excellence in Undergraduate Teaching, which he has received three times ∎

Gary Armstrong

Brief contents

Contents

CHAPTER TWENTY-ONE: RESPONSIBLE MARKETING   822

Preface

The seventh edition of *Marketing* has been specifically written to help you—the reader—learn about, and apply, the concepts and practices of modern marketing science. You may be planning a marketing career with a manufacturing organisation, or a service firm or indeed an entertainment company that is marketing experiences. Or perhaps you intend a career in a government enterprise or a not-for-profit organisation such as the Red Cross. Maybe your future employer will be a domestic or global company; or a small and medium enterprise (SME), or a large business with offices around the globe. Perhaps your employer will mainly use traditional marketing methods. More likely, your employer will use e-marketing methods, even though it may not be a company that has been newly created to operate solely in the online environment. Even if you are already working in one of these areas—this book has been designed to meet your needs.

In each of these organisations it is now necessary to know why and how to define and segment a market, as well as why and how to position the organisation to develop need-satisfying goods, services and experiences—branded *products* in the language of marketing science—for chosen target segments. Each marketing organisation must know how to make and price its offerings to be attractive and affordable, and how to work with intermediaries best suited to ensure that products are available to customers, or to deal directly with customers. And each needs to know how to communicate with customers in such a way as to impart both knowledge and a sense of excitement about the organisation's offerings. Given the wide range of organisations facing diverse groups of people, marketers need a broad range of skills in order to sense, serve and satisfy customer needs.

Approach and objectives

The seventh edition of *Marketing* is significantly different from other texts because it adopts an holistic approach—integrating all aspects of marketing. It integrates online marketing into the fabric of mainstream marketing strategies and tactics. It incorporates and integrates services and product marketing throughout the chapters in the book. It provides a marketing strategy framework which ties all this together with a powerful marketing logic. It incorporates a marketing plan example of a service business which shows how the marketing elements fit together to provide direction and action for growing a business.

Marketing, seventh edition, tells the stories that reveal the drama of modern business. These include: Telstra's major refocus on market-based management to transform its business in the midst of rapid technological change; the challenge to Qantas to maintain profitability during upheavals in the airline industry; the rise to dominance of Google; Speedo's strategies to grow and extend its business into new markets; how HP is reorganising for the digital imaging market; what Woolworths has done to strengthen its position as the leading Australian supermarket chain; Apple's global strategy for entering the digital music business with its highly successful iPod range and iTunes. Smaller companies also feature like Stormy Australia which is building its brand of safety apparel for boating and fishing enthusiasts and global specialist, Cochlear, which has become the world leader in ear implants. These and dozens of other examples and illustrations throughout each chapter reinforce key concepts and bring marketing to life.

Thus, the seventh edition of *Marketing* provides a comprehensive and innovative, managerial and practical insight into marketing. Its style and extensive use of examples and illustrations make the book straightforward, easy to read, and enjoyable.

Changes in the seventh edition

The seventh edition of *Marketing* is a complete and thorough revision of the widely acclaimed 6th edition. It offers important improvements in organisation, content and style. **Part 1** retains its strengths in providing an overview of marketing and the marketing process. Chapter 1 lays the foundation of marketing's role as the focus for creating value and adds new material on 'customers as assets' and the practical challenges of market orientation, while Chapter 2 describes *how* value is created to ensure customer retention and achievement of business profits. Chapter 3 retains its emphasis on the strategic nature of marketing and Chapter 4 on preparing marketing plans. Chapter 4 also contains a marketing plan at the end of the chapter which can be used as a template for marketing planning or as a case study. This marketing plan is constructed for a service business but can equally be applied to product marketing planning. **Part 2** focuses on the marketing environment and analysing marketing opportunities with inclusion of chapters on the global marketing environment, marketing research, consumer behaviour and business-to-business buying behaviour, market analysis and market segmentation. Chapter 6 which covers information management and market research includes new material on marketing intelligence and online market research. Chapter 7 which focuses on consumer behaviour reflects the latest thinking in prospect theory and behavioural economics. Chapter 9 has broadened its coverage of market analysis to incorporate important management decisions about market definition and measurement of market potential as well as demand measurement and forecasting. The strategic nature of segmenting markets and positioning brands are discussed in Chapter 10. **Part 3** presents the reader with the full range of marketing mix elements that are the ingredients for development of marketing strategy which is dealt with later in the book. This important section gives comprehensive attention to marketing goods, services, and experiences in Chapters 11 with new material on branding, and 12 on new products, and the strategies and tactics required for pricing them in Chapter 13. Chapters 14 and 15 discuss the network of firms that must work together to place products in consumers' hands, homes, mouths, minds, or wherever they are required, including wholesalers and retailers. These focus on how value can be delivered to customers through effective channel selection and marketing logistics network management. Marketing communication has been updated in three chapters, 16–18. In particular, Chapter 18 has been further developed to reflect the rapid changes experienced in effective direct and online marketing and updated expenditure patterns as well as the impacts on online marketing of mobility. An international flavour is maintained through every chapter with particular reference to the South-East Asian region. In **Part 4**, chapter 19 on competitive marketing strategy highlights the importance of redefining competitive advantage in terms of value to customers and the role of value innovation which creates both greater differentiation and lower costs. Chapter 20 identifies strategies for tapping global markets and explores the role of alliance strategies in providing access to markets, products and technologies. Ethical and social issues also form the base for several new highlights throughout the book on challenges in marketing research, target marketing, packaging and the environment, pricing, distribution, direct marketing, advertising and personal selling, and many other areas. While ethics and social responsibilities are raised in other chapters, the final chapter of the book, Chapter 21 looks more deeply into this matter. This chapter has been written with input from Eugene Clark, noted legal author and Professor of Law with the University of Canberra.

The seventh edition of *Marketing* includes substantial information on a wide range of other marketing management topics: competitive advantage and differentiating the marketing offer;

customer-driven marketing and developing a marketing culture; customer value and satisfaction; total quality management of marketing products and processes; changing consumer values and lifestyles; changes in brand and category management; product design; direct marketing and single-source *data* systems; retailing strategy; services marketing strategy; marketing ethics and social responsibility; and environmentalism.

The seventh edition has been designed to provide a comprehensive coverage of the marketing of services, consumer goods, experiences, and business-to-business, industrial products of old, promoted through traditional and new interactive media as well as distributed through private and public digital networks. There are examples and cases spread throughout the book, which give particular focus to these matters, in addition to specialist chapters on such topics. Also, the seventh edition presents many examples related to small and medium-sized firms, given their importance in the Australian and New Zealand economies. Tailored case studies have been included—such as Fast Fitness—that relate not only to small business and services marketing, but bring in emerging health issues related to obesity and lack of exercise.

Finally, the seventh edition of *Marketing* contains many new photos and advertisements that illustrate key points and make the text more effective and appealing. Many new chapter-opening examples and marketing highlights illustrate important new concepts with actual business applications. All tables, figures, examples, and references throughout the text have been thoroughly updated.

Twenty-three contributors, in addition to the authors of this text, have prepared twenty-one new case studies. The contributors come from academic institutions and businesses located throughout Australia and New Zealand. All of the case studies are new to this edition and have been selected for their quality and coverage of key marketing issues. The chapter introductions, marketing highlights and case studies help to bring the real world directly into the classroom, while the new aids are designed to make this edition the best resource available for marketing students.

Learning Aids

This text provides a practical, managerial approach to marketing and provides the reader with a rich variety of examples and applications illustrating the major decisions that marketing management faces in its efforts to balance the organisation's objectives and resources against needs and opportunities in the global marketplace. This is achieved by the following:

Visual preface

WEBSITE ADDRESSES

of relevant businesses are listed at the end of the opening examples, encouraging students to use the internet and find out up-to-date information about the opening example and other information in the chapter.

CHAPTER INTRODUCTION/OPENING EXAMPLES

A marketing story introduces every chapter, providing a real-world context for the central themes of the chapter.

CHAPTER OBJECTIVES

Each chapter begins with objectives that prepare the reader for the chapter material and detail learning goals.

MARKETING HIGHLIGHTS

Additional examples and important information are presented in marketing highlight exhibits throughout the text, together with questions for class and individual use.

SELF-CHECK QUESTIONS

are included at the end of each major section in chapters. They are designed to reinforce and check understanding of concepts raised in the chapter. Answers are provided at the end of the text.

COLOUR FIGURES, ADVERTISEMENTS AND ILLUSTRATIONS

Throughout each chapter, key concepts and applications are illustrated with strong, colour visual material.

HIGHLIGHTED DEFINITIONS AND MARGIN NOTES

Throughout each chapter, key terms are highlighted in the text and defined in the margin in colour adjacent to the point at which each term is discussed in the text.

END OF CHAPTER MATERIAL

Each chapter ends with a chapter summary, key terms, a Discussing the Issues section and references.

DISCUSSING THE ISSUES

Each chapter contains a set of questions covering issues arising out of the chapter. They are designed to encourage critical thinking and group discussion.

MARKETING ISSUES

are raised at the end of each chapter. This contains a marketing challenge related to the chapter content and theme.

CASE STUDY

Case studies highlight key ideas, stories and marketing strategies. Cases involve small and medium enterprises (SMEs) as well as large firms—moreover, the cases include branded goods, services, not-for-profit organisations as well as sports marketing and so on. These and dozens of other examples and illustrations throughout each chapter reinforce key concepts and bring marketing to life.

Support Material

A successful marketing course requires more than a well-written book. Today's classroom requires a dedicated teacher and a fully-integrated teaching system. The seventh edition of *Marketing* is supported by an extensive system of supplementary learning and teaching aids with are available upon adoption:

Student learning guide and workbook

This comprehensive study guide has been written and developed by Don Bradmore and Peter Butler. It gives students an overview of the material, summarises the major topics and concepts, and strengthens understanding through Applying the Concepts Exercises, as well as situational exercises involving cases, chapter highlights, and quizzes. Study tips, practice exam questions and a project question run across most chapters of the workbook. It can be used very effectively either as a self-paced study guide or as a weekly supplement to help prepare and reinforce the material presented at lectures and tutorials.

All new Instructor's Manual

The Instructor's Manual has been fully revised. It includes comprehensive teaching notes and in-depth discussion of all text questions, case analyses, chapter overviews, as well as teaching tips for class projects and class debate topics. The material has been updated by Dr Steve Ward (Murdoch University).

PowerPoint lecture slides

Fully revised and updated PowerPoint lecture slides, cover each chapter of the text. Revisions to this edition have been made by Sandra Gountas (La Trobe University).

Classroom response slides (clickers)

These slides allow lecturers to use group and audience response systems—the wireless response technology that lets lecturers gather instant feedback from students and respond to it during class. This edition's questions have been written by Sandra Gountas (La Trobe University).

New Australian marketing video clips

Over 90 minutes of Australian footage, created specifically for the Kotler books is available. Together with several hours of material from other international versions of Kotler, this provides a vast library of video footage.

A brand new suite of Australian video segments has been specially prepared for this edition. Acknowledging the visual learning styles of many of today's students, these video segments illuminate key theories and concepts from the experience of real marketers. Featuring a broad diversity of marketing types, positions and ages, these new videos will help your students connect to marketing through personal stories, challenges, achievements and knowledge.

The DVDs are available to adopters together with a video guide which includes teaching suggestions and questions.

Computerised Test Bank

The Test Bank includes 3500 true, false and multiple choice questions, fully revised, referenced to the text and graded for level of difficulty. This is all accessed via a software program which allows lecturers to select, edit and create their own questions and tests. Revisions to this edition have be carried out by Dr Simon Pervan (University of Bath, United Kingdom).

Technology

Activebook

Every copy of this text comes with an access code—your pathway to a completely integrated live learning environment, activebook™.

An activebook is an online version of the text in which exercises are integrated and interactive, enabling students to learn and revise effectively. Situated within the lecturer's choice of course management platforms, BlackBoard, WebCT or CourseCompass, instructors can:

- customise the activebook for students to access
- connect to students with assessment or communication tools
- highlight sections of the digital text for close student attention, and
- add lecturer notes and links for extra information or specific course requirements.

Student self-testing with instant feedback provides an interactive study guide, including the following features:

- animated versions of selected figures and tables to bring learning to life
- warm-up activities, concept check and end-of-chapter questions which allow students to see their progress immediately and focus on areas for revision, guided by linked pages to the text.

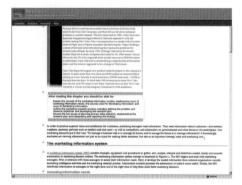

The activebook is co-authored by Jan Charbonneau (Massey University, New Zealand), Jeaney Yip (University of Sydney) and Jeffrey Lim (University of Sydney).

Emarketing @ internet

The second edition of *eMarketing@Internet* by Stewart Adam and Eugene Clark is included in the online course management systems. This user-friendly text on e-marketing is ideal for both personal users of the Internet as well as business users aiming to communicate, distribute and enhance relationships using the Internet's graphical face, the World Wide Web.

Acknowledgments

No book is the work only of its authors. We owe much to the pioneers of marketing who first identified its major issues and developed its concepts and techniques. Our thanks go to our colleagues at Northwestern University; University of Technology, Sydney; Deakin University; Macquarie University and the University of North Carolina at Chapel Hill. The authors would also like to specifically acknowledge Professor Eugene Clark for his major contribution to Chapter 21 on Responsible Marketing.

Many reviewers at other universities provided valuable comments and suggestions. We are indebted to the following colleagues:

Petra Bouvain, University of Canberra
Dawn Birch, University of Southern Queensland
Tony Garrett, University of Otago
Reshmee Gunesh, James Cook University

Laurie Murphy, James Cook University
Karen Fernandez, Macquarie University
Kim Cowley, University of Newcastle
Julian de Meyrick, Macquarie University

Special thanks go to the academics and marketing practitioners throughout Australia and New Zealand who contributed generously of their time and expertise in providing the many case studies and marketing highlights which are a key feature of this seventh edition. They are:

Rodney Arambewela, Deakin University
Chris Baumann, Macquarie University
Rebekah Bennett, Queensland University of Technology
John van Beveren, University of Ballarat and Melbourne Institute of Technology
Jean Boisvert, American University of Sharjah, United Arab Emirates
Mike Brennan, Massey University
Jan Charbonneau, Massey University
David Corkindale, University of South Australia
Barry Duncan, General Manager Outback Queensland Tourism Authority
Andrew Hercus, Christchurch College of Education

Andrew Hughes, Australian National University
Garry Kingshott, Melbourne Convention and Visitors Bureau
Jeffrey Lim, University of Sydney
Wayne MacArthur, Massey University
Peter Moore, Senior Marketing Consultant, Interstrat
Barry O'Mahony, Victoria University
Daniel Prior, Charles Sturt University
Bill Proud, Queensland University of Technology
Martin Quick, General Manager, Aftersales, P&A
Judy Rex, Swinburne University
Margaret Wallace, University of Canberra
Joe Williams, Flinders University
Jeaney Yip, University of Sydney

Special thanks and appreciation also to the authors of the supplements, who are individually referenced with the supplements, who provide invaluable support to both students and academics who select and use the book.

Our thanks also go to the many organisations and their employees who provided photographs and advertisements, many free of charge, for inclusion in this book. They are listed separately in the Photo/Ad Credits at the end of each chapter.

We also owe a great deal to the people at Pearson Education who helped develop this book. Sonia Wilson and Paul Burgess provided much-needed comment and feedback as the book developed; Roisin Fitzgerald skilfully managed the cases through the development process and Rebecca Pomponio provided the detailed editorial support that such a large educational publication demands.

Case study matrix

The case studies developed for this book provide a mechanism to integrate marketing science and practice. They offer readers a broad exposure to a cross section of marketing situations and provide a variety of consumer and business products cases with a selection of consumer and business services marketing challenges. For ease of reference and topic focus a case summary matrix is presented below.

Part	Chapter	Case Study Name	Focus
1			
	1	The adoption of a marketing orientation by the Outback Queensland Tourism Authority	Market orientation
	2	Retaining customers in a small financial planning business: the elusive pursuit of marketing's silver bullet	Customer retention
	3	The Melbourne Convention and Visitors Bureau (MCVB)	Corporate and business strategy
	4	Fast Fitness: planning for a growth business	Marketing planning
2			
	5	The 'alternative' marketplace: marketing wellbeing	Global health trends
	6	Researching complaints: is there a student satisfaction problem?	Research design
	7	Entertain me! Attracting reviewers to reality TV	Consumer behaviour
	8	King Industries: electrical wholesalers	Business buying behaviour
	9	Super Economy Class: the business travellers' class of the future	Analysing the market
	10	There's no other store like David Jones	Segmentation and target marketing
3			
	11	What makes a tourist destination? The trials and tribulations of two regional centres	Product positioning
	12	The automotive industry: new-product challenges	New product development
	13	Trisled: pricing for market expansion	Pricing strategy
	14	Assessing a franchise opportunity	New business assessment
	15	Evolution of camera stores at the beginning of the third millennium	Marketing channels
	16	Government advertising: benefiting society or political parties?	Advertising effectiveness

| Services/Experiences | | Physical Goods | | Online Student Research | Large Enterprise | Small Medium Enterprise |
Consumer	Business	Consumer	Business			
Yes				Yes		Yes
Yes				Yes		Yes
Yes	Yes			Yes		Yes
Yes				Yes		Yes
Yes		Yes		Yes	Yes	Yes
Yes						Yes
Yes				Yes	Yes	
			Yes		Yes	
	Yes			Yes	Yes	
Yes		Yes		Yes	Yes	
Yes		Yes		Yes		Yes
		Yes	Yes		Yes	
		Yes		Yes		Yes
		Yes				Yes
		Yes		Yes		Yes
Yes					Yes	

| Services/Experiences | | Physical Goods | | Online Student Research | Large Enterprise | Small Medium Enterprise |
Consumer	Business	Consumer	Business			
		Yes				Yes
Yes		Yes		Yes	Yes	
Yes	Yes			Yes		Yes
			Yes	Yes		Yes
Yes		Yes		Yes		Yes

PART 1

UNDERSTANDING THE MARKETING PROCESS AND STRATEGIC PLANNING

CHAPTER 1

Marketing: creating value

BMW: www.bmw.com.au

Cisco: www.cisco.com

Clinique: www.clinique.com

Dell: www.dell.com/Australia

eBay: www.ebay.com.au

Ericsson: www.ericsson.com

Google: www.google.com.au

Optus: www.optus.com.au

Telstra: www.telstra.com

Vodafone: www.vodafone.com.au

Marketing has gone through many transformations from village markets where buyers and sellers meet to haggle over price to the mass production of manufactured goods available in shops to the Information Age of buying products and services electronically. In the first decade of the twenty-first century we see these different forms operating side by side but adapting to the changing conditions of modern society. In all these market forms one thing remains the same—a market is created by the connection and exchange between potential buyers looking for ways of satisfying their wants and needs and sellers seeking to provide products and services that will meet buyers' requirements.

Whatever the market form, the role of marketing has one common central theme—to create perceived customer value that is superior to the alternatives available while at the same time creating value to the business. Today, value is created in so many different ways. Think of how communication and relationships between people have been affected by the mobile phone—this multifunction device is for voice communication and much more! It stores and plays music, video and still photo images can be sent to our friends and family, we can get information on sports, entertainment and shopping and use it to order and pay for goods and services. We send SMS messages to our friends all over the world and we can collect our emails—all on one hand-held product. The Information Age has revolutionised how we live and the way in which marketing is performed.

Telecommunications companies like Optus, Telstra and Vodafone, with the help of technology suppliers such as Ericsson and Cisco and customer relationship systems providers like Oracle, have broadened our options for communication and entertainment with VoIP (Voice over Internet Protocol) telephone services, Internet access and content, and interactive TV. eBay has created a huge global electronic marketplace and spawned many businesses that operate only in this electronic marketing environment. Google has become *the* local and global search engine making all types of information accessible including real-time photos of locations around the world and even a close view from space of our very own street and house. Google has become so pervasive that we often say in response to a question about information—'Google it'.

Apple's iPod creates value.

But creating customer value is not enough! Anybody can run a business that gives value to customers by selling at rock bottom prices or by giving the product away. Today's marketers must also be able to create value for the business, which means providing valued products or services to customers while making a profit for the company.

Marketers need to understand how value offered to customers can be translated into profit through appropriate price levels and/or efficient marketing communications and channels to the market. Cosmetic companies such as Clinique have been able to command premium prices for their brands while offering high perceived value to consumers. Dell Computers has found a business and marketing model that is the most efficient means of selling and delivering computers to the business market worldwide, becoming the largest computer vendor with by far the biggest profit in an industry that has struggled for profitability in the last five years. The movie industry now makes as much money from DVDs and the merchandising of related products (such as we have seen with Harry Potter) as well as direct product advertising (the use of big brand products in movies) as it does from movie ticket sales. So, too, the latest-release movie that is experienced on a 'pay-per-view' basis may be customised so that one of a number of endings is experienced.

All of this is occurring in a rapidly changing market environment. Many of the products and services available to consumers during the first decade of the twenty-first century have been in existence only a short time. And for many potential customers such products as digital TV providing for consumer interactivity and computerised toys are seen as 'high tech'. So too are online shopping and gambling, and all manner of new online services such as online education with its 'virtual classroom' facilities and childcare monitoring services. Where wine and travel were once only purchased from a 'bricks and mortar' retail outlet, we now see all manner of online outlets to choose from—reshaping marketing channels. The arrival of successive models of iPods and iTunes has revolutionised the way we select, buy and listen to our favourite music—at home, on the move and in the office.

Moreover, our notion of time is changing. Customers want their wine, books and online-ordered groceries delivered in a matter of hours, their music, software and cash delivered instantaneously and their payments made in 'real time'. BMW is one of several car manufacturers that seeks to custom build its cars in the ordered colour and option configuration, rather than adding to costs by storing a newly made car in the hope that someone will ultimately desire it. Combined with several alliance partners, today's BMW has become an entertainment product with its sound system, Internet access and global positioning system to guide us through unfamiliar city streets to our destination. Customer expectations have risen as wave after wave of new technology has enabled successive generations of businesses to transform the value offered.

Marketing communication is also changing as convergence occurs between entertainment, publishing, telecommunications, old media (newspapers and television) and new media (online channels accessed via the Internet). Where once customers self-elected which television commercials they paid attention to, which newspapers they read, which movies they watched and which direct mail they read, today customers value requested communication more highly than unsought communication. Marketing communication falls into this category. News information sought out by a personal agent, or online robot, will come from many sources and is in effect customised to suit the individual customer.

The continuous changes in products, services, channels and marketing communication mentioned above are enabled and augmented by information technology. In particular, it is the interconnection of commercial and government databases and customers via the Internet which enables marketing organisations to capture people's attention and interact with them, ultimately causing them to remain with the marketing organisation. It is understanding how customer value and business value can be created and retained in the context of these changes that is the exciting challenge of marketing.[1]

After reading this chapter you should be able to:

1. Define marketing and outline the concepts of needs, wants and demands.

2. Discuss marketing management and express the basic ideas of demand management and building profitable customer relationships.

3. List the marketing management philosophies and be able to distinguish between the production concept, the product concept, the selling concept, the marketing concept and the societal marketing concept.

4. Analyse the key marketing challenges of this century, including growth of non-profit marketing, rapid globalisation, the changing world economy, the call for more ethical behaviour and social responsibility and the new marketing landscape.

Many factors contribute to making a business successful: great strategy, dedicated employees, good information systems, excellent implementation. However, today's successful companies at all levels have one thing in common—they are strongly customer focused and heavily committed to marketing. These companies share an absolute dedication to understanding and satisfying the needs of customers in well-defined target markets. They motivate everyone in the organisation to produce superior value for their customers, leading to high levels of customer satisfaction.

Marketing, more than any other business function, deals with customers. Creating customer value and satisfaction are at the very heart of modern marketing thinking and practice. Although we will explore more detailed definitions of marketing later in this chapter, perhaps the simplest definition is this one: Marketing is the delivery of customer value and satisfaction at a profit. The goal of marketing is to attract new customers by promising superior value, and to keep current customers by delivering satisfaction. As Peter Drucker, a leading management thinker, put it:

> Marketing is so basic that it cannot be considered a separate function. It is the whole business seen from the point of view of its final result, that is, from the customer's point of view . . . Business success is not determined by the producer but by the customer.[2]

Some people think that only large business organisations operating in highly developed economies use marketing, but sound marketing is critical to the success of every organisation—whether large or small, for-profit or non-profit, domestic or global. Large for-profit firms such as Coca-Cola, McDonald's, Qantas, Telstra, Mitsubishi, Federal Express, Woolworths, BHP Billiton and many others use marketing. But so do non-profit organisations such as universities, hospitals, museums, art galleries, symphony orchestras and even churches. Moreover, marketing is practised right around the world. Most countries in North and South America, Western Europe and the Far East have well-developed marketing systems. Even in Eastern Europe and the former Soviet republics, where a different ideology prevailed, dramatic political and social changes have created new opportunities for marketing. Business and government leaders in most of these nations, for example Poland, Slovakia, Hungary and Russia, are eager to learn everything they can about modern marketing practices.

You already know a lot about marketing—it's all around you. You see the results of marketing in the abundance of products that line the store shelves in your nearby shopping centre. You see marketing in the advertisements that fill your television screen, magazines, letterbox and computer screen when connected to the Internet. At home, at school, where you work, at leisure—you are exposed to marketing in almost everything you do. Yet there is much more to marketing than meets the consumer's casual eye. Behind it all is a massive network of people and activities competing for your attention and purchasing dollars.

In the remainder of this chapter we give you a complete and formal introduction to the basic concepts and practices of today's marketing. We begin by defining marketing and its core concepts, describing the major philosophies of marketing thinking and practice and discussing some of the major new challenges that marketers now face.

What is marketing?

What does the term *marketing* mean? Many people think of marketing only as selling and advertising. And no wonder—every day we are bombarded with television commercials, newspaper advertisements (ads), direct mail and sales calls by telephone, fax and email. Someone is always trying to sell us something.

You may be surprised, then, to learn that selling and advertising are only the tip of the marketing iceberg. Although they are important, they are only two of many marketing functions that have developed over time, and often not the most important ones. The marketing functions developed as marketing's influence extended into different business sectors. Figure 1.1 shows that marketing has been taken up by a number of areas of business over time. Marketing came to prominence in the 1950s and 1960s at a time when many countries had excess production capacity. The focus at that time was on gaining customers for a multitude of newly developed consumer goods.

Different companies became interested in marketing at different times. Companies such as Coca-Cola saw marketing's potential almost immediately. Marketing spread most rapidly in consumer packaged goods companies, consumer durables companies and industrial equipment companies—roughly in that order. Industrial product manufacturers and producers of such commodities as steel, chemicals and paper adopted marketing later, and many still have a long way to go. In the more recent past, consumer service firms like international relocation companies have adopted modern marketing practices. Marketing has also attracted the interest of insurance and financial services companies.

A feature of developed countries today is the fact that the services sector accounts for over 70% of total value added and over 80% of all employment. As we shall see in later chapters, the marketing of services presents different challenges to marketing organisations. In Chapter 11, for example, we discuss the nature of products and services and some of the implications for marketers. In fact, the latest business groups to adopt the marketing approach are service providers—professionals such as engineers, lawyers, accountants and physicians. The growth in 24-hour medical centres is in response to the need for convenient availability of medical services by a population that is getting older. Also, naturopathic health services which provide a more holistic approach to health, and are growing in number, have adopted marketing approaches to create awareness and attract consumers. Until recently, professional associations did not allow their members to engage in price competition, client solicitation and advertising. But changing legislation and professional codes of conduct have opened competition within the professions. Accountants, lawyers and other professional people now advertise and are prepared to engage in competitive pricing. However, the professions themselves are under threat, with some commentators predicting a shrinking in the demand for professionals

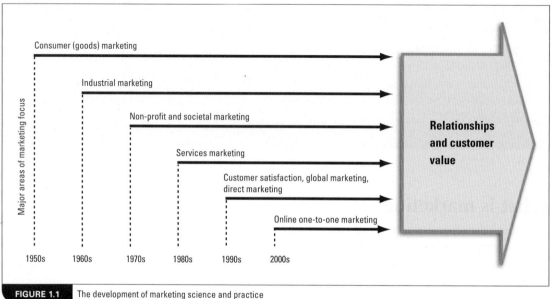

FIGURE 1.1   The development of marketing science and practice
Source: Adapted from Adrian Payne, *The Essence of Services Marketing* © 1993, p. 30. Reproduced by permission of Pearson Education Inc., Upper Saddle River, NJ.

such as lawyers and doctors due to the Information Age and the access to knowledge provided by Internet services.[3]

In the twenty-first century marketing must be understood not in the old sense of making a sale— 'telling and selling'—but in the new sense of satisfying customer needs by creating value through interacting and working with the customer. We live in the age of online one-to-one marketing— tailoring products, services, processes and experiences to individual customers and communicating with them as well as supplying value on an individual basis. Throughout this book you will find reference to online marketing. In Chapter 18, in particular, we illustrate the use of online technologies which permit interaction with customers in 'real time' and confront the issues and opportunities of online marketing.

For now, though, whatever the method used, the marketing organisation that excels in understanding consumer needs, develops products that provide superior value and then prices, distributes and communicates effectively and efficiently should find that their products and services sell very easily. Newer technologies present special challenges to marketing organisations for they bring them into contact with a global marketplace. On the one hand, national borders are no longer hurdles to trade. On the other hand, marketing organisations face greater challenges in trying to decide whether to standardise their offering or tailor their product to particular geographic markets and culture groups. The challenge all marketing organisations face is to retain customers by satisfying their needs, wants and demands. Today, as in the past, the importance of building and maintaining relationships takes on new meaning as it is often a technology, such as super-kiosks or automatic dispensing machines, which stands between a marketing organisation and its customers.

Although selling and advertising are highly visible aspects of marketing practice, they are only part of a larger 'marketing mix'—a set of marketing tools that work together to affect the marketplace. We define **marketing** as an organisational function and a set of processes for creating, communicating, and delivering value to customers and for managing customer relationships in ways that benefit the organisation and its stakeholders. We tend to think of customers gaining value through a process of exchange, where their needs, wants and demands are met. We next examine the following important terms: needs, wants and demands; products; value; satisfaction and quality; exchange, transactions and relationships; and markets. Figure 1.2 (overleaf) shows that these core marketing concepts are linked, with each concept building on the one before it.

> **Marketing** is an organisational function and a set of processes for creating, communicating, and delivering value to customers and for managing customer relationships in ways that benefit the organisation and its stakeholders.

Needs, wants and demands

The most basic concept underlying marketing is that of human needs. Human **needs** are states of felt deprivation. Humans have many complex needs. These include basic *physical* needs for food, clothing, warmth and safety; *social* needs for belonging and affection; and *individual* needs for knowledge and self-expression. These needs are not invented by marketers, they are a basic part of the human make-up. When a need is not satisfied a person will try either to reduce the need or look for an object that will satisfy it. People in less-developed societies might try to reduce their desires and satisfy them with what is available. People in industrial societies might try to find or develop objects that will satisfy their needs.

> **Needs** States of felt deprivation.

Wants are the form taken by human needs as they are shaped by culture and individual personality. A hungry person in Australia, Singapore or Hong Kong might want a hamburger, chips and a cola. A hungry person in the South Pacific might want mangoes, coconuts and beans. Wants are described in terms of objects that will satisfy needs. As a society evolves, the wants of its members expand. As people are exposed to more objects that arouse their interest and desire, producers try to provide more want-satisfying products and services.

> **Wants** The form taken by human needs as they are shaped by culture and individual personality.

People have almost unlimited wants but limited resources. Thus, they want to choose products that provide the most value and satisfaction for their money. When backed by buying power, wants become

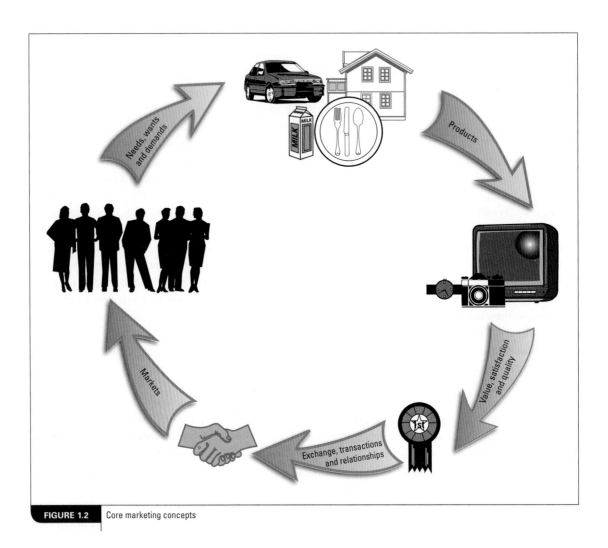

FIGURE 1.2   Core marketing concepts

Demands Human wants that are backed by buying power.

demands. Consumers view products as bundles of benefits and choose products that give them the best bundle for their money. Thus, a Proton car from Malaysia means basic transportation, low price and fuel economy. A Mercedes-Benz or a Lexus means comfort, luxury and status. Given their wants and resources, people demand products with the benefits that add up to the most satisfaction.

Outstanding marketing companies go to great lengths to learn about and understand their customers' needs, wants and demands. They conduct consumer research to find out. They analyse customer complaint, inquiry, warranty and service data. They train salespeople to be on the lookout for unfulfilled customer needs. They observe customers using their own and competing products, and interview them in-depth about their likes and dislikes.[4] Understanding customer needs, wants and demands in detail provides important input for designing marketing strategies.

In these outstanding companies, people at all levels—including top management—stay close to customers in an ongoing effort to understand their needs and wants. For example, top executives from retail chains spend a day or two each week visiting stores and mingling with customers. At Disney's theme parks, at least once in his or her career, every manager spends a day touring the park in a Mickey, Minnie, Goofy or other character costume. Moreover, all Disney theme park managers spend a week each year on the front line—taking tickets, selling popcorn or loading and unloading rides. At Pizza Hut, in addition to surveying customers about their quality needs, analysing customer complaints and studying customer service records, top executives routinely work in outlets to gain better insights into customer needs.

Products

People satisfy their needs and wants with products. A **product** is anything that can be offered to a market to satisfy a need or want. Usually the word *product* suggests a physical object such as a car, a television set or a bar of soap. However, the concept of *product* is not limited to physical objects—anything capable of satisfying a need can be called a product. The importance of physical goods lies not so much in owning them as in the benefits they provide. We don't buy food to look at it but because it satisfies our hunger. We don't buy a microwave to admire it but because it cooks our food.

Marketers often use the expressions *goods* and *services* to distinguish between physical products and intangible ones. However, in Chapter 11 we show that there is a continuum involved and not a clear-cut dichotomy. Moreover, consumers obtain benefits through other vehicles such as people, places, organisations, activities and ideas. Consumers decide which entertainers to watch on television, which places to visit on holiday, which organisations to support through contributions and which ideas to adopt. Thus, the term 'product' covers physical goods, services and a variety of other vehicles that can satisfy consumers' needs and wants. If at times the term does not seem to fit, we could substitute other terms such as 'satisfier', 'resource' or 'offer'.

Many sellers make the mistake of paying more attention to the physical products they offer than to the benefits produced by these products. They see themselves as selling a product rather than providing a solution to a need. A manufacturer of drill bits may think that the customer needs a drill bit, but what the customer really needs is a hole. These sellers may suffer from 'marketing myopia'.[5] They are so taken with their products that they focus only on existing wants and lose sight of underlying customer needs. They forget that a physical product is only a tool to solve a consumer problem. These sellers have trouble if a new product comes along that serves the need better or less expensively. The customer with the same need will want the new product.

Value, satisfaction and quality

Consumers usually face a broad array of products and services that might satisfy a given need. How do they choose between these many products and services? Consumers make buying choices based on their perceptions of the value that various products and services deliver (see Marketing Highlight 1.1).

Customer value is the difference between the values the customer gains from owning and using a product and the costs of obtaining the product. For example, United Parcel Service (UPS) customers gain a number of benefits. The most obvious is fast and reliable package delivery. However, by using UPS, customers might also receive some status and image value. Using UPS usually makes both the package sender and the receiver feel more important. When deciding whether to send a package via UPS, customers will weigh these and other values against the money, effort and psychic costs of using the service. Moreover, they will compare the value of using UPS against the value of using other shippers—FedEx, TNT, DHL or Fastway Global—and select the one that gives them the greatest delivered value.

Customers often do not judge product values and costs accurately or objectively. They act on perceived value. For example, does UPS really provide faster, more reliable delivery? If so, is this better service worth the higher prices UPS charges? Fastway Global would argue that its express service is comparable, and its prices are much lower. However, judging by market share, most consumers

Product Anything that can be offered to a market for attention, acquisition, use or consumption that might satisfy a want or need. It includes physical objects, services, persons, places, organisations and ideas.

Customer value The difference between the values the customer gains from owning and using a product and the costs of obtaining the product.

perceive otherwise. UPS is a growing carrier in Australia with strong positions in the USA, Europe and the UK, and growing influence in Asia.[6] Fastway Global's challenge is to change these customer value perceptions.

Customer satisfaction depends on a product's perceived performance in delivering value relative to a buyer's expectations. If the product's performance falls short of the customer's expectations the buyer is dissatisfied. If performance matches expectations the buyer is satisfied. If performance exceeds expectations the buyer is delighted. Outstanding marketing companies go out of their way to keep their customers satisfied. Satisfied customers make repeat purchases, and they tell others about their good experiences with the product. The key is to match customer expectations with company performance. Smart companies aim to delight customers by promising only what they can deliver, then delivering more than they promise.

Customer satisfaction is closely linked to quality. Many companies have adopted **total quality management (TQM)** programs, designed to improve the quality of their products, services and marketing processes constantly. Quality has a direct impact on product performance and hence on customer satisfaction.

In the narrowest sense, quality can be defined as 'freedom from defects'. But most customer-centred companies go beyond this narrow definition of quality. Instead, they define quality in terms of customer satisfaction. For example, the vice-president of quality at Motorola, a company that pioneered total quality efforts in the USA, says that 'Quality has to do something for the customer . . . Our definition of a defect is "If the customer doesn't like it, it's a defect".'[7] Similarly, the American Society for Quality Control defines quality as the totality of features and characteristics of a product or service that bear on its ability to satisfy customer needs. These customer-focused definitions suggest that a company has achieved total quality only when its products or services meet or exceed customer expectations. Thus, the fundamental aim of today's total quality movement has become total customer satisfaction. Quality begins with customer needs and ends with customer satisfaction. The British TNT subsidiary is an excellent example of a company that has become famous for measuring every aspect of its performance for customers—'If it moves, they measure it'.[8]

Exchange, transactions and relationships

Marketing occurs when people decide to satisfy needs and wants through exchange. **Exchange** is the act of obtaining a desired object from someone by offering something in return. Exchange is only one of many ways people can obtain a desired object. For example, hungry people can find food by hunting, fishing or gathering fruit. They could beg for food or take food from someone else. Or they could offer money, another good or a service in return for food.

As a means of satisfying needs, exchange has much in its favour. People do not have to prey on others or depend on donations. Nor must they possess the skills to produce every necessity for themselves. They can concentrate on making things they are good at making and trade them for needed items made by others. Thus, exchange allows a society to produce much more than it would with any alternative system.

Customer satisfaction
The extent to which a product's perceived performance matches a buyer's expectations. If the product's performance falls short of expectations the buyer is dissatisfied. If performance matches or exceeds expectations the buyer is satisfied or delighted.

Total quality management (TQM)
A recognised system (set in place by the management of a firm) that empowers employees to accept or reject their own output to agreed standards, based on the premise that each work group is a customer of the preceding group, and that continual advancement should be made towards zero defects. Under such a system, statistical process controls allow observation of deviation from agreed standards, and immediate rectification of the process or the product.

Exchange The act of obtaining a desired object from someone by offering something in return.

More than basic transport.

Exchange is the core concept of marketing. For an exchange to take place several conditions must be satisfied. Of course, at least two parties must participate, and each must have something of value to the other. Each party must also want to deal with the other party and each must be free to accept or reject the other's offer. Finally, each party must be able to communicate and deliver.

These conditions simply make exchange possible. Whether exchange actually takes place depends on the parties coming to an agreement. If they agree, we must conclude that the act of exchange has left both of them better off, or at least not worse off. In this sense, exchange creates value just as production creates value. It gives people more consumption possibilities.

Whereas exchange is the core concept of marketing, a **transaction** is marketing's unit of measurement. A transaction consists of a trade of values between two parties. In a transaction, we must be able to say that one party gives X to another party and gets Y in return. For example, you pay Harvey Norman in Sydney or Computer Link in Wellington $1500 for a PC. This is a classic monetary transaction, but not all transactions involve money. In a barter transaction, you might trade your old colour printer and fax in return for a neighbour's second-hand PC.

In the broadest sense, the marketer tries to bring about a response to some offer. The response might be more than simply 'buying' or 'trading' goods and services. A political candidate, for instance, wants a response called 'votes', a church wants 'membership' and a social-action group wants 'idea acceptance'. Marketing consists of actions taken to obtain a desired response from a target audience toward some product, service, idea or other object.

Products do not have to be physical objects. Here the advertisement is promoting services designed to help families cope with childhood cancer.

Transaction marketing is part of the larger idea of relationship marketing. **Relationship marketing** involves creating, maintaining and enhancing strong, value-laden relationships with customers and other stakeholders. Beyond creating short-term transactions, marketers need to build long-term relationships with valued customers, distributors, dealers and suppliers. They must build strong economic and social ties by promising and consistently delivering high-quality products, good service and fair prices. Increasingly, marketing is shifting from trying to maximise the profit on each individual transaction to maximising mutually beneficial relationships with consumers and other parties. The operating assumption is: Build good relationships and profitable transactions will follow.

Markets

The concept of exchange leads to the concept of a market. A **market** is the set of all actual and potential buyers of a product. These buyers share a particular need or want that can be satisfied through exchange. Thus, the size of a market depends on the number of people who exhibit the need, have resources to engage in exchange and are willing to offer these resources in exchange for what they want.

Transaction A trade between two parties that involves at least two things of value, agreed-upon conditions, a time of agreement and a place of agreement.

Relationship marketing The process of creating, maintaining and enhancing strong, value-laden relationships with customers and other stakeholders.

Market The set of all actual and potential buyers of a product.

Delivering customer value profitably

What makes marketing exciting is the challenge of delivering customer value to the market in such a way that the company also benefits in terms of profitability. This involves the decision of how much value will be delivered to customers and how much will be retained by the business—a decision which will be affected by customer perceptions of value delivered by the business compared with all known alternatives and the cost to the business of delivering that value.

Customer delivered value

An underlying premise of marketing is that customers will buy from the firm that they see as offering the highest customer delivered value. *Customer delivered value* is the difference between the prospective customer's evaluation of all the benefits and all the costs of an offering as compared to the perceived alternatives. *Total customer value* is the perceived monetary value of the bundle of economic, functional and psychological benefits customers expect from a given market offering. *Total customer cost* is the bundle of costs customers expect to incur in evaluating, obtaining, using and disposing of the given market offering—see Figure 1.

For example, suppose the buyer for a large media company wants to buy a networked mobile phone communication system from Optus or Vodafone. The competing salespeople carefully describe their respective offers. The buyer wants to use the mobile network in a part of the business where reliability and quality are vital. He would like the system to deliver certain levels of reliability, durability, performance and resale value. He evaluates mobile communication systems and decides that Voafone has a higher product value based on perceived reliability, durability, performance and resale value. He also perceives differences in the accompanying services—delivery, training and maintenance—and decides that Vodafone provides better service and more knowledgeable and responsive personnel. Finally, he places higher value on Vodafone's

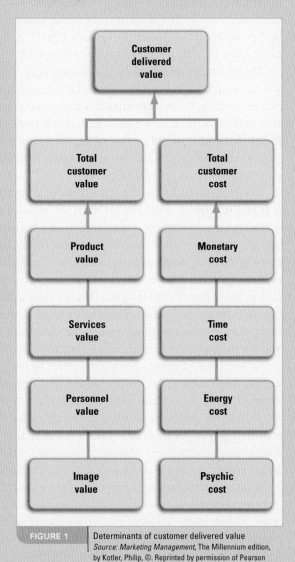

FIGURE 1 Determinants of customer delivered value
Source: Marketing Management, The Millennium edition, by Kotler, Philip, ©. Reprinted by permission of Pearson Education Inc., Upper Saddle River, NJ.

corporate image. He adds all the values from these four sources—product, services, personnel and image—and perceives Vodafone as delivering greater total customer value.

Does he buy the Vodafone system? Not necessarily. He also examines his total cost of transacting with Vodafone versus Optus. The total cost consists of more than the money. As Adam Smith observed over two centuries ago, 'The real price of anything is the toil and trouble of acquiring it'. Total customer cost includes the buyer's time, energy and psychic costs. The buyer evaluates these costs along with the monetary cost to form a total customer cost. Then the buyer considers whether Vodafone's total customer cost is too high in relation to the total customer value Vodafone delivers. If it is, the buyer might choose the Optus system. The buyer will buy from whichever source he thinks delivers the highest perceived customer value after taking account of both perceived benefits and perceived costs.

Vodafone can improve its offer in three ways. First, it can increase total customer value by improving product, services, personnel and/or image benefits. Second, it can reduce the buyer's non-monetary costs by reducing the time, energy and psychic costs. Third, it can reduce its product's monetary cost to the buyer.

Balancing customer value and business value

Suppose Vodafone concludes that the buyer sees its offer as worth $1 000 000. Further, suppose Vodafone's own cost of producing and supplying the mobile phone system is $700 000. This means that Vodaphone's offer potentially generates $300 000 over the company's cost ($1 000 000 minus $700 000). Vodafone needs to charge a price between $700 000 and $1 000 000. If it charges less than $700 000, it won't cover its costs. If it charges more than $1 000 000, it will price itself out of the market.

The price Vodafone charges will determine how much value will be delivered to the buyer and how much will flow to Vodafone. For example, if it charges $900 000, it is creating $100 000 of customer perceived value and keeping $200 000 for itself. The lower Vodafone sets its price, the higher is the customer perceived value and, therefore, the higher is the customer's incentive to purchase. To win the sale, Vodafone must offer more customer perceived value than Optus does. If Vodafone's total customer value is $1 000 000 and total customer cost is $900 000, its customer delivered value is $100 000. If Optus's total customer value is $900 000 and total

customer cost is $850 000, its customer delivered value is $50 000, thus giving Vodafone a customer delivered value advantage of $50 000.

Are customers rational?

Some marketers might argue that the process we've described is too rational. Suppose the customer chose the Optus mobile communication system. How can we explain this choice? Here are three possibilities.

1. The buyer might be under orders to buy at the lowest price. The Vodafone salesperson's task is to convince the buyer's manager that buying on price alone will result in lower long-term profits.

2. The buyer will retire before the company realises that the Optus system is more expensive to operate. The buyer will look good in the short run; he is maximising personal benefit. The Vodafone salesperson's task is to convince other people in the customer company that Vodafone delivers greater customer value.

3. The buyer enjoys a long-term friendship with the Optus salesperson. In this case, Vodafone's salesperson needs to show the buyer that the Optus system will draw complaints from the IT managers and users when they discover its high operating cost and need for frequent repairs.

Implications of customer value

The point of these examples is clear: buyers operate under various constraints and occasionally make choices that give more weight to their personal benefit than to the company's benefit. However, customer delivered value is a useful framework that applies to many situations and yields rich insights. Here are its implications. First, the seller must assess the total customer value and total customer cost associated with each competitor's offer to know how his or her offer rates in the buyer's mind. Second, the seller who is at a customer perceived value disadvantage has two alternatives: to increase total customer value or to decrease total customer cost. The former calls for strengthening or augmenting the offer's product, services, personnel and image benefits. The latter calls for reducing the buyer's

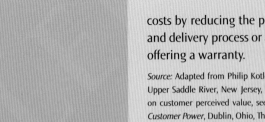

costs by reducing the price, simplifying the ordering and delivery process or absorbing some buyer risk by offering a warranty.

Source: Adapted from Philip Kotler, *Marketing Management,* 11th edition, Upper Saddle River, New Jersey, Prentice Hall, 2003, Chapter 3. For more on customer perceived value, see David C. Swaddling and Charles Miller, *Customer Power,* Dublin, Ohio, The Wellington Press, 2001.

Questions

1 What is the customer delivered value model?

2 Provide your own example of two alternative offers using the customer delivered value model.

3 Do you believe that customers are rational? Give an example of both rational and irrational customer buying behaviour.

4 For more elaboration and examples of customer value, customer satisfaction and customer loyalty see Chapter 2, pp. 40–49.

Originally, the term market stood for the place where buyers and sellers gathered to exchange their goods, such as a village square. Economists use the term market to refer to a collection of buyers and sellers who transact in a particular product class, as in the housing market or the grain market. Marketing organisations, however, see the sellers as constituting an industry and the buyers as constituting a market. The relationship between the industry and the market is shown in Figure 1.3. Sellers and the buyers are connected by four flows. The sellers send products, services and communications to the market; in return, they receive money and information. The inner loop shows an exchange of money for goods; the outer loop shows an exchange of information.

Modern economies operate on the principle of division of labour, where each person specialises in producing something, receives payment and buys needed things with this money. Thus, modern economies abound in markets. Producers go to resource markets (raw-material markets, labour markets, money markets), buy resources, turn them into goods and services and sell them to middlemen, who sell them to consumers. The consumers sell their labour, for which they receive income to pay for the goods and services they buy. The government is another market that plays several roles. It buys goods from resource, producer and middlemen markets; it pays them; it taxes these markets (including consumer markets); and it returns necessary public services. Thus, each nation's economy and the whole world economy consist of complex interacting sets of markets that are linked through exchange processes.

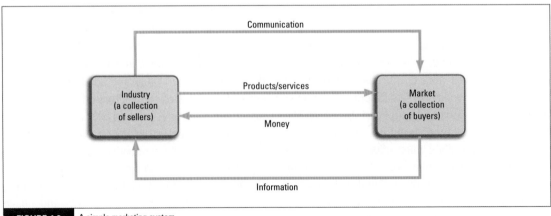

FIGURE 1.3   A simple marketing system

Business people use the term markets to cover various groupings of customers. They talk about need markets (such as the health seekers), product markets (such as the consumer-electronics market), demographic markets (such as teens or the baby boomers) and geographic markets (such as Western Australia or South-East Asia). Or they extend the concept to cover non-customer groupings as well, such as financial markets, labour markets and donor markets.

Marketing

The concept of markets finally brings us full circle to the concept of marketing. *Marketing* means managing markets to bring about exchanges for the purpose of satisfying human needs and wants. Thus, we return to our definition of marketing as a process by which individuals and groups obtain what they need and want by creating and exchanging products and value with others.

Exchange processes involve work. Sellers must search for buyers, identify their needs, design good products and services, set prices for them, promote them and store and deliver them. Activities such as product development, research, communication, distribution, pricing and service are core marketing activities. Although we normally think of marketing as being carried on by sellers, buyers also carry on marketing activities. Consumers do 'marketing' when they search for the goods they need at prices they can afford. Company purchasing agents do 'marketing' when they track down sellers and bargain for good terms.

Figure 1.4 shows the main elements in a modern marketing system. In the usual situation, marketing involves serving a market of end-users in the face of competitors. The company and the competitors send their respective products and messages directly to consumers or through marketing intermediaries (middlemen) to the end-users. All the actors in the system are affected by major environmental forces (demographic, economic, physical, technological, political/legal and social/cultural).

Each party in the system adds value for the next level. Thus, a marketing organisation's success depends not only on its own actions but also on how well the entire value chain serves the needs of the final consumers. Franklins Supermarkets in Australia, The Warehouse in New Zealand or Food Lion in Singapore cannot fulfil their promise of low prices unless their suppliers provide merchandise at low costs. And Ford cannot deliver high quality to car buyers unless its dealers provide outstanding service.

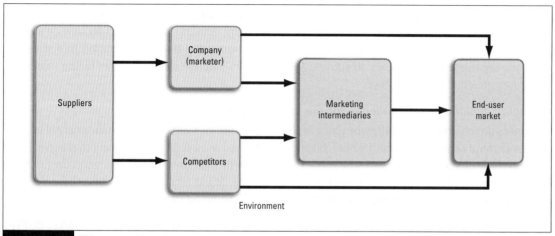

| **FIGURE 1.4** | Main actors and forces in a modern marketing system |

Marketing management

Marketing management
The analysis, planning, implementation and control of programs designed to create, build and maintain beneficial exchanges with target buyers for the purpose of achieving organisational objectives.

We define **marketing management** as the analysis, planning, implementation and control of programs designed to create, build and maintain beneficial exchanges with target buyers for the purpose of achieving organisational objectives. Thus, marketing management involves managing demand, which in turn involves managing customer relationships.

Demand management

Most people think of marketing management as finding enough customers for the company's current output, but this is too limited a view. The organisation has a desired level of demand for its products. At any point in time there may be no demand, adequate demand, irregular demand or too much demand, and marketing management must find ways to deal with these different demand states. Marketing management is concerned not only with finding and increasing demand, but also with changing or even reducing it.

For example, Uluru (Ayers Rock) might have too many tourists wanting to climb it, and Daintree National Park in Queensland can become overcrowded in the tourist season. Power companies sometimes have trouble meeting demand during peak usage periods. In these and other cases of excess demand, the needed marketing task, called **demarketing**, is to reduce demand temporarily or permanently. The aim of demarketing is not to destroy demand but only to reduce or shift it. Thus, marketing management seeks to affect the level, timing and nature of demand in a way that helps the organisation achieve its objectives. A summary of different demand states facing marketers illustrates the challenges involved.

Demarketing
Marketing in which the task is temporarily or permanently to reduce demand.

Managing demand: a key challenge for the marketing manager

Marketers are challenged by different types of demand conditions affected by environmental events, consumer trends and perceptions, fashion, business cycles and seasonality. An industry that experiences many of these different conditions is the travel industry in which airlines, hotels and resort destinations confront these challenges often over a short period of time. Marketers must recognise these demand conditions and the specific marketing challenges that are to be addressed.

1. **Negative demand** A market is in a state of negative demand if a major part of the market dislikes the product and may even pay a price to avoid it. People have a negative demand for vaccinations,

dental work and varicose vein operations. Australian research shows consumers resist replacing the mufflers on their cars until the noise becomes unbearable. These are examples of 'grudge' purchases. The marketing task is to analyse why the market dislikes the product and whether a marketing program consisting of product redesign, improved convenience, lower prices and more positive promotion can change the market's beliefs and attitudes.

2. No demand Target consumers may be unaware of or uninterested in the product. Thus, farmers may not be interested in a new farming method, and students may not be interested in foreign-language courses. The marketing task is to find ways to connect the benefits of the product with the person's natural needs and interests. Early demand for Sony PlayStations was inhibited by a lack of suitable exciting and challenging game software. The marketing task is to understand the factors that are inhibiting demand.

3. Latent demand Many consumers may share a strong need that cannot be satisfied by any existing product. There is a strong latent demand for safer neighbourhoods, more-fuel-efficient cars and buying online. There are still inhibitors to electronic commerce such as security, privacy of information and convenient access by major sections of the business community and consumers. The marketing task is to measure the size of the potential market and develop effective products and services that would satisfy the demand.

4. Declining demand Every organisation, sooner or later, faces declining demand for one or more of its products. Churches have seen their membership decline, and traditional department stores have seen their sales fall. This is often brought about by competition from substitutes.

The marketer must analyse the causes of market decline and determine whether demand can be restimulated by finding new target markets, changing the product's features or developing more effective communication. The marketing task is to reverse the declining demand through creative remarketing of the product.

5. Irregular demand Many organisations face demand that varies on a seasonal, daily or even hourly basis, causing problems of idle or overworked capacity. The Sydney Harbour Bridge has too many lanes during the middle of the day, but too few during peak travel hours in the morning and afternoon. In public transport, much of the equipment is idle during off-peak hours and insufficient during peak travel hours. Museums are undervisited on weekdays and overcrowded on weekends. Supermarkets may be less frequented early in the week and understocked after heavy weekend trading. The marketing task is to find ways to alter the pattern of demand through flexible pricing (early-bird specials), promotion and other incentives like the off-peak rates for telephone calls offered by Telstra and Optus.

6. Full demand Organisations face full demand when they are satisfied with their volume of business and operating at close to current capacity. The marketing task is to maintain the current level of demand in the face of changing consumer preferences and increasing competition. The marketing organisation must maintain or improve its quality and continually measure consumer satisfaction to make sure it is doing a good job.

7. Overfull demand Some organisations face a demand level that is higher than they can or want to handle. Thus, a National Park might attract more tourists than the facilities can handle. The marketing task, called demarketing, requires finding ways to reduce the demand temporarily or permanently. General demarketing seeks to discourage overall demand and consists of such steps as raising prices and reducing promotion and service. Builders adopt this approach when they are overcommitted on existing work. Selective demarketing consists of trying to reduce the demand coming from those

Car manufacturers focus on customer lifetime value.

parts of the market that are less profitable or less in need of the product. Demarketing aims not to destroy demand but only to reduce its level, temporarily or permanently.

8. Unwholesome demand Unwholesome products will attract organised efforts to discourage their consumption. Unselling campaigns have been conducted against cigarettes, alcohol, hard drugs, handguns and pornography on the World Wide Web. An overload of hikers and campers may inflict damage on the environment or its natural inhabitants. The marketing task is to influence people who like something to give it up, using such tools as fear messages, price hikes and reduced availability.

Building profitable customer relationships

Managing demand means managing customers. A marketing organisation's demand comes from two groups: new customers and repeat customers. Traditional marketing science and practice have focused on attracting new customers and making the sale. Today, however, the emphasis is shifting. Beyond designing strategies to *attract* new customers and *create* transactions with them, companies now are going all out to *retain* current customers and build lasting customer *relationships*.

Why the new emphasis on keeping customers? In the past, companies facing an expanding economy and rapidly growing markets could practise the 'leaky-bucket' approach to marketing. Growing markets meant a plentiful supply of new customers. Companies could keep filling the marketing bucket with new customers without worrying about losing old customers through the holes in the bottom of the bucket. However, companies today are facing new marketing realities. Changing demographics, a slow-growth economy, more sophisticated competitors and overcapacity in many industries mean that there are fewer new customers to go round. Many companies are now fighting for shares of flat or fading markets. Thus, the costs of attracting new customers are rising. In fact, it costs five times as much to attract a new customer as it does to keep a current customer satisfied.[9]

Companies are also realising that losing a customer means more than losing a single sale—it means losing the entire stream of purchases that the customer would make over a lifetime of patronage. For Holden, Toyota or Ford, the lifetime value of a customer might well exceed $350 000. Thus, working to retain customers makes good economic sense. A marketing organisation can lose money on a specific transaction, but still benefit greatly from a long-term relationship.

Attracting new customers remains an important marketing management task. However, the focus today is on retaining current customers and building profitable, long-term relationships with them. The key to customer retention is superior customer value and satisfaction. With this in mind, many companies are going to extremes to keep their customers satisfied by providing additional value (see Marketing Highlight 1.1). Chapter 2 explores these relationships in more detail.

SELF-CHECK QUESTIONS

5   Present this text's definition of marketing management.

6   Consider the different demand states. Would you say that the demand for a non-polluting motor vehicle is similar to the demand for safe cigarettes? Are these both examples of latent demand?

7   Select a product or service which is experiencing irregular demand. How would you overcome the irregularity if you were the marketing manager concerned?

Marketing management philosophies

We describe marketing management as carrying out tasks to achieve desired exchanges with target markets. What *philosophy* should guide these marketing efforts? What weight should be given to the interests of the organisation, the customers and the society? Very often these interests conflict.

There are five alternative concepts under which organisations conduct their marketing activities: the *production, product, selling, marketing* and *societal marketing* concepts.

The production concept

The **production concept** holds that consumers will favour products that are available and highly affordable. Therefore, management should focus on improving production and distribution efficiency. This concept is one of the oldest philosophies that guides sellers.

The production concept is still a useful philosophy in two types of situations. The first occurs when the demand for a product exceeds the supply. Here, management should look for ways to increase production. The second situation occurs when the product's cost is too high and improved productivity is needed to bring it down. For example, Henry Ford's whole philosophy was to perfect the production of the Model T so that its cost could be reduced and more people could afford it. He joked about offering people a car of any colour as long as it was black.

For many years, Texas Instruments (TI) followed a philosophy of increased production and lower costs in order to bring down prices. It won a major share of the American hand-held calculator market using this approach. However, companies operating under a production philosophy run a major risk of focusing too narrowly on their own operations. For example, when TI used this strategy in the digital watch market, it failed. Although TI's watches were priced low, customers did not find them very attractive. In its drive to bring down prices, TI lost sight of something else that its customers wanted—namely, affordable, *attractive* digital watches.

Production concept The philosophy that consumers favour products that are available and highly affordable and that management should therefore focus on improving production and distribution efficiency.

The product concept

Another major concept guiding sellers, the **product concept**, holds that consumers will favour products that offer the most quality, performance and innovative features. Thus, an organisation should devote energy to making continuous product improvements. Some manufacturers believe that if they can build a better mousetrap the world will beat a path to their door.[10] But they are often rudely shocked. Buyers may well be looking for a better solution to a mouse problem, but not necessarily for a better mousetrap. The solution might be a chemical spray, an exterminating service or something that works better than a mousetrap. Furthermore, a better mousetrap will not sell unless the manufacturer designs, packages and prices it attractively, places it in convenient distribution channels, brings it to the attention of people who need it and convinces buyers that it is a better product.

Product concept The idea that consumers favour products that offer the most quality, performance and features and that the organisation should therefore devote its energy to making continuous product improvements; a detailed version of the new product idea stated in meaningful consumer terms.

The product concept also can lead to 'marketing myopia'. For instance, railways management once thought that users wanted *trains* rather than *transportation* and overlooked the growing challenge of airlines, buses, trucks and cars. Many universities have assumed that school leavers want a university education and have thus overlooked the increasing challenge of vocational courses provided by TAFE colleges and polytechnics.

The selling concept

Selling concept The idea that consumers will not buy enough of the organisation's products unless the organisation undertakes a large-scale selling and promotion effort.

Many organisations follow the **selling concept**, which holds that consumers will not buy enough of the organisation's products unless it undertakes a large-scale selling and promotion effort. The concept is typically practised with *unsought* goods—those that buyers do not normally think of buying—such as encyclopaedias or insurance. These industries must be good at tracking down prospects and selling them on product benefits. The selling concept is also practised in the non-profit area. A political party, for example, will vigorously sell its candidate to voters as a fantastic person for the job. The candidate works in voting precincts from dawn to dusk—shaking hands, kissing babies, meeting supporters and making speeches. Much money is spent on radio and television advertising, posters and mailings. The candidate's flaws are hidden from the public because the aim is to get the sale, not to worry about consumer satisfaction afterwards.

Most firms practise the selling concept when they have overcapacity. Their aim is to sell what they make rather than make what the market wants. Thus, marketing based on hard selling carries high risks. It focuses on creating sales transactions rather than on building long-term, profitable relationships with customers. It assumes that customers who are coaxed into buying the product will like it. Or, if they don't like it, they will possibly forget their disappointment and buy it again later. These are usually poor assumptions to make about buyers. Most studies show that dissatisfied customers do not buy again. Worse yet, while the average satisfied customer tells three others about their good experiences, the average dissatisfied customer tells 10 others about their bad experiences.[11]

The marketing concept

Marketing concept The marketing management philosophy which holds that achieving organisational goals depends on determining the needs and wants of target markets and delivering the desired satisfactions more effectively and efficiently than competitors.

The **marketing concept** holds that achieving organisational goals depends on determining the needs and wants of target markets and delivering the desired satisfactions more effectively and efficiently than competitors do. The marketing concept has been stated in colourful ways: 'Honda *The Power of Dreams*', 'hp *invent*', 'Gloria Jeans's Coffees *Escape the daily grind*', '*There's no other store like David Jones*', Woolworths *The fresh food people*' and '*Yes, we can*' (Radisson Hotels). JC Penney's motto also summarises the marketing concept: 'To do all in our power to pack the customer's dollar full of value, quality, and satisfaction.'

A steel tablet hangs on the wall of many Toyota employees' offices saying: 'Lest we forget what Oh What a Feeling means. Key thought: Toyota delivers an outstanding sense of ownership satisfaction. For those who forget, the penalties are severe. For those who remember, the rewards are immense.' Worldwide Toyota has replaced its original goal of 10% of the world's market share with 'No. 1 in customer satisfaction' because it believes its market share will follow the satisfaction it delivers to its customers.

The selling concept and the marketing concept are sometimes confused. Figure 1.5 compares the two concepts. The selling concept takes an inside-out perspective. It starts with the factory, focuses on the marketing organisation's existing products, and calls for heavy selling and promotion to obtain profitable sales. It focuses heavily on customer conquest—getting short-term sales with little concern about who buys or why. In contrast, the marketing concept takes an outside-in perspective. It starts with a well-defined market, focuses on customer needs, coordinates all the marketing activities affecting customers and makes profits by creating long-term customer relationships based on customer value and satisfaction. Under the marketing concept, companies produce what consumers want, thereby satisfying consumers and making profits.[12]

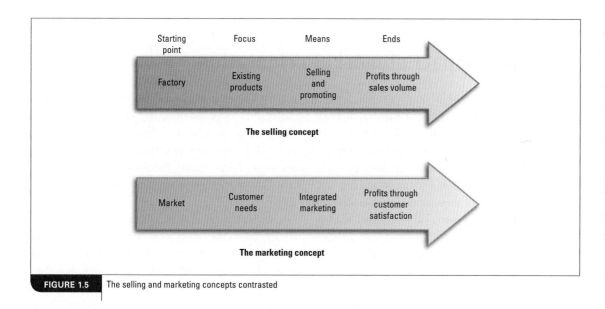

Starting point — Focus — Means — Ends

Factory → Existing products → Selling and promoting → Profits through sales volume

The selling concept

Market → Customer needs → Integrated marketing → Profits through customer satisfaction

The marketing concept

FIGURE 1.5　The selling and marketing concepts contrasted

Many successful and well-known companies have adopted the marketing concept, as well as many lesser known marketing organisations. Singapore Airlines, Nestlé and McDonald's follow it faithfully.

In contrast, many companies claim to practise the marketing concept but do not. They have the forms of marketing, such as a marketing director, marketing manager, group product managers, product managers, marketing plans and marketing research, but this does not mean that they are market-focused and customer-driven companies. The question is whether they are finely tuned to changing customer needs and competitor strategies. Formerly great companies—Burns Philp, AMP, Coles Myer—all lost substantial market share and profitability because they failed to adjust their marketing strategies to the changing marketplace.

Several years of hard work are needed to turn a sales-oriented organisation into a marketing-oriented organisation. The goal is to build customer satisfaction into the very fabric of the firm. Customer satisfaction is no longer a fad. As one marketing analyst notes: 'It's becoming a way of life . . . as embedded into corporate cultures as information technology and strategic planning'.[13]

However, the marketing concept does not mean that a marketing organisation should try to give all consumers everything they want. Marketers must balance creating more value for customers against making profits for the organisation. The purpose of marketing is not to maximise customer satisfaction. As one marketing expert notes: 'The shortest definition of marketing I know is "meeting needs profitably". The purpose of marketing is to generate customer value [at a profit]. The truth is [that the relationship with a customer] will break up if value evaporates. You've got to continue to generate more value for the consumer but not give away the house. It's a very delicate balance.'[14]

Gupta and Lehmann give a compelling case for managing customers as investments and evaluating the profit margins provided by customers, measuring the lifetime value of customers and focusing on strategies that are designed to achieve very high retention rates of the most profitable customers.[15] To put this into practice the business needs to be market oriented. Marketing Highlight 1.2 explores the notion of a market-oriented business and the links to profitability.

The societal marketing concept

The **societal marketing concept** holds that the organisation should determine the needs, wants and interests of target markets. It should then deliver superior value to customers in a way that

Societal marketing concept The idea that the organisation should determine the needs, wants and interests of target markets and deliver the desired satisfactions more effectively and efficiently than competitors in a way that maintains or improves the consumer's and society's well-being.

The profit impact of market orientation

To achieve above-average financial performance a company must first attain a consistently superior performance in the marketplace. To reach this the company must create a sustainable competitive advantage (SCA) which in turn will enable it to create sustainable and superior value for its customers.

The desire to create superior value for customers and attain SCA drives successful business leaders to create and maintain a culture that will produce the necessary behaviours to achieve their goals. Market orientation is the organisational culture that most effectively creates the necessary behaviours for the creation of superior value for buyers and, thus, continuous superior performance for investors.

Narver and Slater published a seminal article in 1990 that examined the effect of market orientation on business profitability. For that article they reviewed three decades of the major conceptual literature on SCA and market orientation to identify the principal common threads. They inferred from the literature that market orientation consists of three behavioural components—customer orientation, competitor orientation and interfunctional coordination—and two decision criteria—long-term focus and profitability.

Customer orientation and competitor orientation include all of the activities involved in acquiring information about buyers and competitors in the target market and disseminating it throughout the business. The third behaviour component, interfunctional coordination, is based on customer and competitor information and comprises the business's coordinated efforts, typically involving more than the marketing department, to create superior value for the buyers.

Customer orientation suggests a thorough understanding of the firm's target customers that enables it to create consistently superior value. A strong customer orientation requires that a seller understand a buyer's entire value chain, not only as it was yesterday or is today but also as it will evolve over time. Specifically, Gupta and Lehmann propose

that customer profitability (i.e. profit derived from customers) is determined by customer retention, margin and acquisition. This requires a detailed understanding of the drivers of customer value and retention. Furthermore, they show that the factors that drive customer profitability directly affect firm value.

Competitor orientation means that a company understands the short-term strengths and weaknesses and long-term capabilities and strategies of both current and potential competitors. The firm must also include the entire set of technologies capable of satisfying the current and expected needs of the target buyers.

The third of the three behavioural components is *interfunctional coordination*—the coordinated leverage of all the resources available to the organisation in creating superior value for customers. Creating value for buyers is too important to delegate it to one department—marketing. Rather, value creation for buyers is analogous to a symphony orchestra in which the contribution of each subgroup is tailored and integrated by a conductor—with a synergistic effect. However, the marketing department must lead the organisation with well-developed marketing knowledge, skills and attitudes.

A market-oriented seller understands that, through the many ways of creating additional benefits for buyers as well as the numerous types of reductions in the buyers' total acquisition and use costs, there are many potential sources of SCA. As a result, a market-oriented business continuously examines these alternative sources of advantage to see how it can be most effective in creating sustainable and superior value for its present and future target buyers.

For example, both Wal-Mart and Nordstrom are retailers who operate throughout the USA. Both companies create superior value for their customers and earn above-average profits for investors. Though their organisations and methods of competition are very different, they both have a very strong market orientation. Wal-Mart's market orientation leads it to focus on the numerous types of reductions in the buyers' total acquisition and use costs as compared to competitive discount retailers, while Nordstrom's market orientation drives it to creating additional benefits for buyers as compared to its high-end competitors. Australian retailers Woolworths, David Jones and Harvey Norman are companies that have been able to create superior value for their customers which has been translated into superior value for shareholders.

Sources: Aaker, David A., *Strategic Market Management*, 2nd edn, New York, John Wiley & Sons, Inc, 1988; Porter, Michael, *Competitive Strategy*, New York, The Free Press, 1980; Narver, John and Stanley F. Slater, 'The Effect of a Market Orientation on Business Profitability', *Journal of Marketing*, October 1990, vol. 54, no. 4, p. 21; Gupta, Sunil and Lehmann, Donald R. *Managing*

Customers as Investments: The Strategic Value of Customers in the Long Run, New Jersey, Pearson Education, Inc., 2005, pp. 53–77, 98–107; see also the 2005 Annual Reports of Woolworths, David Jones and Harvey Norman.

Questions

1 What are the internal building blocks for market orientation in a company?

2 What is the logic that suggests that superior customer value creates superior value for shareholders?

3 Give an example of a company you think provides both superior customer value and superior business performance.

1.2

maintains or improves the consumer's *and the society's* wellbeing. The societal marketing concept is the newest of the five marketing management philosophies.

The societal marketing concept questions whether the pure marketing concept is adequate in an age of environmental problems, resource shortages, rapid population growth, worldwide economic problems and neglected social services. It asks if the firm that senses, serves and satisfies individual wants is always doing what's best for consumers and society in the long run. According to the societal marketing concept, the pure marketing concept overlooks possible conflicts between consumer short-run wants and consumer long-run welfare.

Consider Coca-Cola Amatil. Most people see it as a highly responsible corporation producing fine soft drinks that satisfy consumer tastes. Yet some consumer and environmental groups have voiced concerns that Coke has little nutritional value, can harm people's teeth, contains caffeine and adds to the litter problem with disposable bottles and cans. Also, most people see BHP Billiton, the Australian–South African resources company in steel, minerals and petroleum, and Orica, a fertiliser, plastics and explosives company, as responsible companies. To sustain this image BHP Billiton engages in community education and development programs. Both Orica and BHP Billiton also focus their attention and strategies on environmental pollution as well as employee and community safety. In parts of New Zealand and Australia community concern about the depletion of forests through woodchipping has led timber companies to develop reafforestation programs and to consider the needs and concerns of society.

Such concerns and conflicts led to the societal marketing concept. The societal marketing concept calls on marketers to

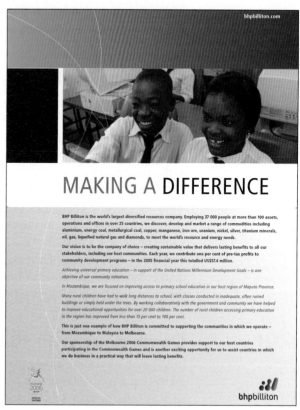

BHP Billiton makes a difference in local communities.

balance three considerations in setting their marketing policies: company profits, consumer wants and society's interests. Originally, most companies based their marketing decisions largely on short-run company profit. Eventually, they began to recognise the long-run importance of satisfying consumer wants, and the marketing concept emerged. Now many companies are beginning to think of society's interests when making their marketing decisions.

One such company is The Body Shop which is widely admired for community and environmental responsibility. The Body Shop's open policy of selling products that do not harm the environment shows a direct concern for societal interests.

However, in practice, companies are under continuing pressure from investors to show both short-term and longer-term financial performance while balancing market, supplier, financial, employee and wider societal stakeholder interests.[16]

SELF-CHECK QUESTIONS

8 Consider the situation where a political party continues to send letters and pamphlets to households that do not support it. Is this an example of the marketing concept in action?

9 Consider the situation where a new industry is developing, such as the satellite-TV industry. If the first companies concentrate on the technology, does this make them product oriented?

10 Should all marketing organisations adopt the societal marketing concept, or should there be exemptions for certain companies? An example might be Optus (now owned by SingTel) which was allowed to install overhead fibre-optic cabling.

11 What approach, if any, could be taken by Australian breweries to practise societal marketing?

Marketing challenges in the twenty-first century

Marketing operates within a dynamic global environment. Every decade calls on marketing managers to think in a fresh way about their marketing objectives and practices. Rapid changes can quickly make yesterday's winning strategies out of date. As management thought-leader, Peter Drucker, once observed, a marketing organisation's winning formula for the last decade will probably be its undoing in the next decade.

What are the marketing challenges at the beginning of the twenty-first century? Today's companies are wrestling with changing customer values and orientations, market maturity in many industries, environmental decline, increased global competition and a host of other economic, political and social problems. However, these problems also provide marketing opportunities. We now look more deeply into several key trends and forces that are changing the marketing landscape and challenging marketing strategy: growth of non-profit marketing, rapid globalisation, information technology, the changing world economy, the call for more socially responsible actions and accountability for marketing performance.[17]

Growth of non-profit marketing

In the past, marketing has been most widely applied in the business sector. In recent years, however, marketing has also become a major component in the strategies of many non-profit organisations such as colleges, hospitals, museums, symphony orchestras and even churches. Consider the following examples:

As hospital costs and room rates soar, many hospitals face under-utilisation, especially in their maternity and paediatrics sections. Many private hospitals in Australia and the United States have taken steps toward marketing their services. One hospital, competing for maternity patients, offered a steak and champagne dinner with candlelight for new parents. Another uses innovative billboards to promote its emergency care service. Other hospitals, in an effort to attract doctors, have installed services such as saunas, chauffeurs and private tennis courts.[18]

Before even opening its doors, one new church hired a research firm to find out what its customers would want. The research showed that people with no current church connection found church boring and church services irrelevant to their everyday lives. They complained that churches were always asking for money. So the church added contemporary music and skits, loosened its dress codes, and presented sermons on topics such as money management and parenting. Its direct mail piece read: 'Given up on the church? We don't blame you. Lots of people have. They're fed up with boring sermons, ritual that doesn't mean anything . . . music that nobody likes . . . [and] preachers who seem to be more interested in your wallet than you . . . Church can be different. Give us a shot.' The results have been impressive. Within the first year of opening, the church attracted nearly 400 members, 80% of whom were not previously attending church.[19]

Similarly, many private schools and, increasingly, universities, facing declining enrolments, rising costs and global competitors are using marketing to compete for students and funds. They are defining target markets, improving their communication and promotion, and responding better to student needs and wants. Many performing arts groups face huge operating deficits that they must cover by more aggressive donor marketing. Finally, many longstanding non-profit organisations—the YMCA, the Salvation Army, the Scouts—have lost members and are now modernising their missions and 'products' to attract more members and donations.[20]

Even government agencies have shown an increased interest in marketing. For example, the Armed Services in many countries have marketing plans to attract recruits. And various government agencies are now designing social marketing campaigns to reward and encourage energy conservation and concern for the environment, to stimulate good corporate behaviour or to discourage smoking, excessive drinking and drug use.

The continued growth of non-profit and public sector marketing presents exciting challenges for marketing managers.

Rapid globalisation

The world economy has undergone radical change during the past 25 years, particularly during the last 10 years. Geographical and cultural distances have shrunk with the advent of jet airliners, fax machines, Internet, computer and telephone links, digital satellite television broadcasting (such as Britain's BSkyB and Japan's PERFECTV) and other technical advances. This has allowed companies to expand their geographical market coverage, purchasing and manufacturing greatly. The result is a vastly more complex marketing environment, for both companies and consumers.

Today, almost every marketing organisation, large or small, is touched in some way by global competition—from the American florist that buys its flowers from Dutch nurseries, to the Melbourne clothing retailer that sources its merchandise in Asia, to the American electronics manufacturer competing in its home markets with giant Japanese rivals, to the Australian consumer goods designer leading the way with new products for international markets.

St. George implements market orientation

Gail Kelly, Managing Director, St. George, states: 'Our on-going focus on providing great customer service through fully engaged people continues to deliver superior shareholder returns—that's what makes us different'.

St. George Bank's share price has grown from $20 in January 2004 to over $30 in January 2006—a 50% increase over this two-year period. This also reflects its growth in profits, which were 15.5% higher in 2005 than in 2004. Its growth in value is in large part a product of a strategy which is driven around a culture of market orientation as reflected in its strategic framework established in 2002 and consistently implemented to the present day. The strategy revolves around:

- Deepening relationships with customers in selected customer segments, in particular its 'middle market' customers (business customers with loans of over $1 million) and 'Gold and private bank' customers as well as its intermediaries such as mortgage brokers and independent financial advisers.
- Creatively differentiating on service.
- Accelerating and empowering relationship selling.
- Developing a team and performance-oriented culture.

During 2005 there was greater focus by St. George on its customer service strategy, which is based on this formula: engaged people + great customer service = superior financial returns. St. George actively invested in 2005 to strengthen this startegy by:

- Implementing a new distribution model to develop a local market focus.
- Embedding a new customer relationship management system to provide frontline staff with information on customers' complete banking arrangements with St George.
- Adding 123 new business bankers to strengthen service and customer focus in the middle market.

St. George focuses on customers' needs.

- Expanding initiatives in the geographic markets of Victoria, Queensland and Western Australia.

St. George pays great attention to recruiting people who have the 'right' atitude as well as skills and aptitude and invests in induction and training and skills courses to instil a market-oriented culture. Its focus is continually to develop a workplace where its people actively seek to provide customers with a superior service experience.

St. George is a good example of implementation of the marketing concept by aligning an internal culture of customer-oriented attitudes with systems and processes and focused marketing strategies which have given it a sustainable differentiated advantage in its chosen target markets.

Source: 'The Things that Make us Different', St. George Concise Annual Report 2005, Managing Director's Report.

Questions

1 How has St George been able to create a customer focus in its business?

2 Why has St George been able to grow its revenue, profits and share price over the last few years?

3 How will St George continue growth in the future?

Like American marketing organisations, Australian and New Zealand companies have been challenged at home by the skilful marketing of European and Asian multinationals. Companies such as Toyota, Siemens, Nestlé, Sony and Samsung are fierce competitors of local companies in the countries they compete in. Similarly, local companies in a wide range of industries have found new opportunities abroad. Companies such as Microsoft, Intel, Sony, Panasonic, General Motors, Exxon, IBM, General Electric, DuPont, Hewlett-Packard, Coca-Cola, HSBC ('The world's local bank') and dozens of others have developed truly global operations, making and selling their products worldwide.

Today, companies are not only trying to sell more of their locally produced goods in international markets, but are also buying more components and supplies abroad. For example, an American fashion designer may choose cloth woven from Australian wool with printed designs from Italy. The designer will design a dress and fax the drawing to a Hong Kong agent who will place the order with a mainland China factory. Finished dresses will be airfreighted to New York where they will be distributed to department and specialty stores around the country.

Many domestically purchased goods and services are 'hybrids' with design, materials purchases, manufacturing and marketing taking place in several countries. Australians who decide to 'buy Australian' might reasonably decide to avoid a Honda Civic and a Mitsubishi Lancer and purchase a Holden Barina. Imagine their surprise when they learn that the Barina is actually a rebadged Opel from GM Europe, and that General Motors is an American company. People wanting an imported car and buying a Toyota Lexcen might be disconcerted to find that the Lexcen is a rebadged Holden Commodore made in Australia. Consumers in many other nations suffer similar surprises. For example, Fox Broadcasting in the USA is owned by an Australian company—News Corporation.

Thus, managers in countries around the world are asking: Just what is global marketing? How does it differ from domestic marketing? How do global competitors and forces affect our business? To what extent should we 'go global'? Many companies are forming strategic alliances with foreign companies, even competitors, who serve as suppliers or marketing partners. The past few years have produced some surprising alliances between competitors such as Ford and Mazda, General Electric and Matsushita, Telstra and News Corporation, and Ericsson and Sony. Winning companies in the twenty-first century may well be those that have built the best global networks.[21]

Information technology and electronic marketing

The information revolution has reached a critical mass where a new information-based infrastructure is being developed through the convergence of telecommunications, computer systems, computer software, information services and media and consumer/professional electronics. The new infrastructure is creating major shifts in markets and competition. As a result, traditional company and industry structures are being transformed and competitive boundaries blurred. This information technology explosion is accelerating the rate of change and the emergence of new global competitors.

Information technology is having a profound impact on every industry in the world. An array of commercial reports available in the marketplace from such organisations as KPMG, Gartner Group, Microsoft and McKinsey strongly indicates that we will observe the law of diminishing returns from traditional marketing. The complexity of information management and marketing processes requires increasing levels of digitisation of information, more powerful processors and larger digital storage capability. These consulting groups suggest that the harnessing and disseminating of information in all its varied forms will be the key to survival and the building of future dominance in the marketplace. It is not that traditional physical marketing will disappear, but rather that powerful new tools are becoming available to implement new relationship-building strategies through online marketing.[22]

The changing world economy

A large part of the world has grown poorer during the past few decades. A sluggish world economy has resulted in more difficult times for both consumers and marketing organisations. Around the world people's needs are greater than ever, but in many areas people lack the means to pay for necessary goods. Markets, after all, consist of people with needs *and* purchasing power. In many cases, the latter is lacking. In many developed countries, although wages have risen real buying power has declined, especially for the less skilled members of the workforce. Many households have managed to maintain their buying power only because both spouses work. Many workers have lost their jobs as companies have 'downsized' and 're-engineered' to cut costs.

Current economic conditions create both problems and opportunities for marketing organisations. Some companies are facing declining demand and see few opportunities for growth. Others, however, are developing new solutions to changing consumer problems. Many are finding ways to offer consumers 'more for less'. The giant retailer Wal-Mart in the USA rose to market leadership on two principles, emblazoned on every Wal-Mart store: 'Satisfaction Guaranteed' and 'We Sell for Less—Always'. When consumers enter a Wal-Mart store they are welcomed by a friendly greeter and find a huge assortment of good-quality merchandise at everyday low prices. The same principle explains the explosive growth of factory outlet stores and discount chains—these days customers want value. This applies even to luxury products: Toyota introduced its successful Lexus luxury automobile with the headline 'Perhaps the First Time in History that Trading a $72 000 Car for a $36 000 Car Could Be Considered Trading Up'. Later advertisements for the smaller ES300 model drove the point home further. Advertisements in the financial press pictured the Lexus in a driveway next door to a parked compact Mercedes. The headline stated, 'Don't just keep up with the Jones. Publicly humiliate them.'

The call for ethical behaviour and social responsibility

A further factor in today's marketing environment is the increased call for companies to take responsibility for the social and environmental impact of their actions and to contribute positively to the communities within which they operate. Many companies have responded to this with specific contributions to their communities, for example, the ANZ bank and its Intensive Care Foundation aiming to raise $10 million to help intensive care units to save more lives. Corporate ethics has become a hot topic in almost every business arena, from the corporate boardroom to the business-school classroom. But the unethical behaviour of executives at Enron led to its collapse and the demise of Arthur Andersen which had audit responsibility, and the accounting anomalies at Worldcom brought this massive company into receivership. And few companies can ignore the well-organised and very demanding environmental movement. The ethics and environmental movements will place even stricter demands on companies in the future.

Consider recent environmental developments. In many Eastern European countries the massive environmental negligence of their former governments has resulted in fouled air, polluted water and soil poisoned by chemical dumping. In the early 1990s representatives from more than 100 countries attended the Earth Summit in Rio de Janeiro to consider how to handle such problems as the destruction of rainforests, global warming, endangered species and other environmental threats. This formalised a focus on conservation issues, world heritage areas and retaining a balance of wildlife and natural forest with ever encroaching urban and rural development. The huge oil spill by the *Exxon Valdez* in 1989 off the Alaskan coast devastated marine life and destroyed the livings of many in the fishing industry. An oil spill in Sydney Harbour in 1999 and the one off the coast of Spain in 2002 as a result of the sinking of the oil tanker *Prestige* threatened other ecological disasters and highlighted the need for corporate responsibility for the environment.[23] Clearly, in the future companies will be held to an increasingly higher standard of environmental responsibility in their marketing and manufacturing activities.

Marketing accountability

The trend towards more ethical corporate behaviour has accompanied a push for stronger corporate governance, more disclosure and accountability for business actions and performance. Marketing is not immune and now corporate management expects marketers to do more than spend the marketing budget—they want to see returns to the business from marketing activities. This means that marketers need to understand how their marketing strategies and programs will yield a return on their investment. The marketer's tools for justifying their actions and returning profit to the business lie in the marketing planning and performance monitoring process which is discussed in detail in Chapter 3.[24]

Implementation of stronger market orientation

All of these trends create pressure on firms to be more responsive, innovative and competitive—which in turn drives them to have a stronger **market orientation**. We see many companies now making it their stated aim to organise their business around the customer as the means of generating profitable growth for the future. Telstra is an excellent example of this with its stated aim of transforming the company to be customer-centric and creating accountability through its segment-based marketing structure for profitability. Marketing Highlight 1.3 describes how St George has created a market-oriented business with impressive results.

Market orientation
A situation in which a business has a strong customer focus and competitor orientation supported by effective interfunctional coordination that enables the business to deliver profitable customer value over time.

The new marketing landscape

The past decade taught business firms everywhere a humbling lesson. Domestic companies learned that they can no longer ignore global markets and competitors. Successful firms in mature industries learned that they cannot overlook emerging markets, technologies and management approaches. Companies of every sort learned that they cannot remain inwardly focused, ignoring the needs of customers and their environment.

The most powerful companies of the late 1980s and early 1990s included General Motors, the Swedish multinational Ericsson, IBM, Hewlett-Packard (HP), Telstra and BHP. But these giant companies appear to have failed at marketing, and today all are having to reinvent themselves with a market focus. Each failed to understand its changing marketplace, its customers and the need to provide value in a different way from the past. Today, General Motors is still trying to work out why so many consumers around the world switched to Japanese and European cars. Mighty Ericsson has lost its way, losing share to both Nokia and Motorola on the one hand, and to Internet players like Cisco on the other.[25] In contrast the global growth of Nokia to lead the mobile communications market has in large measure resulted from effective marketing. IBM has repositioned the entire company as an e-business powerhouse and HP is working hard to incorporate the digital age and build an e-services company. Telstra has faced the prospect of declining fixed line revenue at a rate which cannot be matched by the revenue growth from its mobile, Internet and directory businesses and has had to implement a major business transformation effort. BHP Billiton has had to reinvent itself as a more focused global resources company.

In this new century, companies will have to become customer oriented and market driven in all that they do. It is not enough to be product or technology driven—too many companies still design their products without customer input, only to find them rejected in the marketplace. It is not enough to be good at winning new customers—too many companies forget about customers after the sale, only to lose their future business. The key to success on the rapidly changing marketing landscape will be a strong focus on the marketplace and a total marketing commitment to providing value to customers.[26]

SELF-CHECK QUESTIONS

12 Rapid globalisation is referred to in this section. Does this affect only large international marketing organisations or might smaller firms also be affected?

13 Commentators point to the widening gap that continues to develop between the financially rich and poor. Might being 'information rich' versus 'information poor' be related?

14 It is stated that marketing organisations will need to be even more customer oriented and market driven than they have been. Why is this so?

15 In what ways do you think information technology will impact on marketing in the next three years?

SUMMARY

Although many factors contribute to business success, today's successful organisations share a strong customer focus and a heavy commitment to marketing. The goals of modern marketing are to attract new customers by promising superior value, and to keep current customers by delivering satisfaction. Sound marketing is critical to the success of all organisations, whether large or small, for-profit or non-profit, domestic or global.

Many people think of marketing as only selling or advertising. But, in fact, marketing occurs both before and after the selling event. *Marketing* combines many activities—market research, product development, distribution, pricing, advertising, personal selling and others—designed to sense, serve and satisfy consumer needs while meeting the organisation's goals.

Marketing is a social and managerial process by which individuals and groups obtain what they need and want through creating and exchanging products and value with others. The core concepts of marketing are *needs, wants and demands; products; value, satisfaction and quality; exchange, transactions* and *relationships;* and *markets.*

Marketing management is the analysis, planning, implementation and control of programs designed to create, build and maintain beneficial exchanges with target markets in order to achieve organisational objectives. Marketers must be good at managing the level, timing and composition of *demand.* Managing demand means managing relationships with customers. This involves both attracting new customers and retaining current ones. Recently, marketing managers have been shifting their emphasis towards building profitable, long-term relationships with important customers.

Marketing management can be guided by five different philosophies. The *production concept* holds that consumers favour products that are available at low cost and that management's task is to improve production efficiency and bring down prices. The *product concept* holds that consumers favour quality products and that little promotional effort is thus required. The *selling concept* holds that consumers will not buy enough of the company's products unless stimulated through heavy selling and promotion. The *marketing concept* holds that a marketing organisation gains competitive advantage by understanding the needs and wants of a well-defined target market and doing a superior job of delivering the desired satisfactions. The *societal marketing concept* holds that the marketing organisation should generate customer satisfaction and long-run societal wellbeing as the key to achieving both its goals and its responsibilities.

Marketing operates within a dynamic global environment. Rapid changes can quickly make yesterday's winning strategies obsolete. Marketers will face many new challenges and opportunities in the twenty-first century and leading the way will be electronic marketing. Today's companies are wrestling with the growth of non-profit marketing, increased global competition, a sluggish world economy, a call for greater social responsibility and a host of other economic, political and social challenges. There is also the call by corporate management for marketers to be more accountable for the use of marketing resources and value and profit they return to the business. However, these challenges also offer marketing opportunities. To be successful in the twenty-first century companies will have to be strongly market focused.

MARKETING ISSUE

The marketing concept is a compelling philosophy but there is evidence to show that many companies and business units within corporations do not have a strong market orientation.[27] Why? In part the answer lies in the fact that businesses are driven by many forces such as technological change and stakeholders such as investment analysts and shareholders that favour short-term returns which often take the focus away from customers and the investment required to build longer-term customer value. Very frequently market orientation is inhibited by a lack of marketing knowledge within the marketing group, limited tools and market research to assist an effective customer focus, lack of systematic marketing processes that a disciplined market-oriented approach to business

requires or lack of marketing leadership. If many or all of these conditions exist a company will require a marketing transformation involving restructuring and rebuilding the culture and processes with a market orientation. An example of a company which underook this transformation process in 2006 is Telstra. This involved a massive effort to restructure the marketing function and the business around customer segments, substantial marketing training and process development to build the marketing capability necessary to meet the challenges of a fast-changing and highly competitive industry. As a marketer or student of marketing consider what the challenges might be to strengthen the market orientation of a company with which you are familiar.

KEY TERMS

customer satisfaction	10	marketing	7	relationship marketing	11
customer value	9	marketing concept	20	selling concept	20
demands	8	marketing management	16	societal marketing concept	21
demarketing	16	needs	7	total quality management (TQM)	10
exchange	10	product	9	transaction	11
market	11	product concept	19	wants	7
market orientation	29	production concept	19		

DISCUSSING THE ISSUES

1 Many companies believe they have adopted marketing when they invest heavily in advertising and selling. Explain what a company must focus on to adopt the marketing philosophy fully.

2 Marketing management's main task is to manage demand. Give examples of different types of demand that need to be managed with reference to specific industries or markets.

3 Are large organisations adopting the societal marketing concept? Give examples of how some firms are doing this.

4 Information technology and electronic marketing require changes to the way in which marketing is implemented. Describe how these changes are affecting marketing by the banking and financial services industry.

5 Globalisation is bringing new demands on the marketing approaches of many companies. What factors should companies look at when they are being affected by this force?

6 Marketers are becoming more accountable for the resources they use to deliver value to customers. What new skills do you think marketers need to be effective in this new environment?

REFERENCES

1. Philip Kotler, *Kotler on Marketing: How to Create, Win and Dominate Markets*, New York, The Free Press, 1999, pp. 140–61; for an interesting review of the growth and influence of Google see David A. Vise, *The Google Story*, New York, Bantam Dell, 2005; also a practical overview of marketing is found in Philip Kotler, *According to Kotler*, New York, AMACOM, 2005, Chapter 1.
2. Peter F. Drucker, *Management: Tasks, Responsibilities, Practices*, New York, Harper & Row, 1973, pp. 64–65.
3. See Julie Macken, '20 Years On', *Australian Financial Review Magazine*, Summer 1996, pp. 6–11; Lucinda Schmidt, 'Partner Perfect', *Business Review Weekly*, 31 October–6 November 2002, pp. 66–68.
4. See P. Ranganath Nayak, Albert C. Chen and James F. Reider, 'Listening to Customers', *Prism*, Arthur D. Little, Inc., Second Quarter, 1993, pp. 43–57; Tim Biddlecombe, 'Research: Enter the Third Generation', *B&T Weekly*, 19 July 2002, p. 12.
5. See Theodore Levitt's classic article, 'Marketing Myopia', *Harvard Business Review*, July–August 1960, pp. 45–56.
6. See David Greising, 'Watch Out for Flying Packages', *Business Week*, 14 November 1994, p. 40; David Rocks, 'Going Nowhere Fast in Cyberspace', *Business Week*, Asian Edition, 31 January 2000, pp. 65–66; Amanda Gome, 'Fastway's Fast Fix', *Business Review Weekly*, 27 June–3 July 2002, p. 46; David Smedley, 'DHL Express Gives Imports the Finger', *B&T Weekly*, 7 June 2002, p. 5.
7. Lois Therrien, 'Motorola and NEC: Going for Glory', *Business Week*, special issue on quality, 1991, pp. 60–61.
8. Trevor Merriden, 'TNT Owners Look for Final Link', *Business Review Weekly*, 18 January 1999, pp. 46–47.
9. See Joan C. Szabo, 'Service = Survival', *Nation's Business*, March 1989, pp. 16–24; Kevin J. Clancy and Robert S. Shulman, 'Breaking the Mold', *Sales & Marketing Management*, January 1994, pp. 82–84.
10. Ralph Waldo Emerson offered this advice: 'If a man . . . makes a better mousetrap . . . the world will beat a path to his door'. Several companies, however, have built better mousetraps yet failed. One was a laser mousetrap costing $US1500. Contrary to popular assumptions, people do not automatically learn about new products, believe product claims or willingly pay higher prices.
11. Barry Farber and Joyce Wycoff, 'Customer Service: Evolution and Revolution', *Sales & Marketing Management*, May 1991, p. 47.
12. See Don E. Schultz, 'Traditional Marketers Have Become Obsolete', *Marketing News*, 6 June 1994, p. 11.
13. Howard Schlossberg, 'Customer Satisfaction: Not a Fad, but a Way of Life', *Marketing News*, 10 June 1991, p. 18. Also see Bernard J. Jaworski and Ajay K. Kohli, 'Market Orientation: Antecedents and Consequences', *Journal of Marketing*, July 1993, pp. 53–70.
14. Thomas E. Caruso, 'Kotler: Future Marketers Will Focus on Customer Data Base to Compete Globally', *Marketing News*, 8 June 1992, pp. 21–22.
15. Sunil Gupta and Donald R. Lehmann, *Managing Customers as Investments: The Strategic Value of Customers in the Long Run*, Upper Saddle River, NJ, Pearson Education Inc., publishing as Wharton School Publishing, 2005, Chapter 2, pp. 13–40.
16. An account of how companies need to balance both short-run demands and longer-term strategy is found in Michelle Hannen and Nicholas Way, 'Run the Risk: The Short-Term Demands of the Market Can Undermine a Company's Long-Term Strategy', *Business Review Weekly*, 25–31 July 2002, pp. 49–55.
17. See how these challenges are being addressed in the *Harvard Business Review*, Special issue, The Innovative Enterprise, August 2002.
18. For other examples, and for a good review of non-profit marketing, see Philip Kotler and Alan R. Andreasen, *Strategic Marketing for Nonprofit Organizations*, Englewood Cliffs, NJ, Prentice Hall, 1991.
19. See Cyndee Miller, 'Churches Turn to Research for Help in Saving New Souls', *Marketing News*, 11 April 1994, pp. 1, 2.
20. For more examples, see Philip Kotler and Karen Fox, *Strategic Marketing for Educational Institutions*, Englewood Cliffs, NJ, Prentice Hall, 1985; Bradley G. Morrison and Julie Gordon Dalgleish, *Waiting in the Wings: A Larger Audience for the Arts and How to Develop It*, New York, ACA Books, 1987; Norman Shawchuck, Philip Kotler, Bruce Wren and Gustave Rath, *Marketing for Congregations: Choosing to Serve People More Effectively*, Nashville, TN, Abingdon Press, 1993; and Cyndee Miller, 'Churches Turn to Research for Help in Saving New Souls', *Marketing News*, 11 April 1994, pp. 1, 2.
21. See Andy Reinhardt and Karim Djemi, 'Sony Ericsson: In Big Bloody Trouble', *Business Week*, 4 November 2002, pp. 50–51. For more on strategic alliances see Jordan D. Lewis, *Partnerships for Profit: Structuring and Managing Strategic Alliances*, New York, The Free Press, 1990; Peter Lorange and Johan Roos, *Strategic Alliances: Formation, Implementation, and Evolution*, Cambridge, MA, Blackwell Publishers, 1992; and Frederick E. Webster Jr, 'The Changing Role of Marketing in the Corporation', *Journal of Marketing*, October 1992, pp. 1–17.
22. For a thorough overview on the impacts of information technology on marketing see Rafi Mohammed, Robert Fisher, Bernard Jaworski and Aileen Cahill, *Internet Marketing: Building Advantage in a Networked Economy*, New York, McGraw-Hill/Irwin, 2002.
23. Editorial, *Time*, 23 December 2002, p. 6.
24. Robert Skeffington, 'How Company Boardrooms Are Changing', *Business Review Weekly*, 31 October–6 November 2002, pp. 58–62. See also Tim Ambler, *Marketing and the Bottom Line: The New Metrics of Corporate Wealth*, London, Financial Times Prentice Hall, 2000, Chapter 4.
25. Stanley Reed, Andy Reinhardt and Ariane Sains, 'Saving Ericsson', *Business Week*, 4 November 2002, pp. 48–52.
26. There are many books outlining the new marketing landscape. See Roger J. Best, *Market-Based Management*, 4th edn, New Jersey, Prentice Hall, 2006; see also Peter J. Rosenwald, *Accountable Marketing: The Economics of Data-Driven Marketing*, New York, Thomson Business and Professional Publishing, 2004; Roger Brooksbank, *Hot Marketing, Cool Profits*, Sydney, McGraw-Hill, 2002; Gary Hamel, *Leading the Revolution*, Boston, MA, Harvard Business School Press, 2000; and Deidre Breakenridge, *Cyberbranding: Brand Building in the Digital Economy*, London, Financial Times Prentice Hall, 2001.
27. The Marketing Excellence Survey is a large commercial database measuring marketing attitudes and marketing knowledge. Analysis of its database shows that marketing attitudes (which reflect market orientation) are relatively weak in many organisations. See <www.mesurvey.com/mes_findings.html>.

PHOTO/AD CREDITS

Barry Duncan, General Manager Outback Queensland Tourism Authority and Dr Rebekah Bennett, Queensland University of Technology

CASE STUDY

The adoption of a marketing orientation by the Outback Queensland Tourism Authority

Introduction

The Outback Queensland Tourism Authority (OQTA) is the peak body responsible for the marketing, promotion and development of the tourism industry in Queensland's Outback, which covers some 48% of Queensland. The OQTA services 21 local government authorities and some 230 members, including tour operators, attractions, accommodation and transport providers.

Over a period of four years (1999 to 2003), visitation to Queensland's Outback had declined by 5%. Table 1 shows the source of visitors in 2002. In 2004 the new general manager identified the need to adopt a marketing orientation for the organisation if they were to achieve the goals set.

The goals of OQTA are to:

- Increase total visitation.
- Increase yield to operators. This means focusing on the segments that spend more money during their stay.
- Expand the range of options for visitors to experience in Queensland's Outback, thus making the destination more attractive to visitors.
- Enhance existing tourism product offerings in all locations to ensure applicability to a broader spectrum of visitors.

Marketing activity prior to 2004

Before 2004, while the organisation undertook marketing activities it did not have a fully-embedded marketing orientation. This was as a result of the organisation having undergone a significant restructuring in 2001–2002. As a non-profit organisation the funds were not necessarily available at the time to develop a comprehensive marketing orientation.

Therefore, promotional activity conducted by the OQTA was piecemeal and did not accurately overcome consumer misperceptions about the region. There was inconsistent message delivery with a mass-market approach being used with little segmentation and targeted communication. The approach to marketing Queensland's Outback was heavily focused on mass communication rather than utilising a range of marketing elements. An example of this was the regular airing of brand-building advertising on television and in newspapers.

Marketing activity after 2004

One of the ways the new general manager implemented a marketing orientation was through the segmentation of the market for Outback Queensland. While Queensland's Outback and the attractions that it has to offer had been involved in tourism for a number of years it was not widely recognised as a major tourist destination and would not have been considered even an emerging market. Visitation had primarily been focused on the traditional long-haul grey nomad market during the peak season of May to September with most visitors coming from within Queensland (intrastate) (refer to Figure 1).

However, the amount of money spent per day (yield) by the intrastate segment was less than the amount spent by interstate and international

TABLE 1 Leisure visitors to Outback Queensland				
Year	Number of visitors	Intrastate	Interstate	International
2002	185 000	49%	38%	13%

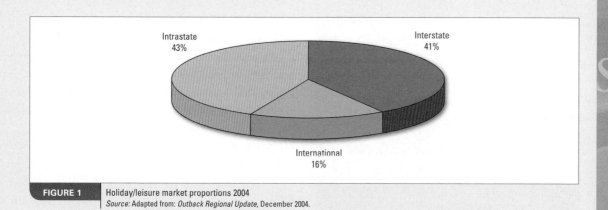

FIGURE 1 Holiday/leisure market proportions 2004
Source: Adapted from: *Outback Regional Update*, December 2004.

visitors. To increase the yield, the OQTA needed to increase the proportion of visitors from these high-yield segments. The grey nomad market, while the traditional market for Queensland's Outback, had a low average yield of between $20 to $30 per person per night compared to markets of couples 45 years and over and young families with children who spent considerably higher amounts per day. In particular, the OQTA wanted to attract high-yield markets and has incorporated the use of younger talent in the promotional material.

Thus as a result of segmenting the market, the communication elements used were more targeted to each group. Television ads were no longer a one-off brand exercise; rather they used a drip-feed frequency that was linked to other marketing activities. A specific campaign was developed aimed at showing people, particularly those from interstate and overseas, the distinct difference of a visit to Queensland's Outback.

The Check Out Queensland's Backyard campaign highlights the diversity of the region—identifying the key reasons visitors should undertake a holiday in Queensland's Outback. The campaign utilises strong images that give visitors a sense of what to experience—the wide open spaces, camping. It also teases them with some of the unexpected—dinosaurs, gorge landscapes with crystal clear water.

The campaign aims to entice a younger market to visit the region through the use of younger talent—there is a suggestion, but no confirmation, that this couple may or may not

have a family—thus attracting the interest of both the family market and couples.

Another aspect of implementing a marketing orientation was the development of alliances with complementary partners to create synergy and increase recall of messages. One of these was with Queensland Rail. Queensland Rail operates three passenger services to Queensland's Outback and the Check Out Queensland's Backyard campaign provided them with the opportunity to ensure the rail component was seen as part of an overall holiday experience rather than simply being a form of transport. Queensland Rail produced advertising to link to the campaign specifics and purchased media in conjunction with the OQTA's buy.

Finally, the communications were made consistent in the messages, the livery and the delivery. Everything from print advertisements to brochures were redesigned to reflect the colours of the outback, the logo of the OQTA, the campaign slogan 'Check out Queensland's backyard' and the people looking over their back fence at one of a series of images of the Outback (see Figure 2 overleaf).

Outcomes of a marketing orientation

One of the changes implemented by the new general manager was the inclusion of marketing metrics. Every aspect of marketing activity was linked to responses and measurable outcomes. For instance, all advertising included a specific URL, <www.adventureoutback.com.au>, allowing

FIGURE 2 OQTA advertising with Queensland's backyard positioning

the OQTA to track visitors to the website and to link this to the placement of advertising in accordance with postcodes. Follow-up marketing activities utilised this information to ensure that timing and activities were more targeted.

The result of this focus on marketing metrics are outcomes that indicate the goals set for 2004–07 are on track and likely to be achieved (refer to Table 2). To date there has been a 21% increase in visitor numbers, which is double the goal.

TABLE 2 Goals, strategy and progress 2004–07

Goal	Goal 2004–07	Strategy	Progress to date
Visitor numbers	Increase total visitor numbers by 10.81%	Targeted marketing activities; strong and consistent market presence	Based on the NVS and IVS statistics, year ended September 2005 saw a 21% increase in visitor numbers over same time in 2004
Yield	Decrease market share of intrastate visitors from 49% to 45%	Maintain traditional markets and grow high-yield markets through more targeted marketing activities—for example, 4X4 market; New Zealand; recreational fishers; educational groups	Increased visitor numbers from New Zealand; 4X4 campaign and activity undertaken; new market segment activities being developed
	Decrease market share of interstate visitors from 38% to 35%		
	Increase market share of international visitors from 13% to 20%		

QUESTIONS

1 Why is a marketing approach useful for non-profit and government organisations?

2 Explain the difference between a marketing orientation and a production orientation using the OQTA as an example.

3 Many visitors to Queensland's Outback are interested in experiencing local characters and life as it is for people who live in local communities. What can the OQTA do to satisfy this need?

4 Why is it necessary for an organisation like the OQTA to utilise marketing metrics when implementing a campaign like Check Out Queensland's Backyard?

5 How can a change in market segmentation provide a boost to the overall tourism industry in a location like Queensland's Outback?

CASE STUDY

CHAPTER 2

Customer retention and business profits

British Airways: www.britishairways.com

Coles Myer: www.colesmyer.com

FedEx: www.fedex.com

Holden: www.holden.com.au

Huawei: huawei.com

ING DIRECT: www.ing.com.au

Noni B: www.nonib.com.au

Wal-Mart: www.walmart.com

Zara: www.zara.com

How do you choose a credit card? Do you still have the first one that was offered to you? Have you taken out a new credit card because a company offered you what looked like at attractive deal? And if, like most people, you have several credit cards, which do you use most? Your answers, and the answers of other customers, are critical for the banks, retailers and credit card companies, which are generating increasing profits from credit cards as consumers pay more and more with credit cards. In response, credit card providers are trying hard to win new customers, offering deals such as low interest rates, discounts at selected outlets and loyalty programs. In the highly competitive Hong Kong market, it's not unusual for consumers to be given gifts such as a free CD or MP3 player when they take out a credit card. Consumers are responding to attractive offers like these by taking out more and more cards, with credit card applications up around 30% in late 2005 compared to the previous quarter. But it's expensive and inefficient for the company if the consumer takes the card and the gift, but then doesn't use the credit card. So companies aim to get more customers, but also to get those customers to use the card more—to increase what's called their 'share of wallet' with a customer.

In an effort to increase usage, most credit card companies offer some form of loyalty program, and there is no doubt that these are attractive to consumers. After all, wouldn't we all prefer to get some form of reward when we pay with a credit card? But for companies, a loyalty program is only useful if it generates additional revenue, over and above the cost of the program, and loyalty programs are expensive to run. So the success of a loyalty program shouldn't be assessed by the number of customers who join, but by whether the loyalty program contributes to increased profits.

For customers too, despite their apparent attractiveness, loyalty programs often come at a price. Financial analysts warn that consumers who don't pay off their balance in time should be looking for cards with low interest rates, rather than cards with attractive programs. Many cards with loyalty programs also charge an annual fee, and for customers it doesn't make sense to pay a fee to collect points if they don't get that value out of the card each year.

Most customers love loyalty programs because they give them a bonus, but the real test of a loyalty program is if it leads to higher profits.

But do customers choose credit cards (or other products) 'rationally' by weighing up what they get for what they pay, and choosing the best product for their needs? Or are some of us swayed to make emotional decisions based on attractive rewards, without really evaluating the downside of our choices? In this chapter we will examine the factors influencing consumer choices, and discuss how marketers aim to understand customers' decision processes, so they can alter their marketing actions to influence customers to buy more regularly.

Sources: Miriam, Hechtman, 'Cardholders Urged to Find Out What's in Store', *The Australian Financial Review,* 6 October, 2005, Special report, p. 12; Tracy Lee, 'Harvey Credit Card on the Way', *The Australian Financial Review,* 19 October, 2005, p. 18; Joyce Moullakis, 'Diminishing Rewards for Card Users', *The Australian Financial Review,* 5 October, 2005, p. 52.

After reading this chapter you should be able to:

1. Define customer value, customer satisfaction and customer retention.

2. Explain why relationships matter in marketing.

3. Explain how marketing organisations retain customers by engendering trust and commitment and totally satisfying them through delivering superior value.

4. Explain the importance of customer orientation in people and processes, including the place of internal marketing and employee retention.

5. Discuss the implementation of quality marketing.

Whether we think about individual customers buying products or services for themselves, or business buyers purchasing for other people, *marketing is a people business*. Customers and marketers are bound together in any service delivery encounter, and each interaction between the two plays a part in determining whether or not the customer is satisfied and remains loyal to the marketer. Jan Carlzon, the former CEO of SAS airlines, responsible for returning the airline to profitability in the 1980s, famously described the importance of each interaction between the customer and the company as a 'moment of truth'.[1] Each contact may be brief (Carlzon estimated that a typical interaction with a customer at SAS lasted around 15 seconds) but he argued that every customer interaction was important, because every interaction will contribute to the customer's assessment of, and attitude towards, the brand. Each interaction, therefore, offers the opportunity to make a customer more loyal, but also offers the threat of dissatisfying the customer, and threatening their future loyalty. So marketing management must consider every interaction, but must also look beyond single transactions and consider how the organisation offers superior *value to the customer* over a period of time, while ensuring that the organisation also *receives a return on its marketing investment* over the *lifetime of its relationship* with each customer.

A number of factors will influence customer loyalty: the value they perceive that they receive from the organisation's offering, their satisfaction with any previous experience and, in some circumstances, their trust in, and relationship with, the selling organisation. This chapter begins by discussing customer value and satisfaction, and then moves on to examine the role of trust and commitment in commercial relationships. The chapter addresses a number of important questions: When are customers satisfied? How do customer perceptions of value and satisfaction influence their purchase intentions? Why do relationships matter in business? Do the customers that the marketer retains the longest provide the greatest profits and lifetime value for the marketing organisation? How do learning organisations organise themselves and their people to deliver high value and satisfaction? How can marketers keep current customers as well as gain new ones?

ING DIRECT offers attractive promotions to acquire new customers.

Customer value and satisfaction

More than 35 years ago management author Peter Drucker observed that a marketing organisation's first task is 'to create customers'. However, 'creating' or attracting customers can be a difficult task, and entails costs in acquiring the customer (such as advertising to get their attention, perhaps special offers to engender interest and sometimes set-up costs in opening a customer account to manage and track purchases). For example, ING DIRECT has sometimes offered promotions where the bank pays customers to open an account. Such short-term costs to acquire customers will only be worthwhile if the customer stays with the company long enough to repay the cost of attracting them, and to contribute to company profits. However, retaining profitable customers is often difficult. Today's customers face a vast array of product and brand choices, prices and suppliers. Every marketing organisation must answer a key question: How do customers make their choices?

One answer is that customers will choose the marketing offer that they believe gives them the most value. Economists express this idea by saying that customers are *value maximisers*. This doesn't mean that customers will always select the product or service which will actually provide them with the highest value, because they usually have limited information. If the decision is important enough, the customer might seek more information in order to make a better decision. Ultimately, however, the customer will make the decision which seems to offer them the best options, given their limited knowledge, mobility and income. They form expectations of the value that they expect to get from different possible purchases, and act upon these expectations. After purchasing, the customer is likely to make some assessment of the value they think they received from the product or service, and this judgment will influence their satisfaction and repurchase behaviour.

Customer value

We introduced the idea of customer delivered value in Chapter 1; given free choice, customers will choose to buy from a firm which they believe offers them the highest delivered value. However, what's important may be very different for different customers, and sometimes a company will provide features that a particular customer doesn't value at all. So when customers decide on the value they get from a particular product or service, they will only factor in those features of the product or service which are important to them.

Consider the teenager who is buying an iPod music player. Some expert reviews have suggested that other competing MP3 players offer better value than the iPod, because they are cheaper, have replaceable batteries and offer features that the iPod doesn't, such as an FM radio. However, the teenager might still prefer the iPod, because the brand is seen as more fashionable than its competitors and iPod dominates the market, with about 60% of sales, well ahead of Creative in second place.[2] Understanding the importance of customer value with regard to the iPod brand is important for its seller, Apple, and also for competitors like Creative. Apple knows that if the teenager values the iPod brand it can charge a premium over other MP3 players. But if Apple charges too much the teenager might decide that the high price of the iPod can't be justified and that a competing MP3 player offers better value. Understanding the teenager's value assessment also tells Creative and other competitors that they are unlikely to be able to sell their product to brand-conscious buyers unless they increase the value of the product (for example, by convincing customers to value their features or by making the brand fashionable) or decrease the price, so the lower price compensates for the perceived lower value of the brand.

Just as customers will choose to buy products which they think provide greater value, so their perceptions of the value of the product or service will influence whether they buy it again next time they have a need. So a customer's perception of the value provided by a product is a strong predictor of purchase. Once they have experience with the product any future choice will be influenced by that experience, and an important part of that experience is their satisfaction with the product.

Customer satisfaction

Once a customer has experience with a product, they will make judgments based on that experience. **Customer satisfaction** is the customer's conscious evaluation of a product or service feature, or of the product or service itself.[3] Customers will form this judgment based on what they have experienced from the company and its competitors in the past, what they think is fair value and what they actually want.

It used to be said that customers were satisfied if a company performed as well as or better than the customer expected, but this isn't the full story. If a customer expects the product to be poor but chooses it anyway (perhaps because there is no other choice), the product may perform better than expected, but the customer may still be dissatisfied, thinking something like 'it was better than I expected, but it still wasn't very good!' Similarly, if a customer has bought from a company

Customer satisfaction
The extent to which a product's perceived performance matches a buyer's expectations. If the product's performance falls short of expectations the buyer is dissatisfied. If performance matches or exceeds expectations the buyer is satisfied or delighted.

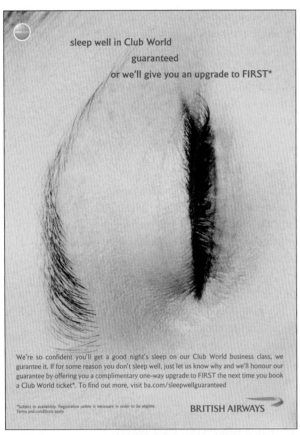

sleep well in Club World
guaranteed
or we'll give you an upgrade to FIRST*

We're so confident you'll get a good night's sleep on our Club World business class, we guarantee it. If for some reason you don't sleep well, just let us know why and we'll honour our guarantee by offering you a complimentary one-way upgrade to FIRST the next time you book a Club World ticket*. To find out more, visit ba.com/sleepwellguaranteed

*Subject to availability. Registration online is necessary in order to be eligible. Terms and conditions apply.

BRITISH AIRWAYS

If the customer can't judge quality, advertising can raise perceptions of quality.

many times in the past (such as a business buyer), they are likely to have very good knowledge of how the company and its products perform. Under these circumstances, it's very difficult to exceed the customer's expectations, but the customer can still be satisfied. If a customer has very high expectations, it's even possible for performance to fall short of those expectations and for the customer still to be satisfied: 'They weren't quite as good as I expected, but they were still very, very good!'

So what influences whether a customer is satisfied or not? Evidence suggests that customers' satisfaction judgments will be influenced by a number of factors. First and foremost, people will be influenced by how well they think the product or service performed. But how do people decide what's 'good', what's 'great' and what's 'bad' performance? It seems that people's satisfaction judgments will be influenced by a number of factors: the customer's past buying experiences (what they expect based on previous experience with the company and its competitors), the information and promises made by marketing organisations and their competitors (what they expect the product or service should provide), and what customers think is fair value based on the price they paid (what the product or service 'should' provide for the cost).[4] However, sometimes customers can't easily evaluate quality themselves. For example, when you use the services of a professional like a dentist or a financial planner, it's difficult for the average customer to judge the quality of the service they receive. When it's hard for customers to judge quality, there is evidence that customers tend to rate the quality higher and will tend to be more satisfied.[5] We also know that advertising can influence customer's perceptions of quality and their satisfaction. So some of today's most successful marketing organisations are raising expectations—and delivering performance to match. These marketers embrace total customer satisfaction. For example, Honda claims, 'One reason our customers are so satisfied is that we aren't'. And British Airways advertises that you will 'sleep well in Club World—guaranteed'.

Advertising like this suggests to the customer that a brand is high quality, and if the customer finds it hard to judge the quality themselves, there is evidence that they are likely to judge a more heavily advertised brand as higher quality.[6] However, marketers must be careful not to create unreasonable expectations by customers, or to draw attention to areas where they don't perform well. Some years ago, ANZ bank offered to pay $5 to any customer who had to wait more than five minutes in line for service in the bank. The result was that many customers waiting in line looked at their watches, and suddenly paid much more attention to how long they were waiting. Even customers who didn't wait five minutes became less satisfied with their waiting time, because it was suddenly more obvious to them. At the same time, another bank found out through its research that while many customers said they didn't mind waiting in line for a short time, one of the things that really annoyed them was seeing staff behind the counter doing something, but not serving customers, while there was a long line of customers. These staff were working (performing operational tasks) but the value of this work wasn't obvious to the customers waiting in line. So the bank reorganised its branches so that staff who weren't serving customers worked in an area not visible to customers. Customer satisfaction increased, although the waiting time was unchanged, because customers couldn't see staff who were apparently ignoring the lines of customers. Similarly, many professional service firms have realised that clients are much less annoyed by waiting if the dentist, doctor or accountant is running late as long as there is something to keep the customer occupied—a range of up-to-date magazines to read and/or toys for children to play with.

So while actual performance (such as waiting time) is obviously important in predicting whether customers will repurchase, customer perceptions of the performance, and satisfaction with that performance, are critical. If a customer is dissatisfied, and they have a choice, then they are more likely to switch to a competitor. However, satisfaction alone isn't enough to ensure repurchase. For example, in the automobile industry 85–95% of customers report that they are satisfied, but only 30–40% re-buy the previous make or model.[7] Another study by the US telecommunications giant AT&T showed that 70% of customers who say they are satisfied with a product or service would still be willing to switch to a competitor.[8]

Customer-centred companies, those that focus on customer outcomes when designing their strategies, strive to achieve both customer satisfaction and customer loyalty. The aim of such customer-centred organisations is to add more value to the core product to improve customer satisfaction, and so strengthen the customer's bond with the company, and thus increase customer loyalty.[9] These and other companies realise that highly satisfied customers produce several benefits for the marketing organisation. They remain customers for a longer period, and they can be less price sensitive. They tend to buy additional products over time as the marketing organisation introduces related products or improvements. Moreover, they are more likely to talk favourably to others about the marketing organisation and its products.[10]

Today's winning companies track customers' perceptions of their performance so they can find out what they are doing well, and where they may be falling behind competitors. Ideally, satisfaction measures are tracked over time to benchmark performance, and to give an early warning of problems. However, customer satisfaction measures can provide false assurance to a company if the measures don't collect information about competitors. For example, a company might be very happy to find that 80% of its customers say they are satisfied with its products. However, if a competitor is achieving 90% customer satisfaction and aiming for 95%, the company might find that it is losing customers to the competitor. Thus, companies must monitor both their own and competitors' customer satisfaction performance. Marketing Highlight 2.1 describes the ways in which companies can track customer satisfaction and loyalty.

Although the customer-centred firm seeks to deliver high customer satisfaction relative to competitors, it does not attempt to maximise customer satisfaction. A marketing organisation might be able to increase customer satisfaction by lowering its price or increasing its services, but this may result in lower profits. In addition to customers, the marketing organisation has many stakeholders or customers, including employees, dealers, suppliers and shareholders. Spending more to increase customer satisfaction might divert funds from increasing the satisfaction of these other stakeholders. Thus, the purpose of marketing is to generate customer value *profitably*. Ultimately, the marketing organisation must strive to deliver a high level of customer satisfaction while at the same time delivering at least acceptable levels of satisfaction to the firm's other stakeholders.

Customer-centred company A company that focuses on customer developments in designing its marketing strategies.

MARKETING 2.1 HIGHLIGHT

Measuring customer satisfaction and loyalty

Tools for assessing, measuring and tracking customer satisfaction and loyalty are continually increasing in sophistication. Here, we examine a number of methods that marketing organisations are using to see whether or not their customers are satisfied and, more importantly, to assess if they will repurchase or recommend the company.

Customer satisfaction and loyalty surveys

Most large companies measure satisfaction and customer loyalty in some way, and one study in 1993 reported that post-purchase research of customers (largely involving customer satisfaction measurement) accounted for one-third of the revenues received by the largest US research firms.[11] Even from this high base, satisfaction research was continuing to increase through the late 1990s.[12] According to the former CEO of Hewlett-Packard, John Young, nine out of ten customers in HP surveys who rank themselves as highly satisfied say they would definitely or probably buy from HP again. Satisfaction research is clearly seen as important by many large organisations, but what are the best things to measure?

A marketing organisation can assess customer satisfaction and loyalty in a number of ways. It can measure overall satisfaction by asking: 'How satisfied are you with this product?' It can measure satisfaction with different attributes (or features) of the service to work out what customers are most satisfied with, and what areas might need attention. For example, car companies typically assess the satisfaction of new car buyers with different features of the purchase process, such as the car's comfort and accessories, the performance of the sales staff and the dealership. See Figure 1 for an extract from a survey of new car buyers.

Effective surveys don't just measure satisfaction because, as we have seen, satisfaction isn't always a good predictor of repurchase, so companies often measure the customer's *repurchase intention* and *willingness to recommend* the marketing organisation and brand to other people. These measures are usually high if satisfaction is high, and are better predictors than satisfaction of repurchase. One large research study across a range of industries showed that the best predictor of a company's growth was customers' answers to the question: 'How likely is it that you would recommend [company x] to a friend or colleague?'[13]

A good satisfaction and loyalty survey will finish by asking respondents if they have any general comments, in order to identify and rectify problems which aren't covered in the rest of the survey, and also to provide customers with the chance to make suggestions.

Complaint and suggestion systems

A customer-centred organisation makes it easy for customers to make suggestions or complaints, so that problems can be identified and hopefully prevented from happening in the future. Hence restaurants and hotels provide forms on which customers can report problems or complaints, and make suggestions for improvements. Some companies set up customer hotlines with toll-free numbers to make it easy for customers to inquire, suggest or complain. Such systems help companies to act more quickly to resolve problems. However, providing a complaints system will create customer expectations of a response; if a customer writes a complaint letter to a company and gets no response, studies suggest that the customer will be less happy than if they had never complained. So if a company can't respond appropriately to complaints and suggestions, it may be better not to encourage them.

While a complaint system can be helpful in allowing an organisation to identify and respond to dissatisfied customers, the absence of complaints doesn't mean that some customers aren't dissatisfied. Studies show that around one in every four purchases results in customer dissatisfaction, but that less than 5% of dissatisfied customers bother to complain—most

How satisfied were you with: *(Please tick whichever box applies)*	Very dissatisfied		Neither satisfied or dissatisfied		Very satisfied
The range of accessories available........................	☐	☐	☐	☐	☐
The ability of the sales staff to explain the accessories available........................	☐	☐	☐	☐	☐

How satisfied were you with the following aspects of the vehicle's delivery?: *(Please tick whichever box applies)*	Very dissatisfied		Neither satisfied or dissatisfied		Very satisfied
Cleanliness and presentation of the vehicle........................	☐	☐	☐	☐	☐
Working order of the vehicle........................	☐	☐	☐	☐	☐
The delivery time from placing your order........................	☐	☐	☐	☐	☐

How satisfied were you with: *(Please tick whichever box applies)*	Very dissatisfied		Neither satisfied or dissatisfied		Very satisfied
The dealership you purchased the vehicle from........................	☐	☐	☐	☐	☐
The salesperson you dealt with........................	☐	☐	☐	☐	☐
The vehicle........................	☐	☐	☐	☐	☐
Your overall purchase experience........................	☐	☐	☐	☐	☐

FIGURE 1 | Extract from a new car buyer satisfaction survey. An effective satisfaction survey will allow the company to assess overall customer satisfaction, and also satisfaction with different features of the product

customers simply switch suppliers. So the most customer-focused organisations monitor their complaints, but also carefully track customer satisfaction and willingness to recommend. They also make every attempt to understand a typical customer experience—sometimes by using mystery shopping.

Mystery shopping and customer interviews

Another way of assessing factors that can result in customer dissatisfaction is to use people to pose as buyers and report their experiences in buying the marketing organisation's and competitors' products. Mystery shoppers are used by retailers like David Jones and banks, and by fast-food chains like McDonald's. These mystery shoppers can even present specific problems to test whether the marketing organisation's personnel handle difficult situations well. For example, mystery shoppers can complain about a restaurant's food to see how the restaurant handles this complaint. Staff themselves can be a valuable source of information on the customer experience. Frontline staff who deal with customers all the time are often more aware of customer problems than senior managers, who are often less closely involved with customers. As a result, some customer-centred organisations insist that all managers spend some time each month directly involved with customers—on the road with salespeople, listening in on customer complaint lines or serving behind counters. Customer contact like this can make managers acutely aware of the problems faced by customers, and by the staff who have to deal with them. Such customer contact can be valuable at every level of the organisation: the Chinese networking and telecommunications company Huawei Technologies advertises that its CEO spends up to 70% of his time listening to customers. Such a customer-focused strategy has enabled Huawei to become one of the top 10 Chinese brands, according to the *Financial Times* 2005 ratings.[14]

Lost customer analysis

Many companies conduct exit interviews with customers who have stopped buying or who have switched to a competitor, to learn why this happened. For example, when IBM loses a customer it mounts a thorough effort to learn how it failed: Was IBM's price too high, its service poor or its products substandard? Not only should the marketing

organisation conduct such *exit interviews*, it should also monitor the *customer loss rate*. A rising loss rate indicates that the marketing organisation is failing to satisfy its customers. Finding out what those who have stopped buying think and feel is often the key to best practice in service delivery, and can provide an early warning of problems.

When customers stop buying, however, it is often too late to do anything to win their business back. The best organisations track possible customer defections and do something before the customer stops buying altogether. For example a changed spending pattern can be an early indicator that a customer is thinking about leaving, and contacting these customers, identifying their concerns and doing something *before* they leave is far more effective than trying to win back their custom after they have switched to a competitor.

Some cautions in measuring customer satisfaction

Customer satisfaction ratings are sometimes difficult to interpret. When customers rate their satisfaction with some element of the marketing organisation's performance, such as delivery, they can vary greatly in how they define good delivery. It might mean early delivery, on-time delivery, order completeness or something else. Yet if the marketing organisation tried to define every element in detail, customers would face a huge questionnaire and most wouldn't bother to fill it in. A good customer survey therefore needs to strike a balance by collecting useful information, without being so long that customers won't want to take the time to fill in the survey.

Satisfaction ratings also don't always reveal the full picture, especially if staff are evaluated according to customer satisfaction ratings. This can encourage people to try and manipulate their ratings on customer satisfaction, by being especially nice to customers just before the survey or by trying to exclude unhappy customers from the survey. So if it is trying to measure satisfaction and loyalty, the organisation needs to make every effort to ensure that the method used is appropriate for its aims.

Huawei uses road shows to display its new products to customers, like this event in Malaysia promoting its new 3G phones.

Questions

1 Management at a major Cairns hotel wants to measure customer satisfaction. It feels that it needs to measure satisfaction levels with the processes customers experience and with the staff. Detail how it might approach such a study.

2 A mobile telephone company wants to find out why it has such a high 'churn' rate. That is, customers are turning to other service providers at the end of their contract rate period. How might the company find out why this is happening?

3 If a study undertaken for the telephone company in Question 2 establishes that existing customers are satisfied, why might others be defecting?

SELF-CHECK QUESTIONS

1 Jane Smith, a marketing manager, starts work as a pharmaceutical company sales manager. Customer satisfaction by specialist doctors with the service of the representatives averages 4.2 on a five-point scale, with 60% of doctors rating themselves at 5 out of 5 (very satisfied). Jane used to work at another company, which sold specialist software to business customers. She knows that the customer satisfaction at that company was 4.6 on a similar five-point scale, with 80% of customers rating themselves at 5 out of 5 (very satisfied). What conclusions (if any) can Jane draw about customer satisfaction at the two companies?

2 Is it appropriate for a private hospital to establish that it has lifted satisfaction levels among those who have had surgery from 65% to 85%? Discuss the meaning of this question, and its implications from a marketing standpoint. Also discuss the question with reference to a well-known brand of breakfast cereal, an international airline and a Ford truck.

Retaining customers

Totally satisfied customers are more likely to be loyal customers.[15] However, the relationship between customer satisfaction and loyalty varies greatly across industries and competitive situations. Satisfaction alone isn't enough to achieve loyalty, and companies which aim for satisfaction without also pursuing loyalty have been said to fall into a 'satisfaction trap'.[16] Many markets have settled into maturity, and there are not many new customers entering most categories. Competition is increasing and the costs of attracting new customers are rising, because it takes a great deal of effort and spending to coax satisfied customers away from competitors. In these markets, it might cost five times as much to attract a new customer as to keep a current customer happy.[17]

Unfortunately, classic marketing theory and practice have for too long focused on attracting new customers, rather than on retaining the most valuable existing customers. This has been called the 'leaky bucket' approach to marketing; just as a bucket with holes constantly loses water and needs to be refilled, so some organisations have accepted that they will inevitably lose customers and have focused on winning new customers. In the twentieth century, when populations were expanding and economies and markets were rapidly growing, this strategy was successful for many organisations.

Today, however, successful marketers recognise the importance of retaining current customers. According to one report, by reducing customer defections by only 5%, companies can improve profits anywhere from 25% to 85%.[18] For example, one study of online customers found that repeat customers spent twice as much in months 24–30 of their relationships as they did in the first six months.[19] New customers, in contrast, cost more early in their relationship, due to the costs of setting up accounts and dealing with their more frequent inquiries. So for most organisations, it is far more efficient to retain current customers than to try and replace them with new customers. Unfortunately, however, many management and financial systems still fail to show the value of retained customers.

Thus, although for many years marketing practice has involved formulating marketing mixes that aimed to create sales and new customers, the reality is that a firm's first line of defence lies in customer retention. And the best approach to customer retention is to deliver high customer satisfaction and value that result in strong customer loyalty and well-developed business relationships.

Customer satisfaction and customer loyalty

Figure 2.1 shows the relationship between customer satisfaction and customer loyalty in five different markets. Not surprisingly, as satisfaction increases, so does loyalty. In highly competitive markets, such as those for cars and computers, there is surprisingly little difference between the loyalty of less satisfied customers and those who are merely satisfied. However, there is a great difference between the loyalty of *satisfied* customers and *completely satisfied* customers.

Even a slight drop from complete satisfaction can create an enormous drop in loyalty. For example, one study showed that completely satisfied customers are nearly 42% more likely to be loyal than merely satisfied customers. Xerox found that its totally satisfied customers are six times more likely to repurchase Xerox products over the next 18 months than its satisfied customers.[20] This means marketing organisations must aim high if they want to hold on to their customers. High customer satisfaction creates an emotional affinity for a product or service, not just a rational preference, and this creates high customer loyalty.

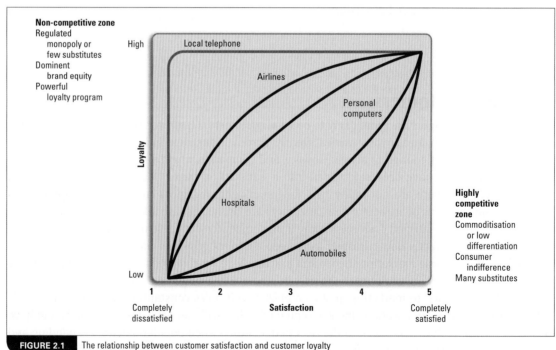

FIGURE 2.1 The relationship between customer satisfaction and customer loyalty

Source: Reprinted by permission of *Harvard Business Review*. From 'Why Satisfied Customers Defect', by Thomas O. Jones and W. Earl Sasser Jr, November–December 1995, p. 91. Copyright © 1995 by the President and Fellows of Harvard College; all rights reserved.

Under some circumstances, however, customer satisfaction is less important. Figure 2.1 shows that in non-competitive markets such as those served by regulated monopolists, or those dominated by powerful patent-protected brands, customers may be loyal no matter how dissatisfied they are. This might seem an ideal situation for the protected or dominant firm. However, such firms can pay a high price for customer dissatisfaction in the long run.

For example, during the 1960s and 1970s, Xerox flourished under the protection of patents on its revolutionary photocopy process. Customers had no choice but to remain loyal to Xerox, and sales and profits soared despite customer dissatisfaction over machine malfunctions and rising prices. In fact, customer dissatisfaction led to even greater short-term profits for Xerox as disgruntled customers were forced to pay for service when machines broke down. But in the 1980s, Xerox paid dearly for its failure to keep its customers satisfied. Japanese competitors skirted patents and brought higher-quality machines to market at lower prices. Dissatisfied customers gleefully defected to the new competitors. Xerox's share of the global copier market plunged from more than 80% to less than 35% in just five years.[21] Thus, even highly successful marketing organisations must pay close attention to customer satisfaction and its relationship with customer loyalty. Xerox has now developed industry-leading, customer-driven quality and customer satisfaction programs. As a result, although it has lost its dominance, it is once again a profitable industry leader.

Relationships in marketing

The importance of customer retention has led to an interest in what has come to be called relationship marketing—proactively creating, developing and maintaining committed, interactive and profitable exchanges with selected customers.[22] Relationship marketing involves a change in focus from the single sales encounter in an attempt to develop a relationship with the customer and to increase customer retention and concomitant growth for the businesses involved.[23] The marketing focus for many organisations has thus moved from attracting customers to retaining the most profitable customers. These profitable customers are often referred to as 'key customers' in consumer markets and 'key accounts' in business markets. The aim is to hold the loyalty of these key customers by totally satisfying them, thereby developing and maintaining their trust by convincing them that the vendor is reliable and has integrity.[24]

Not every customer wants a relationship with an organisation, however.[25] The shopper buying impulse lines typically has neither the time nor inclination to form such relationships with companies, their brands or the retailing intermediaries involved. The organisation needs to apply appropriate levels of customer relationship management in different circumstances.

Customer relationship management

Customer relationship management (CRM) is one of the most important concepts of modern marketing. Until recently, CRM has been defined narrowly as a customer data management activity. By this definition, it involves managing detailed information about individual customers and carefully managing customer 'touchpoints' in order to maximise customer loyalty.

More recently, however, customer relationship management has taken on a broader meaning. In this broader sense, **customer relationship management** is the overall process of building and maintaining profitable customer relationships by delivering superior customer value and satisfaction. It deals with all aspects of acquiring, keeping and growing customers. We will discuss CRM activity further in Chapter 18 when dealing with direct marketing.

Relationships defined There are a number of aspects of a commercial relationship that marketing management can and should focus on. Figure 2.2 (overleaf) presents seven key aspects of relationships, and words used by a number of authors that are aligned to each conceptual category.[26]

Customer relationship management The overall process of building and maintaining profitable customer relationships by delivering superior customer value and satisfaction.

Primary construct	(Other common constructs)
Creation	Attracting, establish, getting
Development	Enhancing, strengthening, enhance
Maintenance	Sustaining, stable, keeping
Interactive	Exchange, mutually, cooperative
Long term	Lasting, permanent, retaining
Emotional content	Commitment, trust, promises
Output	Profitable, rewarding, efficiency

FIGURE 2.2 Relationship constructs

Source: Michael J. Harker, 'Relationship Marketing Defined? An Examination of Current Relationship Marketing Definitions', *Marketing Intelligence and Planning*, vol. 17, no. 1, 1999, p. 14.

When considering relationships in marketing it is important to remember that not all customers have the same relational orientation.[27] A customer's willingness to provide information to, and receive information from, a company will depend partly on individual differences, but also on the importance of the product category for the customer.

The notion of relationship levels It is possible to identify five levels of relationships that can be formed with customers who have purchased a marketing organisation's product, such as a motor vehicle or a piece of industrial machinery:

1 *Basic:* The marketing organisation salesperson sells the product but does not follow up in any way.
2 *Reactive:* The salesperson sells the product and encourages the customer to call whenever they have any questions or problems.
3 *Accountable:* The salesperson phones the customer a short time after the sale to check whether the product is meeting the customer's expectations. The salesperson also solicits from the customer any product improvement suggestions and any specific disappointments. This information helps the marketing organisation to improve its offering continuously.
4 *Proactive:* The salesperson or others in the marketing organisation phone the customer from time to time with suggestions about improved product use or helpful new products.
5 *Partnership:* The marketing organisation works continuously with the customer and with other customers to discover ways to deliver better value.

Figure 2.3 shows that a marketing organisation's relationship marketing strategy will depend on how many customers it has and their individual profitability. For example, companies with many low-margin customers will practise basic marketing. Thus, H. J. Heinz will not phone all its baked beans buyers to express its appreciation for their business. At best, Heinz will be reactive by setting up a customer information service, with a toll-free telephone number. At the other extreme, in markets with few customers and high margins, most sellers will move toward partnership marketing. Boeing and Airbus Industries, for example, will work very closely with customers like Qantas and Singapore Airlines in designing their aeroplanes and ensuring that the planes fully satisfy the airlines' requirements. In between these two extremes, different levels of relationship marketing are appropriate; for example, banks will typically provide customised service, telephone priority and sometimes personal banking for their most valuable customers, and lower levels of service for less valuable customers.

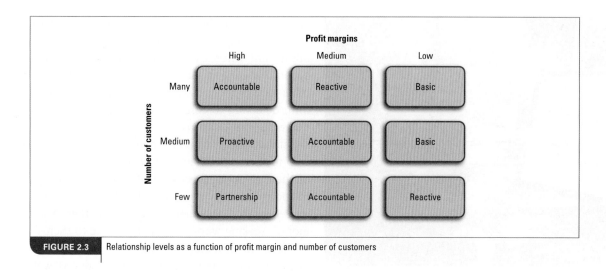

FIGURE 2.3   Relationship levels as a function of profit margin and number of customers

What specific marketing tools can a marketing organisation use to develop stronger customer bonding and satisfaction? It can adopt any of three customer-value-building approaches: financial, social or structural.[28]

Financial benefits The first value-building approach relies primarily on adding financial benefits to the customer relationship. For example, airlines offer frequent-flyer programs, hotels give room upgrades to frequent guests and supermarkets sometimes give discounts on less busy days. Loyalty programs such as Coles Myer Ltd's Fly Buys program encourage customers to sign up for the program in order to gain long-term rewards. In turn, the company obtains information about its customers' shopping habits, and has the opportunity to target customers with particular offers. Such programs are very expensive to run, however, and will only be beneficial to the company if they add value by encouraging customers to spend more. The loyalty program must provide greater revenue than the cost to run the program, and must also provide a better return than any other program that the company could have spent its money on.[29]

Social benefits Although loyalty programs and other financial incentives can build customer preference, they can usually be easily copied by competitors and may thus fail to differentiate the organisation's offer permanently. The second approach is to add social benefits as well as financial benefits. Here marketing organisation personnel work to increase their social bonds with customers by learning individual customers' needs and wants and then individualising and personalising their products and services. For example, employees of Ritz-Carlton hotels are trained to treat customers as individuals, not as nameless members of a mass market. Whenever possible, they refer to guests by name and give each guest a warm welcome. They record guest preferences in a customer database, accessible by all Ritz-Carlton hotels in the worldwide chain. A guest who requests a foam pillow at the Ritz-Carlton in Sydney is likely to be delighted to find one waiting in the room when they check into the Ritz-Carlton in Hong Kong a year later.[30]

Structural ties The third approach to building strong customer relationships is to add structural ties as well as financial and social benefits. For instance, a business marketer might supply customers with special equipment or computer linkages that help them manage their orders, payroll or inventory. For example, Sigma Corporation, a leading pharmaceutical wholesaler in Australia, has invested heavily in its online electronic system to help small pharmacies manage their inventory, their order

In a competitive environment, FedEx uses advanced software solutions to build strong customer relationships.

entry and their shelf space. FedEx uses its FedEx Ship Manager software solution to provide customers additional value by making label creation and account management faster and easier. This and other tools provided by FedEx help to avert customers from defecting to competitors like DHL and UPS. Customer firms can use their computers to check the status of their own deliveries or those that they ship to their customers and manage other aspects of their shipping process. To further enhance its relationships with customers, FedEx polls some of its FedEx Ship Manager software customers each month, seeking ways to improve service to them.[31]

Relationship marketing means that organisations must focus on managing their customers as well as their products. But companies do not want relationships with every customer, and some customers are undesirable because they are too difficult or too expensive to serve. Companies must judge which segments and which specific customers will be profitable.

Retention and customer profitability

Ultimately, marketing is the art of attracting and keeping profitable customers. However, companies often discover that between 20% and 40% of their customers do not represent profitable sales. Further, many companies report that their most profitable customers are not their largest customers, but their mid-size customers. The largest customers sometimes demand greater service and receive the deepest discounts, thereby reducing the marketing organisation's profit level. The smallest customers pay full price and receive less service, but the cost of transacting with small customers reduces their profitability. In many cases, mid-size customers who pay close to full price and receive good service are the most profitable.

A marketing organisation shouldn't necessarily try to pursue and satisfy every customer. However, although customers often make good suggestions, they also suggest actions that a marketing organisation cannot undertake profitably. A market focus means making disciplined choices about which customers to serve and which specific benefits to deliver or deny.[32] For example, if customers of discount airlines like Ryanair or Tiger Airways, which offer cheap flights and no-frills service and whose business design is based on low costs, start asking for frequent-flyer programs and exclusive 'Club' services such as those offered by higher-priced competitors, the no-frills airline should think very carefully. Providing such services will add to costs, and unless it results in substantial increases in revenue, money spent on these services might be better spent in other areas of the airline, or could be used to lower fares to attract more customers.

Measuring and managing return on marketing

Marketing managers must ensure that their marketing dollars are being well spent. In the past, many marketers spent freely on big advertising campaigns and other expensive marketing programs, sometimes without thinking carefully about the financial returns on their spending. But all that is changing. Given today's more competitive economy, marketers face growing pressures to show that they are adding value in line with their costs. Many companies now view marketing as an investment rather than an expense. They expect marketers to account for results, in terms of both market impact and profits. A 2004 US poll of marketing experts found that they thought that understanding marketing metrics and the return on marketing investment (ROMI) was one of the top priorities facing marketers.[33]

In response, marketers are developing better measures of *return on marketing investment*. **Return on marketing investment (ROMI or marketing ROI)** is the net return from a marketing investment divided by the costs of the marketing investment. See Marketing Highlight 2.2 for a discussion of how smart marketers are measuring their lifetime customer value, and managing different customers in different ways, according to that value.

Customer lifetime value

What makes a customer profitable? Marketers refer to *customer lifetime value* where the revenue from each customer (whether a personal or business customer) is calculated over the entire length of that relationship. **Customer lifetime value** is the amount by which revenues from a given customer over time exceed the marketing organisation's costs of attracting, selling to and servicing that customer. This definition emphasises lifetime revenues and costs, not profit from a single transaction.[34]

Understanding the lifetime value of customers is important, because it can help marketers to decide which customers are worth keeping. For example, a university student with a low bank balance may be a low-profit customer for the bank, just like a retired person with limited savings. Examining the profitability of both customer groups might suggest that the bank should increase its fees on the bank accounts of such low-profit customers, in order to increase the return on these customers. However, the potential lifetime value of the two groups is very different; the university students are likely to move on to higher paying positions, and may later become very profitable customers.

Understanding this fact has led marketers to consider the lifetime value of customers in developing marketing programs to attract and retain customers. It's sometimes suggested that long-term customers are more profitable, because they are said to be more loyal, less price sensitive and lower cost to serve. However, there is very little evidence to support these claims.[35] Even after graduation, the university student may remain a low-profit customer, paying off their credit cards on time to minimise interest charges, and going to a competitor for a lower mortgage rate. This reinforces the need for marketers to understand the lifetime customer value of different customer groups, rather than merely focusing on obtaining long-term customers.

In order to understand customer lifetime value better, companies should actively measure individual customer value and profitability. Figure 2.4 shows a useful type of profitability analysis.[36] Customers make up the columns of the figure and products or services make up the rows. Each cell contains a symbol for the profitability of selling a given product or service to a given customer. Customer C1 is very profitable—they buy three profit-making products, products P1, P2 and P3. Customer C2 yields mixed profitability, buying one profitable product and one unprofitable product. Customer C3 generates losses by purchasing one profitable product and two unprofitable ones ('loss leaders'). What can the company do about consumers like C3? First, the company should consider raising the prices of its less profitable products or eliminating them. Second, the company can try to cross-sell its profit-making products to its unprofitable customers. If these actions cause customers like C3 to defect, it may actually be beneficial for the company. In fact, if it can't change their behaviour to make them profitable, the company would benefit by encouraging its unprofitable customers to switch to competitors.

Retaining the most valuable customers invariably involves motivated and knowledgeable employees, and it is to this matter that we now turn.

Return on marketing investment (ROMI or marketing ROI) The net return from a marketing investment divided by the costs of the marketing investment.

Customer lifetime value The amount by which revenues from a given customer over time exceed the company's costs of attracting, selling to and servicing that customer.

MARKETING HIGHLIGHT 2.2

Measuring and managing for customer value

If customers are asked what they want from an organisation, most people would like better value—better quality products and services at lower cost. However, the marketing organisation needs to decide what it can profitably provide to customers, and what marketing actions will be most effective in adding value for customers and for the organisation. Effective marketers are increasingly putting emphasis on measuring the effectiveness of their marketing efforts, and differentiating between customers in the level of service provided. This marketing highlight discusses how organisations are measuring and managing for customer value.

Customer value measurement

If a company can work out the lifetime value of a customer, it has the potential to offer its most valuable customers a higher level of service, and therefore make it more likely that they will stay with the company. This approach is most useful when the costs of serving customers vary, and when the company can offer higher levels of service to some customers. For example, it clearly makes sense for an airline to identify its most profitable customers, and perhaps provide them with priority in answering the phone or with occasional upgrades. These are actions which cost the airline very little, but which might have a big impact on customer loyalty. It's not clear that it will be particularly useful for a company like Pepsi to identify the people who drink Pepsi the most, because it would be difficult (and probably not useful) for Pepsi to treat those individuals differently. However, Pepsi would certainly benefit from identifying its most important sales outlets, and making sure that these critical distributors are satisfied.

So how can a company identify its most valuable customers? Rust, Zeithaml and Lemon have studied what a company needs to know to work out the value of its customers.[37] First, the company needs to decide on a time period for analysis (e.g. one month, one quarter or a year). It then needs information on a number of factors:

- The customer's frequency of purchase in each period.
- The average profit contribution from a purchase of this brand.
- The most recent brand chosen by the customer.
- The customer's estimated probability of choosing each brand on the next purchase.
- The company's cost of capital (because in a low-inflation environment marketing expenditure on acquiring the customer will provide a better return than the same expenditure in a high-inflation environment).
- The cost of maintaining the relationship with this type of customer (including salesperson time, the cost of targeted direct mail, etc.).
- The likely future purchase pattern of this type of customer (e.g. do records show that this sort of customer spends more or less over time?).

When the company has this sort of information it can calculate an estimated lifetime value for the customer—the customer's total contribution to profit in each time period, with future periods discounted, to reflect the fact that future income is worth less than current income.[38]

Once the organisation has calculated the lifetime value of its customers, it has the ability to spend more or less on customers; for example, one catalogue company calculated that a reduction of 31% in marketing investment per customer would increase average profitability by about 29%. In contrast, at another firm, a pharmaceutical company, an estimated 31% reduction in direct marketing activity was estimated to increase average customer profitability by 36%.[39] Knowledge of the different lifetime values of customers means that the organisation also has the ability to offer higher levels of service to its most profitable customers. For example, banks like Citibank offer personal banking services to their most valuable customers, and credit card companies offer 'gold' or 'platinum' credit cards, with associated services such as travel insurance and access to discounted offers. All of these actions cost the organisation money, however, and need to be factored into the customer's lifetime value calculation. There's no point in spending more to keep the highest spending customers than they return in profits.

So from a profit point of view, the most effective actions will be those which the customer values, but which don't cost the marketing organisation much. For example, an airline can offer telephone priority to the high-value customer so they don't have to wait in line on the phone, and might offer an upgrade from time to time to its highest value travellers if there are empty business class seats. The organisation needs to be careful, however, that it doesn't alienate other customers; while it may be beneficial to communicate to some customers that they have priority in telephone calls, advertising this benefit so that customers who don't get priority find out that they need to wait in line longer is likely to decrease their satisfaction. So the very best targeted actions will (1) add value for the customers (2) at low cost to the marketing organisation (3) in a way that isn't obvious to other customers.

Sources: See Roland, T. Rust, Valarie A. Zeithaml and Katherine N. Lemon, *Driving Customer Equity: How Customer Lifetime Value is Reshaping Corporate Strategy*, New York, The Free Press, 2000; Jacquelyn S. Thomas, Werner Reinartz and V. Kumar, 'Getting the Most Out of All Your Customers', *Harvard Business Review*, July–August 2004, pp. 116–23; Fred Feinberg, Aradhna Krishna and Z. John Zhang, 'Do We Care What Others Get? A Behaviorist Approach to Targeted Promotions', *Journal of Marketing Research*, vol. 39, August 2002, pp. 277–291.

Questions

1 What makes you more likely to remain as a customer of an organisation? What makes you less likely? What are the implications for the organisations you deal with?

2 Some organisations will typically only make one sale to a customer. For example, a luxury resort may market itself as a once-in-a-lifetime destination. Does this mean that the concept of customer lifetime value does not apply to the resort? Why or why not?

3 The idea that a customer will have a certain value can result in organisations spending now to maintain the customer, with the hope that the customer's business will more than repay this spending over their lifetime. However, this doesn't always happen. What can an organisation do to ensure that it doesn't spend too much to retain customers who will never repay this investment?

2.2

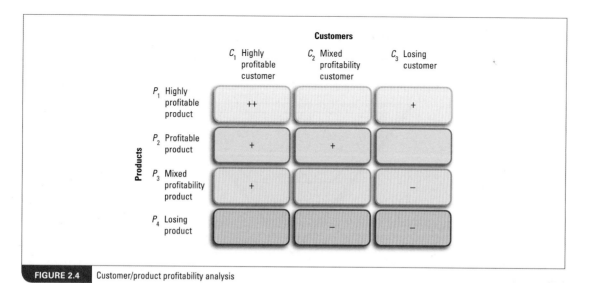

FIGURE 2.4 Customer/product profitability analysis

Customer orientation in people and processes

An important factor in customer satisfaction and retention is retaining valuable and committed employees. There is evidence that employee satisfaction is associated with higher levels of customer satisfaction, which is in turn associated with higher levels of customer retention, and higher customer profitability.[40] A focus on customer retention, therefore, also requires a focus on retaining and satisfying the employees with whom customers interact. This means that the organisation needs to consider its internal marketing practices (see Figure 2.5).

Internal marketing

In almost every interaction with a company, a customer is likely to have direct or indirect interaction with its employees. The interaction may be face-to-face, by phone or by written communications such as letters and emails. Each of these moments of truth, as we called them earlier in the chapter, can be important in the customer's view of, and loyalty to, the organisation. If the employee is unhappy because of poor work conditions, or stressed because of inadequate backup, they are less likely to be able to manage these moments of truth as the company might wish. Marketing Highlight 2.3 discusses how some organisations are focusing on internal marketing, to attract and retain valuable employees.

Internal marketing
One part of a marketing organisation marketing its capabilities to another part of the organisation.

The aim of an **internal marketing** program is to ensure that staff share the organisation's goals, and have sufficient training and power to respond appropriately under different situations. For

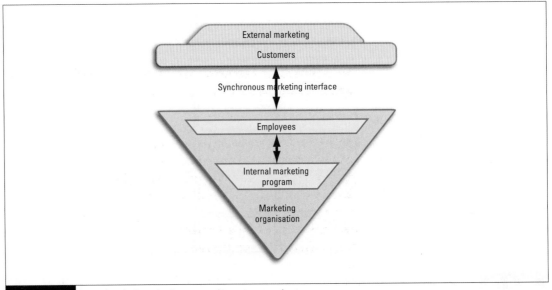

FIGURE 2.5 Internal marketing: orienting personnel to customers and programs

example, Australian car company GM Holden (GMH) knows that all car companies, whatever they do, will at some time have customers who aren't satisfied. As a result, GMH specifically trains its staff to deal with situations where customers aren't happy. 'The whole ethos is to take care of the customer, but there are times when no matter what you do, the customer will not be happy with it. For that reason, we put all our staff through a lot of training to be able to deal with these types of situation on a case-by-case basis' says the Director of Sales, John Nigro.[41] An effective internal marketing program builds on the human resources strategy of the organisation, aiming to recruit, train and retain committed employees. So Coles Myer states that its vision is:

> To be the employer of choice because of the philosophies, values, policies and work practices across all areas of Coles Myer Limited. As a Coles Myer employee, you become part of a living system that fosters achievement of career goals, while leaving you free to pursue your lifestyle choices.[42]

Organisations often use salary and bonuses in an attempt to motivate staff. For example, a restaurant group might pay bonuses when front-of-house staff have served (say) $25 000 of meals, thus recognising when staff have made a significant contribution to the wellbeing of the business.[43] However, retaining satisfied staff requires more than providing good salaries and bonuses linked to performance targets. While inadequate wages can certainly be demotivating, there is evidence that higher salaries and bonuses have limited ability to motivate people.[44] Providing interesting, challenging work is much more effective in motivating staff. Everyone can't have an interesting job, but training, job rotation and recognition can maintain staff motivation, even among lower-level workers. For example, McDonald's trains its staff to perform a variety of jobs. This allows flexibility in staff allocation, and means that the job is less boring for workers. Training doesn't stop in the store, however. McDonald's employees can attend 'Hamburger University' where 16 full-time resident professors teach students from more than 119 countries. Such training schemes, from the top to the bottom of the organisation, have helped McDonald's to develop a reputation for what the company calls QSCV—quality, service, cleanliness and value.

Service quality is a group effort

A marketing organisation's internal marketing program seeks to ensure that there is a common purpose among those who work together—both within sections of the organisation and across the

Deutsche Bank uses its Bank of the Year Award to highlight its service quality.

Service delivery
When customers and representatives of an organisation interact with one another. Such interactions play a large part in determining whether or not the customer is satisfied and remains loyal to the marketer, particularly in service and experiential encounters.

organisation. As Len Berry put it in the context of **service delivery**: 'Service providers must possess the capability and desire to perform the service customers expect. Teamwork enhances both. Delivering service quality is a group effort.'[45]

SELF-CHECK QUESTIONS

5   How important do you think training is? Does it always ensure that employees interface with customers in such a way as to provide good service?

6   Every so often Disney makes its managers dress up as Mickey Mouse or Goofy and spend a day cavorting around the theme parks. They also spend a week each year selling tickets and popcorn, or directing patrons on and off buses. Also, every employee wears a name badge and they address each other on a first-name basis. Why might Disney enshrine such practices?

7   Some marketing organisations now utilise an intranet and allow employees to develop an individualistic 'Home Page'. Such pages include employees' experience and qualifications as well as their current projects and personal likes and dislikes. Why might companies allow such pages to be developed in work time?

Processes in delivering customer value

Customer value and satisfaction are important ingredients in the marketer's formula for success. But what does it take to produce and deliver customer value? To answer this, we return to the processes involved in the marketing organisation's value chain and its value delivery system.

Value chain

Value chain The activities performed to deliver a product to a customer.

Michael Porter put forward the notion of the **value chain** as a major tool for identifying ways to create more customer value (see Figure 2.6).[46] Every commercial endeavour consists of a collection of activities performed to design, produce, market, deliver and support the organisation's products. The value chain envisages the individual business as made up of value-creating activities in an effort to understand the behaviour of costs in the specific business and the potential sources of competitive differentiation. The nine value-creating activities include five primary activities and four support activities.

The primary activities involve the sequence of bringing materials into the business (inbound logistics), operating on them (operations or conversion operations), sending them out (outbound

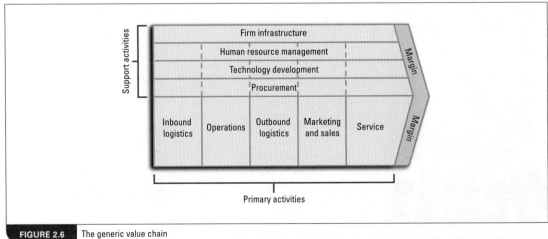

FIGURE 2.6   The generic value chain
Source: Michael E. Porter, *Competitive Advantage: Creating and Sustaining Superior Performance*, New York, Free Press, 1985, p. 37. Reprinted with permission of the Free Press, a division of Simon & Schuster Inc. © 1985, 1998 Michael Porter. All rights reserved.

logistics), marketing them (marketing and sales) and servicing them (service or supporting services). The support activities occur within each of these primary activities. For example, procurement involves obtaining the various inputs for each primary activity—only a fraction of procurement is done by the purchasing department. Technology development and human resource management also occur in all departments. The business's infrastructure covers the overhead of general management, planning, finance, accounting and legal, and government affairs.

Under the value-chain concept, the business should examine its costs and performance in each value-creating activity to identify possible improvements. It should also estimate its competitors' costs and performances as benchmarks.

Benchmarking and blueprinting

If a marketing organisation can perform certain activities better than its competitors, it can achieve a competitive advantage. **Benchmarking** entails comparing the marketing organisation's products and processes with those of competitors and leading firms in other industries to find ways to improve quality and performance. For example, benchmarking would involve a comparison of supply costs with those of competitors, in an attempt to identify and copy best practice. **Service blueprinting** extends the idea of benchmarking by examining the value chain from the customer's point of view. A service blueprint is a type of flowchart, which shows all the stages involved in providing service to a customer. It provides a way to break the service down into its logical components, and to depict the steps or tasks in the process, the means by which the tasks are executed and the evidence of service as the customer experiences it.[47] In this way, unnecessary steps or delays in the process can be identified and eliminated.

Value-chain analysis, benchmarking and service blueprinting can all contribute to customer value and firm profitability by encouraging a coordinated focus, across departments in the organisation, on delivering value to the customer. Without this business-focused view, individual departments will sometimes pursue a goal which makes sense for the department but may not be in the best interests of the business or the customer. For example, a credit department might attempt to reduce bad debts by raising credit standards; meanwhile, salespeople get frustrated and customers might buy elsewhere if they can't get credit. A distribution department might decide to save money by shipping goods by rail; meanwhile, the customer waits. In each case, individual departments have erected walls that impede the delivery of quality customer service.

To overcome this problem companies should place more emphasis on the coordination of core business processes, most of which depend on inputs from many functional departments. Core business processes which must be managed include:

- ⊚ *Product development process:* all the activities involved in identifying, researching and developing new products with speed, high quality and reasonable cost.
- ⊚ *Inventory management process:* all the activities involved in developing and managing the right inventory levels of raw materials, work-in-process and finished goods so that adequate supplies are available while avoiding the costs of high overstocks.
- ⊚ *Order-to-payment process:* all the activities involved in receiving orders, approving them, shipping the goods on time and collecting payment.
- ⊚ *Customer service process:* all the activities involved in making it easy for customers to reach the right parties within the marketing organisation to obtain service, answers and any problem resolution.

Successful companies develop superior capabilities in managing these and other core processes. In turn, mastering core business processes gives these companies a substantial competitive edge.[48] For example, Europe's fastest growing fashion retailer, Zara, has built international success, with over

Benchmarking
Comparison of a company's performance and processes with its competitors and with best-practice companies, using specific measures such as scrap levels, power costs, process waste, order-processing cycle times and productivity measures.

Service blueprinting
Documentation of the stages involved in providing service to a customer.

Gaining a competitive edge requires sophisticated and efficient distribution systems which are often outsourced to specialists with state of the art IT and quality control systems for track and tracing, such as DHL.

700 stores in 53 countries, by addressing each of these four processes. Zara continuously develops new fashion lines, rather than bringing in new lines at the start of each season, the practice used by most of its competitors. This process of rapid new product development, or 'fast fashion', encourages customers to keep coming back to Zara stores, and encourages customers to buy, because, in the words of Zara's parent company's deputy chairman, José Maria Castellano, 'Zara shoppers know that if they see something they like, they must buy it because it will not be in the store the following week.'[49] 'Zara breaks all the rules of fashion' says one commentator. 'The scarcity factor generates demand, instead of discouraging it'.[50]

Zara can only maintain this flow of new fashion lines by sophisticated inventory management and order-to-payment processes; store managers can view available items online, and orders for new stock are sent electronically to the head office of Zara twice a week. Sophisticated demand projection means that production is closely matched to demand (resulting in low levels of inventory) but stock can still be delivered in Europe one or two days after the order is placed, and only slightly later in Asian outlets. The efficient delivery system means that the customer in Zara stores is constantly being presented with new products to buy, and thus encouraged to revisit the store frequently, providing an enjoyable service experience for the fashion-conscious shopper. Store layouts and fittings are redesigned constantly so the stores continue to look fashionable, and the corporate policy of allowing exchange or refund within one month of purchase means that the customer is encouraged to buy, with the knowledge that they can receive a refund if they change their mind.

Value delivery networks

Customer value delivery networks
Marketing channels in which each channel member adds value for the customer.

In its search for competitive advantage, the individual company needs to look beyond its own value chain and into the value chains of its suppliers, distributors and ultimately its customers—the marketing logistics network of which it is a vital component. More companies today are 'partnering' with the other members of the demand chain to improve the performance of the **customer value delivery network**. For example, Campbell Soup operates a qualified supplier program and chooses only the few who are willing to meet its demanding requirements for quality, on-time delivery and continuous improvement. Campbell then assigns its own experts to work with suppliers to constantly improve their joint performance.

One great strength of world-class retailer Wal-Mart is its ability to source products at low costs, and hold low levels of inventory, thus keeping costs low while providing consistent supply. As individual Wal-Mart stores sell their goods, sales information flows not only to Wal-Mart's headquarters, but also to Wal-Mart's suppliers, who ship replacement goods to Wal-Mart stores almost as fast as the products move off the shelf. Goods are frequently delivered and displayed on the pallets on which they are delivered, meaning faster delivery and lower staff costs because shelves don't need to be restocked. This is known as a 'quick response', or 'just-in time' system, in which goods are pulled by demand rather than pushed by supply, resulting in lower inventory costs, which can then be passed on to the customer in lower prices or retained in order to provide greater profits for the company.

Examples like Zara and Wal-Mart show that value can be created for the customer at every stage in the value chain, either by providing a better quality product, or by ensuring lower costs. Today's marketing managers must think not only about selling today's products but also about how to stimulate the development of improved products, how to work actively with other departments in managing core business processes and how to build better external partnerships.[51]

SELF-CHECK QUESTIONS

8 Describe some recent examples where the processes employed by a marketing organisation have led to your or a friend's satisfaction as a customer.

9 Does McDonald's have a unique process in providing customer satisfaction? Describe their process and its importance.

10 Is process simply a matter of gaining advantage through productivity, as in an assembly-line approach to making hamburgers, or is process a more pervasive element in marketing products and services for companies such as McDonald's?

Implementing total quality marketing

Customer satisfaction and company profitability are closely linked to product and service quality. Higher levels of quality result in greater customer satisfaction, while at the same time supporting higher prices. The well-known Profit Impact of Marketing Strategies (PIMS) studies show a high correlation between relative product quality and profitability.[52] The task of improving product and service quality should therefore be a high priority for marketing organisations. Much of the global success of Japanese companies has resulted from building exceptional quality into their products, because most customers will no longer tolerate poor or average quality. Companies today have no choice but to adopt quality concepts if they want to stay in the race, let alone be profitable. According to GE's former chairman, John F. (Jack) Welch Jr: 'Quality is our best assurance of customer allegiance, our strongest defence against foreign competition, and the only path to sustained growth and earnings'.[53]

Quality needn't mean providing more and more features or constantly improving the service to customers. Organisations can, and do, make money offering lower-priced, lower-quality products. For example, airlines like Ryan Air and Southwest Airlines offer only basic services but have remained profitable while airlines offering higher levels of service have experienced losses. The key is in offering customers higher quality at any given price than competitors—thus increasing the value for customers. For example, Westpac's quality program is focused on customer service processes, using a process of 'define, measure, analyse, improve and control' to improve speed of delivery, reduce waste and re-work, and reduce process variation.[54] Quality improvement programs can therefore be aimed at improving actual product quality or at improving the efficiency of the value chain, thus decreasing costs and adding value for the customer.

The American Society for Quality Control defines **quality** as the totality of features and characteristics of a product or service that bear on its ability to satisfy stated or implied needs. This is clearly a customer-centred definition of quality. It suggests that a marketing organisation has delivered quality whenever its product or service meets or exceeds customers' needs, requirements and expectations.

It is important to distinguish between performance quality and conformance quality. Performance quality refers to the level at which a product performs its functions. For example, a (Toyota) Lexus provides higher performance quality than a Toyota Corolla—it has a quieter and smoother ride,

Quality The totality of features and characteristics of a product or service that bear on its ability to satisfy stated or implied needs.

Internal marketing—attracting and retaining valuable employees

More and more businesses are realising that the basis of their success relies on attracting and retaining good employees. This is critical for service organisations, where the customer's experience relies on service personnel. For some organisations the staff actually provide the service (think about doctors, solicitors or accountants). For other organisations staff may be critical in upselling, like the relationship manager for a bank, who provides information about new products to the bank's important business or high-wealth customers. Or staff may be relatively unskilled but still able to contribute to a pleasant or unpleasant service experience for customers, like the room service staff in a hotel or fast-food workers.

But there are fewer workers to go around in most countries, and the problem is likely to get worse. In 2001 alone there were 170 000 new entrants to the workforce in Australia, but estimates suggest that between 2020 and 2030 there will only be 125 000 in total. With low levels of unemployment and an ageing workforce, attracting and retaining new staff is becoming even more important for organisations, especially those which rely on skilled employees, who can make a huge contribution to organisational productivity. One survey showed that finding and retaining staff was by far the highest priority of the top accounting firms in Australia. And the problem of labour shortages isn't just one for Australia. In China, for example, there are vast numbers of unskilled workers, but attracting skilled labour is becoming harder, while in the developed south of the country organisations are complaining that they cannot recruit enough manual workers, pushing up labour costs. The problem is particularly acute for marketing staff, according to the head of China for L'Oréal, the French cosmetics firm, who says that 'to find good people in China is not easy. Technically and in administration they are very good. But in marketing—a crucial discipline—there are just a few people with short experience and everyone is competing for them.'

Even for organisations which can recruit sufficient staff, staff turnover is expensive and recruiting the right staff is important, because an exceptional employee at any level can change a customer's experience from ordinary to exceptional, and can result in a lost customer or in increased loyalty. Staff who are satisfied themselves are more likely to be able to give good service, and staff satisfaction has been shown to correlate highly with total shareholder returns.[55] As a result, smart organisations are putting more effort into attracting the right employees, retaining those employees and providing an environment which encourages employees to perform. For example, Westpac has worked on improving staff morale, and has seen employee retention increase as a result. ANA has guaranteed its older staff the right to work part-time, in order to retain older staff who are closer to the demographic of many of its customers. Freedom Furniture went through an in-depth process where it gathered groups of staff to decide on the values of the business. Freedom then introduced the chosen values into its 72 stores, and uses these values in recruitment, orientation and training. Exercises were developed so that store managers could work with their staff through challenging situations, such as dealing with difficult customers or underperforming staff. An external agency is used to measure cultural and personal values in the organisation on a regular basis.

Similarly, brewer Lion Nathan assessed its work culture, and found an unpleasant work environment. Five core values consistent with the core purpose of Lion Nathan 'making the world a more sociable place' were introduced: facing reality, acting with integrity, passion, achieving together and being sociable. These values were used in key strategic decisions, such as Lion Nathan's decision not to have poker machines in company-owned properties. Following the change, from 1999 to 2004, Lion Nathan saw an upturn in profitability.

Retailer Noni B is another company with a strong emphasis on a supportive staff culture which has achieved lower staff turnover and higher profits. Operating in the highly competitive fashion apparel sector, Noni B's 177 stores have achieved rising sales; in the year to June 2005 the company reported a 41.3% increase in net profits. At the same time the company's competitors have experienced decreased profits and complained of falling consumer spending. What's the secret of Noni B's success? The managing director, Alan Kindl, attributes it to the culture he has created.

It's a family culture, we're very proud of what we do. I'm the guardian of the culture, and we make sure it rubs off right the way down the line because that is our strength . . . We have a saying in our business . . . 'We know that family is the most important thing in your life, and then comes Noni B'. We have to blend the two because if a person is not happy at home, she is not going to perform well.

Kindl once spoke to a national conference of 400 Noni B sales staff, and told them their families should come first. Recalling the occasion, one employee says that some of the staff were in tears. 'You never hear that from employers. We would walk on water for him.' This sort of attitude has resulted in Noni B having a staff turnover of 17%, in an industry where 30–40% is the norm.

Businesses will increasingly need to think, like Noni B, about what can make them an attractive employer to work for. But good businesses have always known that. In the words of David Morgan, CEO of Westpac bank: 'Put simply, a company needs employees who want to work for it . . . Motivated employees strongly and positively influence customer satisfaction.'

Sources: 'China's People Problem', *The Economist*, 16 April 2005, pp. 57–58; Lachlan Colquhoun, 'Skills Shortage Creates Dilemmas for Recruiters', *Financial Times*, 21 July 2005, p. 23; Andrew Heathcote, 'Tough Times, Good Money', *Business Review Weekly*, 3 August 2005, p. 20; Julia May, 'Grow Your Own', *Business Review Weekly*, 14 September 2005, pp. 52–53; Samantha Moran, 'ANZ Promises Places for Mature Staff', *The Financial Review*, 20 September 2005, p. 3; David Morgan, 'Valuing Values at the Heart of the Enterprise Is How You Create Sustainable Profit', *The Age*, 18 August 2005, p. 2; Amita Tandukar, 'Real Values, Real Profits', *Business Review Weekly*, 8 September 2005, pp. 64–65; Jacqui Walker, 'Family in Fashion', *Business Review Weekly*, 8 September 2005, pp. 35–38.

Questions

1 Is attracting and retaining the right employees the responsibility of marketing or the human resources (HR) department?

2 Whatever your answer to Question 1, the HR department is heavily involved in recruitment and retention of staff. What can marketing principles teach the HR department?

3 Is attracting and retaining employees just a matter of paying them more money? Why or why not?

2.3

handles better and lasts longer. It is also much more expensive, but sells to a market with higher means and requirements, and retains its resale value better than its mass-marketed sibling. Conformance quality refers to freedom from defects and the consistency with which a product delivers a specified level of performance. Thus, a Lexus and a Corolla can both be said to offer equivalent conformance quality to their respective markets if each consistently delivers what its market expects. The $25 000 car that meets all its requirements is a quality car; so is a $125 000 car that meets all its requirements. But if the Lexus handles badly, or if the Corolla gives poor fuel efficiency, then both cars have failed to deliver quality, and customer satisfaction suffers accordingly.

Total quality management

Quality philosophies such as total quality management swept the corporate sector during the 1980s. Total quality management (TQM) (see Chapter 1, page 10) is a management philosophy emphasising quality, teamwork and decisions based on data. Many organisations adopted the language of TQM but not the substance. Others viewed TQM as a cure-all for their problems. Still others became obsessed with narrowly defined TQM principles and lost sight of broader concerns for customer value and satisfaction. As a result, many TQM programs begun in the 1980s failed, causing a recent backlash against TQM. Still, when applied in the context of creating customer satisfaction, total quality principles remain a requirement for success. Although many firms don't use the TQM label any more, for most top companies customer-driven quality has become a way of doing business. They apply the notion of 'return on quality (ROQ)', and they make certain that the quality they offer is the quality that customers want. This quality, in turn, results in improved sales and profits.[56] Total quality is the key to creating customer value and satisfaction. Just as marketing is everyone's job, so total quality is everyone's job:

> Marketers who don't learn the language of quality improvement, manufacturing and operations will become as obsolete as buggy whips. The days of functional marketing are gone. We can no longer afford to think of ourselves as market researchers, advertising people, direct marketers, marketing strategists—we have to think of ourselves as customer satisfiers—customer advocates focused on whole processes.[57]

Customer retention and total quality

Marketing management have three responsibilities in a quality-centred marketing organisation. First, marketers bear the major responsibility for correctly identifying customers' needs and requirements and for communicating customer expectations correctly to product designers. Second, marketers must make sure that customers' orders are filled correctly and on time, and must check to see that customers have received proper instructions, training and technical assistance in the use of the product. Third, marketers must stay in touch with customers after the sale to make sure they remain satisfied, and to gather and convey customer ideas for product and service improvements to the appropriate marketing organisation departments.

While marketing strives to create quality and customer retention, one study found that marketing people were responsible for more customer complaints than any other department (35%). Marketing mistakes included cases in which the salesforce ordered special product features for customers but failed to notify manufacturing of the changes; where incorrect order processing resulted in the wrong product being made and shipped; and where customer complaints were not properly handled.[58]

The implication here is that marketers must spend time and effort not only to improve external marketing but also to improve internal marketing. Marketers must be the customer's watchdog or guardian, complaining loudly for the customer when the product or service is not right. If organisations want to retain satisfied customers, marketers must constantly uphold the standard of 'giving the customer the best solution'.

SELF-CHECK QUESTIONS

11 Comment on the following statement: 'Total quality is the key to value creation and customer satisfaction. Total quality is everyone's job. Marketers who do not learn the language of quality improvement, manufacturing and service delivery operations are obsolete.'

12 Describe the role that marketing at all levels plays in total quality management. Illustrate your answer with examples of companies where marketers play such a role.

13 Is internal marketing equally important for all organisations? Why or why not?

SUMMARY

Today's customers face a growing range of choices in the products and services they can buy. They base their choices as to what they buy and what they will re-buy on their perceptions of quality, value and service. *Customer satisfaction* is the customer's fulfilment response regarding a product or service feature or the product or service itself.

To generate *trust*, *commitment* and *total satisfaction*, a marketing organisation must manage its own value chain and the entire *value delivery system* in a *customer-centred* way. The organisation's goal is not only to attract customers but, even more importantly, to identify and retain customers who contribute most to company revenues and profits and to retain their trust and commitment. Customer *relationship marketing* provides the key to retaining customers and involves building financial and social benefits as well as structural ties to customers. Companies must decide the level at which they want to build relationships with different market segments and individual customers, from such levels as basic, reactive, accountable and proactive to full partnership. Appropriate relationship management will consider the *customer's lifetime value* to the organisation, and whether relationship management programs will increase the customer value over and above the costs required to attract and retain that customer.

Marketing organisations also need to look to *internal marketing* to ensure that employees are well trained and motivated to remain oriented towards customers and total organisational goals. Additionally, people and processes must be taken into account in delivering customer satisfaction. *Total quality management* has become a major approach to providing customer satisfaction and marketing organisation profitability. Companies must understand how their customers perceive quality and how much quality they expect. Companies must then do a better job of satisfying their customers' desires than their competitors do. Delivering quality requires total management and employee commitment as well as measurement and reward systems. Marketers play an especially critical role in their marketing organisation's drive toward higher quality.

MARKETING ISSUE

Customer satisfaction is important for universities, as it is for other organisations. If students are satisfied with their lecturers they are more likely to recommend the university to their friends, and to return for postgraduate degrees. More students means more money for the university. Students' ratings of the university are also important in determining the ranking of the university, which in turn is influential in whether future students choose the university. For students, satisfaction with their classes is very important and teaching performance has always been important in the assessment and promotion of academics, but it has been only one factor (research and administration are also evaluated). Research is becoming increasingly important in the recruitment and promotion of academics because governments in many countries are offering more funding to universities which have higher research output. Many staff believe that research is weighted much more heavily in the promotion process, with a common view expressed as 'You can get promoted with good research and ordinary teaching, but you'll never get promoted with good teaching and ordinary research'.

In an effort to reward and encourage good teaching one university is planning to offer academics who obtain high teaching ratings monetary bonuses. There is some concern with the proposal among academics, who argue that they can obtain higher ratings by making courses easy for students and by giving out good grades, and that this isn't in the best interests of the university, or of its current, past and future students. They also argue that it is easier to get good ratings in some subjects, so the system will be inherently unfair.

What do you think are the advantages of the university's plan to pay staff who get higher student ratings a bonus? What are the potential problems with the scheme? Are you aware of other organisations where offering bonuses based on customer satisfaction has both advantages and disadvantages?

KEY TERMS

benchmarking	59	customer satisfaction	41	return on marketing investment (ROMI or marketing ROI)	53
customer-centred company	43	customer value delivery networks	60	service blueprinting	59
customer lifetime value	53	internal marketing	56	service delivery	58
customer relationship management	49	quality	61	value chain	58

DISCUSSING THE ISSUES

1 Recall an activity in which a company went beyond your expectations in providing their offering—either your company, or one of which you were a customer. Was this due to an individual employee, or were business processes involved such that the company could repeat this with all or the most valuable customers?

2 Describe a situation in which you became a 'lost customer'. Did you leave because of poor product quality, poor service quality or both?

3 Consider the commentary on customer lifetime value. Summarise the discussion concerning the lifelong value of subscribers and repertoire customers.

4 Why are relationships discussed in the context of business profitability?

5 Consider your answers to Questions 1 and 2. To what extent was trust influenced? Was commitment to the vendor or brand influenced?

6 To what extent might human interface technologies influence relationships and profits? Provide examples wherever possible.

REFERENCES

1. Jan Carlzon, *Moments of Truth*, Sydney, Harper & Row, 1987.
2. Jake Lloyd-Smith, 'MP3 Slump Hits Creative Technology', *Financial Times*, 29 June 2005, p. 16.
3. Richard L. Oliver, *Satisfaction: A Behavioral Perspective on the Consumer*, Boston, McGraw-Hill/Irwin, 1997.
4. For a discussion of the factors influencing satisfaction see Richard L. Oliver, *Satisfaction: A Behavioral Perspective on the Consumer*, Boston, McGraw Hill/Irwin, 1997.
5. Eugene W. Anderson, Claes Fornell and Donald R. Lehmann, 'Customer Satisfaction, Market Share and Profitability: Findings from Sweden', *Journal of Marketing*, vol. 58, no. 3, 1994, pp. 53–66.
6. Sridhar Moorthy and Hao Zhao, 'Advertising Spending and Perceived Quality', *Marketing Letters*, vol. 11, no. 3, 1995, pp. 221–233.
7. F. Reichheld, *The Loyalty Effect*, Cambridge, MA, Harvard Business School Press, 1996.
8. Richard Whitely, 'Do Selling and Quality Mix?', *Sales & Marketing Management*, October 1993, p. 70.
9. See Annika Ravald and Christian Gronroos, 'The Value Concept and Relationship Marketing', *European Journal of Marketing*, vol. 30, no. 2, 1996, pp. 19–30. For a discussion on value, also see Howard E. Butz and Leonard D. Goodstein, 'Measuring Customer Value: Gaining Strategic Advantage', *Organizational Dynamics*, Winter 1996, pp. 63–77; and Robert W. Woodruff, 'Customer Value: The Next Source of Competitive Advantage', *Journal of the Academy of Marketing Science*, Spring 1997, pp. 139–153.
10. Fred Selnes, 'Antecedents and Consequences of Trust and Satisfaction in Buyer–Seller Relationships', *European Journal of Marketing*, vol. 32, no. 3/4, 1998, pp. 305–322.
11. Kenneth Wylie, 'Customer Satisfaction Blooms: Rivalry at Top Grows', *Advertising Age*, 18 October 1993, pp. S1–S5.
12. Kevin T. Higgins, 'Coming of Age: Despite Growing Pains, Customer Satisfaction Measurement Continues to Evolve', *Marketing News*, vol. 31, no. 22, 1997, pp. 1–12.
13. Frederick F. Reichheld, 'The One Number You Need to Grow', *Harvard Business Review*, December 2003, pp. 46–54.
14. <Huawei.com>, accessed 12 September 2005.
15. See Thomas O. Jones and W. Earl Sasser, 'Why Satisfied Customers Defect', *Harvard Business Review*, November–December 1995, pp. 88–99. Also see Thomas A. Stewart, 'A Satisfied Customer Isn't Enough', *Fortune*, 21 July 1997, pp. 112–113.
16. F. Reichheld, *The Loyalty Effect*, Cambridge, MA, Harvard Business School Press, 1996.
17. See Kevin J. Clancy and Robert S. Shulman, 'Breaking the Mold', *Sales & Marketing Management*, vol. 146, January 1994, pp. 82–84.
18. Frederick F. Reichheld and W. Earl Sasser, Jr, 'Zero Defections: Quality Comes to Services', *Harvard Business Review*, September–October 1990, pp. 301–307.
19. Frederick F. Reichheld and Phil Schefter, 'e-Loyalty: Your Secret Weapon on the Web', *Harvard Business Review*, vol. 78, no. 4, 2000, p. 106.
20. Jones and Sasser, 'Why Satisfied Customers Defect', p. 91. For other examples, see Roger Sant, 'Did He Jump or Was He Pushed?', *Marketing News*, 12 May 1997, pp. 2–21.
21. See Joseph Juran, 'Made in the USA: A Renaissance in Quality', *Harvard Business Review*, July–August 1993, pp. 42–50.

22. Michael J. Harker, 'Relationship Marketing Defined? An Examination of Current Relationship Marketing Definitions', *Marketing Intelligence and Planning*, vol. 17, no. 1, 1999, p. 16.
23. For in-depth examination of relationships in marketing, see Annika Ravald and Christian Gronroos, 'The Value Concept and Relationship Marketing', *European Journal of Marketing*, vol. 30, no. 2, 1996, pp. 19–30; Christian Gronroos, 'From Marketing Mix to Relationship Marketing: Towards a Paradigm Shift in Marketing', *Management Decision*, vol. 32, no. 2, pp. 4–20; Robert M. Morgan and Shelby D. Hunt, 'The Commitment–Trust Theory of Relationship Marketing', *Journal of Marketing*, vol. 58, July 1994, pp. 20–38; and Fred Selnes, 'Antecedents and Consequences of Trust and Satisfaction in Buyer–Seller Relationships', *European Journal of Marketing*, vol. 32, no. 3/4, 1998, pp. 305–22.
24. See, for example, Robert C. Blattberg and John Deighton, 'Interactive Marketing: Exploiting the Age of Addressability', *Sloan Management Review*, vol. 33, no. 1, 1991; Robert C. Blattberg and John Deighton, 'Manage Marketing by the Customer Equity Test', *Harvard Business Review*, vol. 74, July–August 1996, pp. 136–144; Garbarino and Johnson, 1999; and Shankar Ganesan, 'Determinants of Long-Term Orientation in Buyer–Seller Relationships', *Journal of Marketing*, vol. 58, April 1994, pp. 1–19.
25. Ibid., Garbarino and Johnson, 1999.
26. Michael J. Harker, 'Relationship Marketing Defined? An Examination of Current Relationship Marketing Definitions', *Marketing Intelligence and Planning*, vol. 17, no. 1, 1999, p. 14.
27. Ibid., Garbarino and Johnson, 1999.
28. Leonard L. Berry and A. Parasuraman, *Marketing Services: Competing through Quality*, New York, The Free Press, 1991, pp. 136–142.
29. See Grahame R. Dowling and Mark Uncles, 'Do Customer Loyalty Programs Really Work?', *Sloan Management Review*, vol. 38, Summer 1997, pp. 71–82.
30. Edwin McDowell, 'Ritz-Carlton's Keys to Good Service', *New York Times*, 31 March 1993, p. 1.
31. David Greising, 'Watch Out for Flying Packages', *Business Week*, 14 November 1994, p. 40.
32. See Michael J. Lanning and Lynn W. Phillips, 'Strategy Shifts up a Gear', *Marketing*, October 1991, p. 9.
33. Bob Donath, 'Despite Economic Shifts, Biz Marketers Still View ROMI as No. 1 Concern', *Marketing News*, vol. 38, no. 4, 2004, pp. 6–7.
34. See Blattberg and Deighton, 1996.
35. See Werner J. Reinartz and V. Kumar, 'On the Profitability of Long-Life Customers in a Noncontractual Setting: An Empirical Investigation and Implications for Marketing', *Journal of Marketing*, vol. 64, October 2000, pp. 17–35.
36. See Garbarino and Johnson, 1999.
37. Roland T. Rust, Valerie A. Zeithaml and Katherine N. Lemon, *Driving Customer Equity: How Customer Lifetime Value is Reshaping Corporate Strategy*, New York, The Free Press, 2000.
38. For more detail, see Roland T. Rust, Valerie A. Zeithaml and Katherine N. Lemon, *Driving Customer Equity: How Customer Lifetime Value is Reshaping Corporate Strategy*, New York, The Free Press, 2000, pp. 37–49.
39. Jacquelyn S. Thomas, Werner Reinartz and V. Kumar, 'Getting the Most Out of All Your Customers', *Harvard Business Review*, July–August 2004, pp. 116–23.
40. Gary W. Loveman, 'Employee Satisfaction, Customer Loyalty, and Financial Performance', *Journal of Service Research*, vol. 1, no. 1, 1998, pp. 18–31.
41. Simon Lloyd, 'The Price of Loyal Customers', *Business Review Weekly*, 28 July 2005, pp. 56–57.
42. <http://careers.colesmyer.com/content.awp>, accessed September 2005.
43. Frederick F. Reichheld, 'Loyalty-based Management', *Harvard Business Review*, vol. 71, March–April 1993, pp. 64–73.
44. Frederick Herzberg, 'One More Time: How Do You Motivate Employees?' *Harvard Business Review*, vol. 81, no. 1, 2003, pp. 87–96.
45. Leonard L. Berry, *On Great Service: A Framework for Action*, New York, The Free Press, 1995, p. 225.
46. Michael E. Porter, *Competitive Advantage: Creating and Sustaining Superior Performance*, New York, The Free Press, 1985. For more discussion on value chains and strategies for creating value, see Richard Normann and Rafael Ramirez, 'From Value Chain to Value Constellation: Designing Interactive Strategy', *Harvard Business Review*, July–August 1993, pp. 65–77; and 'Strategy and the Art of Reinventing Value', *Harvard Business Review*, September–October 1993, pp. 39–51.
47. Valerie A. Zeithaml and Mary Jo Bitner, *Services Marketing: Integrating Customer Focus Across the Firm*, Boston, McGraw-Hill, 2003.
48. See George Stalk, Philip Evans and Laurence E. Shulman, 'Competing Capabilities: The New Rules of Corporate Strategy', *Harvard Business Review*, March–April 1992, pp. 57–69; and Benson P. Shapiro, V. Kasturi Rangan and John J. Sviokla, 'Staple Yourself to an Order', *Harvard Business Review*, July–August 1992, pp. 113–122.
49. Leslie Crawford, 'Zara Races to Retain Speed of Growth', *Financial Times*, 19 June 2005, p. 8.
50. Leslie Crawford, 'Spain's Fast-Fashion Phenomenon Loses Its Maestro and Maybe Its Way', *The Weekend Australian*, 31 December 2005, p. 29.
51. For more discussion see Frederick E. Webster Jr, 'The Changing Role of Marketing in the Corporation', *Journal of Marketing*, October 1992, pp. 1–17.
52. Robert D. Buzzell and Bradley T. Gale, *The PIMS Principles: Linking Strategy to Performance*, New York, The Free Press, 1987, Chapter 6.
53. 'Quality: The U.S. Drives to Catch Up', *Business Week*, November 1982, pp. 66–80.
54. David James, 'A Question of Quality', *Business Review Weekly*, 28 July 2005, pp. 60–61.
55. Andrew Cornell, 'Banks Need to Keep the Customer Satisfied', *The Australian Financial Review*, 12 December 2005, p. 54.
56. See David Greising, 'Quality: How to Make It Pay', *Business Week*, 8 August 1994, pp. 54–59; and Cyndee Miller, 'TQM Out; Continuous Process Improvement In', *Marketing News*, 9 May 1994, pp. 5, 10.
57. J. Daniel Beckham, 'Expect the Unexpected in Health Care Marketing Future', *The Academy Bulletin*, July 1992, p. 3.
58. Kenneth Kivenko, *Quality Control for Management*, Englewood Cliffs, NJ, Prentice Hall, 1984. Also see Kate Bertrand, 'Marketing Discovers What "Quality" Really Means', *Business Marketing*, April 1987, pp. 58–72.

PHOTO/AD CREDITS

Daniel Prior, Charles Sturt University

CASE STUDY

Retaining customers in a small financial planning business: the elusive pursuit of marketing's silver bullet

After a diverse career path that had already spanned 15 years, John decided to set up a financial planning business in his home town, a small country town on the south coast of New South Wales. The year was 2001 and the baby boomer generation had begun to seriously consider its retirement options. If they had not already retired, they were thinking about it, with many of them opting to retire at a much younger age than 65.

Along with retirement came a whole new lifestyle which, as John had discovered, was accompanied by a move out of the major metropolitan centres like Sydney and Melbourne, to smaller, beach-side towns—otherwise known as a 'sea change'.

What was striking about this generation of retirees was the different set of priorities it had from past generations. Instead of living a simple lifestyle plagued with rationing a meagre income over extended periods (such as their parents' generation had done), the baby boomers had managed to establish a lifestyle with greater access to the pleasures of life. Many of them 'worked to live' rather than 'lived to work', which explained the high growth in the consumption of luxury items and other pleasures that began in the 1970s and which has continued with subsequent generations. All of this meant that retiring baby boomers needed to consider seriously how they were going to fund these extravagances, especially when it came time to retire.

John believed that the answer was sound financial management. John had come to this opinion while studying financial planning in the late 1990s and while working as an assistant financial planner for a medium-sized Sydney financial planning firm. As the logic went, if you began saving early enough, and then invested that money in high-growth superannuation

funds, a much higher likelihood would exist that you would be able to achieve a real income sufficient to maintain your lifestyle from the time you retired until the time of death. However, the fact that the time difference between retirement and death was ever increasing (due to earlier retirement ages and longer expected lifetimes) meant that the saving/investing process had to begin as early as possible and in a concentrated manner.

After much thought and consideration and with a constant yearning to re-settle in his home town, John and his family moved to begin a new chapter in their lives which involved the creation of a new financial planning business in his home town. Prior to their trip, John was aware of at least two couples who fitted John's profile of the ideal customer, and who had recently moved to the area. One of John's first acts of business when he reached town was to make contact with them and see how their moves had gone and if they, or anyone they knew, were in search of any financial planning services. Both couples agreed to meet John and subsequently agreed to become his customers. They also recommended another three couples they knew were interested in obtaining financial planning services.

On an off-chance, John happened to wander into the local pub. The pub was filled with memorabilia from the many successes of the local football club over the years. John hunted through the photographs to find the photos of the 1978 and 1979 grand finals for the under 18s team, the team he captained during that time. While staring at the faded pictures, John was tapped on the back by an old football mate. They began talking and drinking. As the night wore on, it turned out his old football mate knew of some people who were also in need of a financial planner. Subsequently John began to follow up the leads he had recorded.

After frantically building his business for 12 months, John finally felt as though he could take a breather since his list of clients had grown to number around 300. Out of curiosity, he began to scan computer records of his clients. He realised that a number of the couples he had originally gained as clients had not made contact with him for some time. He also realised that he had not made any efforts to contact them either. He wondered how they were progressing towards the goals they had established during their meetings 12 months ago. He decided to give them a call. Out of the 10 clients John called, two had moved on, five did not feel John's services were necessary anymore and three had taken up the services of an alternative financial planner. After doing some calculations, John soon realised that losing these customers was equivalent to losing $50 000 worth of business.

Retaining customers was going to be difficult. If John could not secure long-term clients his business would not be viable. What can be done to help John?

QUESTIONS

1. Why is it important to maintain customers over the long term?

2. What would you suggest are the major success factors in John's situation?

3. Where do you think John should direct his investigations to find out why he lost the customers he did? Suggest action plans that could help John to find out the necessary information.

4. Suggest ways that John could maintain his customer base over the long term and make recommendations for how to implement these.

5. What information would you suggest is necessary to keep about current customers to maximise the potential for customer retention?

CASE STUDY

CHAPTER 3

Strategic planning and marketing

In swimming circles Speedo is synonymous with top performance, reliability and Space Age product development. For example, the development of FastSkins fabrics used by the world champion swimmers at the Athens Olympics in 2004 and the World Swimming Championships in Montreal in 2005 have been based on shark skin features. As a result swimmers can move significantly faster through the water than in ordinary swimsuits.

In early 2001 Speedo realised that although 80% of top performance athletes wear the Speedo brand, the company was losing its appeal to the general marketplace, particularly for the occasional swimmer and the beach goer. The brand was perceived to be cool but only if you were a top performance swimmer or an exercise-conscious person. However, any company that wants to grow and deliver higher profits needs to sell more of its products to existing customers or it must enter new market segments.

Speedo's gaps in its strategic market planning process in 2000 meant that uncompetitive offers and poor value propositions to several of the market segments it was trying to serve were not being effectively addressed. But the team at Speedo, used to competitive situations, knew that the gold medal, whether in the swimming pool or in the marketplace, can only be won through hard work, systematic planning and implementation, and a 'never give-up' attitude.

Speedo watched as its competitors, who were just mere blips in the marketplace, began concentrating on the market segments of the traditional swimmer and the beach goer—markets that had always belonged to Speedo. To ordinary people, who probably constitute 99% of the swimming market in Australia, Speedo's winning performance in the world swimming events did not mean much when it came to making a swimsuit purchasing decision.

Faced with a continuing loss of market share, the Speedo marketing team began the process of developing a new strategic marketing plan. It went through the critical stages of analysing the marketplace and its product portfolio, reassessing its strengths, weaknesses, opportunities and threats, and reviewing its objectives, financial performance and current strategies and tactics.

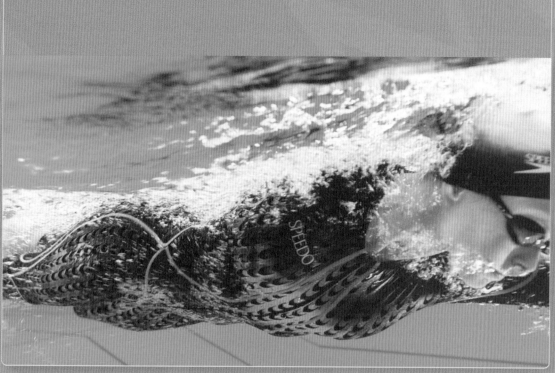

Speedo's Fastskins win gold.

Through the strategic planning process Speedo discovered that it had some products that were poorly positioned in terms of market segment needs and poorly targeted. Only after a critical review and strengthening of its marketing planning process and development of a new marketing plan was the Speedo team able to implement an aggressive new strategy taking into consideration objectives, market analysis and segmentation knowledge.

The impact of the new strategic plan on organisational focus and priorities was felt immediately due to a far better understanding of the relevant market segments and the value propositions needed for success. The Speedo marketing team was able to develop a more focused and differentiated offer for each target market. The strategic plan and process also discovered that there were new segments in the market that Speedo was not targeting. These segments were growing and Speedo had no presence there. The market segmentation, targeting and positioning process (developed as a part of the strategic market plan) enabled Speedo to go after these segments, resulting in far greater sales and profits in 2001 and 2002.

The strategic planning process and its outcome, the strategic market plan, enabled Speedo to reassert its position as the preferred swimming brand in its core market—the performance swimmer—but also to develop more focused offers for those segments where 'performance' is secondary to the primary need for a swimsuit that 'looks good'. Speedo's marketing strategy and plan had a big impact on the market in 2002—several competitors had retreated from Speedo's core markets back to their previous positions, customers were buying more Speedos and shareholders benefited from higher dividends.

In 2003 Speedo conducted a further strategic review and made some significant changes, shutting down its Australian manufacturing and establishing Speedo-specified manufacturing in Asia, streamlining its Australian distribution function and building a stronger product design group. These moves were in response to the need for cost reductions in its supply chain and greater capability in design of new swimwear products for the general beach and leisure market.

A further review in 2005 led Speedo to focus more resources on the beach and leisure swimwear market with particular emphasis on a range of apparel and equipment for men.

Since 2001, Speedo has made a commitment to strategic planning and marketing as the basis for strategic decision making and a commitment of corporate and marketing resources to its growth strategy. Subsequent strategic reviews in 2003 and 2005 have led to strategic decisions on target markets, product lines, manufacturing, warehousing and distribution—all taken with a strong market orientation. As its experience in strategic planning and marketing has evolved Speedo has taken a broader view of its market and widened its opportunities for profitable growth.[1]

After reading this chapter you should be able to:

1. Explain strategic planning, and discuss how it relates to the company mission, objectives and goals.

2. Identify and define methods for designing the business portfolio, developing growth strategies and planning functional strategies.

3. Outline the marketing process, explaining the concepts of target consumers, using marketing strategies for competitive advantage and developing the marketing mix.

4. Evaluate the relevance of electronic business to strategic planning and marketing.

All companies must look ahead and develop long-term strategies to meet the changing conditions in their industries. Each company must find the game plan that makes the most sense given its specific situation, opportunities, objectives and resources. The hard task of selecting an overall company strategy for long-run survival and growth is called *strategic planning*.

Marketing plays an important role in strategic planning. It provides market information and other inputs to help prepare the strategic plan. In turn, strategic planning defines marketing's role in the organisation. Guided by the strategic plan, marketing works with other departments in the organisation to achieve overall strategic objectives.

In this chapter we look first at the organisation's overall strategic planning. Next we discuss marketing's role in the organisation as it is defined by the overall strategic plan. Finally, we explain the marketing management process—the process that marketers undertake to carry out their role in the organisation.

Strategic planning

Most marketing organisations operate according to formal plans. Some, however, do not. In new companies, managers are sometimes so busy that they have no time for planning. In small companies, managers sometimes think that only large corporations need formal planning. In mature companies, many managers argue that they have done well without formal planning and that therefore it cannot be too important. They may resist taking the time to prepare a written plan. They may argue that the marketplace changes too quickly for a plan to be useful, that it would end up collecting dust.

Formal planning can yield many benefits for all types of companies, large and small, new and mature. It encourages management to think ahead systematically. It forces the company to sharpen its objectives and policies, leads to better coordination of company efforts and provides clearer performance standards for control. The argument that planning is less useful in a fast-changing environment makes little sense. In fact, the opposite is true: sound planning helps the company to anticipate and respond quickly to environmental changes, and to prepare for sudden developments more effectively. We could say that in today's world of rapid change those organisations that fail to plan *plan to fail*.

Hamel and Prahalad maintain that the main purpose of strategic planning is to help companies understand how they can compete for the future.[2]

To compete effectively firms not only must continually improve their operations but they frequently need to reinvent themselves to remain differentiated and relevant. The impact of Internet-based companies such as Amazon.com and Expedia.com are forcing booksellers like Dymocks and travel companies such as Flight Centre to redevelop strategies and restructure their businesses. Angus & Robertson, as part of its business strategy, provides the customer with a secure online buying environment, with additional information on new book releases and electronic gift certificates.[3] Also e-paper technology and e-books are making their way to existing PCs and the new Tablet PCs are further redefining traditional markets.[4]

This has brought about a refocus of strategic planning on the process of creating value—shareholder value and customer value. Figure 3.1 depicts a 'value seesaw' in which we see the pendulum swinging between excessive shareholder value and excessive customer value. If shareholder value dominates, as it frequently has with traditional monopolies like energy authorities, customer value is reduced and consumers actively look elsewhere for alternatives. If customer value dominates, the firm is not delivering sufficient value to shareholders in terms of profit, dividends and capital growth. Effective strategic planning assists business to develop strategies that will achieve a longer-term balance.

However, the need for flexibility, quick response and agility with resources and competencies has led to a resurgence in the process of scenario planning as a means of painting pictures of plausible futures that the firm may have to face. Richard Slaughter, a specialist in 'futures' studies, suggests that firms need to develop the capability of strategic foresight.

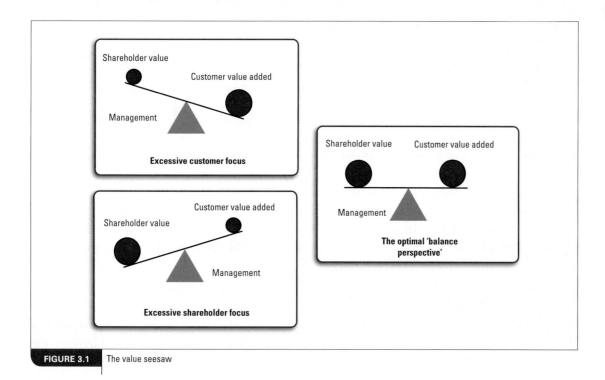

FIGURE 3.1   The value seesaw

Slaughter views foresight not as a process of trying to predict the future, but of projecting the future we want, then shaping our present concepts and actions to move towards it. He explains how institutions and individuals can use analysis and imagination to create a new view of the future. Specifically for companies, he suggests that strategic foresight involves the ability to create and maintain a coherent and functional forward view and to use these insights in useful ways for planning organisational strategy. He outlines a number of methods for developing strategic foresight, and scenario planning is the one most frequently used by business.[5] A scenario is not designed to try to forecast the future but aims to envisage a possible future.

Many leading international organisations such as Shell, Ericsson, Telstra and Fujitsu-ICL undertake scenario planning because of the uncertainty of future operating environments. No single outcome can be accurately forecast in times of turbulence, rapid change and industry convergence. Scenario planning is therefore becoming an essential capability for managing in this present environment. The essential steps in scenario planning are:

- *Familiarisation*: understanding the organisation, key stakeholders, their needs and expectations.
- *Discovery*: gaining an understanding of current trends and events and anticipating possible future discontinuities in the international environment.
- *Scenario building*: developing and progressively upgrading a range of scenarios that reflect events, patterns and discontinuities which together form possible operating environments of the future relevant to targeted overseas markets.
- *Action and integration*: developing appropriate business and marketing strategies which enable the organisation to operate effectively within the scenarios generated. This phase also includes coming to terms with managing the migration, that is, blending the emerging business with the existing business. The most critical part of this phase is to manage the expectations of the key internal and external stakeholders of the organisation.

The significance of scenarios is that each has different implications for marketing strategies in terms of what customers value and where the business value is in the changing value chain. In turn, they imply quite different investments, strategies, alliance partners and people capabilities for success and ongoing growth.

The marketer's task is to be on the leading edge of the industry in target markets as they develop. This will involve a number of components:

- Progressive scenario development which portrays realistic operating environments of the future globally and in target markets.
- Integrated business and marketing strategies which exploit the opportunities and identify the threats in the emerging scenarios.
- Ensuring the process of change is driven by customer considerations rather than technology and internal processes.
- Ensuring cultural and organisation changes are planned and managed effectively to provide capability.

At the operational level, this may be viewed in terms of best case, worst case and most likely scenario of outcomes for a business. For those organisations that use it, scenario planning is a central input to the strategic planning process.

Strategy hierarchy

Companies usually prepare annual plans, long-range plans and strategic plans. The *annual plan* is a short-term marketing plan that describes the current marketing situation, company objectives, the marketing strategy for the year, the action program, budgets and controls. The *long-range plan* describes the major factors and forces affecting the organisation during the next several years. It includes the long-term objectives, the major marketing strategies that will be used to attain them and the resources required. This long-range plan is reviewed and updated each year so that the company always has a current long-range plan.

Whereas the company's annual and long-range plans deal with current businesses and how to keep them going, the strategic plan involves adapting the firm to take advantage of opportunities in its constantly changing environment. We define **strategic planning** as the process of developing and maintaining a strategic fit between the organisation's goals and capabilities and its changing marketing opportunities.

Strategic planning is undertaken at a number of levels depending on the size and structure of the organisation. For the most complex organisations a hierarchy of strategies is required. This is shown in Figure 3.2.

Corporate strategy

At this level decisions concentrate on the scope of the organisation, the portfolio of businesses now and for the future and how resources are to be obtained and allocated. Corporate strategy is concerned with the economic value and financing requirements of the corporation, and the returns required by shareholders. The financial market's perception of the financial health of the organisation is also a key input to corporate strategy and constantly affects the trade-off between short-term profits and longer-term investments. Its role is to develop a vision of the future for the entire business. Marketing Highlight 3.1 describes the critical role of corporate strategy in the airline industry particularly in times of turbulence and upheaval.

At corporate level the focus is on developing strengths that maximise synergy between strategic business units in terms of technology, management experience, specific skills, research and development, and distribution. A **strategic business unit (SBU)** is a unit of the company and each unit has a separate mission and objectives and can be planned independently of other company business. An SBU

Strategic planning The process of developing and maintaining a strategic fit between the organisation's goals and capabilities and its changing marketing opportunities. It relies on developing a clear company mission, supporting objectives, a sound business portfolio and coordinated functional strategies.

Strategic business unit (SBU) A unit of the company that has a separate mission and separate objectives and that can be planned independently of other company businesses. An SBU can be a company division, a product line within a division or sometimes a single product or brand.

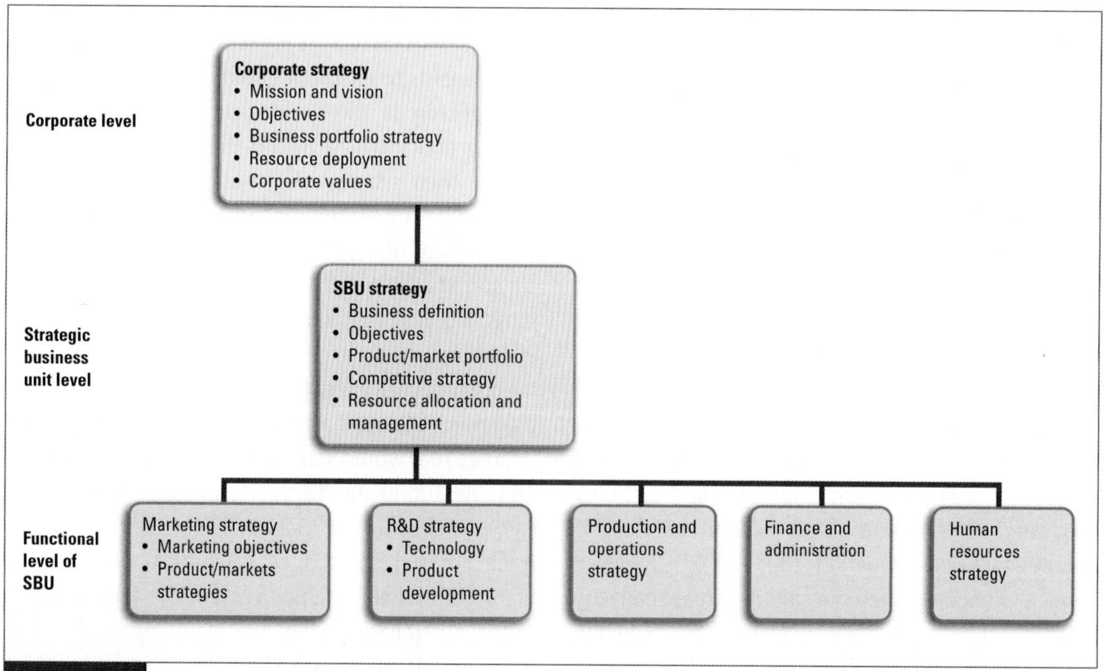

FIGURE 3.2 The strategy hierarchy

Source: L. Brown, *Competitive Marketing Strategy*, Melbourne, Nelson, 1997, p. 10, © Thomson Learning.

Strategic planning in the airline business— Qantas enters the low-end growth market

In an industry in turmoil from economic downturn, skyrocketing fuel costs, perceived threat of terrorism, the potential outbreak of the 'birdflu' virus and massive insurance premiums the international airline industry faces an uncertain and challenging future. With United Airlines, the USA's second largest carrier, filing for bankruptcy in December 2002 and remaining there in 2005 and other airlines scrambling for alliance arrangements and merger possibilities, Qantas has been one of the few airlines to show healthy profits. The six biggest airlines—American, United, Delta, Northwest, Continental and US Airways—collectively lost $US6.9 billion between October 2001 and June 2002. These losses continued in 2004 and 2005 while Qantas survived a potential loss through the collapse of Ansett Airlines in September 2001 and posted a 3% increase in net profit to $428 million for 2001–2002. What's more, Qantas implemented a bold growth strategy in 2004 and 2005 at a time of privatisation of airports and emergence of many growing discount airlines like Ryanair and easyJet.com which have taken market share from traditional full-service airlines over the last five years and wreaked havoc on their profitability. For instance, easyJet.com encompasses 25 destinations in Europe up to seven times daily, handles all bookings through the Internet and offers one class of travel.

To protect Qantas from the impact caused by the potential entry of a third domestic airline in Australia and from the spread of discount airlines into its overseas markets, it has established its domestic and international routes into a series of 'products'. These include the creation of separate international and domestic airlines offering one class and low fares. In addition, Qantas has expanded other related businesses such as travel, catering and freight by acquiring other businesses to expand its existing operations. Over the period 2003–2005 it invested about $13 billion on new aircraft to increase capacity and improve its overall efficiency by reducing maintenance costs. At the same time, Virgin Blue,

which had around 30% of the Australian market in 2005, committed to purchase 10 new Boeing 737s as part of an order of 50 new aircraft over the period to 2010. This $5.4 billion deal puts Virgin among the world's six biggest low-cost carriers. By 2006 it plans to have a third of the Australian market and a slice of the South Pacific market with expansion into routes between Australia and New Zealand, Fiji, Vanuatu and Singapore.

Qantas launched its first low-cost airline, Australian Airlines, a separately operated subsidiary, to focus as a holiday airline on various Asia service routes between Australian holiday centres like Cairns and Japan, Hong Kong, Taiwan and Singapore in October 2002. It offers economy class travel only with its own operations, management and administration based around a low-cost operations model. It followed this move in 2004 with the launch of JetStar, a domestically focused low-cost airline designed to compete with Virgin Blue. In order to compete, JetStar needed carefully to lay out a game plan that would provide some differential advantage against Virgin. One decision that was taken was to eliminate commissions to travel agents to ensure it could offer the lowest possible pricing. It also decided on a non-allocation of seating policy which meant that passengers would choose their seats as they entered the plane. This, coupled with a 30-minute check-in cut-off and non-connectivity of baggage, meant that a low price for consumers came with some real trade-offs. However, in its first year of operations 90% of customers travelled direct to their destination and there has been minimal negative feedback on the other policies. Its biggest challenge has been to build a clear brand strategy that would stand out from the iconic Qantas and the fun-loving British billionaire. The answer came in the form of Magda Szubanski, one of Australia's most respected TV celebrities, whose series of TV commercials helped cement the JetStar brand in the Australian psyche. The planning for the next steps in JetStar's strategy involves the addition of frequent-flyer recognition for Qantas frequent flyers (representing an increased focus on business travellers), pre-boarding for premium ticket holders, new entertainment systems such as video on demand—all without losing its focus on being the all-day every-day low-fares airline. So far so good. JetStar's business performed to plan in its first year to capture over 10% of the domestic airline business and contribute more than $19 million before-tax profit in its first six months.

The need for concise strategic market planning is even more critical when it comes to outside players entering this highly competitive market. One such player is OzJet, backed by Paul Stoddart (owner of the Formula 1 Racing Team, Minardi). OzJet focused on business travellers with a unique offering, planes that had business class seats only, for the price of a full-fare economy ticket on Qantas or Virgin Blue. OzJet's managing director believed he could cut 30% of the normal travel time to get from Melbourne airport to the Sydney CBD for a meeting as travellers could carry on up to three bags on board (no lines to wait in to check bags in then out) and only 60 seats meant faster boarding and disembarking. However, Ozjet closed down in early 2006 after only several months in operation.

These are bold moves in an industry facing intense competition, uncertain political and economic climates and shifting markets. To be confident in its moves and the level of investment to be undertaken, Qantas needs thorough strategic analysis and planning as well as sound marketing strategies, including contingencies and flexibility to allow for unforeseen events that may put its investments at risk or the emergence of new opportunities which make sense as part of Qantas's growth strategies. Over the next few years the belief of current chief executive, Geoff Dixon, that 'our main strength is the flexibility of the management team and board to change tack and take advantage of opportunities' will be put to the test.

Sources: Anonymous, 'Cut-Price Fares Just the Start for JetStar', *The Sydney Morning Herald*, 10 May 2005, accessed at <www.smh.com.au> on 29 September 2005; Stephen Dabkowski, 'JetStar Heads Up-market on Low-cost Route', *The Age*, 10 May 2005, accessed at <www.theage.com.au> on 29 September 2005; Alan Joyce, CEO JetStar, 'Address to National Aviation Press Club, Sydney—Transcript', accessed on <www.jetstart.com/news>; 'JetStar Alienates Travel Agents', Allan Kohler interview with Graham Turner, MD of Flight Centre, *Inside Business*, 30 April 2004, accessed on ABC Online at <www.abc.net.au> on 28 September 2005; Katie Cincotta, 'Domestic Airlines Lure Business Fliers', *B&T Magazine*, 31 March 2005, accessed online at <www.bandt.com/news> on 29 September 2005; Felicia Williams, 'Ozjet in Business to Take Market Share', 27 April 2005, accessed online at <www.bandt.com.au/news> on 29 September 2005.

Questions

1 Should JetStar focus on its core business of low-cost leisure travel or look for new growth opportunities in the business and trans-Tasman markets?

2 What type of planning should be done at JetStar?

3 How important was JetStar's brand planning in achieving a successful company launch?

3.1

can be a company division, a product line within a division or sometimes a single product or brand. Woolworths has a number of SBUs retailing clothes, food, grocery, liquor and consumer electronics in Australia, New Zealand and internationally. Traditionally the units have operated independently, each determining and pursuing its own objectives within those sent down from the corporate centre. Now Woolworth's corporate strategy focuses on the development and exploitation of strengths in technology and distribution across the group in order to strengthen customer relationships. Its mission and vision is stated as follows:

> Woolworths Limited is an Australian retail company made up of a number of businesses all providing our customers with quality, range, value and everyday low prices. We're built on a passion for retail, attention to detail, working hard, ensuring the safety of our customers and our people, and having fun.
>
> Our mission is to deliver to customers a better shopping experience—each and every time. Our vision and values are known as The Woolworths Way. [6]

Figure 3.3 shows Woolworths' SBUs and leading brands such as Dick Smith Electronics, Big W and of course the Woolworths supermarket brand.

The role of corporate strategy is to provide a guiding vision that unifies the group and guides the development of core competencies. Core competencies represent the specific skills and abilities that enable a firm to deliver products or services to its customers, thereby producing an exceptional result—for customers and the firm. The characteristics of core competencies are threefold:

1 They provide access to a wide range of markets.
2 They make a significant contribution to the perceived customer benefits of the end product.
3 They are difficult for competitors to imitate.[7]

Core competencies enable the firm to develop the core products from which entire product ranges evolve. For example, Canon's core competencies have resulted in:

- The camera core product—from competencies in precision mechanics and fine optics.
- The fax core product—from precision mechanics and microelectronics.
- The laser printer core product—from precision mechanics, fine optics and microelectronics.[8]

Sony's competency in miniaturisation has resulted in a wide range of audio products. The value of core competencies is affected by the firm's ability to distribute them across SBUs and to use them to create new markets. This is an important role of strategy at the corporate level.

Sony's new corporate vision extends its business to include digital cameras and electronically distributed images direct to end-users—aiming to displace Kodak's traditional business of film and film processing and courier services such as those provided by UPS and FedEx.

Business strategy

In large organisations the different businesses are usually operated as separate SBUs. At this level the focus is on building, defending and maintaining competitive positions through development and implementation of competitive marketing strategies.

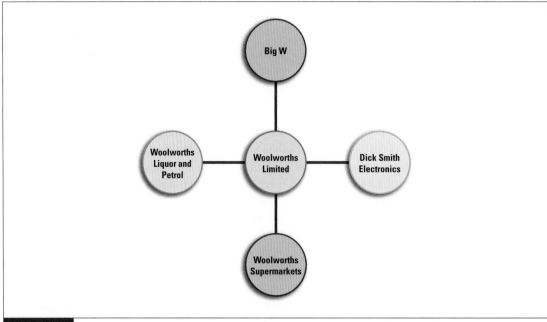

FIGURE 3.3 Woolworths' strategic business units

This requires an assessment of the capabilities of the business and how these best match the needs and wants of its target markets. Since they may not be suitable for all markets in its business area, managers at this level must evaluate and select which markets are appropriate as primary targets and hence the markets in which it will compete. Defining its business in terms of scope and communicating the vision of the business, its objectives and market priorities are important elements of business strategy. The basis of its competitive strategy in terms of differentiation or cost advantages should also be addressed. At the business unit level synergies should be sought across markets to capitalise on competencies and to maximise the effectiveness of resource allocation.

Marketing strategy

Marketing strategy requires the planning and coordination of marketing resources and the integration of the marketing mix to achieve a desired result in the markets selected for targeting by the business. The business's offers are tailored through marketing strategy in terms of product line, communication, distribution and pricing elements to match the perceptions of value of its target market. Similarly, research and development, production, finance and human resources strategies are developed at the functional level to dovetail with and support SBU strategy.[9]

Strategic planning steps

Strategic planning sets the stage for the planning in the firm. It relies on defining a clear company mission, setting supporting company objectives, designing a sound business portfolio and coordinating functional strategies, as shown in Figure 3.4. At the corporate level the company first defines its overall purpose and mission. This mission is then turned into detailed supporting objectives that guide the whole company. Next, corporate head office decides what portfolio of business and products is best for the company and how much support to give each one. In turn, each business and product unit must develop detailed marketing and other departmental plans that support the company-wide plan. Thus, marketing planning occurs at the business-unit, product and market levels. It supports company strategic planning with more detailed planning for specific marketing opportunities.

Defining the company mission

An organisation exists to accomplish something. At first it has a clear purpose or mission, but over time its mission may become unclear as the organisation grows and adds new products and markets. Or the mission may remain clear but some managers may no longer be committed to it. Or the mission may remain clear but may no longer be the best choice given new conditions in the environment.

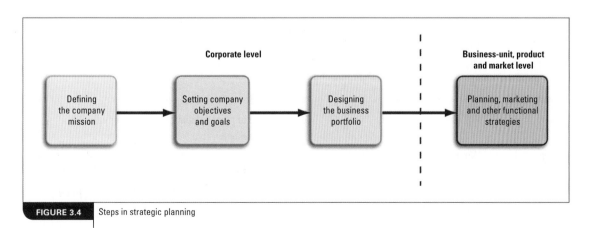

FIGURE 3.4   Steps in strategic planning

When management sense that the organisation is drifting, they must renew their search for purpose. It is time to ask: What is our business? Who is the customer? What do consumers value? What will our business be? What should our business be? These simple-sounding questions are among the most difficult the company will ever have to answer. Successful companies raise these questions continually and answer them carefully and completely.

Mission statement
A statement of
the organisation's
purpose—what it wants to
accomplish in the larger
environment.

Many organisations develop formal mission statements that answer these questions. A **mission statement** is a statement of the organisation's purpose—what it wants to accomplish in the larger environment. A clear mission statement acts as an 'invisible hand' that guides people in the organisation so they can work independently and yet collectively toward overall organisational goals.

Traditionally, organisations have defined their businesses in product terms ('We manufacture furniture') or in technological terms ('We are a chemical-processing firm'). But mission statements should be *market oriented*. Market definitions of a business are better than product or technological definitions. Products and technologies eventually become outdated, but basic market needs may last forever. A market-oriented mission statement defines the business in terms of satisfying basic customer needs. Thus, Telstra is in the communications business, not the telephone business. ANZ defines its business not as issuing credit cards but as allowing customers to exchange value—for virtually anything, anywhere in the world. And 3M does more than just make adhesives, scientific equipment and healthcare products. It solves people's problems by putting innovation to work for them. A typical mission statement found on many corporate websites is reflected in the following statement from Weston Milling of the George Weston Foods Group:

> To provide optimum returns to our stakeholders (employees, shareholders and customers) through the provision of quality products and services to meet our customer needs. This will be done through the involvement, commitment and contribution of all our people and will ensure the nutritional and food safety needs of our consumers, and the health and wellbeing of all who work with us.[10]

Table 3.1 provides several other examples of product-oriented versus market-oriented business definitions.

Table 3.2 provides some examples of mission statements.

Management should avoid making its mission too narrow or too broad. A pencil manufacturer that says it is in the communication-equipment business is stating its mission too broadly. Missions

TABLE 3.1 Product- and market-oriented business definitions

Company	Product-oriented definition	Market-oriented definition
Max Factor	We make lipsticks	We sell lifestyle and self-expression; success and status; memories, hopes and dreams
Sea World	We run a theme park	We provide fantasies and entertainment
Kmart	We run discount stores	We offer products and services that deliver value to middle-Australians
Xerox	We make copying, fax and other office machines	We make businesses more productive by helping them scan, store, retrieve, revise, distribute, print and publish documents
Bunnings	We sell tools and home repair/improvement items	We provide advice and solutions that transform home-owners into Mr and Ms Fixits

should be *realistic*—Qantas would be deluding itself if it adopted the mission to become the world's largest airline. Missions should also be *specific*. Many mission statements are written for public relations purposes and lack specific, workable guidelines. The statement 'We want to become the

---

TABLE 3.2 Examples of mission statements

Carlton United Breweries

OUR VISION

Inspiring Global Enjoyment.

Whether through beer, wine, spirits, leisure or property, Foster's premium products inspire enjoyment around the world.

OUR MISSION

Foster's mission is to work together, respecting each other, our heritage, diversity, skills and knowledge to:

- Build premium quality, first-choice brands,
- Deliver service excellence to customers and consumers,
- Generate superior returns for shareholders,
- Create an inspiring workplace,
- Be welcomed in the communities in which we operate.

Fisher and Paykel

OUR MISSION

To seek profitable growth by designing, manufacturing, and marketing, a range of appliances that care for the needs of our customers around the world, while offering innovation, style and integrity. At the same time we will exploit the sale of technology and form alliances that complement our business.

Canon Australia <www.canon.com.au/about/story_112.html>

CORPORATE MISSION STATEMENT

Canon Australia is a market leading supplier of consumer and business imaging solutions. We are a team committed to our customers' ongoing satisfaction through the empowerment and development of our staff.

To be the preferred supplier we will be easy to deal with and provide quality, value for money, products and services.

To ensure success for all stakeholders we will deliver profitability, growth, job fulfilment and have a positive impact on the community.

Primus Telecom <www.primustel.com.au/PrimusWeb/AboutUs>

OUR MISSION

To provide a competitive advantage to our clients through excellence in total telecommunications, data, Internet and e-Commerce solutions while significantly reducing their overall costs.

Ford Motor Company <www.mycareer.ford.com/OURCOMPANY.ASP?CID=23>

OUR VISION

Our vision is to become the world's leading consumer company for automotive products and services.

OUR MISSION

We are a global family with a proud heritage, passionately committed to providing personal mobility for people around the world. We anticipate consumer needs and deliver outstanding products and services that improve people's lives.

OUR VALUES

The customer is Job 1. We do the right thing for our customers, our people, our environment and our society. By improving everything we do, we provide superior returns to our shareholders.

IBM <www.ibm.com/investor/company/index.phtml>

COMPANY MISSION

At IBM, we strive to lead in the creation, development and manufacture of the industry's most advanced information technologies, including computer systems, software, networking systems, storage devices and microelectronics.

We translate these advanced technologies into value for our customers through our professional solutions and services businesses worldwide.

---

continued

TABLE 3.2 Examples of mission statements

Adelaide Yoshinkai Aikido <www.ojirowashi.com/mission.htm>

MISSION STATEMENT

The mission of Adelaide Yoshinkai Aikido is to work in partnership with the South Australian community:

- to provide students with best quality training, focusing on the promotion of the aikido philosophy and ideals,
- providing an environment that is conducive to practising excellent aikido,
- to practise aikido in a friendly, and non-competitive atmosphere,
- to promote and spread the Yoshinkan style of aikido.

News Corporation <www.newscorp.com/mission.html>

MISSION STATEMENT

A constellation of media businesses, News Corporation's global operations encompass the fields of filmed entertainment, newspapers, pay and free-to-air television, cable network programming, book publishing, magazines and consumer marketing.

Just as our assets span the world, our vision spans art and humor, audacity and compassion, information and innovation—whether in an American television series, an Indian game show, an Australian newspaper, an English sports broadcast or an international box-office hit.

Every day, hundreds of millions of people are entertained and enlightened by the authors and actors, printers and producers, reporters and directors who fulfil our mission. That mission remains unchanged after half a century of expansion and improvement: the creation and distribution of top-quality news, sports and entertainment around the world.

University of Newcastle

MISSION STATEMENT

The University of Newcastle:

- prepares graduates who contribute to society, are adaptable global citizens and are sought out by employers;
- undertakes outstanding research, including creative works and scholarship; and
- contributes to social, economic and cultural enrichment and environmental sustainability.

Master Painters Association of Queensland

Mission Statement

To effectively represent the interests of our members and to encourage in them ever increasing standards.

Body Shop Australia <www.thebodyshop.com.au/infopage.cfm?pageID=53>

MISSION STATEMENT

- Dedicate our business to the pursuit of social and environmental change.
- Creatively balance the financial and human needs of our stakeholders: employees, customers, franchisees, suppliers and shareholders.
- Courageously ensure that our business is ecologically sustainable, meeting the needs of the present without compromising the future.
- Meaningfully contribute to local, national and international communities in which we trade, by adopting a code of conduct which ensures care, honesty, fairness and respect.
- Passionately campaign for the protection of the environment, human and civil rights, and against animal testing within the cosmetics and toiletries industry.
- Tirelessly work to narrow the gap between principle and practice, whilst making fun, passion and care part of our daily lives.

leading company in this industry by producing the highest-quality products with the best service at the lowest prices' sounds good, but it is full of generalities and contradictions. It will not help the company make tough decisions. Missions should fit the *market environment*.

The organisation should base its mission on its *core competencies*. Nestlé could probably enter the computer business, but that would not take advantage of its core competence—providing low-cost food and conveniently packaged food to large groups of customers. Finally, mission statements should be motivating. A company's mission should not be stated as making more sales or profits—profits are only a reward for undertaking a useful activity. A company's employees need to feel that their work is significant and contributes to people's lives. Microsoft's long-term goal has been IAYF—'information at your fingertips'—to put information at the fingertips of every person. This is also translated for the corporate mission: 'To enable people and businesses throughout the world to realize their full potential'. Microsoft's mission is highly motivating.[11]

Missions are best when guided by a *vision*, an almost 'impossible dream'. Lou Gerstner's vision of the world is in the following statement: 'Every day it becomes more clear that the Net is taking its place alongside the other great transformational technologies that first challenged, and then fundamentally changed, the way things are done in the world'.[12] His vision is reflected in IBM's positioning as an electronic business (e-business) company offering 'solutions for a small planet'.

Sony's president, Akio Morita, wanted everyone to have access to 'personal portable sound', and his company created the Walkman. Fred Smith wanted to deliver mail anywhere in the USA before 10.30 am the next day, and he created Federal Express. Sam Walton wanted to bring modern discount principles to small-town Americans, and he created the giant retailer Wal-Mart. A vision that can portray a concise and motivating picture for all employees gives a unifying sense of direction that is actionable.

Talk to the Home Loan Lender of the Year today.

More Convenient Banking ANZ NOW

ANZ is among the world's top 100 banks, and is increasingly servicing its customers online.

Pepsi's 'beat Coke' vision is an example. More closely linked with the societal concept of marketing discussed in Chapter 1 is the vision of The Body Shop:

> To dedicate our business to the pursuit of social and environmental change . . . To tirelessly work to narrow the gap between principle and practice, whilst making fun, passion and care part of our daily lives.[13]

The company's mission statement should provide a vision and direction for the company for the next five to ten years. Companies do not revise their missions every few years in response to each new turn in the environment. Still, a company must redefine its mission if that mission has lost credibility or no longer defines an optimal course for the company.[14]

Drawing from a research project of 18 exceptional and long-lasting companies, Collins and Porras tried to identify what made them different and able to sustain long-term dominance in their markets.[15] The companies included General Electric, 3M, Wal-Mart, Walt Disney, Hewlett-Packard, Proctor & Gamble, Motorola, Sony, Merck and Boeing. Two key principles were identified as internal drivers of those companies that are built to last. First, it is of critical importance to preserve and *protect the company's core ideology*. Core ideology goes beyond making money. For Wal-Mart it is to 'exceed customer expectations', for 3M it is 'respect for individual initiative' and for Boeing it is 'being on the leading edge of innovation; being pioneers'. Second, the company must have a *relentless drive for progress*. This means urging continual change, pushing continual movement towards goals and improvement, expanding the number and variety of possibilities, and being prepared to implement radical change consistent with the company's core ideology.[16] These two principles must be connected to tangible mechanisms. Collins and Porras found that long-lasting companies are distinguished by the following methods:

- ⊙ *BHAGs*. Big Hairy Audacious Goals stimulate progress.
- ⊙ *Cult-like cultures*. The working environment is right for those who buy into the core ideology and rejects those that don't. This preserves the core.
- ⊙ *Experimentation*. Try a lot of things and keep what works. This stimulates progress.
- ⊙ *Home-grown management*. This preserves the core.
- ⊙ *Good enough never is*. Relentless self-improvement stimulates progress.[17]

In their next book, *Good to Great*, they found that making the transition from good to great did not require a high-profile outside CEO or cutting edge technology, but a corporate culture that identified and promoted disciplined people with a blend of personal humility and professional integrity. These companies, defined as those that transitioned from a 10-year fallow period to 15 years of increased profits, were driven by core values and purpose that went beynd simply making money.[18]

Setting company objectives and goals

The company's mission needs to be turned into detailed supporting objectives for each level of management. Each manager should have objectives and be responsible for reaching them. For example, Orica Australia is involved in several businesses: explosives, plastics and fertilisers. The fertiliser division, Incitec, does not say that its mission is to produce fertiliser. Instead, it says that its mission is to 'increase agricultural productivity'. This mission leads to a hierarchy of objectives, including business objectives and marketing objectives (see Figure 3.5). The mission of increasing

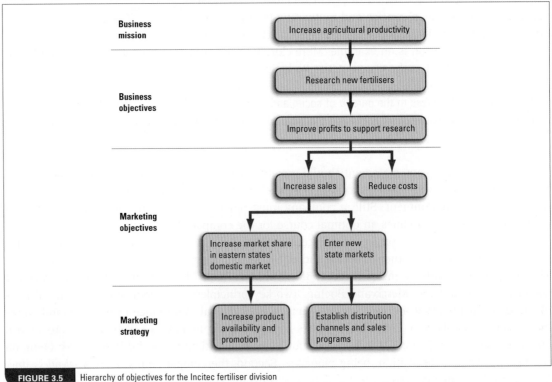

FIGURE 3.5 Hierarchy of objectives for the Incitec fertiliser division

agricultural productivity leads to the company's business objective of researching new fertilisers that promise higher yields. But research is expensive and requires improved profits to reinvest in research programs.

Information technology now plays a major part in reducing costs, improving efficiency of customer access and providing relevant information to help farmers increase agricultural productivity. So the implementation of an electronic marketing strategy can contribute to Ford's mission as well as improving profits, which is a key business objective. Profits can be improved by reducing costs. Cost reductions may be possible through efficiencies achieved in the supply chain from Ford to dealers to customers. For instance, Dell, the computer manufacturer, is leading PC producers in Australia by opening up direct access to end-consumers with the objective of reducing distribution costs. Ford Motor Company in the USA teamed up with Microsoft to deliver the first online build-to-order system to link consumer orders directly with automotive manufacturers' supply and delivery systems.[19]

Profits can also be improved by increasing sales. For Incitec, sales can be increased by improving the company's share of the Australian market, which may involve tapping into farmers who want to buy fertilisers online as well as entering new overseas markets, or both. These goals then become the company's current marketing objectives.

Marketing strategies must be developed to support these marketing objectives. To increase its market share, the company may increase its product's availability by setting up an online presence, promotion and targeting. To enter new overseas markets, the company may use its online information services to target large farms abroad through tailored web page applications, custom tailored pricing and reference to local country distributors. These are its broad marketing strategies. Each broad marketing strategy must then be defined in greater detail. For example, increasing the product's promotion may require more salespeople and more advertising; if so, both requirements must be spelled out. In this way, the company's mission is translated into a set of objectives for the current period. The objectives should be as specific as possible. The objective to 'increase our market share' is not as useful as the objective to 'increase our market share to 30% by the end of the second year'. An example of this hierarchy is shown in Figure 3.5.

SELF-CHECK QUESTIONS

1   List the specific areas of focus in each level of the strategy hierarchy.

2   What is the difference between customer value and business value? Refer to Figure 3.1.

3   Note the important characteristics of a mission statement and evaluate examples you have found in company annual reports. Compare them with the examples in Table 3.2.

4   List examples of business objectives and marketing objectives.

Designing the business portfolio

Guided by the company's mission statement and objectives, management must now plan its **business portfolio**—the collection of businesses and products that make up the company. The most effective business portfolio is the one that best fits the company's strengths and weaknesses to opportunities in the environment. The company must (1) analyse its *current* business portfolio and decide which businesses should receive more, less or no investment; and (2) develop growth strategies for adding *new* products or businesses to the portfolio.

Business portfolio The collection of businesses and products that make up the company.

Analysing the current business portfolio

Portfolio analysis
A tool by which management identify and evaluate the various businesses that make up the company.

Many companies operate several businesses. However, they often fail to define them carefully. The major activity in strategic planning is business **portfolio analysis**, whereby management identify and evaluate the businesses making up the company. The company will want to put strong resources into its more profitable businesses and phase down or shed its weaker ones. For example, in recent years PepsiCo has strengthened its portfolio by selling off what shareholders and management saw as less attractive businesses such as its fast-food business units in Australia—Pizza Hut, KFC and Taco Bell. At the same time, it has invested more heavily in its core soft drink business around the world where its core competencies and capabilities lie. George Stalk, a leading Boston Consulting Group consultant, suggests that winning companies are those that have achieved superior in-company capabilities, not just core competencies.[20] PepsiCo's capabilities are very strong in the soft drink industry but very weak in the fast-food retail industry.

Management's first step is to identify the key businesses making up the company. These are called *strategic business units*. The next step in business portfolio analysis calls for management to assess the attractiveness of its various SBUs and decide how much support each deserves. In some companies this is done informally. Management looks at the company's collection of businesses or products and uses its judgment to decide how much each SBU should contribute and receive.

The purpose of strategic planning is to find ways in which the company can best use its strengths to take advantage of attractive opportunities in the environment. So most standard portfolio-analysis methods evaluate SBUs on two important dimensions—the attractiveness of the SBU's market or industry and the strength of the SBU's position in that market or industry. The best known portfolio-planning methods were developed by the Boston Consulting Group, a leading management consulting firm, and by General Electric.

Growth-share matrix
A portfolio-planning method that evaluates a company's strategic business units in terms of their market growth rate and relative market share. SBUs are classified as stars, cash cows, question marks or dogs.

The Boston Consulting Group approach

Using the Boston Consulting Group (BCG) approach, a company classifies all its SBUs according to the **growth-share matrix** shown in Figure 3.6. On the vertical axis, *market growth rate* provides a measure of market attractiveness. On the horizontal axis, *relative market share* serves as a measure of company strength in the market. By dividing the growth-share matrix as indicated, four types of SBUs can be distinguished:

Question marks
Low-share business units in high-growth markets that require a lot of cash to hold their share or build into stars.

Stars High-growth, high-share businesses or products that often require heavy investment to finance their rapid growth.

Cash cows Low-growth, high-share businesses or products—established and successful units that generate cash, which the company uses to pay its bills and support other business units that need investment.

- ⊙ *Question marks*. Question marks are businesses that operate in high-growth markets but have low relative market shares. Most businesses start off as question marks as the company tries to enter a high-growth market in which there is already a market leader. A question mark requires a lot of cash because the company has to spend money on plant, equipment and personnel to keep up with the fast-growing market, and because it wants to overtake the leader. The term 'question mark' is appropriate because the company has to think hard about whether to keep pouring money into this business. The company in Figure 3.6 operates three question-mark businesses, and this may be too many. The company might be better off investing more cash in one or two of these businesses instead of spreading its cash over all three question marks.
- ⊙ *Stars*. If the question-mark business is successful, it becomes a star. A star is the market leader in a high-growth market. A star does not necessarily produce a positive cash flow for the company. The company must spend substantial funds to keep up with the high market growth and fight off competitors' attacks. In Figure 3.6 the company has two stars. The company would justifiably be concerned if it had no stars.
- ⊙ *Cash cows*. When a market's annual growth rate falls to less than 10%, the star becomes a cash cow if it still has the largest relative market share. A cash cow produces a lot of cash for the company. The company does not have to finance a lot of capacity expansion because the

market's growth rate has slowed down. And since the business is the market leader, it enjoys economies of scale and higher profit margins. The company uses its cash-cow businesses to pay its bills and support its other businesses. The company in Figure 3.6 has two cash cows and is therefore less vulnerable than if it had only one. If either cash cow starts losing relative market share, the company will have to pump enough money back into it to maintain market leadership. If it uses its cash to support its other businesses, one or both of its strong cash cows may devolve into a dog.

● **Dogs.** Dogs are businesses that have weak market shares in low-growth markets. They typically generate low profits or losses, although they may generate some cash. The company in Figure 3.6 holds three dogs, and this may be three too many. The company should consider whether it is holding on to these dog businesses for good reasons (such as an expected turnaround in the market growth rate or a new chance at market leadership) or for sentimental reasons. Dogs often consume more management time than they are worth and need to be phased down or out.

Dogs Low-growth, low-share businesses or products that may generate enough cash to maintain themselves but do not promise to be a large source of cash.

The 10 circles in the growth-share matrix represent a company's 10 current SBUs. The company has two stars, two cash cows, three question marks and three dogs. The areas of the circles are proportional to the SBU's dollar sales. This company is in fair shape, though not in good shape. It wants to invest in the more promising question marks to make them stars, and to maintain the stars so that they will become cash cows as their markets mature. Fortunately, it has two good-sized cash cows whose income helps to finance the company's question marks, stars and dogs. The company should take some decisive action concerning its dogs and its question marks. The picture would be worse if the company had no stars, if it had too many dogs or if it had only one weak cash cow.

Once it has classified its SBUs, the company must determine what role each will play in the future. One of four strategies can be pursued for each SBU. The company can invest more in the business unit in order to *build* its share. Or it can invest just enough to *hold* the SBU's share at the current level. It can *harvest* the SBU, milking its short-term cash flow regardless of the long-term effect. Finally, the company can *divest* the SBU by selling it or phasing it out and using the resources elsewhere.

As time passes, SBUs change their positions in the growth-share matrix. Each SBU has a life cycle. Many SBUs start out as question marks and move into the star category if they succeed. They later

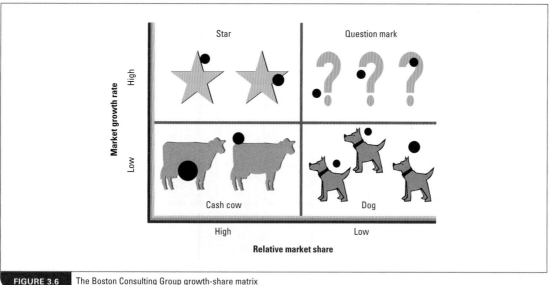

FIGURE 3.6 The Boston Consulting Group growth-share matrix

become cash cows as market growth falls, then finally die off or turn into dogs toward the end of their life cycle. The company needs to add new products and units continually so that some of them will become stars and, eventually, cash cows that will help finance other SBUs.[21]

The General Electric approach

General Electric (GE) introduced a comprehensive portfolio-planning tool called a *strategic business-planning grid* (see Figure 3.7). Like the BCG approach, it uses a matrix with two dimensions—one representing industry attractiveness (the vertical axis) and one representing company strength in the industry (the horizontal axis). The best businesses are those located in highly attractive industries where the company has high business strength.

The GE approach considers many factors besides market growth rate as part of industry attractiveness. It uses an industry attractiveness index made up of market size, market growth rate, industry profit margin, amount of competition, seasonality and cyclicality of demand, and industry cost structure. Each of these factors is rated and combined in an index of industry attractiveness. For our purposes, an industry's attractiveness will be described as high, medium or low. As an example, Kraft has identified numerous highly attractive industries—natural foods, specialty frozen foods, physical fitness products and others. It has withdrawn from less attractive industries such as bulk oils and cardboard packaging.

For business strength, the GE approach again uses an index rather than a simple measure of relative market share. The business-strength index includes factors such as the company's relative market share, price competitiveness, product quality, customer and market knowledge, sales effectiveness and geographic advantages. These factors are rated and combined in an index of business strength, which can be described as strong, average or weak. Thus, Kraft has substantial business strength in food and related industries, but is relatively weak in other industries.

The grid is divided into three different zones. The green cells at the upper left include the strong SBUs in which the company should invest and grow. The purple cells contain SBUs that are medium in overall attractiveness. The company should maintain its level of investment in these SBUs. The three solid red cells at the lower right indicate SBUs that are low in overall attractiveness. The company should give serious thought to harvesting or divesting these SBUs.

The circles represent four company SBUs; the areas of the circles are proportional to the relative sizes of the industries in which these SBUs compete. The pie slices within the circles represent each SBU's market share. Thus, circle A represents a company SBU with a 75% market share in a good-sized, highly attractive industry in which the company has strong business strength. Circle B

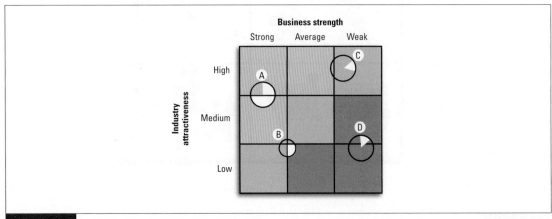

FIGURE 3.7   General Electric's strategic business-planning grid

represents an SBU that has a 50% market share, but the industry is not very attractive. Circles C and D represent two other company SBUs in industries where the company has small market shares and not much business strength. Altogether, the company should build A, maintain B and make some hard decisions on what to do with C and D.

Management would also plot the projected positions of the SBUs with and without changes in strategies. By comparing current and projected business grids, management can identify the major strategic issues and opportunities it faces.

Problems with matrix approaches

The BCG, GE and other formal methods revolutionised strategic planning. However, such approaches have limitations. They can be difficult, time consuming and costly to implement. Management may find it difficult to define SBUs and measure market share and growth. In addition, these approaches focus on classifying *current* businesses but provide little advice for *future* planning. Management must still rely on its own judgment to set the business objectives for each SBU, to determine what resources each will be given and to work out which new businesses should be added.

Formal planning approaches can also lead the company to place too much emphasis on market-share growth or growth through entry into attractive new markets. Using these approaches, many companies plunged into unrelated and new high-growth businesses they did not know how to manage—with very bad results. At the same time, these companies were often too quick to abandon, sell or milk to death their healthy mature businesses. As a result, many companies that diversified too broadly in the past are now narrowing their focus and getting back to the basics of serving one or a few industries they know best.

Another problem with the portfolio approach was that it did not address how value can be created across SBUs, such as the Mars portfolio in snack foods, pet care and Mars Electronics. The only relationship between them was cash. As we have come to learn, the relatedness of businesses is at the heart of value creation in diversified companies. The portfolio matrix also suffers from its assumption that corporations have to be self-sufficient in capital. This implies that they should find a use for all internally generated cash and that they should not raise additional funds from the capital market. This implies that additional funds from the capital market are not available. Both these assumptions are inappropriate. We now see some companies like Bluescope Steel refunding capital to shareholders, with others, like Telstra, continually in the capital market to raise funds.[22] In addition, the growth-share matrix fails to compare the competitive advantage a business receives from being owned by a particular company with the costs of owning it.

Despite these and other problems, and although many companies have dropped formal matrix methods in favour of more customised approaches that are better suited to their situations, most large companies remain firmly committed to strategic planning. Portfolio analysis is no cure-all for finding the best strategy. However, it can help management to understand the company's overall situation, to see how each business or product contributes, to assign resources to its businesses and to orient the company for future success. When used properly, strategic planning is just one important aspect of overall strategic management, a way of thinking about how to manage a business.

Developing growth strategies

Beyond evaluating current business, designing the business portfolio involves finding future businesses and products the company should consider. Igor Ansoff, a pioneer in strategic thinking, introduced the concept of the *planning gap*. Management could readily measure the challenges they faced by charting the expected sales based on no change to current strategies, and then charting potential sales based on an assessment of the full market potential.[23] Figure 3.8 (overleaf) illustrates this gap.

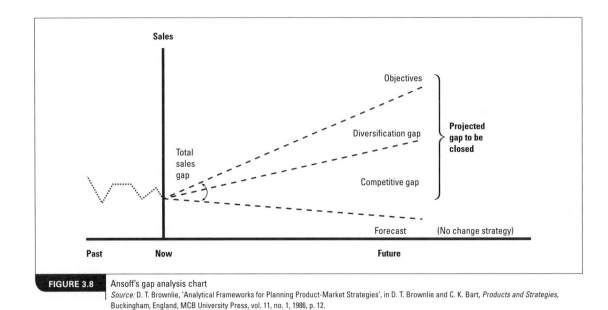

FIGURE 3.8 Ansoff's gap analysis chart
Source: D. T. Brownlie, 'Analytical Frameworks for Planning Product-Market Strategies', in D. T. Brownlie and C. K. Bart, *Products and Strategies*, Buckingham, England, MCB University Press, vol. 11, no. 1, 1986, p. 12.

Product/market expansion grid
A portfolio planning tool for identifying company growth opportunities through market penetration, market development, product development or diversification.

Market penetration
A strategy for promoting company growth by increasing sales of current products to current market segments without changing the product in any way.

Analysis of the gap shows that two gaps exist. A competitive gap indicates the sales potential from the existing business, and a diversification gap is the sales potential from new businesses. One useful device for identifying growth opportunities is the **product/market expansion grid**.[24] This grid is shown in Figure 3.9. Below, we apply it to Unilever Foods.

Market penetration First, Unilever Foods management might consider whether the company's major brands can achieve deeper **market penetration**—making more sales to present customers without changing products in any way. For example, to increase its margarine sales it might cut prices, increase advertising, get its products into more stores or obtain better shelf positions for them. Basically, Unilever management would like to increase usage by current customers and attract customers of other brands to its margarine brands.

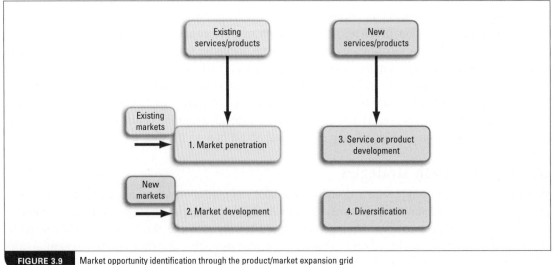

FIGURE 3.9 Market opportunity identification through the product/market expansion grid

Market development Second, Unilever management might consider possibilities for **market development**—identifying and developing new markets for current products. For example, managers at Unilever might review demographic markets for its ice-cream—kids, teenagers, young adults, professionals, families and health-conscious baby boomers—to see if any of these groups could be encouraged to buy, or buy more, of Unilever's Streets ice-cream products. The managers might also look at institutional markets—restaurants, food services, hospitals—to see if sales to these buyers could be increased. And managers could review geographical markets—Indonesia, Thailand, Malaysia—to see if these markets could be developed. All these are market development strategies.

Product development Third, management could consider **product development**—offering modified or new products to current markets. Unilever Food's products could be offered in new sizes, with new ingredients or in new packaging, all representing possible product modifications. Unilever could also launch new brands to appeal to different users or it could launch other food products that its current customers might buy. For example, in Australia the Flora Proactive brand was successfully launched as a new margarine that reduces cholesterol uptake. All these are product development strategies.

Diversification Fourth, Unilever might consider **diversification**. It could start up or buy businesses entirely outside its current products and markets. For example, the company's moves into the growing health and fitness industry, which includes gym equipment, health foods and slimming programs, would represent diversification. Purchase of Jenny Craig and the Fitness First Clubs chain (www.fitnessfirst.com.au) might be an appropriate entry point. Some companies try to identify the most attractive emerging industries. They feel that half the secret of success is to enter attractive industries instead of trying to be efficient in an unattractive industry. But many companies which diversified too broadly, like PepsiCo in the 1990s and Ericsson in the early 2000s, are now narrowing their market focus and getting back to the basics of serving one industry or a few industries they know best.

The strategic and relevant options will depend on the size of the gap and the competitive position in its markets. For instance, a high market share in existing markets, such as Franklins Foods' position in New South Wales, led it to seek growth from new markets such as Queensland and from new product ranges such as fresh fruit and vegetables. The diversification into fresh foods led to unprofitability at Franklins and it was sold in parts to Pick 'n Pay, Woolworths and to independents. However, Woolworths has shown how steady sales and profit growth can be sustained in the retail food sector—see Marketing Highlight 3.2.

The product/market expansion grid provides another point for the development of objectives and strategies. Figure 3.10 indicates alternative directions for growth from the established business where market penetration is the current strategy.

Depending on the firm and its environment, product development, market development or a higher-risk move to diversification may be pursued. TNT, because of strong positions across all main sectors of the Australian transport industry, is offering similar services in new overseas markets.

Sometimes the gap analysis approach will show that the momentum of present strategies will take sales higher than is desirable, given the limited supply capabilities of the firm. Blue Banner Foods, for example, dominates the pickled onion market in Tasmania. Seeking growth in other states, with its limited production capacity, it received complaints from distributors about the unavailability of the product. The momentum of the growth strategy was not supported by supply, and it was necessary to adopt strategies to reduce demand.

Market development
A strategy for promoting company growth by identifying and developing new market segments for current company products.

Product development
A strategy for promoting company growth by offering modified or new products to current market segments; developing the product concept into a physical product in order to assure that the product idea can be turned into a workable product.

Diversification
A strategy for promoting company growth by starting up or acquiring businesses outside the company's current products and markets.

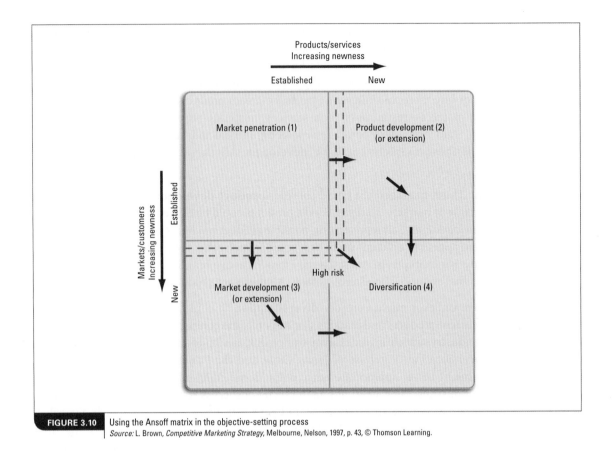

FIGURE 3.10   Using the Ansoff matrix in the objective-setting process
Source: L. Brown, *Competitive Marketing Strategy*, Melbourne, Nelson, 1997, p. 43, © Thomson Learning.

Strategic implications

In general we find that companies have difficulty meeting demand during the rapid-growth stage of the life cycle. Customer complaints, poor service and a decline in quality in an effort to meet demand weaken the company's market position. The significance of these concepts is that market growth should be managed in line with capabilities to achieve realistic objectives.

Gap analysis can be extended to identify the profit gap using the same approach. However, the options are viewed in terms of their provision of profit in the short, medium and longer term. Profit-generating strategies to close the gap must consider both product/market options, as indicated in the growth matrix, and cost and productivity initiatives. A combination of options for closing the profit gap is depicted in Figure 3.11.

Although a simplification of the issues involved, the planning gap and product/market growth concepts are good starting points for identifying the strategic analysis task and providing broad indicators for strategic direction. They can indicate widely different growth or profit expectations from those that are realistic and thus highlight problems to be addressed by management. Brown suggests that the sales or profit gap can be closed by one or a combination of three major strategies. The three main means of closing the gap are sales growth, productivity improvement and redeployment of capital resources by changing the firm's asset base. Figure 3.12 depicts these options.

The rapid growth of electronic connection through the Internet is having a transformational effect on many businesses. For example, the fastest growing computer manufacturer and marketer in the world is Dell Computers, which sells goods online worth more than $US8 million a day. This has

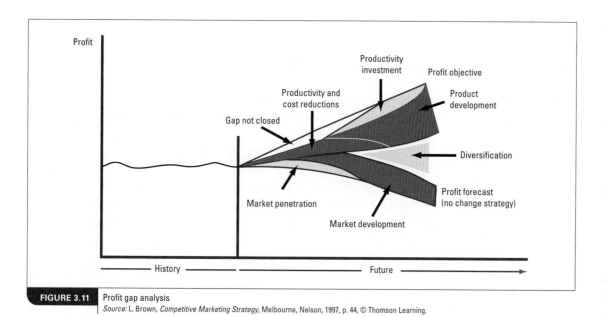

FIGURE 3.11 Profit gap analysis
Source: L. Brown, *Competitive Marketing Strategy,* Melbourne, Nelson, 1997, p. 44, © Thomson Learning.

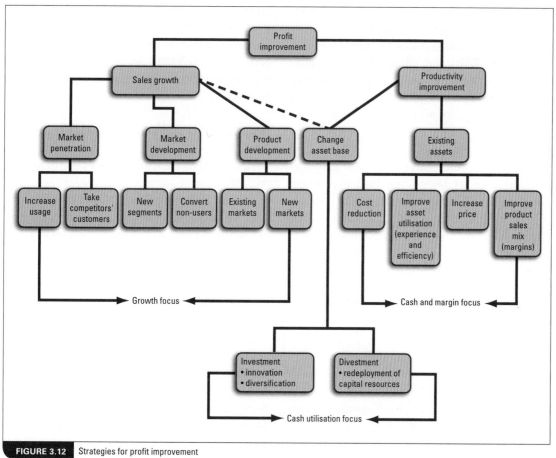

FIGURE 3.12 Strategies for profit improvement
Source: L. Brown, *Competitive Marketing Strategy*, Melbourne, Nelson, 1997, p. 162, © Thomson Learning.

Woolworths' strategy for growth

Why is it that Woolworths has shown consistent sales and profit growth over the last decade and Coles Myer has struggled? Over the six years from June 1999 to June 2005, Woolworths' sales have increased 56% to $31.3 billion with earnings before interest and tax up 88% to $1283 million and net profit up 128% to $791 million. Over the same period Coles Myer showed a similar 56% sales growth to $36.5 billion, but only a small increase in earnings before interest and tax from $751.3 million in 1999 to around $1010 million in 2005.

Consistency of strategy and positioning

Woolworths has implemented a long-term strategy with consistent positioning and communication in each of its businesses of Woolworths Supermarkets, Big W discount stores and Dick Smith Electronics. The supermarkets business has been particularly successful with the differentiated theme of 'the fresh food people', which has positioned that business over the last decade around the primary value of 'fresh' required by a large proportion of supermarket buyers. The conversion of 72 Franklins stores acquired in June 2001 to Woolworths has added increased market coverage.

In contrast Coles Myer has had particular problems with its Myer/Grace Bros department store group with inconsistent positioning throughout the 1990s and declining appeal in the early 2000s. There has also been cannibalisation of the Myer/Grace Bros business by Target, its own discount chain, and inconsistent strategies around decentralised and centralised buying which has led to both internal complexity and confusion in the marketplace.

Management and board stability

Woolworths has had a relatively smooth and fairly infrequent succession of management executives and board members enabling it to implement longer-term strategies and plans effectively. Coles Myer has had a disruptive history of changing chief executives and warring directors that has kept its focus short term and in a reactive 'fix-it' mode of operation.

Synergy of business units

Woolworths has not had to contend with the diversity of businesses managed by Coles Myer. Woolworths has been able to keep its focus on each business unit, recognising its need for independence as well as finding synergies through e-business initiatives applicable across all units. The Coles Myer Board and management have engaged in an ongoing debate over whether the Myer department stores and Target businesses should be floated as a separate stand-alone company. Efforts have been made to find synergies between department stores, discount stores, liquor outlets and office supplies stores, but few have been effective. The shareholder loyalty discount card which applies for shareholders/ consumers across all businesses was phased out in 2004. By late 2005 the Coles Myer Board had made a decision to sell Myer department stores as a separate business.

Competitive vigilance and strategic reactions

While Coles Myer has had much of its energy focused on dealing with internal issues associated with changes of management and directors, Woolworths has been able to maintain competitive vigilance with the arrival of German discount grocery retailer Aldi in Australia in January 2001 and the purchase of much of Franklins by South African chain Pick 'n Pay in June 2001, at the same time expanding its store numbers and market coverage. Woolworths acquired Foodland Limited's New Zealand business plus 22 Australia stores in 2005.

A focused strategy for growth

Woolworths still believes it can grow its market share; according to Dismasi Strategic Research the Australian food, liquor and grocery market is worth approximately $75 billion of which Woolworths holds about 28%, with 50% or more held by the independent retailers. Woolworths plans include rolling out 15–25 supermarkets each year in order to capture more of this market. In addition to market share gains Woolworths is looking to expand its existing categories and branch out into new categories of product offerings. For instance, it is looking to expand into liquor, petrol, consumer electronics and hotels and to expand its existing fresh food formats. One new category in particular that has been a focus over the past few years is the pharmacy market. Woolworths recently released a report showing that an 18% consumer saving could be achieved if the supermarket chain were allowed to distribute non-prescription medical products through its stores.

On the international front Woolworths has been eyeing the Indian market as an appropriate target for its Dick Smith Electronics franchise. It plans to launch 50 stores in 2006 as part of a joint venture with Tata, India's oldest and largest business conglomerate.

Cost savings through productivity and efficiency

Senior management in Woolworths believe that cost savings will continue to be the engine to provide better value for customers and returns to shareholders. 'Project Refresh', announced in August 1999, has three phases. The first has been to reorganise Woolworth's group management structure to eliminate duplication and improve communication with suppliers and customers. In phase two, which began in 2002, the company is investing around $1 billion over a five-year period to improve logistics, supply chain systems and information technology.

Phase three, completed during 2003–2004, provided opportunities to expand using the new technology put in place in phase two. Over the six-year period from 1999 to 2005, about $3.6 billion of savings have been made.

The bottom line

Woolworths is an example of a company with a well thought through strategy and alignment of resources to ensure effective implementation. In the words of CEO Roger Corbett, 'A strategic plan doesn't provide growth, opportunities do; but opportunities are best recognised if you can quantify them and measure them in the matrix of a plan you have done'. The results speak for themselves.

Sources: Simon Lloyd, 'The Wizard of Woolies', *Business Review Weekly*, 12–18 September 2002, pp. 52–58; Adele Ferguson, 'How to Fix Coles Myer', *Business Review Weekly*, 26 September–2 October 2002, pp. 49–55; Andrew Trounson, 'Review 200: Asia's Leading Companies: Australia-Woolworths on a Food High', *Far Eastern Economic Review*, 26 December 2002–2 January 2003, vol. 165, no. 51, pp. 58–59; Anonymous, 'Woolworths Charges Ahead', *Retail World*, 2–13 September 2002, vol. 55, no. 17, p. 8; Sue Mitchell, 'Woolies Attacks Chemists' Prices', *The Australian Financial Review*, 16 June 2005, p. 17; Sue Mitchell, 'Corbett Targets India for Dick Smith Franchise', *The Australian Financial Review*, 8 June 2005, p. 55; Woolworths Annual Results FY 2005, accessed at <www.woolworths.com.au> on 30 September 2005; Coles Myer Annual Results FY 2005, accessed at <www.colesmyer.com.au>; Woolworths Limited Annual Report 2005, pp. 9–24.

Questions

1 What is Coles Myer's biggest inhibitor to successful growth and profitability?

2 How can Coles Myer obtain profit growth in the next 2–3 years?

3 How can Coles Myer obtain sales and profit growth in the next 3–5 years?

3.2

forced market leaders such as Hewlett-Packard to rethink their online strategies in order to be more competitive. However, Dell, having dominated online computer sales, is beginning to compete head on by selectively establishing physical distribution channels such as department stores. But this time it will again be through the capabilities it knows best—by using the Internet kiosks.[25]

Technology-driven environmental shifts like the Internet represent one of the most powerful forces changing the nature of competitive advantage. Shifts like this not only undermine current sources of advantage like Hewlett-Packard's traditionally powerful distribution system but also the whole basis of thinking about strategy. They can rapidly transform a competitive advantage to competitive disadvantage.[26]

Today companies must broaden their strategic planning to encompass the migration of value, which is moving from physical marketing and delivery towards electronic marketing. Referring to Figure 3.12, moves towards electronic marketing strategies can have simultaneous impacts on profit through the potential for productivity improvement, sales growth and the restructuring of the company's asset base.

It is quite possible that electronic marketing strategies can simultaneously affect market penetration and market development strategies, improve asset utilisation through reduced inventories and speed up the cash cycle, as well as creating entirely new product ranges where information is a pivotal factor in creating value for customers. Marketing Highlight 3.3 illustrates the potential application in the wine industry.

Migration planning

Today, most firms must plan strategies based around their traditional market 'place' plus strategies to take them into market 'space'—that is, the virtual world of electronic business. Figure 3.13 depicts the task facing management—developing integrated strategies that link both physical and electronic components. The same planning dimensions apply—markets, people, corporate culture, technology and processes. But blending the different mindsets of place and space marketing, implanting new business processes and upskilling people is an enormous challenge for most businesses. It is the challenge of what Slywotzky refers to as value migration. Objectives and key milestones to measure progress are vital elements in migration planning.[27]

Nowhere is this more apparent than in the media industry. News Corp founder, Rupert Murdoch, who built his empire on 'old media' newspapers, invested more than $US1.3 billion in mid-2005 to purchase Internet gaming and entertainment site, IGN Entertainment and Intermix Media Inc., which controls social networking site MySpace.com and sports online network Scout.com. This was after Microsoft chairman, Bill Gates, forecast Internet advertising revenue would be likely to be $US30 billion annually by 2008. This pointed to an overhaul of News Corp's Internet sites which appealed to an over-30 demographic, not to the younger groups flocking to the Net and wireless digital. Advertising revenues for traditional media are slowing and while News Corp's TV properties like Fox, Fuel and FX already draw the under-30s, sites such as MySpace.com and IGN.com are growing much faster. With the Net, News Corp can also more easily promote its other offerings. For instance, its Fox studio sent out 10 million emails to MySpace users on 1 September 2005 with a trailer for the movie *Transporter 2*.[28]

These issues are dealt with in more detail in Chapter 20.

Strategic planning should therefore involve managing opportunities and capabilities to meet objectives. The setting of appropriate objectives is just as important as selecting appropriate strategies.[29]

Planning functional strategies

The company's strategic plan establishes what kinds of businesses the company will be in and its objectives for each. Then within each business unit more detailed planning must take place. The major functional departments in each unit—marketing, finance, accounting, IT, purchasing, manufacturing, human resources and others—must work together to accomplish strategic objectives.

Each functional department deals with different publics to obtain inputs the business needs—inputs such as cash, labour, raw materials, research ideas, IT infrastructure and manufacturing

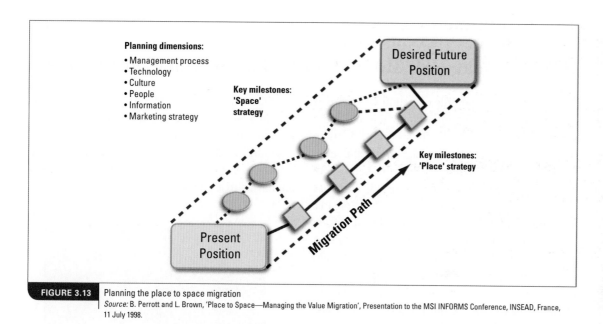

FIGURE 3.13 Planning the place to space migration
Source: B. Perrott and L. Brown, 'Place to Space—Managing the Value Migration', Presentation to the MSI INFORMS Conference, INSEAD, France, 11 July 1998.

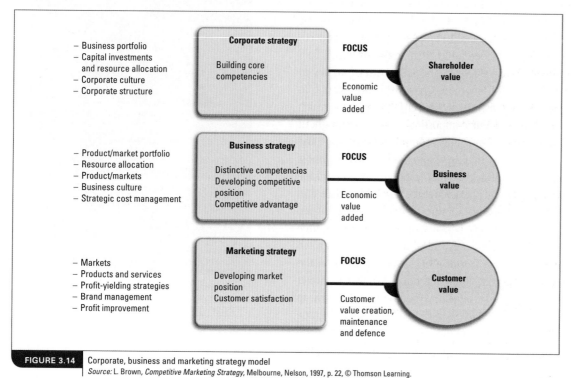

FIGURE 3.14 Corporate, business and marketing strategy model
Source: L. Brown, *Competitive Marketing Strategy*, Melbourne, Nelson, 1997, p. 22, © Thomson Learning.

processes. For example, marketing brings in revenues by negotiating exchanges with consumers. Finance arranges exchanges with lenders and shareholders to obtain cash. Thus, the marketing and finance departments must work together to obtain needed funds. Similarly, the human resources department supplies labour and is concerned with skill development, and the purchasing department obtains materials needed for operations and manufacturing. IT provides the necessary communication platforms for transactions to take place on the Internet and through other electronic channels.

MARKETING HIGHLIGHT

3.3

Organic wine—strategic marketing in 'place' and 'space'

Two unconnected vineyards operating worlds apart have a number of things in common: they are at the vanguard of a small number of specialists focusing on organic wine production; they are viable, even though small by industry standards, because of 'place' and 'space' marketing strategies; each has a long-term strategic plan committed to organic viticulture and the use of high-quality grapes to achieve consistent wine quality over time; and they even have similar names: Frogmore Creek Vineyard in Tasmania operated by vineyard manager and co-owner, Tony Scherer, and Frogpond Farm Vineyard in the Niagara wine region of Canada owned and operated by Jens Gemmrich and Heike Koch.

Frogmore Creek is the first certified organic vineyard in Tasmania. Vineyard manager and co-owner, Tony Scherer, has been an expert in this field for more than 20 years and emphasises that key to the success of Frogmore Creek is healthy plants. To this end, it has initiated a 'Fertility Program' which maintains organic composting practices throughout the vineyard—utilising compost made on the property. This healthy, biologically active compost containing straw, animal manure, winery grape wastes, natural rock minerals, vegetable waste and fish waste ensures a natural form of fertiliser. Aside from the obvious benefits of a grape grown free of chemicals and pesticides, an organically grown grape produces a fruit more 'alive', resulting in the true flavour that nature intended. While a 'healthier wine' is a side benefit, Frogmore Creek aims to distinguish itself by producing a better quality grape from which to produce award-winning wines. Of equal importance is organic viticulture's influence on the health and longevity of the vines and soil.

Frogpond Farm operates with the same philosophy and, in a region that must guard against insects and parasites that can destroy the grapes, Gemmrich has found a natural process of planting between the rows of vines that attracts non-destructive insect and animal life that also protect the vines.

Organic wine from Niagara.

Frogmore's

Organic wine from Tasmania.

Both companies rely on visitors to their vineyards to educate consumers on the benefits of organic wines and their taste and as a means of creating product concept and brand awareness and preference. Farm tours give visitors a tangible feel for what is involved in organic farming. Wine tasting and music events in the vineyard, as occur in the Niagara wine region, draw visitors and create awareness and trial. Follow-up through mailing and electronic marketing supported by their website linkages integrates an important marketing strategy linking 'place' and 'space' strategies.

Frogmore Creek has plans in the development stage for world-class amenities to be built on the property. These include:

- A 3158 square metre winery—projected capacity 45 000 cases
- A 930 square metre restaurant, tasting room and gift shop
- A 12-hectare olive grove—to produce boutique olives, oils and spreads
- Trout-stocked lakes for fishing and boating
- Over 15 kilometres of walking and hiking trails that overlook the vineyard
- Organic vegetable and herb demonstration gardens highlighting the latest advances in organic farming

- The Estates at Frogmore Creek—five premium home sites overlooking the vineyard, Storm Bay and the Tasmanian Sea

Success in the wine growing and processing industry requires a strategic plan—one looking forward with an ambitious vision encompassing many years into the future. Even more important if you are in the fledgling organic wine sector, long-term commitment is required after the early harvests to manage quality and consistency and develop a growing and loyal customer base. As the sector starts to grow the awareness and preference for the specific brand must be a key part of the marketing strategy.

Sources: <www.frogmorecreekvineyards.com>; <www.frogpondfarm.ca>; interview with Jens Gemmrich, Frogpond Farm, 1385 Larkin Road, Niagara-on-the-Lake, Ontario, Canada, August 2005.

Questions

1. What is the product/market growth path being followed by Frogmore Creek?

2. What are the key elements for survival for a vineyard like Frogmore Creek?

3. How might the Internet provide more value for Frogmore Creek's markets?

3.3

The focus of each strategy level differs. As Figure 3.14 illustrates, the primary focus of corporate strategy is to add economic value to the organisation as reflected in shareholder value. Its responsibility is to enhance existing core competencies and to build new ones. A recent addition to corporate strategy is the management of an extended form of organisation referred to as the 'virtual corporation'. Although the task is predominantly to manage the transfer of knowledge throughout the alliances that make up the virtual corporation to the benefit of one company, it is possible that a notion of collective management of core competencies and economic return for part or the whole of the virtual corporation could be part of future corporate strategy. This concept has been expanded, not only to incorporate alliance networks but to embrace cyberspace as the principal business focus of the future. Papows, CEO of Lotus Corporation, proposes that the internal systems linking employees and business processes need to operate in the same environment as the external stakeholders, including alliance partners, shareholders and customers. In this way rapid delivery of value occurs for both internal and external interest groups. He calls this the 'market-facing enterprise' which is constantly connected via information flows within the business and across the extended enterprise of customers, suppliers and other stakeholders. This empowers employees to make rapid decisions which create more value for customers and shareholders.[30] These ideas are discussed in more detail in Chapter 20.

At the business-unit level the focus is on adding economic value to the business, measured in terms of return on investment or **economic value added**. The aim is to build the value of the business utilising distinctive core competencies and developing competitive position and advantage. Extension of these notions to alliances and the market-facing enterprise embraces the new forms of electronically connected companies. This highlights the importance of knowledge and the 'informating' of products and services as critical determinants of both return on investment and economic value creation.

Economic value added
A measure of operating profit (before interest and after tax) less cost of all capital employed to produce the profit. This can be thought of as economic profit which is added to the value of the business as a result of operations. The term EVA (short for economic value added) is a registered trademark of Stern Stewart & Co.

Marketing's role in strategic planning

At the marketing-strategy level the focus shifts to customer value, enhancing the utility of products and services. As noted in Chapter 1, customer value has undergone a major shift related to 'cash-rich, time-poor' market segments in today's developed economies like Australia and New Zealand. Marketing's role is to lead and coordinate the process of customer value creation, maintenance and defence at the product and market level. Its focus is on developing market position and customer satisfaction and retention.

There is much overlap between overall company strategy and marketing strategy. This is now even more visible with the overlap of electronic business strategies (to do with cost reduction, market access and expansion) and electronic marketing strategies which are focused on customer acquisition and retention. Marketing looks at consumer needs and the company's ability to satisfy them; these same factors guide the company mission and objectives. Most company strategy planning deals with marketing variables—market share, market development, growth—and it is sometimes hard to separate strategic planning from marketing planning. In fact, some companies refer to their strategic planning as 'strategic marketing planning'.

Marketing plays a key role in the company's strategic planning in several ways. First, marketing provides a guiding philosophy—the marketing concept—which suggests company strategy should revolve around serving the needs of important customer groups. Second, marketing provides inputs to strategic planners by helping to identify attractive market opportunities and by assessing the company's potential to take advantage of them. For instance, customer wants and demands are changing rapidly towards electronic access via the uniform platform of the Internet and its World Wide Web. Finally, within individual business units, marketing designs strategies for reaching the unit's objectives.

Within each business unit, marketing management must determine the best way to help achieve strategic objectives. Some marketing managers will find that their objective is not necessarily to build sales. Rather, it may be to hold existing sales with a smaller marketing budget, or it may actually be to reduce demand. Thus, marketing management must manage demand to the level decided on by the strategic planning prepared at head office. Marketing helps to assess each business unit's potential but, once the unit's objective is set, marketing's task is to carry it out profitably.

Marketing and the other business functions

Confusion persists about marketing's importance in the company. In some companies it is just another function—all functions count in the company and none takes leadership. At the other extreme, some marketers claim that marketing is the major function of the company. They quote management consultant Peter Drucker, who says, 'The aim of the business is to create customers'.[31] They say it is marketing's job to define the company's mission, products and markets and to direct the other functions in the task of serving customers.

More enlightened marketers prefer to put the customer at the centre of the company. These marketers argue that the company cannot succeed without customers, so the crucial task is to attract and hold them. Customers are attracted by promises and held through satisfaction, and marketing defines the promise and ensures its delivery. However, because actual consumer satisfaction is affected by the performance of other departments, all functions should work together to deliver superior customer value and satisfaction. Marketing plays an integrative role to help ensure that all departments work together toward consumer satisfaction, and identifies how well customer value is being delivered.

Conflict between departments

Each business function has a different view about which interest groups and activities are most important. Manufacturing focuses on suppliers and production; finance is concerned with shareholders and sound investment; marketing emphasises consumers and products, pricing, promotion and distribution. Ideally, all the different functions should work in harmony to produce value for consumers. But, in practice, departmental relations are full of conflicts and misunderstandings. The marketing department takes the consumer's point of view. But when marketing tries to develop customer satisfaction, it often causes other departments to do a poorer job in their terms. Marketing department actions can increase purchasing costs, disrupt production schedules, increase inventories and create budget headaches. Thus, the other departments may resist bending their efforts to the will of the marketing department.

Yet marketers must get all departments to 'think consumer' and to put the consumer at the centre of company activity. This involves the task of breaking down the 'functional silos' that still exist in many businesses and taking the heat out of 'turf wars', which are traditionally based on power struggles in the organisation. Customer satisfaction requires a total company effort to deliver superior value to target customers.

> Creating value for buyers is much more than a 'marketing function'; rather, [it is] analogous to a symphony orchestra in which the contribution of each subgroup is tailored and integrated by a conductor—with a synergistic effect. A seller must draw upon and integrate effectively . . . its entire human and other capital resources . . . [Creating superior value for buyers] is the proper focus of the entire business and not merely of a single department in it.[32]

The DuPont 'Adopt a Customer' program recognises the importance of having people in all its functions who are 'close to the customer'. Through this program, DuPont encourages people on the manufacturing line at many of its plants to develop and maintain a direct relationship with the customer. The manufacturing representatives meet with the assigned customer once a year and interact regularly by phone to learn about the company's needs and problems. Then they represent the customer on the factory floor. If quality or delivery problems arise, the manufacturing representative is more likely to see the adopted customer's point of view and to make decisions that will keep this customer happy.[33]

BHP Steel recognises the importance of having people in all areas 'close to the customer'. For instance, the Steel Division has frequent meetings separately with each of its key customers at which functional heads from all departments in both companies discuss and solve problems, to their mutual benefit. BHP invites the customer team at these meetings to assess its strengths and weaknesses and compares these with its own assessment. These meetings enable the Steel Division to involve people in all its functional departments in focusing on satisfying customer needs.

Lactos, an Australian specialty cheese manufacturer, found there was a problem with the presentation of its cheeses when they arrived in Western Australia from the Tasmanian production plant. Investigation of customer complaints identified the problem in the packing and dispatch department. Employees in this department were sent to Western Australia to receive shipments of their own products, packed by them, to view first-hand the impact of the problem on the customer. The problem was very quickly solved.

Thus, marketing management can best gain support for their goal of consumer satisfaction by working to understand the company's other departments. Marketing managers must work closely with managers of other functions to develop a system of functional plans under which the different departments can work together to accomplish the company's overall strategic objectives.

SELF-CHECK QUESTIONS

5 Compare and contrast the BCG and GE portfolio models.

6 List the advantages and limitations of portfolio models.

7 Describe alternative expansion strategies for a company using the product/market expansion grid. Give examples of companies using different strategies.

8 List the reasons why a company should include electronic marketing in its strategic planning process.

9 Explain the gap analysis concept. Note the alternative ways in which a profit gap can be reduced.

10 List the elements that make up the focus of marketing strategy.

11 What is marketing's role in strategic planning and with other functional departments of a firm?

12 How can marketing provide a rationale for reducing conflicts with other departments?

The marketing process

The strategic plan defines the company's overall mission and objectives. Within each business unit, marketing plays a role in helping to accomplish the overall strategic objectives. Marketing's role and activities in the organisation are shown in Figure 3.15, which summarises the entire **marketing process** and the forces influencing company marketing strategy.

Marketing process The process of (1) analysing marketing opportunities; (2) selecting target markets; (3) developing the marketing mix; and (4) managing the marketing effort.

Target consumers stand in the centre. The company identifies the total market, divides it into smaller segments, selects the most promising segments and focuses on serving and satisfying these segments. It designs a marketing mix made up of factors under its control—product, price, place and promotion.

To find the best marketing mix and put it into action, the company engages in marketing analysis, planning, implementation and control. Through these activities, the company watches and adapts to the marketing environment. We now look briefly at each element in the marketing process. In later chapters we discuss each element in more depth.

Target consumers

To succeed in today's competitive marketplace companies must be customer centred, winning customers from competitors by delivering greater value. But before it can satisfy consumers a company must first understand their needs and wants. Thus, sound marketing requires a careful analysis of consumers. Companies know that they cannot satisfy all consumers in a given market—at least not all consumers in the same way. There are too many different kinds of consumers with too many different kinds of needs. And some companies are in a better position to serve certain segments of

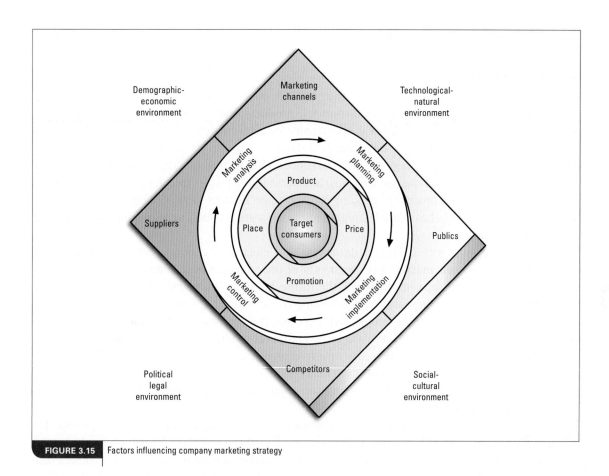

FIGURE 3.15 Factors influencing company marketing strategy

the market. Thus, each company must divide up the total market, choose the best segments and design strategies for profitably serving chosen segments better than its competitors do. This process involves four steps: demand measurement and forecasting, market segmentation, market targeting and market positioning.

Demand measurement and forecasting

Suppose a company is looking at possible markets for a potential new product. First, the company needs to make a careful estimate of the current and future size of the market and its various segments. To estimate current market size, the company would identify all competing products, estimate the current sales of these products and determine whether the market is large enough to support another product profitably.

Equally important is future market growth. Companies want to enter markets that show strong growth prospects. Growth potential may depend on the growth rate of certain age, income and nationality groups that use the product. Growth may also be related to larger developments in the environment, such as economic conditions, the crime rate and lifestyle changes. For example, the future market for Digital Video Discs (DVDs) and Apple's iPod and related products is strongly related to current birthrates, education levels, trends in consumer affluence and projected family lifestyles. Accurately forecasting the effect of these environmental forces is very difficult, but it must be attempted in order to make decisions about the market. The creation of entirely new products requires vision and strategic foresight and the use of tools like scenario planning to assist the forecasting process.

The company's marketing information specialists will probably use a variety of techniques to measure and forecast demand.

Market segmentation

Suppose the demand forecast looks good. The company must now decide how to enter the market. The market consists of many types of customers, products and needs, and the marketer has to determine which segments offer the best opportunity for achieving company objectives. Consumers can be grouped in various ways based on needs and wants. This can be further detailed by analysing geographic factors (countries, regions, cities), demographic factors (sex, age, income, education), psychographic factors (social classes, lifestyles) and behavioural factors (purchase occasions, benefits sought, usage rates). The process of dividing a market into distinct groups of buyers with different needs, characteristics or behaviour who might require separate products or marketing mixes is called **market segmentation**.

Today's technology, with customer databases and electronic communication, enables some companies to break their markets into segments of one. Peppers and Rogers provide numerous examples of how one-to-one marketing is the future for many industries. This can go as far as interacting with customers in real-time and helping consumers design their own product or service from the company's offers.[34] For example, Dell's commercial customers have their own webpage on Dell's Internet site, enabling them to design the computer products and peripherals from the Dell range that meet their needs. It is also easy now to design your own travel itinerary and make hotel reservations and transport arrangements from many travel websites. One-to-one market segmentation puts control into the hands of consumers and can create unique relationships between companies and their individual customers.

Every market has market segments, but not all ways of segmenting a market are equally useful. For example, Blackmores would gain little by distinguishing between male and female users of vitamins if both responded the same way to marketing efforts. A **market segment** consists of consumers who respond in a similar way to a given set of marketing efforts. In the car market, for example, consumers who choose the biggest, most comfortable car regardless of price make up one market segment. Another market segment would be customers who care mainly about price and operating economy. It would be difficult to make one model of car that was the first choice of every consumer. Companies are wise to focus their efforts on meeting the distinct needs of one or more market segments.

Market targeting

After a company has defined market segments, it can enter one or many segments of a given market. **Market targeting** involves evaluating each market segment's attractiveness and selecting one or more segments to enter. A company should target segments in which it can generate the greatest customer value and sustain it over time. A company with limited resources might decide to serve only one or a few special segments. This strategy limits sales, but can be very profitable. Or a company might choose to serve several related segments—perhaps those with different kinds of customers but with the same basic wants. Or a large company might decide to offer a complete range of products to serve all market segments.

Most companies enter a new market by serving a single segment, and if this proves successful they add segments. Large companies eventually seek full market coverage. They want to be the 'Telstra' of their industry. Telstra says that it has a service to suit every person's communication needs and budget. The leading company normally has different products designed to meet the special needs of each segment.

Market segmentation
Dividing a market into direct groups of buyers who might require separate products or marketing mixes; the process of classifying customers into groups with different needs, characteristics or behaviour.

Market segment
A group of consumers who respond in a similar way to a given set of marketing stimuli.

Market targeting
Evaluating each market segment's attractiveness and selecting one or more segments to enter.

Market positioning

When a company has decided which market segments to enter, it must decide what 'positions' it wants to occupy in those segments. A product's position is the place the product occupies relative to competitors in consumers' minds. If a product is perceived to be exactly like another product on the market, consumers would have no reason to buy it.

Market positioning is arranging for a product to occupy a clear, distinctive and desirable place in the minds of target consumers relative to competing products. Thus, marketers plan positions that distinguish their products from competing brands and give them the greatest strategic advantage in their target markets. Consider the positioning statement of Coopers based on its strength as a boutique beer company compared to large mass market beer companies: 'Breweries should never be run by accountants. Breweries should be run by brewers' (Maxwell Cooper, chairman until 2002). This philosophy is continued by current executive chairman and marketing director, Glenn Cooper, and Dr Tim Cooper as managing director with qualifications in brewing and medicine (see www. coopers.com.ao/aboutus/).

LexisNexis's (Butterworths Publishers) positioning of 'information being delivered directly from the source' implies differentiation by allowing users to stay ahead of their competitors by having access to all necessary intelligence directly via their email inbox. This is not a general source of information but specific information for those who appreciate it and really need it. Such deceptively simple statements form the backbone of a product's marketing strategy.

In positioning its product, the company first identifies possible competitive advantages on which to build the position. To gain competitive advantage, the company must offer greater value to chosen target segments, either by charging lower prices than competitors do or by offering more benefits to justify higher prices. But if the company positions the product as offering greater value, it must then deliver that greater value. Thus, effective positioning begins with actually differentiating the company's marketing offer so that it gives consumers more value than they are offered by the competition. Once the company has chosen a desired position, it must take strong steps to deliver and communicate that position to target consumers. The company's entire marketing program should support the chosen positioning strategy.

Market positioning
Arranging for a product to occupy a clear, distinctive and desirable place relative to competing products in the minds of target consumers; formulating competitive positioning for a product and creating a detailed marketing mix.

Marketing strategies for competitive advantage

To be successful, a marketing organisation must do a better job of satisfying target consumers than its competitors. Thus, marketing strategies must be geared to the needs of consumers and also to the strategies of competitors. Based on its size and industry position, the company must decide how it will position itself relative to competitors in order to gain the strongest possible competitive advantage.

Designing competitive marketing strategies begins with thorough competitor analysis. The company constantly compares the value and customer satisfaction delivered by its products, prices, channels and promotion with that of its close competitors. In this way it can discern areas of potential advantage and disadvantage. The company must formally or informally monitor the competitive environment to answer these and other important questions: Who are our competitors? What are their objectives and strategies? What are their strengths and weaknesses? How will they react to different competitive strategies we might use?

The competitive marketing strategy a company adopts depends on its industry position. A firm that dominates a market can adopt one or several market-leader strategies. Well-known leaders include CocaCola (soft drinks), McDonald's (fast food), Starbucks (coffee), Kodak (photographic film), Orica (explosives) and Hewlett-Packard (printers). Market challengers are runner-up companies that aggressively attack competitors to get more market share. For example, Pepsi challenges Coke, Lexmark challenges Hewlett-Packard, Optus challenges Telstra. The challenger might attack the market leader, other firms its own size or smaller local and regional competitors.

Some runner-up firms will choose to follow rather than challenge the market leader. Firms using market-follower strategies seek stable market shares and profits by following competitors' product offers, prices and marketing programs. In the electronic environment National Australia Bank has followed online banking innovators such as Westpac. Smaller firms in a market, or even larger firms that lack established positions, often adopt market-niche strategies. For instance, Coopers and Heineken adopt niche strategies, avoiding direct competition with large mainstream beer brands. They specialise in serving market niches that major competitors overlook or ignore. 'Nichers' avoid direct confrontation with the majors by specialising along market, customer, product or marketing-mix lines. Through smart niching, low-share firms in an industry can be as profitable as their larger competitors. We discuss competitive marketing strategies more fully in Chapter 19.

Developing the marketing mix

Marketing mix The set of controllable marketing variables that the company blends to produce the response it wants in the target market.

Once the company has decided on its overall competitive marketing strategy, it is ready to begin planning the details of the marketing mix. The marketing mix is one of the major concepts in modern marketing. We define **marketing mix** as the set of controllable marketing variables that the firm blends to produce the response it wants in the target market. The marketing mix consists of everything the firm can do to influence the demand for its product. The many possibilities can be collected into four groups of variables known as the marketing mix, or the 'four Ps': product, price, place and promotion. In recent years, the marketing mix has been extended. Services-marketing scientists and practitioners have distinguished features of service encounters, whether discrete transactions such as catching a plane or continuous as in subscribing to a mobile phone network, which have led to the additional Ps shown in Figure 3.16.

The four Ps are not a scientific explanation of marketing. They are a form of shorthand designed to assist marketing scientists and practitioners.

Product means the 'goods-and-service' combination the company offers to the target market. Whenever we refer to branded goods and/or services in marketing we refer to 'products'. Thus, a Ford Falcon 'product' consists of nuts and bolts, spark plugs, pistons, headlights and thousands of other parts. Ford offers several Falcon styles and dozens of optional features. The car comes fully serviced and with a comprehensive warranty that is as much a part of the product as the exhaust pipe.

Price is the amount of money customers have to pay to obtain the product. Ford calculates suggested retail prices that its dealers might charge for each Falcon. But Ford dealers rarely charge the full advertised price. Instead, they negotiate the price with each customer, offering discounts, trade-in allowances and credit terms to adjust for the current competitive situation and to bring the price into line with the buyer's perception of the car's value.

Placement involves company logistics and marketing activities concerned with making and distributing the finished product to

Marketing positioning—LexisNexis's statement is 'information being delivered directly from the source'.

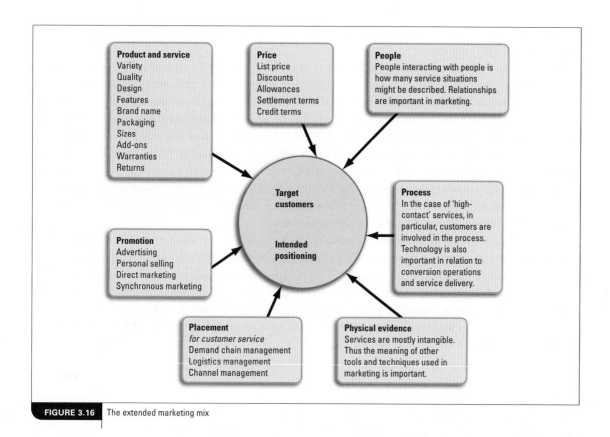

Product and service
Variety
Quality
Design
Features
Brand name
Packaging
Sizes
Add-ons
Warranties
Returns

Price
List price
Discounts
Allowances
Settlement terms
Credit terms

People
People interacting with people is
how many service situations
might be described. Relationships
are important in marketing.

**Target
customers**

**Intended
positioning**

Process
In the case of 'high-
contact' services, in
particular, customers are
involved in the process.
Technology is also
important in relation to
conversion operations
and service delivery.

Promotion
Advertising
Personal selling
Direct marketing
Synchronous marketing

Placement
for customer service
Demand chain management
Logistics management
Channel management

Physical evidence
Services are mostly intangible.
Thus the meaning of other
tools and techniques used in
marketing is important.

FIGURE 3.16 The extended marketing mix

target consumers. Ford maintains factories all over the world that now act in concert to make cars with inbuilt customer value. The company maintains a large body of independently owned dealerships that sell the company's many different models. Ford selects its dealers carefully and supports them strongly. The dealers keep an inventory of Ford automobiles, demonstrate them to potential buyers, negotiate prices, close sales and service the cars after the sale. More than physical product flows through the demand chain that links suppliers, Ford, the dealer network and the final customer. Marketing communication, information, money and credit are some of the other flows involved.

Promotion means activities that communicate the merits of the product and persuade target customers to buy it. Ford spends millions of dollars around the world each year on advertising to tell consumers about the company and its products. Dealership salespeople assist potential buyers and persuade them that Ford is the best car for them. Ford and its dealers offer special promotions—sales, cash rebates, low financing rates—as added purchase incentives. Ford also uses direct marketing tools and techniques to maintain a relationship with its buyers before, during and between purchases.

The extended marketing mix includes people, process and physical evidence. People are especially important in marketing—particularly in marketing services where there is a high degree of intangibility and where service delivery can entail high variability if people are poorly trained or are not adequately motivated to deliver service.

Process is also important in marketing, and not just the process of making the car. Both Ford cars and Optus's Internet service involve the customer in the consumption process. The customer who has a bad experience during the delivery phase or who is treated poorly during a regular car service makes a bad ambassador for the company. If Optus's Internet service breaks down or becomes clogged with calls, or an Internet user notices a slow delivery of information, then the process is not providing customer value. Customers migrate to other service providers when the process is poorly managed and lets them down.

When we say that an organisation such as a university exceeds its customers' expectations, we are saying, on the one hand, that the university has managed the customers' expectations and, on the other hand, that the students perceived that their needs had been met or exceeded. But, in the case of a service such as education, how does a student's employer who has paid the student's fees know that the student's needs have been met? The employer was not there to experience the education delivered and must therefore use other 'evidence'. Managing physical evidence entails examining every aspect that customers use in their perceptual field to assess such a service. This might include, for a university, its buildings, location, subject notes, lecture theatres, computer labs and audiovisual equipment. Often the customer requires assistance in deciding just which criteria to use in judging the service. This too is part of marketing.

An effective marketing program blends all the marketing mix elements into a coordinated program designed to achieve the company's marketing objectives by delivering value to consumers. The marketing mix constitutes the company's tactical tool kit for establishing strong positioning in target markets. However, note that the Ps of marketing as expressed represent the seller's view of the marketing tools available for influencing buyers. From a consumer viewpoint, each marketing tool is designed to deliver a customer benefit. One marketing expert suggests that companies should view the four Ps in terms of the customer's four Cs.[35]

Four Ps	*Four Cs*
Product	Customer needs and wants
Price	Cost to the customer
Placement	Convenience
Promotion	Communication

The context of the marketing mix also requires consideration when operating in the electronic marketing environment. Additional complexity faces the marketer in interpreting the extended marketing mix in a highly technical communications infrastructure. What exactly is the product? Who pays for it? How is it promoted and distributed? In addition, new processes and different kinds of physical evidence—often without the presence of people or any human interaction—are now major challenges.

Thus, winning companies will be those that can meet customer needs economically and conveniently and with effective communication.

SELF-CHECK QUESTIONS

13 Provide a brief description of each of the factors that influence company marketing strategies.

14 Describe the elements of the extended marketing mix using a service business example.

15 Interpret the extended marketing mix for the service discussed in Question 14 above when promoted and distributed via the Internet.

SUMMARY

Strategic planning involves developing a strategy for long-run survival and growth. Marketing helps in strategic planning, and the overall strategic plan defines marketing's role in the company. Not all companies use formal planning or use it well, yet formal planning offers several benefits. Companies develop three kinds of plans: annual plans, long-range plans and strategic plans. Additionally, strategic planning is undertaken on a hierarchical basis: at corporate level, SBU level and at the functional level.

Strategic planning sets the stage for the rest of company planning. The strategic planning process consists of developing the company's mission, objectives and goals, business portfolio and functional plans. Developing a sound *mission statement* is a challenging undertaking. The mission statement should be market oriented, feasible, motivating and specific if it is to direct the company to its best opportunities. The mission statement then leads to supporting objectives and goals.

From here, strategic planning calls for an analysis of the company's *business portfolio* and a decision about which businesses should receive more or fewer resources. The company might use a formal portfolio-planning method like the Boston Consulting Group *growth-share matrix* or the General Electric strategic business grid. But most companies are now designing more customised portfolio-planning approaches that suit their unique situations better.

Beyond evaluating current strategic business units, management must plan for growth into new businesses and products. The product/market expansion grid shows four avenues for growth: *market penetration*, *market development*, *product development* and *diversification*. Part of this evaluation requires management to look for profit improvement strategies which may come from sales growth, productivity improvement or asset restructuring. This process is affected greatly by the emergence of sophisticated information technology which enables companies to transform their products, processes and customer value by employing electronic business strategies. Now companies must provide access to their internal systems to suppliers, alliance partners and customers, thus revealing previously confidential strategies. The companies that do this are the new market-facing enterprises.

Each of the company's functional departments provides inputs for strategic planning. Once strategic objectives have been defined, management within each business must prepare a set of functional plans that coordinates the activities of the marketing, finance, IT, manufacturing and other departments. Each department has a different idea about which objectives and activities are most important. The marketing department stresses the consumer's point of view. Marketing managers must understand the points of view of the company's other functions and work with other functional managers to develop a system of plans that will best accomplish the company's overall strategic objectives.

To fulfil their role in the organisation, marketers engage in the marketing process. Consumers are at the centre of the *marketing process*. The company divides the total market into smaller segments and selects the segments it can serve best. It then designs its *marketing mix* to differentiate its marketing offer and positions this offer in selected target segments. To find the best mix and put it into action, the company engages in marketing analysis, marketing planning, marketing implementation and marketing control.

MARKETING ISSUE

In large businesses—whether they be financial institutions, industrial manufacturers or professional service firms—there appear to be many forces at work against long-term strategic planning and marketing:

- ⊚ Shareholders demanding a focus on performance in the short run—each quarter is a challenge for publicly listed companies.
- ⊚ 'Politics' at play as middle and senior managers 'jockey' for position as they move up the hierarchy.

- ⊚ Conflicts between sales and marketing when sales compensation plans drive a short-term focus.
- ⊚ Relatively short tenure of CEOs.
- ⊚ Turf wars between departments to hold or increase their influence in the company.

What do successful large companies do to overcome these issues to ensure integrated strategic plannning and marketing can occur?

KEY TERMS

business portfolio	85	market positioning	105	product development	91
cash cows	86	market segment	104	product/market expansion grid	90
diversification	91	market segmentation	104	question marks	86
dogs	87	market targeting	104	stars	86
economic value added	100	marketing mix	106	strategic business unit (SBU)	75
growth-share matrix	86	marketing process	102	strategic planning	75
market development	91	mission statement	80		
market penetration	90	portfolio analysis	86		

DISCUSSING THE ISSUES

1 Should companies develop strategic plans in a turbulent environment? What are the pros and cons for a company like Telstra which is experiencing major upheavals?

2 Many mission statements seem to be very general statements of purpose. What makes a mission statement meaningful and actionable?

3 Some critics argue that portfolio models restrict marketing thinking by narrowing the focus to current businesses and markets. How are portfolio models best used for strategic decision making?

4 Many companies have strategic plans at the corporate, business-unit and product-market levels but they do not seem to connect. This is particularly the case in technology-driven or financially driven companies. What role can marketing play to ensure realistic marketing strategies are embedded in strategic plans?

5 As companies become more customer and marketing oriented, many departments find that they must change their traditional way of doing business. This is a particular challenge as businesses use electronic networks to connect with suppliers, customers and partners. List several ways that a company's finance, IT, accounting and engineering departments can help the company become more marketing oriented in an increasingly electronic world.

6 Most companies today have some type of marketing process. What do you think are the main gaps in marketing processes which limit a business in its marketing orientation? Comment according to your experience or from business cases you have studied.

REFERENCES

1. Interviews with Tim Lees, Marketing Director, Speedo Australia, January and November 2005.
2. Gary Hamel and C. K. Prahalad, *Competing for the Future*, Boston, Harvard Business School Press, 1994, Chapter 1; Simon London, 'The Next Core Competence Is Getting Personal', *Financial Times*, 13 December 2002, p. 14. Also see Lori Schlottman, 'Competing for the Future', *Futurics*, vol. 25, no. 1/2, 2001, pp. 101–102.
3. Angus & Robertson, <www.angusrobertson.com.au>; Rich Barton, 'Expedia', *Business Week*, 13 January 2003, issue 3815, p. 68.
4. Olga Kharif, 'Tomorrow's Paper-Thin Screen Gems', *Business Week*, 18 June 2002, accessed 28 January 2003, <www.business week.com/technology/content/jun2002/tc20020617_5587.htm>; Patricia O'Connell, 'Chewing the Sashimi with Jeff Bezos', *Business Week*, 15 July 2002, accessed 29 January 2003, <www.businessweek.com/bwdaily/dnflash/jul2002/nf20020715_5066.htm>; Australian Virtual Publishing, <www.avp-online.com/>.
5. R. Slaughter, *The Foresight Principle*, Westport, CT, Praeger Publishers, 1995; Robert E. Morgan, 'Determining Marketing Strategy: A Cybernetic Systems Approach to Scenario Planning', *European Journal of Marketing*, vol. 36, no. 4, 2002, p. 450.
6. <www.goodmanfielder.com.au/GF_CorProfile_A1.htm>, accessed 29 September 1999.
7. Hamel and Prahalad, op. cit.
8. Anonymous, 'CANON: Canon Named Global Innovation Leader by Reuters Business Insight; Canon Ranked as One of the World's "Innovation Elite" along with Honda, NEC, Samsung and Microsoft', *M2 Presswire*, 12 July 2002, p. 1. Also see Gary Hamel and C. K. Prahalad, *Competing for the Future*, Boston, Harvard Business School Press, 1994, Chapter 1.
9. This section draws heavily from Linden Brown, *Competitive Marketing Strategy*, Melbourne, Nelson, 1997, Chapter 1. Also, for a more detailed discussion of corporate and business-level strategic planning as they apply to marketing, see Phillp Kotler, *Marketing Management: Analysis, Planning, Implementation, and Control*, 9th edn, Englewood Cliffs, NJ, Prentice Hall, 1998, Chapters 3 and 4. Also see Ramiro Montealegre, 'A Process Model of Capability Development: Lessons from the Electronic Commerce Strategy at Bolsa de Valores de Guayaquil', *Organization Science*, September/October 2002, vol. 13, no. 5, pp. 514–524.
10. <www.austarab.com.au/westonmilling/westonmilling_mission.html>, accessed September 1999.
11. <www.microsoft.com/mscorp/articles/mission_values.asp>, accessed 3 February 2003.
12. See Table 3.2 for IBM's mission statement; <www.ibm.com/lvg/>, accessed October 1999.
13. <www.thebodyshop.com/web/tbsgl/about_reason.jsp>, accessed 4 February 2003; <www.the-body-shop.com/aboutus/index.htm>, accessed October 1999.
14. Anonymous, 'Fine-tune Your Marketing Know-how', *Journal of Accountancy*, vol. 195, no. 1, January 2003, p. 26. For more on mission statements, see David A. Aker, *Strategic Market Management*, 4th edn, New York, Wiley, 1998; A. A. Thompson Jr and A. J. Strickland III, *Strategic Management*, 10th edn, Boston, Irwin/McGraw-Hill, 1998, Chapter 2; M. S. S Elnamaki, 'Creating a Corporate Vision', *Long Range Planning*, vol. 25, no. 6, 1992, pp. 25–29; Laura Nash, 'Mission Statements—Mirrors and Windows', *Harvard Business Review*, March–April 1988, pp. 155–156; Fred R. David, 'How Companies Define Their Mission Statements', *Long Range Planning*, vol. 22, no. 1, 1989, pp. 90–97; David L. Calfee, 'Get Your Mission Statement Working!', *Management Review*, January 1993, pp. 54–57.
15. J. C. Collins and J. I. Porras, *Built to Last: Successful Habits of Visionary Companies*, New York, Harper Business, 1994, p. 3. See also Michael Skapinker, 'Time to Revisit What Really Makes Your Company Work', *Financial Times*, 5 August 2002, p. 9; and Michael Skapinker, 'Living Long in Dangerous Waters', *Financial Times*, 29 January 2001, p. 13.
16. J. C. Collins and J. I. Porras, *Built to Last: Successful Habits of Visionary Companies*, New York, Harper Business, 1994, Chapter 4.
17. Ibid., p. 44.
18. J. C. Collins and J. I. Porras, *Good to Great: Why Some Companies Make the Leap . . . and Others Don't*, New York, HarperCollins, 2001.
19. Barbara Gengler, 'Ford Customs Site for US', *The Australian*, 28 September 1999, p. 49; Anonymous, 'Plumtree Software: Plumtree and Microsoft Extend Global Strategic Alliance with Integration of Plumtree Corporate Portal and SharePoint Portal Server', *M2*, 1 June 2001, p. 1; Saul Hansell, 'G.M. Proposes an Online Site for Car Sales', *New York Times*, 12 August 2000, Late Edition (East Coast), p. C.1.
20. George Stalk, Philip Evans and Lawrence E. Shulman, 'Competing Capabilities: The New Rules of Corporate Strategy', *Harvard Business Review*, March–April, 1992, pp. 57–69.
21. Ghanima K. Al-Sharrah, 'Planning an Integrated Petrochemical Business Portfolio for Long-Range Financial Stability', *Industrial & Engineering Chemistry Research*, 29 May 2002, vol. 41, no. 11, p. 2798.
22. D. J. Collins and C. A. Montgomery, 'Competing on Resources: Strategy in the 1990s', *Harvard Business Review*, July–August 1995.
23. I. Ansoff, *Corporate Strategy*, London, Pelican, 1968. Also see Igal Karin, 'Strategic Marketing Models for a Dynamic Competitive Environment', *Journal of General Management*, vol. 27, no. 4, 2002, p. 63.
24. H. Igor Ansoff, 'Strategies for Diversification', *Harvard Business Review*, September–October 1957, pp. 113–124.
25. N. Shoebridge, 'Speed and Agility Let Dell Give Customers Exactly What They Want', *Business Review Weekly*, 16 November 1998, p. 195; Anonymous, 'Dell Tests Retail Waters with Sears Deal', TechWeb News, *Information Week*, 30 January 2003, p. 1; Kathryn Jones, *The Dell Way*, February 2003, <www.business2.com/articles/mag/0,1640,46293,00.html>, accessed 8 February 2003.
26. E. K. Clemons, 'Technology Driven Environmental Shifts and the Sustainable Competitive Disadvantage of Previously Dominant Companies', in G. S. Day and D. J. Reibstein (eds), *Wharton on Dynamic Competitive Strategy*, New York, John Wiley, 1997, Chapter 4.
27. See A. J. Slywotzky and D. J. Morrison, *The Profit Zone*, New York, Times Business Book, 1997, Chapter 3; A. J. Slywotzky, *Value Migration*, Boston, HBR Press, 1996, Chapter 1.
28. Ronald Grover, 'Murdoch's Web Gambit', *Business Week*, 10 October, 2005, pp. 35–36.
29. A. A. Thompson Jr and A. J. Strickland III, *Strategic Management*, 10th edn, Boston, Irwin/McGraw-Hill, 1998, Chapter 2.
30. J. Papows, *Enterprise.Com: Market Leadership in the Information Age*, London, Nicholas Brealey Publishing, 1999, Chapter 5.
31. Peter F. Drucker, *Management, Tasks, Responsibilities, Practices*, Harper & Row, New York, 1973, p. 64.
32. John C. Narvar and Stanley F. Slater, 'The Effect of a Market Orientation on Business Profitability', *Journal of Marketing*, October 1990, pp. 20–35.
33. See Brian Dumaine, 'Creating a New Company Culture', *Fortune*, 15 January 1990, p. 128.
34. D. Peppers and M. Rogers, *The One to One Future*, New York, Doubleday, 1996.
35. Robert Lauterborn, 'New Marketing Litany: Four P's Passé; C-Words Take Over', *Advertising Age*, 1 October 1990, p. 26.

PHOTO/ADS CREDITS

Barry O'Mahony, Victoria University, and Garry Kingshott, Melbourne Convention and Visitors Bureau

CASE STUDY

The Melbourne Convention and Visitors Bureau (MCVB)

The Melbourne Convention and Visitors Bureau (MCVB) is a not-for-profit public company with revenues derived from both public and private sources, including the state of Victoria, the Melbourne Exhibition and Convention Centre (MECC), member fees, advertising sales, cooperative promotions and hotel sales commissions. Headquartered in Melbourne, with representation offices in London, New York and Sydney, the MCVB markets Melbourne as a business events destination.

MCVB vision

To make Melbourne one of the world's most successful business events destinations.

MCVB mission

To maximise the benefits to the Victorian economy from business events (meetings, incentives, conventions and exhibitions).

MCVB corporate goals

- Position Melbourne as a premier business events destination.
- Attract and secure high-value business events.
- Maximise yield and dispersal from business events.
- Build a sustainable revenue base.
- Create and sustain a high-performance organisation.

MCVB objectives

- To attract national and international business events (meeting, incentive, convention and exhibition) to Melbourne.

- To maximise yield from business events through the promotion of longer stays, higher delegate expenditure and delegate recruitment.

MCVB target markets

- International association conventions, meetings and exhibitions
- International government conventions and meetings
- International corporate and incentive conventions and meetings
- National association conventions and meetings

The majority of the MCVB's international business is currently sourced from Europe and North America. The MCVB believes, however, that the growing incentive segment out of Asia is lucrative and has a high potential for Australia and in particular for Melbourne. As a result, the MCVB has attempted to source some of this business for Melbourne. The results, however, have been far from favourable with fewer than 10 meetings worth $7 million in direct delegate expenditure secured. At the same time, the Sydney Convention and Visitors Bureau (SCVB) has seen incentives from Asia grow from less than 5% of its business to over 25%, securing 11 Asian incentive meetings worth $27 million in direct expenditure in 2004.[1]

A national report into the business events market shows the destinations that attracted most incentive business to Australia in recent years.[2] As Table 1 highlights, Melbourne received far less than several other national destinations in terms of market share.

---

1   Sydney Convention and Visitors Bureau Annual Report 2003/04.
2   National Business Events Study 2003, Incentive Travel Sector, CRC.

TABLE 1 Incentive destinations (Multi-destination programs account for the sum of cases being greater than 100%)

Destination	n	% of cases	Destination	n	% of cases
Sydney	98	39.4	ACT/Canberra	12	4.8
Gold Coast	50	20.1	Ayers Rock	11	4.4
Brisbane	39	15.7	NT	10	4.0
Cairns	39	15.7	Darwin	8	3.2
NSW	38	15.3	Hobart	8	3.2
Blue Mountains	35	14.1	Broome	8	3.2
Port Douglas	31	12.4	Kakadu	4	1.6
Melbourne	31	12.4	Whitsundays	4	1.6
Queensland	23	9.2	Tasmania	4	1.6
Perth	23	9.2	Victoria	4	1.6
Barossa Valley	15	6.0	Perth	4	1.6
Adelaide	14	5.6			

QUESTIONS

1. It is clear from the introduction that the MCVB understands the competitive environment and has engaged in formal strategic planning to achieve defined goals. Based on the background information provided create a hierarchy of objectives for the MCVB.

2. Having assessed the MCVB's corporate strategy and portfolio of businesses it is obvious that a vision has been developed for the business as a whole. While the majority of the MCVB's business strategies are successful, the incentives area is considered to be underperforming. Why should the MCVB set up a separate strategic business unit (SBU) for the Asian incentives market?

3. Given the current level of incentives business that the MCVB secures and their position behind their competitors in the incentives market highlighted in Table 1, what Boston matrix description would best describe the MCVB's incentives sector?

4. Once the MCVB has classified a new SBU for the incentive market it must pursue one of four SBU strategies. Should the MCVB build, hold, harvest or divest?

5. Given that Melbourne and Victoria are core attributes of the MCVB's incentives product, what growth evaluation strategies could the MCVB use to develop future business?

CHAPTER 4

Marketing plans

Apple iPod: www.apple.com/ipod

Braun: www.braun.com

CoverGirl: www.covergirl.com

Gillette: www.gillette.com

Hugo Boss fragrances:

www.hugofragrances.com

Proctor & Gamble: www.pg.com

Every day, hour and minute, consumers are bombarded with more choices and offers to satisfy their needs and wants. This comes in the form of new products and services, product extensions and product revivals. However, only a handful of competitors in a given market or market segment are successful over a sustained period of time. They fail to make a memorable or profitable impact in the market and are gradually, or even abruptly, phased out. The failures are everywhere—they occur in small businesses and in large corporations. One of the most talked about Australian product failures was One.Tel Telephone Company where profits simply did not eventuate. Similarly, the large American company Burger King's European and Japanese market development failed due to poor customer acceptance and a highly competitive environment. However, there are also great success stories such as Apple Computer's iPod where the company executed its offer through a carefully managed and implemented marketing plan and achieved dominance of the portable music market.

Achievement of marketing and business objectives comes only from well-researched and implemented business and marketing plans. As discussed in Chapter 12, a large proportion of products and services marketed fail in the marketplace. The managers responsible for these 'failed' products and services often say that their product did not perform to their expectations due to unrealistic goals, lack of customer interest, poor market conditions or simply because of too powerful competing offers. But what makes the remaining ones succeed in the market?

The answer to this is a well-researched, created and implemented marketing plan. A well-developed and implemented marketing plan can in most cases save a company from these failures by correcting elements of the offer before a major commitment. A good example of a company that first experienced major declines in its business and then bounced back to its former market position is Procter and Gamble (P&G)—a company with a product portfolio that includes CoverGirl, Hugo Boss Fragrances, Oral-B, Lactose, Max Factor and Braun Shavers.

In 2000 the company had missed its earnings targets, products were losing their customer appeal and market share and the stock price almost halved. The company was perceived to be an old marketer with a weakening marketing culture and not so 'cool' products.

However, by refocusing on its marketing planning efforts, P&G management turned the company around. The company undertook a rigorous and coordinated marketing planning process. Jim Stengel, the Global Marketing Officer, implemented what was called 'Marketing Framework 3.0' in order to build a systematic planning process and common marketing skills. As a result P&G regained its market share and sales in all geographical segments and businesses between 2003 and 2006 (three consecutive years of growth) and achieved share growth in markets where previously P&G lagged behind its major rivals. Accomplishing these results came about by creating an integrated marketing focus with emphasis on realistic but challenging marketing objectives and plans. By identifying key strengths, weaknesses, opportunities and threats the marketers were able to overcome key weaknesses and threats and build on their opportunities and strengths.

ASIC's $92 million damages claim against the founders of One.Tel resulted in high profile appearances in the NSW Supreme Court.

The company now engages in more focused marketing planning which encompasses not only marketing but also finance, logistics, operations, HR and shareholder value considerations when developing and implementing its marketing plans. Its powerful marketing and financial performance over this period enabled the company to acquire its best performing rival, the Gillette Company, as a means of maintaining its market share growth and corporate objectives for the future.

Effective marketing planning is no different for small or medium-sized businesses. These businesses need to pause, regroup and rethink their marketing efforts and engage in a systematic marketing planning approach. This also applies to the Sydney-based fitness company, Fast Fitness. It takes its marketing planning seriously by continuously looking for business opportunities in the light of the current market conditions and then systematically focusing on providing superior customer value to its customers.[1]

After reading this chapter you should be able to:

1. Describe the marketing process.
2. Identify the sections of a marketing plan and specify the contents of each section.
3. Discuss the marketing implementation process.
4. Identify the approaches to marketing an organisation.
5. Explain the ways in which marketing organisations control and evaluate their marketing performance.

M anagement in every marketing organisation want to design and put into action the marketing mix that will best achieve their objectives in their target markets. This involves marketing management in a cycle of activities that we call the **marketing process**—analysing marketing opportunities, researching and selecting target markets, designing marketing strategies, planning marketing programs, implementing (which includes organising) and controlling the marketing effort. In Chapter 3 we began our discussion of marketing management and planning by examining the hierarchical nature of strategic planning. In this chapter we begin by briefly revisiting the levels within the organisation where planning is undertaken, then proceed to examine the nature of the marketing plan. Finally, we discuss analysis further, as well as the marketing management functions not already covered in our examination of the marketing plan— implementation and control.

Marketing process The process of (1) analysing marketing opportunities; (2) selecting target markets; (3) developing the marketing mix; and (4) managing the marketing effort.

Marketing management and planning

Most large organisations consist of four organisational levels: the corporate level, the divisional level, the business-unit level and the product level. A marketing organisation's head office is responsible for designing a corporate strategic plan to guide the whole enterprise into a profitable future; it makes decisions on how much resource support to allocate to each division, as well as which businesses to start or eliminate. In reality this is not entirely a top-down approach as divisions and their business units have a deep knowledge of the marketplace and a vested interest in seeking the optimal corporate strategy. Each division establishes a divisional plan covering the allocation of funds to each business unit within the division. For instance, the James Hardie Building Products division for Australasia allocates funds to the Australian and New Zealand business units. The International division allocates funds to James Hardie Philippines and to the other Southeast Asian business units. Each business unit develops a business-unit strategic plan to carry that business unit into a profitable future. Finally, each product level (product line, brand) within a business unit develops a product plan for achieving its objectives in its product market. In part, it is the aggregation of these detailed product plans that we recognise as a marketing plan.

The marketing plan operates at two levels. The strategic marketing plan develops the broad marketing objectives and strategy based on an analysis of the current market situation and opportunities. The tactical marketing plan outlines specific marketing tactics, including advertising, merchandising, pricing, channels, service and so on.

The marketing plan is the central instrument for directing and coordinating the marketing effort. In today's organisations the marketing department does not set the marketing plan by itself. Rather, today's plans are developed by teams, with inputs and sign-offs from every important function. These plans are then implemented at the appropriate levels of the organisation. Results are monitored and corrective actions are taken when necessary. The complete planning, implementation and control cycle is shown in Figure 4.1. Through implementation, the company turns the strategic and marketing plans into actions that will achieve the company's strategic objectives. Marketing plans are implemented by people in the marketing organisation who work with others both inside and outside the company. Control consists of measuring and evaluating the results of marketing plans and activities and taking corrective action to make sure objectives are being reached. Marketing analysis provides information and evaluations needed for all the other marketing activities.

A marketing plan or a business plan?

Comprehensive global surveys by Jean-Claude Larreche at INSEAD and the Corporate Strategy Board in the USA found that most companies have developed marketing planning capabilities and set their

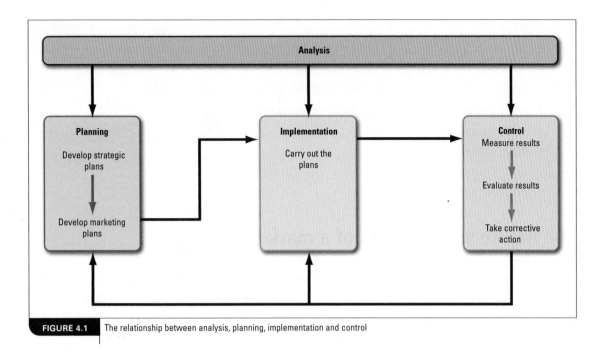

FIGURE 4.1   The relationship between analysis, planning, implementation and control

purpose as that of acquiring and satisfying customers rather than producing goods or services. Business plans are oriented more to customers and competitors, and better reasoned and more realistic than they were in the past. The plans draw more inputs from all the functions and are team developed. Marketing executives increasingly see themselves as professional managers first and specialists second. Senior management are more involved in making and/or approving marketing decisions. Planning is now a continual process throughout the year to respond to rapidly changing market conditions.[2]

However, marketing planning procedures and content vary considerably between companies. The plan is variously called a 'business plan', a 'marketing plan' and sometimes an 'operating plan'. But there are differences between business plans and marketing plans. The business plan incorporates the plans of all functions—production, R&D, finance, human resources, IT and marketing.

As discussed in more detail in Chapter 3 and depicted in Figure 3.14, the business plan looks at higher-level decision making which involves allocation of resources such as financial and HR and instilling a business-wide culture in the organisation, while the marketing plan has its focus on customer acquisition and retention through creation of customer value. It utilises all resources required to do this effectively using a variety of marketing programs. It will include the resources needed to implement specific marketing functions such as selling, advertising, sales promotion and market research. Most marketing plans cover one year, but some cover several years, most commonly three years. Plans vary in their length, from under 10 pages to over 100. Some companies take their plans very seriously, whereas others see them as only a rough guide to action. The most frequently cited shortcomings of current marketing plans, according to marketing executives, are lack of realism, insufficient competitive analysis, weak financial justification and a short-run focus.[3]

We next examine how marketing planning is carried out at the product level, and what a marketing plan includes. We later return to the marketing management process after gaining a perspective on the nature of the marketing plan.

The nature and contents of a marketing plan

The marketing plan is one of the most important outputs of the marketing process. It relies very heavily on an analysis of the industry, the business and the product situation. But what does a marketing plan look like? What does it contain? Regardless of how marketing plans might be structured in different companies, a complete marketing plan has several important sections, and these are listed in Table 4.1. Throughout the discussion, we illustrate the sections of the plan with an example of a real Australian company—Fast Fitness. To preserve confidentiality, financial figures and some facts have been disguised. The Fast Fitness marketing plan is shown as a single document at the end of this chapter and is available as both a pro-forma marketing plan example and a case study for use for an individual or team project.*

Here is an abbreviated example using the Fast Fitness case.

TABLE 4.1 Contents of a marketing plan

Section	Description
I Executive summary and table of contents	Present a brief overview of the proposed plan
II Current marketing situation	Presents relevant background data on the market, product, competition, distribution and macro-environment
III SWOT and issue analysis	Identifies the main opportunities/threats, strengths/weaknesses and issues facing the product line
IV Objectives	Define the plan's financial and marketing goals in terms of sales volume, market share and profit
V Marketing strategy	Presents the broad marketing approach that will be used to achieve the plan's objectives
VI Action programs	Present the special marketing programs designed to achieve the business objectives
VII Projected profit-and-loss statement	Forecasts the plan's expected financial outcomes
VIII Controls	Indicate how the plan will be monitored

---

* The Fast Fitness marketing plan and case study was developed by Peter Moore, University of Technology, Sydney. The author wishes to thank Phil Murray, owner of Fast Fitness, for his involvement and major contribution.

Company background

In this section a brief description of the company background is given.

Fast Fitness is a personal-training-focused company operating in three locations across Sydney. The company provides more personalised training to that offered by large gyms where individuals develop their own training routine. Fast Fitness is doing what is usually being done by individual personal trainers but it does it in a more professional manner with clearly visible locations as opposed to 'one-man' personal trainers that need to be booked over the telephone to arrive at a mutually convenient location for fitness training. Fast Fitness offers a new concept in personal training. It prices its offer below the rates of individual trainers who can charge between $65 and $90 per hour. Fast Fitness charges $80 per week rather than per hour (including GST), with members attending on average three sessions per week.

Executive summary

The marketing plan should open with an **executive summary**, a brief summary aimed at the senior management to enable them to grasp the plan's major thrust.

There is an opportunity for Fast Fitness to improve its market position in 2006. Currently the market shows positive growth across the industry of around 14% per annum indexed. In line with this trend and based on its strategy it is estimated that Fast Fitness will be able to grow its market share from 2.12% to 2.52% of its local market, representing an 18.9% increase. It can also increase its profitability in line with this proposed growth. Its financial and marketing objectives and its strategy for 2006 are detailed below.

Executive summary
The opening section of the marketing plan that presents a short summary of the main goals and recommendations to be presented in the plan.

The calm before the storm—a Fast Fitness studio.

Financial objectives

- To earn an annual rate of return on sales over the next three years of at least 28% before interest and taxes.
- To produce a net marketing contribution of $1 014 731 in 2006.
- To produce a net operating profit (before interest and taxes) of $514 727 in 2006.

Marketing objectives

- To grow distribution/current locations from two to four by October 2006.
- To increase the number of personal training memberships to 498 per annum by December 2006.
- To grow market share from 2.15% in 2005 to 2.52% by December 2006 in the Sydney North and South combined market.
- To grow sales revenue from $1356 million in 2005 to $1832 million in 2006.

Marketing strategy

The Fast Fitness strategy is to position itself as a personal training specialist with quality services delivered at affordable prices—an average price of $80 per weekly membership (price includes GST). This is expected to be an appealing offer since competitors' prices range from $65 to $90 per hour. Fast Fitness will continue to grow its business continuing to focus on the northern and southern regions of Sydney. The company will selectively increase its marketing expenditure from 1.6% to 3.9% of revenue based on the competitor benchmarked marketing spending. Additionally in 2006, there will be an increased focus on market research and building the customer base through a focused marketing initiative including multimedia channels such as the Internet and TV channels.

Current marketing situation

This section presents relevant background data on the target market, product, competition, distribution and the macro-environment. The data are drawn from a product fact book or database maintained by the product manager.

Market situation

In this section, data are presented on the target market. The size and growth of the market (in units and/or dollars) are shown for several past years and by market and geographical segments. Data on customer needs, perceptions and buying behaviour trends are also presented.

Nations such as America and Australia and countries of Western Europe have become labelled as the 'fat' nations of the world. The USA holds the label as the 'Fattest Nation'. Stress is widespread in Australia which is evidenced by the fact that it is one of the world leaders in consumption of stress-related medications. Additionally, over seven million adult Australians have adverse health effects from being overweight and the average lifespan of Australians is not near the top-ranking countries.

Exercise has long been cited as a way of improving one's health and quality of life. But in recent years the data about the specific benefits of physical activity has grown to what is now a breathtaking list: lower cholesterol and blood pressure; a reduced risk of heart disease, stroke, osteoporosis, diabetes and colon cancer; strengthening of bones, joints and muscle; and an improvement from reduced anxiety and depression.

The Centre for Disease Control and Prevention in the USA estimates that getting inactive Americans exercising could save that country around $80 billion a year in cost otherwise spent on treating chronic disease. The same trends are evident in Australian society. Insurance agencies such as AMP and Mercantile Mutual are beginning to conduct risk-assessment studies for future insurance claims and to develop appropriate premiums based on the level of fitness. Large companies are also becoming concerned with their CEOs' and senior managers' fitness/health levels, since poor health and fitness often correlate with early retirements and poor business and market performance. Corporate 'wellness' is a rapidly expanding market within the fitness industry. A number of companies in Australia, such as Medifit, Health Fitness Corporation and Corporate Fitness Works, provide on-site management and staffing to corporate wellness facilities. Companies are increasing their corporate wellness programs due to the favourable cost–benefit equation related to healthier employees. Memberships in gyms, sports clubs and fitness centres are being subsidised by health funds like Medibank Private, MBF and HCF with a view to reducing future insurance.

The growth of focus on a healthy lifestyle is evident through the rapid growth in sales of fast-moving consumer goods companies which are developing and marketing a host of products focusing on 'healthy living' and fat-reduced diet. Sport and exercise now play a greater role in people's lives and Australian society as a whole. Exercising is no longer associated with specific age groups, even extreme sports like triathlons, marathons and the Australian Ironman. According to the Iron Man website in 2005 it attracted over 1500 entries with age brackets ranging from 18 to 75 for both men and women <http://www.ironmanoz.com/>, accessed 20 December 2005.

There are a number of clear sectors that have emerged in the Australian market. The two main sectors are as follows:

1   Health gyms (mass exercising with limited trainer–trainee interaction)—these are large bulk membership gyms.
2   Personal training (greater interaction between trainer and trainee)—a premium-priced product with a smaller but more personalised service with focused management of the exercise regime.

There is now a newly emerging group hitting the gyms—baby boomers—who are reaching their late 40s and 50s. The number of health clubs, personal trainers and personal fitness businesses are growing exponentially. Membership for the upper age bracket has risen fourfold since the 1990s, from 220 000 members in 1993 to 635 000 members in 2004. It is estimated by IHRSA (International Health, Raquet & Sportsclub Association) that by 2010 there will be around 3 000 000 registered members (FitnessAustralia, 'One Million Members by 2010', from the corporate website, accessed 20 December 2005, http://www.fitnessaustralia.com.au/_uploads/res/243_2135.pdf). No longer is the fitness industry being dominated by the 18 to 34 age group, but is shifting to a more mature demographic—one which has a higher disposable income and health considerations.

Additionally there is growth in the exercise equipment industry. Sales of treadmills, exercise bicycles, weight benches and other apparatus to households reached $US5.8 billion in the USA in 2000 versus $US1.9 billion in 1990. It is estimated that this will grow at around 5% per annum between 2006 and 2010. The same growth is occurring in Australia (Jordana Willner, 'Fitness: Health Clubs Discover That It's More Than Just Tight Abs', *Information Week*, Manhasset, 23 April 2001, no. 834, p. 105).

The health and fitness market shows good profit potential and business opportunities in Australia in the coming years. Based on a recent Australian Bureau of Statistics labour force survey, cultural and recreation services had the second highest employment growth in the period February 1998 to February 2001 of 17 industry groupings. This growth trend also holds true for the year 2005 and beyond. Some of the statistics are as follows:

- There are 217 500 employees.
- There are 11 000 registered businesses.
- Goods and services production is valued at $12 billion.
- The contribution to Gross Domestic Product (GDP) is 1.2% (the same as the motor vehicle manufacturing industry).

▸ Thirty-three per cent of Australians aged 15 years and older are involved in sport.

▸ The fitness market (gyms and personal trainers) is estimated to be 3200 businesses in Australia.

We discuss the marketing environment, demand analysis and forecasting further in Chapters 5 and 9; the marketing research and information systems that lie at the heart of such situation analyses are discussed in Chapter 6.

Product situation

Here the sales, product prices, contribution margins and profits are shown for Fast Fitness for several past years (see Case Study Table 1).

CASE STUDY TABLE 1 Fast Fitness annual profit statements

Variable	Rows	2002	2003	2004	2005	2006–Plan
1 Industry sales in memberships (ea)		702 000	745 000	851 000	969 000	1 100 000
2 Membership sales in Sydney (ea)		189 540	179 000	229 770	261 630	297 000
3 Sales in North & South Sydney (ea)		66 339	62 650	80 420	91 571	103 950
4 Sales in Sydney North and South ($)		46 437 300	49 281 750	56 293 650	64 099 350	72 765 000
5 Sales Sydney ($)		132 678 000	125 300 000	160 839 000	183 141 000	207 900 000
6 Industry growth rate (%)			6.13%	14.23%	13.87%	13.52%
7 Company's market share (%)		1.62%	2.01%	1.95%	2.12%	2.52%
8 Average membership price ($)		3 000	3 000	3 000	3 300	3 680
9 Variable unit cost		250	265	268	255	285
10 Units gross contribution margin ($)	(8–9)	2 750	2 735	2 732	3 045	3 395
11 Sales volume (in units)		250	330	365	411	498
12 Sales revenues ($)	(8 × 11)	750 000	990 000	1 095 000	1 356 300	1 832 640
13 Gross contribution margin ($)	(10 × 11)	687 500	902 550	997 180	1 251 495	1 690 710
14 Advertising and promotion expenditure ($)		7 500	9 900	10 950	13 563	54 979
15 Trainers (salesforce) ($)		250 000	330 000	350 000	410 000	609 600
16 Marketing research ($)		6 000	5 000	8 800	7 000	11 400
17 Net marketing contribution ($)	(13–14–15–16)	424 000	557 650	627 430	820 932	1 014 731
18 Overheads ($)		160 000	160 000	250 000	450 000	500 004
19 Net operating profit ($)	(17–18)	264 000	397 650	377 430	370 932	514 727
20 Profit growth rate (%)			50.63%	−5.08%	−1.72%	38.77%

Row 1 in [Case Study Table 1] shows the total industry sales by number of fitness club/gym memberships. Row 2 splits up the market to show the total sales in the Sydney area. Fast Fitness operates in the northern and southern areas of Sydney and row 3 shows the size of that market. It is estimated that in the northern and southern Sydney area there were approximately 91 571 gym memberships in 2005. The number of memberships has grown on average by 14% annually except in 2003 when the growth declined to 6.1% per annum. Row 7 shows the Fast Fitness market share hovering around 1.98%, although it reached 2.12% in 2005. Row 8 shows the average price for Fast Fitness being stable and then rising about 10% in 2005. Row 9 shows variable costs—materials, equipment, power—rising each year. Row 10 shows that the gross contribution margin per unit— the difference between price (row 8) and unit variable cost (row 9)—was relatively steady over 2002 and 2004, then rose by over 10% in 2005. Rows 11 and 12 show sales volume in units and dollars, and row 13 shows the total gross contribution margin, which increased every year. Rows 14, 15, 16 and 17 show marketing expenditures on advertising and promotion, trainers and marketing research. Row 17 also shows net marketing contribution margin, which had increased by 48% between 2002 and 2004. Row 18 shows that overheads remained constant during 2002 and 2003, then nearly doubled in 2004 and again in 2005, owing to an increase in capacity. Finally, row 19 shows net operating profit after marketing expenses. The picture is one of increasing profits until 2004, then in 2005 a fall in relation to increased revenue levels compared to that of 2003 was recorded. Clearly, Fast Fitness needs to find a strategy for 2006 that will restore healthy growth in sales and profits to the business.

Competitive situation

Here the major competitors are identified and described in terms of their size, goals, market share, product quality, marketing strategies and other characteristics that are needed to understand their intentions and behaviour.

Competition for the fitness market comprises 3500 registered businesses in Australia. The area of Sydney has 27% of the total fitness market in Australia (945 businesses). The Sydney market is divided into five key competitive geographic areas (North, East, Inner City, South and West). The biggest number of fitness businesses are in the areas of North and South Sydney. It is estimated that the combined North and South cover around 35% of the fitness market in Sydney. There are around 330 businesses operating in this area. Case Study Table 2 [overleaf] breaks down the competition in terms of market share, product quality and future intentions.

The market is very fragmented in this industry with a bulk of the market share being held by 'home business' (a fitness trainer without any business-owned facilities) operations offering personal training. Due to the fragmentation of the market, Fast Fitness has different smaller competitors in each of its three locations. Its key location is in the Sydney suburb of Harbord. However, in 2006, with the service provided by Fast Fitness there are three distinctive competitors that between them hold 37% of the personal fitness market.

Distribution situation

This section presents data on the size and importance of each marketing (distribution) channel.

Fast Fitness currently operates from three studio outlets located in the south and north of Sydney. Customers currently attend on average three personal training sessions per week. Access is relatively easy for customers and parking is readily available nearby.

| CASE STUDY TABLE 2 Competitor shares and market positions |||
Brand/Company	Market share %	Competitor market position
URCoach	20	• Offers personal training at an hourly rate of $50 • Employs known personalities to endorse/advertise the product • It is the premium product in the market • Plans to grow its business to at least 40% of the market
Executive Fitness	11	• Provides a competitively priced offer and charges a membership fee • Its personal training sessions are starting on the hour and the membership is pre-booked three months in advance. Wants to grow
Coaching Pro	6	• Is also positioned as a premium product but is purely based on high price as the differentiator. Wants to grow
Fast Fitness	2.2	• Charges a weekly fee of $80 (includes GST) for an unlimited number of one-hour training sessions • Works with small groups (up to 10 individuals) rather than on a one-to-one basis • Creates a closely linked community for local business people and their families for personal training
Individual personal trainers (others)	60	• Work on one-to-one basis • Priced at a premium between $60 to $75 per one-hour session • Do not have their own facilities and often work in hired gyms or at customer locations

Macroenvironment situation

This section gives a brief summary of broad macroenvironmental trends—demographic, technological, economic, political/legal and sociocultural—that bear on the product line's future.

About 15% of Australians and New Zealanders between the ages of 18 and 55 actively participate in fitness activities. The health and exercise market is growing while the time available to exercise is getting shorter. This results in people wanting shorter and more intense exercise programs without regular pre-set training session times due to other time commitments and pressures. They seek flexibility in times and pricing offers. Market growth is steady at 14%.

There are new trends emerging in the marketplace that combine a series of fitness techniques such as walking, weights, nutritional control, cardiovascular aerobics and most recently Cardio Yoga.

Strength, opportunity and issue analysis

After summarising the current marketing situation, the product manager proceeds to identify the major strengths/weaknesses, opportunities/threats and issues facing the product line.

SWOT analysis

Strengths/weaknesses analysis (internal) In this section the manager needs to identify product strengths and weaknesses. The main strengths and weaknesses facing Fast Fitness are as follows:

Strengths

- High brand awareness and good-quality image in local studio area and surrounding neighbourhoods.
- Location of fitness gyms—next to coffee shop and shops (compatible with target market lifestyles).
- Very competitive pricing.
- Non-intimidating atmosphere.
- High level of professionalism, expertise and experience of the instructors.
- Flexibility of times clients can attend plus custom-made programs for clients with specific needs.
- Instructor's high rapport with their clients.

Weaknesses

- Not enough space (location) to run Cardio Yoga classes and personal training side by side.
- No showers or large change room.
- No child-minding facilities.
- Management/instructors are both time deficient, so are never able to expand on the education of their clients with regard to nutritional and specific program aspects.

Opportunities/threats analysis (external) Here the marketer identifies the main opportunities and threats facing the business.

The main opportunities and threats facing Fast Fitness are as follows:

Opportunities

- A market opportunity for increasing the appeal of Cardio Yoga.
- Opportunity for geographic expansion.
- Consumer need for wider range of services in one convenient 'shop'.
- Opportunity for a more holistic service to be provided to a 'fitness/nutritional/dietary' segment.
- Consumer need for access to information on nutrition/diet and programs to meet holiday/travel needs.

Threats

- Management/instructor burnout.
- Competitors copying Cardio Yoga concept.
- Large fitness chains entering the personal coaching scene with substantial capital backing.

Issues analysis

In this section of the marketing plan, the product manager uses the strengths/weaknesses analysis to define the main issues that the plan must address.

The company must consider the following basic issues:

- Should Fast Fitness stay in the personal business? Can it compete effectively?
- If Fast Fitness stays in the business, should it continue with its present products, distribution channels and price and promotion policies?
- Should Fast Fitness switch to high-growth channels (Cardio Yoga and the Internet)? Can it do this and retain the loyalty of its current customers?
- Should Fast Fitness increase its advertising and promotion expenditures to grow its business's awareness?
- Should Fast Fitness pour money into R&D to develop advanced features, such as Internet communities and new products and services?

Objectives

After the product manager has summarised the issues involved with the product line, they must decide on the plan's objectives. Two types of objectives must be set: financial and marketing.

Financial objectives

Fast Fitness's financial objectives are:

- To earn an annual rate of return on sales over the next three years of at least 28% before interest and taxes.
- To produce a net marketing contribution of $1 014 731 in 2006.
- To produce a net operating profit (before interest and taxes) of $514 727 in 2006.

Marketing objectives

Fast Fitness's marketing objectives are:

- To increase the number of personal training memberships to 498 per annum by December 2006.
- To grow market share from 2.15% in 2005 to 2.52% by December 2006 in the Sydney North and South combined market.
- To grow sales revenue from $1356 million in 2005 to $1832 million in 2006.

Marketing strategy

Marketing strategy The marketing logic by which the business unit hopes to achieve its marketing objectives. Marketing strategy consists of specific strategies for target markets, marketing mix and marketing expenditure level.

The product manager now outlines the broad **marketing strategy** or 'game plan' that they will use to accomplish the plan's objectives. It is here that the gap analysis model presented in Chapter 3 can be used to evaluate the alternative marketing strategy options. The marketing strategy is often presented in list form after the inclusion of a positioning strategy statement as follows.

Fast Fitness is positioned as an affordable personal fitness service, aimed at health-conscious and active individuals in the 40–55 age group.

Positioning strategy

Target market:	Health-conscious and exercise active market with emphasis on business executive buyer.
Product positioning:	Personal training with no contracts and at your own pace where you pay for what you use.
Product line:	Add one product extension (Cardio Yoga) and two higher-priced products for the primary market.
Price:	Price somewhat below personal trainers and below large city gyms. The current price of $80 (including GST) per week is still highly competitive.
Communication:	Increase advertising in local newspapers. Use website to communicate detailed benefits of the offer to potential new customers.
Salesforce:	Maintain high calibre of trainers to build personal rapport.
Service:	Personalised, convenient, flexible and quickly available.
Advertising:	Develop a new advertising program that supports the positioning strategy; emphasise personal program yielding tailored benefits with lower price than competitors. Increase advertising to 3.9% of sales revenues.
Sales promotion:	Increase the sales-promotion budget by 20% to develop a point-of-purchase display and to participate to a greater extent in local shops. Develop an

	information package on personal training and the importance of exercise in stress relief.
Synchronous:	Develop a new website that supports the positioning strategy; show all products; provide information on each; run a consumer sales promotion in each Sydney geographical area that exhibits relevant market characteristics. Create a website that addresses our target market's interests. This might include 'How to stay fit and healthy' and current developments in fitness and stress relief.
Research and development:	Increase expenditures by 30% to develop new product lines that appeal to the target market. Work on modern/contemporary gym layout.
Marketing research:	Increase expenditures to improve knowledge of consumer-choice process and to monitor competitor moves. Place special emphasis on the Internet environment.

In developing the strategy, the marketing manager needs to talk with the other functional managers to make sure they provide enough resources to meet the required sales-volume levels. The manager must also 'sell' to the sales manager to obtain the planned salesforce support, and to the financial officer to make sure enough advertising and promotion funds will be available to support the marketing strategy.

Action programs

The marketing plan must specify the broad marketing programs designed to achieve the business objectives. Each marketing strategy element must now be elaborated to answer: What will be done? When will it be done? Who will do it? How much will be spent?

February. Fast Fitness will advertise in local newspapers the fact that a free Exercise Planner can be downloaded from its website, available to everyone. Joanne B. will handle this project at a planned cost of $2760.

March–June. Website development to communicate the offer and and attract new customers. Cost $9000.

April. Fast Fitness will participate in the Good Health and Fitness Trade Show in Manly by offering a half-price workout to local residents. The expected cost is $4100 and will be managed by Phil M.

June. Launch new Cardio Yoga classes. Offer BOGOF (buy one get one free) classes in July for existing members. Cost $6000. This will be handled by Phil M.

July. Provide fitness calculators to existing and new members to build up recall and recognition of Fast Fitness to increase the number of visits. Cost $2500. Joanne B. will be in charge of this project.

August. A sales contest will be conducted over the website with the winner receiving two memberships to Fast Fitness for a year (four memberships on offer). The aim of this is to build a profile of potential customers for future sales leads. The contest will be handled by Vanessa M. at a planned cost of $4200.

September–October. Fast Fitness will re-advertise in local newspapers the fact that a free Exercise Planner can be downloaded from its website and will be available to everyone. Joanne B. and Vanessa M. will handle this project at a planned cost of $3960.

October. Launch the new range to the 40–45-year-old market in the first week of the month. This is a high period for the need for personal training and weight loss and is to meet the pre-summer fitness frenzy. Provide brochures outlining the services offered. Total cost $1650.

November. A sales contest will be conducted over the website with the winner receiving two memberships to Fast Fitness for a year (six memberships on the offer). Additionally T-shirts will be provided to existing and new members promoting Fast Fitness. The contest and merchandise will be handled by Vanessa M. at a planned cost of $4900.

January–December. Have 'open day' sessions (free sessions) every week (Mondays) in the idle periods between 3–5 pm for trialling Fast Fitness services. Cost $10 000. To be managed by Phil M.

Projected statement of financial performance

Action plans allow the product manager to build a supporting budget. On the revenue side, this budget shows the forecast sales volume in units and the average price. On the expense side, it shows the cost of production, physical distribution and marketing broken down into finer categories. The difference between revenues and sales is the projected profit. Case Study Table 3 shows the projected financial plan for Fast Fitness indicating variations from month to month affected by seasonality.

Once the budget has been prepared, senior management will review it and approve or modify it. If the requested budget is too high, the product manager will have to make some cuts. Once approved, the budget is the basis for developing plans and schedules for material procurement, production scheduling, employee recruitment and marketing operations.

CASE STUDY TABLE 3 Fast Fitness financial plan

1 P&L January 2006–Dec 2006		January	February	March	April
2 Average membership price ($)		3 680	3 680	3 680	3 680
3 Variable unit cost ($)		285	285	285	285
4 Units gross contribution margin ($)	(2–3)	3 395	3 395	3 395	3 395
5 Sales volume (in units-memberships)		42	35	49	38
6 Sales revenues ($)	(2 × 6)	154 560	128 800	180 320	139 840
7 Gross contribution margin ($)	(4 × 5)	142 590	118 825	166 355	129 010
8 Advertising & promotion ($)		4 637	3 864	5 410	4 195
9 Trainers (salesforce) ($)		50 800	50 800	50 800	50 800
10 Marketing research ($)		950	950	950	950
11 Net marketing contribution ($)	(7–8–9–10)	86 203	63 211	109 195	73 065
12 Overheads ($)		41 667	41 667	41 667	41 667
13 Net operating profit ($)	(11–12)	**44 536**	**21 544**	**67 528**	**31 398**

Controls

The last section of the marketing plan outlines the controls for monitoring the plan's progress. Typically, the goals and budget are spelled out for each month or quarter. Senior management can review the results of each period and identify businesses that are not attaining their goals. Managers of lagging businesses must explain what is happening and the actions they will take to improve plan fulfilment.

Some control sections include contingency plans. A contingency plan outlines the steps that management would take in response to specific adverse developments, such as price wars or strikes. The purpose of contingency planning is to encourage managers to think about difficulties that might lie ahead.

SELF-CHECK QUESTIONS

5   List the major sections in a marketing plan.

6   The current marketing situation is a major section in the marketing plan. What information does this section provide?

7   List and describe the aspects detailed in the marketing plan under the heading SWOT analysis.

8   Using the Procter and Gamble (P&G) example in the chapter opening, present two typical marketing objectives and briefly describe strategies that a company such as P&G might employ to achieve these objectives.

May	June	July	August	September	October	November	December	TOTAL
3 680	3 680	3 680	3 680	3 680	3 680	3 680	3 680	**3 680**
285	285	285	285	285	285	285	285	**285**
3 395	3 395	3 395	3 395	3 395	3 395	3 395	3 395	**3 395**
34	43	36	40	39	51	54	37	**498**
125 120	158 240	132 480	147 200	143 520	187 680	198 720	136 160	**1 832 640**
115 430	145 985	122 220	135 800	132 405	173 145	183 330	125 615	**1 690 710**
3 754	4 747	3 974	4 416	4 306	5 630	5 962	4 085	**54 979**
50 800	50 800	50 800	50 800	50 800	50 800	50 800	50 800	**609 600**
950	950	950	950	950	950	950	950	**11 400**
59 926	89 488	66 496	79 634	76 349	115 765	125 618	69 780	**1 014 731**
41 667	41 667	41 667	41 667	41 667	41 667	41 667	41 667	**500 004**
18 259	**47 821**	**24 829**	**37 967**	**34 682**	**74 098**	**83 951**	**28 113**	**514 727**

Analysing market opportunities

Because of its importance in the marketing planning process, we return here to the marketing management function of analysing market opportunities. The first task facing the Fast Fitness marketing manager, and indeed any marketing manager, is to analyse the long-run opportunities in the market so as to improve the business unit's performance. There is usually an abundance of opportunities in most markets, and the burgeoning health fitness field is no exception. The convergence of a number of technologies and high investment in this area is likely to continue in coming decades.

Fast Fitness's long-run goal might be to become a complete health fitness marketer. At present, however, it must come up with a plan for improving its product line. Within the personal fitness market there are still many opportunities.

To evaluate its opportunities, Fast Fitness needs to operate a reliable marketing information system (see Chapter 6). Marketing research is an indispensable marketing tool—companies can serve their customers well only by researching their needs and wants, their locations, their buying practices and so on. At the very least, Fast Fitness needs a good internal accounting system that reports current sales by product line, segment, location, salesperson and distribution channel. In addition, Fast Fitness managers should continually be collecting market intelligence on competitors and end-users. The marketing people should conduct formal research by running focus groups and conducting telephone, mail and personal surveys. By analysing the collected data using advanced statistical methods and models, the company will gain useful information on how sales are influenced by various marketing forces.

The purpose of market research is to gather significant information about the marketing environment. Fast Fitness's micro-environment consists of all the players who affect the company's ability to produce and deliver its service, suppliers, marketing intermediaries, customers and competitors. Fast Fitness's macro-environment consists of demographic, economic, physical, technological, political/legal and sociocultural forces that affect its sales and profits. An important part of gathering environmental information includes measuring market potential and forecasting future demand (see Chapter 9).

Fast Fitness sells its services to consumers and therefore it needs to understand consumer markets (see Chapter 7). It needs to know, for example: How many consumers buy fitness sessions? Who buys and why do they buy? What are they looking for in the way of attributes and prices? Where do they exercise? What are their images of different brands?

Fast Fitness also sells to institutional markets, including corporations, and businesses who are focusing on executive fitness (see Chapter 8). Large organisations use purchasing agents or buying committees who are skilled at evaluating products. Fast Fitness needs to gain a full understanding of how organisational buyers buy. Fast Fitness must also pay close attention to its competitors, anticipating their moves and knowing how to react quickly and decisively. It may want to initiate some surprise moves, in which case it needs to anticipate how its competitors will respond.

Once Fast Fitness has analysed its market opportunities, it is ready to select target markets. Modern marketing practice calls for dividing the market into major market segments, evaluating each segment and selecting and targeting those market segments that the company can serve best (see Chapter 10).

Evaluating the marketing plan

How does your marketing plan measure up? Before implementing the marketing plan it can be useful to evaluate it by answering the following questions:

◉ Do your marketing objectives relate directly to the company's strategic initiatives?

⊛ Do your marketing objectives relate directly to what you learned in your situational analysis?

⊛ Do your marketing objectives relate directly to the capacity of your current marketing mix to handle them?

⊛ Do your marketing objectives relate directly to your business's strengths and to the opportunities available?

⊛ Do your marketing objectives relate directly to your business's weaknesses and to the threats that endanger it?

⊛ Are your marketing objectives clear, measurable statements of what is to be achieved?

⊛ Do your marketing objectives, strategies and tactics relate to each other?

⊛ Does each strategy in your marketing plan contain a cost–benefit evaluation?

⊛ Is every person involved in implementation included in the marketing planning process in some way?

⊛ Is the plan clearly visible on your desk every day?

⊛ Is your business's vision truly a 'shared vision'?

If you can answer all these questions positively you have a powerful marketing plan ready for implementation.[4]

SELF-CHECK QUESTIONS

9 When analysing market opportunities, some aspects require continual market scanning, whereas others need only periodic examination. Provide examples of each for Qantas.

10 Suggest aspects of the competitive environment facing Qantas that it should monitor.

11 Are there aspects of the macro-environment that Qantas should monitor? If so, what are they?

Implementing the marketing plan

Analysis and incorporation of clear strategies into the marketing plan are only a start toward successful marketing. A brilliant marketing strategy counts for little if the company fails to implement it properly. **Marketing implementation** is the process that turns marketing strategies and plans into marketing actions in order to accomplish strategic marketing objectives. Implementation involves day-to-day, month-to-month activities that effectively put the marketing plan to work. Whereas marketing planning addresses the what and why of marketing activities, implementation addresses the who, where, when and how.

Many managers think that 'doing things right' (implementation) is as important, or even more important, than 'doing the right things' (strategy). The fact is that both are critical to success. This can be seen in the success story of Splenda—see Marketing Highlight 4.1. However, companies can gain competitive advantages through effective implementation. One firm can have essentially the same strategy as another, yet win in the marketplace through faster or better execution. Still, implementation is difficult—it is often easier to think up good marketing strategies than it is to carry them out.

A clear strategy and well thought out supporting program may be useless if the firm fails to implement them carefully. Indeed, strategy is only one of seven elements, according to the McKinsey Consulting Firm, that the best managed companies exhibit.[5] According to the McKinsey 7-S framework for business success, the first three elements—strategy, structure and systems—are considered the 'hardware' of success. The next four—style, staff, skills and shared values—are the 'software'.

Marketing implementation
The process that turns marketing strategies and plans into marketing actions in order to accomplish strategic marketing objectives.

Splendid taste for Splenda sales—made from sugar so it tastes like sugar

It is hard to believe how an unknown product can turn around an industry and become a market leader in just under four years.

Some industry experts say that the product is heading towards 'iconic status' with sales of over $A250 million. Today in an era of multiple competition and oversupply, the company is actually turning away new customers until it can increase its production capacity to meet demand.

Splenda is a trademark name given to a sucralose sweetener. This sweetener is produced by Tate & Lyle, an English firm known for making sugar cubes.

Sucralose was discovered when a researcher misunderstood the word 'test' during a laboratory experiment and tasted a substance that was not supposed to be ingested. The researcher's accidental discovery was that of a formulation which is 600 times sweeter than sugar, and yet is not absorbed by the human body as a carbohydrate. These properties mean that it has no effect on weight. Subsequent research has also showed that the product with-

Splenda provides a sweet alternative.

stands high temperature and therefore it can be used in cooking and baking. Splenda can also be formulated to resemble the look and feel of sugar meaning that it measures cup for a cup like sugar.

Armed with this discovery Tate & Lyle teamed up with Johnson & Johnson Pharmaceutical Company to market the product in a multitude of markets. The marketing team was formulated and embarked on a detailed study of market conditions, possible market segments and communication messages. The marketing plan was created in line with the company's goals and objectives. The initial marketing plan focused on specific market segments that showed particular interest in these types of products. The first target market was the diabetics' segment. The diabetic community had the powerful word-of-mouth network so needed in creating product awareness. Over one million units were sold over the Internet in less than a year.

The early success in the diabetic segment enabled Splenda's marketing team to reformulate its marketing plan to target the next most appealing segments. Part of the marketing plan was to create a series of campaigns with copy such as 'Splenda and Spice and Everything Nice' or 'Made from Sugar so it Tastes Like Sugar' to better position the product in the marketplace. Positioning of the product as a more natural alternative was created and the product was able to challenge sugars head on.

Another segment in Splenda's marketing plan was the beverage market. Companies such as Coca-Cola and Pepsi Cola were easily converted to use Splenda.

As at December 2005 Splenda had become an ingredient in more than 3000 marketed foods and drinks. Splenda has now surpassed Equal as Number One sweetener in the market.

Even McDonald's has replaced another artificial sweetener, 'Sweet 'N Low', with Splenda's yellow sachets. But McDonald's is not an isolated case. When Starbucks started stocking Splenda in late 2004 some employees reportedly kept Splenda's yellow sachets behind the counter so that the customers would not take handfuls.

In the USA the sales of Splenda has passed those of top sugar brands. Additionally, during 2004 the combined sales of Equal and Sweet 'N Low were dwarfed by Splenda's $US250 million in retail sales alone.

However, the years 2006 and 2007 will become even more challenging for Splenda. Although there are in excess of 30 patents guarding the process of making sucralose, the sucralose itself is not patented and some of these closely guarded patents will begin to expire in early 2007. This will give a window of opportunity for generics to emerge. NutraSweet, the former Number One player in the sweeteners market, is now working on a sucralose-based product to hit the shelves in 2007. Splenda's marketing team needs to revisit its marketing planning as the competition is just around the corner. Focusing on new segments and new product uses together with brand loyalty will become crucial in sustaining its leading position in the marketplace.

Sources: Splenda website, <www.splenda.com/page.jhtml?id=splenda/pressctr/starbucks.inc>, accessed 17 January 2006; Elizabeth Esfahani, 'Finding Sweet Spot by Starting Small but Thinking Big, Sugar Substitute Splenda Pulled Off One of the Most Successful Consumer Product Launches in History', *Business 2.0*, vol. 6, p. 49.

Questions

1 Which market segments should Splenda focus on next?

2 What would be one of the key marketing objectives needed to be achieved by Splenda's marketing team?

3 How can the company fend off the competition?

4 Are there any associations or industry bodies like the Diabetics Society that can be a catalyst for increasing sales of the product?

5 Visit Splenda's website (www.splendastore.com). Based on the information on the website, what objectives could you set for Splenda to follow for 18 months from today?

4.1

The first 'soft' element, style, means that company employees share a common way of thinking and behaving. Thus everyone at McDonald's smiles at the customer, and Optus employees are very professional in their customer dealings. The second, skills, means that the employees have the skills needed to carry out the company's strategy. The third, staffing, means that the company has hired able people, trained them well and assigned them to the right jobs. The fourth, shared values, means that the employees share the same guiding values. When these soft elements are present, companies are usually more successful at strategy implementation.[6]

These elements have been expanded by Peter Senge, suggesting that challenges now and in the future will be focused on an organisation's ability to learn. While the concept of a learning organisation is not new, its relevance to today's business is heightened by the magnitude of change impacting on organisations. Senge proposes that a **learning organisation** needs a number of dimensions or disciplines that are associated with its ability to innovate and change:

Learning organisation
A learning organisation is defined by its ability to innovate, adopt and change in line with its changing environment.

- Systems thinking
- Personal mastery
- Mental models
- Shared vision
- Team learning

Systems thinking consists of observing patterns, interrelationships and causal links and reinforcing or changing those patterns effectively in the light of experience or new thinking.

Personal mastery emphasises the need for individuals to focus on the alignment of learning with personal vision, thus gaining proficiency through creativity. Senge's concept of personal learning is one of expanding individual capacity to create the desired results and choosing to make a commitment to achieve the desired results. From an organisational perspective this means creating an environment in which all individuals can develop themselves to achieve the goals they chose. Collectively, individuals make up departments, teams and organisation.

People carry notions and assumptions that form their world-view or mental models. Many of these notions are untested—they are self-generated beliefs. Through a series of processes, these beliefs reinforce actions. The mental-model concept can be extended from individuals to groups. Powerful organisational mental models may enhance or hinder development and change in an organisation. These models create shared visions, beliefs and attitudes that may be untested but can form the basis for the development of new business and marketing strategies in the business unit.

The characteristics of an effective learning organisation include a decentralised, flat, team-focused structure with parallel information from multiple sources. Team learning is a basis for organisational learning as groups work together to achieve profit and business objectives. This encourages new thinking about problems and creates new ways of doing things.[7]

New areas of marketing capability will be demanded by developments in electronic business. New individual and team knowledge and skills will be needed to deal successfully with the strategies and tactics of electronic marketing.

Reasons for poor implementation

What causes poor implementation? Why do so many companies have trouble getting their marketing plans to work effectively? Several factors cause implementation problems.

Isolated planning

A company's strategic plans are often set by top management or high-level 'professional planners' who have little direct contact with the marketers who must implement the plan. Central strategic planning can provide benefits—strong central leadership, better coordination of strategies across business units and more emphasis on long-term strategic thinking and performance. But central planning also leads to problems. Top-level managers and planners are concerned with broad strategy and can prepare plans that are too general. They might not understand the practical problems faced by line managers and so produce unrealistic plans. Or lower-level managers who did not prepare the plans might not fully understand them. Finally, managers who face day-to-day operations can resent what they see as unrealistic plans made up by 'ivory tower' planners.

Many companies have realised that high-level managers and planners cannot plan strategies for marketing managers. Instead, planners must help marketing managers to find their own strategies. Many companies have cut down on their planning role and given more planning responsibility to lower-level managers. In these companies, top management and strategy planners are not isolated—they work directly with line managers to design more workable strategies.

Trade-offs between long-term and short-term objectives

Company marketing strategies often address long-run activities for the next three to five years. But the marketing managers who implement these strategies are usually rewarded for short-run sales, growth or profits. When choosing between long-run strategy and short-run performance, managers in the Western world usually favour one of the more rewarding short-run results. One study found many examples of such harmful trade-offs. For example, one company designed a marketing strategy that stressed product availability and customer service. But to increase short-term profit, operating managers cut costs by reducing inventories and service staff. These managers met short-run performance goals and received high evaluations, but their actions hurt the company's long-run strategy.[8]

Sydney's Amlab Technology, an innovative instrumentation company, went into receivership in April 1998 when its venture capital backer withdrew $2 million because it failed to meet sales and profit goals. Its longer-term objective of instrumentation product leadership did not deliver sufficient revenue in the short term to maintain the support of its financiers. Revived in August 1998, it developed a realistic business plan for sales and profit growth in both the short and medium term.[9]

Some companies are taking steps to maintain a better balance between short- and long-run goals. They are making managers more aware of strategic goals, evaluating managers on both long- and short-run performance and rewarding managers for reaching long-run objectives. The Japanese have taken this long-term approach in the application of their marketing strategies to penetrate international markets by rewarding managers on meeting market share and customer satisfaction milestones along the way, in line with the requirements for establishing new markets.

Natural resistance to change

As a rule, the company's current operations have been designed to implement past plans and strategies. New strategies requiring new company patterns and habits might be resisted. And the more different the new strategy from the old, the greater the resistance to implementing it. Singapore Airlines had to plan and continuously implement a very different strategy if it was to survive in the Australian and global air carrier market and find growth opportunities for the future—see Marketing Highlight 4.2.

For very different strategies, implementation might cut across traditional organisation lines within the company. For example, when one company tried to implement a strategy of developing new markets for an old product line, its established salesforce resisted strongly because of lack of familiarity with new customers and the level of service required to satisfy them. The company was forced to create an entirely new sales division in order to develop the new markets.

Lack of financial and marketing integration

There is often a lack of integration between finance and marketing at the business strategy level. The disciplines of financial analysis and marketing analysis have not been effectively brought together to develop business strategies. Financial analysts too frequently do not understand market realities and uncertainties, while marketing analysts have limited experience in evaluating the financial impacts of proposed marketing strategies.

Overemphasis on the document

Frequently, too much emphasis is given to 'the plan' (the document), rather than to the marketing planning process. Stories abound of plans evaluated on the basis of size or weight ('It must weigh at least two kilos to pass the test!'), coloured pictures or politically correct contents ('That's what I want to hear!'). A marketing plan should be concise, clear and directional.

Factors for successful implementation

Some marketing plans are poorly implemented because the planners fail to include enough detail about the action required. They leave the details to managers and the result is poor implementation or no implementation at all. Planners cannot simply assume that their plans will be carried out. They must prepare a detailed implementation plan that shows the specific activities needed to put it into action. They must develop timetables and assign major implementation tasks to individual managers.

Make money in the air—Singapore Airlines shows how

World travel is back. International tourist travel soared in 2005 to an all-time record. This represented an annual increase of 10% and was the largest jump in 20 years, according to the World Tourism Organization. Pent-up demand is just one factor fuelling this recovery. Another is a desire for new destinations, particularly in Asia and the Pacific, which recorded the largest increase at 29%.

The popularity of Asian destinations has brought more competition to these local markets traditionally serviced by Singapore Airlines (SIA). Full service US-, European- and Australian-based carriers, while protecting their markets, are expanding rapidly to markets such as Vietnam, China, Malaysia, Cambodia and Singapore. Such popularity has meant that new entrants of discount (budget) carriers are beginning to make strong inroads in the tourist and business travel markets.

Competition from discounters has prompted the major carriers to slash fares on the most popular routes. Many carriers are feeling the pinch and are beginning to reduce non-essential services to remain profitable such as the quality of food and quality of service. Despite such stern competition Singapore Airlines has not reduced service to its customers but remains profitable. In addition, SIA can still boast 30 years of continuing profit success, even excelling during periods of travel industry downturn.

Singapore Airlines maintains its innovative edge.

Its marketing success is clear when listing the myriad of awards won. SIA is regularly voted:

- Best business class
- Best cabin service
- Best air cargo
- Best in-flight food
- Best in punctuality and safety
- Asia's mostly admired company

In 2002 alone SIA achieved a total of 67 international awards.

How has this level of success been sustained for so long? SIA instils a customer-oriented culture that pervades the whole spectrum of the airline's operations. The marketing team focuses on customer service excellence while at the same time being aware that all the marketing initiatives need to be cost efficient. This awareness is shared by all employees. Holistic training methods drive the message home as does the fact that bonuses and other rewards are very much dependent upon profits earned. Not surprisingly, staff at all levels work to stop resources being wasted.

Market leaders don't stay at the top for 30 years by standing still. Innovation is vital and SIA excels in this aspect of business. The company believes that all innovations have a limited life and is not afraid to discontinue those that no longer bring competitive advantage. But surely this type of innovation must be a costly strategy? Not so, as SIA also implements a continuous program of minor and incremental improvements. Doing this enables the airline always to remain marginally superior to rivals in what it offers the passenger. The keyword here is marginally.

But how does this benefit the company? By this incremental approach, smaller improvements equal lower costs while still producing value for the customer. The importance of this strategy cannot be underestimated as cost efficiency here frees up resources for more major investments.

SIA's marketing strategy revolves around the customer's unmet wants and needs and develops its future programs around it. For example, when

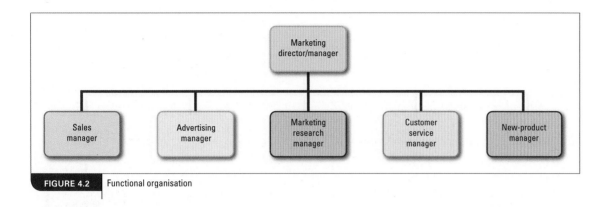

| **FIGURE 4.2** | Functional organisation |

or districts. Geographic organisation allows salespeople to settle into a territory, get to know their customers and work with a minimum of travel time and cost. Figure 4.3 depicts this structure.

Companies with many different products or brands often create a product management organisation. Using this approach, a product manager develops and implements a complete strategy and marketing program for a specific product or brand. Product management first appeared in the American company Procter and Gamble in 1929. A new company soap, Camay, was not doing well and a young P&G executive was assigned to give his exclusive attention to developing and promoting this product. He was successful and the company soon added other product managers.[11]

Since then many firms, especially in the food, soap, toiletries and chemical industries, have set up product management organisations. Today, the product management system is firmly entrenched. Figure 4.4 (overleaf) outlines this organisation. However, recent dramatic changes in the marketing environment have caused many companies to rethink the role of the product manager.

For companies that sell one product line to many different types of markets with different needs and preferences, a market management organisation might be best. Many companies are organised

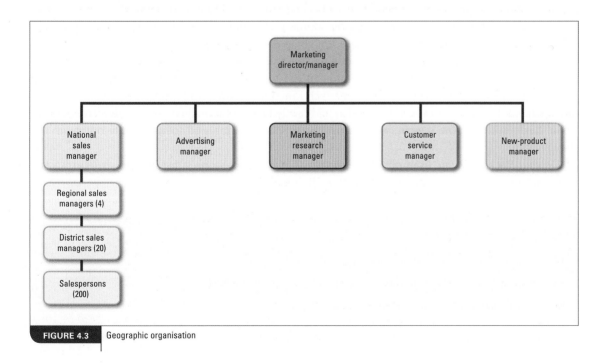

| **FIGURE 4.3** | Geographic organisation |

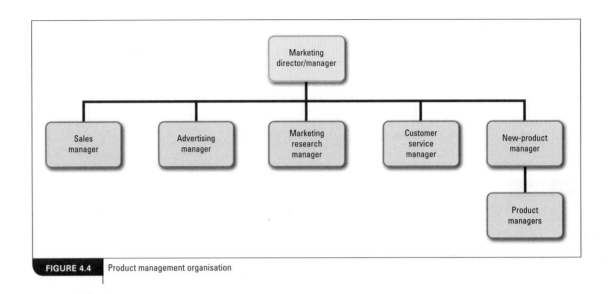

FIGURE 4.4 Product management organisation

along market lines. A market management organisation is similar to the product management organisation. Market managers are responsible for developing long-range and annual plans for the sales and profits in their markets. This system's main advantage is that the company is organised around the needs of specific customer segments.

In recent years we saw major changes in marketing organisation as companies formed alliances to access new markets. The marketing or product manager became part of an alliance team both in developing marketing plans and implementing them. For example, an AMP product manager developing insurance products would need to work with channel partners such as accountants and insurance brokers to formulate and implement marketing programs. At the same time, because of the integral nature of information technology (IT) in the communication and delivery of information about its products, the AMP manager would also need to work closely with IBM, which manages all AMP's IT assets and staff as part of a major outsourcing agreement. This form of 'virtual' organisation is becoming more prevalent and is discussed in some detail in Chapter 20.

Large companies that produce many different products flowing into many different geographic and customer markets use some combination of the functional, geographic, product, market and virtual organisation forms. This ensures that each function, product and market receives its share of management attention. However, it can also add costly layers of management and reduce organisational flexibility. Still, the benefits of organisational specialisation and focus usually outweigh the drawbacks.[12]

Hewlett-Packard is one example of a company that has undergone substantial restructuring and reorganisation in recent years—see Marketing Highlight 4.3.

SELF-CHECK QUESTIONS

12 Define marketing implementation in terms of what is involved.

13 List and describe the key elements involved in successful implementation.

14 Compare different forms of marketing organisation.

Controlling and evaluating performance

Because many surprises occur during the implementation of marketing plans, the marketing department must practise constant marketing control. **Marketing control** involves evaluating the results of marketing strategies and plans and taking corrective action to ensure that objectives are attained. It involves the four steps shown in Figure 4.5. Management first sets specific marketing goals. It then measures its performance in the marketplace and evaluates the causes of any differences between expected and actual performance. Finally, management takes corrective action to close the gaps between its goals and its performance. This may require changing the action program or even changing the goals.

Operating control involves checking ongoing performance against the annual plan and taking corrective action when necessary. Its purpose is to ensure that the company achieves the sales, profits and other goals set out in its annual plan. It also involves determining the profitability of different products, territories, markets and channels. Strategic control involves looking at whether the company's basic strategies are well matched to its opportunities. Marketing strategies and programs can quickly become outdated, and each company should periodically reassess its overall approach to the marketplace. A major tool for such strategic control is a marketing audit. The **marketing audit** is a comprehensive, systematic, independent and periodic examination of a company's environment, objectives, strategies and activities to determine problem areas and opportunities. The audit provides good input for a plan of action to improve the company's marketing performance.[13]

The marketing audit covers all major marketing areas of a business, not just a few trouble spots. It is normally conducted by an objective and experienced outside party who is independent of the marketing department. Table 4.2 on page 144 shows the kinds of questions the marketing auditor might ask. The findings may come as a surprise—and sometimes as a shock—to management. Management then decides which actions make sense and how and when to implement them.

Marketing control The process of measuring and evaluating the results of marketing strategies and plans, and taking corrective action to ensure that marketing objectives are attained.

Marketing audit A comprehensive, systematic, independent and periodic examination of a company's environment, objectives, strategies and activities to determine problem areas and opportunities and to recommend a plan of action to improve the company's marketing performance.

SELF-CHECK QUESTIONS

15 What does marketing control involve? Is it simply measuring variance between plans and marketing outcomes?

16 Describe operating control.

17 Discuss the nature of strategic control.

18 How important is the marketing audit in the marketing process?

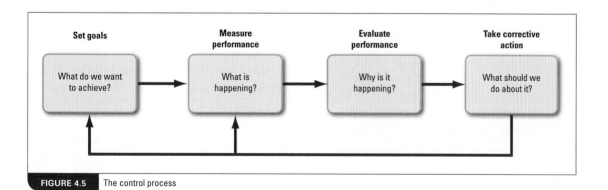

Set goals	Measure performance	Evaluate performance	Take corrective action
What do we want to achieve?	What is happening?	Why is it happening?	What should we do about it?

FIGURE 4.5 The control process

MARKETING HIGHLIGHT

4.3

The new HP reorganises again . . . and again

In 1939 two engineers, Bill Hewlett and David Packard, started Hewlett-Packard in a Palo Alto garage to build test equipment. At the start Bill and Dave did everything themselves, from designing and building their equipment to marketing it. As the firm grew out of the garage and began to offer more types of test equipment, Hewlett and Packard could no longer make all the necessary operating decisions themselves. They hired functional managers to run various company activities. These managers were relatively autonomous, but they were still closely tied to the owners.

By the mid-1970s Hewlett-Packard's 42 divisions employed more than 30 000 people. The company's structure evolved to support its heavy emphasis on innovation and autonomy. Each division operated as an independent unit and was responsible for its own strategic planning, product development, marketing programs and implementation.

Hewlett-Packard's humble garage beginnings.

HP's unrestrictive structure and high degree of informal communication (its style of management by walking around (MBWA)) fostered autonomy by decentralising decision-making responsibility and authority. The approach became known as the 'HP Way', a structure that encouraged innovation by abolishing rigid chains of command and putting managers and employees on a first-name basis. But by the mid-1980s, although still profitable, HP had begun to encounter problems in the fast-changing personal computer and minicomputer markets. In a new climate that required its fiercely autonomous divisions to work together in product development and marketing, HP's famed innovative culture—with its heavy emphasis on autonomy and entrepreneurship—became a hindrance. Thus, HP moved to bring its structure and culture in line with its changing situation. It established a system of committees to foster communication within and across its many divisions and to coordinate product development, marketing and other activities.

The new structure seemed to work well—for a while. However, the move toward centralisation soon got out of hand. Committees multiplied and soon every decision was made by committee. By the late 1980s the 'HP Way' was completely bogged down by unwieldy bureaucracy. Entering the 1990s HP had no fewer than 38 in-house committees that made decisions on everything from technical specifications for new products to the best cities for staging product launches. Instead of enhancing communication, this suffocating structure pushed up costs and increased HP's decision-making and market-reaction time. For example, in one case it took almost 100 people over seven weeks just to come up with a name for the company's New Wave Computing Software. As one frustrated marketing manager noted, to overcome the bureaucracy it required the philosophy: 'Don't ask for permission—ask for forgiveness'.

In the fast-paced workstation and personal computer markets, HP's sluggish decision making put it at a serious disadvantage against such nimble competitors as Compaq Computer Corporation and Sun Microsystems. Top management finally took action. Bill Hewlett and Dave Packard themselves stepped in to help break the bureaucracy and restore a measure of decentralisation. The result was a sweeping reorganisation that wiped out HP's committee structure and flattened the organisation.

New CEO, Carly Fiorina, appointed in July 1999, faced the challenge of propelling HP into the Internet age without sacrificing the things that had made it great. After declining sales and inconsistent profits in 1997 and 1998, its new e-services thrust is attacking the position taken by IBM. However, with 130 different product groups, the HP bureaucracy was overwhelming. In a move to streamline the company, the Test and Measurement unit was separated from the rest of HP. Then CEO-like powers were given to four divisional heads—covering inkjet imaging, enterprise computing, laserjet imaging and PCs. This approach has helped HP put together a Net strategy. HP's traditional method of selling stand-alone products is not effective in the Internet age. Customers want a vision of a future and integrated suites of products to solve particular needs, like e-commerce.

This was further complicated when, in 2002, HP went through a bruising merger process to absorb Compaq to create a mega-corporation to compete with IBM and Dell. The strength of Compaq's PCs, notebooks and computer systems combined with HP's traditional strength in imaging and printers has created a competitive powerhouse. The 'hp invent' brand positioning launched in 2002 is having an impact on building its corporate brand image and position as an e-services business. Its 'One Voice' marketing communications program was launched in mid-2003. This was accompanied by another restructure to create four major divisions:

1 Image and Printing Group—commercial and consumer markets

2 Enterprise Systems Group—computer systems and storage for large enterprises

3 Personal Systems Group—PCs, notebooks and personal digital assistants for business and consumer markets

4 HP Services—network services and consulting

The Asia–Pacific Japan (APJ) region is one of three HP marketing centres along with the Americas and EMEA—Europe, Middle East and Africa. In Singapore, product managers responsible for profit and pricing of product lines are supported by market development managers in each country like Australia. These, in turn, aim to understand market segmentation and customer needs at the local level.

In 2005 its high-profile CEO Carly Fiorina was dumped by the board and a new chief executive, Mark Hurd, was hired to focus on creating a more stable business in terms of profitability and ensure effective execution of HP's strategy. One of his earliest actions in July 2005 was to eliminate the Customer Solutions Group (CSG) which housed the key customer-facing functions including marketing and sales. This was replaced with a new Chief Marketing Officer (CMO) with a broader function plus newly empowered marketing within the major lines of business. Several months after his appointment he restructured HP again by separating the imaging and printing business from the PC business. The three HP

hp connectivity

product lines are now Technology Solutions Group, which focuses on the enterprise market, the Personal Systems Group (includes PCs) and the Imaging and Printing Group.

Thus, in less than a decade HP's structure has evolved from the highly decentralised and informal 'HP Way' to a highly centralised committee system and back again to a point in between. It has restructured its lines of business through hiving off businesses and acquiring new ones. HP is not likely to find a single best structure that will satisfy all its future needs. Rather, it must continue adapting its structure to suit the requirements of its ever-changing environment.

Sources: Nicole C. Wong and Dean Takahashi, 'HP's CEO Takes Low Profile at Electronics Show', *San José Mercury News*, 5 January 2006 (www. mercurynews.com/mld/mercurynews/business/13560080.htm); Richard Vancil, 'Marketing Evolution at HP', Event Flash IDC, December 2005, IDC #34692, vol. 1; Pimm Fox, 'Leaders Need Vision', *Computerworld*, 17 February 2003, vol. 37, no. 7, p. 18; Carly Fiorina, 'Lessons We Shouldn't Forget', *Information Week*, 27 January 2003, no. 924, p. 14; Grant Buckler, 'HP Looks for a New Way', *The Journal of Business Strategy*, September/October 2001, vol. 22, no. 5, p. 22; Barbara Buell, Robert D. Hof and Gary McWilliams, 'Hewlett Packard Rethinks Itself', *Business Week*, 1 April 1991, pp. 76–79; Alan Deutschman, 'How HP Continues to Grow and Grow', *Fortune*, 2 May 1994, pp. 90–100; P. Burrows and P. Elstrom, 'The Boss', *Business Week*, 2 August 1999, pp. 76–84.

Questions

1 Has HP found the ideal organisational structure with the advent of its more decentralised organisation and four lines of business? Why or why not?

2 Why do you think that organisational structure is important in meeting customers' needs?

3 Have you encountered a marketing organisation where a 'simple, flexible structure' is in place? If so, is the organisation successful in the sense that it enjoys sales and profit growth or gives evidence of this by being in business for a long time?

4.3

TABLE 4.2 Marketing audit questions

Marketing environment audit

The macro-environment
1. Demographic. What major demographic trends pose threats and opportunities for this company?
2. Economic. What developments in income, prices, savings and credit will affect the company?
3. Natural. What is the outlook for costs and availability of natural resources and energy? Is the company environmentally responsible?
4. Technology. What technological changes are occurring? What is the company's position on technology?
5. Political. What current and proposed laws will affect company strategy?
6. Cultural. What is the public's attitude toward business and the company's products? What changes in consumer lifestyles might have an impact?

The task environment
1. Markets. What is happening to market size, growth, geographic distribution and profits? What are the major market segments?
2. Customers. How do customers rate the company on product quality, service and price? How do they make their buying decisions?
3. Competitors. Who are the major competitors? What are their strategies, market shares, and strengths and weaknesses?
4. Channels. What main channels does the company use to distribute products to customers? How are they performing?
5. Suppliers. What trends are affecting suppliers? What is the outlook for the availability of key production resources?
6. Publics. What key publics provide problems or opportunities? How should the company deal with these publics?

TABLE 4.2 Marketing audit questions

Marketing environment audit

Marketing strategy audit

1. Business mission. Is the mission clearly defined and market oriented?
2. Marketing objectives. Has the company set clear objectives to guide marketing planning and performance? Do these objectives fit with company opportunities and resources?
3. Marketing strategy. Does the company have a sound marketing strategy for achieving its objectives?
4. Budgets. Has the company budgeted sufficient resources to segments, products, territories and marketing mix elements?

Marketing organisation audit

1. Formal structure. Does the chief marketing officer have adequate authority over activities affecting customer satisfaction? Are marketing activities optimally structured along functional, product, market and territory lines?
2. Functional efficiency. Do marketing and sales communicate effectively? Is the marketing staff well trained, supervised, motivated and evaluated?
3. Interface efficiency. Does the marketing staff work well with manufacturing, R&D, purchasing, human resources and other non-marketing areas?

Marketing systems audit

1. Marketing information system. Is the marketing intelligence system providing accurate and timely information about marketplace developments? Are company decision makers using marketing research effectively?
2. Marketing planning system. Does the company prepare annual, long-term and strategic plans? Are they used?
3. Marketing control system. Are annual plan objectives being achieved? Does management periodically analyse the sales and profitability of products, markets, territories and channels?
4. New-product development. Is the company well organised to gather, generate and screen new-product ideas? Does it carry out adequate product and market testing? Has the company succeeded with new products?

Marketing productivity audit

1. Profitability analysis. How profitable are the company's different products, markets, territories and channels? Should the company enter, expand or withdraw from any business segments? What would be the consequences?
2. Cost-effectiveness analysis. Do any marketing activities have excessive costs? How can costs be reduced?

Marketing function audit

1. Products. Has the company developed sound product-line objectives? Should some products be phased out? Should some new products be added? Would some products benefit from quality, style or feature changes?
2. Price. What are the company's pricing objectives, policies, strategies and procedures? Are the company's prices in line with customers' perceived value? Are price promotions used properly?
3. Distribution. What are the distribution objectives and strategies? Does the company have adequate market coverage and service? Should existing channels be changed or new ones added?
4. Advertising, sales promotion and publicity. What are the company's promotion objectives? How is the budget determined? Is it sufficient? Are advertising messages and media well developed and received? Does the company have well-developed sales promotion and public relations programs?
5. Salesforce. What are the company's salesforce objectives? Is the salesforce large enough? Is it properly organised? Is it well trained, supervised and motivated? How is the salesforce rated relative to those of competitors?

SUMMARY

Corporate head office is responsible for setting into motion the strategic planning process. The corporate strategy establishes the framework within which the division and business units prepare their strategic plans.

The *marketing process* consists of four steps: analysing market opportunities; developing marketing strategies; planning marketing programs, which entails choosing the marketing mix (the four Ps of product, price, place and promotion); and organising, implementing and controlling the marketing effort.

Each product level within a business unit must develop a marketing plan for achieving its goals. The marketing plan is one of the most important outputs of the marketing process and it should contain the following elements: an *executive summary* and table of contents; an overview of the current marketing situation; an analysis of the opportunities and issues facing the product; a summary of the plan's financial and marketing objectives; an overview of the *marketing strategy* to be used to achieve the plan's objectives; a description of the action programs to be implemented to achieve the plan's objectives; a projected statement of financial performance; and a summary of the controls to be used in monitoring the plan's progress.

Successful implementation also requires careful human resources planning. The company must recruit, allocate, develop and maintain good people. The firm's company culture can also make or break implementation. Company culture guides people in the company; good implementation relies on strong, clearly defined cultures that fit the chosen strategy.

Most of the responsibility for implementation goes to the company's marketing department. Modern marketing departments are organised in a number of ways. The most common form is the functional marketing organisation, in which marketing functions are directed by separate managers who report to the marketing vice-president. The company might also use a geographic organisation in which its salesforce or other functions specialise by geographic area. The company may also use the product management organisation, in which products are assigned to product managers who work with functional specialists to develop and achieve their plans. Another form is the market management organisation, in which major markets are assigned to market managers who work with functional specialists.

Marketing organisations carry out marketing control. Operating control involves monitoring current marketing results to make sure that the annual sales and profit goals will be achieved. It also calls for determining the profitability of the firm's products, territories, market segments and channels. Strategic control makes sure that the company's marketing objectives, strategies and systems fit with the current and forecast marketing environment. It uses the *marketing audit* to determine marketing opportunities and problems and to recommend short- and long-run actions to improve overall marketing performance. Through these activities, the company watches and adapts to the marketing environment.

Marketing plans in many businesses are well-researched plans that are never implemented. Here's what happens! As a well-trained marketing graduate, new to the company or new to the marketing position, you are asked to write the marketing plan for a product or market segment. Senior management provides some guideline objectives for market share and profit. You gather all of the business data and carefully craft a realistic marketing plan. This, however, does not meet the required objectives, which appear to be unrealistic and unattainable. Senior management rejects your plan and asks for one that will meet their objectives.

You look for creative ways to cut costs and increase revenues but feel that this will be very difficult to achieve. However, with some compromise on objectives, strategy and budget a plan is finalised.

In the first quarter it seems clear that the objectives are not being achieved, resources are cut and the marketing plan is used as a door-stop (i.e. placed on your library shelf) and short-term actions are taken to increase sales without reference to your plan.

How can you overcome this type of problem?

KEY TERMS

executive summary	119	marketing implementation	131
learning organisation	133	marketing process	116
marketing audit	141	marketing strategy	126
marketing control	141		

DISCUSSING THE ISSUES

1 A product manager, reporting to you, wonders how a large, detailed marketing plan can be condensed into a useful one-page executive summary. Suggest what should go into the executive summary. What should be left out?

2 Describe some of the threats and opportunities facing the department store business. How might a major chain such as Myer respond to these threats and opportunities?

3 Overall, which is the most important part of the marketing management process: analysis, planning, implementation or control? Discuss whether a company that 'does things right' is more or less likely to succeed than a company that 'does the right things'.

4 Which is easier to change, organisation structure or company culture? Which do you think has a greater impact on how well plans are implemented?

5 How important is having adequate marketing resources to the implementation of a marketing plan? What needs to change in a plan if resources are suddenly reduced substantially?

6 eBay sells a wide range of products all through the Internet to individuals and organisations around the world. Suggest and justify the form of organisation eBay might use for its marketing department—functional, geographic, product management, market management or some other organisation. Why?

REFERENCES

1. Jack Neff, 'Well Balanced Plan Allows P&G to Soar', *Advertising Age*, Chicago, 12 December 2005, vol. 76, no. 50, p. S2. For a detailed explanation of the marketing planning process see Malcolm McDonald, *Marketing Plans*, 5th edn, London, Butterworth-Heinemann, 2002.

2. J. C. Larreche, *The MECA Reports on the Competitive Fitness of Global Firms*, London, Pitman Publishing, 1998; also see five annual reports entitled *Measuring the Competitive Fitness of Global Firms*, Financial Times Prentice Hall, 1998–2002; Corporate Strategy

Board, *Unbroken Growth: Salient Insights from Inaugural Research*, The Advisory Board Company, Washington DC, December 1997; Joan Llonch, 'Measures of Marketing Success: A Comparison between Spain and the UK', *European Management Journal*, August 2002, vol. 20, no. 4, p. 414; Charles P. Griffin, 'Strategic Planning for the Internal Marketing and Communication of Facilities Management', *Journal of Facilities Management*, November 2002, vol. 1, no. 3, p. 237.

3. Marisa D. Jacobson, *The Marketing Plan: How to Prepare and Implement It*, 3rd edn, Santa Barbara, *The Journal of Consumer Marketing*, 2003, vol. 20, no. 1, p. 73.

4. J. A. McComb, 'Marketing by Design', *Bank Marketing*, vol. 29, no. 1, 1997, pp. 14–20; Philip R. Harris, 'Marketing Plans: How to Prepare Them, How to Use Them (5th edn)', *European Business Review*, 2002, vol. 14, no. 6, p. 450; Andrew Kay, 'World-Class Marketing Plans', *Pharmaceutical Executive*, May 2001, p. 42.

5. See Thomas J. Peters and Robert H. Waterman Jr, *In Search of Excellence: Lessons from America's Best-Run Companies*, New York, Harper & Row, 1982, pp. 9–12. The same framework is used in Richard Tanner Pascale and Anthony G. Athos, *The Art of Japanese Management: Applications for American Executives*, New York, Simon & Schuster, 1981. See also E. Rasiel, *The McKinsey Way*, New York, McGraw-Hill, 1999.

6. See Terrence E. Deal and Allan A. Kennedy, *Corporate Cultures: The Rites and Rituals of Corporate Life*, Reading, MA, Addison-Wesley, 1982; 'Corporate Culture', *Business Week*, 27 October 1980, pp. 148–160; Lyndon Simkin, 'Tackling Implementation Impediments to Marketing Planning', *Marketing Intelligence & Planning*, vol. 20, no. 2, 2002, p. 120; Stanley M. Davis, *Managing Corporate Culture*, Cambridge, MA, Ballinger, 1984; John P. Kotter and James L. Heskett, *Corporate Culture and Performance*, New York, The Free Press, 1992; Lyndon Simkin, 'Barriers Impeding Effective Implementation of Marketing Plans—a Training Agenda', *The Journal of Business & Industrial Marketing*, vol. 17, no. 1, 2002, p. 8.

7. P. M. Senge, *The Fifth Discipline*, Sydney, Random House, 1992; R. C. Blattberg, R. Glazer, J. D. C. Little (eds), *The Marketing Information Revolution*, Boston, MA, Harvard Business School Press, 1994; Carol Reineck, 'Leadership's Guiding Light, Part 2: Create a Learning Organization', *Nursing Management*, October 2002, vol. 33, no. 10, p. 42; I. Chaston, 'The Internet and e-Commerce: An Opportunity to Examine Organisational Learning in Progress in Small Manufacturing Firms?', *International Small Business Journal*, January–March 2001, vol. 19, no. 2, p. 13.

8. A. A. Thompson Jr and A. J. Strickland III, *Strategic Management*, 10th edn, Boston, MA, Irwin/McGraw-Hill, 1998, pp. 36–39; Echo Montgomery Garrett, 'Outsourcing to the Max', *Small Business Reports*, August 1994, pp. 9–14.

9. M. Harvey, 'Virtual Monitoring Gets Real', *Business Review Weekly*, 3 September 1999, pp. 50–51.

10. J. Collins and J. Porras, *Built to Last*, New York, Harper Business, 1994.

11. Joseph Winski, 'One Brand, One Manager', *Advertising Age*, 20 August 1987, p. 86.

12. For more complete discussions of marketing organisation approaches and issues see Robert W. Ruekert, Orville C. Walker Jr and Kenneth J. Roering, 'The Organisation of Marketing Activities: A Contingency Theory of Structure and Performance', *Journal of Marketing*, Winter 1985, pp. 13–25; and Ravi S. Achrol, 'Evolution of the Marketing Organization: New Forms for Turbulent Environments', *Journal of Marketing*, October 1991, pp. 77–93.

13. For details see Philip Kotler and Kevin Lane Keller, *Marketing Management*, 12th edn, Upper Saddle River, NJ, Prentice Hall, 2006, Chapter 22, pp. 719–721. Also see P. Kotler, *Kotler on Marketing: How to Create, Win and Dominate Markets*, New York, The Free Press, 1999, Chapter 10, pp. 185–202.

PHOTO/AD CREDITS

115. AAP Image/Dean Lewins; **132.** Image provided by Dreamstime.com; **136.** Courtesy of Singapore Airlines; **142.** Reproduced with the permission of Hewlett Packard Australia; **143.** Reproduced with the permission of Hewlett Packard Australia.

CASE STUDY
Fast Fitness: planning for a growth business

Peter Moore, Senior Marketing Consultant, Interstrat

The Fast Fitness marketing plan is reproduced from this chapter for your reference to a marketing plan as a single document. Marketing plans vary in their structure and content but this document is a useful reference point for the structure, content and flow of most marketing plans. The Fast Fitness marketing plan can also be used as a case study by addressing the questions posed at the end of the plan.

1 Company overview

Fast Fitness is a personal-training-focused company operating in three locations across Sydney. The company provides more personalised training to that offered by large gyms where individuals develop their own training routine. Fast Fitness is doing what is usually being done by individual personal trainers but it does it in a more professional manner with clearly visible locations as opposed to 'one-man' personal trainers that need to be booked over the telephone to arrive at a mutually convenient location for fitness training. Fast Fitness offers a new concept in personal training. It prices its offer below the rates of individual trainers who can charge between $65 and $90 per hour. Fast Fitness charges $80 per week rather than per hour (including GST), with an average member attending three sessions per week.

Fast Fitness was launched by Phil Murray in December 2000. Prior to that Phil had been trading as Muz Personal Training for around eight years but then saw the opportunity to create a strong identity around his unique fitness training concept with a professional studio to match in Sydney's Northern and Southern Beaches area. After his early years of training people in squash and boxing Phil gained his personal training qualifications through the Australian Council of Health and Physical Education and Recreation (ACHPER) and started Muz Personal Training. In those early years, he operated in a number of studios and realised the importance of customer relationships, service, new training concepts and fitness trends as well as strong business management. He developed a strong marketing orientation and by the time he launched Fast Fitness he had the marketing knowledge and business skills required to build a professional operation. From Christmas 2000 the business took off and with an astute balance of investment and consolidation had grown sizeably by the third quarter of 2005. It was then that Phil began crafting his marketing plan for 2006.

2 Executive summary

There is an opportunity for Fast Fitness to improve its market position in 2006. Currently the market shows positive growth across the industry of around 14% per annum indexed. In line with this trend and based on its strategy it is estimated that Fast Fitness will be able to grow its market share from 2.12% to 2.52% of its local market, representing an 18.9% increase. It can also increase its profitability in line with this proposed growth. Its financial and marketing objectives and its strategy for 2006 are detailed below.

Financial objectives
- To earn an annual rate of return on sales over the next three years of at least 28% before interest and taxes.
- To produce a net marketing contribution of $1 014 731 in 2006.
- To produce a net operating profit (before interest and taxes) of $514 727 in 2006.

Marketing objectives
- To grow distribution/current locations from three to four by October 2006.
- To increase the number of personal training memberships to 498 per annum by December 2006.
- To grow market share from 2.15% in 2005 to 2.52% by December 2006 in the Sydney North and South combined market.

◉ To grow sales revenue from $1356 million in 2005 to $1832 million in 2006.

Marketing strategy

The Fast Fitness strategy is to position itself as a personal training specialist with quality services delivered at affordable prices—an average price of $80 per weekly membership (price includes GST). This is expected to be an appealing offer since competitors' prices range from $65 to $90 per hour. Fast Fitness will continue to grow its business continuing to focus on the northern and southern regions of Sydney. The company will selectively increase its marketing expenditure from 1.6% to 3.9% of revenue based on the competitor benchmarked marketing spending. Additionally in 2006, there will be an increased focus on market research and building the customer base through a focused marketing initiative including the multimedia channels such as the Internet and TV channels.

TABLE OF CONTENTS

3 Situation analysis (current marketing situation)

3.1 Market situation

Nations such as America, Australia and countries of Western Europe are being labelled as the fat nations on the face of the earth, with the USA maintaining the label as the 'Fattest Nation' on earth. Every day due to working and the general environment, stress is becoming a real epidemic in Australia. Australia is one of the world leaders in consumption of stress-related medications. Additionally over seven million adult Australians are affecting their health by being overweight. Despite the country spending over $100 million on healthcare, the average lifespan of Australians is nowhere near the top-ranking countries.

Exercise has long been cited as a way of improving one's health and quality of life. But in recent years the data about the specific benefits of physical activity have grown to what is now a breathtaking list: lower cholesterol and blood pressure; a reduced risk of heart disease, stroke, osteoporosis, diabetes and colon cancer; strengthening of bones, joints and muscle; and an improvement from reduced anxiety and depression.

The Centre for Disease Control and Prevention in the USA estimates that getting inactive Americans exercising could save that country around $80 billion a year in cost otherwise spent on treating chronic disease. The same trends are evident in Australian society. Insurance agencies such as AMP and Mercantile Mutual are beginning to conduct risk-assessment studies for future insurance claims and to develop appropriate premiums based on the level of fitness. Large companies are also becoming concerned with their CEOs' and senior managers' fitness/health levels, since poor health and fitness often correlates with early retirements and poor business and market performance. Corporate 'wellness' is a rapidly expanding market within the fitness industry. A number of companies in Australia, such as Medifit, Health Fitness Corporation and Corporate Fitness Works, provide on-site management and staffing to

corporate wellness facilities. Companies are increasing their corporate wellness programs due to the favourable cost–benefit equation related to healthier employees. Memberships in gyms, sports clubs and fitness centres are being subsidised by health funds like Medibank Private, MBF and HCF with a view to reducing future insurance.

The growth of focus on a healthy lifestyle is evident through the rapid growth in sales of fast-moving consumer goods companies which are developing and marketing a host of products focusing on 'healthy living' and fat-reduced diet. Sport and exercise now play a greater role in people's lives and Australian society as a whole. Exercising is no longer associated with specific age groups, even extreme sports like triathlons, marathons and the Australian Ironman. According to the Iron Man website in 2005 it attracted over 1500 entries with the age brackets ranging from 18 to 75 for both men and women (source: <http://www.ironmanoz.com/>, accessed December 2005).

There are a number of clear sectors that have emerged in the Australian market. The two main sectors are as follows:

1 Health gyms (mass exercising with limited trainer–trainee interaction)—these are large bulk membership gyms.
2 Personal training (greater interaction between trainer and trainee)—a premium-priced product with a smaller but more personalised service with focused management of the exercise regime.

There is now a newly emerging group hitting the gyms—baby boomers—who are reaching their late 40s and 50s. The number of health clubs, personal trainers and personal fitness businesses are growing exponentially. Membership for the upper age bracket has risen fourfold since the 1990s from 220 000 members in 1993 to 635 000 members in 2004. It is estimated by IHRSA (International Health, Raquet & Sportsclub Association) that by 2010 there will be around 3 000 000 registered members (Fitness Australia, 'One Million Members by 2010', from the corporate website, accessed 20 December 2005, www.fitnessaustralia.com.au/_uploads/res/243_2135.pdf.) No longer is the fitness industry being dominated by the 18 to 34 age group, but is shifting to a more mature demographic—one which has a higher disposable income and health considerations.

Additionally there is growth in the exercise equipment industry. Sales of treadmills, exercise bicycles, weight benches and other apparatus to households reached $US5.8 billion in the USA in 2000 versus $US1.9 billion in 1990. It is estimated that this will grow at around 5% per annum between 2006 and 2010. The same growth is occurring in Australia (Jordana Willner, 'Fitness: Health Clubs Discover That It's More Than Just Tight Abs', *Information Week*, Manhasset, 23 April 2001, issue 834, p. 105).

The health and fitness market shows good profit potential and business opportunities in Australia in the coming years. A recent Australian Bureau of Statistics labour force survey indicated that cultural and recreation services had the second highest employment growth in the period February 1998 to February 2001 of 17 industry groupings. Some of the statistics are as follows (this growth trend also holds true for the years 2005 and beyond):

- There are 217 500 employees.
- There are 11 000 registered businesses.
- Goods and services production is valued at $12 billion.
- The contribution to Gross Domestic Product (GDP) is 1.2% (the same as the motor vehicle manufacturing industry).
- Thirty-three per cent of Australians aged 15 years and older are involved in sport.
- The fitness market (gyms and personal trainers) is estimated to be 3200 businesses in Australia.

3.2 The product

Fast Fitness is a personal training health club offering a new pricing and value concept for fitness and weight management. At Fast Fitness clients do not sign up for a lengthy contract and do not need to sign any membership papers. Members only pay for the workouts they have used.

CASE STUDY

Each session is designed to meet each individual's needs. The workouts last for around one hour at a weekly cost of $80 with an average annual membership of $3680 based on 46 weeks' member annual attendance. On average the client will have three training sessions per week. Because the products are specifically designed for each individual and because it is done in small managed groups there are no delays for use of equipment to complete each individual workout—it is managed by the trainer during the session.

The product offerings and related programs are: fat burning, strength building, toning and definition, self-defence, and stretching and flexibility. The benefits include a feeling of wellbeing, general fitness, health and confidence.

3.3 Product/service situation

The product sales, costs and margins across the local industry are shown in Table 1.

Row 1 in Table 1 shows the total industry sales by number of fitness club/gym memberships. Row 2 splits up the market to show the total sales in

TABLE 1 Fast Fitness annual profit statements

Variable	Rows	2002	2003	2004	2005	2006–Plan
1 Industry sales in memberships (ea)		702 000	745 000	851 000	969 000	1 100 000
2 Membership sales in Sydney (ea)		189 540	179 000	229 770	261 630	297 000
3 Sales in North & South Sydney (ea)		66 339	62 650	80 420	91 571	103 950
4 Sales in Sydney North and South ($)		46 437 300	49 281 750	56 293 650	64 099 350	72 765 000
5 Sales Sydney ($)		132 678 000	125 300 000	160 839 000	183 141 000	207 900 000
6 Industry growth rate (%)			6.13%	14.23%	13.87%	13.52%
7 Company's market share (%)		1.62%	2.01%	1.95%	2.12%	2.52%
8 Average membership price ($)		3 000	3 000	3 000	3 300	3 680
9 Variable unit cost		250	265	268	255	285
10 Units gross contribution margin ($)	(8–9)	2 750	2 735	2 732	3 045	3 395
11 Sales volume (in units)		250	330	365	411	498
12 Sales revenues ($)	(8 × 11)	750 000	990 000	1 095 000	1 356 300	1 832 640
13 Gross contribution margin ($)	(10 × 11)	687 500	902 550	997 180	1 251 495	1 690 710
14 Advertising and promotion expenditure ($)		7 500	9 900	10 950	13 563	54 979
15 Trainers (salesforce) ($)		250 000	330 000	350 000	410 000	609 600
16 Marketing research ($)		6 000	5 000	8 800	7 000	11 400
17 Net marketing contribution ($)	(13–14–15–16)	424 000	557 650	627 430	820 932	1 014 731
18 Overheads ($)		160 000	160 000	250 000	450 000	500 004
19 Net operating profit ($)	(17–18)	264 000	397 650	377 430	370 932	514 727
20 Profit growth rate (%)			50.63%	−5.08%	−1.72%	38.77%

CASE STUDY

the Sydney area. Fast Fitness operates in the northern and Southern areas of Sydney and row 3 shows the size of that market. It is estimated that in the northern and southern Sydney area there were approximately 91 571 gym memberships in 2005. The number of memberships has grown on average by 14% annually except in 2003 when the growth declined to 6.1% per annum. Row 7 shows the Fast Fitness market share hovering around 1.98%, although it reached 2.12% in 2005. Row 8 shows the average price for Fast Fitness being stable and then rising about 10% in 2005. Row 9 shows variable costs—materials, equipment, power—rising each year. Row 10 shows that the gross contribution margin per unit—the difference between price (row 8) and unit variable cost (row 9)—was relatively steady over 2002 and 2004, then rose by over 10% in 2005. Rows 11 and 12 show sales volume in units and dollars, and row 13 shows the total gross contribution margin, which increased every year. Rows 14, 15, 16 and 17 show marketing expenditures on advertising and promotion, trainers and marketing research. Row 17 also shows net marketing contribution margin, which had increased by 48% between 2002 and 2004. Row 18 shows that overheads remained constant during 2002 and 2003, then nearly doubled in 2004 and again in 2005, owing to an increase in capacity. Finally, Row 19 shows net operating profit after marketing expenses. The picture is one of increasing profits until 2004, then in 2005 a fall in relation to increased revenue levels compared to that of 2003 was recorded. Clearly, Fast Fitness needs to find a strategy for 2006 that will restore healthy growth in sales and profits to the business.

3.4 Competitive situation (competitor analysis)

Competition for the fitness market comprises 3500 registered businesses in Australia. The area of Sydney has 27% of the total fitness market in Australia (945 businesses) (see Figure 1). The Sydney market is divided into five key competitive geographic areas (North, East, Inner City, South and West). The biggest number of fitness

businesses are in the areas of North and South Sydney. It is estimated that the combined North and South cover around 35% of the fitness market in Sydney. There are around 330 businesses operating in this area.

Out of the 330 businesses operating in the North and South areas, the fitness market is further subdivided into three key segments:

1 Fitness gyms 30% (99 businesses)
2 Personal fitness 20% (66 businesses)
3 Individual trainers 50% (165 businesses)

The market is very fragmented in this industry with a bulk of the market share being held by 'home business' (a fitness trainer without any business-owned facilities) operations offering personal training (see Figure 2). Due to the fragmentation of the market, Fast Fitness has different smaller competitors in each of its three locations. Its key location is in the Sydney suburb of Harbord. However, in 2006, with the service provided by Fast Fitness there are three distinctive competitors that between them hold 37% of the personal fitness market. Table 2 (overleaf) breaks

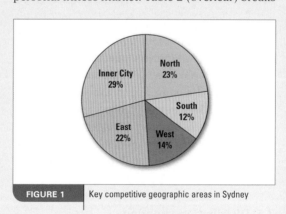
FIGURE 1 Key competitive geographic areas in Sydney

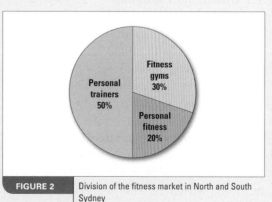
FIGURE 2 Division of the fitness market in North and South Sydney

CASE
STUDY

TABLE 2 Competitor share and market position

Brand/Company	Market share %	Competitor market position
URCoach	20	• Offers personal training at an hourly rate of $50 • Employs known personalities to endorse/advertise the product • It is the premium product in the market • Plans to grow its business to at least 40% of the market
Executive Fitness	11	• Provides a competitively priced offer and charges a membership fee • Its personal training sessions are starting on the hour and the membership is pre-booked three months in advance. Wants to grow
Coaching Pro	6	• Is also positioned as a premium product but is purely based on high price as the differentiator. Wants to grow
Fast Fitness	2.2	• Charges a weekly fee of $80 (includes GST) for an unlimited number of one-hour training sessions • Works with small groups (up to 10 individuals) rather than on a one-to-one basis • Creates a closely linked community for local business people and their families for personal training
Individual personal trainers (others)	60	• Work on one-to-one basis • Priced at a premium between $60 to $75 per one-hour session • Do not have their own facilities and often work in hired gyms or at customer locations

down the competition in terms of market share, product quality and future intentions.

The two top competitors (in terms of market share) spend a significant amount of their revenues to advertise their product and to conduct market research. In some instances they spend as much as 10% of their sales on advertising and research compared to Fast Fitness's expenditure of 3.9%.

3.5 Distribution situation

Fast Fitness currently operates from three studio outlets located in the south and north of Sydney. Customers currently attend on average three personal training sessions per week. Access is relatively easy for customers and parking is readily available nearby.

3.6 Macro-environment situation

About 15% of Australians and New Zealanders between the ages of 18 and 55 actively participate in fitness activities. The health and exercise market is growing while the time available to exercise is getting shorter. This results in people wanting shorter and more intense exercise programs without regular pre-set training session times due to other time commitments and pressures. They seek flexibility in times and pricing offers. Market growth is steady at 14%.

There are new trends emerging in the marketplace that combine a series of fitness techniques such as walking, weights, nutritional control, cardiovascular aerobics and most recently Cardio Yoga.

3.7 SWOT analysis (micro-analysis)

3.7.1 Strengths

● High brand awareness and good-quality image in local studio area and surrounding neighbourhoods.

● Location of fitness gyms—next to coffee shop and shops (compatible with target market lifestyles).

● Very competitive pricing.

- Non-intimidating atmosphere.
- High level of professionalism, expertise and experience of the instructors.
- Flexibility of times clients can attend plus custom-made programs for clients with specific needs.
- Instructor's high rapport with their clients.

3.7.2 Weaknesses

- Not enough space (location) to run Cardio Yoga classes and personal training side by side.
- No showers or large change room.
- No child-minding facilities.
- Management/instructors are both time deficient, so are never able to expand on the education of their clients on nutritional and specific program aspects.

3.7.3 Opportunities

- A market opportunity for increasing the appeal of Cardio Yoga.
- Opportunity for geographic expansion.
- Consumer need for wider range of services in one convenient 'shop'.
- Opportunity for a more holistic service to be provided to a 'fitness/nutritional/dietary' segment.
- Consumer need for access to information on nutrition/diet and programs to meet holiday/travel needs.

3.7.4 Threats

- Management/instructor burnout.
- Competitors copying Cardio Yoga concept.
- Large fitness chains entering the personal coaching scene with substantial capital backing.

3.7.5 Issue analysis

The company must consider the following basic issues:

- Should Fast Fitness stay in the personal business? Can it compete effectively?
- If Fast Fitness stays in the business, should it continue with its present products, distribution channels and price and promotion policies?
- Should Fast Fitness switch to high-growth channels (Cardio Yoga and the Internet)?

Can it do this and retain the loyalty of its current customers?

- Should Fast Fitness increase its advertising and promotion expenditures to grow its business's awareness?
- Should Fast Fitness pour money into R&D to develop advanced features, such as Internet communities and new products and services?

4 Objectives

4.1 Financial objectives

- To earn an annual rate of return on sales over the next three years of at least 28% before interest and taxes.
- To produce a net marketing contribution of $1 014 731 in 2006.
- To produce a net operating profit (before interest and taxes) of $514 727 in 2006.

4.2 Marketing objectives

- To grow distribution/current locations from three to four by October 2006.
- To increase the number of personal training memberships to 498 per annum by December 2006.
- To grow market share from 2.15% in 2005 to 2.52% by December 2006 in the Sydney North and South combined market.
- To grow sales revenue from $1356 million in 2005 to $1832 million in 2006.

5 Marketing strategy

5.1 Positioning strategy

Fast Fitness is positioned as an affordable personal fitness service, aimed at health-conscious and active individuals in the 40–55 age group.

Positioning strategy

Target market: Health-conscious and exercise active market with emphasis on business executive buyer.

Product positioning: Personal training with no contracts and at your own pace where you pay for what you use.

Product line: Add one product extension (Cardio Yoga) and two higher-priced products for the primary market.

CASE STUDY

Price: Price somewhat below personal trainers and below large city gyms. The current price of $80 (including GST) per week is still highly competitive.

Communication: Increase advertising in local newspapers. Use website to communicate detailed benefits of the offer to potential new customers.

Salesforce: Maintain high calibre of trainers to build personal rapport.

Service: Personalised, convenient, flexible and quickly available.

Advertising: Develop a new advertising program that supports the positioning strategy; emphasise personal program yielding tailored benefits with lower price than competitors. Increase advertising to 3.9% of sales revenues.

Sales promotion: Increase the sales-promotion budget by 20% to develop a point-of-purchase display and to participate to a greater extent in local shops. Develop an information package on personal training and the importance of exercise in stress relief.

Synchronous: Develop a new website that supports the positioning strategy; show all products; provide information on each; run a consumer sales promotion in each Sydney geographical area that exhibits relevant market characteristics. Create a website that addresses our target market's interests. This might include 'How to stay fit and healthy' and current developments in fitness and stress relief.

Research and development: Increase expenditures by 30% to develop new product lines that appeal to the target market. Work on modern/contemporary gym layout.

Marketing research: Increase expenditures to improve knowledge of consumer-choice process and to monitor competitor moves. Place special emphasis on the Internet environment.

6 Action programs

February. Fast Fitness will advertise in local newspapers the fact that a free Exercise Planner can be downloaded from its website available to

TABLE 3 Fast Fitness financial plan					
1 P&L January 2006–Dec 2006		January	February	March	April
2 Average membership price ($)		3 680	3 680	3 680	3 680
3 Variable unit cost ($)		285	285	285	285
4 Units gross contribution margin ($)	(2–3)	3 395	3 395	3 395	3 395
5 Sales volume (in units-memberships)		42	35	49	38
6 Sales revenues ($)	(2 × 6)	154 560	128 800	180 320	139 840
7 Gross contribution margin ($)	(4 × 5)	142 590	118 825	166 355	129 010
8 Advertising & promotion ($)		4 637	3 864	5 410	4 195
9 Trainers (salesforce) ($)		50 800	50 800	50 800	50 800
10 Marketing research ($)		950	950	950	950
11 Net marketing contribution ($)	(7–8–9–10)	86 203	63 211	109 195	73 065
12 Overheads ($)		41 667	41 667	41 667	41 667
13 Net operating profit ($)	(11–12)	**44 536**	**21 544**	**67 528**	**31 398**

everyone. Joanne B. will handle this project at a planned cost of $2760.

March–June. Website development to communicate the offer and and attract new customers. Cost $9000.

April. Fast Fitness will participate in the Good Health and Fitness Trade Show in Manly by offering a half-price workout to local residents. The expected cost is $4100 and will be managed by Phil M.

June. Launch new Cardio Yoga classes. Offer BOGOF (buy one get one free) classes in July for existing members. Cost $6000. This will be handled by Phil M.

July. Provide fitness calculators to existing and new members to build up recall and recognition of Fast Fitness to increase the number of visits. Cost $2500. Joanne B. will be in charge of this project.

August. A sales contest will be conducted over the website with the winner receiving two memberships to Fast Fitness for a year (four memberships on offer). The aim of this is to build a profile of potential customers for future sales

leads. The contest will be handled by Vanessa M. at a planned cost of $4200.

September–October. Fast Fitness will re-advertise in local newspapers the fact that a free Exercise Planner can be downloaded from its website and will be available to everyone. Joanne B. and Vanessa M. will handle this project at a planned cost of $3960.

October. Launch the new range to the 40–45-year-old market in the first week of the month. This is a high period for the need for personal training and weight loss and is to meet the pre-summer fitness frenzy. Provide brochures outlining the services offered. Total cost $1650.

November. A sales contest will be conducted over the website with the winner receiving two memberships to Fast Fitness for a year (six memberships on the offer). Additionally T-shirts will be provided to existing and new members promoting Fast Fitness. The contest and merchandise will be handled by Vanessa M. at a planned cost of $4900.

January–December. Have 'open day' sessions (free sessions) every week (Mondays) in the idle periods between 3–5 pm for trialling Fast

May	June	July	August	September	October	November	December	TOTAL
3 680	3 680	3 680	3 680	3 680	3 680	3 680	3 680	**3 680**
285	285	285	285	285	285	285	285	**285**
3 395	3 395	3 395	3 395	3 395	3 395	3 395	3 395	**3 395**
34	43	36	40	39	51	54	37	**498**
125 120	158 240	132 480	147 200	143 520	187 680	198 720	136 160	**1 832 640**
115 430	145 985	122 220	135 800	132 405	173 145	183 330	125 615	**1 690 710**
3 754	4 747	3 974	4 416	4 306	5 630	5 962	4 085	**54 979**
50 800	50 800	50 800	50 800	50 800	50 800	50 800	50 800	**609 600**
950	950	950	950	950	950	950	950	**11 400**
59 926	89 488	66 496	79 634	76 349	115 765	125 618	69 780	**1 014 731**
41 667	41 667	41 667	41 667	41 667	41 667	41 667	41 667	**500 004**
18 259	**47 821**	**24 829**	**37 967**	**34 682**	**74 098**	**83 951**	**28 113**	**514 727**

Fitness services. Cost $10 000. To be managed by Phil M.

7 Projected profit and loss statement

Table 3 on the previous page shows the projected profit and loss statement for the 12 months of 2006 showing the impact of seasonality in the financial plan.

Sources: The major source for this case came from interviews and documents provided by Phil Murray, owner of Fast Fitness. The author wishes to express his appreciation for the time and contribution made by Mr Murray.

QUESTIONS

1. Review the Fast Fitness marketing plan and develop realistic objectives, marketing strategy and action programs for 2007.

2. Define what specific market research you would implement to measure customer satisfaction with the Fast Fitness offer and also measure the effectiveness of information and services provided via the Internet.

3. Specifically, what market measures would you use to gauge the marketing performance of Fast Fitness?

PART 2

MARKET ANALYSIS, TARGETING AND POSITIONING

CHAPTER 5

The global marketing environment

ABS: www.abs.gov.au

Google: www.google.com

Interbrand: www.interbrand.com

Lenovo: www.lenovo.com

New Zealand Statistics:

www.stats.govt.nz

How much time does it take to create a global brand? Less and less, it seems, if we look at the history of some of the companies that have arisen from the Internet boom. Most global brands start out in one country, and slowly expand as they become successful. But the Internet is making it possible for a few very successful companies to become truly global brands in a very short time. Consider Google, which started in 1998 when two students raised $US1 million in funding from family, friends and investors to launch what is becoming one of the most influential communications companies in the world.[1] Since launching on the stock market in August 2004 at around $US85, Google's share price has rocketed and today, with a share price of over $US400, the company is more valuable than long time brand leaders like McDonald's, General Motors and Disney.[2] And Google continues to get bigger, despite spending only $US5 million on marketing in 2004, a fraction of the amount spent by its competitors.[3] For example, Yahoo, Google's closest competitor, spends around 28% of its revenue on sales and marketing, while Google spends 11%. But Google keeps gaining market share from Yahoo and its other competitors, and its revenue is growing twice as fast as Yahoo's.[4]

Google's model is unique, as it is based on giving away free access to its sophisticated search engine, and providing millions of users with searches which, from Google's inception, were much more specific than its competitors. (Google was the first search engine to rate sites on both content and by the links to those sites, with the result that its searches were much more likely to put highly relevant results at the top of the search list.) So far, Google would seem to follow conventional marketing wisdom: develop a better product than competitors, and try to make money selling the innovation. But Google didn't try to sell its innovative search ability, beyond offering personalised search services for corporate clients—it gave access to searches away, and Google's search was such an improvement on its competitors' that people recommended Google to their friends, colleagues and families. So Google rapidly became the most popular search engine worldwide. But how can you make money out of something you give away free? By selling advertising which is highly targeted to the search, and which is therefore most likely to be relevant to buyers, Google's model of 'selling eyeballs' (exposure to readers) is a model long used by newspapers; although buyers pay for a newspaper, the prime source of revenue for newspapers is advertising, leading the former editor of Australia's largest newspaper to say: 'What you've got to understand is [the newspaper] is an advertising business with a news wrap-around.'

Like the newspapers before them, Google has become successful by selling advertising, but it can only sell that advertising in large amounts if it creates a service attractive enough to draw millions of potential viewers for the advertisers. Google's particular innovation was to make its advertising highly relevant by positioning it beside related searches, thereby increasing the likelihood that potential buyers would click on advertising links to take them to the advertiser's site. Google also

Google's ability to attract users by novel offerings, coupled with its ability to sell targeted advertising, has resulted in it becoming a major brand without any advertising expenditure.

allows users to customise their searches by country, so the site is just as relevant for searchers in Australia or Switzerland or India (just a few of the countries where Google is the number one search engine) with the result that Google has become a truly global brand, with over 50% of its traffic from outside the USA.[5]

If Google was just a (very successful) search engine, it would be a major concern for other online advertisers. But as the largest online advertiser, and growing faster than any of its competitors, Google is worrying many big companies. Its enormous profits and motivated staff (fuelled by free catering, dry cleaning and lunchtime bands at Google's famous headquarters, its 'Googleplex') keep churning out new ideas which make the brand more and more attractive to consumers (and thus to advertisers).[6] There's Google News (competing with traditional media outlets), Google G-Mail (competing with Hotmail.com), Google Blogger (the world's most popular blog page), Google Froogle, an e-commerce search engine, Google Base, which looks as if it may take on ebay and, most recently, Google Earth, which allows visitors to zoom in on their corner of the world with satellite imaging. How's that for catering to a variety of customer needs?

Google's huge size and prominence create what economists call 'network effects'; because so many people are using Google, it keeps getting better and better, and it will be very hard for any competitor to threaten its prominence. Instead, Google is threatening the dominance of large off-line organisations, such as book publishers. Google has announced plans to scan and allow users to search through any printed book, and the large publishers are taking Google to court to challenge what they claim threatens violation of their copyright.[7] Some critics suggest that Google's size will allow it to obtain a stranglehold on the Internet, and drive smaller operations out of business.[8]

Most great brands are built on the back of massive advertising, but Google has largely grown on the strength of word-of-mouth, and its brand reputation has followed. In fact, the company doesn't do any conventional brand building: 'Google does not participate in traditional marketing activities,' says spokeswoman Eileen Rodriguez.[9] Instead, Google keeps getting free publicity and word-of-mouth with innovations like Google Earth, which doesn't generate revenue, but which is a way of drawing new users to the site and getting existing users to come back more often. Google has created the ultimate customisation of an Internet site; the user can sit at home, zoom in on pictures of their local area, blog, search for information, store their email at Google G-Mail and pay nothing for the services (except by exposing themselves to Google's advertising—which, because it is targeted, is less intrusive and sometimes even attractive for a consumer). In some regions (and the number of sites is likely to grow), Google will even let you browse the Web free of charge; the company offers free wireless access in Silicon Valley and San Francisco, which allows it to sell targeted local advertising, since it then knows where users are located.[10] We're going to hear more and more about Google; the company has developed a powerful business by creating a customised experience for its users worldwide, and it's likely to keep getting bigger and bigger.

After reading this chapter you should be able to:

1. List and discuss the importance of the elements of the marketing organisation's microenvironment, including the marketing organisation, marketing intermediaries, customers, competitors and publics.

2. Explain the broad concept of the organisation's macroenvironment.

3. Outline the key changes occurring in the organisation's macroenvironment, including shifts in the demographic, economic, technological, political, cultural and natural environments.

Marketing environment The actors and forces outside marketing that affect marketing management's ability to develop and maintain successful transactions with its target customers.

Microenvironment The forces close to the organisation that affect its ability to serve its customers—the organisation, marketing channel firms, customer markets, competitors and publics.

Macroenvironment The larger societal forces that affect the whole microenvironment—demographic, economic, natural, technological, political and cultural forces.

Although we often think of marketing as being involved in selling something, 'marketing' is practised by many different forms of organisation ranging from small partnerships to large public organisations, and on to 'corporatised' sections of government and government services. Newer forms of marketing organisations range from the networked organisations we see in the airline industry (Star Alliance and OneWorld), to the franchise organisations that form marketing alliances through legal and financial arrangements (Harvey Norman department franchises) and virtual organisations such as Verisign or Ariba operating in the Internet environment, linking a variety of suppliers and customers. The **marketing environment** facing both new and old marketing organisations consists of the actors and forces that affect marketing management's ability to develop and maintain successful transactions with its target customers. To be successful, an organisation must adapt its marketing mix to trends and developments in this environment.

The changing and uncertain marketing environment deeply affects the organisation. Instead of changing slowly and predictably, the environment can produce major surprises and shocks. How many managers at Heinz foresaw that the baby-boom numbers would fall away so rapidly? Who would have predicted that the Internet would result in new businesses like Google? How many were able to predict that SMS and cameras would become almost essential features of phones, or that phones would be marketed for their ability to store and play music? The marketing environment offers both opportunities and threats, and the organisation must use its marketing research and marketing intelligence systems to analyse, and react to, the changing environment.

The marketing environment is made up of a microenvironment and a macroenvironment. The **microenvironment** consists of the forces close to the organisation that affect its ability to serve its customers—the organisation, marketing channel firms, customer markets, competitors and publics. The **macroenvironment** consists of the larger societal forces that affect the whole microenvironment—demographic, economic, natural, technological, political and cultural forces. We look first at the organisation's microenvironment and then at its macroenvironment.

The marketing organisation's microenvironment

Marketing management has the task of attracting and building relationships with customers by creating customer value and satisfaction. However, marketing management does not accomplish this task alone. Its success will depend on other actors in the organisation's microenvironment—other departments, marketing intermediaries, customers, competitors and various publics (see Figure 5.1).

The marketing organisation

In designing marketing plans, marketing management takes other groups in the organisation into account—groups such as top management, finance, research and development (R&D), purchasing, manufacturing and accounting. All these interrelated groups form the internal environment (see Figure 5.2).

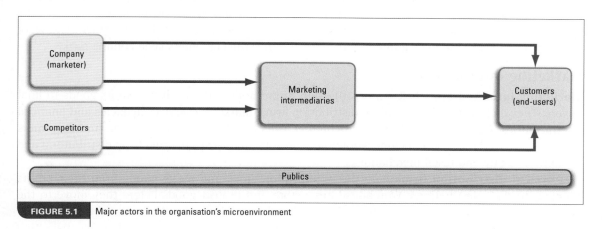

FIGURE 5.1 Major actors in the organisation's microenvironment

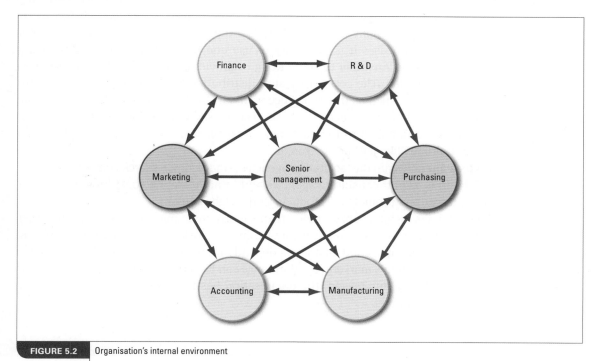

FIGURE 5.2 Organisation's internal environment

Senior management sets the organisation's mission, objectives, broad strategies and policies. Marketing managers must make decisions consistent with the plans made by senior management, and marketing plans must be approved by senior management before they can be implemented.

Marketing managers must also work closely with other departments in the organisation. The finance department is concerned with finding and using funds to carry out the marketing plan. R&D focuses on the problems of designing safe and effective products, as well as the processes used. Purchasing concerns itself with getting supplies and materials, and manufacturing is responsible for producing the desired amount of finished product. In service organisations such as retailers, we refer to operations rather than manufacturing. Operations management has the task of ensuring that stores stock and sell the merchandise wanted by customers, and the human resources department ensures the organisation takes on sufficient personnel with the appropriate skills. Accounting and finance measure revenues and costs so as to help marketing know how well it is achieving its sales and profit objectives. Together these sections of the organisation have an impact on the marketing department's plan and actions. Organisations that adopt the marketing concept must 'think customer', and work together to deliver value to customers, thus ensuring that the customers keep coming back.

Marketing intermediaries

Marketing intermediaries help an organisation to promote, sell and distribute its goods to final buyers. They include resellers, physical distribution firms, marketing services agencies and financial intermediaries. **Resellers** are distribution channel firms that help the organisation find customers or make sales to them. These include wholesalers (in some industries referred to as distributors) and retailers who buy and resell merchandise.

Physical distribution firms help the organisation stock and move goods from their points of origin to their destinations. Warehouse firms store and protect goods before they move to the next destination. Transportation firms include railroads, trucking organisations, airlines, shipping organisations and others that specialise in moving goods from one location to another. The marketing organisation must determine the best ways to store and ship goods, balancing such factors as cost, delivery, speed and safety. In many instances there is a trade-off between costs and customer service levels involved. In other cases it is necessary to use one transport mode—such as flying chilled lobster tails from Western Australia to Hong Kong or providing broadband Internet services to remote rural regions by satellite. The costs of physical distribution became a critical obstacle for many failed Internet businesses, such as Internet grocers adMart in Hong Kong and Webvan in the USA.[11] In contrast, online distribution has been the basis of successful new businesses, such as music download sites like iTunes, and added to the efficiency of existing businesses, for example online ticket sales by discount airlines like JetStar or Ryanair.

Marketing services agencies are the facilitating agencies—marketing research companies, advertising agencies, media firms, export consulting agencies and local marketing consulting firms—that help the organisation target and promote its products to the right markets.

Financial intermediaries include banks, credit organisations, insurance organisations and other businesses that help to finance transactions or insure against the risks associated with the buying and selling of goods. Most companies and customers depend on financial intermediaries to finance their transactions. The organisation's marketing performance can be seriously affected by rising credit costs, limited credit or both. For this reason, the organisation has to develop strong relationships with important financial institutions.

Customers

The marketing organisation must study its customer markets closely. The organisation can operate in five types of customer markets, shown in Figure 5.3.

Marketing intermediaries Firms that help the organisation to promote, sell and distribute its goods to final buyers; they include resellers, physical distribution firms, marketing services agencies and financial intermediaries.

Resellers Distribution channel firms that help the organisation find customers or make sales to them.

Physical distribution firms Warehouse, transportation and other firms that help the organisation stock and move goods from their points of origin to their destinations.

Marketing services agencies Marketing research companies, advertising agencies, media firms, marketing consulting agencies and other service providers that help the organisation target and promote its products to the right markets.

Financial intermediaries Banks, credit companies, insurance companies and other businesses that help finance transactions or insure against the risks associated with the buying and selling of goods.

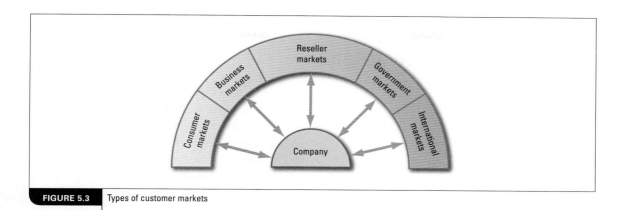

FIGURE 5.3 | Types of customer markets

1   *Consumer markets:* individuals and households that buy goods and services for personal or household consumption.
2   *Business markets:* organisations that buy goods and services for further processing or for use in their production process.
3   *Reseller markets:* organisations that buy goods and services in order to resell them at a profit.
4   *Government markets:* government agencies that buy goods and services in order to produce public services or transfer these goods and services to others who need them.
5   *International markets:* overseas buyers including consumers, producers, resellers and governments.

Each market type has special characteristics that call for careful study by the seller.

Competitors

Every organisation faces a wide range of competitors. The marketing concept states that, to be successful, an organisation must provide greater customer value and satisfaction than its competitors. Thus, marketers must do more than simply adapt to the needs of target consumers. They must also gain strategic advantage by positioning their offerings against competitors' offerings in the minds of consumers.

No single competitive marketing strategy is best for all organisations. Each marketer should consider its own size and industry position compared with those of its competitors. Large companies with dominant positions in an industry can use certain strategies that smaller companies cannot afford. But small companies can often be more flexible, and able to offer personalised services in a way that large organisations cannot, allowing them to use strategies that give them better rates of return than large companies.[12] Increasingly, organisations are facing competition from international competitors, but also opportunities as international markets open up to them. Marketing Highlight 5.1 discusses the growth of the Chinese economy, which has contributed to strong growth in Southeast Asian economies over the past few years, but which also presents challenges to many organisations.

Publics

The organisation's marketing environment also includes various publics. A **public** is any group that has an actual or potential interest in, or impact on, an organisation's ability to achieve its objectives. Every organisation is involved with seven types of publics (see Figure 5.4 on page 168):

1   *Financial publics.* Financial publics influence the organisation's ability to obtain funds. Banks, investment houses and shareholders are the major financial publics.

Public Any group that has an actual or potential interest in, or impact on, an organisation's ability to achieve its objectives.

Chasing the Chinese dragon

Transport company DHL is just one firm expanding to tap into growth in China.

China has become the market that everyone wants to be in. It's the world's fastest growing economy, surging by around 9.3% in 2005, way ahead of the global growth rate of 3.2%. China's economic growth is so fast, according to the Organization for Economic Co-operation and Development, that it 'represents one of the most sustained and rapid economic transformations seen in the world'. This Chinese growth is driving increasing levels of globalisation, as China imports raw materials and exports an increasing amount of manufactured goods which are consumed by more developed economies. In 2005, total world exports of about $US10.3 trillion dollars in goods and services amounted to nearly 24% of the world gross domestic product (GDP), three times the level of exporting in the early part of the twentieth century. More and more marketing organisations are becoming major exporters to China, and/or importers from China, and are learning to operate in very different markets. For some, Chinese growth means that a long-standing national brand can become

Chinese; in 2004 Chinese computer company Lenovo paid $US1.5 billion for IBM's personal computer division, obtaining the right to sell IBM-branded computers made by Lenovo for five years. The deal made Lenovo the third biggest PC maker in the world, behind Dell and Hewlett-Packard. Lenovo's move is just one example of a cashed-up Chinese company attempting to acquire a global brand by acquisition. And the run of Chinese takeovers won't be limited to consumer brand names; in 2005 an even bigger bid of $US18.5 billion by the China National Offshore Oil Corporation (CNOOC) for California's Unocal oil company was withdrawn after what was described by one US analyst as 'anti-China hysteria' in the USA. CNOOC withdrew its bid, and Unocal accepted a lower offer from a domestic rival, Chevron.

Whether it's coping with new Chinese ownership, moving manufacturing to China, exporting to the growing China market or reacting to lower-cost Chinese competitors, China is changing the environment for many organisations. For example, rapidly rising growth in sales in the Asia–Pacific, particularly in China and India, is behind the rapid growth in the mobile phone market, as growth in developed markets tails off. This growing Chinese market seems to have the potential to sustain growth for all sorts of firms which are facing falling demand in their home market. Hong Kong-based fashion chain Giordano, one of Asia's largest clothing retailers, was one of the first retailers to set up in mainland China, and had 671 outlets in China by the end of 2004, providing more than 20% of the group's income, with a 17% increase in profits from Chinese sales. Europe's largest perfume chain, Marrionaud, was bought by another Hong Kong-based firm in 2004, with plans to open more than 1000 shops in China by 2010, with sales of perfume in China forecast to rise by more than 50% by 2010. The Chinese growth is also fuelling optimism and growth in nearby economies, with people in India, Hong Kong and New Zealand ranked as the most optimistic in the world about their job prospects in a 2005 study.[13]

Doing business in China sometimes poses unusual problems, however. For example, the Boral Lafarge joint venture, producing plasterboard for the Chinese building boom, was informed by the Shanghai government that a road was being built through the middle of their factory. Doug Anderson, the former head of Boral's operations in China, said 'They have been given two choices: move or move'. And Australia Post moved its logistics hub from Guangzhou to Shanghai after their Chinese manager was kidnapped when he asked the landlords of their building for improvements. (He escaped.)

Setbacks like this aren't going to dampen the enthusiasm of the many multinationals setting up in China, however. The next big rush is likely to come in 2007, when China's banking system is opened up, giving foreign banks the chance to compete in the Chinese market. Many foreign firms invested heavily in China in the 1990s, failed to make money and, after suffering heavy losses, wound back their China investments. Beer manufacturers Fosters and Lion Nathan and lawyers Mallesons Stephen Jacques are just three which suffered losses for years before scaling back their China operations. Some of these companies are going back, however. And there are also successes for some firms who stuck in China during some uncertain early years, and then during the Asian financial crisis in 1998; for example, former BHP business BlueScope has been in China since the 1990s and has grown more than sixfold, and China's huge demand for raw materials is largely responsible for a resources boom for Australian companies like BHP Billiton and Rio Tinto.

Competing in China remains tough for many companies; it's a different industrial relations, legal and political environment, presenting particular challenges for expatriate managers who don't speak the language and who need to learn the local customs. Up till 2003, foreign companies investing in China were required to use a joint venture structure, but since China joined the World Trade Organization they can now go it alone. And most analysts agree that China is too big a market to ignore. The executive Director of Macquarie Bank's central executive group, Warwick Smith, says that 'Everyone needs to have a China strategy, because of the huge impact the country's rise is having on markets in Asia and more broadly. There is no substantial bank in the world that is not involved in some way with China'. Think he's only talking about banks, and it won't affect your organisation? Think again. The price of cheese rose by twice the cost of inflation in 2005, driven by a record export price for cheese, as Asians increasingly eat Western fast food, especially pizza and hamburgers. That's good news for dairy farmers, but bad news for the fast-food industry (especially the pizza chains) since about a third of the cost of a pizza is in the cheese. And if your business is tourism, watch out for the wave of Chinese tourists. Projections are that Chinese tourists, who currently mostly visit Hong Kong and Macau, will become the largest source of inbound tourists for other regions. Anyone for Mandarin classes?

Sources: Clay Chandler, 'Does This Look Like a Slowdown?', *Fortune*, 11 July 2005, pp. 11–13; Economist Intelligence Unit, 'China: Country Outlook', 29 December 2005, p. 5; Phil Ruthven, 'Reaching Out', *Business Review Weekly*, 14 July 2005, pp. 37–43; 'Giving China a Bloody Nose', *The Economist*, 6 August 2005, pp. 49–50; 'Champ or Chump?', *The Economist*, 11 December 2004, pp. 52–53; Mark Odell, 'Annual Mobile Phone Sales "to top 1bn units in 2009"', *Financial Times*, 20 July 2005, p. 21; 'Scents and Sensibility', *The Economist*, 22 January 2005, p. 57; David James, 'Along the Silk Road', *Business Review Weekly*, 28 September 2005, pp. 37–48; Bridie Smith, 'Asia's Taste for Pizza has Cheese Costs Whey out of Line', *The Sydney Morning Herald*, 21 November 2005, p. 3; Narelle Hooper, 'Companies Learn from the Past's Fumbles', *The Financial Review*, 1 October 2005, p. 39; Colleen Ryan, 'Asian Dragon's hot . . . but not too hot', *The Australian Financial Review*, 1 October 2005, p. 46.

Questions

1 What do you think might be some of the challenges for foreign companies setting up in China?

2 Most Westerners don't speak Mandarin, the national language of China (or Putonghua, as it is also known), unless they come from an Asian background. Chinese culture is also very different. Do you think that this is a problem for companies doing business in China, or is it just a minor inconvenience that can be solved with the use of interpreters?

3 Many large companies have lost substantial amounts of money operating in China. Is the Chinese market too risky for small or medium enterprises to take on? If not, what might they do to manage the risk?

5.1

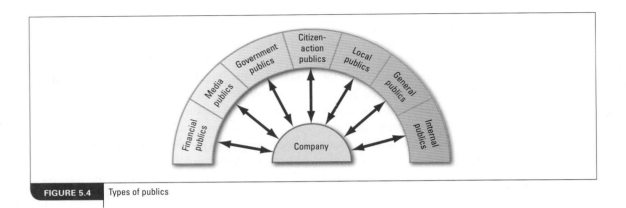

Types of publics

2 *Media publics.* Media publics are those that carry news, features and editorial opinion. They include newspapers, magazines and radio and television stations.

3 *Government publics.* Management must take government requirements into account. Marketing management often needs to consult the organisation's lawyers on issues of product safety, truthful advertising, resellers' rights and other matters.

4 *Citizen-action publics.* An organisation's marketing decisions may be questioned by consumer groups, environmental groups, minority groups and other public interest groups.

5 *Local publics.* Every organisation has local publics such as neighbourhood residents and community protection organisations. Large organisations may appoint a community relations officer to deal with the community, attend meetings, answer questions and contribute to worthwhile causes.

6 *General publics.* A marketing organisation needs to be concerned about the general public's attitude toward its products, services and activities. The public's image of the organisation affects its buying behaviour.

7 *Internal publics.* An organisation's internal publics include its employees, volunteers, managers and the board of directors. Large organisations use newsletters and other means to inform and motivate their internal publics. When employees feel good about their organisation, this positive attitude spills over to external publics.

An organisation can prepare marketing plans for its major publics as well as its customer markets. Suppose the organisation wants a specific response from a particular public—such as goodwill, favourable word-of-mouth or perhaps donations of time or money. The organisation would have to design an offer to this public attractive enough to produce the desired response. Although the desired outcome in some cases may not be sales, any attempt to influence attitude or behaviour is another example of an exchange process that must be well managed to achieve the desired outcome.

SELF-CHECK QUESTIONS

1 Are each of these publics equally important for every organisation? Why or why not?

2 Advertising agencies are one example of a service agency. List and describe two others.

3 Marketing organisations usually prepare marketing plans for their customer markets. Should they do this for internal publics?

The marketing organisation's macroenvironment

The organisation and its suppliers, marketing intermediaries, customers, competitors and publics all operate in a larger macroenvironment of forces that shape opportunities and pose threats to the organisation. The organisation must carefully watch and respond to these forces. The macroenvironment consists of the six major forces shown in Figure 5.5. The remaining sections of this chapter examine these forces and show how they affect marketing plans.

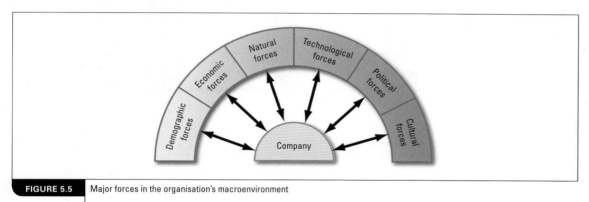

| FIGURE 5.5 | Major forces in the organisation's macroenvironment |

Demographic environment

Demography is the study of human populations in terms of size, density, location, age, sex, race, occupation and other statistics. The demographic environment is of major interest to marketers because it involves people, and people make up markets. The world's population is now over 6.4 billion people and is predicted to exceed 8 billion by 2028, with most of that growth coming from a small number of countries such as China, India and Brazil.[14] This makes these regions highly attractive markets, promising population growth which will not be achieved in more developed economies.[15] In contrast, the opposite trend is occurring in Europe, with an ageing population and population shrinkage in some rural areas.[16] Here we discuss some of the important demographic trends in domestic and important international markets.

> **Demography** The study of human populations in terms of size, density, location, age, sex, race, occupation and other statistics.

Changing age structure of the population

The global population is ageing, in a way which the United Nations has described as 'unprecedented'. By 1998, in most developed nations, the number of older people (aged over 60) exceeded the number of younger people (those under 15) for the first time in history. It is estimated that by 2050 the number of older people in the world will exceed the young for the first time in history.[17] Figure 5.6 shows the changing age structure of the world population. In Japan, which has the oldest median age (at 41 years), this is leading to huge changes in retailing. In department stores, which rely on the housewife buying everything for the family, sales are falling, but sales at convenience stores (whose typical customer is a childless 30-year-old man) are growing by 15% a year.[18]

The population of Australia was estimated to be 20.55 million in May 2006, and to be increasing by 1.2% per year, consistent with past years (Figure 5.7). The Australian Bureau of Statistics estimates that the Australian population changes are based on:
- one birth every 2 minutes and 4 seconds
- one death every 3 minutes and 52 seconds
- a net gain of one international migrant every 4 minutes and 11 seconds

which will lead to an overall total population increase of one person every 2 minutes and 9 seconds.[19]

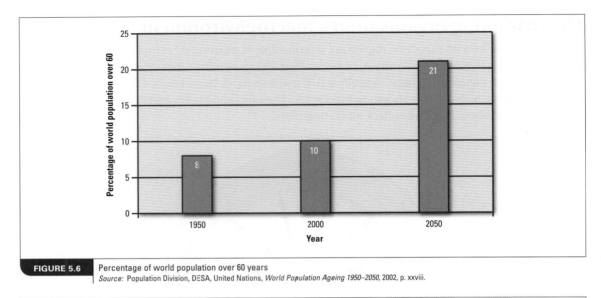

FIGURE 5.6 Percentage of world population over 60 years
Source: Population Division, DESA, United Nations, *World Population Ageing 1950–2050*, 2002, p. xxviii.

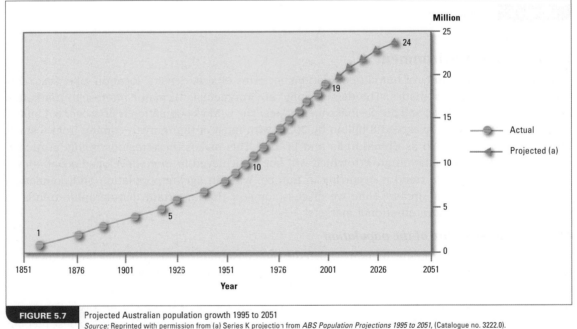

FIGURE 5.7 Projected Australian population growth 1995 to 2051
Source: Reprinted with permission from (a) Series K projection from *ABS Population Projections 1995 to 2051*, (Catalogue no. 3222.0).

This means that Australia is a relatively small market, with less than half a per cent of the world population. In contrast, China is the country with the largest number of people, with 20.4% of the world's population. Japan, with a population of 128 million, and 1.9% of the world's population, is the largest developed economy in the Asia–Pacific region.[20] The area covered by Australia, New Zealand and Oceania is shown in Figure 5.8 (overleaf) and the countries included in Asia are shown in Figure 5.9 on page 173.

Like many other developed countries, while its total population is continuing to grow, Australians are becoming older, on average, because Australian women are having fewer babies. Table 5.1 compares the population structure, fertility rates and life expectancy for a range of countries. The

TABLE 5.1 Population age structure: international comparison

Selected countries	2000 Aged 0–14 years %	Aged 15–64 years %	Aged 65 years and over %	Median Age years	2005[a] Aged 0–14 years %	Aged 15–64 years %	Aged 65 years and over %	Median Age years	Total fertility rate[b] rate	Life expectancy[c] years
Australia	**20.7**	**66.9**	**12.4**	**35.4**	**19.5**	**67.4**	**13.1**	**36.7**	**1.8**	**79.2**
Canada	19	68.4	12.6	36.9	17.3	69.4	13.2	38.9	1.5	79.3
China (exl. SARs and Taiwan)	24.8	68.3	6.8	30	21.8	70.6	7.5	32.4	1.8	71
France	18.8	65.2	16	37.6	18.4	65.3	16.3	38.9	1.9	79
Greece	15.1	67.4	17.5	39.1	14.3	66.7	19	40.8	1.3	78.3
Hong Kong (SAR of China)	16.6	72.7	10.6	36.1	14.6	73.9	11.4	38.6	1	79.9
India	34.1	60.9	4.9	23.4	31.9	62.8	5.3	24.5	3	63.9
Indonesia	30.9	64.3	4.8	24.6	28.7	65.9	5.5	26.2	2.4	66.8
Italy	14.3	67.6	18.1	40.2	13.9	66.6	19.6	42.2	1.2	78.7
Japan	14.6	68.2	17.2	41.3	14	66.3	19.7	42.8	1.3	81.6
Korea, Republic of	20.9	72	7.1	31.8	19.4	71.8	8.8	34.4	1.4	75.5
Malaysia	33.7	62.2	4.1	23.6	32.3	63.1	4.6	24.8	2.9	73.1
New Zealand	22.9	65.3	11.8	34.5	21.8	66	12.1	36	2	78.3
Papua New Guinea	41.5	56.1	2.4	19.1	40.3	57.2	2.5	19.7	4.1	57.6
Philippines	37.5	58.9	3.5	20.9	35	61.1	3.9	22.2	3.2	70
Singapore	21.8	71.1	7.2	34.5	19.6	72	8.4	37.5	1.4	78.1
South Africa	34	62.3	3.7	22.6	32.2	63.5	4.2	23.3	2.6	47.7
Sweden	18.3	64.3	17.4	39.6	17	65.3	17.7	41	1.6	80.1
United Kingdom	19.1	65.1	15.9	37.7	17.9	66.1	15.9	38.8	1.6	78.2
United States of America	21.8	65.9	12.3	35.2	21.2	66.5	12.3	35.9	2.1	77.1
Vietnam	33.4	61.3	5.3	23.1	29.4	65.2	5.4	24.9	2.3	69.2

a International data are United Nations medium variant projections. Australian data are ABS medium series (Series B) projections. United Nations medium variant projections for the period 2000–2005.
b Births per woman. United Nations medium variant projections for the period 2000–2005.
c Life expectancy at birth. United Nations medium variant projections for the period 2000–2005, for males and females combined.
Source: United Nations World Population Prospects, 2002 Revision; ABS, Estimated Resident Population; ABS, Population Projections, Australia, 2002 to 2101 (Catalogue no. 3222.0).

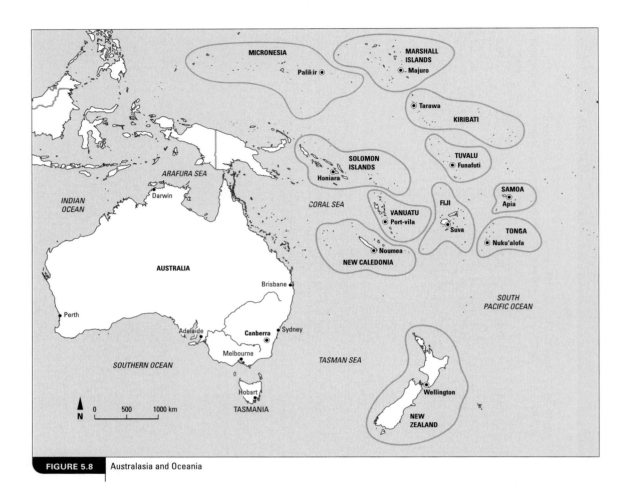

FIGURE 5.8 | Australasia and Oceania

Australian age structure is similar to that of New Zealand and the USA. European countries and Japan tend to have smaller proportions of younger people, and higher percentages of older people than Australia, while the developing Southeast Asian countries of Vietnam, India and Malaysia tend to have more young people.

Australia has one of the world's lowest population densities, with only 2.6 people per square kilometre, compared to 336 per square kilometre in Japan, and 476 per square kilometre in Korea.[21] However, this statistic does not reflect that Australia, like New Zealand, is highly urbanised, with 92% of Australians (and 85.9% of New Zealanders) living in urban areas. Both countries are far less urbanised, however, than some nearby Southeast Asian countries, such as Singapore and Macau, both with 100% of the population living in urban areas.[22]

One of the most important demographic trends in developed countries is the changing age structure of the population. Lower birth rates and increasing life expectancies are combining to create ageing populations. This effect is highest in countries with a low birth rate (such as Hong Kong) and a high life expectancy (such as Japan), as shown in Table 5.1 on page 173.[23] This ageing population will have obvious implications for businesses, including changing demand for products and services, and an increasing shortage of employees as older workers retire.

As well as paying attention to major demographic trends, marketers must take demographic groups into account. These groups may emerge through the impact of historical events such as war

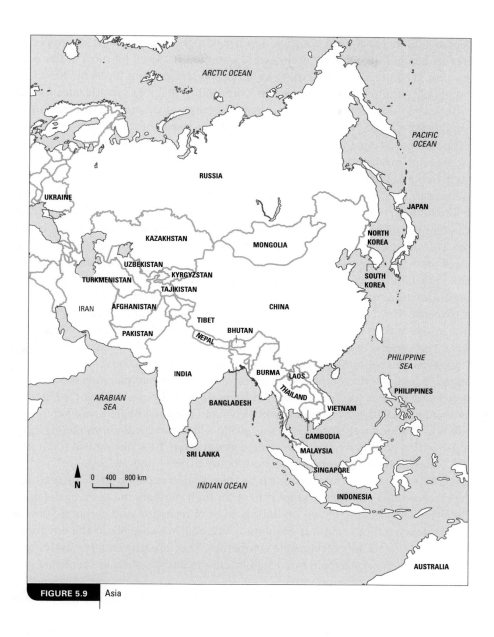

FIGURE 5.9 | Asia

and other catastrophes, or through the changing composition of a country's population over time. The **baby boom** that followed World War II and ran through the period from 1946 to 1964 is one such major demographic group. This 'bulge' in the age distribution has had many effects, and will continue to have an effect in the future—the percentage of Australians aged over 60 will have risen from 11.9% at the 1996 census to 29.9% by 2050 or up to nearly 6 million people (depending on which ABS or United Nations statistics for immigration level projection are used).[24]

The baby boom was followed by a 'birth dearth', and by the mid-1970s the birthrate had fallen sharply in countries such as Australia and New Zealand. This decrease was caused by smaller family sizes resulting from a desire to improve personal living standards, the increased number of women working outside the home and improved birth control. This pattern is characteristic of developed countries; fertility rates by women in developed countries are typically below replacement level,

Baby boom The major increase in the annual birthrate following World War II and lasting until the early 1960s. The 'baby boomers' are a prime target for marketers.

and life expectancy is increasing. In contrast, fertility is highest in the least developed countries, which account for most of the increase in the world's population. Even for most of these developing countries, the United Nations expects fertility to fall below replacement levels by 2050.[25]

The changing age structure of the population will result in different growth rates for various age groups over the next decade, and these differences will strongly affect marketers' targeting strategies. The growth trends for six age groups are summarised below for Australia.

1 *Children*. The number of Australian preschoolers stood at 6.3% of the population in 2004, creating a valuable market of under five year olds.[26] Smaller family sizes and a high percentage of working parents have resulted in a booming market for child care and products aimed at children. For example, Sony and Seiko and other electronics firms are now offering products designed for children, and many retailers are opening separate children's clothing chains.

2 *Youths*. The number of 10 to 19 year olds dropped through the early 1990s, but is increasing again now. This age group consists of 2.6 million consumers who buy or strongly influence purchases of products ranging from health and beauty aids, clothing and food to stereo equipment, cars, family travel, entertainment and secondary and tertiary education. Organisations are finding that there is a new youth segment emerging aged between 10 and 14 called 'Tweens'. The Tweens market is perceived as maturing much more quickly and seeking the goods and services previously reserved for the 19–21-year-old markets.[27]

3 *Young adults*. This group declined during the 1990s as a result of the reduced fertility of the 1970s. Marketers who sell to the 20 to 34 age group—furniture makers, life insurance organisations, banks, sports equipment, footwear and apparel manufacturers—can no longer rely on increasing market size for increases in sales. They will have to work for bigger shares of smaller markets. Soft drink companies like Pepsi and personal hygiene marketers such as Gillette are now realigning themselves to this group's lifestyles for their marketing campaigns.[28] The younger of this group are sometimes called **generation Y**, to distinguish them from the group who preceded them, **generation X**, born between 1965 and 1976.[29]

The generation Xers are defined as much by their shared experiences as by their age. Increasing divorce rates and higher employment for their mothers made them the first generation of latchkey kids. Having grown up during times of recession and corporate downsizing, they have developed a more cautious economic outlook. They care about the environment and respond favourably to socially responsible companies. They are cautious romantics who want a better quality of life and are more interested in job satisfaction than in sacrificing personal happiness and growth for promotion.

As a result, the generation Xers are a more sceptical bunch, cynical of frivolous marketing pitches that promise easy success. Says one marketer, 'Marketing to Gen Xers is difficult, and it's all about word of mouth. You can't tell them you're good, and they have zero interest in a slick brochure that says so. You have to rely on somebody they know and trust to give you instant credibility. They have a lot of "filters" in place.'[30] However, generation X has also created a growing market for luxury products; an American Express survey showed that the average generation Xer spent 18% more on luxury goods than an average baby boomer.[31]

Generation X was succeeded by generation Y, born between 1977 and 1994. The children of the baby boomers, gen Y, as they are often called, typically grew up with fewer brothers and sisters than the baby boomers and gen X, but with more affluent parents, and higher disposable income themselves, as their parents (typically both working) gave gen Y children more pocket money than they had enjoyed themselves. Markets for teens' toys and games, clothes, furniture and food have enjoyed a boom, and gen Y members are highly influential in family spending, influencing what the family buys (DVDs, plasma screens and holidays) and

Generation Y The children of the baby boomers, born between 1977 and 1994.

Generation X The people born between 1965 and 1976 in the 'birth dearth' following the baby boom.

also the brands bought. Designers and retailers have created new lines, new products and even new stores devoted to children and teens—Tommy Hilfiger, DKNY and Gap are all brands which have become successful catering to gen Y. New media have appeared that cater specifically to this market: *Time*, *Sports Illustrated* and *People* have all started new editions for kids and teens. Banks have offered banking and investment services for young people, including investment camps.[32] Like the trailing edge of the generation Xers ahead of them, one distinguishing characteristic of generation Y is their utter fluency and comfort with computer, digital and Internet technology. They are an impatient, now-oriented bunch. 'Blame it on the relentless and dizzying pace of the Internet, 24-hour cable news cycles, cell phones, and TiVo for creating the on-demand, gotta-get-it-now universe in which we live,' says one observer. 'Perhaps nowhere is the trend more pronounced than among the gen Y set.'[33]

BT uses the former Australian rugby captain to appeal to the early middle age and empty nesters—the same age group as John Eales.

4   *Early middle age and empty nesters.* The baby-boom generation will continue to move into the late 40s and 50s age group, and the older generation Xers are moving into middle age, creating huge increases in this age segment. This group is a major market for larger homes, renovations, new cars, clothing, entertainment and investments. Many of this group are now 'empty nesters'—meaning parents whose youngest child has left home. According to research company Asian Demographics Ltd, empty nesters are now at the peak of their careers and, newly dependent free, constitute a fast-growing group in powerful economies such as Hong Kong, Singapore, Korea and Taiwan. The forecasts indicate that this group will grow by 30% to 10.9 million in these countries in the next decade. Meanwhile, the youth market will shrink by 10% to 11.4 million in the same decade, according to the research company.[34]

5   *Late middle age.* The 50 to 64 age group had grown by 26% by the end of the twentieth century, as the baby boomers aged. This group is a major market for eating out, travel, clothing, recreation and financial services. 'There's a bulge of people around 55 to 60 who have finished with their children', says one consultant. 'They have plenty of money and they know how to enjoy life.'[35]

6   *Retirees.* In 2003 this group included only 12.8% of all Australians.[36] By 2031 it will make up approximately 27% of the population.[37] This group requires smaller housing, retirement communities, quieter forms of recreation, lifecare and healthcare services, and leisure travel.[38]

Thus the changing age structure of the population strongly affects potential markets. In particular, the baby-boom generation will continue to be a prime target for marketers, albeit with changing marketing strategies.

The changing family

The traditional image of a two-children, two-car suburban family is becoming less common. Both marriage and remarriage rates (per 1000 of unmarried population) fell steeply during the 1980s and 1990s, reaching the lowest level in 2001. Since 2001 the number of marriages has increased each year, but people are marrying later, with a median age of 29 years for men and 28 years for women for the first marriage, up from 25 years and 23 years in 1984.[39] Couple families with children are still the most common household type in Australia, but are becoming less common, as fewer families have children or have only one child.[40] An increasing number of families with children under 15 have only one income—23% in 2004, up from 17% in 1994.[41]

The number of working women and working mothers has also increased. The female workforce participation rate increased from 45.0% in 1983–84 to 55.6% in 2003–04. Over the same period, the male participation rate fell from 76.5% to 71.6%.[42] Women earn less than men, on average earning two-thirds of the salary of men, a proportion that has been relatively constant for 15 years. This difference is partly because women work in lower paid jobs; when the earnings of average adult non-managerial employees are compared, female earnings are 92% of male earnings.[43] Women's incomes contribute over 40% of their household income, on average, and influence the purchase of higher-quality goods and services. Marketers of products as diverse as tyres, motor vehicles, insurance, travel and financial services are increasingly directing their advertising to working women. All this activity is accompanied by a shift in the traditional roles and values of husbands and wives, with the husband assuming more domestic functions such as shopping and childcare. As a result, husbands are becoming more of a target market for food and household appliance marketers.

Finally, both the total number of dwellings and the number of non-family households are increasing. The number of households in Australia has increased by an average of 2.4% per year, compared with an average yearly increase of 1.6% in the population.[44] The average number of people in each household is decreasing, however, as families have fewer children, people live longer and more people live alone. Single-parent households are among the fastest-growing categories of households; between 1994 and 2004 the proportion of one-parent families with children under 15 increased from 17% to 23%.[45] These groups have their own special needs. For example, they need smaller homes, more flexible childcare arrangements, inexpensive and smaller appliances, furniture and furnishings, and food that is packaged in smaller sizes.

Geographic shifts in population

Australians are a mobile people, with a large number of people moving each year. Among the major trends are the following.

- ◉ *Movement between states.* While New South Wales remains the most populous state, accounting for one-third of the total population in 2003, Queensland has the fastest growth rate of Australian states, growing by 22% between 1993 and 2003.[46] Population shifts interest marketers because people in different regions buy differently. For example, the movement north to Queensland will lessen the demand for warm clothing and home heating equipment and increase the demand for air conditioning and for new apartments and furnishings in the north.

- ◉ *Movement from rural to urban areas.* Australians have been moving from rural to metropolitan areas for more than a century. In 1901, 64% of Australians lived outside capital cities. By 2003, this proportion had reversed, with 64% of Australians living in capital cities.[47] The metropolitan areas have a faster pace of living, more commuting, higher incomes and greater variety of goods and services than can be found in the small towns and rural areas that dot the country. The largest cities account for most of the sales of expensive apparel, perfumes, luggage and works of art. These cities also support the opera, ballet and other forms of 'high culture'.

- ◉ *Movement from the city to the suburbs.* In the 1960s Australians made an exodus from the inner cities to the suburbs. The Australian Bureau of Statistics breaks these sprawling urban areas into statistical clusters. Organisations use these clusters in researching the best geographical segments for their products and in deciding where to buy advertising space and use direct marketing campaigns. Australians living in the suburbs engage in more casual, outdoor living and greater interaction with neighbours and have higher incomes and younger families.

A better educated and more-white-collar population

Table 5.2 shows the highest educational levels obtained by people aged 25–64 in a number of countries.[48] As Table 5.2 shows, while only a minority of people in every country have a university education, the population in all developed countries is becoming more educated. For example, between 1994 and 2004 the proportion of Australian 25–64 year olds with a vocational or higher education qualification rose from 44% to 58%, continuing a trend seen for many decades. The proportion of people aged 25–64 with a higher education qualification increased from 13% to 22%. This was more than double the increase in the proportion of people whose highest qualification was a vocational qualification, which rose from 31% to 35% over the same period.[49]

TABLE 5.2 Highest educational level for 25–64 year olds

Country	Reference year	Below upper secondary education[a] %	Upper secondary education and post-secondary non-tertiary education[b] %	Tertiary type B education[c] %	Tertiary type A and advanced research programs[d] %	Total[e] %
Australia	2002	39	30	11	20	100
Canada	2002	18	40	22	21	100
France	2002	35	40	12	12	100
Greece	2002	47	34	6	13	100
Indonesia	1999	77	18	2	3	100
Italy	2002	53	36	[f]	10	100
Japan	2002	16	47	16	20	100
Korea (Republic of)	2002	30	45	8	18	100
Malaysia	1998	65	27	–	8	100
New Zealand	2002	24	47	15	15	100
Sweden	2002	18	49	15	18	100
United Kingdom	2002	16	56	8	19	100
United States of America	2002	13	49	9	29	100

[a] International Standard Classification of Education (ISCED) levels 0, 1 and 2. For Australia this includes Preschool, Primary School and lower Secondary School levels as well as the Basic Vocational level

[b] International Standard Classification of Education (ISCED) levels 3 and 4. For Australia this includes Year 12 completion as well as the Skilled Vocational level

[c] International Standard Classification of Education (ISCED) level 5B. For Australia this includes Associate Diplomas and Undergraduate Diplomas

[d] International Standard Classification of Education (ISCED) levels 5A and 6. For Australia this includes Bachelor degree level or higher

[e] Component totals when added may not equal 100% due to rounding.

[f] Data included in Tertiary Type A and advanced research programs

Source: Organisation for Economic Co-operation and Development 2004, Education at a Glance: OECD Indicators, 2004, OECD, Paris.

Source: Australian Bureau of Statistics (2005) Year Book Australia, Australian Social Trends, International comparisons, Education.

MTV Global—music is the universal language

Some say love is the universal language. But for MTV the universal language is *music*. In 1981, MTV began offering its unique brand of programming for young music lovers across the USA. The channel's quirky but pulse-thumping line-up of shows soon attracted a large audience in its target 12–34 age group. MTV quickly established itself as the nation's youth-culture network, offering up 'everything young people care about'.

With success in the USA secured, MTV went global in 1986, and the network has experienced phenomenal global growth ever since. MTV now offers programming in 166 countries. It recently became the first US cable network to provide round-the-clock programming in China. The result of this global expansion? Today, MTV reaches twice as many people around the world as CNN, and 80% of MTV viewers live outside the USA. Altogether, MTV reaches into an astounding 384 million households in 19 different languages on 37 different channels and 17 websites.

What is the secret of MTV's roaring international success? Of course, it offers viewers around the globe plenty of what made it so popular in the USA. Tune in to the network anywhere in the world—Paris, Beijing, Moscow or Tierra del Fuego—and you'll see all of the elements that make it uniquely MTV. You'll feel right at home with the global MTV brand symbols, fast-paced format, veejays, rockumentaries and music, music, music.

But rather than just offering a carbon copy of its US programming to international viewers, MTV carefully localises its fare. Each channel serves up a mix that includes 70% local programming tailored to the specific tastes of viewers in local markets. A *Business Week* analyst notes:

> [MTV is] shrewd enough to realize that while the world's teens want American music, they really want the local stuff, too. So, MTV's producers and veejays scour their local

markets for the top talent. The result is an endless stream of overnight sensations that keep MTV's global offerings fresh. Colombian rock singer Shakira was unknown outside Latin America until 1999, when she recorded an MTV Unplugged CD—the acoustic live concerts recorded by MTV. Her CD has now gone platinum, and she's won a US Grammy and two Latin Grammy awards.

MTV's push for local content has resulted in some of the network's most creative shows. Another MTV analyst observes:

> MTV Russia now has a show called '12 Angry Viewers', in which intellectuals and others debate music videos. In Brazil, 'Mochilao', a backpack travel show, is hosted by a popular Brazilian model. In China, MTV Mandarin broadcasts 'Mei Mei Sees MTV,' which features a 'virtual video jockey'. And MTV India screens 'Silly Point', which is made up of short films poking fun at how cricket gear can be used in everyday life. In Australia, MTV launched the MTV Australian Video Music Awards in March 2005, using international stars such as Ozzy and Sharon Osbourne to host and publicise the event, firmly establishing MTV as a presence in the Australian musical scene.

At the centre of MTV's global growth machine is Bill Roedy, president of MTV Networks International. He's a non-stop ambassador on a mission to make MTV available in every last global nook and cranny. According to *Business Week*:

> To give kids their dose of rock, [Roedy] has breakfasted with former Israeli Prime Minister Shimon Peres, dined with Singapore founder Lee Kuan Yew, and chewed the fat

with Chinese leader Jiang Zemin. [He] even met with El Caudillo himself—Cuban leader Fidel Castro—who wondered if MTV could teach Cuban kids English. Says Roedy: 'We've had very little resistance once we explain that we're not in the business of exporting American culture.'

If MTV's business model was only based on its TV show, it might not be doing so well. TV audiences in the USA in 2005 have been down 22% on 2004 figures, but MTV's broadband channel, Overdrive, is thriving, with more than 11 million video downloads of show segments. The station also has a thriving business in providing ringtones in a partnership which brings traffic to the MTV site, publicity for the artist and profits for both. For example, in late 2005 Madonna debuted her new single as a ring tone on mtv.com, creating publicity and interest even before the single's release. MTV's content is seen as such an indicator of what is wanted by young consumers that it is watched very carefully by other communications businesses: in Australia, phone networks developing their new 3G networks (which offer a vast array of Internet content which can be downloaded to mobile phones) see MTV downloads as an important indicator of what their young audiences want from 3G.

MTV's unique blend of international and local programming is not only popular, it's also highly profitable. The network's hold on a young, increasingly wealthy population makes its programming especially popular with advertisers. Altogether, its mix of local and international content, combined with early entry in international markets, makes it tough to beat. 'MTV Networks International makes buckets of money year after year from a potent combination of cable subscriber fees, advertising, and, increasingly, new media,' says the analyst. Meanwhile, the competition struggles just to break even. VIVA, MTV's strongest competitor in Europe, has yet to turn a profit.

Thus, in only two decades, MTV has joined the ranks of the global brand elite, alongside such icons as Coke, Levi's and Sony. Concludes the analyst: 'MTV's version of globalization rocks.'

Sources: Excerpts from Kerry Capell, 'MTV's World: Mando-Pop. Mexican Hip Hop. Russian Rap. It's All Fueling the Biggest Global Channel,' *Business Week*, 18 February 2002, pp. 81–84; and Charles Goldsmith, 'MTV Seeks Global Appeal', *Wall Street Journal*, 21 July 2003, p. B1. Also see 'MTV to Begin 24-Hour Service in Part of China', *New York Times*, 27 March 2003, p. C.13; the MTV website, <www.mtv.com/mtvinternational>; Emma Connors, 'Sweet Music as Ringtones Rake in a Festive Bonus', *The Australian Financial Review*, 10 December 2005, p. 3; Beverley Head, 'Hip Pocket Rockets', *The Sydney Morning Herald*, 11 May 2005, p. 13; Paul Mcintyre, 'TV Takes a Loss but Broadband Is Climbing', *The Age*, 3 October 2005, p. 3; Simon Yeaman, 'Summer Television Isn't Boring Any More, If You Are Prepared to Pay for Your . . .', *The Advertiser*, 19 January 2005, p. DO2.

MTV has joined the ranks of the global brand elite. It reaches into an astounding 384 million households in 19 different languages on 37 different channels and 17 websites.

Questions

1 MTV has created global stars out of music artists who 20 years ago would have been unlikely to become well known outside their home country. What do you think are the implications for music marketing?

2 MTV says that 'we're not in the business of exporting American culture', but music shows like MTV showcase American music, clothing and behaviour. To what extent do you think shows like this are influential in changing behaviour in other countries?

3 MTV is enormously popular among its target market of 12–34 year olds, but in most developed countries this age group constitutes a diminishing proportion of the population. Given this demographic shift, should MTV change as its current market ages? Why or why not?

5.2

Increasing ethnic diversity

A significant component of the growth in the Australian population is accounted for by overseas migration; in 2002–03 overseas migration accounted for just over half of Australia's population growth for the year.[50] The total number of migrants who have come to Australia since the end of World War II is some 5 million, and around 58% of the population are second-generation Australians. The major origins of immigrants have varied over the years; for example, in 1982–83, 28% of immigrants to Australia were born in the UK, 9% were born in Vietnam and 7% were born in New Zealand. Immigrants from the UK have decreased, while those from China and India have increased, respectively contributing 7% and 6% of all immigrants in 2002–03, compared with only 1% and 2% in 1982–83.[51]

Each national group has specific wants and different buying habits. Many marketers of food, clothing, furniture and other products have targeted specially designed products and promotions at one or more of these groups. However, the growth of global companies like MTV, catering to the youth segment in different markets with partly customised offerings, increasingly means that what is popular with one national group has the potential to spread quickly to other international markets—see Marketing Highlight 5.2.

All these demographic developments, along with lifestyle and other changes in the population, have transformed the Australian marketplace from a mass market into more fragmented micromarkets differentiated by age, sex, geography, lifestyle, ethnic background, education and other factors. Each group has strong preferences and consumer characteristics and can be reached through more narrowly focused media. Many organisations are abandoning 'shotgun' approaches aimed at the mythical 'average consumer' and are instead designing products and marketing programs targeting specific micromarkets.

Demographic trends are highly reliable for the short and intermediate term. There is little excuse for an organisation being suddenly surprised by a demographic development. Organisations can easily list the major demographic trends and then spell out what the trends mean for them.

Economic environment

Economic environment
Factors that affect consumer buying power and spending patterns.

The **economic environment** consists of factors that affect consumer buying power and spending patterns. Markets require buying power as well as people. Total buying power depends on current income, prices, savings and credit. Marketers should be aware of major trends in income and of changing consumer spending patterns.

Changes in income

Australia experienced a period of economic growth between 1994–95 and 2000–01 and, in 'real' terms (i.e. after adjustment for changes in prices), disposable household income for all people, on average, increased by 12% (from $419 to $469 per week).[52] There is some indication of increasing inequality in incomes, however, with measures of income inequality increasing each year from 1996–97. For example, the real mean income of high-income people increased, on average, by 14% from 1996–97 to 2000–01 (from $792 to $903 per week) while the income of low-income people only increased by 8% over the same period.[53] The more affluent group demands higher quality and better service—and they are willing and able to pay for it. They spend more on time-saving products, services and luxury-branded products. The comfortable and most numerous group—the middle socioeconomic class—is somewhat careful about its spending but can still afford the good life some of the time. However, commentators suggest that there is a division occurring in what was once thought of as a homogeneous middle class. High-income earners (with a household income of $83 000 per annum or more) are becoming more numerous, while at the other end of the spectrum the lower-income-earning households are also becoming more numerous (households with less than $22 000 per annum). The net effect is that the number of households with incomes of between $27 000 and $83 000 has shrunk from 65% to 40% of all households.[54] This creates very different economic groups: an increasingly well off group and a lower socioeconomic class which frequently struggles to cover the basics of food, clothing and shelter.

With increasing inequality in incomes, value marketing has become the goal for many marketers looking for ways to offer today's more financially cautious buyers greater value—the right combination of product quality and good service at a fair price. At the same time, luxury products are enjoying a growing market, as the economic prosperity of the last 10 years encourages the more comfortably off to spend increasing amounts of money on themselves.[55]

Rising income levels mean that consumers are spending more on themselves.

Changing consumer spending patterns

Figure 5.10 shows the average weekly household expenditure on goods and services. In 2003–04, the largest broad category of household expenditure was food and non-alcoholic beverages, with an average expenditure per household of $153 per week, equating to 16% of total expenditure on goods and services. The next highest was transport, with $139 per week (17.3% of the total) and housing costs, $136 per week (or 15.3% of the total).

When compared to five years earlier, Australians are now spending less on clothing and footwear (down 13.3%), tobacco (down 12.7%) and more on medical care and health expenses (up 12.6%) and on housing costs (up 9.9%).

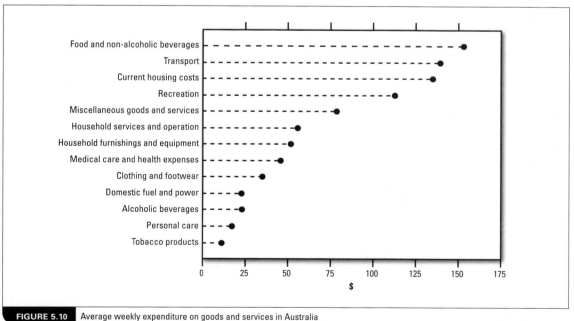

FIGURE 5.10 | Average weekly expenditure on goods and services in Australia
Source: Australian Bureau of Statistics, *Household Expenditure Survey, Australia: Summary of Results,* Catalogue no. 6530.0, August 2005.

Household income directly affects the composition of a household's expenditure. In 2003–04, food and non-alcoholic drinks comprised 18.6% of the expenditure on goods and services of households in the lowest income quintile, and 16.7% for the top income quintile. In general, the proportion spent on housing, household services and domestic fuel and power also declined as household income rose, while the proportion spent on transport, recreation, clothing and footwear, and alcohol increased.[56]

Figure 5.11 shows that the size and the blend of household income and expenditure relates to social and demographic characteristics of the members in the household. The households in the lowest income quintile were more likely to be lone-person households and to rely on government pensions and allowances as their main source of income. The highest income quintile mainly represents couples with two incomes.

There is substantial evidence that consumers at different income levels have different spending patterns. Some of these differences were noted more than a century ago by Ernst Engel, who studied how people shifted their spending as their incomes rose. Engel found that as family income rises, the percentage spent on food declines, the percentage spent on housing remains constant (except for utilities such as gas, electricity and public services, which decrease), and both the percentage spent on other categories and that devoted to savings increase. These patterns, often described as **'Engel's laws'**, have generally been supported by later studies.

Changes in such major economic variables as income, cost of living, interest rates, and savings and borrowing patterns have a large impact on the marketplace. Organisations watch these variables using economic forecasting, so they can anticipate, and respond to, changes in economic demand.

Natural environment

The **natural environment** involves natural resources which are needed as inputs by marketers or which are affected by marketing activities. During the 1960s public concern about damage to the natural environment began to grow. Popular books raised concerns about shortages of natural resources and about the damage to water, earth and air caused by the industrial activities of modern

Engel's laws
Differences noted more than a century ago by Ernst Engel regarding family spending patterns in response to increased income; categories studied included food, housing, transportation, healthcare and other goods and services.

Natural environment
Natural resources which are needed as inputs by marketers or which are affected by marketing activities.

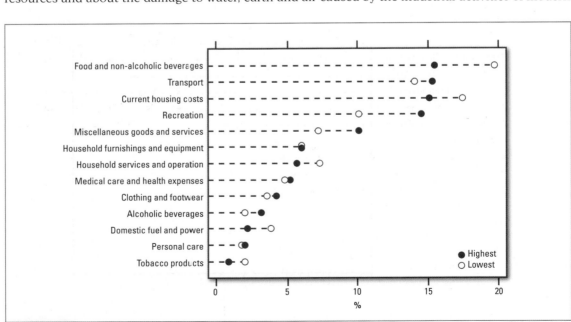

FIGURE 5.11 Proportion of expenditure allocated to goods and services by the lowest and highest income quintile groups in Australia
Source: Australian Bureau of Statistics, *Household Expenditure Survey, Australia: Summary of Results*, Catalogue no. 6530.0, August 2005.

nations. Watchdog groups such as Greenpeace and Friends of the Earth sprang up, and legislators proposed measures to protect the environment.

Environmental concerns have continued to grow over the past two decades. Some trend analysts believe that the decade after 2010 will be seen as the 'Earth Decade' and protection of the natural environment will be the major worldwide issue facing business and the public. The Earth Summit held in Johannesburg in 2002 saw the world and its leaders concentrating on environmental and sustainable development economics issues, and many countries have responded with increasing regulation of business.[57] For example, in some European countries, cars that are more than 10 years old cannot be re-registered. Concern continues to mount about the depletion of the earth's ozone layer and the resultant 'greenhouse effect', a dangerous warming of the earth's atmosphere. Already about 40% of the world's population has insufficient water for sanitation and hygiene, and 2.2 million people die each year from diseases linked to inadequate sewerage or contaminated drinking water. Each day, about two million tonnes of waste are dumped into the world's rivers and lakes.[58] Marketers should be aware of four trends in the natural environment as their products can be boycotted if they do not comply with government and/or community standards.[59]

Increased concern about the environment, and legislative changes, are creating a growing market for green products.

1. Shortages of raw materials

Air and water may seem to be infinite resources, but some groups see a long-run danger. Environmental groups have successfully lobbied for a ban on propellants such as chlorofluorocarbon (formerly used in aerosol cans and motor vehicle air conditioning) because of their potential damage to the ozone layer. Water shortages are already a concern in some parts of Australia, South Africa, the Middle East and other parts of the world. There have been 37 violent conflicts involving water between nations in the past 50 years.[60]

Non-renewable resources, such as oil, coal and various minerals, also pose a serious problem. Companies making products that require these increasingly scarce minerals face large cost increases even if the materials do remain available, and these companies may not find it easy to pass these costs on to the consumer.

2. Increased cost of energy

One non-renewable resource, oil, has created the most serious problem for future economic growth. The major industrial economies of the world depend heavily on oil, and until economical energy substitutes can be developed oil will continue to dominate the world political and economic picture. Large increases in the price of oil during the 1970s (from $US2 per barrel in 1970 to $US34 per barrel in 1982) created a frantic search for alternative forms of energy. The Gulf Wars in 1991 and 2003 also caused large increases in the price of oil and prompted many organisations to search for practical ways to harness solar, nuclear, wind, wave and other forms of energy. For example, BP, Europe's largest oil company, has created a new business unit that will invest $US1.8 billion a year on solar, wind, and hydrogen energy and carbon sequestration, in what a spokesperson described as 'responding to climate change by making a business'.[61]

3. Increased pollution

Industry will almost always damage the quality of the natural environment. Consider the disposal of chemical and nuclear wastes, the quantity of DDT and other chemical pollutants in the soil and food supply, and the littering of the environment with non-biodegradable bottles, plastics and other packaging materials.

Public concern with pollution creates a marketing opportunity for some organisations. It results in a market for pollution-control solutions such as smoke-stack scrubbers, recycling centres, high-temperature incinerators and landfill systems. It leads to a search for new ways to produce and package goods that do not cause environmental damage. Concern for the natural environment has also contributed to the growth of the 'Green movement'. Increasing numbers of consumers have begun doing more business with ecologically responsible organisations and avoiding those whose actions harm the environment. They buy 'environmentally friendly' products, even if these products cost more.[62] Many industries are also improving their environmental performance, fearing that unless they self-regulate they will face government legislation. For example, the Australian mobile phone industry has attempted to increase recycling of mobile phones by providing consumers with information about where phones can be recycled, under threat of regulation by the government if recycling levels remain low.[63]

4. Government intervention in natural resource management

The governments of different countries vary in their concern and efforts to promote a clean environment. International concern with the environment was shown by the signing of the Kyoto Protocol, an international treaty on climate change, which requires all countries which sign up to meet agreed targets for emissions of carbon dioxide and five other greenhouse gases, or trade these emissions with other countries. The agreement, which as of June 2006 has been signed by all developed countries except the USA and Australia, has created an enormous increase in demand for alternative energy, such as wind power. It will also create increasing foreign investment between signatories to the protocol in so-called 'carbon sinks' which allow countries that do not meet their emissions reduction targets to invest in other countries. For example, the Dutch government has bought into forestry in New Zealand, and Spain is allocating 205 million euros ($A358 million) to offset its emissions.[64] The Kyoto Protocol has been criticised as an inadequate solution to global warming, as it does not provide sanctions for countries that do not reach their targets, and does not impose targets for developing nations.[65] However, the international recognition that global warming is a problem which must be addressed is likely to result in ongoing and increasing pressure on businesses in developed countries to reduce pollution and to meet renewable energy targets.

Technological environment

Technological environment
Forces that affect new technologies, creating new product and market opportunities.

The **technological environment** is perhaps the most dramatic force now shaping our destiny. Technology has released such wonders as penicillin, organ transplants, biotechnology and the computer. It has also released such horrors as the machine gun, nuclear submarines, hydrogen bombs, nerve gas, cruise missiles and 'smart bombs'. Our attitude towards technology depends on whether we are more impressed with its wonders or its blunders.

Every new technology replaces an older technology. The car hurt the railroads, xerography hurt the carbon-paper business, xerography is being hurt by laser photocopiers, emails are hurting postal services and videoconferencing is hurting the airline industry. When old industries fought or ignored new technologies, their businesses declined. The Internet emergence created a new web-hosting and web-design industry, and mobile phones with Internet capabilities have created a 'new media' communication industry. The marketer should watch the following trends in technology.

Fast pace of technological change

Many of today's common products were not available even 20 years ago. Who would have predicted in 1967 that the network developed to facilitate effective American military communications—Arpanet—would develop into the Internet, and ultimately be enhanced to run World Wide Web server and browser software and thus become the information, entertainment and commercial tool that it is today?[66] Organisations that do not keep up with technological change will soon find their products out of date. And they will miss new product and market opportunities.

Scientists are currently working on a wide range of new technologies that will revolutionise our products and production processes. The most exciting work is being done in biotechnology, converging microcomputing and communications technologies, miniature electronics, robotics and materials science.[67] Scientists are working on promising new products and services that range from practical solar and wave energy generation applications to tiny devices that will clean our arteries to voice-controlled automatic dispensing machines for money and other products. The challenge in each case is not only technical but commercial—to make practical, affordable products which do not breach ethical considerations and which are attractive to consumers.

High R&D budgets

The largest spending on R&D occurs in the USA, where R&D spending reached an estimated $291 billion in 2004.[68] In terms of the proportion of GDP, however, the Scandinavian countries of Sweden and Finland spend the highest percentage on R&D, as shown in Table 5.3. Every other country lags far behind the USA in R&D spending, and in Australia the federal and state governments are striving to encourage organisations to spend more on R&D and thereby create export earnings to counter the large trade deficits of the past decade. The Australian federal and state governments funded 42% of R&D in Australia in 2002–03 (down from 50% 10 years before).[69] However, government also provides as much as 175% of R&D expenditures as tax breaks and other funding. For example, Glaxo Australia was one of the first to obtain Australian government's funding under the Factor F scheme for the pharmaceutical industry. It also gained benefits under the Victorian government's Strategic Firm Assistance Scheme, such as a grant for the construction of new laboratories in the Eastern Melbourne suburb of Boronia. Under these schemes, Glaxo Australia increased its exports eightfold in five years.[70]

Increased regulation

As products become more complex, the public needs to know that they are safe. Thus government agencies investigate and ban potentially unsafe products. For example, Australia's National Health and Medical Research Council has set up complex regulations for testing new drugs, and the state Consumer Protection Agencies set safety standards for consumer products and penalise organisations that fail to meet them. Such regulations have resulted in much higher research costs and in longer times between new product ideas and their introduction. For example, it took nearly 20 years for Ralph Sarich's Orbital engines to reach market commercialisation. Marketers should be aware of these regulations when seeking and developing new products.[71]

Marketers need to understand the changing technological environment and the varying ways new technologies can serve human needs. They need to work closely with R&D people to encourage more market-oriented research and they must be alert to any aspects of an innovation that might harm users or arouse opposition.

Political environment

Marketing decisions are strongly affected by developments in the political environment. The **political environment** consists of laws, government agencies and pressure groups that influence and limit various organisations and individuals in a given society.

Political environment
Laws, government agencies and pressure groups that influence and limit various organisations and individuals in a given society.

TABLE 5.3 R&D spending by different countries

	Business %	Government %	Higher Education %	All sectors[a] %
Sweden[b]	3.32	0.12	0.83	4.27
Finland	2.41	0.36	0.66	3.46
Japan	2.32	0.3	0.43	3.12
Iceland	1.77	0.76	0.5	3.09
Korea	2.18	0.39	0.3	2.91
United States of America	1.87	0.24	0.42	2.67
Denmark[b]	1.75	0.18	0.58	2.52
Germany	1.75	0.35	0.43	2.52
France	1.37	0.37	0.43	2.2
Belgium[b]	1.6	0.13	0.42	2.17
Austria	n.a.	n.a.	n.a.	1.93
Canada	1.05	0.22	0.63	1.91
Netherlands[b]	1.1	0.27	0.51	1.89
United Kingdom	1.26	0.17	0.42	1.88
Australia	**0.87**	**0.33**	**0.45**	**1.69**
Norway	0.96	0.26	0.45	1.67
Czech Republic	0.79	0.3	0.2	1.3
New Zealand[b]	0.43	0.39	0.36	1.18
Ireland[b]	0.8	0.09	0.26	1.15
Italy[b]	0.55	0.2	0.36	1.11
Spain	0.56	0.16	0.31	1.03
Hungary	0.36	0.34	0.26	1.02
Portugal	0.32	0.18	0.33	0.93
Greece[b]	0.21	0.14	0.29	0.65
Poland	0.13	0.26	0.2	0.59
Slovak Republic	0.37	0.15	0.05	0.58
Mexico[b]	0.12	0.15	0.12	0.39

a Includes private non-profit.
b Data for 2001–02.
Sources: OECD 2004; Australian Bureau of Statistics, *Year Book Australia 2006, Science and Innovation.*

Legislation regulating business

Legislation affecting business has increased steadily over the years to protect organisations from each other, and to protect consumers from unscrupulous businesses. So laws are passed to define and prevent unfair competition. These laws are enforced in Australia by the Australian Competition and Consumer Commission (or ACCC, but usually known as the A Triple C) and the Foreign Investment Review Board if a foreign organisation is involved. Even the Australian Constitution is involved. Section 93 of the Constitution affects most organisations positively by ensuring that they can trade freely between the states. In some cases, however, individual state legislation such as Weights and Measures Acts and Regulations can be invoked to cause an organisation manufacturing in one state to cease marketing until it modifies its packaging sizes to conform with legislation in another state. Organisations mounting sales promotions such as 'Scratch this Label and Win a Free Trip' are also affected by different state laws governing gaming and lotteries. (For example, in South Australia entrants to a competition can't be forced to attach a label or labels as 'proof of purchase'.)

The federal Trade Practices Act is the law which has the greatest impact on marketers. The Act does not lend itself to a precise summary and is discussed in more detail in Chapter 21. Suffice it to say here that the Act is divided into a number of parts, two of which are quite major:

- Part IV, which deals with anti-competitive practices
- Part V, which deals with consumer protection:
    Division 1—unfair practices
    Division 1A—product safety and information
    Division 2—conditions and warranties
    Division 2A—actions against manufacturers/importers.[72]

The Act protects consumers from unfair business practices, and also protects the interests of society against unrestrained business behaviour. Marketers need to know about the major laws protecting competition, consumers and society. The main federal law is discussed in Chapter 21, but marketers should also know the state and local laws that affect their local marketing activity.[73]

Increased emphasis on ethics and socially responsible actions

Written regulations cannot possibly cover all potential marketing abuses, and existing laws are often difficult to enforce. However, beyond written laws and regulations, business is also governed by social codes and rules of professional ethics. Enlightened organisations encourage all employees to act ethically. These socially responsible marketing organisations seek out ways to protect consumers and the environment.

Although most organisations act legally and ethically, a string of high-profile business scandals over the past few years, such as the collapse of insurance company HIH and of US trading and energy giant Enron (named by *Fortune* magazine as 'America's Most Innovative Company' six years in a row), with executives from both firms sent to gaol, have spurred renewed interest in ethics and social responsibility. As a result, many industrial and professional trade associations have suggested codes of ethics, and many companies are now developing policies and guidelines to deal with complex social responsibility issues.

Large organisations have also been increasingly influenced by public interest groups operating at the national, state and local levels over the past two decades. These groups can draw unfavourable attention to organisations, even if they are engaging in legal behaviour. For example, pressure by environmental groups before the opening of Disneyland Hong Kong forced Disneyland hotels to remove shark fin soup from their restaurant menus, by drawing attention to the cruel treatment of the sharks. Other hotels in Hong Kong commonly serve shark fin soup without criticism, but the unwelcome publicity and threats of consumer boycotts created strong pressure for Disneyland to give in to the lobby groups.[74] Coca-Cola recently said it had been banned from a second American university, the University of Michigan, one of its largest university accounts, because of concerns about the soft drink

In 2006, former Enron CEO Ken Lay was found guilty on six counts of conspiracy and fraud over the collapse of Enron in 2001. Lay faced 20–30 years in gaol but died before sentencing.

maker's labour practices in Columbia and environmental actions in India. While Coca-Cola has denied the allegations, it has admitted that the boycott has damaged its reputation.[75]

Cultural environment

Cultural environment
Institutions and other forces that affect society's basic values, perceptions, preferences and behaviours.

The **cultural environment** is made up of institutions and other forces that affect society's basic values, perceptions, preferences and behaviours. People grow up in a particular society that shapes their basic beliefs and values. They absorb a world-view that defines their relationships between themselves and others. The following cultural characteristics can affect marketing decisions.

Persistence of cultural values

People in a given society hold many beliefs and values. Their core beliefs and values have a high degree of persistence. For example, Australians and New Zealanders are said to value equality and a 'fair go' for others. These beliefs shape more specific attitudes and behaviours found in everyday life. Core beliefs and values are passed on from parents to children and are reinforced by schools, churches, business and government. Marketing Highlight 5.3 discusses issues that arise for businesses in interacting with other cultures.

Secondary beliefs and values are more open to change. Believing that celebrating with friends is a good thing is a core belief; believing that people should drink champagne when they celebrate is a secondary belief. Marketers have some chance of changing secondary values but little chance of changing core values. For example, family planning marketers could argue more effectively that people should get married later rather than arguing that they should not get married at all.

Subcultures

Each society contains subcultures—groups of people with shared value systems based on common life experiences or situations. Catholics, teenagers and working women all represent separate subcultures whose members share common beliefs, preferences and behaviours. When subcultural groups show different wants and buying behaviour, marketers can choose to target different subcultures with different products. For example, banks in the UK such as Lloyds and HSBC have recently started to offer products which conform with Islamic law, or shari'a, which prohibits paying or charging interest.[76]

Shifts in secondary cultural values

Although core values are fairly persistent, cultural swings do take place. Consider the impact of popular music groups, movie personalities and other celebrities on young people's hairstyles, clothes and sexual norms. Marketers want to predict cultural shifts in order to spot new opportunities or threats. Several organisations offer 'futures' forecasts in this connection. For example, the marketing research firm Roy Morgan Research Centre tracks cultural values such as 'anti-bigness', 'mysticism', 'living for today', 'away from possessions' and 'sensuousness' as part of its readership surveys. The centre describes the percentage of the population who share such attitudes.

The major cultural values of a society are expressed in people's views about organisations, society, nature and the universe.

- *People's views of themselves.* People vary in the emphasis they place on serving themselves versus serving others. Some people seek personal pleasure, wanting fun, change and escape. Others seek self-realisation through religion, recreation or the avid pursuit of careers or other life goals.

  Many people use products, brands and services as a means of self-expression. They wear and/or aspire to expensive, conspicuously branded products because the brand says something about who they are. They spend more time in outdoor health activities (jogging, tennis) and on luxury items. The leisure industry (camping, boating, arts and crafts, and sports) faces good growth prospects in a society in which people seek self-fulfilment. The market for services which aim to bring people closer to their ideal view of themselves (such as spas, massages and self-improvement training) is also increasing, as economic success allows more people to spend larger amounts of money on themselves.

⊚ *People's views of others.* Technologies such as email, text messaging, chat rooms and blogs are allowing increasing contact and transfer of information between people, without even requiring face-to-face contact. Information and fashions can be spread around the world much faster than ever before, especially by the technologically savvy generation Y. In such an environment, some people (variously called the innovators, market mavens or those just labelled 'cool') will be most influential in determining fashions, resulting in market success for some products and failure for others. Marketers are increasingly trying to identify and target the most influential individuals, and encourage them to spread positive word-of-mouth about products, using a technique which is called 'buzz marketing' or 'viral marketing'. We will discuss this technique more in Chapter 16.[78]

⊚ *People's views of organisations.* People vary in their attitudes towards corporations, government agencies, trade unions, universities and other organisations, although most people expect organisations to treat their employees, customers and the community fairly. There has been, however, a decline in organisational loyalty and trust of large organisations. The late 1980s saw a sharp decrease in confidence in and loyalty toward business and political organisations and institutions, and this loss of confidence has been exacerbated by high-profile corporate collapses and by unfavourable publicity about high executive salaries, even in organisations which are retrenching workers. In the workplace, there has been an overall decline in organisational loyalty. Many people today see work not as a source of satisfaction but as a required chore to earn money to enjoy their non-work hours. This trend suggests that organisations need to find new ways to win consumer and employee confidence.

⊚ *People's views of society.* People vary in their attitudes towards their society, from patriots who defend it, to reformers who want to change it, to discontents who want to leave it. Both national success (such as sporting victories) and times of national stress (such as threats of terrorism) tend to result in increased patriotism, which will often be expressed by a greater tendency to buy national products. For example, Australia and China have both experienced huge increases in national pride and increased interest in national products and services after being chosen to host the Olympic Games. American patriotism surged after the 2001 terrorist attacks. No matter which country we examine, people's orientation to their society influences their consumption patterns, levels of savings and attitudes towards the marketplace. Marketers need to watch consumers' changing social orientations and adapt their strategies accordingly.

⊚ *People's views of nature.* People vary in their attitudes towards the natural world. Some feel ruled by it, others feel in harmony with it and still others seek to master it. A long-term trend has been people's growing mastery over nature through technology and the belief that nature is bountiful. More recently, however, people have recognised that nature is finite and fragile—that it can be destroyed or spoiled by human activities.

Love of nature is leading to an increasing market for 'green' products, which are seen as environmentally friendly, and to increased demand for products which allow people to experience nature, such as hiking, boating and active holidays. Food producers have found growing markets for 'natural' and organic products. Marketing communicators are using appealing natural backgrounds in advertisements for their products.

MARKETING HIGHLIGHT

5.3

International marketing manners— when in Rome, do as the Romans do

Picture this: Consolidated Amalgamation, Inc. thinks it's time that the rest of the world enjoyed the same fine products it has offered consumers in its home country for two generations. It dispatches its General Manager, Bruce Slicksmile, on a world tour to explore the territory. Bruce stops first in London, where he makes short work of some bankers, ringing them up on the phone to introduce his company. He handles Parisians with similar ease. After securing a table at La Tour d'Argent, he greets his lunch guest, the director of an industrial engineering firm, with 'Call me Bruce, Jacques'.

In Germany, Bruce is a powerhouse. Whisking through a lavish, state-of-the-art marketing presentation, complete with flip charts and audiovisuals, he shows them that this boy from down under *knows* how to make money. Heading on to Milan, Bruce strikes up a conversation with the Japanese businessman sitting next to him on the plane. He touches the man's arm to show his sincerity, puts his card on the man's meal tray and slips the man's card into his novel as a bookmark.

Bruce next visits Saudi Arabia, where he presents a potential client with a multimillion-dollar proposal in a classy pigskin binder. He offers a firm handshake to the man, a Muslim. His final stop is Beijing, where he talks business over lunch with a group of Chinese executives. After completing the meal, he stabs his chopsticks into his bowl of rice and presents each guest with an elegant Tiffany's clock as a reminder of his visit.

A great tour, sure to generate a pile of orders, right? Wrong. Six months later, Consolidated Amalgamation has nothing to show for the trip but a stack of bills. Unfortunately, his potential customers weren't wild about Bruce.

This hypothetical case has been exaggerated for emphasis. Businesspeople are rarely so culturally unaware. But experts say success in international business has a lot to do with knowing the territory and its people. By learning English and extending themselves in other ways, businesspeople from Asia and Europe have met English-speaking businesspeople more than halfway. In contrast, English-speaking executives too often do little except assume that others will behave the same way they do.

Poor Bruce tried, all right, but in all the wrong ways. The British do not generally do deals over the phone as much as some other nationalities. A proper Frenchman neither likes instant familiarity—questions about family, church or alma mater—nor refers to strangers by their first names. 'That poor fellow, Jacques, probably wouldn't show anything, but he'd recoil. He'd *not be* pleased,' explains an expert on French business practices. 'It's considered poor taste,' he continues. 'Even after months of business dealings, I'd wait for him or her to make the invitation [to use first names] . . . You are always right, in Europe, to say "Mister".'

Bruce's flashy presentation would probably have been a flop with the Germans, who dislike overstatement and showiness, says one German expert. He says that calling secretaries by their first names would also be considered rude: 'They have a right to be called by their surname. You'd certainly ask—and get—permission first.' In Europe, people tend to address each other formally and correctly—for example, in Germany, someone with two doctorates (which is fairly common) must be referred to as 'Herr Doktor Doktor'.

When Bruce Slicksmile touched his new Japanese acquaintance on the arm, the executive probably considered him disrespectful and presumptuous. Japan, like many Asian countries, is a 'no-contact culture' in which even shaking hands is a strange experience. Bruce made matters worse by casually putting his business card on the man's tray. Japanese people revere the business card as an extension of self and as an indicator of rank. They do not *hand* it to people, they *present* it—with both hands. In addition, the Japanese are sticklers about rank. Unlike Americans, they don't heap praise on subordinates in a room; they will praise only the highest-ranking official present.

To the Saudi Arabians, the pigskin binder would have been considered vile. An American salesman who really did present such a binder was unceremoniously tossed out and his company was blacklisted from working with Saudi businesses. For some Muslims, shaking hands with a non-Muslim (especially one of the opposite sex) is considered unacceptable, so it is wise to follow their lead. In China, Bruce stabbing his chopsticks could have been misinterpreted as an act of aggression. Stabbing chopsticks into a bowl of rice and leaving them signifies death to the Chinese. The clocks Bruce offered as gifts might have confirmed such dark intentions. To 'give a clock' in Chinese sounds the same as 'seeing someone off to his end'.

To compete successfully in global markets, or even to deal effectively with international firms in their home markets, companies must help their managers to understand the needs, customs and cultures of international business buyers. 'When doing business in a foreign country and a foreign culture—particularly a non-Western culture—assume nothing,' advises an international business specialist. 'Take nothing for granted. Turn every stone. Ask every question. Because cultures really are different, and those differences can have a major impact.' So the old advice is still good advice: when in Rome, do as the Romans do.

Sources: Portions adapted from Susan Harte, 'When in Rome, You Should Learn to Do What the Romans Do', *The Atlanta Journal-Constitution*, 22 January, 1990, pp. D1, D6. Additional examples can be found in David A. Ricks, *Blunders in International Business Around the World*, Malden, MA, Blackwell Publishing, 2000; Terri Morrison, Wayne A. Conway and Joseph J. Douress, *Dun & Bradstreet's Guide to Doing Business*, Upper Saddle River, NJ, Prentice Hall, 2000; Jame K. Sebenius, 'The Hidden Challenge of Cross-Border Negotiations', *Harvard Business Review*, March 2002, pp. 76–85; Daniel Joseph, 'Dangerous Assumptions', *Ceramic Industry*, January 2003, p. 120; and information accessed at <www.executiveplanet.com>, January 2005.

Questions

1 Ford Australia and AMP insurance company both say that they use their diverse workforce to get ideas about what might appeal to different cultural groups.[77] Can an organisation use its workforce to prevent the sorts of mistakes that Bruce made? How? What else can an organisation do to prepare its staff for contact with other cultures?

2 Talk to classmates who come from, or who have lived in, other countries. What are some of the differences in accepted behaviour in different countries?

3 With increasing cultural diversity in most societies, even organisations that don't send staff overseas interact with many cultures in their home countries. Do you think that most organisations use the diversity in their workforce to understand different customer preferences?

5.3

⊛ *People's views of the universe.* Finally, people vary in their beliefs about the origin of the universe and their place in it. Although most Australians report that they belong to a religious group, religious conviction and practice has been decreasing, and church attendance has fallen steadily. As people lose their religious orientation, they seek to enjoy life on earth as fully as possible. They seek goods and experiences which provide immediate satisfaction. Some futurists, however, have noted an emerging renewal of interest in religion, perhaps as part of a broader search for a new inner purpose. At the same time, some religious groups are using marketing concepts to examine what they offer their members, and to consider the best way to communicate with current and potential members.

Responding to the marketing environment

Someone once observed: 'There are three kinds of companies: those who make things happen, those who watch things happen, and those who wonder what's happened'.[79] Many companies view the marketing environment as an uncontrollable element to which they must react and adapt. They passively accept the marketing environment and do not try to change it. They analyse the environmental forces and design strategies that will help the company avoid the threats and take advantage of the opportunities the environment provides.

Other companies take a *proactive* stance toward the marketing environment. Rather than simply watching and reacting, these firms take aggressive actions to affect the publics and forces in their marketing environment. Such companies hire lobbyists to influence legislation affecting their industries and stage media events to gain favourable press coverage. They run advertorials (ads expressing editorial points of view) to shape public opinion. They press lawsuits and file complaints with regulators to keep competitors in line, and they form contractual agreements to control their distribution channels better.

Often, companies can find positive ways to overcome seemingly uncontrollable environmental constraints. For example:

> Cathay Pacific Airlines . . . determined that many travellers were avoiding Hong Kong because of lengthy delays at immigration. Rather than assuming that this was a problem they could not solve, Cathay's senior staff asked the Hong Kong government how to avoid these immigration delays. After lengthy discussions, the airline agreed to make an annual grant-in-aid to the government to hire more immigration inspectors—but these reinforcements would primarily service the Cathay Pacific gates. The reduced waiting period increased customer value and thus strengthened [Cathay's competitive advantage].[80]

Marketing management cannot always control environmental forces. In many cases, it must settle for simply watching and reacting to the environment. For example, a company would have little success trying to influence geographic population shifts, the economic environment or major cultural values. But whenever possible, smart marketing managers will take a *proactive* rather than a *reactive* approach to the marketing environment.

SELF-CHECK QUESTIONS

4 Why is immigration a factor to consider when examining a country's demography?

5 Do you agree that there is an identifiable generation X, separate from generation Y? Why or why not?

6 Are you a member of a special-interest group such as Greenpeace? Why are such groups important to marketing organisations?

SUMMARY

The organisation must start with the *marketing environment* in searching for opportunities and monitoring threats. The marketing environment consists of all the actors and forces that affect the organisation's ability to transact effectively with the target market. The organisation's marketing environment can be divided into the *microenvironment* and the *macroenvironment*.

The *microenvironment* consists of five components. The first is the organisation's internal environment—its several departments and management levels—as it affects marketing management's decision making. The second component includes the marketing channel firms that cooperate to create value and marketing intermediaries (resellers, physical distribution firms, marketing services agencies, financial intermediaries). The third component consists of the five types of markets in which the organisation can sell: the consumer, business-to-business, reseller, government and international markets. The fourth component consists of the competitors facing the organisation. The fifth component consists of all the publics that have an actual or potential interest in or impact on the organisation's ability to achieve its objectives: financial, media, government, citizen action, and local, general and internal publics.

The organisation's *macroenvironment* consists of major forces that shape opportunities and pose threats to the organisation: demographic, economic, natural, technological, political and cultural.

The demographic environment shows a changing age structure in the population, changing family patterns, geographic population shifts, a better educated and more-white-collar population, and increasing ethnic diversity. The economic environment shows changing real income and changing consumer spending patterns. The natural environment shows impending shortages of certain raw materials, increased energy costs, increased pollution levels and increasing government intervention in natural-resource management. The technological environment shows rapid technological change, innovation opportunities, concentration on minor improvements rather than major discoveries and increased regulation of technological change. The political environment shows increasing business regulation, strong government agency enforcement and the growth of public-interest groups. The cultural environment shows long-run trends toward the use of branded products as a means of self-expression, decreasing organisational loyalty, an increasing appreciation for nature and a search for more meaningful and enduring values.

MARKETING ISSUE

World trade has tripled from the early part of the twentieth century. Businesses which used to provide goods and services for the domestic market are now earning a large percentage of their income from overseas, either by operating in those markets (for example, Australia Post's logistic services in China), by exporting to those markets (like iron ore exporters Rio Tinto) or by catering to demand from those markets (like Australian universities which receive a substantial amount of income from foreign students). Yet most companies have no formal policy to equip their staff for working in foreign countries, or for familiarising their staff with the customs of customers' cultures. Multinationals have traditionally employed expatriates in senior positions (at high cost), and located them in foreign markets to manage operations. These expatriates often live in communities frequented by other expatriates, mix with other expatriates and typically don't learn the local language or only learn a few key phrases. Perhaps this is understandable given the demands on the time of busy executives, but does it create a problem? After all, in a multinational company, most people speak English, don't they? Well, maybe not . . .

1. Have you lived or worked overseas? What are the challenges you found in surviving in a different culture? Talk to a classmate who comes from another country. What are some of the differences in buying behaviours between countries?

2 Given that one of the mantras of marketing is to 'know your customer', can an expatriate manager understand local customers if they don't speak the language and/or understand the culture?

3 Ideally, all employees of an organisation (including expatriates) would speak the same language. However, that will never happen for large Western organisations operating in emerging markets such as China. Does it matter? What, if anything, can an organisation do to improve the communication between employees who speak multiple languages?

KEY TERMS

baby boom	173	Generation X	174	natural environment	182
cultural environment	188	macroenvironment	162	physical distribution firms	164
demography	169	marketing environment	162	political environment	185
economic environment	180	marketing intermediaries	164	public	165
Engel's laws	182	marketing services agencies	164	resellers	164
financial intermediaries	164			technological environment	184
Generation Y	174	microenvironment	162		

DISCUSSING THE ISSUES

1 To what extent should cultural differences be considered in the international marketing environment?

2 Look at the websites of Qantas, BHP Billiton and News Corporation and evaluate them in terms of their appeal as companies that bridge the global marketing environment.

3 Imagine that you are the communications director for an alternative medicines health company. What publics might be affected by a news report that your organisation had not tested its products for potential side effects? How would you respond to this report?

4 How can Australian firms minimise the inconvenience to their international operations when foreign governments act as regulators of international commercial involvement within their borders?

5 Recent lifestyle studies have identified a growing attitude that 'meal preparation should take as little time as possible'. What products and businesses are being affected by this trend? What future marketing opportunities does this trend suggest?

6 The Internet is a channel that transcends national boundaries. How can firms use this medium to advantage in emerging markets like China?

REFERENCES

1. <www.google.com.au/profile.html>.
2. Background Briefing, 'Googlemania', 18 December 2005, <www.abc.net.au/rntalks/bbing/stories/s1534898.htm>; Sean Aylmer, 'Google Races Past $US400 as GM Goes Backward', *The Australian Financial Review*, 19 November 2005, p. 46.
3. Robert Berner and David Kiley, 'Global Brands', *Business Week*, 5 September 2005, pp. 56–63.
4. Saul Hansell, 'Google Profit Soars Again. Beyond High Expectations', *The New York Times*, 22 July 2005, p. 3.
5. <www.google.com.au/profile.html>.
6. Steve Lohr, 'Lots of Happy Campus at Googleplex', *The Australian Financial Review*, 7 December 2005, p. 10.
7. Claudia Parsons, 'Publisher to Go Digital to Block Google', *The Australian Financial Review*, 14 December 2005, p. 48.
8. Dan Mitchell, 'Mind-Googling Expansion Sparks Protest', *The Australian Financial Review*, 28 November 2005, p. 47; Richard Waters and Chris Nuttal, 'Google Seeks to Calm "Gatekeeper" Fears', *Financial Times*, 28 June 2005, p. 22.
9. Al Ehrbar, Abraham Lustgarten, Julie Schlosser, Corey Hajim, Matthew Boyle and Julia Boorstin, 'Breakaway Brands: How Ten Companies, Making Products from Drills to Waffles, Took Good Brands and Made Them Much, Much Better', *Fortune*, 31 October 2005, pp. 153–154.

10. David A. Vise, 'Googling Google', *Newsbytes News Network*, 15 December 2005.

11. Suzan Burton, 'Where Are All the Shoppers', *E-tailing Lessons for the Asia-Pacific*, vol. 3, no. 4, 2002, pp. 331–342.

12. Andrall E. Pearson, 'Tough-minded Ways to Get Innovative', *Harvard Business Review*, vol. 80, no 8, August 2002, p. 117; John Seeley Brown, 'Research that Reinvents the Corporation', *Harvard Business Review*, vol. 80, no. 8, August 2002, p. 105.

13. ACNielsen, 'Consumers in Asia–Pacific—Our Confidence, Spending Intentions and Major Concerns', 2005, available at <www2.acnielsen.com/reports/index_consumer.shtml>, accessed 20 January 2006.

14. <www.census.gov/ipc/www/worldpop.html>, accessed 31 December 2005; US Census Bureau, POPclock, <www.census.gov>, accessed 31 December 2005—this website provides continuously updated figures for world and US populations.

15. Sally D. Goll, 'Marketing: China's (Only) Children Get the Royal Treatment', *Wall Street Journal*, 8 February 1993, pp. B1, B3.

16. Anonymous, 'The "greying" of Europe', *Business Europe*, 30 October 2002, vol. 42, no. 21, p. 1.

17. United Nations, *World Population Ageing 1950–2050*, available at <www.un.org/esa/population/publications/worldageing1950 2050/pdf/62executivesummary_english.pdf>.

18. Ibid.; David, Turner, 'Why Selling to Little People Is No Longer Child's Play', *Financial Times*, 6 June 2005, p. 14.

19. See the 'Population Clock' at <www.abs.gov.au/websitedbs/d3310114.nsf/Home/Popular%20Statistics>, accessed May 2006.

20. See United Nations, *World Population Prospects: The 2004 Revision, Highlights*, Department of Economic and Social Affairs, 2005.

21. See Australian Bureau of Statistics, *Year Book Australia, Population, Households and Families*, 2005; and *Australia Now, Measures of Australia's Progress, Population*, 2004.

22. United Nations, *World Urbanisation Prospects: The 2003 Revision, Data Table and Highlights*, Department of Economic and Social Affairs, 2004.

23. Australian Bureau of Statistics, *Population by Age and Sex, Australian States and Territories*, Catalogue no. 3201.0, 17 December 2004.

24. United Nations Population Division, *Annex Tables—World Population Prospects: The 2002 Revision*, Table 7—Percentage Distribution of Population in Selected Age Groups by Country 2000–2050 (medium variant), p. 57.

25. See United Nations, *World Population Prospects: The 2004 Revision, Highlights*, Department of Economic and Social Affairs, 2005.

26. Australian Bureau of Statistics, *Population by Age and Sex, Australian States and Territories*, Catalogue no. 3201.0, 17 December 2004.

27. Robert Dwek, 'The Toyshop—No Place for Children?', *Marketing Week*, 13 June 2002, p. 21; Anonymous, 'Toronto Star Section Targets Tweens', *Marketing Magazine*, 27 January 2003, vol. 108, no. 3, p. 15; Sonia Reyes, 'Tony's Takes New Tack Targeting Pizza to Tweens', *Brandweek*, 13 January 2003, vol. 44, no. 2, p. 5.

28. Christina Cheddar Berk, 'Pepsi Bets on a "Limited Edition" for a Mountain Dew Rollout', *Wall Street Journal*, 12 March 2003, Eastern edition, p. B.9.A; Mark Kleinman, 'Right Guard Links with Extreme Sports Event', *Marketing*, 27 February 2003, p. 6.

29. Dori R. Perrucci, 'Talking 'bout my Generation', *Newsweek*, 24 March 2003, vol. 141, no. 12, p. 61; Anonymous, 'Understanding the GenX Market', *Pension Benefits*, vol. 11, no. 11, November 2002, p. 2; Skip Corsini, 'Bridging the Boomer–Xer Gap', *Training*, vol. 39, no. 11, November 2002, p. 84. See Nathan Cobb, 'Agent X', *Boston Globe*, 28 November 1994, pp. 35, 40.

30. 'Mixed Success: One Who Targeted Gen X and Succeeded—Sort Of,' *Journal of Financial Planning*, February 2004, p. 15.

31. Deborah Hope, 'The I-Want It Now Years', *The Australian*, 31 December 2005, p. 15.

32. See Ken Gronback, 'Marketing to Generation Y,' *DSN Retailing Today*, 24 July 2000, p. 14; and Joanna Krotz, 'Tough Customers: How to Reach Gen Y,' accessed at <www.bcentral.com>, 21 March 2003.

33. Tobi Elkin, 'Gen Y Quizzed about On-Demand', *Advertising Age*, 14 February 2003, p. 37. Also see Pamela Paul, 'Getting Inside Gen Y', *American Demographics*, September 2001, pp. 43–49; Rebecca Gardyn, 'Born to be Wired', *American Demographics*, April 2003, pp. 14–15; 'Teens Spent $175 Billion in 2003', press release, Teenage Research Unlimited, 9 January 2004, accessed at <www.teen-research.com>; and Bernard Salt, 'Slippery Little Suckers', *Business Review Weekly*, 8 December 2005, p. 58.

34. Cris Prystay and Sarah Ellison, 'Time for Marketers to Grow Up?', *Wall Street Journal*, 27 February 2003, Eastern edition, p. B1.

35. David Turner, 'Why Selling to Little People Is No Longer Child's Play', *Financial Times*, 6 June 2005, p. 14.

36. Australian Bureau of Statistics, *Year Book Australia*, 2005.

37. Australian Bureau of Statistics, *Population Projections, Australia, 2002–2101*, 2003.

38. Kathleen Murray, 'Selling to Aging Baby Boomers', *The Australian Financial Review*, 17 January 1996, p. 13.

39. Australian Bureau of Statistics, *Marriages, Australia*, Catalogue no. 3306.0.55.001, 2004.

40. Australian Bureau of Statistics, *Year Book Australia, Population, Households and Families*, 2005.

41. Australian Bureau of Statistics, *Australia Now, Measures of Australia's Progress: Summary Indicators*, 2005.

42. Australian Bureau of Statistics, *Year Book Australia, Labour, Labour Force*, 2005.

43. Australian Bureau of Statistics, *Year Book Australia, Australian Social Trends, Economic Resources, Female/Male Earnings*, 2005.

44. Australian Bureau of Statistics, *Year Book Australia, Population, Households and Families*, 2005.

45. Australian Bureau of Statistics, *Australia Now, Measures of Australia's Progress: Summary Indicators*, 2005.

46. Australian Bureau of Statistics, *Year Book Australia, Population, Geographic Distribution of the Population*, 2005, and Australian Bureau of Statistics, *Australia Now, Measures of Australia's Progress: Summary Indicators*, 2005.

47. Australian Bureau of Statistics, *Year Book Australia, Population, Geographic Distribution of the Population*, 2005.

48. Australian Bureau of Statistics, *Year Book Australia, Australian Social Trends, International Comparisons, Education*, 2005.

49. Australian Bureau of Statistics, *Australia Now, Measures of Australia's Progress: Summary Indicators*, 2005.

50. Australian Bureau of Statistics, *Year Book Australia, Population, International Migration*, 2005.

51. Ibid.

52. Australian Bureau of Statistics, *Year Book Australia, Income and Welfare, Household Income and Wealth*, 2005.

53. Ibid. Also see this catalogue for an explanation of one measure of income equality, the Gini coefficient.

54. See Australian Bureau of Statistics, *Average Weekly Earnings, Australia*, February 2002, Catalogue no. 6302.0.

55. Deirdre Macken, 'As Good as It Gets—Life in the Wealthy Country', *The Australian Financial Review*, 22 October 2005, pp. 17–20; Emma-Kate Symons, 'The Art of Selling Luxury', *The Australian*, 8 July 2005, p. 18.

56. Australian Bureau of Statistics, *Household Expenditure Survey, Australia: Summary of Results*, Catalogue no. 6530.0, August 2005.

57. Rosalie Gardiner, 'Towards Earth Summit Briefing Paper', June 2002, <www.earthsummit2002.org/Es2002.PDF>.

58. Anonymous, 'Nor Any Drop to Drink', Economist.com/Global Agenda, 5 March 2003, p. 1.

59. For more discussion see Michael E. Porter and Claas van der Linde, 'Green and Competitive: Ending the Stalemate', *Harvard Business Review*, September–October 1995, pp. 120–134; William S. Stavropoulos, 'Environmentalism's Third Wave', *Executive Speeches*,

August/September 1996, pp. 28–30; and Stuart L. Hart, 'Beyond Greening: Strategies for a Sustainable World', *Harvard Business Review*, January–February 1997, pp. 67–76.

60. Anonymous, 'Nor Any Drop to Drink', Economist.com/Global Agenda, 5 March 2003, p. 1.
61. Bill Murray, 'BP Doubles Spending on Green Power', *The Australian Financial Review*, 30 November 2005, p. 14.
62. Luke Collins, 'The New Consumers', *The Australian Financial Review*, 14 October 2005, p. 46.
63. Rachel Lebihan, 'Phone Recycling Effort Gets Another Go', *The Australian Financial Review*, 5 December 2005, p. 46.
64. Rachel Lebihan, 'Kyoto, Coming Ready or Not', *The Sydney Morning Herald*, 27 December 2004.
65. Rachel Lebihan, 'Time to Look Well Beyond Kyoto', *The Australian Financial Review*, 16 February 2005.
66. David Stodder, 'Customers Turn the Tides', *Intelligent Enterprise*, 12 August 2002, vol. 5, no. 13, p. 14; Dae-Young Choi, 'Enhancing the Power of Web Search Engines by Means of Fuzzy Query', *Decision Support Systems*, April 2003, vol. 35, no. 1, p. 31. See M. Hanlon, 'The Internet Catalyses a New Renaissance', *Australian Professional Marketing*, December 1995/January 1996, p. 8.
67. Douglas Mulhall, 'The Short Path from Fiction to Science', *The Futurist*, vol. 37, no. 1, January/February 2003, p. 20; Brad Edenn, 'Digital Future: Strategies for the Information Age', *Reference & User Services Quarterly*, vol. 42, no. 1, Fall 2002, p. 89; Gene Bylinsky, 'Technology in the Year 2000', *Fortune*, 18 July 1988, pp. 92–98; and see Bill Gates, *The Road Ahead* (book and CD-ROM), New York, Viking Books, 2001.
68. See 'Increased U.S. R&D Spending Expected in 2004', *Journal of Metals*, vol. 56, no. 3, March 2004, p. 7.
69. Australian Bureau of Statistics, *Year Book Australia, Science and Innovation*, 2006.
70. Matthew Stevens, 'Glaxo Punts on Australian Research', *Business Review Weekly*, 10 April 1992, pp. 60–62; and Gavin Gilchrist, 'Our Gift to the World: A Flu Drug that Works', *The Sydney Morning Herald*, 3 February 1996, p. 1.
71. Anonymous, 'Ucal Ties up with Australian Co for Fuel Injection Tech', *Businessline*, 13 February 2003, p. 1; David Fowler, 'Clean, Lean and Direct', *The Engineer*, vol. 289, no. 7504, 19 May 2000, p. 28.
72. Rhonda L. Smith, 'Possible Implications of the Dawson Inquiry for the ACCC', *The Australian Economic Review*, vol. 35, no. 4, December 2002, p. 446; *Summaries of the Trade Practices Act and the Prices Surveillance Act*, Belconnen, ACT, Commonwealth of Australia, November 1995. Commonwealth of Australia copyright.
73. See Eugene Clark and John Livermore, *Australian Marketing Law*, Sydney, The Law Book Company, 1994.
74. Keith Bradsher, 'Hong Kong Disneyland Is in the Soup', *International Herald Tribune*, 16 June 2005, p. 1.
75. See 'Statement of The Coca-Cola Company to the University of Michigan Board of Regents', <www2.coca-cola.com/presscenter/viewpointsmichigan_bor.html>, accessed 28 January 2006; 'US Universities Boycott Coke', *The Sydney Morning Herald*, 2 January 2006, p. 19.
76. Shelley Emling, 'Banks Vie for Islamic Customers', *Fortune*, 5 September 2005, pp. 16–17.
77. See Diversity Australia case studies at <www.diversityaustralia.gov.au/employer/03.htm>, accessed 28 January 2006.
78. For a discussion of the causes and results of consumer buzz see Malcolm Gladwell, *The Tipping Point*, London, Abacus, 2000; and Emanuel Rosen, *Anatomy of Buzz: Creating Word-of-Mouth Marketing*, New York, Profile Books, 2001.
79. P. Kotler, *Marketing Insights from A to Z*, Hoboken, NJ, John Wiley & Sons, 2003, pp. 23–24.
80. Howard E. Butz Jr and Leonard D. Goodstein, 'Measuring Customer Value: Gaining the Strategic Advantage', *Organizational Dynamics*, Winter 1996, pp. 66–67.

PHOTO/AD CREDITS

CASE STUDY

The 'alternative' marketplace: marketing wellbeing

From Feng Shui, crystal healings, psychic readings and yoga to mind power exercises and organic products, the annual 'Mind, Body, Spirit Festival' in Sydney and Melbourne features a myriad of 'alternative living options' (<www.mbsfestival. com.au>, accessed 10 January 2006) that cater to the wellbeing of consumers. The Vitality Expo, a sister festival especially catering to the health and lifestyle needs of 'today's urban women' (<www.vitalityexpo.com.au>, accessed 10 January 2006), features a variety of fitness, beauty and health solutions targeted to a primary market of professional urban women aged 25–45. These two festivals are evidence of an 'alternative' marketplace so diverse and loose that it is difficult to define its boundaries and characteristics.

Holistic health therapies such as naturopathy and aromatherapy, alternative health treatments such as kinesiology and Ayurveda, personal growth products from Anthony Robbins and Deepak Chopra on realising one's potential in life and even Christian books that are popular secularly such as Rick Warren's *A Purpose-driven Life* are indicative of a thriving industry which caters to the contemporary consumer— a consumer who is not only concerned with quality of life and wellbeing, but is willing to

experiment with alternative options rather than sticking to traditional mainstream medicine. Baby boomers, generation Xers (those born between 1965 and 1976) and females tend to make up the consumers in this type of market.

Global trends: a cultural change to health

Research conducted in the USA indicates that more Americans are now visiting holistic rather than general practitioners (Macgregor, 2001). Holistic therapies such as chiropractic, oriental medicine and homeopathy are among the most common ones used. This trend is also occurring in the UK where legislation has been passed to include osteopathy and chiropractic in the National Health Scheme (Australian Pharmacy Trade, 2001). A research report also found more and more UK patients moving towards holistic therapies after becoming disenchanted with medical practitioners. These trends are mirrored in Australia where around 60% of Australians use alternative healthcare (Miraudo, 2002) after failing to find mainstream avenues effective. These statistics are indicative of a much larger shift in the cultural environment. Consumers' values, mindsets and attitudes towards quality of life and wellbeing have shifted somewhat from a traditional reliance on science and medicine to 'naturalness', 'holistic', 'organic' and 'wholesome' experiences that seek to fulfil the mind, body and spirit. A report issued by Grey Worldwide (cited in Plaskitt, 2004) found that Australians want more spiritual fulfilment and meaning in their lives, and are willing to spend more money on relaxation. It is frequently a common characteristic of a modern society like Australia that has enjoyed sophisticated technologies and a high quality of life achieved through hard work that its people now want to spend more time relaxing and finding meaning through the use of 'alternative' treatments. Despite the lack of a

Source: <www.vitalityexpo.com.au>; the company behind the exhibition is DMG World Media Australia Pty Ltd, <www.dmgworldmedia.com.au>, accessed on 13 January 2006.

CASE
STUDY

scientific base (*The Australian*, 2002) and the 'loose' regulations governing the practice of herbal and alternative therapies, many consumers believe that natural medicines are 'less toxic' (Miraudo, 2002) and there is constant tension between what is reported 'medically' and what is 'naturally claimed'.

The industry

The industry comprises several sectors, while other sectors previously not operating within the industry have jumped at the opportunity to capitalise on the growing emphasis on health and wellbeing. The dynamics of the industry are discussed below.

Health retailers and practitioners

The alternative therapy industry in Australia is reported to be growing at a rate of 30% each year (Owens, 2005), accompanied by a $1 billion spend by Australian consumers, and is used by half of the population (*Choice*, 2001). This is backed up by health retailers such as Go Vita and GNC, where figures show that the alternative retail sector is growing strongly (Nichols, 2005). The industry consists of health stores that typically stock vitamins and healthcare products, organic produce stores that often stock vitamins as well as offering services like massage and iridology, New Age stores that stock crystals, spells and jewellery, and independent clinics/centres that provide specific services such as kinesiology, chiropractic and Feldenkrais. Stores can also be found online, coupled with portals and informational websites. Aside from vitamins, they stock herbal and/or natural products ranging from common garlic to more exotic products such as Tahitian noni juice (www.tahitiannoni. com), New Zealand Manuka Honey (www. comvita.com), Hawaiian spirulina (www.nutrex-hawaii.com) and Chinese ganoderma mushrooms (www.concordhealth.com.au).

Day spa service providers

Even the spa industry, which is technically part of the leisure industry (Benton and Jordan, 2000), has branched out to offer more holistic aspects

Keturah Day Spa in Perth offers day spa services ranging from stone therapy, Russian steam bath, Dead Sea mud wrap, the ancient Ayurvedic practice of Shirodhara, flotation tanks and Hawaiian Lomi Lomi massage.
Source: <www.keturah.com.au>, accessed 13 January 2006.

of healthcare combined with a pampering experience to help busy executives de-stress. The concepts of a 'day spa' (for example, <www. keturah.com.au> in Perth, <www.angsanaspa. com> in Sydney and worldwide) and 'health retreats' (www.goldendoor.com.au) continue to gain popularity among consumers with their hybrid mix of alternative health treatments, beauty regimes like cold/hot stone therapy, aromatherapy and massage, including traditional Thai, Japanese Shiatsu, Swedish and Hawaiian Lomi Lomi.

Spa and health retreats

The popularity of day spas has extended to more elaborate 'spa destinations' in which players overseas have capitalised on this lucrative market opportunity. The internationally renowned spa, Chiva-Som (www.chivasom.com) in Hua Hin, Thailand, has an 'academy' that offer courses in spa management as well as training that enables its graduates to practise on customers with health problems (Siripunyawit, 2004). 'Health trips', 'beauty holidays' and even 'anti-ageing holidays' are also reportedly on the increase among Europeans and residents of other industrialised, developed and economically advanced countries where millions are being spent in pursuit of 'good health' (Muqbil, 2004). Many providers of these holidays are to be found in Asian countries like Indonesia, Sri Lanka, Thailand, China and India which are famous for their massage and ancient therapies such as Ayurveda, Qi-Gong and Yoga.

Spiritual providers

A slightly different sector of the industry focuses more on the spiritual and/or motivational and personal growth aspects of a person. This sector is situated in the domain of religion and spirituality which is targeted towards the holistic wellbeing of the 'soul'. Players in this sector include Deepak Chopra (www.chopra.com), Gary Zukav (www.zukav.com), Anthony Robbins (www.anthonyrobbins.com) and Shakti Gawain (www.shaktigawain.com). The spread of Eastern religious traditions in the West has also seen the burgeoning growth of such practices as Yoga and meditation, often perceived as 'alternative' in a foreign culture.

In summary, the trends are positive in fuelling demand for these alternative treatments and services. There is, however, concern over the lack of regulations and scientific evidence for many of these natural medicine and alternative treatments. For example, the medical profession has questioned the practice of 'ear candling', stating that there is no medical evidence to support the claims it is effective, and that it could be dangerous (Hunter, 2005). Alternative health therapists in Indonesia range from licensed acupuncturists to paranormal healers who often are not endorsed by the Ministry of Health (Kennedy, 2004). These practices can be dangerous or misleading but still continue to attract customers. Cultural reasons are often cited as the main motivator, as many of these practices have long been part of the local culture and history blended with ancient teachings and religious practices. And many of these practices still prove popular, even when imported to a foreign country.

In Australia, the National Herbalists Association claims to have evidence showing the effec-

tiveness and safety of alternative medicine when used by a trained practitioner (*The Australian*, 2002). The importance of accreditation of practitioners (e.g. with the Australian Traditional Medicine Society), being covered by insurance and discouraging people from trying to treat themselves without seeking professional help (Australian Institute of Holistic Medicine, cited in Miraudo 2002) is being advocated to help ensure safe practice within the industry. In spite of these reservations, this eclectic industry is currently thriving and seems to be appealing to the modern consumer who would like to manage their health and wellbeing.

Conclusion

If this trend continues, what are the implications for marketers who are already in this industry and others who may enter? In this 'alternative' marketplace 'wellbeing', 'health management', 'disease prevention', 'holistic living' and 'living to your full potential' are marketed, to take advantage of the underlying shift in consumers' mindsets and attitudes. Ancient health practices from other cultures, New Age practices that tap into the spiritual and a mix of beauty and soul therapies are proving popular with today's 'alternative' consumer. This has given rise to an industry filled with eager players taking advantage of changing trends.

Sources: 'Alternative Therapies: Do They Help?', *Choice*, 1 September 2001, p. 18; N. Benton and D. Jordan, 'Spa Turn', *Australian Leisure Management*, 1 October 2000, pp. 32–33; 'Concern Lingers over Herb Therapies', *The Australian*, 28 February 2002, p. 4; E. Hunter, 'Worth Waxing Lyrical About?', *The Herald*, 7 February 2005, p. 10; D. Kennedy, 'Traditional Approach to Healing Ripe for Change', *The Jakarta Post*, 21 March 2004, p. 6; 'Lords See Alternative for NHS', *Australian Pharmacy Trade*, 8 February 2001, p. 8; J. Macgregor, 'The Alternative Reality', *The Age*, 22 October 2001, p. B4; N. Miraudo, 'A $1b Natural High', *The Sunday Times*, 3 March 2002, p. 15; I. Muqbil, 'Soul Searching: Stressed Fat Cats Fuel New Industry', *The Bangkok Post*, 4 April 2004, p. 3; S. Nichols, 'A Retail Sector That's Full of Vim and Vigour', *The Australian Financial Review*, 24 February 2005, p. 13; S. Owens, 'Alternative Treatment Is in the Pink of Health', *The Australian Financial Review*, 25 June 2005, p. L8; S. Plaskitt, 'Tapping into Wellbeing', *B&T Weekly*, 23 April 2004, p. 4; S. Siripunyawit, 'Preparing for Spa Success; Entrepreneurs: New Entrant Bases Business Model on Careful Market Research and Professionalism', *The Bangkok Post*, 29 March 2004, p. B12.

CASE STUDY

QUESTIONS

1. How could marketers of other products take advantage of this cultural shift towards wellbeing? List two opportunities.

2. Why do you think enhancing one's wellbeing through alternative means is a popular trend?

3. Do you think this new emphasis on wellbeing is related to the other environments (e.g. demographic, economic, technological or political)?

4. How has this cultural shift towards wellbeing influenced the way consumers view themselves? Organisations? Nature?

5. What do you think is the typical profile of an 'alternative' consumer?

CHAPTER 6

Information management and marketing research

ACNielsen: www.acnielsen.com

Hitwise: www.hitwise.com

Jupiter Research:
www.jupiterresearch.com

LexisNexis: www.lexisnexis.com

Perhaps the two most famous market research failures of all time both relate to the Coca-Cola Company, and they tell us a lot about potential problems in market research. The first dates back to 1985, when Coca-Cola famously dropped its original formula Coke and replaced it with the sweeter tasting New Coke. Coke was responding to a steady drift of market share to Pepsi, and to Pepsi's successful ads featuring the 'Pepsi Challenge', a series of televised taste tests showing that consumers preferred the sweeter taste of Pepsi. By early 1985, although Coke led in the overall market, Pepsi led in share of supermarket sales by 2%. (That doesn't sound like much, but 2% of the huge soft drink market amounts to $US960 million in retail sales.) Coca-Cola had to do something to stop the loss of its market share, and the solution appeared to be a change in Coke's taste.

Coca-Cola began the largest new-product research project in the company's history. It spent more than two years and $US4 million on research before settling on a new formula. It conducted some 200 000 taste tests—30 000 on the final formula alone. In blind tests, 60% of consumers chose New Coke over the old, and 52% chose it over Pepsi. Research showed that New Coke would be a winner and the company introduced it with confidence.

At first, New Coke sold well. But sales soon went flat as a stunned public reacted. Coke began receiving sacks of mail and more than 1500 phone calls each day from angry consumers. A group called 'Old Cola Drinkers' staged protests, handed out T-shirts and threatened a class action suit unless Coca-Cola brought back the old formula. After just three months Coca-Cola gave in and brought old Coke back, at first labelled 'Coke Classic', selling side by side with New Coke on supermarket shelves. The company said that New Coke would remain its 'flagship' brand, but consumers had a different idea. By the end of 1985 Classic was outselling New Coke in supermarkets by two to one. By mid-1986 the company's two largest 'postmix' (that is, mixed after selling) accounts, McDonald's and KFC, had returned to serving Coke Classic in their restaurants, and some time later New Coke was dropped from Coke's product line.

Why was New Coke introduced in the first place? What went wrong? Many analysts blame the blunder on poor marketing research. Looking back, we can see that Coke's marketing research was too narrowly focused.

The research only looked at taste; it did not explore consumers' feelings about dropping the old Coke and replacing it with a new version. It took no account of the intangibles—Coke's name, history, packaging, cultural heritage and image. For many of its buyers, Coke stands alongside baseball, hotdogs and apple pie as an American institution, and represents the very fabric of America. Coke's symbolic meaning turned out to be more important to many consumers than its taste. More complete marketing research would have detected these strong emotions.

Coke's managers may also have used poor judgment in interpreting the research and planning strategies around it. For example, they took the finding that 60% of consumers preferred New Coke's taste to mean that the new product would win in the marketplace—as when a political candidate wins with 60% of the vote. But it also meant that 40% still

Some bottled water is purified tap water, and some is spring water. Dasani in the UK had problems trying to sell purified tap water.

liked the old Coke. By dropping the old Coke, the company trampled on the taste buds of the large core of loyal Coke drinkers who didn't want a change. The company might have been wiser to leave the old Coke alone and introduce New Coke as a brand extension, as was later done successfully with Cherry Coke and Coke with vanilla.[1]

New Coke might be just an interesting historical example, if Coke hadn't stumbled again badly in 2004, launching a new brand of bottled water, Dasani, in the UK. Like Dasani in the USA, the Dasani was purified tap water, not the spring water that Europeans are used to drinking. But Coke did market research and its focus groups told the company that consumers would pay for purified tap water. That may have been true, except the British media realised there was a story, and headlines appeared in British newspapers highlighting the fact: 'The Real Sting' said the *Sun*, and 'Coke sells tap water' headlined the *Mirror*. Coke may have been able to ride out the massive bad publicity, but was hit again by a health scandal when it was discovered that the 'pure water' was contaminated with the chemical bromate, which could increase the risk of cancer. Coke was forced to recall all its stock, and withdrew the brand from the UK market. Plans to launch in France and Germany (where the product would have been sourced from springs) were shelved, though Coke hasn't ruled out reintroducing the drink to the UK at a later date.[2]

Faced with falling sales of soft drinks, Coke will have to relaunch a water in the UK at some stage. But meanwhile, its profits have fallen, and in the latest indignity its share price fell to almost $US41 in December 2005 (down from $US88 in 1998) with the result that the market capitalisation of Pepsi became larger than Coke.[3]

The Coca-Cola Company has one of the largest, best managed and most advanced marketing research operations in America. Good marketing research has kept the company atop the rough-and-tumble soft drink market for decades. But marketing research is far from an exact science. If Coca-Cola can make a large marketing research mistake, and then another one some years later, any company can, and its dual failure emphasises the importance of good design of market research and information systems. In this chapter we discuss the principles underlying the collection and interpretation of relevant marketing information, hopefully helping other companies to avoid problems like Coca-Cola's!

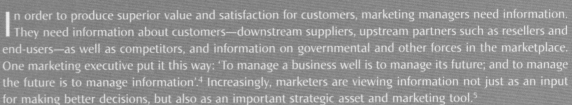

After reading this chapter you should be able to:

1. Explain the concept of the marketing information system, emphasising ways of assessing information needs, the sources used for developing information and ways of distributing information.

2. Outline the marketing research process, including defining the problem and research objectives and developing the research plan.

3. Discuss the key issues of planning primary data collection, implementing the research plan and interpreting and reporting the findings.

In order to produce superior value and satisfaction for customers, marketing managers need information. They need information about customers—downstream suppliers, upstream partners such as resellers and end-users—as well as competitors, and information on governmental and other forces in the marketplace. One marketing executive put it this way: 'To manage a business well is to manage its future; and to manage the future is to manage information'.[4] Increasingly, marketers are viewing information not just as an input for making better decisions, but also as an important strategic asset and marketing tool.[5]

For most of the twentieth century the majority of marketing organisations were small and knew their customers first-hand. Managers picked up marketing information by being around people, observing them and asking questions. During the latter part of the twentieth century, however, competition increased, and the growing use of computers resulted in the need for more and better information. This trend is accelerating as the new millennium progresses. As marketing organisations become national or international in scope, they need more information on larger, more distant markets. As incomes increase and buyers become more selective, sellers need better information about how buyers respond to different products and appeals. As sellers use more complex marketing approaches and face more competition, they need information on the effectiveness of their marketing tools. Finally, in today's rapidly changing environments, managers need more up-to-date information to make timely decisions.

The supply of information has also increased greatly. In fact, today's managers sometimes receive too much information. For example, one study found that with all the marketing organisations offering data, and with all the information now available through supermarket scanners, a packaged goods product manager can be bombarded with one million to one billion new numbers each week.[6] As Naisbitt points out: 'Running out of information is not a problem, but drowning in it is'.[7]

Yet marketers frequently complain that they lack information of the right kind or have too much of the wrong kind. Or marketing information is so widely spread throughout the organisation that it takes great effort to locate even simple facts. Subordinates may withhold information they believe will reflect badly on their performance. Important information often arrives too late to be useful, or on-time information is not accurate. So marketing managers need more and better information. Marketing organisations have greater capacity to provide managers with information but often have not made good use of it. Many marketing organisations are now studying their managers' information needs and designing information systems to meet those needs.

The marketing information system

A **marketing information system (MIS)** consists of people, equipment and procedures to gather, sort, analyse, evaluate and distribute needed, timely and accurate information to marketing decision makers. The marketing information system concept is illustrated in Figure 6.1. The MIS begins and ends with marketing managers. First, it interacts with these managers to assess their information needs. Next, it develops the needed information from internal organisation records, marketing intelligence activities and the marketing research process. Information analysis processes the information to make it more useful. Finally, the MIS distributes information to managers in the right form and at the right time to help them make better marketing decisions.

Marketing information system (MIS) People, equipment and procedures to gather, sort, analyse, evaluate and distribute needed, timely and accurate information to marketing decision makers.

Assessing information needs

A good MIS balances the information managers would like to have against what they really need and what it is feasible to acquire or monitor. The organisation begins by interviewing managers to find out what information they would like. Figure 6.2 (on page 207) lists a useful set of questions. But managers do not always need all the information they ask for, and they may not ask for all they really need. Moreover, the MIS cannot always supply all the information managers request.

Some managers will ask for whatever information they can get without thinking carefully about what they really need. Collecting and analysing information can be expensive in staff time and money, and if there is too much information the most important information may be overlooked. The presentation of the data often affects their use, and if information is easily available and well presented it can assist greatly in interpretation (see Marketing Highlight 6.1). This is one reason for the rise of 'distributed data processing', whereby software on desktop computers is now more widely used to capture and manipulate data and then later to present them to other managers.

Sometimes managers may not know to ask for some information they should have. For instance, how does a manager know to ask consumers what they think about a competitor's new product if there has been no monitoring of the competitor's activity, and the organisation is unaware of the new product? The MIS must watch the marketing environment and provide decision makers with information they should have in order to make key marketing decisions. Such an early warning

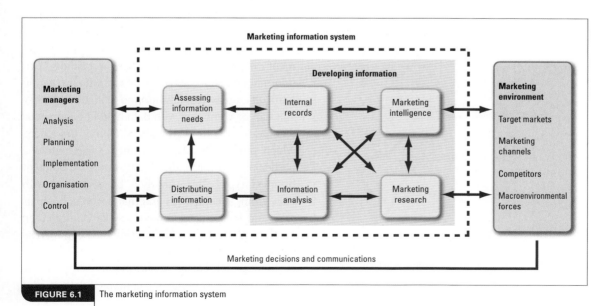

FIGURE 6.1 The marketing information system

Show me the data!

Executive information systems rely on computers to gather data, manipulate the data and then present the output as information that can help executives to make better decisions. Perhaps you are thinking of setting up a new childcare centre or restaurant, and are trying to decide between a few potential locations which are all available at approximately the same price. What would help you to decide? Well, it would be useful to know who lives near your possible locations—their age, number of children, income. You'd also like to know how easy it would be for customers from outside the immediate vicinity to get there—how about knowing who lives within a 15 minute driving distance. And of course, you'd like to know where your competitors are.

Government statistical departments and a range of private providers like ACNielsen, MapData Sciences and Channel Marketing Decisions provide raw data, and also visual representation of much of the information needed by decision makers to plot customer and competitor location. Data like these are invaluable in order to estimate potential competition and demand, decide on locations, and on which locations to expand and which locations might not be worth long-term investment. These sort of data are used by a range of organisations to locate and plan their services. Car companies use these data to locate dealerships and customer service centres, maximising market coverage while also allowing the dealers to maximise revenue and profits. Banks and fuel companies use these data to locate their outlets close to changing catchment areas for their target markets.

Graphical analysis of information can also do much more. It can be used to decide on the best location for outdoor advertising, to maximise the number of people who drive or walk past billboards. It can be used in customer service centres to locate customers on the basis of their postcode, to identify their nearest service location and to provide driving instructions. Using a service such as MapData Sciences, a company can provide a map on its website, and allow a customer to obtain personalised driving directions to visit the business.

Need to know where the next delivery load is? The use of location technology, such as geo satellite applications and RFID (radio frequency identification devices), combined with data visualisation services, allows tracking of deliveries and components within a delivery. Visualisation services can be used for route planning for delivery drivers or to provide driving instructions in a rental car.

So where does the data come from? Data in mapping systems come from a range of sources: census data are obtained from the relevant government department of statistics, providing rich information about the type of people who live within particular areas (usually around 250 households). This can be combined with data held in commercial databases such as LexisNexis or Dun & Bradstreet, which provide details on business types within a particular area and indicative turnover for different business types. This can then be combined with data from a company's internal records, such as sales and service data. Companies like MapInfo then combine all the types of data using their commercial software and visually present them to their clients, customised for each specific inquiry. Why is one outlet underperforming? The combined data sources

Private providers sell a variety of data on customer characteristics and behaviour.

Source: MapData Sciences Pty Ltd: <www.mapds.com.au>

can be used to look for patterns, to identify problems and to suggest solutions. A fast-food outlet might appear to be well located, but may be located near another outlet which provides more convenient access. Perhaps the area doesn't get much passing traffic, so not many people in the area are aware of it. Awareness of the outlet could be increased by a letter-box drop of a discount coupon, and the result assessed. If the problem is lack of awareness, a coupon offer is likely to result in increased business and a sustained increase in business after the expiry of the coupon offer. If the problem is lack of convenient access, a coupon is less likely to be successful and less likely to result in an ongoing increase in business.

The use of data visualisation is continuing to increase, as computer power improves. Google Maps (www.maps.google.com) already allows visual searching and location of businesses for North American customers, and is likely to be rolled out to other locations before too long. With Google's huge computing power and investment in research and development, Google may soon be providing powerful competition to the other mapware companies.

Marketing information systems can take many forms and use many types of input data. One thing is certain though—staying connected with customers in the future will mean greater use of all sorts of visualisation systems.

Sources: Kath Walters, 'Position Perfect', *Business Review Weekly*, 18 August 2005, p. 26; MapInfo Corporation, <www.mapinfo.com> (see the MapXtreme demonstration at <www.ithacamaps.org>); Channel Marketing Decisions, <www.channelmarketing.com.au>; MapData Sciences, <www.mapds.com.au/>; Australian Bureau of Statistics, <www.abs.gov.au>; Statistics New Zealand, <www.stats.govt.nz/>; <www.earth.google.com>; <www.maps.google.com>.

Questions

1 Use of data by companies often raises privacy concerns. What actions could a company take to prevent and/or respond to customer concerns about privacy?

2 Why is visualising data seemingly so important to decision makers, when similar data can be obtained from spreadsheets? What are the advantages and disadvantages of visual displays versus detailed spreadsheets?

6.1

1. What types of decisions are you regularly called upon to make?
2. What types of information do you need to make these decisions?
3. What types of information do you regularly get?
4. What types of special studies do you periodically request?
5. What types of information would you like to get that you are not now getting?
6. What information would you want daily? Weekly? Monthly? Yearly?
7. What magazine and trade reports would you like to see on a regular basis?
8. What specific topics would you like to be kept informed of?
9. What types of data analysis programs would you like to see made available?
10. What do you think would be the four most helpful improvements that could be made in the present marketing information system?

FIGURE 6.2 Questions for assessing marketing information needs

and monitoring system is sometimes called an executive information system (EIS) (see Marketing Highlight 6.1).

Sometimes the organisation cannot provide the needed information because it is not available or because of MIS limitations. For example, a product manager might want to know how much competitors will change their advertising budgets next year and how these changes will affect industry market shares. The information on planned budgets is probably not available. Even if it is, the organisation's MIS may not be advanced enough to forecast resulting changes in market shares.

Finally, the organisation must decide whether the benefits of having an item of information are worth the costs of providing it, and both value and cost are often hard to assess. By itself, information has no worth—its value comes from its use. Although methods have been developed for calculating the value of information, decision makers must often rely on subjective judgment.[8] Similarly, although an organisation can total the costs of an MIS or the costs of a marketing research project, working out the cost of a specific information item may be difficult.

The costs of obtaining, processing, storing and delivering information can mount quickly. In many cases additional information will do little to change or improve a manager's decision, or the costs of the information will exceed the returns from the improved decision. For example, suppose an organisation estimates that launching a new product without any further information will yield a profit of $500 000. The manager believes that additional information will improve the marketing mix and allow the organisation to make $525 000. Paying $40 000 for the extra information would be foolish.

Developing information

Information needed by marketing managers can be obtained from internal organisation records, marketing intelligence and marketing research. The information analysis system then processes this information to make it more useful to managers.

Internal records

Most marketing managers use internal organisation records and reports regularly, especially for making day-to-day planning, implementation and control decisions. Each section of an organisation typically keeps records which can help marketing managers make better decisions. The organisation's accounting department prepares financial statements and keeps detailed records of sales and orders, costs and cash flows. The operations department reports on production schedules, inward and outward stock and work-in-progress movements and inventories. The salesforce reports on reseller reactions and competitor activities. Information on service quality levels and reported service difficulties are recorded by the customer service centre or department. The marketing department maintains a database or electronic links to a database of customer demographics, psychographics and buying behaviour. Research studies done for one department may provide useful information for several others. Managers can use information gathered from these and other sources within the organisation to evaluate performance and to detect problems and opportunities.

Consider the following example of the use of internal records by the global snackfoods marketer Frito-Lay:

Frito-Lay uses its sophisticated internal information system to analyse daily sales performance. Each day, Frito-Lay's salespeople report their day's efforts via hand-held computers into Frito-Lay head office. Twenty-four hours later, Frito-Lay's marketing managers have a complete report analysing the previous day's sales of Doritos and other brands. The system helps marketing managers make better decisions and makes the salespeople more effective. It greatly reduces the number of hours spent filling out reports, giving salespeople extra time for selling. Frito-Lay's sales might thus increase without the addition of a single salesperson.

Internal records can usually be obtained more quickly and cheaply than other information sources, but they also present some problems. Because internal records contain information collected for other purposes, they may be incomplete or in the wrong form for making marketing decisions. For this reason, the information may offer little competitive advantage unless it is summarised and presented in a form which is accessible to, and useful for, decision makers. For example, the accounting department uses sales and cost data to prepare financial statements; however, this information must be adapted for use by marketers who are evaluating product, salesforce or channel performance. In addition, large organisations produce vast amounts of information and keeping track of it all is difficult. The MIS must gather, organise, process and index this mountain of information so that managers can find it easily and quickly.

Internal records
Information gathered from sources within the company to evaluate marketing performance and to detect marketing problems and opportunities.

Marketing intelligence

Marketing intelligence is the systematic collection and analysis of publicly available information about competitors and developments in the marketplace. The goal of marketing intelligence is to improve strategic decision making, assess and track competitors' actions and provide early warning of opportunities and threats.

Marketing intelligence
Systematic collection and analysis of publicly available information about competitors and developments in the marketplace.

Marketing intelligence can be gathered from many sources. Much intelligence can be collected from the organisation's own personnel—executives, purchasing agents and the salesforce. But these people are often busy and may fail to pass on important information. The organisation must 'sell' its people on their importance as intelligence gatherers, train them to spot new developments and urge them to report intelligence back to the organisation. The organisation must also get suppliers, resellers and customers to pass along important intelligence. This can be made easier and faster by modern extranets, where customers and suppliers are linked via web-based technology to secure websites.

The organisation can learn about competitors from what others say about them in business publications and at trade shows. Or the organisation can watch what competitors do—including buying and analysing their products, monitoring their sales and checking for new patents. Competitors may also reveal intelligence about themselves through their annual reports, business publications, trade show exhibits, press releases, advertisements and web pages. The Internet is proving to be a vast new source of competitor-supplied information. Most companies now place volumes of information on their websites, providing details to attract customers, partners, suppliers or franchisees. Using Internet search engines, marketers can search specific competitor names, events or trends and see what turns up.[9]

Marketing organisations also buy intelligence information from outside suppliers. For example, the ACNielsen company sells data on brand shares, retail prices and percentages of stores stocking different brands. It also sells reports on weekly movements of brand shares, size, prices and deals. For a fee, marketing organisations can subscribe to online databases or information search services. For example, Nielsen Media Research (www.nielsenmedia.com.au) provides information such as radio ratings and direct mail activity, while OzTAM (www.oztam.com.au) is the official source of metropolitan television audience ratings data in Australia. Marketing organisations can use these data to assess their own and competitors' advertising strategies and styles, shares of advertising space, media usage and ad budgets.

Service firms such as Marketing Channels collect demographic data from the Australian Census and then add their own demographic projections by state, city or postcode. Marketing organisations can use this information to measure markets and develop segmentation strategies. Sensis provides the Yellow Pages Online (www.yellowpages.com.au), which contains listings of the nation's telephone numbers as well as separate listings of subscribing company website URLs. Firms such as Hungry Jack's might use these databases to count McDonald's restaurants in different geographical locations or search for websites maintained by competitors. A readily available online database exists to fill almost any marketing information need. For a fee, companies can subscribe to any of more than 3000 online databases and information search services such as Dialog, DataStar, LexisNexis, Dow Jones News Retrieval, UMI ProQuest and Dun & Bradstreet's Online Access.

Some companies have even rifled their competitors' garbage, which is legally considered abandoned property once it leaves the premises. In one garbage snatching incident, Oracle was caught rifling through rival Microsoft's waste bins. In another case, Procter & Gamble (P&G) admitted to 'dumpster diving' at rival Unilever's headquarters. The target was Unilever's haircare products, which compete with P&G's Pantene, Head & Shoulders and Pert brands. 'Apparently, the operation was a big success,' notes an analyst. 'P&G got its mitts on just about every iota of info there was to be had about Unilever's brands.' However, when news of the questionable tactics reached top P&G managers, they were shocked. They immediately stopped the project, voluntarily informed Unilever and set up negotiations to right whatever competitive wrongs had been done. Although P&G claims it broke no laws, the company reported that the dumpster raids 'violated our strict guidelines regarding our business policies.'[10]

The intelligence game goes both ways. Facing determined marketing intelligence efforts by competitors, most companies are now taking steps to protect their own information. For example, Unilever has begun widespread competitive intelligence training. According to a former Unilever staffer, 'We were told how to protect information, as well as how to get it from competitors. We were warned to always keep our mouths shut when travelling . . . We were even warned that spies from competitors could be posing as drivers at the mini-cab company we used.' Unilever even performs random checks on internal security. Says the former staffer, 'At one [internal marketing] conference, we were set up when an actor was employed to infiltrate the group. The idea was to see who spoke to him, how much they told him, and how long it took to realize that no one knew him. He ended up being there for a long time.'[11]

The growing use of marketing intelligence raises a number of ethical issues. Although most of the preceding techniques are legal, and some are considered to be shrewdly competitive, some may involve questionable ethics. Clearly, companies should take advantage of publicly available information. But with all the legitimate intelligence sources now available, a company does not have to break the law or accepted codes of ethics to get good intelligence.

Marketing research

Managers cannot always wait for information to arrive in bits and pieces from the MIS. They often require formal studies of specific situations. For example, HP wants to know how many and what kinds of people or marketing organisations will buy its servers and desktops. Australian universities need to know what percentage of their domestic and overseas target markets have heard of them, what they know, how they heard about the university and how they feel about it. In such situations the MIS will not provide the detailed information needed. Managers will need formal marketing research such as that provided by Hitwise (www.hitwise.com.au) that allows them to see where their website visitors came from and where they went after viewing a particular website.

Marketing research The function that links the consumer, customer and public to the marketer through information— information used to identify and define marketing opportunities and problems; to generate, refine and evaluate marketing actions; to monitor marketing performance; and to improve understanding of the marketing process.

We define **marketing research** as the function that links the consumer, customer and public to the marketer through information. It is used to identify and define marketing opportunities and problems; to generate, refine and evaluate marketing actions; to monitor marketing performance; and to improve understanding of the marketing process.[12] Marketing research provides the information needed to address marketing issues, and involves designing the method for collecting information, managing and implementing the data collection process, analysing the results and communicating the findings and their implications to decision makers.

An organisation can do marketing research itself or have some or all of it done outside. Most large marketing organisations have their own marketing research departments, but even large marketing organisations with their own departments often use outside groups to do special research tasks or special studies.

Many people think of marketing research as a lengthy, formal process carried out by large marketing organisations. While small businesses may say that they are not involved in marketing research, almost any organisation can find informal, low-cost alternatives to the formal and complex marketing research techniques used by research experts in large firms. If there is a weakness in the use of marketing research, however, it is the difficulty of relating marketing performance and financial outcomes to specific expenditure on marketing research.[13]

Information analysis

Information gathered by the company's marketing intelligence and marketing research systems often requires more analysis, and sometimes managers need more help to apply the information to their marketing problems and decisions. This help may include advanced statistical analysis to learn more about both the relationships within a set of data and their statistical reliability. Such analysis allows managers to answer such questions as:

- What are the major variables affecting my sales and how important is each one?
- What are the best variables for segmenting my market, and how many segments exist?
- What are the best predictors of which consumers are likely to buy my brand versus my competitor's brand?
- If I raised my price 10% and increased my advertising expenditure 20%, what would happen to sales?

Information analysis might also involve a collection of mathematical models that will help marketers make better decisions. Each model represents some real system, process or outcome. These models can help answer the questions of 'what if?' and 'which is best?'. During the past 20 years marketing scientists have developed numerous models to help marketing managers make better marketing mix decisions, design sales territories and sales-call plans, select sites for retail outlets, develop optimal advertising mixes and forecast new-product sales.[14]

Distributing information

Marketing information has no value until managers use it to make better marketing decisions. The information gathered through marketing intelligence and marketing research must be distributed to the right marketing managers at the right time. Most companies have centralised MISs that provide managers with regular performance reports and intelligence updates and reports. Managers need these routine reports for making regular planning, implementation and control decisions. But marketing managers might also need non-routine information for special situations and on-the-spot decisions. For example, a sales manager having trouble with a large customer may want a summary of the account's sales and profitability over the past year. Or a retail store manager who has run out of a best-selling product may want to know the current inventory levels in the chain's other stores. Increasingly, therefore, modern marketing organisations have **distributed marketing information systems** which involve entering information into databases and making it available in a user-friendly and timely way.

Many firms use a company *intranet* to facilitate this process. The intranet provides ready access to research information, stored reports, shared work documents, contact information for employees and other stakeholders, and more. For example, one catalogue and web retailer integrates incoming customer service calls with up-to-date database information about customers' web purchases and

Distributed marketing information systems Internal and external information can be obtained, over digital networks, even around the world.

email inquiries. By accessing this information on the intranet while speaking with the customer, the service representatives can get a well-rounded picture of each customer's purchasing history and previous contacts with the company.

In addition, companies are increasingly allowing key customers and value-network members to access account, product and other data on demand through *extranets*. Suppliers, customers, resellers and select other network members may access a company's extranet to update their accounts, arrange purchases and check orders against inventories to improve customer service. For example, one insurance firm allows its 200 independent agents access to a web-based database of claim information covering one million customers. This allows the agents to avoid high-risk customers and to compare claim data with their own customer databases. And Wal-Mart stores around the globe use the Retail Link system, which provides suppliers with up to two years worth of data on how their products have sold in Wal-Mart stores.[15]

Thanks to modern technology, today's marketing managers can gain direct access to the information system at any time and from virtually any location. They can tap into the system while working at a home office, from a hotel room or wherever they can turn on a laptop and link up. Such systems allow managers to get the information they need directly and quickly and to tailor it to their own needs. From just about anywhere, they can obtain information from company or outside databases, analyse it using statistical software, prepare reports and presentations, and communicate directly with others in the network.

SELF-CHECK QUESTIONS

1 Internal records can supply information quickly, but do they always provide a complete picture of the marketplace?

2 Marketing intelligence is everyday information about developments in the marketing environment. How useful are employees such as salespeople in gathering this information?

3 if it's not illegal to go through competitors' rubbish, why do you think P&G stopped doing this and apologised to Unilever?

The marketing research process

The marketing research process (see Figure 6.3) consists of four steps: defining the problem and the research objectives, designing the research, implementing the research plan and interpreting and reporting the findings.

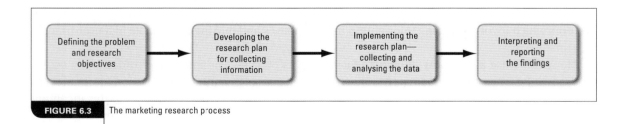

FIGURE 6.3   The marketing research process

Defining the problem and the research objectives

The marketing manager and the researcher must work closely together to define the problem carefully and agree on the research objectives. The manager best understands what information is needed; the researcher best understands marketing research and how to obtain the information.

Managers must know enough about marketing research to help in the planning and interpretation of research results. If they don't know much about marketing research they may ask for information that costs too much, obtain the wrong information or accept wrong conclusions. Experienced marketing researchers who understand the manager's problem should also be involved at this stage. The researcher must be able to help the manager define the problem and suggest ways that research can help the manager make better decisions.

Defining the problem and the research objectives is often the hardest step in the research process. The manager may know that something is wrong without knowing the specific causes. For example, managers of a retail chain store may decide that falling sales are due to poor advertising and order research to test the organisation's advertising. If this research showed that current advertising is reaching the right people with the right message, the managers would need to look elsewhere for the solution to their declining sales. It may be that the chain is not delivering the products, prices and services that the advertising promises. For example, an overly tight creditor payment policy might cause suppliers to withhold supply, and thereby cause negative views among customers who can't buy what they want. Careful problem definition might have avoided the cost and delay of advertising research and would have suggested research on the real problem—consumer reactions to the products, services and prices offered in the chain's stores. The latter might have been uncovered by informal market research or 'MBWAC' (management by wandering among customers).

After the problem has been carefully defined, the manager and researcher must set the research objectives. A marketing research project might have one of three types of objectives. Sometimes the objective is **exploratory**—to gather preliminary information that will help define the problem and suggest hypotheses. For example, Unilever, which makes Streets ice-cream, might want to find out if a new adult flavour will add to their Magnum brand ice-cream sales and profits, or cannibalise existing sales. Sometimes the objective is **descriptive**—to describe things such as the market potential for a product or the demographics and attitudes of consumers who buy the product. Volkswagen, for example, might wish to obtain a profile of their most likely buyers so they can locate dealerships in the most appropriate geographical locations. Managers often start with exploratory research and later follow with descriptive or **causal research**, to test hypotheses about cause and effect relationships. For example, a bank might want to test the effect of a follow-up call to new home mortgage customers. Does it increase sales of other products by higher satisfaction and cross-selling compared to a follow-up letter or a control group? See Marketing Highlight 6.2 for more detail on how marketers are using experimentation to test cause and effect relationships.

Designing the research

The second step of the marketing research process calls for determining the information needed, developing a plan for gathering it efficiently and presenting the research design to marketing management in the form of a plan. The plan outlines sources of secondary data and spells out the specific research approaches, contact methods, sampling plans and instruments that researchers will use to gather primary data.

Determining specific information needs

Research objectives must be translated into specific information needs. For example, suppose Uncle Tobys decides to do research to find out how consumers would react to the company replacing the

Exploratory research
Marketing research to gather preliminary information that will help to define problems better and suggest hypotheses.

Descriptive research
Marketing research to describe marketing problems, situations or markets better—such as the market potential for a product or the demographics and attitudes of consumers.

Causal research
Marketing research to test hypotheses about cause and effect relationships.

Scientific experimentation comes to marketing

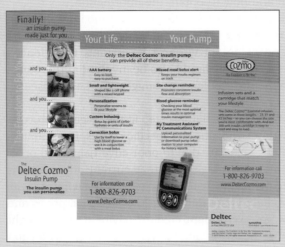

The push for marketers to demonstrate their effectiveness has led to a sharp increase in direct mail because its effect is easy to measure.

Every aspect of marketing depends on collecting information and using it to make better decisions. Market research helps a company decide what features potential customers want and what price they will pay, and provides information about sales to help manage staffing and stocking. Analysis of the information helps managers to continually refine their marketing programs to determine the best combination of customer value and company profits. But deciding on the best action isn't easy, and marketers are drawing more and more on the principles of scientific experimentation. Let's look at how experimentation is being used in market research to increase responses to direct mail.

Most of us receive large amounts of direct mail, offering products like credit cards, phone and Internet deals. If it is correctly targeted, direct mail like this can be very effective, allowing organisations to offer products to those who are most likely to be interested. For example, a bank can target students with offers of deferred interest loans and people in their thirties with information on home mortgages. However, direct mail can be expensive and ineffective if not many people respond. Many years ago direct marketers used to say that about 3%

of people would respond to a direct mail campaign, meaning that 97% of direct mail was ineffective and thus wasted marketing expenditure. Today, the biggest direct marketer in the world, Otto Versand in Germany, says that it can predict with almost 80% accuracy whether an individual will respond, so it can avoid sending mail to people who are less likely to respond. So how can an organisation increase the effectiveness of its marketing effort?

The best organisations are using what is often called a 'test and learn' approach to improve their direct mail campaigns. The approach is based on scientific experiments, to try and ensure that the person really did respond to the campaign (and wouldn't have bought the product anyway) and to improve a campaign continually in order to maximise the response rate. Here's how it typically works.

Suppose an organisation like a bank wants to encourage customers to take up a credit card. The bank uses its best information to work out which customers are most likely to respond; perhaps those who don't have a credit card with the bank, and who have recently had a salary increase (the bank is likely to know this because for most salary earners their salary will be paid directly into their bank account).

The bank develops a mail package, explaining the benefits of the credit card (perhaps a low interest rate and/or an attractive loyalty program, or a long interest-free period). In the first stage of the test and learn strategy, the bank draws a list of likely prospects from its databases. If the campaign is still being tested, this group might be fairly small, perhaps as few as 100 potential customers. We'll call this group the target group. At the same time, the bank obtains another list of names, chosen on the same criteria as the target group, from its database. This is the 'control group'. The bank then sends out the offer to the target group and waits to see how many of them take up the offer.

If the bank later finds that 10% of the target group have taken out the credit card, is the campaign a success? It might sound good, but that's where the importance of the control group comes in. The success of the campaign can only be evaluated if the success rate of the target group is compared to that of the control group. Perhaps 8% of the control group took up the credit card, even without receiving the direct mail offer (perhaps after seeing some other advertising). This means that instead of achieving a 10% response rate, the mail campaign only provided 2% more customers than the control group. Is the campaign then a success? Well, it depends on how much the whole campaign costs, including designing and sending out the direct mail, staff time, etc., and on the average profitability of customers of the credit card. Two per cent more customers seems better than nothing, but it's not worth getting these customers if it costs more to get them than they return in profits.

However, the 'test and learn' strategy doesn't stop there; for example, the bank might decide that the reason the campaign didn't provide many more customers than the control group may have been because the mail offer wasn't personalised, or because the graphics in the brochure looked boring. Using the same experimental approach, the bank can try different approaches (different paper, different pictures, different accompanying letters) to work out which is the most effective offer to send to target customers. And the ultimate measurement of the campaign effectiveness is always whether it delivers sufficient extra customers, over and above a control group, to pay for all of the costs of the campaign and, in addition, to give the bank an acceptable profit on its marketing expenses. The use of such 'test and learn' strategies to improve the targeting of direct mail campaigns has resulted in direct mail campaigns where around 15–20% of customers take up the offer. That's still a lot of waste, but it's a lot better than the old claims that a successful campaign was one where around 3% of customers responded!

Source: Jacquelyn S. Thomas, Werner Reinartz and V. Kumar, 'Getting the Most Out of All Your Customers', *Harvard Business Review*, July–August 2004, pp. 116–23.

Questions

1 Suppose that a marketing manager says that they don't want to wait for the results of a 'test and learn' strategy but wants to run a full campaign now. What would be your response?

2 Can a 'test and learn' campaign be applied to other communications methods such as (a) telephone sales (b) advertising? How?

3 What are the advantages of a 'test and learn' strategy? Do you see any disadvantages with the strategy?

6.2

cardboard box that holds its breakfast oats with new single serve plastic containers. These would cost more but would allow consumers to heat the rolled oats in a microwave oven and eat them without using bowls. This research might call for the following specific information:

- The demographic, economic and lifestyle characteristics of current breakfast eaters. (Busy working couples might find the convenience of the new packaging worth the price; families with children might want to pay less and wash the saucepan and bowls.)
- Consumer usage patterns for cereal—how much breakfast cereal they eat, where and when. (The new packaging might be ideal for adults in a hurry but less convenient for parents feeding breakfast to several children.)
- The number of microwave ovens in consumer and commercial markets. (The number in homes and offices will influence the demand for the new containers.)
- Retailer reactions to the new packaging. (Failure to get retailer support could hurt sales of the new package.)

○ Consumer attitudes towards the new packaging. (The familiar breakfast cereal box has become an institution—will consumers accept the new packaging?)

○ Forecasts of sales of both new and current packages. (Will the new packaging increase profits?)

Uncle Tobys' managers will need these and many other types of information to decide whether or not to introduce the new packaging.

Gathering secondary information

Secondary data
Information that already exists somewhere, having been collected for another purpose.

Primary data Information collected for the current research purpose.

To meet the manager's information needs the researcher can gather secondary data, primary data, or both. **Secondary data** consist of information that already exists somewhere, having been collected for another purpose. **Primary data** consist of information collected for the current research purpose.

Researchers usually start by gathering secondary data. Figure 6.4 shows some of the many secondary data sources available from external sources.[16] Secondary data can usually be obtained more quickly and at a lower cost than primary data. Today, much of it is free or inexpensive, and much of it is available online (see Table 6.1). For example, electronic access to commercial databases or to government statistics might provide some of the information Uncle Tobys needs on household and microwave oven usage at almost no cost. In contrast, a study to collect primary information might take weeks or months and cost thousands of dollars. Secondary sources can sometimes provide data an individual organisation cannot collect on its own—information that is not directly available or which would be too expensive to collect. For example, it would be too expensive for Uncle Tobys to conduct an ongoing retail store audit to find out about the market shares, prices and displays of competitors' brands. But it can buy ACNielsen's ScanTrack service, which provides this information using scanner data from supermarkets, chemists and mass merchants.

Secondary data may, however, present problems. The desired information may not exist—researchers can't usually obtain all the data they need from secondary sources. For example, Uncle Tobys will not find information about consumer reactions to new packaging that is not yet available on the market. Even when data can be found, they might not be very usable. The researcher must evaluate secondary information to make certain it is *relevant* (fits the research project needs), *accurate*

Commercial data

Here are just a few of the dozens of commercial research houses selling data to subscribers:

○ ACNielsen Scan Track provides data on household purchasing (ACNielsen/Homescan consumer panels), supermarket scanner data (Nielsen), data on television audiences (Nielsen and Medica Research) and others.

○ The Roy Morgan Research Centre provides annual reports covering television markets and geodemographic data by sex, income, age and brand preferences (selective markets and media reaching them).

○ Specialist researchers, such as PAXUS, provide data on motor vehicle sales, while IDC provides feedback on such industries as the information technology industry.

○ Others, such as BIS Shrapnel, undertake syndicated research on the food services industry and the construction industry, as well as general economic forecasting studies.

○ Firms such as Access Economics undertake econometric studies of the type that governments and opposition parties use, for example, to model such inputs/outputs as the effects of particular policy changes—such as taxation changes—on household income and expenditure.

FIGURE 6.4 Commercial sources of secondary data

TABLE 6.1 Selected online secondary data sources

For business data:

ACNielsen Corporation (www.acnielsen.com) provides supermarket scanner data on sales, market share and retail prices; data on household purchasing; and data on television audiences.

Nielsen Media Research (www.nielsenmedia.com) provides media reports for a range of countries.

Information Resources, Inc. (www.infores.com) provides supermarket scanner data for tracking grocery product movement and new product purchasing data.

Arbitron (www.arbitron.com) provides local-market and Internet radio audience and advertising expenditure information, among other media and ad spending data.

NDC Health Information Services (www.ndchealth.com) reports on the movement of drugs, laboratory supplies, animal health products and personal care products.

Simmons Market Research Bureau (www.smrb.com) provides detailed analysis of consumer patterns in 400 product categories in selected markets.

Dun & Bradstreet (www.dnb.com) maintains a database containing information on more than 50 million individual companies around the globe.

ComScore Networks (www.comscore.com) provides consumer behaviour information and geodemographic analysis of Internet and digital media users around the world.

Thomson Dialog (http://library.dialog.com) offers access to ABI/INFORM, a database of articles from 800+ publications and to reports, newsletters and directories covering dozens of industries.

LEXIS-NEXIS (www.lexisnexis.com) features articles from business, consumer and marketing publications plus tracking of firms, industries, trends and promotion techniques.

CompuServe (www.compuserve.com) provides access to databases of business and consumer demographics, government reports and patent records, plus articles from newspapers, newsletters and research reports.

Factiva (www.factiva.com) specialises in in-depth financial, historical and operational information on public and private companies.

Hoovers Online (www.hoovers.com) provides business descriptions, financial overviews and news about major companies around the world.

For government data:

The Australian Bureau of Statistics (www.abs.gov.au)

The Year Book Australia, updated annually, and available online from the Australian Bureau of Statistics, provides summary data on the Australian economy, demographics and society.

Statistics New Zealand (www.stats.govt.nz)

Statistics Singapore (www.singstat.gov.sg)

The Census and Statistics Department, Hong Kong (www.info.gov.hk/censtatd)

Department of Statistics, Malaysia (www.statistics.gov.my)

For Internet data:

ClickZ Stats/CyberAtlas (www.clickz.com/stats) brings together a wealth of information about the Internet and its users, from consumers to e-commerce.

Interactive Advertising Bureau (www.iab.net) covers statistics about advertising on the Internet.

Jupiter Research (www.jupiterresearch.com) monitors Web traffic and ranks the most popular sites.

Less focus on focus groups—anthropological market research

Focus groups have been a long-standing feature of market research, but many companies are now turning to other research methods. 'You don't really learn anything insightful [from focus groups],' says Jim Stengel, Procter & Gamble's chief marketing officer. Stengel argues that P&G and its competitors have met consumers' obvious needs, and today's opportunities lie in meeting needs that consumers may not be able to articulate. P&G isn't the only company moving away from focus groups. 'My research department doesn't know it, but I'm killing all our focus groups,' says Cammie Dunaway, chief marketing officer at Yahoo!.

For companies that understand their customers like P&G and Yahoo!, focus groups may not provide many new ideas. Worse, focus group participants may try to please the people who are providing the focus group, and unintentionally or intentionally give wrong answers. 'If you give someone £100 and some beer, they'll say anything you want them to say,' says Tyler Brûlé, the founder of *Wallpaper* magazine, and European trend forecaster. For example, focus group research told Best Western motels that it was the men in couples who made the decision when to turn off the highway and where to stay. However, when Best Western paid couples to allow them to put cameras in their cars as they drove around America, the tapes showed that it was the women who made the decision, providing Best Western with better information to plan their advertising.

So what are marketers using instead of focus groups? Many companies are spending more time on observational research, watching consumers in their own environments, using hidden cameras like Best Western or head-mounted cameras to track customer eye movement, or just following consumers around and observing what they do. The method is so new that it goes by different names, but it's often called anthropological or ethonographic market research, drawing on the methods of anthropologists and sociologists for studying people in their natural settings. For example, Intel employs four anthropologists, four psychologists and two interaction designers in its People and Practices division. Intel's research staff travel the globe, observing, photographing and talking to consumers in their homes and offices, to try to understand people's uses of technology. One of the products that has come out of its Asian research is an 'education PC' for the Chinese market, with a lock and key function so that parents can stop their children wasting time on the Internet or playing games.

Similarly, P&G's marketers are spending more and more time watching consumers. In 2000, the average brand marketer spent less than four hours a month with consumers, and according to Jim Spengel 'It's at least triple that now'. P&G opened a nappy-testing laboratory so it could watch how mothers actually used their nappies, Pampers. Pamper's mission was 'we want the driest diapers' but the company learnt that while dryness is important for babies, parents of toddlers get frustrated with how long it takes to toilet train their children. As a result, P&G launched a new line, Pampers Feel 'n Learn, designed to stay wet for two minutes, to encourage toddlers to use the toilet. Pampers new mission now reflects its new focus on customers, not on its products: 'helping moms with baby's development'. This new focus has been reflected in sales, with Pampers gaining market share from its rival, Kimberly-Clark's Huggies, for the first time in a decade.

Some companies are using what is called 'neuromarketing', scanning consumers' brains to try to understand which brands and advertising their brains react to. In one study, for example, consumers were asked to blind taste test Coke and Pepsi, and were evenly split on which they preferred. But when the subjects were told which cola they were drinking, a different area of the brain lit up on the MRIs (magnetic resonance images of the brain) and three-quarters of the subjects said they preferred Coke. The researchers interpreted this as concrete evidence of the effect of branding.

Other companies are still using focus groups, but supplementing them with other methods. Ford suffered a disastrous launch of the AU Falcon in 1998, after the car was partly styled based on the results of focus groups but flopped in the market. Ford again used focus groups and customer clinics to test its new Territory model, launched in early 2005, but also did extensive testing with 5000 pre-production test drives in 300 vehicles built specially for market research. The Territory was a big success, winning a car of the year award, and dominating the popular SUV (sports utility vehicle) segment.

So is the focus group likely to disappear? That's not likely any time soon. Focus groups can still be useful if the marketer doesn't understand the market well, or to get reactions to different product or promotional concepts. However, results from focus groups are never conclusive, and are likely to be most useful if combined with other methods. Particularly for products and services that consumers use when they are alone, it may be most effective to do one-on-one research with customers, preferably by watching them use the product or by asking them their opinion when they can't be influenced by the opinions or presence of others.

Sources: 'Inside the Mind of the Consumer', *The Economist*, 12 June 2004, p. 11; Fiona Buffini, 'The Ethnographer', *The Australian Financial Review*, 8 April 2005, p. 54–55; Josh Gliddon, 'Wheel of Fortune: Secrecy Is Out and Openness Is in When Trying to Capture the Public's Imagination', *The Bulletin*, 22 February 2005; Gerry Khermouch, 'See Me Consume', *Business Review Weekly*, 23 March 2001, p. 47; David Kiley, 'Shoot the Focus Group', *Business Week*, 14 November 2005, pp. 120–121; Julian Lee, 'Brand on the Run', *The Sydney Morning Herald*, 2 August 2005, p. 14; Paul McIntyre, 'Great New Trick: Wiring the Brain of the Consumer', *The Sydney Morning Herald*, 24 February 2005, p. 27; Jill Mahoney, 'The Brave New World of Neuromarketing: Researchers Tap into the "Black Box" of the Human Brain to Unlock Secrets of Why We Buy', *The Globe and Mail*, 10 September 2005, p. A10; David Meagher, 'Are You Experienced?', *The Australian Financial Review*, 27 August 2004, p. 68; Patricia Seller, 'P&G: Teaching an Old Dog New Tricks', *Fortune*, 31 May 2004, pp. 59–65.

Questions

1 Many companies are turning to online market research, paying consumers to give their opinions, as an alternative to focus groups. What do you think are the advantages and disadvantages of this method?

2 The increasing interest in brain scanning techniques to understand consumer reactions has led to opposition on the grounds that consumers may be manipulated if marketers understand how they respond. Do you agree with these concerns? Why or why not?

3 Under what circumstances are focus groups likely to be most useful? When are they likely to be least useful?

6.3

(reliably collected and reported), *current* (sufficiently up to date for current decisions) and *impartial* (objectively collected and reported). Secondary data provide a good starting point for research and often help to define problems and research objectives. Because the data are available to all firms, they often do not provide competitive advantage when used as a single source of information. In most cases, secondary sources cannot provide all the needed information, and the organisation must collect primary data.

Planning primary data collection

Good decisions require good data. Just as researchers must carefully evaluate the quality of secondary information they obtain, so they must also take great care in collecting primary data to ensure that they provide marketing decision makers with relevant, accurate, current and unbiased information. Table 6.2 shows that designing a plan for primary data collection calls for a number of decisions on research approaches, contact methods, sampling plan and research instruments. The research plan is typically summarised in a written proposal. This proposal is especially important when the research project will be large and complex or when an outside firm carries it out. The proposal should cover

TABLE 6.2 Planning primary data collection			
Research approaches	**Contact methods**	**Sampling plan**	**Research instruments**
Observation	Mail	Sampling unit	Questionnaire
Survey	Telephone	Sample size	Mechanical instruments
Experiment	Personal	Sampling procedure	

the problems being addressed and the research objectives, the information to be obtained, the sources of secondary information or methods for collecting primary data, and the way the results will help management decision making. The proposal should also include research costs. A written research plan or proposal makes sure that the marketing manager and researchers have considered all the important aspects of the research and that they agree on why and how the research will be done.

Observational research
The gathering of primary data by observing relevant people, actions and situations.

Research approaches Observational research is the gathering of primary data by observing relevant people, actions and situations. Observational research can be used to obtain information that people are unwilling or unable to provide. In some cases observation may be the only way to obtain the needed information. See Marketing Highlight 6.3 for examples of observational research. However, some things cannot be observed—things such as feelings, attitudes and motives. Private, long-term or infrequent behaviour is also difficult to observe. Because of these limitations, researchers often combine information they get from observation with other data collection methods to make predictions about consumer behaviour.

Survey research The gathering of primary data by asking people questions about their knowledge, attitudes, preferences and buying behaviour.

Survey research is the approach best suited to gathering descriptive information. When an organisation wants to know about people's knowledge, attitudes, preferences or buying behaviour, it can often find out by asking them directly. For example, political surveys, or polls, aim to find out how voters feel about political parties and their attitudes on specific issues, and ultimately who they intend to vote for. Survey research can be structured or unstructured. Structured surveys use formal lists of questions asked of all respondents in the same way. Unstructured surveys let the interviewer probe respondents and guide the interview according to their answers.

Survey research may be direct or indirect. In the direct approach, the researcher asks direct questions about behaviour or thoughts—for example, 'Why don't you buy clothes at Country Road?'. By contrast, the researcher might use the indirect approach by asking, 'What kinds of people buy clothes at Country Road?'. From the response to this indirect question, the researcher may be able to discover why some consumers might avoid Country Road clothing—in fact, it may suggest reasons consumers are not consciously aware of or are unwilling to admit to themselves.

Survey research is the most widely used method for primary data collection, and it is often the only method used in a research study. The major advantage of survey research is its flexibility. It can be used to obtain many different kinds of information in different marketing situations. Depending on the survey design, it may also provide information more quickly and at lower cost than observational or experimental research.

However, survey research also presents some problems. Sometimes people are unable to answer survey questions because they cannot remember or have never thought about what they do and why. Or people may be unwilling to respond to unknown interviewers or to questions about things they consider private. Busy people may not take the time. Respondents may answer survey questions even when they do not know the answer in order to appear smarter or more informed. Or they may try to help the interviewer by giving pleasing answers. Careful survey design can help to minimise these problems.

Whereas observation is best suited for exploratory research and surveys for descriptive research, **experimental research** is best suited to gathering causal information. Experiments involve selecting matched groups of subjects, giving them different treatments, controlling unrelated factors and checking for differences in group responses, in order to understand cause and effect relationships. So researchers at Red Rooster might use experiments before adding a new item such as a Chicken Wrap to the menu to answer such questions as:

- How much will the new menu item increase Red Rooster store sales?
- How will the new menu item affect the sales of other menu items?
- Which advertising approach would have the greatest effect on sales of the menu item?
- How would different prices affect the sales of the product?
- Should the new item be targeted towards adults, children or both?

Experimental research
The gathering of primary data by selecting matched groups of subjects, giving them different treatments, controlling unrelated factors and checking for differences in group responses.

For example, to test the effects of two different prices, Red Rooster could set up a simple experiment. It could introduce the new food item at one price in its restaurants in one city and at another price in restaurants in another demographically similar city. If all other marketing efforts for the product are the same, then differences in sales in the two cities could be related to the price charged. More complex experiments could be designed to test the effect of other variables and other locations.

Contact methods Information can be collected by mail, telephone, personal interview or online. Table 6.3 shows the strengths and weaknesses of each of these contact methods.

Mail questionnaires have many advantages. They can be used to collect large amounts of information at a low cost per respondent. Respondents may give more honest answers to personal questions on a mail questionnaire than to an unknown interviewer in person or over the phone. No interviewer is involved to bias the respondent's answers, and measures can be collected and tracked over time, for example to estimate customer satisfaction and willingness to recommend a product.

However, mail questionnaires also have some disadvantages. They are not very flexible—they require simple and clearly worded questions, all respondents answer the same questions in a fixed order, and the researcher cannot adapt the questionnaire based on earlier answers. The response rate—the number of people returning completed questionnaires—is often very low and has been decreasing, possibly due to the growth in junk mail. Companies will often use rewards, such as a chance to win tickets to watch the Australian Formula One Grand Prix in Melbourne, to induce a higher response rate. However, offering an incentive like this could introduce a bias in the response rate, because a high proportion of motor-sport lovers might reply, resulting in underrepresentation of non-enthusiasts.

TABLE 6.3 Strengths and weaknesses of contact methods				
	Mail	**Telephone**	**Personal**	**Online**
Flexibility	Poor	Good	Excellent	Good
Quantity of data that can be collected	Good	Fair	Excellent	Good
Control of interviewer effects	Excellent	Fair	Poor	Fair
Control of sample	Fair	Excellent	Fair	Poor
Speed of data collection	Poor	Excellent	Good	Excellent
Response rate	Fair	Good	Good	Good
Cost	Good	Fair	Poor	Excellent

Source: Adapted with permission of Macmillan Publishing Company from *Marketing Research: Measurement and Method*, 6th edn, by David S. Tull and Del I. Hawkins, copyright © 1993 Macmillan Publishing Company.

Focus groups are an effective way of gaining insight into consumer thoughts and feelings.

Telephone interviewing is the best method for gathering information quickly, and provides greater flexibility than mail questionnaires. Interviewers can explain questions that are not understood. Depending on the respondent's answers, they can skip some questions or probe further on others. Telephone interviewing also allows greater sample control. Interviewers can ask to speak to respondents with the desired characteristics or even by name, and response rates tend to be higher than with mail questionnaires.

However, telephone interviewing also has drawbacks. The cost per respondent is higher than with mail questionnaires, and people may not want to discuss personal questions with an interviewer. Using an interviewer increases flexibility but also introduces interviewer bias. The way interviewers talk, small differences in how they ask questions and other differences may affect respondents' answers. Finally, different interviewers may interpret and record responses differently, and under time pressures some interviewers might even cheat by recording answers without asking questions.

Focus group A group of six to ten people brought together for a few hours with a trained interviewer to talk about a product, service or organisation. The interviewer 'focuses' the group discussion on important issues.

A **focus group** consists of six to ten people brought together for a few hours with a trained interviewer to talk about a product, service or organisation. The interviewer needs objectivity, knowledge of the subject and industry and some understanding of group and consumer behaviour. The participants are normally paid a small sum for attending. The meeting is held in a pleasant place and refreshments are served to foster an informal setting. The interviewer starts with broad questions before moving to more specific issues, and encourages free and easy discussion, hoping that group interactions will bring out people's feelings and thoughts. At the same time, the interviewer 'focuses' the discussion. The comments are recorded as written notes or on audiotapes and videotapes that are studied later.

Focus groups have become one of the major marketing research tools for gaining insight into consumer thoughts and feelings. However, focus group studies usually employ small sample sizes to keep time and costs down, and it may be hard to generalise from the results. If a dominant individual in the group expresses a strong view, other people in the group may be influenced by their view or unwilling to speak out and oppose them, so the focus group may not represent the opinions of all individuals involved. Because interviewers have more freedom in personal interviews, the problem of interviewer bias is greater. See Marketing Highlight 6.3 for the techniques some firms are exploring as alternatives to focus groups.

Short point-of-sale surveys using a device like the 'Tracka' can be used to rapidly obtain customer data and feedback.
Source: <southafrica.com>

Advances in computers and communications have had a signficant impact on market research techniques. For example, most research firms now use computer-assisted telephone interviewing, or CATI. Professional interviewers call respondents around the country, often using phone numbers drawn at random to ensure that even people who aren't listed in the phone book have a change of being interviewed. When the respondent answers, the interviewer reads a set of questions from a video screen and types the respondent's answers directly into the computer. In an attempt to ensure that they survey all types of people, other research firms set up terminals in shopping centres and respondents sit down at a terminal, read questions from a screen and type their own answers into the computer.

Other technological developments are making it easier and faster for companies to collect and collate customer feedback. For example, the Barbeques Galore chain uses a small electronic device called a 'Tracka' to collect survey data from customers. The small hand-held wireless device is located at the cash register, and customers can be asked about their perceptions of the store's service as their sale is being completed, using a keypad to enter their responses. The data are electronically transmitted to the technology provider, which compiles the data and provides weekly reports to Barbeques Galore, allowing each store to track and benchmark customer perceptions and compare the effect of the environment, for example allowing the store to compare service when the store is busy and when it is quiet.[17]

Online marketing research Increasingly, marketing researchers are collecting primary data through **online marketing research**—using *Internet surveys, experiments* and *online focus groups.*

Web research offers some real advantages over traditional surveys and focus groups. The most obvious advantages are speed and low costs. Online focus groups require some advance scheduling, but results are practically instantaneous. For example, one soft drink company recently conducted an online survey to test teenagers' opinions of new packaging ideas. The 10- to 15-minute Internet survey included dozens of questions along with 765 different images of labels and bottle shapes. Some 600 teenagers participated over a three- to four-day period. Detailed analysis from the survey was available just five days after all the responses had come in—lightning quick compared with offline efforts.[18]

Internet research is also relatively low in cost. Participants can dial in for a focus group from anywhere in the world, eliminating travel, lodging and facility costs. For surveys, the Internet eliminates most of the postage, phone, labour and printing costs associated with other approaches. 'A survey on the Internet is only 10 or 20 percent as expensive as mail, telephone, or in-person surveys,' says one researcher. Moreover, notes another, sample size has little influence on costs. 'There's not a huge difference between 10 and 10 000 on the Web,' he says.

Online surveys and focus groups are also excellent for reaching the hard-to-reach—the often-elusive teen, or single, affluent and well-educated audiences. It's also good for reaching working mothers and other people who lead busy lives. They respond to it in their own space and at their own convenience. The Internet also works well for bringing together people from different parts of the country, especially those in higher-income groups who can't spare the time to travel to a central site.

Using the Internet to conduct marketing research does have some drawbacks. For one, restricted Internet access can make it difficult to get a broad cross-section of consumers. Another major problem is controlling who's in the sample. 'If you can't see a person with whom you are communicating,' says a research executive, 'how do you know who they really are?'

Even when you reach the right respondents, online surveys and focus groups can lack the dynamics of more personal approaches. The online world is devoid of the eye contact, body language and direct personal interactions found in traditional focus group research. And the Internet format—running, typed commentary and online 'emoticons' (punctuation marks that express emotion, such as :-) to signify happiness)—greatly restricts respondent expressiveness. 'You're missing all of the key things that make a focus group a viable method,' says the executive. 'You may get people online to talk to each other and play off each other, but it's very different to watch people get excited about a concept.'

Online (Internet) marketing research
Collecting primary data through Internet surveys and online focus groups.

To overcome such sample and response problems, many online research firms use opt-in communities and respondent panels. Advances in technology—such as the integration of animation, streaming audio and video and virtual environments—also help to overcome these limitations.

Perhaps the most explosive issue facing online researchers concerns consumer privacy. Some fear that unethical researchers will use the email addresses and confidential responses gathered through surveys to sell products after the research is completed. They are concerned about the use of electronic agents (called Spambots or Spiders) that collect personal information without the respondents' consent.[19] Failure to address such privacy issues could result in angry, less cooperative consumers and increased government intervention. Despite these concerns, online research is now estimated to account for 20% of marketing research in Australia, and most industry insiders predict healthy growth.[20]

Response rates and costs of different survey methods There have been conflicting results about whether mail or online surveys result in higher response rates. Online data collection response levels reportedly vary from 6% to 76%—most achieving less than 20%—while postal survey response levels reportedly vary from 16% to 75%.[21] Some studies have reported higher response rates with online surveys,[22] while others have reported that the highest response to a web survey was achieved if the instructions and an incentive were sent by mail.[23] In practice, the best way to maximise the response rate may be to offer respondents a choice, and let them use the method which they prefer. One comparison of survey methods found that the best response rate was achieved by sending a letter and the survey to participants, but also by giving them the opportunity to respond online if they wished.[24]

Costs vary between different survey methods, with face-to-face interviews being the most expensive. For example, in 2005 Telstra commissioned a survey of 16 000 small-business owners. Research experts estimated that face-to-face interviews would cost $1.2 million, telephone interviews would cost $800 000 and an online survey would cost $100 000.[25]

SELF-CHECK QUESTION

4   Would you be more prepared to answer (a) a phone survey about your shopping behaviour, (b) a mail survey about your shopping behaviour, (c) an online survey or (d) a personal interview in a shopping centre? Why? What are the advantages or disadvantages of each method for a marketer attempting to obtain information about consumers' shopping habits?

Sampling plans Marketing researchers usually draw conclusions about large groups of consumers by studying a small sample of the total consumer population. A **sample** is a segment of the population that has been selected to represent the population as a whole. The sample should be representative of the group the researcher is interested in (the population) so that the researcher can make accurate estimates of the thoughts and behaviour of the larger population.

Designing the sample requires three decisions. First, who is to be surveyed (what sampling unit)? The answer to this question is not always obvious. For example, to study the decision-making process for a family car purchase, should the researcher interview the husband, wife, other family members, dealership salespeople or all of these? In the case of a business vehicle, should the researcher interview just the fleet manager, managing director or other senior manager—or should the users also be interviewed? The researcher must determine what information is needed and who is most likely to have it. Second, how many people should be surveyed (what sample size)? Large samples give more reliable results than small samples. However, it is not necessary to sample the entire target market

Sample A segment of the population selected for marketing research to represent the population as a whole.

or even a large portion to get reliable results. If well chosen, samples of less than 1% of a population can give good reliability.

Third, how should the people in the sample be chosen (what sampling procedure)? Table 6.4 describes different types of samples. To obtain a representative sample the researchers should draw one of the three types of probability samples. But when probability sampling costs too much or takes too much time, marketing researchers often draw non-probability samples. These varied ways of drawing samples have different costs and time limitations, as well as different accuracy and statistical properties. Which method is best depends on the needs of the research project.

Sampling presents particular problems with online consumer surveys, as the population of Internet users is not representative of the general population. The aim is to ensure that the respondents are representative of the group being investigated, and that the survey format doesn't introduce biases or other unintended errors.[26] Inviting a sample of individual subscribers (such as football club members) or a sample of businesses drawn from an up-to-date list (such as a D&B list) to visit a survey questionnaire website is an appropriate use of online surveys. In contrast, intercepting unidentifiable online passers-by and enticing them to respond to an online survey is likely to result in **sampling error**, because the results won't be indicative of the general population and are therefore likely to be misleading.

Sampling error Error in the results of a survey which occurs if the sample is not representative of the group being investigated.

Research instruments In collecting primary data, marketing researchers have a choice of two main research instruments—the questionnaire and mechanical devices.

The questionnaire is by far the most common instrument, both in Australia and overseas. Broadly speaking, a questionnaire consists of a set of questions presented to a respondent for their answers. The questionnaire is very flexible—there are many ways to ask questions. Questionnaires must be carefully developed and tested before they can be used on a large scale. A carelessly prepared questionnaire usually contains several errors (see Figure 6.5).

In preparing a questionnaire the marketing researcher must decide what questions to ask, the form of the questions, the wording of the questions and the ordering of the questions. Questionnaires frequently leave out questions that should be included and include questions that cannot be answered, will not be answered or need not be answered. Each question should be considered very carefully before it is used to see that it contributes to the research objectives.

TABLE 6.4 Types of samples	
Sample type	**Description**
Probability sample	
Simple random sample	Every member of the population has a known and equal chance of selection.
Stratified random sample	The population is divided into mutually exclusive groups (such as age-groups), and random samples are drawn from each group.
Cluster (area) sample	The population is divided into mutually exclusive groups (such as blocks), and the researcher draws a sample of the groups to interview.
Non-probability sample	
Convenience sample	The researcher selects the easiest population members from which to obtain information.
Judgment sample	The researcher uses his or her judgment to select population members who are good prospects for accurate information.
Quota sample	The researcher finds and interviews a prescribed number of people in each of several categories.

Suppose that the principal of a private school had prepared the following questionnaire to use when interviewing the parents of prospective students. How would you assess each question?

1. What is your income to the nearest hundred dollars?

   People don't usually know their incomes to the nearest hundred dollars nor do they want to reveal their income that closely. Moreover, a researcher should never open a questionnaire with such a personal question.

2. Are you a strong or weak supporter of overnight excursions for your children?

   What do 'strong' and 'weak' mean?

3. Do your children behave themselves well on school excursions?

   Yes ( ) No ( )

'Behave' is a relative term. Furthermore, are 'yes' and 'no' the best responses to allow for this question? Besides, will people want to answer this? Why ask the question in the first place?

4. How many schools mailed literature to you last term? This term?

   Who can remember this?

5. What are the most salient and determinant attributes in your evaluation of schools for your children?

   What are 'salient' and 'determinant' attributes? Don't use big words on me!

6. Do you think it is right to deprive your child of the opportunity of growing into a mature person through the experience of attending a private school?

   A loaded question. Given the bias, how can any parent answer 'yes'?

FIGURE 6.5 A 'questionable' questionnaire

The form of the question can also influence the response. Marketing researchers distinguish between closed and open-ended questions. Closed questions include all the possible answers, and subjects make choices from them. Table 6.5A shows the most common forms of closed questions as they might appear in an airline's survey of passengers. Open-ended questions allow respondents to answer in their own words. The main forms are shown in Table 6.5B. Open-ended questions often reveal more than closed questions because respondents are not limited in their answers. Open-ended questions are especially useful in exploratory research where the researcher is trying to find out *what* people think, but is not measuring *how many* people think in a certain way. Closed questions, on the other hand, provide answers that are easier to interpret and tabulate.

Researchers should also use care in the wording and ordering of questions. They should use simple, direct, unbiased wording. Questions should be arranged in a logical order. The first question should create interest if possible, and difficult or personal questions should be asked last so that respondents do not become defensive.

Although questionnaires are the most common research instrument, mechanical instruments are also used. Several marketing organisations sell information collected through mechanical observation. For example, OzTAM attaches 'people meters' to television sets in the homes of panel members to record who watches which programs. Mechanical observation such as this is more accurate than the old method of asking people to record what they watched in a diary, but accurate information on who is watching still relies on members of the consumer panel accurately recording when they are watching TV (for example, noting when someone enters or leaves the room). The viewing data are automatically uploaded to OzTAM, and the company then provides summaries of the size and demographic make-up of audiences for different television programs.[27] The television networks use these ratings to judge program popularity and to set charges for advertising time. Advertisers use the ratings when selecting programs for their commercials.

Checkout scanners in retail stores also provide mechanical observation data. These laser scanners record consumer purchases in detail. Consumer products marketing organisations and retailers use

TABLE 6.5 Types of questions

A. Closed questions

Name	Description	Example
Dichotomous	A question offering two answer choices.	'In arranging this trip, did you personally phone Rex?' Yes ☐ No ☐
Multiple choice	A question offering three or more answer choices.	'With whom are you travelling on this flight?' No one ☐ Children only ☐ Spouse ☐ Business associates/friends/relatives ☐ Spouse and children ☐ An organised tour group ☐
Likert scale	A statement with which the respondent shows the amount of agreement/disagreement.	'Small airlines generally give better service than large ones' Strongly disagree 1 ☐ Disagree 2 ☐ Neither agree nor disagree 3 ☐ Agree 4 ☐ Strongly agree 5 ☐
Semantic differential	A scale is inscribed between two bipolar words, and the respondent selects the point that represents the direction and intensity of his or her feelings.	*Rex Airlines* Large X__: __: __: __: __: __: __ Small Experienced __: __: __: __: __: X__: __ Inexperienced Modern __: __: __: X__: __: __: __ Old-fashioned
Importance scale	A scale that rates the importance of some attribute from 'not at all important' to 'extremely important'.	'Airline food service to me is' Extremely important 1 _____ Very important 2 _____ Somewhat important 3 _____ Not very important 4 _____ Not at all important 5 _____
Rating scale	A scale that rates some attribute from 'poor' to 'excellent'.	'Rex's food service is' Excellent 1 _____ Very good 2 _____ Good 3 _____ Fair 4 _____ Poor 5 _____
Intention-to-buy scale	A scale that describes the respondent's intentions to buy.	'If in-flight telephone services were available on a long flight, I would' Definitely buy 1 _____ Probably buy 2 _____ Not certain 3 _____ Probably not buy 4 _____ Definitely not buy 5 _____

B. Open-ended questions

Name	Description	Example
Completely unstructured	A question that respondents can answer in an almost unlimited number of ways.	'What is your opinion of Rex Airlines?'
Word association	Words are presented, one at a time, and respondents mention the first word that comes to mind.	'What is the first word that comes to your mind when you hear the following?' Airline_____ Rex_____ Travel _____
Sentence completion	Incomplete sentences are presented, and respondents are asked to complete them.	'When I choose an airline, the most important consideration in my decision is _____
Picture completion	A picture of two characters is presented, with one making a statement. Respondents are asked to identify with the other and fill in the empty balloon.	 Fill in the empty balloon.
Thematic Apperception Tests (TATs)	A picture is presented, and respondents are asked to make up a story about what is happening or may happen in the picture.	 Make up a story about what you see.

scanner information to assess and improve product sales and store performance. Some marketing research firms now offer **single-source data systems** that electronically monitor both consumers' purchases and their exposure to various marketing efforts in an attempt to evaluate better the link between the two.

Single-source data systems Electronic monitoring systems that link consumers' exposure to television advertising and promotion (measured using television meters) with what they buy in stores (measured using checkout scanners).

Another group of mechanical devices measures subjects' physical responses. For example, eye cameras are used to study respondents' eye movements to determine at what points their eyes focus first and how long they linger on a given item. IBM is developing an 'emotion mouse' that will try to determine users' emotional states by measuring pulse, temperature, movement and galvanic skin response. Using such inputs, an Internet marketer might offer a different screen display if it senses that the user is frustrated.

Implementing the research plan

The researcher next puts the marketing research plan into action. This involves collecting, processing and analysing the information. Data collection can be carried out by the organisation's marketing research staff or by outside firms. The organisation keeps more control over the collection process and data quality if it conducts the research itself. However, outside firms specialising in data collection can often do the job more quickly and at lower cost. For example, a specialist third-party firm that conducts regular telephone surveys using CATI can often add questions to its regular surveys at much lower cost than conducting a separate survey.

The data collection phase of the marketing research process is generally the most expensive and the most subject to error. Researchers should watch closely to make sure that the plan is implemented correctly. They must guard against problems with contacting respondents, with respondents who refuse to cooperate or who give biased answers, and with interviewers who make mistakes or take shortcuts.

The collected data must be processed and analysed to isolate important information and findings. Data from questionnaires are checked for accuracy and completeness and coded for computer analysis. The researcher then uses survey or statistics programs to summarise the results and to understand what might predict the outcomes of interest. For example, if a bank has asked its customers how satisfied they are with the bank's service, and has also asked how many accounts the customer has with the bank and with its competitors, a regression model can be applied to determine the extent to which satisfaction predicts (and perhaps causes) behaviour. By adding more information to the model (such as information about the customer's age and income) sophisticated models can be developed which allow the bank to understand what influences their customers' behaviour, and what the bank can do to influence that behaviour.

Interpreting and reporting the findings

The researcher must now interpret the findings, draw conclusions and report them to management. The researcher should not try to overwhelm managers with numbers and complex statistical techniques. Rather, the researcher should present major findings that are useful for the main decisions faced by management.

Interpretation should not be left only to the researchers, however. They are often experts in research design and statistics, but the marketing manager knows more about the problem and the decisions that must be made. In many cases findings can be interpreted in different ways, and discussions between researchers and managers will help point to the best interpretations. The manager will also want to check that the research project was properly carried out and that all the necessary analysis was completed. Or, after seeing the findings, the manager may have additional questions that can be answered through further sifting of the data. Finally, the manager is the one who must ultimately decide what actions are suggested by the results of the research.

Interpretation is an important phase of the marketing process. The best research is meaningless if the manager accepts wrong interpretations from the researcher. Similarly, managers may have biased interpretations—managers (like other people) tend to accept research results that show what they expected and reject those they did not expect or hope for. Thus, managers and researchers must work together when interpreting research results, and must both share responsibility for the research process and resulting decisions.[28]

Other marketing research considerations

This section discusses marketing research in two special contexts: marketing research by small businesses and non-profit organisations, and international marketing research. Finally, we look at public policy and ethics issues in marketing research.

Marketing research in small businesses and non-profit organisations

Like larger firms, small organisations need market information. But managers of small businesses and non-profit organisations often think that marketing research can only be done by experts in large companies with big research budgets. However, many of the marketing research techniques discussed in this chapter can also be used by smaller organisations in a less formal manner and at little or no expense.

Managers of small businesses and non-profit organisations can obtain good marketing information simply by observing things around them. For example, retailers can evaluate new locations by observing vehicle and pedestrian traffic. They can visit competing stores to check on facilities and prices. They can evaluate their customer mix by recording how many and what kinds of customers shop in the store at different times. Competitor advertising can be monitored by collecting advertisements from local media. Managers can conduct informal surveys using small convenience samples, or by randomly sampling their business or supplier customer base. Retail salespeople can talk with customers visiting the store; managers in a hospital can interview patients and/or their relatives. Restaurant managers might make random phone calls during slack hours to interview consumers about where they eat out and what they think of various restaurants in the area. Managers can also conduct their own simple experiments. For example, by changing the themes in regular mailings and watching the results, a manager can test which marketing strategies work best. By varying newspaper advertisements, a store manager can learn the effects of things such as ad size and position, price coupons and media used.

In summary, secondary data collection, observation, surveys and experiments can all be used effectively by small organisations with small budgets. Although these informal research methods are less complex and less costly, they must still be conducted carefully. Managers must think carefully about the objectives of the research, formulate questions in advance, recognise the biases introduced by smaller samples and less skilled researchers and conduct the research systematically.[29]

International marketing research

International marketing researchers follow the same steps as domestic researchers, from defining the research problem and developing a research plan to interpreting and reporting the results. However, these researchers often face more and different problems. Different geographic markets often vary greatly in their levels of economic development, cultures, customs and buying patterns.

In many foreign markets, the international researcher has a difficult time finding good secondary data. Even when secondary information is available, it may need to be obtained from many different sources on a country-by-country basis, making the information difficult to combine or compare. Because of the scarcity of good secondary data, international researchers must often collect their own primary data. Here, again, researchers face problems not found domestically. For example, they may find that it is difficult to develop good samples. Researchers can use current telephone directories, census tract data and any of several sources of socioeconomic data to construct samples. However, such information is sometimes lacking in developing countries.

Once the sample is drawn, the researcher in developed countries can usually reach most respondents easily by telephone, by mail or in person. Reaching respondents is often not so easy in other parts of the world. In some countries few people have telephones—there are only 117 telephones and 54 PCs per thousand people in Mexico, and in Ghana the numbers drop to 11 phones and 3 PCs per 1000 people.[30] And even if they can be reached by phone, people who have phones in these areas aren't representative of the population. In multilingual countries like China, even deciding on the language for a mail or telephone survey can pose a problem, because people in different areas will speak different languages or dialects, and may not speak the national language. In other countries the postal system is notoriously unreliable. In Brazil, for instance, one estimate was that around 30% of the mail is never delivered. In many developing countries poor roads and transportation systems make certain areas hard to reach, making personal interviews difficult and expensive. Even when respondents are willing to respond to a written survey, they may not be able to because of high functional illiteracy rates.

Differences in culture and language from country to country cause additional problems for international researchers. For example, questionnaires must be prepared in one language and then translated into the languages of each country researched. Responses must then be translated back into the original language for analysis and interpretation. This adds to research costs and increases the risk of error. In addition, accurately translating a questionnaire from one language to another is often difficult. Many idioms, phrases and statements mean different things in different cultures. For example, a Danish executive noted: 'Check this out by having a different translator put back into English what you've translated from English. You'll get the shock of your life. I remember [an example in which] "out of sight, out of mind" had become "invisible things are insane".'[31] As a result, standard practice is to use what is called 'back translation' for research which involves translation. The survey is developed in one language (for example, English, if the company's head office is in an English-speaking country). It is then translated to the target language. Another translator is used to translate it back to English (hence 'back translation'). This version can then be compared with the original version, to try to ensure that the foreign language version really says what it was developed to say.

Buying roles and consumer decision processes vary greatly from country to country, further complicating international marketing research. Consumers in different countries also vary in their attitudes toward marketing research. People in one country may be very willing to respond; in other countries non-response can be a major problem. For example, customs in some Islamic countries prohibit people from talking with strangers—a male researcher may not be allowed to speak by phone with women about brand attitudes or buying behaviour, and mixed-gender focus groups are taboo, as is videotaping female-only focus groups.[32] In certain cultures research questions are often considered too personal. For example, in many Latin American countries people may feel embarrassed to talk with researchers about their choices of shampoo, deodorant or other personal care products. And middle-class people in developing countries often make false claims in order to appear well off. For example, in a study of tea consumption in India, over 70% of middle-income respondents claimed that they used one of several national brands. However, the researchers had good reason to doubt these results—more than 60% of the tea sold in India is unbranded generic tea.

Despite these problems, the recent growth of international marketing has resulted in a rapid increase in the use of international marketing research. Global companies have little choice but to conduct such research. Although the costs and problems associated with international research may be high, the costs of not doing it—in terms of missed opportunities and mistakes—might be even higher. Once recognised, many of the problems associated with international marketing research can be overcome or avoided.

Public policy and ethics in marketing research

When properly used, marketing research benefits both the sponsoring company and its customers. It helps the company to make better marketing decisions, which in turn result in products and services that meet the needs of consumers better. However, when misused, marketing research can also abuse and annoy consumers.

Intrusions on consumer privacy

Privacy legislation is being increasingly strengthened due to intrusions by marketing researchers and direct response marketing organisations.[33] Both consumers and business entities are becoming more resentful of unsolicited phone calls, and as a result do-not-call registers are becoming increasingly common. These registers allow consumers to list themselves and ban commercial market researchers from contacting these people. In late 2005, the Australian government released a discussion paper to invite comment on whether such a register should be developed in Australia, and legislation creating a do-not-call register was presented to the Australian parliament in 2006.[34]

Misuse of research findings

Research findings can be powerful persuasion tools; companies often use such findings as claims in their advertising, particularly with pharmaceutical products. Great care must be taken when using results in this way. Many opportunities exist to stretch the truth or omit certain qualifying statements that would put a different slant on the claim being made, and misleading or deceptive advertising is illegal in most countries, with heavy penalties for companies which do it.

Codes of practice

Most countries have codes of practice which regulate market research activities. For example, the Australian Association of Market and Social Research Organisations (AMSRO) has developed a code which governs the handling of information about the subjects of research for all AMSRO member organisations.[35]

In Europe, the ICC/ESOMAR International Code of Marketing and Social Research Practice regulates the professional activities of marketing researchers. The code sets out what is meant by 'marketing and social research, including opinion research' and emphasises that such research must always be clearly distinguished from other forms of marketing activities—many of which are regulated by their own separate code of practice and, in certain cases, legislative controls. The code outlines researchers' responsibilities to the general public, states that researchers should make their names and addresses available to participants, and bans companies from misrepresenting direct selling or database compilation activities as marketing research.[36]

SELF-CHECK QUESTIONS

5   The marketing research process consists of four steps. What are these four steps?

6   Why do marketers seek to use single-source marketing research?

7   Would there be a difference in the research instruments used by large marketing organisations and those used by small and medium enterprises (SMEs)? If so, list and describe these differences.

SUMMARY

In carrying out their marketing responsibilities, marketing managers need a great deal of information. Despite the growing supply of information, managers often lack enough information of the right kind or have too much of the wrong kind. To overcome these problems, many companies are taking steps to improve their marketing information systems.

A well-designed *marketing information system* (MIS) begins and ends with the user. The MIS first assesses information needs by interviewing marketing managers and surveying their decision environment to determine what information is desired, needed and feasible to offer.

The MIS next develops information and helps managers to use it more effectively. *Internal records* provide information on sales, costs, inventories, cash flows and accounts receivable and payable. Such data can usually be obtained quickly and cheaply, but must often be adapted for marketing decisions. The marketing intelligence system supplies marketing executives with everyday information about developments in the external marketing environment. Intelligence can be collected from company employees, customers, suppliers and resellers or by monitoring published reports, conferences, advertisements, websites, competitor actions and other activities in the environment. *Marketing research* involves collecting information relevant to a specific marketing problem facing the company.

Finally, the MIS distributes information gathered from internal sources, marketing intelligence and marketing research to the right managers at the right times. More and more companies are decentralising their information systems through networks that allow managers to have direct access to information.

Every marketer needs marketing research, and most large companies have their own marketing research departments. Marketing research involves a four-step process. The first step consists of the manager and researcher carefully *defining the problem* and setting the research *objectives*. The objective may be *exploratory*, *descriptive* or *causal*. The second step consists of *developing the research plan* for collecting data from *primary* and *secondary sources*. Primary data collection calls for choosing a research approach (*observation*, *survey*, *experiment*); choosing a *contact method* (mail, telephone, personal); designing a *sampling plan* (whom to survey, how many to survey and how to choose them); and developing *research instruments* (questionnaire or mechanical instruments). The third step consists of implementing the marketing research plan by collecting, processing and analysing the information. The fourth step consists of interpreting and reporting the findings. Further information analysis helps marketing managers to understand and apply the information through the use of statistical procedures and models.

Marketing research can also be conducted effectively by small organisations with small budgets. International marketing researchers follow the same steps as domestic researchers but often face more and different problems. All organisations need to understand the major public policy and ethics issues surrounding marketing research.

One of the principal methods of market research over the past 40 years has been the telephone interview. It's used to test a variety of consumer attitudes and behaviours and marketing effectiveness. For example, a telephone survey might be used to test advertising effectiveness (by testing ad recall), attitudes (for example, to brands or in political research) and to examine the frequency of behaviour. Telephone interviewing usually targets people at home on a fixed-line phone, when they are most likely to be prepared to answer questions. Because some people have an unlisted number, random number diallers are typically used, to try to ensure that everyone with a fixed-line phone has an equal chance of being called.

However, research is only useful if the people who respond are representative in some way of the population of interest, and changes in phone patterns are creating some concerns among market researchers. As people get busier, and as telephone selling is becoming more common, more people are refusing to answer telephone market research questions, because they see unwanted phone calls at home as an intrusion on their time. In addition, as cheaper mobile phones encourage more people (especially young people) to abandon the use of fixed lines and to have only a mobile phone, telephone interviews run the risk of not being representative of the population, because busy, mobile and single people may be less likely to have a fixed-line phone. The fixed-line phone, which used to be a way to contact people of all ages from all walks of life, may be becoming a channel which does not reach a growing segment of the population.

1 What are the problems for market research if telephone surveys aren't reaching certain segments of the population?

2 Is the answer to include mobile phone numbers in market research studies? What would be the advantages and disadvantage of this?

3 What can marketers do to overcome this potential source of sampling error?

KEY TERMS

DISCUSSING THE ISSUES

1 Is marketing research becoming difficult to undertake and are valid and reliable results difficult to obtain? Do you think that marketers have been their own worst enemy in this regard? For example, how many of your classmates, or their families, use caller ID or answer phones to screen calls in the evenings? Why?

2 What are your views concerning marketing intelligence? Is it merely snooping, or might it be unethical or in some situations illegal?

3 When will you answer a mail or online survey or agree to a personal interview? When won't you? What are the implications for market research if you think that lots of people are like you?

4 Salespeople who call on industrial accounts learn a lot that helps decision makers within their own (vendor) company. What kinds of information do salespeople typically pass on to their company? How might they decide whether something is worth reporting?

5 Focus group are widely used, but are also a widely criticised research technique. What are the advantages and disadvantages of focus groups? Describe the kinds of issues that might be investigated using focus groups.

6 What type of research would be appropriate in the following situations? Why?

(a) Uncle Tobys wants to investigate the degree of influence young children have on parents' decisions to buy breakfast foods.

(b) A football club wants to learn more about the perceptions of the football club held by various classes of supporters, for example past members, new members, long-term members and potential members.

(c) Red Rooster is considering where to locate a new outlet in a fast-growing suburb.

(d) Gillette wants to determine whether a new line of quadruple blade shaver for women will be profitable.

REFERENCES

1. For more detail on New Coke's failure, see 'Coke "Family" Sales Fly as New Coke Stumbles', *Advertising Age*, 17 January 1986, p. 1; Jack Honomichl, 'Missing Ingredients in "New" Coke's Research', *Advertising Age*, 22 July 1985, p. 1; Rick Wise, 'Why Things Go Better with Coke', *The Journal of Business Strategy*, January–February 1999, pp. 15–19; Catherine Fredman, 'Smart People, Stupid Choices', *Chief Executive*, August/September 2002, pp. 64–68; 'Top-10 U.S. Carbonated Soft Drink Companies and Brands for 2003', special issue, *Beverage Digest*, 5 March 2004, accessed at <www.beverage-digest.com/pdf/top-10_2003.pdf>; and 'The Real Story of New Coke', accessed online at <www2.coca-cola.com/heritage/cokelore_newcoke.html>, 22 January 2006.

2. For the story of Dasani's disastrous entry into the UK see Jo Johnson and Adam Jones, 'Coke Cans Plans for Dasani in France', *Financial Times*, 25 March 2004, p. 1; 'Water Wars', *The Guardian*, 3 March 2004, p. 6; 'Chopping Brands', *Marketing Week*, 10 June 2004, p. 22; 'Coca-Cola: Bubbles and Troubles', *Business and Finance*, 1 July 2004; Dominic Rushe, 'Coke's Latest Idea Falls Flat', *The Sunday Times*, 14 November 2004, Business, p. 15.

3. Paula L. Stepankowsky, 'In Market Cap, Pepsi Proved to be the Real Thing After All', *The Sydney Morning Herald*, 15 December 2005, p. 29.

4. Marion Harper Jr, 'A New Profession to Aid Management', *Journal of Marketing*, January 1961, p. 1.

5. Rashi Glazer, 'Marketing in an Information-Intensive Environment: Strategic Implications of Knowledge as an Asset', *Journal of Marketing*, October 1991, pp. 1–19.

6. 'Harnessing the Data Explosion', *Sales & Marketing Management*, January 1987, p. 31; and Joseph M. Winski, 'Gentle Rain Turns Into Torrent', *Advertising Age*, 3 June 1991, p. 34.

7. John Naisbitt, *Megatrends: Ten New Directions Transforming Our Lives*, New York, Warner Books, 1984, p. 16.

8. Donald S. Tull and Del I. Hawkins, *Marketing Research: Measurement and Method*, 4th edn, New York, Macmillan, 1987, pp. 40–41, 750–760.

9. Adapted from information in Ellen Neuborne, 'Know Thy Enemy', *Sales & Marketing Management*, January 2003, pp. 29–33. Also see Gina Rollins, 'Cast Deep to Sell', *Selling Power*, June 2003, pp. 26–28; and Deborah Lynne Wiley, 'Super Searchers on Competitive Intelligence: The Online and Offline Secrets of Top CI Researchers', *Online*, May–June 2004, p. 62.

10. Andy Serwer, 'P&G's Covert Operation', *Fortune*, 17 September, 2001, pp. 42–44.

11. See James Curtis, 'Behind Enemy Lines', *Marketing*, 21 May 2001, pp. 28–29; and Mei Fong, 'The Enemy Within', *Far Eastern Economic Review*, 22 April 2004, pp. 34–38.

12. The American Marketing Association officially adopted this definition in 1987.

13. See Susan Hart and Adamantios Diamantopolous, 'Marketing Research Activity and Company Performance: Evidence from Manufacturing Industry', *European Journal of Marketing*, vol. 27, no. 5, 1992, pp. 54–72.

14. For more on statistical analysis consult a standard text, such as Gilbert A. Churchill and Dawn Iacobucci, *Marketing Research: Methodological Foundations*, Mason, Thomson, 2005. For a review of marketing models see Gary L. Lilien, Philip Kotler and Sridhar Moorthy, *Marketing Models*, Englewood Cliffs, NJ, Prentice Hall, 1992.

15. Ravi Kalakota and Marcia Robinson, *E-Business: Roadmap for Success*, Reading, MA, Addison-Wesley, 1999; 'Maximizing Relationships', *Chain Store Age*, August 2001, pp. 21A–23A; and Pacific Research Consulting, 'Seiyu Implementing Wal-Mart's Real-Time Sales/Inventory System', *Innovative New Packaging in Japan*, 25 February 2004, p. 1.

16. For more information on secondary sources of business and marketing data see Gilbert A. Churchill and Dawn Iacobucci, *Marketing Research: Methodological Foundations*, Mason, Thomson, 2005.

17. Simon Sharwood, 'Making Service Sizzle', *The Sydney Morning Herald*, 22 November 2005, Next, p. 3. See also <www.cfs-southafrica.com/>, accessed 22 January 2006.

18. This and other examples and quotes in this section, unless otherwise noted, are from 'Market Trends: Online Research Growing', accessed at <www.greenfieldcentral.com/research_solutions/rsrch_solns_main.htm>, June 2003; Noah Shachtman, 'Web Enhanced Market Research', *Advertising Age*, 18 June 2001, p. T18; Thomas W. Miller, 'Make the Call: Online Results Are a Mixed Bag', *Marketing News*, 24 September 2001, pp. 30–35; 'Cybersurveys Come of Age', *Marketing Research*, Spring 2003, pp. 32–37; and Richard Lee, 'Stamford, Conn.Based Market Research Firm Able to Reach Millions', *Knight Ridder Tribune Business News*, 6 May 2004, p. 1. Also see Catherine Arnold, 'Not Done Net', *Marketing News*, April 2004, p. 17.

19. For more on Internet privacy, see James R. Hagerty and Dennis K. Berman, 'Caught in the Net: New Battleground over Web Privacy', *Wall Street Journal*, 27 August 2004, p. A1; and 'The Spies in Your Computer', *Wall Street Journal*, 18 February 2004, p. A18.

20. Neil Shoebridge, 'Online Surveys Gaining Pace', *The Australian Financial Review*, 14 November 2005, p. 51.
21. Heath McDonald and Stewart Adam, 'A Comparison of Online and Postal Data Collection Methods in Marketing Research', *Marketing Intelligence and Planning*, vol. 27, no. 2, 2003, pp. 85–95.
22. See, for example, Derek Glover and Tony Bush, 'The online or e-survey: A Research Approach for the ICT Age', *International Journal of Research & Method in Education*, 28(2), pp. 135–146.
23. Jeremy P. Birnholtz, Daniel B. Horn, Thomas A. Finholt and Sung Joo Bae, 'The Effects of Cash, Electronic, and Paper Gift Certificates as Respondent Incentives for a Web-Based Survey of Technologically Sophisticated Respondents', *Social Science Computer Review*, vol. 22, no. 3, pp. 355–362.
24. Linda J. Sax, Shannon K. Gilmartin and Alyssa N. Bryant, 'Assessing Response Rates and Nonresponse Bias in Web and Paper Surveys', *Research in Higher Education*, vol. 44, no. 4, pp. 409–433.
25. Neil Shoebridge, 'Online Surveys Gaining Pace', *The Australian Financial Review*, 14 November 2005, p. 51.
26. Don A. Dillman, *Mail and Internet Surveys: The Tailored Design Method*, New York, Wiley, 2000.
27. For information on how television ratings are estimated, based on a sample of the population, see 'The Ratings Process' available at <www.oztam.com.au/pdf/tv_ratings/ratingsprocess.pdf>, accessed 8 November 2005.
28. For a discussion of the importance of the relationship between market researchers and research users, see Christine Moorman, Gerald Zaltman and Rohit Deshpande, 'Relationships between Providers and Users of Market Research: The Dynamics of Trust within and between Organizations', *Journal of Marketing Research*, August 1992, pp. 314–328; Christine Moorman, Rohit Deshpande and Gerald Zaltman, 'Factors Affecting Trust in Market Research Relationships', *Journal of Marketing*, January 1993, pp. 81–101.
29. For some good advice on conducting market research in a small business see 'Marketing Research . . . Basics 101', accessed at <www.onlinewbc.gov/docs/market/mkt_res_basics.html>, June 2004; and U.S. Small Business Administration, 'Researching Your Market', accessed at <www.sba.gov/library/pubs/mt-8.doc>, June 2004.
30. Phone, PC and other country media stats are from <www.nationamaster.com>, accessed July 2004.
31. Subhash C. Jain, *International Marketing Management*, 3rd edn, Boston, PWS-Kent, 1990, p. 338. Also see Alvin C. Burns and Ronald F. Bush, *Marketing Research*, 3rd edn, Upper Saddle River, NJ, Prentice Hall, 2000, pp. 317–318; and Debra L. Vence, 'Leave It to the Experts', *Marketing News*, 28 April 2003, p. 37.
32. Steve Jarvis, 'Status Quo = Progress', *Marketing News*, 29 April 2002, pp. 37–38; and Catherine Arnold, 'Global Perspective', *Marketing News*, 15 May 2004, p. 43.
33. Australian Privacy Commissioner's website, <www.privacy.gov.au>, accessed 22 January 2006.
34. See <www.dcita.gov.au/tel/do_not_call>, accessed 22 January 2006; Neil Shoebridge, 'Do-not-call Register off Hold', *The Australian Financial Review*, 22 May 2006, p. 50.
35. The code can be downloaded at <www.amsro.com.au/index.cfm?p=1635>, accessed 22 January 2006.
36. 'ICC/ESOMAR International Code of Marketing and Social Research Practice', accessed at <www.iccwbo.org/home/menu_advert_marketing.asp>, June 2004; for more on codes of practice regarding online marketing research also see the websites for the Marketing Research Society of Australia, <www.mrsa.org.au>, and the New Zealand Marketing Research Society, <www.nzmrs.org.nz>.

PHOTO/AD CREDITS

Dr Rodney Arambewela, Deakin University

CASE STUDY
Researching complaints: is there a student satisfaction problem?

The background

Sitting in his office overlooking the courtyard leading to lecture theatres, Professor Damian Murphy, the Director of Research of a leading Australian university, with a large intake of culturally diverse international and domestic students each year, was thinking about his research projects for the new academic year. Over the years, he has established a well-planned research program to monitor student satisfaction towards the university's educational services and was pleased with the results achieved by his university against several measures. He was, however, uncertain about how much his research program had contributed towards understanding the underlying causes of student satisfaction and dissatisfaction (C/SD). He was also not impressed with the number of students participating in these evaluation studies. This was a major concern and he was wondering whether the results produced in previous studies conveyed the true position of the university's standing against these measures. Another concern was the low number of complaints or feedback received from students on university educational and administrative services. Some *ad hoc* studies his office had conducted revealed the possibility of a strong reluctance or unwillingness on the part of the students to complain. This had not been confined to international students but was also evident among domestic Australian students. He was aware that some researchers, however, had commented on the cultural influences on complaint behaviour. Another indication he received from these *ad hoc* studies was that student awareness regarding the facilities for complaints and policies for complaint handling was extremely low.

Deciding on a new approach

Having thought about these issues, Damian decided to take an entirely different path in assessing student experiences with university services. To this end he felt that a study on student complaint behaviour would be useful in understanding C/SD as well as managing it. A study therefore was planned to investigate whether or not students complain and, if they do, how and why they complain. He considered that this aspect was of strategic importance to the university in terms of the strong relationship between complaint behaviour and student satisfaction. The outcome he expected from the study was the improvement of service quality in which feedback from students, irrespective of whether it was positive or negative, would be crucial. He knew from other external research findings that encouraging customers to complain is beneficial to an organisation because complaining facilitates successful venting of negative effects, leading to reduced level of negative word-of-mouth (WOM) activity (Nyer and Gopinath, 2005). He also knew that such a study would allow the university to discover gaps in the delivery of its services and take corrective action. He was convinced that this study would be able to supplement the existing knowledge on student satisfaction.

Damian decided to seek the assistance of a PhD student (as a research assistant) to undertake an extensive literature review on complaint behaviour that would allow the university to decide the direction of the proposed research.

Results of past research

The review of literature relevant to past research studies indicated that complaint behaviour is influenced by many factors, including:

1 The attitude towards complaining. This is the individual's disposition to seek redress when dissatisfied. People with a positive attitude towards complaining seem to possess a greater propensity to complain (Nyer and Gopinath, 2005).

2 The likely success of a complaint. It is the perceived probability that the service provider will remedy the problem without protest (Oh, 2004).

3 Difficulty of complaining to seek redress. This relates to the issue of whether it is worthwhile to complain.

4 The more negative a customer's perception of the service provider's responsiveness to complaints, the more likely the individual was to engage in negative WOM behaviour (Singh, 1990).

5 Importance of service to the customer. This is the relative worth that individuals place on a product or service. As the investment in a product or service increases so does the propensity to complain (Grambois et al., 1977).

6 Relationship between loyalty and complaining behaviour. The more loyal the customer is to an organisation and its products/services, the greater the propensity to complain (Grambois et al., 1977).

Next steps

Given the importance of the inquiry, Professor Murphy decided that the university should commit to a major study involving both qualitative and quantitative phases. He asked the research assistant to plan the research project and both agreed that undergraduate students enrolled in all disciplines should be targeted for information.

Sources: D. Grambois, J. D. Summers and G. C. Frazier, *Correlates of Consumer Expectation and Complaining Behavior in Consumer Satisfaction and Dissatisfaction and Complaining Behavior*, edited by R. L. Day, Indiana University Press, 1977; M. Guolla, 'Assessing the Teaching Quality to Student Satisfaction Relationship: Applied Customer Satisfaction Research in the Classroom', *Journal of Marketing Theory and Practice*, vol.7, no. 3, 1999, pp. 87–97; B. Harvis and P. A. Voyer, 'Word of Mouth Processes within a Services Purchase Decision Context', *Journal of Service Research*, vol. 3, no. 2, 2000, pp. 166–177; P. U. Nyer and M. Gopinath, 'Effects of Complaining Versus Negative Word of Mouth on Subsequent Changes in Satisfaction: The Role of Public Commitment', *Psychology & Marketing*, vol. 22, no. 12, 2005, pp. 937–953; Don-Geun Oh, 'Complaining Behavior of Academic Library Users in South Korea', *Journal of Academic Librarianship*, vol. 30, no. 2, 2004, pp. 136–144; J. Singh, 'Voice, Exit, Negative WOM Behaviors: An Investigation across Three Service Categories', *Journal of The Academy of Science*, vol. 18, 1990, pp. 1–15.

QUESTIONS

1 Define the management problem and the marketing research problem based on the information provided in the case study. What research questions would be appropriate for the proposed study?

2 In your opinion, how should the research design for the proposed study be formulated?

3 How would the results of earlier research be used to assist with your research design and the types of questions to be asked?

4 What research approaches/techniques for gathering data are relevant to this study?

5 What sampling frame and sampling unit would be relevant to this study? What sampling strategy would be appropriate for this research?

6 What steps should be followed in designing a questionnaire? In your opinion what would be an acceptable presentation format for a questionnaire of this nature?

CHAPTER 7

Consumer behaviour

Every company wants to be number one in its market. Number one almost invariably has higher awareness, more customers that it can sell and resell to and bigger budgets for market research and marketing promotions. But large or small, understanding customers is critical, and can still be hard, even for the largest companies, which might be expected to be the best at marketing. Think about Telstra, Australia's largest telephone company, which has the largest market share in Australia and, after a recent merger of its Hong Kong venture, CSL, with rival New World PCS, will be part of the biggest mobile business in the Hong Kong market.

While being big has advantages in any market, it can also bring problems which need to be addressed by smart strategy and marketing. For example, Telstra's size can make it inefficient in its marketing efforts; a small business broadband user might have four separate divisions of Telstra trying to communicate with them: consumer and marketing, business, Countrywide and the Internet arm, BigPond. Telstra's size and long history mean that new divisions and systems have developed to respond to a rapidly changing telecommunications market, resulting in a plethora of product lines often developed in isolation by different divisions and hundreds of billing systems, with an inability to offer any customer a single bill. Its history as a monopoly provider of telephone services also means that a large number of consumers have had a poor experience with Telstra at some stage. Of course, they have also had good experiences, but customers tend to remember bad experiences, and newer operators like Optus and Vodafone aren't burdened with Telstra's association with the poor service offered by its bureaucratic, government-owned predecessor. Following deregulation of the Australian telecommunications market in 1997, the Australian market has become very competitive. Telstra has retained many of its former customers, due to customer inertia and the company's strategy of offering selective discounts, making it difficult for customers to compare prices. But revenue from fixed-line services is declining as customers switch to mobiles and Internet phone calls, and to maintain profitability Telstra has to do more than keep its existing customers; it needs to convince them to use more of new higher profit services, like mobile Internet. But the high-profit customers for these sorts of services are less likely to be Telstra customers, and are also being aggressively targeted by other

Vodafone is working hard to woo traditional Telstra customers.

phone companies. Worse, some competitors like Vodafone and Optus are large players in other markets, so despite small marketing budgets relative to Telstra they can draw on experience and partnerships based in other markets to develop the Australian market (particularly important as all the companies roll out their 3G networks, where access to attractive content is critical). For example, Vodafone's substantial size in overseas markets allows it to offer good deals on handsets, and obtain access to prime online content for its new 3G service. As if competition from other telcos wasn't bad enough, Telstra is facing competition from outside the industry, with Microsoft announcing that it is developing an Internet telephone service. The combination of intensive competition in the mobile, business and broadband markets and falling fixed-line revenue has led Telstra to warn of falling profits and a falling share price.

So a big part of Telstra's strategy to improve its image and performance is based on marketing; Telstra's new boss, Sol Trujillo, has said that the company's future will be heavily interwoven with the tastes, habits and needs of its customers. With the biggest market research budget of any of the telcos in Australia, Telstra is aiming to know its customers better than they know themselves—to micro-segment and target its customers based on their individual tastes and practices, to tempt customers with new products and to persuade those customers to spend more time using Telstra products and to buy more products from Telstra. So Telstra is aiming to have 80% of its Internet customers on broadband by the end of 2008, and 25% of customers using its 3G network.[1]

Will Telstra succeed in its strategy of convincing customers to stay with it and, even more importantly, spend more on new services? Its success will largely depend on the company's understanding of its customers and its ability to respond with smarter marketing than its competitors.

After reading this chapter you should be able to:

1. Name the elements in the stimulus–response model of consumer behaviour.

2. Outline the major characteristics affecting consumer behaviour, and list some of the specific psychological, personal, cultural and social factors that influence consumers.

3. Explain the buyer decision process and discuss the importance of problem recognition, information search, evaluation of alternatives, the purchase decision and post-purchase behaviour.

4. Identify and define the consumer buying roles of initiator, influencer, decider, buyer and user.

5. Illustrate different types of buying decision behaviour, including complex, dissonance-reducing, habitual and variety-seeking buying behaviour.

6. Identify the key components of prospect theory, and the implications for marketers.

Consumer market
All the individuals and
households who buy
or acquire goods and
services for personal
consumption.

Buying behaviour is never simple, yet understanding it is the essential task of marketing management. This chapter and the next explore the dynamics of individual and group behaviour in the commercial context. In this chapter, we examine the **consumer market**—all the individuals and households who buy or acquire goods and services for personal consumption.

Consumers vary widely in age, income, education level and tastes. And they buy an incredible variety of goods and services. How consumers make their choices among these products takes us into a fascinating field composed of personal, cultural and social influences.

A model of consumer behaviour

Consumers make buying decisions every day. And they make many different types of purchases. Marketers can study actual consumer purchases to find out what they buy, where and how much. But learning about the *whys* of consumer buyer behaviour is not so easy—the answers are often locked deep within the consumer's head.

Penetrating the dark recesses of the consumer's mind is no easy task. Often, consumers themselves don't know exactly what influences their purchases. 'Ninety-five percent of the thought, emotion, and learning [that drive our purchases] occur in the unconscious mind—that is, without our awareness,' notes one consumer behaviour expert.[2]

The central question for marketers is: how do consumers respond to various marketing efforts the company might use? The starting point for the answer is the stimulus–response model of buyer behaviour shown in Figure 7.1. This figure shows that marketing and other stimuli enter the consumer's 'black box' and produce certain responses. Marketers must figure out what is in the buyer's black box.[3]

On the left of this figure, we see marketing stimuli represented and that these consist of the extended marketing mix elements—product, price, placement and promotion, together with the people and processes involved. Other stimuli include major forces and events in the buyer's environment—economic, technological, political and cultural. These stimuli make themselves felt by their combined action in the buyer's 'black box'. They result in a set of observable buyer responses shown on the right of the figure—product category selection, brand selection, dealer choice, reseller selection, purchase timing, repurchase intervals and purchase amount.

Marketers want to understand how the stimuli are changed into responses within the consumer's mind. First, the buyer's individual characteristics influence how they perceive and react to the stimuli. Second, the buyer's decision process itself affects the buyer's behaviour. This chapter looks first at buyer characteristics as they affect buying behaviour, and then discusses the buyer decision process.

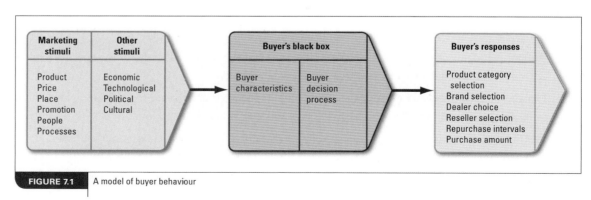

FIGURE 7.1   A model of buyer behaviour

Characteristics influencing consumer behaviour

Consumer purchases are strongly influenced by two groups of factors, shown in Figure 7.2. On the one hand there are internal characteristics that determine our behaviour: psychological and personal. And then there are external influences that represent the environment in which the individual behaviour takes place: cultural and social. Consumers themselves often aren't aware of all the factors that influence their behaviour, but marketers can influence some components of the individual's environment through their marketing programs (see Marketing Highlight 7.1). Other aspects of the individual's behaviour can't be influenced by the marketer but must be taken into account, for example by developing different products and services to meet the desires of different cultural groups.

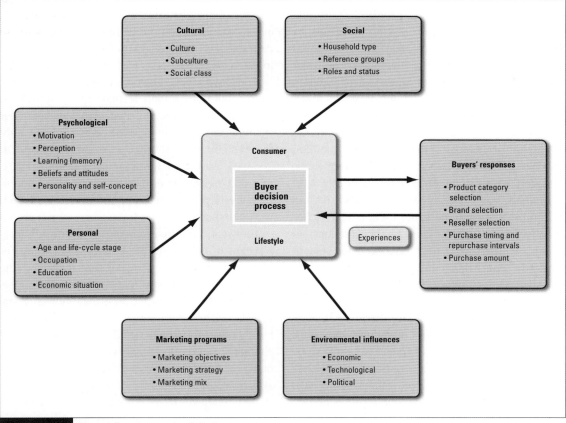

FIGURE 7.2   Factors influencing consumer behaviour

Shoes—fashion statement or mark of individualism?

Ask someone why they bought their last pair of shoes and you're likely to get a wide range of answers. Some answers will reflect the most basic level of need, 'My old ones wore out and these ones fitted the best', some might reflect variety-seeking behaviour, 'I like having different shoes for different occasions', and some might reflect the perceived value of the shoe, 'I think these have the best shock absorption, and I wanted them for running/walking/aerobics'. Some responses suggest a rational approach: 'I compared them with the other brands and I think these are the best value for money'; and others seem more emotional: 'I just like the way they look'.

However, consumers themselves often don't recognise the influences on their behaviour, which is what makes good market research more complex than just asking the consumer why they bought something. For example, most people don't say that they bought shoes because of the advertising or because a shoe was fashionable, but Nike moved from a struggling brand to the largest footwear company in the world after it signed Michael Jordan in 1985 and developed a range of sports shoes based on his nickname, Air. Teenagers around the world bought Nike Air shoes, even though American basketball barely rated at the time outside the USA, and Michael Jordan was just a name for many of the teenagers who bought Air Jordans. Suddenly, Nike Air were the shoes to have. Twenty years on, Nike and its competitors continue to do multi-million dollar deals with sports stars to endorse their products. In a highly competitive market, celebrity endorsement provides some differentiation between brands, so Nike sponsors sporting stars like Tiger Woods, Serena Williams and the Socceroos, while its major competitor Adidas sponsors David Beckham, Cricket Australia and the Australian Commonwealth Games team. And it can work; sports fans who aspire to be like their sporting idol often respond emotionally, even though deep down we know that wearing Nike won't make us any more like our sporting heroes. However, the sponsorship also allows the consumer

to claim a rational decision: 'If it's good enough for Tiger Woods, it must be good enough for me'.

If they think about it, consumers know that celebrities like Tiger Woods get paid to use a product, so the big brands also do everything they can to make sure that lesser known, but influential, people are wearing or using their products. Companies like Nike, Motorola and iRiver provide free products to sports people, entertainment stars and anyone who is likely to be in the media or at the right places, to make their brand look cool, desirable and the brand to buy. Celebrity endorsement draws attention to the product, and if the celebrity is well liked, liking for the celebrity can be transferred to the products they use, in what's called the 'halo effect'. Celebrity endorsement also reduces the risk in a purchase; if a brand is worn by the latest celebrity it signals that this brand must be socially acceptable, and perhaps even high status, and this will make the brand more desirable, even if most consumers won't reveal this in market research.

Consumers will also be affected by external factors, but don't usually recognise the effect of the external environment on their own behaviour; for example, global running shoe sales slumped after the September 2001 attacks in the USA, and in 2004–05 Australian footwear sales dropped 5.9% in a slowing consumer market. People shop more if they are happy, relaxed and optimistic about their work situation.

Footwear can also be a means of self-expression—a means of enhancing the buyer's self-concept. For some, this can mean showing that they have the latest, most fashionable footwear. For others, this means using footwear to express their individualism, so Nike allows consumers to customise their shoes by choosing the colours and adding personalised components, like their name written across the back of the shoe. (Nike reserves the right to refuse requests, after a well-publicised series of emails when a college student wanted to have 'sweatshop' emblazoned on his shoes, in protest at Nike's labour practices.)

Nike has been offering customisation since 1999, but relaunched the site <www.nikeid.com> in 2005 with more styles and greater ability to customise, hoping to tap into the growing number of consumers who will pay more for something unique.

Not to be outdone, Adidas allows users to order customised measurements of its Mi Adidas, using a fitting system in the Athlete's Foot stores. The system measures the length and width of a person's foot, allows users to select the colours and pick up their custom-made shoe three weeks later, for a premium of $AUD60. Herbert Hainer, the chief executive of Adidas, says that 'It is mainly an image tool. It shows that Adidas is the most innovative brand in the market.' In line with its positioning as the most innovative sportswear brand ('not a fashion brand', says Hainer), Adidas Australia launched Adidas 1 in 2005, a shoe that contains a computer chip that adjusts its cushioning level to the surface it is running or walking over. The shoes were priced at $450, and Adidas distributed just 500 pairs, but most of these were sold within three weeks.

Despite all the brand building by the major companies, there is a segment which is rebelling against the commercialism (and accusations of unethical labour practices) of the major sports shoe companies. Blackspot is one example of an emerging 'anti-brand'—purchasers of its sneakers are rejecting major brands, either as a sign of individuality and/or in protest against actions of the large corporations. Blackspot sneakers are produced by the Canadian not-for-profit organisation, Adbusters, using labour practices which are certified to treat workers well. The design is based on Converse, the world's oldest sports shoe brand and a popular US street brand, since bought by Nike. Reinforcing the brand's anti-Nike positioning, the Blackspot shoes have white

The Adbusters site promotes its 'anti-brand' shoe.

hand-painted circles which resemble a smudged-out swoosh (the Nike tick) and a small red spot on each toe, symbolising kicking the backside of Phil Knight, the CEO of Nike. One design is called the 'unswoosher'.

So brands can allow you to express your personality by wearing them, or you can express your individuality by wearing a customised version of the brand, or by not wearing a brand at all. How's that for catering to all segments?

Questions

1 Why do you think consumers are often more likely to buy a product which is endorsed by a celebrity? Do you think it is a rational or an emotional decision?

2 What might be some of the disadvantages in using a celebrity to endorse a product?

3 Ask your friends or family why they bought their last pair of shoes. Based on their answers, to what extent do you think that consumers are aware of the influences on their buying behaviour?

7.1

Psychological factors

As marketers we are intent on predicting buyer behaviour. The study of psychology has contributed to our present understanding of consumer behaviour. We begin by examining how a person's buying choices are influenced by five major psychological factors—motivation, perception, learning, beliefs and attitudes, and personality and self-concept.

Motivation

When consumers express interest in buying a product there are a number of questions we might ask. Why? What is the person really seeking? What needs are they trying to satisfy?

A person has many needs at any given time. Some needs are biological, arising from states of tension such as hunger, thirst or discomfort. Other needs are psychological, arising from the need for recognition, esteem or belonging. Most of these needs will not be strong enough to motivate the person to act at a given point in time. A need becomes a motive when it is aroused to a sufficient level of intensity. A **motive (or drive)** is a need that is sufficiently pressing to direct the person to seek satisfaction. Two of the most popular psychological theories, developed by Sigmund Freud and Abraham Maslow, have helped to increase our understanding of consumers' behaviour.

Sigmund Freud was one of the first to realise that people themselves often aren't aware of the reasons for their behaviour. In fact Freud assumed that people are largely unconscious of the real psychological forces shaping their behaviour. He saw the person as growing up and repressing many urges. According to his theory, these urges are never eliminated or under perfect control; they emerge in dreams, in slips of the tongue, in neurotic and obsessive behaviour or ultimately in psychoses.

Although much of Freud's work has been challenged, his work does support current understanding that a person's buying decisions are affected by subconscious motives that even the buyer may not fully understand. Thus, an ageing baby boomer who buys a sporty BMW convertible might explain that he simply likes the feel of the wind in his thinning hair. At a deeper level, he may be trying to impress others with his success. At a still deeper level, he may be buying the car to feel young and independent again. If the marketer understands this, they may advertise the car in a setting which is consistent with the potential buyer's motives.

The term *motivation research* refers to qualitative research designed to probe consumers' hidden, subconscious motivations. Motivation research evolved from Freudian ideas, using in-depth information from small samples of consumers to uncover the deeper motives for their product choices. The techniques range from sentence completion, word association and inkblot or cartoon interpretation tests, to having consumers describe typical brand users or form daydreams and fantasies about brands or buying situations.[4]

Like Freud, Abraham Maslow sought to explain why people are driven by particular needs at particular times.[5] Why does one person spend much time and energy on personal safety and another on gaining the esteem of others? Maslow's answer is that human needs are arranged in a hierarchy, from the most pressing to the least pressing. Maslow's hierarchy of needs is shown in Figure 7.3. In order of importance, they are physiological needs, safety needs, social needs, esteem needs and self-actualisation needs. The theory suggests that a person tries to satisfy the most important need first. When that important need is satisfied, it ceases to act as a motivator and the person will try to satisfy the next most important need.

For example, a starving person (with physiological needs) will not take an interest in the latest happenings in the art world (which serve self-actualisation needs), or in how they are seen or esteemed by others (social or esteem needs), or even in whether they are breathing clean air (safety needs). But as each important need is satisfied, the next most important need will come into play. Marketers tap into these needs, by reminding consumers of how their product will satisfy the needs. For example, advertising for insurance plays on peoples' need for security, and luxury branded goods are often sold with the suggestion that they will contribute to a person's status.

Perception

A motivated person is ready to act. How the person acts is influenced by their perception of the situation. Two people with similar motivation and in the same situation might act quite differently

Motive (or drive) A need that is sufficiently pressing to direct the person to seek satisfaction of the need.

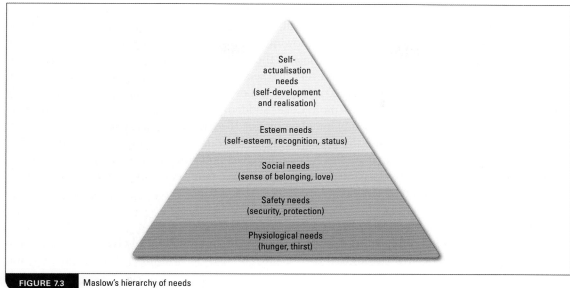

FIGURE 7.3   Maslow's hierarchy of needs
Source: Adapted from *Motivation and Personality*, 3rd edn, by Abraham H. Maslow. Copyright © 1987 by Abraham H. Maslow. Reprinted by permission of Pearson Education Inc., Upper Saddle River, NJ.

because they perceive the situation differently. One buyer of a home theatre system might consider a fast-talking salesperson loud or insincere. Another buyer might consider the same salesperson to be intelligent and helpful.

Why do people perceive the same situation differently? We all learn from the flow of information through our five senses: sight, sound, smell, touch and taste. However, each of us receives, organises and interprets this sensory information in an individual way using short- and long-term memory as part of the process. **Perception** is the process by which people select, organise and interpret information to form a meaningful picture of the world.

People can form different perceptions of the same stimulus because of three perceptual processes: selective exposure, selective distortion and selective retention.

Selective exposure   People are exposed to a great number of stimuli every day. For example, the average person might be exposed to more than 5000 ads a day.[6] It is impossible for a person to pay attention to all these stimuli; most will be screened out. Selective exposure means that marketers must work especially hard to attract the consumer's attention. Their offer will be lost on most people who are not in the market for the product. Even people who are in the market may not notice the offer unless it stands out from the many other offers.

Selective distortion   Even stimuli that consumers do notice do not always come across in the intended way. Each person tries to fit incoming information into an existing mindset. Selective distortion describes the tendency of people to adapt information to personal meanings. People tend to interpret information in a way that will support what they already believe. Selective distortion means that marketers must try to understand the mindsets of consumers and how they will affect interpretations of advertising and sales information.

Selective retention   People will also forget much of what they learn. They tend to retain information that supports their attitudes and beliefs.

These three perceptual factors—selective exposure, distortion and retention—mean that marketers have to work hard to get their messages through. This explains why marketers use so much drama

Perception The process by which people select, organise and interpret information to form a meaningful picture of the world.

and repetition in sending messages to their market. Interestingly, although most marketers worry about whether their offers will be perceived at all, some consumers are worried that they will be affected by marketing messages without even knowing it—through so-called 'subliminal' advertising. In 1957, a researcher announced that he had flashed the phrases 'Eat popcorn' and 'Drink Coca-Cola' on a screen in a New Jersey movie theatre every five seconds for 1/300th of a second. He reported that although viewers did not consciously recognise these messages, they absorbed them subconsciously and bought 58% more popcorn and 18% more Coke. Suddenly advertisers and consumer-protection groups became intensely interested in subliminal perception. People voiced fears of being brainwashed, and California and Canada declared the practice illegal. Although the researcher later admitted to making up the data, and numerous studies by psychologists and consumer researchers have found no link between subliminal messages and consumer behaviour, many consumers still fear, incorrectly, that they can be manipulated by subliminal messages.[7]

Learning

Learning Changes in an individual's behaviour arising from experience.

When people act, they learn. **Learning** describes changes in an individual's behaviour arising from experience. Learning occurs through the interplay of drives, stimuli, cues, responses and reinforcement.

It was suggested earlier that the buyer of a sports car may seek to satisfy a need, or drive, for self-esteem. A drive is a strong internal stimulus that calls for action. A drive becomes a motive when it is directed towards a particular stimulus object, in this case a sports car. A buyer's response to the idea of buying a sports car is conditioned by the surrounding cues. Cues are minor stimuli that determine when, where and how the person responds. Seeing a BMW ad in a magazine, hearing that a friend has bought one and being encouraged by friends are all cues that can influence a person's response to the impulse to buy a sports car.

Suppose a person buys an AIWA brand MP3 player. If the experience is rewarding the probability is that the player will be used more and more. The buyer's response will be reinforced. Then the next time the person buys a radio or portable television or a similar entertainment product, the probability is greater that an AIWA will be purchased. We say that the person generalises their response to similar stimuli.

The reverse of generalisation is discrimination. Suppose an AIWA buyer examines an MP3 player marketed under the Sony brand and sees that the Sony range has more features than the AIWA range. The buyer has learned to discriminate between brands, that is, recognise differences in sets of products, and may then adjust their response accordingly.

The practical significance of learning theory to marketers is that they can build demand for a product by associating it with strong drives, using motivating cues and providing positive reinforcement. A new company can enter the market by appealing to the same drives as competitors and providing similar cues because buyers are more likely to transfer loyalty to similar brands than to dissimilar ones (showing generalisation). Or it may design its brand to appeal to a different set of drives and offer strong cue inducements to switch (encouraging discrimination).

Beliefs and attitudes

Belief A descriptive thought or conviction that a person holds about something.

Brand image The set of beliefs consumers hold about a particular brand.

Through doing and learning, people acquire beliefs and attitudes. These, in turn, influence their buying behaviour. A **belief** is a descriptive thought that a person has about something. Beliefs may be based on real knowledge, opinion or faith, and may or may not carry an emotional charge. Marketers are interested in the beliefs that people formulate about specific products and services, because these beliefs make up product and **brand images** that affect buying behaviour. If some of the beliefs are wrong and prevent purchase, the marketer will want to launch a campaign to correct them.

People have attitudes regarding religion, politics, clothes, music, food and almost everything else. **Attitude** describes a person's relatively consistent evaluations, feelings and tendencies towards an object or idea. Attitudes put people into a frame of mind of liking or disliking things, of moving towards or away from them. A digital camera buyer may hold attitudes such as 'Buy the best', 'The Japanese make the best electronics products in the world', and 'Creativity and self-expression are among the most important things in life'. If so, the Nikon camera would fit well into the consumer's existing attitudes.

Because attitudes are usually developed over a long time, attitudes are difficult to change. Thus, a company should usually try to fit its products into existing attitudes rather than attempt to change attitudes. It may even be easier to alter the person's behaviour, without trying to change the attitude. This is often one reason why cut-price specials or sales are offered for particular products whose sales levels are not as high as the marketer desires; the person may be encouraged to buy because of a lower than expected price, and then if it performs well their attitude towards the product is likely to change.

Personality and self-concept

Each person's distinct personality influences their buying behaviour. Personality is perhaps the most complex of all aspects of human make-up. **Personality** refers to the unique psychological characteristics that lead to relatively consistent and lasting responses to one's own environment. Personality is closely tied to motivation and is usually described in terms of traits, with the five most important traits being neuroticism, extraversion, openness to experience, agreeableness/antagonism and conscientiousness–undirectedness.[8] Personality can be useful in analysing consumer behaviour for certain product or brand choices.[9] For example, coffee marketers have discovered that heavy coffee drinkers tend to be high on sociability. Thus, to attract customers Starbucks and other coffee shops create environments in which people can relax and socialise over a cup of coffee.

Many marketers use a concept related to personality—a person's self-concept (also called self-image) (see Marketing Highlight 7.1). The basic self-concept premise is that people's possessions contribute to and reflect their identities; that is, 'we are what we have'. So marketers develop what are called 'brand personalities' in their marketing communications, with the belief that consumers are more likely to choose brands whose personalities match their own. A **brand personality** is the specific mix of human traits that are attributed to a particular brand.

Personal factors

A buyer's decisions are also influenced by personal characteristics such as the buyer's age and life-cycle stage, occupation and economic situation.

Age and life-cycle stage

People change the goods and services they buy over their lifetimes. Tastes in food, clothes, furniture and recreation are often age related. Buying is also shaped by the stage of the *family life cycle*—the stages through which families might pass as they mature over time. Marketers often define their target markets in terms of life-cycle stage and develop appropriate products and marketing plans for each stage.

Traditional family life-cycle stages include young singles and married couples with children. Today, however, marketers are increasingly catering to a growing number of alternative, non-traditional stages such as unmarried couples, singles, childless couples, same-sex couples, single parents, extended parents (those with young adult children returning home) and others. In addition, every developed country is experiencing an increasing proportion of older consumers, as shown in

Attitude A person's relatively consistent evaluations, feelings and tendencies towards an object or an idea.

Personality A person's distinguishing psychological characteristics that lead to relatively consistent and lasting responses to their own environment.

Brand personality The specific mix of human traits that are attributed to a particular brand.

Figure 7.4. These older consumers are often healthy, and financially more secure than older consumers in the past, and have created a growing market for goods and services which suit their lifestyle.

Sony recently overhauled its marketing approach in order to target products and services to consumers based on their life stages. It created a new unit called the Consumer Segment Marketing Division, which has identified seven life-stage segments. They include, among others, generation Y (under 25), young professionals/DINKs (double income no kids, 25 to 34), families (35 to 54) and zoomers (55 and over). A recent Sony ad aimed at zoomers, people who have just retired or are close to doing so, shows a man living his dream by going into outer space. The ad deals not just with going into retirement, but with the psychological life-stage changes that go with it. 'The goal is to get closer to consumers,' says a Sony segment marketing executive.[10]

Occupation

A person's occupation affects the goods and services bought. Manual workers tend to buy more work clothes, work shoes and lunch boxes and enjoy sports like motor racing, whereas those involved in information-intensive industries tend to buy more business shirts and ties and would be more likely to have a home computer. Marketers try to identify and target the occupational groups that are most likely to be interested in their products and services. A company can even specialise in making products needed by a given occupational group. For example, computer software companies will design specialist products for accountants, engineers and doctors.

Economic situation

A person's economic situation will affect product choice, and some marketers target consumers who have lots of money and resources, charging prices to match. For example, Rolex positions its luxury

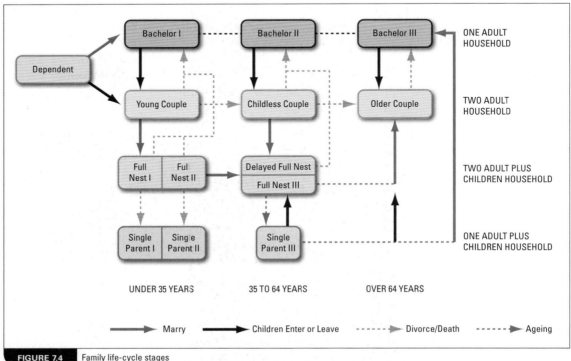

FIGURE 7.4 Family life-cycle stages

Source: Robert E. Wilkes, 'Household Life-cycle Stages, Transitions, and Product Expenditures', *Journal of Consumer Research*, vol. 22, June 1995, p. 29. Published by the University of Chicago Press. Used with permission.

watches as 'a tribute to elegance, an object of passion, a symbol for all time'. Other marketers target consumers with more modest means, such as the discount airlines like JetStar and Southwest Airlines. Marketers of income-sensitive goods—such as cars—closely watch trends in personal income, savings and interest rates. If economic indicators point to a recession, marketers will often take steps to redesign, reposition and reprice their products, or reduce stock and the number of outlets.

Cultural factors

Cultural factors exert the broadest and deepest influence on consumer behaviour. Marketers need to take into account the consumer's culture, subculture and social class.

Culture

Culture is a major influence on a person's wants and general behaviour. Much of human behaviour is learned. Growing up in a particular society, children learn basic values, perceptions, wants and responses from the family unit, their peers and other important institutions.[11] Global marketers must be fully aware of the underlying cultures in each market where sales are sought, and adapt their marketing strategy accordingly.

Marketers are always trying to spot cultural shifts in order to conceive and develop new products that might be wanted. For example, the cultural shift towards greater concern about health and fitness has created a large industry for exercise equipment, specialised apparel, lighter and more natural foods, exercise gyms and fitness services. Marketing Highlight 7.2 discusses how a growing number of coffee outlets have responded to, and reinforced, the growing leisure practice of meeting in coffee shops.

Culture The set of basic values, perceptions, wants and behaviours learned by a member of society from family and other important institutions.

Subculture

The dominant cultures in Australia and New Zealand are similar. Their cultures developed mainly from an Anglo-Saxon base followed by a European influence. But in both countries there are many **subcultures**, or smaller groups of people with shared value systems based on common life experiences and situations. Subcultures such as Chinese, Italian and Middle Eastern communities have distinctly different tastes and interests. This has led to a blending with previous aspects of the dominant culture, notably in restaurant fare and street wear. Marketers need to design products and marketing programs tailored to the wants and desires of these segments. For example, many marketers are developing new products that cater to the expanding Muslim market; Nokia has developed a phone, the Ikon i800, which directs users towards Mecca and tells them when to pray. Heineken, best known for its beers, has released a non-alcoholic malt drink, Fayrouz, and Lloyds bank is introducing Islamic banking services. (Muslims are not allowed to pay or accept interest.)[12]

Subculture A group of people with shared value systems based on common life experiences and situations.

The interest of buyers in various goods and services will be influenced by their subcultural background and their religion, race and geographical situation, or those of their partners, family and associational groups. These factors affect food preferences, clothing choices, recreational pursuits and even aspirations, such as career goals. For example, Asians like their milk thicker and sweeter than Western consumers, and New Zealand's largest dairy, Fonterra, has successfully developed milk drinks for the Asian market featuring flavours such as lemongrass, and has promoted vitamin D enriched milk products by installing two dozen bone scanners in supermarkets, to show Asian consumers that their bones would benefit from vitamin D.[13]

Social class

Social classes are relatively permanent and ordered divisions in a society whose members share similar values, interests and behaviours. Almost every lifeform and society has some kind of pecking order or social class structure, though in most societies people can move between classes. For example,

Social classes Relatively permanent and ordered divisions in a society whose members share similar values, interests and behaviours.

MARKETING HIGHLIGHT

7.2

The rise and rise of the café culture

What do the USA, Australia, China, Korea and a host of other countries have in common? A boom in out-of-home coffee sales, as chains like Starbucks, Gloria Jeans and Pacific Coffee fight for leadership in their local markets. What's behind this fundamental change in consumer behaviour, where millions of consumers are acquiring the habit of a daily (or more often) latte or cappuccino from their local coffee shop? The rise in coffee consumption shows the interplay between effective marketing, distribution and changing social patterns, which have combined to create new consumer habits and a hugely growing market in catering to those habits.

The rise in coffee consumption also reflects a change in choice of beverage; Asian consumers have long been tea drinkers, but Starbucks chairman Howard Schulz told analysts in 2004 that 'we have turned them into coffee drinkers'. He may be exaggerating the change, but there is no doubt that coffee consumption is rising, partly at the expense of tea; since 1992–93, consumption of tea in Australia has fallen by 22.5%, while coffee consumption has increased by 4.2%. Out-of-home coffee consumption is growing much faster, up by about 15% per year. But what's behind this change? Consumer preferences aren't enough to explain such a rapid growth in coffee consumption in Asian countries like China, Singapore and Korea, which are traditionally tea drinking cultures, but which, like most Western countries, are seeing a boom in out-of-home coffee sales. The rise in coffee chains shows a more fundamental shift in consumer behaviour—the coffee shop has become the new meeting place, a 'third place', separate from both home and office, and for many consumers a home away from home. The growth of the coffee shop is one indication of an increasing tendency to spend money on quick gratification. This steady change in consumer behaviour also reflects a highly effective strategy by Starbucks and the other chains to create a daily habit by consumers to buy a coffee. The growth in coffee shops responds to this growing consumer habit, as more coffee shops open up to cater to the growing market. The large number of coffee shops also reinforces the coffee habit, by providing a constant reminder of the ability to escape the daily grind of work or life by a fix of caffeine, or by a retreat to the soft lounges of the local coffee store.

Starbucks hopes to do for coffee what McDonald's did for hamburgers, and it already dominates most of the markets in which it operates. The strategy relies on convenient location of coffee outlets, and Starbucks is well on the way to its aim of a store on every corner, with nearly 9000 locations operating around the world, and plans to grow this number to 30000 in the next 10 years. Starbucks has been less successful in entering the established coffee market of Australia, where it has suffered criticisms that its coffee is unappealing to the more demanding Australian coffee drinker, and with 59 stores it lags behind its rival Gloria Jeans, with 259 stores. Both chains, however, represent only a small proportion of the total Australian market of around 5000 independent coffee shops, and account for only an estimated 3% of coffee sales in Australia. While the competition is intense in every market, most operators realise that the growing visibility of the chains is increasing sales for everyone; as Michael Wu, Managing Director of Maxim's, the Hong Kong Starbucks operator, says: 'We're opening ten stores a year and I cannot see that slowing . . . The pie is getting bigger for the coffee market.'

Starbucks itself says that it doesn't just sell coffee, it sells an 'experience', and the most loyal of its regulars return around 18 times a month. Particularly for the fast-growing Asian market, the experience often seems more important than a coffee fix. The Asian coffee chains' menus offer a far wider range of non-coffee drinks than the US outlets, and often offer extras like newspapers, magazines and, for the outlets of Pacific Coffee, computers with free Internet access.

There are also other important differences between the countries in consumer behaviour.

Australian and US stores tend to do most business in the morning, particularly in takeaway sales, as commuters grab a cup of coffee on the way to work. The Asian stores tend to do more business later in the day. Philippine branches of the Coffee Bean and Tea Leaf chain do their biggest business on Friday and Saturday nights, as people meet up with friends and family.

The coffee chains are well on the way to creating a new consumer habit, and Starbucks, with 34 million customers a week, is now the most frequently visited retailer in the world. It's capitalising on this store traffic by aiming for incremental revenue, and is now one of the largest music retailers in the USA. It is slowly expanding its music sales throughout its global outlets, striking arrangements with record companies to jointly develop albums and digital downloads, most of which are pitched at its prime demographic of over 30. It's a trend that is being watched very carefully by the music industry. Will Starbucks expand the market, as it did for coffee, or steal sales away from the traditional outlets? Whatever happens, the coffee shops are likely to remain a lasting component of our lifestyles.

Sources: Simon Bowers, 'Coffee Bar Chain to Tackle the Land of Tea', *The Sydney Morning Herald*, 29 August 2005, p. 24; Mark Chipperfield, 'Coffee Wars', *The Sydney Morning Herald*, The Sydney Magazine, 22 September 2005, p. 72; Barrie Dunstan, 'Starbucks Snaps the Sands Man Wide Awake', *The Australian Financial Review*, 4 November 2005, p. 32; Neil Gough, 'City's Romance with Coffee Gives Grounds for Optimism', *South China Morning Post*, 29 April 2005, p. 2; Neil Shoebridge, 'Starbucks to Continue with Daily Grind', *The Australian Financial Review*, 18 April 2005, p. 50; Neil Shoebridge, 'Starbucks Brewing Up Different Tune', *The Australian Financial Review*, 20 October 2005, p. 3; Neil Shoebridge, 'Starbucks Lacking in Musical Muscle', *The Australian Financial Review*, 31 October 2005, p. 49; Robert Stockdill, 'Starbucks Back on Track', *Foodweek*, 6 May 2005; Leanne Tolra, 'Drinking to the Caffeine Connection', *The Age*, 15 November 2005, p. 12; Cris V. Paraso, 'Tapping the Filipino's Unique Penchant for Gourmet Coffee', *BusinessWorld*, 20 May 2005, p. S4/9; Gretchen Weber, 'Preserving the Counter Culture', *Workforce Management*, vol. 84, no. 2, 2005, pp. 28–34; <www.pacificcoffee.com/eng/home.php>; <www.gloriajeans.com>; <www.starbucks.com>; Australian Bureau of Statistics, *Apparent Consumption of Foodstuffs, Australia, Preliminary*, Catalogue no. 4315.0, November 1998.

Questions

1 How important is the taste of the coffee to the success of a coffee chain, or are these chains selling an 'experience' in which the coffee itself is relatively unimportant?

2 Which is your favourite coffee shop or chain? Why? What does this suggest about consumer preferences?

3 Do you think Starbucks poses a danger to music outlets? Why or why not?

7.2

completing tertiary education may give rise to a better occupation and movement up the social scale. Other factors, such as losing a prestigious position, may cause one to slide back down the social scale.

Social class is not determined by a single factor. A number of classification schemes have been developed, ranging from those using occupation and education to those based on a combination of occupation, income, education, source of income, house type and dwelling area.[14] Marketers are interested in social class because people within a given social class tend to exhibit similar buying behaviour. Social classes show distinct product and brand preferences in areas such as clothing, home furnishings, leisure activity and cars.[15]

Social factors

A consumer's behaviour is also influenced by social factors, such as the consumer's household type and reference groups, social roles and status. Because these social factors can strongly affect consumer responses, companies must take them into account when designing their marketing strategies.

Household types

The members of a person's household can strongly influence buyer behaviour. We can distinguish between three household types in the buyer's life. The buyer's parents make up the family of orientation. From parents a person acquires an orientation towards religion, politics, leisure pursuits, economics and a sense of personal ambition, self-worth and love. Even if the buyer no longer interacts very much with their parents, the parents can still significantly influence the buyer's unconscious behaviour. In countries where parents continue to live with their children their influence can be significant.

The family of procreation—the buyer's spouse and children—exert a more direct influence on everyday buying behaviour. The family is the most important consumer buying organisation in society and it has been researched extensively. Marketers are interested in the roles and relative influence of the husband, wife and children on the purchase of a large variety of products and services.

Husband–wife involvement varies widely by product category and by stage in the buying process. And buying roles change with evolving consumer lifestyles. The wife has traditionally been the main purchasing agent for the family, especially in the areas of food, household products and clothing. But this is changing with the increased number of working wives and the willingness of husbands to do more of the family purchasing. Whereas women make up just 40% of drivers, they now influence more than 80% of car-buying decisions. Men now account for about 40% of all food shopping dollars. In all, women now make almost 85% of all purchases, spending $6 trillion each year.[16]

In the case of expensive products and services, husbands and wives engage more in joint decision making. And their joint decisions often differ from those they would make as individuals. The marketer needs to determine how family members interact to reach decisions and how much influence each has on the purchase of a particular product or service. Understanding the dynamics of husband–wife decision making can help marketers to aim the best marketing strategies towards the right family members.

Where a married person buys household appliances such as air conditioning, the spouse will play an influencer role. They may have an opinion about buying a camera and the kind of camera to buy, although one member of the couple is often the primary decider, purchaser and user.

Groups

Reference groups Groups that have direct (face-to-face) or indirect influence on a person's attitudes or behaviour.

Membership groups Groups that have a direct influence on a person's behaviour and to which a person belongs.

Aspirational groups Groups to which an individual wishes to belong.

Opinion leaders People who exert influence on others' opinions and buying behaviour.

A person's behaviour is influenced by many small groups. **Reference groups** serve as direct (face-to-face) or indirect points of comparison or reference in forming a person's attitudes or behaviour. Groups to which a person belongs which have a direct influence on the person's behaviour are called **membership groups**. But people are often influenced by reference groups to which they do not belong. For example, an **aspirational group** is one to which the individual wishes to belong, as when a teenage football player hopes to play some day for the Wallabies or the Socceroos. Marketers try to identify the reference groups of their target markets. Reference groups expose a person to new behaviours and lifestyles, influence the person's attitudes and self-concept and create pressures to conform that may affect the person's product and brand choices.

The importance of group influence varies across products and brands. It tends to be strongest when the product is visible to others whom the buyer respects. Manufacturers of products and brands subjected to strong group influence must figure out how to reach **opinion leaders**—people within a reference group who, because of special skills, knowledge, personality or other characteristics, exert influence on others. One expert calls them *the influentials*. 'They drive trends, influence mass opinion and, most importantly, sell a great many products,' he says. 'These are the early adopters who had a digital camera before everyone else and who were the first to fly again after September 11. They are the 10 percent . . . who determine how the rest consume and live by chatting about their likes and dislikes.'[17] We'll talk more about new methods of marketing to these influential opinion leaders in Chapter 16.

Roles and status

A person belongs to many groups—family, clubs, organisations. The person's position in each group can be defined in terms of both role and status. A role consists of the activities people are expected to perform according to the persons around them. Each role carries a status reflecting the general esteem given to it by society. People usually choose products appropriate to their roles and status. Consider the various roles a working mother plays. In her company she might play the role of a brand manager; in her family she plays the role of wife and mother; at her favourite sporting events she plays the role of avid fan. As a brand manager, she will buy the kind of clothing that reflects her role and status in her company.

Roles in the buying process

The marketer needs to know which people are involved in the buying decision and what role each person plays. Identifying the decision maker in many transactions is fairly easy. For example, both men and women normally choose their own shoes. Other products, however, involve group decisions. Consider the selection of a family car. The suggestion to buy a new car might come from the oldest child. A friend might advise the family on the kind of car to buy. The husband might choose the make. The wife might have a definite opinion regarding the car's style. The husband and wife might then make the final decision jointly. And the wife might end up using the car more than her husband.

IT'S YOUR WATCH THAT
TELLS MOST ABOUT WHO YOU ARE.

Premier   SXD774P $1300.
ANALOGUE. SAPPHIRE GLASS. 48 DIAMONDS.
MOTHER OF PEARL DIAL. STAINLESS STEEL.
100M WATER RESISTANT.

SEIKO
www.seiko.com.au

Purchases of items which are publicly visible, such as jewellery and watches, are likely to be influenced by others.

Figure 7.5 shows that people might play any of several roles in a buying decision:

- ◉ initiator—the person who first suggests or thinks of the idea of buying a particular product or service

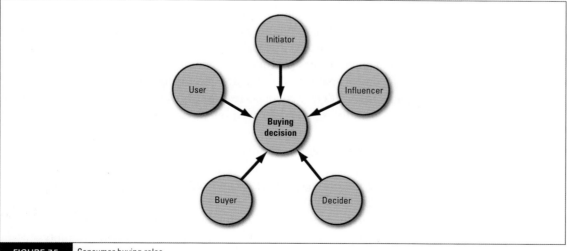

FIGURE 7.5   Consumer buying roles

⊚ influencer—a person whose views or advice carry some weight in making the final buying decision

⊚ decider—the person who ultimately makes a buying decision or any part of it—whether to buy, what to buy, how to buy or where to buy

⊚ buyer—the person who makes an actual purchase

⊚ user—the person who consumes or uses a product or service.

A company needs to identify who occupies the various roles because this information affects product design and advertising message decisions. If Ford finds that husbands make buying decisions for the family four-wheel-drive car, it will direct most of its advertising for these models towards husbands. Even if Ford targets its ads for four-wheel drives towards men, the ads are likely to include wives, children and others who might initiate or influence the buying decision. And the company will design its station wagons with features that meet the needs of those buying-decision participants. Knowing the main participants and the roles they play helps the marketer fine-tune the marketing program.

SELF-CHECK QUESTIONS

3 Behavioural scientists argue about the extent to which our behaviour is the result of our genetic make-up or what we learn. How does this impact on the science of marketing?

4 Personality and self-concept are at the root of our individuality. How might these factors influence a consumer's decision-making process?

5 Which group(s) do you feel have had the most influence in determining the beliefs and attitudes you hold about major brands of mobile phones and banks? Why?

Consumer lifestyle

Lifestyle A person's pattern of living as expressed in their activities, interests and opinions.

Psychographics The technique of measuring lifestyles and developing lifestyle classifications; it involves measuring the major AIO dimensions (activities, interests, opinions).

People coming from the same subculture, social class and occupation might have quite different lifestyles. **Lifestyle** indicates a pattern of living and consumption and describes how people allocate their time and money. While people who have similar lifestyles tend to band together, it is not possible to describe these groups by demographic profiles alone. They may be similar in age, gender, income and where they live, but still live quite different lifestyles. To fill this information gap, marketers use what is called **psychographics**, whereby consumers' major AIO dimensions—activities, interests and opinions—are ascertained and used in marketing appeals. Lifestyle captures something more than the person's social class or personality. It profiles a person's pattern of acting and interacting in the world.

In Australia, the Roy Morgan Research Centre conducts research into consumer opinions and trends. It has established what it calls 10 'value segments' based on consumers' values and fundamental ways of approaching the world:

1 Basic Needs (usually associated with people who have reduced their needs in line with reduced income).

2 Real Conservatism (tend to be mature-age people, in mid-career, and those in rural locations who hold conservative and ethical views).

3 Conventional Family Life (generally suburban life, centred on raising their children).

4 Traditional Family Life (the older segment of 'conventional family life', generally empty-nesters or extended families).

5 Young Optimism (tend to be those who are mainly city dwellers and starting out on professional careers).

6 Something Better (usually those who are after the next big deal; usually carrying debt).

7 Look At Me (generally those who are directed by their peer group, watch a lot of TV, always on the move).

8 A Fairer Deal (usually blue-collar workers, who left school early, feel life has let them down somewhat).

9 Socially Aware (generally those who absorb information, like new gadgets, think like the highest socioeconomic group).

10 Visible Achievement (usually associated with those who feel they have made it, and can reflect this achievement in their homes, cars and choice of holiday location) (see Figure 7.6).

Over the last 20 years, Roy Morgan Research has been able to illustrate that these mindsets have a theoretical base that reflects the choices that people make, and the changes that people experience,

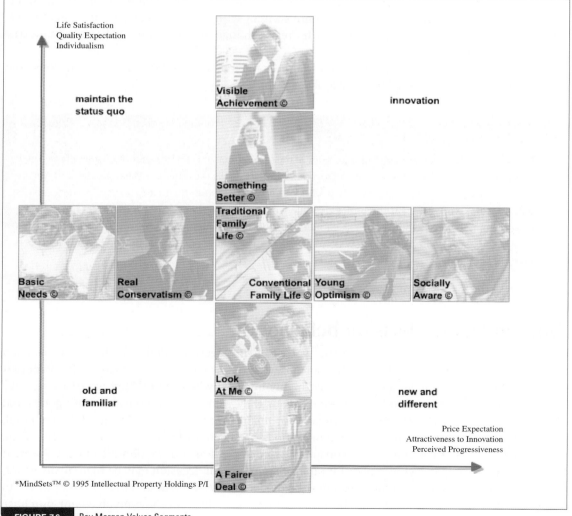

FIGURE 7.6 | Roy Morgan Values Segments
Source: <www.roymorgan.com>. Reproduced courtesy of Roy Morgan Pty Ltd. Roy Morgan Values Segments are developed in conjunction with Colin Benjamin of the Horizons Network.

in their lives. Psychographic classifications will also profile the activities that different groups engage in, the brands they choose and the media they consume.[18]

Psychographics is commonly used by companies like beer brewers to update their image and improve sales. When a brewer such as Lion Nathan is developing its marketing strategy for a product like Becks (a premium imported beer) psychographic studies will typically be used to profile the target customers, work out their preferences and interests and reflect that in the brand positioning or brand personality, to make the beer most attractive to target drinkers. The ads might feature images of the financial sector of the city with scenes of 'young optimists' having fun and working hard.

No psychographic classification is universal and different lifestyle groups have been identified in other countries. For example, McCann-Erickson London found the following British lifestyles: avant guardians (interested in change), pontificators (traditionalists, very British), chameleons (follow the crowd) and sleepwalkers (contented underachievers). Backer Spielvogel Bates Worldwide found five global lifestyles that they believe span country borders and cultural systems: strivers (young, active people seeking instant gratification), achievers (more successful, affluent people who value status and quality), the pressured (people bogged down by life's daily problems), adapters (older consumers who live comfortably and are content with their lives) and traditionals (people who represent the old values and culture, who resist change and who are loyal to tried and true products).[19]

When used carefully, the lifestyle concept can help the marketer understand changing consumer values and how they affect buying behaviour.

SELF-CHECK QUESTION

6   Two households are situated on opposite sides of the same street, in the same suburb of your city or town. One male head of household is a self-employed truck driver, while the other is a Malaysian-born university professor. Each household comprises two adults and two children in their early teens. The truck driver's wife does not work, whereas the professor's wife works as a laboratory assistant in a local hospital. The gross income before tax for each household is $100 000 per annum. What do you think are the likely lifestyles for each household, and how do you think these would impact on the buying behaviour of each household member?

Types of buying decision behaviour

Involvement The importance of the product for the consumer. High-involvement purchases are typical of important, risky, infrequently purchased goods. Low-involvement products are typically frequently purchased, low-cost, low-risk purchases.

Consumer decision making varies with the type of buying decision. Purchase decisions are often classified according to the importance of the purchase to the consumer, or the consumer's **involvement** with the product. Consumers are likely to be highly involved when the product is expensive, risky and important to them or to others whose opinions they value.[20] Cars, houses, luxury goods and education are all likely to be high involvement for a consumer. In contrast, frequently purchased, low-risk purchases like fast-moving consumer goods are likely to be low involvement. The same product may be high involvement for a consumer on one occasion and low or moderate involvement on another. For example, a choice of restaurant for an important occasion may be high involvement, the choice of a restaurant for a nice meal may be moderate involvement and the choice of where to eat for a quick meal after work may be low involvement. High- and low-involvement purchase situations result in different types of decision making, as shown in Figure 7.7.

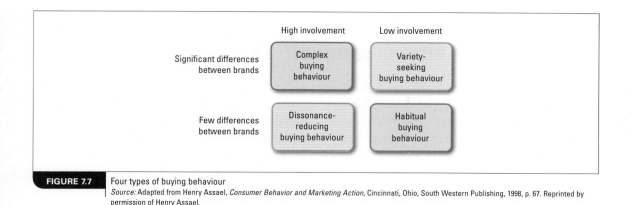

FIGURE 7.7 | Four types of buying behaviour
Source: Adapted from Henry Assael, *Consumer Behavior and Marketing Action*, Cincinnati, Ohio, South Western Publishing, 1998, p. 67. Reprinted by permission of Henry Assael.

Complex buying behaviour

Consumers will typically undertake **complex buying behaviour** when the purchase is high involvement, and when they believe that there are significant differences between brands. For example, a personal computer buyer may not even know what attributes to consider. Many product features carry no real meaning to the consumer, for instance a '3.4 GHz Pentium processor', 'super VGA resolution', or '2 GB SDRAM memory'. The buyer will pass through a learning process, first developing beliefs about the product, then attitudes and then making a considered purchase choice. Marketers of high-involvement products must understand the information-gathering and evaluation behaviour of high-involvement consumers. They need to help buyers learn about product-class attributes and their relative importance. They need to differentiate their brand's features, perhaps by describing the brand's benefits using print media. They must motivate store salespeople and the buyer's acquaintances to influence the final brand choice. However, even with complex buying behaviour, consumers don't always make what economists would think is the 'best' decision, as Marketing Highlight 7.3 shows.

Complex buying behaviour Consumer buying behaviour in situations characterised by high consumer involvement in a purchase and significant perceived differences between brands.

Dissonance-reducing buying behaviour Consumer buying behaviour in situations characterised by high involvement but few perceived differences between brands.

Dissonance-reducing buying behaviour

Dissonance-reducing buying behaviour occurs when consumers are highly involved with an expensive, infrequent or risky purchase, but see little difference between brands. For example, consumers buying carpeting may face a high-involvement decision because carpeting is expensive and self-expressive. Yet these buyers might consider most carpet brands in a given price range to be the same. In this case, because perceived brand differences are not large, buyers might shop around to learn what is available but buy relatively quickly. They might respond primarily to a good price or to purchase convenience. After the purchase, consumers might experience post-purchase dissonance (after-sale discomfort) when they notice certain disadvantages of the purchased carpet brand or hear favourable things about brands not purchased. To counter such dissonance, the

Philips encourages purchase by providing the buyer with a money-back guarantee, thus allowing the customer to anticipate, and avoid, post-purchase dissonance.

Utility The satisfaction or pleasure that an individual derives from the consumption of a good or service.

Prospect theory A theory that describes how people make decisions when the outcome is uncertain.

Are consumers always rational?

We saw in Chapter 1 that if they have a choice customers will buy a product or service that they believe offers them the highest value. This is a basic idea of both economics and marketing, though economists tend to use the term **utility** rather than 'value' to describe the happiness or pleasure that people try to achieve from any transaction. The idea that people's behaviour can be explained by their attempt to get the best value or utility dates back to nineteenth-century economist William Stanley Jevons, and has led to a fundamental economic principle that people will aim to 'maximise their utility'. This means that people will try to get the best outcome or value from their actions, including from their purchases. Such behaviour is said to be 'rational'. Of course as we saw in Chapter 1, this doesn't always mean that people make the best choice; for example, they might not know that a better alternative is available, and they won't keep searching for a better alternative if they don't think it is worth their time. Even if they know what is available, people will sometimes be unable to judge which is the best product or service. This led Nobel prize winning economist Herb Simon to propose the idea of 'bounded rationality': the principle that people have limited ability to collect and process information, and so their choices will often be imperfect. Despite this, the underlying principle that people will be rational in their buying behaviour—will seek to get the best value, and will be happier when they get better value—is a very good guide to how people will buy and how they will make judgments about the results of purchases. Bounded rationality is also the basis for the idea that consumers will engage in complex buying behaviour if the purchase is high involvement, and they think there are differences between brands; if it's worth the effort, people will put the effort in to try and make the best decision.

Prospect theory

Some recent research, however, suggests that people don't always act 'rationally'; they sometimes make decisions which don't seem to be in their best interest, and make judgments which don't seem to be rational. This work, which is often described as **prospect theory**, led to Daniel Kahneman being awarded the Nobel Prize for economics in 2002. Results from many studies investigating prospect theory show that people tend to make decisions with particular biases, and understanding those biases provides fascinating insights into what influences consumer decisions. Along with researchers Amos Tversky and Richard Thaler, Kahneman's work identifies a number of mental shortcuts or 'heuristics' which are often used by consumers to make decisions. We list some of the most important mental shortcuts here, and their implications for marketing.

Mental accounting

Richard Thaler first used the term 'mental accounting' to show how people seem to think about money. Rather than thinking purely about the monetary cost and value of different options, Thaler suggests that people think about the same sum of money differently at different times. He gives an example to illustrate this principle:

> Mr and Mrs L go on a fishing trip, and catch some salmon. The fish are lost by the airline on the way home, and Mr and Mrs L receive $300 in insurance. They take the money and go out to dinner at an upmarket restaurant, spending $225 on the meal. They have never spent this amount before in a restaurant.[21]

Why would Mr and Mrs L suddenly spend more money on a meal than they ever have before? Traditional economic theory doesn't explain this well; it would say that if they have never before seen the value of spending $225 on a restaurant meal, there is no reason they would do so now (assuming they could have afforded to spend the money, if they wished, before). However, Thaler's idea of mental accounting says that instead of just looking at the

exquisite **tastes**

2005/2006
hampers and
gift packs

Mental accounting shows that a windfall gain (such as a gift voucher) will often be spent on items that people often wouldn't buy for themselves.

cost of purchases, consumers often treat money as if it came from different bank accounts, and spend it differently. So an unexpected gain (a 'windfall gain') is treated differently, and Mr and Mrs L are prepared to spend this money on something they never have before.

Effective marketers can capitalise on this mental accounting. For example, since we know that unexpected gains are often spent on things that people wouldn't usually buy, luxury items can effectively be promoted to consumers when they have unexpected extra income—for instance at the time of the year when lots of people get tax returns, or at Christmas or Chinese New Year, when people are often given money or gift vouchers to spend.

Segregation and integration

Another aspect of mental accounting is that people don't seem to think just about the monetary aspect or value of an outcome as traditional theory would suggest, but instead appear to think about outcomes in terms of 'losses' and 'gains'. Thaler gives two examples to illustrate this:

- Mr A was given two lottery tickets. He won $50 in one and $25 in the other.
- Mr B was given a single lottery ticket. He won $75.

Who is happier: A, B, or no difference?

- Ms A received a letter from the tax department, saying that she had made a minor arithmetical error on her tax return, and owed $100. On the same day, she received a letter from the state tax department, saying she owed $50.
- Ms B received a letter from the tax department, saying that she had made a minor arithmetical error, and owed $150.

Who is more upset: A, B, or no difference?

Most people answer A in both cases. However, from the point of view of traditional economic theory, there should be no difference between the two cases. In the first two cases both A and B are $75 better off, and in the next two both have lost $150. But most people don't just think about the money; they think about what they have won or 'gained' and what they have lost, and two gains seem better than one of the same size, just as two losses seem worse than one of the equivalent size.

An understanding of how people think about gains and losses leads to some important implications for selling products. Since we know that people are less upset by one larger loss than several smaller losses which result in the same total loss, marketers can make people more willing to pay by combining many small losses into one larger loss (or *integrating* losses). The consumer then notices one loss, which they won't like, but they don't dislike this one large loss as much as regular small losses. So a clever marketer encourages a consumer to have a regular payment (for example, a gym membership) charged directly to their credit card. This means that consumers will typically pay less attention to the monthly charge, because it is just one of many charges on the monthly bill. Automatic debit cards are another way for marketers to integrate losses. For example, Hong Kong users of public transport usually pay with a cash card, the Octopus Card, which is swiped to pay

Using the **Octopus Card**

Credit and debit cards like the Octopus Card encourage consumers to spend more by combining many small charges into one.

for bus, train or ferry trips. The Octopus Card can also be used for a wide range of other goods and services, such as groceries or entry to swimming pools. The commuter tops up the Octopus Card with value from time to time (one loss) but is then less likely to pay attention to intermittent charges which are debited from their Octopus Card. Electronic passes for tollways have the same effect; the consumer typically pays less attention to a debit from the toll pass than they would if they had to pay with coins each time, so tollway usage typically increases when people have an electronic tag.

In contrast to their preference for integrated losses, consumers value separate (or segregated) gains more than one equivalent gain. So instead of giving price discounts, marketers will sometimes have a cash back offer. Although the gain is the same, prospect theory suggests that consumers will notice and value the cash back offer more than they would an equivalent price discount.

Losses are weighted more heavily than gains

The previous examples show that people think about losses and gains from a given position, not as the final monetary outcome. A substantial amount of research also shows that people notice, and are more upset by, losses than they are pleased by equivalent gains. Two more examples show this.

- Mr A bought his first lottery ticket and won $100. On the same day, he damaged the carpet in his apartment, and had to pay the landlord $80.
- Mr B bought his first lottery ticket and won $20.

Who is happier: A, B, or no difference?

Again, classical economics would say there should be no difference; both A and B are $20 better off than they were at the start of the day. However, most

people say that B is happier, because B has had a gain which has not been offset by a loss. This finding and other related research show strong evidence that people notice and dislike losses more than they value equivalent gains. Economists partly express this by saying that consumers are typically 'risk averse', but it seems that consumers are 'loss averse' rather then risk averse (which suggests they don't like variability). Marketers can use this knowledge to position or 'frame' their offerings to suggest either a gain or a loss. For example, one study compared the response of consumers to two promotional messages by a company selling insulation. The first framed the product as a gain which could be achieved by insulation:

- 'If you insulate your home fully, you will save 75c every day.'

The second message framed the same offer as a loss, which could be avoided by insulation.

- 'If you fail to insulate your home fully, you will lose 75c every day.'

Significantly more customers took up insulation after hearing of the second offer, just as would be predicted by prospect theory.

This consumer dislike of losses has strong implications for service delivery. If consumers are used to a particular service, and the service is taken away, consumers are likely to notice and be dissatisfied. Marketers will often try to compensate for taking away one service by offering something in return, thereby offsetting the loss with a gain. However, prospect theory suggests that while it is better to offset a loss with a gain than do nothing at all, consumers will tend to pay more attention to what they have lost than to what they have gained. This suggests that if the company is planning on introducing a new service, if the new service can't be maintained it may be better not to start at all rather than offer a service, create expectations of that service and then take it away, even if something is offered to consumers in return.

So where does all this discussion leave the old idea that consumers are rational in their buying behaviour? Most authors accept that consumers strive to be rational but that this rationality is limited. As Simon first argued, it's limited by our capacity to gather and process information, but also because we all tend to make judgments based on our own (often unconscious) biases and mental shortcuts. Understanding these mental shortcuts can help a marketer to understand consumers' decision processes and present offers so they are likely to be more acceptable to consumers.

Sources: R. Thaler, 'Mental Accounting and Consumer Choice', *Marketing Science*, vol. 4, no. 3, 1985, pp. 199–214; S. Yates, Using Prospect Theory to Create Persuasive Communications about Solar Water Heaters and Insulation, unpublished doctoral dissertation, University of California, Santa Cruz, CA; Daniel Kahneman and Amos Tversky, 'Choices, Values and Frames', *American Psychologist*, vol. 39, no. 4, 1983, pp. 341–350; Daniel Kahneman and Amos Tversky, 'Prospect Theory: An Analysis of Decision under Risk', *Econometrica*, vol. 47, no. 2, 1979, pp. 263–291; A. Tversky and D. Kahneman, 'The Framing of Decisions and the Psychology of Choice', *Science*, vol. 211, 1981, pp. 453–458.

Questions

1 An Australian bank decided to introduce a cash-handling fee for its small-business customers. This meant that business customers who deposited cash into their bank accounts were charged an extra sum each month on top of the monthly account fee, thereby segregating the customer's loss in fees. Customers were very angry, and complained bitterly to the bank. Can you think of another way for the bank to raise its charges without angering customers so much?

2 Qantas recently changed its method of calculating the value of frequent-flyer points. The airline argued that customers would get more points on some routes (a gain) and fewer points on others (a loss). What would prospect theory predict would be the effect on customer satisfaction with this new strategy?

3 Some products are advertised as including numerous extras; if you buy a set of steak knives you get an extra carving knife plus a knife sharpener. But such extras cost money, and the company selling the knives could instead decrease the price of the knives, and sell the extras separately to those who value them. Explain, using prospect theory, why such promotions are used so often.

7.3

marketer's after-sale communications should provide evidence and support to help consumers feel good about their brand choices.

Habitual buying behaviour

Habitual buying behaviour occurs when the purchase is low involvement and the consumer doesn't think there are significant differences between brands. For example, take salt. Most consumers have little involvement in this product category—they simply go to the store and reach for a brand. If they keep reaching for the same brand, it is generally out of habit rather than strong brand loyalty. Consumers appear to have low involvement with most low-cost, frequently purchased products.

In such cases, consumers do not search extensively for information about the brands, evaluate brand characteristics and make weighty decisions about which brands to buy. Instead, they passively receive information as they watch television or read magazines. Ad repetition creates *brand familiarity* rather than *brand conviction*. In these circumstances, consumers do not form strong attitudes towards a brand; they select the brand because it is familiar. Because they are not highly involved with the product, consumers may not evaluate the choice even after purchase, except very fleetingly.

Because buyers aren't usually highly committed to low-involvement products, marketers of low-involvement products with few brand differences often use price and sales promotions to stimulate

Habitual buying behaviour Consumer buying behaviour in situations characterised by low consumer involvement and few significant perceived brand differences.

product trial. In advertising for a low-involvement product, ad copy should stress only a few key points. Visual symbols and imagery are important because they can be remembered easily and associated with the brand. Ad campaigns should include high repetition of short-duration messages. Television is usually more effective than print media because it is a low-involvement medium suitable for passive learning.

Variety-seeking buying behaviour

Variety-seeking buying behaviour Consumer buying behaviour in situations characterised by low consumer involvement but significant perceived brand differences.

Consumers undertake **variety-seeking buying behaviour** in situations characterised by low involvement but significant perceived brand differences. In such cases, consumers often do a lot of brand switching. For example, when buying biscuits a consumer might hold some beliefs, choose a biscuit brand without much evaluation, then evaluate that brand during consumption. But the next time the consumer might pick another brand out of boredom or simply to try something different. With low-involvement products, brand switching often occurs for the sake of variety rather than because of dissatisfaction.

In such product categories, the marketing strategy of the market leader will often be different from that of the minor brands. The market leader will try to encourage habitual buying behaviour by dominating shelf space, keeping shelves fully stocked and running frequent reminder advertising. Challenger firms will encourage variety seeking by offering lower prices, special deals, coupons, free samples and advertising that presents reasons for trying something new.

SELF-CHECK QUESTIONS

7   Discuss the differences between high-involvement and low-involvement products.

8   If a consumer is in a buying situation where there is a high-involvement product and few perceived differences between the brands, the consumer may exhibit behaviour designed to reduce the anxiety. What is the term used to describe this anxiety-reducing behaviour?

9   Habitual buying behaviour occurs under conditions of low consumer involvement and where there are major brand differences. Do you agree with this statement? If so, why? If not, why not?

The buyer decision process

Now that we have looked at the influences that affect buyers, we are ready to look at how consumers make buying decisions. Figure 7.8 shows the consumer as passing through five stages: problem recognition, information search, evaluation of alternatives, purchase decision and post-purchase behaviour. Clearly, the buying process starts long before actual purchase and continues long after. Marketers need to focus on the entire buying process rather than on just the purchase decision.

The figure implies that consumers always pass through all five stages with every purchase. But in low-involvement purchases, consumers often skip or reverse some of these stages. Someone who

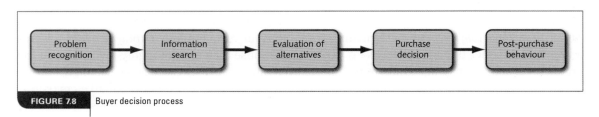

FIGURE 7.8 Buyer decision process

has run out of toothpaste might recognise the need and go right to the purchase decision, skipping information search and evaluation, beyond a fleeting information search of memory to establish which brand they bought last time, or perhaps some limited evaluation of alternatives if a brand or size is on special. However, we use the model in Figure 7.8 because it shows all the considerations that arise when a consumer faces a new and complex purchase situation, and even when a consumer faces a new low-involvement purchase situation, for example when their regular toothpaste is not available and they need to choose a replacement.

Problem recognition

The buying process starts with **problem recognition**—with the buyer recognising a problem or need. A buyer senses a difference between their actual state and some desired state. The need can be triggered by internal stimuli when one of the person's normal needs—hunger, thirst, sex—rises to a level high enough to become a drive. A need can also be triggered by external stimuli. For example, a person passing a bakery might find that the smell of freshly baked bread stimulates hunger; passing a neighbour's new car might spark admiration; or watching a television commercial for a Club Med holiday might generate interest. The marketer needs to understand what consumer problems exist, in order to work out how the consumer can be convinced that the marketer's product is a solution for the consumer's problem.

Problem recognition
The first stage of the buyer decision process in which the consumer recognises a problem or need.

Information search

An interested consumer may or may not search for more information. If the consumer's drive is strong and a satisfying product is near at hand, the consumer is likely to buy it then. If not, the consumer may undertake an **information search** related to the problem or need. For example, once you've decided you need a new car, at the least you will probably pay more attention to car ads, cars owned by friends and conversations about cars. Or you may search the Internet, phone friends and gather information in other ways. The amount of searching you do will depend on a number of factors, such as the strength of your drive, the amount of information you start with, the ease of obtaining more information, the value you place on additional information and the satisfaction you get from searching.

Information search
The stage of the buyer decision process in which the consumer is aroused to search for more information; the consumer may simply have heightened attention or may go into active information search.

Consumers can obtain information from any of several sources. These include *personal sources* (family, friends, neighbours, acquaintances), *commercial sources* (advertising, salespeople, dealers, packaging, displays), *public sources* (mass media, consumer-rating organisations), and *experiential sources* (handling, examining, using the product). The relative influence of these information sources varies with the product and the buyer, but personal sources appear to be particularly important in influencing the purchase of services because there is no physical evidence on which to base a purchase decision.[22]

Generally, the consumer receives the most information about a product from commercial sources—those controlled by the marketer. The most effective sources, however, tend to be personal. Commercial sources normally *inform* the buyer, but personal sources *legitimise* or *evaluate* products for the buyer. For example, doctors normally learn of new drugs from commercial sources, but turn to other doctors for evaluative information.[23]

As more information is obtained, the consumer's awareness and knowledge of the available brands and features increase. In your car information search, you may learn about several brands which might suit your requirements. The information might also help you to drop certain brands from consideration. A company must design its marketing mix to make prospects aware of and knowledgeable about its brand. It should carefully identify consumers' sources of information and the importance of each source.

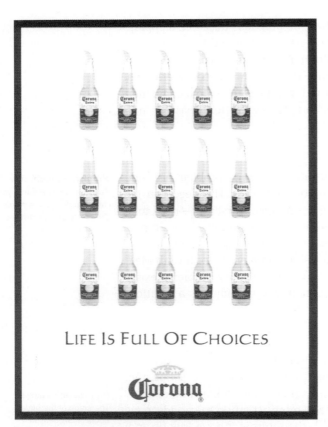

LIFE IS FULL OF CHOICES

Corona®

Corona's ad uses humour to suggest that the consumer shouldn't even consider other alternative drinks.

Evaluation of alternatives

We have seen how the consumer uses information to arrive at a set of final brand choices. How does the consumer choose between the alternative brands? The marketer needs to know about **alternative evaluation**—that is, how the consumer processes information to arrive at brand choices. Unfortunately, consumers do not use a simple and single evaluation process in all buying situations. Instead, several evaluation processes are at work.

How consumers go about evaluating purchase alternatives depends on the individual consumer and the specific buying situation. In some cases, consumers use careful calculations and logical thinking. At other times, the same consumers do little or no evaluating; instead they buy on impulse and rely on intuition. Sometimes consumers make buying decisions on their own; sometimes they turn to friends, consumer guides or salespeople for buying advice.

Suppose you've narrowed your car choices to three brands. And suppose that you are primarily interested in four attributes— styling, operating economy, warranty and price. By this time, you've probably formed beliefs about how each brand rates on each attribute. Clearly, if you think that one car rates best on all the attributes, the choice would be easy, and we could confidently predict that you would choose it if you buy any brand. However, the brands will no doubt vary in performance on the different attributes. You might base your buying decision on only one attribute, and your choice would be easy to predict.

Alternative evaluation
The stage of the buyer decision process in which the consumer uses information to evaluate alternative brands in the choice set.

If you wanted styling above everything else, you would buy the car you think has the best styling. But most buyers consider several attributes, each with different importance. If we knew the importance of the weights you assigned to each of the four attributes, we could predict your car choice more reliably.[24]

Marketers should study buyers to find out how they actually evaluate brand alternatives. If they know what evaluative processes go on, marketers can take steps to influence the buyer's decision.

Purchase decision

In the evaluation stage, the consumer ranks brands and forms purchase intentions. Generally, the consumer's **purchase decision** will be to buy the most preferred brand, but two factors can come between the purchase *intention* and the purchase *decision*. The first factor is the *attitudes of others*. If someone important to you thinks that you should buy the lowest priced car, then the chances of your buying a more expensive car are reduced.

Purchase decision
The stage of the buyer decision process in which the consumer actually buys the product.

The second factor is *unexpected situational factors*. The consumer may form a purchase intention based on factors such as expected income, expected price and expected product benefits. However, unexpected events may change the purchase intention. For example, the economy might take a turn for the worse, a close competitor might drop its price or a friend might report being disappointed in your preferred car. Thus, preferences and even purchase intentions do not always result in actual purchase choice.

Post-purchase behaviour

The marketer's job does not end when the product is bought. After purchasing the product the consumer will engage in **post-purchase behaviour**. They will assess the product's performance (though perhaps only fleetingly for low-involvement products, or only if there is a problem). They may discuss the product with others, and recommend it to others or complain about it.

Almost all major purchases result in some **cognitive dissonance**, or discomfort caused by post-purchase conflict.[25] After the purchase, consumers may be satisfied with the benefits of the chosen brand and glad to avoid the drawbacks of the brands not bought. However, every purchase involves compromise. Consumers will often feel uneasy about acquiring the drawbacks of the chosen brand and about losing the benefits of the brands not purchased. The marketer can reduce post-purchase dissonance by good product performance, good after-sales service and even by advertising. For example, the famous Toyota 'Oh what a feeling' campaign was partly aimed at decreasing any post-purchase dissonance by recent car buyers, in order to make them more likely to recommend the brand to others.

By studying the overall buyer decision, marketers may be able to find ways to help consumers move through it. For example, if consumers are not buying a new product because they do not perceive a need for it, marketing might launch advertising messages that trigger the need and show how the product solves customers' problems. If customers know about the product but are not buying because they hold unfavourable attitudes towards it, the marketer must find ways either to change the product or change consumer perceptions.

Post-purchase behaviour The stage of the buyer decision process in which consumers take further action after the purchase, based on their satisfaction or dissatisfaction.

Cognitive dissonance Buyer discomfort caused by post-purchase conflict.

SELF-CHECK QUESTIONS

10 Describe at least two buying situations where a buyer might not pass through each of the five steps mentioned in arriving at a purchase decision.

11 What are the likely differences (if any) at the information search stage when purchasing household groceries compared with buying a 3G video-capable mobile telephone?

12 Why would advertising have any effect on post-purchase dissonance?

Consumer behaviour across international borders

Understanding consumer behaviour is difficult enough for companies marketing within the borders of a single country like Australia where there are differences between subcultures. For companies operating in many countries, understanding and serving the needs of consumers can be daunting. Although consumers in different countries may have some things in common, their values, attitudes and behaviours often vary greatly. International marketers must understand such differences and adjust their products and marketing programs accordingly.

Sometimes the differences are obvious. For example, in Australia and New Zealand, where many people eat cereal regularly for breakfast, Kellogg's focuses its marketing on persuading consumers to select a Kellogg's brand rather than a competitor's brand. In France, however, where most people prefer croissants and coffee or no breakfast at all, Kellogg's advertising simply attempts to persuade people that they should eat cereal for breakfast. Its packaging includes step-by-step instructions on how to prepare cereal.

Often, differences across international markets are more subtle. They may result from physical differences in consumers and their environments. For example, Remington makes smaller electric shavers to fit the smaller hands of Japanese consumers, and battery-powered shavers for the British market, where many bathrooms don't have electrical outlets.

Marketers must decide on the degree to which they will adapt their products and marketing programs to meet the unique cultures and needs of consumers in various markets. On the one hand, they want to standardise their offerings in order to simplify operations and take advantage of cost economies. On the other hand, adapting marketing efforts within each country results in products and programs that satisfy the needs of local consumers better. The question of whether to adapt or standardise the marketing mix across international markets has created a lively debate in recent years.

SELF-CHECK QUESTIONS

13 How might you address the situation where a new electronic auto-flushing toilet released in the South Korean market is not selling because women in that country tend to flush the toilet immediately before or during use due to extreme modesty?

14 In Thailand it is unacceptable to show feet in a television commercial. What alternatives are open to the marketer of an inner sole for shoes in Thailand?

SUMMARY

Markets have to be understood before marketing strategies can be developed. The consumer market buys goods and services for personal consumption. Consumers vary tremendously in age, income, education, tastes and other factors. Marketers must understand the influences on consumers' buying responses, including the buyer's characteristics and the buyer's decision process. Buyer characteristics include four major factors: *cultural*, *social*, *personal* and *psychological*.

Culture is the most basic determinant of a person's wants and behaviour. It includes the basic values, perceptions, preferences and behaviours that a person learns from family and other key institutions. *Subcultures* are 'cultures within cultures' with their own distinct values and lifestyles. People with different cultural and subcultural characteristics will often have different product and brand preferences. Marketers may want to focus their marketing programs on the special needs of certain groups.

¡*Social factors* also influence a buyer's behaviour. A person's *reference groups*—family, friends, social organisations—strongly affect product and brand choices. Although many of these factors cannot be controlled by marketers, they are useful in identifying and understanding the consumers that marketers are trying to influence.

The buyer's age, life-cycle stage, occupation and economic circumstances are *personal factors* which influence their buying decisions. Consumer lifestyles—the whole pattern of acting and interacting in the world—are also an important influence on buyers' choices.

Consumer buying behaviour is also influenced by five major psychological factors—the consumer's *motivations*, *perception*, *learning*, *beliefs* and *attitudes*, and *personality* and *self-concept*. Each of these factors provides a different perspective for understanding the workings of the buyer's mind.

Some buying decisions involve only one *decision maker*. Other decisions may involve several participants who play such roles as *initiator*, *influencer*, *decider*, *buyer* and *user*. The marketer tries to identify the people who influence the buying decision, their buying criteria and their level of influence on the buyer.

The number of buying participants and the amount of buying effort increase with the importance of the buying situation, or the buyer's *involvement* with the product. There are four types of buying decision behaviour based on the degree of buyer involvement and the degree of differences between brands: *complex* buying behaviour, *dissonance-reducing* buying behaviour, *habitual* buying behaviour and *variety-seeking* buying behaviour.

In buying something, the buyer goes through a decision process consisting of *problem recognition*, *information search*, *evaluation of alternatives*, *purchase decision* and *post-purchase behaviour*. The marketer's job is to understand the buyer's behaviour at each stage and the influences that are operating. This allows the marketer to develop significant and effective marketing programs for the target market.

Understanding consumer behaviour is difficult enough for companies marketing within the borders of a single country. For companies operating internationally, however, understanding and serving the needs of consumers can be even more difficult. Consumers in different countries can vary dramatically in their values, attitudes and behaviours. International marketers must understand such differences and adjust their products and marketing programs accordingly.

MARKETING ISSUE

Jane isn't having a good flight. She's flying from Sydney to Perth with a major Australian airline. Jane's work entails a lot of flying, and she is an airline club member and gold-level frequent flyer. She's travelling economy, which is what the firm will pay for. The airline won't allow her to upgrade her discount economy ticket even though she has hundreds of thousands of frequent-flyer points. The plane is due to depart at 12.25, and passengers are called to board at 12.05. Jane has been very, very busy at work, and wants a lunchtime glass of wine in the club before the plane leaves at 12.25. When she arrives at the club, signs say that the bar opens at 1 pm, so she can't get a drink. Boarding is announced at 12.05, so Jane rushes to the departure lounge, somewhat stressed because she appears to be the last passenger to board. After walking past the boarding desk, however, she finds that there is a long, slow line of passengers on the air bridge waiting to board. She finally gets to her seat, but after some delay the captain announces that departure has been delayed by 25 minutes, so the passengers sit on the plane waiting to leave. Jane thinks wistfully of the drink which she could have had if they had let customers wait in the lounge. There is also a problem with the sound system; the man sitting behind Jane is trying to listen to classical music, but is getting different channels through his earpieces. A cabin attendant resets the sound system without any explanation to the surrounding people, so Jane (who didn't have a problem) now loses sound for around 15 minutes, and the man sitting behind her still has a problem with the sound. No crew members check to see if the problems have been sorted out. Finally, the man complains and is given a drink to compensate.

After a further delay, the plane finally takes off and lunch is served. However, there seems to be some problem with allocation of special meals. Staff are walking down the aisles, calling out names, trying to find passengers who have ordered a special meal, and the staff have difficulty finding Jane's pre-ordered vegetarian meal. Jane finally gets her meal, which has been assigned to seat 40D, even though she is sitting (as originally assigned) in 27B, but gets the feeling the staff think it's her fault they couldn't find her meal.

The captain has announced that there is a movie, but doesn't say what channel it is on. When the overhead screen starts, Jane can't find the appropriate channel for the soundtrack. As an experienced traveller, Jane knows that main cabin sound is usually on channel 1 or channel 2, but there is no sound on either channel. Jane checks the movie guide in the onboard magazine, but the movie channel isn't listed. She asks one of the staff. He doesn't know, but says he will find out. After some delay, he tells Jane it is channel 9. (It isn't; channel 9 is a radio channel.) Jane finally finds it herself, on channel 16. However, there is a British sit-com before the movie, so Jane doesn't listen. The sound disappears for several minutes, then returns, apparently at random. The sit-com and its sound finish, so Jane reads a paper, waiting for the movie to start. After some time, Jane realises that the movie has started, but there is now no sound on channel 16. She pushes her call button to ask the staff if there is a problem with the movie sound track. None of the staff respond to the call button, but after some experimentation she finds that the movie soundtrack is now on channel 1, even though the sound for the preceding program was on channel 16. Since Jane has now missed a considerable portion of the movie, she abandons the movie and works on her laptop.

Jane's frustration with the level of service increases when she goes to the toilets. The drain in one is blocked and the sink is half full of waste water, and there is no toilet paper. Jane is not surprised; she often encounters this on the airline's flights, since the staff seem to check the condition of toilets far less often than their overseas competitor airlines. Jane travels about four times a year to Hong Kong and/or to Europe, and she has always experienced excellent service with overseas airlines, but they don't fly within Australia. In Australia, she can fly with a local competitor but they don't have a lounge, and Jane is a life member of the major Australian airline. Jane asks herself, yet again, if she can avoid travelling on this airline.

Many business travellers, like Jane, are reluctant to switch to competitors, even though they are unhappy with the service they are getting, because their frequent-flyer status or airline lounge membership gives them privileges they won't get from a competitor. What (if anything) could competitors do to win over customers like this?

1 Do you think that Jane's experience is unusual? Do you think that the airline's management are aware of problems like hers? If not, what could they do to find out, and prevent, such problems? If management are

aware, why do you think these sorts of problems aren't fixed?

2 Do you think Jane's problems are the fault of the staff on the flight, or indicative of deeper problems within the airline? What do you think it might be like to work in customer contact positions for an organisation where customers are continually experiencing problems?

KEY TERMS

DISCUSSING THE ISSUES

1 Consumers sometimes aren't consciously aware of their motivation for buying some products, and sometimes don't like publicly expressing their motivations for buying other products. What does this suggest about the role that motivational research has to play in gaining an understanding of consumer motives in such situations?

2 Does it matter to marketing scientists and/or marketing practitioners that there is no firm resolution concerning the degree to which human behaviour is determined by internal characteristics, such as our physiological and psychological make-up, or is a matter of learned cultural and social responses?

3 Researchers may use triangulation to assure themselves that they have a valid view of the consumers they are studying. For example, marketers might use observation, surveys (self-reports) and projective techniques to gain an insight into why some consumers buy some products, while others are not motivated to buy these products. Describe examples of this approach from your recent reading or experience.

4 Think about a recent very good or bad experience you have had with a product (goods, services or experiences). Discuss how this shaped your beliefs about this product. How long do you think these beliefs will last?

5 Consumers play different roles in the buying process: initiator, influencer, decider, buyer and user. Name the person in your household who would adopt each of these roles when buying the following items: snack food, a new DVD player and a newly released movie on DVD that you are hiring.

6 How does the concept of bounded rationality contribute to an explanation of the differences in consumer decision making between low- and high-involvement products?

7 Most consumers would claim that they are logical or 'rational' in their purchases, but prospect theory shows that they often make decisions which economists wouldn't call rational. How would you explain this?

REFERENCES

1. Information from Tony Boyd, 'Trujillo: How I'll Turn Telstra Around', *The Australian Financial Review*, 15 November 2005, pp. 1, 7; Garry Barker, '3G Key as Telco Battle Goes Down to the Wireless', *The Age*, 18 October 2005, p. 1; Garry Barker, 'At Telstra, the Micro-segment Comes First', *The Age*, 16 November 2005, p. 2; Julian Bajkowski, 'Keep Marketing Away from IT Strategy or Lose Customers, *Computerworld*, 31 October 2005; John H. Roberts, 'Defensive Marketing', *Harvard Business Review*, vol. 83, no. 11, pp. 150–157; Michael Sainsbury and Simon Canning, 'Image Problems', *The Australian*, 23 July 2005, p. 33; Michael Sainsbury and Glenda Korporaal, 'Telstra in $2.1bn HK Mobile Merger', *The Australian*, 10 December 2005, p. 33; David Teather, 'Microsoft Picks up on Internet Telephone Calls', *The Australian Financial Review*, 2 September 2005, p. 70.
2. Brad Weiners, 'Getting Inside—Way Inside—Your Customer's Head', *Business 2.0*, April 2003, pp. 54–55.
3. Several models of the consumer buying process have been developed by marketing scholars. The most prominent models are those of John A. Howard and Jagdish N. Sheth, *The Theory of Buyer Behavior*, New York, John Wiley, 1969; Francesco M. Nicosia, *Consumer Decision Processes*, Englewood Cliffs, NJ, Prentice Hall, 1966; James F. Engel, Roger D. Blackwell and Paul W. Miniard, *Consumer Behavior*, 9th edn, New York, Holt, Rinehart & Winston, 2001; and James R. Bettman, *An Information Processing Theory of Consumer Choice*, Fort Worth, TX, Harcourt College Publishers.
4. See Annetta Miller and Dody Tsiantar, 'Psyching Out Consumers', *Newsweek*, 27 February 1989, pp. 46–47; and Rebecca Piirto, 'Words that Sell', *American Demographics*, January 1992, p. 6.
5. Abraham H. Maslow, *Motivation and Personality*, 2nd edn, New York, Harper & Row, 1970, pp. 80–106. Also see Rudy Schrocer, 'Maslow's Hierarchy of Needs as a Framework for Identifying Emotional Triggers', *Marketing Review*, February 1991, pp. 26, 28.
6. Charles Pappas, 'Ad Nauseam', *Advertising Age*, 10 July 2000, pp. 16–18.
7. Bob Garfield, '"Subliminal" Seduction and Other Urban Myths', *Advertising Age*, 18 September 2000, pp. 4, 105. Also see 'We Have Ways of Making You Think', *Marketing Week*, 25 September 2003, p. 14; and Si Cantwell, 'Common Sense: Scrutiny Helps Catch Catchy Ads', *Wilmington Star-News*, 1 April 2004, p. 1B.
8. See R. R. McCrae and P. T. Costa, 'Validation of the Five-Factor Model of Personality across Instruments and Observers', *Journal of Personality and Social Psychology*, vol. 52, 1987, pp. 81–90; and R. R. McCrae and P. T. Costa Jr, 'Toward a New Generation of Personality Theories: Theoretical Contexts for the Five-Factor Model', in J. S. Wiggins (ed.), *The Five-Factor Model of Personality: Theoretical Perspectives*, New York, Guilford, 1996, pp. 51–87.
9. For more on personality see Michael R. Solomon, *Consumer Behavior: Buying, Having, and Being*, Upper Saddle River, NJ, Pearson Prentice Hall, 2004, Chapter 6.
10. Tobi Elkin, 'Sony Marketing Aims at Lifestyle Segments', *Advertising Age*, 18 March 2002, pp. 3, 72; and Kenneth Hein, 'When Is Enough Enough?', *Brandweek*, 2 December 2002, pp. 26–28.
11. There is growing evidence that while genes are critical in influencing behaviour, parental behaviour and the family environment is in fact less important than has previously been thought. See Judith Rich Harris, *The Nurture Assumption: Why Children Turn Out the Way They Do*, New York, The Free Press, 1998.
12. Meg Carter, 'Muslims Offer a New Mecca for Marketers', *Financial Times*, 11 August 2005, p. 6.
13. Chris Prystay, 'Getting a Taste for Milk', *The Asian Wall Street Journal*, 9 August 2005, p. A5.
14. See R. P. Coleman, 'The Continuing Significance of Social Class to Marketing', *Journal of Consumer Research*, 10 December 1983, pp. 265–280.
15. For more on social class see Terrell G. Williams, 'Social Class Influences on Purchase Evaluation Criteria', *Journal of Consumer Marketing*, vol. 19, no. 2/3, 2002, pp. 248–276; Michael R. Solomon, *Consumer Behavior*, 5th edn, Upper Saddle River, NJ, Prentice Hall, 2002, Chapter 13; and Leon G. Schiffman and Leslie L. Kanuk, *Consumer Behavior*, 8th edn, Upper Saddle River, NJ, Prentice Hall, 2004, Chapter 11.
16. See Darla Dernovsek, 'Marketing to Women', *Credit Union Magazine*, October 2000, pp. 90–96; Sharon Goldman Edry, 'No Longer Just Fun and Games', *American Demographics*, May 2001, pp. 36–38; Hillary Chura, 'Marketing Messages for Women Fall Short', *Advertising Age*, 23 September 2002, pp. 4, 14–15; and Jennifer Pendleton, 'Ford at 100: Targeting the Female Market', *Advertising Age*, 31 March 2003, pp. F38–F40.
17. See Edward Keller and Jonathan Berry, *The Influentials*, New York, The Free Press, 2003; 'The Chattering Class', *Fast Company*, January 2003, p. 48; and John Battelle, 'The Net of Influence', *Business 2.0*, March 2004, p. 70.
18. For more on the Roy Morgan Values Segments, see <www.roymorgan.com/products/values-segments/values-segments.cfm>.
19. See 'Ad Agency Finds Five Global Segments', *Marketing News*, 8 January 1990, pp. 9, 17.
20. Judith Lynne Zaichkowsky, 'Measuring the Involvement Construct', *Journal of Consumer Research*, vol. 12, no. 3, 1985, pp. 341–352.
21. Examples adapted from R. Thaler, 'Mental Accounting and Consumer Choice', *Marketing Science*, vol. 4, no. 3, 1985, pp. 199–214.
22. Keith B. Murray, 'A Test of Services Marketing Theory: Consumer Information Acquisition Theory', *Journal of Marketing*, January 1991, pp. 10–25.
23. Everett M. Rogers, *Diffusion of Innovations*, New York, The Free Press, 2003.
24. For more on consumers' mental models see James R. Bettman, N. Capon and R.J. Lutz, 'Cognitive Algebra in Multi-attribute Models', *Journal of Management Science*, vol. 12, May 1975, pp. 151–164; and James R. Bettman and M. A. Zinns, 'Constructive Processes in Consumer Choice', *Journal of Consumer Research*, vol. 4, September 1977, pp. 75–85.
25. See Leon Festinger, *A Theory of Cognitive Dissonance*, Stanford, CA, Stanford University Press, 1957.

CASE STUDY

Entertain me! Attracting viewers to reality TV

Big Brother, the *Amazing Race*, *Australian Idol*, *The Apprentice*, *Fear Factor*, *Survivor* . . . reality TV at its finest. Real people, in real situations, making real decisions, facing real challenges—or as real as it can be with cameras recording 24/7 and producers editing into one-hour chunks.

Reality TV shows are not new, dating back to 1948 when *Candid Camera* used hidden cameras to record unsuspecting participants' reactions to staged practical jokes. It was in 2000 that reality TV went mainstream when 'The Tribe Spoke', evicting the first *Survivor* contestant at Tribal Council. Reality TV programs now represent an increasing proportion of television offerings. Shows such as *Dancing with the Stars* and *Big Brother* have spawned countless international spin-offs. *Idol*, as one example, is produced in 32 territories, attracting over 110 million viewers who have cast over 1.7 billion votes (fremantlemedia.com). Even Iraq has its own reality TV show, *Labour and Materials*, where war-ravaged homes are rebuilt using viewer-donated materials and appliances, all counting as *zakak*, the charitable donations required of all Muslims. There is even a dedicated reality TV television channel, watched by more than 35 million subscribers in 125 territories around the globe and reality TV now warrants its own category at America's Emmy and Australia's Logie Awards.

Despite some slippage in the ratings, television networks continue their love affair with reality TV. Why? Reality TV costs less to produce per hour than scripted dramas like *CSI: Crime Scene Investigation* or comedies like *Friends*—even after factoring in licensing fees such as the reported $US2 million per episode commanded by Mark Burnett, creator of *Survivor* and *The Apprentice* (Meade and Brook, 2002). Reality TV also delivers advertising revenue. In 2004, CBS was able to increase its rate from *Survivor 1*'s $US100000 to $US428000 per 30-second spot on *Survivor: All Stars*. Shows like *Big Brother* and the *Idol* franchise which air multiple times per week over multiple

months are powerful earners. In 2004, 30-second spots on *American Idol 3* each cost $US415000, generating over $US260 million in advertising revenue for the Fox network (Patsuris, 2004). Is it any surprise then that an estimated 60% of Fox's programming is now 'unscripted'—in other words, reality TV.

Advertisers pay these fees to gain access to millions of viewers, most in the coveted 18–49 demographic—the prime purchasers of goods and services in today's marketplace. While down from the 50 million viewers internationally who watched the finale of *Survivor 1*, *Survivor* finales regularly deliver in excess of 20 million viewers worldwide. In 2004, *Australian Idol* and *Big Brother* finales beat the AFL Grand Final and the Melbourne Cup, claiming the two top ratings spots, each drawing almost three million viewers. Even though sport won out in 2005, *Big Brother* and *Dancing with the Stars* finales still drew well over two million viewers in Australia.

These millions of viewers see more than just contestants, challenges and advertisements—they see hours of programming where brands can be promoted, used and seamlessly woven (or as marketers say 'integrated') into the everyday existence of each show's 'real world'. And because brands are 'embedded' into the programming, the risk of viewers hitting 'fast forward' and missing the brand message, as they often do with advertisements, is reduced. Contestants on *Survivor* and *Fear Factor* routinely compete for the latest 'yet to be released' automobile, *Big Brother* housemates eat, drink and lounge on sponsoring companies' products, and *The Apprentice*'s Donald Trump 'wanna-be's' compete to create new toys for Mattel or in-store catalogues for Levi's jeans.

Product placement, however, is not cheap. Brands appearing on *The Apprentice* pay in the range of $US1–4 million per episode for what amounts to an hour long infomercial (Schiller, 2005). While the fees may be high, so too can be

Jan Charbonneau and Mike Brennan, Department of Marketing, Massey University

the results. When General Motors used a 2005 episode of *The Apprentice* to announce a national early-order program for its new Solstice, the car's full production sold out in 10 days. In the two weeks following the show, Burger King sold 1.2 million of the Western Angus steak burgers created by the winning *Apprentice* team.

For reality TV to continue attracting advertising and product placement dollars it must continue to attract viewers. So . . . what is it that attracts viewers to reality TV? Early American research (2001) found the thrill of guessing winners and losers to be the number one reason, followed by seeing others facing challenging situations and thinking about how they would perform in similar challenges. Older viewers (35+) focused more on contestant strategies while younger viewers (18–34) tuned in for the conflict.

Contrast this with results from a major late 2005 New Zealand general public survey conducted by the authors (1000 respondents, most aged 18–55, watching an average of 1–5 hours of reality TV per week). Pure entertainment was judged the most important reason for watching reality TV, followed by seeing participants face challenging situations. Interestingly, lack of choice was judged the third most important reason, followed by the thrill of guessing the outcome, team work or situations outside contestant control.

The results in Table 1 would suggest that romance, group living and physical improvement shows are losing ground, with New Zealand viewers preferring reality TV shows featuring home/garden improvements, community service, pets or celebrities. Why might this be? Perhaps with the wealth of reality TV on offer, the novelty of the competitive formats of adventure and group living shows has worn off, with viewers preferring to see celebrities, rather

TABLE 1 Results of a 2005 general public survey regarding viewing habits of reality TV shows

Reality TV shows	Male		Female		Total	
	Regular	Never	Regular	Never	Regular	Never
Romance (e.g. *The Bachelor*)	23%	78%	43%	57%	34%	66%
Adventure (e.g. *Survivor*)	56%	44%	59%	41%	58%	42%
Family (e.g. *Trading Spouses*)	32%	68%	58%	42%	43%	57%
Group living (e.g. *Big Brother*)	21%	79%	23%	77%	22%	78%
Personal advancement (e.g. *The Apprentice*)	54%	46%	66%	34%	60%	40%
Physical improvement (e.g. *The Swan*)	29%	71%	47%	53%	29%	71%
Home/Garden (e.g. *The Block*)	72%	28%	81%	19%	77%	23%
Pet (e.g. *The Zoo*)	60%	40%	68%	32%	65%	35%
Community service (e.g. *Border Patrol*)	77%	23%	70%	30%	73%	27%
Celebrity (e.g. *Dancing with the Stars*)	57%	43%	69%	31%	64%	36%

Regular includes regular and occasional viewership.

than traditional contestants, 'out of their comfort zone'.

Notice the differences between male and female viewer, with females being the main viewers of romance, family and physical improvement shows. Both males and females regularly watch community service and home/ garden improvement shows, with males favouring community service and females home/garden shows. Important information for advertisers!

Psychologists have suggested that social comparison theory could be used to explain the attractions of reality TV—with viewers using contestants or participants as a basis for personal comparisons. With upward comparisons, viewers look to reality TV participants as role models, learning from their mistakes, repeating for themselves behaviours that proved productive for contestants, learning vicariously how to strategise, cooperate and assert themselves. With downward comparisons, viewers are able to feel better about their own situations, especially when compared to contestants voted off by their peers or rejected by the show's love interest. The philosopher Aristotle believed in the power of downward comparison, suggesting that individuals could be both entertained and emotionally cleansed by art forms portraying the woes of others—via a process he called catharsis. Perhaps this is why some psychologists have referred to reality TV as 'cinematherapy'.

Interestingly, for the New Zealand general public, identifying with strategies/abilities/ opinions and learning from mistakes were judged only as somewhat important reasons for viewing, with feeling better about own situation and copying productive behaviours judged even less important.

Early American research suggested that viewers, particularly males, tune in to see attractive contestants. The New Zealand general public though doesn't agree, with over 50% of males and 70% of females judging seeing physically attractive contestants as not at all important. While attractive contestants are appealing, viewers want to see people with whom they can identify, who look and behave like they do. According

to one reality TV fan 'If we wanted fake, we'd be watching sitcoms.' (Anonymous, 2001). This was supported by research conducted in 2004 at Sydney University with teenage girls. These teens, who account for the lion's share of voting in shows like *Big Brother* and *Australian Idol*, want to see potential friends—honest, down-to-earth girls with good senses of humour (Tsavdardis, 2004).

One benefit noted by marketers is that regular reality TV viewers exhibit a high level of commitment, inviting contestants into their homes and lives on a daily basis, providing multiple exposures to ads and product placements. Many reality TV shows try to encourage regular viewing by allowing viewers to participate actively in the outcome (e.g. voting for *Australian Idol*) or via membership-only websites providing a range of interactive features, contests and 'behind the scenes' information. According to research conducted by the Australian Film, Television and Radio School, *Big Brother* fans spent an average of 12 minutes per visit on the show's official website in 2004 (containing live feeds, program-linked tasks and contests), compared to seven minutes on regular sites, with 80% stating the website enhanced their enjoyment of the television show (Tuohy, 2004).

Reality TV show winners receive fortune ($A1 million for *Big Brother 4*), love (newlyweds Trista and Ryan from *The Bachelorette*) or careers (*The Apprentice*). But in reality TV land, even losers can extend their '15 minutes of fame'. Reality TV has created a new crop of 'celebrities' available for publicity, celebrity reality TV shows and use as product endorsers. These new 'celebrities' often sign on with talent agents such as Australia's Harry M Miller Personality Management company, ensuring they don't disappear from our television screens.

Reality TV has generated its share of controversy by continuing to 'push the envelope'. In Australia in 2005 *Big Brother*'s nudity and sexually explicit behaviour was discussed in parliament, and in the UK in 2005 a pregnant contestant gave birth (off camera) in the *Big Brother* house. And 2006 saw a British Member of Parliament acting like a cat, licking milk from

CASE STUDY

an ageing actress's hands in the UK's *Celebrity Big Brother*. While much has been written about its demise, even with controversy—or perhaps because of the controversy—reality TV continues to generate viewer numbers.

As long as viewers keep watching, advertisers will keep advertising, brands will pay for product placements, contestants will become instant 'celebrities' and networks will keep producing programs. And, if the New Zealand general public survey is any indication, as long as reality TV shows continue to entertain, viewers will continue to watch.

Sources: Gail Schiller, 'Win, Draw for Burnett Branding', *The Hollywood Reporter*, 1 June 2005; Wendy Tuohy, 'Not Drowning, Thriving', *The Age*, 25 November 2004; Steve Brennan, 'Viewers Worldwide Are Tuning in to Reality TV', *MSNBC.com*, 5 January 2004; Penelope Patsuris, 'The Most Profitable Reality TV Shows', *Forbes*, 7 September 2004; Amanda Meade and Stephen Brook, 'Grabbing a Slice of the Action', *The Australian*, 20 June 2002; Anonymous, 'The Tribe Has Spoken', *American Demographics*, 1 September 2001; Cynthia Frisby, 'Getting Real with Reality TV', *USA Today*, vol. 133, no. 2712, September 2004; Dora Tsavdardis, 'Reality Cuties Curse', *The Courier–Mail*, 21 October 2004.

QUESTIONS

1. Why are reality TV shows so popular with television networks and marketers?

2. How might a consumer behaviourist explain the popularity of reality TV shows? Make reference to the internal characteristics (psychological and personal) and external characteristics (cultural and social) that influence consumer behaviour.

3. It would appear that what attracts viewers to reality TV has changed over the years. Why might that be? Does it matter to marketers? If the New Zealand general public survey was conducted in Australia, do you think the results would differ?

4. Many reality TV show concepts like *Big Brother* and *Idol* were developed and market tested in Europe then exported to America and Australia. Do you think a reality TV formula can be exported to any country or are there cultural factors to be considered?

5. Is reality TV a fad, using up its own '15 minutes of fame', or is it now an established television genre such as situation comedies or drama? Discuss the impact of your answer on reality TV's use in promotion strategies.

CHAPTER 8

Business-to-business behaviour

Ariba: www.ariba.com

Intel: www.intel.com

Loctite: www.loctite.com

Mitsubishi: www.mitsubishi.com.au

Toyota: www.toyota.com.au

TNT: www.tnt.com

Wal-Mart: www.walmart.com

Ever dreamt that one day you might own your own business? What about a consultancy business specialising in marketing advice? A good business degree with a strong marketing emphasis and some experience working in a marketing role might be enough to get started. After all, there are lots of companies out there which don't employ marketing staff which might be able to benefit from your advice. But is it that easy? Think about what is required to get your first few customers in a business that provides a service, with all of its intangibilities and inherent risks—for the customer and for the consultant. How would a business customer decide to use your services? First, of course, the customer must have a need for your services. But often companies don't know what a consultant can do for them. Perhaps you could talk to companies to convince them that they could benefit from your help. But who should you talk to? Even if companies know they have a problem, how would they get to know about your services? You could advertise, but advertising is expensive, and it isn't easy to decide where to advertise.

Even if a need is identified, many questions are likely to go through a manager's mind before they select a consultant: Who does the company manager know who can help? Did the manager have a good experience last time a consultant was used? Does the manager feel comfortable using a consultant to fill this need, or do they fear using outside help will make them look inadequate? What if the manager authorises payment of $100 000 for this project and the consultant doesn't provide much value? How can the manager be sure that the consultant is the right one? As you can see, getting noticed, considered and chosen by potential business buyers can present considerable challenges for businesses. There are fewer business buyers than consumer buyers, so mass advertising usually isn't an option. The business selling to other businesses needs to be targeted in their approach, and to have a good understanding of the needs and behaviours of business customers. In this chapter, we will discuss the different types of business buying, and the factors which influence business buying.

Oracle offers its business customers services and products aimed at meeting specific business needs.

After reading this chapter you should be able to:

1. List the characteristics of business-to-business markets, explaining market structure and demand, the nature of the buying unit and the decision process.

2. Outline the model of business buyer behaviour.

3. Discuss business buyer behaviour, types of buying situations, participants in the business buying process and major influences on business buyers.

4. Identify and define the steps in the business buying process and compare and contrast these with the consumer market.

5. Identify the differences between business markets, institutional markets and government markets.

In one way or another, most large companies sell to other organisations. Many companies, such as Dell, Ford, Pacific Dunlop and countless others, sell most of their products to other businesses—that is, they engage in business-to-business marketing. Even large consumer-products companies, which make products used by final consumers, must first sell their products to other businesses. For example, Nestlé makes many familiar consumer products—coffee, ice-cream, chocolate, yoghurt, prepared single-serve meals and others. But to sell these products to consumers, Nestlé must first sell them to the wholesalers and retailers that serve the consumer market. Nestlé also sells products directly to other businesses which in turn use the products to make their own finished product.

For example, Nestlé supplies KFC with coatings for its chicken pieces, made to KFC's recipe. Nestlé also sells catering or bulk packs of its products to some customers, as well as single-serve packs to other business customers—including sometimes different sections of the one customer. For example, a company canteen might use bulk tins of coffee or vending machines, the external visitors meeting room might use single-serve packs of coffee and the boardroom might require ground coffee.

The business-to-business market, or **business market** as it is termed for convenience, consists of all the organisations that buy goods and services to use in the production of other products and services that are sold, rented or supplied to others. It also includes retailing and wholesaling firms that acquire goods for the purpose of reselling or renting them to others at a profit. The **business buying process** is the decision-making process by which business buyers establish the need for purchased products and services and identify, evaluate and choose between alternative brands and suppliers. Marketing organisations that sell to other businesses and institutions must do their best to understand business markets and business buyer behaviour.

Business market All the organisations that buy goods and services to use in the production of other products and services or for the purpose of reselling or renting them to others at a profit.

Business buying process The decision-making process by which business buyers establish the need for purchased products and services and identify, evaluate and choose between alternative brands and suppliers.

Industrial market All the individuals and organisations acquiring goods and services that enter into the production of other products and services that are sold, rented or supplied to others.

Reseller market All the individuals and organisations that acquire goods for the purpose of reselling or renting them to others at a profit.

Government market Governmental units—federal, state and local—that purchase or rent goods and services for carrying out the main functions of government.

Institutional market Schools, hospitals, nursing homes, prisons and other institutions that provide goods and services to people in their care.

Business-to-business markets

The business-to-business market is very large and is characterised by complex products and complex business structures. Although, strictly speaking, the institutional market (such as schools and hospitals) and government market (such as the Department of Health) are non-business markets, much of the discussion on business-to-business marketing also applies in marketing to government and institutional buyers. This grouping means that business markets involve much more volume in terms of dollars and items than do consumer markets. When you think about the large number of business transactions involved in the production and sale of a single product, such as a set of Pirelli tyres, it is easier to comprehend the size of the business market. Various suppliers sell Pirelli the rubber, steel, equipment and other goods that it needs to produce the tyres. Pirelli then sells the finished tyres to wholesalers who sell them to retailers, who in turn sell them to consumers. Thus, many sets of business purchases are made for only one consumer purchase. In addition, Pirelli sells tyres as original equipment to manufacturers who install them on new vehicles, and as replacement tyres to companies that maintain their own fleets of company cars, trucks and buses.

The **industrial market** consists of all the individuals and organisations acquiring goods and services that are used in the production of other goods and services. The **reseller market** consists of all the individuals and organisations that acquire goods for the purpose of reselling or renting them to others, usually at a profit. The **government market** consists of government units at all levels—federal, state and local government—that purchase or rent goods used in carrying out their functions. Governments also buy directly, or indirectly through funding, for the use of government-owned institutions—schools, colleges, universities, hospitals, nursing homes, prisons and other institutions. Government buying is thus part of the **institutional market**, which also includes the private and not-for-profit organisations running non-government institutions such as schools, hospitals and universities.

Industry classification schemes

Business markets are characterised by a wide diversity in customer types and products. To obtain some order in this seeming chaos, industries are classified according to the **International Standard Industrial Classification (ISIC)**. Standardisation of the industrial system began in the USA in the 1930s, in order to promote uniformity and comparability of data collected and published by agencies within the US government, state agencies, trade associations and research organisations.[1] The increasing need for a standard international system led to the United Nations developing the International Standard Industrial Classification of all Economic Activities (ISIC) in the late 1940s. The latest revision, ISIC Rev. 4, breaks industries down into 21 broad major industry sections, with each industry section broken down into divisions, each with a two-digit code. Each industry division is further subdivided into groups, designated by a three-digit code, and groups are divided into four-digit classes. For example, Section K covers financial and insurance activities, and is divided into different divisions. Table 8.1 shows one of these, Division 65, which is broken into three groups, insurance, reinsurance and pension funding. The insurance group is further divided into two classes of insurance.

Since the 1930s, the ISIC has been revised continuously to reflect the emergence of new industries, and many countries have developed a related classification system which reflects their own industry situation. For example, the USA and Canada use NAICS, the North American Industry Classification System, and Australia and New Zealand use the **Australian and New Zealand Standard Industrial Classification (ANZSIC)**. Most of these classifications are very similar to ISIC, and use a similar four-digit classification system, but may include more detail in some levels and collapse others that are less relevant for the country. For example, the 2006 revision of the ANZSIC classification breaks down one ISIC section, trade, into wholesale and retail trade, and as a result of this and other differences has 19 industry groups at the broadest level of classification, as opposed to the 21 ISIC sections. To reflect these differences, there are also differences in terminology. So the broadest division of the ANZSIC classification is 'divisions' (not the ISIC 'sections'). These sections are divided into two-digit subdivisions. Subdivisions are divided into three-digit groups, which are in turn divided into four-digit classes. Figure 8.1 (overleaf) shows the 19 ANZSIC divisions in the newest classification system.

As new industry groups appear, the classification systems need to be updated to include them. So the latest ANZSIC revision, ANZSIC06, which replaces the classification dating from 1993, has 19 divisions and 86 subdivisions, while the previous ANZSIC system had 17 divisions and 53 subdivisions.[2] For each four-digit class, the Australian Bureau of Statistics (ABS) and its New Zealand counterpart report on such information as the number of establishments subclassified by location, number of employees, annual sales and net worth.[3]

International Standard Industrial Classification (ISIC) International classification system for industry types.

Australian and New Zealand Standard Industrial Classification (ANZSIC) System of classifying industry into 19 major groups and 86 subdivisions.

TABLE 8.1 Extract from International Standard Industrial Classification

Section	Division	Groups	Classes
K Financial and insurance activities	65 Insurance, reinsurance and pension funding	651 Insurance	6511 Life Insurance
		652 Reinsurance	6512 Non Life Insurance
		653 Pension funding	

Source: <http://unstats.un.org/unsd/cr/registry/regct.asp?Lg=1>.

A	Agriculture, forestry and fishing	K	Financial and Insurance Services
B	Mining	L	Retail, Hiring and Real Estate Services
C	Manufacturing	M	Professional, Scientific and Technical Services
D	Electricity, Gas, Water and Waste Services	N	Administrative and Support Services
E	Construction	O	Public Administration and Safety
F	Wholesale Trade	P	Education and Training
G	Retail Trade	Q	Health Care and Social Assistance
H	Accommodation and Food Services	R	Arts and Recreation Services
I	Transport, Postal and Warehousing	S	Other Services
J	Information Media and Telecommunications		

FIGURE 8.1 | ANZSIC 2006 industry classification
Source: Australian Bureau of Statistics, *Information Paper: ANZSIC 2006 Development,* Catalogue no. 1294.0, released 9 September 2004.

Using physical descriptions such as these allows segmentation of the business market into broad groups, or 'macrosegmentation'. Classifying business products in such a scheme enables input–output analysis for the purpose of calculating market potential based on characteristics of the buyer's geographical location, size and industry group. It also assists marketers in 'microsegmentation', or in gaining an understanding of who may be involved in purchasing the products, and what marketing factors are likely to affect the buying decision.

Characteristics of business markets

In some ways business markets are similar to consumer markets. Both involve people who assume buying roles and make purchase decisions to satisfy needs. However, business markets also differ in many ways from consumer markets.[4] The main differences discussed in this section involve market structure and demand, the types of decisions and the decision process involved.

Market structure and demand

We defined the business market as consisting of all the organisations that acquire goods and services used in the production of other products or services that are sold, rented or supplied to others. The major industries making up the business market are agriculture, forestry and fisheries; mining; manufacturing; construction; transportation; communication; public utilities; banking, finance and insurance; distribution and services.

Business markets have several characteristics that contrast sharply with consumer markets. There are *fewer,* but *larger buyers,* and *close relationships* develop between buyers and sellers because of greater dependency between them.[5] An important difference between the business and consumer markets, which partly explains the dependency between buyer and seller, is the fact that in business markets demand for the seller's products is derived from demand by end-consumers for the product. As a result, business buying also tends to be less affected by price than consumer purchases. Another major difference is that, where consumers can sometimes be quite vague in describing the product they want to buy, professional **procurement managers and officers** are very specific and use very precise terminology. After all, their jobs often depend on making the right purchase decision. Consequently, they are more likely to deal with a salesperson or a procurement website (an electronic network connection between buying and selling organisations) than rely on mass media advertising or publicity. Businesses also buy directly from suppliers in most instances, rather than relying on retailing intermediaries.

Procurement managers and officers Business managers responsible for buying company supplies, raw materials and capital items, directly from suppliers in most instances.

Now let us examine the characteristics of the business-to-business market in more detail.

⊜ *Fewer buyers*. The business marketer normally deals with far fewer buyers than the consumer marketer. For example, the Dunlop division of Pacific Dunlop, which produces tyres, depends critically on getting an order from one of the three Australian car makers to provide tyres for new cars. But when Dunlop sells replacement tyres to consumers, it faces a potential domestic market of many million Australian car owners, as well as a global market of millions of other car owners. To sell to these customers, Dunlop first has to ensure that its tyres are stocked by the largest tyre outlets, like Bob Jane T-Marts and Beaurepaires.

Mitsubishi works closely with TNT to ensure timely delivery of all the components needed in its factories.

⊜ *Larger buyers*. Many business markets are characterised by a high buyer-concentration ratio. A few large buyers do most of the purchasing in industries such as steel construction, commercial jets and government buying.

⊜ *Close supplier–customer relationships*. Because of the smaller customer base and the importance and power of the larger customers, we observe close relationships between customers and suppliers in business markets. Suppliers are frequently expected to customise their offerings to individual business customer needs. Contracts go to those suppliers who cooperate with the buyer on technical specifications and delivery requirements. For example, TNT logistics and car maker Mitsubishi cooperate so closely that Mitsubishi has effectively handed over control of its logistics function in Australia to TNT. Mitsubishi gives TNT a production schedule and TNT controls, monitors and transports raw materials from the supplier to Mitsubishi's factory, delivering products just in time, but also in the order they will be used on the assembly line, in a process called sequencing. The system relies on an advanced logistics system which tracks all parts through the supply chain, allowing TNT to detect and fix potential bottlenecks or shortages in the supply chain before they can affect Mitsubishi, so the Mitsubishi production line can continue without interruptions.[6] Systems like this are light years away from a conventional supply contract. They mark a commitment between two corporations, not between a salesperson and a purchasing agent. Marketing Highlight 8.1 shows how the mutual dependency between supplier and buyer results in buyers and sellers working together for mutual benefit at Wal-Mart and Honda.

⊜ *Geographically concentrated buyers*. More than two-thirds of Australian business buyers are concentrated in two cities: Sydney and Melbourne. Industries such as petroleum, rubber and steel show an even greater geographical concentration. This geographical concentration of producers helps to reduce selling costs. At the same time, business marketers need to monitor regional shifts of certain industries.

⊜ **Derived demand**. The demand for business goods is ultimately derived from the demand for consumer goods. Thus animal hides are purchased because consumers want to buy shoes, handbags and other leather goods. If the demand for these consumer goods slackens, so will the demand for all the business goods entering into their production. For this reason, the business marketer must closely monitor the buying patterns of ultimate consumers. For

Derived demand
Organisational demand that ultimately comes from (derives from) the demand for consumer goods.

The business buying process—not just 'purchasing', it's 'supplier development'

The largest retailer (and corporation) in the world, Wal-Mart, sells more than a quarter of a trillion dollars worth of goods each year. But before it can sell products to customers, it must first *purchase* them from suppliers. The giant retailer can't rely on spot purchases from suppliers which might be available when needed. Wal-Mart must systematically develop a robust network of supplier partners who will efficiently and reliably provide the tremendous volume of goods that it sells.

Wal-Mart doesn't have a Purchasing Department, it has a Supplier Development Department, which seeks out qualified suppliers and helps guide them through the complex Wal-Mart buying process. The department offers a Supplier Proposal Guide and maintains a website providing advice to suppliers wishing to do business with Wal-Mart. The retailer supports its suppliers in other ways. For example, it works actively with suppliers to test new products and marketing programs in its stores. And it lets major suppliers use its voluminous point-of-sale databases to analyse customers' regional buying habits. Proctor & Gamble, for example, learned that its liquid Tide sells better at Wal-Mart stores in the north and northeast of the USA, while Tide powder sells better in the south and southwest. P&G uses such data to tailor its product availability to specific regions. By sharing information with suppliers like this, Wal-Mart helps them sell more products which, in turn, brings in more sales for Wal-Mart.

Wal-Mart's enormous size, as the world's largest retailer, gives it enormous buying power.

Like Wal-Mart, buyers in a wide range of industries are evolving from 'purchasing' to 'supplier development', identifying, developing and supporting suppliers to ensure a dependable supply of products and materials they will use in making their own products or resell to others. They know that what's good for suppliers is also good for the company. So they partner with suppliers to help make them more effective. Consider Honda, part of the heavily supplier dependent automobile industry. Honda purchases parts and materials from hundreds of suppliers. More than a decade ago, Honda established a rigorous supplier relations program, which provides extensive supplier development and support. Honda doesn't just buy from its suppliers—it helps to train them as well. For example, Honda offers more than 160 training classes for suppliers, on topics ranging from improving quality and reducing costs to developing frontline leadership. Honda also hosts twice yearly events in which quality teams from as many as 100 suppliers meet to share ideas on improving manufacturing processes. 'Our intent is to strengthen supplier business operations,' says one Honda executive. 'The whole family organization is only as strong as the weakest link,' says another. 'So we have to perform together.'

Competitor Toyota also seeks out quality suppliers and helps to train them. For example, Toyota's Supplier Support Centre spent three years teaching managers at supplier Ernie Green Industries about the Toyota Production System before issuing the first purchase order. Similarly, Toyota sent several consultants to supplier Summit Polymers' plant every day for four months to help Summit implement the Toyota system. Such supplier development activities have produced dramatic results. On average, Toyota has helped its suppliers increase productivity by 123%. Of course, Toyota expects to benefit in return. 'We've grown quickly with . . . Toyota, and we're profitable,' says Carl Code, a vice-president at Ernie Green Industries. 'But it's no gravy train. They want suppliers to make enough money to stay in business, grow, and bring them innovation.'

What does the shift from purchasing to supplier development mean for business-to-business marketers? It means that major business buyers are no longer looking only for 'suppliers' from which to purchase goods and services. They are seeking 'supplier partners' with which they can develop mutually beneficial supply relationships. But such relationships are a two-way street. Just as buyers are partnering with and supporting their suppliers, the suppliers must be worthy partners in return. They must work closely with the customers to meet their supply needs better.

Sources: Katherine Zachary, 'Honda Goes Beyond Philosophy in Supplier Efforts', *Ward's Auto World*, 1 July 2003, accessed at <www.wardsauto.com/ar/auto_honda_goes_beyond_2/index.htm>; Jeffrey H. Dyer and Nile W. Hatch, 'Using Supplier Networks to Learn Faster', *MIT Sloan Management Review*, Spring 2004, pp. 77–84; 'BJ's Knows . . . Our System Is Their Solution', *Insights,* March 2002, p. 1; Robert Sherefkin and Amy Wilson, 'Why the Big 3 Can't Be Japanese', *Automotive News*, 10 February 2003; David Hannon, 'Suppliers: Friend or Foe?', *Purchasing*, 6 February 2003, pp. 25–30; 'Delphi: Parts Maker Helps Suppliers Shape Up', *Information Week*, 19 April 2004; 'Supplier Information: Your Guide to Becoming a Wal-Mart Supplier', accessed at <www.walmartstores.com>, January 2005; 'Fortune Global 500', *Fortune*, 25 July 2005, pp. F1–12.

Questions

1 If companies like Wal-Mart and Honda spend money on developing suppliers, this might also benefit their competitors, if those suppliers switch to, or simultaneously supply, Wal-Mart's and Honda's competitors. Is this a problem? If so, what could Wal-Mart or Honda do to minimise the problem?

2 Wal-Mart is often criticised as imposing harsh conditions on its suppliers, such as requiring cost cuts which threaten the margin of their suppliers. None of Wal-Mart's suppliers are as big as Wal-Mart. What are the advantages and disadvantages of supplying to a much larger company?

3 A Honda executive says that 'The whole family organization is only as strong as the weakest link'. Is this always true of supplier–buyer relationships? If so, why don't more companies work closely with their suppliers like Honda?

8.1

instance, magnesium is used in the manufacture of cars, motor bikes, aircraft, machinery and cans, but its use in automobiles accounts for about 88% of the magnesium market.[7] If consumer demand for cars drops, so does the demand for magnesium and for all the other products used to make cars. Therefore, business marketers sometimes promote their products directly to final consumers to increase business demand. For example, glass container manufacturers will advertise the benefits of keeping milk or other beverages in glass as opposed to plastic or aluminium cans. Marketing Highlight 8.2 shows how Intel successfully created derived demand for its microprocessors by marketing to end-users, as well as to its direct customers, the computer manufacturers.

- *Inelastic demand.* The total demand for many business goods and services is inelastic—that is, not much affected by price changes. So drug manufacturers such as Bayer or Roche (which use sulphur in the production of drugs) are not going to buy much more sulphur if the price falls. Nor are they going to buy much less if the price of sulphur rises, unless they can find satisfactory sulphur substitutes. Demand is particularly inelastic in the short run because producers cannot make quick changes in their production methods. Demand is also inelastic for business goods that represent a small percentage of the item's total cost. For example, an increase in the price of shoelaces is unlikely to affect the total demand for shoelaces. However, shoe manufacturers may switch suppliers in response to price differences.

- *Fluctuating demand.* The demand for business goods and services tends to be more volatile than the demand for consumer goods and services. This is especially true of the demand for new plant and equipment. A given percentage increase in consumer demand can lead to a much

Intel inside and the buyer outside?

Intel invented the first microprocessor in 1971 and for 35 years has dominated the chip market for desktop computers. In 2005, Intel chips powered 81% of personal computers, with its nearest rival, AMD (Advanced Micro Devices), trailing far behind with a market share of 18% (and by August 2005, losses for three consecutive quarters, despite offering lower prices than Intel). Few companies dominate an industry like Intel, especially those which supply only one component in a finished product. Intel's rising fortune is all the more remarkable when it is contrasted with the original developer of the personal computer, IBM. Despite its early dominance of personal computers, IBM saw profits from its computers fall in the 1990s as a host of competitors copied its PCs and launched lower cost models, and in 2004 IBM quit the PC manufacturing business, licensing its brand to Chinese manufacturer Lenovo to manufacture and market Lenovo PCs under the IBM brand. Over the same period, Intel's sales and brand value have soared, and the brand has been labelled the world's fifth most powerful brand by brand marketing consultancy Interbrand. How has Intel managed to gain increasing profits while IBM lost out to clone machines? By very clever marketing to its business customers, and to their customers.

In mid-1991 Intel launched its 'Intel Inside' advertising campaign to sell personal computer buyers on the virtues of Intel microprocessors, the small chips that serve as the brains of personal computers. This was a radical move by a component manufacturer; after all, computer buyers can't buy a microprocessor chip, and at the time few computer buyers would have known what a microprocessor was or known that Intel made them. But by co-branded advertising with its business customers (the ones who bought the chips and made the computers) the 'Intel Inside' logo suddenly became salient for the final consumers. Most probably didn't know what a microprocessor was, but the simple Intel message on the computer ads, and the logo on the computer, suggested that 'Intel Inside' offered higher quality;

after all, otherwise why would anyone advertise it? And so began the steady growth of Intel. By 2005, Intel and its partners had spend $US7 billion on co-branded advertising, making the Intel logo one of the most recognisable in computing. In Australia, in addition to ongoing co-branded advertising with computer manufacturers and sellers, Intel co-sponsors the Indy 300 race with Acer computers, showcasing Intel and Acer products by offering a tent where visitors can experience Acer and Intel wireless technology by playing a V8 supercar game against other visitors. Many computer buyers still don't know what 'Intel Inside' actually means, but wouldn't buy a computer that didn't have it. After all, it must be important, mustn't it, because nearly all the computers advertise it?

Demand for microprocessors is derived demand—it comes from demand for products that contain microprocessors. Before Intel made its brand so salient, consumers would buy computers and take whatever brand of chip the computer manufacturer chose to include. Traditionally, component manufacturers such as Intel would market only to the manufacturers who buy their products. In contrast, the 'Intel Inside' campaign appeals directly to computer buyers—Intel's customers' customers. By making the Intel brand salient and important for these consumers, Intel chips became more attractive to computer manufacturers. With its campaign, Intel was able to rewrite the equation of organisational buying: the end-customer became an integral influencer on the organisation's buying team. And by offering co-branded advertising with computer manufacturers, Intel was able to partner directly with members of the buying organisation to jointly reach the final consumer.

This well-executed marketing strategy has resulted in a steady increase in sales, and rewarded Intel with constant large profits. As a result, Intel has the ability to spend far more on R&D than its competitors, releasing a steady stream of faster chips; the latest Pentium 4 series chips run at clock speeds of over

3–3.6 gigahertz (the exact speed depending on the model). With a market share of over 80%, demand for Intel products might appear saturated. So Intel needs to work on developing new markets for its chips, and increasing repurchase rates for computers by offering newer, faster technology, which builds demand for the computers made by Intel's business customers, and creates more sales of Intel chips. Intel's chief operating officer, Paul Otellini, says that the average replacement cycle for a PC is three to four years, so by continually offering chip upgrades, Intel can stimulate demand and bring that repurchase time down. Most recently, the Centrino chip, which offers the ability for notebook users to work wirelessly, has boosted demand for new wireless-enabled laptops (of course, at the same time boosting the demand for Intel chips!).

Intel also works closely with its component suppliers, with customers such as major PC manufacturers Dell, HP and Acer and with software and network developers like Sun Microsystems, to continue to ensure that it is the supplier of choice. Intel needs to make sure that each time the process of 'straight rebuy' or 'modified rebuy' takes place it has plenty of opportunities to sell additional products. To do this, Intel has developed a suite of products aimed at providing a 'systems sell' to its client. For example, Intel is working on chips for mobile phones, and possibly for some computers, that extend battery life. Extending battery life means a trade-off in performance, in some cases decreasing a chip's speed by half. But Intel knows that for some products battery life is much more important for consumers than speed. Its innovative products and related services enable Intel to be seen as a partner and systems seller for all important information technology processing needs. It seems that in this business-to-business buying scenario everyone is a winner—the chip maker, since customers demand Intel processors, PC manufacturers, because they know that customers will demand products with Intel chips, and software manufacturers, because they can develop software based on the new microprocessor architecture. All these industry groups have successfully combined to grow the computer market, as consumers respond to the improved performance of new computers and electronic devices by upgrading their old machines.

Sources: <www.intel.com/museum/corporatetimeline>, accessed 6 December 2005; Jack Robertson and Faith Hung, 'Intel Maintains Chipset Grip as It Readies Centrino', *EBN*, 10 March 2003, p. 3; Don Clark, 'Intel Bets on Wi-Fi in Start-Ups and New Chips', *Wall Street Journal*, 10 March 2003, Eastern edition, p. B.4; Jack Robertson, 'Intel Plants Stake in Wi-Fi Market with Centrino—Customers Hedge Bets with Rival Chipsets', *EBN*, 17 March 2003, p. 1; 'Intel 6xx Series Hardware', *APC Magazine*, 17 May 2005; Laurie Flynn, 'Intel to Reduce Drain on Battery Life', *The Australian Financial Review*, 22 September 2005, p. 20; Brad Howarth, 'Intel Searches for the Next Silver Lining', *Business Review Weekly*, 15 August 2005, p. 41; Amanda Swinburn, 'Technology Firms Focus on Making Brands Experiential', *B & T Weekly*, 14 October 2005, p. 8; Julia Talevski, 'Builders See AMD Sales Pick Up', *Australian Reseller News*, 15 November 2005.

Questions

1. Demand for Intel's chips could be said to be derived demand. Explain what is meant by this statement.

2. Visit a computer shop, or a retailer such as Harvey Norman, and note how many computers carry the 'Intel Inside' logo? Why do they do this? Isn't the computer brand name the most important feature to the buyer?

3. Why has Intel chosen to use marketing communications with consumer markets—the end-users—rather than simply concentrating on those who use its chips and motherboards in their finished computers?

8.2

larger percentage increase in the demand for plant and equipment necessary to produce the additional output. Economists refer to this effect as the acceleration effect. Sometimes a rise of only 10% in consumer demand can cause as much as a 200% rise in businesses' demand for products in the next period, and a 10% fall in consumer demand may cause a complete collapse in businesses' demand. This sales volatility has led many business marketers to diversify their products and markets to achieve more balanced sales over the business cycle.

Nature of the buying unit

The business buying unit differs from consumer purchases in several ways, reflecting that there is more purchasing procurement effort and more people influencing the buying process. Often buying committees made up of technical experts are responsible for decisions involving complex products and processes.

- *Professional purchasing.* Business goods are often purchased by trained purchasing agents, who must follow the organisation's purchasing policies, constraints and requirements. Many of the steps in buying—for example, requests for quotations, proposals and purchase contracts—are not typically found in consumer buying.

  Professional buyers spend their professional lives learning how to buy better. They go to seminars and conferences to learn about new purchasing/procurement technologies. They are also trained to evaluate technical information that leads to more cost-effective buying. In response, selling organisations need to become expert at selling. Business marketers have to provide greater technical data about their product and its advantages compared to competitors' products. For example, Xerox uses what they call 'major account managers' who look after the relationship with Xerox's 300 largest corporate customers. They need to be experts in the art and science of selling; everything from analysis of document flow through organisations to outsourcing of document imaging, archiving and retrieval, in order to successfully manage the relationship with their customers.[8]

- *Several buying influences.* Typically, more people influence business buying decisions than consumer buying decisions. Buying committees consisting of technical experts and even senior management are common in the purchase of major goods or services. Consequently, business marketers need well-trained sales representatives and often sales teams to deal with the well-trained buyers. Although advertising, sales promotion and publicity play an important role in the business promotional mix, personal selling usually serves as the main marketing tool. For example, an industrial chemicals company might pursue an 'account management approach', with a dedicated sales team assigned to a major client in an attempt to reach all the people who influence its customers' buying decisions. Marketing Highlight 8.3 discusses one example which highlights the importance of identifying and targeting the important influencers and decision makers in the buying process.

Types of decisions and the decision process

Business buyers face more complex decisions than consumers, and the process is more formalised. Quite apart from helping their customers, salespeople in the business-to-business field are at pains to develop long-term relationships so as to lock the parties together.[9] Another difference between consumer and business buying is that direct purchasing is prevalent. Business buyers often buy directly from manufacturers rather than through intermediaries, especially those items that are technically complex and/or expensive (such as medical equipment, construction and high-tech equipment). Reciprocity is also often important in the decision process; business buyers often select suppliers who also buy from them. For example, a telecommunications company might give preference to handset suppliers which use that telco for their own business needs.

Another difference is that rather than make outright purchases businesses will often lease products. Leasing is particularly common with computers, shop machinery, packaging equipment, heavy-construction equipment, machine tools and motor vehicles. The lessee gains a number of advantages: conserving capital, getting the seller's latest products, receiving better service and evening out cash flow. The lessor often ends up with a larger net income and the chance to sell to customers who could not afford outright purchase.

Business buyer behaviour

At the most basic level, marketers want to know how business buyers will respond to various marketing stimuli. Figure 8.2 shows a model of business buyer behaviour. In this model, marketing and other stimuli affect the buying organisation and produce certain buyer responses. As with consumer buying, the marketing stimuli for business buying consist of all the elements of the marketing mix: product, price, place, promotion, people and processes.

Other stimuli include major forces in the environment: economic, technological, political, cultural and competitive. These stimuli influence the organisation's operating environment, and in turn influence the buyers' responses: product or service choice, supplier choice, order quantity, and delivery, service and payment terms. In order to design effective marketing mix strategies the marketer must understand what factors within the organisation influence the purchase (or non-purchase) response of potential customers.

Within the organisation, buying activity consists of two major parts: the buying centre, made up of all the people involved in the buying decision, and the buying decision process. The model shows that the buying centre and the buying decision process are influenced by internal organisational, interpersonal and individual factors, as well as by external environmental factors.

The model in Figure 8.2 suggests four questions about business buyer behaviour: What buying decisions do business buyers make? Who participates in the buying process? What are the major influences on buyers? How do business buyers make their buying decisions?

Major types of buying situations

There are three major types of buying situations as shown in Figure 8.3 (overleaf).[10] At one extreme is the straight rebuy, which is a fairly routine decision. At the other extreme is the new task, which may call for thorough research. In the middle is the modified rebuy, which requires some research.

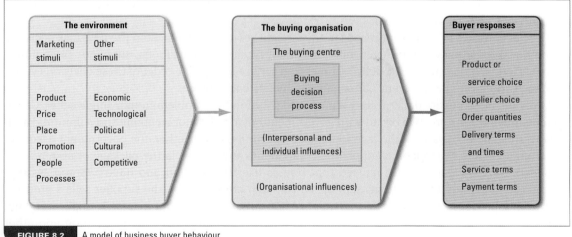

FIGURE 8.2 A model of business buyer behaviour

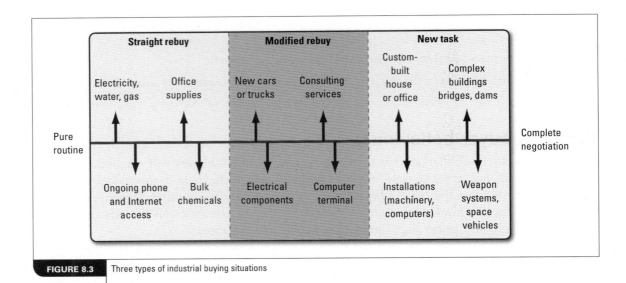

FIGURE 8.3 | Three types of industrial buying situations

Straight rebuy
An industrial buying
situation in which the
buyer routinely reorders
something without
modification.

Where a **straight rebuy** occurs, the buyer reorders items without any modifications. It is usually handled on a routine basis by procurement officers. Based on past buying satisfaction, the buyer simply chooses from the various suppliers on its list. 'In' suppliers try to maintain product and service quality. They often propose automatic reordering systems so that the purchasing agent will save reordering time. The 'out' suppliers try to offer something new or exploit dissatisfaction so that the buyer will consider them. They try to get their foot in the door with a small order and then enlarge their purchase share over time.

Modified rebuy An
industrial buying situation
in which the buyer
wants to modify product
specifications, prices,
terms or suppliers.

In a **modified rebuy**, the buyer wants to modify product specifications, prices, terms or suppliers. The modified rebuy usually involves more decision participants than the straight rebuy. The 'in' suppliers may become nervous and feel pressured to put their best foot forward to protect an account. 'Out' suppliers may see the modified rebuy situation as an opportunity to make a better offer and gain new business.

New task An industrial
buying situation in which
the buyer purchases a
product or service for
the first time.

A company buying a product or service for the first time faces a **new-task** situation. In such cases, the greater the cost or risk, the larger the number of decision participants and the greater their efforts to collect information will be. The new-task situation is the marketer's greatest opportunity and challenge. The marketer not only tries to reach as many key buying influences as possible, but also provides help and information.

The buyer makes the fewest decisions in the straight rebuy and the most in the new-task decision. In the new-task situation, the buyer must decide on product specifications, suppliers, price limits, payment terms, order quantities, delivery times and service terms. The order of these decisions varies with each situation, and different participants influence each choice.

Systems buying Buying
a packaged solution to
a problem, which avoids
making all the separate
decisions involved in
buying each item or
service separately.

Many business buyers prefer to buy a packaged solution to a problem from a single seller. Called **systems buying**, this practice began with government buying of major weapons and communication systems. Instead of buying all the components and putting them together, the government asked for bids from suppliers which would supply the components and assemble the package or system.

Sellers have increasingly recognised that buyers like this method and have adopted systems selling as a marketing tool. Systems selling is a two-step process. First, the supplier sells a group of interlocking products. For example, the supplier not only sells glue, but also sells applicators and dryers. Second, the supplier sells a system of production, inventory control, distribution and other services to meet the buyer's need for a smooth-running operation.

Systems selling is a key business marketing strategy for winning and holding accounts. The contract often goes to the firm that provides the most complete system to meet the customer's needs. For example, the Victorian government requested bids to build an electronic services website for its 'consumable' supplies procurement. A Dutch firm's proposal included choosing the hardware, designing the architecture, hiring the support crew, developing the database and turning the finished system over to the Victorian government. An Australian/American firm's proposal included all these services, plus hiring and training the government workers to run the website services, and the ability to scale this web service to other government departments. Although the Australian firm's proposal cost more, it won the contract. The Australians viewed the project not just as one of building a website services system (the narrow view of systems selling) but instead as one of providing a system that would contribute to the government's overall consistency and cross-organisational efficiencies. They took the broadest view of the customer's needs. This is true systems selling.[11]

Participants in the business buying process

Who does the buying of the billions of dollars worth of goods and services needed by business organisations? The decision-making unit of a buying organisation is called its **buying centre**, defined as all the individuals and units that participate in the business decision-making process.[12]

The buying centre includes all members of the organisation who play any of five roles in the purchase decision process.[13]

- **Users** are members of the organisation who use the product or service. In many cases, users initiate the buying proposal and help define product specifications.
- **Influencers** affect the buying decision. They often help to define specifications and also provide information for evaluating alternatives. Technical personnel are particularly important influencers.
- **Buyers** have formal authority to select the supplier and arrange terms of purchase. Buyers may help shape product specifications, but they play their major role in selecting vendors and in negotiating. In more complex purchases, buyers might include high-level officers participating in the negotiations.
- **Deciders** have formal or informal power to select or approve the final suppliers. In routine buying, the buyers are often the deciders, or at least the approvers.
- **Gatekeepers** control the flow of information to others. For example, purchasing agents often have authority to prevent salespersons from seeing users or deciders. Other gatekeepers include technical personnel and even personal assistants and executive secretaries.

Some organisations have a buying centre which purchases everything for the organisation—raw materials, office supplies, outsourced services and travel. However, in many cases the buying centre is not a fixed and formally identified unit within the buying organisation. It is a set of buying roles assumed by different people for different purchases. Within the organisation, the size and make-up of the buying centre will vary for different products and for different buying situations. For some routine purchases, one person—perhaps a procurement officer—may assume all the buying centre roles and serve as the only person involved in the buying decision. For more complex purchases, the buying centre may include 20 or 30 people from different levels and departments in the organisation. One study of business buying showed that the typical business equipment purchase involved seven people from three management levels representing four different departments.[14]

Major influences on business buyers

Business buyers are subject to many influences when they make their buying decisions. Some marketers assume that the major influences are economic. They think buyers will favour the supplier

Buying centre All the individuals and units that participate in the organisational buying decision process.

User The person who consumes or uses a product or service.

Influencer A person whose view or advice carries some weight in making a final buying decision.

Buyer The person who makes an actual purchase.

Decider The person who ultimately makes a buying decision or any part of it—whether to buy, what to buy, how to buy or where to buy.

Gatekeeper The person in the organisation's buying centre who controls the flow of information to others.

Who is the customer?

Henkel Loctite Corporation manufactures and markets a broad range of high-performance adhesives, sealants and coatings used in products like computers, cars, planes, vacuum cleaners, mobile phones and medical devices. The company's website states that it is 'in the business of solving customers' problems', and when the company launched a new product branded the RC-660, management was confident that it would be a great new-product success. In one customer test, one 6-ounce (170-gram) tube of RC-660 saved 800 hours of machine downtime. The product, today referred to as Quick Metal 660, is a creamy, non-running gel which is applied onto cylindrical parts to fill surface imperfections and repair worn areas. It contains no metal, but once assembled hardens to a strength that often doubles that of a press fit. It is used to salvage worn metallic parts or to keep machinery running until new parts arrive. The history of RC-660's launch reveals important lessons for marketers in targeting the right customer.

At the time of its market introduction, though production engineers were believed to be sceptical of using a gel-like plastic to repair critical machine parts, Loctite's marketing strategy was to target this scepticism head on. Sales literature and advertising copy were created in technical detail in order to document convincingly the strength and engineering characteristics of RC-660.

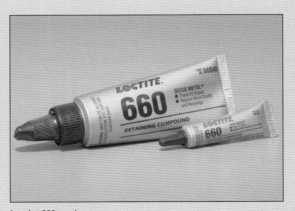

Loctite 660 packs.

The price of RC-660 was designed to be attractive and not present a barrier to trial usage. With a price of less than $10 per 6-ounce (170-gram) tube, the new product team felt there should be little opposition to trying the new Loctite product. While the unit cost was under $3, the net margin was less than it would appear since Loctite products are sold through a distributor sales organisation and Loctite has to pay commission on all sales. The product provided an inexpensive solution to machine downtime when a part broke or needed repair. What more could the target customer want?

But the RC-660 marketing strategy failed. After several months of marketing effort, Loctite distributors were requesting refunds on unsold RC-660 inventory. Though the product worked reliably, the market failed to accept it, even at a low price. RC-660 was removed from the market less than one year after its market launch.

After several months of internal speculation, a market research project was commissioned to determine why the market rejected RC-660. The market research uncovered the fact that production engineers were risk averse and wanted proven solutions. The low price created suspicions about the product's reliability and quality. The market research also revealed that the real target customer was the maintenance worker, not the production engineer or supervisor. Maintenance workers were more open to new ideas, preferred pictures of how things worked and could purchase supplies such as RC-660 when they cost under $25. With this market intelligence a revised target market strategy was initiated. The new marketing strategy for Quick Metal 660 was formulated around the maintenance workers' product needs, and every aspect of the marketing mix was customised to meet the target customers' needs:

- The name was changed from RC-660 to Quick Metal 660 to better communicate the primary benefits of the product (speed and strength).
- The price was raised to $18.95 to capture more

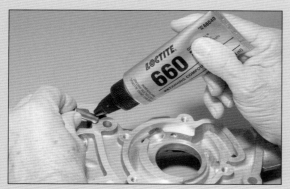

Loctite repairs worn parts.

based upon finding the right target customer and then building the entire marketing strategy around the needs of that target customer. Even though the initial RC-660 strategy was somewhat customised to the needs of a target customer, production engineers were not the target customer. Quick Metal 660 continues today to be one of Loctite's most successful products in Australia and around the world.

Sources: Information provided by David Marshall, Advertising and Public Relations Manager, Henkel Engineering Adhesives, Sydney, and historical facts reproduced from Roger Best, *Market Based Management: Strategies for Growing Customer Value and Profitability,* 2nd edn, Upper Saddle River, NJ, Prentice Hall, 2000, Chapter 7, pp. 153–154; Loctite websites, <www.loctite.com.au> and <www.loctite.com>, accessed 6 December 2005; Alison Dunn, 'Industrial Strength Sealants Help Steel Company Avoid Costly Crack Ups', *PEM,* vol. 26, no. 2, April 2002, p. 34; Frederic B. Jueneman, 'Stick it to 'em', *Research & Development,* vol. 43, no. 11, November 2001, p. 9; Joe Jancsurak, 'Accelerating Time to Market for Adhesives', *Appliance Manufacturer,* vol. 47, no. 6, June 1999, p. 44; Anonymous, 'Loctite Launches Education Effort', *Appliance Manufacturer,* vol. 48, no. 7, July 2000, p. 20.

of the value created by the product while also keeping the purchase decision within the sole discretion of the target customer (the maintenance worker).

- ⊙ The advertising copy and promotional literature featured maintenance workers using the product and featured the value proposition, 'keeps the machinery running until the new part arrives'.
- ⊙ A logo was created along with new packaging that featured a metallic coloured tube and a box with bold lettering.
- ⊙ Promotional samples were provided to stimulate trial usage by target customers, the maintenance workers.

The revised target customer strategy was a huge market success. The success, however, was solely

Questions

1 Why is it important to identify clearly who the customer is? Explain, using reference to Loctite.

2 What causes a firm to launch a new product, then, when it fails, conduct market research? Isn't something out of sequence here?

3 Can you think of other examples like Loctite where it is possible to target the 'wrong' customer? Illustrate your example.

8.3

who offers the lowest price, or the best product, or the most service. They concentrate on offering strong economic benefits to buyers. However, business buyers actually respond to both economic and personal factors. Far from being cold, calculating and impersonal, business buyers are human and social as well. They react to both reason and emotion.

When suppliers' offers are very similar, business buyers have little basis for strictly rational choice. Because they can meet organisational goals with any supplier, buyers can allow personal factors to play a larger role in their decisions. However, when competing products differ greatly, business buyers are more accountable for their choice and tend to pay more attention to economic factors. Figure 8.4 (overleaf) lists various groups of influences on business buyers—environmental, organisational, interpersonal and individual.[15]

Environmental factors

Business buyers are influenced heavily by factors in the current and expected economic environment, such as the level of primary demand, the economic outlook and the cost of money. As economic

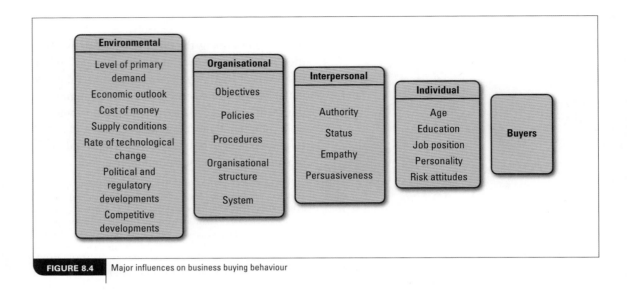

FIGURE 8.4 | Major influences on business buying behaviour

uncertainty rises, business buyers tend to cut back on new investments and attempt to reduce their inventories.

An increasingly important environmental factor is shortages in key materials. Many companies now are more willing to buy larger inventories of scarce materials or commit to long-term agreed price contracts in order to ensure adequate supply. Business buyers are also affected by technological, political and competitive developments in the environment. Culture and customs can strongly influence business buyer reactions to the marketer's behaviour and strategies, especially in the international marketing environment. The business marketer must watch these factors, determine how they will affect the buyer and try to turn these challenges into opportunities.

Organisational factors

Each buying organisation has its own objectives, policies, procedures, structure and systems which must be understood by the business marketer. An astute marketer will try to determine how many people are involved in the buying decision and who they are and try to find out their evaluative criteria and any company policies and limits on its buyers. In addition, the business marketer should be aware of the following organisational trends in the purchasing area.

Upgraded purchasing Procurement personnel have often occupied a lowly position in the management hierarchy, even though they may manage more than half the company's costs. With the advent of e-business and the Internet, many companies have upgraded their procurement sections. Several large corporations have elevated the heads of procurement to the position of general manager or vice-president. Some companies have combined several functions—such as purchasing, inventory control, production scheduling and traffic—into a high-level function called strategic materials management. Procurement sections in many multinational companies have responsibility for purchasing materials and services around the world. Companies also require a good pool of technology-savvy procurement personnel to drive cost-effective purchasing. This has driven many companies to turn to online procurement systems, such as that provided by Ariba, an online procurement and sourcing website that helps companies to manage their purchasing with what Ariba calls its 'Spend Management Solutions'.[16]

Centralised purchasing In companies consisting of many divisions with differing needs, much of the procurement is carried out at the division level. However, some large companies have recentralised purchasing. Headquarters identifies materials purchased by several divisions and buys them centrally. Centralised purchasing gives the company more purchasing clout, which can produce substantial savings. For the business marketer, this development means dealing with fewer, higher-level buyers. Instead of using regional salesforces to sell to a large buyer's separate plants, the seller may use a national account salesforce to service the buyer. For example, in the USA, Xerox uses national account managers who each handle one to five large national accounts across many scattered locations. The national account managers coordinate the efforts of an entire Xerox team—specialists, analysts, salespeople for individual products—to sell to and service important national customers. National account selling is challenging and demands both a high-level salesforce and a sophisticated marketing effort.

Business buying on the Internet Over the past few years, advances in information technology have brought significant changes to business-to-business marketing. Online purchasing, often called *e-procurement*, is growing rapidly. In a recent survey, almost 75% of business buyers indicated that they use the Internet to make at least some of their purchases. Another study estimates that e-procurement accounted for 13% of company total direct materials purchases in 2004, up from 2% in 2003.[17] In addition to their own web pages on the Internet, companies are establishing extranets that link a company's communications and data with its regular suppliers and distributors.

Business-to-business e-procurement yields many benefits. A web-powered purchasing program eliminates the paperwork associated with traditional requisition and ordering procedures, so it shaves transaction costs and results in more efficient purchasing for both buyers and suppliers. For example, Owens Corning estimates that e-procurement has shaved 10% off its annual purchasing bill of $US3.4 billion. And Microsoft recently reduced its purchasing costs by $US700 million after implementing its MS Market e-procurement system. Beyond the cost and time savings, e-procurement frees purchasing people to focus on more strategic issues. For many purchasing professionals, going online means reducing drudgery and paperwork and spending more time managing inventory and working creatively with suppliers. 'That is the key,' says one HP executive. 'You can now focus people on value-added activities. Procurement professionals can now find different sources and work with suppliers to reduce costs and to develop new products.'[18]

So far, most of the products bought online are MRO materials—maintenance, repair and operations. The actual dollar amount spent on MRO materials bought online pales in comparison to the amount spent for items such as airplane parts, computer systems and steel tubing. Yet, MRO materials make up 80% of all business orders and the transaction costs for order processing are high. Thus, companies have much to gain by streamlining the MRO buying process on the Web. General Electric, one of the world's biggest purchasers, plans to be buying *all* of its general operating and industrial supplies online within the next few years.

Many business marketers also offer a host of web-based procurement options to their customers. When using such systems, the seller links customers' computers to its own, allowing customers to order needed items instantly by entering orders directly into the computer. Orders are transmitted automatically to the supplier, instantly updating the production, storage and distribution requirements along the entire value chain. A good example of a small company using a procurement website is Harris Technology, which supplies hardware and software to business and consumer customers. Harris Technology buys and sells online, and is able to procure an item without holding a large inventory (their aim is to have zero or close to zero inventory) or experiencing long supply lead times.[19] This means that Harris Technology can lower its own costs (and thus keep prices low for its customers),

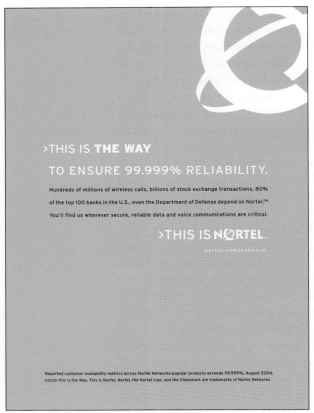

>THIS IS **THE WAY**

TO ENSURE 99.999% RELIABILITY.

Hundreds of millions of wireless calls, billions of stock exchange transactions, 80% of the top 100 banks in the U.S., even the Department of Defense depend on Nortel.™ You'll find us wherever secure, reliable data and voice communications are critical.

>THIS IS N⊘RTEL

nortel.com/enhance

Reported customer availability metrics across Nortel Networks popular products exceeds 99.999%, August 2004. ©2005 This is the Way. This is Nortel, Nortel, the Nortel logo, and the Globemark are trademarks of Nortel Networks.

Business sellers will often highlight the possible risk of lower quality products, to encourage a choice of an apparently superior product.

because it doesn't have to hold large amounts of inventory, but at the same time it can rapidly supply its customers when an order is placed. Time savings are particularly dramatic for companies with many overseas suppliers. Adaptec, a leading supplier of computer storage, used an extranet to tie all of its Taiwanese chip suppliers together in a kind of virtual family. Now messages from Adaptec flow in seconds from its headquarters to its Asian partners, and Adaptec has reduced the time between the order and delivery of its chips from as long as 16 weeks to just 55 days—the same turnaround time for companies that build their own chips.

Online purchasing also takes place through online auctions and on public and private online trading exchanges (or e-marketplaces). However, many of these e-marketplaces, or B2B hubs, have failed to operate profitably. Suppliers questioned the business model, which imposed an intermediary between the seller and the buyer, leading in some cases to higher costs than direct sourcing. One of the highest profile e-marketplaces, Covisint, established by a consortium of car companies with the aim of decreasing their supply costs, cost its founders a reported $US500 million but failed to offer the expected returns, and after years of losses the company was sold. It has now closed its auction service and electronic parts catalogue, but it continues to operate, offering access to services such as web services and portal development.[20]

The rapidly expanding use of e-purchasing, however, also presents some problems for businesses. For example, at the same time that the Web makes it possible for suppliers and customers to share business data and even collaborate on product design, it can also erode decades-old customer–supplier relationships. Many firms are using the Web to search for better suppliers.

E-purchasing can also create potential security disasters. More than 80% of companies say security is the leading barrier to expanding electronic links with customers and partners. Although email and home banking transactions can be protected through basic encryption, the secure environment that businesses need to carry out confidential interactions is still often lacking. Companies are spending millions for research on defensive strategies to keep hackers at bay. Cisco Systems, for example, specifies the types of routers, firewalls and security procedures that its partners must use to safeguard extranet connections. Cisco goes even further—it sends its own security engineers to examine a partner's defences and holds the partner liable for any security breach that originates from its computer.

Purchasing performance evaluation Some companies are setting up incentive systems to reward purchasing managers for especially good purchasing performance, in much the same way that salespeople receive bonuses for especially good selling performance. These systems should lead purchasing managers to increase their pressure on sellers for the best terms.

Just-in-time production systems Over the past 15 years businesses around the world have adopted several innovative production concepts, such as just-in-time (JIT) production, early supplier involvement, value analysis, quality management, quality at source and flexible manufacturing. These practices greatly affect how business marketers sell to and service their customers. For example, JIT means that production materials arrive at the customer's factory exactly when needed for production, rather than being stored by the customer until used. It calls for close coordination between the production schedules of supplier and customer so that neither has to carry much inventory. Dell uses JIT coupled with an online-ordering concept with its clients and calls it 'just in order' where the PC is not manufactured until the customer places the order. This way the customer always has the latest PC and Dell doesn't have any inventories or holding costs and is able to pass on the cost savings to its customers. As a result Dell has been able to become the largest computer manufacturer in the world.[21]

Interpersonal factors

The buying centre usually includes many participants who influence each other. The business marketer often finds it difficult to determine what kinds of interpersonal factors and group dynamics enter into the buying process. As one writer notes: 'Managers do not wear tags that say "decision maker" or "unimportant person". The powerful are often invisible, at least to vendor representatives.'[22] Nor does the buying centre participant with the highest rank always have the most influence. Participants may have influence in the buying decision because they control rewards and punishments, are well liked, have special expertise or have a special relationship with other important participants. Interpersonal factors are often very subtle. Whenever possible, business marketers must try to understand these factors and design strategies that take them into account.

Individual factors

Each participant in the business buying decision process brings in personal motives, perceptions and preferences. These individual factors are affected by personal characteristics such as age, income, education, professional identification, personality and attitudes toward risk. Also, buyers have different buying styles. Some may be technical types who make in-depth analyses of competitive proposals before choosing a supplier. Other buyers may be intuitive negotiators who are adept at pitting the sellers against one another for the best deal.

The business buying process

The buying decision process in business-to-business marketing is more deliberate and differs from the decision process in consumer markets, as Table 8.2 (overleaf) illustrates.[23] The purchase decision will vary with the importance of the buying decision, and with the size of the business. However, buyers who face a new-task buying situation usually go through all stages of the buying process, even though the process may be less formal for small businesses. Buyers making modified or straight rebuys may skip some of the stages. We will examine these steps for the typical new-task buying situation.

Problem recognition

Similar to consumer buying, the business buying process begins when someone in the company recognises a problem or need that can be met by acquiring a specific good or service. **Problem recognition** can result from internal or external stimuli. Internally, the company may decide to launch a new product that requires new production equipment and materials. Or a machine may break down and need new parts. Perhaps a purchasing manager is unhappy with a current supplier's product quality, service or prices. Externally, the buyer may get some new ideas at a trade show, see an ad or receive a call from a salesperson who offers a better product or a lower price. Business marketers often create problem recognition by alerting customers to potential problems in their advertising or sales calls, and then show how their products provide solutions.

Problem recognition
The first stage of the buyer decision process in which the consumer recognises a problem or need.

TABLE 8.2 Comparison of the business and consumer buying process in relation to major buying situations (motor vehicles)

Buying step	Business-to-business	Consumer
1. Problem recognition	Anticipates and plans for purchase on a routine basis	Reacts to needs when they arise
2. General need description	Extensive, objective cost–benefit analysis	Limited analysis of benefits; concern with total cost
3. Product specification	Precise, technical description using techniques such as value analysis	Description more in terms of benefits
4. Information/supplier search	Extensive search that extends to the search for supplier	Limited search—geographically and in terms of sources
5. Proposal solicitation	Formal, such as in a tender process if large volumes or values involved	May be verbal
6. Supplier selection	Made after extensive analysis of objective information	Limited analysis, with subjective and anecdotal information influencing the decision
7. Order-routine specification	Routinised calculation of reorder points as well as time and place of delivery	Not routinised
8. Post-purchase performance review	Extensive comparison made and feedback given; concern with quality management at source	Little basis for comparison

Sources: Adapted from Patrick J. Robinson, Charles W. Faris and Yoram Wind, *Industrial Buying and Creative Marketing,* Boston, Allyn & Bacon, 1967), p. 14; and G. David Hughes, *A Planning Approach to Marketing Management,* Reading, Massachusetts, Addison Wesley Publishing, 1980, p. 187.

General need description

Having recognised a need, the buyer next prepares a **general need description** that describes the characteristics and quantity of the needed item. For standard items, this process presents few problems. For complex items, however, the buyer may have to work with others—engineers, users, consultants—to define the item. The team may rank the importance of reliability, durability, price and other attributes desired in the item. In this phase, the alert business marketer can help the buyers define their needs and provide information about the value of different product characteristics.

Product specification

The buying organisation next develops the item's technical **product specifications**, often with the help of a value analysis engineering team. **Value analysis** is an approach to cost reduction in which components are studied carefully to determine whether they can be redesigned, standardised or made by less costly methods of production. The team decides on the best product characteristics and specifies them accordingly. Sellers, too, can use value analysis as a tool to help secure a new account. Many buyers are now considering, and business sellers are now pointing out, the long-term costs and value of a product, using a concept known as 'total cost of ownership' (TCO). For example, for the purchase of a software package, TCO includes licence fees, training, support, maintenance, hardware, customisation, integration and even end-of-life data migration and archiving.[24] In this way a seller can often justify a higher initial price, by showing that the long-term cost is lower than competing offers.

Supplier search

The buyer now conducts a **supplier search** to find the best vendors. The buyer can compile a list of qualified suppliers by reviewing trade directories, doing a computer search or phoning other companies for recommendations. The newer the buying task, and the more complex and costly the item, the greater the amount of time the buyer is likely to spend searching for suppliers. The challenge for the supplier is therefore to get listed in major directories and build a good reputation in the marketplace, so they stand the best chance of coming to the attention of potential buyers. Salespeople should watch for companies in the process of searching for suppliers and make certain their firm is considered.

Proposal solicitation

In the **proposal solicitation** stage of the business buying process, the buyer invites qualified suppliers to submit proposals. In response, some suppliers will send only a catalogue or a salesperson. However, when the item is complex or expensive, the buyer will usually require detailed written proposals or formal presentations from each potential supplier.

Business marketers must be skilled in researching, writing and presenting proposals in response to buyer proposal solicitations. Proposals should be marketing documents, not just technical documents. Presentations should inspire confidence and should make the marketer's company stand out from the competition.

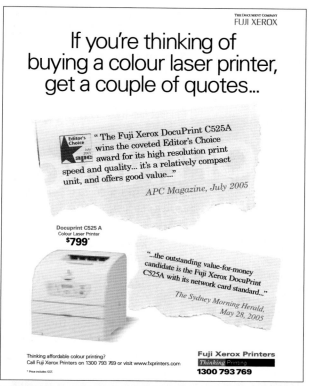

Fuji Xerox's ad encourages the potential buyer to include Fuji Xerox in the supplier search.

Supplier selection

The members of the buying centre now review the proposals and select a supplier or suppliers. During **supplier selection**, the buying centre will often draw up a list of the desired supplier attributes and their relative importance. In one survey, purchasing executives listed the following attributes as most important in influencing the relationship between supplier and customer: quality products and services, on-time delivery, ethical corporate behaviour, honest communication and competitive prices.[25] Other important factors include repair and servicing capabilities, technical aid and advice, geographic location, performance history and reputation. The members of the buying centre will sometimes rate suppliers against these attributes and identify the best suppliers. They often use a supplier evaluation form similar to the one shown in Table 8.3 (overleaf). The supplier in this example rates as excellent on quality, service, responsiveness and reputation, but only as fair on price and delivery. The buyer will now have to decide how important the two weaknesses are and compare these ratings with those of other possible suppliers. The ratings could be redone using importance weightings for the seven attributes.

The importance of various supplier attributes depends on the type of purchase situation the buyer faces.[26] One study of 220 purchasing managers showed that economic criteria were most important in situations involving routine purchases of standard products. Performance criteria became more important in purchases of non-standard, more complex products. However, the supplier's ability to adapt to the buyer's changing needs was important for almost all types of purchases.[27] Buyers might attempt to negotiate with preferred suppliers for better prices and terms before making the final

Supplier search The stage of the industrial buying process in which the buyer tries to find the best vendors.

Proposal solicitation The stage of the industrial buying process in which the buyer invites qualified suppliers to submit proposals.

Supplier selection The stage of the industrial buying process in which the buyer reviews proposals and selects a supplier or suppliers.

TABLE 8.3 An example of supplier analysis

Supplier attribute	Rating				
	Very poor (1)	Poor (2)	Fair (3)	Good (4)	Excellent (5)
Price competitiveness			X		
Product quality, reliability					X
Service and repair capabilities					X
On-time delivery			X		
Quality of sales representatives				X	
Overall responsiveness to customer needs					X
Overall reputation					X
Average score = 4.29					

Order-routine specification The stage of the industrial buying process in which the buyer writes the final order with the chosen supplier(s), listing the technical specifications, quantity needed, expected time of delivery, return policies, warranties and so on.

selections. In the end, they may select a single supplier or a few suppliers. Many buyers prefer multiple sources of supplies to avoid being totally dependent on one supplier and to allow comparisons of the prices and performance of several suppliers over time.

Order-routine specification

The buyer now prepares an **order-routine specification**. It includes the final order with the chosen supplier or suppliers and lists items such as technical specifications, quantity needed, expected time of delivery, return policies and warranties. In the case of maintenance, repair and operating items, buyers may use blanket contracts rather than periodic purchase orders. A blanket contract creates a long-term relationship in which the supplier promises to resupply the buyer as needed at agreed prices for a set time period. The seller holds the stock and the buyer's computer system automatically prints out an order to the seller when stock is needed. A blanket order eliminates the expensive process of renegotiating a purchase each time stock is required. It also allows buyers to write more but smaller purchase orders, resulting in lower inventory levels and carrying costs.

Blanket contracting leads to more single-source buying and to buying more items from that source. This practice locks the supplier in more tightly with the buyer and makes it difficult for other suppliers to break in unless the buyer becomes dissatisfied with prices or service.

Performance review

In this stage, the buyer reviews supplier performance. The buyer might contact users and ask them to rate their satisfaction. The

Sun highlights its lower price, relative to alternative systems.

performance review may lead the buyer to continue, modify or drop the arrangement. The seller's job is to monitor the same factors used by the buyer to make sure that the seller is delivering the expected level of performance.

We have described the stages that would typically occur in a new-task buying situation. The eight-stage model provides a simple view of the business buying decision process. The actual process is usually much more complex. In the modified rebuy or straight rebuy situations, some of these stages would be compressed or bypassed. Each organisation buys in its own way, and each buying situation has unique requirements. Different buying centre participants may be involved at different stages of the process. Although certain buying process steps usually do occur, buyers do not always follow them in the same order, and they may add other steps. Often, buyers will repeat certain stages of the process. For example, the supplier selection stage may reveal that no proposal addresses all the desired criteria, and the buyer may decide to seek more proposals from different suppliers.

> **Performance review**
> The stage of the industrial buying process in which the buyer rates its satisfaction with suppliers, deciding whether to continue, modify or drop the relationship.

SELF-CHECK QUESTIONS

3 What are the major groups of influences on business buyer behaviour?

4 Why are there differences between the buyer behaviour of businesses and consumers?

Institutional and government markets

We now turn our attention to institutional and government markets. In this final section we again clarify the terms used, and then address the special features of institutional and government markets.

Institutional markets

The institutional market consists of schools, colleges, universities, hospitals, nursing homes, prisons and other institutions that provide goods and services to people in their care. Many institutional markets are characterised by low budgets and captive patrons. For example, hospital patients have little choice but to eat whatever food the hospital supplies. A hospital procurement officer has to decide on the quality of food to buy for patients. Because the food is provided as part of a total service package, the buying objective is not profit. Nor is strict cost minimisation the goal—patients receiving poor quality food will complain to others and damage the hospital's reputation. Thus, the hospital procurement officer must search for institutional food vendors whose quality meets or exceeds a certain minimum standard and whose prices are low.

Many marketers set up separate divisions to meet the special characteristics and needs of institutional buyers. For example, Arnotts (a member of the Campbells group) produces, packages and prices its biscuits, snacks and other products differently so as to serve the requirements of hospitals, colleges and other institutional markets more effectively.

Government markets

In every country, the government market comprises a significant proportion of business activity. For example, in Australia the government market comprises around 17% of business activity.[28] The government market therefore offers vast selling opportunities for many companies. Government buying and business buying are similar in many ways. But there are also differences that must be understood by companies that wish to sell products and services to governments. To succeed in the government market, sellers must locate key decision makers, identify the factors that affect buyer behaviour and understand the buying decision process.

In Australia, federal, state and local governments contain many separate buying units. Federal government buying units operate in both the civilian and military sectors. Various government departments, administrations, agencies, boards, commissions, executive offices and other units carry out federal civilian buying. Many, like the Department of Finance and Administration, provide information and guidelines for potential suppliers. Departmental guidelines provide Commonwealth procurement guidelines and best practice guidance covering efficiency and effectiveness, accountability, transparency and ethics. Federal military buying is carried out by the Defence Department on behalf of the Army, Navy and Air Force. In an effort to reduce costly duplication, the department buys and distributes supplies used by all military services. It operates supply centres, which specialise in construction, electronics, fuel, personnel support, business products and general supplies. State and local buying agencies include schools, transport departments, hospitals, housing agencies and many others. Each has its own buying process that sellers must master. The growth of the Internet now provides opportunities for both suppliers and government departments to reduce costs and improve effectiveness in sourcing supplies.[29]

Major influences on government buyers

Like consumer and business buyers, government buyers are affected by environmental, organisational, interpersonal and individual factors. One unique thing about government buying is that it is carefully watched by outside publics, ranging from parliament to a variety of private groups interested in how the government spends taxpayers' money. Because their spending decisions are subject to public review, and there are many levels of bureaucracy, there is often a higher level of documentation and delay before purchases are approved. Non-economic criteria also play a growing role in government buying. Government buyers are sometimes asked to favour locally made products, depressed business firms and areas, small businesses, minority-owned firms and companies that avoid race, sex or age discrimination. Sellers need to keep these factors in mind when deciding to seek government business.

Because of the size of many government purchases, governments can impose particular requirements on their suppliers. For example, to sell to many sections of the Australian government, suppliers of information technology, major office machines and office furniture must be pre-approved, or what the government calls 'pre-qualified'.[30] Pre-qualification allows the government to ensure that suppliers meet a certain level of quality, and simplifies the buying process for repeat purchases.

Government organisations typically require suppliers to submit bids, or tenders as they are often called, and contracts are normally awarded to the lowest bidder who meets the specified standards. In some cases, however, government buyers make allowances for superior quality or for a company's reputation for completing contracts on time. Governments will also buy on a negotiated contract basis for complex projects that involve major R&D costs and risks, or when there is little effective competition. Governments will sometimes tend to favour domestic suppliers over foreign suppliers, which is a major complaint of international businesses.

Despite these potential disadvantages in selling to government, there are also advantages. Governments are often much more open than private businesses about their criteria for selection of suppliers. For example, the Australian government maintains a website with details on government buying at <www.finance.gov.au/ctc> and displays all current tenders at <www.tenders.gov.au>. These processes mean that government buying is often more transparent and straightforward than selling to private organisations.

Government buyer decision process

Government buying practices often seem complex and frustrating to suppliers, who have voiced many complaints about government purchasing procedures. These include too much paperwork and bureaucracy, needless regulations, emphasis on low bid prices, decision-making delays, frequent shifts in buying personnel and too many policy changes. Yet despite such obstacles, selling to the government can often be mastered in a short time. The government is generally helpful in providing information about its buying needs and procedures. Government is often as eager to attract new suppliers as the suppliers are to find customers. It does this by providing information services to potential suppliers informing them of the procedures for joining the tender list and other pertinent information.

More companies are now setting up separate marketing departments for government marketing efforts. These companies want to coordinate bids and prepare them more systematically, and to propose projects to meet government needs rather than just respond to government requests. They also want to gather competitive intelligence and prepare communications which best describe the company's competence.[31]

SELF-CHECK QUESTIONS

5   What are the main characteristics of the institutional market that impact on sellers to this market?

6   Why is it that most government departments require potential suppliers to engage in bidding or tender processes to win business? What might be some advantages and disadvantages of a tender system?

SUMMARY

The business-to-business market is vast. In many ways business markets are like consumer markets, but business markets usually have fewer, larger buyers who are more geographically concentrated. Business demand is *derived*, largely *inelastic* and *more fluctuating*. More people are usually involved in the business buying decision, and business buyers are better trained and more professional than consumer buyers. In general, business purchasing decisions are more complex, and the buying process is more formal than consumer buying.

The *business market* includes firms that buy goods and services in order to produce products and services to sell to others. It also includes retailing and wholesaling firms that buy goods in order to resell them at a profit. Because aspects of business-to-business marketing apply to *institutional markets* and *government markets*, we group these together. Business buyers make decisions that vary with the three types of buying situations: *straight rebuys*, *modified rebuys* and *new tasks*.

The decision-making unit of a buying organisation—*the buying centre*—might consist of many people playing many roles. The business marketer needs to know the following: Who are the major participants? In what decisions do they exercise influence? What is their relative degree of influence? What evaluation criteria does each decision participant use?

The business marketer also needs to understand the major environmental, interpersonal and individual influences on the buying process. The business buying decision process itself consists of eight stages: *problem recognition*, *general need description*, *product specification*, *supplier search*, *proposal solicitation*, *supplier selection*, *order-routine specification* and *performance review*. As business buyers become more sophisticated, business marketers must keep in step by upgrading their marketing accordingly.

The *institutional market* consists of schools, hospitals, prisons and other institutions that provide goods and services to people in their care. These markets are typically characterised by low budgets and captive patrons. The *government market* is also vast. Government buyers purchase products and services for defence, education, public welfare and other public needs. Government buying practices are highly specialised and specified, with open bidding or negotiated contracts characterising most of the buying. Government buyers operate under the watchful eye of parliament and many private watchdog groups. Hence, they tend to require more documentation and respond more slowly when making decisions.

MARKETING ISSUE

Businesses often use sponsorship and corporate events such as golf days to attempt to influence their customers. At events such as this, the purchasing manager of an organisation would be invited to the event, and would typically have a very pleasant day (perhaps watching the Australian Open tennis or the cricket from a corporate box, constantly supplied with good food and alcohol). If you were the purchasing manager, would such an event influence your judgment? Most purchasing managers would say no, but if this is true, why would smart marketers spend large amounts of money on entertaining corporate customers?

1 What are the advantages and disadvantages of corporate entertaining from the supplier's point of view?

2 What the advantages and disadvantages of corporate entertaining from the customer's point of view?

3 How might smart marketers maximise the effectiveness of corporate entertaining?

KEY TERMS

DISCUSSING THE ISSUES

1 Many companies that were formerly vertically integrated, producing their own materials or parts, are now using outside suppliers to produce them instead (outsourcing). Are there any longer-term dangers in outsourcing? What if the company outsources to the same company that produces for its closest competitor? What are your thoughts?

2 Many companies are working to improve quality and reduce delivery times of their components by employing quality techniques such as total quality managment, quality at source and Six Sigma. A major element in these approaches is feedback when defects are discovered. List some of the ways using continuous improvement might affect the relationship and information flow between buyers and suppliers.

3 Businesses prefer dealing with suppliers that offer them a product or service that is solving more than just the obvious need. They prefer buyers who engage in systems or solutions selling. Give examples of companies that take this approach and describe what they do.

4 Business markets are usually less affected by price fluctuations than consumer markets. Why does this happen? Give examples.

5 Could a small Australian business employing fewer than five employees become a part of the supply chain of global businesses? Can an online procurement system such as Ariba help or are these businesses still too small to be considered as a part of such a group? What should they do?

6 Online buying and selling means that businesses may buy from organisations without actually speaking to anyone at the organisation. Do you think that this inevitably means that relationships will become less important in business buying? Why or why not?

REFERENCES

1. 'Development of NAICS', <www.census.gov/epcd/www/naicsdev.htm>, accessed 16 October 2005.

2. Australian Bureau of Statistics, *Information Paper: ANZSIC 2006 Development*, Catalogue no. 1294.0, 9 September 2004.

3. See <www.abs.gov.au> and <www.stats.govt.nz/default.htm>.

4. For discussions of similarities and differences in consumer and business marketing see Wolfgang Ulaga, 'Customer Value in Business Markets: An Agenda for Inquiry', *Industrial Marketing Management*, vol. 30, no. 4, May 2001, pp. 315–319; Jean L. Johnson, 'The Interplay of Task Allocation Patterns and Governance Mechanisms in Industrial Distribution Channels', *Industrial Marketing Management*, vol. 31, no. 8, November 2002, p. 665; Edward F. Fern and James R. Brown, 'The Industrial/Consumer Marketing Dichotomy: A Case of Insufficient Justification', *Journal of Marketing*, Fall 1984, pp. 68–77.

5. Swinder Janda, 'Manufacturer–Supplier Relationships: An Empirical Test of a Model of Buyer Outcomes', *Industrial Marketing Management*, vol. 31, no. 5, August 2002, p. 411; Christian Homburg, 'Customer Satisfaction in Transnational Buyer–Supplier

Relationships', *Journal of International Marketing*, vol. 10, no. 4, 2002, p. 1; D. L. Blenkhorn and H. F. MacKenzie, 'Interdependence in Relationship Marketing', *Asia-Australia Marketing Journal*, vol. 4, no. 1, December 1996, pp. 25–30. See also Alan Weber, 'Selling to Both Businesses and Consumers', *Zip/Target Marketing*, vol. 22, no. 10, October 1999, pp. 164–170.

6. James Thomson, 'Moving and Shaking', *Business Review Weekly*, 6 October 2005, pp. 56–57.

7. <www.Hydromagnesium.com>, accessed 16 October 2005.

8. Simon London, 'Xerox Runs Off a New Blueprint', *Financial Times*, 23 September 2005, p. 10.

9. See R. Bertodo, 'Some Developing Trends in Manufacturer–Supplier Relationships', *International Journal of Manufacturing Technology and Management*, vol. 4, no. 1, 2, 2002, p. 21; Swinder Janda, 'Manufacturer–Supplier Relationships: An Empirical Test of a Model of Buyer Outcomes', *Industrial Marketing Management*, vol. 31, no. 5, August 2002, p. 411; Fred Selnes and Kjell Gonhaug, 'Effects of Supplier Reliability and Benevolence in Business Marketing', *Journal of Business Research*, vol. 49, no. 3, September 2000, pp. 259–271; Roger Best, *Market Based Management*, 2nd edn, Prentice Hall, 2000, Chapter 8; James C. Anderson and James A. Narus, 'Business Marketing: Understand What Customers Value', *Harvard Business Review*, November–December 1998, pp. 53–65; Lawrence A. Crosby, Kenneth R. Evans and Deborah Cowles, 'Relationship Quality and Services Selling: An Interpersonal Influence Perspective', *Journal of Marketing*, July 1990, pp. 68–81; Minda Zetlin, 'It's All the Same to Me', *Sales & Marketing Management*, February 1994, pp. 71–75; and Rahul Jacob, 'Why Some Customers Are More Equal than Others', *Fortune*, 19 September 1994, pp. 215–224.

10. David A. Reid, 'The Impact of Purchase Situation on Salesperson Communication Behaviors in Business Markets', *Industrial Marketing Management*, vol. 31, no. 3, April 2002, p. 205; Regina McNally, 'Simulating Buying Center Decision Processes: Propositions and Methodology', *Journal of Business & Industrial Marketing*, vol. 17, no. 2/3, 2002, p. 167; Patrick J. Robinson, Charles W. Faris and Yoram Wind, *Industrial Buying Behavior and Creative Marketing*, Boston, Allyn & Bacon, 1967. Also see Erin Anderson, Weyien Chu and Barton Weitz, 'Industrial Purchasing: An Empirical Exploration of the Buyclass Framework', *Journal of Marketing*, July 1987, pp. 71–86.

11. For more examples of systems selling visit IBM's Australia website, <www-7.ibm.com/ebusiness/au/case_studies>, accessed 8 February 2002; see also Susan Avery, 'E-procurement Delivers for FedEx', *Purchasing*, vol. 130, no. 2, 18 October 2001, pp. 72–75.

12. Jae H. Pae, 'Managing Intraorganizational Diffusion of Innovations: Impact of Buying Center Dynamics and Environments', *Industrial Marketing Management*, vol. 31, no. 8, November 2002, p. 719; Frederick E. Webster Jr and Yoram Wind, *Organisational Buying Behavior*, Englewood Cliffs, NJ, Prentice Hall, 1972, p. 6. See also Jeffrey E. Lewin, 'The Effects of Downsizing on Organizational Buying Behavior: An Empirical Investigation', *Journal of the Academy of Marketing Science*, vol. 29, no. 2, Spring 2001, pp. 151–164. For more reading on buying centres, see Geok-Theng, Mark Goh and Shan Lei Phua, 'Purchase-related Factors and Buying Center Structure: An Empirical Assessment', *Industrial Marketing Management*, vol. 28, no. 6, November 1999, pp. 573–587; Thomas V. Bonoma, 'Major Sales: Who Really Does the Buying', *Harvard Business Review*, May–June 1982, pp. 111–119; and Donald W. Jackson Jr, Janet E. Keith and Richard K. Burdick, 'Purchasing Agents' Perceptions of Industrial Buying Centre Influence: A Situational Approach', *Journal of Marketing*, Fall 1984, pp. 75–83.

13. Webster and Wind, op. cit., pp. 78–80; Christian Homburg, 'Customer Satisfaction in Industrial Markets: Dimensional and Multiple Role Issues', *Journal of Business Research*, vol. 52, no. 1, April 2001, p. 15.

14. Regina McNally, 'Simulating Buying Center Decision Processes: Propositions and Methodology', *Journal of Business & Industrial Marketing*, vol. 17, no. 2/3, 2002, p. 167; Wesley J. Johnson and Thomas V. Bonoma, 'Purchase Process for Capital Equipment and Services', *Industrial Marketing Management*, vol. 10, 1981, pp. 258–259. Also see Philip L. Dawes, Grahame R. Dowling and Paul G. Patterson, 'Factors Affecting the Structure of Buying Centres for the Purchase of Professional Advisory Services', *International Journal of Research in Marketing*, August 1992, pp. 269–279; and Robert D. McWilliams, Earl Naumann and Stan Scott, 'Determining Buying Centre Size', *Industrial Marketing Management*, February 1992, pp. 43–49.

15. Webster and Wind, op. cit., pp. 33–37.

16. Ariba.com accessed 17 October 2005.

17. Unless otherwise noted, quotes and spending information in this section are from Michael A. Verespej, 'E-Procurement Explosion', *Industry Week*, March 2002, pp. 24–28; 'E-Procurement Still Less Popular than Paper Orders', *Supply Management*, 13 March 2003, p. 10; Jennifer Baljko, 'Online Purchasing Activity on the Rise—But OEM Cost-Cutting Initiatives Are Limiting Process Changes', *EBN*, 21 April 2003, p. 6; 'Online Purchasing Still on the Rise', *Industrial Distribution*, December 2004, p. 24; and C. Subramaniam and M. Shaw, 'The Effects of Process Characteristics on the Value of B2B E-Procurement', *Information Technology and Management*, January–April 2004, p. 161.

18. See Verespej, 'E-Procurement Explosion', pp. 25–28; 'E-Procurement: Certain Value in Changing Times', *Fortune*, 30 April 2001, pp. S2–S3; and Susan Avery, 'Microsoft Moves Entire PC Buy Online, Saves 6%', *Purchasing*, 16 January 2003, pp. 14–18.

19. <www.ht.com.au>, accessed 2 January 2006.

20. Andrew Dietderich, 'Covisint Sees Growth in New Markets', *Automotive News*, vol. 79, no. 6150, 30 May 2005, p. 28; Kate Maddox, 'The fall and rise of b-to-b', *B to B*, vol. 90, no. 7, p. 19.

21. See <www.dell.com>, accessed 16 October 2005.

22. Thomas V. Bonoma, 'Major Sales: Who Really Does the Buying?', *Harvard Business Review*, May–June 1982, p. 114. Also see Ajay Kohli, 'Determinants of Influence in Organisational Buying: A Contingency Approach', *Journal of Marketing*, July 1989, pp. 50–65.

23. Patrick J. Robinson, Charles W. Faris and Yoram Wind, *Industrial Buying and Creative Marketing*, Boston, Allyn & Bacon, 1967, p. 14.

24. See Julie Smith, David Schuff and Robert St Louis, 'Managing Your It Total Cost of Ownership', *Communications of the ACM*, vol. 45, no. 1, January 2002, pp. 101–106; Paul Bleicher, 'How Do I Buy Software? Let Me Count the Ways', *Applied Clinical Trials*, vol. 13, no. 6, 2004, pp. 34–38.

25. Alan S. Mitchell, 'Do You Really Want to Understand Your Customer?', *Journal of Consumer Behaviour*, September 2002, vol. 2, no. 1, p. 71; Vijay R. Kannan, 'Supplier Selection and Assessment: Their Impact on Business Performance', *Journal of Supply Chain Management*, vol. 38, no. 4, Fall 2002, p. 11; see 'What Buyers Really Want', *Sales & Marketing Management*, October 1989, p. 30.

26. Jacques C. Verville, 'A Qualitative Study of the Influencing Factors on the Decision Process for Acquiring ERP Software', *Qualitative Market Research*, vol. 5, no. 3, 2002, p. 188; Donald R. Lehmann and John O'Shaughnessy, 'Decision Criteria Used in Buying Different Categories of Products', *Journal of Purchasing and Materials Management*, Spring 1982, pp. 9–14.

27. Rui Vinhas Da Silva, 'Assessing Customer Orientation in the Context of Buyer/Supplier Relationships Using Judgmental Modelling', *Industrial Marketing Management*, vol. 31, no. 3, April 2002, p. 241. For another study of 1000 purchasing managers in the global

context see Laura M. Birou and Stanley E. Fawcett, 'International Purchasing: Benefits, Requirements, and Challenges', *International Journal of Purchasing and Materials Management*, vol. 29, no. 2, Spring 1993, pp. 27–37. See also Tom Stundza, 'Steel Buyers Slash Suppliers, Tighten Quality', *Purchasing*, vol. 130, no. 19, 4 October 2001, pp. 33–37.

28. Phil Ruthven, 'Down Every Street', *Business Review Weekly*, 28 July 2005, pp. 28–29.

29. For a good source on the latest developments in government procurement initiatives and current government tenders, go to the Department of Finance and Administration website, <www.finance.gov.au/ctc/>, accessed 2 January 2006.

30. See <www.finance.gov.au/ctc/> for a detailed discussion of the process of government buying, accessed 17 October 2005.

31. Mylene Mangalindan and Michael Totty, 'Slumping Tech Companies Go to Washington to Seek Sales', *Wall Street Journal*, 4 October 2002, Eastern edition, p. B.1.

PHOTO/AD CREDITS

Judy Rex, Swinburne University

CASE STUDY

King Industries: electrical wholesalers

King Industries* is a leader in value-added business-to-business distribution services. The company is a wholesaler of electrical and safety products, and has about 160 strategically located branches across Australia in both metropolitan and regional areas.

King Industries Australia forms part of a global business-to-business group with revenues in excess of $US16 billion. It employs over 15 000 staff in 60 countries. The mission of King Industries is to be a leading distributor of electrical and safety products and services to the construction markets in the USA, Europe and the Asia–Pacific region.

The main market for King Industries is the domestic electrical and safety market, with SME electrical contractors being the primary target market for Kings. King Industries has two main competitors, Hagemeyer and Rexell, who are both multinational companies that distribute electrical and safety products, and Protector Alsafe is the major competitor for safety products.

King Industries source their products in two different ways—from local suppliers and via a Home Brand Program. The distribution network for King Industries is shown in Figure 1.

Figure 1 shows that for King Industries the products can be distributed in three ways. The first distribution channel involves the three stages from wholesaler, through the branch network, to the customers. Other products are distributed straight from the suppliers to the branch network, while in a small number of instances products go straight from the suppliers to the end-users.

Figure 1 also shows that there are three main customers for the electrical and safety products that King Industries distributes:

- consumers
- electricians
- small industrial customers.

King Industries' trade outlets only stock fast-moving items and they rely on the distribution centres to hold stock of the slower moving items. The distribution centres need to be able to supply these items rapidly when they are ordered. This means that King Industries needs an efficient network of distribution centres to supply the trade outlets. About 70% of the stock required for the trade outlets is replenished direct from the suppliers' distribution centres (DCs), and the remaining 30% of stock comes direct from the King Industries DCs.

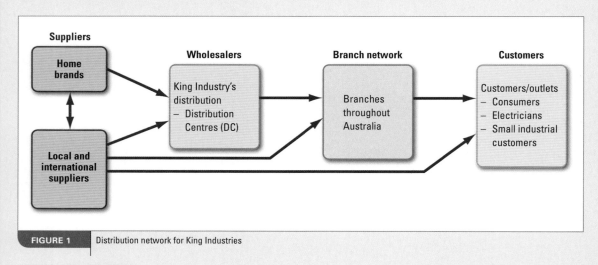

| FIGURE 1 | Distribution network for King Industries |

* Not the real name.

The procurement for the trade outlets is characterised by the following factors:

- About 25% of customers represent 80% of total sales.
- Most orders are placed by the installer/tradesperson.
- Most of the orders are small and frequent.
- They have a close relationship with their customers.
- Most of the customers are geographically concentrated in the capital cities and larger rural centres.

King Industries has over 30 000 customers who are spread across many different industries and their staff pride themselves on the close relationship they have with these customers. Most of their customers have very specific product and delivery requirements, and King Industries relies on its branch managers and major account managers to manage the customer relationships. King Industries promotes its products to end-customers by using catalogues and bi-monthly specials, to increase business demand. Speed of fulfilment and inventory availability are key components of the customer service proposition.

Demand for the domestic electrical and safety products distributed by King Industries is largely dependent on the building industry and the state of the economy. If the economy and/or the building industry decline, this will have a severe impact on this industry. In addition, demand is driven by product availability, the relationships the branch managers have with their customers and consistency of pricing, as King's customers need to be competitive when quoting prices to their customers.

King Industries has about 250 000 different product lines or SKUs (stock keeping units) and this increases the complexity of the buying decision process. Most purchases are a straight rebuy; however, depending on the nature of the job, purchases can be a new purchase or a modified rebuy. For example, if a contractor wins a new job they may require different kinds of electrical and safety products from the ones they have used in the past.

King Industries has long-term relationships with many of its customers, and it works hard to maintain these relationships. It also conducts marketing research regularly using customer satisfaction surveys, and internal staff surveys once a year. One important aspect of its marketing is incentive programs which include free giveaways and conference travel. These incentive programs are designed to reward customer loyalty and to increase procurement by individual customers.

King Industries operates a successful business in a very competitive and price-driven market that is largely driven by the state of the economy and the state of the building industry. It has to work hard to maintain customer loyalty and to promote its high levels of service quality rather than relying on selling just on price alone.

QUESTIONS

1. Describe the buying process for King's customers.

2. King Industries has a complex distribution system. What kinds of potential problems could the distribution system raise?

3. How does the B2B procurement process for King Industries differ from the B2C process that you have learned about in other sections of this book?

4. Which environmental factors are most likely to affect King's day-to-day business operations?

5. What kinds of incentive programs do you think King Industries could use? How would these incentive programs help it to achieve its marketing objectives?

CHAPTER 9

Market analysis and applications

Forecasting Principles:
www.forecastingprinciples.com
Kodak: www.kodak.com
McDonalds: www.mcdonalds.com
Pacific Brands:
www.pacificbrands.com.au

F ew companies have seen their market change as radically in the past 10 years as Kodak. The bulk of Kodak's profits in the past 20 years have come from sales of film and paper, but Kodak's own invention of the digital camera in the early 1970s was the beginning of the end for the film market that Kodak had dominated for so long. Even then, Kodak anticipated that sales of photographic film would decline slowly, giving the company time to develop new products and new markets to replace its lost film sales. But the market for film has declined faster than Kodak anticipated. Even in emerging markets like China, affluent consumers are buying digital cameras, just like consumers in Kodak's more longstanding markets. Kodak responded by announcing a series of job cuts; 15000 in 2004 and 10000 in 2005. But even these drastic cuts were not enough to save the company from a second quarter loss in 2005 of $US146 million, compared to earnings of $US136 million the previous year, and the share market wiped 33% off the value of Kodak shares in response.

Knowing that demand for its core product, film, was shrinking, Kodak had earlier announced plans to transform itself into a digital company, but admitted in 2005 that it was 'somewhat behind' in its plans. 'I don't think anyone had any idea how fast the uptake would be in digital photography, and how fast the falloff might be in silver halide around the world,' said Steve Sasson, the inventor of the digital camera, still working for Kodak in 2005. (Silver halide is a key ingredient in traditional film processing.) 'Kodak was doing modelling about this as much as they could, but nobody really had the insight.'

The changing market has caught Kodak on many fronts; while it still makes money from camera sales, Kodak is facing new competitors like Nokia and Motorola, which sell camera phones in numbers that Kodak can only dream of, and these companies are more accustomed than Kodak to rapid product life cycles and aggressive pricing. Worse, Kodak's primary target customers have always been women, because the company knew that women took the bulk of pictures, and it had reflected this target with a focus on the emotional importance of photos, or 'Kodak moments'. This strategy had been rewarded with the company capturing the number one market share position for camera sales to women (with 20% of the

Digital cameras have led to changes in who takes pictures, what people photograph, and what photos get printed.

market), but only number four (with 11%) among men. With increased use of digital cameras, men were suddenly taking more pictures, and Kodak's research showed that men were far more likely than women to keep pictures on the computer and never print them. The Photo Marketing Association estimates that women print 35% of their digital pictures, while men print only 20%. And women are far more likely to print and give away multiple copies.

Kodak has had to make big changes to capture more revenue from consumers to replace the plummeting film market. It has developed new digital cameras, such as the EasyShare camera, which provides a larger viewing screen, storage for 1000 pictures and the ability to connect to a wireless network, allowing users to email pictures to an online photo-sharing business or to a friend. The company has also developed compact printers which can be directly attached to a camera, to allow home printing, because the company's research told it that women were more likely to print photos if they didn't have to compete with a partner or children for the use of the family computer. Responding to the sentimental importance of photos for women, and increasing concerns that changes in technology and unstable inks in home printers might lead to fading and loss of family photos, Kodak has touted the advantages of its own brand of paper, which it claims will last for 100 years without fading (though the claims have been disputed by other printer and paper manufacturers). Another part of the company's strategy is to make it very easy for its customers to print their photos professionally; Kodak has produced thousands of photo-printing booths, which it leases to all sort of outlets—discount stores, pharmacies, cruise ships and hospitals—hoping that women will buy digital prints the way they always have, in retail locations.

The company also bought online photo storage leader Ofoto in 2001, and despite increasing business, decided in 2005 to replace the well-known Ofoto brand with 'Kodak EasyShare Gallery' in 2005. This allows people to post their photos online, and send emails telling friends that the photos are available for viewing and purchase.

Despite these measures, Kodak's transition to a digital company is, the organisation admits, incomplete, and in 2005 marketing consultancy Interbrand wiped 55% off the value of the brand compared to the previous year.

However, there is some evidence that Kodak's strategy is working. In its largest US market, the proportion of prints made in digital stores rose to 35% of the market, up from 21% the previous year. It remains to be seen whether Kodak will succeed in this new market. But it won't be for want of trying.[1]

After reading this chapter you should be able to:

1. Name the different ways of defining the market.

2. Discuss measuring current market demand, and look at the differences between the market-buildup method and the market-factor index method.

3. List and explain several ways of forecasting future demand, including a survey of buyers' intentions, composites of salesforce opinions or expert opinions, test marketing, time-series analysis, leading indicators and statistical demand analysis.

When a marketing organisation finds an attractive market it must estimate the market's current size and future potential carefully. Established organisations must continue to assess changes in demand or they risk, like Kodak, being unprepared for major changes in their market. Any marketing organisation can lose a lot of profit by overestimating or underestimating the market. This chapter presents the principles and tools for measuring and forecasting market demand.

Demand can be measured and forecast on many levels—Figure 9.1 shows 75 possible types of demand measurement! For example, Sony Ericsson might measure demand for five different product levels: demand for its new W900 phone (demand at the product item level); demand for its entire range of mobile phones (the product line); demand for the combined sales of Sony Ericsson and all other competing brands (the product category); demand for its total sales of telephones and other related products and services (company sales); demand for the combined sales of all the mobile phone manufacturers in the market (industry sales). Note that the definition of product category is quite important, for if Sony considers that camera manufacturers compete with camera phones, then Sony Ericsson would need to estimate its market share relative to camera manufacturers like Kodak. Sony Ericsson might also measure demand for five different geographic levels (customer, territory, region, country and world). Finally, Sony Ericsson might prepare its forecasts covering three different time levels (short range, medium range and long range).

Each type of demand measurement serves a specific purpose. Sony Ericsson might forecast short-range demand for mobile phones in Asia and Southeast Asia as a basis for ordering raw materials, planning production and scheduling short-run financing. Or it might forecast long-range demand in this geographic market for its digital telephone and Internet access products as a basis for designing a market expansion strategy.

Defining the market

Market-demand measurement calls for a clear understanding of the market involved. The term market has acquired many meanings over the years. In its original meaning a market was a physical place where buyers and sellers gathered to exchange goods and services. Today's market, however, is no longer restricted to physical locations. To an economist, a market describes all the buyers and sellers who transact over some good or service. Thus, the soft drink market consists of sellers such as Coca-Cola and Pepsi, plus all the consumers who buy soft drinks.

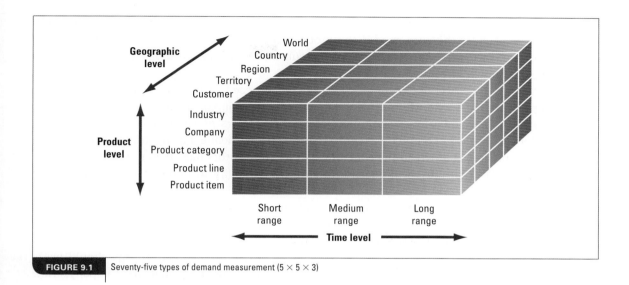

FIGURE 9.1 Seventy-five types of demand measurement (5 × 5 × 3)

To a marketer, a **market** is the set of all actual and potential buyers of a product. A market is the set of buyers, and an **industry** is the set of sellers. The size of a market, then, hinges on the number of buyers who might exist for a particular market offer, and the frequency of their purchases. Those who are in the market for something have four characteristics: interest, income, access and qualifications. The starting point is to develop an operational definition of a market. This requires definition of a product type and a market around a defined need for which the marketer's product is one solution. Figure 9.2 shows the process of building up a market definition.

To obtain a working definition of the market, a business must identify current customers, the product need they have and the product or 'solution' they seek. The product market is defined when

Market The set of all actual and potential buyers of a product.

Industry A group of firms that offer a product or class of products that are close substitutes for each other; the set of all sellers of a product.

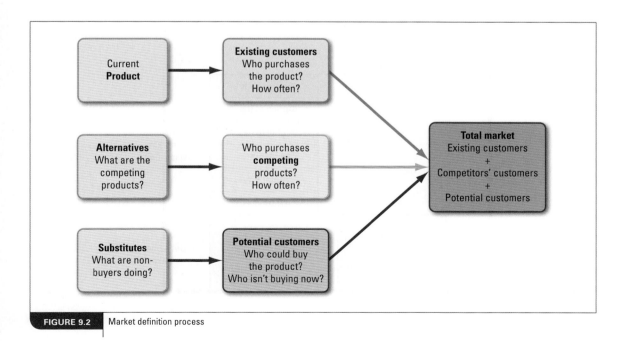

FIGURE 9.2 Market definition process

customers are also included for the competing alternatives. Substitutes are the solutions customers will consider that meet the core need if the product and its direct alternatives are unavailable. A combination of the specific product market and substitutes provides a broader definition of the total market, as shown in Figure 9.2.

At any point in time overall demand for a product or service is fixed. This means that there is a set number of customers who will purchase the product at specific price levels—creating a level of market demand. The number of existing and potential customers provides an organisation with a specific size of the business opportunity. Potential customers help define the opportunity while existing customers show the level at which the company and its competitors have penetrated the market.

The success of the business will depend, in part, on its ability to understand and predict the following:

What is the current level of market potential and market demand?

What is the rate of replacement purchases and new customer purchases?

What is our existing and potential market share?[2]

In order not to limit the capability for seizing new opportunities, organisations should use a broader rather than narrower market definition. A narrow market definition limits the company's view of potential and may result in lost opportunities or ending up in a narrow market which is declining. A broad market then allows a business manager to look differently at the opportunities. For example, if Kodak sees itself as competing in the film and camera market, it will see itself as competing against other camera and film manufacturers, and may not investigate the growing market in online photo storage, sharing and ordering.

Once a market definition is established, the marketer should determine how well that defined market is being served by existing companies and how many potential customers have not yet become a part of that market. Marketing Highlight 9.1 discusses how McDonald's introduced a new product range to respond to changes in demand in its core market. At any point in time the market may have not reached its full potential, indicating that there is an untapped opportunity. Untapped potential exists because the maximum market potential is impacted on and influenced by a number of factors, as shown in Figure 9.3.

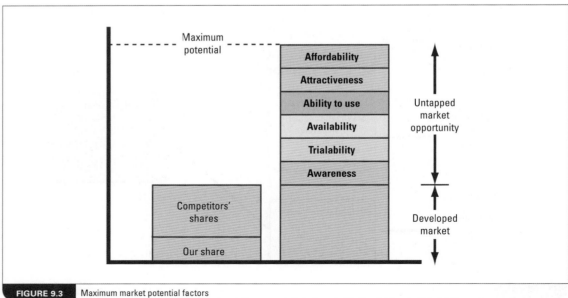

FIGURE 9.3 Maximum market potential factors
Source: Adapted from Roger Best, *Market Based Management*, 3rd edn, Upper Saddle River NJ, Prentice Hall, 2004, Chapter 3.

- *Awareness.* The customers may not be aware of the product, or they may not be able to understand the benefits and features the product is offering because the organisation was not able to inform them effectively. For example, customers may be aware of some of the features of a new phone—such as picture messaging—but they may not fully understand the benefits. With complex products or services, some benefits may be understood only after use of the product or service.

- *Trialability.* Here the potential customers are aware of the product but require the opportunity to try out (or have a demonstration of) the product. This is often the case with expensive goods and also with some food items which customers are more likely to purchase if they have been given a sample. As a result, marketers will often use samples to create awareness, interest and trial. For example, when McDonald's introduced its new sandwich range it created rapid awareness and trial by offering free samples, using a post-it prominently positioned on the front page of daily newspapers.

- *Availability.* This refers to the availability of the product and/or availability of product service. Here the potential customers may not purchase the product due to the lack of availability of the product in their geographical area. For example, a company selling wireless broadband services like Unwired, iBurst or BigPond may lose sales because the service isn't available for some customers, or even because customers incorrectly perceive that the service may not be available in areas where they are likely to visit.

Even books can be promoted by sampling: Hodder and Stoughton gave away miniature books containing Chapter 1 to publicise this book.

- *Ability to use/ease of use.* Inability to use the product or its key features can also impact on the market. For example, the uptake of personal digital organisers like the Palm Pilot and Blackberry has suffered because the devices require some learning by the user. In contrast, iPod sales have benefited, because the iPod is very easy for someone to learn to use.

- *Attractiveness.* Here the attractiveness of the offer inhibits the degree of market potential. For some consumers the set of benefits offered by the product are not attractive enough to buy the product. For example, customers may resist purchasing a full music CD if they only like one song on it, but many more people may be willing to purchase one or a few songs from the CD if they can download the music from a service such as iTunes or Sony Music and load it on to their MP3 player.

- *Affordability.* A customer may like a product, but decide it is too expensive for them. A narrowly focused business will simply forgo this type of customer. But smarter marketers will try to develop products that are affordable for different customers within this market. For example, if a customer can't afford the top of the range 60 GB iPod at $598, they can buy the iPod shuffle at $149. In the business market, Intel develops products such as the premium-priced Core™ 2 Duo processors for buyers who want maximum speed and performance, and lower-priced versions of the Celeron processor for the more price-sensitive segment of the market.

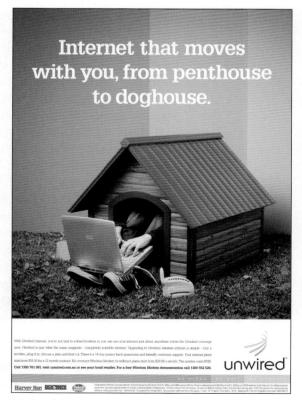

Wireless Internet providers attempt to build demand by promoting mobile availability.

MARKETING 9.1 HIGHLIGHT

Turning around a giant

For a long time it looked as if McDonald's could do no wrong. The company just kept growing bigger and bigger. McDonald's dominates the fast-food market in most countries, with 42% market share in its largest market, the USA. Ronald McDonald, the company symbol, is said to be the second most recognised character by children worldwide, after Santa Claus.

However, signs were emerging through the 1990s of deep problems within McDonald's, particularly in the USA. The chain rated lowest in customer satisfaction among the fast-food chains for every yearly rating of the American Customer Satisfaction Index during the 1990s. The McDonald's motto of 'quality, service, cleanliness and value' was starting to sound hollow, with growing complaints about dirty restaurants and indifferent staff. Same store sales fell, as the company lost market share to its major competitors, Burger King and Wendy's, resulting in franchisee discontent, as the company's policy of opening new stores ate into the profits of existing franchisees. Rising public concerns about obesity meant that rival fast-food chain, Subway—positioned as offering healthier alternatives to hamburgers—was also eating into the market of all three fast-food chains. In 2002 McDonald's recorded its first quarterly loss since 1954.

Spurred on by falling profits, McDonald's began its turnaround strategy, called 'Plan to Win', in 2003 under then CEO Jim Cantalupo. The company knew that it had to do something to revitalise its market, while at the same time maintaining the fast service it was famous for and that customers expected. A previous attempt in the late 1990s to introduce a new, healthier range called 'made for you', featuring custom-made sandwiches and freshly toasted buns, had failed. The menu had led to delays in service, franchisee resistance to kitchen fit-out costs and, worst of all, continuing loss of market share to competitors. McDonald's feared that it was losing ground and relevance in an increasingly diet-conscious world.

McDonald's problems were highlighted by the release of the 2004 movie *Super Size Me*, detailing film-maker Morgan Spurlock's growing weight and health problems after a month of eating solely at McDonald's. The film became one of the most successful documentaries ever in Australia, and McDonald's responded aggressively, stating that it was unhealthy to eat only at McDonald's. It also announced it would end 'super-sizing' (offering jumbo sizes of food and soft drinks) in its US markets. (Supersizing wasn't offered in the Asia–Pacific markets.) However, the association between McDonald's and unhealthy food seemed to be deeply established; the then CEO of McDonald's, Charlie Bell, seemed to sum up McDonald's problems when he said in 2004 that a lot of companies get 'fat, dumb and happy and take their eye off the ball'. Customer sentiment was reflected by Australian McDonald's CEO Peter Bush using quotes from customers revealed in its market research: 'The world has changed and McDonald's hasn't' and 'I grew up and McDonald's hasn't'.

So this time McDonald's engaged in extensive business analysis, market research and testing before introducing its new menus. Following its research, McDonald's famously introduced a new menu, introducing new products such as salads and sandwiches, including a 'meal for grownups' promoted by Oprah Winfrey's personal trainer, consisting of a salad and bottled water, and including a book of walking tips and a pedometer. In the USA, the company has tried to improve service by better training, and by improving employee morale by measures such as introducing medical benefits for staff and incentives for those who stay with the company for a set period. The company is refurbishing restaurants and cafés, and continuing to broaden the menu. The changes haven't been easy; the new menu items have required substantial investments by franchisees to refit their outlets, and have a lower profit margin than McDonald's traditional products because they are more labour intensive. But the changes have generally been welcomed by franchisees because customers and profits are up. In Australia, after an increase in sales of just 2% in 2002, sales climbed 6% in 2003, 10% in 2004 and again increased strongly in 2005. One franchisee expressed the need for change as follows: 'I've been in the system for 12 years. We needed to change. If I was selling the same products now as I was then, I wouldn't have survived.'

But McDonald's isn't relaxing after the success of its deli range. The company is testing an expanded menu which will include what the Australian CEO, Guy Russo, calls 'proper dinners'. But it's hard going when customers are used to almost instant delivery of cheap food from McDonald's. In the words of Guy Russo (interviewed by Jennifer Byrne):

> We're working at the moment with customers—unbranded, not in a McDonald's store—and saying: 'Here is the food'. So they do just what you've just done then'—that is, push the food around my lunch-plate, and cut off the bits I don't like the look of—'Give that a tick, no, can you get rid of that piece there, reduce the fat.' The next part after we get customer acceptance on the food is we then say: 'What would you pay for it?' So they go; 'Somewhere between $15 and $20', and then we do the next part. We put an M in front of it. Same food they've loved, told me they'd pay $20, and all of a sudden perceptions change. 'Oh, McDonald's'. Now it could be exactly the same food but they'll start saying: 'Hang on, it doesn't taste as good, we think' or 'That's better than we would have expected of you and we really believe it's worth about $7'. The same food . . . and their expectation of delivery time is about 60 seconds.

To stay successful, McDonald's will have to continue to change. Ray Kroc, McDonald's founder, famously observed that he didn't know what McDonald's would sell in the future, except that the company would sell the most of it. McDonald's still dominates the fast-food market in the USA, its largest market, but in other parts of the world it has fallen behind other chains which are positioned as offering healthier choices. In Australia, Subway now has more outlets than McDonald's, with 123% growth since 2001. But McDonald's is still the largest seller of hamburgers, and as it continues its push to be seen as offering healthy alternatives, it may still eat into the sandwich market. The company's goal is to increase the number of transactions in McDonald's stores by 30% by early 2011. Don't give up on them yet . . .

Sources: Jennifer Byrne, 'Lunch with Jennifer Byrne: Guy Russo', *The Bulletin*, 12 May 2004, pp. 28–29; David Stires, 'Fallen Arches, McDonald's has had six straight earnings disappointments. Its stock is down 42%. And we can't even remember the jingle! What happened?' *Time*, 29 April 2002, pp. 74+; 'Big Mac's Makeover', *The Eonomist*, 16 October 2004, pp. 61–63; Andrew Hough and Sam Holmes, 'Fast Food Giant Being Beaten into SuBMission by a Club Sandwich', *The Advertiser*, 2 July 2005, p. 48; Jacqui Walker, 'The Menu Planner, *Business Review Weekly*, 14 July 2005, pp. 34–36; Peter Wilmoth, 'Super Resize Me', *Sunday Age*, 12 June 2005, p. 11.

Questions

1 Do you think that McDonald's healthier range is increasing the market potential, or increasing their market share? Why? Why is the distinction important?

2 Subway doesn't sell hamburgers, and sandwiches are only a minor portion of McDonald's sales. So is Subway a serious competitor for McDonald's?

3 What are the potential problems for McDonald's in moving into what it calls 'dinner solutions'? What can it do to avoid these problems?

9.1

Another way of looking at the potential market is to use the consumer market for motorbikes as an illustration. We must first estimate the number of consumers who have a potential interest in owning a motorbike. To do this, a market researcher could contact a random sample of consumers and ask: 'Do you have an interest in buying and owning a motorbike?'. If one person out of 10 said yes, the makers could assume that 10% of the total number of consumers would constitute the

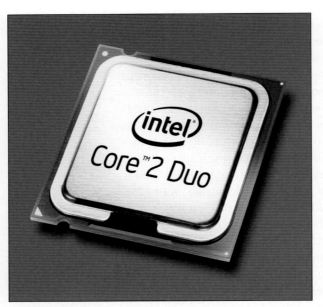

For price-sensitive customers Intel serves a wide section of the market with premium-priced products such as the Core™ Duo processor as well as more affordable options.

potential market for motorbikes. The *potential market* is the set of consumers who profess some level of interest in a particular product or service.

However, consumer interest alone is not enough to define the motorbike market. Potential consumers must have enough income to afford the product. They must be able to answer yes to the following question: 'Can you afford to buy a motorbike?'. The higher the price, the fewer the number of people who can answer yes to this question. Thus, market size depends on both interest and income. Yet further barriers reduce motorbike market size. If motorbike producers do not distribute their products in some countries because of high shipping costs, potential consumers in those areas are not available as customers. The *available market* is the set of consumers who have interest in, income for and access to a particular product or service.

In some countries motorbikes can't be ridden by those under 18 years of age. So young potential buyers would not qualify because of their age. The remaining adults make up the *qualified available* market—the set of consumers who have interest in, income for, access to and qualifications for the product or service.

The marketing organisation now has the choice of pursuing the whole qualified available market or concentrating on selected segments. The *served market* (also called the *target market*) is that part of the qualified available market the organisation decides to pursue. A motorbike distributor, for example, might decide to concentrate its marketing and distribution efforts on Indonesia and Vietnam, where motorbike sales are high. This then becomes its *served market*.

The marketing organisation and its competitors will end up selling a certain number of motorbikes in their served markets. The *penetrated market* is the set of consumers who have already bought motorbikes. These definitions of a market are useful tools for marketing planning. If the marketing organisation is not satisfied with current sales, it can consider a number of actions. It can try to attract a larger percentage of buyers from its served market. It can lobby for lower qualifications of potential buyers. It can expand to other available markets. It can lower its price to expand the size of the available market. It can try to increase the frequency of purchase by customers, by encouraging customers to trade in their bikes for new models. Or it can try to expand the potential market by increasing its advertising to convert non-interested consumers into interested consumers.

SELF-CHECK QUESTIONS

1 The set of consumers who have interest in, income for, access to and qualifications for the product or service is the qualified available market. Provide an example to illustrate the meaning of this term.

2 The penetrated market is the set of consumers who have already bought a particular product. Why is it necessary to identify the penetrated market?

3 Define what is meant by market potential and untapped opportunity.

Defining and measuring market demand

We now turn to some further concepts that are important in understanding the steps involved in estimating current market demand.

Defining our terms in demand measurement

The major concepts in demand measurement are *market demand* and *company demand*. Within each, we distinguish between a *demand function*, a *sales forecast* and a *potential*.

Market demand for a product or service is the total volume that would be bought by a defined consumer group in a defined geographical area during a defined time period in a defined marketing environment under a defined level and mix of industry marketing effort.

Total market demand is not a fixed number but rather a function of the stated conditions. This is why it is often called the market demand function. For example, next year's total market demand for wireless broadband in any geographic market will depend on the marketing effort put behind all the competing brands like BigPond, Unwired and iBurst. It will also depend on environmental factors, such as the number of laptops sold, the number of competing devices like Internet-enabled phones, the level of technology use in the community and overall economic conditions.

The relationships between total market demand and these market conditions are shown in Figure 9.4A. The horizontal axis shows possible levels of industry marketing expenditure during a given time period. The vertical axis shows the resulting demand level. The curve represents the estimated level of market demand for varying levels of industry marketing expenditure. Some minimum level of sales (called the market minimum) would take place without any marketing expenditures. Greater marketing expenditures would yield higher levels of demand, first at an increasing rate and then at a decreasing rate. Marketing expenditures above a certain level would not cause much more demand, suggesting an upper limit to market demand called **market potential**. The industry market forecast shows the level of market demand corresponding to the planned level of industry marketing expenditure in the given environment.

The distance between the market minimum and the market potential shows the overall sensitivity of demand to marketing efforts. We can think of two extreme types of markets, the *expandable* and the *non-expandable*. The size of an expandable market, such as the market for MP3 players, is strongly affected by the level of industry marketing expenditures. In terms of Figure 9.4A, the distance between

Market demand The total volume of a product or service that would be bought by a defined consumer group in a defined geographic area in a defined time period in a defined marketing environment under a defined level and mix of industry marketing effort.

Market potential The upper limit of market demand.

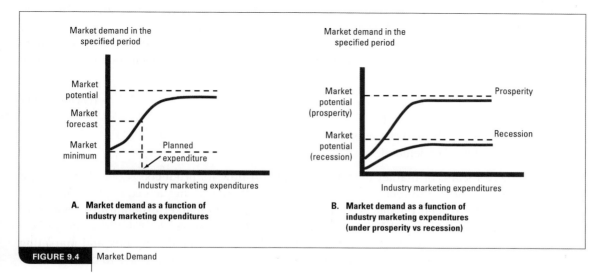

A. Market demand as a function of industry marketing expenditures

B. Market demand as a function of industry marketing expenditures (under prosperity vs recession)

FIGURE 9.4 Market Demand

the market minimum and the market potential would be fairly large. The size of a non-expandable market, such as the market for babies' cots (largely a function of the birthrate) is not affected to any significant degree by the level of marketing expenditures; the distance between market minimum and market potential would be fairly small. Organisations selling in a non-expandable market can take **primary demand**—total demand for all brands of a given product or service—as given. They concentrate their marketing resources on building **selective demand**, demand for the brand of the product or service. For example, in Australia and New Zealand, where it faces a mature and largely non-expandable total soft drink market, Coca-Cola directs most of its marketing effort towards maintaining consumer preference for Coke, Diet-Coke, Sprite and its other brands. However, in Indonesia, where a market of over 200 million people drink some 3% of the Australian per capita consumption of Coke, Coca-Cola Amatil—the Australian franchisee operating a joint venture in Indonesia—attempts to build the primary demand for soft drinks, as well as preference for its own brands.

Different marketing environments mean that different demand curves result. For example, the market for cars is stronger during prosperity than it is during recession. The relationship of market demand to the environment is shown in Figure 9.4B. A given level of marketing expenditure will always result in more demand during prosperity than it will during a recession. The point is that marketers should carefully define the situation for which they are estimating market demand. Such knowledge is important for marketers because it enables them to develop appropriate strategies for increasing company demand among various market segments, depending on the opportunities they foresee.

Only one level of industry marketing expenditure will actually occur. The estimated market demand is called the *market forecast*. The market forecast shows expected market demand, not maximum market demand. To estimate maximum market demand the marketer needs to estimate the level of market demand for a 'very high' level of industry marketing expenditure, where further increases in marketing effort would have little effect in stimulating further demand. *Market potential* is the limit approached by market demand as industry marketing expenditures approach infinity, for a given marketing environment.

The phrase 'for a given market environment' is crucial in the concept of market potential. Market analysts distinguish between the position of the market demand function and movement along it. Companies cannot do anything about the position of the market demand function, which is determined by the marketing environment. However, companies influence their particular location on the function when they decide how much to spend on marketing.

We are now ready to define company demand. *Company demand* is the company's estimated share of market demand at alternative levels of company marketing effort in a given time period. It can be expressed as:

$$Q_i = s_i Q$$ (Formula 9.1)

where Q_i = company i's demand
s_i = company i's market share
Q = total market demand

The company's share of market demand depends on how its products, services, prices and communications are perceived relative to its competitors'. If other things are equal, the company's market share would depend on the size and effectiveness of its market expenditures relative to its competitors'. Marketing model builders have developed *sales-response functions* to measure how a company's sales are affected by its marketing expenditure level, marketing mix and marketing effectiveness.[3] Once marketers have estimated company demand, their next task is to choose a level

Primary demand The level of total demand for all brands of a given product or service, for example the total demand for motorbikes.

Selective demand The demand for a given brand of a product or service, for example the demand for a Honda motorbike.

of marketing effort. The *company sales forecast* is the expected level of company sales based on a chosen marketing plan and an assumed marketing environment. Marketing Highlight 9.2 shows how Bonds increased its sales and market share in the highly competitive underwear market by in-depth market analysis and effective marketing, despite increasing its prices.

Too often the relationship between the company forecast and the marketing plan is confused. One frequently hears that the company should develop its marketing plan on the basis of its sales forecast. This forecast-to-plan sequence is valid if 'forecast' means an estimate of national economic activity or if company demand is non-expandable. The sequence is not valid, however, where market demand is expandable or where 'forecast' means an estimate of company sales. The company sales forecast should not be used to decide what to spend on marketing. On the contrary, the sales forecast is the result of an assumed marketing expenditure plan.

A *sales quota* is the sales goal set for a product line, company division or sales representative. It is primarily a managerial device for defining and stimulating sales effort. Management set sales quotas on the basis of the company sales forecast and the psychology of stimulating its achievement. Generally, sales quotas are set slightly higher than estimated sales in order to encourage the salesforce's effort.

A *sales budget* is an estimate of the expected volume of sales and is used primarily for making current purchasing, production and cash flow decisions. The sales budget considers the sales forecast and the need to avoid excessive risk. Sales budgets are generally set slightly lower than the sales forecast.

Company sales potential is the sales limit approached by company demand as company marketing effort increases relative to competitors'. The absolute limit of company demand is, of course, the market potential. The two would be equal if the company achieved 100% of the market. In most cases, company sales potential is less than market potential, even when company marketing expenditures increase considerably relative to competitors'. The reason is that each competitor has a hard core of loyal buyers who are not very responsive to other companies' efforts to woo them.

To illustrate the use of the above terms, we will use Figure 9.5 and the market for motor vehicles in Australia. It is not possible to show the complex modelling and information system used in this simple

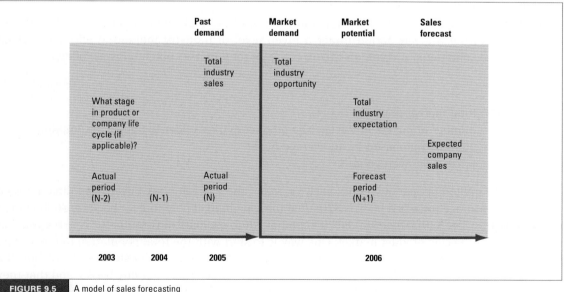

FIGURE 9.5 | A model of sales forecasting

illustration. However, we do see that there is a three-stage process involved. First an *environmental forecast* is made, followed by an *industry forecast* and finally a *company sales forecast*.

For an individual company trying to forecast motor vehicle sales for 2006, the starting point would be to determine market demand. As already noted, market demand is a function of the marketing environment as well as the industry marketing effort. The total demand for cars and trucks in Australia in 2005 was 988 269 vehicles.[4] If the market had been growing at around 2% per annum for a number of years, modelling might show continued growth at this level—giving market demand of 1 008 034 for 2006. Market potential, or industry expectation, might be determined to be some 950 000, based on expected lower industry marketing effort and fewer new models being released in 2006. A company such as Mazda, which might be releasing two new models during 2006, might expect that it will gain market share due to increased marketing effort. This being the case, it estimates company demand at 10%, even though it achieved only a 6.7% market share in 2005.[5] Thus Mazda's sales forecast is their expected sales level based on estimates of market demand, company demand and their chosen level of marketing effort.

SELF-CHECK QUESTIONS

4   Why is it necessary when forecasting sales to be specific about aspects such as the geographic area, time period, marketing environment and marketing effort?

5   Describe the difference in meaning between the terms 'market demand' and 'market potential'.

6   Is it possible for a company's market share to equal market potential? If it is, describe such a situation.

Estimating current demand

We are now ready to examine practical methods for estimating current market demand. Marketing executives want to estimate total market potential, area market potential and total industry sales and market shares.

Total market potential

Total market potential is the maximum amount of sales that might be available to all the firms in an industry during a given period under a given level of industry marketing effort and given environmental conditions. A common way to estimate total market potential is as follows:

$$Q = nqp \hspace{4cm} \text{(Formula 9.2)}$$

where Q = total market potential
   n = number of buyers in the specific product market under the given assumptions
   q = quantity purchased by an average buyer
   p = price of an average unit

Thus if 10 million people buy books each year, and the average book buyer buys three books a year, and the average price of a book is $20, then the total market potential for books is $600 million (= 10 000 000 × 3 × $20). The most difficult component to estimate in Formula 9.2 is n, the number of buyers in the specific product market. One way is to start with the total population in the nation, say 20 million people. The next step is to eliminate groups that obviously would not buy the product. Let us assume that illiterate people and children under 12 do not buy books, and that they constitute 20% of the population. This means that only 80% of the population, or approximately

16 million people, would be in the *suspect pool*. We might do further research and find that people with low income and low education do not read books, and that they constitute over 30% of the suspect pool. Eliminating them, we arrive at a *prospect pool* of approximately 11 200 000 book buyers. We would use this number of potential buyers in Formula 9.2 to calculate total market potential. The difference between the estimated total market potential and the population may also give the marketer ideas on how to expand the market potential by thinking about why some people *aren't* buying the product. For example, Marketing Highlight 9.3 discusses how companies are increasingly turning their attention to lower socioeconomic groups, and making money by selling to this relatively neglected segment of the market.

A variation is the *chain-ratio method*. This method involves multiplying a base number by several adjusting percentages. Suppose a brewery is interested in estimating the market potential for a new light beer. An estimate can be made by the following calculation.[6]

$$
\begin{array}{l}
\text{Demand} \\
\text{for the} \\
\text{new light} \\
\text{beer}
\end{array}
=
\begin{array}{l}
\text{Population} \times \text{Personal discretionary income per capita} \\
\times \text{Average percentage of discretionary income spent on} \\
\text{food} \times \text{Average percentage of amount spent on food} \\
\text{that is spent on beverages} \times \text{Average percentage of} \\
\text{amount spent on beverages that is spent on alcoholic} \\
\text{beverages} \times \text{Average percentage of amount spent on} \\
\text{alcoholic beverages that is spent on beer} \times \text{Expected} \\
\text{percentage of amount spent on beer that will be spent} \\
\text{on light beer}
\end{array}
$$

This simple chain of calculations would provide only a rough estimate of potential demand. However, more detailed chains involving additional segments and other qualifying factors would yield more accurate and refined estimates.[7]

Estimating area market demand

Marketing organisations face the problem of selecting the best sales territories and allocating their marketing budget optimally between these territories. To make good selections, they need to estimate the market potential of different cities, states and countries. Two major methods are available: the *market-buildup method*, used primarily by industrial goods firms, and the *market-factor index method*, used primarily by consumer goods firms.

Market-buildup method

The **market-buildup method** calls for identifying all the potential buyers in each market and estimating their potential purchases. This method can produce accurate results if we have a list of potential buyers and a good estimate of what each will buy. Needless to say, this information is not always easy to gather. The total company demand is therefore estimated on an industry-by-industry basis. We will work through an example—Wilco Pty Ltd, a manufacturer and marketer of wood lathes—to gain an appreciation of the steps involved in estimating not only current demand but also future demand. The steps are shown in Table 9.1 (on page 324). A suggested source of information is also shown at each step.

Market-buildup method
A forecasting method that calls for identifying all the potential buyers in each market and estimating their potential purchases.

Wilco must first identify all the potential buyers of wood lathes before proceeding to establish its share of the projected demand in the period ahead. Zero-based sales forecasting is appropriate for the industrial goods manufacturer because demand is derived from the demand for the products by the companies using the wood lathes. It is not appropriate for Wilco to attempt to become an expert in forecasting the sales of the myriad of products that its customers make. The solution is to

Modernising an icon—the repositioning of Bonds

Bonds has been an icon brand in Australia for over 70 years, but the brand was famous for men's underwear and for the decidedly unsexy Cottontails underpants favoured by older women. The story of how Pacific Brands repositioned Bonds from a rather dull traditional brand to a sexy young brand (and tripled sales as a result) is a story of marketing success. However, it's more than that; it's the story of a company that examined its market, and used and developed the expertise in its staff to create one of the most effective relaunches of a brand in recent years, establishing Bonds firmly as number one in the Australian underwear market.

Up until 2001 the Bonds brand was owned by Pacific Dunlop, in its later years a cash-strapped conglomerate which didn't invest heavily in building the brand. The Bonds line was sold to private equity investors in 1979, becoming part of the Pacific Brands group, together with other well-known brands such as Berlei, Holeproof, Antz Pantz, Stubbies and King Gee.

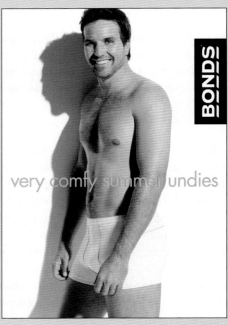

very comfy summer undies

BONDS

Bonds has successfully repositioned its brand by reviewing every aspect of its strategy.

A key part of the strategy of Pacific Brands CEO Paul Moore was to build a company which valued and developed the talent of its staff, and which encouraged collaboration and knowledge sharing. And since the company estimates that about 80% of the people who buy underwear are women, or are influenced by women, the company's growing use of women in senior management makes a lot of sense. Sue Morphet, the Group General Manager, says that 'Gone are the days of females in middle management and men in the senior ranks . . . [We are] very much more people and performance focused, and that attracts more women.' It's a change from the old days at Pacific Dunlop. Mary Keely, General Manager for People and Performance, says that when she joined the company she was amused and surprised to be the only woman at a lengthy presentation by the man running the Berlei business (which sells bras), but not to be asked for comment. 'I thought they might ask me one question . . . All these men talking about Berlei—I found it bizarre.'

Pacific Brands' turnaround relied on reviewing all aspects of strategy. There was an emphasis on supply chain efficiencies, removing duplication, rationalising sourcing and leveraging off scale in manufacturing and distribution. The company invested heavily in intensive training of staff to enhance their understanding of how good marketing delivers dividends. The company developed a framework to peer-review their branding strategy. It set out to create a pull model, with consumers demanding the products in store, rather than Pacific Brands having to push the products to retailers. But that required a substantial and effective advertising campaign, to establish these brands firmly in consumers' minds, and to develop new segments. Total advertising for Pacific Brands rose by 37% to $62 million in 2003–2004 (up from just a few million when Bonds was managed by Pacific Dunlop).

Relaunching Bonds to a new segment was a key part of Pacific Brands' strategy. The brand was very strong in men's underwear, but sales were very poor in the most attractive segment—females aged 18–35, who buy underwear more often and who are prepared to spend more on attractive underwear. The brand was 'traditionally dominated by men's underwear', admits Sue Morphet. 'We wanted to refresh it and make it more contemporary and appealing to young women.' So Bonds has developed new lines which are more attractive to younger females, using bright colours and younger styles, and started producing coordinated bras and underpants. It hired Sarah O'Hare, the well-known model and wife of media mogul Lachlan Murdoch as the face of the brand. The new Bonds line was launched in 2001 at Melbourne's high-profile Fashion Week, generating large amounts of publicity. This was supplemented with TV, radio and magazine ads, and backed up by in-store promotion and swing tickets showing Sarah O'Hare. A public relations campaign was used to generate ongoing coverage in women's magazines and newspapers, and sales boomed. Bonds' share of the underwear market went from 6% in 2000 to 18% in 2002, despite an average price rise of 17.7% for the range, in a very competitive market. From 2003 to 2004 sales continued to rise, increasing 9% on the previous year's results. Consumer tracking showed that unprompted awareness of the Bonds brand, and attitude towards the brand, rose substantially. Evaluation of the campaign showed that for every dollar spent on marketing, a return on investment of $13.24 was generated for the period of 2000–01.

But Bonds isn't standing still. A year after relaunching the women's underwear market, former tennis star Pat Rafter was signed as the face of Bonds men's singlets, and sales increased by 25%. Sarah O'Hare has become a mother, and the company is planning a new range of underwear aimed at women aged 28–35. It is also pursuing innovation in other areas, working with a supplier to develop a new environmentally friendly fabric partly made from bamboo. And it's developing new lines, such as the Love Kylie range, endorsed by Kylie Minogue, for which sales have increased by up to 300% per year.

And those private investors who bought the underperforming brands from Pacific Dunlop? They received a handsome return on their investment when the brand was publicly listed in 2004 in Australia's largest private equity listing. The float was oversubscribed, and widely praised in the media. But CEO Paul Moore was modest about the success; 'It wasn't overly difficult. We don't build rockets. We just make undies. All we've done is grow profit by doing things better.' It's amazing what a good strategy and good marketing can achieve!

Sources: Catherine Fox, 'A Pacific Revolution', *The Australian Financial Review*, 11 February 2005, p. 20; Teresa Ooi, 'Stars Show off Their Undies', *The Australian*, 26 January 2005, p. 36; Craig Roberts, 'Ideas from Everywhere', *Business Review Weekly*, 16 June 2005, pp. 70–71; Deborah Tarrant, 'Brand on the Run', *The Australian*, 1 December 2004, p. 28; C. Thomas, (ed.). 'Bonds: The Totally Integrated Marketing Campaign that Revitalized an Australian Icon', in *Effective Advertising 7: Casebook of the AFA Advertising Effectiveness Awards*, Sydney, Advertising Federation of Australia.

Questions

1 Do you think the underwear market is an expandable market or a non-expandable market. Why?

2 Do you think Bonds grew the market or increased their market share? Does your answer depend on your answer to Question 1?

3 Figure 9.4 shows that sales will be higher under economic prosperity. How then can Bonds establish whether its increase in sales was due to its own marketing activities or whether the sales growth was due to external factors such as the economic environment?

9.2

use information supplied by the network of customers. The task is made less complex in this case because Wilco makes lathes that are considered too large to be sold to the home lathe user. This cuts out the need to approach hardware retailers.

The first piece of research which can help Wilco to understand its potential market is to identify the types of industries that would use wooden lathes. This can be done by consulting the appropriate

TABLE 9.1 Zero-based sales forecast for a wood lathe manufacturer, Wilco Pty Ltd	
Steps	**Source**
1. Market identification Define market for wood lathes. Check off all four-digit-code industries that would use such lathes (see Tables 9.2A and 9.2B).	ANZSIC manual (Australian and New Zealand Standard Industrial Classification) and the ABS Manufacturing Survey)
2. Market diagnosis (a) Diagnose the basis for estimating the likely number of lathes used in each industry #2921 = 10 lathes for every $1 million customer sales. (b) Establish extent of market saturation: • user industry • number of competitors • market growth rate.	Past experience or mail survey to establish usage for each user industry (see Table 9.2)
3. Market demand In this case, market demand for the past 12 months would not necessarily be indicative of the future. Industrial markets are notable for the fact that it is much more difficult to undertake trend analysis in each product market, e.g. the construction industry is cyclical and zero-based budgeting is usually undertaken. Industry associations which gather sales and other data for benchmarking purposes perform a useful function by publishing surveys of buyer intent and confidence. They can also provide information on market demand by this method.	
4. Market potential (a) Compute area market potential as shown for the Sydney example in Table 9.3. (b) Compute total market potential: (Sydney + Melbourne + Adelaide etc.) = 2000 units for 2007.	
5. Sales potential Estimate the total replacement sales potential from survey carried out at 2(a) as well as sales potential to new manufacturers from trend analysis of past years' sales results (industry and/or company): = 500 units	ABS Manufacturing Survey, and mail survey data
6. Compare market potential with sales potential Provides information on replacement rates for future planning periods. (NB: Does not indicate unsatisfied demand for period immediately ahead.)	
7. Sales forecast (a) Estimate market share positions of competitors (and own firm if continuing). (b) Assess competitors' marketing effort—expenditure and quality.	Survey or sales team Judgment based on your observations and reports from the marketplace by salespeople.
(c) Set company's marketing strategy. (d) Forecast company's market share for period ahead (e.g. 5%). (e) Forecast company sales (e.g. sales potential × 5% = 25 lathes). (f) Prepare detailed sales forecast—product type × month and so on. (g) Incorporate sales forecast in business-unit plan for period ahead.	Mail survey and expected results of implementation of chosen marketing strategy.

industry classification list (for example, the Australian and New Zealand Standard Industrial Classification (ANZSIC), discussed in Chapter 8). ANZSIC classifies all businesses into major industry groups or divisions. Each division is further broken down into 53 subdivisions, each with a two-digit code. So subdivision 29 in Table 9.2 is 'Other manufacturing'. This classification scheme gives us a point of entry in identifying potential customers as well as competitors.

As discussed in Chapter 8, each industry subdivision is further subdivided into groups designated by a three-digit code. For example, Group 292 is Furniture manufacturing. In turn, each group is broken down into four-digit classes. Class 2921 is Wooden furniture and upholstered seat manufacturing. This class is one that would be of interest to Wilco Pty Ltd.

For each four-digit class, the Australian Bureau of Statistics (ABS) and its New Zealand counterpart Statistics New Zealand report on such information as the number of establishments subclassified by location, number of employees, annual sales and net worth, so Wilco can find out information on the number of customers, and gain some indication of their size.

To use the ANZSIC system, Wilco must first determine the four-digit code that represents businesses which are likely to require lathes. For example, lathes would be used by manufacturers in class 2921—Wooden furniture and upholstered seat manufacture—as well as by those included in class 2323—Wooden structural component manufacturing.

To get a full picture, Wilco could proceed by one or more of the following methods:

1 Look to past sales (if any) and determine the ANZSIC numbers of past customers.
2 Go through the ANZSIC manual and check all the four-digit industries that, in management's judgment, would use such lathes.
3 Carry out a mail or telephone survey to establish which companies express an interest in wood lathes and the number used in relation to factors such as sales turnover or number of employees.

TABLE 9.2 ANZSIC: Extract from Division C

Division C—Manufacturing

Subdivision 21— Food, beverages and tobacco
- Group 211 Meat and meat product manufacturing
  212 Dairy product manufacturing
  213 Vegetable processing
  214 Oil and fat manufacturing
  215 Flour mill and cereal food manufacturing
  216 Bakery product manufacturing
  217 Other food manufacturing
  218 Beverage and malt manufacturing
  219 Tobacco product manufacturing

Subdivision 22— Textile, clothing, footwear and leather manufacturing

Subdivision 23— Wood and paper product manufacturing
- Group 232 Other wood product manufacturing
  Class 2323 Wooden structural component manufacturing

Subdivision 29— Other manufacturing
- Group 292 Furniture manufacturing
  Class 2921 Wooden furniture and upholstered seat manufacturing

Source: Australian and New Zealand Standard Industrial Classification, 1993, Canberra, ABS, Catalogue no. 1292.0; Department of Statistics, New Zealand, Catalogue no. 19.005.0092.

Once Wilco has identified the ANZSIC classifications relevant to its wood lathes, the next step is to determine an appropriate base for estimating the likely number of lathes. Either through industry experience or using the responses to the mail survey of companies within the industry groups suggested in Step 2 in Table 9.1, Wilco must establish the most appropriate base, whether this is lathes related to turnover or perhaps lathes used in relation to the number of employees. This enables data such as that set out in Table 9.3 for the Sydney market to be constructed for each geographic market, and ultimately the overall market potential can be computed using the Australian census of manufacturers. If we take the market potential for Australia to be a hypothetical 2000 units, Sydney therefore accounts for 10% of the market potential. This does not mean that 10% of all marketing effort will be expended there by the industry or companies concerned. Additional information would be required to make such a decision, for example the extent of market saturation, the number of competitive lathe manufacturers and growth rates expected for the various geographical markets.

Wilco next sets out to establish the sales potential for the forthcoming 12-month period. Industry sales, and ultimately Wilco's share of these sales, is information which invariably depends on the sales projections being made by the end-user companies. Where consumer goods companies and retailers have access to up-to-date sales and market share information from scan data, the industrial marketer is often faced with the task of zero-based budgeting. That is, the past is not a good prediction of the future. This is because many industries such as the construction industry are faced with cyclical economic conditions. The constructor has customers who will only build when debt financing is cheap and the overall economy is healthy. Additionally, various sectors perform differently at different times. The pharmaceutical industry may be performing well when the office-construction industry is in tatters. To circumvent the many pitfalls, Wilco must include as part of the survey used in Step 2 of Table 9.1 a number of questions relating to:

- intentions to purchase within 3 months, 6 months and 12 months
- brands and models intended for purchase.

Responses to this type of questionnaire provide an indication of the size of the replacement market in the next 12 months. However, this method will not yield information on the size of the market attributable to new manufacturers starting up in the 12 months ahead. This must be estimated from the growth in the number of firms in the relevant four-digit ANZSIC class over the past few years under similar national and global economic circumstances. Here, we will assume that the replacement market sales potential for the year ahead amounts to 475 units, whereas the new market amounts to 25 units, giving a total sales potential of 500 units.

The comparison of *market potential* and *sales potential* in Step 6 in Table 9.1 shows the replacement rates for wood lathes in the various industry groups which use the product. In this example, Wilco

TABLE 9.3 Sydney market potential for wood lathes				
(1) ANZSIC	(2) No. of establishments	(3) Annual sales ($ millions) customer sales	(4) Potential sales in units per $ millions	Market potential (col. 2 × 3 × 4)
2323	3	1	5	15
	1	5	5	25
2921	6	1	10	60
	2	5	10	100
Total				200

must gain a share of a market which amounts to 500 units. To compute its likely share, Wilco must have knowledge of competitors' current market penetrations—which customers currently use what brand and who is satisfied with that brand. The mail survey used in Step 2 could also be used for this purpose. Likewise, internal sales records would have enabled a profile of many customers to be built up over time, together with knowledge of penetration by competitive companies, and the approximate timing of replacement.

Since industrial marketers rely much more than other marketers on personal selling, the quality of the marketing effort is going to revolve heavily around product quality and salespeople quality. So in Step 7 Wilco must also assess the marketing effort of competitors, both in terms of level and quality. Having done all this, Wilco should be in a good position to set its own marketing strategy and forecast its likely market share and sales level. Any environmental factors, such as the reintroduction of some form of investment allowance for Australian-made goods or tariffs for imported equipment, would need to be taken into account. A detailed sales forecast is prepared, broken down by model and/or size of lathe. The sales forecast then forms part of a business plan for the ensuing period.

Market-factor index method

Consumer goods companies also have to estimate area market potential. Consider the following example: an importer of men's dress shirts wishes to evaluate its sales performance relative to market potential in several major market areas, starting with New South Wales. It estimates the total national potential for dress shirts at about $100 million. The company's current nationwide sales are $30 million, about a 30% share of the total potential market. Its sales in the metropolitan areas of Sydney are $9 million. It wants to know whether its share of the Sydney market is higher or lower than its national 30% market share. To find out, the company must first calculate market potential in the Sydney area.

A common method of calculating area market potential is the **market-factor index method**, which identifies market factors that correlate with market potential and combines them into a weighted index. Using this method requires establishing a *buying-power index*. This can be done using 'household expenditure' information, or via specially syndicated consumer research. Such a survey estimates the buying power for each geographic region. A buying-power index is usually based on three factors: the area's share of the nation's disposable personal income, retail sales and population. The buying-power index published in the USA each year by Sales and Marketing Management in its 'Survey of Buying Power' uses the following formula for a specific area:[8]

> **Market-factor index method** A forecasting method that identifies market factors that correlate with market potential and combines them into a weighted index.

$$B_i = 0.5y_i + 0.3r_i + 0.2p_i \qquad \text{(Formula 9.3)}$$

where B_i = percentage of total national buying power in area i
y_i = percentage of national disposable personal income in area i
r_i = percentage of national retail sales in area i
p_i = percentage of national population in area i

The three coefficients in the formula reflect the relative weights of the three factors. The exact weightings might be estimated by manufacturers or purchased from market research agencies who collect these sorts of data and sell them to many businesses. Using such an index, the importer looks up Sydney and finds that this market has, say, 20% of the nation's disposable personal income, 23% of the nation's retail sales and 25% of the nation's population. Thus, it calculates the buying-power index for Sydney as follows:

$$B_i = 0.5(20) + 0.3(23) + 0.2(25) = 21.9$$

That is, Sydney should account for 21.9% of the nation's total potential demand for dress shirts. Because the total national potential is $100 million each year, total potential in Sydney equals $21 900 000 ($100 million × 0.219). Thus, the company's sales in Sydney of $9 million amount to a 41.1% share ($9 000 000/$21 900 000) of area market potential. Comparing this with the 30% national share, the company appears to be doing better in Sydney than it is in other parts of the country.

Use of a buying power index can therefore provide a useful benchmark for marketers to assess their current sales and potential. However, the buying power index also has some limitations, because the weights used in the index are somewhat arbitrary. They apply mainly to consumer goods that are neither low-priced staples nor high-priced luxury goods. Other weights can be used. The importer can adjust the market potential for additional factors such as the level of competition in the market, local promotion costs, seasonal changes in demand and unique local market characteristics. Many companies compute additional area demand measures. Marketers can refine city-by-city measures down to census districts or postcode centres. Census districts are small areas about the size of a neighbourhood (approximately 250 households), and postcode areas are larger areas. Information on population size, family income and other characteristics is available for each type of unit. Marketers can use these data for estimating demand in neighbourhoods or other geographical areas.

Estimating industry sales and market shares

Besides estimating total and area demand, a marketing organisation will want to know the actual industry sales in its market. Thus, it must identify its competitors and estimate their sales.

Industry trade associations often collect and publish total industry sales, although they might not list individual company sales separately. In this way, each marketing organisation can evaluate its performance against the industry as a whole. Suppose the marketing organisation's sales are increasing at 5% per year and industry sales are increasing at 10%. This marketing organisation is actually losing its relative standing in the industry.

Another way to estimate sales is to buy reports from a marketing research firm that audits total sales and brand sales. The various industries use different marketing research firms which monitor their particular industry. So as discussed in Chapter 6, ACNielsen provides consumer marketers with store scanner data—ScanTrack and information on individual consumer purchase patterns using panel data, BrandScan. BIS Shrapnel is one of the best known sources for construction, infrastructure and property information, and firms such as Forrester and the Gartner Group are best known for information on information technology. Using sources such as these, a company can thus obtain data on total product category sales and brand sales. It can compare its performance with that of the total industry or with any particular competitor.

SELF-CHECK QUESTIONS

7 Illustrate the use of the chain-ratio method of assessing total market potential with an example other than the one provided.

8 Why might the methods of assessing area market potential differ for consumer products and business-to-business or industrial products?

9 Standard industrial classification schemes such as ANZSIC are vital to the use of the market-buildup model. Describe another situation where an industrial marketer might use such a scheme.

10 How might an industry association assist a small or medium enterprise (SME) to find out the size of a market, its growth (if any) and the enterprise's relative standing?

Forecasting future demand

Having looked at ways to estimate current demand, we now examine ways to forecast future market demand. **Forecasting** is the art of estimating future demand by anticipating what buyers are likely to do under a given set of conditions. Forecasting is an important part of a marketing manager's job: one study found that 99% of companies prepared formal forecasts when they developed written marketing plans.[9] However, very few products or services lend themselves to easy forecasting. Those that do generally involve a product with steady sales or sales growth in a stable competitive environment. However, most markets do not have stable total and company demand, and so good forecasting becomes a key factor in company success. Poor forecasting can lead to overly large inventories, costly price markdowns or lost sales due to items being out of stock. The more unstable the demand, the more the marketing organisation needs accurate forecasts and elaborate forecasting procedures. As we saw in Figure 9.5, marketing organisations commonly use a three-stage procedure to arrive at a sales forecast. First, they make an environmental forecast, which is followed by an industry forecast and finally by a company sales forecast. The environmental forecast calls for estimating factors such as inflation, unemployment, interest rates, consumer spending and saving, business investment, government expenditures, net exports and other environmental events important to the company. The result is a forecast of gross national product, which is used along with other indicators to forecast industry sales. The company then prepares its sales forecast by assuming that it will win a certain share of industry sales.

Companies can use many techniques to forecast their sales.[10] Many of these techniques are listed in Table 9.4 and are described in the following paragraphs.[11] All forecasts are built on one of three information bases: what people say, what people do or what people have done. The first basis—what people say—involves surveying the opinions of buyers or those close to them, such as salespeople or outside experts. Information is gathered using three methods: surveys of buyer intentions, composites of salesforce opinions and expert opinion. Building a forecast of what people do involves another method: that of putting the product into a test market to assess buyer response. The final basis—what people have done—involves analysing records of past buying behaviour or using time-series analysis or statistical demand analysis. Often different forecasts will be used: all forecasts involve some uncertainty, and even experts tend to be overconfident.[12] After a review of the evidence on different forecasting methods, Armstrong and Green recommend that when forecasting is being made in situations with high uncertainty, more than one forecasting method should be used, and the results from different forecasts combined.[13]

Survey of buyers' intentions

One way to forecast what buyers will do is to ask them directly. Surveys of buyers are most useful under six conditions where:

Forecasting The art of estimating future demand by anticipating what buyers are likely to do under a given set of conditions.

TABLE 9.4 Common sales forecasting techniques	
Based on	**Methods**
What people say	Surveys of buyers' intentions Composite salesforce opinions Expert opinion
What people do	Test markets
What people have done	Time-series analysis Leading indicators Statistical demand analysis

1   Responses can be obtained.
2   The behaviour is important to the respondent.
3   The behaviour is planned.
4   The plan is reported correctly.
5   The respondent is able to fulfil the plan.
6   The plan is unlikely to change.[14]

Several research organisations conduct periodic surveys of consumer buying intentions. These organisations ask questions such as: Do you intend to buy a motor vehicle in the next six months? This is called a *purchase probability scale*. In addition, other surveys ask about the consumer's present finances and their expectations about their job security, financial security and general buying intentions. The various bits of information are combined into a *consumer sentiment measure* or a *consumer confidence measure*. Some banks carry out such surveys and report the results in the financial press. Consumer durable goods companies subscribe to such indexes to help them anticipate major shifts in consumer buying intentions so that they can adjust their production and marketing plans accordingly. For industrial buying, various companies such as BIS Shrapnel conduct regular surveys concerning planned purchases of plant, equipment and materials.

Composite of salesforce opinions

When buyer interviewing is impractical, the marketing organisation may base its sales forecasts on information provided by the salesforce. The marketing organisation typically asks its salespeople to estimate sales, by product, for their individual territories. It then adds up the individual estimates to arrive at an overall sales forecast.

Few companies use their salesforce's estimates without making some adjustments. Salespeople are biased observers. They may be naturally pessimistic or optimistic, or they may go to one extreme or another because of recent sales setbacks or successes. Furthermore, they are often unaware of larger economic developments and do not know how their organisation's marketing plans will affect future sales in their territories. They may understate demand so that the marketing organisation will set a low sales quota. They may not have the time to prepare careful estimates or they may not consider them worthwhile.

Assuming that these biases can be countered, a number of benefits can be gained by involving the salesforce in forecasting. Salespeople may have better insight into developing trends than any other group in the marketing organisation. After participating in the forecasting process, the salespeople may have greater confidence in their quotas and more incentive to achieve them. In addition, 'grassroots' forecasting provides estimates broken down by product, territory, customer and salesperson.[15]

Expert opinion

Companies can also obtain forecasts by turning to experts. Experts include dealers, distributors, suppliers, marketing consultants and trade associations. Thus, car companies survey their dealers periodically for forecasts of short-term demand. Dealer estimates, however, are subject to the same strengths and weaknesses as salesforce estimates.

Many companies buy economic and industry forecasts from well-known organisations such as Access Economics, BIS Shrapnel, IBIS or Syntec. These forecasting specialists are in a better position than many marketing organisations to prepare economic forecasts, because they have more data available and more forecasting expertise.

Occasionally, companies put together a special group of experts to make a particular kind of forecast. The experts may be asked to exchange views and come up with a group estimate (group discussion method). Or they may be asked to supply their estimates individually, after which the analyst combines them into a single estimate (pooling of individual estimates). Or they may supply individual estimates and assumptions that are reviewed by a marketing organisation analyst, revised and followed by further rounds of estimation (called the Delphi method).[16] The Delphi method has been shown to be more accurate than combined forecasts from unaided judgments.[17]

Experts can provide good insights upon which to base forecasts, but they can also be wrong. For example, in 1943 IBM Chairman Thomas J. Watson predicted: 'I think there's a world market for about five computers'. And in 1946 Daryl F. Zanuck, head of 20th Century Fox, announced that 'TV won't be able to hold on to any market it captures after the first six months. People will soon get tired of staring at a plywood box every night'.[18] Where possible, the marketing organisation should back up experts' opinions with estimates obtained using other methods.

Test-market method

Where buyers do not plan their purchases carefully or are inconsistent in carrying out their intentions, or where experts are not good guessers, the marketing organisation may want to conduct a direct test market. A direct test market is especially useful in forecasting sales of a new product or of an established product in a new distribution channel or territory. Test marketing is discussed further in Chapter 12.

Time-series analysis

Many firms base their forecasts on past sales, assuming that the causes of past sales can be uncovered through statistical analysis. The causal relations can then be used to predict future sales. A **time-series analysis** of a product's past sales involves separating them into four major components—trend, cycle, season and erratic components—then recombining these components to produce the sales forecast.

A *trend* is the long-term, underlying pattern of growth or decline in sales resulting from basic changes in population, economic activity and technology. It is found by fitting a straight or curved line through past sales. *Cycle* captures the medium-term, wave-like movement of sales resulting from changes in general economic and competitive activity. Cyclical swings, however, are difficult to predict because they do not occur on a regular basis. *Season* refers to a consistent pattern of sales movements within the year. The term 'season' describes any recurrent hourly, weekly, monthly or quarterly sales pattern. The seasonal component may be related to weather factors, holidays and trade customs, and the seasonal pattern thus provides a norm for forecasting short-range sales. Finally, *erratic events* include unforeseeable events such as fads, strikes, floods and other erratic disturbances to the market. These components are by definition unpredictable and should be removed from past data to see the more normal behaviour of sales.

Time-series analysis
Breaking down past sales of a product or service into its trend, cycle, season and erratic components, and then recombining these components to produce a sales forecast.

Leading indicactors

Many companies try to forecast their sales by finding one or more **leading indicators**—other factors that change in the same direction but in advance of company sales. For example, a plumbing supply company might find that its sales lag behind the housing starts index by about four months. The number of housing starts or approvals to build would then be a useful leading indicator of changes in demand. Some suppliers to the construction industry have noted that, on the way into a recession, architects are the first to lose work. Conversely, when an economic upswing is in the offing, we would expect architects to be the first to experience a lift in demand for their services. The time lag in this case might be 12 months or more.

Leading indicators
Factors that change in the same direction but in advance of company sales.

MARKETING HIGHLIGHT 9.3

Marketing to the bottom of the pyramid

Marketing has typically involved segmenting markets, and targeting products to the most attractive customer segments. The most attractive segments are often considered to comprise consumers with high disposable income, because these consumers will often pay higher prices, and thus allow higher profit margins for organisations which sell to them. It's easy to think of companies who are renowned for targeting higher-wealth individuals—makers of luxury items, spa holidays, but also service providers offering high-priced products (such as American Express's high-prestige black card, offered only to individuals with very high personal wealth).

Targeting high-wealth individuals who will pay a price premium can appear to be an attractive strategy, but if competitors have the same idea, the high-wealth segments can be very competitive, with many competitors targeting the same customers. In contrast, the larger number of lower-wealth individuals can constitute a less competitive, potentially profitable segment. Several years ago, banks realised that many low-account-balance customers were unprofitable, and decided to target higher-wealth individuals, who are more likely to use low-cost channels (such as Internet banking), have higher balances and thus provide higher profit for the banks. In contrast, the Commonwealth Bank (CBA), which had a large number of less wealthy individuals among its customer base, developed a strategy of making money from these customers. CBA didn't focus solely on low-value customers, because it still aimed to make money from higher-wealth customers, but the bank changed its pricing and systems to encourage lower-value customers to switch to lower-cost accounts, thus allowing the bank to make money from all its customers.

US academic C. K. Prahalad has developed this idea in his widely discussed book *The Fortune at the Bottom of the Pyramid*. Prahalad points out that there are more than four billion people in the world with an income of less than $US1500 per year. Large organisations have generally regarded these people as an unattractive segment, without the income to purchase products beyond bare essentials. However, Prahalad argues that while margins cannot be high when selling to this segment, unit sales are very high, so with effective marketing organisations can make money catering to the needs of this segment and at the same time improve the living standards of these people by providing them with access to useful products.

Marketing to the people at the bottom of the economic pyramid, however, requires radical new thinking within organisations. Traditional marketing theory would suggest that selling products to people with very low incomes requires lower-quality, lower-cost products. Instead, Prahalad argues that organisations need radical innovation in their products and systems, so that they can make money serving this huge market segment.

Prahalad gives numerous examples of companies that are making money by refocusing efforts on consumers at the bottom of the pyramid. For example, India's largest soap company, Hindustan Lever Limited (HLL), was experiencing falling market share and profits in its traditional markets, where soap sales were stagnant and competition was high. The company reformulated its soaps to make them cheaper, and thus more affordable to people on low wages. Through market research, it found low levels of hand washing in poor families, contributing to higher levels of diseases. HLL cooperated with a UNICEF program to teach the benefits of hygiene and hand washing, and refocused its advertising on the prevention of diarrhoea and skin and eye infections by the use of soap. By reaching out to consumers with a strong brand, the company's 'Lifebuoy' soap, and by building a customer habit of buying that brand, HLL can create strong loyalty, benefiting the company, but also contributing to better health. In the words of a company spokesperson:

> We're not shying away from the fact that Lifebuoy is going to benefit or we're trying

to get soap consumption up. We're being up-front about it. But we're also telling them that we're doing something for the good of the community and it's there for you to see yourself. And that's the reason we're actually going into schools and schools are giving us permission to go in. Because they believe that what we're saying is actually making sense. I'm trying to develop the category because I believe soaps can reduce diarrheal incidents by 40%. And if you believe it's true, there's no reason why you should dispute this program.

Higher socioeconomic groups represent the core customers for many organisations. But with efficient market analysis, more companies like HLL will be able to make money in these less obvious market segments at the 'bottom of the pyramid'.

Sources: C. K. Prahalad, 'The Bottom of the Pyramid', *Siliconindia*, vol. 5, no. 10, October 2001, pp. 76–77; C. K. Prahalad, 'Strategies for the Bottom of the Economic Pyramid', *Reflections*, vol. 3, 2005, p. 4; C. K. Prahalad, *The Fortune at the Bottom of the Pyramid*, Upper Saddle River, NJ, Wharton School Publishing.

Questions

1 How could HLL go about estimating total market potential for soap sales?

2 Do you think that organisations which are used to targeting middle and upper class customers have the skills to target lower-value customers successfully?

3 Could marketing to individuals with lower income be accused of being unethical? Why or why not?

9.3

Statistical demand analysis

Time-series analysis treats past and future sales as a function of time rather than as a function of any real demand factors. But many real factors affect the sales of any product. **Statistical demand analysis** is a set of statistical procedures used to discover the most important factors affecting sales and their relative influences. The factors most commonly analysed are prices, income, population and promotion.

Statistical demand analysis consists of expressing sales (Q) as a dependent variable and trying to explain sales as a function of a number of independent demand variables $X_1, X_2, ..., X_n$. That is:

$$Q = f(X_1, X_2, ..., X_n) \qquad \text{(Formula 9.4)}$$

Using statistical techniques such as multiple regression analysis, various equation forms can be statistically fitted to the data in the search for the best predicting factors and equation.[19]

For example, a US soft drink company found that the per capita sales of soft drinks by state were well explained by:[20]

$$Q = -145.5 + 6.46X_1 - 2.37X_2$$

where X_1 = mean annual temperature of the state (Fahrenheit)
X_2 = annual per capita income in the state (in thousands)

For example, New Jersey had a mean annual temperature of 54°F and an annual per capita income of 24 (in thousands). Using the immediately preceding equation, the company would predict per capita soft drink consumption in New Jersey to be as follows:

$$Q = -145.5 + 6.46(54) - 2.37(24) = 146.6$$

Actual per capita consumption was 143. If the equation predicted this for other states as well, it would serve as a useful forecasting tool. Marketing management would predict next year's mean

Statistical demand analysis A set of statistical procedures used to discover the most important factors affecting sales and their relative influence; the most commonly analysed factors are prices, income, population and promotion.

temperature and per capita income for each state and use the above equation to predict next year's sales.

Statistical demand analysis can be very complex, and the marketer must take care in designing, conducting and interpreting such analysis. Yet constantly improving computer technology has made statistical demand analysis an increasingly popular approach to forecasting.[21]

SELF-CHECK QUESTIONS

11 How likely is it that buyers will state their purchase intentions for the next 12 months? And how accurate might such a statement of intention be?

12 Why might salespeople overestimate or underestimate future sales?

13 Explain why the Wilco example states that it is more difficult to use statistical techniques to predict sales of industrial goods than sales of consumer goods.

SUMMARY

To carry out their responsibilities marketing managers need measures of current and future market size. We define a *market* as the set of all actual and potential consumers of a market offer. Consumers in the market have *interest, income, access* and *qualifications for* the market offer.

One task is to *estimate current demand*. Total market demand is not a fixed number, but a function of the marketing environment and the level and mix of industry marketing effort. Marketers can estimate total market potential through the chain-ratio method, which involves multiplying a base number by successive percentages. Area market demand can be estimated by the market-buildup method or the market-factor index method. Estimating actual industry sales requires identifying competitors and using some method of estimating the sales of each. Finally, companies estimate the market shares of competitors to judge their relative performance.

For *estimating future demand*, the company can use one or a combination of seven possible forecasting methods, based on what consumers say (buyers' intentions surveys, composite of salesforce opinions, expert opinion), what consumers do (test marketing) or what consumers have done (time-series analysis, leading indicators and statistical demand analysis). The best method to use depends on the purpose of the forecast, the type of product and the availability and reliability of data.

MARKETING ISSUE

The chapter has discussed ways in which organisations can estimate market demand, but it also gives examples where so called 'experts' have been embarrassingly wrong in their forecasts. Before the launch of the iMac in 1998, Apple, the former market share leader, had suffered eight consecutive quarters of annual losses. Its market share had shrunk to approximately 3% of the US market, and the company's future was uncertain. The launch of the iMac rescued Apple from what seemed like an impending failure, but few people, if anyone, predicted that Apple would return to dominate a very different market with a very different product, the iPod (and its variations) and the related music sales. In contrast, Sony, which dominated the personal music device market with its Walkman products, has seen its share of the personal music market shrink.

1 Could market forecasting have helped Apple or Sony to forecast their contrasting fortunes in the personal music market and react accordingly?

2 Under what circumstances might market forecasting be most accurate? When is it likely to be least accurate?

KEY TERMS

forecasting	329	market-buildup method	321	primary demand	318
industry	311	market demand	317	selective demand	318
leading indicators	331	market-factor index method	327	statistical demand analysis	333
market	311	market potential	317	time-series analysis	331

DISCUSSING THE ISSUES

1 Why is it important to define the market? What different market definitions should be considered and why?

2 In market measurement and forecasting, which is the more serious problem, to overestimate demand or to underestimate it?

3 List some expandable and non-expandable markets. Can you think of any markets that have expanded even though they were once considered non-expandable? What caused the unexpected expansion?

4 Many long-term trends occur because of changes in technology or the environment. What effect might the Internet have on real estate agents, given that consumers can list their property with an Internet service provider and show real-time images of the interior and exterior of the home?

5 People are generally less responsive to marketing efforts during a recession than when the economy is booming. Does this imply that marketers should cut back on advertising and other marketing efforts during recessions?

6 What approaches to forecasting should companies adopt when trying to enter emerging markets?

REFERENCES

1. William M. Bulkeley, 'In Digital Age, a Tiff over Fading Photos', *The Asian Wall Street Journal*, 5 April 2005, p. A6; William, Bulkeley, 'With a Sharper Focus on Women, Kodak Improves Digital Picture', *The Asian Wall Street Journal*, 7 July 2005, p. 1; Rochelle Burbury, 'Brand New Day', *The Australian Financial Review*, 29 April 2005, p. 104; John Davidson, 'Kodak Finds a Place in Today's Picture', *The Australian Financial Review*, 6 October 2005, p. 25; Amy Yee, 'Kodak Axes 10,000 More Jobs as Digital Takes off in China, *Financial Times*, 21 July 2005 p. 15.
2. Roger Best, *Market Based Management*, 3rd edn, Upper Saddle River, NJ, Prentice Hall, 2004, Chapter 3.
3. For further discussion see Gary L. Lilien, Philip Kotler and K. Sridhar Moorthy, *Marketing Models*, Englewood Cliffs, NJ, Prentice Hall, 1992; Peter S. H. Leeflang, Dick Wittink, Michel Wedel and Philippe Naert, *Building Models for Marketing Decisions*, Boston, Kluwer Academic, 2000.
4. Peter Roberts, 'Small Cars Ride High as Sales Hit Record', *The Australian Financial Review*, 6 January 2006, p. 4.
5. Ibid.
6. See Russell L. Ackoff, *A Concept of Corporate Planning*, New York, Wiley Interscience, 1970, pp. 36–37.
7. For more on forecasting total market demand see F. William Barnett, 'Four Steps to Forecasting Total Market Demand', *Harvard Business Review*, July–August 1988, pp. 28–34; and 'Forecasting the Potential for New Industrial Products', *Industrial Marketing Management*, no. 4, 1989, pp. 307–312.
8. For more on using this survey see 'A User's Guide to the Survey of Buying Power', *Sales & Marketing Management*, 30 August 1993, pp. A4–A19.
9. D. J. Dalrymple, 'Sales Forecasting: Methods and Accuracy', *Business Horizons*, vol. 18, 1975, pp. 69–73.
10. For a review of the evidence on different forecasting methods, see J. Scott Armstrong and Kesten C. Green, 'Demand Forecasting: Evidence-based Methods', in Luiz Moutinho and Geoff Southern (eds), *Strategic Marketing Management: A Business Process Approach* (also available as Monash University Working Paper 25–05), forthcoming.
11. For a listing and analysis of these and other forecasting techniques see David M. Georgoff and Robert G. Murdick, 'Manager's Guide to Forecasting', *Harvard Business Review*, January–February 1986, pp. 110–120; and Donald S. Tull and Del I. Hawkins, *Marketing Research: Measurement and Method*, 6th edn, New York, Macmillan, 1990, Chapter 21.
12. M. R. Arkes, 'Overconfidence in Judgmental Forecasting', in J. S. Armstrong (ed.), *Principles of Forecasting*, Norwell, MA, Kluwer Academic Publishers, 2001, pp. 495–515.
13. J. Scott Armstrong and Kesten C. Green, 'Demand Forecasting: Evidence-based Methods', in Luiz Moutinho and Geoff Southern (eds), *Strategic Marketing Management: A Business Process Approach* (also available as Monash University Working Paper 25–05), forthcoming.
14. V. Morwitz, 'Methods for Forecasting from Intentions Data', in J. S. Armstrong (ed.), *Principles of Forecasting*, Norwell, MA, Kluwer Academic Publishers, 2001, pp. 33–56. See also J. Scott Armstrong and Kesten C. Green, 'Demand Forecasting: Evidence-based Methods', in Luiz Moutinho and Geoff Southern (eds), *Strategic Marketing Management: A Business Process Approach* (Monash University Working Paper 25–05), forthcoming.
15. For more on the salesforce composite method see Tull and Hawkins, *Marketing Research: Measurement and Method*, pp. 705–706.
16. See Norman Dalkey and Olaf Helmer, 'An Experimental Application of the Delphi Method to the Use of Experts', *Management Science*, April 1963, pp. 458–467; see also Roger J. Best, 'An Experiment in Delphi Estimation in Marketing Decision Making', *Journal of Marketing Research*, November 1974, pp. 447–452. Software for using the Delphi model is available at <www.forecastingprinciples.com>, accessed January 2006.

17. R. Rowe and G. Wright, 'Expert Opinions in Forecasting Role of the Delphi Technique', in J. S. Armstrong (ed.), *Principles of Forecasting*, Norwell, MA, Kluwer Academic Publishers, 2001, pp. 125–144.

18. See 'Sometimes Expert Opinion Isn't All It Should Be', *Go*, September–October 1985, p. 2.

19. See Tull and Hawkins, *Marketing Research: Measurement and Method*, pp. 686–691; and Alvin C. Burns and Ronald F. Bush, *Marketing Research*, 2nd edn, Upper Saddle River, NJ, Prentice Hall, 1998, pp. 586–596.

20. See 'The Du Pont Company', in Harper W. Boyd Jr, Ralph Westfall and Stanley Stasch (eds), *Marketing Research: Text and Cases*, 3rd edn, Homewood, IL, Irwin, 1977, pp. 498–500.

21. For detail on some of the complex statistical techniques and how they are applied in marketing see G. L. Lilien and A. Rangaswamy, *Marketing Engineering*, Upper Saddle River, NJ, Prentice Hall, 2003; and G. L. Lilien, P. Kotler and K. S. Moorthy, *Marketing Models*, Englewood Cliffs, NJ, Prentice Hall, 1992.

PHOTO/AD CREDITS

Chris Baumann, Macquarie University

CASE STUDY

Super Economy Class: the business travellers' class of the future?

Introduction

The airline industry is dynamic and competitive. Over the past few decades major brands have disappeared, for example Pan American and Eastern in the USA, Ansett in Australia and Swissair in Europe, while new ones have only recently emerged. New entrants are predominantly low or no frills airlines, such as EasyJet and Ryanair in Europe, AirAsia in Southeast Asia, and Jetstar in Australia, which offer discount travel.

The airline industry has always been exposed to global economic conditions and is seen as a business subject to a range of unique international and domestic risk factors. President Reagan's deregulation of the US airline industry in the 1980s resulted in a more competitive industry, making the entry of new carriers easier, and also resulted in a challenge to the cost structure of the established brands. In the last decade, the global airline industry faced rising oil prices, a world economy in recession, terrorist attacks and other major crises such as SARS that impacted negatively on the airline business. The industry itself has also undergone major changes in its distribution systems, generating larger proportions of sales on the Internet and by direct phone bookings. Consequently, it has become very easy for customers to compare fares between carriers, while previously they had relied largely on information from travel agents. In particular, the leisure segment such as tourist and student travel has taken advantage of these new means and increased their bookings using e-tools. This customer segment has always been fairly price sensitive, but it was only in the 1980s and 1990s, when the corporate world focused more strongly on cost cutting, that 'price' also became a major issue for corporate travellers. Corporate travel policies have changed, forcing many top executives to switch from First to Business Class travel, and more and more mid-level managers have had to become familiar with Economy Class flying. Airlines are trying to maintain the loyalty of frequent flyers and have introduced sophisticated membership programs that offer 'perks' such as miles collection, upgrades and airport pre-departure lounge access.

Super Economy—a new product

As a reaction to a market situation where fewer travellers fly First and Business Class, some airlines have abolished First Class altogether (for example, Air Canada only offers Executive First Class, which is a type of Business Class) or have introduced a mid-range product between Business and Economy Class—the Super Economy Class. British Airways (BA) calls it 'World Traveller Plus', Scandinavian Airlines (SAS) labels it 'Economy Extra', and United Airlines (UA) names it 'Economy Plus'. The common characteristic of this relatively new concept is that the prices are substantially lower than for Business Class tickets, yet it offers more space than Economy

In the Australian domestic market, Virgin Blue is a strong competitor of Qantas and its affiliated airlines.

Class. For example, there is extra legroom, seats are wider and there is more seat recline. The meal and beverage service, however, is the same or very similar to that served in Economy Class.

Not all airlines believe in this relatively new concept of introducing a Super Economy Class. In the USA, for example, American Airlines (AA) terminated its Super Economy Class in 2005 (launched only in 2000), replacing these seats with regular Economy Class and generating $US100 million in extra revenue each year. On the other hand, United Airlines upgraded its First Class, and is now the only major US carrier to offer the Super Economy concept throughout its fleet. United Airlines expects an additional $US50 million in revenue from selling its Economy Plus service, and believes that offering this product adds to its brand image. Thus, United is pursuing a very different marketing strategy to AA and other major US competitors which are currently cost cutting and reducing services.

Australian domestic airline market

The Australian air travel market is smaller than the American market, with fewer key players sharing the pie such as Qantas, Jetstar Airways and Virgin Blue Airlines. Qantas had a market share of 80% of the domestic and 36% of the Australia inbound and outbound market in 2004. However, market shares have been shifting since Qantas itself launched its low-cost subsidiaries Australian Airlines in 2002 and Jetstar Airways in May 2004. Virgin Blue, a member of Sir Richard Branson's Virgin Group, started offering its services in Australia in 2000, and reported that it had achieved a 30% market share of all Australian domestic traffic in 2003. Virgin Blue has thus become a strong competitor of Qantas and its affiliated airlines. Virgin Blue operates their planes on a one-class-only basis but offers a 'Blue Zone', where passengers enjoy some extended leg room for a small fee. Qantas offers

Business and Economy Class on most domestic flights while Jetstar has only Economy Class, but plans to introduce an 'Enhanced Economy' product 'StarClass' on international flights but not on domestic flights.

In late 2005, a new airline, OzJet, was established that offered Business Class-only flights between Sydney and Melbourne. At the time, OzJet also intended to include Adelaide, Brisbane and Canberra in 2006. However, the venture was not successful and OzJet had to suspend their flights between Melbourne and Sydney in March 2006. The airline now offers charter flights only and has reduced its workforce.

No airline in Australia has so far (in 2006) introduced a Super Economy Class for domestic services, although there may be a market segment of cost-conscious business travellers who could be interested in such a product. Qantas is known to offer a high-priced Business Class with few discount options, while Jetstar and Virgin Blue do not have a Business Class at all. Wealthy domestic and international travellers touring Australia as well as senior citizens could potentially be interested in a mid-range product that offers a few perks, but is more affordable than the traditional Business Class offered by Qantas.

Your task for this case study is to further investigate the Super Economy Class concept in relation to the Australian airline industry for its domestic market. The questions below offer aspects that need to be considered when conducting the market analysis and developing suggestions.

Sources: Susan Carey, 'United Charts Odd Course: Luxury', *The Wall Street Journal Asia*, vol. xxx, no. 95, 2006, pp. 14–15; United Airlines, <www.united.com/page/article/0,6722,1314,00.html?navSource= AwardsBar&linkTitle=Award04_Economy_Plus&pos=2>, accessed 23 February 2006; Datamonitor, Company Profile on Qantas Airways, Reference Code 13069, July 2004; Virgin Blue, Media Release, 17 December 2003; OzJet, <http://www.ozjet.com.au/flight/#1>, accessed 23 February 2006; OzJet, <http://www.ozjet.com.au/index.htm>, accessed 15 March 2006.

QUESTIONS

1. Investigate the websites of airlines offering a Super Economy Class (e.g. British Airways, United Airlines and Scandinavian Airlines) and summarise the key features of the Super Economy Class. On which type of routes is this product offered?

2. Outline the market segments that could be targeted for a Super Economy Class product on Australian routes, and provide evidence for your arguments based on research into the Australian air travel market.

3. On the basis of your analysis of the market segments, suggest what information could be collected to estimate the potential market size.

4. For Australian airlines such as Qantas, Jetstar Airways and Virgin Blue Airlines, discuss whether offering a Super Economy Class could be a profitable strategy for their domestic market. (Note that Jetstar plans to introduce an enhanced economy class 'StarClass' on international flights but not on domestic flights.)

5. Outline how the airlines discussed in Question 4 could test a Super Economy Class product prior to introduction to the market. For example, on which routes would test marketing ideally be conducted, and why?

6. What type of competitive response would you expect if one of the major Australian airlines were to introduce a Super Economy Class product in the domestic market?

CHAPTER 10

Market segmentation, targeting and positioning

Orca: www.orca.co.nz

Softride: www.softride.com

Xterra: www.xterraplanet.com/

Ironman Triathlon:

www.ironmanlive.com/

Have you ever wondered whether an additional 1 mm of wetsuit thickness will improve your ocean swimming by two minutes over 1500 metres or whether a 250 gram weight saving would save you five minutes on a bike ride, or perhaps whether a new endurance formula will help you sustain your running effort by an extra half an hour? Welcome to the world of the competitive 'age group' triathlete. Many of us have swum at the beach, gone for a ride at the local park or a run on the treadmill at the gym—but what about completing all three activities back to back? The triathlon is a relatively new sport, originating in the late 1970s with the introduction of the Hawaiian Ironman. Since 2000, it has become one of the fastest growing sports for men and women across the globe and across many age groups. The sport has evolved over time to become a subsegment of the three major sports it involves—swimming, cycling and running. For many years it was too small a market for the traditional major sport manufacturers to entertain seriously as a separate business. But in the last 10 years many of these suppliers of sports apparel and equipment have been forced to look at the specific needs of triathletes as new specialist companies with a focus on this segment have started to encroach on their business.

The growth in the triathlon segment has seen the development of triathlon-specific wetsuits, designed with extra rubber and flexibility around the shoulders for flotation and ease of stroke. Companies such as Orca and Ironman Wetsuits (now Blue Seventy) were the pioneers and more recently have been joined by traditional wetsuit manufacturers like O'Neill (from surfing origins). Bikes are now made specifically for triathlon competitors, and are designed to be lighter and more aerodynamic to cut through the wind resistance which slows down triathletes on the bike portion of the race. Triathlon-specific running shoes are light and easy to put on, and are made with elastic laces. For triathletes they assist the speed required through their transition from the bike to the final running leg.

Understanding the unique needs of this segment has been critical to the success of manufacturers targeting this market. Larger manufacturers that have ignored these needs are now playing catch-up in a market that is growing faster than any other subsegment. In particular, women are underpinning this growth. In the USA, overall membership has grown from less than 16 000 members in 1993 to more than 40 000 in 2002. Whereas women made up only 9% of the membership in 1990, in 2005 they comprised 29%. The attractiveness of this segment is no surprise when you consider that 57% of triathletes in the USA have an annual income of more than $70 000. The statistics in Australia follow a similar pattern. Triathletes are generally goal-oriented individuals who want to challenge themselves and enjoy the 'rush' that comes from competing in a physically challenging sport.

Astute companies have targeted the triathlete market with specifically designed performance clothing.

One company in particular that has successfully targeted the triathlon market for many years is Orca. Scott Unsworth was competing in triathlons at an elite level during the late 1980s and realised there was no performance clothing designed specifically for triathletes. After an injury forced Unsworth out of competition he started work on a speed suit that would provide an advantage to triathletes in the swimming leg of the triathlon. When his first design turned out to be faster than anything else available on the market, Orca was born. Orca is now a leading maker of triathlon-specific wetsuits and athletic wear. Unsworth understood the triathlon market early on and understood that triathletes would pay a premium for any products that would provide them with a competitive edge. Orca's understanding of the triathlon segment has allowed it to ride the growth of the sport for the past 15 years.

In emerging markets like the triathlon, an analysis of segments, identification of targets and focused market positioning are the basis for development of a range of triathlete-targeted solutions. These solutions have emerged not just in triathlon-specific equipment but in triathlon-specific travel agencies, women-triathlon-specific events and even variations on the triathlon event theme such the Xterra Series (off-road triathlons).[1]

Visit the websites of some of the companies targeting this market to see what they are offering and how they are segmenting their markets.

After reading this chapter you should be able to:

1. Explain market segmentation, and identify several possible bases for segmenting consumer markets and international markets.

2. Distinguish between the requirements for effective segmentation: measurability, accessibility, substantiality, actionability.

3. Outline the process of evaluating market segments and suggest some methods for selecting market segments.

4. Illustrate the concept of positioning for competitive advantage by offering specific examples.

5. Discuss choosing and implementing a positioning strategy, and contrast positioning based on product, service, personnel and image differentiation.

The triathlon industry gives us clear examples of how markets can be segmented and targeted by firms in order to meet the needs of different customer groups or segments more effectively—the subject of this chapter.

Markets

Organisations that sell to consumer and business markets recognise that they cannot appeal to all buyers in those markets, or at least not to all buyers in the same way. Buyers are too numerous, too widely scattered and too varied in their needs and buying practices. And different companies vary widely in their abilities to serve different segments of the market. Rather than trying to compete in an entire market, sometimes against superior competitors, each company must identify the parts of the market that it can serve best.

Sellers have not always practised this philosophy. Marketing has passed through three stages:

1 *Mass marketing.* In mass marketing, the seller mass produces, mass distributes and mass promotes one product to all buyers. At one time, Sony produced only one type of television set for the whole market, hoping it would appeal to everyone. The argument for mass marketing is that it should lead to the lowest costs and prices and create the largest potential market.

2 *Product-variety marketing.* Here, the seller produces two or more products that have different features, styles, quality, sizes and so on. Later, Sony produced several television sets with different screen sizes and outside frame (casing) colours. They were designed to offer variety to buyers rather than to appeal to different market segments. The argument for product-variety marketing is that consumers have different needs that change over time. Consumers seek variety and change.

3 *Target marketing.* Here, the seller identifies market segments, selects one or more of them, and develops products and marketing mixes tailored to each. For example, Sony now produces television sets for the home entertainment segment (rear projection TVs), the fashion segment (plasma screens), the convenience segment (small TVs as a second set in the home) and the technology enthusiasts (digital TVs).

Micromarketing
A form of target marketing in which companies tailor their marketing programs to the needs and wants of narrowly defined geographic, demographic, psychographic or behaviour, or benefit, segments.

Today's companies are moving away from mass marketing and product-variety marketing and toward target marketing. Target marketing can help sellers to find their marketing opportunities more efficiently. Sellers can develop the right product for each target market and adjust their prices, distribution channels and advertising to reach the target market efficiently. Instead of scattering their marketing efforts (the 'shotgun' approach), they can focus on the buyers who have greater purchase interest (the 'rifle' approach).

As a result of the increasing fragmentation of Australian mass markets into hundreds of micro-markets, each with different needs and lifestyles, target marketing is increasingly taking the form of micromarketing. Using **micromarketing**, companies tailor their marketing programs to the needs and wants of narrowly defined geographic, demographic, psychographic or behaviour, or benefit, segments. The ultimate form of target marketing is *customised marketing* in which the company adapts its product and marketing program to the needs of a specific customer or buying organisation.

Market segmentation
Dividing a market into direct groups of buyers who might require separate products or marketing mixes; the process of classifying customers into groups with different needs, characteristics or behaviour.

Figure 10.1 shows the three major steps in target marketing. The first is **market segmentation**—dividing a market into distinct groups of buyers with different needs, characteristics or behaviour who might require separate products or marketing mixes. The company identifies different ways to segment the market and develops profiles of the resulting market segments. The second step is

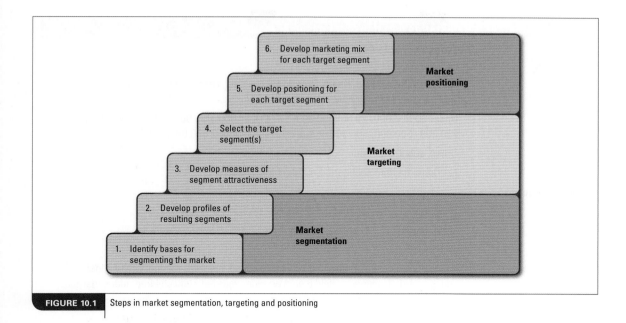

FIGURE 10.1 | Steps in market segmentation, targeting and positioning

market targeting—evaluating each market segment's attractiveness and selecting one or more of the market segments to enter. The third step is **market positioning**—setting the competitive positioning for the product and creating a detailed marketing mix.

Market segmentation

Markets consist of buyers, and buyers differ in one or more ways. They may differ in their wants, resources, locations, buying attitudes and buying practices. Because buyers have unique needs and wants, each buyer is potentially a separate market. Ideally, then, a seller might design a separate marketing program for each buyer. For example, Boeing and its closest rival, Airbus Industries, manufacture aeroplanes for only a few buyers and customise their products and marketing programs to satisfy each specific customer.

However, most sellers face larger numbers of smaller buyers and do not find complete segmentation worthwhile. Instead, they look for broad *classes* of buyers who differ in their product needs or buying responses. For example, Toyota has found that high- and low-income groups differ in their car-buying needs and wants. It also knows that young consumers' needs and wants differ from those of older consumers. So, Toyota has designed specific models for different income, age and lifestyle groups. In fact, it sells models for segments with varied *combinations* of age and income. For instance, Toyota designed its brand Avalon for older customers, its Lexus for higher-income consumers and its Corolla for younger, lower-income consumers. Age and income are only two of many bases that companies use for segmenting their markets.

Bases for segmenting consumer markets

There is no single way to segment a market. A marketer has to try different segmentation variables, alone and in combination, to find the best way to view the market structure. Table 10.1 (overleaf) outlines the major variables that might be used in segmenting consumer markets. Here we look at the major *geographic, demographic, psychographic* and *behavioural variables*. Then we consider a different form of segmentation being used for Internet address (domain location) registration.[2]

Market targeting
Evaluating each market segment's attractiveness and selecting one or more segments to enter.

Market positioning
Arranging for a product to occupy a clear, distinctive and desirable place relative to competing products in the minds of target consumers; formulating competitive positioning for a product and creating a detailed marketing mix.

TABLE 10.1 Market segmentation variables for consumer markets

Variable	Typical breakdowns
Geographic	
Region	Far North Queensland, South-Eastern Queensland, Far North Coast of NSW, NSW Tablelands, Western NSW, Lakes District—Victoria
City size	Under 5000; 5000–20 000; 20 000–50 000; 50 000–100 000; 100 000–250 000; 250 000–500 000; 500 000–1 000 000; 1 000 000–2 000 000; 2 000 000 or over
Density	Urban, suburban, rural
Climate	Northern, Eastern seaboard, Southern and Western
Demographic	
Age	Under 6, 7–11, 12–19, 20–34, 35–49, 50–64, 65+
Sex	Male, female
Family size	1–2, 3–4, 5+
Family life cycle	Young, single; young, married, no children; young, married, youngest child under 6; young, married, youngest child 6 or over; older, married, with children; older, married, no children under 18; older, single; other
Income	Under $10 000; $10 000–$15 000; $15 000–$20 000, $20 000–$30 000; $30 000–$50 000; $50 000 and over
Occupation	Professional and technical; managers, officials and proprietors; clerical, sales; craftspeople, supervisors; operatives; farmers; retired; students; homemakers; unemployed
Education	Primary school or less; some high school; high school graduate, some TAFE college; TAFE college graduate; some university; university graduate
Religion	Catholic, Protestant, Orthodox, Jewish, Muslim, other
Nationality	Australian, British, New Zealander, American, Chinese, French, German, Scandinavian, Italian, Greek, Middle Eastern, Japanese, Taiwanese, Vietnamese, South African
Psychographic	
Socioeconomic	Quintiles: AB, C, D, E, FG
Status	Where education, income and occupation levels are used in combination to indicate status
Values, attitudes and lifestyle groupings	Visible Achievement, Something Better, Young Optimists, Socially Aware, Look at Me, A Fairer Deal, Basic Needs, Real Conservatism, Traditional Family Life and Conventional Family Life
Personality	Compulsive, gregarious, authoritarian, ambitious
Behavioural	
Purchase occasion	Regular occasion, special occasion
Benefits sought	Quality, service, economy
User status	Non-user, ex-user, potential user, first-time user, regular user
Usage rate	Light user, medium user, heavy user
Loyalty status	None, medium, strong, absolute
Buyer-readiness stage	Unaware, aware, informed, interested, desirous, intending to buy
Attitude towards product	Enthusiastic, positive, indifferent, negative, hostile

Geographic segmentation

Geographic segmentation calls for dividing the market into different geographical units such as nations, regions, states, municipalities, cities or neighbourhoods. A company may decide to operate in one or a few geographical areas, or to operate in all areas but pay attention to geographical differences in needs and wants.

Incitec, the Australian fertiliser arm of Orica, practises geographic segmentation for its range of crop-protection products by emphasising the right products in the right geographic areas at the right times. To extend its share of the farm-crop-protection market into other states it became proactive in predicting where and when different protection methods and systems were required.

Many companies today are 'regionalising' their marketing programs—localising their products, advertising, promotion and sales efforts to fit the needs of individual regions, cities and even suburbs.

However, some companies are changing the nature of geographic segmentation by using the Internet to widen their markets. For example, Hewlett-Packard has found that it is necessary to have country-specific websites such as <hewlettpackard.com.fr> to satisfy its French online buyers in terms of country-specific computer packages, pricing, features, delivery and service.

Geographic segmentation Dividing a market into different geographical units such as nations, regions, states, municipalities, cities or neighbourhoods.

Demographic segmentation

Demographic segmentation consists of dividing the market into groups based on variables such as age, gender, family size, family life cycle, income, occupation, education, religion, race and nationality. Demographic factors are the most popular bases for segmenting customer groups. One reason is that consumer needs, wants and usage rates often vary closely with demographic variables. Another is that demographic variables are easier to measure than most other types of variables. Even when market segments are first defined using other bases, such as personality or behaviour, their demographic characteristics must be known in order to assess the size of the target market and to reach it efficiently.

Demographic segmentation Dividing the market into groups based on demographic variables such as age, sex, family size, family life cycle, income, occupation, education, religion and nationality.

Age and life-cycle stage Consumer needs and wants change with age. Some companies use **age and life-cycle segmentation**, offering different products or using different marketing approaches for different age and life-cycle groups. Many companies now use different products and appeals to target teens, generation Xers (twenty-somethings), baby boomers or mature consumers. For example, IKEA stores sometimes target their self-assembly furniture at the 30–45-year-old inner city dwellers, using contemporary advertising cues—single man invites single woman for dinner but needs quickly to buy a dining table. IKEA stores come to the rescue. In contrast, Nick Scali, a Sydney-based Italian furniture retailer, aims its offer at older and more affluent buyers, using elegance, classical music and the pitch of furniture with style and Italian heritage to which a 'successful' person should aspire. McDonald's targets children,

Age and life-cycle segmentation Dividing a market into different age and life-cycle groups.

IKEA blends in with modern living.

Norganic addresses the health crunch.

teens, adults and seniors with different ads and media. Its ads to teens feature dance-beat music, adventure and fast-paced cutting from scene to scene; ads to seniors are softer and more sentimental.

However, marketers must be careful to guard against stereotypes when using age and life-cycle segmentation. Although you might find some 70 year olds in wheelchairs, you will find others on tennis courts. Similarly, while some 40-year-old couples are sending their children off to college, others are just beginning new families. Thus, age is often a poor predictor of a person's life-cycle stage, health, work or family status, needs and buying power.

Gender segmentation

Dividing a market into different groups based on sex.

Gender **Gender segmentation** has long been used in clothing, cosmetics and magazines. Recently, other marketers have noticed opportunities for gender segmentation. For example, most financial services are used by men and women alike. However, firms such as National Australia Bank have discovered the young, single female market. The National has advertised its credit card services in magazines such as *Cosmopolitan*. These ads are clearly designed for women and the bank is promoting heavily to convert this market to depositors. The Toyota website, 'Toyota Avenue', was designed specifically for women drivers.[3] Toyota Australia also launched Safe & Savvy—a program to provide women with vehicle maintenance knowledge that will foster confidence and heighten safety on the roads. Toyota created the Safe & Savvy series of car know-how nights to help provide basic automotive information to a primarily female audience. Safe & Savvy is an extension of Toyota Avenue, a program designed to provide women with automotive advice. Also, in the 'ready-to-drink' market Smirnoff is positioning Smirnoff Ice as an alternative to beer for young women.

The car industry also uses gender segmentation extensively. Women have different frames, less upperbody strength and greater safety concerns. To address these issues, car makers are designing cars with hoods and boots that are easier to open, seats that are easier to adjust and seat belts that fit women better. They've also increased their safety focus, emphasising features such as air bags and remote door locking.

In another example of gender segmentation, GM-H pitched the Holden Barina—a rebadged Suzuki Swift—at young women, as did Mazda with its 'jellybean'-shaped Mazda 121.

Norganic Foods Australia has specialised in providing natural and organic ingredients in their breakfast cereals and snacks. Since its inception its target has always been the health conscious consumer segment.[4]

In advertising, more and more car manufacturers are targeting women directly. In contrast to the car advertising of past decades, ads today portray women as competent and knowledgeable consumers who are interested in what a car is all about, not just the colour.

Income segmentation

Dividing a market into different income groups.

Income **Income segmentation** has long been used by the marketers of such products and services as cars, boats, clothing, cosmetics and travel. Many companies target affluent consumers with luxury goods and convenience services. Stores such as Tiffany's and Louis Vuitton in Sydney offer expensive perfumes, jewellery, bags and fine fashion to affluent consumers.

But not all companies using income segmentation target the affluent. Many companies, such as Bi-Lo and Best for Less supermarkets, profitably target low-income consumers. Income alone, however, does not always predict the customers for a given product. You might think that blue-collar workers would continue to rent videos while executives would subscribe to Pay-TV. Yet the opposite has occurred. Blue-collar workers were among the first purchasers of colour television sets; it was cheaper for them to buy a set than to go out to the movies or restaurants. Bargain shops like 'Crazy Prices' in Sydney do not only attract low-income earners, just as buyers of brand-name goods are not always affluent.[5]

Multivariate demographic segmentation Most companies will segment a market by combining two or more demographic variables. Consider the market for toilet soaps. The top-selling soap brands are used by many different kinds of consumers, but two demographic variables—gender and age—coupled with geographic region are the most useful in distinguishing the users of one brand from those of another.

Men and women differ in their soap preferences. Top men's brands include Palmolive, Imperial Leather and Safeguard—these brands account for over 30% of the total men's soap market. Women, in contrast, prefer Lux, Imperial Leather and Dove, which account for 23% of the total women's soap market. The leading soaps also appeal differently to different age segments, and preferences differ by region. Thus, no single demographic variable captures all the different needs and preferences of toilet soap buyers. To define important market segments more precisely, soap marketers must use *multivariate demographic segmentation.*

Psychographic segmentation

In **psychographic segmentation** buyers are divided into different groups based on socioeconomic status, lifestyle or personality characteristics. People in the same geodemographic group can have very different psychographic profiles.

Psychographic segmentation
Dividing a market into different groups based on social class, lifestyle or personality characteristics.

Socioeconomic status We described the socioeconomic classes in detail in Chapter 7. Socioeconomic status has a strong effect on preferences in cars, clothing, home furnishings, leisure activities, reading habits and store choice. Many companies design products or services for specific socioeconomic classes.

Lifestyle We also described lifestyle in more detail in Chapter 7. People's interest in many goods is affected by their lifestyle and many goods they buy are expressions of their lifestyle. Marketers are increasingly segmenting their markets by consumer lifestyles. Products such as frozen dinners are targeted to singles with the theme 'Are you looking after yourself?' hoping to reflect a healthy lifestyle of which parents and friends would approve. Boston Market, a McDonald's-owned chain, positions its offer so that you 'never want to cook at home again'. The advertising portrays families *and* a couple enjoying the food at Boston Market. This chain is designed to appeal to consumers in the lifestyle segment who do not have time to cook themselves a wholesome, roast dinner anymore, but want good quality, affordable home-style meals.[6]

Personality Marketers have also used personality variables to segment markets, giving their products personalities that correspond to consumer personalities. Successful market segmentation strategies based on personality have been used for products like cosmetics, cigarettes, insurance, liquor and online share trades. For instance, e*trade targets individuals, especially educated women, who want to be in control and are confident in making their own financial decisions.[7]

Behavioural segmentation

Behavioural segmentation
Dividing a market into groups based on consumers' knowledge of, attitude towards, uses for and responses to a product.

Behavioural segmentation divides buyers into groups based on their knowledge of the product, their attitude towards it, the way they use it and their responses to it. Many marketers believe that behaviour variables are the best starting point for building market segments.

Occasion segmentation
Dividing the market into groups according to occasions when buyers get the idea, make a purchase or use a product.

Purchase occasions Buyers can be grouped according to the occasions when they get the idea to buy, actually make the purchase or use the purchased item. **Occasion segmentation** can help firms build up product usage. For example, milk is most often consumed at breakfast, but milk producers have promoted milk as a healthy and refreshing drink at other times of the day. The *Yellow Pages* advertising campaign in its Australian market attempts to increase its usage by promoting Yellow Pages Emergency—where *can* you get *pizza* delivered at 7 am on a Sunday morning? Some special days, such as Mother's Day, Valentine's Day and Secretary's Day, were originally promoted partly to increase the sale of chocolates, flowers, cards and other gifts. Turkey growers would like Christmas to occur more often, and greeting-card marketers have come up with cards for almost every human event and condition as a means of increasing sales. Marketing Highlight 10.1 describes how Apple created a new mass market for digital music and then followed a segment-based strategy to grow the market and retain its dominance.

Kodak and Fuji use occasion segmentation in designing and marketing single-use cameras. The customer simply snaps off the roll of pictures and returns the film, camera and all, to be processed. By mixing lenses, film speeds and accessories, Kodak and Fuji have developed special versions of the camera for almost any picture-taking occasion, from underwater photography to baby pictures.

Benefit segmentation
Dividing the market into groups according to the different benefits that consumers seek from the product.

Benefits sought A powerful form of segmentation is to group buyers according to the different *benefits* they seek from the product. **Benefit segmentation** requires finding out the major benefits that people look for in the product class, the kinds of people who look for each benefit and the major brands that deliver each benefit. One of the best examples of benefit segmentation was conducted in the toothpaste market. There were four main benefit segments: economic, protective, cosmetic and taste benefits. Each benefit group had special demographic, behavioural and psychographic characteristics. For example, decay-prevention seekers tended to have large families, were heavy toothpaste users and were conservative.

Each segment also favoured certain brands. Most current brands appeal to one of these segments: Tartar Control Colgate Fluorigard toothpaste stresses protection and appeals to the family segment; Colgate Herbal White is directed at those who want no artificial ingredients; Rexona's Close-up appeals to the segment of consumers wanting breath freshness (the cosmetic segment); Colgate's Whitening is aimed at those wanting white teeth, as is Macleans. Colgate Total is aimed at the individuals wanting complete 12-hour teeth protection.

Thus, companies can use benefit segmentation to clarify the segment to which they are appealing, its characteristics and the major competitive brands. They can also search for new benefits and launch brands that deliver them.[8]

Great whites. treatment

Colgate Fluoriguard has strengthened more teeth and helped prevent more cavities than any other toothpaste in Australia. Only your dentist can give you a better fluoride **treatment**.

Colgate

Benefit segmentation: Colgate's Fluoriguard is designed to appeal to families.

User status Many markets can be segmented into non-users, ex-users, potential users, first-time users and regular users of a product. High-market-share companies are particularly interested in attracting potential users, whereas smaller firms will try to attract regular users. Potential users and regular users may require different kinds of marketing appeals. For example, active job seekers would frequently use placement services such as TMP or Drake Personnel when looking for frequent updated information on jobs of interest. Currently employed prospective candidates would need to be contacted and their interest raised through selling activities by the placement agency.[9]

Usage rate Markets can also be segmented into light-, medium- and heavy-user groups. Heavy users are often a small percentage of the market but account for a high percentage of total buying. Swimming represents such a market. Swimsuit manufacturers such as Speedo have in their product range swimsuits that can improve swimmers' performance/speed by up to 20%. Speedo's brand, Fastskins, has been developed for elite competition swimmers and is targeted towards all swimmers who want—and can afford—a high-performance swimsuit. These swimmers train and compete constantly and form the heavy-user group in the swimming market. If the heavy-user group accounts for 87% of Speedo's Fastskins purchased, almost seven times as much as the light-user group, it is easy to see why Speedo would prefer to attract one heavy user to its brand than several light users. Thus, most swimsuit companies target the heavy users, using appeals such as Speedo's 'Are you swimming your best?'.

Loyalty status A market can also be segmented by consumer loyalty. Consumers can be loyal to brands (Coca-Cola), products (iPod), stores (Target) and companies (Apple). Buyers can be divided into groups according to their degree of loyalty. Some consumers are completely loyal—they buy one brand all the time. Others are somewhat loyal—they are loyal to two or three brands of a given product or favour one brand while sometimes buying others. Still other buyers show no loyalty to any brand. They either want something different each time they buy or always buy a brand on special.

Each market is made up of different numbers of each type of buyer. A brand-loyal market is one with a high percentage of buyers showing strong brand loyalty. The toothpaste market and the beer market seem to be fairly high brand-loyal markets. Companies selling in a brand-loyal market have a hard time gaining more market share, and companies trying to enter such a market have a hard time getting in.

A company can learn a lot by analysing loyalty patterns in its market. It should start by studying its own loyal customers. Colgate finds that its loyal buyers are more middle class, have larger families and are more health conscious. These characteristics pinpoint the target market for Colgate. By studying its less loyal buyers, the company can detect which brands are most competitive with its own. If many Colgate Total buyers also buy GlaxoSmithKline's Macleans, Colgate can attempt to improve its positioning against Macleans. By looking at customers who are shifting away from its brand, the company can learn about its marketing weaknesses. As for non-loyal people, the company may attract them by putting its brand on special.

Companies must be careful when using brand loyalty in their segmentation strategies. What appear to be brand-loyal purchase patterns might reflect little more than *habit, indifference, a low price* or *unavailability* of other brands. Thus, frequent or regular purchasing may not be the same as brand loyalty—marketers must examine the motivations behind observed purchase patterns.

Buyer-readiness stage At any time, people are in different stages of readiness to buy a product. Some people are unaware of the product; some are aware; some are informed; some are interested; some want the product; and some intend to buy. The relative numbers make a big difference in designing the marketing program. For example, Deakin University is offering self-paced degree courses via personal computer. Students can log onto the university's mid-range computer through their personal computers at any time and from any location to complete their lessons or 'talk' to their instructors

MARKETING HIGHLIGHT

10.1

The iPod odyssey—has digital music finally landed?

Apple launched its first foray into the digital music market in 2001 with the introduction of the first-generation Apple iPod. Until that point Apple had been a niche-focused computer company with a very loyal base of customers so passionate about Apple that many refused ever to entertain any other computer hardware regardless of any advantages it may have over Apple.

When Apple first launched its breakthrough product the market was idling along with a number of low-profile manufacturers (mainly from the computer memory industry), such as Rio, Sandisk and Creative Technology, focused on comparatively low-capacity (in terms of digital music storage) 'flash' devices. Apple's strategy was to develop a portable, stylish, easy to use, high-capacity music player which would lead a company revival by breaking into the mainstream market. The result was a 'killer' product for all people wanting to take advantage of the benefits of digital music. The offer was a single product targeted at the mass market for digital music, a single segment strategy so to speak.

With a creative advertising campaign designed to stand out and rapidly promote brand and product awareness, Apple quickly dominated the

market and has continued to grow exponentially ever since. According to the NDP Group, Apple held 74% market share for digital music devices as of July 2005. The first three quarters of 2006 showed sales of more than 30 million units. Amazingly, this topped the company's lifetime iPod sales to mid-2005 of 27 million units! The additional growth is expected to be driven by Apple's increasingly segment-driven approach. Since the release of the original iPod, Apple has developed a number of variations of the product designed to target evolving segments of the market. First, a segment emerged that wanted a more portable digital music player. These customers liked the high capacity but wanted something smaller and easier to carry while travelling on a train or bus or perhaps flying from one destination to another. Apple's answer was the iPod Mini, a smaller version of the original with only a minor trade-off in capacity. Following this launch, Apple received feedback from another segment of potential customers who wanted more from their device. Music was one thing but what about digital photos and a calendar so the iPod could be more central to their day-to-day activities and they would no longer need multiple devices? As a result Apple

Apple iPod—more than digital music.

introduced the Photo iPod with a larger capacity and a colour screen that could be used to show photos as well as play music and keep appointments, provide a 'to do' list and other features. At the same time an emerging segment of consumers wanting a simple ultraportable music device that could be used when exercising and on the move was developing. Apple released the iPod Shuffle in early 2005 to target this group with a small, sleek, easy to use plug and play music player without a screen to keep the user experience simple. As consumers continued to demand smaller devices that were more feature rich and increasing numbers of vendors began entering the market, Apple announced another new model. In September 2005, the iPod Nano, a pencil-thin version of the popular iPod Mini, was released. Apple's vice-president commented 'we shipped more of the Nanos than any product in memory'. It would be oversimplifying Apple's strategy to focus on the devices alone. Although Apple's devices are undoubted 'killer' products, it has been Apple's focus on the customer's overall digital music experience that has kept it in the lead for so long. Consumers in this market are not only interested in the player but also the ability to access the latest music in a cost-effective and easy manner. This is where Apple's iTunes software and website have dominated the market. Apple's customers can easily download the latest songs from iTunes for 99 cents a song; they can create playlist, read song reviews, get free bonuses, burn music to CDs and manage their entire music collection. It has been Apple's ability to provide a complete experience and satisfy varying customer segment demands that have allowed it to be at the forefront of the digital music revolution. This continued razor focus on the emerging segments has kept it ahead of its competition for the past four years, but for how long can it continue setting the pace?

Source: Jefferson Graham, 'Looks Like the New iPod's a Hit', *USA Today*, 18 September, 2005; <www.apple.com> (see Investor Relations).

Questions

1 What segmentation criteria should a new entrant to the digital music player category use to develop new segment opportunities?

2 What elements of marketing are the keys to success in the high-growth, Apple-dominated digital music player market?

3 What impact will mobile phones that double as digital music players have on Apple's dominance and how should Apple respond to such a potential threat?

10.1

via electronic mail. At first, potential students will be unaware of the new program. The initial marketing effort should thus employ high awareness-building advertising and publicity using a simple message. If successful in building awareness, the marketing program should shift focus in order to move people into the next readiness stage—say, interest in the program—by stressing the benefits of the 'electronic university'. Facilities should be readied for handling the large number of people who may be moved to enrol in the courses. In general, the marketing program must be adjusted to the changing distribution of buyer readiness.

Attitude towards product People in a market can be enthusiastic, positive, indifferent, negative or hostile towards a product. Door-to-door workers in a campaign such as Australia's republic referendum use a given voter's attitude to determine how much time to spend with that voter. They thank enthusiastic voters and remind them to vote; they spend little or no time trying to change the attitudes of negative and hostile voters. They reinforce those who are positive and try to win the votes of indifferent or undecided voters. In such marketing situations, attitudes can be effective segmentation variables.

Internet address segmentation/domain names and ISP

Every Internet user has an electronic address which includes an Internet service provider (ISP) identification such as BigPond, Optus, IHUG or a workplace network address, and various abbreviations. For instance, edu represents an educational institution, gov means a government organisation, com a commercial enterprise and au a country (Australia). ISPs such as BigPond and Optus have their assigned ISP numbers, and marketers might infer that a BigPond user who is subscribing to a premium service may be interested in a range of information-related services such as those provided by BigPond's information partner Sensis. Alternatively, a user of <www.optus.home.net> may have different product and service requirements. It is possible for the web marketer to know from which service provider the prospective customer is originating and thus it is able in real-time to customise a premium offer for a BigPond user and a different offer for an Optus user.

Consider this! You are a university student in the computer lab searching for information for your next skiing trip to Perisher. The Lodge at Perisher has signed an advertising contract with Anzwers (Australia and New Zealand Web Enquiry Research System, <www.anzwers.com.au>, to show banner ads with special discount offers to university students. Its key target market for the ski season is university students, and from other students who have booked accommodation it knows exactly what package will interest you. From the banner ad you are immediately linked to The Lodge's website for booking, payment and organisation of transport and gear.[10]

Bases for segmenting business markets

Industrial markets can be segmented using many of the same variables used in consumer market segmentation. Industrial buyers can be segmented geographically or by benefits sought, user status, usage rate, loyalty status, readiness state and attitudes..Yet new variables also come into play. As Figure 10.2 shows, these include industrial customer demographics, operating characteristics, purchasing approaches, situational factors and personal characteristics.[11]

Figure 10.2 lists major questions that industrial marketers should ask in determining which customers they want to serve. By going after segments instead of the whole market', a company has a much better chance of delivering value to consumers and of receiving maximum rewards for its close attention to segment consumer needs. Thus, Pirelli and other tyre companies should decide which *industries* they want to serve. Manufacturers seeking original equipment tyres vary in their needs. Makers of luxury and high-performance cars like Mercedes-Benz want tyres of a higher grade than makers of economy models. The tyres needed by aircraft manufacturers must meet much higher safety standards than tyres needed by farm tractor manufacturers.

Within the chosen industry, a company can further segment by *customer size* or *geographical location*. The company might set up separate systems for dealing with larger or multiple-location customers. For example, computer equipment distributors, such as Tech Pacific, first segment corporate customers into industries, including banking, insurance and electronics. Next, company salespeople might work with independent resellers to handle smaller, local or regional customers in each segment. But many national multiple-location customers or potential customers, such as the ANZ Bank, have special needs that may reach beyond the scope of individual dealers. So Tech Pacific does what Telstra and other suppliers do—it uses national accounts managers to help its dealer networks handle its national accounts.

Within a certain target industry and customer size, the company can segment by *purchase approaches and criteria*. For example, government, university and industrial laboratories like the CSIRO typically differ in their purchase criteria for scientific instruments. Government labs need low prices (because they have difficulty in getting funds to buy instruments) and service contracts (because they can easily get money to maintain instruments). University labs want equipment that needs little regular

Demographic

Industry: Which industries that buy this product should we focus on?

Company size: What size companies should we focus on?

Location: What geographical areas should we focus on?

Operating variables

Technology: What customer technologies should we focus on?

User/non-user status: Should we focus on heavy, medium or light users or non-users?

Customer capabilities: Should we focus on customers needing many services or few services?

Purchasing approaches

Purchasing function organisation: Should we focus on companies with highly centralised or decentralised purchasing organisations?

Power structure: Should we focus on companies that are engineering dominated, financially dominated or marketing dominated?

Nature of existing relationships: Should we focus on companies with which we already have strong relationships or simply go after the most desirable companies?

General purchase policies: Should we focus on companies that prefer leasing? service contracts? systems purchases? sealed bidding/tenders?

Purchasing criteria: Should we focus on companies that are seeking quality? service? price?

Situational factors

Urgency: Should we focus on companies that need quick and sudden delivery or service?

Specific application: Should we focus on certain applications of our product rather than all applications?

Size of order: Should we focus on large or small orders?

Personal characteristics

Buyer–seller similarity: Should we focus on companies whose people and values are similar to ours?

Attitudes towards risk: Should we focus on risk-taking or risk-avoiding customers?

Loyalty: Should we focus on companies that show high loyalty to their suppliers?

FIGURE 10.2 | Major segmentation variables for industrial markets
Source: Adapted from Thomas V. Bonoma and Benson P. Shapiro, *Segmenting the Industrial Market,* Lexington, Mass, Lexington Books, 1983.

service because they don't have service people on their payrolls. Industrial labs need highly reliable equipment because they cannot afford downtime.

In general, industrial companies do not focus on one segmentation variable but use a combination of many. One aluminium company used a series of four major variables. It first looked at which *end-use* market to serve: motor vehicle, residential or beverage containers. Choosing the residential market, it determined the most attractive *product application*: semi-finished material, building components or mobile homes. Deciding to focus on building components, it next considered the best *customer size* to serve and chose large customers. The company further segmented the large-customer, building components market. It saw customers falling into three *benefit* groups: those who bought for price, those who bought for service and those who bought for quality. Because the company offered excellent service, it decided to concentrate on the service-seeking segment of the market.

Segmenting international markets

Few companies have either the resources or the will to operate in all, or even most, of the countries that dot the globe. Although some large companies, such as Coca-Cola, Nestlé and Nokia, sell products in more than 150 countries, most international firms focus on a smaller set. Operating in many countries presents new challenges. The different countries of the world, even those that are close together, can vary dramatically in their economic, cultural and political make-up. Thus, just as they do within their domestic markets, international firms need to group their world markets into segments with distinct buying needs and behaviours.

Companies can segment international markets using one or a combination of several variables. They can segment by *geographic location*, grouping countries by regions such as Southeast Asia, Western Europe, the Pacific Rim, the Middle East or Africa. In fact, countries in many regions already have organised geographically into market groups or 'free-trade zones' such as the European Union, the European Free Trade Association and the North America Free Trade Agreement. These associations reduce trade barriers between member countries, creating larger and more homogeneous markets.

Geographic segmentation assumes that nations close to one another will have many common traits and behaviours. Although this is often the case, there are many exceptions. For example, although the USA and Canada have much in common, both differ culturally and economically from the USA's neighbour Mexico. Even within a region, consumers can differ widely. For example, until recently many international marketers thought that all Asian countries were the same. However, Indonesia is no more like the Philippines than Italy is like Sweden.[12]

World markets can be segmented on the basis of *economic factors*. For example, countries might be grouped by population income levels or by their overall level of economic development. Some countries, such as the so-called Group of Seven (G7)—the USA, Britain, France, Germany, Japan, Canada and Italy—have established highly industrialised economies. Other countries have newly industrialised or developing economies (Singapore, Taiwan, Korea, Mexico). Still others are less developed (China, India). A company's economic structure shapes its population's product and service needs and therefore the marketing opportunities it offers.

Countries can be segmented by *political and legal factors* such as the type and stability of government, receptivity to foreign firms, monetary regulations and the amount of bureaucracy. Such factors can play a crucial role in a company's choice of which countries to enter and how. *Cultural factors* can also be used, grouping markets according to common languages, religions, values and attitudes, customs and behavioural patterns.

Segmenting international markets on the basis of geographic, economic, political, cultural and other factors assumes that segments should consist of clusters of countries. However, many companies use a different approach, called **intermarket segmentation**. Using this approach, they form segments of consumers who have similar needs and buying behaviour even though they are located in different countries. For example, Mercedes-Benz targets the world's well-to-do, regardless of their country. And Pepsi uses ads filled with kids, sports and rock music to target the world's teenagers. Its introduction of sugar-free Pepsi Max in 16 countries, including Britain, Australia and Japan, was with a single set of ads aimed at teens who like to live on the wild side.[13]

Similarly, an agricultural chemicals manufacturer like Incitec, based in Queensland, might focus on small farmers in a variety of developing countries:

> Whether from Thailand or Indonesia or Kenya or India, these small farmers appear to represent common needs and behaviour patterns. Most of them till the land using bullock carts and have very little cash to buy agricultural inputs. They lack the education . . . to appreciate fully the value of using fertiliser and depend on government help for such things as seeds, pesticides and fertiliser. They acquire farming needs from local suppliers and count on word-of-mouth to learn and accept new things and ideas. Thus, even though these farmers are in different countries continents apart, and even though they speak different languages and have different cultural backgrounds, they may represent a homogeneous market segment.[14]

Intermarket segmentation
Forming segments of consumers who have similar needs and buying behaviour even though they are located in different countries.

Marketing Highlight 10.2 illustrates the importance of segmentation in the maturing mobile phone market.

Requirements for effective segmentation

Clearly, there are many ways to segment a market—but not all segmentations are effective. For example, buyers of table salt could be divided into blonde and brunette customers. But hair colour obviously does not affect the purchase of salt. Furthermore, if all salt buyers bought the same amount of salt each month, believed all salt was the same and wanted to pay the same price, the company would not benefit from segmenting this market.

To be useful, market segments must have the following characteristics:

- Measurability—the degree to which the size and purchasing power of the segments can be measured. Certain segmentation variables are difficult to measure. For example, there is a significant proportion of left-handed people in Australia, yet few products are targeted towards this left-handed segment. Check how many left-handed computer mouses exist in your computer lab or office work area. The major problem may be that the segment is hard to identify and measure. There are no data on the demographics of lefties, and the Australian Bureau of Statistics does not keep track of lefthandedness in its surveys. Private data companies keep reams of statistics on other demographic segments, but not on left-handers.[15]

- Accessibility—the degree to which the segments can be reached and served. Suppose a perfume company finds that heavy users of its brand are single women who stay out late and socialise a lot. Unless this group lives or shops at certain places and is exposed to certain media, it will be difficult to reach.

- Substantiality—the degree to which the segments are large or profitable enough. A segment should be the largest possible homogeneous group worth going after with a tailored marketing program. It would not pay, for example, for a car manufacturer to develop cars for people whose height is less than 122 centimetres. However, the economics of segmentation is changing with the development of mass customisation and the low cost of consumer access using the Internet. This is particularly the case for products and services that can be provided electronically.

   For instance, it is feasible to download your favourite CD tracks and 'burn' your own CD with only your favourite artists. It is easy to design your own holiday by combining packages promoted online by <www.travel.com.au>. But it also applies to some products. You can configure your own PC, peripherals and maintenance service arrangement at <www.dell. com.au>.

- Actionability—the degree to which effective programs can be designed for attracting and serving the segments. For example, although one small airline identified seven market segments, its staff was too small to develop separate marketing programs for each segment.

Segmenting the Australian market

By international standards, Australian consumers and industrial buyers are very sophisticated. They are attracted by products that meet their particular needs. With a population of only 20 million, this buyer expectation often presents a problem. The marketer must determine whether or not it is feasible and economic to reach a small market segment. Sometimes the only way an Australian supplier can meet overseas competition in reaching a small market segment is by marketing this segment on an international basis and in this way gain economies of scale.

MARKETING HIGHLIGHT

10.2

Targeting the youth segment to drive growth in the maturing mobile phone market

As the mobile phone market matures many carriers and phone manufacturers are having to examine their segmentation schemes and reorient their marketing efforts towards the fastest growing and most profitable target groups. Telstra in particular recently undertook a major segmentation project and has realigned its marketing efforts in its consumer marketing division into a focus on three distinct segments: youth, consumer and small business. The youth segment in particular was identified as a market in which Telstra needed to improve its performance and a shift from a product-focused approach to a customer-segment-focused approach was necessary in order to improve Telstra's share of this highly competitive market. With a seemingly endless array of features and services being offered in the once humble mobile phone, the challenge for the carriers and manufacturers targeting the youth segment is to decide on which of these will provide the most value to these customers and at what price. Mobile phones can now double as digital cameras, digital music players, radio players, diaries, alarm clocks, stop watches and the list goes on. Carrier

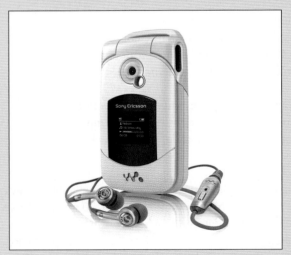

With the W300i ClamShell Walkman Phone, Sony Ericsson allows users to transfer their favourite CDs to their mobile phone and enjoy them anywhere, anytime, without missing a call.

offerings that enable SMS, MMS, GPS, online mobile games, email, new ring tones and Internet browsing are added to a dizzying raft of options now available to the youth market. Telstra's approach has been to address the high price perception many customers have by communicating aggressive offers specifically targeting the youth market such as a product that offers 50 free SMS messages. Telstra has also reviewed its corporate sponsorship programs and is moving away from corporate brand awareness sponsorship towards more grassroots-focused sponsorship that aligns better with its target segments.

One of Telstra's key competitors in the youth segment is Virgin Mobile. Virgin entered the market in 2001 through an agreement with Optus and has no long-term contracts, no monthly access fees, no minimum monthly spends, voicemail is free and calls are billed by the second. It is an offering that is very appealing to the youth market which typically prefers pre-paid offerings. In addition to Virgin's value proposition, its brand speaks directly to the youth market. Virgin also positions itself as the champion of the consumer against the bigger players like Telstra, Vodafone and Optus. Virgin has also been innovative in its understanding of customer needs. 'Rescue ring' is a service it offers its subscribers who may need to get out of a tricky situation. For example, if a Friday night date is not going well or you are caught up in a store by a pushy salesperson, simply pre-program the phone to ring you (rescue ring) and you can make an excuse to remove yourself from the situation. In the USA, there is even a rescue droid on the other end that happily relays a message: 'Now get out of there and start having a better day!'. Virgin's other focus is on providing the youth segment with relevant content such as horoscopes, top 10 music, ring tones, gossip, entertainment and sport. It is with this type of needs-based segmentation that Virgin has been able to grow to more than 600 000 customers in Australia in less than five years.

Sources: Neil Shoebridge, 'Renovating Telstra', *The Australian Financial Review Boss Magazine,* <www.boss.afr.com.au/printmagazine.asp?doc_id=23379>, accessed 28 September 2005; Anonymous, *Citigroup/Smith Barney Report,* 22 November 2004, Telecommunications Services: Aust/NZ Report,' p. 58; Richard Rapaport, 'Virgin's Version', Forbes.com, 7 October 2002, <www.forbes.com/asap/2002/1007/058_print.html>, accessed 28 September 2005; Virgin Mobile website, <www.virginmobile.com.au/companyinfo/aboutus/companybackground.html>, accessed 29 September 2005.

Questions

1 What is the difference between product segmentation and needs-based segmentation in the mobile phone market?

2 What do you think are the most appealing elements to the youth market (age 15–19) in the mobile phone offers?

3 Which of Teltsra and Virgin Mobile has the most appealing offer to this segment? Why?

10.2

SELF-CHECK QUESTIONS

1   Explain market segmentation. What is its role in marketing?

2   Consider a bank targeting the consumer market. Propose a number of possible segmentation bases.

3   Consider CSR targeting the building materials market in the Philippines. What bases of segmentation might be relevant?

4   Explain the requirements for effective segmentation of the airline business market by Singapore Airlines.

5   Explain the requirements for effective segmentation of the Chinese market for marketing education.

6   How is online marketing changing the feasibility of segmentation on a single-customer basis? Provide examples of products and services where mass customisation is occurring.

Market targeting

Marketing segmentation reveals the market segment opportunities facing a firm. The firm now has to evaluate the various segments and decide on the number of segments to cover and the ones to serve. This section looks at how companies evaluate and select target segments.

Evaluating market segments

In evaluating different market segments, a company must look at three factors: segment size and growth, segment structural attractiveness, and company objectives and resources.

Segment size and growth

The company must first collect and analyse data on current dollar sales, projected sales growth rates and expected profit margins for the various segments. It wants to select segments that have the right size and growth characteristics, but 'right size growth' is a relative matter. Some companies will want to target segments with large current sales, a high growth rate and a high profit margin. However, the largest, fastest growing segments are not always the most attractive ones for every company. Smaller companies may find that they lack the skills and resources needed to serve the larger segments or that these segments are too competitive. Such companies may select segments that are smaller and less attractive, in an absolute sense, but that are potentially more profitable for them. A case in point—credit unions such as the Teachers Credit Union and the Builders Credit Union which target quite specific niche markets avoid confrontation with the large players such as the major banks.

Segment structural attractiveness

A segment might have desirable size and growth and still not be attractive from a profitability point of view. The company must examine several major structural factors that affect long-run segment attractiveness.[16] For example, the company should appraise the impact of current and potential *competitors*. A segment is less attractive if it already contains many strong and aggressive competitors. Marketers should also consider the threat of *substitute products*. A segment is less attractive if actual or potential substitutes for the product already exist. Substitutes place a limit on the potential prices and profits that can be earned in a segment. The relative *power of buyers* also affects segment attractiveness. If the buyers in a segment possess strong or increasing bargaining power relative to sellers, they will try to force prices down, demand more quality or services and set competitors against one another, all at the expense of seller profitability. Finally, segment attractiveness depends on the relative *power of suppliers*. A segment is less attractive if the suppliers of raw materials, equipment, labour and services in the segment are powerful enough to raise prices or reduce the quality or quantity of ordered goods and services. Suppliers tend to be powerful when they are large and concentrated, when few substitutes exist or when the supplied product is an important input.

For instance, the Australian container market for liquid products, such as soft drinks, is supplied by glass, plastic, tetra and aluminium manufacturers. There are relatively few large buyers of these products and with the potential entry of global competitors the power of the container manufacturers (the suppliers) is low, with consequent impact on profit and segment attractiveness.

Company objectives and resources

Even if a segment has positive size and growth and is structurally attractive, the company must consider its own objectives and resources in relation to that segment. Some attractive segments could be quickly dismissed because they do not mesh with the company's long-run objectives. Although they might be tempting segments in themselves, they might divert the company's attention and energies away from its main goals.

If a segment fits the company's objectives, the company must then decide whether it possesses the skills and resources needed to succeed in that segment. Each segment has certain success requirements. If the company lacks and cannot readily obtain the strengths needed to compete successfully in a segment, it should not enter that segment. But even if the company possesses the *required* strengths, this is not enough. If it is really going to win in a market segment it needs to employ skills and resources *superior* to those of the competition. The company should only enter segments where it can offer superior value and gain advantages over competitors.

Target market A set of buyers sharing common needs or characteristics that the company decides to serve.

Selecting market segments

After evaluating different segments, a company hopes to find one or more market segments worth entering. It must then decide which and how many segments to serve. This is the problem of *target market selection*. A **target market** consists of a set of buyers sharing common needs or characteristics that the company decides to serve. The company can adopt one of three market-coverage strategies: *undifferentiated marketing*, *differentiated marketing* or *concentrated marketing*. These strategies are shown in Figure 10.3 and are discussed below.

Undifferentiated marketing A market-coverage strategy in which a company might decide to ignore market segment differences and go after the whole market with one market offer.

Undifferentiated marketing

Using an **undifferentiated marketing** strategy, a company might decide to ignore market segment differences and go after the whole market with one market offer. It focuses on what is *common* in the

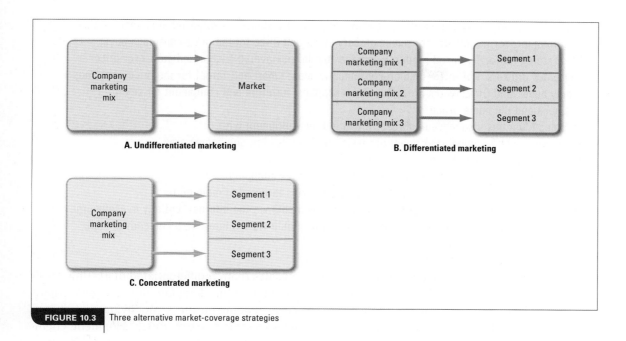

FIGURE 10.3   Three alternative market-coverage strategies

needs of consumers rather than on what is *different*. The company designs a product and a marketing program that appeals to the largest number of buyers. It relies on mass distribution and mass advertising, and aims to give the product a superior image in people's minds.

Undifferentiated marketing provides cost economies. The narrow product line keeps down production, inventory and transportation costs. The undifferentiated advertising program keeps down advertising costs. The absence of segment marketing research and planning lowers the costs of marketing research and product management.

Most modern marketers, however, have strong doubts about this strategy. Difficulties arise in developing a product or brand that will satisfy all consumers. Companies using undifferentiated marketing typically develop an offer aimed at the largest segments in the market. When several companies do this, heavy competition develops in the largest segments and less satisfaction results in the smaller ones. The result is that the larger segments may be less profitable because they attract heavy competition. Recognition of this problem has resulted in companies being more interested in smaller segments of the market.

Differentiated marketing

Using a **differentiated marketing** strategy, a company decides to target several market segments, and designs separate offers for each. Toyota tries to produce a car for every 'purse, purpose and personality'. By offering product and marketing variations, it hopes for higher sales and a stronger position within each market segment. It hopes that a stronger position in several segments will strengthen consumers' overall identification of the company with the product category. And it hopes for greater repeat purchasing because the company's offer matches the customer's desire more exactly.

A growing number of firms have adopted differentiated marketing. Coles Myer's segmentation strategy is a good example. Coles Myer uses different store formats and types to meet the needs of different customer segments:

Differentiated marketing A market-coverage strategy in which a company decides to target several market segments and designs separate offers for each.

Coles Myer's merchandising strategy attempts to provide a store for every kind of shopper: Coles Supermarkets for the quality-conscious grocery buyer and Bi-Lo for the price-conscious buyer, Myer stores for family mixed-product purchases by the risk-averse, Liquorland stores for price-conscious drinkers, Katies for fashion-conscious women, Kmart and Target for the price-conscious family buyer, and Officeworks providing office supplies, furniture and equipment for small business and the home office.

Coles Myer has also moved aggressively into direct fulfilment with:

- Myer Direct—a wide assortment of fashion apparel, leisure and homewares
- South Cape—high-quality casual sportswear
- The Footy Store—AFL merchandise via Internet online shopping
- Harry Day—lifestyle golfing apparel and accessories targeted at male golfers
- Coles Online—full range of 40 000 food items available via the Internet, initially in Melbourne
- Harris Technology—50 000 computer products available via the Internet, a call centre, mail order or at a local store.[17]

Differentiated marketing typically creates more total sales than undifferentiated marketing. Lever & Kitchen (Unilever) gets a higher total market share with a multitude of laundry detergent brands than it could with only one. But it also increases the costs of doing business. Modifying a product to meet different market segment requirements usually involves some research and development, engineering or special tooling costs. A company usually finds it more expensive to produce, say, 10 units of 10 different products than 100 units of one product. Developing separate marketing plans for the separate segments requires extra marketing research, forecasting, sales analysis, promotion planning and channel management. And trying to reach different market segments with different advertising increases promotion costs. If this involves different brands, as with Unilever, the marketing costs are much higher. Thus, the company must weigh increased sales against increased costs when deciding on a differentiated marketing strategy.

Concentrated marketing

Concentrated marketing A market-coverage strategy in which a company goes after a large share of one or a few submarkets.

A third market-coverage strategy, **concentrated marketing**, is especially appealing when company resources are limited. Instead of going after a small share of a large market, the company goes after a large share of one or a few submarkets. Many examples of concentrated marketing can be found. In computers, Dell concentrates on computer re-purchasers but avoids first-time users; IBM focuses on large interconnected supercomputers; Sony targets the user who wants enriched multimedia; and Toshiba focuses on pocket PCs. Golden Door Health Retreats concentrate on the market for upmarket, health-conscious individuals. Concentrated marketing provides an excellent way for small new businesses to get a foothold against larger, highly resourced competitors.

Through concentrated marketing, the company achieves a strong market position in the segments it serves because of its greater knowledge of the segments' needs and the special reputation it acquires. And it enjoys many operating economies because of specialisation in production, distribution and promotion. If the segment is well chosen, the company can earn a high rate of return on its investment. At the same time, concentrated marketing involves higher than normal risks. If a company has 'all its eggs in one basket' and the market takes a downturn, or a larger competitor takes an attacking position, the company may lose out.

Choosing a market-coverage strategy

Many factors must be considered when choosing a market-coverage strategy. This strategy has gone through a number of transitions. First, from mass marketing to direct marketing—an attempt to build a direct relationship with a person who will ultimately buy. Then to one-to-one marketing—'we have your credit card number and buying history and we want to sell you more because you already trust us'. Now we have **permission marketing**—a kind of reverse targeting which is a process of converting strangers into friends and friends into customers.

Internet marketing pioneer and father of permission marketing, Seth Godin, believes that the most effective targeting occurs in reverse—prospective customers give their permission for you to communicate with them! Hence permission must be granted (not presumed), its basis is consumer benefit (people grant permission when there is something for them), it can be revoked (if the quality of the interaction is poor) and it cannot be transferred.

Godin suggests four tests for permission marketing:

1 Does every marketing effort you create facilitate a learning relationship with your customer? That is, does it enable customers to 'raise their hands' and begin communicating?

2 Do you have a permission database—do you track the number of people who have agreed to communicate with you?

3 If permission is granted, do you have a script to educate people about your products or services?

4 Once an individual becomes your customer, do you work to deepen your permission to communicate with them?

Consider Amazon.com. It has built a 'permission' asset. It has overt permission to track which books you browse and buy and also explicit permission to send you promotional email messages. Amazon is building special-interest communities of its customers who talk to each other about books and areas of interest.

The significant payoff will come the day that Amazon decides to publish books. This is the area of biggest profitability since Amazon is in the best position to leverage its permission asset. A book costs around $A4 to produce and then retails for $40 in the bookshop. This is a huge gap, but unfortunately most of this money disappears in the value-chain activities such as distribution, advertising and, in particular, the shredding of unsold books. What if you could remove all these activities? What if Amazon.com sends a note to each of the one million people who bought a mystery novel from their site last year? It costs them virtually nothing to do this, since email is free. In the email they could ask if you would like to buy the next Robert Ludlum mystery novel, which will be available first from Amazon. And let's assume that 30% of those customers respond and say yes.

Now Amazon can make this fantastic offer to Robert Ludlum: 'We would like you to write the book. Don't worry about the editing and typesetting. We will also ship it directly to the 333 000 people who have pre-ordered it. Amazon will deduct its costs and still have a million dollars left over to pay you.' By any standard, this is a lot of money for writing a mystery novel but Amazon can still make $4 million in profit from just one book. By extrapolating this thinking to the thousands of books Amazon sells each year, and the use of permission marketing, Amazon can fundamentally reshape the entire book industry. It will disintermediate and combine every step of the value chain until there remain only the two key elements: Amazon.com and the writer.

This is the best way to visualise the power and potential of permission marketing.

Now consider Pepsi. It has a new interactive website aimed at Pepsi's key target segment of 18 to 24 year olds. It resists the temptation to be just another vehicle for branding, but taps into the music, entertainment and recreational needs of its customers. Users can play video games, chat to entertainment personalities in a virtual chatroom, enter competitions and talk to each other. Pepsi believes effective interactivity and relevance to the teen market are the most important things.

Permission marketing
A process of converting strangers into friends and friends into customers.

Building global communities and permission marketing go hand in hand as electronic neighbourhoods become the incubators of trends and future opportunities for marketers that have already gained permission![18]

Which strategy is best depends on *company resources*. When the firm's resources are limited, concentrated marketing makes the most sense. The best strategy also depends on the degree of *product variability*. Undifferentiated marketing is more suited to uniform products, such as grapefruit or steel. Products that can vary in design, such as cameras and cars, are more suited to differentiation or concentration. The product's *stage in the life cycle* must also be considered. When a firm introduces a new product it is practical to launch only one version, and undifferentiated marketing or concentrated marketing makes the most sense. In the mature stage of the product life cycle, however, differentiated marketing begins to make more sense. Another factor is *market variability*. If most buyers have the same tastes, buy the same amounts and react the same way to marketing efforts, undifferentiated marketing is appropriate. Finally, competitors' *marketing strategies* are important. When competitors use segmentation, undifferentiated marketing can be suicidal. Conversely, when competitors use undifferentiated marketing, a firm can gain by using differentiated or concentrated marketing.

SELF-CHECK QUESTIONS

7   Describe the process for evaluating and selecting market segments for targeting.

8   What types of marketing strategies could be used in targeting the computer market?

Market positioning

Once a company has decided which segments of the market it will enter, it must decide which 'positions' it wants to occupy in those segments.

What is market positioning?

Product position The way the product is defined by consumers on important attributes—the place the product occupies in consumers' minds relative to competing products.

Product position is the way the product is *defined by consumers* on important attributes—the place the product occupies in consumers' minds relative to competing products. Thus, Drive is positioned as an all-purpose, family washing detergent; Cold Power is positioned as a cold-water washing detergent; and Unilever's Snuggle is positioned as a washing detergent for delicate fabrics such as wool. Holden is positioned as Australia's own car; Volvo is positioned on safety; Subaru is positioned on road handling; Mercedes and Lexus are positioned on luxury; BMW is positioned on excellence and quality embodied in 'sheer driving pleasure'.

Consumers are overloaded with information about products and services. They cannot re-evaluate products every time they make a buying decision. To simplify buying decision making, they organise products into categories—they 'position' products, services and companies in their minds. A product's position is the complex set of perceptions, impressions and feelings that consumers hold for the product compared with competing products. Consumers position products with or without the help of marketers, but marketers do not want to leave their products' positions to chance. They *plan* positions that will give their products the greatest advantage in selected target markets, and they *design* marketing mixes to create the planned positions.[19]

Positioning strategies

Marketers can follow several positioning strategies.[20] They can position their products on specific *product* attributes—Hyundai Excel advertises its low price; Peugeot promotes on the basis of performance; Saab advertises style and engineering (it also manufactures aircraft jet engines). Products can be positioned on the needs they fill or on the *benefits* they offer—Colgate Sensitive reduces pain associated with sensitive teeth; Macleans triple stripe provides three benefits at once (fresh breath, cavity protection and calcium for bone strength).[21] Or products can be positioned according to *usage* occasions—in the summer, Gatorade can be positioned as a beverage for replacing athletes' body fluids; in the winter, it can be positioned as the drink to use when the doctor recommends plenty of liquids. Another approach is to position the product for certain classes of users—Procter & Gamble improved the market share for its Head and Shoulders shampoo by repositioning the product as suitable for everyday use rather than as a medicated shampoo; they even added a variant with conditioner to reinforce this point.

A product can also be positioned directly *against a competitor*. For example, in advertisements for their database products, Oracle has at times directly compared its offerings with IBM. Oracle claims its database is faster than IBM's and is being used by a larger number of Fortune 100 companies. GlaxoSmithKline (makers of Panadol) advertised directly against Herron and Dick Smith has raised the ire of Kellogg's with ads comparing the sugar levels of Smith's product with Nutri-Grain.[22]

In its famous 'We're number two, so we try harder' campaign, Avis rental cars successfully positioned itself against the larger Hertz. A product may also be positioned *away from competitors*; Virgin Mobile became the number four mobile service provider when it was positioned as the 'no hidden costs, pay for the second and not for the 30 second block alternative' to the 'overcharging' of Telstra and Optus.[23]

Finally, the product can be positioned for different *product classes*. For example, some margarines are positioned against butter, others against cooking oils. Dove hand soap (with moisturiser) is positioned with bath oils rather than with soap. Marketers often use a *combination* of these positioning strategies. Thus, Johnson & Johnson's Baby brand is positioned as a product gentle enough for baby's care (product class *and* user).[24] And Arm & Hammer—the major US brand of baking soda—has been positioned as a deodoriser for refrigerators and carpet spills cleaner (product class *and* usage situation).

Marketing Highlight 10.3 describes how positioning works to create a 'position' in the mind and the challenge involved using the Internet.

Choosing and implementing a positioning strategy

Some firms find it easy to choose their positioning strategy. For example, a firm that is well known for quality in certain segments will go for this position in a new segment if it sees enough buyers seeking quality. But, in many cases, two or more firms will go after the same position. Then, each will have to find other ways to set itself apart, such as promising 'high quality for a lower cost' or 'high quality with more technical service'. That is, each firm must differentiate its offer by building a unique bundle of competitive advantages that appeal to a substantial group within the segment.

Identifying a positional direction

The positioning task consists of three steps: identifying a set of possible competitive advantages upon which to build a position, selecting the right competitive advantages, and effectively communicating and delivering the chosen position to the market.

A cornerstone of brand marketing strategy is the concept of brand positioning—identifying the 'position' of a brand in the mind of customers. One type of analysis to do this is known as *perceptual mapping.* At the company, product range or individual product level, depending on the brand context, existing or prospective customers are asked to rate brands against each other in terms of similarity or dissimilarity. The result is a multidimensional map which identifies factors that discriminate between brands. It is then necessary for the analyst to give relevant descriptors to the factors.

The two-dimensional map of department store brand positions constructed in Figure 10.4 makes the assumption that a high percentage of the explanation of perceived similarities and differences between companies lies in two dimensions. These dimensions need to be interpreted—here shown as personal service, and quality and status. Once the positions are identified, decisions are made to support the current position or reposition the brand. In Figure 10.4 it is assumed that the service and quality dimensions encapsulate the important market-position criteria.

The high levels of perceived quality, status and service reflected in David Jones's position may also reflect perceptions of high price and exclusivity. Kmart's market position at the other end of the spectrum may also reflect an image of low price and commodity products.

This mapping technique is a useful tool for plotting moves over time by competitors as well as the results of a firm's own brand-positioning strategy. For example, if David Jones decides to reposition to appeal to a broader market by reducing its perception of quality and status, shown by the arrow in Figure 10.4, and Target moves to upgrade its image of quality, Myer may be caught in a positioning squeeze, losing customers trading up to DJs or trading down to Target. Under these conditions it would be essential for Myer to have a very clear brand-positioning strategy in order to reinforce or improve its market position.

Another use of perceptual mapping is to see the relative positions of different product forms. This is particularly relevant to dominant businesses which may be clear leaders in one or two product forms but not so dominant in other forms. Substitution between forms is a strategic issue which has implications for brand extension and multibranding. A narrow industry focus by Australia Post on its dominant mail and courier brands may overlook performance benefits provided by other forms of

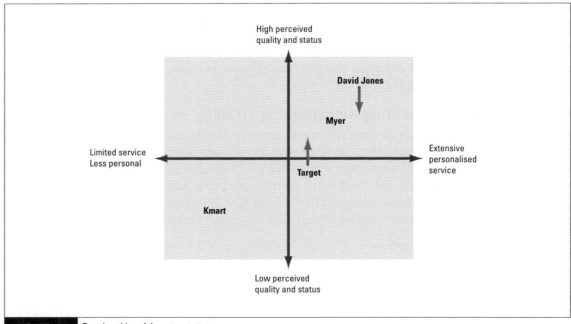

FIGURE 10.4 Brand position of department stores

interpersonal communication such as email, facsimile and multimedia. A view of potential growth opportunities in these electronic media has led the traditional dominant postal businesses to launch brands into these markets.

To make brand strategy decisions using perceptual maps it is also necessary to know the ideal combination of attributes for each market segment. This enables brand-positioning strategies to be directed towards those segments that are attractive. Figure 10.5 shows the repositioning moves necessary for Kmart and Target to appeal more closely to specific segments.

Identifying possible competitive advantages

Consumers typically choose products and services that give them the greatest value. Thus, the key to winning and keeping customers is to understand their needs and buying processes better than competitors and to deliver more value. If a company can position itself as providing superior value to selected target markets—either by offering lower prices than competitors or by providing more benefits to justify higher prices—it gains **competitive advantage**.[25] But solid positions cannot be built on empty promises. If a company positions its product as *offering* the best quality and service, it must then *deliver* the promised quality and service. Thus, positioning begins with actually *differentiating* the company's marketing offer so that it will give consumers more value than a competitor's offer (see Marketing Highlight 10.3).

Not every company finds many opportunities for differentiating its offer and gaining competitive advantage. Some companies find many minor advantages that are easily copied by competitors. The solution for these companies is to keep identifying new potential advantages and introduce them one by one to keep competitors off balance. These companies do not expect to gain a single major permanent advantage, but rather many minor ones that can be introduced to win market share over a period of time.

In what specific ways can a company differentiate its offer from those of competitors? A company or market offer can be differentiated along lines of *product, services, personnel* or *image*.

Competitive advantage
An advantage over competitors gained by offering consumers greater value, either through lower prices or by providing more benefits that justify higher prices.

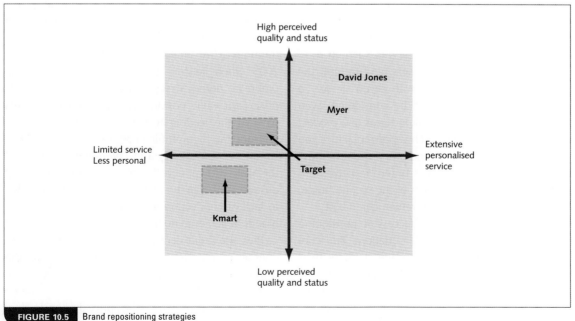

FIGURE 10.5   Brand repositioning strategies

Positioning and branding—it's virtually in the mind

Although marketers understand well the process of segmenting markets, targeting those they can best serve and then positioning their product and service for competitive advantage, it is instructive to look back to the origins of the notion of *positioning*. The term has been taken into marketing folklore following popularisation by two advertising executives, Al Ries and Jack Trout. Their definition reads as follows:

> Positioning starts with a product. A piece of merchandise, a service, a company, an institution, or even a person . . . But positioning is not what you do to a product. Positioning is what you do to the mind of a prospect.

Ries and Trout argue that products are positioned in consumers' minds such that there is a perception of brands such as Yellow Pages, Harvey Norman, Coca-Cola and Cadbury as being best in their category. In effect, they own these positions and it is very hard for a competitor to muscle in on these positions.

Marketers recognise that consumers filter the many hundreds of communications they receive daily. Ries and Trout suggest how essentially similar brands can acquire distinctiveness in such an over-communicated world. Consumers tend to limit the brands they actively consider to seven or so. So only seven soft drinks would be considered. Even then, consumers tend to think in terms of a *product ladder,* such as Coke/Pepsi/Schweppes cola. Ries and Trout observed that the second brand usually enjoys half the business of the first brand and the third brand enjoys half the business of the second brand. Furthermore, the top brand is remembered best.

Trout also suggests that successful positioning must be based around differentiation. But consumers see differentiation according to how their decision-making process works, usually with one of four functions prevailing—thinking, intuition, sensing and feeling. 'Thinkers' are logical, precise and analytical and make decisions about differentiation on facts. BMW's positioning of 'the ultimate driving machine' would appeal to this group when facts like ergonomic design, manoeuvrability and expert reviews are used to support it. 'Intuitives' look at the big picture and are influenced by differentiation based on the next generation product which we may see advertised by Apple with its iPod Nano. 'Sensors' see things as they are, absorb detail and can put things in context. Aussie Homeloans differentiating message against the banks is 'we'll save you'. It is an effective program for sensors because they already know that the banks are expensive and there is a good chance Aussie Homeloans will save them money. To them it makes sense that Aussie will save them. 'Feelers' are people oriented and are interested in the feelings of others. They respond to emotion and differentiation strategies like those presented by exotic drinks such as Tequila and Bacardi in sexually charged social situations. Understanding the target market's 'mind' is important to determining the positioning message and how it is presented.

Some companies have chosen to modify their brand names to achieve new positioning. For instance, the Commonwealth Bank decided to call its share trading service Commonwealth Securities (Commsec). A similar example occurred early in 2005 when Telstra launched 'T-time' as a retail umbrella brand designed to counter the high-price/poor value positioning that many consumers have of the leading telecommunications provider. A group of high-profile magazines, namely *Time, Fortune, People, Money* and *Entertainment*, went all the way with a new brand, Pathfinder. This was unsuccessful due to lack of recognition and due to lack of connection to these famous print media brands. It achieved no positioning.

Ries and Trout deal with the psychology of positioning or repositioning a current brand in the consumer's mind. They acknowledge that adoption of a particular strategy may entail making cosmetic changes to the product's name, price and packaging, in the interests of securing a worthwhile position in the prospect's mind. Many other marketers would add greater emphasis to *real positioning* where they work up every tangible aspect of a new product to capture a position. Psychological positioning must be supported by real positioning—after all, it is not just a mind game.

But when it comes to the virtual world, a lot of the tangibility that exists in the physical world is absent and brand, product, distribution and payment become virtual, particularly when applied to banking, music, software and entertainment. Branding and positioning is literally 'virtually' in the mind!

Sources: Al Ries and Jack Trout, *Positioning: The Battle for Your Mind,* New York, Warner Books, 1982; Neil McGrath, 'Drive to Expand Brings Applause', *Asian Business,* May 1994, p. 26; Tony Barrett, 'Al Ries: Consumer Viewpoint Is Crucial', *Professional Marketing,* August–September 1999, pp. 15–16; Neil Shoebridge, 'The Big Golden Book Continues to Explore Beyond the Printed Page', *Business Review Weekly,* 3 August 1998, pp. 60–63; Jack Trout with Steve Rivkin, *Differentiate or Die: Survival in Our Era of Killer Competition,* New York, Wiley, 2000; Jack Trout, *Trout on Strategy: Capturing Mindshare, Conquering Markets,* New York, McGraw-Hill, 2004, Chapter 2, pp. 13–33; Neil Shoebridge, 'Renovating Telstra', *The Australian Financial Review Boss Magazine,* at <www.boss.afr.com.au/printmagazine.asp?doc_id=23379>, accessed 28 September 2005.

Questions

1 Provide an example of a brand strategy that illustrates a strengthening of one's own position.

2 Provide an example of a brand strategy that illustrates a repositioning of the brand.

3 Identify two brands that have been extended to the Web—one using the same brand name and the other using a modified brand name. How effective do you think are the strategies of each? Give reasons for your conclusions.

10.3

Product differentiation A company can differentiate its physical product. At one extreme, some companies offer highly standardised products that allow little variation: chicken, steel, aspirin. Yet even here, some meaningful differentiation is possible. For example, Steggles claims that its branded chickens are better—more meat, less fat—and gets a price premium based on this differentiation—see Steggles Chicken and Steggles the Chook at <www.steggles.com.au>.

Other companies offer products that can be highly differentiated, such as motor cars, commercial buildings and furniture. Here, the company faces an abundance of design parameters. It can offer a variety of standard or optional features not provided by competitors. Thus, Volvo provides new and better safety features; Cathay Pacific offers high-level in-flight service. Companies can also differentiate their products on *performance*. Fisher and Paykel designs its two-drawer dishwasher to be more innovative than others on the market. Milton formulates NapiSan to get nappies cleaner and whites whiter. *Style and design* can also be important differentiating factors. Thus, many car buyers pay a premium for Volvo car design because of its extraordinary safety record, even though Volvo may have a poor perception on performance parameters when compared with other cars in its class. Similarly, companies can differentiate their products on such attributes as *consistency, durability, reliability, performance* or *repairability*.

Services differentiation In addition to differentiating its physical product, the company can also differentiate the services that accompany the product. Many possibilities exist. Some companies gain competitive advantage through speedy, reliable or careful *delivery*. Orica Chemicals, for example, has built an impressive reputation for shipping out stock with additional 'safety in use' information and procedures (beyond government regulation requirements) when compared to its competitors. *Installation* can also differentiate one buyer from another. IBM Global Services, for example, is known for its quality installation service. It delivers all pieces of purchased equipment to the site at one time rather than sending individual components to sit waiting for others to arrive. And when asked

Dishdrawers provide two dishwashers in one.

to move IBM equipment and install it in another location, IBM Global Services often moves competitors' equipment as well. IBM is moving further in this direction and wants to be seen as a services company that just happens to supply hardware, rather than the other way round.[26] Companies can further distinguish themselves through their *repair* services. Many a car buyer would gladly pay a little more and travel a little further to buy a car from a dealer that provides topnotch repair service.

Some companies differentiate their offers by providing *customer training service*. General Electric not only sells and installs expensive X-ray equipment in hospitals, it also trains the hospital employees who will use this equipment. Other companies offer free or paid *consulting* services—data, information systems and advising services that buyers need. For example, Sigma Corporation, a major pharmaceuticals wholesaler, consults with its independent pharmacists to help them set up accounting, inventory and computer ordering systems. By helping its customers compete better, Sigma gains greater customer loyalty and sales.

Companies can find many other ways to add value through differentiated services. In fact, they can choose from a virtually unlimited number of specific services and benefits on which to differentiate themselves from their competitors. McDonald's provides one of the best examples of a company that has gained competitive advantage through superior and consistent service.

Personnel differentiation Companies can gain a strong competitive advantage by hiring and training better people than their competitors. Thus, Singapore Airlines enjoys an excellent reputation, largely because of the beauty and grace of its cabin crews; McDonald's employees are courteous and Hewlett-Packard employees are professional and knowledgeable; David Jones has differentiated its department stores in Australia by employing 'people greeters' who welcome shoppers and give advice on where to find items.

Personnel differentiation requires a company to select its customer-contact people carefully and train them well. These personnel must be competent; they must possess the required skills and knowledge. They need to be courteous, friendly, respectful and considerate. They must perform the

The Singapore girl differentiates Singapore Airlines.

service with consistency and accuracy. And they must make an effort to understand customers, to communicate clearly with them and to respond quickly to their requests and problems.

Image differentiation Even when competing companies offer the same products and accompanying services, buyers may perceive a difference based on company or brand images. Thus, companies work to establish *images* that differentiate them from competitors. A company or brand image should convey a singular and distinctive message that communicates the product's major benefits and positioning. Developing a strong and distinctive image calls for creativity and hard work. A company cannot implant an image in the public's mind overnight using only a few advertisements. If 'David Jones means service', this image must be supported by everything the company says and does.

Symbols can provide strong company or brand recognition and image differentiation. Companies design signs and logos that provide instant recognition. They associate themselves with objects or characters that symbolise quality or other attributes, such as the Apple Computer apple, the Qantas red kangaroo or the McDonald's 'M' (the golden arches). The company might build a brand around some famous person, such as Weight Watchers with Sara Ferguson (Fergie of British royalty fame), Speedo (Michael Klim) and Adidas (Ian Thorpe). Some companies even become associated with colours, such as IBM (blue) or Ferrari (red).

The chosen symbols must be communicated through advertising that conveys the company or brand's personality. The ads attempt to establish a story line, a mood, a performance level—something distinctive about the company or brand. The atmosphere of the physical space in which the organisation produces or delivers its products and services can be another powerful image generator. Hyatt hotels have become known for their atrium lobbies. A bank that wants to distinguish itself as the 'friendly bank' must choose the right building and interior design, layout, colours, materials and furnishings.

A company can also create an image through the types of events it sponsors. Perrier, the bottled water company, became known by laying out exercise tracks and sponsoring health sports events. Other organisations, such as Telstra and BMW, have identified themselves with cultural events, such as symphony performances, opera and art exhibits. Still other organisations support popular causes—Microsoft supports the Starlight Foundation which grants wishes to seriously ill children.

Another way to look at positioning is to use surrogates or metaphors. For instance, 'Use our vitamin mix because it was created by a leading health expert'. This is saying the product differs because of its designer. Figure 10.6 (overleaf) gives examples of surrogate positioning alternatives currently being used. No doubt there are many others awaiting discovery. For each, the definition is given, followed by one or more examples. The surrogates are listed in order of popularity in use.

Selecting the right competitive advantages

Suppose a company is fortunate enough to discover several potential competitive advantages. It must now choose the ones upon which it will build its positioning strategy. It must decide *how many* differences to promote and which ones.

How many differences to promote? Many marketers think that companies should aggressively promote only one benefit to the target market. Rosser Reeves, for example, said that a company should develop a *unique selling proposition* (USP) for each brand and stick to it. Each brand should pick an attribute and position itself as 'number one' on that attribute. Buyers tend to remember 'number one' better, especially in an overcommunicated society. Thus, Fujitsu Air-conditioning uses Mark Taylor (former Australian cricket captain) to promote the reliability of its product, and BMW promotes its great automotive engineering. What are some of the 'number one' positions to promote? The major ones are 'best quality', 'best service', 'lowest price', 'best value' and 'most advanced technology'. A company

Nonpareil	… because the product has no equal; it is the best (the Jaguar car and Nissan 300ZX, the 'convertible of convertibles').
Parentage	… because of where it comes from, who makes it, who sells it, who performs it, and so on. The three ways of parentage positioning are brand (Le Temps Chanel timepieces); company ('everything we know about peanut butter is now available in jars' for Reese's peanut butter), ('No one potpourri like Glade' for the new Peachpouri), (new 'Adventures in Wonderland' TV show that has no features in its advertising but clearly comes from Disney); and person (the RL2000 chair, designed by Ralph Lauren; *Turning Point*, a new book by Hugh Mackay).
Manufacture	… because of how the product was made. This includes process (Hunt's tomatoes are left longer on the vine), ingredients (Fruit of the Loom panties are pure cotton) and design (Audi's engineering).
Target	… because the product was made especially for people or firms like you. Four ways are end use (Vector tyre designed especially for use on wet roads), demographic (several airlines have service specially designed for the business traveller), psychographic (Michelob Light for 'the people who want it all') and behavioural (Hagar's Gallery line for men who work out a lot, 'fit for the fit').
Rank	… because it is the best-selling product (Hertz and Blue Cross/Blue Shield); not very useful on a new item unless also positioned under parent brand.
Endorsement	… because people you respect say it is good. May be expert (the many doctors who prescribed DuoFilm wart remover when it was prescription-only) or a person to be emulated (NEC cellular phone keys were designed for Mickey Spillane).
Experience	… because its long and frequent use attests to its desirable attributes. Modes are other market (Nuprin's extensive use in the prescription market), bandwagon (Stuart Hall's Executive line of business accessories are 'the tools business professionals rely on') and time (Bell's Yellow Pages).
	The last two of these are of limited use on new products.
Competitor	… because it is just (or almost) like another product that you know and like (new RPS air service, just like the leading competitor, only cheaper).
Predecessor	… because it is comparable (in some way) to an earlier product you liked (Hershey's new Solitaries addition to Golden line).

FIGURE 10.6 Surrogate positioning—alternatives and examples

Source: Merle C. Crawford, *New Product Management*, 5th edn, 1997, p. 348. Reproduced with the permission of McGraw-Hill Companies.

that hammers away at one of these positions and consistently delivers on it will probably become best known and remembered for it.

Other marketers think that companies should position themselves on more than one differentiating factor. This may be necessary if two or more firms are claiming to be the best on the same attribute. Volvo is still regarded as the 'safest' and 'most durable' car—if you are in an accident, it is better to be in a Volvo. When Volvo found that Mercedes had also adopted a safety and durability stance, it decided to change to a more performance- and lifestyle-oriented pitch of style and safety with the new S40 model and comfort and safety with the S80 model. Although these two benefits are compatible—a very safe car should also be very durable—it benefits neither car maker if positions become blurred when the same two differentiating factors are used by competitors.

Today, in a time when the mass market is fragmenting into many small segments, companies are trying to broaden their positioning strategies to appeal to more segments. For example, GlaxoSmith-

Kline promotes its Macleans Triple Stripe toothpaste as offering a variety of benefits such as 'long-lasting taste', 'patented fluoride protection' and 'antiplaque protection'. Clearly, many people want all three benefits, and the challenge is to convince them that the brand delivers all three. The company's solution was to promote a toothpaste that squeezed out of the tube in three colours, thus visually confirming the three benefits. In doing this, Macleans attracted three segments instead of one.

However, as companies increase the number of claims for their brands, they risk disbelief and a loss of clear positioning. In general, a company needs to avoid three major positioning errors. The first is *underpositioning—failing* really to position the company at all. Some companies discover that buyers have only a vague idea of the company or that they do not really know anything special about it. The second positioning error is *overpositioning—giving* buyers too narrow a picture of the company. Thus, a consumer might think that David Jones is expensive compared with its competitors because of its hound's-tooth packaging and the imagery and personalities in its advertising, and not hear the line that it will not knowingly be beaten on price. Finally, companies must avoid *confused positioning*—leaving buyers with a confused image of a company. For example, Hungry Jack's (the Burger King franchise in Australia) struggled for years to establish a profitable and consistent position. Since 1991, however, it has adopted a consistent 'resistance is useless' advertising message and based its campaign on 1960s music, thereby giving greater focus to its identity. This is not unlike the position of Burger King in the USA. Now Hungry Jack's more recent slogan, 'the burgers taste better at Hungry Jack's', has been supplemented by 'we're all about fresh at Hungry Jack's'.[27]

Which differences to promote? Not all brand differences are meaningful or worthwhile. Not every difference is a differentiator. Each difference has the potential to create company costs as well as customer benefits. Therefore, the company must carefully select the ways in which it will distinguish itself from its competitors. A difference is worth establishing to the extent that it satisfies the following criteria. It must be:

- *Important:* The difference delivers a highly valued benefit to target buyers.
- *Distinctive:* Competitors do not offer the difference, or the company can offer it in a more distinctive way.
- *Superior:* The difference is superior to other ways that customers might obtain the same benefit.
- *Communicable:* The difference is communicable and visible to buyers.
- *Pre-emptive:* Competitors cannot easily copy the difference.
- *Affordable:* Buyers can afford to pay for the difference.
- *Profitable:* The company can introduce the difference profitably.

Many companies have introduced differentiations that failed one or more of these tests. The Westin Stamford hotel in Singapore advertises that it is the world's tallest hotel, a distinction that is not important to many tourists—in fact, it turns many off. In Australia and the USA the Iridium satellite phones were unsuccessful. Being able to talk anywhere, even in the desert, did not have sufficient appeal to customers in relation to the phone's high cost—especially when traditional networks cover 98% of Australia's inhabitable regions. Polaroid's Polarvision, which produced instantly developed home movies, also failed. Although Polarvision was distinctive and even pre-emptive, it was inferior to another way of capturing motion, namely video cameras.

Some competitive advantages can be quickly ruled out because they are too slight, too costly to develop or too inconsistent with the company's profile. Suppose that a company is designing its positioning strategy and has narrowed its list of possible competitive advantages to four. The company needs a framework for selecting the one advantage that makes the most sense to develop. Table 10.2 (overleaf) shows a systematic way to evaluate several potential competitive advantages and to choose the right one.

TABLE 10.2 Finding competitive advantage

Competitive advantage	Company standing (1–10)	Competitor standing (1–10)	Importance of improving standing (H-M-L)	Affordability and speed (H-M-L)	Competitor's ability to improve standing (H-M-L)	Recommended action
Technology	8	8	L	L	M	Hold
Cost	6	8	H	M	M	Watch
Quality	8	6	L	L	H	Watch
Service	4	3	H	H	L	Invest

In Table 10.2 the company compares its standing on four attributes—technology, cost, quality and service—with the standing of its major competitor. Let's assume that both companies stand at 8 on technology (1 = low score, 10 = high score), which means they both have good technology. The company questions whether it can gain much by improving its technology further, especially given the high cost of new technology. The competitor has a better standing on cost (8 instead of 6), and this can hurt the company if the market becomes more price sensitive. The company offers higher quality than its competitors (8 instead of 6). Finally, both companies offer below-average service.

At first glance it appears that the company should go after cost or service to improve its market appeal relative to the competitor. However, it must consider other factors. First, how important are improvements in each of these attributes to the target customers? The fourth column shows that cost and service improvements would both be highly important to customers. Next, can the company afford to make the improvements? If so, how fast can it complete them? The fifth column shows that the company could improve service quickly and affordably. But if the firm decided to do this, would the competitor be able to improve its service also? The sixth column shows that the competitor's ability to improve service is low, perhaps because the competitor doesn't believe in service or is strapped for funds. The final column then shows the appropriate actions to take on each attribute. It makes the most sense for the company to invest in improving its service. Service is important to customers; the company can afford to improve its service and do it fast; and the competitor probably can't catch up.

Communicating and delivering the chosen position

Once it has chosen a position, the company must take strong steps to deliver and communicate the desired position to target consumers. All the company's marketing mix efforts must support the positioning strategy. Positioning the company calls for concrete action, not just talk. If the company decides to build a position on better quality and service, it must first *deliver* that position. Designing the marketing mix—product, price, place and promotion—essentially involves working out the tactical details of the positioning strategy. Thus, a firm that seizes upon a 'high-quality position' knows that it must produce high-quality products, charge a high price, distribute through high-class dealers and advertise in high-quality media. It must hire and train more service people, find retailers who have a good reputation for service and develop sales and advertising messages that broadcast its superior service. This is the only way to build a consistent and believable high-quality, high-service position.

Companies often find it easier to come up with a good positioning strategy than to implement it. Establishing a position or changing one usually takes a long time. On the other hand, positions that have taken years to build can quickly be lost. Once a company has built the desired position, it must take care to maintain the position through consistent performance and communication. The position must be closely monitored and adapted over time to match changes in consumer needs and competitors' strategies. However, the company should avoid abrupt changes that might confuse consumers. Instead, a product's position should evolve gradually as it adapts to the ever-changing marketing environment.

SELF-CHECK QUESTIONS

9 Explain the concept of market positioning.

10 What forms of differentiation can be achieved by different positioning strategies? Describe each form with reference to the market for pay-TV.

11 What factors should be considered when deciding on the market positioning to communicate?

SUMMARY

Sellers can take three approaches to a market. *Mass marketing* is the decision to mass produce and mass distribute one product and attempt to attract all kinds of buyers. *Product-variety marketing* is the decision to produce two or more market offers differentiated in style, features, quality or sizes, designed to offer variety to the market and to set the seller's products apart from competitor's products. *Target marketing* is the decision to identify the different groups that make up a market and to develop products and marketing mixes for selected target markets. Sellers today are moving away from mass marketing and product differentiation towards target marketing because this approach is more helpful in spotting market opportunities and developing more effective products and marketing mixes.

The key steps in target marketing are market segmentation, market targeting and market positioning. *Market segmentation* is the act of dividing a market into distinct groups of buyers who might merit separate products or marketing mixes. The marketer tries different variables to see which give the best segmentation opportunities. For consumer marketing, the major segmentation variables are geographic, demographic, psychographic and behavioural. Business markets can be segmented by business consumer demographics, operating characteristics, purchasing approaches, situational factors and personal characteristics. The effectiveness of segmentation analysis depends on finding segments that are *measurable*, *accessible*, *substantial* and *actionable.*

Next, the seller has to target the best market segments. The company first evaluates each segment's size and growth characteristics, structural attractiveness and compatibility with company resources and objectives. It then chooses one of three market-coverage strategies. The seller can ignore segment differences (*undifferentiated marketing*), develop different market offers for several segments (*differentiated marketing*) or go after one or a few market segments (*concentrated marketing*). Much depends on company resources, product variability, product life-cycle stage and competitive marketing strategies.

Once a company has decided what segments to enter, it must decide on its *market positioning* strategy—on which positions to occupy in its chosen segments. It can position its products on specific product attributes, according to usage occasion, for certain classes of users or by product class. It can position either against or away from competitors. The positioning task consists of three steps: identifying a set of possible competitive advantages on which to build a position, selecting the right competitive advantages, and effectively communicating and delivering the chosen position to the market.

MARKETING ISSUE

In practice many business-to-business marketers primarily segment their markets on business demographics using criteria such as size of customer (in terms of assets or employees), how much money they spend in the area of interest or what industry they represent. As a result they group their customers into corporate, government and SMEs (small and medium businesses). Two issues commonly arise from this.

First, corporate and government customers are frequently dealt with on an individual basis and each offering is formulated to provide a unique solution for that specific customer. While this may be considered 'good marketing', it often overlooks the common needs and benefits requirements of specific groups of customers which would enable repeatable solutions to be developed with positive impacts on profitability and identification of viable new opportunities. Benefits-based segmentation, rather than demographic segmentation as the primary segmentation scheme, typically will require new reporting systems to be developed by the company to capture the relevant data for evaluating sales and profit potential and making the appropriate marketing decisions. This change also requires a different mindset as well as time and investment to implement it effectively.

Second, the SME market is usually not just one segment. It is made up of several segments, each having different needs and benefits requirements in terms of applications, service, costs and quality. However, many large businesses treat SMEs as one market and provide generalised offerings which do not fully satisfy any particular subsegment.

Orica, the Australian-based chemicals and explosives company, is an example of one large business that has been able to segment its markets according to needs and benefits differences and has shown consistent profitability growth since doing so.

What do you think is required for an industrial company to move from demographics-based to benefits-based segmentation as the primary driver of its segmentation approach?

KEY TERMS

age and life-cycle segmentation	347	gender segmentation	348	micromarketing	344
behavioural segmentation	350	geographic segmentation	347	occasion segmentation	350
benefit segmentation	350	income segmentation	348	permission marketing	363
competitive advantage	367	intermarket segmentation	356	product position	364
concentrated marketing	362	market positioning	345	psychographic segmentation	349
demographic segmentation	347	market segmentation	344	target market	360
differentiated marketing	361	market targeting	345	undifferentiated marketing	360

DISCUSSING THE ISSUES

1 Market segmentation is built around identifying differences in needs between different groups of customers. How does National Australia Bank account for those different needs and segment its consumer market?

2 How effectively do companies segment their markets? Compare service industries like insurance and entertainment. Give examples from your own experience—which do it best and which worst?

3 The factors that make segments attractive are often different for large firms and small businesses. Large companies are attracted to large growth markets while small ones are drawn to more specialised niche market segments. Describe this for the swimwear industry or the wine industry.

4 Some industrial suppliers are able to command a premium price by offering service, selection and reliability. This has occurred in markets for chemicals and building supplies. How can these suppliers segment the market to find customers who are willing to pay more for these benefits?

5 What roles do product attributes and perceptions of attributes play in positioning a product? Can an attribute held by several competing brands be used in a successful positioning strategy? Give an example of this in the airline industry.

6 Describe how Coca-Cola has moved from mass marketing to product-variety marketing to target marketing. Can you think of other examples of companies whose marketing approaches have evolved over time?

REFERENCES

1. Sources: <www.slowtwitch.com/mainheadings/features/state03.html>, accessed 26 September 2005; Dan Empfield, 'Women Are Quietly Fueling Triathlon's Growth', 5.9.03, <www.fairchildmanagementgroup.com/about>, accessed 26 September 2005; S. J. Croft, C. C. Gray and J. F. Duncan, 'Motives for Participating in Triathlon—An Investigation between Elite and Non-Elite Competitors in an Australian setting', <www.geocities.com/CollegePark/5686/su99p12.htm?200526>, accessed 26 September 2005; 'The Orca Story', <www.betterebydesign.org.nz/stories/orca/step1.php>, accessed 26 September 2005.

2. See how customers play a key role in segmenting emerging markets in Stefan Thomke and Eric von Hippel, 'Customers as Innovators: A New Way to Create Value', *Harvard Business Review*, April 2002, pp. 74–81. See also Jim Sterne, *World Wide Web Marketing*, New York, Wiley, 1999, Chapter 11. See also a commentary on the trends in segmentation in Philip Kotler, *According to Kotler*, New York, AMACOM, 2005, pp. 48–51.

3. Toyota Avenue website, <http://toyotaavenue.com.au>, accessed 10 March 2003.

4. See the products offered by Norganic at <www.norganic.com>. For the process of identifying and measuring market segments refer to Malcolm McDonald and Ian Dunbar, *Market Segmentation: How to do it, How to profit from it*, Oxford, Elsevier Butterworth-Heinemann, 2004.

5. Mike Duff, 'Deep Discount Garners Interest Outside of Dollar Store Realm', *DSN Retailing Today*, New York, vol. 41, no. 18, 23 September 2002, p. 5; Cecile B. Corral, 'Dollar Express Readies for Growth', *Discount Store News*, vol. 38, no. 8, 19 April 1999, p. 3. Also see AP Dow Jones, 'Private-Label Goods Change European Retailing Scene', *The Australian Financial Review*, 22 October 1992, p. 32.

6. See <www.bostonmarket.com/media/index.jsp>, accessed 12 March 2003; also Kate MacArthur, 'Boston Market Ads Make Dinner a Focus', *Advertising Age*, Midwest region edition, vol. 74, no. 3, 20 January 2003, p. 34; Daniel Rogers, 'Can Mac Fight Back?', *Marketing*, 17 October 2002, p. 22; Neil Shoebridge, 'Food Retailers in a Rush to Gobble up the Heat-and-Eat Market', *Business Review Weekly*, 9 November 1999.

7. See Frank R. Kardes, *Consumer Behavior and Managerial Decision Making*, Reading, Mass., Addison Wesley, 1999, pp. 117, 172–173.

8. See <www.colgate.com/cp/global.class/showcasetool/templates/displayAllProducts.jsp?catid=12&id=122&pid=8>, accessed 5 March 2003. For more reading on benefit segmentation see George Belch and Michael Belch, *Introduction to Advertising and Promotion: An Integrated Marketing Communication Perspective*, 3rd edn, New York, Richard Irwin Publishers, 1995, p. 137; Russell I. Haley, 'Benefit Segmentation: Backwards and Forwards', *Journal of Advertising Research*, February–March 1984, pp. 19–25.

9. TMP, <http://au.tmp.com>, accessed 7 March 2003; and Drake Personnel, <www.drakeintl.com/>, accessed 7 March 2003. Also see Saul Hansell, 'Once an Acquirer, TMP Worldwide Decides to Divide', *New York Times*, Late Edition (East Coast), 18 February 2003, p. C.1; Narelle Hooper, 'Employment: Headhunters Sit This One Out', *Business Review Weekly*, 9 July 1999.

10. See Rafi Mohammed, Robert J. Fisher, Bernard Javorski and Aileen Cahill, *Internet Marketing: Building Advantage in the Networked Economy*, Boston, McGraw-Hill, 2002, Chapter 10; Jim Sterne, *World Wide Web Marketing*, New York, Wiley, 1999, Chapter 11, pp. 283–284; Margo Komenar, *Electronic Marketing*, New York, John Wiley, 1997, Chapter 2, pp. 80–88, and Chapter 3, pp. 89–112.

11. Sally Dibb, 'Segmentation Analysis for Industrial Markets: Problems of Integrating Customer Requirements into Operations Strategy', *European Journal of Marketing*, vol. 36, no. 1/2, 2002, p. 231; Paul Millier, 'Intuition Can Help in Segmenting Industrial Markets', *Industrial Marketing Management*, vol. 29, no. 2, 2000, p. 147. See Subhash C. Jain, *Marketing Planning and Strategy*, 5th edn, Cincinnati, Ohio, South-Western College Publishing, 1997, pp. 116–117; Thomas V. Bonoma and Benson P. Shapiro, *Segmenting the Industrial Market*, Lexington, Mass., Lexington Books, 1983. For examples of segmenting business markets, see Kate Bertrand, 'Market Segmentation: Divide and Conquer', *Business Marketing*, October 1989, pp. 48–54.

12. See Reuters, 'Net Remains Privilege of Argentinean Elite', 11 August 1999, <www.nua.ie/surveys/index.cgi?f=VS&art_id=905355182&rel=true>; Boston Consulting Group, 'Brazil Driving Latin American E-commerce', 27 July 1999, <www.nua.ie/surveys/index.cgi?f=VS&art_id= 905355057&rel=true>; Marlene L. Rossman, 'Understanding Five Nations of Latin America', *Marketing News*, 11 October 1985, p. 10, as quoted in Subhash C. Jain, *International Marketing Management*, 3rd edn, Boston, PWS–Kent Publishing Company, 1990, p. 366.

13. Charles R. Taylor, 'Emerging Issues in Marketing', *Psychology & Marketing*, vol. 17, no. 6, June 2000, p. 441; Shawn Tully, 'Teens: The Most Global Market of All', *Fortune*, 16 May 1994, pp. 90–97.

14. Subhash C. Jain, *International Marketing Management*, 3rd edn, Boston, PWS–Kent Publishing Company, 1990, pp. 370–371.

15. Anonymous, 'Web Site for Left Handed People Launched', *Internet Business News*, 24 May 2000, p. 1; <www.anythinglefthanded.co.uk/>, accessed 12 March 2003. Also see American Psychological Association, 'Who Are Left-Handed People?', <www.apa.org/monitor/apr97/leftside.html>, accessed 5 November 1999; and Joe Schwartz, 'Southpaw Strategy', *American Demographics*, June 1988, p. 61.

16. See Carl Shapiro and Hal R. Varian, *Information Rules: A Strategic Guide to the Network Economy*, Boston, Mass., Harvard Business School Press, Chapter 6; Michael Porter, *Competitive Advantage*, New York, The Free Press, 1985, pp. 4–8, 234–236. For a discussion on optimising competitiveness using operations strategy, see Danny Samson, *Manufacturing and Operations Strategy*, Sydney, Prentice Hall Australia, 1991, Chapter 1.

17. James Kirby (Cover Story) 'Part Two: Online's Top 10', *Business Review Weekly*, 17 September 1999; Robert Gottliebsen (Editorial Comment) 'Retailers Shape Up over the Net', *Business Review Weekly*, 5 April 1999; Rafi Mohammed, Robert J. Fisher, Bernard Javorski and Aileen Cahill, *Internet Marketing: Building Advantage in the Networked Economy*, Boston, McGraw-Hill, 2002, Chapters 7 and 12.

18. Seth Godin, *Permission Marketing, Turning Strangers into Friends and Friends into Customers*, New York, Simon and Schuster, 1999; J. Hagel and A.G. Armstrong, *Net.Gain: Expanding Markets through Virtual Communities*, Boston, Harvard Business School Press, 1997; Kate Lyons, 'Web Sites that Work', *Professional Marketing*, April/May 1998, p. 24; Neil Gross, 'Building Global Communities', *Business Week ebiz*, 22 March 1999, pp. 22–23.

19. For more reading on positioning, see Carl Shapiro and Hal R. Varian, *Information Rules: A Strategic Guide to the Network Economy*, Boston, Harvard Business School Press, 1999, Chapter 1; Yoram Wind, 'New Twists for Some Old Tricks', *The Wharton Magazine*, Spring 1980, pp. 34–39; David A. Aaker and J. Gary Shansby, 'Positioning Your Product', *Business Horizons*, May–June 1982, pp. 56–62; and Regis McKenna, 'Playing for Position', *INC*, April 1985, pp. 92–97. For more reading on positioning in service industries see Linden Brown, *Competitive Marketing Strategy*, Melbourne, Thomas Nelson Australia, 1990, Chapter 5.

20. Jack Trout with Steve Rivkin, *The New Positioning*, New York, McGraw-Hill, 1995.
21. See <www.gsk.com.au/gskinternet/publishing.nsf/Content/Macleans+Triple+Stripe>.
22. See the advertisement in *Business Week*, 5 March 2003, p. 66, and the advertisement in *Business Week*, 17 June 2002, p. 70.
23. See <www.virgin.com/redirect.html?content=http://www.virgin.com/international/australia/index.shtml>, accessed 5 March 2003.
24. See <www.johnsonsbaby.com/pro_shampoo.asp>, accessed 5 March 2003.
25. For a good discussion of the concepts of differentiation and competitive advantage and methods for assessing them, see Michael Porter, *Competitive Advantage*, Chapter 2; George S. Day and Robin Wensley, 'Assessing Advantage: A Framework for Diagnosing Competitive Superiority', *Journal of Marketing*, April 1988, pp. 1–20; and Philip Kotler, *Marketing Management*, 9th edn, Englewood Cliffs, NJ, Prentice Hall, 1997, Chapter 11.
26. Amy Rogers, 'Ties that Bind?', *CRN*, no. 1006, 5 August 2002, p. 16. Also see Beverley Head, 'Fine Line for IBM Aust', *The Australian Financial Review*, 19 October 1992, p. 38; Tony Thomas, 'Working for the World in a New Way of Outsourcing', *Business Review Weekly*, 25 January 1999; Brad Howarth, 'Big Three under Challenge', *Business Review Weekly*, 29 October 1999.
27. Matt Balogh, 'Cracking the Kids Marketing Code', *B & T Weekly*, 7 August 2002; also see Mark Landler and Gail DeGeorge, 'Tempers Are Sizzling over Burger King's New Ads', *Business Week*, 12 February 1990, p. 33. See also <www.hungryjacks.com.au/Home.aspx>, accessed 8 November 2005.

PHOTO/AD CREDITS

Margaret Wallace, University of Canberra

CASE STUDY

There's no other store like David Jones

'There's no other store like David Jones' is the slogan of this retailer and there is some truth in it: David Jones, founded in 1838, is the oldest department store in the world still trading under its original name. It has 37 stores spread across every Australian state except Tasmania and the Northern Territory. Typically, the stores are located in central business districts and in major suburban malls—for example, Chatswood Chase or Bondi Junction in Sydney, and Civic Mall and Woden Mall in Canberra. The stores themselves are continually refurbished in prestigious style, and the new Adelaide store won an international design award.

David Jones offers a wide range of services: a bridal registry, florist, interior decorator, beauty treatments (there is a day spa in the flagship Elizabeth Street store in Sydney) and an online wine club. At the Elizabeth Street store there is even a women's health screening clinic. David Jones's customers can arrange to have gift hampers delivered to the UK and the USA as well as within Australia. Corporate clients are invited to use the Gift Card service as a convenient way to reward employees and individual customers can also purchase gift voucher cards if they are looking for an easy solution to gift shopping. Counter staff are trained to help and advise customers and to address them by name.

The David Jones credit card is an important contributor to company earnings: about one-third of company profits came from this source in 2005. The card charges no annual fee and offers up to 56 days' interest-free credit. Holders are eligible for special offers on 'selected quality products' and receive invitations to special events, fashion parades, cosmetic launches and exclusive shopping nights.

Unlike its rival, Myer, David Jones rarely holds sales, relying on its half-yearly clearances, and advertises relatively infrequently on television.[1] Its

main communication tools are print advertising in publications like *Good Weekend* (which targets upmarket readers) and catalogues delivered to the mailboxes of its target customers. The catalogues are expensively produced on good quality paper and lavishly illustrated with full-page colour photos, often including Asian models. The Summer 2005 catalogue was shot on the Italian Amalfi Coast and features Italian brands such as Bulgari, Fendi, Zegna and Ferragamo as well as Australian designers. Typical prices are $575 for a pair of shoes and $1795 for a man's suit. Younger consumers are catered for by brands such as Diesel, Sass & Bide, Tommy Hilfiger and Marcs Baby Doll. The company also has its own David Jones clothing brand, which offers a limited range of medium-priced items such as tee shirts and knitwear.

In spite of the focus on spacious, luxurious décor and upmarket international brands, David Jones has a Price Promise: 'It costs no more to shop at David Jones'. If a customer can find a product at a cheaper price elsewhere, David Jones will match the competitor's price.

In addition to men's and women's clothing, cosmetics, accessories and footwear, David Jones also stocks furniture and electrical goods, manchester, toys, books and stationery. Some stores also have gourmet food halls.

Recently there has been an increase in the use of Brand Concept Areas. These resemble individual boutiques within the store, each dedicated to a leading brand and staffed by specialists in that brand. This is in keeping with David Jones's image as a brand-based store, with many brands exclusive to David Jones.

The department store dilemma

Globally, as well as in Australia, there is concern that department stores are becoming the dinosaurs of retail. Their market share in many categories is being taken over by specialty stores. For example, a consumer who would once have bought white goods from a department store may

---

1   However, in August 2005 Coles Myer announced that it would sell its Myer stores, and subsequently David Jones began to imitate Myer's strategy of frequent sales advertised in full page newspaper ads.

now prefer to buy them from a retailer like Harvey Norman. When department stores originated in the nineteenth century there were no shopping malls so consumers welcomed the one-stop shopping offered by department stores. Now that shopping malls can outdo department stores by offering a huge range of specialty goods under one roof, can the department store survive? Coles Myer evidently has its doubts: in late 2005 the company announced that it would be selling its Myer stores, after numerous failed attempts to improve their performance.

Yet David Jones has bucked the trend: in spite of a slowdown in consumer spending in 2005, David Jones achieved a record profit after tax of $77.9 million, representing 19.2% growth on the previous year. The company now plans to buy a number of the Myer stores.

Target marketing by David Jones

David Jones appears to have been targeting the higher end of the market successfully, which has helped boost sales and profits. The upmarket marketing mix seems to be positioned to appeal to customers from the AB demographic quintile. The quintile system is a tool for segmenting customers by socioeconomic status (SES) into five groups, each representing 20% of the population, with AB as the highest, followed by C, D E and FG. To be classified in the AB quintile, a customer needs to score at least 125 points based on education, income and occupation. For example, a doctor earning $80 000 would score 60 for education, 52 for income and 59 for occupation, a total of 171 points. A salesperson who had completed secondary school and earns $29 000 would be placed in the D quintile with a score of 30 for

education, 20 for income and 39 for occupation, totalling 89.

The socioeconomic quintile system of segmentation is now being challenged by an alternative approach developed by Ross Honeywill and Verity Byth of the Centre for Customer Strategy. In *The New Consumer Landscape in Australia—2004* these authors propose a new category of even more desirable high-value consumers, the Neo Consumers (NEOs). Although some ABs can also be classified as NEOs, in the Big Spender category we find that 54% are NEOs but only 42% are ABs. To qualify as a NEO a consumer must have a high-spending propensity and a high-spending capacity—features with important implications for marketers. NEOs read more magazines than ABs and use more commercial radio and television. Australia has 3.8 million NEOs, most of whom live in Sydney or Melbourne. They may be found in all age groups, but are most highly represented among 25–39 year olds. Ross Honeywill believes that 72% of David Jones's customers are NEOs.

Attractive though the AB segment may have been to David Jones in the past, it would be understandable if the company's focus were now shifting to the NEOs as its primary target market.

Sources: ABC Radio National, 'Specialty Outlets Lay Siege to Department Stores', *Inside Business*, 3 April 2005; ABC Radio National, *Saturday Extra*, 4 February 2006; David Jones, Chairman's and Chief Executive Officer's Address, 2 December 2005; David Jones, *Annual Report 2005*; Fairfax, Readership—September 2002, Media Release. Michelle Innes, 'Trouble in Store', *The Age*, 14 December 2005, p. 10; Mitchells, 'What Are Quintiles', <http://mitchells.au/media/faqs/quintiles>, accessed 3 January 2006; Roy Morgan Research, 'The New Consumer Landscape in Australia—2004'; Roy Morgan Research, 'ABs Challenged as the Media Holy Grail', Article No. 363, 8 December 2004; Amanda Swinburne, 'Sale-mania Year Round for Retail Giants', *B & T*, 17 June 2005, p. 14; <www.davidjones.com.au>, accessed 3 December 2005.

QUESTIONS

1. What is the relationship between segmentation, targeting and positioning? Illustrate you answer with reference to David Jones.

2. Analyse and evaluate David Jones's marketing strategy.

3. David Jones appears to be targeting younger customers with brands like Diesel and Sass & Bide. Why? In your experience, how successful is this strategy?

4　Visit a website like <http://mitchells.com.au/media/faqs/quintiles> and calculate your quintile now and in five years' time. Do the same for your parents. Do your findings suggest that there is a positive relationship between the AB quintile and a tendency to shop at David Jones?

5　What would be useful segmentation variables for identifying target segments for a department store?

6　Why might marketers wish to target ABs or NEOs?

7　Refer to Figure 10.4. Is the positioning of David Jones relative to its competitors consistent with the information provided in the case about the likely needs of the store's target customers for quality, status and service levels?

PART 3

WORKING WITH THE EXTENDED MARKETING MIX

CHAPTER 11

Products: goods, services and experiences

Australia Post: www.auspost.com.au

Disney: www.disney.com.hk

Hong Kong Tourism Board:
www.khta.org

Interbrand: www.interbrand.com

Traditional marketing theory divides offerings into goods, services and experiences. But the boundaries are increasingly becoming blurred. In their best selling book *The Experience Economy* (one of the four finalists for the American Marketing Association book of the year award in 2003), authors Joseph Pine and James Gilmore argue that leading-edge companies can achieve higher value by providing experiences that customers will readily pay for, rather than by thinking about selling goods and services. Pine and Gilmore quote a range of companies which have transformed services into experiences—the Hard Rock cafés, Nike superstores and Disney theme parks.

Pine and Gilmore's book makes a convincing argument that companies need to differentiate their offerings, but if you are a Disney theme park or a theme restaurant it is obviously easier to create an 'experience' than if you are offering a product which is more mundane—for example, if you're a bank, insurance company or supermarket. However, this doesn't mean that 'experiences' marketing is only relevant for some companies. Let's look at one of the newest big experiences around, Disneyland Hong Kong, which opened in late 2005, and its effect on other businesses.

On any criteria, Disneyland qualifies as an experience; its very slogan 'the magical kingdom' reflects Disney's aim of providing park visitors with an escape from their normal routine. But what works in the USA doesn't always work overseas. After a very successful opening in Tokyo, Disneyland famously suffered large losses when it opened in France, as Europeans protested at the arrival of American culture. The park struggled to attract visitor numbers, and those who went spent less than expected. So Disneyland conducted substantial research into what might work well in the Hong Kong park. Experts in the Chinese tradition of feng shui—the belief that harmonious energy and fortune can be achieved by correct design—were consulted in the design of the park. Mulan, a Chinese animated film heroine, is featured in the park, located in the Fantasy Gardens, with lots of picture spots to accommodate the higher frequency of photo taking by Chinese visitors. However, trying to combine the Disney experience with traditional Chinese practices also created unexpected problems; Disneyland hotels were confronted with worldwide protests after news that the hotels would serve shark fin soup, a traditional Chinese delicacy. Environmentalists protested that the practice was environmentally unsound, with some species of sharks being fished to extinction, and cruel, since sharks are often thrown back into the water to die after their fin is sliced off. The publicity led to threats of consumer boycotts of Disneyland Hong Kong, and (after some delay) the hotels agreed to take shark fin soup off the menus.

However, the marketing implications of Disneyland Hong Kong reach far beyond the park itself. The financing of the park, and its impact on the Hong Kong economy, shows the interconnection between businesses and

Even a popular experience like Disneyland needs smart marketing—research, planning and attention to detail.

government in delivering a major experience to the public. The Hong Kong government has invested heavily in bringing Disneyland to Hong Kong in its largest ever infrastructure project, spending $HK25 billion (around $A4.3 billion) to develop the site and related infrastructure, for a 57% majority ownership in the park. Projects like Disneyland have a huge effect on local economies; the project has generated around 14 000 job opportunities in construction, and is expected to result in around 36 000 ongoing direct or indirect jobs at the park and from flow-on effects on local businesses. Don Robinson, the Group Managing Director of Hong Kong Disneyland, estimates that the park will receive around 5.6 million tourists in the first year of its opening, around one-third locals, one-third from China and the rest from other Asia–Pacific countries. Many of those visitors wouldn't have come to Hong Kong without the park, and many will stay in Hong Kong for a few more nights, fuelling the opening of new hotels and higher occupancy rates for established hotels. Visitors will fly to Hong Kong with Cathay Pacific, ride on Hong Kong's new train line, visit its new cable car, shop in local shops and eat at local restaurants (perhaps even shark fin soup, though not at a Disneyland hotel!). The park also has flow-on effects for nearby economies; there is some concern in Singapore that increased numbers of tourists in Hong Kong will mean fewer visitors to Singapore, but Hong Kong is already looking nervously towards the future opening of Disneyland in Shanghai. Construction on the Shanghai park hasn't started, and there is no date for completion, but it's likely that Disney will go ahead with a mainland theme park, and that sooner or later Hong Kong Disneyland will be competing with another newer Disneyland park in Asia. But meanwhile, Disneyland offers one more attraction for potential visitors to Hong Kong, and marketing Disneyland means marketing Hong Kong, with huge flow-on opportunities for Hong Kong businesses. Experiences are big business, even for firms which aren't selling the experience themselves.[1]

After reading this chapter you should be able to:

1 Describe the nature of product in marketing management.

2 Explain the concept of the goods–services spectrum.

3 Define the term product, including the core, actual and augmented product.

4 Explain product classifications, and contrast the differing types of consumer products and business-to-business products.

5 Explain services classifications and discuss the marketing of services.

6 Discuss an extended notion of product which includes marketing persons, experiences, events, places, political ideas, causes, non-profit services and fundraising endeavours.

7 Outline the range of individual product decisions marketers make, discussing the product attributes of quality, features and design.

8 Discuss branding, and contrast the differences between line extensions, brand extensions, multibrands and new brands.

9 Illustrate product line and product mix decisions, describing stretching and filling the product line length.

10 List some of the considerations marketers face in making international product decisions, including whether or not to standardise or adapt product and packaging.

This chapter begins with a deceptively simple question: what is a product? We then look at ways to classify products in consumer and industrial markets and links between types of products and types of marketing strategies. At the broadest level of 'product', marketers may sell commodities, goods, services and experiences. Table 11.1 summarises differences between them; 'commodities are fungible (i.e. they are interchangeable), goods tangible (they can be touched and felt), services intangible, experiences memorable and transformations are effectual, long-lasting and "the customer is the product"'.[2] In this chapter, we see that each type of product involves decisions that go beyond basic product design, such as branding, packaging and labelling, and product support services. Finally, we move from decisions about individual products to decisions about building product lines and product mixes.

Product Anything that can be offered to a market for attention, acquisition, use or consumption that might satisfy a want or need. It includes physical objects, services, persons, places, organisations and ideas.

Fast-moving consumer goods (FMCG) Products such as weekly grocery items which are consumed in a single use or on a few usage occasions.

What is a product?

When most people think about products, they think about physical objects. However, in a marketing context a Slazenger tennis racquet, a performance by a singer like Missy Higgins, a holiday in Bali or a Vodafone phone service are all products. Marketing scientists and practitioners define a **product** as anything that can be offered to a market for attention, acquisition, use or consumption that might satisfy a want or need.

Many products are physical goods, such as cars, shoes, eggs and this book. We refer to products which are used over an extended period of time (such as refrigerators and motor cars) as *durable products*. Products such as weekly grocery items which are consumed in a single use or on a few usage occasions are referred to as non-durable products, or **fast-moving consumer goods (FMCG)**. But

TABLE 11.1 Economic distinctions between commodities, goods, services, experiences and transformations

Economic offering	Commodities	Goods	Services	Experiences	Transformations
Economy	Agrarian	Industrial	Service	Experience	Transformation
Economic function	Extract	Make	Deliver	Stage	Guide
Nature of offering	Fungible	Tangible	Intangible	Memorable	Effectual
Key attribute	Natural	Standardised	Customised	Personal	Individual
Method of supply	Stored in bulk	Inventoried after production	Delivered on demand	Revealed over a duration	Sustained through time
Seller	Trader	Manufacturer	Provider	Stager	Elicitor
Buyer	Market	Customer	Client	Guest	Aspirant
Factors on demand	Characteristics	Features	Benefits	Sensations	Traits

the broad term 'product' also includes services which are sold by marketers. In practice, the sale of many physical products includes some service, and many services include some physical products. Most market offerings lie on a continuum between the two extremes and involve a combination of physical products and services as shown in Figure 11.1. At the physical end of the continuum lie such products as self-service petrol and groceries. They are purchased with little or no service. At the other end of the continuum lie products which are experienced during their delivery. A cruise to the Barrier Reef, a workout in a health club and childcare services fall towards this end of the continuum. These

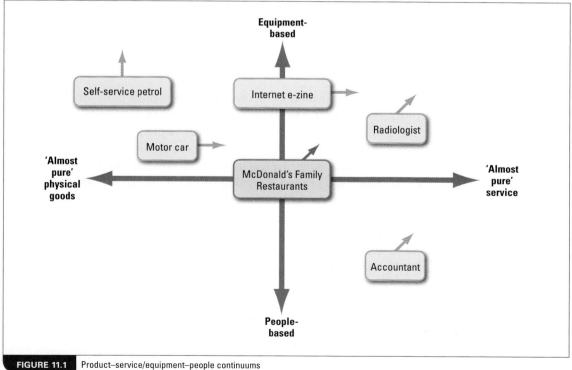

FIGURE 11.1   Product–service/equipment–people continuums

'almost pure' services are activities or benefits offered for sale which are intangible, inseparable from the consumer, perishable in that they are experiential and do not result in ownership of anything.[3] These aspects are elaborated on under the 'Services classifications' heading later in this chapter.

A product from McDonald's is shown in Figure 11.1 as lying midway along the (horizontal) goods–service continuum.[4] It is positioned on this continuum in such a way as to reflect our thinking that burgers, fries and shakes are the physical components, whereas service components tend to be experiential—such as fast and reliable service at the counter, freshly made burgers, cleanly dressed crew and so on. By alluding to many services as experiential, we are reflecting the fact that the customer is more involved in the process of making and consuming the service than is the case with most physical products. This is, however, also true for some physical products, such as Volvo in Europe, which allows customers to help build their car. McDonald's is also shown midway along a second (vertical) continuum in this schematic model—the people–equipment continuum. The continuum shows the greater or lesser reliance on people or processes of different market offerings. We discuss this aspect in more detail under the heading of 'Services classifications' in this chapter. Suffice it to say here that McDonald's is reliant on both its people and its processes to provide the value customers seek. A perfectly cooked burger depends on the correct performance of its equipment and crew, just as the service aspect depends on the communication system between the front of the store and the mini-manufacturing operation at the back of store.

In Figure 11.1 we also see arrows that indicate a movement over time—for a variety of products— towards the equipment end of the vertical continuum, and in many cases towards the service end of the horizontal continuum. Many service organisations are trying to decrease the variability and costs in people-reliant service delivery, by using technology to reduce costs, improve quality and bring services to customers more quickly.[5] So airline customers are encouraged to book online, and banks encourage their customers to bank online rather than going into a bank branch.

Figure 11.1 also reflects that with increasing use of technology in most businesses, equipment and/or technology is increasingly involved in encounters with service providers. This is why the figure shows movement towards the equipment end of the people–equipment continuum. After we purchase a car, we tend to judge the vehicle on its service delivery—its ability to start and transport us safely to our destinations. Thus, we see an arrow pointing towards the service end of the continuum for the motor car.

Core product The problem-solving services or core benefits that consumers are really buying when they obtain a product.

Product planners need to think about the product on three levels. The most basic level is the **core product**, which addresses the question: what is the buyer really buying? As illustrated in Figure 11.2, the core product stands at the centre of the total product. It consists of the problem-solving services or core benefits that consumers obtain when they buy a product. A woman buying lipstick buys more than lip colour. Charles Revson of Revlon saw this when he first stated: 'In the factory, we make cosmetics; in the store, we sell hope'. Thus, when designing products, marketers must first define the core benefits the product will provide to consumers. For example, with an airline like Qantas, illustrated in Figure 11.3, the core benefit or service is 'time-critical transport'.[6]

Actual product A product's parts, styling, features, brand name, packaging and other attributes that combine to deliver core product benefits.

The product planner must next design an **actual product** around the core product. Actual products may have as many as five characteristics: a quality level, features, styling, a brand name and packaging. For example, a Qantas air ticket to Singapore is an actual product. The Qantas brand name, air terminal layout and services, plane seating configuration, crew uniform styling, booking system, features such as in-flight movies, food and beverage service and their quality levels have all been carefully combined to deliver the core benefit or service.

Augmented product Additional consumer services and benefits built around the core and actual products.

Finally, the product planner must build an **augmented product** around the core and actual products by offering additional consumer services and benefits. Qantas must offer more than a flight to Singapore—it must provide consumers with a product that customers value before, during and

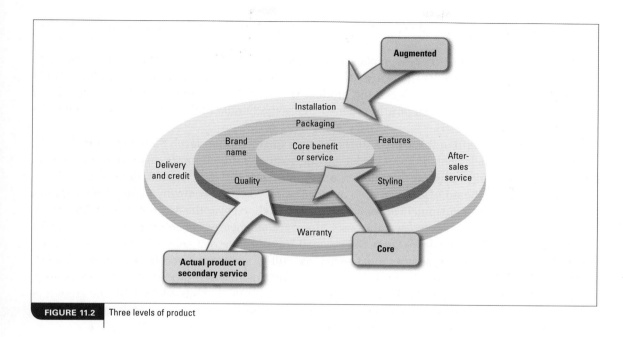

FIGURE 11.2   Three levels of product

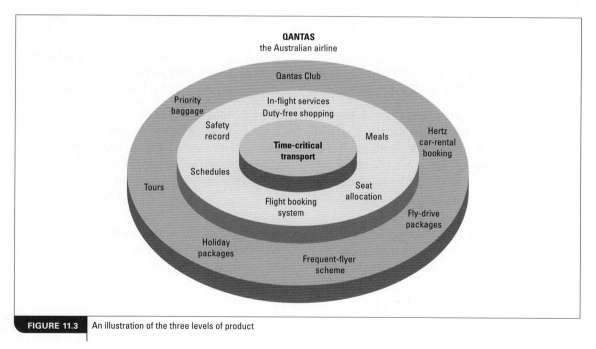

FIGURE 11.3   An illustration of the three levels of product

after the flight. Thus, when consumers buy a Qantas flight, they receive more than just the ticket and a seat on a plane. Some consumers require greater service levels than others—they may require vegetarian meals in-flight. Some expect service before the flight and join the Qantas Club. Some expect to be able to arrange packaged tours to holiday destinations. Some like the idea of receiving a bonus in points from flying with Qantas, so they join the airline's frequent-flyer scheme. To the consumer, these augmentations (and the costs and value they add to the core product) become an important part of the total product, and will contribute to their choice of airline for their flight (see Figure 11.3).

Thus, a product is more than a simple set of tangible features. Consumers tend to see products as complex bundles of benefits that satisfy their needs. When developing products, marketers must first identify the core consumer needs the product will satisfy. They must then design the actual product and find ways to augment it in order to create the bundle of benefits that will provide the greatest value for consumers.

Today, most competition takes place at the product augmentation level. So many companies try to add benefits to their offers that add value for the customer; hotel guests might find a chocolate on the pillow, a bowl of fruit on the table or a DVD player and DVDs; Virgin Airlines even offers a masseuse service on board.[7] However, each augmentation costs the company money. The marketer has to ask whether their customers are willing to pay enough to cover the extra cost, or whether they will make sufficient extra sales to cover the costs. Moreover, augmented benefits soon become expected benefits. Many hotel guests now expect DVDs, small trays of toiletries and other amenities in their rooms. This means that competitors must search for still more features and benefits to distinguish their offers. Finally, as companies raise the prices of their augmented products, some competitors can go back to offering a more basic product at a much lower price. Thus, along with the growth of five-star hotels such as the Four Seasons, we see the emergence of lower-cost hotels and motels for clients who want only basic room accommodation.

SELF-CHECK QUESTIONS

1 In Figure 11.1, Internet e-zines (electronic magazines such as *Salon*) are placed midway on the product–service continuum, and closer to the equipment end of the people–equipment continuum. Do you agree with this positioning? What is the significance of this placement from a marketing mix viewpoint?

2 A hotel chain researching its service quality levels issued tickets with an 11-point (0 to 10) survey question assessing each stage of the customer's stay with the hotel. For example, a ticket issued at the check-in counter asked customers to rate the speed of check-in and the courteousness of staff. Other tickets related to room service and check-out. Completed tickets could be exchanged for a free drink in any of the hotel chain's bars. Comment on the possible research findings and their implications for product design.

The core, actual and augmented service offered by organisations will also change over time. Marketing Highlight 11.1 shows how Australia Post now offers much more than its old core product (mail delivery) and as a result has been able to prosper in a shrinking market for postal services.

Product classifications

In order to develop marketing strategies marketers often divide products and services into two broad classes based on the types of consumers that use them—consumer products and industrial products. Each category is further divided into finer categories to reflect how consumers buy and/or use them.

Consumer products

Consumer products
Products bought by final consumers for personal consumption.

Consumer products are those bought by final consumers for personal consumption. Marketers classify these products further based on how consumers go about buying them. Consumer products include convenience, shopping, specialty and unsought products (see Table 11.2).[8]

TABLE 11.2 Marketing considerations for consumer products

Marketing considerations	Type of consumer product			
	Convenience	**Shopping**	**Specialty**	**Unsought**
Customer buying behaviour	Frequent purchase, little planning, little comparison or shopping effort, low customer involvement	Less frequent purchase, much planning and shopping effort, comparison of brands on price, quality, style	Strong brand preference and loyalty, special purchase effort, little comparison of brands, low price sensitivity	Little product awareness, knowledge (or if aware, little or even negative interest)
Price	Low price	Higher price	High price	Varies
Distribution	Widespread distribution, convenient locations	Selective distribution in fewer outlets	Exclusive distribution in only one or a few outlets per market area	Varies
Promotion	Mass promotion by the producer	Advertising and personal selling by both producer and resellers	More carefully targeted promotion by both producer and resellers	Aggressive advertising and personal selling by producer and resellers
Examples	Toothpaste, magazines, laundry detergent	Major appliances, televisions, furniture, clothing	Luxury goods, such as Rolex watches or fine crystal	Life insurance, Red Cross blood donations

Convenience products are consumer goods and services that people usually buy frequently, immediately and with a minimum of comparison and buying effort. They are usually low priced and widely available. Examples include milk, bread, soap and newspapers. Convenience products can be further divided into staples, impulse products and emergency products. *Staples* are products that consumers buy on a regular basis, such as tea, coffee and toothpaste. *Impulse products* are purchased with little planning or search effort. These products are normally available in many different places because consumers are more likely to buy them on impulse when they see them. So chocolate bars and magazines are placed next to checkout counters to encourage customers to buy on impulse. Some, like CC's corn chips, might be a planned purchase for later impulse consumption. *Emergency products* are purchased when a need is urgent, for example umbrellas during a rainstorm. Manufacturers of emergency products will try to locate them in many outlets to avoid losing a sale when the customer needs them.

Shopping products are consumer goods and services that the customer, in the process of selection and purchase, usually compares on bases such as suitability, quality, price and style. When purchasing shopping products, consumers typically spend considerable time and effort gathering information and making comparisons. Examples include furniture, clothing, used cars and major appliances. Shopping products can be divided into *uniform* and *non-uniform* products. The buyer sees uniform shopping products as similar in quality but different enough in price to justify shopping comparisons. The seller has to 'talk price' to the buyer. But in shopping for clothing, furniture and other non-uniform products, product features are often more important to the consumer than the price. If the buyer wants a new suit, the cut, fit and look are likely to be more important than small price differences. The seller of non-uniform shopping products must therefore carry a wide assortment to satisfy individual tastes and must have well-trained salespeople to give information and advice to customers.

Convenience products
Consumer goods and services that the customer usually buys frequently, immediately and with the minimum of comparison and buying effort.

Shopping products
Consumer goods and services that the customer, in the process of selection and purpose, characteristically compares on such bases as suitability, quality, price and style.

MARKETING HIGHLIGHT

11.1

Much more than letters—the evolution of Australia Post

To maintain profitability in light of its shrinking letter business, Australia Post has had to develop new markets.

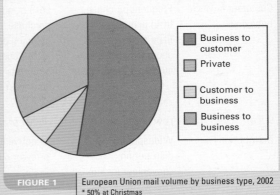

- Business to customer
- Private
- Customer to business
- Business to business

FIGURE 1 | European Union mail volume by business type, 2002
* 50% at Christmas
Source: Adapted from *The Economist*, 22 January 2005.

Post offices all over the world are facing plummeting demand for their core service of over 100 years—letters. After all, who writes letters any more, in an age of email, text messaging and Internet phone calls? Figure 1 shows that personal letters now constitute only a small percentage of postal services (7.5%), and most of that is at Christmas. When demand for your core service is shrinking, the best strategy is to sell the business off and get out, right? However, if you are a postal service, in most countries saddled with what is called a 'universal service obligation'—the requirement to deliver a standard letter at a fixed price to any address within the country—you don't have the option to sell out (and after all who wants to buy a shrinking business?). Even worse, most countries are reducing subsidies to their postal services, opening some classes of mail (such as bulk business mail) to private competitors, and demanding that their

postal services be self-sufficient. One commentator expressed the challenge facing Australia Post as: 'In the age of fax machines, couriers, parcel companies, modems, the Internet and electronic mail, how can Australia Post hope to survive?'. So post offices all over the world are faced with redefining their businesses, and developing a whole new range of products and services for new target segments. The postal services that the average consumer sees are just a tiny portion of postal business, and there's a lot of action in the postal business these days.

Australia Post began the long road of redesigning itself in the early 1990s, by introducing modern retailing décor, barcode scanners and training customer-focused sales assistants. The stores started selling a range of items, such as stationery, cards, computer and telephone consumables—even items of Australiana. Like a supermarket, merchandise most likely to be bought on impulse was placed in bins near the sales counters to catch customers' attention (and sales) while they waited in line. With over 4000 outlets around Australia, Australia Post is the largest physical retail network in the country, and has become a powerful retailing presence.

The retail market is crowded, however, and selling stationery and related items will never generate enough income to replace the lost income from the shrinking personal mail business. And unless there is a reason for customers to go into its stores, Australia Post can't capture any impulse sales. In order to decrease its costs and increase its business, Australia Post invested substantially in information technology to handle over-the-counter transactions, and developed what has become Australia's largest electronic bill paying service, EPOS (after an investment of $70 million). EPOS processes around 160 million transactions per year for a range of third parties such as the utility companies, councils and telcos, all the while earning commissions for Australia Post, and giving customers a reason to come into the stores. Australia Post also started to offer retail banking facilities on behalf of financial institutions, and now handles around 34 million transactions each year for banks and other financial institutions. This move has enabled banks such as Citibank to gain a street-front presence without the recurrent and capital investment many other banks have faced, and at the same time exposes customers to all the retail merchandise that Australia Post is selling.

At the same time, Australia Post moved to replace a stagnant letter market with a growing product—direct mail. Consumer mail has been steadily falling and tends to be concentrated at Christmas, but by investment in technology Australia Post was able to bring down the cost of direct mail, and offered bulk packages to business buyers to encourage them to use direct mail. It used competitions to recruit customers who were prepared to be contacted by commercial organisations, and developed a business selling those customer contacts. It developed a new product, EDIPost, which enables businesses to send invoices, statements or direct marketing electronically to a postal centre which prints them, puts them in envelopes and delivers them. As a consequence, the total amount of mail, while not increasing, has not fallen, as business mail replaces dwindling private mail. Even this portion of Australia Post's business remains under pressure, however, as more and more businesses move to electronic substitution—electronic delivery and payment of bills.

The organisation also moved to increase efficiencies in its operations. It closed branches and offered licences to sell its merchandise and services to sub-branches, which could be run more efficiently by independent operators. Australia Post had always had an extensive delivery network to deliver mail five days a week all around Australia. It extended this service into what became its Post Logistics service, offering a range of integrated logistics services from warehousing to order acceptance, picking, packing, dispatch and distribution, while offering sophisticated tracking and reporting systems at every stage. This investment in logistics has offered Australia Post the opportunity to serve new markets; for example, refrigerated Australia Post trucks deliver groceries ordered online from Coles Supermarkets. More recently, Australia Post has begun a joint venture with a Chinese logistics company and opened logistics centres in China to support Australian businesses importing from China. It's also working on a deal to sell Jetstar tickets at Australia Post shops, in a move which has been said to have the potential to add millions to its profits.

A range of measures like this have seen Australia Post deliver increasing profits to its sole shareholder, the Australian government, despite falling profits in its letter division. In 2004–2005, Australia Post paid the government a dividend of $286.2 million (75% of profits), up from $220 million the year before. It's a great success story of a former government bureaucracy which anticipated its changing environment, developed new products and services to serve a growing business market, and which has profitably expanded in the growing areas of direct mail and logistics. While the backbone of postal services, the consumer letter, may soon be a rarity, it seems postal services will be around for a long time yet.

Sources: Mark Fenton-Jones, 'Call to Curtail Australia Post', The Australian Financial Review, 6 September 2005, p. 47; Damien Lynch, 'Postal Franchisees Sought', The Australian Financial Review, 8 November 2005, p. 56; Ben Potter and Sophie Loras, 'Internet Erodes Letter Profits', The Australian Financial Review, 13 October 2005, p. 3; 'Pulling the Envelope', The Economist, 22 January 2005, pp. 63–65; Australia Post Annual Report, 2005, available at <www.auspost.com.au/annualreport2005/download_entire.asp>, accessed 11 January 2006.

Questions

1 Is Australia Post selling goods, services or experiences? Justify your answer.

2 What do you think is Australia Post's core product? Actual product? Augmented product? How have these changed over the years?

3 Customers frequently complain that when they want to buy stamps or send a package, they need to wait in line behind people paying bills. How should Australia Post respond to this sort of complaint?

11.1

Specialty products
Consumer goods and services with unique characteristics or brand identification for which a significant group of buyers is willing to make a special purchase effort.

Specialty products are consumer goods and services that have unique characteristics or brand identification for which a significant group of buyers is willing to make a special purchase effort. Examples include specific brands and types of cars, high-priced photographic equipment and men's suits. A Mercedes-Benz car, for example, is a specialty good because buyers are usually willing to travel to buy one. Buyers do not normally compare specialty products. They invest only the time needed to reach dealers carrying the wanted products. Although dealers do not need convenient locations, they must let buyers know where to find them.

Unsought products
Consumer goods and services that the consumer either does not know about or knows about but does not normally think of buying.

Unsought products are consumer goods and services that the consumer either does not know about or knows about but does not normally think of buying, such as life insurance. New products such as smoke detectors and MP3 players are unsought products until the consumer is made aware of the need they satisfy—often due to marketing communication. Because consumers do not see the need for them, unsought products require a lot of advertising, personal selling and other marketing efforts, and some of the most advanced personal selling methods have developed out of the challenge of selling unsought products.

Industrial products

Industrial products
Goods bought by individuals and organisations for further processing or for use in conducting a business.

Industrial products are those purchased for further processing or for use in conducting a business. Thus, the distinction between a consumer good and an industrial good is based on the purpose for which the product is purchased. If a consumer buys a Skil chainsaw for use around the home, the chainsaw is a consumer good. If the same consumer buys the same Skil chainsaw for use in a landscaping business or a Jim's landscaping franchise, the chainsaw is an industrial good.

Industrial products can be classified according to how they enter the production process and according to what they cost. The three groups of industrial products are: *materials and parts*, *capital items*, and *supplies and services* (see Figure 11.4).

Materials and parts
Industrial goods that enter the manufacturer's product completely, including raw materials and manufactured materials and parts.

Materials and parts are industrial goods that become part of the buyer's product. They fall into two classes: raw materials and manufactured materials and parts.

Raw materials include farm products (wheat, cotton, livestock, fruit, vegetables) and natural products (fish, timber, crude petroleum, iron ore, liquefied petroleum gas). Each is marketed somewhat differently. Farm products are supplied by many small producers, who turn them over to marketing intermediaries who process and sell them. They are rarely advertised and promoted, but there are some exceptions. From time to time grower groups will launch campaigns to promote their products—such as the very successful campaigns launched by the Australian Banana Growers' Council positioning bananas as energy foods. Alternatively, a producer can attempt to differentiate the product by increasing the quality (such as super-fine wool, which

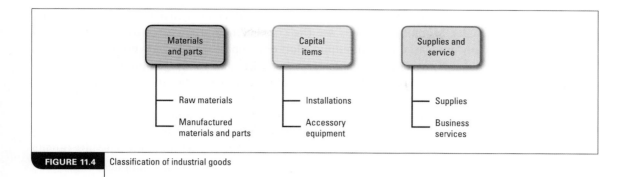

FIGURE 11.4 Classification of industrial goods

commands much higher prices than normal wool) and/or by branding (such as oranges labelled with a brand like Sunkist).

Natural products (or commodities) such as iron ore and coal are often limited in supply. They are usually bulky, have low unit value and require lots of transportation to move them from producer to user. Producers are fewer and larger, and they tend to market natural products directly to industrial users. Because the users depend on these materials, long-term supply contracts are common. Because there are multiple sources of supply, and users will typically choose cheaper sources, producers of these products will typically concentrate on lowering prices, rather than on actions to increase the use of the product, and thus increase demand. Price and delivery are the major factors affecting the selection of suppliers.

Manufactured materials and parts include component materials (iron, yarn and cement) and component parts (small motors, tyres and castings). Component materials are usually processed further—for example, pig iron is made into steel, and yarn is woven into cloth. The uniform nature of component materials usually means that price and supplier reliability are the most important purchase factors. Component parts enter the finished product completely with no further change in form, as when small motors are installed in vacuum cleaners and tyres are added to new cars. Most manufactured materials and parts are sold directly to industrial users. Price and service are the major marketing factors, and branding and advertising tend to be less important.

Capital items are industrial goods and services that aid in the buyer's manufacturing or service operations. They include two groups: installations and accessory equipment.

Installations consist of buildings (factories, offices) and fixed equipment (generators, mainframe computers and lifts). Installations are major purchases. They are usually bought directly from the producer after a long decision period. The producers use technical salesforces which often include sales engineers. The producers must be willing to design to specification and to supply after-sales service. They use some advertising, but rely much more on personal representation, enhanced by electronic communication.

Accessory equipment includes portable factory equipment and tools (hand tools, lift trucks) and office equipment (personal computers, paperclips and desks). These products do not become part of the finished product. They simply aid in the production process. They have a shorter life than installations but a longer life than operating supplies. Most accessory equipment sellers use resellers because the market is spread out geographically, the buyers are numerous and the orders are small. Quality, features, price and service are major factors in supplier selection. The salesforce tends to be more important than advertising, although advertising can be used effectively.

Supplies and services are industrial goods and services that do not enter the finished product at all.

Capital items Industrial goods and services that enter the finished product partly, including installations and accessory equipment.

Supplies and services Industrial goods and services that do not enter the finished product at all.

Supplies include operating supplies (lubricants, coal, typing paper, pencils) and maintenance and repair items (paint, nails, brooms). Supplies are the convenience products of the industrial field because they are usually purchased with minimum effort or comparison. They are normally marketed through resellers because of the low unit value of the products and the large number of customers spread out around the country. Price and service are important factors because suppliers are quite similar and brand preference is not high.

Business services include maintenance and repair services (window cleaning, computer maintenance and repair) and business advisory services (legal, management consulting, advertising). These services are usually supplied under contract. Business advisory services are normally new-task buying situations, and the industrial buyer will choose the supplier on the basis of the supplier's reputation and personnel.

SELF-CHECK QUESTIONS

3   What is the main feature that distinguishes a consumer product from an industrial product (used in business-to-business marketing)?

4   It is often said that products such as corn chips are a planned purchase for impulse consumption. Explain the meaning of this statement.

5   At one time, an American Express card would have been an 'unsought product'. Explain why.

Services classifications

Services Any activity or benefit that one party can offer to another that is essentially intangible and does not result in the ownership of anything.

Services involve one party offering something that is essentially intangible and where the interaction does not result in the ownership of anything. Modern economies are increasingly dependent on the sale of services; services are responsible for 68% of 'total value added' and 75% of total employment in Australia;[9] the figures are higher still in some countries. The comparable figures for the much larger US economy are 74% and 82% respectively.[10]

Our examination of services in this chapter begins with an overview of the industries involved, and then moves on to a more detailed discussion of the characteristics of services before examining an extension of the product concept.

Service industries

In discussing the marketing of services, one starting point is an examination of the industries that make up the services sector. Here, we use as an example the Australian and New Zealand Standard Industrial Classification (ANZSIC) divisions:

- electricity, gas, water and waste services (ANZSIC Division D)
- construction (ANZSIC Division E)
- wholesale trade (ANZSIC Division F)
- retail trade (ANZSIC Division G)
- accommodation and food services (ANZSIC Division H)
- transport, postal and warehousing (ANZSIC Division I)
- information media and telecommunications services (ANZSIC Division J)
- financial and insurance services (ANZSIC Division K)
- rental hiring and real estate services (ANZSIC Division L)
- professional, scientific and technical services (ANZSIC Division M)

- administrative and support services (ANZSIC Division N)
- public administration and safety (ANZSIC Division O)
- education and training (ANZSIC Division P)
- healthcare and social assistance (ANZSIC Division Q)
- arts and recreation services (ANZSIC Division R)
- other services (ANZSIC Division S).[11]

Thus, out of 19 divisions which cover all industries in the Australian and New Zealand economies, the 16 listed are concerned primarily with services and experiences. As manufacturing has declined in modern economies, services sectors such as health, hospitality and personal services have grown. They have also provided an increasing proportion of jobs, as manufacturing industries have moved to greater use of technology. In contrast, services industries (such as education, retailing and tourism) are typically much more labour intensive than manufacturing, so more and more jobs have shifted to services industries.

Services characteristics

Earlier, a classification scheme was introduced whereby physical goods and services were shown to lie on a continuum (Figure 11.1). This scheme also indicates that some services are highly capital intensive, while others are more people based. This is shown by the range of alternative transaction methods that financial services marketers offer consumers. When using a savings bank product, consumers may use High Street retail outlets and deal with a human teller (people based). Alternatively, consumers might elect to use an automatic teller machine (ATM), telephone banking or the Internet (equipment based).

Services are distinguished from physical goods by a number of features: *intangibility*, *inseparability*, *variability* and *perishability*. We look at each feature of services below.

Service intangibility

Service intangibility means that services cannot be seen, tasted, felt, heard or smelled before they are bought. For example, people undergoing cosmetic surgery cannot see the result before the purchase. Airline passengers have nothing but a ticket and the promise that they and their luggage will arrive safely at the intended destination, hopefully at the same time. To reduce uncertainty, buyers look for 'signals' of service quality. They draw conclusions about quality from the place, people, price, equipment and communications they can see.

Therefore, the service provider's task is to make the service tangible in one or more ways and to send the right signals about quality. One analyst calls this *evidence management*, in which the service organisation presents its customers with organised, honest evidence of its capabilities.[12]

Service intangibility
Almost pure services, such as a haircut, may be distinguished from almost pure physical products, such as coffee, in that there is no physical element.

Service inseparability

Service inseparability means that services cannot be separated from their providers, whether the providers are people or machines. If a service employee provides the service, then the employee is a part of the service. Because the customer is also present as the service is produced, *provider–customer interaction* is a special feature of services marketing. Both the provider and the customer affect the service outcome.

Service inseparability
Services cannot be separated from their providers, whether the providers are people or machines.

Service variability

Because services often depend on the actions of individuals, services are more variable than physical products. The customer's reaction to the service may therefore depend on the actions of any individual with whom they come in contact. As discussed in Chapter 2, Jan Carlzon, former chief executive of

Scandinavian Airline Systems (SAS), famously called the many interactions between customers and SAS 'moments of truth' to describe the potential importance of each of these encounters. Carlzon pointed out that 'each of our 10 million customers comes into contact with approximately five SAS employees, and this contact lasted an average of 15 seconds each time. Thus SAS is "created" 50 million times a year, 15 seconds at a time. These 50 million "moments of truth" are the moments that ultimately determine whether SAS will succeed or fail as a company'.[13]

Another reason for **service variability** is that any number of unexpected situations can arise which can influence the service; staff may call in sick, customers may have unusual requests or there may be unexpected problems caused by weather or equipment failure. In such cases, staff may need to respond in ways which haven't been anticipated. Under such circumstances, empowering service staff to respond appropriately may be critical to managing the moments of truth. So SAS was reorganised to enable its staff to make decisions, and thus avoid delays which had been caused by the old requirement to consult management.

Technology is increasingly used in services as a means of reducing service variability and reducing costs. However, technology can be a twin-edged sword. If human contact is removed by forcing customers to use telephone menus, ATMs and Internet sites, some consumers will be alienated. If such technology is complex to use or introduces new and different variability to the service encounter, customers may simply move on. As a response, many organisations such as airlines and banks offer customers a choice of self-service technologies (such as booking tickets online) or personal service (such as banking service in a bank branch) but will charge a higher price for people-based services. For example, Qantas charges fewer frequent-flyer points for a rewards ticket which is booked online than for one booked through its call centre. This sort of customer self-segmentation can be one way to continue to offer personal services to customers who want it, and who are prepared to pay for it, while capturing the cost benefits of technology for those customers who won't pay extra for personal service.

Service perishability

Service perishability means that services cannot be stored for later sale or use. So some doctors charge patients for missed appointments because the service value existed only at that point and disappeared when the patient did not show up. The perishability of services is not a problem when demand is steady. However, when demand fluctuates service firms often have difficult problems. For example, because of rush-hour demand, public transport services have to have much more capacity than they would if demand was steady throughout the day. Thus, service firms often design strategies for producing a better match between demand and supply. Hotels and resorts charge lower prices in the off-season to attract more guests, and restaurants hire part-time employees to serve during peak periods.

Managing service quality

Because services are intangible and variable, it is difficult for service providers to measure the quality of their services, or to convince customers that those services will be high quality. One of the major ways a service firm can differentiate itself is by delivering consistently

Service variability
Almost pure services, such as a restaurant or cruise line experience, involve interaction between a patron/guest and customer service personnel. There is the potential for service variability in what have been termed 'moments of truth'.

Service perishability
Almost pure services, such as a rock concert, may be distinguished from almost pure physical products, such as coffee, in that there is no stored physical inventory. Once the concert is over, there is only the memory of it.

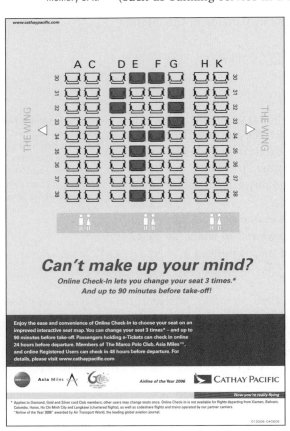

Cathay Pacific uses technology to allow customers to choose their seat online.

higher quality than its competitors do. Like manufacturers before them, most service industries have now joined the customer-driven quality movement. And like product marketers, service providers need to identify what target customers expect concerning service quality.

Unfortunately, service quality is harder to define and judge than is product quality. For instance, it is harder to agree on the quality of a haircut than on the quality of a hair dryer. Customer retention is perhaps the best measure of quality—a service firm's ability to hang onto its customers depends on how consistently it delivers value to them.[14]

Top service companies set high service quality standards. They watch service performance closely, both their own and that of competitors. They do not settle for merely good service; they aim for 100% defect-free service. A 98% performance standard may sound good, but using this standard 64 000 FedEx packages would be lost each day, 10 words would be misspelled on each printed page, 400 000 prescriptions would be wrong each day and drinking water would be unsafe 8 days a year.[15]

Unlike product manufacturers which can adjust their machinery and inputs until everything is perfect, service quality will always vary, depending on the interactions between employees and customers. As hard as they try, even the best companies will have an occasional late delivery, burned steak or grumpy employee. However, good service recovery can turn angry customers into loyal ones. Therefore, companies should take steps not only to provide good service every time but also to recover from service mistakes when they do occur.

The first step is to empower frontline service employees—to give them the authority, responsibility and incentives they need to recognise, care about and tend to customer needs. At Marriott, for example, well-trained employees are given the authority to do whatever it takes, on the spot, to keep guests happy. They are also expected to help management ferret out the cause of guests' problems and to inform managers of ways to improve overall hotel service and guests' comfort.

SELF-CHECK QUESTIONS

6   In Pine and Gilmore's terms (see Table 11.1), what is the key attribute of a service?

7   What other attributes are ascribed to services in the section 'Services classifications'?

8   Is there any inconsistency between the views of services portrayed in Questions 6 and 7?

Extending the goods and services classification

When Beijing stages the 2008 Olympic Games, or when Bob Geldof organised the Live 8 concerts for famine relief in Africa, these too are products. People, ideas, causes and other services are also marketed as products. Products may be non-profit oriented—a charitable group markets the idea of giving to an appeal to help victims of war in Iraq or famine in Africa. We examine some of the issues in marketing non-traditional services in the next section.

Event marketing

Event marketing combines elements of marketing physical products with those of services, particularly the experiential aspects of sporting, entertainment and other staged events delivered over a period of time. The Olympic Games combines elements of the physical with those of a service. Such events deserve our attention separately because they may involve two or three types of sponsorships. On the one hand, they may be a special event; on the other, they may be considered a sporting event.

Event marketing
Combines elements of marketing physical products with those of services, particularly the experiential aspects of sporting, entertainment and other staged events delivered over a period of time.

The Olympic Games is also an example of cause-related marketing as it brings countries together in peaceful, non-political competition. Finally, in the case of attendance at any single games event, the experience is the product on offer. Official sponsor companies try to reinforce positive buyer attitudes by being associated with helping a nation's athletes to develop and compete. Some non-sponsoring organisations engage in what is called 'ambush marketing' when they attempt to connect their products with events like the Olympic Games, despite not being official sponsors.

Political marketing

Political candidates and parties are marketed, not in the sense that we 'buy' them, but in the sense that we give them attention, vote for them and support their policies. Political parties adopt many of the same market research techniques used in the commercial world. Focus groups, telephone surveys and other polls are used to help determine marketing and communications strategy, particularly when nearing elections. Political parties are some of the largest users of both mass communications and direct marketing. Each of the major political parties maintains sophisticated databases recording voter names, ages and any political affiliation revealed by past communication. If a voter writes to a politician supporting or objecting to a particular policy, this information about the voter attitude is likely to be added to the database. In this way, targeted communications can be sent to voters, carrying the message which the political party's communication team believes is most likely to influence the undecided or swinging voter.

Cause marketing

An organisation such as the Red Cross is a marketing organisation which aims to ensure that we feel positively towards it and support it. To succeed in its goals, the Red Cross must market itself as a product, as well as marketing the idea of helping others by giving blood or by giving money. Even ideas or social causes, such as saving water, avoiding drink-driving or catching public transport to and from work, are marketed.[16]

Non-profit marketing

Non-profit marketing involves activities by organisations not motivated by profit which ultimately lead to a donation, bequest or some other contribution. Organisations like the RSPCA want people to donate money or time, leave a bequest or offer a home for animals destined to be put down. While such organisations are not profit driven, they still need to achieve a surplus so they can continue their activities and thus are paying more attention to conducting their businesses in more efficient ways and investigating new ways to raise money.[17] As a result, non-profit organisations are becoming increasingly sophisticated at marketing, and increasing their use of direct mail to target past and prospective donors.

Experiences marketing

Experiences marketing involves adding value for customers buying products and services through customer participation and connection by managing the environmental aspects of the relationship. The new Hong Kong Disneyland is marketed by Disney, the Hong Kong government and by other organisations (such as hotels and travel agents) which stand to profit when Disneyland is chosen as a holiday destination. The product that customers buy is the experience of visiting Disneyland, perhaps shopping in Hong Kong and the excitement of a holiday.

Walt Disney calls buyers of experiences at its theme parks 'guests' and acknowledges that they 'value what the company reveals over a duration of time'.[18] Authors Pine and Gilmore suggest that, whether we consider an image chain such as Hard Rock Cafe or an ocean cruise aboard the 2600 berth

Disney Magic, customers want engaging experiences.[19] For example, travellers on the Disney Magic find that the restaurant themes change every 30 minutes. Most companies can't develop the multi-million special effects of Disney, but Pine and Gilmore suggest that in both consumer and business marketing customers want engaging experiences. 'Experiences are inherently personal, existing only in the mind of an individual who has been engaged on an emotional, physical, intellectual, or even spiritual level', point out Pine and Gilmore.[20] So Nike superstores have turned the idea of a store selling sportsware into an experience, with giant screens and the opportunity to try out sporting equipment. A coffee chain like Pacific Coffee in Hong Kong sells coffee and snacks, but also provides a relaxing environment, with free computers and Internet access, newspapers, magazines and armchairs, so the process of buying coffee becomes a sought-after experience. Ironically, at the same time coffee shops in Seattle are limiting or removing their wireless Internet access, because they have decided that large numbers of solo computer users are detracting from the experience of the café as a social venue.[21]

SELF-CHECK QUESTIONS

9 Businesses usually measure the effect of marketing by sales and profits. How can the effectiveness of cause marketing and not-for-profit marketing be measured?

10 Who pays for political marketing? Who is the target of the marketing?

11 Do you agree with the statement that, in some ways, experiences marketing is an umbrella concept that embraces many of the other services categories (such as events, people, causes)?

Individual product decisions

Having discussed product and service classifications and illustrated that in marketing parlance the term 'product' embraces more than just physical commodities, we now look at decisions relating to the development and marketing of individual products. Figure 11.5 shows the important decisions. We focus on decisions about product attributes, branding, packaging, labelling and product-support services.

Product attribute decisions

Developing a product or service involves defining the benefits that will be offered to the marketplace. These benefits are communicated and delivered by product attributes such as quality, features and design. Decisions about these attributes greatly affect consumer reactions to a product. Below, we discuss the issues involved in each decision.

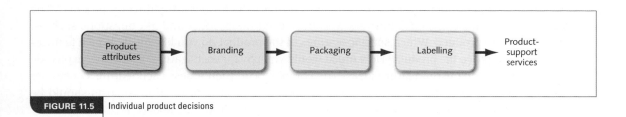

| Product attributes | → | Branding | → | Packaging | → | Labelling | → | Product-support services |

FIGURE 11.5 Individual product decisions

Product quality

Product quality The ability of a product to perform its functions; it includes the product's overall durability, reliability, precision, ease of operation and repair, and other valued attributes.

Quality is one of the marketer's major positioning tools. Quality has two dimensions—level and consistency. In developing a product, the marketer must first choose a quality level that will support the product's position in the target market. Here, **product quality** means the ability of a product to perform its functions. It includes the product's overall durability, reliability, precision, ease of operation and repair and other valued attributes. For services in particular, where variability is higher than with physical products, high quality also means consistently delivering the targeted level of quality to consumers. Although some of these attributes can be measured objectively, from a marketing point of view quality should be measured in terms of buyers' perceptions. Companies rarely try to offer the high levels of quality that are found in products such as a Rolls-Royce car or a Rolex watch. Instead, companies choose a quality level that matches the expectations of the target market or the quality levels of competing products.

To some companies, improving quality means using better quality control to reduce defects that annoy consumers. For others, quality means better training of service staff to provide a more consistent service experience. For still others, it may require empowering staff to make decisions without having to ask permission in order to resolve a customer problem rapidly. Quality can be a potent strategic weapon. Strategic quality involves gaining an edge over competitors by consistently offering products and services that give customers better quality, at a given price, than their competitors.

This doesn't mean that organisations constantly need to offer higher quality, if customers won't pay for it. Over the last 10 years, the fastest growing airlines have been budget operators such as Southwest and Ryanair. Airlines like these offer lower levels of service to customers at lower prices, and have succeeded by offering higher value for many customers than their higher service, higher priced competitors. But Southwest and Ryanair still strive for quality: consistency in on-time departures, a good service experience (even if customers need to pay for food and drink) and efficient baggage handling. Every organisation needs to decide what quality of experience it can provide to its customers, but customers will always prefer an organisation that gives them the highest value—the highest quality for a given price. Marketing Highlight 11.2 shows how even low-cost innovation in service delivery can be used by service businesses to provide a higher quality experience for customers.

Product features

A product can be offered with varying features. A 'stripped-down' model, one without any extras, is often the starting point. The company can then create higher-level models by adding more features. Features are a competitive tool for differentiating the company's product from competitors' products, and being the first producer to introduce a valued new feature is one of the most effective ways to compete. Selling features separately can also be a way to offer a cheaper price to customers who don't want to pay more, and to charge more to those who will. So car companies offer base models and then sell options such as sunroofs, seats with memory, electric adjustable suspensions, fuzzy-logic gearboxes and so on.

How can a company identify new features and decide which ones to add to its product? The company should periodically survey buyers who have used the product and ask questions such as: How do you like the product? Which specific features of the product do you like most? Which features could we add to improve the product? How much would you pay for each feature? The answers provide the company with a rich list of feature ideas. The company can then assess each feature's customer value against its company cost. Features that customers value little in relation to costs should be dropped; those that customers value highly in relation to costs should be added.

Product design

Another way to add product distinctiveness is through **product design**. Some companies have reputations for outstanding design: Apple for computers and more recently for its iPod range, Sony for electrical products and Intel for silicon chip technology. Design can be one of the most powerful competitive weapons in a company's marketing arsenal. For example, Sunbeam (which makes kitchen appliances such as toasters and kettles) has redesigned and updated its range to look more modern and fashionable. The company has won design awards for its styles, emphasises its stylish design in its advertising and thus has increased sales dramatically.

Product design The process of designing a product's style and function: creating a product that is attractive; easy, safe and inexpensive to use and service; and simple and economical to produce and distribute.

Branding

Consumers view a brand as an important part of the product, and branding can add value to a product by allowing a company to charge higher prices. For example, most consumers would perceive a shapely bottle of Jean-Paul Gaultier perfume in its distinctive metal can as a high-quality, expensive product. But the same perfume in an unmarked bottle would probably be viewed as lower in quality, even if the fragrance were identical.

Branding has become a major issue in product strategy requiring a number of decisions (see Figure 11.6). Developing a branded product requires a great deal of long-term marketing investment,

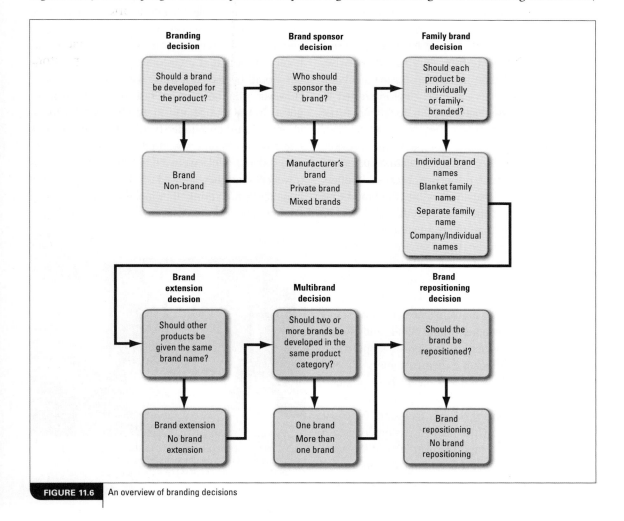

FIGURE 11.6   An overview of branding decisions

Customer-focused marketing

Good marketing has always been about understanding customers and what they want, but a recent *Harvard Business Review* article argues that rather than segmenting the market into groups of customers, and then designing products for 'average' customers, companies need to understand what customers *really* want from those products. Authors Clayton Christensen, Scott Cook and Taddy Hall quote the CEO of Procter & Gamble (P&G), A.G. Lafey, who recently said that 'We need to reinvent the way we market to consumers. We need a new model.' P&G invented one of its most successful new products, Whitestrips (do-it-yourself whitening strips), when it realised that people wanted the benefit of white teeth but hated going to the dentist.

P&G is big enough to be able to develop real innovations like Whitestrips, but Patrick Barwise, Professor of Marketing at London Business School, argues that customers are much less interested in breakthrough technologies than in quality products, good service, on-time delivery and other such generic benefits that any company can provide. 'Usually,' says Barwise, 'the reality is that customers rarely buy a product or service because it offers something unique. Usually, they buy the brand that they expect to meet their basic needs a bit better or more conveniently than the competition. What they usually want are products and services that are not more differentiated, but simply better.'

And what does 'better' mean? Christensen and his co-authors argue that customers buy products to do a job for them, and so marketers need to understand the job that a customer wants done, and design a product and associated experiences in purchase and use to do that job, and then customers will buy the product. To show what is meant by a product-focused rather than a customer-focused approach, they give the example of Quicken Financial Planner, a product which helped customers create a retirement plan. It captured over 90% of the sales in its product category, but annual revenue never passed $2 million and the product was pulled from the market. Why? It's never really clear why products fail, but the price wasn't high ($49), and the most likely reason for the product's failure is that most people don't actually see the need for, or get around to, creating a financial plan. In other words, the marketing would have had to convince customers to buy a product to do a job that they didn't seem to see the need for. That's a hard marketing sell.

So Christensen and his co-authors argue that marketers need to design products that do the jobs that customers want, rather than just improve existing products. This will often need very good understanding of just what different customers want. For example, Sheraton hotels has long followed quality practices, and strives to improve its performance. At one stage, the standard in one of its hotel bars was that a customer who arrived in the bar would be served a drink within three minutes. However, the hotel used researchers to observe guests in the lounge and to watch their behaviour, in order to try and understand if this standard was really what customers wanted. Some of the people who ordered drinks were alone, apparently business travellers, and they showed all the signs of waiting impatiently for a drink. They looked around, watched the bar staff and didn't seem to relax until they got

High-quality services such as the JW Marriott hotel chain need to design their product to meet the needs of their target customers, but also customise features to respond to different guest preferences.

their drink. For these people, sitting alone, without anything to distract them, three minutes seemed like a long time. In contrast, other customers came in groups, many apparently groups of friends who came in together after work. The observers noticed something quite different about these groups. They were talking to each other, often laughing and talking across tables they had pulled together. These sorts of groups seemed to pay much less attention to the progress of their drink orders, and if the drinks came within the three-minute standard the interruption of the server to put down the drinks actually seemed to interrupt their conversations. So the hotel changed its serving standard at this hotel; single guests were to be served as fast as possible, because for them the drink was a way of relaxing, since lots of people don't feel very comfortable in a bar by themselves. The standard for the groups of customers was changed to five minutes, because for the customers in groups the job of the drink was to allow them to catch up with friends, and it was less important for the drink to arrive fast. That's low-cost, customer-centred innovation by really understanding what customers want.

Hans Snook, the former CEO of Orange, argues that customer-centred innovations often fail because there isn't enough focus on the customer: 'Often it is the finance department that's the killer of innovation because it does all the sums and says "If we do it that way, we're not going to make more money",' Mr Snook said. 'Typically they're wrong, but unfortunately a lot of companies let that be the overriding consideration because the champion of whatever new product or idea it may be is not always in the higher echelons of the company. And if the CEO doesn't really get involved and make sure that everybody in the company understands the customer is king, it's not going to happen.'

Understanding the job that the customer wants done, and doing it better, can even be more efficient. For example, hotel chains have to cope with customers who speak a variety of languages. In Hong Kong, a typical visitor to the five-star JW Marriott (the top level of the Marriott chain) may ring room service and make a request in English, Cantonese or Mandarin (or Putonghua, as it is called locally). Though Hong Kong is officially bilingual (English and Cantonese) it's hard to get staff who are truly trilingual, let alone who can cope with visitors who speak other languages. Under the traditional hotel system, a customer might ring room service, the front desk, the restaurant or housekeeping, and staff would need to be able to respond in whatever language the guest spoke. As a result, the Marriott chain developed a simple innovation; instead of ringing each department with a request, the customer has one button on their phone, labelled 'At your service'. All requests are made to this one extension, and the staff member on the 'At your service' line sorts out the guest problem. The hotel staff would identify the primary language of each guest, the call will be directed and answered by a member of staff who speaks that language. The hotel doesn't need trilingual people answering phones in each of its departments, and the hotel guest is almost always answered by someone fluently speaking their language. This is a dedicated service which shows an understanding of what the customer wants—an easy solution to their request, without having to struggle to explain their request to someone who doesn't speak their language well.

So why don't more organisations provide truly great service? Perhaps because it's difficult. Hans Snook says that 'If you really start talking about customer issues in a very deep way, you have to transform your corporate culture, and that isn't always easy. It isn't just having a good marketing department or research department or customer service department that's going to solve the problem; it's everybody in the organisation having to believe that, ultimately, what they're doing is in the best interests of the customer.'

Sources: P. Barwise and S. Meehan, Simply Better: Winning and Keeping Customers by Delivering What Matters Most, Boston, Harvard Business School Press, 2004; C. M. Christensen, S. Cook and T. Hall, 'Marketing Malpractice', Harvard Business Review, vol. 83, no. 12, 2005, pp. 74–83; Richard Tomkins, 'The Art of Keeping Customers Happy', Financial Times, 17 June 2005, p. 8; Richard Tomkins, 'Old Products Scrub Up Well in New Guises', Financial Times, 17 June 2005, p. 8.

Questions

1 Do you agree with A. G. Lafey that 'We need to reinvent the way we market to consumers'? Why or why not?

2 Why do you think customers so often receive poor service?

3 Do you agree with Barwise that customers are 'much less interested in breakthrough technologies than in quality products, good service, on-time delivery and other such generic benefits that any company can provide'? Why or why not? Give an example.

especially for advertising, promotion and packaging. Manufacturers sometimes find it easier and less expensive simply to make the product and let others do the brand building. Chinese computer company Lenovo has done this by buying the right to use the IBM computer brand for five years. Lenovo will build the computers, but sell them to consumers under the well-known IBM brand, and avoid the expense of trying to convince consumers of the value of its own brand. At the same time, the gradually increasing knowledge in the market that IBM computers are made by Lenovo is likely to lead to an increase in value of the Lenovo brand and the prospect that Lenovo branded computers will eventually be accepted by consumers.

What is a brand?

> **Brand** A name, term, sign, symbol or design, or a combination of these, intended to identify the goods or services of one seller or group of sellers and to differentiate them from those of competitors.

Perhaps the most distinctive skill of professional marketers is their ability to create, maintain, protect and enhance brands. A **brand** is a name, term, sign, symbol or design, or a combination of these, intended to identify the goods or services of one seller or group of sellers and to differentiate them from those of competitors.[22] Thus, a brand identifies the maker or seller of a product or service. But brands do far more than this; powerful brand names can command strong consumer loyalty, and result in customers demanding these brands and refusing substitutes, even if the substitutes are offered at somewhat lower prices.

Some analysts see brands as *the* major enduring asset of a company, outlasting the company's specific products and facilities. John Stewart, co-founder of Quaker Oats, once said, 'If this business were split up, I would give you the land and bricks and mortar, and I would keep the brands and trademarks, and I would fare better than you.' A former CEO of McDonald's agrees:[23]

> A McDonald's board member who worked at Coca-Cola once talked to us about the value of our brand. He said if every asset we own, every building, and every piece of equipment were destroyed in a terrible natural disaster, we would be able to borrow all the money to replace it very quickly because of the value of our brand. And he's right. The brand is more valuable than the totality of all these assets.

Thus, brands are powerful assets that must be carefully developed and managed. Below we examine the key strategies for building and managing brands.

Brand equity

Brands are more than just names and symbols. Brands represent consumers' perceptions and feelings about a product and its performance—everything that the product or service *means* to consumers. Thus, the real value of a strong brand is its power to capture consumer preference and loyalty.

Brands vary in the amount of power and value they have in the marketplace. Some brands—such as Coca-Cola, Nike, Disney and others—become icons that maintain their power in the market for years, even generations. 'These brands win competitive battles not [just] because they deliver distinctive benefits, trustworthy service, or innovative technologies,' notes a branding expert. 'Rather, they succeed because they forge a deep connection with the culture.'[24]

A powerful brand has high *brand equity.* **Brand equity** is the value of a brand, based on the extent to which it has high brand loyalty. A measure of a brand's equity is the extent to which customers are willing to pay more for the brand. One study found that 72% of customers would pay a 20% premium for their brand of choice relative to the closest competing brand; 40% said they would pay a 50% premium. Heinz lovers were willing to pay a 100% premium, loyal Coke drinkers a 50% premium and Volvo users a 40% premium.[25]

A brand with strong brand equity is a very valuable asset. *Brand valuation* is the process of estimating the total financial value of a brand. Measuring such value is difficult. However, according to one estimate the brand value of Coca-Cola is almost $67 billion, Microsoft $61 billion and IBM $54 billion.

High brand equity provides a company with many competitive advantages. A powerful brand enjoys a high level of consumer awareness and loyalty. Because consumers expect stores to carry the brand, the company has more leverage in bargaining with resellers. Because the brand name carries high credibility, the company can more easily launch line and brand extensions, as when Coca-Cola uses its well-known brand to introduce new varieties such as Vanilla Coke and Coke with Lemon. A powerful brand offers the company some defence against fierce price competition.[26]

Above all, a powerful brand forms the basis for building strong and profitable customer relationships. Therefore, the fundamental asset underlying brand equity is *customer* equity—the value of the customer relationships that the brand creates. A powerful brand is important, but what it really represents is a profitable set of loyal customers. Marketing Highlight 11.3 compares the top 20 global and Australian brands, and examines some of the factors behind their success.

> **Brand equity** The value of a brand, based on the extent to which it has high brand loyalty, name awareness, perceived quality, strong brand associations and other assets such as patents, trademarks and channel relationships.

Brand strategy

Branding poses challenging decisions to the marketer. Figure 11.7 shows that the major **brand strategy** decisions involve brand positioning, brand name selection, brand sponsorship and brand development.

> **Brand strategy** Entails decisions on brand positioning, brand name, brand sponsorship and brand development (see Figure 11.7).

Brand positioning Marketers need to position their brands clearly in target customers' minds. They can position brands at any of three levels. At the lowest level, they can position the brand on *product attributes*. Thus, marketers of Colgate toothpaste can talk about the product's innovative ingredients and good taste. However, attributes are the least desirable level for brand positioning. Competitors can easily copy attributes. More important, customers are not interested in attributes as such; they are interested in what the attributes will do for them.

Brand positioning	**Brand name selection**	**Brand sponsorship**	**Brand development**
Attributes Benefits Beliefs and values	Selection Protection	Manufacturer's brand Private brand Licensing Co-branding	Line extensions Brand extensions Multibrands New brands

FIGURE 11.7 Major brand strategy decisions

MARKETING HIGHLIGHT

11.3

The star brands (and a few falls)

Coca-Cola, Microsoft, IBM, Nokia, Disney and McDonald's are familiar brand names for nearly everyone. GE and Intel, which make the majority of their sales to consumers through other businesses, aren't quite as well known in the general community. Yet together they make up the world's top eight brands.

Companies around the world invest billions of dollars each year to create preference for these and hundreds of other major brands. The reason is clear—powerful brand names provide strong competitive advantage. Interbrand, a brand consultancy, assesses the top global brands each year, and the results, and changes in brand value, reflect the marketing success of these organisations. Table 1 lists the top 20 global and Australian brands and their value according to the latest Interbrand reports.

It's hard to make any brand stand out among the clutter of competition; after all, there are 32 brands of shampoo and 16 types of toothpaste on Australian supermarket aisles alone. So what makes these great brands stand out? Branding is all about promise, and then keeping those promises. When a brand loses the trust it has engendered, its value soon declines. Australian bank NAB experienced this in 2004, when it suffered poor publicity following $360 million in losses in unauthorised staff trading and a 20% fall in profits, yet rewarded its resigning CEO with a $14 million payout.[27] In the subsequent brand valuation list, Interbrand decreased NAB's brand valuation by 14% or $400 million.

In contrast, looking at the top performers on the two lists, it's easy to see some of the indicators of a healthy brand: a sustained emphasis on communicating a message to consumers, and on making the brand relevant for those consumers. The five largest improvements in brand value in the global 2005 brand list were Google (a new entrant, following its share listing), ebay, HSBC, Samsung and Apple. It's easy to see why Google, ebay, Samsung and Apple are on the list; all four companies are renowned for innovation, and for

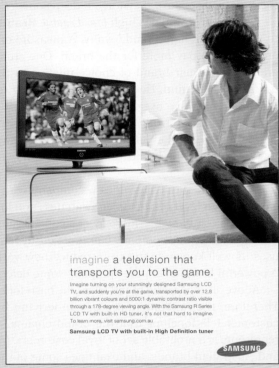

A few brands like Samsung have shown continual growth through strong branding and research and development, which offers customers continually improving quality.

providing products that consumers love. Notably, they also aren't among the heaviest advertisers in the top brands list; Google and ebay don't even advertise in traditional media, but dominate their categories with innovative new business models. Apple, Samsung and HSBC, however, show the benefits of superb branding in competitive markets. Each has risen to dominate powerful competitors, with a consistent communication message in their advertising worldwide. The list of top brands also shows that with powerful marketing, top brands can be grown very rapidly. Ten years ago Google and ebay didn't exist, and Samsung was a minor electronics company outside Korea, manufacturing under a variety of names. Realising that it had to develop consumer confidence in its products, Samsung ditched its old brands like Wiseview and

TABLE 1 Top 20 ranked brands—global and Australian companies

Top 20 ranked brands—global companies					Top 20 ranked brands—Australian companies				

Rank 2005/2004			2005 Brand value $millions	Percent change 2004–05	Rank 2004/2002			2004 Brand value $millions	Percent change 2002–04
1	1	Coca-Cola	67 525	0%	1	1	Telstra	9300	−4%
2	2	Microsoft	59 941	−2%	2	2	CBA	4000	8%
3	3	IBM	53 376	−1%	3	3	Westpac	3600	16%
4	4	GE	46 996	7%	4	4	ANZ	2900	7%
5	5	Intel	35 588	6%	5	5	Woolworths	2500	39%
6	8	Nokia	26 452	10%	6	8	NAB	2400	−14%
7	6	Disney	26 441	−2%	7	6	Billabong	1100	20%
8	7	McDonald's	26 014	4%	8	7	St George	1000	23%
9	9	Toyota	24 837	10%	9	NA	Macquarie Bank	830	NA
10	10	Marlboro	21 189	−4%	10	NA	Qantas	820	NA
11	11	Mercedes-Benz	20 006	−6%	11	9	Australia Post	780	11%
12	13	CITI	19 967	0%	12	19	Harvey Norman	420	223%
13	12	Hewlett-Packard	18 866	−10%	13	12	Crown	390	26%
14	14	American Express	18 559	5%	14	11	Nine Network	380	19%
15	15	Gillette	17 534	5%	15	10	Ansell	360	−12%
16	17	BMW	17 126	8%	16	15	Suncorp	350	94%
17	16	Cisco	16 592	4%	17	NA	Virgin Blue	330	NA
18	44	Louis Vuitton	16 077	NA	18	15	Flight Centre	320	78%
19	18	Honda	15 788	6%	18	NA	Bunnings	320	NA
20	21	Samsung	14 956	19%	18	18	Network Ten	320	100%

Sources: Robert Berner and David Kiley, 'Global Brands', *Business Week*, 5 September 2005, pp. 56–63; Simon Lloyd, 'Brand Values Surge', *Business Review Weekly*, 18 November 2004, pp. 12–15.

Tantus and adopted a single brand strategy under the Samsung name, backed up by research to build top-quality products. In particular, the brand pushed its mobile phones, because in the words of its North American marketing head, 'We wanted the brand in users' presence 24/7'. The strategy has been so successful that Samsung's brand value surged 186% in 2005, surpassing its rival Sony, whose brand value slipped 16% over the same period.

Comparing brand values from year to year also shows that successful companies can't afford to relax, with big falls in brand value for stalwarts like Sony, Volkswagen, Levi's and Hewlett-Packard. Even with huge budgets for research, these companies have failed to capitalise on their brand value, and have been surpassed by smaller, more innovative competitors. For example, Sony developed the Walkman and mini-disc technologies, but allowed Apple to revolutionise MP3 technology, instead investing in films, where its brand adds little value and where it faces strong competition from other content providers.

Every successful and unsuccessful brand has a different story, but if there is a common theme among the successful brands it seems to be avoiding complacency: making that brand important for consumers in both products and communications and being constantly vigilant even when you are successful.

Sources: <www.interbrand.com>; Robert Berner and David Kiley, 'Global Brands', *Business Week*, 5 September 2005, pp. 56–63; Rochelle Burbury, 'Brand New Day', *The Australian Financial Review Magazine*, 29 April 2005, pp. 104–106; Simon Lloyd, 'Brand Values Surge', *Business Review Weekly*, 18 November 2004, pp. 12–15; Mark Ritson, 'The Bigger the Brand, the Easier It Falls', *Marketing* (UK), 9 September 2004, p. 23.

Questions

1 Ask colleagues, classmates or friends to rate—on a scale of 0 (low) to 10 (high)—the top 20 global brands and the top 20 brands in your country. Does the list align with the 20 brands listed in Table 1? If not, why not?

2 Do you think that it makes any difference to the value of a brand if the name of the parent company is also the global brand name?

3 Why does Coca-Cola rank so consistently highly in almost every brand study? Is there a lesson for other companies?

A brand can be better positioned by associating its name with a desirable *benefit*. Thus, Colgate marketers can go beyond the brand's ingredients and talk about the resulting cavity prevention or teeth whitening benefits. Some successful brands positioned on benefits are Singapore Airlines (service), Harley-Davidson (adventure), FedEx (guaranteed on-time delivery), Nike (performance) and Lexus (quality).

The strongest brands go beyond attribute or benefit positioning. They are positioned on strong *beliefs and values*. These brands pack an emotional wallop. Thus, Colgate's marketers can talk not just about ingredients and cavity-prevention benefits, but about how these give customers 'healthy, beautiful smiles for life'. Brand experts are increasingly relying less on a product's tangible attributes and more on creating surprise, passion and excitement surrounding a brand.

When positioning a brand, the marketer should establish a mission for the brand and a vision of what the brand must be and do. A brand is the company's promise to deliver a specific set of features, benefits, services and experiences consistently to the buyers. It can be thought of as a contract to the customer regarding how the product or service will deliver value and satisfaction. The brand contract must be simple and honest. Motel 6, for example, offers clean rooms, low prices and good service but does not promise expensive furniture or large bathrooms. In contrast, Ritz-Carlton offers luxurious rooms and a truly memorable experience but does not promise low prices.

Brand name selection A good name can add greatly to a product's success. However, finding the best brand name is a difficult task. It begins with a careful review of the product and its benefits, the target market and proposed marketing strategies. Desirable qualities for a brand name include:

- It should suggest something about the product's benefits and qualities. Examples: Beautyrest, Navigator (Netscape's browser and Ford Lincoln's US 4×4 wagon), Sunkist, Spray & Wipe, Unwired.
- It should be easy to pronounce, recognise and remember. Short names help. Examples: Tide, Aim, Total. But longer ones are sometimes effective. Examples: 'I can't believe it's not butter' (a butter substitute) and 'Love My Carpet' carpet cleaner.
- The brand name should be distinctive. Examples: Exxon, Mach 3 (Gillette's three-blade shaving system), Prado, Taurus, Kodak.
- The name should translate easily into foreign languages. Before spending $US100 million to change its name to Exxon, Standard Oil of New Jersey tested the name in 54 languages in

more than 150 foreign markets, and found that one of the names it was considering, Enco, referred to a stalled engine when pronounced in Japanese.

⊛ The name should be capable of registration and legal protection.

A brand name cannot be registered if it infringes on existing brand names. Also, brand names that are merely descriptive or suggestive may be unprotectable. For example, the Miller Brewing Company registered the name Lite for its low-calorie beer and invested millions in establishing the name with consumers. But the courts later ruled that the terms lite and light are generic or common descriptive terms applied to beer and that Miller could not use the Lite name exclusively.[28]

Once chosen, the brand name must be protected. Many firms try to build a brand name that will eventually become identified with the product category. Brand names such as Frigidaire, Kleenex, Levi's, Scotch Tape, Formica and Fibreglass have succeeded in this way. However, their very success may threaten the company's rights to the name. Many originally protected brand names, such as cellophane, aspirin, nylon, kerosene, linoleum, yo-yo, trampoline, escalator, thermos and shredded wheat, are now names that any seller can use.

Brand sponsor decision A marketing organisation has four sponsorship options. The product may be launched as a manufacturer's brand (also called a national brand). Or the manufacturer may sell the product to intermediaries who give it a house brand or a private label. Or the manufacturer may follow a mixed brand strategy, selling some output under its own brand names and some under private labels. Kellogg's and Samsung sell almost all their output under their own (manufacturer's) brand names. On the other hand, chicken processors, such as Inghams, sell their fresh and frozen chicken under brands such as Inghams, Coles' 'Farmland' and 'Savings' brands, and Woolworths/Safeways' house brands and generic brands. Many other marketers do not create their own brands but rather pay licence fees to use the brands of others. Some co-brand products, so that two well-known brands are combined on the one product. We examine these different branding decisions below.

Manufacturers' brands versus private labels **Manufacturers' brands** have long dominated the retail scene. In recent times an increasing number of department stores, supermarkets, service stations, clothiers, chemists and appliance dealers have launched private labels.

Private brands, or **private labels**, are often hard to establish and costly to stock and promote, but can be much more profitable for their distributors than manufacturers' brands, because intermediaries can often locate manufacturers with excess capacity which will produce the private label at a low cost, resulting in a higher profit margin for the intermediaries. This has led supermarket chains, in particular, to extend their private label ranges, and decrease the number of manufacturers' brands they carry.[29]

The competition between manufacturers' and intermediaries' brands is sometimes called the 'battle of the brands'. In this battle, intermediaries have many advantages. The retailers control scarce shelf space—many manufacturers, especially the newer and smaller ones, cannot get the shelf space needed to introduce products under their own name. The retailers charge suppliers a fee to stock new products. They can give better display space to their own brands and ensure that those brands are better stocked. Intermediaries' brands are often priced lower than comparable manufacturers' brands, thus appealing to budget-conscious shoppers. And most shoppers know that the private label products are often made by one of the larger manufacturers. Thus, the dominance of manufacturers' brands has weakened somewhat. Some marketers predict that intermediaries' brands will eventually knock out all but the strongest manufacturers' brands.

In the Asia–Pacific market private labels are more commonly known as house brands and generics. House brands and generics have traditionally operated at the bottom end of the market in this region,

Manufacturers' brand (or national brand) A brand created and owned by the producer of a product or service.

Private brand (or house brand) A brand created and owned by a reseller of a product or service.

and have captured only a small portion of the market. However, the big Australian supermarkets hope to change that; Coles supermarket has recently launched three tiers of housebrands: 'George J Coles', 'You'll love Coles' and 'Coles $mart buy'. The George J Coles label will be the highest quality, while the Coles $mart buy will be the cheapest.[30] By offering a range of house brands, Coles hopes to obtain 30% of its sales from private labels by 2007.[31]

To fend off private brands, leading brand marketers will have to invest in R&D to bring out new brands, new features and continuous quality improvements. They must design strong advertising programs to maintain high awareness and preference. They must find ways to partner with major distributors in a search for distribution economies and improved joint performance. For example, in the USA Proctor & Gamble has assigned 20 of its managers to Wal-Mart headquarters in Bentonville, Arkansas, to work alongside Wal-Mart managers in a search for ways to improve their joint cost and competitive performance.

Licensing Most manufacturers take years and spend millions to create their own brand names. However, some companies license names or symbols previously created by other manufacturers, names of well-known celebrities or characters from popular movies and books; for a fee, any of these can provide an instant and proven brand name. Apparel and accessories sellers pay large royalties to adorn their products—from blouses to ties, and linens to luggage—with the names or initials of fashion innovators such as Calvin Klein, Gucci or Armani. Sellers of children's products attach an almost endless list of character names to clothing, toys, school supplies, dolls, lunch boxes, cereals and other items. The character names range from such classics as Disney and Barbie to more recent television characters with more adult appeal such as the Simpsons.

The fastest-growing licensing category is corporate brand licensing, renting a corporate trademark or logo made famous in one category and using it in a related category. More and more for-profit and not-for-profit organisations are licensing their names to generate additional revenues and brand recognition. Coca-Cola, for example, has some 320 licensees in 57 countries producing more than 10 000 products, ranging from baby clothes and boxer shorts to earrings, a Coca-Cola Barbie doll and even a fishing lure shaped like a tiny Coke can. Each year, licensees sell more than $1 billion worth of licensed Coca-Cola products.[32]

Co-branding Although companies have been co-branding products for many years, there has been a recent resurgence in co-branded products. **Co-branding** occurs when two established brand names of different companies are used on the same product. In most co-branding situations, one company licenses another company's well-known brand to use in combination with its own.

Co-branding The practice of using the established brand names of two different companies on the same product.

Co-branding offers many advantages. Because each brand dominates in a different category, the combined brands create broader consumer appeal and greater brand equity. Co-branding also allows a company to expand its existing brand into a category it might otherwise have difficulty entering alone. For example, we see co-branded credit cards carrying such familiar brands as Telstra, Visa and Qantas.

Co-branding also has its limitations. Such relationships usually involve complex legal contracts and licences. Co-branding partners must carefully coordinate their advertising, sales promotion and other marketing efforts. Finally, when co-branding, each partner must trust that the other will take good care of its brand. As one Nabisco manager puts it, 'Giving away your brand is a lot like giving away your child—you want to make sure everything is perfect'.[33]

Brand development A company has four choices when it comes to developing brands (see Figure 11.8). It can introduce *line extensions* (existing brand names extended to new forms, sizes and flavours of an existing product category), *brand extensions* (existing brand names extended to new product categories), *multibrands* (new brand names introduced in the same product category) or *new brands* (new brand names in new product categories).

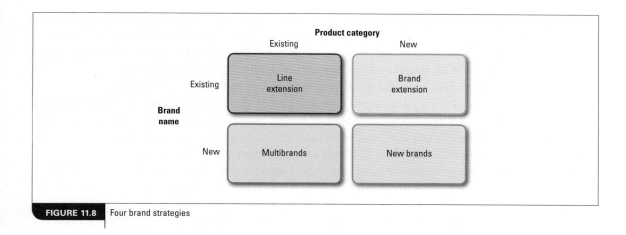

FIGURE 11.8 Four brand strategies

Line extensions **Line extensions** occur when a company introduces additional items in a given product category under the same brand name, such as new flavours, forms, colours, ingredients or package sizes. Thus, yogurt marketers have introduced several line extensions, including new yogurt flavours, fat-free yogurt and large 'economy-size' packaging.

The vast majority of new product activity consists of line extensions. A company might introduce line extensions for several reasons. It might want to respond to a consumer desire for variety or it might recognise a latent consumer want and try to capitalise on it. Excess manufacturing capacity might drive the company to introduce additional items, or the company might want to match a competitor's successful line extension. Some companies introduce line extensions simply to command more shelf space from resellers.

Line extensions also involve some risks. An overextended brand name might lose its specific meaning. In the past, when consumers asked for a Coke they received a small bottle of the classic beverage. Today the seller might ask: Regular, Diet or Zero? Caffeine or caffeine-free? Bottle or can? Another risk is that many line extensions will not sell enough to cover their development and promotion costs. Or, even when they sell enough, the sales may come at the expense of other items in the line. A line extension works best when it takes sales away from competing brands, rather than cannibalising the company's other items.[34]

Brand extensions A **brand extension** involves the use of a successful brand name to launch new or modified products in a new category. So Honda uses its company name to cover such different products as its cars, motorcycles, lawn mowers, marine engines and snowmobiles.

A brand-extension strategy offers many advantages. A recent study found that brand extensions capture greater market share and realise greater advertising efficiency than individual brands.[35] A well-regarded brand name helps the company enter new product categories more easily and gives a new product instant recognition and faster acceptance. Sony puts its name on most of its new electronic products, creating an instant perception of high quality for each new product. Brand extensions also save the high advertising cost usually required to familiarise consumers with a new brand name.

At the same time, a brand-extension strategy involves some risk. Brand extensions such as Bic pantyhose, Life Savers gum and Victa light aircraft met early deaths. If an extension brand fails, it may harm consumer attitudes toward the other products carrying the same brand name. And a brand name may lose its special positioning in the consumer's mind through overuse. *Brand dilution* occurs when consumers no longer associate a brand with a specific product or even highly similar products. Companies that are tempted to transfer a brand name must research how well the brand's associations fit the new product.[36]

Line extension Using a successful brand name to introduce additional items in a given product category under the same brand name, such as new flavours, forms, colours, added ingredients or package sizes.

Brand extension A new or modified product launched under an already successful brand name.

Multibranding
A strategy under which
a seller develops two or
more brands in the same
product category.

Product category
A grouping of products,
often at retail level, which
may be substituted for
each other or which in
some way supplement
each other.

Multibrands **Multibranding** offers a way to establish different features and appeal to different buying motives, by introducing additional brands in the same category. A **product category** is a grouping of products, often at retail level, which may be substituted for each other or which in some way supplement each other. Thus, Colgate-Palmolive markets many different brands of toothpaste, within an oral hygiene category that includes pre-rinses, dental floss and other related products.

Multibranding also allows a company to command more shelf space. Or the company may want to protect its major brand by setting up flanker or fighter brands. For example, Seiko uses different brand names for its higher-priced watches (Seiko Lasalle) and lower-priced watches (Pulsar) to protect the flanks of its mainstream Seiko brand. Sometimes a company inherits different brand names in the process of acquiring a competitor, and each brand name has a loyal following. Thus, Electrolux, the Swedish multinational, owns a stable of acquired brand names for its appliance lines—Frigidaire, Kelvinator, Westinghouse, Zanussi, White and Gibson and McCulloch. Finally, companies sometimes develop separate brand names for different regions or countries, perhaps to suit different cultures or languages. For example, Procter & Gamble (P&G) dominates the US laundry detergent market with Tide, which in all its forms captures more than a 31% market share. In Europe, however, P&G leads with its Ariel detergent brand.

A major drawback of multibranding is that each brand might obtain only a small market share, and none may be very profitable. The company could end up spreading its resources over many brands instead of building a few brands to a highly profitable level. These companies should reduce the number of brands they sell in a given category and set up tighter screening procedures for new brands. Ideally, a company's brands should cannibalise competitors' brands and not its own, and net profits from multibranding should be larger, even if some cannibalism occurs.

New brands A company might create a new brand name when it enters a new product category for which none of the company's current brand names are appropriate. Or the company might believe that the power of its existing brand name is waning and a new brand name is needed. The company might also obtain new brands in new categories through acquisitions.

As with multibranding, offering many new brands can result in a company spreading its resources too thinly. And in some industries, such as consumer packaged goods, consumers and retailers have become concerned that there are already too many brands, with too few differences between them. Thus, large consumer-product marketers like P&G, Unilever and Nestlé are now pursuing megabrand strategies—weeding out weaker brands and focusing their marketing dollars only on brands that can achieve the number one or two market-share positions in their categories.[37]

Brand repositioning However well a brand is initially positioned in a market, the company might have to reposition it later. A competitor might launch a brand positioned next to the company's brand and cut into its market share. Or customer wants might shift, leaving the company's brand with less demand. Marketers should consider repositioning existing brands before introducing new ones. In this way, they can build on existing brand recognition and consumer loyalty.

Brand repositioning
Because of competitive
action, or due to
implementation of a new
strategy, a marketer
might need to change
both the product and its
image to meet customer
expectations with its
brand(s) better.

Brand repositioning might require changing both the product and its image. For example, Kentucky Fried Chicken changed its name to KFC and changed its menu, adding lower-fat skinless chicken and non-fried items such as chicken burgers to reposition itself towards more health-conscious fast-food consumers. A brand can also be repositioned by changing only the product's image. Kraft repositioned Velveeta from a 'cooking cheese' to a 'good tasting, natural and nutritious' snack cheese. Although the product remained unchanged, Kraft used new advertising appeals to change consumer perceptions of Velveeta. When repositioning a brand, the marketer must be careful not to lose or confuse current loyal users. When shifting Velveeta's position, Kraft made certain that the product's new position was compatible with its old one. Thus, Kraft kept loyal customers while attracting new users.[38]

Managing brands

Companies must manage their brands carefully. First, the brand's positioning must be continuously communicated to consumers. Major brand marketers often spend huge amounts on advertising to create brand awareness and to build preference and loyalty. For example, McDonald's spends more than $500 million each year to promote its brand.[39]

Such advertising campaigns can help to create name recognition, brand knowledge and maybe even some brand preference. However, the fact is that brands are not maintained by advertising but by the *brand experience*. Today, customers come to know a brand through a wide range of contacts with the brand, sometimes known as 'touchpoints'. These touchpoints include advertising, but also personal experience with the brand, word-of-mouth, personal interactions with company people, telephone interactions, company web pages and many others. The company must put as much care into managing these touchpoints as it does into producing its ads.

The brand's positioning will not take hold fully unless everyone in the company lives the brand. Therefore the company needs to train its people to be customer centred. Even better, the company should carry on internal brand building to help employees to understand and be enthusiastic about the brand promise. Many companies go even further by training and encouraging their distributors and dealers to serve their customers well.

As a result, some companies are now setting up brand asset management teams to manage their major brands, rather than assigning responsibility for the brand to a (usually less senior) brand manager. For example, Colgate-Palmolive appoints *brand equity managers* to maintain and protect its brands' images, associations and quality, and to prevent short-term actions by over-eager brand managers from hurting the brand. Similarly, Hewlett-Packard has appointed a senior executive in charge of the customer experience in each of its two divisions, consumer and business-to-business (B2B). Their job is to track, measure and improve the customer relationship with Hewlett-Packard products. They report directly to the presidents of their respective divisions.

Finally, companies must periodically audit their brands' strengths and weaknesses.[40] They should ask: Does our brand excel at delivering benefits that consumers truly value? Is the brand properly positioned? Do all of our consumer touchpoints support the brand's positioning? Do the brand's managers understand what the brand means to consumers? Does the brand receive proper, sustained support?

The brand audit may turn up brands that need to be repositioned because of changing customer preferences or new competitors. Some cases may call for completely rebranding a product, service or company. For example, in 2004, 27 Grace Brothers department stores in NSW and the ACT were rebranded from the 119-year-old Grace Brothers name to Myer, to bring the stores' name into line with the other department stores owned by Myer, 15 years after Myer bought the Grace Brothers chain. The company refused to reveal the cost of rebranding, but it was estimated to be a multimillion dollar exercise, partly aimed at rejuvenating the store's image with younger shoppers.[41] However, the large cost of rebranding was followed, just over a year later, by an announcement that the Myer stores could be up for sale, following estimates that 20 of the 61 Myer stores were making a loss, due to inappropriate locations, high rents and/or too large a footprint.[42]

The challenge of branding, and the driving force behind a brand audit, is to develop a deep set of meanings for the brand. The most lasting meanings of a brand are its values and personality. They define the brand's essence. Thus, Mercedes stands for 'high achievers and success'. The company must build its brand strategy around creating and protecting this brand personality.

Packaging

Many products offered to the market have to be packaged. **Packaging** includes the activities of designing and producing the container or wrapper for a product. The package may include the

Packaging The activities of designing and producing the container or wrapper for a product.

product's primary container (the bottle holding Old Spice After-Shave Lotion or the metal can containing the shapely bottle of Jean-Paul Gaultier perfume), a secondary package that is thrown away when the product is about to be used (the cardboard box containing the bottle of Old Spice) and the shipping package necessary to store, identify and ship the product (a corrugated box carrying six dozen bottles of Old Spice). Labelling is also part of packaging and consists of printed information appearing on or with the package.

Traditionally, packaging decisions were based primarily on cost and production factors; the primary function of the package was to contain and protect the product. In recent times, packaging has become an important marketing tool. An increase in self-service means that packages must now perform many sales tasks—from attracting attention, to describing the product, to meeting legal requirements concerning the contents, to making the sale. Companies are realising the power of good packaging to create instant consumer recognition of the company or brand. For example, in an average supermarket, which stocks 15 000 to 17 000 items, the typical shopper passes by some 300 items per minute, and more than 60% of all purchases are made on impulse. In this highly competitive environment, the package may be the seller's last chance to influence buyers. It becomes a 'five-second commercial'.[43]

Innovative packaging can give a company an advantage over competitors. Liquid detergents quickly attained a healthy share of the heavy-duty detergent market partly because of the popularity of the containers' innovative drip-proof spout and cap. The first companies to put their fruit drinks in airtight foil and paper cartons, and their toothpastes in pump dispensers, attracted many new customers. In contrast, poorly designed packages can cause headaches for consumers and lost sales for the company.

In recent years product safety has also become a major packaging concern. After a number of product tampering threats during the 1990s and in 2000 (e.g. Arnott's, Herron and Panadol), most drug producers and food makers are now putting their products in tamper-resistant packages.

Music store Sanity differentiates its gift voucher by its packaging, presenting the voucher in a CD jewel case.

Developing a good package for a new product requires many decisions. The first task is to establish the packaging concept. The packaging concept states what the package should be or do for the product. Should the main functions of the package be to offer product protection, introduce a new dispensing method, suggest certain qualities about the product or the company or something else? Decisions must then be made on specific elements of the package, such as size, shape, materials, colour, text and brand mark. These various elements must work together to support the product's position and marketing strategy. The package must be consistent with the product's advertising, pricing and distribution.

Companies usually consider several different package designs for a new product. To select the best package, they test the various designs to find the one that stands up best under normal use, is easiest for dealers to handle and receives the most favourable consumer response. After selecting and introducing the package, the company should check it regularly in the face of changing consumer preferences and advances in technology. In the past, a package design might last for 15 years before it needed changes. However, in today's rapidly changing environment some experts advise that companies should recheck their packaging every two or three years.[44]

In making packaging decisions, the company must also heed growing environmental concerns about packaging, and make decisions that serve society's interests as well as immediate customer and company objectives. Increasingly, companies will be asked to take responsibility for the environmental costs of their products and packaging.

Labelling

Labels may range from simple tags attached to products to complex graphics that are part of the package. They perform several functions, and the seller has to decide which ones to use. At the very least, the label identifies the product or brand, such as the name Sunpack stamped on oranges. The label might also grade the product. The label might describe several things about the product—who made it, where it was made, when it was made, its contents, how it is to be used and how to use it safely. Finally, the label might promote the product through attractive graphics.

In most countries, labelling, especially for food and drugs, is strongly regulated, but the requirements vary between countries. Some countries require labels to include unit pricing (stating the price per unit of standard measure), use-by date (stating the expected shelf life of the product) and nutritional labelling (stating the ingredients and nutritional values of the product). Other legislation regulates the use of health-related terms such as low fat, light and high fibre. Sellers must ensure that their labels contain all the information required in the countries in which the products will be sold.

Labels May range from simple tags attached to products to complex graphics that are part of the package.

Product-support services

Customer service is another element of product strategy. As pointed out earlier in this chapter, a marketing organisation's offer to the marketplace usually includes some augmenting services. These services can be a minor or a major part of the total offer. Here, we discuss product-support services—services that augment the product offering. More and more companies are using product-support services as a major tool in gaining competitive advantage.

Good customer service is good for business. It costs less to keep the goodwill of existing customers than it does to attract new customers or woo back lost customers. Companies that provide high-quality service usually outperform their less-service-oriented competitors. A study comparing the performance of businesses that had high and low customer ratings of service quality found that the high-service businesses managed to charge more, grow faster and make more profits.[45] Clearly, marketers need to think carefully about their service strategies.

A company should design its product-support services to meet the needs of target customers. Customers vary in the value they assign to different services. Thus, the first step in deciding which product-support services to offer is to determine the services valued by target consumers and then the relative importance of these services. The company should periodically survey its customers to get ratings of current services as well as ideas for new ones. For example, car makers hold regular focus group interviews with owners and carefully watch complaints that come into their dealerships. The car makers have learned that buyers are very upset by repairs that are not done correctly the first time. As a result, the companies have set up systems directly linking dealerships with groups of engineers who can help guide mechanics through difficult repairs. This in turn impacts on market performance.[46]

Products can often be designed to reduce the amount of required servicing. Thus, companies need to coordinate their product design and service mix decisions. For example, the Canon home copier uses a disposable toner cartridge that greatly reduces the need for service calls. Kodak and 3M are designing products that can be 'plugged in' to a central diagnostic facility that performs tests, locates problems and fixes equipment over telephone lines. Thus, a key to successful service strategy is to design products that are easily installed, or that rarely break down and are easily fixable with little service expense.

Given the importance of customer service as a marketing tool, many companies have set up strong customer service operations to handle complaints and adjustments, credit service, maintenance service, technical service and consumer information. For example, many companies have set up toll-free customer service hotlines. By keeping records on the types of requests and complaints, the customer service group can press for needed changes in product design, quality control and marketing efforts. An active customer service operation coordinates all the company's services, creates consumer satisfaction and loyalty and helps the company to set itself further apart from competitors.

SELF-CHECK QUESTIONS

12 Distinguish between the attributes of a product and its benefits. Use an example in your explanation.

13 Why is it stated in the text that perhaps the most distinctive skill of professional marketers is their ability to create, maintain, protect and enhance brands?

14 Explain how distinctive packaging might give a marketing organisation an advantage over competitors. Use an example to illustrate your answer.

Product line decisions

Product line A group of products that are closely related because they function in a similar manner, are sold to the same customer groups, are marketed through the same types of outlets or fall within given price ranges.

We have looked at product strategy decisions—branding, packaging, labelling and services—for individual products. But product strategy also calls for building a product line. A **product line** is a group of products that are closely related because they function in a similar manner, are sold to the same customer groups, are marketed through the same types of outlets or fall within given price ranges. Thus, the Holden car company produces a range of cars, and Nokia produces several lines of mobile phones. In developing product line strategies, marketers face a number of tough decisions on product line length.

Product line length

Product line managers have to decide on the product line length. The line is too short if the manager can increase profits by adding items; the line is too long if the manager can increase profits by dropping items. Product line length is influenced by company objectives. Companies that want to be positioned as full-line companies or that are seeking high market share and market growth usually carry longer lines. They are less concerned when some items fail to add to profits. Companies that are keen on high profitability generally carry shorter lines consisting of selected items.

Product lines tend to lengthen over time. The product line manager feels pressure to add new products to use up excess manufacturing capacity. The salesforce and distributors might be pressured by the manager for a more complete product line to satisfy customers. The product line manager might want to add items to the product line to increase sales and profits.

However, as the manager adds items, several costs rise: design and engineering, inventory carrying, manufacturing changeover, order processing, transportation and promotional costs. Eventually someone calls a halt to the mushrooming product line. Top management may freeze things because of insufficient funds or manufacturing capacity. Or the brand manager may question the line's profitability and call for a study. The study will probably show a number of unprofitable items, and they will be pruned from the line in a major effort to increase profitability. A pattern of uncontrolled product line growth followed by heavy pruning is typical and may repeat itself many times.[47]

The company must therefore plan product line growth carefully. It can systematically increase the length of its product line in two ways: by stretching its line and by filling its line. Every company's product line covers a certain range of the products offered by the industry as a whole. Product line stretching occurs when a company lengthens its product line beyond its current range. As shown in Figure 11.9, the company can stretch its line downward, upward or both ways.

Downward stretch

Many companies initially locate at the high end of the market and later stretch their lines downward. A company may stretch downward for any number of reasons. It may find faster growth taking place at the low end. Or it may have first entered the high end to establish a quality image and intended to roll downward. The company may add a low-end product to plug a market hole that would otherwise attract a new competitor. Or it may be attacked at the high end and respond by invading the low end. Mercedes-Benz has traditionally marketed high-priced vehicles in competition with luxury models marketed by BMW, Volvo and Audi. Now it, too, markets a small car priced at less than $A50 000, the A160, to allow it to compete in this segment.

In making a downward stretch, a company faces some risks. The low-end item might provoke competitors to counteract by moving into the higher end. Or the company's dealers may not be willing or able to handle the lower-end products. Or the new low-end item might cannibalise higher-end items, leaving the company worse off.

Upward stretch

Companies at the lower end of the market might want to enter the higher end. They may be attracted by a faster growth rate or higher margins at the higher end, or they may simply want to position themselves as full-line manufacturers. Sometimes, companies stretch upward in order to add prestige to their current products. In the late 1990s, LG was barely known outside Korea, and produced low-priced goods under the Goldstar brand. The company ditched the Goldstar brand, renamed itself LG and produced an Internet-capable fridge. The fridge was prominently displayed in whitegoods departments, and received extensive media coverage. Hardly anyone bought the fridge (does anyone want an Internet fridge?), but it was very effective in contributing to LG's positioning as an innovative

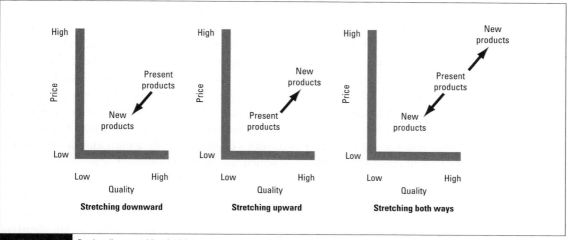

FIGURE 11.9 | Product line stretching decision

producer of electrical products, because most people wouldn't expect such a high-end product to be produced by a low-quality brand.

An upward-stretch decision can, however, be risky. The higher-end competitors are not only well entrenched but may strike back by entering the lower end of the market. Prospective customers might not believe that the newcomer can produce quality products. Finally, the company's salespeople and distributors may lack the talent and training to serve the higher end of the market.

Two-way stretch

Companies in the middle range of the market might decide to stretch their lines in both directions. Apple has done this very successfully in its iPod market, introducing its first iPod in the middle of the market. As imitative competitors moved in with lower-priced models, Apple stretched downwards with an iPod Mini, and then an iPod Shuffle, catering for people who could not afford the higher-priced iPods, as well as for those who valued the Shuffle's small size. At the same time, to add lustre to its lower-priced models and to attract more affluent consumers, Apple stretched the iPod line upwards, with a video-capable iPod. Using this two-way stretch strategy, Apple now dominates the personal stereo market, and builds follow-on sales through its iTunes site.

Product line filling

A product line can also be extended by adding more items within the current range of the line. Thus, Apple has added accessories to its iPod range, including arm bands to carry the iPod, docking stations and accessories to allow the iPod to be connected to a stereo.

However, line filling is overdone if it results in cannibalisation and customer confusion. The company should ensure that new items are noticeably different from current items.

SELF-CHECK QUESTIONS

15 Provide another example of a company that has stretched its product line both upwards and downwards.

16 Provide at least three reasons why a company might lengthen its product line by adding more items within the present range of the line.

Product mix decisions

Product mix (or product assortment)
The set of all product lines and items that a particular seller offers for sale to buyers.

An organisation with several product lines has a product mix. A **product mix** (also called product assortment) is the set of all product lines and items that a particular seller offers for sale. Avon's product mix consists of four major product lines: cosmetics, jewellery, fashion and household items. Each product line consists of several sub-lines. For example, cosmetics breaks down into lipstick, blusher, powder and so on. Each line and sub-line has many individual items. Altogether, Avon's product mix includes 1300 items. A large supermarket handles as many as 17 000 items; a typical Kmart store stocks 15 000 items; and companies such as General Electric manufacture as many as 250 000 items.

A company's product mix can be described as having a certain breadth, length, depth and consistency. These concepts are illustrated in Table 11.3, which lists selected Unilever consumer products. The breadth of Unilever's product mix refers to the number of different product lines the company carries. Table 11.3 shows a product mix width of seven broad lines. (In fact, Unilever produces many more.) The length of Unilever's product mix refers to the total number of items the company carries. In Table 11.3 the total number is 40; however, this is by no means the complete listing. The depth of Unilever's product mix refers to the number of versions offered of each product in the line. Thus, if

TABLE 11.3 Product mix breadth and product line length shown for selected major Unilever products						
Product mix breadth						
Detergents and softeners	**Cleansers**	**Toothpaste**	**Bar soap**	**Personal care**	**Food**	**Beverages**
Drive	Ajax	Aim	Lux	Rexona	Rosella	Bushells
Omo and	Jif		Sunlight	Norsca	Continental	Robert Timms
Omo Micro	Domestos		Velvet	Brut	Streets	Lan-Choo
Rinso			Dove	Pears	Flora	Liptons
Persil				Impulse	Keens	
Lux					Fray Bentos	
Surf					Oxo	
Fab					Stork	
Huggie					Daffodil	
Comfort					John West	
					Seakist	
					Ally	
					Plumes	
					Copha	

Aim toothpaste comes in three sizes and two formulations (paste and gel), Aim has a depth of six. By counting the number of versions within each brand we can calculate the average depth of Unilever's product mix. The consistency of the product mix refers to how closely related the various product lines are in end use, production requirements, distribution channels or some other way. Unilever's product lines are consistent insofar as they are consumer products that go through the same distribution channels. The lines are less consistent in that they perform different functions for buyers.

The breadth, length, depth and consistency of the product mix provide the handles for defining the company's product strategy. The company can increase its business in four ways. It can add new product lines, thus widening its product mix. In this way, its new lines build on the company's reputation. Or the company can lengthen its existing product lines to become a more full-line company. Or the company can add more product versions to each product and thus deepen its product mix. Finally, the company can pursue more product line consistency—or less—depending on whether it wants to have a strong reputation in a single field or in several fields.

SELF-CHECK QUESTIONS

17 What are the four important dimensions of a company's product mix?

18 Is the term 'product mix' different from the term 'product assortment'?

International product decisions

International marketers face special product and packaging challenges. First, they must work out what products to introduce and in which countries. Then, they must decide how much to standardise or adapt their products for world markets. Standardisation helps a company to develop a consistent worldwide image. It also results in lower manufacturing costs and eliminates duplication of research and development, advertising and product design efforts. However, consumers around the world differ in their cultures, attitudes and buying behaviours. And markets vary in their economic conditions, competition, legal requirements and physical environments. Usually companies must respond to these differences by adapting their product offerings. Something as simple as an electrical outlet can create big product problems:

> Those who have travelled to Europe know the frustration of electrical plugs, different voltages, and other annoyances of international travel . . . Philips, the electrical appliance manufacturer, has to produce 12 kinds of irons to serve just its European market. The problem is that Europe does not have a universal [electrical] standard. The ends of irons bristle with different plugs for different countries. Some have three prongs, others two; prongs protrude straight or angled, round or rectangular, fat, thin, and sometimes sheathed. There are circular plug faces, squares, pentagons and hexagons. Some are perforated and some are notched. One French plug has a niche like a keyhole; British plugs carry fuses.[48]

Packaging also presents new challenges for international marketers. The US company Penn Racquet Sports found this out when it attempted to launch its line of tennis balls in Japan in its usual threeball can. After netting an initial 8% market share, Penn's Japanese sales quickly plummeted to less than 1%. The problem: poor packaging. Whereas Americans play with three balls, the Japanese use only two. Explained one Penn manager: 'The Japanese thought a three-ball can was a discount, and they passed us over. Our big mistake was that we didn't know the market.' Penn redesigned its package and sales recovered. It now designs its containers to fit the needs of each market: Japan gets a two-ball can, whereas Australia and Europe receive four-ball plastic tubes.[49]

Packaging issues can be subtle. For example, names, labels and colours may not translate easily from one country to another. A firm using yellow flowers in its logo might fare well in the USA, but meet with disaster in Mexico, where a yellow flower symbolises death or disrespect. A firm located at 104 High Street in a Western country might find such a number connotes death to those of Chinese extraction. Similarly, although 'Nature's Gift' might be an appealing name for gourmet mushrooms in America, it would be deadly in Germany, where 'gift' means 'poison'. Consumers in different countries vary in their packaging preferences. Europeans like efficient, functional, recyclable boxes with understated designs. In contrast, products in Japan are often carefully packaged to be given as gifts. Thus, in Japan, Unilever packages its Lux soap in stylish gift boxes. Packaging may even have to be tailored to meet the physical characteristics of consumers in various parts of the world. For instance, soft drinks are sold in smaller cans in Japan to suit the smaller Japanese hand.

Companies may have to adapt their packaging to meet specific regulations regarding package design or label contents. For instance, some countries ban the use of any foreign language on labels; other countries require that labels be printed in two or more languages. Labelling laws vary greatly from country to country:

> In Saudi Arabia . . . product names must be specific. 'Hot Chilli' will not do, it must be 'Spiced Hot Chilli'. Prices are required to be printed on the labels in Venezuela, but in Chile it is illegal to put prices on labels or in any way suggest retail prices. Coca-Cola ran into a legal problem in Brazil with its Diet Coke. Brazilian law interprets 'diet' to have medicinal qualities. Under the law, producers must give daily recommended consumption on the label of all medicines. Coke had to get special approval to get around this restriction.[50]

Thus, although product and package standardisation can produce benefits, companies must usually adapt their offerings to serve the unique needs and requirements of specific international markets.

In summary, whether domestic or international, product strategy calls for complex decisions on product mix, product line, branding, packaging and service strategy. These decisions must be made not only with a full understanding of consumer wants and competitors' strategies but also with increasing attention to the growing public policy affecting product and packaging decisions.

SELF-CHECK QUESTIONS

19 International marketers have long had to decide whether to standardise or adapt their product offerings in different countries. Maxwell House uses red packaging on its coffee labelling in all its markets except Japan. Does Maxwell House standardise or adapt its product offering? Why does Maxwell House use white rather than red on its packaging in Japan alone?

20 Cite two examples where cultural requirements have necessitated product adaptation.

SUMMARY

Product is a complex concept that must be defined carefully. Most importantly, the term 'product' includes services. Products can be viewed as being on a continuum between 'almost pure' physical products and 'almost pure' services. Most products are a combination of a physical good and a service. The chapter examines a number of factors that are often cited as distinguishing a service from a physical good: *intangibility, high involvement* and *personal nature of services, variability of service encounters* and *perishability*.

Also examined are additional classification schemes that help manage the marketing of services. In particular, the marketing of *experiences* is highlighted as it embraces such aspects as *event, political* and *cause* and *not-for-profit* marketing. In each of these situations, product strategy calls for making coordinated decisions on product items, product lines and the product mix.

Each product item offered to customers can be viewed on three levels. The *core product* is the essential benefit the customer is buying. The *actual product* includes the features, styling, quality, brand name and packaging of the product. The *augmented product* is the actual product plus the various services offered with it, such as warranty, installation, maintenance and free delivery.

There are six basic types of *product classifications. Durable* products are used over an extended period of time. *Non-durable* products are more quickly consumed. *Services* are activities or benefits offered for sale which are intangible, inseparable from the consumer, and perishable in that they are experiential and do not result in ownership of anything. Each of these products can be bought by either consumer or industrial customers. *Consumer products* are sold to the final end-user for personal consumption. *Industrial products* are bought by individuals and other organisations to use in their administrative or processing operations and consist of consumables such as paper clips or raw materials that are converted to finished products.

Marketers make individual product decisions for each product, including *product attribute decisions* and *brand, packaging, labelling* and *product-support* services decisions. Product attributes deliver benefits through tangible aspects of the product including features and design, as well as through intangible features such as quality and experiential aspects. A *brand* is a way to identify and differentiate goods and services through use of a name or distinctive design element, resulting in long-term value known as brand equity. The *product package* and *labelling* are also important elements in the product decision mix, as they both carry brand equity through appearance and affect product performance with functionality. The level of product-support services provided can also have a major effect on the appeal of the product to a potential buyer.

Product strategy goes a step beyond individual product decisions, requiring that offerings be built into a logical portfolio through *product line decisions*. A product line is a group of products that are closely related because of similar function, customers, channels of distribution or pricing. A key dimension of the product line is the number of items it contains, referred to as the *product line length*. The product line length can be increased by *upward stretch, downward stretch* or *stretching both ways*. Profits can sometimes be increased by *product line filling*, adding more items within the present range of the line.

Marketing organisations manage multiple product lines through *product mix decisions*. An organisation's product mix has four basic dimensions: *breadth, length, depth* and *consistency*. The *breadth* of a product mix refers to the number of different types of product lines that a company offers. Product mix *length* is the total number of items that the company carries. *Depth* pertains to the number of versions, such as colours or flavours, offered for each product in a line. *Consistency* is a measure of how closely related different product lines are to each other. Consistency can be judged on end use, channels of distribution or production methods.

Marketers face complex considerations in *international product decisions*. First there must be a decision about what products to introduce in what countries. After this decision is made, the organisation must decide whether or not to *standardise* the product and packaging, or whether to adapt them to local conditions.

Overall, developing products and brands is a complex and demanding task. There are no firm rules to assure success in these decisions. Careful consideration of all issues in these decisions, and maintaining consistency with broad organisational objectives, is necessary for long-term success.

MARKETING ISSUE

Their mobile phone is important for most people. But what are they really buying when they buy a new handset, as it's called in the phone business? Certainly, the customer chooses a particular style of phone, and since it's so visible the look of the handset is important; a few years ago, flat 'candy bar' style handsets were the most common variety sold, but today flip phones or 'clamshells' are by far the most popular seller, and the slickest new designs are 'sliders' where the keyboard slips out from under the phone.[51] So getting the right style is important.

But revenue from the phone sale is only a small part of the total telecommunications revenue. Services like SMS and the use of the phone to download ring tones are well established, but these days the phone companies want you to use your phone more, and to use it for newer services. So the phone companies are pushing a range of services such as MMS (picture messaging) and mobile Internet services, which allow the consumer to download content such as horoscopes, music, weather and news reports, and entertainment such as mini-dramas specially developed for phones. But uptake of these newer services has been slow; most consumers haven't tried them and many of those who have seem to get bored, with the level of usage falling off for most people. No one really knows why; perhaps it's the limitation of the small phone screens, the cost or because people are used to using their computers to download Internet content. But the companies are going to keep pushing, hoping that it will just take time, and that picture messaging and mobile Internet use will take off just as SMS and the Internet did.

1   What techniques could a telecommunications company use to understand the limited take-up and use of new services such as mobile Internet?

2   What methods could be used to increase consumers' spending on telecoms' services? How should the effect of any marketing efforts be measured?

KEY TERMS

DISCUSSING THE ISSUES

1. What are the core, tangible and augmented components of the Disneyland experience discussed in the chapter introduction?

2. Would you classify email, instant messaging and SMS/MMS as non-durable goods or as services? Why?

3. Consumers buy from self-service intermediaries such as Aldi, Coles Supermarkets and Woolworths/Safeway, where they deal with few people other than at the checkout. What part might relationships play in marketing these outlets? Might consumers form relationships with the brands themselves?

4. Take the situation where two premium brands, two competing housebrands and two competing generic labelled brands of tinned tomatoes are produced in batches to the same formula on the same continuous production line by the one manufacturer. Would many people be willing to pay more for the branded products than for unbranded products? What does this tell you about the value of branding? Is this situation ethical? Is the situation legal?

5. For many years there was one type of Coca-Cola, one type of Omo and one type of Colgate toothpaste. Now we find Coke in several varieties, different versions of Omo and varieties of toothpaste with stripes, colours and packaging. What issues do these brand extensions raise for manufacturers, retailers and consumers?

6. Car companies monitor consumers' perceptions of their models (brands) and the perceived benefits they offer over time. However, there is usually a long delay before the consumer purchases again. Under these circumstances, would you expect the customer experience to vary? How might this impact on what the marketer should measure, and how they should act?

REFERENCES

1. Joseph B. Pine, II and James H. Gilmore, *The Experience Economy: Work is Theatre and Every Business a Stage*, Boston, Harvard Business School Press, 1999; Keith Bradsher, 'Hong Kong Disneyland is in the Soup', *International Herald Tribune*, 16 June 2005, p. 1; Keith Bradsher, 'A Trial Run Finds Hong Kong Disneyland Much Too Popular for its Modest Size', *The New York Times*, 8 September 2005, p 1; Dennis Eng, 'Disney Hotels Built with a Local Touch; Fung Shui and Superstitions are as Evident as Mickey Mouse', *South China Morning Post*, 10 August 2005, p. 3; Leslie Kwoh and Cannix Yau, 'SAR May Sell Disney Stake', *The Standard*, 3 November 2005; Min Lee, 'Hong Kong Disneyland is a Feng Shui Fantasia', *Vancouver Sun*, 24 September 2005, p. D7; Christie Lohchristie, 'Lure of the Magic Kingdom: Will Mickey Give Hong Kong an Edge over S'pore in the Fight for Visitors?', *Today* (Singapore), 10 September 2005, p. 1; Merissa Marr and Geoffrey A. Fowler, 'Will Chinese Share the Dream? Disney's Hong Kong Park Walks Cultural Tightrope, with an Eye on the Paris Experience', *The Wall Street Journal Europe*, 16 June 2005, p. A5; Benjamin Tan 'The Eat Ethical diet', *Straits Times*, 2 October 2005.

2. Joseph B. Pine II and James H. Gilmore, 'Welcome to the Experience Economy', *Harvard Business Review*, July–August 1998, p. 98.

3. See Christopher Lovelock, Paul G. Patterson and Rhett H. Walker, *Services Marketing*, 2nd edn, Sydney, Pearson Education Australia, 2001.

4. See <www.mcdonalds.com>, last accessed January 2006.

5. Lovelock et al., *Services Marketing*, Sydney, Pearson Education Australia, 2001.

6. See <www.qantas.com>, last accessed 3 November 2002.

7. See <www.fly.virgin.com/atlantic>.

8. For more information on product classifications see Patrick E. Murphy and Ben M. Enis, 'Classifying Products Strategically', *Journal of Marketing*, July 1986, pp. 24–42.

9. Australian Bureau of Statistics, *Year Book, 2005*.

10. See Ronald Henkoff, 'Service is Everybody's Business', *Fortune*, 27 June 1994, pp. 48–60; Valarie Zeithaml and Mary Jo Bitner, *Services Marketing*, 3d edn, New York, McGraw-Hill, 2002, pp. 8–9; and Margaret Popper, 'Services: Slowed but Still Strong', *Business Week*, 12 December 2002, accessed online at <www.businessweek.com>. For more on the importance of services to marketing and the economy, see Robert F. Lusch and Stephen L. Vargo, 'Evolving to a New Dominant Logic for Marketing', *Journal of Marketing*, January 2004, p. 1.

11. Australian Bureau of Statistics, *ANZSIC 2006 Development*, 1294.0, Information paper, 2004.

12. Adapted from information in Leonard Berry and Neeli Bendapudi, 'Clueing in Customers', *Harvard Business Review*, February 2003, pp. 100–106.

13. Jan Carlzon, *Moments of Truth*, Cambridge, MA, Ballinger Publishing, 1987, p. 3.

14. For discussions of service quality, see Valarie A. Zeithaml, A. Parasuraman and Leonard L. Berry, *Delivering Quality Service: Balancing Customer Perceptions and Expectations*, New York, The Free Press, 1990; Zeithaml, Berry and Parasuraman, 'The Behavioral Consequences of Service Quality', *Journal of Marketing*, April 1996, pp. 31–46; Thomas J. Page Jr, 'Difference Scores Versus Direct Effects in

Service Quality Measurement', *Journal of Service Research*, February 2002, pp. 184–192; and Y. H. Hung, M. L. Huang and K. S. Chen, 'Service Quality Evaluation by Service Quality Performance Matrix', *Total Quality Management & Business Excellence*, January 2003, pp. 79–89.

15. See James L. Heskett, W. Earl Sasser Jr and Christopher W. L. Hart, *Service Breakthroughs*, New York, The Free Press, 1990.
16. For a discussion of cause and not-for-profit marketing see V. Kasturi Rangan, Sohel Karim and Sherly K. Sandberg, 'Do Better at Doing Good', *Harvard Business Review*, May–June 1996, pp. 42–54.
17. See Willian P. Ryan, 'The New Landscape for Nonprofits', *Harvard Business Review*, January–February 1999, pp. 127–136.
18. Joseph B. Pine II and James H. Gilmore, 'Welcome to the Experience Economy', *Harvard Business Review*, July–August 1998, p. 99.
19. B. Joseph Pine, II and James H. Gilmore, *The Experience Economy: Work is Theatre and Every Business a Stage*, Boston, Harvard Business School Press, 1999.
20. Pine and Gilmore, op. cit., p. 99.
21. Chris Nuttall, 'Seattle WiFi Users Wake up and Smell the Coffee', *Financial Times*, 13 June 2005, p. 14.
22. See Peter Bennett, *Dictionary of Marketing Terms*, Chicago, American Marketing Association, 1988.
23. See 'McAtlas Shrugged', *Foreign Policy*, May–June 2001, pp. 26–37; and Philip Kotler, *Marketing Management*, 11th edn, Upper Saddle River, NJ, Prentice Hall, 2003, p. 423.
24. Douglas Holt, 'What Becomes an Icon Most?', *Harvard Business Review*, March 2003, pp. 43–49.
25. David C. Bello and Morris. B. Holbrook, 'Does an Absence of Brand Equity Generalize across Product Classes?', *Journal of Business Research*, October 1995, p. 125; and Scott Davis, *Brand Asset Management: Driving Profitable Growth through Your Brands*, San Francisco, Jossey-Bass, 2000. Also see Kevin Lane Keller, *Building, Measuring, and Managing Brand Equity*, 2nd edn, Upper Saddle River, NJ, Prentice Hall, 2003, Chapter 2; and Kusum Ailawadi, Donald R. Lehman and Scott A. Neslin, 'Revenue Premium as an Outcome Measure of Brand Equity', *Journal of Marketing*, October 2003, pp. 1–17.
26. See Roland Rust, Katherine Lemon and Valarie Zeithaml, 'Return on Marketing: Using Customer Equity to Focus Marketing Strategy', *Journal of Marketing*, January 2004, p. 109.
27. Alan Kohler, 'The Buck Starts with Frank', *The Sydney Morning Herald*, 3 February 2004, p. 1.
28. Thomas M. S. Hemnes, 'How Can You Find a Safe Trademark?', *Harvard Business Review*, March–April 1985, p. 44.
29. Lyn White, 'Size Isn't Everything', *Food Week*, 25 March 2005.
30. Varun Mudgil, 'Coles' Housebrand Strategy Axes Existing Private Labels', *Retail World*, 4 April 2005.
31. Anonymous, 'Coles Launches House Brands . . . Modestly', *Food Week*, 1 July 2005.
32. See Laura Petrecca, '"Corporate Brands" Put Licensing in the Spotlight', *Advertising Age*, 14 June 1999, p. 1; and Bob Vavra, 'The Game of the Name', *Supermarket Business*, 15 March 2001, pp. 45–46.
33. Kim Cleland, 'Multimarketer Melange an Increasingly Tasty Option on the Store Shelf', *Advertising Age*, 2 May 1994, p. S10.
34. For more on line extensions, see Kevin Lane Keller and David A. Aaker, 'The Effects of Sequential Introduction of Line Extensions', *Journal of Marketing Research*, February 1992, pp. 35–50; and Srinivas K. Reddy, Susan L. Holak and Subodh Bhat, 'To Extend or Not to Extend: Success Determinants of Line Extensions', *Journal of Marketing Research*, May 1994, pp. 243–262.
35. Daniel C. Smith and C. Whan Park, 'The Effects of Brand Extensions on Market Share and Advertising Efficiency', *Journal of Marketing Research*, August 1992, pp. 296–313.
36. For more on the use of brand extensions and consumer attitudes towards them see David A. Aaker and Kevin L. Keller, 'Consumer Evaluations of Brand Extensions', *Journal of Marketing*, January 1990, pp. 27–41; Julie Liesse, 'Brand Extensions Take Center Stage', *Advertising Age*, 8 March 1993, p. 12; and Susan M. Broniarczyk and Joseph W. Alba, 'The Importance of Brand in Brand Extension', *Journal of Marketing Research*, May 1994, pp. 214–228.
37. See Ira Teinowitz, 'Brand Proliferation Attacked', *Advertising Age*, 10 May 1993, pp. 1, 49; and Jennifer Lawrence, 'P&G Strategy: Build on Brands', *Advertising Age*, 23 August 1993, pp. 3, 31.
38. See Christopher Power, 'And Now, Finger-Lickin' Good for Ya?', *Business Week*, 18 February 1991, p. 60; and Gary Strauss, 'Building on Brand Names: Companies Freshen Old Product Lines', *USA Today*, 20 March 1992, pp. 1, 2.
39. 'Top 200 Megabrands', accessed at <www.adage.com>, June 2004.
40. See Kevin Lane Keller, 'The Brand Report Card', *Harvard Business Review*, January 2000, pp. 147–157; Keller, *Strategic Brand Management*, pp. 766–767; and David A. Aaker, 'Even Brands Need Spring Cleaning', *Brandweek*, 8 March 2004, pp. 36–40.
41. Simon Canning, 'Local Shoppers Not Buying Store's Name Change', *The Australian*, 6 February 2004.
42. Australian Associated Press Financial News Wire, 'Coles Says Myer may be for Sale after Strategic Review', 16 August 2005. Michael West and Kevin Andrusiak, '$1bn in Retail Assets on Block', *The Australian*, 9 November 2005; James McCullough and Jeff Turnbull, 'Retail Myer Chief Pledges a Tough Fight: Can This Dinosaur Become a Dynamo?', *The Advertiser*, 20 August 2005.
43. Kate Fitzgerald, 'Packaging Is the Capper', *Advertising Age*, 5 May 2003, p. 22.
44. See Alicia Swasy, 'Sales Lost Their Vim? Try Repackaging', *The Wall Street Journal*, 11 October 1989, p. B1.
45. Bro Uttal, 'Companies that Serve You Best', *Fortune*, 7 December 1987, pp. 98–116. Also see Barry Farber and Joyce Wycoff, 'Customer Service: Evolution and Revolution', *Sales & Marketing Management*, May 1991, pp. 44–51.
46. Bro Uttal, 'Companies that Serve You Best', p. 116.
47. For a discussion of product line expansion issues see John A. Quelch and David Kenny, 'Extend Profits, Not Product Lines', *Harvard Business Review*, September–October 1994, pp. 153–160.
48. Philip Cateora, *International Marketing*, 8th edn, Homewood, IL, Irwin, 1993, p. 270.
49. David J. Morrow, 'Sitting Pretty: How to Make Your Package Stand out in a Crowd', *International Business*, November 1991, pp. 30–32.
50. Philip R. Cateora, *International Marketing*, 9th edn, Chicago, Irwin, 1996, p. 426.
51. Karen Keller, 'The Secret Life of a Cellphone', *Fortune*, 19 September 2005, pp. 100–101.

PHOTO/AD CREDITS

Daniel Prior, Charles Sturt University

CASE STUDY

What makes a tourist destination?
The trials and tribulations of two regional centres

Contributing around $7.6 billion to Australia's GDP (2004) and employing between 5% and 6% of the Australian workforce, the Australian tourism industry is one of the largest industries in Australia. The economic benefits of tourism permeate the entire Australian economy with retailers, transport providers, accommodation providers and entertainment providers all owing at least some of their income to tourism. The benefits of tourism are manifold but can be primarily defined as economic and social. As such, increasing the incidence of tourism in any one location provides a luring bounty to those who stand to benefit either directly or indirectly from tourism.

Jack Wilson was the marketing and promotions manager for the city of Dubbo from 1998 to 2004. Located in the central west of New South Wales, Dubbo at that time supported a population of around 25 000 residents. Jack was given a brief to identify and promote Dubbo as a tourist destination. Tourists tended to go to Dubbo for only a few main reasons. These included visiting friends and/or family, for business, to visit the Western Plains Zoo or to tour the wineries. The largest single reason was visiting friends and family. As far as Jack could tell, these reasons had endured for at least 20 years as the primary reasons for travel to Dubbo and tourism had remained virtually stagnant for almost as long. The peak times had been when the Western Plains Zoo had recruited a new animal or a rare animal had been born at the zoo.

After reviewing the situation, Jack began rethinking the tourism 'product', as it was called in the industry. He was of the belief that Dubbo, and surrounding districts, offered a number of additional tourist lures that could also be exploited. Jack believed that tourists often were in search of an experience that included visiting a number of tourist destinations, eating good food and drinking good wine, staying in appropriate accommodation and travelling to Dubbo in a comfortable and quick manner.

Subsequently, Jack began to develop a number of major initiatives designed to attract greater numbers of tourists, to make them stay in the region for longer periods of time and to increase spending while in the region. The first of these initiatives was to develop a number of tourist packages that encompassed tours of the region, accommodation, meals and entertainment—all of which were provided by local suppliers. Four major types of package were created, including the Western Plains Zoo package (a tour of the zoo, a wildlife tour and accommodation near the zoo), the gourmet traveller's package (a tour of local wineries, fresh produce suppliers, good quality restaurants and accommodation at upmarket bed and breakfasts), the adventurer's package (a hiking/camping package around some of the Dubbo bushland) and the history package (a tour of significant historical sites around the region). Transport to these sites was supplied by local operators. The second of these initiatives involved promoting the newly created tours to key stakeholder groups. This step was multifaceted and involved launching the packages at a major event in Sydney. This was followed up with a road show that saw Jack and his team tour many of the larger towns and cities throughout New South Wales.

The last of these steps was to maintain promotions throughout the year through public relations activities and advertisements in local and national newspapers and ensure that packages all ran according to plan.

As a result of Jack's efforts, inbound tourism to the region increased from around 100 000 unique visits per year to just over 220 000.

Jack decided it was time to move on. In 2005, Jack was appointed to the position of marketing and tourism manager for the city of Wagga Wagga, a town about twice the size of Dubbo and located approximately 400 km to the south of Dubbo. Wagga Wagga presented a cast of new challenges in that it had a population of around 57 000, and relatively little inbound tourism. Inbound tourists numbered around 180 000. Jack discovered that the major reasons for travel to Wagga Wagga were for business and family, and not much else. The largest influx of tourists was generated by the local defence bases, with Kapooka Army Barracks being the primary training facility for new recruits into the Australian Army. The most significant other reasons included visits to family and friends, and to study at the local university.

Jack's employer, the local council, was of the firm belief that tourism to the area could be increased and that all it would take would be some advertising. Jack's position had only recently been created by a council vote, so not much experience existed within the organisation as to what was involved in successfully creating and promoting a tourism product.

Being a hardened veteran of the tourism industry, Jack began a campaign to re-educate members of the council as well as other members of the community as to what would improve the city's tourism. He began by explaining the components of the city's tourism product, suggesting that it was lacking in a number of major areas. While plenty of accommodation existed in town, significant attractions for non-business and non-family/friends tourists to the town did not exist. It would be a challenge to develop this product further before even thinking of advertising.

Jack knew the road ahead would be long and arduous. Many challenges were on the horizon in terms of developing Wagga Wagga's tourism product and promoting it to the wider community. How can we help Jack?

Please note: While loosely based on actual events, the figures and events in this case study are entirely fictitious unless indicated otherwise.

Source: Australian Bureau of Statistics, *Australian National Accounts: Tourism Satellite Account*, Catalogue no. 5249.0, 2003–04.

QUESTIONS

1. Define the product characteristics of tourism products. Is tourism really just one product/service? Explain your answer.

2. What is the core benefit of tourism for the tourist? Is this the same for all tourists and tourist products?

3. Is an 'experience', as outlined in the case study, a product or a service? Explain your answer.

4. What are the differences between the Dubbo tourist product and the Wagga Wagga tourism product as outlined in the case study?

5. Using concepts in this chapter, suggest what Jack should do with the Wagga Wagga tourism product.

CHAPTER 12

New products

Kodak: www.kodak.com
Hewlett-Packard: www.hp.com
Dell: www.dell.com
Sony: www.sony.com
Canon: www.canon.com
Samsung: www.samsung.com

The consumer electronics industry is a continuous hot-bed of new-product innovation. In recent years new technology has enabled the consumer electronic giants to develop new flat screen televisions, wireless stereo speaker systems and personal video recorders that record live TV on a hard disk drive enabling users to pause and rewind while they watch. The digital camera category, in particular, has spawned new growth opportunities for the major players and attracted new vendors to a market growing exponentially. In fact it seems like there is a new digital camera launched every day with more mega-pixels, a sleeker design, pencil-thin profiles and a larger viewing screen. This new-product market has appeared so attractive that non-traditional still-camera makers from the consumer electronics industry such as Samsung and Sony have joined the traditional camera players like Canon, Nikon and Kodak in a fight for a share of this new market.

The digital camera has been a breakthrough product category as the technology has improved the consumer's experience of photography by eliminating the risk associated with taking a bad photograph. This reduction in risk means that people are taking more photos than ever before and photography's popularity has boomed. This popularity has meant that manufacturers have invested heavily in research and development to continually improve the technology and offerings available to capture as much of the market as possible and keep at least one step ahead of competitors. Cameras have been developed in four major categories, the ultra-portable for those wanting a pocket-sized camera for all occasions, the portable for those wanting a convenient-sized easy-to-use camera for travel and special occasions, the fully automatic for the enthusiast who wants a better picture and more features and the digital SLR for the professional wanting the most flexibility and highest picture quality.

The digital camera phenomenon has driven the growth in digital film processing and associated accessories such as digital film. Digital film or memory cards have replaced the need for traditional film development. The digital film allows users to easily transfer images from one digital device to another. For instance, HP has developed stand-alone photo printers where users can simply take their digital film

So many choices in digital cameras.

straight out of their cameras, place it in the photo printer and proceed to select the images they want printed. Many large supermarket and computer store chains now have digital photo processing kiosks which allow consumers without photo printers simply to insert their digital film and produce photographic prints.

Why would you buy a stand-alone digital camera when you already have one in something else? The immense popularity of digital cameras has meant that manufacturers have begun building this technology into other devices. Many mobile phones now have in-built digital cameras, as well as laptop computers, video cameras, PDAs and digital music players. This creates confusion for consumers wondering how many cameras do they really need?

Today, new-product management has become a very important field in business and marketing. The importance of new products is that they can be the answer to many organisations' ability to compete profitably. Low-cost competitors do damage in the marketplace when there is little differentiation and when competitors have a product that customers value. Revenues and profits suffer when customers no longer want our products and prefer our competitors' products at lower prices. Also, new competitors have an impact when they enter the market with lower prices and additional features. It is a competitive world and it means that we must offer something of better overall value than our competitors to stay in front.

A major shift in a marketplace such as that which has occurred in the camera business can have a crippling effect on the incumbents of that industry as Kodak has discovered. In 2004, for the first time more digital cameras were sold than film-based cameras, which was not good news for Kodak, a 125-year-old company that has been one of the leaders in the film processing business. In fact the film business has been declining by 25% annually, which is more than three times the expected rate, and although Kodak has managed to establish a leadership position in the new digital camera market (holding 22% of the US market) it has come at a great cost. The growth and intensity of competition has meant that Kodak's margins on digital cameras have been lower than expected and it is not able to make up for the shortfall in its declining film business. Organisations, no matter how big or small or how successful in the past, need to be careful and must have effective new-product processes so that there is a blend of new products that generate future profitability. Perhaps Kodak could have avoided some of its current woes if it had acted sooner and more aggressively in the digital camera market.[1]

After reading this chapter you should be able to:

1 Identify the challenges companies face in creating a new-product development strategy.

2 List different sources for ideas generation, and discuss how an idea moves ahead through ideas screening, concept development and concept testing.

3 Outline how a potential product advances from a concept to a product through marketing strategy development, business analysis and product development.

4 Explain the purpose of test marketing, and distinguish between standard, controlled and simulated test markets.

5 Express the basics of the buyer decision process for new products and identify stages in the adoption process, individual differences in the adoption of innovation, and the influence of product characteristics on the rate of diffusion of innovation.

6 Evaluate the product life-cycle theory, detailing the extent to which you accept the sequence of the introduction, growth, maturity and decline stages.

A company has to be good at developing new products. It must also manage them in the face of changing tastes, technologies and competition. Every product seems to go through a life cycle—it is born, goes through several phases and eventually dies as newer and better products come along.

This product life cycle presents two major challenges. First, because all products eventually decline, the firm must find new products to replace ageing ones (the problem of *new-product development*). Second, the firm must understand how its products age and adapt its marketing strategies as products pass through life-cycle stages (the problem of *product life-cycle strategies*). Chapter 11 described products and services lying along a product–service continuum. In this chapter when we use the term 'product' it can equally be applied to a product or a service. We first look at the problem of finding and developing new products and then at the problem of managing them successfully over their life cycles.

What is a new product?

Before we start looking at the process of new-product development and management we should consider just what is a new product. Table 12.1 provides a summary of different categories of new products. This provides a checklist for the new product from a developer's view which can be useful when marketers are considering repositioning options. Can we tell our customers that this is a new product just by repositioning it and telling them it is something else? Sometimes yes, as the example in Table 12.1 shows.

The new category in Table 12.1 also explores the issue of an organisation having an imitation or 'me-too' product. If a firm introduces a new brand of web-authoring software identical to the features already on the market, is it a new product? According to Table 12.1, yes. It is new to the firm. It is a new product from that firm's perspective.

The other categories in Table 12.1 from new to the world to additions to the line and improvements are commonly regarded as new products. The further down the list the category lies the less expensive and difficult the challenge. Each type of new product brings with it different challenges and strategic implications for the marketer.

TABLE 12.1 Categories of new product	
Categories	**Description**
New to the world	*This category represents inventions.* The product is new to the world. For example, first car, PDA, laser printer, antibiotic.
New category entries	*Products that take the firm into a category which is new to it.* Here products are not new to the world. For example, Johnson & Johnson's first insect spray, Hewlett-Packard's first Internet server.
Additions to product lines	*This category represents products that are line extensions in the firm's current markets.* For example, Cascade Light beer, BMW 4WD vehicle, Canon digital camera.
Product improvements	*This category represents existing products that have been made better.* Almost every product in the marketplace has been or will be improved one or several times in the course of its life cycle.
Repositioning	*This category is reserved for products that are retargeted for new use, application or to a new user.* A classic example is the Arm and Hammer baking soda that was repositioned several times from baking, to deodorant, fridge deodorant and carpet cleaner.
Variations of the above	Variations such as new to the country, new to the channel, packaging improvements and different methods of manufacturing *are not* commonly accepted as new products.

New-product development strategy

Given the rapid changes in tastes, technology and competition, a company cannot rely solely on its existing products. Customers want and expect the new and improved products that competition will do its best to provide. Every company needs a new-product development program.

A company can obtain new products in two ways. One is through acquisition—buying a whole company, a patent or a licence to produce someone else's product. Companies such as Microsoft, Oracle, Coca-Cola or McDonald's use such methods. For example, in order to appeal to the health-conscious market Coca-Cola has acquired Mount Franklin water and other various fruit juice brands. Similarly, McDonald's, in order to compete in the growing premium takeaway food segment, has acquired the Boston Market brand. Oracle acquired PeopleSoft in June 2005 and Siebel Systems in early 2006 to consolidate its software business.

The other is through **new-product development** in the company's own research and development department. As the costs of developing and introducing major new products have climbed, many large companies have decided to acquire existing brands rather than create new ones. Others have saved money by copying competitors' brands or by reviving old brands. For example, when Sanitarium Foods challenged Kellogg's on the basis of high sugar content in Kellogg's products, the Kellogg's Cornflakes brand was revived to reduce this threat. Volkswagen revived the VW Beetle brand of the 1960s to appeal to baby boomers' sentiments in the early 2000s.[2] Marketing Highlight 12.1 gives more examples of new-product strategy options.

By *new products* we mean original products, product improvements, product modifications and new brands that the company develops through its research and development efforts. In this chapter we concentrate on new-product development.

New-product development The development of original products, product improvements, product modifications and new brands through the company's own R&D efforts.

New-product success and failure

Innovation can be very risky. Ford lost $US350 million on its Edsel car; RCA lost $US580 million on its SelectaVision videodisc player; Texas Instruments lost $US660 million before withdrawing from

New-product strategies

The average cost of developing and introducing a major new product from scratch has jumped to well over $US100 million. If a new technology is involved, the cost is much more. What's worse, many of these costly new products fail. So companies are now pursuing new-product strategies that are less costly and less risky than developing completely new brands. These strategies include *acquiring new brands*, *developing 'me-too' products* and *reviving old brands*.

Acquiring new products

Instead of building its own new products, a company can buy another company and its established brands. In October 2005 Proctor & Gamble bought the Boston-based shaving superpower, Gillette, the first major fast-moving consumer goods industry acquisition since the 1990s. The IT industry in most recent years has been setting the pace on acquisitions, in 2005 and 2006 with Oracle (the Enterprise Software company) buying PeopleSoft and Siebel within one year and eBay purchasing the VoIP (voice over Internet protocol) software developer Skype.

Such acquisitions can be tricky. The company must be certain that the acquired products blend well with its own current products, and that the firm has the skills and resources needed to continue to run the acquired products profitably. Acquisitions can also run into snags with government regulators. For example, under an ACCC ruling in 1999, regulators did not allow Cable & Wireless Optus to acquire AAPT. Finally, such acquisitions have high price tags as the $US57 billion Procter & Gamble paid for Gillette demonstrates.

History tells us that brands last much longer than their creators. Only one in three of the top 500 Australian enterprises of the 1980s survived to celebrate New Year's Eve of 1999. Between 1982 and 1998 54% of the top 500 left the list. Of the 34 deletions among the biggest 100 of the top 500, Petersville has been taken over six times—most recently by Pacific Dunlop, then Simplot and now Nestlé. Among the 54% (268) departures, most of the brand names have survived.

But despite high initial outlays, buying established brands or new-product technologies may be cheaper in the long run than paying the enormous costs of trying to create well-known brand names from scratch. And acquiring proven winners eliminates almost all the risks of new-product failure. Acquisition also provides a quick and easy way to gain access to new markets or to strengthen positions in current markets. For example, by acquiring Gillette, Procter & Gamble moved immediately into the shaving market.

Developing 'me-too' products

In recent years many companies have used 'me-too' product strategies—introducing imitations of successful competitors' products. Thus, Compaq, Dell, HP and many others produce IBM-compatible personal computers. Me-too products have also hit the fragrance industry. Several companies now offer smell-alike 'knock-offs' of popular, high-priced perfumes such as Poison, Opium and Georgio at a fifth of the originals' prices. The success of knock-off fragrances has also inspired a wave of look-alike designer fashions and imitative versions of prestige cosmetics and hair-care brands. Imitation is now fair play for products ranging from soft drinks and food to clothing and house designs.

Me-too products are often quicker and less expensive to develop. The market leader pioneers the technology and bears most of the product development costs. The imitative products sometimes give consumers even more value than the market-leading originals: the copycat company can build on the leader's design and technology to create an equivalent product at a lower price, or an even better product at the same or a higher price. Me-too products are also less costly and risky to introduce—they enter a proven market already developed by the market leader. Thus, James Hardie invested millions to develop its fibre cement walling product and cultivate a housing market; while the clone makers such as CSR and Humes rode on James Hardie's coat-tails.

However, a me-too strategy also has some drawbacks. The imitating company enters the market late and must battle a successful, firmly entrenched competitor. Some me-too products never take much business from the leader. Others succeed broadly and end up challenging for market leadership. Still others settle into small but profitable niches in the market created by the leader.

Reviving old products

Many companies have found 'new gold in the old' by reviving once-successful brands that are dead or dying. Many old and tarnished brand names still hold magic for consumers. Often, simply reviving, reformulating and repositioning an old brand can give the company a successful 'new' product at a fraction of the cost of building new brands. Hollywood has proven this many times over, bringing back to life old stories and heroes in movies such as *Batman Returns, Oceans 12, Charlie and the Chocolate Factory* and *Star Wars—Revenge of the Sith* in 2004–05.

Sometimes, a dead product rises again with a new name, as happened with Nestlé's New Cookery brand of low-fat, low-sugar, low-salt entrées. Some years ago, Nestlé withdrew the product when it failed in the test market. But New Cookery was well suited to today's health-conscious consumers, and Stouffer, a Nestlé company, revived the line under the Lean Cuisine brand. Lean Cuisine proved a resounding success.

Sources: Jenn Abelson, 'An Era Ends: Goodbye, Gillette Hello, Procter & Gamble', *The Boston Globe, The (MA)*, 10 January 2005; Phil Ruthven, 'Brands Endure, Empires Go', *Business Review Weekly*, 21 December 1998; Pat Sloan, 'Knock-Offs Deliver Blows to Fragrance Market', *Advertising Age*, 2 March 1987, p. S14; Arthur Bragg, 'Back to the Future', *Sales and Marketing Management*, November 1986, pp. 61–62; Michael Oneal, 'The Best and Worst Deals of the '80s', *Business Week*, 15 January 1990, pp. 52–58; and Neil Shoebridge, *Business Review Weekly*, 13 December 1991, p. 69.

Questions

1 Provide a recent example of a company buying another company's brands. Explain the logic behind the acquisition.

2 What are the advantages and disadvantages of a 'me-too' strategy?

3 Look for an example of an old brand that has been revitalised. What did the company do to achieve this?

12.1

the home computer business; and Boo.com, an Internet fashion merchant, lost $US300 million on its virtual fashion model technology leading to its bankruptcy. Compaq's Concerto notebook with a detachable keyboard that could double as a notepad ended up on the junk heap—in part because Compaq priced this black and white model too high just as colour portables were going mainstream.[3]

Inghams/Amatil lost more than $10 million on a roast chicken range in Australia, which Holly Farms, a $US1.5 billion a year US chicken producer, also lost heavily on. In both cases, consumer research gave a false reading. Holly Farms claimed it did not go far enough in educating supermarket meat managers on how to handle a short-shelf-life product such as this, but the Australian case was more complex.

However, the United Kingdom poultry group D.B. Marshalls, among others, was successful with the identical product sold through supermarkets such as Marks and Spencer in Britain and France. Other costly product failures from sophisticated companies include:

- Coles Myer (MyCar Superstores)
- Homer Hudson ice-cream (Streets)
- New Coke (Coca-Cola Company)

- Birdseye frozen meals
- Polarvision instant movies (Polaroid)
- Décoré Hold That Colour Shampoo and Colorants (Décoré)
- Satellite Phone (Iridium)
- Internet groceries (Webvan.com)
- Dairy Farmers (Franklins Fresh)
- Grilled Chicken Burger (McDonald's)
- Firestone SUV tyre (Bridgestone/Firestone North American Tire, LLC)
- Burger King expansion into Poland and Japan (closure of all outlets at the end of 2001)

New products continue to fail at a disturbing rate. One recent study estimated that new consumer packaged goods (consisting mostly of line extensions) fail at a rate of 80%. Another study found that about 33% of new industrial products fail at launch.[4] According to one marketing expert: 'If companies can improve their effectiveness at launching new products, they could double their bottom line. It's one of the areas left with the greatest potential for improvement.'[5]

Another study found that the new-product failure rate was 40% for consumer products, 20% for industrial products and 18% for services. A study of 700 consumer and industrial firms found an overall success rate for new products of only 65%. Still another source estimates that, of the 2500 new products introduced each year, some 90% survived less than three years![6]

Why do so many new products fail? There are several reasons (see Table 12.2). A high-level executive might push a favourite idea in spite of poor marketing research findings. Or, although an idea may be good, the market size may have been overestimated. Perhaps the actual product was not designed as well as it should have been. Or maybe it was incorrectly positioned in the market, priced too high or advertised poorly. Sometimes the costs of product development are higher than expected, and sometimes competitors fight back harder than expected.

Because so many new products fail, companies are anxious to learn how to improve their odds of new-product success. One way is to identify successful new products and find out what they have in common. One study of 200 moderate-to-high-technology new-product launches, which looked for factors shared by successful products but not by product failures, found that the number one success factor is a *unique superior product*, one with higher quality, new features and higher value in use. Specifically, products with a high product advantage succeed 98% of the time, compared with products with a moderate advantage (58% success) or minimal advantage (18% success). Another key success factor is a *well-defined product concept* prior to development, for which the company carefully defines and assesses the target market, the product requirements and the benefits before proceeding.[7] From an overview of new-product success and failure, Gruenwald reports that top management commitment to developing new business is a key to success coupled with the factors of a longer-range perspective, recognition for technological creativity and encouragement of entrepreneurship.[8] In all, to create successful new products, a company must understand its consumers, markets and competitors and develop products that deliver superior value to customers.

Successful new-product development may be even more difficult in the future. Keen competition has led to increasing market fragmentation—companies must now aim at smaller market segments rather than at the mass market, with the probable results of smaller sales and profits for each product. New products must meet growing social and governmental constraints, such as consumer safety and ecological standards. The costs of finding, developing and launching new products will rise steadily because of rising manufacturing, media and distribution costs. Many companies cannot afford or cannot raise the funds needed for new-product development—they emphasise product modification and imitation rather than true innovation. Even when a new product is successful, rivals are so quick to follow suit that the new product is typically fated to a happy but short life. Thus, IBM finds dozens

TABLE 12.2 Reasons for new-product failure

1. *Market segment too small*
   Although a segment with differentiated needs has been identified, demand is inadequate to make the product profitable.

2. *Poor match with company capabilities*
   There is little synergy with the company's technical, marketing, production and financial skills and experience. The product does not build on the organisation's distinctive competence.

3. *Not unique*
   Even though the new product is technically or physically different, it is not new from the customer's point of view.

4. *Lacks superior quality*
   The product does not reliably meet specifications that lead to high perceived quality.

5. *Little benefit relative to competition*
   The product does not provide significant performance advantages over alternatives already available to customers.

6. *Poor positioning*
   The product is poorly positioned because management misunderstood customers' perceptions, relative importance weights and price trade-offs.

7. *Inadequate support from channel*
   Channel members are not motivated to provide requisite distribution intensity or support.

8. *Forecasting error*
   Sales potential and/or rate of diffusion have been overestimated.

9. *Competitive response*
   Competition copies and/or improves product rapidly, and the company has an inadequate strategy or insufficient resources to wage and survive a competitive battle.

10. *Changes in consumer tastes*
    There is a shift in preferences while the product is being developed or launched.

11. *Changes in environment*
    Tax changes, fluctuations in the prices of raw materials and shifts in social attitudes, for example, make a product design obsolete.

12. *Ineffective launch*
    Selling, distribution, advertising or delivery are not executed as planned.

13. *Insufficient profitability*
    Sales are good, but margins are poor because of higher-than-anticipated costs or lower-than-expected prices.

14. *Organisational problems*
    Intra-organisational conflicts and poor management practices exist.

Source: Glen L. Urban and Steven H. Star, *Advanced Marketing Strategy: Phenomena, Analysis, Decisions,* © 1991, p. 287. Reprinted by permission of Prentice Hall, Englewood Cliffs, New Jersey.

of imitators offering IBM-compatible computers, and Hewlett-Packard finds foreign 'knock-offs' of its inkjet printers being sold in some Asian countries. Cisco had its software and training manuals copied by a Chinese company.[9] Record labels are finding that the more successful the product is, the more chance of it being pirated. Record labels have won the wars with music swapping websites such as Napster; however, because the opportunity exists, newcomers will try to make a success of copying others' hard work.[10]

Similarly, large pharmaceutical companies are finding that their winning products are being turned into generic medications. Currently large drugmakers are being threatened by Indian drugmakers who make 'legal' copies and generics of their patent-expired market-leader products.[11]

The new-product dilemma

So companies face a problem—they must develop new products, but the odds weigh heavily against success. The solution lies in strong new-product planning. Top management is ultimately accountable for the new-product success record. It cannot simply ask the new-product manager to come up with great ideas. Top management must define the business domains and product categories that the company wants to emphasise.

It must establish specific criteria for new-product idea acceptance, especially in large multidivisional companies in which all kinds of projects bubble up as favourites of various managers. These criteria vary with the specific *strategic role* the product is expected to play. The product's role might be to help the company maintain its industry position as an innovator, to defend a market-share position or to get a foothold in a future new market. Or the new product might help the company take advantage of its special strengths or exploit technology in a new way. For example, a typical global company might set the following acceptance criteria for new products aimed at exploiting a technology in a new way:

- The product can be introduced within three years.
- The product has a market potential of at least $50 million and a 15% growth rate.
- The product will provide at least 10% return on sales and 30% on investment.
- The product will achieve technical or market leadership.

Another major decision facing top management is how much to budget for new-product development. New-product outcomes are so uncertain that using normal investment criteria for budgeting is difficult. Some companies solve this problem by encouraging and financing as many projects as possible, hoping to achieve a few winners. Other companies set their R&D budgets by applying a conventional percentage-to-sales figure or by spending as much as the competition spends. Still other companies decide how many successful new products they need and work backwards to estimate the required R&D investment.

Another important factor in new-product development work is to set up effective organisational structures for nurturing and handling new products. Table 12.3 outlines the most common organisational arrangements—product managers, new-product managers, new-product committees, new product departments and venture teams.

Thus, successful new-product development requires a total company effort. The most successful innovating companies make a consistent commitment of resources to new-product development, design a new-product strategy that is linked to their strategic planning process, and set up formal and sophisticated organisational arrangements for managing the new-product development process.

A new way of speeding up product development

Product failure rates can be reduced when organisations begin to think of customers as innovators. Today both

The Starbucks concept has changed the way consumers drink coffee at the same time as providing a new venue for business meetings and Internet access on every street corner.

TABLE 12.3 Ways companies organise for new-product development

Product managers

Many companies assign responsibility for new-product ideas to their product managers. Because these managers are close to the market and competition, they are ideally situated to find and develop new-product opportunities. In practice, however, this system has several faults. Product managers are usually so busy managing their product lines that they give little thought to new products other than brand modifications or extensions. They also lack the specific skills and knowledge needed to evaluate and develop new products.

New-product managers

General Foods and Johnson & Johnson have new-product managers who report to group product managers. This position 'professionalises' the new-product function. On the other hand, new-product managers tend to think in terms of product modifications and line extensions limited to their current product and markets.

New-product committees

Most companies have a high-level management committee charged with reviewing and approving new-product proposals. It usually consists of representatives from marketing, manufacturing, finance, engineering and other departments. Its function is not developing or coordinating new products so much as reviewing and approving new-product plans.

New-product departments

Large companies often establish a new-product department headed by a manager who has substantial authority and access to top management. The department's major responsibilities include generating and screening new ideas, working with the R&D department, and carrying out field testing and commercialisation.

New-product venture teams

The 3M Company, Dow and Westinghouse often assign major new-product development work to venture teams. A venture team is a group brought together from various operating departments and charged with developing a specific product or business. Team members are relieved of their other duties, and given a budget and a time frame. In some cases, this team stays with the product long after it is successfully introduced.

business and customers demand fast development cycles and competition comes from well beyond the local country. Now there is less room for error. Customers want the latest, the newest and often the lowest-cost products and services. The flavouring industry, for example, supplies consumer brands such as Nestlé, Pizza Hut and Heinz with a process for developing a perfect flavour for the next frozen dinner, packet of Mentos or Skittles sweets, or banana or tropical yogurt. Such a process is a laborious, costly, time-consuming series of iterations resulting in many meetings between a supplier and the customer (not consumers). Traditionally, suppliers (flavour producers) were exposed to many samples and iterations before the customer finally accepted the new flavour. Traditionally, costs associated with this process were on the borderline of profit and loss. However, there is a way of speeding up this process while making the customer happier and more involved. It all lies in the provision of the necessary tools for a customer to take charge.

Figure 12.1 (overleaf) depicts the product development process as a traditional sequential approach led by the supplier. In this process the majority of the work and interacting lies with the supplier. The supplier is responsible for product development, designing of the product, creating a series of prototypes and then communicating the prototype to the customer. The customer then assesses whether the prototype fits in with the perception held in the customer's mind. If the product prototype is not what the customer expects then the supplier will go back to the product design phase and alter the prototype through a series of product iterations and intense meetings with the customer. This, in most cases, takes at least a dozen attempts before the product is 'signed off'—making this process very costly for the supplier. It is costly because the customer usually expects to pay for the final product and not the prototypes. For example, in the flavouring industry, when a customer requests a new

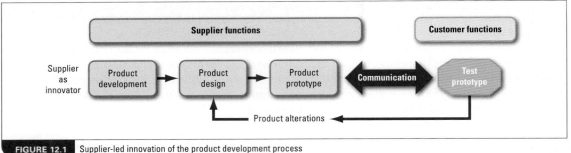

flavour from the supplier it may describe the key traits of the flavour as a 'smoky, woody, fresh taste with a light hint of bacon'. While this description is very meaningful to the customer, the supplier can easily attribute different meanings. Usually the flavour supplier will come up with a series of flavour variations hoping that the customer likes one of them. In many cases this is not so, requiring additional samples and further iterations between the supplier and customer.

However, there is a new-product development process with much more customer involvement, as shown in Figure 12.2. This process enables the customer to be a part of the product generation process by actively participating in product development. Provision of a software simulation tool allows the customer to review the new-product prototype in real-time and then make or suggest necessary changes. The simulation tool assists the customer to develop the product prototype they like and it also limits the effort on the part of the supplier to 'second-guess' what the customer may be thinking. In the case of the flavouring industry, for example, customers are able to design and redesign their flavour alterations on their own PCs. Then their new sample requests can be created instantly at the supplier's site and couriered back for customer assessment. In doing so the time spent by the supplier and customer in explaining, adjusting and redesigning prototypes is cut back significantly. The added bonus is that the customer feels more empowered and reassured that what they get is exactly what they wanted rather than achieving a 'rational compromise'. The final flavour becomes only as good as the customer's tastes and consumer market research that goes into creating it.

The flavouring industry is not alone in the process of empowering customers as a part of new-product development. The same occurs now where advertising agencies produce print media for product and job advertisements. Here, rather than providing customers with a sample of the advertisement, the customer can view the work-in-progress in real-time and then make any necessary changes or suggestions such as colour, font, size and copy adjustments, rather than waiting for a finished product before making suggestions. This way the product development (number of versions) and lengthy

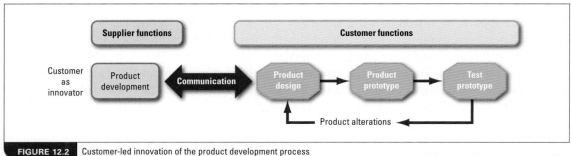

bipartisan meetings are avoided and the advertisement hits the market much faster. The message for business today is—involve the customer much more in the new-product development process.

Decision dimensions

A high degree of complexity and a multitude of decisions are trademarks of product innovation. In order to succeed, new-product managers must be more than just administrators—they must orchestrate, for there is rarely a simple new-product procedure. In every major new-product development, dozens of individuals are involved and, for many of them, a new product simply means more work. As one new-product manager at a fast-moving consumer goods company commented: 'We have some great people working for us, but I need to make sure that no milk will be spilt'. He feared that slip-ups could easily occur even when very capable people were doing the work.

Another trademark of the new-product development field is the fact that all product innovations—such as the Internet, email or online shopping—must be 'followed through' or simply pushed through. Innovation, which involves change, means that we often have to overcome embedded human traits that resist change. The same is true for business organisations. The phrase 'If it ain't broke, don't fix it' depicts the dilemma that new-product managers often have to face. They may spend a major proportion of their time and energy just opening up the organisational mindset. An American car maker, Chrysler, developed and marketed a new fold-down child's seat which became so popular that cars were being sold on the basis of whether they contained the seat or not. Quickly, the demand for cars with the fold-down seat outstripped supply. It was a new-product success. But it had taken the new-product manager several years to get top management interested in the idea and then an additional four years to overcome internal resistance to production.

Crawford and Di Benedetto[12] compiled a list of phrases that act as roadblocks for managers in the new-product process. It includes comments like 'It simply won't work' or 'It is good, but impractical' or 'That won't work in our market' or 'Where are you going to get the money for that?'. Such phrases reflect the almost insurmountable blocks to innovation that can occur. Managers need to be sensitive to such comments and then work around them so that new products can be launched. Typically, the new-product development process discussed in this chapter can help in overcoming such biases.

Another experience in product innovation is the conflicting set of management demands that product innovators must comply with. Figure 12.3 depicts the innovators' dilemma. First, the product

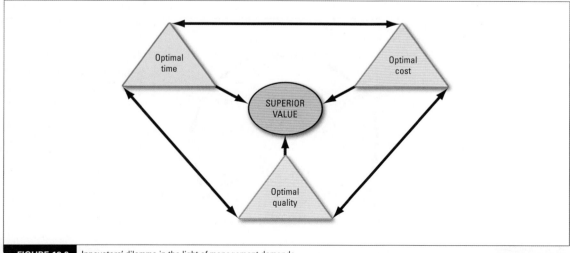

FIGURE 12.3   Innovators' dilemma in the light of management demands

must have some valuable attributes that meet end-users' needs, then it must be high on design quality, low in production cost (compared with competitors) and finally it must get to market quickly. Often such dimensions can work in tandem. For example, some firms have discovered that for them the ability to produce goods quickly is most effective, while others find that by making products with higher design quality they can lower the real cost of production. However, these demands can also conflict. The new-product manager's ultimate task is to optimise the set of relationships shown in Figure 12.3 for each new-product situation.

SELF-CHECK QUESTIONS

1 If experience shows that a high proportion of new products fail, why do companies introduce new products?

2 What are the main reasons for new-product failure?

The new-product development process

The new-product *development process* for finding and growing new products consists of eight major steps. These steps are shown in Figure 12.4.

Idea generation

Idea generation
The systematic search for new product ideas.

New-product development starts with **idea generation**, the systematic search for new-product ideas. A company must usually generate many ideas in order to find a few good ones.

The search for new-product ideas should be systematic rather than haphazard. Top management should define carefully its new-product development strategy. It should state which products and markets to emphasise. It must indicate what the company wants from its new products—high cash flow, market share or some other objective. It must indicate the effort to be devoted to developing original products, changing existing products and imitating competitors' products. Without this information, the company might find many ideas but most will not be suitable for its type of business.

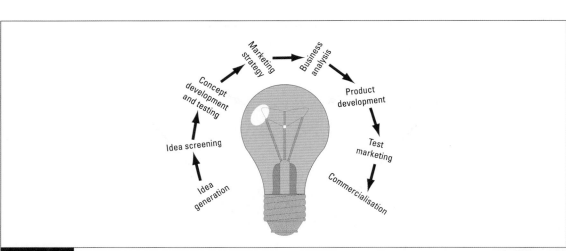

FIGURE 12.4   Major issues in new-product development

To obtain a flow of new-product ideas, the company can tap many idea sources, including:

◉ *Internal sources.* One study found that more than 55% of all new-product ideas come from within the company.[13] The company can find new ideas through formal research and development. It can pick the brains of its scientists, engineers and manufacturing people. Or company executives can brainstorm new-product ideas. The company's salespeople are another good source because they are in daily contact with customers. Toyota claims that employees submit two million ideas annually—about 35 suggestions per employee—and that more than 85% of them are implemented.

◉ *Customers.* Almost 28% of all new-product ideas come from watching and listening to customers. Consumer needs and wants can be obtained from consumer surveys. The company can analyse customer questions and complaints for new-product indications that will solve consumer problems more effectively. Company engineers or salespeople can meet with customers to get suggestions. NEC's Video Products Division (part of its Home Electronics business) has its design engineers talk with final consumers to get ideas for new home-electronics products. Ford has a product application centre where company engineers work with automotive customers to discover customer needs that might require new products. Finally, consumers often create new products on their own, and companies can benefit by finding these products and putting them on the market.[14]

◉ *Competitors.* About 30% of new-product ideas come from analysing competitors' products. The company can watch competitors' ads and other communications to pick up clues about their new products. Companies buy competing new products, take them apart to see how they work, analyse their sales and decide whether the company should bring out a new product of its own. For example, when designing its highly successful Taurus, Ford in the USA tore down more than 50 competing models, layer by layer, looking for things to copy or improve upon. It copied the Audi's accelerator pedal 'feel', the Toyota Supra fuel gauge, the BMW 528e tyre and jack storage system and 400 other such outstanding features.[15]

◉ *Distributors and suppliers.* Resellers are close to the market and can pass along information about consumer problems and new-product possibilities. Suppliers can tell the company about new concepts, techniques and materials that can be used to develop new products.

◉ *Other sources.* Other idea sources include trade magazines, shows and seminars; government agencies; new-product consultants; advertising agencies; marketing-research firms; university and commercial laboratories; and inventories.

A wide range of systematic techniques—such as brainstorming, adaptation and aggregation—is available to provide momentum to the idea-generation process.[16]

Idea screening

The purpose of idea generation is to create a large number of ideas. The purpose of the succeeding stages is to *reduce* that number. The first idea-reducing stage is **idea screening**. The purpose of screening is to spot good ideas and drop poor ones as soon as possible. Product development costs rise greatly in later stages. The company wants to go ahead only with the product ideas that will turn into profitable products.

Most companies require their executives to write up new-product ideas on a standard form that can be reviewed by a new-product committee. The write-up describes the product, the target market and the competition, and makes some rough estimates of market size, product price, development time and costs, manufacturing costs and rate of return. The committee then evaluates the idea against a set of general criteria. At Kao Company of Japan, specialising in personal and household hygiene,

Idea screening
Screening new product ideas in order to spot good ideas and drop poor ones as soon as possible.

for example, the committee asks questions such as these: Is the product truly useful to consumers and society? Is this product good for our particular company? Does it mesh well with the company's objectives and strategies? Do we have the people, skills and resources to make it succeed? Is its cost performance superior to competitive products? Is it easy to advertise and distribute?[17] Surviving ideas can be further screened using a simple rating process such as the one shown in Table 12.4.

The first column lists factors required for the successful launching of the product in the marketplace. In the next column management rate these factors on their relative importance. Thus, management believe that marketing skills and experience are very important (0.20) and purchasing and supplies competence is of minor importance (0.05). Next, on a scale of 0.0 to 1.0, management rate how well the new-product idea fits the company's profile on each factor. Here management feel that the product idea fits very well with the company's marketing skills and experience (0.9) but not too well with its purchasing and supplies capabilities (0.5). Finally, management multiply the importance of each success factor by the rating of fit to obtain an overall rating of the company's ability to launch the product successfully. Thus, if marketing is an important success factor and this product fits the company's marketing skills, this will increase the overall rating of the product idea. In the example, the product idea scored 0.78, which places it at the low end of the 'good idea' level.

The checklist promotes a more systematic product-idea evaluation and basis for discussion; however, it is not designed to make the decision for management.

Concept development and testing

Attractive ideas must now be developed into product concepts. It is important to distinguish between a *product idea*, a *product concept* and a *product image*. A **product idea** is an idea for a possible product that the company can see itself offering to the market. A **product concept** is a detailed version of the idea stated in meaningful consumer terms. A **product image** is the way consumers perceive an actual or potential product.

Product idea An idea for a possible product that the company can see itself offering to the market.

Product concept The idea that consumers favour products that offer the most quality, performance and features and that the organisation should therefore devote its energy to making continuous product improvements; a detailed version of the new product idea stated in meaningful consumer terms.

Product image The way consumers perceive an actual or potential product.

TABLE 12.4 Product-idea rating process

New-product success factors	(A) Relative importance	(B) Fit between product idea and company capabilities											(A × B) Idea rating
		.0	.1	.2	.3	.4	.5	.6	.7	.8	.9	1.0	
Company strategy and objectives	.20									X			.160
Marketing skills and experience	.20										X		.180
Financial resources	.15								X				.105
Channels of distribution	.15									X			.120
Production capabilities	.15									X			.120
Research and development	.10								X				.070
Purchasing and supplies	.05						X						.025
Total	1.00												.780*

* Rating scale: .00–.49, poor; .50–.75, fair; .76–1.00, good, Minimum acceptance level: .70

HP's Compaq branded tablet PC.

Concept development

Suppose a computer manufacturer works out how to design a personal computer—called a Tablet PC— that can recognise handwriting and keyboard strokes and functions also like any conventional PC. The manufacturer estimates that the handwriting-recognition PC's operating costs will be about two-thirds of that of a standard PC and the usage occasions of this system will be double that of standard PCs.

This is a product idea. Customers, however, do not buy a product idea; they buy a product concept. The marketer's task is to develop this idea into some alternative product *concept*, find out how attractive each concept is to customers and choose the best one.

The following product concepts might be created for the Tablet PC:

- *Concept 1*—an inexpensive compact Tablet PC designed to be used as a second PC for people on the move (ideal for taking notes at meetings and replying to emails while on the move).
- *Concept 2*—a medium-cost, and medium-sized, Tablet PC designed to be a laptop PC substitute.
- *Concept 3*—a medium-cost contemporary design with high processing capabilities with the latest features appealing to young people.
- *Concept 4*—a premium-cost, desktop substitute with all the mobility features for people who prefer handwriting and do not have high typing skills. The user does not want to take the same note twice.

Concept testing

Concept testing calls for testing these concepts with a group of target consumers. The concepts may be presented through word or picture descriptions.[18] Here is concept 1:

> An efficient, fun-to-use, handwriting-capable compact PC that can be used by anyone. Great for meetings, school, trips and customer visits. Costs a third less to operate than keyboard-only based PCs. Operates for 12 hours before recharging and with a processor speed of 4 GigaHertz. Priced, fully equipped, at $3000.

Concept testing Testing new product concepts with a group of target consumers to find out if the concepts have strong consumer appeal.

Consumers may then be asked to react to this concept by answering the questions in Table 12.5. The answers will help the company decide which concept has the strongest appeal. The last question asks about the consumer's intention to buy. Suppose 15% of the surveyed consumers said they 'definitely' would buy and another 5% said 'probably' *and* a further 35% 'probably not'. The company could project these figures to the population size of this target group to estimate sales volume and additionally work on the 'probably not' group to find out their reason for being unsure. Of course, even then the estimate is uncertain, because people do not always carry out their stated intentions.[19]

Marketing strategy development

Marketing strategy development Designing an initial marketing strategy for a new product based on the product concept.

Suppose concept 1 for the Tablet PC tests out best. The next step is **marketing strategy development**: designing an initial marketing strategy for introducing this Tablet PC into the market.

The *marketing strategy statement* consists of three parts. The first part describes the target market, the planned product positioning and the sales, market-share and profit goals for the first few years. Thus:

> The target market is people who need a versatile PC for meetings and/or trips where substantial note taking takes place and where the use of a keyboard is deemed difficult or inappropriate. The Tablet PC will be positioned as more economical and versatile to buy and operate and more fun to operate than PCs currently available to this market. The company aims to sell 70 000 units in the first year, at a loss of not more than $10 million. The second year's objective is for sales of 230 000 units with a profit of $276 million.

The second part of the marketing strategy statement outlines the product's planned price, distribution and marketing budget for the first year:

> The Tablet PC will be offered in four colours (titanium, purple, black and yellow) and will have an optional DVD ROM burning drive and speech-recognition software built in. It will sell at a retail price of $4000, with 15% off the list price to dealers. Dealers who sell more than 10 Tablet PC units per month will get an additional discount of 5% on each Tablet PC sold that month. An advertising budget of $12 million will be split 50–50 between national and local advertising. Advertising will emphasise the Tablet PC's versatility, benefits and fun. During the first year $150 000 will be spent on marketing research to find out who is buying the Tablet PC and to determine their satisfaction levels.

TABLE 12.5 Questions for the Tablet PC concept test
1. Do you understand the concept of a Tablet PC?
2. What do you see as the benefits of a Tablet PC compared with a conventional PC?
3. Do you believe the claims about the Tablet PC performance?
4. Would the Tablet PC meet all your computing needs?
5. What improvements can you suggest in the Tablet PC features?
6. Would you prefer a Tablet PC to a conventional PC? For what uses?
7. What do you think the price of the Tablet PC should be?
8. Who would be involved in your purchase decision for such a Tablet PC? Who would use it?
9. Would you buy a Tablet PC? (Definitely, probably, probably not, definitely not).

The third part of the marketing strategy statement describes the planned long-run sales, profit goals and marketing mix:

> The company intends to capture a 23% long-run share of the total Tablet PC market and realise an after-tax return on investment of 20%. To achieve this, product quality will start high and be improved over time. Price will be raised in the second and third years if competition permits. The total advertising budget will be raised each year by about 10%. Marketing research will be reduced to $70 000 per year after the first year.

Business analysis

Once management have decided on their product concept and marketing strategy, they can evaluate the business attractiveness of the proposal. **Business analysis** involves a review of the sales, costs and profit projections to find out whether they satisfy the company's objectives. If they do, the product can move to the product-development stage.

To estimate sales, the company should look at the sales history of similar products and should survey market opinion. It should estimate minimum and maximum sales to learn the range of risk. After preparing the sales forecast, management can estimate the expected costs and profits for the product. The costs are estimated by the R&D, manufacturing, accounting and finance departments. The planned marketing costs are included in the analysis. The company then uses the sales and costs figures to analyse the new product's financial attractiveness.

Business analysis
A review of the sales, costs and profit projections for a new product to find out whether these factors satisfy the company's objectives.

Product development

If the product concept passes the business test, it moves into **product development**. Here, R&D or engineering develops the product concept into a physical product. So far, the product has existed only as a word description, a drawing or perhaps a crude mock-up. The product development step, however, now calls for a large jump in investment. It will show whether the product idea can be turned into a workable product.

The R&D department will develop one or more physical versions of the product concept. It hopes to design a prototype that not only will satisfy and excite consumers but also can be produced quickly and at budgeted costs.

Developing a successful prototype can take days, weeks, months or even years. The prototype must have the required functional features and also convey the intended psychological characteristics. The Tablet PC, for example, should strike consumers as being well built and reliable and quick to use. Management must learn how consumers decide how well built a Tablet PC is. Some consumers tap the casing, others assess whether there is a definite 'plastic' look and feel about it, others compare the weight of some components and others perform their favourite computing tasks and compare these with their existing PC. If the Tablet PC does not have a 'solid-sounding' casing these consumers will think it is poorly built.

When the prototypes are ready, they must be tested. Functional tests are then conducted under laboratory and field conditions to make sure that the product performs safely and effectively. The new Tablet PC must start up well; it must be intuitive to use and it must be able to perform key tasks without hanging up or freezing up. Consumer tests are conducted in which consumers test-drive the Tablet PC and rate its attributes.

When designing products, the company should look beyond simply creating products that satisfy consumer needs and wants. Too often, companies design their new products without enough concern about how the designs will be produced—their main goal is to create customer-satisfying products. The designs are then passed along to manufacturing, where engineers must try to find the best ways

Product development
A strategy for promoting company growth by offering modified or new products to current market segments; developing the product concept into a physical product in order to ensure that the product idea can be turned into a workable product.

to produce the product. Recently, however, many companies have adopted a new approach towards product development called *design for manufacturability and assembly* (DFMA). Using this approach, companies work to fashion products that are *both* satisfying to consumers *and* easy to manufacture. This often results not only in lower costs but also in higher quality and more reliable products. For example, using DFMA analysis, Texas Instruments recently redesigned an infra-red gun-sighting mechanism that it supplies to the Pentagon: the redesigned product required 75 fewer parts, 78% fewer assembly steps and 85% less assembly time. The new design not only reduced production time and costs, it also worked better than the previous, more complex version. Thus, DFMA can be a potent weapon in helping companies to get products to market sooner and to offer higher quality at lower prices.[20]

Today, the pace of change demands a much faster product development process. Using alliances and internal networks for faster product development, many companies make use of computer-managed systems of networks to assist parallel technical and marketing processes.[21]

Test marketing

If the product passes functional and consumer tests, the next step is test marketing. **Test marketing** is the stage at which the product and marketing program is introduced into more realistic market settings.

Test marketing lets the marketer get experience with marketing the product, find potential problems and learn where more information is needed before going to the great expense of full introduction. The basic purpose of test marketing is to test the product itself in real market situations. But test marketing also allows the company to test its entire marketing program for the product—its positioning strategy, advertising, distribution, pricing, branding and packaging, and budget levels. The company uses test marketing to learn how consumers and dealers will react to handling, using and repurchasing the product. Test marketing results can be used to make better sales and profit forecasts. Thus, a good test market can provide a wealth of information about the potential success of the product and marketing program.

The amount of test marketing needed varies with each new product. Test marketing costs can be enormous, and test marketing takes time during which competitors may gain advantages. When the costs of developing and introducing the product are low or when management is already confident that the new product will succeed, the company may do little or no test marketing. Minor modifications of current products or copies of successful competitor products might not need testing. Colgate-Palmolive introduced its Total toothpaste without test marketing, and Cadbury Schweppes rolled out its ice-cream bars in New Zealand with no standard test market. But when introducing the new product requires a large investment, or when management is not sure of the product or marketing program, the company may do a lot of test marketing. For example, Reckitt and Colman uses the Australian market to test market its Mortein insecticides before it rolls out a new product in the rest of the Asian and European markets. In fact, some products and marketing programs are tested, withdrawn, changed and retested many times over a period of several years before they are finally introduced. The costs of such test marketing are high, but they are often small compared with the costs of making a major mistake.

Thus, whether a company test markets, and the amount of testing it does, depends on the investment cost and risk of introducing the product on the one hand, and on the testing costs and time pressures on the other. Test-marketing methods vary with the type of product and market situation, and each method has advantages and disadvantages.[22]

When they do use test marketing, consumer-products companies usually choose one of three approaches—standard test markets, controlled test markets or simulated test markets.

Standard test markets

Standard test markets test the new consumer product in situations like those it would face in a full-scale launch. The company finds a small number of representative test cities where the company's salesforce tries to persuade resellers to carry the product and give it good shelf space and promotional support. The company puts on a full advertising and promotion campaign in these markets and uses store audits, consumer and distributor surveys and other measures to gauge product performance. The results are used to forecast national sales and profits, to discover potential product problems and to fine-tune the marketing program.

Standard market tests have some drawbacks. First, they take a long time to complete—sometimes from one to three years. If it turns out that the testing was unnecessary, the company will have lost many months of sales and profits. Second, extensive standard test markets may be very costly. Finally, standard test markets give competitors a look at the company's new product well before it is introduced nationally. Many competitors will analyse the product and monitor the company's test market results. If the testing goes on too long, competitors will have time to develop defensive strategies and may even beat the company's product to the market. Furthermore, competitors often try to distort test market results by cutting their prices in test cities, increasing their promotion or even buying up the product being tested. Despite these disadvantages, standard test markets are still the most widely used approach for major testing. But many companies today are shifting towards quicker and cheaper controlled and simulated test-marketing methods.

Controlled test markets

Several research firms keep controlled panels of stores that have agreed to carry new products for a fee. The company with the new product specifies the number of stores and geographical locations it wants. The research firm delivers the product to the participating stores and controls shelf location, amount of shelf space, displays and point-of-purchase promotions and pricing, according to specified plans. Sales results are tracked to determine the impact of these factors on demand.

Controlled test markets take less time than standard test markets (six months to a year) and usually cost less. However, some companies are concerned that the limited number of small cities and panel consumers used by research services may not be representative of their products' markets or target consumers. And, as in standard test markets, controlled test markets allow competitors to get a look at the company's new product.[23] There are several methods of testing which can help to overcome the release of early warning information on new products to competitors. These include controlled buying situations in which consumers purchase their normal basket of goods and new ones released for test (without customer knowledge) in a supermarket laboratory environment.[24]

Simulated test markets

Companies can also test new products in a simulated shopping environment. The company or research firm shows a sample of consumers the ads and promotions for a variety of products, including the new product being tested. The consumers are given a small amount of money and are invited into a real or laboratory store where they may keep the money or use it to buy items. The company notes how many consumers buy the new product and competing brands. This simulation provides a measure of trial purchase and assesses the commercial's effectiveness against competing commercials. Consumers are then asked the reasons for their purchase or non-purchase. Some weeks later they are interviewed by phone to determine product attitudes, usage, satisfaction and repurchase intentions. Sophisticated computer models are used to project national sales from results of the simulated test market. A laboratory store is operated at the University of Indiana in the USA in which a sample of consumers does their weekly supermarket shopping. New products are introduced and evaluated as are special point-of-sale promotions of new brands, based on consumer buying behaviour.

Simulated test markets overcome some of the disadvantages of standard and controlled test markets. They usually cost much less than standard test markets and can be run and evaluated in a few weeks. And the new product is kept out of competitors' view. Yet, because of their small samples and simulated shopping environments, many marketers do not think that simulated test markets are as accurate or reliable as larger, real-world tests. Still, simulated test markets are widely used, often as 'pre-test' markets. Because they are fast and inexpensive, one or more simulated tests can be run to quickly assess a new product or its marketing program. If the pre-test results are strongly positive, the product might be introduced without further testing. If the results are very poor, the product might be dropped or substantially redesigned and retested. If the results are promising but indefinite, the product and marketing program can be tested further in controlled or standard test markets.[25]

Test marketing business products

Business marketers use different methods for test marketing their new products. For example, they may conduct *product-use tests*. Here, the industrial marketer selects a small group of potential customers who agree to use the new product for a limited time. The manufacturer's technical people watch how these customers use the product. From this test the manufacturer learns about customer training and servicing requirements. After the test, the marketer asks the customer about purchase intent and other reactions.

New industrial products can also be tested at *trade shows*. These shows draw a large number of buyers who view new products in a few concentrated days. The manufacturer sees how buyers react to various product features and terms, and can assess buyer interest and purchase intentions.

Fine Australian lagers like Hahn are winning gold medals that attest to their successful commercialisation.

The industrial marketer can also test new industrial products in *distributor and dealer display rooms*, where they may stand next to other company products and possibly competitors' products. This method yields preference and pricing information in the normal selling atmosphere for the product.

Finally, some industrial marketers use *standard or controlled test markets* to measure the potential of their new products. They produce a limited supply of the product and give it to the salesforce to sell in a limited number of geographical areas. The company gives the product full advertising, sales promotion and other marketing support. Such test markets let the company test the product and its marketing program in real market situations.

In the Internet environment, testing and commercialisation become blurred. In October 1994 Netscape posted a Beta version of Navigator on its home page. By downloading the Beta, trying it out and filing their complaints, customers served as Netscape's virtual quality assurance team. By the middle of November 1994 users had downloaded 1.5 million copies of Navigator. Once the final version of Navigator-1.0 was ready to ship, Netscape continued to use the Web as the major vehicle for distribution. By March 1998 users had downloaded 94 million copies of Navigator via the Web. Web-based testing and distribution are now commonplace.[26]

Another aspect of testing is used by Amazon.com through the comments and book reviews it receives from early adopters of new books. Perrott and Moore have found this feedback directly influencing its promotional and pricing decisions for all new products.[27]

Commercialisation

Test marketing gives management the information needed to make a final decision about whether to launch the new product. If the company goes ahead with **commercialisation**—introducing the new product into the market—it will face high costs. The company will have to build or rent a manufacturing facility. And it may have to spend, in the case of a new consumer packaged good, $2 million to $10 million for advertising and sales promotion alone in the first year. In the highly competitive Australian beer market, dominated by Fosters Brewing Group and Lion Nathan, up to $10 million is spent on new brand introductions like Hahn and $5 million on maintaining an existing brand like Tooheys.[28]

Commercialisation
Introducing a new product into the market.

Companies such as Toyota might spend up to $200 million a year on promotion in Australia depending on whether it is an Olympic Games year and on how many launches are involved. In February 2003 advertisers paid on average $US4.2 million for one 30-second commercial spot during the Superbowl—the prime American football grand final.[29]

Commercialisation of products related to the Internet is occurring at an ever-increasing rate. Four major areas for Net commercialisation appear to be:

1 communications, gathering and processing information, publishing, product development collaborative teams
2 networked applications, database applications and methods for sharing information within an organisation
3 real-time multimedia, distance learning and education, entertainment and video/audio conferencing
4 electronic commerce (buying/selling online), virtual marketplaces and store fronts, and new distribution channel intermediaries such as portals.[30]

The company launching a new product must make four decisions.

When?

The first decision is whether the time is right to introduce the new product. If the Tablet PC will eat into the sales of the company's other PCs, its introduction may be delayed. Or if the Tablet PC can be improved further, or if the economy is down, the company may wait to launch it the following year.

Where?

The company must decide whether to launch the new product in a single location, a region, several regions, the national market or the international market. Few companies have the confidence, capital and capacity to launch new products into full national distribution. They will develop a planned *market rollout* over time. In particular, small companies may select an attractive city and conduct a blitz campaign to enter the market. They may then enter other cities one at a time. Larger companies with national distribution networks, such as car companies, often launch their new models in the national market.

Companies with international distribution systems may introduce new products through global rollouts. Colgate-Palmolive uses a 'lead-country' strategy. For example, it launched its Palmolive Optims shampoo and conditioner first in Australia, the Philippines, Hong Kong and Mexico, then rapidly rolled it out into Europe, Asia, Latin America and Africa. International companies are increasingly introducing their new products in swift global assaults. Procter & Gamble (P&G) did this with its Pampers Phases line of disposable nappies. In the past, P&G typically introduced a new product in the US market. If it was successful, overseas competitors would copy the product in their home markets before P&G could expand distribution globally. With Pampers Phases, however, the company introduced the new product into global markets within one month of introducing it in the USA. It planned to have the product on the shelf in 90 countries within just 12 months of introduction. Such rapid worldwide expansion solidified the brand's market position before foreign competitors could react. P&G has since mounted worldwide introductions of several other new products.[31]

Australia is considered by Citigroup to be one of the best countries for conducting e-commerce pilot projects. Because many of the e-commerce products being developed by Citigroup are in English they expect Australia to be one of the first countries for launch. In September 1999 Citigroup launched the first of several products from its new e-Citi division, including an Internet banking product Citibank f/i (for financial interactive). Soon after it planned to launch e-wallet, which allows customers to store and submit information that is regularly requested by online merchants. When shopping online e-wallet allows consumers to call up automatically the information required by Internet merchants. Citibank Mortgage Plus was introduced into the Australian market in October 2005 as a bundled product with a revolving line of credit, a Citibank Gold Visa card and linkage to savings accounts to reduce interest costs for the consumer. This is part of the Citigroup's focus on growing its business in the Australian retail market.[32] Pepsi Cola and Miller breweries use Canada as a test market for future product launches in the USA.[33]

To whom?

Within the rollout markets, the company must target its distribution and promotion to the best prospect groups. The company has already profiled the prime prospects in earlier test marketing. It must now fine-tune its market identification, looking especially for early adopters, heavy users and opinion leaders.

How?

The company must also develop an action plan for introducing the new product into the selected markets. It must spend the marketing budget on the marketing mix and various other activities. Thus, the Tablet PC's launch may be supported by a publicity campaign and then by offers of gifts to draw more people to the showrooms. The company needs to prepare a separate marketing plan for each new market.

Sequential product development A new-product development approach in which one company department works individually to complete its stage of the process before passing the new product along to the next department and stage.

Simultaneous product development An approach to developing new products in which various company departments work closely together, overlapping the steps in the product development process to save time and increase effectiveness.

Sequential versus simultaneous new-product development

Many companies organise their new-product development process into an orderly sequence of steps, starting with idea generation and ending with commercialisation. Under this **sequential product development** approach, one company department works individually to complete its stage of the process before passing the new product along to the next department and stage. This orderly, step-by-step process can help bring control to complex and risky projects. But it can also be dangerously slow. In fast-changing, highly competitive markets, such slow-but-sure product development can cost the company potential sales and profits at the hands of more nimble competitors. Today, in order to get their new products to market more quickly, many companies are dropping the sequential product development approach in favour of the faster, more flexible **simultaneous product development** approach. Under the new approach, various company departments work closely together, overlapping the steps in the product development process to save time and increase effectiveness.

In Marketing Highlight 12.2 we see the challenges faced by Microsoft in developing new products for a market new to the company which is already dominated by large global competitors. It illustrates the need for recognition of the corporate cultural requirements and the major commitment needed to succeed. While this relates the story of a large company there are lessons to be learned by much smaller Australasian businesses when facing the challenge of entering a new market with a new product.

SELF-CHECK QUESTIONS

3 Describe the steps in the new-product development process.

4 What are the disadvantages of test marketing? How can these disadvantages be minimised?

5 What are the advantages and disadvantages of using the Internet for (a) testing new products or services, (b) speed to market, (c) correcting new-product defects?

The buyer decision process for new products

We have looked at the stages of new-product development and commercialisation. We now look at how buyers approach the purchase of new products. From a consumer perspective, a **new product** is a good, service or idea that is perceived by some potential customers as new. It may have been around for a while, but our interest is in how consumers learn about products for the first time and make decisions on whether to adopt them. We define the **adoption process** as the mental process through which an individual passes from first learning about an innovation to final adoption, and adoption as the decision by an individual to become a regular user of the product.[34]

New product A good, service or idea that is perceived by some potential customers as new.

Adoption process The mental process through which an individual passes from first learning about an innovation to final adoption.

Stages in the adoption process

Consumers go through five stages in the process of adopting a new product:

1 *Awareness*. The consumer becomes aware of the new product, but lacks information about it.
2 *Interest*. The consumer seeks information about the new product.
3 *Evaluation*. The consumer considers whether trying the new product makes sense.
4 *Trial*. The consumer tries the new product on a small scale to improve their estimate of its value.
5 *Adoption*. The consumer decides to make full and regular use of the new product.

Individual differences in the adoption of innovations

People differ greatly in their readiness to try new products. In each product area there are those who like to live on the 'leading edge' and who are considered to be early adopters. Other individuals adopt new products much later. People can be classified into the adopter categories shown in Figure 12.5 on page 456. After a slow start, an increasing number of people adopt the new product. The number of adopters reach a peak and then drop off as fewer non-adopters remain. Innovators are defined as the first 2.5% of the buyers to adopt a new idea (those beyond two standard deviations from mean adoption time); the early adopters are the next 13.5% (between one and two standard deviations); and so forth.

The five adopter groups have differing values. Innovators are venturesome—they try new ideas at some risk. Early adopters guide by virtue of the respect others have for them—they are **opinion leaders** in their communities and adopt new ideas early but carefully. The early majority are deliberate—although they are rarely leaders, they adopt new ideas before the average person. The late majority are sceptical—they adopt an innovation only after a majority of people have tried it.

Opinion leaders People who exert influence on others' opinions and buying behaviour.

Getting into the hardware business—how Microsoft developed the Xbox games console

The 2001 introduction of the Xbox by Microsoft is a notable example of the way in which a company can successfully launch a new product into a new market—typically a very high risk strategy but one that can pay big dividends if executed effectively. Microsoft was not known as a hardware company although it did have a hardware division responsible for mice, joysticks and keyboards. With the announcement of the network-enabled Sony Play Station 2 in March 1999, Microsoft woke up to the threat of being squeezed out of the living-room by Sony.

Two opposing product concepts vied for management attention: one was a WebTV offering with gaming capability and the other a dedicated game console. Eventually, it was concluded that it had to be a game console, superior rather than equal to the Play Station 2.

Since that initial launch Microsoft has sold 20 million consoles worldwide and has become the clear second player ahead of Sega and Nintendo. However, it is a distant second player to Sony, which sold 80 million Play Station 2 consoles in addition to the 100 million original play station consoles it sold before Microsoft entered the market.

The challenge for Microsoft for the past three and a half years has been how to develop and launch the next Xbox product. The initial Xbox, although successful from a sales point of view, is yet to return any profit. The games business model is a risky one. Hardware is sold at a loss in the hope of profits from taking a cut of the game sales. So far this has not happened for Microsoft. In fact a billion dollars in hardware losses is not easy to sustain and emphasises the importance of the new-product development process being successful with the next generation of products. In fact this is all part of Microsoft's master plan—the first Xbox was needed to get a shot at making the next one.

Why is this product so important to Microsoft? The answer lies in the fact that technology is turning our living rooms into a digital wireless, networked command centre where TV, movies, music and pictures can be enjoyed and Microsoft wants to make sure it is front and centre.

Developing the new Xbox: Microsoft the right place financially but the wrong culture

Microsoft is a company that has been more known for its bullying, aggressive business tactics than technological innovation and, while it certainly is the right place to provide financial backing to a major R&D effort like the development of the next Xbox, it does not necessarily have the right culture. It is not known for being nimble and quick, radically innovative or very good at partnering. This last point is critical in terms of managing good relationships with the developers of the games software that will run on the Xbox platform. In addition to this it is not an experienced hardware manufacturer. The solution to this cultural dilemma has been to set up a separate division that is physically as well as culturally different from the rest of Microsoft.

Designing the new Xbox 360

The first challenge for Microsoft was to design the look and feel of the new Xbox in a way that broadens its appeal beyond the hard-core gaming segment. Microsoft's approach to this was its first example of un-Microsoft thinking. It decided to contract a sculptor from the Rhode Island School of Design to brief several of the best industrial design firms in the world to each come up with a design for the new Xbox. The result was an entirely different looking console—much sleeker and more slimline than the last with a snap-off face plate for customisation. The seminal moment came when researchers tested the concept with focus groups and the feedback was that this looked like a product designed by Apple or Sony.

The gaming experience

The next challenge was to enhance the gaming experience well beyond anything available in the market. The console was the first to be developed with all games to run in high definition, wide-screen mode with Dolby 5.1 surround sound. The results can be seen in the Xbox's flagship game—Tiger Woods PGA golf. The old version showed grass like a green carpet, the new game shows every blade of grass swaying individually.

What about the digital living room?

Microsoft is well aware of the changes in technology and consumer behaviour occurring around digitally based entertainment. In fact it describes these changes as the 'Digital Entertainment Lifestyle', the notion that all media are becoming digital and that this is changing how consumers will use and integrate them. This is why the new Xbox can play and burn CDs, connect to your iPod and play music, and play DVD movies, as well as connecting to your digital camera and via wireless to your computer to access whatever music and picture you have stored there.

But the capabilities don't end there. Unlike Sony or Nintendo, Microsoft has developed an online service called Xbox live, which allows current Xbox owners to chat live with other gamers over the Internet. With the Xbox 360 this will extend to email, instant messages and even videoconferencing, taking this product well beyond just games and into communications.

So what's the big picture here? Microsoft, primarily known for making business software, has just moved into the living room with a device that replaces your CD and DVD player and perhaps in the future your telephone. It works with your iPod, digital camera, flat-screen TV, PC and laptop, and the Internet. The Xbox 360 is front and centre and this creates the opportunities that Microsoft is really

Xbox 360—for entertainment and communication.

interested in—becoming the *de facto* standard living room platform for digital entertainment.

The challenge going forward will be for Microsoft to walk the tightrope between having an open platform and being too proprietary. An open platform reduces the opportunity for profits, while a proprietary system typically fades away as nobody uses it. Its new product development process will again be critical, ensuring Microsoft becomes the centrepiece of the digital command centre.

Sources: Lev Grossman, 'Out of the Xbox', *Time Canada*, vol. 165, no. 21, 23 May 2005, pp. 30–39.

Questions

1 What are the features of the new-product development process at Microsoft?

2 Which is the most important part of this process?

3 Where could competitors have the greatest impact on Microsoft in their new-product development process?

12.2

Finally, laggards are tradition bound—they are suspicious of changes and adopt the innovation only when it has become something of a tradition itself. The dynamics of the adoption process and diffusion of an innovation over time underpin the concept of the product life cycle and the relevant strategies at different stages. This is discussed in the last section of this chapter.

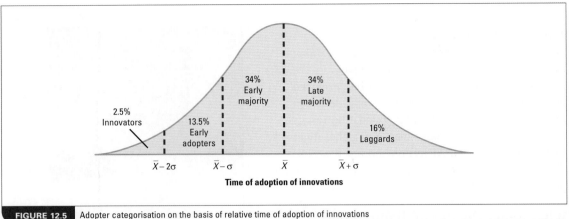

FIGURE 12.5 Adopter categorisation on the basis of relative time of adoption of innovations
Source: Redrawn with the permission of the Free Press, a division of Simon and Schuster Adult Publishing Group, from *Diffusion of Innovations*, 4th edn, by Everett M. Rogers. Copyright © 1962, 1971, 1983 by the Free Press.

This adopter classification suggests that an innovating firm should research the characteristics of innovators and early adopters and direct marketing efforts to them. In general, innovators tend to be relatively younger, better educated and higher in income than later adopters and non-adopters. They are more receptive to unfamiliar things, rely more on their own values and judgment, and are more willing to take risks. They are less brand loyal and more likely to take advantage of special promotions such as discounts, coupons and samples.

Influence of product characteristics on rate of adoption

The characteristics of the new product affect its rate of adoption. Some products are adopted almost overnight (Internet—50 million users worldwide in four years, and 530 million in 20 years), some are fast in gaining acceptance (mobile telephones), others take longer to gain acceptance (personal computers—50 million users worldwide in 16 years and 600 million PCs in 20 years and expected to double by 2007).[35] By way of comparison, radio took 38 years to gain 50 million listeners worldwide, and TV took 13 years to gain 50 million viewers. Five characteristics are especially important in influencing an innovation's rate of adoption. For example, consider the characteristics of World Wide Web technology in education and the rate of adoption by educators and students:

1 *Relative advantage:* the degree to which an innovation such as a PC connected to a Web-based subscription to an encyclopaedia appears superior to existing products such as a multimedia CD-ROM encyclopaedia. The greater the perceived relative advantage of using the Web—say, in easier access to information—the sooner such technology will be adopted.

2 *Compatibility:* the degree to which the innovation fits the values and experiences of potential consumers. Using educational websites, for example, is highly compatible with the lifestyles found in middle-class homes—the Conventional Young Family Life in terms of Roy Morgan's values segments (see Chapter 7).

3 *Complexity:* the degree to which the innovation is difficult to understand or use. Small businesses (those employing fewer than 20 people) have found the issue of online business quite complex, costly and often unsuited to their product category. For these reasons, and also because of security concerns, they have therefore taken more time to add online transactions and/or relationship management to their business model than larger firms.

4 *Divisibility:* the degree to which the innovation may be tried on a limited basis. Web access is expensive when one includes a multimedia PC, ongoing broadband access and perhaps Web

hosting or ancillary equipment such as a router. To the extent that people can lease them with an option to buy, or have the PC cost bundled in with the monthly service charge (so-called free PCs) their rate of adoption will increase.

5 *Communicability*: the degree to which the results of using the innovation can be observed or described to others. Because the Web lends itself to demonstration and description, computer use for this purpose has spread faster among consumers than many other technologies. This is particularly so because educators—who might be regarded as opinion leaders—have recommended the use of such technology to their students.[36]

Other characteristics influence the rate of adoption, such as initial and ongoing costs, risk and uncertainty, and social approval. The new-product marketer has to research all these factors when developing the new product and its marketing program.

SELF-CHECK QUESTIONS

6 Everett M. Rogers made the point that an innovation is any new device or way of doing things as perceived by the user. What are the implications arising from this notion that 'newness' is in the 'eyes of the beholder'?

7 The adopter categories shown in Figure 12.5 were derived from studies involving the adoption of new chemicals by farmers, where there was almost 100% adoption over time. What are the implications where there is a lower adoption rate, such as where only 25% of the population adopt mobile telephones?

Product life-cycle strategies

After launching the new product, management want the product to enjoy a long and successful life. Although they do not expect the product to sell forever, management want to earn a good profit to cover all the effort and risk that went into it. Management are aware that each product will have a life cycle, although the exact shape and length is not known in advance.

The product life cycle

The sales and profit patterns in a typical **product life cycle (PLC)** are shown in Figure 12.6 (overleaf). The product life cycle is marked by five distinct stages:

1 *Product development* begins when the company finds and develops a new-product idea. During product development, sales are zero and the company's investment costs add up.

2 *Introduction* is a period of slow sales growth as the product is being introduced in the market. Profits are non-existent in this stage because of the heavy expenses of product introduction.

3 *Growth* is a period of rapid market acceptance and increasing profits.

4 *Maturity* is a period of slowdown in sales growth because the product has achieved acceptance by most potential buyers. Profits level off or decline because of increased marketing outlays to defend the product against competition.

5 *Decline* is the period when sales fall off and profits drop.

Not all products follow this S-shaped product life cycle. Some products are introduced and die quickly. Others stay in the mature stage for a long, long time. Some enter the decline stage and are then cycled back into the growth stage through strong promotion or repositioning.

Product life cycle (PLC)
The course of a product's sales and profits during its lifetime. It involves five distinct stages: product development, introduction, growth, maturity and decline.

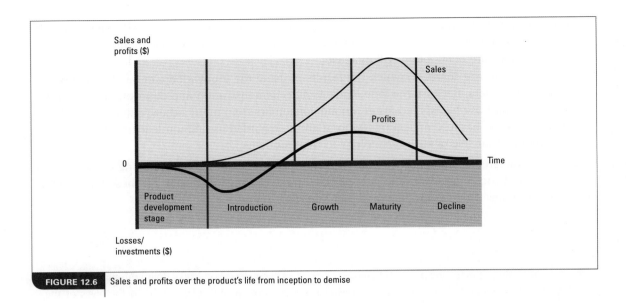

The PLC concept can describe a *product class* (petrol-powered cars), a *product form* (sports car) or a *brand* (the Holden Commodore SV8). The PLC concept applies differently in each case. Product classes have the longest life cycles. The sales of many product classes stay in the mature stage for a long time. Product forms, on the other hand, tend to have the standard PLC shape. Product forms such as the 'dial telephone' and 'cream deodorants' passed through a regular history of introduction, rapid growth, maturity and decline. A specific brand's life cycle can change quickly because of changing competitive attacks and responses.

The PLC concept can also be applied to what are known as styles, fashions and fads. Their special life cycles are shown in Figure 12.7.

Style A basic and distinctive mode of expression.

A **style** is a basic and distinctive mode of expression. For example, styles appear in homes (colonial, Style A basic and distinctive federation), clothing (formal, casual) and art (realistic, surrealistic, abstract). Once a style is invented, its mode of expression may last for generations, coming in and out of vogue. A style has a cycle showing several periods of renewed interest.

Fashion A currently accepted or popular style in a given field.

A **fashion** is a currently accepted or popular style in a given field. By the early 1980s the baby boomers were ageing and their tastes were changing with their waistlines—they bought fewer jeans

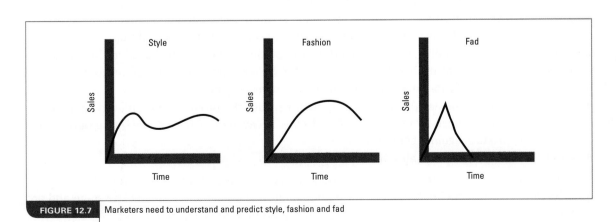

FIGURE 12.7 Marketers need to understand and predict style, fashion and fad

and wore them longer. Meanwhile, the 18–24-year-old segment, the group traditionally most likely to buy jeans, was shrinking. Levi Strauss found itself fighting for share in a fading jeans market. By 1998 baby boomers were continuing to buy jeans, but younger shoppers, particularly teenagers, had drifted to surfwear and streetwear brands such as Mambo, Stussy, Hot Tuna and Fila.[37] In 2006 we see the shifting fashion and style statements in personal electronic gadgets such as mobile phones, digital cameras and iPods.

Fashions pass through many stages. First, a small number of consumers take an interest in something new to set themselves apart. Then other consumers become interested out of a desire to copy the fashion leaders. Next, the fashion becomes popular and is adopted by the mass market. Finally, the fashion fades away as consumers start moving towards other fashions that are beginning to catch their eye. Thus, fashions tend to grow slowly, remain popular for a while and then decline slowly.

Fads are fashions that enter quickly, are adopted with great zeal, peak early and decline very fast. They last only a short time and tend to attract only a limited following. Fads often have a novel or quirky nature, as when people started buying Rubik's Cubes, Trivial Pursuit games, Cabbage Patch dolls or yo-yos. Recent fads include LiveSTRONG yellow wristbands (worn as a fashion statement) initiated by Tour de France six-time winner Lance Armstrong as a way to raise money for cancer research, the Atkins low carb diet and reality TV shows. Fads appeal to people looking for excitement, a way to set themselves apart or something to talk about to others. Fads do not survive for long because they do not normally satisfy a strong need or satisfy it well.

> **Fads** Fashions that enter quickly, are adopted with great zeal, peak early and decline fast.

Technology-adoption cycle

A modification of life-cycle theory has been proposed as the *technology-adoption cycle* for discontinuous innovations based on new technologies. The 'landscape' of this cycle is divided into six zones, described as follows:

1   *The early market*—a time of excitement when customers are technology enthusiasts and visionaries looking to be first to use it.
2   *The chasm*—a time of despair, when the early-market's interest disappears but the mainstream market is still not accepting the immaturity of the solutions available.
3   *The bowling alley*—a period of niche-based adoption in advance of the general marketplace, driven by compelling customer needs and the willingness of suppliers to design niche-specific whole products.
4   *The tornado*—a period of mass-market adoption, when the general marketplace switches over to the new technology.
5   *Main street*—a period of further development, when the basic technology infrastructure has been deployed and the goal now is to extend its potential.
6   *End of life*—a time that can come very soon with high-tech innovations because price and performance are driven to unheard-of levels, enabling wholly new formats to come to market and supplant the original.

Experience with high-technology products highlights the discontinuity occurring at different stages of the life cycle—particularly 'the chasm', when acceptance does not take place, and 'the bowling alley', which involves niche-specific solutions that need to be progressively broadened to appeal to a wider marketplace (see Marketing Highlight 12.3). Successful broadening of the conditions for general-purpose solutions encourages the pragmatist to adopt the product or service, resulting in 'the tornado' of rapid market growth.[38]

MARKETING 12.3 HIGHLIGHT

A giant leap by Xerox and HP to cross the chasm

Where new technologies are concerned, the chasm is crossed and the tornado entered when a 'killer application' is found that delivers so much value that pragmatic and cost-sensitive customers—the mainstream market—feel compelled to buy. For the PC it was the spreadsheet, then word processing. For digital music it was the Apple iPod in conjunction with the iTunes music download service. For digital cameras it was the ability to share and print on demand with no risk. For the World Wide Web it was email. When it comes to conducting business using the Internet, most businesses are at the chasm—or in it! For instance, Woolworths Homeshop and Coles Online are struggling for viability. Woolworths has taken a share of Greengrocer.com.au to improve its online economics and Coles Myer operates Shopfast. com.au as its established online grocery store.

The stakes are high in technology markets. Digital technology convergence is bringing together the copier and printer markets. What were once distinct markets with separate buyers, users and competitors are rapidly converging to put Xerox, the dominant copier company, and Hewlett-Packard (HP), the dominant printer company, in a head-to-head battle for the same market—digitally produced documents. Both Xerox and HP are competing in what is now referred to as the MFD (multi-function device) market which provides the user with a capability of printing, copying, scanning and faxing documents—all in a single piece of equipment.

In Australia this market is evolving, with mono (black and white) MFDs just beyond the chasm and colour MFDs about to take the leap across the chasm. Xerox has been the leading player in taking mono MFDs across the chasm. Initially its deal-driven approach created early acceptance and now its 'whole product' approach targeted at niche markets is achieving penetration in a number of specific industry niches.

Consider Xerox's latest strategy. Xerox has transferred its copier leasing model to the MFD market and prices on a cost per page basis. It offers full service maintenance agreements and thoroughly investigates the customer's print environment. It works towards centralising volumes onto MFDs by consolidating devices and replacing HP printers with Xerox MFDs. Printers are being dumped and not replaced. Companies are leasing copier devices and adding print capabilities. Xerox is organised to provide an integrated focus with offerings to the large-enterprise market. Xerox targets vertical industries such as finance, health, legal, manufacturing and education with a focus on major accounts. With more than 100 salespeople nationally to focus directly on large accounts, it aims to own the relationship and lock up customers with a time-based lease offer with usage being monitored to enable up-selling and contract renewals. This strategy integrates hardware and supplies supported by a focused salesforce. Xerox presents integrated suites of solutions involving document input, document processing and management and output. In 2003 Xerox had about 15 products in its range for the high end of the market.

But the large-scale complex photocopier market is also under attack by HP as its traditional printer market is being eroded by MFDs. It is responding with its own range of multi-function products with the objective of moving the business customer mindset away from the large centralised photocopying facility to smaller, more flexible devices liberally spread throughout the offices of large companies. Its focus is on balancing user productivity with cost reduction and it is a message that is being heard by its larger customers which are concerned that too much centralisation of equipment will cause printing backlogs for end-users just trying to get on with their day-to-day jobs. It is also targeting small and medium businesses which have a need for flexible communicating and imaging appliances. But how will HP change the traditional mindset of big business? Will Xerox win the battle? Here is a clash of the titans with either HP or Xerox gaining leadership.

Sources: Interview with Christopher Brown, National Marketing Manager, HP Australasia, October 2004; Larry Downes and Chunka Mui, *Unleashing the Killer Applications: Digital Strategies for Market Dominance*, Boston, Harvard Business School Press, 1998, pp. 13–20; D. Dixon, D. Haueter and P. Grant, 'US Offfice Output Trends', *Focus Report*, 3 December 2001.

Questions

1 Can you think of a product or service that is in the chasm? Explain why you believe this is the case.

2 Which segments could HP focus on in the early growth phase?

3 Describe how HP might approach the challenge of crossing the chasm with its new MFD colour products.

12.3

Lead users

It is often assumed that technological and product innovations are developed by technology or product manufacturers. Urban and von Hippel show that for industrial markets the innovation process is distributed across users, manufacturers and suppliers.[39] In some areas, such as scientific instruments, they showed that users of innovations were the prime innovators. These users were also the primary instigators of diffusion of their innovations.

In the Australian context, Telstra, as a user of Ericsson's telecommunications exchange networks, has been an innovator in many applications of the network technology and now markets its innovations and know-how internationally.

The concept of lead users

The concept of lead users has relevance to marketing when related to the task of researching and evaluating needs for new products by analysing prospective users. In the relatively slow changing world of building materials, such as steel or fibreboard, new products do not differ much from their earlier versions and the typical user can provide useful feedback on new-product acceptability and appeal. However, in high-technology industries, change is so rapid that related real-world experience and visualisation of ordinary users is inadequate in helping the marketer to form a picture of likely acceptance and diffusion. In these situations, Urban and von Hippel suggest that lead users do have real-world experience with novel product or service needs and are essential to the development of a useful picture through market research.[40]

The definition of lead users includes two characteristics:

1 They have needs that are general in a market, but confront them months or years before most of the marketplace encounters them.

2 They are positioned to gain substantial benefits by obtaining a solution to those needs.[41]

The advantages for the marketer of focusing on lead users in an overseas market are threefold:

A novel product from Sony—the 26 gram, water resistant, digital audio player equipped with a built-in 1 GB flash memory and a FM tuner.

1 They are users whose present strong needs are likely to become general in a market in the future.
2 They can serve as a need-forecasting benchmark for market research.
3 They can provide new-product concept and design data to manufacturers because of their own attempts to satisfy their need.

As Herstatt and von Hippel found in a lead user study of 'low-tech' industrial products, joint development of new-product concepts by a manufacturer with lead users can reduce the costs of development and enhance success.[42]

The challenge of today's high-technology environment for many marketers is to identify lead users in their targeted markets as an input in the adoption and diffusion processes.

In the Internet world noted earlier in this chapter, Hagel and Armstrong propose the concept of the virtual community—a group of interconnected consumers with a common interest and similar needs.[43] In this online interconnected community, they contend, power shifts from suppliers to consumers as the virtual community identifies its own needs and actively seeks solutions from a wide range of potential vendors. The lead-user concept as applied to virtual communities is likely to play an important role in the adoption and diffusion of new innovations.

The PLC concept

The PLC concept can be applied by marketers as a useful framework for describing how products and markets work. But using the PLC concept for forecasting product performance or for developing marketing strategies presents some practical problems.[44] For example, managers may have trouble identifying which stage of the PLC the product is in, pinpointing when the product moves into the next stage, and determining the factors that affect the product's movement through the stages. In practice, it is difficult to forecast the sales level at each PLC stage, the length of each stage and the shape of the PLC curve.

Using the PLC concept to develop marketing strategy can also be difficult because strategy is both a cause *and* a result of the product's life cycle. The product's current PLC position suggests the best marketing strategies, and the resulting marketing strategies affect product performance in later life-cycle stages. Yet, when used carefully, the PLC concept can help in developing good marketing strategies for different stages of the PLC.

We looked at the product development stage of the PLC in the first part of the chapter. We now look at strategies for each of the other life-cycle stages.

Introduction stage

Introduction stage The product life-cycle stage when the new product is first distributed and made available for purchase.

The **introduction stage** starts when the new product is first launched. Introduction takes time, and sales growth is apt to be slow. Such well-known products as instant coffee, frozen orange juice and powdered coffee creamers lingered for many years before they entered a stage of rapid growth.

In this stage, profits are negative or low because of the low sales and the high distribution and promotion expenses. Much money is needed to attract distributors and build their inventories. Promotion spending is relatively high. The goals now are to inform consumers of the new product and get them to try it. Because the market is not generally ready for product refinements at this stage, the company and its few competitors produce basic versions of the product. These firms focus their selling on those buyers who will most readily buy—usually the higher-income groups.

A company might adopt one of several marketing strategies for introducing a new product. It can set a high or low level for each marketing variable such as price, promotion, distribution and product quality. Considering only price and promotion, for example, management might launch the new product with a high price and low promotion spending. The high price helps recover as much gross profit per unit as possible, and the low promotion spending keeps marketing spending down. Such a strategy makes sense when the market is limited in size, when most consumers in the market know about the product and are willing to pay a high price, and when there is little immediate potential competition.

On the other hand, a company might introduce its new product with a low price and heavy promotion spending. This strategy promises to bring the fastest market penetration and the largest market share. It makes sense under these conditions: the market is large; potential buyers are price sensitive and unaware of the product; potential competition is strong; and the company's unit manufacturing costs fall with the scale of production and accumulated manufacturing experience.

A company, especially the *market pioneer*, must choose its launch strategy carefully. It should realise that the initial strategy is just the first step in a grander marketing plan for the product's entire life cycle. If the pioneer chooses its launch strategy to make a 'killing', it will be sacrificing long-run revenue for the sake of short-run gain. As the pioneer moves through later stages of the life cycle, it will continually have to formulate new pricing, promotion and other marketing strategies. It has the best chance of building and retaining market leadership if it plays its cards correctly from the start.

Growth stage

If the new product satisfies the market, it will enter a **growth stage** in which sales will start climbing quickly. The early adopters will continue to buy, and later buyers will start following their lead, especially if they hear favourable word-of-mouth. Attracted by the opportunities for profit, new competitors will enter the market. They will introduce new product features and the market will expand. The increase in competitors leads to an increase in the number of distribution outlets, and sales jump just to build reseller inventories. Prices remain where they are or fall only slightly. Companies keep their promotion spending at the same or a slightly higher level: educating the market remains a goal, but now the company must also meet the competition.

In high-tech markets, the early growth stage is typified by niche strategies with customer-tailored solutions. For example, spreadsheet packages were first targeted at financial professions only. Early word-processing packages were targeted at law firms, government agencies and consultancies. During rapid growth, strategies change towards more-mass-market solutions involving a common standard infrastructure. For instance, the enormous growth in laser and inkjet printers to a $30 billion industry led by Hewlett-Packard reflects this. Hewlett-Packard geared up for huge production and extended distribution channels and kept driving for lower price points.

Profits increase during this growth stage, as promotion costs are spread over a large volume and unit manufacturing costs fall. The company uses several strategies to sustain rapid market growth as long as possible. It improves product quality and adds new product features and models. It enters new market segments and new distribution channels. It shifts some advertising from building product awareness to building product conviction and purchase, and it lowers prices at the right time to attract more buyers.

The company with a product in the growth stage faces a trade-off between high market share and high current profit. By spending a lot of money on product improvement, promotion and distribution, it can capture a dominant position. But it gives up the maximum current profit in the hope of making this up in the next stage.

Maturity stage

At some point a product's sales growth will slow down, and the product will enter a **maturity stage**. This maturity stage normally lasts longer than the previous stages, and it poses strong challenges to marketing management. Most products are in the maturity stage of the life cycle, and therefore most marketing management deals with the mature product.

Growth stage The product life-cycle stage at which a product's sales start climbing quickly.

Maturity stage The stage in the product life cycle in which sales growth slows or levels off.

High-tech products require a change in strategy toward more customised solutions focusing on specific adaptations of the infrastructure for added value through mass customisation. Market extension occurs through more targeted niche-based strategies. For example, Hewlett-Packard now targets home users with a low-cost inkjet printer. It also conducts niche campaigns promoting its compact, portable printer to appeal to those with limited space, its office jet fax/copier for those who do not have a fax, and its higher-performance colour printer for people needing to create their own promotional material. Its latest thrust is colour printers specifically for digital photographs.

The slowdown in sales growth results in many producers with many products to sell. In turn, this overcapacity leads to greater competition. Competitors begin marking down prices, increasing their advertising and sales promotions, and increasing their R&D budgets to find better versions of the product. These steps mean a drop in profit. Some of the weaker competitors drop out, and eventually the industry contains only well-established competitors.

Product managers should not simply defend the product. Attack is the best defence. They should consider modifying the market, the product and the marketing mix.

Market modification During this stage the company tries to increase consumption of the current product. It looks for new users and market segments, as when Johnson & Johnson targeted the adult market with its baby powder and shampoo. The product manager also looks for ways to increase usage among present customers. Campbell does this by offering recipes and convincing consumers that 'soup is good food'. Or the company may want to reposition the brand to appeal to a larger or faster-growing segment. Baileys modified its market by targeting the 19–25 singles segment with its positioning as a sexy drink.

Product modification The product manager can also change a product's characteristics—such as product quality, features or style—to attract new users and more usage.

A strategy of *quality improvement* aims at increasing product performance: durability, reliability, speed, taste. This strategy is effective when the quality can be improved, when buyers believe the claim of improved quality and when enough buyers want higher quality.

A strategy of *feature improvement* adds new features that expand the product's usefulness, safety or convenience. Feature improvement has been successfully used by Japanese makers of watches, calculators and copying machines. For example, Seiko keeps adding new styles and features to its line of watches.

A strategy of *style improvement* aims to increase the attractiveness of the product. Thus, car manufacturers restyle their cars to attract buyers who want a new look. The makers of consumer food and household products introduce new flavours, colours, ingredients or packages to revitalise consumer buying.

Marketing mix modification The product manager can also try to improve sales by changing one or more marketing mix elements. Prices can be cut to attract new users and competitors' customers. A better advertising campaign can be launched. Aggressive sales promotion (trade deals, cents-off, premiums, contests) can be used. The company can also move into larger market channels, using mass merchandisers, if these channels are growing. Finally, the company can offer new or improved services to the buyers.

Decline stage

Decline stage The product life-cycle stage at which a product's sales decline.

The sales of most product forms and brands eventually dip. The decline may be slow, as in the case of oatmeal cereal, or rapid, as for video games. Sales may plunge to zero or they may drop to a low level where they continue for many years. This is the **decline stage**.

Sales decline for many reasons, including technological advances, shifts in consumer tastes and increased competition. As sales and profits decline, some companies withdraw from the market. Those remaining might reduce the number of their product offerings, drop the smaller market segments and marginal trade channels, or cut the promotion budget and reduce their prices further.

Carrying a weak product can be very costly to a firm, and not just in profit terms. There are many hidden costs—the weak product may take up too much of management's time. It often requires frequent price and inventory adjustments. It requires advertising and salesforce attention that might be better used to make 'healthy' products more profitable. Its failing reputation can cause customer concerns about the company and its other products. The biggest cost may well lie in the future. Keeping weak products delays the search for replacements, creates a lopsided product mix, hurts current profits and weakens the company's foothold on the future.

For these reasons, companies need to pay more attention to their ageing products. The first task is to identify those products in the decline stage by regularly reviewing the sales, market shares, cost and profit trends; then, for each declining product, management must decide whether to maintain, harvest or drop it.

Management may decide to *maintain* their brand without change in the hope that competitors will leave the industry. For example, Procter & Gamble made good profits by remaining in the declining liquid-soap business as others withdrew. Or management may decide to reposition the brand in the belief that it will move back into the growth stage of the PLC.

Management may decide to *harvest* the product, which means reducing various costs (plant and equipment, maintenance, R&D, advertising, salesforce) and hoping that sales hold up. If successful, harvesting will increase the company's profits in the short run. Or management may decide to *drop* the product from the line. It can sell it to another firm or simply liquidate it at salvage value. If the company plans to find a buyer, it will not want to run down the product through harvesting.[45]

The key characteristics of each stage of the PLC are summarised in Table 12.6 (overleaf). The table also lists the marketing responses made by companies in each stage.[46]

SELF-CHECK QUESTIONS

8 Compare the traditional PLC concept with the recently proposed technology-adoption cycle.

9 What are the characteristics and role of lead users for high-technology products?

10 Describe the nature of the chasm and the kinds of strategies that are relevant to move a product beyond the chasm.

11 What are the relevant strategies at each stage of the product life cycle?

12 Is there a difference between product life cycle and brand life cycle? If so, what are the key differentiating factors?

TABLE 12.6 Summary of product life-cycle characteristics, objectives and strategies

	Introduction	Growth	Maturity	Decline
Characteristics				
Sales	Low sales	Rapidly rising sales	Peak sales	Declining sales
Costs	High cost per customer	Average cost per customer	Low cost per customer	Low cost per customer
Profits	Negative	Rising profits	High profits	Declining profits
Customers	Innovators	Early adopters	Middle majority	Laggards
Competitors	Few	Growing number	Stable number beginning to decline	Declining number
Marketing objectives				
	Create product awareness and trial	Maximise market share	Maximise profit while defending market share	Reduce expenditure and milk the brand
Strategies				
Product	Offer a basic product	Offer product extensions, service, warranty	Diversify brand and models	Phase out weak items
Price	Use cost-plus	Price to penetrate market	Price to match or better competitors	Cut price
Distribution	Build selective distribution	Build intensive distribution	Build more intensive distribution	Go selective: phase out unprofitable outlets
Advertising	Build product awareness among early adopters and dealers	Build awareness and interest in the mass market	Stress brand differences and benefits	Reduce to level needed to retain hard-core loyals
Sales promotion	Use heavy sales promotion to entice trial	Reduce to take advantage of heavy consumer demand	Increase to encourage brand switching	Reduce to minimal level

Source: Philip Kotler and Kevin Lane, *Marketing Management*, 12th edn, 2006, p. 332. Reprinted by permission of Pearson Education Inc., Upper Saddle River, NJ.

SUMMARY

Organisations must develop new products and services. Their current products face limited lifespans and must be replaced by newer products. But new products can fail—the risks of innovation are as great as the rewards. The key to successful innovation lies in a total company effort, strong planning and a systematic *new-product development process*.

The new-product development process consists of eight stages: *idea generation, idea screening, concept development and testing, marketing strategy development, business analysis, product development, test marketing* and *commercialisation*. The purpose of each stage is to decide whether the idea should be developed further or dropped. The company wants to minimise the chances of poor ideas moving forward and good ideas being rejected.

With regard to new products, consumers respond at different rates, depending on the consumer's characteristics and the product's characteristics. Manufacturers try to bring their new products to the attention of potential early adopters, particularly those with opinion-leader characteristics.

Each product has a *life cycle* marked by a changing set of problems and opportunities. The sales of the typical product follow an S-shaped curve made up of five stages. The cycle begins with the *product development stage* when the company finds and develops a new-product idea. The *introduction stage* is marked by slow growth and low profits as the product is being pushed into distribution. If successful, the product enters a *growth stage* marked by rapid sales growth and increasing profits. During this stage the company tries to improve the product, enter new market segments and distribution channels and reduce its prices slightly. Then comes a *maturity stage* in which sales growth slows down and profits stabilise. The company seeks strategies to renew sales growth, including market, product and marketing mix modification. Finally, the product enters a *decline stage* in which sales and profits dwindle. The company's task during this stage is to identify the declining product and decide whether it should be maintained, harvested or dropped. If dropped, the product can be sold to another firm or liquidated for salvage value.

A variation of the classic life-cycle model is the technology-adoption cycle. This highlights the challenge of crossing the chasm from innovator buyers to early adopters. The role of lead users is important in gaining acceptance of new high-technology products, and the company introducing a new technology needs to nurture its lead users.

MARKETING ISSUE

There is a huge and growing market for beauty products used by plastic surgeons to neutralise the results of the ageing process. You are the marketing manager for a new product about to be introduced with claims of enhancement effects for women. This particular product range is not required to have clearance by the health and drug administration. University tests have shown that this new product might have damaging physical side effects. However, consumer testing shows promising results with most early users singing the praises of your new product. An isolated number of clients have experienced negative side effects after using your product. You have found through further product testing a product ingredient that seems to cause this, but it involves prohibitive cost to eliminate it. You are under pressure from plastic surgeons to release the product. Would you go ahead and launch the product?

KEY TERMS

DISCUSSING THE ISSUES

1 New products are highly risky and often fail. Why don't companies involve customers much more in the new-product development process? How could they do this?

2 One of the issues today with new products is getting them to market fast. How can the process be improved so that a new product acceptable to the target market reaches it faster?

3 Health through diet and exercise is a strong trend in Australasian society. Why do organic fruit and vegetables still have relatively low penetration of the market? Which adopter categories are most important for achieving a rapid increase in the rate of penetration?

4 How can a company distinguish products with long life cycles from current fads and fashions? What products on the market now do you think are fads or fashions that will soon disappear?

5 What have digital cameras done to the product life cycle of traditional film-based cameras? What approaches can producers of film-based cameras adopt to revitalise their markets?

6 Companies organise for new-product development in different ways—there are various versions of new-product departments and new-product management structures. What skills are required in the product development team to encompass an effective process?

REFERENCES

1. Anonymous, 'Digital Camera Market Poised for More Growth', *Electronic News* (North America), vol. 51 no. 9, 28 February 2005; and David Henry, 'A Tense Kodak Moment', *Business Week*, no. 3955, 17 October 2005, pp. 84–85.

2. For more on Sanitarium and Kellogg see Bo Emerson, 'Health-Food Beginnings', *The Atlanta Journal—Constitution*, 7 March 2002, p. C.3. For details of Volkswagen Beetle see Anonymous, '1998–2002 Volkswagen New Beetle', *Consumer Guide*, vol. 696, April 2003, p. 247; Theresa Howard, 'Nostalgia Helps Beetle Score; Convertible Ads Get Good Marks', *USA Today*, 24 February 2003, p. B.05; Don Fernandez, 'Buyers Are Lining up for Beetle Convertible', *The Atlanta Journal—Constitution*, 23 February 2003, p. JJ.1.

3. Charles Cooper, 'Our Favorite Tech Flops: The Can't-misses—That Did', *Zdnet*, 12 February 2001, <www.zdnet.com/anchordesk/stories/story/0,10738,2684197,00.html> accessed 10 March 2003.

4. Bruce Tait, 'The Failure of Marketing "Science"', *Brandweek*, vol. 43, no. 14, 8 April 2002, p. 20; Eric Berggren, 'Introducing New Products Can Be Hazardous to Your Company: Use the Right New-Solutions Delivery Tools', *The Academy of Management Executive*, vol. 15, no. 3, August 2001, p. 92; Eriik Hultnik, Suzan Hart, Henry Robben and Abbie Griffin, 'Launching New Products in Consumer and Industrial Markets: A Multi Country Empirical International Comparison', *Proceedings of the Product Development and Management Association International Research Conference*, Monterey, CA, 1997, pp. 94–125; Eric H. Kessler, Paul E. Bierly III and Shanthi Vasa Gopalakrishnan, 'Syndrome: Insights from a 17th-Century New-Product Disaster', *Academy of Management Executive*, vol. 15, no. 3, pp. 80–91; George M. Chryssochoidis and Veronica Wong, 'Rolling Out New Products Across Country Markets: An Empirical Study of Causes of Delays', *JPIM*, vol. 15, no. 1, January 1998, pp. 16–41; William H. Redmond, 'An Ecological Perspective on New Product Failure: The Effects of Competitive Overcrowding', *JPIM*, vol. 12, no. 3, June 1995, pp. 200–213. Also see *New Product Management for the 1980s*, New York, Booz, Allen & Hamilton, 1982; C. Merle Crawford, 'New Product Failure Rates: A Reprise', *Research Management*, July–August 1987, pp. 20–24; and Lois Therrien, 'Want Shelf Space at the Supermarket? Ante Up', *Business Week*, 7 August 1989, pp. 60–61.

5. See J. Goldenberg, R. Horowitz, A. Levav and D. Mazursky, 'Finding Your Innovation Sweet Spot', *Harvard Business Review*, March 2003; Daryl McKee, 'An Organizational Learning Approach to Product Innovation', *JPIM*, vol. 9, no. 3, September 1992, pp. 232–245; Abbie Griffin and Albert L. Page, 'PDMA Success Measurement Project: Recommended Measures for Product Development Success

and Failure', *JPIM*, vol. 13, no. 6, November 1996, pp. 478–496; Leigh Lawton and A. Parasuraman, 'So You Want Your New Product Planning to be Productive', *Business Horizons*, December 1980, pp. 29–34.

6. Victoria Story, Gareth Smith and Geoff Callow, 'Characteristics of Successful New Product Development: Findings from a Survey of UK Automotive Component Suppliers', *International Journal of Automotive Technology and Management*, vol. 1, 2001, pp. 196–216; Eric Berggren and Thomas Nacher, 'Why Good Ideas Go Bust', *Management Review*, vol. 89, no. 2, February 2000, pp. 32–36; Suzan Hart, 'Dimensions of Success in New Product Development: An Exploratory Investigation', *Journal of Marketing*, vol. 9, 1993, pp. 23–41; Kevin J. Clancy and Robert S. Shulman, *The Marketing Revolution: A Radical Manifesto for Dominating the Marketplace*, New York, Harper Business, 1991, p. 6; and Robert G. Cooper, 'New Product Success in Industrial Firms', *Industrial Marketing Management*, 1992, pp. 215–223. Also see Gary Strauss, 'Building on Brand Names: Companies Freshen Old Product Lines', *USA Today*, 20 March 1992, pp. B1, B2.

7. Victoria Story, 'Characteristics of Successful New Product Development: Findings from a Survey of UK Automotive Component Suppliers', *International Journal of Automotive Technology and Management*, vol. 1, 2001, p. 196. See Christopher Power, 'Flops', *Business Week*, 16 August 1993, pp. 76–82; see also Eric Berggren and Thomas Nacher, 'Why Good Ideas Go Bust', *Management Review*, vol. 89, no. 2, February 2000, pp. 32–36.

8. Max Sutherland, Editorial: 'For Effective Strategy Pre-empt Resistance', *Journal of Brand Management*, vol. 9, no. 2, November 2001, p. 85; Eric Berggren and Thomas Nacher, 'Introducing New Products Can Be Hazardous to Your Company: Use the Right New Solutions Delivery Tools', *The Academy of Management Executive*, vol. 15, no. 3, August 2001, pp. 92–101; George Gruenwald, *How to Create Profitable New Products: From Mission to Market*, Chicago, NTC Business Books, 1997, pp. 28–32; and Robert G. Cooper and Elko J. Kleinschmidt, *New Product: The Key Factors in Success*, Chicago, American Marketing Association, 1990.

9. Bruce Einhorn, 'China: Too Fast a Learner?', *Business Week*, 3 February 2003.

10. Steve Hamm, 'Startups May Die, But Not Their Bright Ideas', *Business Week*, 20 March 2003, pp. 52–53; Jane Black, 'The Keys to Ending Music Piracy', *Business Week*, 27 January 2003.

11. Bruce Einhorn, Manjeet Kripalani and Kerry Capell, 'India's Little Drugmakers that Could', *Business Week*, 3 March 2003, p. 20.

12. Merele Crawford and Anthony Di Benedetto, *New Product Management*, 7th edn, New York, McGraw/Irwin, 2003. See Lisa C. Troy, David M. Szymanski and P. Rajan Varadarajan, 'Generating New Product Ideas: An Initial Investigation of the Role of Market Information and Organizational Characteristics', *Journal of the Academy of Marketing Science*, vol. 29, no. 1, Winter 2001, pp. 89–101; Eric von Hippel, 'Get New Products from Consumers', *Harvard Business Review*, March–April 1982, pp. 117–122.

13. Anonymous, 'From Those Who Know Best', *Small Business Reports*, vol. 18, no. 11, November 1993, p. 8. For a comprehensive approach to generating new ideas see Linda Rochford, 'Generating and Screening New Product Ideas', *Industrial Marketing Management*, vol. 20, 1991, pp. 287–296; Rajesh Sethi, Daniel C. Smith and C. Whan, 'Cross-functional Product Development Teams, Creativity, and the Innovativeness of New Consumer Products', *Journal of Marketing Research*, vol. 38, no. 1, February 2001, pp. 73–85.

14. Russell Mitchell, 'How Ford Hit the Bullseye with Taurus', *Business Week*, 30 June 1986, pp. 69–70; and 'Copycat Stuff? Hardly!', *Business Week*, 14 September 1987, p. 112.

15. For more on idea generation see George Gruenwald, *How to Create Profitable New Products: From Mission to Market*, Chicago, NTC Business Books, 1997, pp. 225–238; Dorothy Leonard and Jeffrey F. Rayport, 'Spark Innovation through Empathic Design', *Harvard Business Review*, November–December 1997, pp. 102–108; Bryan W. Mattimore, 'Eureka! How to Invent a New Product', *Futurist*, vol. 29, no. 2, March/April 1995, pp. 34–38; and Tom W. White, 'Use Variety of Internal, External Sources to Gather and Screen New Product Ideas', *Marketing News*, 16 September 1983, sec. 2, p. 12.

16. Ely Dahan and Haim Mendelson, 'An Extreme-Value Model of Concept Testing', *Management Science*, vol. 47, no. 1, January 2001, pp. 102–116; Paul E. Green, Abba M. Krieger and Terry G. Vavra, 'Evaluating New Products', *Marketing Research: A Magazine of Management & Applications*, vol. 9, no. 4, Winter 1997, pp. 12–21. For more on product idea evaluation and concept testing see William L. Moore, 'Concept Testing', *Journal of Business Research*, vol. 10, 1982, pp. 279–294; and David A. Schwartz, 'Concept Testing Can Be Improved—and Here's How', *Marketing News*, 6 January 1984, pp. 22–23.

17. For Kao's corporate mission see <www.kao.co.jp/e/corp_e/profile/kihon/index.html>, accessed 3 March 2003.

18. See Otis Port, 'Pssst! Want a Secret for Making Superproducts?', *Business Week*, 2 October 1989, pp. 106–110.

19. Iris Poliski, 'Gate-Based System Tracks Product Development', *Research & Development*, vol. 43, no. 10, October 2001, p. 15; Suzan J. Hart and Michael J. Baker, 'The Multiple Convergent Processing Model of New Product Development', in Suzan Hart, *New Product Development: A Reader*, London, The Dryden Press, 1996, pp. 151–165; and Vijay Mahajan and Jerry Wind, 'New Product Models: Practice, Shortcomings and Desired Improvements', in Suzan Hart, op. cit., pp. 178–179.

20. Marc Puich, 'Are You Up to the Cycle-Time Challenge?', *IIE Solutions*, vol. 33, no. 4, April 2001, pp. 24–29; Viswanathan Krishnan, Steven D. Eppinger and Daniel E. Whitney, 'A Model-Based Framework to Overlap Product Development Activities', *Management Science*, vol. 43, no. 4, April 1997, pp. 437–451; Madhav N. Segal and J. S. Johar, 'On Improving the Effectiveness of Test Marketing Decisions', in Suzan Hart, op. cit., pp. 377–384.

21. For more on controlled test markets see Felix Kessler, 'High-Tech Shocks in Ad Research', *Fortune*, 7 July 1986, pp. 58–62; Chad Rubel, 'Researcher Praises On-line Methodology', *Marketing News*, vol. 30, no. 12, 3 June 1996, p. H18.

22. See Philip Kotler and Kevin Lane, *Marketing Management*, 12th edn, Upper Saddle River, NJ, Prentice Hall, 2006, pp. 654–655, and A. Merele Crawford and C. A. Di Benedetto, *New Product Management*, 6th edn, Chicago, Irwin, 2000, Chapter 20; Gary S. Lynn, Mario Mazzuca, Joseph G. Morone and Albert S. Paulson, 'Learning Is the Critical Success Factor in Developing Truly New Products', *Research-Technology Management*, vol. 41, no. 3, May/June 1998, pp. 45–51.

23. Lynne M. Sallot, 'Simulated Test Marketing: Technology for Launching Successful New Products', *Public Relations Review*, vol. 24, no. 2, Summer 1998, pp. 253–254; Robert Mendenhall, 'Ways to Sidestep New-Product Traps', *Business Marketing*, vol. 80, no. 4, April 1995, p. 23. For more on simulated test markets see Kevin Higgins, 'Simulated Test Marketing Winning Acceptance', *Marketing News*, 1 March 1985, pp. 15, 19; and Howard Schlossberg, 'Simulated vs Traditional Test Marketing', *Marketing News*, 23 October 1989, pp. 1–2.

24. A. Merele Crawford and C. A. Di Benedetto, op. cit., Chapter 20.

25. Ibid.

26. David Yoffie and Michael Cusumano, 'Judo Strategy: The Competitive Dynamics of Internet Time', *Harvard Business Review*, January–February 1999, p. 74; Anonymous, 'Mintel Chooses Internet Delivery', *Information World Review*, vol. 71, July/August 2001, p. 6; Rick Whiting, 'Virtual Focus Group', *Information Week*, vol. 848, 30 July 2001, pp. 53–58.

27. Bruce Perrott and Peter Moore, 'Consumer Connections 99', Market Strategy and Technology Group (MSAT), UTS Presentation to the National Retailers Conference, Sydney, 21–22 June 1999.

28. Simon Lloyd, 'Beer War Goes Upmarket', *Business Review Weekly*, 22 October 1999, pp. 58–59; Catherine Penn, 'Media Vary by Product Type and Focus', *Beverage Industry*, vol. 91, no. 5, May 2000, pp. 14–18; Anonymous, 'Media Spending Carefully Allocated', *Beverage Industry*, vol. 90, no. 3, March 1999, p. 40; Dave Curtin, 'Beer-Money Brouhaha Brewing at Area Schools: Some Colleges Passing up Booze Funds at Sports Events', *Denver Post* (Rockies edition), 3 October 1999, p. B.01; Gerry Khermouch, 'Popping the Price Cap in Beer', *Brandweek*, vol. 40, no. 9, 1 March 1999, p. 1.

29. Polly Devaney, 'Bowled over by the $2m Slots on "Super Sunday"', *Marketing Week*, 6 February 2003, p. 30.

30. Walid Mugayar, *Opening Digital Markets*, New York, McGraw-Hill, 1997; Sally Mesner, 'Macleans Strikes First Internet Ad Deal', *Marketing*, 13 September 2001, p. 8; Paul Travis, 'Enterprise Portals: The Current Big Thing', *Information Week*, vol. 847, 23 July 2001, p. 74.

31. Jennifer Lawrence, 'P&G Rushes on Global Diaper Rollout', *Advertising Age*, 14 October 1991, p. 6; Bill Saporito, 'Behind the Tumult at P&G', *Fortune*, 7 March 1994, pp. 75–82; Laurel Wentz, 'P&G Loses in Scandinavia', *Advertising Age*, vol. 71, no. 51, 11 December 2000, p. 20; Christine Bittar, 'Diaper Rash', *Brandweek*, vol. 41, no. 35, 11 September 2000, pp. 1, 8.

32. Gayle Bryant, 'Just the Place for a Global Village', *Business Review Weekly*, 10 September 1999, pp. 126–127. See also <www.citibank.com.au>, accessed 9 November 2005.

33. Merele Crawford and Anthony Di Benedetto, *New Product Management*, 7th edn, McGraw/Irwin, 2003, p. 455.

34. The following discussion draws heavily on Everett M. Rogers, *Diffusion of Innovations*, 4th edn, New York, The Free Press, 1995. Also see Hubert Gatignon and Thomas S. Robertson, 'A Propositional Inventory for New Diffusion Research', *Journal of Consumer Research*, March 1985, pp. 849–867.

35. Computer Industry Almanac, Inc., <www.c-i-a.com>, accessed 23 October 2002; and also see 'The Rapid Impact of the Internet', *Marketing Week*, 20 January 2000.

36. See Stewart Adam, 'Previous Practice Effects on Educator Adoption of Discontinuous Innovation', Competitive Paper, Australian and New Zealand Marketing Academy (ANZMAC 99), Sydney, 29 November to 1 December 1999.

37. David Lawn, 'Jeans Retailer Finds the Fit That Gives It Room to Grow', *Business Review Weekly*, 26 October 1998, pp. 82–84; David Benady, 'Rejeaneration', *Marketing Week*, 12 April 2001, pp. 30–32; Stacy Baker, 'Sun Apparel: The Meaning of Jeans Fashion', *Apparel Industry Magazine*, vol. 60, no. 1, January 1999, p. 74.

38. Phillip Lay, 'Making Partnering Work along the Technology Adoption Life Cycle', *Software Developer & Publisher*, July/August 1997; see also G. A. Moore, *Inside the Tornado*, New York, Harper Business, 1995, Chapter 2, pp. 13–26.

39. G. L. Urban and E. von Hippel, 'Lead Users Analysis for the Development of New Industrial Products', *Management Science*, vol. 34, no. 5, May 1988.

40. Ibid.

41. Ibid.

42. C. Herstatt and E. von Hippel, 'From Experience: Developing New Product Concepts Via the Lead User Method: A Case Study in a "Low Tech" Field', *Journal of Product Innovation Management*, vol. 9, 1992, pp. 200–212.

43. J. Hagel and A. G. Armstrong, *Net.Gain: Expanding Markets through Virtual Communities*, Boston, Harvard Business School Press, 1997.

44. See 'A Simple Approach for Short Product Lifecycle Forecasting', *Journal of Business Forecasting*, vol. 20, no. 1, Spring 2001, pp. 18–20; George S. Day, 'The Product Life Cycle: Analysis and Applications Issues', *Journal of Marketing*, Fall 1981, pp. 60–67; John E. Swan and David R. Rink, 'Fitting Marketing Strategy to Varying Life Cycles', *Business Horizons*, January–February 1982, pp. 72–76; and Sak Onkvisit and John J. Shaw, 'Competition and Product Management: Can the Product Life Cycle Help?', *Business Horizons*, July–August 1986, pp. 51–62.

45. See Laurence P. Feldman and Albert L. Page, 'Harvesting: The Misunderstood Market Exit Strategy', *Journal of Business Strategy*, Spring 1985, pp. 79–85; Alex Tullo, 'An Abandoned Business', *Chemical & Engineering News*, 8 October 2001, vol. 79, no. 41, p. 20; Hans Van Kranenburg, Myriam Cloodt and John Hagedoorn, 'An Exploratory Study of Recent Trends in the Diversification of Dutch Publishing Companies in the Multimedia and Information Industries', *International Studies of Management & Organization*, vol. 31, no. 1, Spring 2001, pp. 64–86.

46. For a more comprehensive discussion of marketing strategies over the course of the product life cycle, see Philip Kotler and Kevin Lane, *Marketing Management*, 12th edn, Upper Saddle River, NJ, Prentice Hall, 2006, Chapter 10, pp. 321–335.

PHOTO/AD CREDITS

CASE STUDY

The automotive industry: new-product challenges

Dr Martin Quick, General Manager, Aftersales, P&A

1. Industry overview

The automotive industry is the largest manufacturing sector in the world, in which over 50 million cars are sold each year. In Australia over 900 000 new cars are sold each year and there are over 300 products to choose from. Continued growth and increased competition, however, has led to the industry becoming increasingly efficient and consolidated in ownership (Holden/Daewoo, Renault/Nissan, Ford/Volvo), product platforms (multiple models produced on a single manufacturing line) and manufacturing bases in emerging consumer markets (China, India).

Figure 1 shows an increase of over 50% in new car sales and 25% in new products during the past 10 years in Australia. This growth has been primarily due to the reduction of tariffs and growth of imported products, which today account for more than 75% of the market.

The balance of the market consists of only six Australian-produced products (Falcon, Territory, Commodore, Camry, Avalon and 380).

In this environment, accountable market and product strategy development and PLC planning are critical for both short- and long-term success. This is particularly important given the shorter product life cycles and the high cost of introducing new products into the market such as Mitsubishi 380 ($600 million) and Ford Territory ($500 million). Furthermore, the marketing of automotive products today exceeds $500 million per annum, and continues to place cost pressures on overall product design, specifications, margins and return on investment.

2. Key product challenges

The globalisation of the automotive industry has brought with it many challenges. Perhaps the most challenging is the consolidation of product development centres for the world market. This approach has led to few products being designed in Australia and provides additional risks for product planners in terms of locally adapting products for segmentation, product name, design, specifications and pricing. For example, Australia

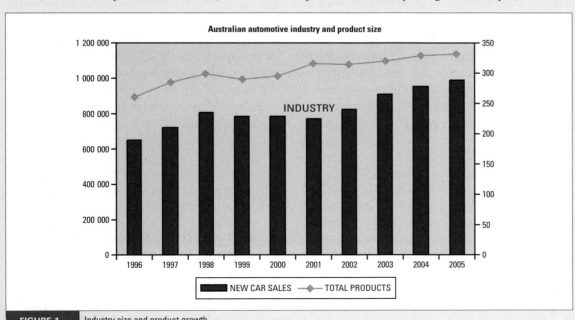

FIGURE 1   Industry size and product growth
Source: Polk Australia, VFACTS, December 2005.

CASE
STUDY

represents only 2% of the world automotive market and as a result products are often designed and priced to suit the larger American and European markets, with only minor changes for Australia. Consequently, Australian products are often not optimally specified or priced, which, together with increased competition, has led to the increased use of price discounts and incentives to reach sales targets. This continued sales approach is likely ultimately to reduce product and brand equity levels.

A key decision for any product planner is therefore whether the new product will deliver incremental or substitutional sales and whether the product will enhance the overall brand image. Critical questions should also be what are the company objectives—sales, market share, profit or all of these—and are these objectives shared globally? While many Australian company objectives are profit and market share, sales may later become the major priority (at the expense of profit) to meet global production objectives. Answers to the above questions are critical prior to determining product specification, pricing and marketing expenditure.

For example, the introduction of additional products does not always yield incremental volume. Hyundai expanded their product range from four to ten products during the late 1990s but sales reduced. This decline was due to exchange rate changes (reduced buying power), increased competition and the challenges of managing an expanded product range from a media perspective. Another example is Ford, which launched Territory in 2004 but lost Falcon sales as a direct result. Forecasting sales for new products can therefore depend on the integration of the product into the current model range and other internal and external factors. The measurement of product, sales and marketing requirements and performance (marketing metrics) is therefore essential to ensure product success.

Product planning decisions are thus likely to be made by corporate, market, sales and product development divisions. The challenge for automotive companies, however, is which division should be held accountable for a product's short- and long-term success? The tactical view of marketing has been traditionally based on the four Ps (product, price, promotion and place), but in recent years has been extended to include segmentation and targeting, which are likely to require multidivisional responsibility. For this reason many companies use product taskforces comprised of corporate, product, sales, marketing, service, parts and finance personnel to manage new-product market development. The product's success will depend upon the collaborative efforts of all departments in both long- (conceptual) and short-term (tactical) planning.

Another challenge is determining the effects of increased competition on PLCs, which have become increasingly shorter and hence a higher risk on investment. The pace with which a product progresses through its evolution will depend on competition, sales expectancies and global product strategies including product and brand equity integration. In this environment, product planners must therefore decide to follow the trends and develop 'me-too products' (perceived low risk), pioneer new segments (high risk like Ford Territory), acquire companies to expand the product range (Holden/Daewoo) or revive maturing products with 'value added' or price point strategies. The continued use of incentives, however, at the maturity stage is likely to reduce resale values and customer perceived value of the brand. Recent examples include the product 'run-out' promotions of ageing models such as Magna, Commodore and Falcon, which were priced considerably lower than the new model. Whichever product strategy is chosen, planners should consider the PLC short- and long-term effects of the new product on its replacement and the overall brand.

3. Competitive product value analysis

Many companies use product value analysis measures to determine a product's competitive 'value' in the market. This value analysis is generally used to measure and determine specifications, pricing and promotions for new and ongoing products. Table 1 shows an example of a typical value analysis measure.

In Table 1, product A is $500 better value (cheaper) for a customer than product B even though it has a higher retail price. This value analysis may additionally be adjusted to increase or discount an overall value based on market share or brand equity. Value analysis is generally conducted monthly for all products and graphed against sales performance to measure overall product competitive value and performance. The interpretation of this model, however, should always be tempered against the initial retail price, which is the 'perceived value' the customer initially sees in the media prior to their information gathering and decision-making process.

The value of these measures should also be considered against some unique automotive characteristics such as the extended times between each purchase and increased service intervals. This means that customers are likely to spend time investigating product specifications and overall value in newspapers and on the Web prior to purchase. Sometimes, however, the best value products do not always result in sales because customers are not prepared to pay for the additional value. As a result, companies generally use price-leader products initially to attract customers into showrooms and up-sell them into more expensive products.

4. Mitsubishi campaign

Value analysis is critical for product and market planners to measure overall perceived customer value and achieve long-term product differentiation on specification and price. Figure 2 (overleaf) shows an example of a new-product advertisement where the retail price was above both the product it replaced and its major competitor's promotional price. To meet this challenge, the company launched an extensive six-month media campaign prior to the launch. The campaign, which was known as 'Better Built Better Backed', was centred on engineering excellence, product quality and customer support to differentiate the brand prior to the launch of the new product. The campaign raised the brand profile and together with the new product's improved quality and specifications helped win 'Australia's Best Car' award.

The example in Figure 2 shows that it is not just the traditional product planning criteria such as specifications, pricing and positioning that were important in its success. It was also the overall perceived value proposition including warranty and customer retention programs that differentiated the Mitsubishi product and encouraged the customer to continue servicing with the brand and repeat purchase. Nurturing this relationship is critical given the extended periods of time between each purchase.

The extended periods between each purchase, however, also bring with them additional challenges. Over time consumers age, income and lifestyles are likely to change and subsequent purchases may differ from previous purchases (average product retention in the automotive industry is 20%). As a result product planners should consider designing product ranges which reflect these changing consumer lifestyles and focus product strategies on brand retention and customer lifetime value.

As products continue to become more aligned in design, quality, price and specifications (the

TABLE 1 Competitive value analysis			
	Product A	**Competitor B**	
Retail price	$20 990	$19 990	
Specifications	($2 000)	0	Standard versus optional air conditioning
Campaign offer	($500)	($1 000)	$500 petrol versus $1000 cashback
Total value	$18 490	$18 990	

FIGURE 2 Mitsubishi 380 new-product campaign focused on value
Source: Mitsubishi Australia, January 2006.

traditional product planning focus), companies will need to extend the product planning focus towards this customer lifetime concept. This has implications for product planners, who will need to consider these effects on PLCs, value analysis measures and providing an integrated product, sales, marketing and service solution to customer acquisition and retention.

QUESTIONS

1. How should regional product planners manage global product development strategies?

2. How should product development be held accountable?

3. Discuss the internal and external factors that may influence product strategies.

4. Do increased product ranges always increase sales? Discuss the challenges faced in managing an increased product range.

5. Discuss the value analysis measurement used by automotive companies.

6. Discuss the Mitsubishi 380 product advertisement—does the wider value proposition differentiate the product from the competition?

CHAPTER 13

Pricing considerations and approaches

OSS World Wide Movers:
www.ossworldwidemovers.com

Four Winds: www.fourwindsint.com.au

Grace Removals Group:
www.grace.com.au

King and Wilson:
www.kingandwilson.com.au

Movements International Movers:
www.movementsinternational.com

New Zealand Van Lines:
www.nzvanlines.co.nz

Have you ever dreamed of naming your own price for a night's accommodation in the centre of Sydney or perhaps for a weekend flight to the Gold Coast? Well, consumers in the North American market have been doing this for the past eight years through a dot.com service that first emerged in the late 1990s in the form of priceline.com. Just what is Priceline? In essence, it's an online consumer clearinghouse of excess travel inventory—hotel rooms, flights, packages and rental cars. Big discounts are possible through Priceline. But there's a catch to those big discounts. Unlike other travel discount programs where you browse through availabilities and pick the one you want, Priceline requires a commitment to a particular category and price before you even know what's available. That's right. With Priceline you pick your category, location and class of travel, name the price you want to pay, dole out your credit card details and then commit irrevocably to accepting whatever Priceline finds within your parameters. That's just a bit scary when you aren't sure what you can end up with. However, these trade-offs allow travellers to gain four-star accommodation in cities like San Francisco, Chicago and LA for no more than $60 per night when the usual rack rates can be three to four times that amount.

Priceline.com adds value to the consumer experience by empowering users to set pricing. There are trade-offs for the consumer but many are willing to accept these trade-offs as the benefit can be substantial savings.

Pricing strategies in the film/TV industry versus the music industry provide a good example of different approaches to pricing of similar entertainment products. One of the reasons for the differences is that movie studios release far less product each year than the music record labels, with major film releases numbering in the 100s as against the 25 000 or so annual CD releases. So this means the studios must really extract the most value from their limited releases each year.

The movie pricing model is a dynamic one where the same movie passes through a release cycle beginning with the highest value release methods targeting the highest value consumers and ending with the lowest value consumers. A movie typically begins with a theatrical release in movie theatres, then

Priceline lets you set the price!

moves to pay-per-view, followed by premium cable (like Foxtel). After the premium cable run has begun (or ends) is the time when typically DVDs are released for sale/rental. Eventually, movies make their way to free-to-air broadcast TV.

DVD sales do not rely on a static pricing model. They are initially released at a price point consistent with expected demand. After a short period of time, prices drop, and in some cases significantly. A recent DVD release illustrates this strategy. The Seinfeld Collection (Seasons 1 and 2, and Seasons 3 and 4) were originally released on 29 November 2004, at a price of $49.99 at retail. As the Christmas holidays approached, prices were reduced to $44.99. Shortly after the holidays, prices dropped as low as $39.99. Then towards the end of March a number of retailers were advertising both sets for $29.95 each.

DVD pricing is dynamically set based on popularity (demand) and age (supply). The older a release is, the greater its availability on the secondary markets. Older movies, such as *Shrek* and *Ice Age*, are all approximately $10 today. More recent films, such as *Finding Nemo* or *Shrek 2* are approximately $14.99. Films fresh out of the theatres, such as *The Incredibles*, are approximately $20.

But it's not just a function of age: certain older titles never seem to drop below $10—recent films of acclaim like *Pulp Fiction* and *Saving Private Ryan* or older classics like *Ben Hur* and *Ten Commandments*— despite their age. It is also a function of demand or popularity of the movie titles.

Ironically, many of the films mentioned here now sell for less than their soundtracks. Two hours (or longer) of a movie, plus additional audio commentary, a documentary of the making of the film, out-takes, special features and so on all cost less than a mere 45-minute audio of songs from the film.

Consumers have very quickly worked out that CDs now offer a weak value propostion. Is it any surpise that CD sales have slid while DVD sales have grown explosively? Maybe the reason is the industries' different pricing approaches?

By pricing DVDs more strategically, in a manner that better reflects the value being derived by consumers, the film/TV industry captures marginal sales and maximises revenue. The only comparable pricing structure in the music industry is for low-cost or budget CDs. These lower priced CDs are usually much older than the equivalent DVDs, that is, several years old versus perhaps several months for DVDs. Typically, they are packaged differently and specifically marketed as the 'budget line'—with less desirable cover art and labelling.

Compare the differing approaches the two industries take:

⊙ DVD sales are dynamically priced and retailers are aware that they have price-sensitive consumers. They offer the exact same product—albeit on a less timely basis.

⊙ CD sales are static, maintaining the same price over the life of a disk. On those select disks when price discounts do occur (budget line), the industry purposefully makes changes to make the product less desirable.

These examples illustrate the variety of approaches taken to pricing products and services in dynamic, competitive marketplaces.[1]

After reading this chapter you should be able to:

1. Explain how marketing objectives, marketing mix strategy and costs and other company factors affect pricing decisions.

2. List and discuss factors outside the company that affect pricing decisions.

3. Explain how price setting depends on consumer perceptions of price and on the price–demand relationship.

4. Compare the five general pricing approaches.

5. Describe the major strategies for pricing new products.

6. Explain how companies find a set of prices that maximises the profits from the total product mix.

7. Explain how companies adjust their prices to take into account different types of customers and situations.

8. Explain why companies decide to change their prices.

All profit organisations and many non-profit organisations must set prices on their products or services. *Price* goes by many names:

> Price is all around us. You pay *rent* for your apartment, *tuition* for your education, and a *fee* to your doctor or dentist. The airline, railway, taxi and bus companies charge you a *fare*; the local utilities call their price a tariff or *rate*; and the local bank charges you *interest* for the money you borrow. The price for driving your car through the Sydney Harbour Tunnel is a *toll*, and the company that insures your car charges you a *premium*. The guest lecturer charges an *honorarium* to tell you about a government official who took a *bribe* to help a shady character steal *dues* collected by a trade association. Fitness clubs or societies to which you belong may make a special *assessment* to pay unusual expenses. Your lawyer may ask for a *retainer* to cover her services. The 'price' of an executive is a *salary*, the price of a salesperson may be a *commission*, and the price of a worker is a *wage*. Finally, many of us feel that *income taxes* are the price we pay for the privilege of making money.[2]

Price The amount of money charged for a product or service, or the sum of the values consumers exchange for the benefits of having or using the product or service.

Simply defined, **price** is the amount of money charged for a product or service. More broadly, price is the sum of the values consumers exchange for the benefits of having or using the product or service.

How are prices set? Historically, prices were usually set by buyers and sellers bargaining with each other. Sellers would ask for a higher price than they expected to get, and buyers would offer less than they expected to pay. Through bargaining, they would arrive at an acceptable price. Individual buyers paid different prices for the same products, depending on their needs and bargaining skills.

Today, most sellers set *one* price to *all* buyers. This idea was helped along by the development of large-scale retailing during the 1940s and 1950s. Woolworths Variety Stores and G. J. Coles first advertised a 'strictly one-price policy' because they carried so many items and had so many employees. Even the penny arcade of old was just that—a one-price amusement parlour. Today we find bargain stores selling all items in their stores for $5 or less. A shop at Manly, a popular Sydney tourist destination, sells all its items for $2 each.

Historically, price has been the major factor affecting buyer choice. This is still true in poorer nations, among poorer groups and with commodity products. However, non-price factors have become more important in buyer choice behaviour in recent decades.

Price is the only element in the marketing mix that produces revenue; all other elements represent costs. Furthermore, pricing and price competition are generally regarded as one of the key practical problems facing marketing executives. Yet many companies do not handle pricing well. The most common mistakes are pricing that is too cost oriented; prices that are not revised often enough to reflect market changes; pricing that does not take the rest of the marketing mix into account; and prices that are not varied enough for different product items and market segments.

This chapter looks at the factors marketers must consider when setting prices and at general pricing approaches, and examines pricing strategies for new-product pricing, product-mix pricing, initiating and responding to price changes, and adjusting prices for buyer and situational factors.[3]

A company sets not a single price but rather a *pricing structure* that covers different items in its line. This pricing structure changes as products move through their life cycles. The company adjusts product prices to reflect changing costs and demand and to account for variations in buyers and situations. As the competitive environment changes, the company considers initiating price changes at times and responding to them at others. This chapter examines the major dynamic pricing strategies available to management. In turn, we look at *new-product pricing strategies* for products in the introductory stage of the product life cycle, *product-mix pricing strategies* for related products in the product mix, *price-adjustment strategies* that account for customer differences and changing situations, and *strategies for initiating and responding to price changes.*[4]

Factors to consider when setting prices

A company's pricing decisions are affected by many internal company factors and external environmental factors. These factors are shown in Figure 13.1 (overleaf). *Internal factors* include the company's marketing objectives, marketing mix strategy, costs and organisation. *External factors* include the nature of the market and demand, competition and other environmental factors.

Internal factors affecting pricing decisions

Marketing objectives

Before setting price the company must decide on its strategy for the product. If the company has selected its target market and positioning carefully, then its marketing mix strategy, including price, will be fairly straightforward. For example, Mercedes-Benz made the decision to produce a new medium-priced A class model to compete with Japanese cars and lower-priced European cars such as Audi and low-end BMW models. Lexus was developed by Toyota to compete with Mercedes in the luxury car market and to enable the company to achieve a positioning of a motor vehicle in an

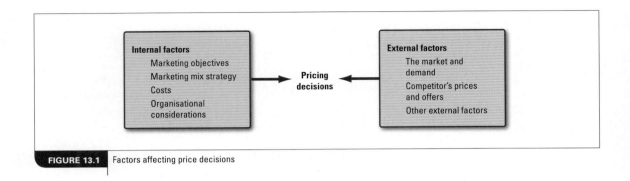

entirely different price space when compared with its Toyota brand. Thrifty has positioned itself as a rental car company for budget-minded travellers; this position requires charging a low price. Lexmark printers are priced below the market leader Hewlett-Packard for more price-conscious consumers. Thus, pricing strategy is largely determined by past decisions on market positioning.

At the same time, the company may seek additional objectives. The clearer a firm is about its objectives, the easier it is to set price. Examples of common objectives are *survival*, *current profit maximisation*, *market-share maximisation* and *product-quality leadership*.

Survival Companies set *survival as* their major objective if they are troubled by too much capacity, heavy competition or changing consumer wants. To keep a plant going, a company may set a low price, hoping to increase demand. In this case, profits are less important than survival. In recent years many car dealers have resorted to pricing below cost or offering large-price-rebate programs in order to survive. Similarly, independent petrol stations frequently price at survival levels to compete with the large oil companies' retail outlets. As long as their prices cover variable costs and some fixed costs, they can stay in business until conditions change or other problems are corrected.

Current profit maximisation Many companies want to set a price that will maximise current profits. They estimate what demand and costs will be at different prices and choose the price that will produce the maximum current profit, cash flow or return on investment. In all cases, the company wants current financial outcomes rather than long-run performance.

Market-share leadership Other companies want to obtain the dominant market share. They believe that the company with the largest market share will enjoy the lowest costs and highest long-run profit. To become the market-share leader, they set prices as low as possible. A variation of this objective is to pursue a specific market-share gain. Say the company wants to increase its market share substantially in one year. It will search for the price and marketing program that will achieve this goal. Pizza Hut Australia implemented this strategy in the Australian market by reducing its prices from $16 to $6 and sometimes as low as $4. While this resulted in a prolonged price war with Domino's and other pizza chains it retained its dominant share position.[5]

Product-quality leadership A company might decide it wants to have the highest quality product on the market. This normally entails charging a high price to cover the high product quality and high cost of R&D. For example, Fisher and Paykel, the New Zealand-based white goods manufacturer, seeks product innovation leadership. Fisher and Paykel makes the most innovative of dishwashers, refrigerators and washing machines. By offering the highest quality and modern design, Fisher and Paykel caters for the high-quality end of the white goods market. Sony's Vaio brand is priced at a premium to project and reinforce the image of a high-quality computer laptop product.

Other objectives A company might also use price to attain other more specific objectives. It can set prices low to prevent competition from entering the market or set prices at competitors' levels to stabilise the market. Prices can be set to keep the loyalty and support of resellers or to avoid government intervention. Prices can be temporarily reduced to create excitement for a product or to draw more customers into a retail store. This is one reason why Bi-Lo Supermarkets periodically promotes milk and bread wars. One product may be priced to help the sales of other products in the company's line. This also reinforces Bi-Lo's price positioning as the 'cheapest' supermarket. Thus, pricing may play an important role in helping to accomplish the company's objectives at many levels. Qantas sets a recommended retail price of an airline ticket on its website to protect its relationship with travel agents and to reduce possible distribution channel conflicts.

Marketing mix strategy

Price is only one of the marketing mix tools that the company uses to achieve its marketing objectives. Price decisions must be coordinated with product design, distribution and promotion decisions to form a consistent and effective marketing program. Decisions made for other marketing mix variables may affect pricing decisions. For example, producers who use many resellers who are expected to support and promote their products may have to build larger reseller margins into their prices. The decision to develop a high-quality position will mean that the seller must charge a higher price to cover higher costs.

The company often makes its pricing decision first and then bases other marketing mix decisions on the price it wants to charge. For example, Yamaha, a traditional marketer of high-quality specialised music equipment, designed a mini stereo system in order to compete with Sony and Philips. It had discovered a market segment for affordable stereos and designed models to sell within the price range that the segment was willing to pay. Here, price was a crucial product-positioning factor that defined the product's market, competition and design. The intended price determined what product features could be offered and what production costs could be incurred.

Many firms support such price-positioning strategies with a technique called *target costing*, a potent strategic weapon. Target costing reverses the usual process of first designing a new product, determining its cost and then asking 'Can we sell it for that?'. Instead, it starts with a target cost and works back. Compaq Computer Corporation, now part of Hewlett-Packard, calls this process 'design to price'. After being battered for years by lower-priced rivals, Compaq used this approach to create its highly successful, lower-priced Prolinea personal computer line. Starting with a price target set by marketing, and with profit-margin goals from management, the Prolinea design team determined what costs *had* to be in order to charge the target price. From this crucial calculation everything else followed. To achieve target costs, the design team negotiated doggedly with all the company departments responsible for different aspects of the new product, and with outside suppliers of needed parts and materials. Compaq engineers designed a machine with fewer and simpler parts, manufacturing overhauled its factories to reduce production costs and suppliers found ways to provide quality components at needed prices. By meeting its target *costs*, Compaq was able to set its target *price* and establish the desired price position. As a result, Prolinea sales and profits soared.[6]

This was followed by its equally successful Presario range for retail consumers and the home office. Its Prosignia was designed, using the same philosophy, for SMEs and the Armada range for corporate clients.

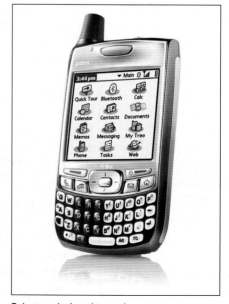

Palm treo designed to a price.

Other companies de-emphasise price and use other marketing mix tools to create *non-price* positions. Often, the best strategy is not to charge the lowest price but rather to differentiate the marketing offer to make it worth a higher price. For example, for years Johnson Controls, a producer of climate-control systems for office buildings, used initial price as its primary competitive tool. However, research showed that customers were more concerned about the total cost of installing and maintaining a system than about its initial price. Repairing broken systems was expensive, time consuming and risky. Customers had to shut down the heat or air conditioning in the whole building, disconnect a lot of wires and face the dangers of electrocution. Johnson decided to change its strategy. It designed an entirely new system called Metasys. To repair the new system, customers need only pull out an old plastic module and slip in a new one—no tools required. Metasys costs more to make than the old system, and customers pay a higher initial price, but it costs less to install and maintain. Despite its higher asking price, the new Metasys system brought in $500 million in revenues in its first year.[7]

Total cost of ownership TCO includes all costs associated with purchasing and using a product over its life.

Research conducted by the Gartner Group revealed that the average **total cost of ownership** (TCO) of hand-held computers in the USA is reaching $US6000 per user per year, going up to $US8554 when combined with a separate wireless modem. This TCO dwarfs the purchase price of many pocket-size personal digital assistants (PDAs), which can be as little as $US300. There are many associated costs of usage and maintenance which people do not think of on their own, such as the hidden costs of training and IT support. Therefore many IT managers do not look only at the product's price but at its associated costs of ownership when making their corporate purchases. Similarly, a study of the TCO for a desktop running Windows 2000 is just above $US5000 per year, whereas the TCO for a fully functioning laptop running Windows 2000 is nearly $US8000 per year. When you compare these with the actual prices of hardware of $US2000 per desktop and $US4000 per laptop it is clear that the bulk of cost resides elsewhere.[8] This remains the case today as we consider the costs of Internet access, program upgrades and capacity additions which are now necessities for functioning in an interconnected world.

Thus, the marketer must consider the total marketing mix when setting prices. If the product is positioned on non-price factors, then decisions about quality, promotion and distribution will strongly affect price. If price is a critical positioning factor, then price will strongly affect decisions made about the other marketing mix elements. In most cases, the company will consider all the marketing mix decisions together when developing the marketing program.

Costs

Costs set the floor for the price that the company can charge for its product. The company wants to charge a price that covers all its costs for producing, distributing and selling the product, and also delivers a fair rate of return for its effort and risk. A company's costs may be an important element in its pricing strategy. Many companies work to become the 'low-cost producers' in their industries. Companies with lower costs can set lower prices, which results in greater sales and profits.

Fixed costs Costs that do not vary with production or sales level.

Types of costs A company's costs take two forms: fixed and variable. **Fixed costs** (also known as overhead expenses) are costs that do not vary with production or sales level. Thus, a company must pay bills each month for rent, heat, interest and executive salaries whatever the company's output. Fixed costs go on no matter what the production level. However, firms want high unit sales because, although fixed costs in total are not affected, on a single-unit basis each unit carries a lower share of the fixed costs.

Variable costs Costs that vary directly with the level of production.

Variable costs vary directly with the level of production. That is, if we add the costs of wires, plastic, packaging and other materials that go into producing every Sharp calculator we come up with variable costs. The costs are the same for each calculator, but if we make and sell fewer calculators then we have lower variable costs. If we make and sell more, we have higher variable costs. Total variable costs vary with the number of units produced.

Total costs are the sum of the fixed and variable costs for any given level of production. Management wants to charge a price that will at least cover the total production costs at a given level of production. The company must watch its costs carefully. If it costs the company more than its competitors to produce and sell its product, the company will have to charge a higher price or make less profit, putting it at a competitive disadvantage.

Costs at different levels of production To price wisely, management needs to know how its costs vary with different levels of production. For example, suppose Fisher and Paykel has built a plant to produce 1000 washing machines per week. Figure 13.2A shows the typical short-run average cost curve (SRAC). It shows that the cost per machine is high if Fisher and Paykel's factory produces only a few per week. But as production approaches 1000 washing machines per week, the average cost falls. This is because fixed costs are spread over more units, with each unit bearing a smaller fixed cost.

Fisher and Paykel can try to produce more than 1000 washing machines per week, but average costs will increase because the plant becomes inefficient. Workers have to wait for machines, the machines break down more often and workers get in each other's way. If Fisher and Paykel believed it could sell 2000 washing machines per week, it should consider building a larger plant. The plant would use more efficient machinery and work arrangements, and the unit cost of producing 2000 units per week would be less than that of 1000 units per week, as shown in the long-run average cost (LRAC) curve (Figure 13.2B). In fact, a 3000-capacity plant would be even more efficient, according to Figure 13.2B. But a 4000 capacity plant would be less efficient because of increasing diseconomies of scale—too many workers to manage, increased paperwork slowing things down and so on. Figure 13.2B shows that a 3000 per week production plant is the best size to build if demand is strong enough to support this level of production.

Costs as a function of production experience Suppose Fisher and Paykel runs a plant that produces 3000 washing machines per week. As it gains experience in producing the machines, it learns how to do it better. Workers learn shortcuts and become more familiar with their equipment. With practice, the work becomes better organised, and Fisher and Paykel finds better equipment and production processes. With higher volume, it becomes more efficient and gains economies of scale. As a result, average cost tends to fall with accumulated production experience. This is shown in Figure 13.3 (overleaf) where accumulated production is drawn on a semi-log scale so that equal distances

Total costs The sum of the fixed and variable costs for any given level of production.

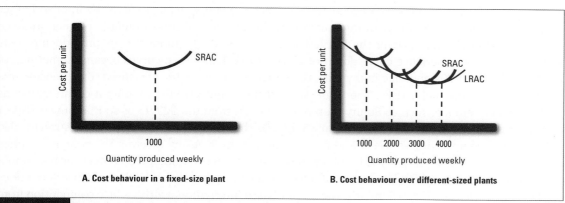

A. Cost behaviour in a fixed-size plant

B. Cost behaviour over different-sized plants

FIGURE 13.2 Cost per unit at different levels of production per period

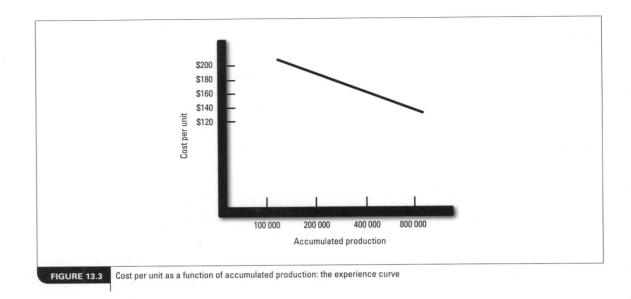

represent the same percentage increase in output.[9] Thus the average cost of producing the first 100 000 washing machines is $200 per unit. When the company has produced the first 200 000 washing machines, the average cost has fallen to $180. After its accumulated production experience doubles *again* to 400 000, the average cost is $160. This drop in the average cost with accumulated production experience is called the **experience curve** (or the *learning curve*).

Experience curve (or learning curve) The drop in the average per-unit production cost that comes with accumulated production experience.

If a downward-sloping experience curve exists, this is highly significant for the company. Not only will the company's unit production cost fall, it will fall faster if the company makes and sells more during a given period. But the market has to stand ready to buy the higher output. And to take advantage of the experience curve, Fisher and Paykel must get a large market share early in the product's life cycle. This suggests the following pricing strategy. It should price its washing machines low; its sales will then increase, and its costs will decrease through gaining more experience, and then it can lower its prices further.

Some companies have built successful strategies around the experience curve. For example, during the past 10 years James Hardie & Company rationalised production plants and injected technology into its Building Boards Division to reduce the costs of its wall-cladding products. This has enabled it to expand sales and hold a low-cost position against imported products. A dramatic example of learning-experience cost reductions is silicon memory chips produced by Intel and other chip manufacturers. Andy Grove of Intel maintains that the cost of chips in relation to performance has halved each 18 months over the last few years.[10] Yet a single-minded focus on reducing costs and exploiting the experience curve does not always work. Experience curves became something of a fad during the 1970s and, like many fads, the strategy was sometimes misused. Experience-curve pricing carries some major risks. The aggressive pricing might give the product a cheap image, as happens when retailers such as Sanity drop prices on CDs from the $29.95 or so that buyers expect to pay for the latest chart busters to about $5 for CDs that were never in vogue.[11] The strategy also assumes that competitors are weak and not willing to fight it out by meeting the company's price cuts. Finally, while the company is building volume under one technology, a competitor may find a lower-cost technology which lets it start at lower prices than the market leader, which still operates on the old experience curve.[12] Similarly, Australian-based international airlines face competition from some Asia–Pacific-based airlines which operate from a lower cost base.

The economics of information-based products

Information goods, which are those that can be distributed in digital form like software, books, movies and music, have a different cost structure from tangible products. A book publisher, for instance, will spend thousands or even millions of dollars acquiring, editing and designing a manuscript, and getting the first run printed. The cost of printing an additional copy is very small. Most of the costs of a movie are committed upfront for script, actors, film crew and direction for the first copy to be produced. Subsequent copies for distribution and production in DVD format cost very little. In both examples most of the costs are fixed and the variable costs are very low for each additional copy produced. In fact most of the fixed costs are 'sunk' costs—being costs that are not recoverable if production is stopped. For example, if a music CD does not sell, the sunk costs have already been lost. What this means is that the unit cost of producing an additional copy of an information product can be close to zero—when produced digitally. There are also dangers in this. Copies of information in digital form, such as CDs and DVDs, can be reproduced at very low cost and are subject to piracy.

The economics of information-based products is skewed towards fixed costs with very large economies of scale. The more that are produced, the lower the average unit cost of production. Capacity is almost unlimited. Sales volume is the key to profitability. Microsoft with its dominance of computer operating system software is very profitable and achieves huge gross margins. The downside is that for companies that do not achieve dominance and large sales, losses can be substantial. If competitors force a business to lower its prices to a level near its marginal production costs, the company will never be able to recover its original investments. This happened to the publishers of CD phone books.[13]

The implications for pricing are clear. Information-based products with large sunk costs need to be priced for volume so that rapid penetration of the available market can be achieved in the shortest possible time.

Organisational considerations

Management must decide who within the organisation should set prices. Companies handle pricing in a variety of ways. In small companies, prices are often set by top management rather than by the marketing or sales department. In large companies, pricing is typically handled by divisional or product line managers. In industrial markets, salespeople may be allowed to negotiate with customers within certain price ranges; even so, top management set the pricing objectives and policies and often approve the prices proposed by lower-level management or salespeople.[14] In industries in which pricing is a key factor (couriers, airlines, chemical companies), companies will often have a pricing department to set the best prices or to help others in setting them. This department reports to the marketing department or top management. Others who have an influence on pricing include sales managers, production managers, finance managers and accountants.

External factors affecting pricing decisions

The market and demand

Costs set the lower limits of prices, whereas the market and demand set the upper limit. Both consumers and industrial buyers balance the price of a product or service against the benefits of owning it. Thus, before setting prices, the marketer must understand the relationship between price and demand for its product.

In this section we explain how the price–demand relationship varies for different types of markets and how buyer perceptions of price affect the pricing decision. We then discuss methods for measuring the price–demand relationship.

Pricing in different types of markets The seller's pricing freedom varies with different types of markets. Economists recognise four types of markets, each presenting a different pricing challenge.

Pure competition
A market in which many buyers and sellers trade in a uniform commodity—no single buyer or seller has much effect on the going market price.

Under **pure competition**, the market consists of many buyers and sellers trading in a uniform commodity such as wheat, vegetables or financial securities. No single buyer or seller has much effect on the going market price. A seller cannot charge more than the going price because buyers can obtain as much as they need at this price. Nor would sellers charge less than the market price because they can sell all they want at that price. If price and profits rise, new sellers can easily enter the market. In a purely competitive market, marketing research, product development, pricing, advertising and sales promotion play little or no role. Thus, sellers in these markets do not spend much time on marketing strategy.

Monopolistic competition A market in which many buyers and sellers trade over a range of prices rather than a single market price.

Under **monopolistic competition**, the market consists of many buyers and sellers who trade over a range of prices rather than a single market price. A range of prices occurs because sellers can differentiate their offers to the buyers. Either the physical product can be varied in quality, features or style, or the accompanying services can be varied. Buyers see differences in sellers' products and will pay different prices. Sellers try to develop differentiated offers for different customer segments and, in addition to price, freely use branding, advertising and personal selling to set their offers apart. Because there are many competitors, each firm is less affected by competitors' marketing strategies than in oligopolistic markets. For example, Maggi and Continental national brands of noodles and gravies compete with other regional and local brands, all differentiated by price and non-price factors.

Oligopolistic competition A market in which there are a few sellers who are highly sensitive to each other's pricing and marketing strategies.

Under **oligopolistic competition**, the market consists of a few sellers who are highly sensitive to each other's pricing and marketing strategies. The product can be uniform (paper, aluminium) or non-uniform (cars, dishwashers). The sellers are few because it is difficult for new sellers to enter the market. Each seller is alert to competitors' strategies and moves. If Comalco slashes its aluminium price by 10%, buyers will quickly switch to this supplier. The other aluminium processors must respond by lowering their prices or increasing their services. An oligopolist is never sure that it will gain anything permanent through a price cut. On the other hand, if an oligopolist raises its price, its competitors might not follow this lead. The oligopolist would then have to retract its price increase or risk losing customers to competitors.

Pure monopoly
A market in which there is a single seller—it may be a government monopoly, a private, regulated monopoly or a private non-regulated monopoly.

A **pure monopoly** consists of one seller. The seller may be a government monopoly (Australia Post—monopolises stamp-based postal services), a private, regulated monopoly (a power company) or a private, non-regulated monopoly (Argyle Diamonds, a division of Rio Tinto plc). Pricing is handled differently in each case. A government monopoly can pursue a variety of pricing objectives. It might set a price below cost because the product is important to buyers who cannot afford to pay full cost. Or the price might be set either to cover costs or to produce good revenue. Or it might be set quite high to slow down consumption. In a regulated monopoly, the government permits the company to set rates that will yield a 'fair return', one that will let the company maintain and expand its operations as needed. Non-regulated monopolies are free to price at what the market will bear. However, they do not always charge the full price, for a number of reasons: desire not to attract competition, desire to penetrate the market faster with a low price, or fear of government regulation.

Consumer perceptions of price and value In the end, the consumer will decide whether a product's price is right. When setting prices, the company must consider consumer perceptions of price and how these perceptions affect consumers' buying decisions. Pricing decisions, like other marketing mix decisions, must be buyer oriented:

Pricing requires more than technical expertise. It requires creative judgment and awareness of buyers' motivations . . . The key to effective pricing is the same one that opens doors . . . in other marketing functions: a creative awareness of who buyers are, why they buy and how they make their buying decisions. The recognition that buyers differ in these dimensions is as important for effective pricing as it is for effective promotion, distribution or product development.[15]

When consumers buy a product they exchange something of value (the price) to get something of value (the benefits of having or using the product). Effective, buyer-oriented pricing involves understanding how much value consumers place on the benefits they receive from the product and then setting a price that fits this value. Such benefits include both actual and perceived benefits. For example, calculating the cost of ingredients in a meal at an upmarket restaurant is relatively easy. But assigning a value to other satisfactions such as taste, environment, relaxation, conversation and status is very hard. And these values will vary both for different consumers and for different situations. Many mobile phone users, the early adopters, knowingly pay more for early releases of new models. They place a higher value on use of the latest, best or smallest phones than others who wait. Thus, a company will often find it hard to measure the values customers will attach to its product. But the consumer does use these values to evaluate a product's price. If consumers perceive that the price is greater than the product's benefits, they will not buy the product. If consumers perceive that the price is below the product's benefits, they will buy it, but the seller loses profit opportunities.[16]

Marketers must therefore try to understand the consumer's reasons for buying the product and then set a price according to consumer perceptions of the product's value. Because consumers vary in the values they assign to different product features, marketers often vary their pricing strategies for different price segments. They offer different sets of product features at different prices. For example, television manufacturers offer small, inexpensive models for consumers who want basic sets and larger, higher-priced models loaded with features for consumers who want the extras.

Buyer-oriented pricing means that the marketer cannot design a product and marketing program and then set the price. Good pricing begins with analysing consumer needs and price perceptions. Price must be considered along with the other marketing mix variables before the marketing program is set.[17]

Pricing and consumption There is evidence to suggest that consumption of a product or service increases at the time when consumers actually pay for it. This is related to the psychology of feeling like we are getting value for the purchase. A study of health club records showed that consumption closely followed the timing of payments. Whether members paid annual or quarterly payments, use of the club was highest in the months immediately following payment, then declined steadily until the next payment. Members who paid monthly used the gym consistently. The same has been found with the sale of season tickets for live shows. The bundling of ticket prices reduces consumption (i.e. high 'no-shows' are experienced) whereas the no-show rate for people who have bought tickets for just one performance is very low. Another related finding is that the extent to which customers use a product or service they have paid for determines whether they will repeat the purchase.[18]

A conclusion to be drawn from this is that the timing of customer payments should be made as close to the consumption period as possible as this is likely to stimulate further consumption and repeat buying.

Analysing the price–demand relationship Each price the company might charge will lead to a different level of demand. The relation between the price charged and the resulting demand level is shown in the familiar **demand curve** in Figure 13.4A (overleaf). The demand curve shows the number of units the market will buy in a given time period, at different prices that might be charged. In the normal case, demand and price are inversely related: that is, the higher the price, the lower the demand. Thus, the company would sell less if it raised its price from P_1 to P_2. In short, consumers with limited budgets will probably buy less of something if its price is too high.

Demand curve A curve that shows the number of units the market will buy in a given time period, at different prices that might be charged.

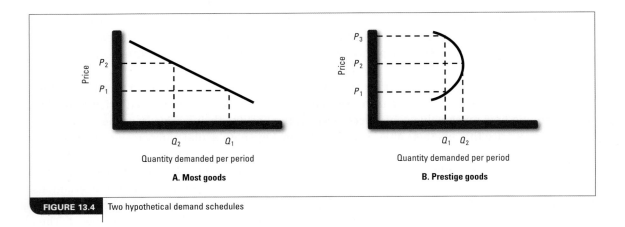

FIGURE 13.4   Two hypothetical demand schedules

Most demand curves slope downward in either a straight or a curved line, as in Figure 13.4A. But for luxury goods the demand curve sometimes slopes upward, as in Figure 13.4B. For example, one perfume company found that by raising its price from P_1 to P_2, it sold more perfume rather than less; consumers thought the higher price meant a better or more desirable perfume. However, if the company charges too high a price (P_3), the level of demand will be lower than at P_2.

Most companies try to measure their demand curves. The type of market makes a difference. In a monopoly the demand curve shows the total market demand resulting from different prices. If the company faces competition, its demand at different prices will depend on whether competitors' prices stay constant or change with the company's own prices. Here, we assume that competitors' prices remain constant. Later in this chapter we discuss what happens when competitors' prices change. To measure a demand curve requires estimating demand at different prices. Figure 13.5A shows the estimated demand curve for foreign touring sedans. Demand rises as the price is lowered from $42 500 to $40 000. The percentage reduction in price of 6.25% shows a 21.4% increase in quantity demanded.

The demand curve for the BMW 318 in Figure 13.5B shows a different relationship. Here a 6.25% reduction in price results in only a 10% increase in quantity demanded.

In measuring the price–demand relationship, the market researcher must not allow other factors affecting demand to vary. For example, if importers of foreign sedans also raised their advertising budgets at the same time as lowering prices, we would not know how much of the increased demand was due to the lower price and how much to the increased advertising.

Economists show the impact of non-price factors on demand through shifts in the demand curve rather than movements along it. Suppose the initial demand curve is D_1 in Figure 13.6 (overleaf). The seller is charging P and selling Q_1 units. Now suppose the economy suddenly improves or the seller doubles its advertising budget. The higher demand is reflected through an upward shift of the demand curve from D_1 to D_2. Without changing the price P, the seller's demand is now Q_2.

Price elasticity
A measure of the sensitivity of demand to changes in price.

Price elasticity of demand   Marketers also need to know **price elasticity**—how responsive demand will be to a change in price. Consider the two demand curves in Figure 13.7 (overleaf). In Figure 13.7A a price increase from P_1 to P_2 leads to a relatively small drop in demand from Q_1 to Q_2. In Figure 13.7B the same price increase leads to a large drop in demand from Q'_1 to Q'_2. If demand hardly changes with a small change in price, we say the demand is *inelastic*. If demand changes greatly, we say the demand is *elastic*. The price elasticity of demand is given by the following formula:

$$\text{price elasticity of demand} = \frac{\text{per cent change in quantity demanded}}{\text{per cent change in price}}$$

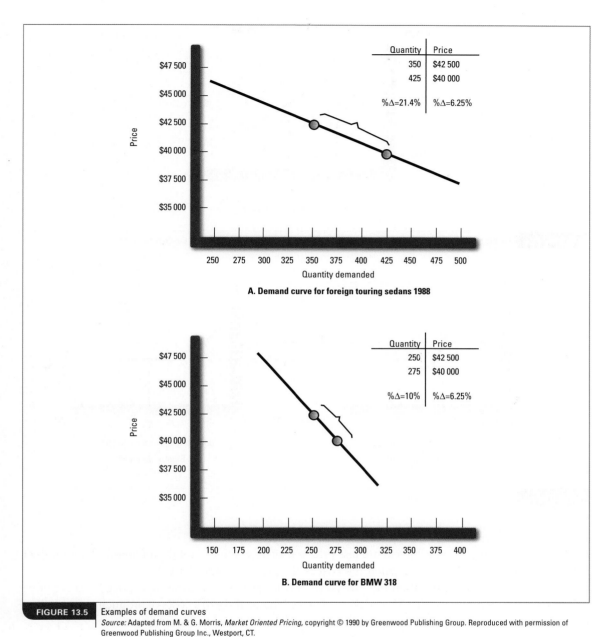

Quantity	Price
350	$42 500
425	$40 000
%Δ=21.4%	%Δ=6.25%

A. Demand curve for foreign touring sedans 1988

Quantity	Price
250	$42 500
275	$40 000
%Δ=10%	%Δ=6.25%

B. Demand curve for BMW 318

FIGURE 13.5   Examples of demand curves

Source: Adapted from M. & G. Morris, *Market Oriented Pricing,* copyright © 1990 by Greenwood Publishing Group. Reproduced with permission of Greenwood Publishing Group Inc., Westport, CT.

Suppose demand falls by 10% when a seller raises its price by 2%. Price elasticity of demand is therefore –5 (the negative sign confirms the inverse relation between price and demand) and demand is elastic. If demand falls by 2% with a 2% increase in price, then elasticity is –1. In this case, the seller's total revenue stays the same: the seller sells fewer items but at a higher price that preserves the same total revenue. If demand falls by 1% when price is increased by 2%, then elasticity is –0.5 and demand is inelastic. The less elastic the demand, the more it pays for the seller to raise the price.

What determines the price elasticity of demand? Buyers are less price sensitive when the product they are buying is unique or when it is high in quality, prestige or exclusiveness. They are also less price sensitive when substitute products are hard to find or when they cannot easily compare the

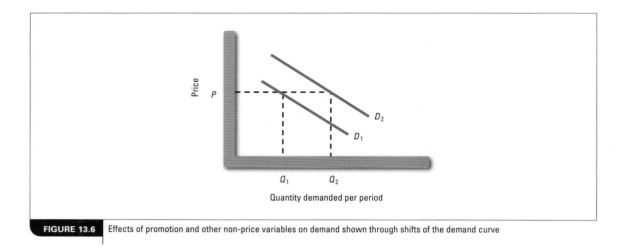

FIGURE 13.6 Effects of promotion and other non-price variables on demand shown through shifts of the demand curve

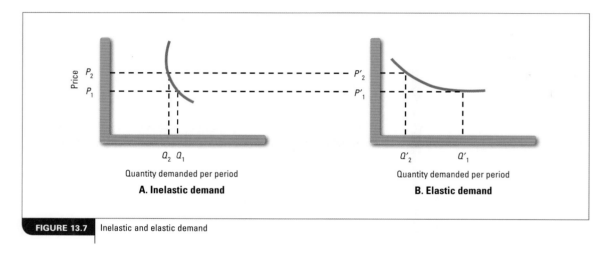

FIGURE 13.7 Inelastic and elastic demand

quality of substitutes. Finally, buyers are less price sensitive when the total expenditure for a product is low relative to their income or when the cost is shared by another party.[19]

If demand is elastic rather than inelastic, sellers will consider lowering their price. A lower price will produce more total revenue. This makes sense as long as the extra costs of producing and selling more do not exceed the extra revenue.

Competitors' prices and offers

Another external factor affecting the company's pricing decisions is competitors' prices and their possible reactions to the company's own pricing moves. A consumer considering buying a Nokia 6020 mobile phone through Virgin Mobile will evaluate Nokia's price and value against the prices and values of comparable products such as Sony Ericsson K500i, Panasonic VS2, Motorola V220 and Samsung D500. In addition, the company's pricing strategy may affect the nature of the competition it faces. If Nokia follows a high-price, high-margin strategy, it may attract competition. A low-price, low-margin strategy, however, may stop competitors or drive them out of the market.

The company needs to learn the price and quality of each competitor's offer. Nokia might do this in several ways. It can send out comparison shoppers to price and compare Sony Ericsson, Motorola and other competitors' products. It can get competitors' price lists and buy competitors' equipment and take it apart. It can ask buyers how they view the price and quality of each competitor's phones. It must also review the pricing strategies and tactics of its channel partners such as Virgin Mobile, Telstra and Optus.

Once Nokia is aware of competitors' prices and offers, it can use them as a starting point for its own pricing. If Nokia's phones are similar to Motorola's, the firm will not be able to charge as much. If Nokia's products are better than Motorola's, it can charge more. Basically, Nokia will use price to position its offer relative to competitors'.

Other external factors

When setting prices, the company must also consider other factors in its external environment. For example, *economic conditions* can have a strong impact on the outcomes of the company's pricing strategies. Economic factors such as inflation, boom or recession and interest rates affect pricing decisions because they affect both the costs of producing a product and consumer perceptions of the product's price and value.

The company must consider what impact its prices will have on other parties in its environment. How will *resellers* react to various prices? The company should set prices that give resellers a fair profit, encourage their support and help them to sell the product effectively. The *government* is another important external influence on pricing decisions. Marketers need to know the laws affecting price and make sure their pricing policies are legal. The Trade Practices Act prohibits price fixing, resale price maintenance and particular forms of price discrimination, as well as predatory pricing by monopolistically positioned competitors and deceptive pricing. The Australian Competition and Consumer Commission (ACCC) plays a major role in investigating possible breaches.[20] Hoechst, the pharmaceutical giant, was fined $US12 million for monochloroacetic acid price fixing in 2003.[21]

SELF-CHECK QUESTIONS

1   'Price is only one element of the marketing mix.' Discuss the implications of this statement.

2   'Too many companies set their prices based on internal factors.' Discuss this statement by reviewing the internal elements that affect pricing and assess their implications.

3   Companies such as Toyota use target costing as a method of formulating marketing strategy. Why is this used and what are the implications of this approach?

4   In considering the external factors affecting pricing decisions, discuss under what conditions external factors should dominate price setting. When should internal factors be the main drivers of price formulation?

5   In the car market, some segments are price inelastic, whereas other segments are highly elastic. Explain this with reference to examples in the car industry.

General pricing approaches

The price the company charges will be between one that is too low to produce a profit and one that is too high to produce any demand. Figure 13.8 (overleaf) summarises the major considerations in setting price. Product costs set a floor to the price; consumer perceptions of the product's value set the ceiling. The company must consider competitors' prices and other external and internal factors to find the best price between these two extremes.

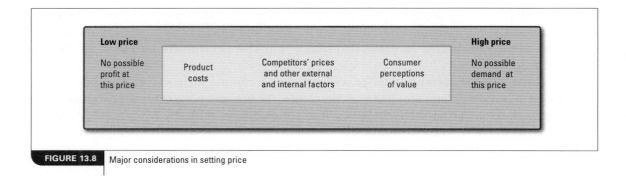

FIGURE 13.8 | Major considerations in setting price

Companies set prices by selecting a general pricing approach that includes one or more of these five sets of factors: the *cost-based approach* (cost-plus pricing, break-even analysis and target profit pricing), the *buyer-based approach* (perceived-value pricing), the *competition-based approach* (going-rate and sealed-bid pricing), *performance-based approach* (pricing tied to delivery performance) and the *relationship approach* (involving alliances).

Cost-based pricing

Cost-plus pricing

Cost-plus pricing
Adding a standard mark-up to the cost of the product.

The simplest pricing method is **cost-plus pricing**—adding a standard mark-up to the cost of the product. Construction companies, for example, submit job bids by estimating the total project cost and adding a standard mark-up for profit. Lawyers, accountants and other professionals typically price by adding a standard mark-up to their costs. Some sellers tell their customers that they will charge cost plus a specified mark-up; for example, components and parts suppliers price this way to car manufacturers.

To illustrate mark-up pricing, suppose a toaster manufacturer had the following costs and expected sales:

Variable cost per unit	$10
Fixed cost	$300 000
Expected unit sales	50 000

Then the manufacturer's cost per toaster is given by:

$$\text{Unit cost} = \text{variable cost} + \frac{\text{unit fixed costs}}{\text{unit sales}}$$

$$= \$10 + \frac{\$300\,000}{50\,000}$$

$$= \$16$$

Now suppose the manufacturer wants to earn a 20% mark-up on sales. The manufacturer's mark-up price is given by:

$$\text{Mark-up price} = \frac{\text{unit cost}}{(1 - \text{desired return on sales})} = \frac{\$16}{1 - 0.2} = \$20$$

The manufacturer would charge retailers $20 per toaster and make a profit of $4 per unit. The retailers in turn will mark up the toaster's price. If retailers want to earn 50% on the sales price they will mark up the toaster to $40 ($20 + 50% of $40). This number is equivalent to a *mark-up on cost* of 100% ($20/$20).

Mark-ups vary considerably between different goods. Mark-ups are smallest on staples such as bread and milk, which consumers can buy for almost the same price anywhere. They are high on products such as fresh chicken (around 50%), which is high in demand and has few substitutes as far as white meats go, and where a retailer's brand such as Coles' Farmland can command a premium. Mark-ups are generally higher on seasonal items and perishables (to cover the risk of not selling), specialty items, slower-moving items, items with high storage and handling costs and items with inelastic demand.

Does using standard mark-ups to set prices make logical sense? Generally, no. Any pricing method that ignores current demand and competition is not likely to lead to the best price. Suppose the toaster manufacturer charges $20 but only sells 30 000 toasters instead of 50 000. Then the unit cost is higher because the fixed costs are spread over fewer units, and the realised percentage mark-up on sales is lower. Mark-up pricing only works if that price actually brings in the expected level of sales.

Still, mark-up pricing remains popular for many reasons. First, sellers are more certain about costs than about demand. By tying the price to cost, sellers simplify pricing—they do not have to make frequent adjustments as demand changes. Second, when all firms in the industry use this pricing method, prices tend to be similar and price competition is thus minimised. Third, many people believe that cost-plus pricing is fairer to both buyers and sellers. Sellers earn a fair return on their investment but do not take advantage of buyers when buyers' demand becomes great.[22]

Break-even analysis and target profit pricing

Another cost-oriented pricing approach is **break-even pricing** or a variation called *target profit pricing*. The company tries to determine the price at which it will break even or make the target profit it is seeking. Target pricing is used by many Australian importers as a means of setting prices to yield a given profit on investment. This pricing method is also used by public utilities, which are constrained to make a fair return on their investment.

Target pricing uses the concept of a *break-even chart*. A break-even chart shows the total cost and total revenue expected at different sales volume levels. Figure 13.9 (overleaf) shows a break-even chart for the toaster manufacturer previously discussed. *Fixed costs* are $300 000 regardless of sales volume. *Variable costs* are added to fixed costs to form total costs, which rise with volume. The total revenue curve starts at zero and rises with each unit sold. The slope of the total revenue curve reflects the price of $20 per unit.

The total revenue and total cost curves cross at 30 000 units. This is the *break-even volume*. At $20, the company must sell at least 30 000 units to break even, that is, for total revenue to cover total cost. Break-even can be calculated using the following formula:

$$\text{Break-even volume} = \frac{\text{fixed cost}}{\text{unit sell price} - \text{unit variable cost}}$$

$$= \frac{\$300\,000}{\$20 - \$10} = 30\,000$$

If the company wants to make a target profit, it must sell more units at $20 each. Suppose the toaster manufacturer has invested $1 million in the business and wants to set a price that will earn a 20% return, or $200 000. It must sell at least 50 000 units at $20 each. If the company charges a higher price, it will not need to sell as many toasters to achieve its target return. But the market may not buy even this lower volume at the higher price. Much depends on the price elasticity and competitors' prices.

The manufacturer should consider different prices and estimate break-even volumes, probable demand and profits for each. This is shown in Table 13.1 (overleaf). The table shows that as price

Break-even pricing (target profit pricing)
Setting price to break even on the costs of making and marketing a product, or to make the desired profit.

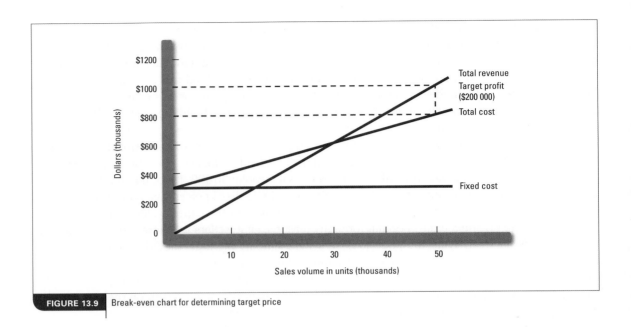

FIGURE 13.9   Break-even chart for determining target price

TABLE 13.1 Break-even volume and profits at different prices					
(1)	**(2)**	**(3)**	**(4)**	**(5)**	**(6)**
Price	Unit demand needed to break even	Expected unit demand at given price	Total revenues (1) × (3)	Total costs*	Profit (4) − (5)
$14	75 000	71 000	$ 994 000	$1 010 000	$ − 16 000
16	50 000	67 000	1 072 000	970 000	102 000
18	37 500	60 000	1 080 000	900 000	180 000
20	30 000	42 000	840 000	720 000	120 000
22	25 000	23 000	506 000	530 000	− 24 000

Note: *Assumes fixed costs of $300 000 and constant unit variable costs of $10.

increases, break-even volume drops (column 2). But as price increases, demand for the toasters also falls off (column 3). At the $14 price, because the manufacturer clears only $4 per toaster ($14 less $10 in variable costs), it must sell a very high volume to break even. Even though the low price attracts many buyers, demand still falls below the high break-even point, and the manufacturer loses money. At the other extreme, with a $22 price the manufacturer clears $12 per toaster and must sell only 25 000 units to break even. But at this high price, consumers buy too few toasters, and profits are negative. The table shows that a price of $18 yields the highest profits. Note that none of the prices produce the manufacturer's target profit of $200 000. To achieve this target return, the manufacturer will have to search for ways to lower fixed or variable costs, thus lowering the break-even.

It is important to consider this analysis within a competitive context. The impacts of cost on profit sensitivity are apparent when break-even analysis is conducted for two competitors.

The typical dominant competitor has a high-fixed-cost structure and high break-even volume. Its profit is directly affected by changes in volume and price—a fall in volume below the break-even point yields substantial losses because most of its costs (namely fixed costs) remain unchanged. In contrast, the typical challenger has a lower break-even volume and its profit is more directly affected by variable costs as well as price movements. A fall in volume below the break-even point yields only small losses. Of course, the opposite also applies. An increase in sales above the break-even point by the dominant competitor delivers large profits—and for the other competitor, much smaller profits.

The sensitivity of marketing mix changes to profits is illustrated in Figure 13.10.

An analysis of the numbers in Figure 13.10 would show the profit vulnerability of a dominant competitor to adverse changes in volume and price. For the non-dominant competitor vulnerability lies mainly in its variable-cost management. A review of break-even volumes of each competitor and the impact of price competition on each would indicate the vulnerability of the high-fixed-cost dominant firm. This analysis also reveals how important pricing is in its impact on the profit of each competitor. As a guideline, when considering the average income statement of an S&P 1500 company, a price rise of 1%—if volumes remain stable—would generate an 8% increase in operating profit. This impact is nearly 50% greater than a 1% fall in variable costs and more than three times greater than a 1% increase in volume.[23]

Value-based pricing

An increasing number of companies are basing their prices on the product's perceived value. **Value-based pricing** uses buyers' perceptions of value, not the seller's cost, as the key to pricing. The company uses the non-price variables in the marketing mix to build up perceived value in the buyers' minds. Price is set to match the perceived value.

Consider the various prices different restaurants charge for the same items. A consumer who wants a Japanese sushi may pay $5.50 at a supermarket, $7.00 at a food hall, $9.50 at a local restaurant, $15.00 at an upmarket Japanese restaurant and $22.00 at an international hotel. Each succeeding venue can charge more because of the value added by the atmosphere and service. Telstra has found that even with commodity-like call services such as STD and IDD, different market segments view price differently. Telstra achieved increased usage of its IDD call service between Australia and China by pricing at 88 cents per minute—the number 8 being perceived as a lucky number in Chinese culture.

Cost-based pricing is product driven. The company designs what it considers to be a good product, totals the costs of making the product and sets a price that covers costs plus a target profit. Marketing must then convince buyers that the product's value at that price justifies its purchase. If the price

Value-based pricing
Setting price based on buyers' perceptions of value rather than on the seller's cost.

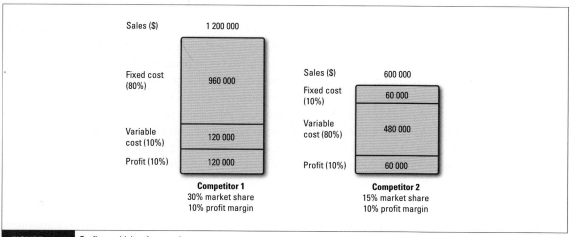

FIGURE 13.10 Profit sensitivity of competitors

turns out to be too high, the company must settle for lower mark-ups or lower sales, both resulting in disappointing profits.

Value-based pricing reverses this process. The company sets its target price based on customer perceptions of the product value. The targeted value and price then drive decisions about product design and what costs can be incurred. As a result, pricing begins with analysing consumer needs and value perceptions, and price is set to match consumers' perceived value. Marketing Highlight 13.1 compares the logics of cost-based and value-based pricing.

The company using value-based pricing must find out the value in the buyers' minds for different competitive offers. In the sushi example, consumers could be asked how much they would pay for the same sushi in the different surroundings. In the case of Telstra, customers do not know telephone service price levels and the differences with SingTel's Optus. Other key value indicators are used as benchmarks in their minds against which to compare prices—such as the per minute call rate between Sydney and Melbourne.

Sometimes consumers could be asked how much they would pay for each benefit added to the offer. If the seller charges more than the buyers' perceived value, the company's sales will suffer. Many companies overprice their products, and their products sell poorly. Other companies underprice. Underpriced products sell very well, but they produce less revenue than they could if prices were raised to the perceived-value level.[24] In the USA and Australia insurance providers such as IAG and ACE were underpricing medical professional liability products in previous years due to low claims arising from malpractice claims. However, in 2003 there was a large increase in claims leading to substantial price hikes to bring pricing to market reality levels.[25]

Marketing Highlight 13.2 illustrates how value is added to enable premium pricing to match customer-perceived value.

Competition-based pricing

Economic-value pricing

For many industrial products the costs perceived by customers extend well beyond the price charged. An industrial purchaser perceives the cost of equipment as including installation, maintenance, training and use of consumables, as well as the basic purchase price. Equipment purchases are evaluated over their economic lives and comparisons between competitors go beyond straight price assessment, as illustrated in Figure 13.11. Although the purchase price from supplier 2 (in Figure 13.11) is higher than that of supplier 1, total cost to the customer is lower and provides an economic advantage to the customer over its competitor's offer.

This same concept of economic value applies to products used in a customer's production process. For example, the packaging supplier Vacuum Seal offered packaging material that in one instance cost more than competing materials. Its packaging did, however, reduce its client's overall packaging costs, as Table 13.2 demonstrates. Although it offered materials at a 37% price premium, Vacuum Seal still saved those customers who used corrugated inserts some $1 per shipment.

Using its economic-value advantage, Vacuum Seal can develop a pricing strategy that positions its product against alternative packaging materials (see Figure 13.12 overleaf). This approach enables industrial firms to move away from price comparisons to differentiating their products on the basis of economic value to customers. The aircraft tyre manufacturer that prices its tyres to airline companies on the basis of cost per 100 landings, instead of cost per tyre, is adopting a similar approach.

Going-rate pricing

Going-rate pricing
Setting price based largely on following competitors' prices rather than on company costs or demand.

In **going-rate pricing** the company bases its price largely on competitors' prices, with less attention paid to its *own* costs or demand. The company might charge the same, more or less, than its major

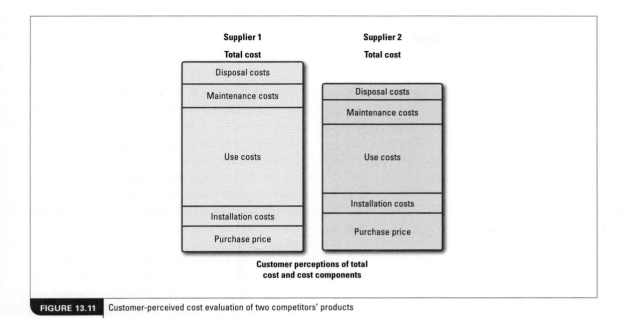

FIGURE 13.11 Customer-perceived cost evaluation of two competitors' products

TABLE 13.2 Vacuum Seal: economic value in packaging material

Value comparison

Cost component	Corrugated inserts	Vacuum seal
Carton	$0.60	$0.60
Packaging material	0.80	1.10
Labour	0.90	0.10
Freight	2.70	2.20
Total cost	$5.00	$4.00
Economic value		$1.00

competitors. In oligopolistic industries that sell a commodity such as steel, paper or fertiliser, companies normally charge the same price for the same grade or quality. The smaller firms follow the leader: they change their prices when the market leader's prices change, rather than when their own demand or cost changes. Some firms may charge a bit more or less, but they hold the amount of difference constant. Thus minor paper manufacturers usually charge a few cents less than the major manufacturers, without letting the difference increase or decrease.

Going-rate pricing is quite popular. When demand elasticity is hard to measure, companies feel that the going price represents the collective wisdom of the industry concerning the price that will yield a fair return. They also feel that holding to the going price will avoid harmful price wars.

Sealed-bid/tenders

Competition-based pricing is also used when companies *bid* for jobs. Using **sealed-bid pricing**, a company bases its price on how it thinks competitors will price rather than on its own costs or demand. The company wants to win a contract, and winning the contract requires pricing lower than other companies.

Sealed-bid pricing
Setting price based on how the firm thinks competitors will price rather than on its own costs or demand— used when a company bids for jobs.

The logics of pricing

There is a world of difference between cost-based pricing logic and customer-perceived value pricing. The cost model shown in Figure 1 is typical of many industrial marketing businesses. The product designers total up the cost of the features they want on a product, work out which supplier provides each part at what price and add a margin of 50%, which then represents the price to channel intermediaries. This price is marked up by another 25% to establish the price to end-buyers.

Customer-value pricing starts in a different place as shown in Figure 2. Managers must decide what they want the end-price to be, given the target market's perception of value for competing alternatives.

This end-price will be set within a value band that represents the market's perception of the additional net value (taking account of benefits and price) offered by the product. Then a dealer mark-up is deducted, and also a gross margin for the manufacturer. The manager then instructs departments of materials procurement, engineering, manufacturing, logistics and marketing to resolve among themselves how to allocate the remaining costs to make the product.

This process of value pricing was understood by Pfizer when it introduced its erectile dysfunction medication Viagra, which was selling for $80 per tablet, four times as much as a treatment from its competitor, Pharmacia. Conventional wisdom was

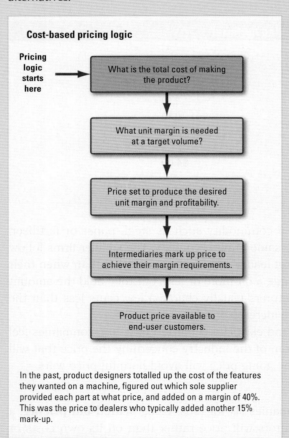

Cost-based pricing logic

Pricing logic starts here →

What is the total cost of making the product?

↓

What unit margin is needed at a target volume?

↓

Price set to produce the desired unit margin and profitability.

↓

Intermediaries mark up price to achieve their margin requirements.

↓

Product price available to end-user customers.

In the past, product designers totalled up the cost of the features they wanted on a machine, figured out which sole supplier provided each part at what price, and added on a margin of 40%. This was the price to dealers who typically added another 15% mark-up.

| FIGURE 1 | Cost-based pricing |

Value pricing logic

Cost targets are set to meet profit objectives.

↑

Target margin is set based on profit goals.

↑

Net price, after distribution costs, is determined.

↑

Price discounted to intermediaries to achieve margin requirements.

↑

Pricing logic starts here →

Price set relative to customer needs, competition, product position and customer value.

Now the process is reversed. Managers must decide what they want the end price to be, based on competitive factors. Then they assume a dealer mark-up, subtract a gross profit margin—about 30% today—and instruct departments of materials, engineering and marketing to resolve among themselves how to allocate the remaining costs to make the product.

| FIGURE 2 | Value pricing |

that the second one in, Pfizer, should price 10% below. But Viagra had substantially greater perceived benefits because of fewer side effects, ease of use and greater dosage convenience. It was introduced at a price premium over Pharmacia's product and still gained undisputed market leadership.

Similarly, Giorgio Armani can charge 10 times more for its business suit than Pierre Cardin because of the perceived benefits that customers associate with wearing it and being seen in it. ANA hotel charges three times the price you would expect to pay for a drink, but the ambience, the fortieth-floor view of Sydney and courteous service make patrons perceive this as good value.

Customer-value-based pricing reduces the risk of underpricing in relation to customers' perception of value. It also lowers the risk of overpricing, which would result in lower than desired sales.

Source: Robert Dolan and Herman Simon, *Power Pricing: How Managing Price Transforms the Bottom Line*, New York, The Free Press, 1996, pp. 7–14. See also M. Morris and G. Morris, *Market Oriented Pricing: Strategies for Management*, Westport, CT, Quorum Books, an imprint of Greenwood Publishing Group, Inc., 1990.

Questions

1 Compare the cost-based and value-based pricing logics.

2 What are the advantages of a cost-based pricing approach?

3 What are the advantages of adopting a value-based pricing approach?

13.1

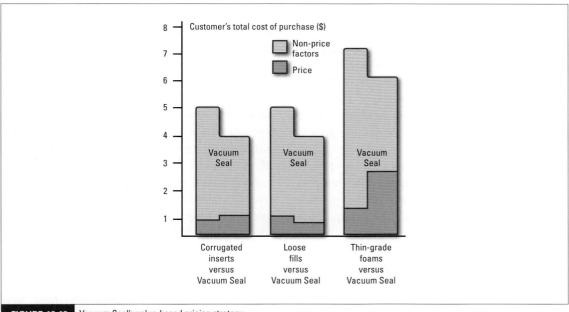

FIGURE 13.12 Vacuum Seal's value-based pricing strategy

Yet the company cannot set its price below a certain level. It cannot price below cost without harming its position. On the other hand, the higher it sets its price above its costs, the lower its chance of getting the contract.

The net effect of the two opposite pulls can be described in terms of the *expected profit* of the particular bid (see Table 13.3 overleaf). Suppose a bid of $9500 would yield a high chance (say 0.81) of getting the contract, but only a low profit (say $100). The expected profit with this bid is therefore

MARKETING HIGHLIGHT

13.2

Innovator faces stormy future

Stormy is braced for all competitive conditions!

One of Australia's favourite sports is fishing—particularly on dangerous rock shelves. It is not unusual to see hardened fishermen and women in small boats, on bridges, rock ledges and Australia's beaches and lakes trying to catch fish. But fishing brings with it a large number of drownings each year. Why? Because people do not wear a life jacket when fishing. Add to this boating accidents through lack of knowledge and experience and the number of drownings escalates.

Stormy Australia was established in Hobart, Tasmania, in 1993 as a simple import/retail business. The company has evolved and all its products are now manufactured and tested in its purpose-built factory and National Association of Testing Authorities (NATA) accredited laboratory. Stormy Australia is a unique business built around the compelling mission of saving lives at sea. It designs, manufactures and distributes a range of inflatable clothing which have rugged wind and waterproof outer shells with integrated inflation systems that can be inflated instantly in an emergency via CO_2 cylinder or orally. On inflation, the comfortable attractive outer-wear is instantly transformed into a personal flotation device (PFD).

The Stormy slogan 'worn not stowed' was developed because of the loss of life due to people not wearing a life jacket—it was typically left in the locker. Its new slogan and strapline launched in 2005 is 'Not without my Stormy'. Stormy's comfortable and attractive PFD is designed for people to wear the product as a well-fitted jacket. Both professionals and amateurs wear Stormy products whether fishing from an ocean-going vessel, 'tin dishes' or the rocks. The list of Stormy's Australian and international customers includes:

- Professional and recreational fishermen
- Racing and cruising sailors
- Sea pilots
- Marine safety and rescue authorities
- Ferry operators
- Enforcement agencies including Water Police and Fisheries officers
- Jet boat and water ski racers
- Maritime colleges and schools
- Australian Antarctic Division.

Its products include inflatable PFDs and wind-proof, water-resistant jackets and vests, wet-weather pants and boat shorts. It also has an Australian-standards-approved testing facility where it safety tests products of other suppliers as well as its own. Stormy distributes its products through local sales offices in Victoria and NSW and is moving into South Australia. It also has direct 'custom' business from Australian and overseas companies requiring specialised designs for specific needs. Since 1999 its sales have doubled each year to 2002 with growth around 20% occurring in 2005. But it does have Australian-based competition from the traditional life jacket manufacturers—Safety Marine and RFD. It also faces more direct competition from New Zealand company Hutchwilco and Canadian firm Mustang Survival.

In mid-2005 a new competitive threat emerged for Stormy. A large credible Australian importer had taken Stormy's design to China and arranged offshore production of similar jackets and apparel at a much lower cost. These were introduced to the Australian market in late 2005 at prices substantially below Stormy's traditional wholesale and retail price structure. Therefore, Stormy was faced with a number of pricing options:

- Match the importer's prices with a significant negative consequences for profit.
- Price below the importer with an objective of driving it out of the market.
- Reduce prices to just above the importer's, holding a small price premium.
- Leave prices unchanged and risk substantial reductions in volume.

Sources: Interview with John Nanscawen, Sales Manager, Stormy Australia, 10 November 2005; Stormy Australia: <www.stormyaustralia.com>.

Questions

1 What challenges face an innovator like Stormy Australia when pricing its new products?

2 What should Stormy's main marketing objective be in the light of its new competition?

3 What pricing strategy should it implement to achieve its objective?

13.2

TABLE 13.3 Effect of different bids on expected profit

Company's bid	(1) Company's profit	(2) Probability of winning with this bid (assumed)	Expected profit (1) × (2)
$ 9 500	$ 100	0.81	$ 81
10 000	600	0.36	216
10 500	1 100	0.09	99
11 000	1 600	0.01	16

$81. If the firm bid $11 000, its profit would be $1600, but its chance of getting the contract might be reduced to 0.01. The expected profit would be only $16. Thus, the company might bid the price that would maximise the expected profit. According to Table 13.3, the best bid would be $10 000, for which the expected profit is $216.

Using expected profit as a basis for setting price makes sense for the large company that makes many bids. By playing the odds, the company will make maximum profits in the long run. But a company that bids only occasionally or needs a particular contract badly will not find the expected profit approach useful. The approach, for example, does not distinguish between a $100 000 profit with a 0.10 probability and a $12 500 profit with an 0.80 probability. Yet the company that wants to keep production going would prefer the second contract to the first.

Performance-based pricing

This pricing approach is an arrangement in which the seller is paid on the basis of actual performance of its offer. This trend is occurring in some of the service industries like professional services (legal), transport and contract construction. This can act as protection for both the seller and the buyer. If the seller provides the full contracted service, they are entitled to full payment. The buyer is also protected by the fact that they will not be paying for aspects of the service which may be promised but are not delivered. Another big advantage of performance-based pricing is that it forces the parties to discuss their objectives, limitations and issues and to expose the uncertainties and assumptions underlying a proposed contract. This enhances communication and often leads to the next type of pricing discussed—relationship pricing.

Relationship pricing

Relationship marketing is a major trend that is discussed in other chapters. The implementation of relationship strategies requires a particular approach to pricing which incorporates shared risk and reward. Priess, Goldman and Nagel propose a three-level model which captures different degrees of a supplier–customer relationship with different risk and reward pricing elements.[26] This is shown as Figure 13.13.

1. Special relationship

At this level, supplier and customer share a special relationship. There is no significant change in the flow of money between organisations, but they work together to reduce time and costs while increasing quality. This is a stretching of single arm's length transactions into a close relationship over time. For example, Orica's Chloralkali Division constantly meets customers to explore ways of enhancing value to both businesses. This is done by joint design projects and agreed 'just-in-time' deliveries with prices based on large volumes, while allowing for variation in the specifics of orders.

2. Enrichment

At the enrichment level, deeper relationships are formed that take advantage of interactivity. For example, BHP Billiton will help its customers to find a saving of $5 million through an innovative engineering solution which reduces a customer's production costs. The system will be installed for the customer without a fee in exchange for 50% of their savings in the first year.

This pricing strategy is particularly effective when customers are afraid of innovative new approaches which appear risky and are not yet proven.

3. Shared risk and reward

This relationship level ties the supplier and customer closely together in an alliance, or even joint venture, in which both the risks and rewards are shared. BHP Billiton Petroleum has a number of alliance partner customers where the cost risks and benefits of oil exploration and processing are shared with their downstream customers. These alliances, discussed in some detail in Chapter 20, require pricing strategies which enable partners to take advantage of time-based opportunities and share the risks and rewards that go with them. A high order of trust, shared ethics and corporate values are required for success.[27]

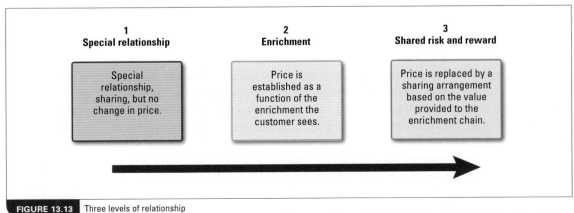

FIGURE 13.13 Three levels of relationship

Source: Adapted from K. Priess, S. L. Goldman and R. N. Nagel, *Co-operate to Compete*, New York, Van Nostrand Reinhold, 1996, p. 145. This material is used by permission of John Wiley & Sons, Inc.

New-product pricing strategies

Pricing strategies usually change as the product passes through its life cycle. This is because the constraints on the company's freedom to price a product differ in each stage. The introductory stage is especially challenging. In this section we consider the strategies applicable in the introductory stage in the life cycle. It is important to note that these strategies are available only to products that are truly innovative. These products must be distinguished from products that are simply new versions, or forms, of existing products. We can distinguish between pricing a real product innovation that is patent protected and pricing a product that imitates existing products.

Pricing an innovative product

Companies bringing out an innovative, patent-protected product tend to adopt either *market-skimming pricing* or *market-penetration pricing* strategies.

Market-skimming pricing

Many companies that invent new products set high prices initially to 'skim' revenues layer by layer from the market. Sony is a prime user of **market-skimming pricing**. On its original Walkmans it charged the highest price it could, given the benefits of its new product over other products customers might buy. Sony set a price that made it just worthwhile for some segments of the market to adopt the new product. After the initial sales, it lowered the price to draw in the next price-sensitive layer of customers. Sony used the same approach with its digital camera. It introduced it at a very high price, $1500. After about a year, it began bringing out lower-priced versions to draw in new segments. In this way, Sony skimmed a maximum amount of revenue from the various segments of the market.[28]

> **Market-skimming pricing** Setting a high price for a new product to skim maximum revenue from the segments willing to pay the high price; the company makes fewer but more profitable sales.

Similarily, Yakult, a fermented milk drink, contains a very high concentration of a unique, beneficial bacterium called *Lactobacillus casei* Shirota strain. This is exclusive to Yakult and the company was able to skim the price since there were no competitors directly challenging the product. Yakult has, however, been directly challenged by the introduction of Farmland's Pro-B drink which is sold in fivepacks of small, foil-topped bottles with red and white packaging similar to that of Yakult.

Market skimming can be effective only under certain conditions. First, the product's quality and image must be consistent with a high price. Second, there must be enough buyers to purchase the product at that price and the costs

Yakult commands a premium price for its differentiated product.

of producing a small volume must not be so high that there is an inadequate margin. This strategy assumes that there are different price-market segments, thereby appealing to those buyers who have a higher range of acceptable prices. For these customers, demand is assumed to be inelastic. A market-skimming strategy is also appropriate when the firm has a new product that is patent protected, like many new ethical drugs, or contains design benefits that are not easily emulated by competitors.

Market-penetration pricing

Rather than setting a high initial price to *skim* small but profitable market segments, other companies set a low initial price in order to *penetrate* the market quickly and deeply—to attract a large number of buyers quickly. Microsoft uses **market-penetration pricing**. With the global introductions of iPod Shuffle and iPod Nano, Apple set its prices as low as possible to win a large market share for these new releases.[29] Once it realised falling costs it could then cut its costs even further. Netscape, now part of Times Warner AOL, first introduced its Netscape browser as a beta version for free. Once it captured 80% of the market it introduced better versions for a low price to retain its customer base. Warehouse stores and discount retailers also use penetration pricing. They charge low prices to attract high volume; the high volume results in lower costs which, in turn, let the discounter keep prices low. Many Internet-based competitors—like Oxycom.com, which sells a wide range of consumer products in the Australian market and worldwide—adopt the price-penetration model.[30]

Several conditions favour setting a low price. The market must be sensitive to different price levels so that a low price produces more rapid market trial and more market growth. Production and distribution costs must fall as sales volume increases. This strategy enables the firm to achieve a market leadership position, assuming that competitors are likely to enter the market quickly. The low price may also help to keep out or delay the competition.

Pricing an imitative new product

A company that plans to develop an imitative new product faces a product-positioning problem. It must decide where to position the product on quality and price. Figure 13.14 shows nine possible price/quality strategies. If the existing market leader has taken Box 1 by producing the premium product and charging the highest price, then the newcomer might prefer to use one of the other strategies. It could design a high-quality product and charge a medium price (Box 2), design a

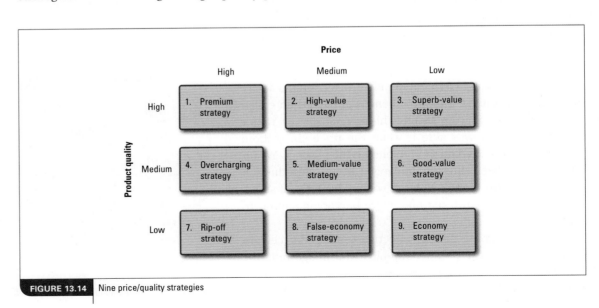

FIGURE 13.14 | Nine price/quality strategies

medium-quality product and charge a medium price (Box 5), and so on. The newcomer must consider the size and growth rate of the market in each box and the competitors it would face.

Product mix and service mix pricing strategies

The strategy for setting a price on an offer often has to be changed when the product or service is part of a mix. In this case, the firm looks for a set of prices that maximises the profits on the total product/service mix. Pricing is difficult because the various products or services have related demand and costs, and face different degrees of competition. We now take a closer look at five *product mix and service mix pricing* situations, summarised in Table 13.4.

Product/service-line pricing

Companies usually develop product lines rather than single products. For example, Fujitsu General Australia makes many different air conditioners, ranging from standard versions priced from $999 to $1199 to elaborate and stylish models that circulate the air more efficiently, have anti-allergy filters and are super-quiet, costing $2700. Each successive air conditioner in the line offers more features. In **product-line pricing**, management must determine what price steps to set between the various models of air conditioner.

The price steps should take into account cost differences between the air conditioners, customer evaluations of their different features and competitors' prices. If the price difference between two successive air conditioners is small, buyers will frequently buy the more advanced model, which increases company profits if the cost difference is smaller than the price difference. If the price difference is large, customers will generally buy the less advanced model.

Optional product/service pricing

Many companies use **optional product/service pricing**—offering to sell optional or accessory products or services along with their main product. This is used as a way of allowing some customers to personalise their vehicles while keeping the base vehicle pricing accessible for other customers. Ever-changing technological and styling enhancements can be incorporated into each customer's purchase, depending on their individual preferences. A car buyer can order electric windows, alloy wheels, spoilers and weather shields. Pricing these options is a sticky problem. Car companies must decide which items to build into the base price and which to offer as options. Each vehicle range's entry-level offering comes with a varying range of accompaniments—depending on range, price point and accepted community standards at the time. For example, the majority of cars now include air conditioning whereas 10 years ago this was not the case. Typical of most manufacturers, Ford's normal pricing strategy is to advertise its basic Ford Focus model for $20 990 in order to pull people into showrooms, and then devote most of the showroom space to option-loaded cars. For instance,

Product-line pricing
Setting the price steps between various products in a product line based on cost differences between the products, customer evaluations of different features and competitors' prices.

Optional product/service pricing The pricing of optional or accessory products along with a main product.

TABLE 13.4 Product/service mix pricing strategies	
Strategy	**Description**
Product/service line pricing	Setting price steps between product and service line items.
Optional product/service pricing	Pricing optional or accessory products and services sold with the main product or service.
Captive product/service pricing	Pricing products and services that must be used with the main product or service.
By-product pricing	Pricing low-value by-products or services to get rid of them.
Product/service-bundle pricing	Pricing bundles of products or services sold together.

a Focus Zetec model with slimline weather shields, alloy wheels, bonnet protector, rear spoiler, boot liner and central locking comes to $27 490. If you want all the accessories available the price is $30 990 for the Focus Ghia (<www.ford.com.au>—accessed 10 November 2005, configure your Ford). However, customers do have the choice to include accessories in their purchase or not. They also have the choice to include them at a later stage which takes customers back into dealerships thereby enabling dealers to develop longer term relationships with customers. Rental car companies like Hertz and Avis also provide options such as car telephones and GPS positioning systems to customers who value these extra services.

Captive product/service pricing

Captive product pricing
The pricing of products that must be used along with a main product, such as blades for a razor and film for cameras.

Companies that make products that must be used along with a main product use **captive product pricing**. Examples of captive products are inkjet printers and lifts. Producers of inkjets often price them low and set high mark-ups on the consumables. Companies that produce lifts and other 'people moving' equipment price their products at or below cost. They make profit on the servicing of the equipment because no other company is permitted to conduct the servicing. Insect-repelling appliances that are connected to an electricity outlet and use a repelling pellet are also priced so that no profit is made on the initial sale. The profit comes from the future sale of the pellets, which carry a very high mark-up. The same principle applies to Nintendo and Sega computer games—the equipment is relatively inexpensive and the companies make their profit on the software.

Two-part pricing
A strategy for pricing services in which price is broken into a fixed fee plus a variable usage rate.

In the case of services, this strategy is called **two-part pricing**. The price of the service is broken into a *fixed fee plus variable usage rate*. Hotels that may be competitively priced for accommodation seek to make their profit on food and beverages and the mini bar. Casinos in Australia that put on subsidised entertainment and food, and often provide free drinks, make a profit on the poker machine 'sales' at the end. Hotels like Conrad Jupiter, which has a casino that provides free service for the high-flying gambler, expect profit from the expected losses at the gaming table. The service firm must decide how much to charge for the basic service and how much for the variable usage. The fixed amount should be low enough to induce usage of the service. Profit can be made on the variable usage fees.

By-product pricing

In the production of processed meats, petroleum products, chemicals and other products, there are often by-products. If the by-products have no value and getting rid of them is costly, this will affect the pricing of the main product. Abattoirs selling offal and unwanted protein to pet food manufacturers ensure that the costs they recover reduce the costs and the final price of meat eaten by humans. Feathers and tallow are two by-products of chicken processing that are used in feed production, thereby reducing the cost of animal protein to you and me. Using **by-product pricing**, the manufacturer will seek a market for these by-products and should accept any price that covers more than the cost of storing and delivering them. This practice allows the seller to reduce the main product's price to make it more competitive.

By-product pricing
Setting a price for by-products in order to make the main product's price more competitive.

In the removals industry, used boxes and materials available after the completion of a furniture removal service are sold as a by-product. In the food industry, Blue Banner Pickles, a Tasmanian manufacturer of pickled onions, sells its by-product onion peelings to Lactos which reprocesses them into its popular 'pickled onion cheese'.

Product/service-bundle pricing

Product-bundle pricing
Combining several products and offering the bundle at a reduced price.

Using **product-bundle pricing**, sellers combine several of their products and offer the bundle at a reduced price. Thus, theatres and sports teams sell season tickets at less than the cost of single tickets and car companies sell attractively priced options packages. Airlines provide various packages which include rental car and accommodation for both business and leisure travellers. Price bundling can promote the sale of products consumers might not otherwise buy, but the combined price must be low enough to get them to buy the bundle.[31]

SELF-CHECK QUESTIONS

8 Foxtel has introduced a new self-select (on demand) movie service accessible through its satellite service. Should it adopt a market-skimming or market-penetration pricing strategy? Evaluate the pros and cons of each option.

9 Give examples of companies marketing on the Internet using penetration pricing strategies. Are they succeeding?

10 Country Link rail service has a number of service mix options for travellers. Give examples of these options.

Price-adjustment strategies

Companies usually adjust their basic prices to account for various customer differences and changing situations. Marketing Highlight 13.3 illustrates how this is managed in the removals industry.

Table 13.5 summarises seven price-adjustment strategies: *discount pricing and allowances, segmented pricing, psychological pricing, promotional pricing, value pricing, geographical pricing* and *international pricing*.

Discount pricing and allowances

Most companies adjust their basic price to reward customers for certain responses, such as early payment of bills, volume purchases and buying off-season. These price adjustments are called *discounts and allowances*.

Cash discounts

A **cash discount** is a price reduction to buyers who pay their bills promptly. A typical example is '2/10, net 30', which means that, although payment is due within 30 days, the buyer can deduct 2%

Cash discount A price reduction to buyers who pay their bills promptly.

TABLE 13.5 Product and service adjustment strategies	
Strategy	**Description**
Discount pricing and allowances	Reducing prices to reward customer responses such as paying early or promoting the product or service.
Segmented pricing	Adjusting prices to allow for differences in customers, services, products or locations.
Psychological pricing	Adjusting prices for psychological effect.
Promotional pricing	Temporarily reducing prices to increase short-run sales.
Value pricing	Adjusting prices to offer the right combination of quality and service at a fair price.
Geographical pricing	Adjusting prices to account for the geographic location of customers.
International pricing	Adjusting prices for international markets.

MARKETING HIGHLIGHT

13.3

Moving house?

Most of us move house several times during our years with our family, as a student and in different jobs in the workforce. If we have accumulated some furniture and household appliances we will probably have the need for a furniture removals service. Some of us, particularly as students, opt to hire a truck and make the move ourselves—with a little help from our friends. But if the move is overseas for an extended period it is likely that the services of an international moving company will be needed. One of the challenges faced by moving companies is how to price their services.

A complex network of removals companies, local and interstate carriers, specialist storage depots and international shipping companies and airlines operate to move items from origin to destination. Throughout Australia there are several hundred companies that coordinate the movement of furniture and household goods. The international removals sector has additional dimensions such as shipping documentation, containerisation for international movements, bond facilities and customs procedures in Australia and other countries. These different

requirements have led the national removalists to establish separate international divisions to deal specifically with overseas removals. Also a number of companies have set up specifically to service this sector of the market.

The product offering of the international removalist includes the removal of furniture, household items, baggage and personal effects from a dwelling in one country to a location in another. This encompasses removal of items from Australia to another country, referred to as exports, or from an overseas country to Australia, denoted as imports. Modes of transportation to and from Australia are shipping and air transport. The services provided in this overall offering are listed below.

- *Export from Australia.* Components include pickup, packing, transportation, storage, shipping, insurance, documentation, clearance at destination port by overseas agent, delivery to home, unpacking and removal of empty boxes and rubbish.
- *Import to Australia.* Components include pickup, packing and transportation to Australia, clear-

OSS offers a complete international moving service.

ance through customs, storage, delivery to the home in Australia, unpacking and removal of empty boxes and rubbish.

A number of separate service packages can be provided, such as:

- Storage, awaiting shipment or delivery
- Consignment to destination port for client-organised clearance (export)
- Completion of documentation for client
- Organised clearance in Australia (import)
- Consignment door to door involving the full range of removalist services.

International removalists usually have a complex pricing formula which adds all the components of the offer to take account of storage, packing, shipping, insurance and documentation to arrive at a total price. They price for a total bundled 'end-to-end' service with a final price that incorporates all the elements. However, not all market segments want this complete service. OSS World Wide Movers, with bases in Sydney, Melbourne, Brisbane and Perth, recognised that some customers want to do some of the move themselves and devised a simple pricing approach based on cost per cubic metre and provided a measurement tool to enable customers to measure their cubic volume and price the consignment themselves.

This 'do-it-yourself' concept allowed the customer to pack their own consignment, deliver it to the OSS depot and organise clearance in the destination country—saving a substantial amount on the move. In this way OSS unbundled the offer and provided several offer/price packages depending upon the level of involvement required by the customer and the speed with which they wanted it delivered to their destination. Pricing was personalised for each job and the customised approach differentiated OSS from its competitors. A key point of differentiation here for OSS is pricing flexibility—not based on competitive pricing, but on different customised value packages to the customer. OSS has a business model which enables it to be flexible with its pricing and use many of the price-adjustment strategies discussed in this section.

Sources: Linden Brown, co-founder of OSS with Richard Overton. Detailed information on the international moving industry and the OSS World Wide Movers strategy is found in Linden Brown, *Competitive Marketing Strategy*, 2nd edn, Melbourne, Nelson ITP, 1997, pp. 328–347.

Questions

1. What are the main internal factors international removalists need to consider in their pricing?

2. What types of price-adjustment strategies are possible in the international removals industry?

3. How can OSS add more value for consumers and avoid price wars that are common in this market?

13.3

if the bill is paid within 10 days. The discount cannot be reserved for favoured customers; it must be granted to all buyers meeting these terms. Such discounts are customary in many industries; they help improve the seller's cash flow, reduce bad debts and lower credit-collection costs.

Quantity discounts

A **quantity discount** is a price reduction to buyers who buy large volumes. A typical example might be '$10 per unit for less than 100 units, $9 per unit for 100 or more units'. Like cash discounts, quantity discounts must be offered to all customers and they must not exceed the seller's cost savings associated with selling large quantities. Such quantity discounts go by many names. The software company talks of licences for multiple users, which have price discounts attached to the various 'packs' or numbers of users to be catered for. These savings include lower selling, inventory and transportation expenses. Discounts provide an incentive to the customer to buy more from a given seller rather than buying from many sources.

Quantity discount
A price reduction to buyers who buy large volumes.

Functional discounts

Functional discount (or trade discount)
A price reduction offered by the seller to trade channel members who perform certain functions, such as selling, storing and record keeping.

A **functional discount** (also called a *trade discount*) is offered by the seller to trade channel members—retailers and wholesalers—who perform certain functions such as selling, storing and record keeping. Manufacturers may offer different functional discounts to different trade channels because of the varying services they perform, but manufacturers must offer the same functional discounts within each trade channel.

Seasonal discounts

Seasonal discount
A price reduction to buyers who buy merchandise or services out of season.

A **seasonal discount** is a price reduction to buyers who buy merchandise or services out of season. Seasonal discounts allow the seller to keep production steady during an entire year. Ski manufacturers offer seasonal discounts to retailers in the spring and summer to encourage early ordering. Hotels, movie theatres and airlines offer seasonal discounts in their slow periods.

Allowances

Allowance
Promotional money paid by manufacturers to retailers in return for an agreement to feature the manufacturer's products in some way.

Allowances are other types of reductions from the list price. For example, **trade-in allowances** are price reductions given for turning in an old item when buying a new one. Trade-in allowances are most common in the car industry but are also given for some other durable goods. **Promotional allowances** are payments or price reductions to reward dealers for participating in advertising and sales support programs.

Trade-in allowance
A price reduction given for turning in an old item when buying a new one.

Promotional allowance
A payment or price reduction to reward dealers for participating in advertising and sales support programs.

Segmented pricing
Selling a product or service at two or more prices, where the difference in prices is not based on differences in costs.

Segmented pricing

Companies often adjust their basic prices to allow for differences in customers, products and locations. In **segmented pricing**, the company sells a product or service at two or more prices, even though the difference in prices is not based on differences in costs. Segmented pricing takes several forms:

- ◉ *Customer segment* pricing—different customers pay different prices for the same product or service. Museums, for example, often charge a lower admission for students and senior citizens.
- ◉ *Product-form* pricing—different versions of the product are priced differently but not according to differences in their costs. Panasonic prices its most expensive DVD recorder with 400GB hard drive at $3299, which is $2300 more than its next most expensive DVD with 200GB hard drive. The top model has many extra features yet these do not cost as much as the price difference.
- ◉ *Location* pricing—different locations are priced differently even though the cost of offering each location is the same. For instance, a theatre varies its seat prices because of audience preferences for certain locations. Airlines charge different prices for first class, business and economy seats.
- ◉ *Time* pricing—prices are varied seasonally, by the month, by the day and even by the hour. Public utilities vary their prices to commercial users by time of day and weekend versus weekday. Telstra, Optus and Telecom NZ offer lower 'off-peak' charges, and resorts give seasonal discounts.

For segmented pricing to be an effective strategy for the company, certain conditions must exist. The market must be segmentable and the segments must show different degrees of demand. Members of the segment paying the lower price should not be able to turn around and resell the product to the segment paying the higher price. Competitors should not be able to undersell the firm in the segment being charged the higher price. Nor should the costs of segmenting and matching the market exceed the extra revenue obtained from the price difference. The practice should not lead to customer resentment and ill will. Finally, the differentiated pricing must be legal.

With the deregulation of certain industries, such as airlines and telecommunications, companies in these industries have used more segmented pricing. Consider the pricing used by airlines. The passengers on a plane bound from Sydney to Auckland may pay as many as 10 different round-trip fares for the same flight—first class, business class, full economy, child, standby, SuperSaver or one of several discount fares that carry various restrictions. These return fares range from $388 to $1934! Travellers who check carefully benefit from the competition between different carriers flying this route and different fare options.

Psychological pricing

Price indicates something about the product. For example, many consumers use price to judge quality. A $100 bottle of perfume may contain only $3 worth of scent, but some people are willing to pay $100 because this price indicates something special.

In using **psychological pricing**, sellers consider the psychology of prices and not simply the economics. For example, one study of the relationship between price and quality perceptions of cars found that consumers perceive higher-priced cars as having higher quality.[32] By the same token, higher-quality cars are perceived to be even higher priced than they actually are! When consumers can judge the quality of a product by examining it or by calling on past experience with it, they use price less to judge quality. But when consumers cannot judge quality because they lack the information or skill, price becomes an important quality signal.[33]

Another aspect of psychological pricing is **reference prices**. These are prices that buyers carry in their minds and refer to when they look at a given product. The reference price might be formed by noting current prices, remembering past prices or assessing the buying situation. Sellers can influence or use these consumers' reference prices when setting price. For example, a company could display its product next to more expensive ones in order to imply that it belongs in the same class. Department stores often sell women's clothing in separate departments differentiated by price: clothing found in the more expensive department is assumed to be of better quality. David Jones Sydney city store reserves its top floor for its most expensive designer labels of women's clothing. Companies can also influence consumers' reference prices by stating high manufacturer's suggested prices, or by indicating that the product was originally priced much higher, or by pointing to a competitor's higher price.

Even small differences in price can suggest product differences. Consider a DVD recorder priced at $400 compared with one priced at $399. The actual price difference is only one dollar, but the psychological difference can be much greater. For example, some consumers will see the $399 as a price in the $300 range rather than the $400 range. Although the $399 will more likely be seen as a bargain price, the $400 price suggests more quality. Some psychologists argue that each digit has symbolic and visual qualities that should be considered in pricing. Thus, 8 is round and even and creates a soothing effect, and 7 is angular and creates a jarring effect.

Promotional pricing

With **promotional pricing**, companies temporarily price their products below list price, and sometimes even below cost. Promotional pricing takes several forms. Supermarkets and department stores often price a few products as *loss leaders* to attract customers to the store in the hope that they will buy other items at normal mark-ups, and to reward existing customers for their loyalty. Sellers also use *special event pricing* in certain seasons to draw more customers. Thus, linens are promotionally priced every January to attract weary Christmas shoppers back into stores.

Manufacturers sometimes offer *cash rebates* to consumers who buy the product from dealers within a specified time, as Microsoft did with Access, and car makers such as Holden and Ford have often done. The manufacturer sends the rebate directly to the customer. Rebates have recently been popular with cars, durable goods and small-appliance producers. Some manufacturers offer *low-interest financing*, *longer warranties* or *free maintenance* to reduce the consumer's 'price'. This practice

Psychological pricing A pricing approach that considers the psychology of prices and not simply the economics—the price is used to say something about the product.

Reference prices Prices that buyers carry in their minds and refer to when they look at a given product.

Promotional pricing Temporarily pricing products below the list price, and sometimes even below cost, to increase short-run sales.

has recently become a favourite of the car industry. Or, the seller may simply offer *discounts* from normal prices to increase sales and reduce inventories. Some home maintenance service companies now offer promotional prices at certain times when their tradespeople are all working together in a particular suburban area.

Value pricing

Value pricing Offering just the right combination of quality and good service at a fair price.

Value pricing starts with the customer and the benefits the product creates relative to key competitors. Based on a combination of customer benefits, price is set relative to competition to provide superior customer value. Price adjustments can be made which either increase or reduce customer value within a price band, every point of which provides superior value. So long as superior value exists there is room for price adjustments that either increase value to the customer or increase value to the business.

Geographical pricing

A company must also decide how to price its products to customers in different parts of the country. Should the company risk losing the business of more distant customers by charging them higher prices to cover the higher shipping costs? Or should the company charge the same to all customers regardless of location? Following are five geographical pricing strategies for this hypothetical situation:

> Kimberly Clark of Australia (KCA) is located in Sydney and sells paper products to customers across Australia. The cost of freight is high and affects the companies from whom customers buy their paper. KCA wants to establish a geographical pricing policy. It is trying to determine how to price a $1000 order to three specific customers: Customer A (Sydney), Customer B (Melbourne) and Customer C (Perth).

FOB-origin pricing

FOB-origin pricing A geographical pricing strategy in which goods are placed free on board a carrier, and the customer pays the freight from the factory to the destination.

On the one hand, KCA can ask each customer to pay the shipping cost from the Sydney factory to the customer's location. All three customers would pay the same factory price of $1000, with Customer A paying, say, $100 for shipping, Customer B $150 and Customer C $250. Called **FOB-origin pricing**, this practice means that the goods are placed *free on board* (hence, FOB) a carrier, at which point the title and responsibility pass to the customer, who pays the freight from the factory to the destination.

Because each customer picks up its own cost, supporters of FOB pricing feel that this is the fairest way to assess freight charges. The disadvantage, however, is that KCA will be a high-cost firm to distant customers. If KCA's main competitor happens to be in Perth, this competitor will no doubt outsell KCA in Perth. In fact, the competitor would outsell KCA in all the west, while KCA would dominate the eastern states. A vertical line could actually be drawn on a map connecting the cities where the two companies' prices plus freight would be roughly equal. KCA would have the price advantage east of this line, and its competitor would have the price advantage west of this line, ignoring back-freight costs from Perth to the east.

Uniform delivered pricing

Uniform delivered pricing A geographical pricing strategy in which the company charges the same price plus freight to all customers regardless of their location.

Uniform delivered pricing is the exact opposite of FOB pricing. The company charges the same price plus freight to all customers regardless of their location. The freight charge is set at the average freight cost. Suppose this is $150. Uniform delivered pricing therefore results in a high charge to the Sydney customer (who pays $150 freight instead of $100) and a lower charge to the Perth customer (who pays $150 instead of $250). The Sydney customer would prefer to buy paper from another local paper company that uses FOB-origin pricing. On the other hand, KCA has a better chance of winning the Perth customer. Other advantages are that uniform delivered pricing is fairly easy to administer and lets the firm advertise its price nationally.

Zone pricing

Zone pricing falls between FOB-origin pricing and uniform delivered pricing. The company sets up two or more zones. All customers within a given zone pay a single total price, and this price is higher in the more distant zones. For example, KCA might set up an East Zone and charge $100 freight to all customers in this zone, a Central Zone in which it charges $150 and a West Zone where it charges $250. In this way, the customers within a given price zone receive no price advantage from the company. Customers in Sydney and Brisbane pay the same total price to KCA. The complaint, however, is that the Sydney customer is paying part of the Brisbane customer's freight cost. In addition, even though they may be within a few kilometres of each other, a customer located just on the west side of the line dividing East and Central pays more than one just on the east side of the line.

Basing-point pricing

Using **basing-point pricing**, the seller selects a given city as a 'basing point' and charges all customers the freight cost from that city to the customer location regardless of the city from which the goods are actually shipped. For example, KCA might set Melbourne as the basing point and charge all customers $1000 plus the freight from Melbourne to their locations. This means that a Sydney customer pays the freight cost from Melbourne to Sydney even though the goods may be shipped from Sydney. Using a basing-point location other than the factory raises the total price to customers near the factory and lowers the total price to customers far from the factory. This may be used as a basis if KCA's key customers and competitors are located in Melbourne.

If all sellers used the same basing-point city, delivered prices would be the same for all customers and price competition would be eliminated. Such industries as sugar, cement, steel and cars used basing-point pricing for many years, but this method is less popular today. Some companies set up multiple basing points to create more flexibility: they quote freight charges from the basing-point city nearest to the customer.

Freight-absorption pricing

Finally, the seller who is eager to do business with a certain customer or geographical area might use **freight-absorption pricing**. This involves absorbing all or part of the actual freight charges in order to get the business. The seller might reason that if it can get more business, its average costs will fall and more than compensate for its extra freight cost. Freight-absorption pricing is used for market penetration and also to hold on to increasingly competitive markets.

International pricing

Companies that market their products internationally must decide what prices to charge in the different countries in which they operate. In some cases, a company can set a uniform worldwide price. For example, Boeing sells its jet-liners at about the same price everywhere, whether in the USA, Europe, Australia or a Third World country. However, most companies adjust their prices to reflect local market conditions and cost considerations.

The price that a company should charge in a specific country depends on many factors, including economic conditions, competitive situations, laws and regulations, and development of the wholesaling and retailing system. Consumer perceptions and preferences may also vary from country to country, calling for different prices. Or the company may have different marketing objectives in various world

Zone pricing
A geographical pricing strategy in which the company sets up two or more zones—all customers within a zone pay the same total price, and this price is higher in the more distant zones.

Basing-point pricing
A geographical pricing strategy in which the seller designates a city as a basing point and charges all customers the freight cost from that city to the customer location, regardless of the city from which the goods are actually shipped.

Freight-absorption pricing A geographical pricing strategy in which the company absorbs all or part of the actual freight charges in order to get the business.

markets which require changes in pricing strategy. For example, Sony might introduce a new product into mature markets in highly developed countries with the goal of quickly gaining mass-market share—this would call for a penetration pricing strategy. In contrast, it might enter a less developed market by targeting smaller, less price sensitive segments—in this case, market-skimming pricing makes sense.

Costs play an important role in setting international prices. Travellers overseas are often surprised to find that goods that are relatively inexpensive at home may carry outrageously high price tags in other countries. An Oroton bag selling for $90 in Australia goes for about $130 in Tokyo and $180 in Paris. A McDonald's Big Mac selling for a modest $2.55 here costs $5.75 in Moscow. And an Oral-B toothbrush selling for $2.70 in Australia costs 90 cents in China. Conversely, a Gucci handbag going for only $150 in Milan, Italy, fetches $500 in Australia. In some cases, such *price escalation* may result from differences in selling strategies or market conditions. In most instances, however, it is simply a result of the higher costs of selling in foreign markets—the additional costs of modifying the product, higher shipping and insurance costs, import tariffs and taxes, costs associated with exchange-rate fluctuations, and higher channel and physical distribution costs.

SELF-CHECK QUESTIONS

11 What kind of price-adjustment strategies are relevant to the marketing of Dell computers, which are sold direct to end-customers? Give illustrations of the strategies you propose.

12 BMW and Mercedes-Benz have introduced a range of lower-priced models in recent times. How would you describe this pricing strategy?

Price flexibility on the Net

Pricing products and services on the Internet provides opportunities to test prices, segment customers and adjust to changes in supply and demand. All products have an 'indifference band' where prices within that band are not seen to be different and have little impact on customers' buying decisions. Being at the top of this band rather than in the middle or at the bottom can have a big impact on profitability. In the financial services sector the 'indifference band' is narrow at around 2% in setting interest rates for personal loans, but a typical financial services business that moves from the middle to the top would increase operating profits by around 11%.[34]

Working out the borders of this indifference band for products and services sold through physical channels is expensive and time consuming. But in the virtual world prices can be tested continually and customers' responses can be analysed instantly. For example, a business can test a price increase of 5% with every twentieth visitor to the site and check if this is within or outside the band by comparing purchase behaviour. In this way the top and bottom of the indifference band can be established and monitored. This provides the marketer with far greater precision in pricing to impact on profits positively without losing sales and share.

Another advantage of pricing on the Net is the speed with which prices can be changed. This can yield huge benefits for companies selling perishable products like hotel rooms and airline seats. Prices can be changed hourly as load factors change and maximum yields can be achieved through flexible pricing.

Conventional theories suggest that the Internet will in most cases drive down prices but there is divided evidence indicating that online prices are not always lower than offline stores. This may be because organisations embark on the process of value pricing where the assessment of benefits and features associated with shopping in this way offers opportunities for value-added pricing. However, whether premium prices are charged or discounted products are on offer, the Internet gives rise to many opportunities. Organisations should be exploring the possibilities for leveraging pricing strategies, conducting instant research and testing capabilities. Customer segmentation, dynamic pricing, product differentiation can be explored. This is particularly well demonstrated by eBay and Priceline.com. They have developed pricing models and infrastructure which offer real-time pricing, thus allowing companies to adjust or revise their suggested prices to reflect current demand and customer price and demand elasticities.

Price changes

Initiating price changes

After developing their price structures and strategies companies may face occasions when they will want either to cut or to raise prices.

Initiating price cuts

Several situations may lead a firm to consider cutting its price. One is excess capacity. The firm needs more business and cannot get it through increased sales effort, product improvement or other measures. In the late 1990s many companies dropped 'follow-the-leader pricing'—that is, charging about the same price as their leading competitor—and aggressively cut prices to boost their sales. But as the airline, construction equipment and other industries have learned in recent years, cutting prices in an industry loaded with excess capacity may lead to price wars as competitors try to retain market share.

Prices are flexible at eBay.

Source: <http://www.ebay.com>. These materials have been reproduced with the permission of eBay Inc. Copyright © eBay Inc. All rights reserved.

Another situation is falling market share in the face of strong price competition. Several Australian industries, such as motor vehicles and consumer electronics, have been losing market share to Japanese competitors, whose high-quality products carry lower prices than their Australian counterparts. Holden and Ford have resorted to more aggressive pricing action.

Companies may also cut prices in a drive to dominate the market through lower costs. Either the company starts with lower costs than its competitors or it cuts prices in the hope of gaining market share that will cut costs through larger volume. St George Bank and the National Australia Bank tend to be aggressive interest-rate cutters.

Initiating price increases

On the other hand, many companies have had to *raise* prices in recent years. They do this knowing that the price increases may be resented by customers, dealers and their own salesforce. Yet a successful price increase can greatly increase profits. For example, if the company's profit margin is 3% of sales, a 1% price increase will increase profits by 33% if sales volume is unaffected.

A major factor in price increases is cost inflation. Rising costs squeeze profit margins and lead companies to regular rounds of price increases. Companies often raise their prices by more than the cost increase in anticipation of further inflation. Companies do not want to make long-run price agreements with customers—they fear that cost inflation will eat into profit margins. Another factor leading to price increases is over-demand: when a company cannot supply all its customers' needs it can raise its prices, ration products to customers or both. This is particularly the case in professional service businesses in which capacity and skills may be constrained.

Companies can increase their prices in a number of ways to keep up with rising costs.[35] Prices can be raised almost invisibly by dropping discounts and adding higher-priced units to the line. Or prices can be pushed up openly. In passing on price increases to customers, the company needs to avoid the image of price gouger. The price increases should be supported by a company communication program telling customers why prices are being increased. The company salesforce should help customers find ways to economise.

When possible, the company considers ways to meet higher costs or demand without raising prices. For example, it can shrink the product instead of raising the price, as chocolate manufacturers often do. Or it can substitute less expensive ingredients, or remove certain product features, packaging or services. Or it can 'unbundle' its products and services, removing and separately pricing elements that were formerly part of the offer. Telstra, for example, now offers communications equipment maintenance as a separately priced service. Many restaurants offer 'à la carte' pricing as well as fixed-price menus.

Buyer reactions to price changes

Whether the price is raised or lowered, the action will affect buyers, competitors, distributors and suppliers, and may interest government as well. Customers do not always put a straightforward interpretation on price changes. They may view a price cut in several ways. For example, what would you think if Hewlett-Packard suddenly cut its printer prices in half? You might think that these printers are about to be replaced by newer models, or that they have some fault and are not selling well. You might think that Hewlett-Packard is in financial trouble and may not stay in the business long enough to supply future parts. You might believe that quality has been reduced. Or you might think that the price will come down even further and that it will pay to wait and see.

Similarly, a price *increase*, which would normally lower sales, may have some positive meanings for buyers. What would you think if Hewlett-Packard *raised* the price of its latest printer model? You might think that the item is very 'hot' and may be unobtainable unless you buy it soon. You might think that the printer is unusually good value or that Hewlett-Packard is charging what the market will bear. Similar reactions may occur when an airline changes its basic prices for particular service routes.

Competitor reactions to price changes

A firm considering a price change has to worry about competitors' as well as customers' reactions. Competitors are most likely to react when the number of firms involved is small, when the product is uniform and when the buyers are well informed, as for domestic airline travel in Australia.

How can the firm work out the likely reactions of its competitors? Assume that the firm faces one large competitor. If the competitor tends to react in a set way to price changes, that reaction can be anticipated. But if the competitor treats each price change as a fresh challenge and reacts according to its self-interest, the company must analyse the competitor's self-interest each time.

The problem is complex because the competitor can interpret a company price cut in many ways. It might think that the company is trying to grab a larger market share, that the company is doing poorly and trying to boost its sales, or that the company wants the whole industry to cut prices to increase total demand.

When there are *several* competitors, the company must guess *each* competitor's likely reaction. If all competitors behave alike, this amounts to analysing only a typical competitor. However, if the competitors do not behave alike—perhaps because of differences in size, market shares or policies— then separate analyses are necessary. On the other hand, if some competitors will match the price change, there is good reason to expect that the rest will also match it.

Responding to price changes

Now let's reverse the question and ask how a firm should respond to a price change by a competitor. The firm needs to consider several issues. Why did the competitor change the price? Was it to take more market share, to use excess capacity, to meet changing cost conditions or to lead an industry-wide price change? Does the competitor plan to make the price change temporary or permanent? What will happen to the company's market share and profits if it doesn't respond? Are other companies going to respond? And what are the competitor's and other firms' responses likely to be to each possible reaction?

Besides these issues, the company must make a broader analysis. It must consider its own product's stage in the life cycle, its importance in the company's product mix, the intentions and resources of the competitor, and possible consumer reactions to price changes.

The company cannot always make an extended analysis of its alternatives at the time of a price change. The competitor may have spent much time preparing this decision, but the company may have to react within hours or days. About the only way to cut down reaction time is to plan ahead for possible competitor's price changes and possible responses. Figure 13.15 (overleaf) shows one company's price-reaction program for meeting a competitor's possible price cut. Reaction programs for meeting price changes are most often used in industries in which price changes occur often and quick reactions are important. Examples can be found in the airline, meat and oil industries.

SELF-CHECK QUESTIONS

13 Aussie's value proposition is an offer of lower home mortgage costs as a result of them doing the 'shopping around'. What are the implications for customers, competitors and the organisation itself?

14 How might Singapore Airlines respond to a cut in business-class fares by Qantas?

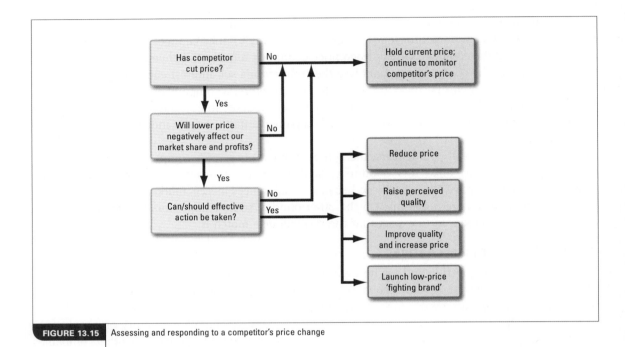

FIGURE 13.15 Assessing and responding to a competitor's price change

Steps to effective pricing

The following process of steps is a useful guide to making and monitoring the results of pricing strategies and tactics.

1 Start by determining what value the target market places on the product or service. This will involve assessing the perceived benefits and cost and comparing this with the value perception of competing offers.

2 Assess the differences in value placed on the offer by different market segments. This allows for customisation of price packages for different segments according to perceived value.

3 Determine price sensitivity in different market segments. This involves an estimation of price elasticity.

4 Identify the best pricing structure. Marketers need to decide whether to price individual components of the offer or bundle different elements together at particular prices for each 'bundle' of benefits.

5 Take account of likely competitors' reactions. This needs to allow for the impact of our price on a competitor's sales, share, margins and competitive position and how a competitor's likely reaction would impact on our business.

6 Measure and monitor the net prices obtained in the market. Marketers should know the effects of tactical price changes, discounts, rebates and terms of trade allowances and their impact on the net prices realised.

7 Assess customers' emotional responses to prices. This takes account of how customers 'feel' about the supplier relationship as a result of price changes. This is particularly important for large customers where special relationships exist and a bond of mutual value needs to be maintained and kept in balance over time.

8 Determine whether the market segment or key customer provides sufficient returns in relation to costs to serve. Periodically each segment or major customer should be assessed in terms of their attractiveness to the business—and in particularly their longer-term profitability.[36]

SUMMARY

Despite the increased role of non-price factors in the modern marketing process, price remains an important element in the marketing mix. Many internal and external factors influence the company's pricing decisions. *Internal factors* include the company's *marketing objectives, marketing mix strategy, costs* and *organisation for pricing*.

The pricing strategy is largely determined by the company's *target market and positioning objectives*. Common pricing objectives include survival, current profit maximisation, market-share leadership and product-quality leadership.

Price is only one of the marketing mix tools the company uses to accomplish its objectives, and pricing decisions affect and are affected by product design, distribution and promotion decisions. Price decisions must be carefully coordinated with the other marketing mix decisions when designing the marketing program.

Costs set the floor for the company's price—the price must cover all the costs of making and selling the product, plus a fair rate of return. Management must decide who within the organisation is responsible for setting price. In large companies, some pricing authority may be delegated to lower-level managers and salespeople, but top management usually set pricing policies and approve proposed prices. Production, finance and accounting managers also influence pricing.

External factors that influence pricing decisions include the nature of the market and demand, competitors' prices and offers, and other factors such as the economy, reseller needs and government actions. The seller's pricing freedom varies with different types of markets. Pricing is especially challenging in markets characterised by monopolistic competition or oligopoly.

In the end, the consumer decides whether the company has set the right price. The consumer weighs the price against the perceived values of using the product—if the price exceeds the sum of the values, consumers will not buy the product. Consumers differ in the values they assign to different product features, and marketers often vary their pricing strategies for different price segments. When assessing the market and demand, the company estimates the demand schedule, which shows the probable quantity purchased per period at alternative price levels. The more *inelastic* the demand, the higher the company can set its price. *Demand* and *consumer value perceptions* set the ceiling for prices.

Consumers compare a product's price with the prices of competitors' products. A company must learn the price and quality of competitors' offers and use them as a starting point for its own pricing.

The company can select one or a combination of five general pricing approaches: the *cost-based approach* (cost-plus or break-even analysis and target profit pricing), the *value-based approach* (buyer's perceived value), the *competition-based approach* (economic-value, going-rate or sealed-bid pricing), *performance-based approach* and the *relationship price approach*.

Pricing strategies usually change as a product passes through its life cycle. The company can decide on one of several price-quality strategies for introducing an imitative product. In pricing innovative new products, it can follow a *skimming policy* by initially setting high prices to 'skim' the maximum amount of revenue from various segments of the market. Or it can use *penetration pricing* by setting a low initial price to win a large market share.

When the product is part of a product mix, the firm searches for a set of prices that will maximise the profits from the total mix. The company decides on *price steps* for items in its product line and on the pricing of *optional products, captive products, by-products* and *product bundles*.

Companies apply a variety of *price-adjustment strategies* to account for differences in consumer segments and situations. One is *discount pricing and allowances*, in which the company establishes cash discounts, quantity discounts, functional discounts, seasonal discounts and allowances. A second is *segmented pricing*, in which the company sets different prices for different customers, product forms, places or times. A third is *psychological pricing*, in which the company adjusts the price to communicate more effectively a product's intended position. A fourth is *promotional pricing*, in which the company decides on loss-leader pricing, special-event pricing and psychological discounting. A fifth is *value pricing*, in which the company offers just the right combination of quality and good service at a fair price. A sixth is *geographical pricing*, in which the company decides how to price to distant customers, choosing from such alternatives as FOB pricing, uniform delivered pricing, zone pricing, basing-point pricing and freight-absorption pricing. A seventh is *international pricing*, in which the company adjusts its price to meet different conditions and expectations in different world markets.

The Internet provides many opportunities for price experimentation and determining price elasticities enabling companies to price more closely to perceived value. Prices can also be changed much faster when using the Internet channel.

When a firm considers initiating a *price change*, it must consider customers' and competitors' reactions. Customers' reactions are influenced by the meaning customers see in the price change. Competitors' reactions flow from a set reaction policy or a fresh analysis of each situation. The firm initiating the price change must also anticipate the probable reactions of suppliers, middlemen and government.

The firm that faces a price change initiated by a competitor must try to understand the competitor's intent as well as the likely duration and impact of the change. If a swift reaction is desirable, the firm should pre-plan its reactions to different possible price actions by competitors. When facing a competitor's price change, the company might sit tight, reduce its own price, raise perceived quality, improve quality and raise price or launch a fighting brand.

MARKETING ISSUE

The dominant incumbent national telecoms around the world—such as Telstra in Australia, Telecom NZ, Bell Canada, BT (Britain) and France Telecom—all face major strategic pricing decisions which will affect their revenue streams and net earnings for years to come. Their sources of revenue and profit have primarily come from local and long-distance calls from fixed lines and from mobile phone call plans. These revenue streams are about to be destroyed by VoIP—voice over Internet protocol. The Internet is increasingly being used for voice calls using computers. A free service offered by Skype has fuelled growth of this form of voice communication and at November 2005 as many as 3.5 million Skype users could be detected online at any point in time. The rapid growth of prepaid long-distance call cards offering overseas calls at a fraction of 'normal' long-distance rates has been made possible by third-party service providers using VoIP technology.

The bottom line? Telephone calls are rapidly migrating from traditional fixed line networks and mobile networks towards the Internet network and many users are starting to believe that telephone calls should be free or 'next to free'! Management of this migration by the telecoms has become a strategic corporate issue as these companies attempt to move from their traditional telecommunications model to an IP model. Marketing and strategic pricing are at the heart of this challenge as the telecoms will need to develop new offers of value at attractive price packages to retain their customers or lose them to the new wave of competitors entering a progressively deregulated marketplace.

KEY TERMS

allowance	510	going-rate pricing	496	pure monopoly	486
basing-point pricing	513	market-penetration pricing	504	quantity discount	509
break-even pricing (target profit pricing)	493	market-skimming pricing	503	reference prices	511
		monopolistic competition	486	sealed-bid pricing	497
by-product pricing	506	oligopolistic competition	486	seasonal discount	510
captive product pricing	506	optional product/service pricing	505	segmented pricing	510
cash discount	507			total cost of ownership	482
cost-plus pricing	492	price	478	total costs	483
demand curve	487	price elasticity	488	trade-in allowance	510
experience curve (learning curve)	484	product-bundle pricing	506	two-part pricing	506
		product-line pricing	505	uniform delivered pricing	512
fixed costs	482	promotional allowance	510	value-based pricing	495
FOB-origin pricing	512	promotional pricing	511	value pricing	512
freight-absorption pricing	513	psychological pricing	511	variable costs	482
functional discount (trade discount)	510	pure competition	486	zone pricing	513

DISCUSSING THE ISSUES

1 Toshiba's newest laptop computer will be lighter than its competitors' but have more interconnection capability to mobile Internet and printing. What factors should Toshiba consider in setting a price for this new product?

2 Sales of McLaren Vales' Tatachilla red wines *increased* when prices were raised 50% over a two-year period. What does this tell you about the demand curve and the elasticity of demand for Tatachilla wines? What does this suggest about using perceived-value pricing in marketing alcoholic beverages?

3 Describe which strategy, market skimming or market penetration, the following companies use in pricing their new products and services:

(a) Jetstar

(b) Sony

(c) Cadbury Schweppes

Are these the right strategies for these companies? Why or why not?

4 A clothing store sells women's jackets at three price levels—$295, $395 and $495. If shoppers use these price points as reference prices in comparing different jackets, what would be the effect of adding a new line of jackets priced at $595? Would you expect sales of the $495 jackets to increase, decrease or stay the same?

5 The consumer paper industry comprising facial tissues, toilet rolls and paper napkins is dominated in Australia by two companies. If one company drops its price, the other usually matches the price reduction. There is a strong orientation to competitor-based pricing. Are there any other options to price matching as a means of holding or growing market share?

6 The formula for mineral water is very similar for all brands. Perrier charges a premium price for this product, yet remains an unchallenged price leader. Discuss what this implies about the value of a brand name. Are there ethical issues involved in this type of pricing?

REFERENCES

1. David Koeppel, 'For Those of You Who Wonder How That TV Show Began', *New York Times*, 21 March 2005, <www.nytimes.com/2005/03/21/business/media/21dvd.html>; Ethan Smith, 'What's on the Flip Side of That CD? Increasingly, a DVD', *The Wall Street Journal*, 21 March 2005, p. B1, <http://online.wsj.com/article/0,,SB111135876878284547,00.html>; Robert Levine, 'The Music Goes on Side A and the Flip Side is a DVD', *New Yoork Times*, 21 March 2005, <www.nytimes.com/2005/03/21/business/media/21dual.html>.

2. See David J. Schwartz, *Marketing Today: A Basic Approach*, 3rd edn, New York, Harcourt Brace Jovanovich, 1981, pp. 270–273.

3. For a thorough account of market-based pricing and pricing strategies at different stages of the product life cycle see Roger Best, *Market-Based Management: Strategies for Growing Customer Value and Profitability*, 3rd edn, Upper Saddle River, Prentice Hall, 2004, Chapter 8, pp. 195–221.

4. For a comprehensive description and comparison of various pricing strategies see Michael V. Marn, Eric V. Roegner and Craig C. Zawada, *The Price Advantage*, New York, John Wiley & Sons, 2004; also see Gerald J. Tellis, 'Beyond the Many Faces of Price: An Integration of Pricing Strategies', *Journal of Marketing*, October 1986, pp. 146–160.

5. Neil Shoebridge, 'Brand-Name Bravery Brings Domino's through the Pizza Wars', *Business Review Weekly*, 18 January 1999, pp. 59–62.

6. Christopher Farrell, 'Stuck! How Companies Cope When They Can't Raise Prices', *Business Week*, 15 November 1993, pp. 146–155. Also see John Y. Lee, 'Use Target Costing to Improve Your Bottom Line', *CPA Journal*, January 1994, pp. 68–71.

7. Brian Dumaine, 'Closing the Innovation Gap', *Fortune*, 2 December 1991, pp. 56–62.

8. John R. Brandt, 'Competing Beyond Quality', *Industry Week*, vol. 252, no. 1, January 2003, p. 23.

9. For information on the white goods industry refer to Neil Shoebridge, 'Email–Southcorp Merger Spurs Old Market Leader into White Goods Action', *Business Review Weekly*, 29 March 1999.

10. Andrew Grove, *Only the Paranoid Survive—How to Exploit the Crisis Points that Challenge Every Company and Career*, New York, Doubleday, 1996.

11. Neil Shoebridge, 'Sanity's Cool-for-Kids Style Drives Competition Crazy', *Business Review Weekly*, 25 May 1998, pp. 196–199.

12. For more on experience-curve strategies see Pankaj Ghemawat, 'Building Strategy on the Experience Curve', *Harvard Business Review*, March–April 1985, pp. 143–149; George S. Day and David B. Montgomery, 'Diagnosing the Experience Curve', *Journal of Marketing*, Spring 1983, pp. 44–58; and William W. Alberts, 'The Experience Curve Doctrine Reconsidered', *Journal of Marketing*, July 1989, pp. 36–49.

13. For an account of the positioning and pricing of information-based products see Carl Shapiro and Hal Varian, 'Versioning: The Smart Way to Sell Information', *Harvard Business Review*, November–December 1998, pp. 106–114.

14. See P. Ronald Stephenson, William L. Cron and Gary L. Frazier, 'Delegating Pricing Authority to the Sales Force: The Effects on Sales and Profit Performance', *Journal of Marketing*, Spring 1979, pp. 21–28.

15. Thomas T. Nagle, 'Pricing as Creative Marketing', *Business Horizons*, July–August 1983, p. 19.

16. An extensive analysis of customer-perceived value using value maps can be found in Bradley T. Gale, *Managing Customer Value*, New York, The Free Press, 1994, pp. 25–47 and 217–221.

17. See Thomas T. Nagle and Reed K. Holden, *The Strategy and Tactics of Pricing*, 2nd edn, Englewood Cliffs, NJ, Prentice Hall, 1995, pp. 1–9.

18. John Gourville and Dilip Soman, 'Pricing and the Psychology of Consumption', *Harvard Business Review*, September 2002, pp. 90–96.

19. Nagle and Holden, op. cit. (note 17).

20. For more examples of price fixing refer to Marc S. Reisch, 'Wielding a Big Stick', *Chemical & Engineering News*, vol. 81, no. 3, 20 January 2003, p. 12.

21. Anonymous, 'News briefs', *Chemical Week*, vol. 165, no. 6, 12 February 2003, p. 5.

22. The arithmetic of mark-ups and margins can be found in Roger Best, *Market-Based Management: Strategies for Growing Customer Value and Profitability*, 3rd edn, Upper Saddle River, Prentice Hall, 2004, pp. 207–213. See also Philip Kotler, *Marketing Management*, 9th edn, Englewood Cliffs, NJ, Prentice Hall, 1997, Appendix 1.

23. Michael V. Marn, Eric V. Roegner and Craig C. Zawada, 'The Power of Pricing', *The McKinsey Quarterly*, no. 1, 2003, p. 32.

24. For more on value-based pricing see Peter Doyle, *Value-Based Marketing: Marketing Strategies for Corporate Growth and Shareholder Value*, New York, John Wiley & Sons, 2000, Chapter 8, pp. 262–270; and Ely S. Lurin, 'Make Sure Product's Price Reflects Its True Value', *Marketing News*, 8 May 1987, p. 8.

25. Phil Zinkewicz, 'Med Mal in Crisis Mode', *Rough Notes*, vol. 145, no. 9, September 2002, p. 66.

26. K. Priess, S. L. Goldman and R. N. Nagel, *Co-operate to Compete*, New York, Van Nostrand Reinhold, 1996, pp. 139–146.

27. Ibid, pp. 145–146.

28. For more details on product pricing strategies see Robert Dolan and Hermann Simon, *Power Pricing*, New York, The Free Press, 1996, pp. 79–111; Thomas T. Nagle, *The Strategy and Tactics of Pricing*, Englewood Cliffs, NJ, Prentice Hall, 1987, pp. 116–117.

29. Jefferson Graham, 'Looks Like the New iPod's a Hit', *USA Today*, 18 September 2005.

30. Raymond Frost and Judy Strauss, *Marketing on the Internet*, Englewood Cliffs, NJ, Prentice Hall, 1999, pp. 141–142; Ravi Kalakota and Andrew Whinston (eds), *Readings in Electronic Commerce*, Reading, MA, Addison-Wesley, 1997, pp. 202–211.

31. See Tellis, op. cit. (note 4), p. 155; and Nagle, op. cit. (note 28), pp. 170–172.

32. Gary M. Erickson and Johny K. Johansson, 'The Role of Price in Multi-Attribute Product Evaluations', *Journal of Consumer Research*, September 1985, pp. 195–199.

33. See Nagle, op. cit. (note 27), pp. 66–68; and Tellis, op. cit. (note 4), pp. 152–153.

34. Walter Baker, Mike Marn and Craig Zawada, 'Price Smarter on the Net', *Harvard Business Review*, February 2001, pp. 122–127.

35. Norman H. Fuss Jr, 'How to Raise Prices—Judiciously—to Meet Today's Conditions', *Harvard Business Review*, May–June 1975, p. 10; and Mary Louise Hatten, 'Don't Get Caught with Your Prices Down', *Business Horizons*, March–April 1982, pp. 23–28.

36. These steps are based on the article by Robert J. Nolan, 'How Do You Know When the Price Is Right?', *Harvard Business Review*, September–October 1995, pp. 174–183.

PHOTO/AD CREDITS

500. © Photographer: Jeff Gynane, Agency: Dreamstime.com.

Dr John Van Beveren, University of Ballarat and Melbourne Institute of Technology

CASE STUDY

Trisled: pricing for market expansion

Trisled is a small business that designs, manufactures, assembles and retails two- and three-wheel recumbent cycles. It is owned and operated by Ben Goodall, who started the business in 1995 from his parents' garage and since 1999 has relocated to a factory in the Dromana industrial estate.

Over the past decade Trisled has grown to be a recognised brand in the Australian cycling market especially among human-powered vehicle enthusiasts and racing professionals. A lot of marketing effort has been required to establish Trisled against strong competition from cheaper domestic and imported recumbent cycles.

Much of the effort has gone into branding the products. A company logo, website (www.trisled. com.au) and standardised advertising text have been created. The Trisled logo is featured on all products, leaflets, the website and 'give-aways' like caps and fridge magnets. Over the past 10 years, Ben has raced the Trisled in many events such as the Adelaide International Pedal Prix, Wonthaggi Pedal Prix and Australian Human Powered Vehicle Association races. At these events he has won numerous first and second places for the race and for the design and construction of the cycles. Trisleds are also raced by other competitors who have purchased the cycles. These events have provided good exposure of the brand. The Trisled website is used to promote the products to the touring segment of the market. Customers of Trisled are encouraged to send in their stories and photos from their touring adventures, which are featured on the website.

Ben recognises the importance of promotion and advertising. In addition, he has actively sought to have his products featured and reviewed in cycling magazines and alternative-lifestyle magazines. These articles are written as a critique of the product, its attributes, features and performance. Only products that are well built and perform well get good reviews. Not only are the reviewers for these magazines critical

when evaluating these products but so are the enthusiasts and racing professionals. Ben is aware of this and spends a lot of time and effort in the design and development of his products. He has gathered a lot of market research from the discussion boards, chat rooms and bloggs on the Internet where enthusiasts for human-powered vehicles and racing often discuss what they like and dislike about the recumbent cycles they have used. Ben continually makes refinements and improvements to the latest models of his products. Trisled is better than most of the competitors' products because Trisleds have better geometry and ergonomics, which makes them more technologically advanced, efficient and comfortable to ride.

Trisled cycles are expensive compared to the competitors' cycles. Despite the price difference many customers have recognised the better level of quality in Trisleds and have been prepared to pay more for them. But the number of customers who can afford a Trisled in Australia is limited. This has restricted the growth of Trisled to be slow and steady. Ben wants to expand his business, but he can't unless he can expand his markets. He sees the opportunities to do this in two ways—offer a less expensive product in the domestic market and offer his products in larger markets such as the USA where there are more enthusiasts for human-powered vehicles and racing professionals.

Reducing the price of Trisleds means reconsidering how the business operates; in particular finding ways to reduce cost while maintaining quality. As the design of the recumbent cycles has been improved the number of parts used in the manufacture of the Trisled models has increased and many of these are provided from numerous suppliers. Many of the suppliers were chosen because of the level and reliability of service they provide. For example, the rims are sourced from a company who agreed to assemble wheels by hand, which produces

better quality than by machine as other suppliers tend to do. Local suppliers are also chosen where possible over other suppliers because communicating with them is easier and logistics is usually simpler.

Recently Ben went to the USA to attend 'Interbike', which is the largest Bicycle Traders Association trade show in North America. It is an event for suppliers, wholesalers and manufacturers. While at Interbike, he discovered that American consumers are more price sensitive than Australian consumers and are even more savvy when evaluating each model of cycles. There are more manufacturers of recumbent cycles in the American market than in Australia. This has provided American consumers with more choice and a greater range of cycles compared to Australia. Manufacturers in America compete on price as well as quality. If Ben wants to compete with the American manufacturers he will need to reduce the price of the Trisled Gizmo, which would retail in the USA for $US3500. This is against comparable models, the Wizwheelsteratrike and the Catike Speed, priced at $US1800 and $US2300 respectively. If Ben is to reduce the price of Trisleds to compete against the competitors' products then the number of recumbent cycles he would need to sell would be at least 200 per year and this volume would mean he would have to rethink his production capacity and methods.

After all the effort of branding his product in Australia, Ben is wondering whether reducing the price of Trisled would have a negative impact on what he has done to create a high-value branded product. In addition, the larger production capacity required to export to the USA could cause problems for Ben with regards to quality control. There is also a large amount of financial risk in increasing his production and having so many cycles in the market with perhaps long delays before he gets paid. Perhaps Ben should try to extend what he currently does in Australia for the US market. One way he can reduce the risk is to adopt a focus strategy based on small volumes and a higher price position, creating less pressure on capacity and positioning the brand

around the specialised position. Managing risk is a very important factor for Ben.

When Ben established the business he normally ordered the components he required as orders were placed. This was done mainly to reduce the amount of finance outlaid on stock and the risk of holding stock that might not be used in future enhancements of the products. Today, Ben buys components in bulk so that he can gain the discounts offered by many suppliers for larger orders. As the Trisled business has grown so has Ben's confidence that there is a demand for his product.

During the first year of operation the price of chromium molybdenum tubing, which is the main material used in the manufacture of the Trisled frames, was reduced by 30% as the result of a price war between the suppliers. Chromium molybdenum tubing is mainly sourced from Japan by a few importers. For some reason they decided to slash the price they were charging for the material. This provided Ben with an opportunity, and he was able to produce his recumbent cycles at a cost level that meant he could sell the Trisleds for a price compatible with imported recumbent cycles. Most of the imported cycles came from Taiwan, which is the world's centre for bike manufacturing.

Ben selects components for his cycles based on their engineering specifications and performance. He has been diligent in selecting components that positively contribute to the performance, robustness and durability of his products. Ben had been using Winzip brakes on his cycles but while in America he found that most retailers were not interested in that particular brand because they had previously been used in the assembly of low-end bikes. This is an important consideration for Ben if he is to enter the American market.

Although Ben has been careful to select good-quality components for his products there have been times when the components were not right. About 12 months ago Ben had to recall about 12 of the Trisleds he had sold. The reason for the recall was that the axles he had used were not hardened sufficiently to withstand the forces placed on them under certain conditions. Although these conditions were not likely to occur with normal use of the cycles and new axles cost hundreds of dollars, Ben decided to replace the axles with more suitable ones from another supplier, at no charge to the customers. Fortunately Ben had the contact details of these customers and was able to contact them for the recall. But he does not have all of his customers' contact details. He realised that this is a problem not just in the case of recalls but also because many of his customers do not return as the product is of high quality and there is usually no need to complain.

QUESTIONS

1. What is the marketing objective of Trisled?

2. How does the strategy of Trisled determine the pricing strategy adopted?

3. Ben wants to expand his business and has been looking at his competitors' prices. What pricing strategy might he adopt to be competitive?

4. Can Ben simply reduce the price of his recumbent cycles to be competitive?

5. Marketing to foreign markets is one option that Ben is considering to expand his market size. Assuming that Ben finds agents that will import his products, what pricing options does he have? (Discuss them.)

CASE STUDY

CHAPTER 14

Marketing logistics networks

Today, you would be hard pressed to find a distribution company that does not incorporate the word 'logistics' in its corporate brand name or in the positioning statement that adorns every truck in its fleet in Australia, New Zealand and increasingly Asia. One of the largest in the Asia region, Toll Holdings, makes this clear in its vision statement: 'To be the most successful provider of integrated total logistics solutions in the Asian region'. This is testimony to the company's recognition that they are part of a network system that ensures that end-users get their favourite brands of products when and where they want them, and at prices they can afford. In between the growers, producers and importers of input materials and the final consumers lie all manner of manufacturers and organisations which support them—including such logistics companies as Toll which are involved in marketing logistics network management. By using the word 'integrated' in their vision statement, Toll Holdings are indicating that they offer integrated services.

On a close inspection we see that such networks of marketing organisations are not confined to branded consumer goods, but also serve business markets, and are prominent in the delivery of services and experiential products. On the one hand we see that container ships ply the world carrying all manner of commodities, semi-finished and finished products destined for business and consumer markets. These commodities range from iron ore to oil and liquified natural gas. We also see that services are delivered by many means ranging from courier services that Toll offer, through to electronic services by organisations such as Australia Post and numerous telecommunications companies.

If you were one of the many punters who lined up behind Australia's totalisator self-service wager processing terminals on Melbourne Cup day, you saw first hand such a marketing logistics network in action—in this case involving an experiential product. Perhaps you contributed to the millions of impressions logged on the wager processing web servers in your country because you placed your wager online. Or perhaps you placed your wager over the telephone—even to the point of interacting with a voice-recognition equipped computer.

Toll Holdings generates in excess of $8 billion in consolidated revenue from its integrated transport and logistics services in the Asian region.

Whichever method punters use to place their wagers, and in whichever part of the world they live, today's consumers interact with a network of marketing organisations that include: racecourses like Flemington, which hosts the annual Melbourne Cup; horse owners, trainers, jockeys and stable hands from a host of countries; sponsors who collectively put up over $20 million each year; the television network which broadcasts the race in Australia and forwards the images via satellite to some 700 million people worldwide; telecommunications companies; public transportation organisations; fashion houses and milliners who clothe the 120 000 race goers on the day and 350 000 for the Victorian Spring carnival week; bookmakers and 'turf accountants'; marquee suppliers; vintners and caterers; and many more.

Like goods and services generally, horse racing is but one experiential product that entails coordination of a network of sometimes competing and sometimes cooperative organisations. For some, such as the big-spending punters and bookmakers, who can win or lose heavily on the Melbourne Cup, the product is transformational. For all involved, the aim is to manage a complex marketing logistics network to deliver satisfaction to a broad array of target markets in a variety of locations—no easy matter, regardless of the industry sector involved.[1]

After reading this chapter you should be able to:

1. Describe the nature of marketing logistics networks.
2. Explain the importance and goals of marketing logistics networks, as well as identify the major decision areas.
3. Describe the nature of marketing channels, and explain why marketing intermediaries are used.
4. Discuss marketing channel behaviour and organisation.
5. Outline the basic elements of channel design decisions by analysing consumer service needs and setting channel objectives and constraints.
6. Identify the major channel alternatives open to marketing organisations.
7. Illustrate how marketing organisations select, motivate and evaluate channel members.

I n this chapter we examine the changing marketing logistics networks for manufacturers, service providers, intermediaries such as wholesalers and retailers and, of course, end-consumers. After a discussion on the nature of marketing logistics network management, we will work our way through the various logistics networks decision areas before turning to an examination of the nature of marketing channels and the distribution of goods and services. In the following chapter we examine a major aspect of marketing logistics networks in more detail—retailing and wholesaling.

The nature of marketing logistics network management

Marketing logistics networks System of efficiently and effectively making and getting products and services to end-users.

We use the term **marketing logistics networks** when describing the system of efficiently and effectively making and getting goods and services to end-users. It will soon become evident why this term is used. At the downstream or output end of these networks are customers—end-users and intermediaries—who pull products through the network. At the upstream or input end of such networks are the many suppliers of raw materials and components used in the conversion process that leads to finished products. In between lie the conversion operations of the manufacturer (see Figure 14.1), the service provider (see the legal service provider example in Figure 14.2) and the experiential product provider (see the experiential broadcaster example in Figure 14.3).

Looking back to the mid-1990s we would see that marketing science and practice tended to focus on physical distribution between the supplier, intermediary and end-customer, almost to the exclusion of the upstream elements covered by the broader perspective taken in this chapter. **Physical distribution** is nevertheless important, and starts at the link between the marketing organisation and its intermediaries—often retailers. It ends with the end-customer taking title to manufactured and imported goods. However, distribution need not involve traditional transport of goods, for, as we know, a client may be engaged in a service encounter that involves receiving legal advice via a facsimile or email and businesses and households receive free-to-air and cable news and entertainment—

Physical distribution The tasks involved in planning, implementing and controlling the physical flow of materials and final goods from points of origin to points of use to meet the needs of customers at a profit.

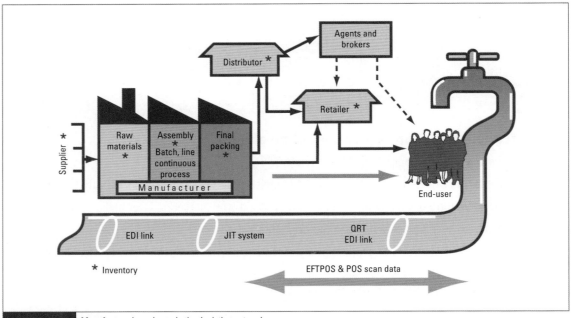

FIGURE 14.1 | Manufactured goods marketing logistics network

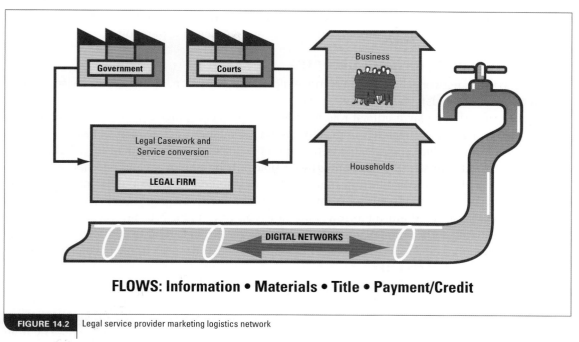

FLOWS: Information • Materials • Title • Payment/Credit

FIGURE 14.2 Legal service provider marketing logistics network

FLOWS: Information • Materials • Payment/Credit

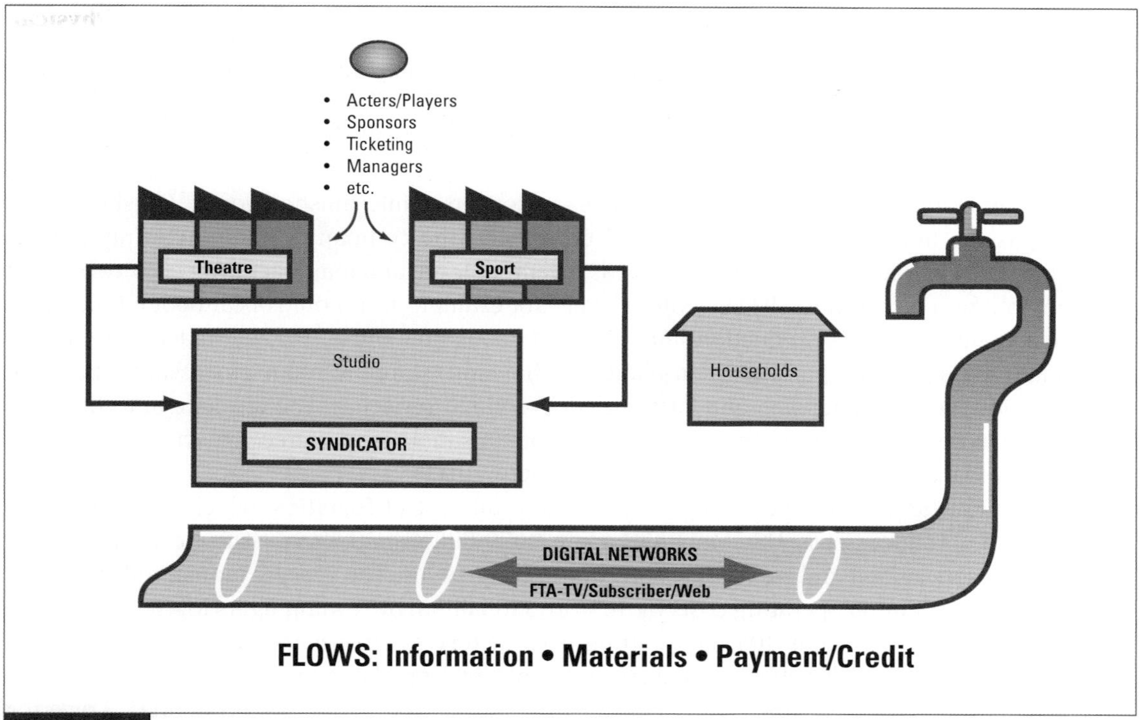

FIGURE 14.3 Experiential product marketing logistics network

experiential products. Universities distribute their results to students via SMS on mobile phone networks, for example. In the case of goods, management select warehouses (stocking points) or cross-docking points and transportation carriers that will deliver finished goods to final destinations

Cross-docking Picking shipments received from suppliers then reloading onto transport without any storage in a warehouse.

in the desired time and/or at the lowest total cost. **Cross-docking** involves picking shipments received from suppliers then reloading onto transport without any storage in a warehouse.

Flows in marketing logistics networks

Marketing logistics networks involve bidirectional flows of information, materials or service content, title (in the case of goods), payment and/or credit.

Information systems play a critical role in managing marketing logistics networks. Major gains in logistical efficiency have resulted from information technology such as point-of-sale terminals, readers of uniform product codes, satellite tracking of transport, electronic data interchange (EDI) and electronic funds transfer (EFT), intranets (accessible only by employees and internal customers), extranets (accessible by both internal markets and customers) and the public Internet. These developments have made it possible for companies to make or require promises such as 'the product will be at dock 25 at 10.00 am tomorrow' and 'now you have paid, you have access to the new software immediately for a period of 24 hours by clicking on this link', and to control such promises through information systems. As Marketing Highlight 14.1 illustrates, electronic payments lie at the heart of modern logistics networks.

Marketing logistics networks decisions, including those related to marketing channels, are among the most important facing management today. Decisions such as whether to sole source or not, operations decisions such as where to locate a plant and the type of electronic storage and delivery process to use, and scheduling decisions such as whether to supply from inventory or directly from production are among many of the most critical decisions an organisation can make. Such process design decisions are critical because they affect every other decision.

Marketing logistics network management Managing the network of players providing customer fulfilment ranging from providers of inputs (raw materials, components and capital equipment) and extending to conversion operations, and including marketing channel intermediaries and those involved in physical movement of product.

Marketing logistics network management involves several activities. The first input decision is sales forecasting, on the basis of which the company schedules production and inventory levels and organises distribution. Production plans indicate the materials that the purchasing department must order. These materials arrive through inbound transportation, enter the receiving area and are stored in raw-materials inventory. Raw materials are converted into finished goods. Finished-goods inventory is the link between the customers' orders and the company's manufacturing activity. Customers' orders draw down the finished-goods inventory level, and manufacturing activity builds it up, or maintains a just-in-time (JIT) inventory level—for example, four hours of car boot lids adjacent to the car manaufacturer's production line. Finished goods flow out of the manufacturing process and usually pass through packaging, in-plant warehousing, shipping-room processing, outbound transportation, field warehousing and customer delivery and servicing. The ultimate aim though is to reduce this dependency on forecasting as more organisations aim to receive synchronously an order and produce to meet it—the intent behind adopting JIT.

Logistics The process of planning, implementing and controlling the efficient, cost-effective flow and storage of material, in-process inventory, finished goods and related information from point of origin to point of consumption for the purpose of conforming to customer requirements.

Management have become concerned about the total cost of **logistics**, which can amount to 30–40% of the product's cost. US companies spent $670 billion—10.5% of GDP—to wrap, bundle, load, unload, sort, reload and transport goods in the early 1990s. The grocery industry alone thinks it can decrease its annual operating costs by 10%, or $30 billion, by revamping its logistics. A typical box of breakfast cereal spends 104 days getting from factory to supermarket, chugging through a labyrinth of wholesalers, distributors, brokers and consolidators.[2] With expensive inefficiencies like these, it's no wonder that experts have called logistics 'the last frontier for cost economies'. Lowering logistics costs permits lower prices and yields higher profit margins, or both.

Though the cost of coordination can be high, a well-planned marketing logistics network management program can be a potent tool in competitive marketing. Companies can attract additional customers by offering better service, faster cycle time or lower prices through logistics improvements.

What happens if a company's logistics systems are not set up properly? Companies lose customers when they fail to supply goods on time. Kodak made the mistake of launching its national advertising campaign for its instant camera in the USA before it had delivered enough cameras to the stores. Customers found that it was not available and bought Polaroid cameras instead.

The direct linking of the manufacturer and retailer, initiated between Wal-Mart and Procter & Gamble in the USA in 1985, has now extended to many others around the world, including Lever-Rexona and Coles Supermarkets in Australia, and is a direct outcome of technological change and a willingness to see advantage in marketing logistics network management.[3] As Figures 14.1, 14.2 and 14.3 illustrate, while products flow from the supplier end to the end-user, as does advertising information and direct selling information, title to the goods and payments flow in the opposite direction. Figure 14.1 also illustrates that there are various marketing channels that can be used to ensure that products reach their final destination and thus satisfy demand and customer service requirements. Marketing logistics networks can be likened to a pipeline delivering water to businesses and household dwellings, for the intent is as far as possible to supply on demand rather than carry inventories of finished goods.

As the chapter opening vignette illustrates, **services marketing logistics** addresses the issue of coordinating activities necessary to provide a service in a cost-efficient way and to provide the service quality expected. Among many other services, the coordination of the many organisations involved in the provision of legal services, as graphically depicted in Figure 14.2, increasingly relies on private and public electronic networks between government and businesses. So too does the provision of experiential products, one of which is depicted in Figure 14.3.

Services marketing logistics Coordinating non-material activities necessary to provide a service in a cost-efficient way and to provide the service quality expected.

SELF-CHECK QUESTIONS

1   Why is the focus on 'marketing logistics networks' in this book rather than 'physical distribution' alone?

2   Provide an example of how a marketing organisation might make productivity gains from adopting a marketing logistics networks perspective rather than the older fragmented view of physical distribution.

3   Marketing logistics network management is concerned with flows within the pipeline that extend from end-users back down through intermediaries, the marketing organisation and on to its suppliers. List and describe the flows within the marketing logistics networks.

Marketing logistics objectives

Many marketing organisations state their marketing logistics objective as 'getting the right goods to the right places at the right time for the least cost'. Unfortunately, this objective provides little practical guidance. No market-oriented logistics system can simultaneously maximise customer service and minimise logistics costs. Maximum customer service implies large inventories, premium transportation and multiple warehouses, all of which raise logistics costs. Minimum logistics cost implies least-cost transportation, low stock levels and few warehouses.

An organisation cannot achieve logistics efficiency by asking each manager in the logistics system, or marketing logistics network, to minimise their own costs. Logistics costs interact and are often negatively related. Consider this example:

The traffic manager favours rail shipment over air shipment because rail reduces the company's freight bill. However, because the railways are slower, rail shipment ties up working capital longer,

Electronic payments make the world go round

The banking sector continually faces threats. As the Information Age impacts on the financial services industry, a range of electronic services are ousting plastic cards as we know them—and even cash itself. There are stored-value cards where a small magnetic strip stores a sum of money that is accessed at point of sale until the value of the card is exhausted. Cards with on-board silicon chips—'smart cards'—augment the service level one step further by allowing more data to be held on the card than simply storing a sum of money. Such a card might store passport details, medical information, financial information, criminal record or simply be used to access the Internet and download digital cash from one's chosen bank or other financial institution. Smart cards mean that we need never visit a bank again now that alliances such as Microsoft and Visa have overcome the security and other issues involved in electronic transactions over the Internet.

The Mondex system, now owned by MasterCard, might be regarded as neither a credit card nor a conventional smart card. Money can be 'loaded' to the card over the phone or over the Internet, and transactions can even be conducted 'chip-to-chip', thanks to the electronic locking system provided by the on-board Hitachi microchip. One advantage of the Mondex card is its ability to be reloaded with money, and the fact that micro payments can be made over the Internet. Australia's four main banks have joined other banks from around the globe in examining this technology, but have yet to commercialise its use. One question that arises with the diffusion of such smart cards is whether or not we will see the retail bank sector shrink, or if banks will reinvent themselves as this paradigm shift takes hold.

Turning back the pages of time, we see that the credit card industry had its origins in the USA in 1951 when Franklin National Bank of Long Island issued its customers a card with their account number on it. Franklin's customers could buy products using the card, but only from merchants who also held accounts with the bank. The bank charged the merchants a fee for processing the transaction. By 1959 approximately 150 banks offered credit cards, but they required their customers to pay off the balances in a month or two. Then they began to extend the repayment time period if the customer paid a monthly finance charge.

In the mid-1960s banks began to form voluntary alliances and offered cards with a common label. BankAmericard started the trend, becoming Visa in 1977. Mastercharge evolved into MasterCard in 1979. Visa and MasterCard were thus non-profit associations made up of member banks. Each association had a board of directors to set policies to guide member banks' issuance of its cards. Many individual banks were members of both Visa and MasterCard. The banks themselves decided which cards to issue. American Express, a separate entity, entered the market in 1958.

Today there is such a wide variety of cards that consumers might be said to be overserviced, and the banks have seen their 'licence to print money' somewhat eroded. Co-branded cards that provide their holders with points that can be transferred to airline frequent-flyer schemes are popular; however, the issues surrounding credit card charges are problematic for cardholders, card issuers and the banking sector in general in Australia. Banks have also made gains by reducing their face-to-face banking costs, particularly in rural areas, until consumers finally made plain their feelings on the matter. Nevertheless, the minimal costs of online banking have helped maintain bank margins and also kept some customer groups very satisfied indeed.

Sources: Jeremy Flint, 'Credit Cards Need a New Pitch', *The Australian Financial Review*, 29 March 1999, p. 36; Bill Saporito, 'Who's Winning the Credit Card War?', *Fortune*, 2 July 1990, pp. 66–71; 'Credit Cards: Plastic Profits Go Pop', *The Economist*, 12 September 1992, p. 92; Gary Levin, 'Co-Branding Trend Takes Credit Cards', *Advertising Age*, 11 November 1991, p. 69; Wanda Cantrell, 'The Party's Over for Bank Cards', *Bank Management*, June 1992, pp. 84–86; Adam Bryant, 'Raising the Stakes in a Plastic War', *New York Times*, 13 September 1992, section 3, p. 13; Adam Bryant, 'GM's Bold Move into Credit Card', *New York Times*, 10 September

1992, section D, p. 5; Andrew Cornell, 'The Great Credit Card Cull: Now for the War', *The Australian Financial Review*, 9 September 1994, pp. 1–2; Ben Mitchell, 'Amex: More Leave Home Without It', *Sunday Age*, 21 August 1994, p. 14; Andrew Cornell, 'New Bank Battle Looms on EFTPOS', *The Australian Financial Review*, 15 August 1994, pp. 1, 4; Andrew Cornell, 'Women Find Gold's a Help in Search for Equality', *The Australian Financial Review*, 15 April 1996, p. 3; 'Visa and Microsoft Promise Safer Credit Card Transactions', *The Straits Times*, Singapore, 28 September 1995, p. 38; Fred Brenchley, 'Cashless World Gets Closer', *The Australian Financial Review*, 28 June 1996, p. 48. See the Hitachi website, <www.hitachi.co.jp/Div/nfs/products/index>. also see the Mondex website, <www.mondex.com/img/mondex>, accessed 5 January 2006.

Questions

1 What are the main benefits from credit card use, and who are the beneficiaries?

2 Do credit cards aid business users more than consumers and, if so, how?

3 Consider the situation where a co-branded smart card such as an adapted Mondex card is used that allows people to travel on any transport within Australia and New Zealand up to the stored value. Assume that included in the attributes of this modified card's primary function is its ability to act as the person's passport and thus contains such information as entry permits and to hold the equivalent of money in five world currencies. The card is accessed by simply walking between two sensors and does not need to be inserted into a machine as did transaction cards of old. What are the pros and cons of such a card and for whom?

14.1

delays customer payment and might cause customers to buy from competitors who offer faster service.

The shipping department uses cheap containers to minimise shipping costs. Cheaper containers lead to a high rate of damaged goods in transit and loss of customer goodwill.

The inventory manager favours low inventories to reduce inventory cost. However, this policy increases stockouts, back orders, paperwork, special production runs and high-cost fast-freight shipments.

Given that logistics activities involve strong trade-offs, decisions must be made on a total system or integrated basis.

The starting point for designing the logistics system is to study what the customers require and what competitors are offering. Customers are interested in on-time delivery, supplier willingness to meet emergency needs, careful handling of merchandise, supplier willingness to take back defective goods and resupply them quickly, and supplier willingness to carry inventory. The company must then research the relative importance of these service outputs.

The company must also take into account competitors' service standards. It will normally want to offer at least the same service level as competitors. But the objective is to maximise profits, not sales. The company has to look at the costs of providing higher levels of service. Some companies offer less service and charge a lower price. Other companies offer more service and charge a premium price.

The company ultimately has to establish marketing logistics networks objectives to guide its planning. For example, Coca-Cola wants to 'put Coke within an arm's length of desire'. Starbucks wants to put a coffee within a one-block walk of its customers in the cities within which it operates. Some companies go even further, defining standards for each service factor.

An appliance manufacturer might establish the following service standards: to deliver at least 95% of the dealer's orders within seven days of order receipt, to fill the dealer's orders with 99% accuracy, to answer dealer inquiries on order status within three hours, and to ensure that damage to merchandise in transit does not exceed 1%.

A fast-moving marketing logistics network in action

In this example, we can see that Figure 1 depicts the flows involved in the marketing logistics network involved in bringing a product to market where the principles of MRP (materials resource planning), JIT (just-in-time), ERP (enterprise resource planning) and ECR (efficient consumer response) have been brought to bear and where EDI (electronic data interchange) and/or telesales have been used in the order process between the marketer and retailing intermediaries. The process is depicted in order to illustrate the use of these technological interface enhancements, before examining the situation where the Web is brought to bear. The product in this instance is a fresh, ready to eat food product with 10 days' shelf-life at 0–4 degrees Celcius. The stepwise flows are as follows:

1 A 10-week materials planning period means

that dressed chicken is available for conversion from its raw state to cooked portion controlled product in a tailor-made Melbourne production facility.

2 A telesales team of four contacts every A-class retail store in Sydney twice each week, and smaller stores once each week, to take orders from chilled food department operatives. Orders from Monday are processed on that day in Melbourne as orders are transmitted via a leased line to a central computer in Melbourne. The central computer translates orders to production computers interfaced with high-speed weigh-labellers which are capable of weighing, printing and applying variable weight labels with pricing applicable to each store (e.g. capital cities and regional cities by state and by retail chain).

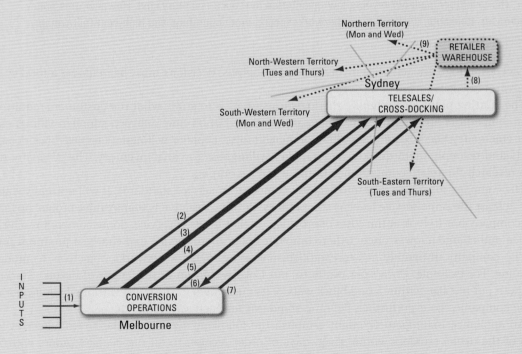

3   Figure 1 Marketing logistics flows for a short-shelf-life consumer product

3 Product is despatched to Sydney by 5.00 pm on day of order, via overnight road transport, and if ordered and produced on a Monday, arrives on a Tuesday.

4 Picking slips are generated by the central computer in Melbourne and printed in Sydney.

5 Load summaries and drop schedules are printed in Sydney.

6 In some operations of this nature, picking slips may be printed in Sydney at step five, and on verification of receipt of exactly configured product, invoices are printed.

7 Invoices are printed in Sydney in drop sequence so that product may be delivered store to store into the territories (geographic areas) shown twice per week. For example, orders taken on a Monday are delivered to store on a Wednesday in Sydney (or Tuesday in Melbourne). While product is delivered store to store at step seven in this case, the reality is that there is a limit to how many trucks can be accommodated by store docking stations, just as there is an upper limit to how many drops a truck can make in a day in cities like Melbourne (30 drops per day), and Sydney (25 drops per day due to a greater number of traffic lights). It is, therefore, more likely that product that has a longer shelf-

life is ordered by a central warehouse through the retail chain head office using EDI. Finished product is then delivered to a central warehouse at a price from which a distribution allowance is deducted by the retailer, as the retailer takes the responsibility for delivery store to store.

In the example depicted in Figure 1, there are two interface technologies discussed, namely telephone and EDI. The case study involves goods rather than services. However, the flows of information other than that provided to the consumer by way of advertising and other marketing communication are clearly evident.

Source: Stewart Adam, The Role of the Web in Marketing and Organisational Performance, unpublished doctoral thesis, Deakin University, 2004, pp. 83–85.

Questions

1 Would least cost be the primary objective in the case of the fast-moving marketing logistics network discussed?

2 What advantages might the use of telesales offer companies such as the fresh food producers in this case?

3 Is forecasting still an important task when producing to order?

14.2

Given its marketing logistics objectives, the company must design a system that will minimise the cost of achieving these objectives. Each possible logistics system will lead to the following cost:

$$M = T + FW + VW + S \qquad \text{(Formula 14.1)}$$

where M = total logistics cost of proposed system
T = total freight cost of proposed system
FW = total fixed warehouse cost of proposed system
VW = total variable warehouse costs (including inventory) of proposed system
S = total cost of lost sales due to average delivery delay under proposed system

Choosing a logistics system calls for an understanding of the total cost (M) associated with different proposed systems and selecting the system that minimises it. If it is hard to measure S, the company should aim to minimise $T + FW + VW$ for a target level of customer service.

Cross-functional teams

The coordination of logistics activities may take a number of forms and require different methods to ensure that an integrated logistics system is in place. In many marketing organisations the responsibility for logistics activities falls to differing functional units. In one company sales might have the responsibility; in another, it might be operations which accounts for the logistics system activities. The difficulty with this approach is that each functional unit might be tempted to optimise its own performance to the detriment of the customer, and therefore to the detriment of the company as a whole. The alternative is to 'harmonise' all the company's distribution decisions. Procter & Gamble has done this by creating 'supply managers' for each of its product categories.[4] Such 'harmonising' might be done either by creating a position at a very senior level or by setting up cross-functional teams to ensure that logistics does indeed 'grease the wheels' between functions and that the company satisfies its customers while doing so with reasonable cost levels. In fact, according to one logistics expert, three-quarters of all major wholesalers and retailers in the USA and a third of major manufacturers have senior logistics officers at the vice-president level or higher.[5]

Building channel partnerships

The members of a marketing logistics network are inexorably linked. One member's distribution network is another member's supply network. Channel partnerships may take many forms, ranging from the location of supplier operatives on the premises of its customers. Alcatel, Siemens, Ericsson and others do this in partnering with Telstra Corporation. Such partnerships also take the form of information sharing and continuous inventory replenishment systems. Companies manage their marketing logistics networks through information. This sharing may involve EDI or it may involve the use of an intranet which is set up and managed by the supplier.

Third-party logistics

Most marketing organisations perform their own logistics functions. Some outsource, or contract out, this role to other companies. Why outsource logistics activities to companies such as P&O Cold Logistics, Mayne Logistics, Fedex or UPS Worldwide Logistics? The main answer is that third-party service organisations can often do it faster and are less expensive. The services these companies provide to their customers may include marketing logistics network management, customised information technology, inventory management, warehousing, transportation management, customer service and fulfilment, freight auditing and control. According to a recent study, outsourcing warehousing alone typically results in 10–15% cost savings.[6] Second, outsourcing logistics activities free the company to focus on its core business. Last, integrated logistics companies have a better understanding of the increasingly complex logistics environment. For example, marketing organisations in European markets face a bewildering array of environmental restrictions which affect logistics, including packaging standards, truck size and weight limits, and noise and pollution controls on emissions. By outsourcing its logistics activities, a company can gain a complete Pan-European distribution network without incurring the costs, delays and risks associated with setting up its own network.[7]

Marketing logistics decisions

The more traditional notion of a trade-off in the five logistics variables when meeting the customer's service requirements is illustrated in Figure 14.4. Customer service in this context might mean that the customer requires all major brands of a range to be delivered into their distribution centre within 24 hours of order placement, and minor brands to be delivered with greater time tolerances. In the case of an entertainment service such as a live PJ Harvey concert, the patrons' experiences cannot be stored. Thus it is meaningless to talk of inventory. Or is it? In addition to the commentary in Chapter 11 on this matter, it is to be noted that the experience at an entertainment centre also requires supporting products such as food and beverages which must be stored so that they will be

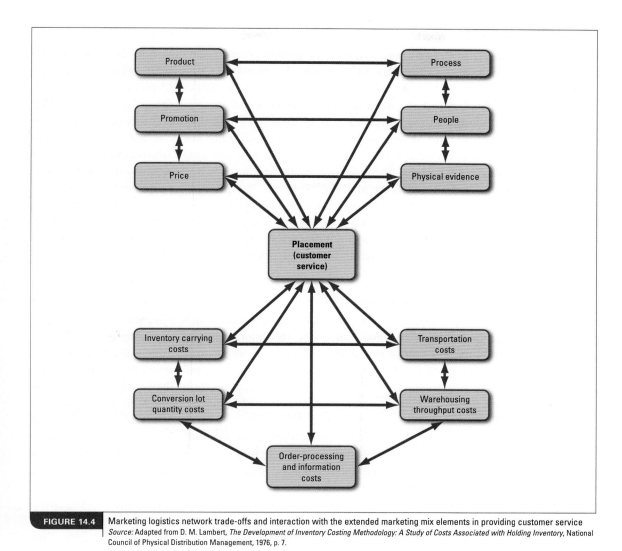

FIGURE 14.4 Marketing logistics network trade-offs and interaction with the extended marketing mix elements in providing customer service
Source: Adapted from D. M. Lambert, *The Development of Inventory Costing Methodology: A Study of Costs Associated with Holding Inventory*, National Council of Physical Distribution Management, 1976, p. 7.

available to meet the need of the concert patrons. These latter items are part of the service encounter or experiential aspect of consuming a service.

The trade-offs occur because management seek an optimal result in terms of achieving a customer service level acceptable to the customer at a cost that gives an optimal profit and cash flow result to the company. In achieving these outcomes, several decisions are involved. Marketing logistics networks decisions involve the following:

- cycle-time reduction
- conversion operations location
- manufacturing and operations process decisions such as product scheduling (lot sizes and costs)
- order processing and costs
- warehouse numbers and costs
- inventory levels and costs
- transport and costs.

Cycle-time reduction decisions

In managing a marketing organisation to a winning market position one important factor is the time it takes to design new products, as well as the time it takes to manufacture and distribute the finished commercialised product. Computer-aided design (CAD) and computer-aided manufacturing (CAM) tools have come to the fore in assisting to build into products and processes those features the market desires, with a minimum of time involved. Just-in-time (JIT) manufacturing techniques assist in reducing manufacturing time, inventory levels, inventory and other costs, as well as reducing the opportunity for defects to occur. Such manufacturing techniques range from simple pull tickets through to sophisticated computer-aided production systems, as used by companies such as Inghams Chickens, Mars, Uncle Ben's of Australia and Simplot. It is also a vital aspect of marketing management—and other management areas—to ensure there is minimal delay between the time an order is received and the time the goods are delivered and paid for. If the marketing organisation is a service provider, such as an airline or a holiday resort, they want to be able instantaneously to advise the customer of seat or room availability and price. Herein lies the path to competitive advantage for the service provider.

Conversion operations location decisions

Conversion operations
Includes services production and physical product manufacturing operations.

Placing a manufacturing plant, or a service centre—each a **conversion operation**—close to raw materials makes economic sense for some companies. This might mean that the bottler of geothermal spring water locates its plant close to the water source. It might mean that a financial services provider places its interaction centre close to where operators are readily available such as Hobart (see Chapter 17 as to why interaction centre is a more appropriate term than call centre). For the spring water bottler there would be low transport costs into the plant as a single logistics (pipeline) system would suffice. However, it might also mean that it would be necessary to have a finished goods warehouse, or at the very least a cross-docking point, located in each major capital city, with inventory in each warehouse so as to meet demand more readily. Also, a separate order-entry system may need to be maintained for each warehouse, resulting in higher order-entry costs, unless a single national electronic system is used.

Although the input materials transport costs will be minimised in this instance, the finished goods transport will be higher—but not as high as if small quantities were shipped store-to-store from one central location. Shipping in semi-trailer loads to each warehouse is possible in this case, thus allowing for staging before breaking down the inventory into delivery loads for each retail outlet.

For each company there is a different set of equations that permits an optimal set of decisions. Each industry is different in regard to the relationship between time and space, and the cost levels that customers will accept. Customers booking a flight from Melbourne to Brisbane with Qantas or Virgin Blue will want an immediate reply on seat availability. Happily for the airline and its customers, such sophisticated information systems coupled to electronic interaction centres exist. Customers buying a new car do not expect the same turnaround time on availability and delivery, with most buyers overstating the time it takes to make a car. Online buyers may have fast turnaround expectations; however, those using eBay have learnt to expect time delays when they have to be verfied by PayPal (eBay's subsidiary company that handles small payments between buyers and sellers), or because incorrect bank account numbers are entered, or simply because the seller is slow to despatch goods.

Manufacturing and operations process decisions

Conversion operations and service-level decisions also impact on every other aspect of marketing and may form part of a company's strategy. The choice of manufacturing process may not be an option for many firms. It may not be possible to use a continuous-flow process in a particular industry; rather, batch processing might be the only process that can be used (see Table 14.1 for configurations of process technology). The moving assembly line for car manufacturing is an example of a now ill-regarded line process—Fordism—whereas the mixing of separate ingredients in a cake production plant—in separate bowls in separate rooms within the plant—is an example of batch processing. In truth, most operations are a mixture of process types.

Even the car makers batch produce engines for later fitting on a moving assembly line. The reduction of manufacturing time by reducing the length of the production line and/or using a pull ticket system—the kanban system—can often lead to advantageous marketplace positioning. So too can the simplification that group technology has allowed.[8] There are many other gains from timely production, mainly related to reduction of inventory costs and reduction of defects.

Order processing decisions

Conversion operations and/or distribution of finished goods begin with a customer order—or at least that is the aim. Some orders are placed by people on the retail floor, while others are inititated by an order department which prepares invoices and sends them to various suppliers. Items out of stock are back-ordered. Shipped items are accompanied by shipping and invoicing documentation with copies going to various internal departments. Orders can be placed in a variety of ways—by mail, telephone (voice or fax), through salespeople and, increasingly, via online methods such as the use of EDI, as this Kmart example illustrates:

> One Kmart quick-response program calls for selected suppliers to manage the retailer's inventory replenishment for their products. Kmart transmits daily records of product sales to the vendor, who analyses the sales information, comes up with an order, and sends it back to Kmart through EDI. Once in Kmart's system, the order is treated as though Kmart itself created it. Says a Kmart executive, 'We don't modify the order, and we don't question it . . . Our relationship with those vendors is such that we trust them to create the type of order that will best meet our inventory needs.'[9]

The steps that most firms follow in **order processing**—those activities involved in receiving, processing and fulfilling orders—are order entry, picking, verification, transport loading, delivery and invoicing (see Marketing Highlight 14.2 for a fast-moving consumer good example).

As already indicated, the use of EDI has resulted in many changes in the way title passes to the customer and payment is received. For example, invoicing may be dispensed with altogether, and payments are made directly into company accounts, as already happens when customers pay for products using bank account access cards (see Figure 14.5 overleaf).

The marketer and customers benefit when the order-processing steps are carried out quickly and accurately. Ideally, orders should be received daily. The order department quickly processes these

Order processing All of the activities involved in receiving, processing and fulfilling sales-order information.

TABLE 14.1 Process technology configurations	
Process	**Example**
Project	Development and commercialisation of the i486 chip by Intel
Job shop	Panel-beater shop
Batch	Mixing a 200-litre batch of bread dough
Line	Moving assembly line for motor vehicles
Continuous process	Oil refinery producing petroleum products

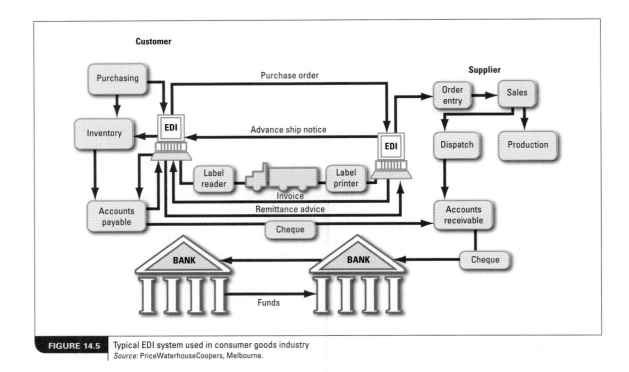

FIGURE 14.5 Typical EDI system used in consumer goods industry
Source: PriceWaterhouseCoopers, Melbourne.

orders and the warehouse sends out the goods on time according to the steps outlined earlier. Invoices go out as soon as possible. The computer is often used to speed up the order–shipping–invoicing cycle. For example, some companies operate computer-based systems that, upon receipt of a customer's order, check the customer's credit standing and whether and where the items are in stock. The computer then issues an order to ship, invoices the customer, updates the inventory records, sends a production order for new stock and relays the message back to the salesperson that the customer's order is on its way—all in less than 15 seconds. Online marketers are already reaping the efficiencies to be gained from using private and public networks.

Warehousing decisions

Every marketing organisation must store its goods while they wait to be sold. A storage function is needed because production and consumption cycles rarely match. Taking the food-processing company SPC Ardmona, wholly owned by Coca-Cola Amatil Ltd, as our example, we can see that

SPC Ardmona picks and packs fresh produce.

fruit and vegetables need to be picked and converted to canned and bottled products, soup, condiments and powdered ingredients in other foodstuffs, according to the growing cycle and not according to demand. The storage function in this instance overcomes differences in needed quantities and timing.

The companies must decide on the best number of stocking locations. The more stocking locations, the more quickly goods can be delivered to customers. However, warehousing costs go up. The company must balance the level of customer service against distribution costs.

Some company stock is kept at or near the plant with the rest in warehouses around the country. The company might own private warehouses, rent space in public warehouses, or both. Owning warehouses gives the company more control, but it ties up capital and is less flexible if desired locations change. Public warehouses, on the other hand, charge for the rented space and provide additional services (at a cost) for inspecting goods, packaging them, shipping them and invoicing them. By using public warehouses, companies also have a wide choice of locations and warehouse types.

Companies may use either storage warehouses or distribution centres. Storage warehouses store goods for moderate to long periods. **Distribution centres**, such as those operated by major retailers, are designed to move goods rather than just store them. They are large and highly automated warehouses designed to receive goods from various plants and suppliers, take orders, fill them efficiently and deliver goods to individual stores as quickly as possible.

Warehousing facilities and equipment technology have improved greatly in recent years. Older multistorey warehouses with slow lifts and outdated materials-handling methods are facing competition from newer single-storey automated warehouses with advanced materials-handling systems under the control of a central computer. In these warehouses, only a few employees are necessary. The computer reads orders and directs lift trucks, electric hoists or robots to gather goods, move them to loading docks and issue invoices. These warehouses have reduced worker injuries, labour costs and theft and breakage, and have improved inventory control.

Distribution centre
A large and highly automated warehouse designed to receive goods from various plants and suppliers, take orders, fill them efficiently and deliver goods to customers as quickly as possible.

Inventory decisions

A major aim of effective marketing logistics network management is the reduction of inventory and its associated costs.[10] The term **inventory** usually refers to finished goods stored as a buffer or warehoused between production and intermediaries such as wholesalers and retailers. There are, however, other inventories, or stocks, that firms seek to reduce and so free capital for other investment activities such as research and development on processes and products. Figure 14.1 illustrates that stocks of raw materials may be held by suppliers or within the manufacturer's plants. Furthermore, some of the input supplies may have already been converted to work-in-process. At close of business on any day, various workstations throughout a production plant will hold inventories at varying levels. If left to its own devices, each station would probably decide on its own safety margin stock, which would result in a ballooning of inventory costs. Among other reasons, this is why inventory must be managed from a wider perspective.

Inventory (sometimes referred to as stocks)
There are three kinds of inventory: raw materials or input supplies to a conversion process; work-in-process and finished goods.

Inventories held by suppliers and as input supplies—whether raw materials or components—can be reduced by good design, as well as by effective management. Good design means building in as few components or sub-assemblies as possible. The same applies to reducing work-in-process, except that good process design is the key.

Finished goods inventory is the most expensive to hold, since it now consists of the original cost plus all of the direct and indirect labour costs involved in making the item, as well as overheads such as factory depreciation and administrative costs. The longer they sit in a warehouse, the more such finished goods will eventually cost, because of mounting inventory carrying costs.

Because the annual carrying cost of inventory can be as high as 20–40% of the materials cost involved, management seek to reduce inventory wherever possible.[11] However, a keen eye must be kept on customer service levels; severely reducing inventory can result in lost sales in the short term and worse in the longer term. Marketers would like their companies to carry enough stock to fill all customer orders right away. However, it costs too much for a company to carry that much inventory.

Inventory costs rise at an increasing rate as the customer service level approaches 100%. To justify larger inventories, management need to know whether sales and profits will increase accordingly.

Inventory decisions involve knowing when to order and how much to order. In deciding when to order, the company balances the risks of running out of stock against the costs of carrying too much. In deciding how much to order, the company needs to balance order-processing costs against inventory carrying costs. Larger average-order size means fewer orders and lower order-processing costs, but it also means larger inventory carrying costs.

Transport decisions

Marketers are involved in their company's transportation decisions. The choice of transportation carriers affects the pricing of the products, delivery performance and condition of the goods when they arrive—all of which affect customer service levels and satisfaction.

In shipping goods to its warehouses, dealers and customers, the company can choose from five transportation modes: rail, road, water, pipeline and air. The characteristics of each transportation mode are summarised in Table 14.2 and discussed in the following paragraphs. **Intermodal transportation methods** are also employed whereby two (or more) transport modes are used—such as Pacific National's Trailerail (illustrated) that involves truck trailers on rail cars, enabling a fast changeover from road wheels to rail bogies on these trailers.

We should not forget, however, that many firms are marketing services and that, in doing so, they rely on the coding, decoding and transmission of voice, data and images using satellites, fibre-optic cable, copper wires and microwave beams. Australian organisations such as Optus and Telstra are involved in the logistics and distribution of such services as the integrated services digital network (ISDN—a digital communications network that can transmit voice, data, text and image) and cellular telephone services. Foxtel and Austar are involved in transmitting news and entertainment over digital networks. In other countries similar organisations are involved in delivering these services.

> **Intermodal transportation methods** Method of transportation whereby two (or more) modes of transport are used, for example piggybacking truck trailers on rail cars.

TABLE 14.2 Transport modes in Australia					
Comparison factors	**Airlines** %	**Motor** %	**Pipeline** %	**Railways** %	**Water** %
Freight hauled (1)	0.01	31	6	31	32
Cost (2)	1	2	4	3	5
Speed (3)	1	2	5	3	4
Reliability (4)	3	2	1	4	5
Capability (5)	4	3	5	2	1
Flexibility (6)	3	1	5	2	4
Capacity (tonnes) (7)	4	5	1	3	2
	5 to 125	10 to 25	30 000 to	50 to	1000 to
			2 500 000	12 000	60 000
Average length of haul	900 km	86 km	na	270 km	2100 km

(1) Freight hauled is based on moving 1 net tonne 1 kilometre; (2) 1 = most costly; (3) 1 = fastest; (4) 1 = most reliable in terms of meeting schedules on time; (5) 1 = best ability to transport various products; (6) 1 = most flexible in terms of door-to-door delivery and number of geographic points served; (7) 1 = ability to carry highest amount of tonnes in one trip.

Source: Reprinted with permission from David J. Bloomberg and Adrian Murray, *The Management of Integrated Logistics: A Pacific Rim Perspective*, Sydney, Prentice Hall Australia, 1996, p. 56.

Like Malaysia, where there were only two large telecommunications organisations from 1987 to 1994 (Telekom Malaysia Bhd and Bina Sat Com. Sdn Bhd [Maxis]), Australia's telecommunications services have been broadened by legislation aimed at providing greater competitiveness and enhanced service quality. In Australia, multi-mode communications companies Telstra and Optus now compete with a number of new entrants such as giant mobile telephone operator Vodafone, which uses a range of technologies to distribute voice, data and images. Other organisations such as General Electric are involved in 'value-added' networks handling EDI on a global basis.

Pacific National's Trailerail system enables a time-saving changeover from road to rail transport.

Rail Between World War II and when fuel price increases affected road transport costs in 2005, railways progressively lost market share because of outdated work practices, inadequate reinvestment in rolling stock and track infrastructure, and the difficulties that arise as a result of different rail gauges used in different parts of the country. Improvements in the interstate road network continue to be a negative influence on rail; however, fuel costs dominate the thoughts of road transport carriers. Private rail system gains—mainly the bulk ore carriers—offset the public sector decline that occurred during the early 1990s to the point where rail now carries about one-third of Australia's freight. Pacific National's Coal Division (illustrated) accounts for a growing proportion of this tonnage. Thus, rail remains one of the most cost-effective modes for transporting large amounts of bulk products— coal, sand, minerals, farm and forest products—over long distances.

With the growing recognition of a national need for improvement in infrastructure, rail is likely to be a major beneficiary of new investment funds. This should result not only in faster and more cost-effective services but also in the introduction of new rolling stock to cater for special needs. Australia's railways continue towards achieving best practice as volumes grow.[12]

Road transport This transport mode continued to increase its share of transportation until recent times. Road trucks still account for the largest portion of transportation within cities mainly because they are are highly flexible in their routing and time schedules. They can move goods door to door, saving shippers the need to transfer goods from truck to rail and back again at a loss of time and risk of theft or damage. Trucks are efficient for short hauls of high-value merchandise. In many cases, their rates are still more competitive than railway rates, and trucks can usually offer faster service.

Technology has also come to the aid of road transport professionals in the form of routing technology and scheduling systems and satellite

Pacific National's Coal Division is a significant bulk ore carrier.

Liquefied natural gas (LNG) carriers transport millions of tonnes each year to help power trading partners China and Japan.

systems to monitor and manage truck performance. Companies such as Foster's Brewing and their transport managers, Linfox, use such a routing system to provide customer service by way of flexible transport scheduling and cost minimisation. In this routing system, the road maps of large capital cities have been photographed by robotic cameras and stored on CD-ROM laser disk. Computer software is then used to determine optimum routes on a day-by-day basis, taking into account 'as you drive' rather than 'as you fly' distances, as well as traffic densities by time of day. This system can also be integrated with a firm's existing pick–load–invoice system. It is yet another tool to assist in achieving faster and more accurate movement of products through the marketing logistics networks.

Water As a major trading nation whose largest customer is Japan, Australia is very dependent on shipping links with the rest of the world. The cost of water transportation is very low for shipping bulky, low-value, non-perishable products such as sand, coal, grain, oil, liquefied natural gas (see illustration) and metallic ores. On the other hand, water transportation is the slowest mode and is sometimes affected by the weather. Until recently, restrictive work practices and a general malaise in waterfront industrial relations meant that Australian costs on the waterfront were substantially higher than those incurred in countries such as Singapore and Hong Kong that compete with each other as Southeast Asian trade hubs. That gap has steadily closed as more container terminals are built, and ship turnaround times continue to decrease.

Pipeline Pipelines are a specialised means of shipping petroleum, natural gas and chemicals from sources to markets. Pipeline shipment of petroleum products costs less than rail shipment but more than water shipment.

Air Although air carriers transport less than 1% of the nation's goods, they are becoming more important as a transportation mode. Air freight rates are much higher than rail or truck rates, but air freight is ideal when speed is needed or distant markets have to be reached. Among the most frequently air-freighted products are perishables (lobster tails, fresh fish, cut flowers) and high-value, low-bulk items (technical instruments, jewellery). Companies find that air freight reduces inventory levels, warehouse numbers and packaging costs. Kodak Australia exports its valuable products via air freight, making it one of the heaviest users of this transport mode.

Choosing transportation modes The cost factors associated with different transport modes determine in large measure which mode is used and thus have

Australia's gas pipelines.

a major impact on competitiveness. However, in choosing a transportation mode costs are not the only factor and shippers consider the criteria that you see in Table 14.2. Thus, if a shipper needs speed, air and truck are the prime choices. If the goal is low cost, then water and pipeline might be best. Trucks appear to offer the most advantages—a fact that explains their growing share of the transportation market.

Thanks to containerisation shippers are increasingly combining two or more modes of transportation. **Containerisation** consists of putting goods in boxes or trailers that are easy to transfer between two transportation modes. Piggyback describes the use of rail and trucks; fishyback, water and trucks; trainship, rail and water; and airtruck, air and trucks. Each combination offers advantages to the shipper. For example, piggyback is not only cheaper than trucking alone but also provides flexibility and convenience.

Containerisation
Putting goods in boxes or trailers that are easy to transfer between two transportation modes. They are used in 'multimode' systems commonly referred to as piggyback, fishyback, trainship and airtruck.

SELF-CHECK QUESTIONS

4   Marketing logistics networks objectives typically involve service standards. Does this mean that marketing logistics network management is solely concerned with the services sector?

5   List and discuss three of the marketing logistics networks' decisions.

6   It has been said that manufacturing and services conversion operations are reliant on each other. Discuss this statement.

7   Discuss the relationships between the extended marketing mix elements and the logistics trade-offs shown in Figure 14.4.

8   What is your view of the statement that it might not be possible for the services sector to compensate for the loss of manufacturing employment in some Western countries? For example, might such an outcome be due solely to companies moving manufacturing to emerging economies where wages are lowest?

9   What is your view of manufacturing (conversion operations) in your country? Do you feel that working in the manufacturing sector is not as acceptable among your peers and family as working in the services sector, or is it the other way round?

The nature of marketing channels

A major part of any marketing logistics network is the intermediaries used to bring the goods and services to the marketplace. These intermediaries are connected by marketing organisations so as to form a marketing channel. A **marketing channel** is a network of interdependent organisations— intermediaries—involved in the process of making a product or service available for use or consumption by the consumer or industrial user.[13]

Marketing channels
A set of interdependent organisations involved in the process of making a product or service available to users.

Why are marketing intermediaries used?

Why do producers give some of the selling jobs to intermediaries? Doing so means giving up some control over how and to whom the products are sold. But producers gain certain advantages from using intermediaries. These advantages are described below.

Many producers lack the financial resources to carry out direct and online marketing. For example, Holden and Ford sell their cars through a number of independent franchise dealers. Even locally, much less worldwide, the car makers would be hard pressed to raise the cash to buy out its dealers.

Direct and online marketing would require many producers to have the resources that intermediaries must use in order to achieve mass-distribution economies for their products. For example, the pie maker Four 'n Twenty would not find it practical to set up small retail pie shops around the country, or to sell its meat pies door to door or by mail order. It would have to sell pies along with many other small products and would end up in the milk bar and food store business. The company finds it easier to work through a network of privately owned distributors. Likewise, Microsoft could not handle the volume of installation work, training and other services that intermediaries provide on a global basis, even though they could easily sell their software over the Web.

Even producers who can afford to set up their own channels can often earn a greater return by increasing their investment in their main business. If a company earns a 20% rate of return on manufacturing and foresees only a 10% return on retailing, it will not want to do its own retailing.

The use of intermediaries largely boils down to their greater efficiency in making products available to target markets. Through their contacts, experience, specialisation and scale of operation, intermediaries usually offer the vendor firm more than it can achieve on its own.

Figure 14.6 shows one way that using intermediaries can provide economies. Part A shows three producers, each using direct marketing to reach three customers. This system requires nine different contacts. Part B shows the three producers working through one distributor, who contacts the three customers. This system requires only six contacts. In this way, intermediaries reduce the amount of work that must be done by both producers and consumers.

From the economic system's point of view, the role of intermediaries is to transform the assortment of products made by producers into the assortments wanted by consumers. Producers make narrow assortments of products in large quantities. But consumers want broad assortments of products in small quantities. In the distribution channels, intermediaries buy large quantities from many producers and break them down into the smaller quantities and broader assortments wanted by consumers. Thus, intermediaries play an important role in matching supply and demand.

Marketing channel functions

Members of the marketing channel move products from producers, importers and aggregators, among others, to end-consumers. This overcomes the major time, place and possession gaps that separate

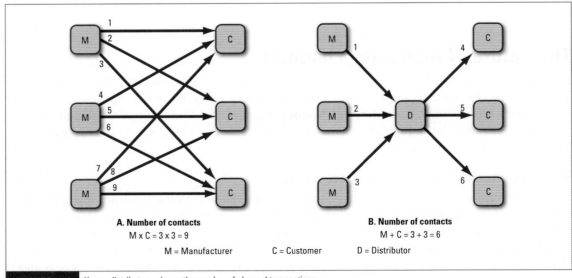

A. Number of contacts
$M \times C = 3 \times 3 = 9$

B. Number of contacts
$M + C = 3 + 3 = 6$

M = Manufacturer   C = Customer   D = Distributor

FIGURE 14.6 | How a distributor reduces the number of channel transactions

goods and services from those who would use them. Members of the marketing channel perform many key functions:

- Information—gathering and distributing marketing research and intelligence information about actors and forces in the marketing environment needed for planning and aiding exchange.
- Promotion—developing and spreading persuasive communications about an offer.
- Contact—finding and communicating with prospective buyers.
- Matching—shaping and fitting the offer to the buyer's needs, including such activities as manufacturing, importing, grading, assembling and packaging.
- Negotiation—reaching an agreement on price and other terms of the offer so that ownership or possession can be transferred.
- Physical distribution—transporting and storing goods.
- Financing—acquiring and using funds to cover the costs of the channel work.
- Risk taking—assuming the risks of carrying out the channel work.

The first five functions help to complete transactions; the last three help to fulfil the completed transactions.

The question is not whether these functions need to be performed—they must be—but rather who is to perform them. All the functions mentioned have three things in common—they use up scarce resources, they can often be performed better through specialisation and they can be transferred between channel members. Where the manufacturer performs them, its costs go up and its selling prices have to be higher. By the same token, when some functions are shifted to intermediaries, the manufacturer's costs and selling prices are lower, but now the intermediaries must add a charge to cover their work. In dividing the work of the channel, the various functions should be assigned to the channel members who can perform them most efficiently and effectively to provide satisfactory assortments of products to target consumers—noting that it is both goods and service that are involved.

Number of channel levels

Marketing channels can be described by the number of channel levels. Each layer of intermediaries that performs some work in bringing the product and its ownership (or usage in the case of services and experiential products) closer to the final buyer is a **channel level**. Because the producer and the end-consumer both perform some work, they are part of every channel. We describe the length of a marketing channel in terms of the number of intermediary levels. Figure 14.7A (overleaf) shows several consumer distribution channels of different lengths.

Channel 1, called a **direct marketing channel**, has no intermediary levels. It consists of a manufacturer, or producer, selling directly to consumers. For example, Avon sells its products door to door, the Franklin Mint sells collectibles through mail order, and private health insurance companies sell their resources through their own outlets or person to person. Channel 2 contains one intermediary level. In consumer markets, this level is typically a retailer. For example, large retailers such as Big W and Kmart sell televisions, cameras, tyres, furniture, appliances and many other products that they buy directly from manufacturers. Channel 3 contains two intermediary levels. In consumer markets, these levels are typically a wholesaler and a retailer. This channel is often used by small manufacturers of food, pharmaceutical, hardware and other products. Channel 4 contains three intermediary levels. In the giftware industry, for example, jobbers often come between wholesalers and retailers. The jobber buys from wholesalers and sells to smaller retailers who are not generally served by the larger wholesalers.

Distribution channels with more levels are sometimes found, but less often. From the producer's point of view, a greater number of levels means less control. And, of course, the more levels, the

Channel level A layer of middlemen that performs some work in bringing the product and its ownership closer to the final buyer.

Direct marketing channel A marketing channel that has no intermediary levels.

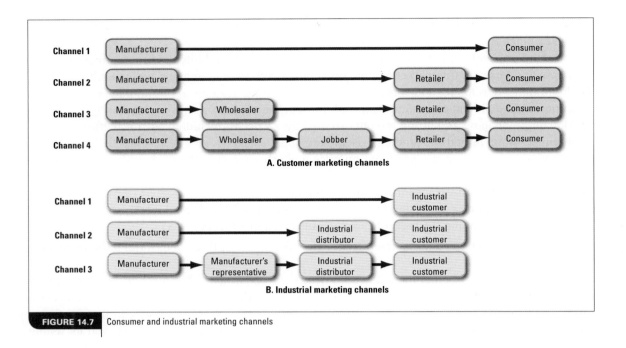

FIGURE 14.7 Consumer and industrial marketing channels

greater the channel's complexity. In Japan, for example, retail products often flow through many levels, thus making it more difficult for suppliers from Australia and New Zealand to understand and influence the market (see Marketing Highlight 14.3).

Figure 14.7B shows some common business-to-business marketing channels. The industrial goods producer can use its own salesforce to sell directly to industrial customers. It can also sell to industrial distributors who in turn sell to industrial customers. It can sell through manufacturer's representatives or its own sales branches to industrial customers, or use them to sell through industrial distributors. Thus zero-, one- and two-level distribution channels are common in industrial goods markets.

All the institutions in the channel are connected by several types of flows. These include the product flow of goods and services, the flow of ownership, payment flow, information flow and promotion flow. These flows can make channels with even only one or a few levels very complex.

Channels in the service sector

The concept of marketing channels is not limited to the distribution of goods. Producers of services and ideas also face the challenge of making their output available to target markets. Utilities such as electricity, natural gas as well as water and sewerage involve marketing channels that are both technology oriented (computer-based systems involving wires, pipelines, metering and billing) and people oriented (retail outlets). Governments develop 'educational distribution systems' (e.g. the UK's Open Learning University, and Open Learning Australia) as well as 'health delivery systems'. Each of these organisations must determine agencies and locations for reaching their widely spread markets.

Hospitals must be located in geographic space to serve the people with complete medical care, and schools must be built close to the children who have to learn. Fire stations must be located to give rapid access to potential fires, and voting booths must be placed so that people can cast their ballots without expending unreasonable amounts of time, effort or money to reach the polling stations. Many of our universities face the problem of locating branch campuses to serve burgeoning populations that are underprovided with educational opportunities. We must create and locate playgrounds for the children in cities and towns. Many overpopulated countries must assign birth-control clinics to reach the people with contraceptive and family planning information.

SELF-CHECK QUESTIONS

10 Provide an example of a marketing organisation that uses both a direct marketing channel and intermediaries to distribute its products and/or services.

11 Does it always follow that goods and services cost more in marketing channels where there are more intermediaries involved?

Channel behaviour and organisation

Marketing channels are more than simple clusters of organisations tied together by various flows. They are complex behavioural networks in which people and companies interact to accomplish individual, company and channel goals. Some channel networks consist only of informal interactions between loosely organised firms; others consist of formal interactions guided by strong organisational structures. And channel networks do not stand still—new types of intermediaries surface and whole new channel networks evolve. In Chapter 18 we describe new types of businesses that have evolved just as network theory suggests they might. Here we look at channel behaviour and at how members in this downstream section of the marketing logistics network organise to do the work of the channel.

Channel behaviour

A marketing channel consists of dissimilar organisations that have networked for their common good. Each channel member is dependent on the others. Ideally, because the success of individual channel members depends on overall success of the network, all channel firms should work together smoothly. They should understand and accept their roles, coordinate their goals and activities and cooperate to attain overall channel goals. By cooperating, they can more effectively sense, serve and satisfy the target market.

However, individual channel members may not take such a broad view. They may be more concerned with their own short-run goals and their dealings with those firms closest to them in the network. Cooperating to achieve overall channel goals sometimes means giving up individual company goals. Although channel members are dependent on one another, they often act alone in their own short-run best interests. They often disagree on the roles each should play, on who should do what and for what rewards. Such disagreements over goals and roles generate **channel conflict**.

Horizontal conflict is conflict between firms at the same level of the channel. Such conflict might be due to rivalry between insurance agents encroaching on each other's territories or customers. Franchisees of large fast-food chains might complain about pricing or other not-so-sound practices by other franchisees in the same image chain. If claims such as cheating on ingredients are made, then this must be investigated by the franchisor. Some car dealers complain about other dealers stealing sales from them by being too aggressive in their pricing and advertising.

Vertical conflict is even more common and refers to conflicts between different levels of the same channel. For example, when Kmart started in Australia, some paint manufacturers were wary about supplying them with the manufacturer's branded product because of the potential backlash that

Channel conflict
Disagreement among marketing channel members on goals and roles—on who should do what and for what rewards.

MARKETING HIGHLIGHT

14.3

Profits flow from sharp marketing logistics management

Retailers in Australia and New Zealand have much smaller markets to contend with than their overseas cousins like Wal-Mart in the USA, and Marks and Spencer (M&S) in the UK. Nevertheless, they look to their overseas counterparts for ideas on how to increase revenues and profits. Coles Group Ltd looked to UK M&S at one point in time. M&S was renowned for initiating new-product development with its suppliers, a feat that CML has not quite mastered, but may do so through a concerted effort to introduce house brands in their supermarket operations, having earlier dropped such house brands as Reserve from the now nationally named Myer department store chain.

Arguably, Coles has looked longingly at how the M&S brand is lauded by consumers in terms of quality. When M&S was slow to change in the 1990s and profits tumbled, no doubt Coles Myer looked elsewhere—certainly in terms of the US management that CEO John Fletcher has brought in to oversee a turnaround that is targeted to lead to an $800 million profit by the reporting season for the 2005/06 financial year. Part of this profit increase is coming from demand chain improvements that include information technology, internal culture, loyalty programs and the spread of supermarket house brands such as *Coles Smart Buys*, *You'll Love Coles* and *George G Coles* across most categories.

However, these gains are dwarfed by fierce competitor Woolworths' (Woolworths-Safeway) earnings before interest, tax depreciation and amortisation which for this period will pass $1.5 billion—all the more significant since Woolworths does not operate department stores. Based on the CGL experience, this might be one reason that Woolworths does so well.

Woolworths has looked to Wal-Mart for inspiration for many years. Woolworths set out to reduce logistics costs in August 1999, while at the same time making their customers' shopping experience more pleasurable, and the program they instituted continues today. Its advertising has variously depicted its logistics technology, dedicated people and suppliers to highlight the fact that they are a great Australian company that focuses on the backend processes and their demand chain (née supply chain), to keep costs down and to ensure that they remain the 'fresh food people'.

However, while Woolworths' performance is not affected by operating departments stores, as is the CML experience, it does increasingly come from their marketing logistics expertise in liquor. Woolworths might be regarded as a retailing conglomerate with such major storefront brands as Woolworths, Safeway, Food For Less, Dick Smith Electronics and PowerHouse, Tandy, Woolworths Liquor, BWS (Beer Wine Spirits) liquor outlets, First Estate, Dan Murphy's, Plus Petrol, BIG W and Woolworths Ezy Banking, and online outlets, Woolworths HomeShop and GreenGrocer. While liquor sales have grown dramatically through acquisitions, the supermarkets division contributes the lion's share of revenue and profit.

In an endeavour to reduce costs, Woolworths CEO Roger Corbett instigated what came to be called 'Project Refresh'—a marketing logistics program without peer in Australian retailing until CML later

Woolworths has a number of major storefront brands.

followed suit on a somewhat smaller scale. The first phase of the Woolworths' program saw the business reorganised as a national retailer, although the Safeway supermarket brand has been retained in Victoria rather than adopt the Woolworths brand. The second phase introduced a restructure of the company's logistics operations, which reportedly cut some $2.5 billion from the company's costs, a figure that represents 2.85% of sales revenue. As part of this program, the company introduced a high-tech automated warehouse re-ordering system (Stocksmart) and an automated store re-ordering system (AutoStockR) to cover all 700 supermarkets in the chain. The company then entered the third phase whereby some 200 new house-brand items continue to be rolled out. This will see Woolworths undertaking the marketing for their own brands and thus be able to position their brands at a lower cost than any single manufacturer might do. It is reported that US house brands cost between 25% and 50% less than comparable manufacturer brands.

While there is much more to this story of the fortunes of Australia and New Zealand's two largest retailers, particularly since it is an unfinished tale, it should be very clear that marketing logistics management features strongly. One only has to look at the retail operations of Wal-Mart to see that both retailers will not rest until they can bring their logistics strengths to bear in the retailing of pharmacy lines (so far vetoed by the Australian government), furniture, homewares and travel services, to mention only some of the more obvious product lines they will pursue.

Sources: Neil Shoebridge, 'On the House', *Business Review Weekly*, 14 July 2005, <brw.com.au/fearticle.aspx?relID=14651>, accessed 7 January 2006; Simon Lloyd, 'Woolies Returns Fire', *Business Review Weekly*, 28 October 2004, <brw.com.au/fearticle.aspx?relID=10420>, accessed 8 January 2006; James Thomson, 'Costs: Low Fat, High Profit', *Business Review Weekly*, 29 April 2004, <brw.com.au/fearticle.aspx?relID=7718>, accessed 8 January 2006; Anonymous, 'Coles Myer: Back in the Game', *Business Review Weekly*, 29 April 2004, <brw.com.au/fearticle.aspx?relID=7717>, accessed 8 January 2006.

Questions

1 Why does marketing logistics management seem to feature so prominently in the marketing strategies employed by retailers?

2 Would you agree with the proposition that business success in any sphere is little different from retailing in terms of the reliance on prowess in marketing logistics network management?

3 According to Neil Plumridge, VP with consulting firm AT Kearney, there are only two ways to cut costs—from labour costs and/or suppliers. What are your opinions on this view of cutting costs? How does it align with those Woolworths seem to be achieving?

14.3

would occur from other retailers who stocked the brand. This concern was also evident when both Coles and Woolworths-Safeway supermarket chains began an aggressive expansion of their own brands to the exclusion of manufacturers' brands in 2005.[14]

Some conflict in the channel takes the form of healthy competition. This competition can be good for the channel—without it the channel could become reactive and not innovate in terms of products and processes. Sometimes conflict can damage the channel. For the channel as a whole to perform well, each channel member's role must be specified and channel conflict must be managed. Cooperation, assigning roles and conflict management in the channel are attained through strong channel leadership. The channel will perform better if it contains a firm, agency or mechanism that has the power to assign roles and manage conflict.

In a large company, the formal organisation structure assigns roles and provides the needed leadership. But in a marketing channel made up of independent firms, leadership and power are not formally set. Traditionally, such channels have lacked the leadership needed to assign roles and manage conflict. In recent years, however, new types of channel organisations have appeared that provide stronger leadership and improved performance.

Channel organisation

Historically, marketing channels have been loose collections of independent companies, each showing little concern for overall channel performance. These conventional distribution channels have lacked strong leadership and have been troubled by damaging conflict and poor performance.

Vertical marketing networks

One of the biggest recent channel developments has been the vertical marketing networks that have emerged to challenge conventional marketing channels. Figure 14.8 contrasts the two types of channel arrangements.

A conventional marketing channel consists of one or more independent producers, wholesalers and retailers. Each is a separate business seeking to maximise its own profits, even at the expense of profits for the network as a whole. No channel member has much control over the other members, and no formal means exist for assigning roles and resolving channel conflict. By contrast, a **vertical marketing network (VMN)** consists of producers, wholesalers and retailers acting as a unified network. It is usually the case that one member owns the others, has contracts with them or wields so much power that they all cooperate. The VMN can be dominated by the producer, wholesaler or retailer. VMNs came into being to control channel behaviour and manage channel conflict. They achieve economies through size, bargaining power and elimination of duplicated services.

We look now at the three major types of VMNs shown in Figure 14.9. Each type uses a different means for setting up leadership and power in the channel. In a corporate VMN coordination and conflict management are attained through common ownership at different levels of the channel. In a contractual VMN they are attained through contractual agreements between channel members. In an administered VMN leadership is assumed by one or a few dominant channel members.

Corporate VMN A **corporate VMN** combines successive stages of production and distribution under single ownership. For example, a manufacturer of paint may operate its own outlets catering for the professional painter and paint trade. In such corporate networks, cooperation and conflict management are managed through regular organisational channels.

Vertical marketing network (VMN)
A distribution channel structure in which producers, wholesalers and retailers act as a unified network—either one channel member owns the others, has contracts with them, or wields so much power that they all cooperate.

Corporate VMN
A vertical marketing network that combines successive stages of production and distribution under single ownership—channel leadership is established through common ownership.

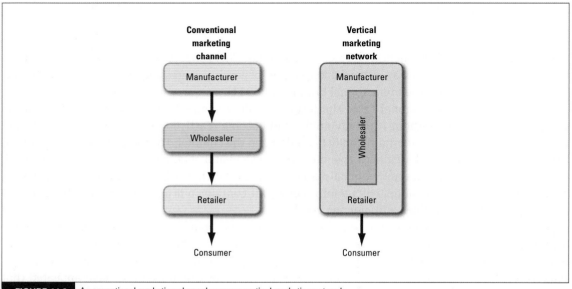

FIGURE 14.8   A conventional marketing channel versus a vertical marketing network

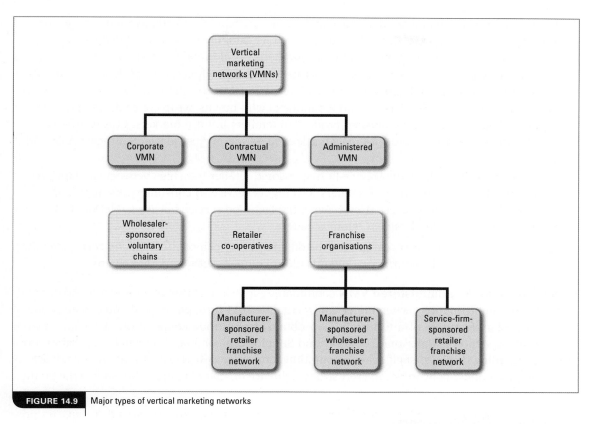

FIGURE 14.9 Major types of vertical marketing networks

Contractual VMN A **contractual VMN** consists of independent firms at different levels of production and distribution who join together through contracts to obtain more economies or sales impact than they could achieve alone. Contractual VMNs have expanded rapidly in recent years. There are three types of contractual VMNs.

Wholesaler-sponsored voluntary chains are networks in which wholesalers organise voluntary chains of independent retailers to help them compete with large chain organisations. The wholesaler develops a program in which independent retailers standardise their selling practices and achieve buying economies that let the group compete effectively with chain organisations. Examples include Sigma Pharmaceutical's AMCAL, AMCAL MAX and Guardian Chemist banner groups.[15]

Retailer co-operatives are networks in which retailers organise a new, jointly owned business to carry on wholesaling and possibly production. Members buy most of their goods through the retailer co-op and plan their advertising jointly. Profits are passed back to members in proportion to their purchases. Non-member retailers may also buy through the co-op but do not share in the profits.

In **franchise organisations** a channel member called a franchisor links several stages in the production–distribution process. Franchising has been the fastest-growing retailing form in recent years. In the USA, more than 500 000 franchise operations account for about one-third of all retail sales, and were predicted to account for one-half by the year 2000.[16] Almost every kind of business has been franchised—from motels and fast-food restaurants to dentists and dating services, from wedding consultants and diet services to funeral homes and bath tub and tile refinishers. Although the basic idea is an old one, some forms of franchising are quite new.

There are three forms of franchises.

Contractual VMN
A vertical marketing network in which independent firms at different levels of production and distribution join together through contracts to obtain more economies or sales impact than they could achieve alone.

Wholesaler-sponsored voluntary chains Contractual vertical marketing networks in which wholesalers organise voluntary chains of independent retailers to help them compete with large corporate chain organisations.

Retailer co-operatives
Contractual vertical marketing network in which retailers organise a new, jointly owned wholesale business.

Franchise organisation
A contractual vertical marketing network in which a channel member called a franchisor links several stages in the production–distribution process.

1 The first form is the manufacturer-sponsored retailer franchise network, as found in the car industry. Ford, for example, licenses dealers to sell its cars; the dealers are independent businesspeople who agree to meet various conditions of sales and service.

2 The second type of franchise is the manufacturer-sponsored wholesaler franchise network, as found in the soft drink industry. Coca-Cola's international distribution strategy, for example, is to license bottlers (wholesalers) in various markets who buy its syrup concentrate and then carbonate, bottle and sell the finished product to retailers in local markets. CCA (Coca-Cola Amatil Ltd) is the largest of Coca-Cola's bottlers operating in Australasia, Southeast Asia and Europe.

3 The third franchise form is the service-firm-sponsored retailer franchise network, in which a service firm licenses a network of retailers to bring its service to consumers. Examples are found in the car rental business (Hertz, Avis), the fast-food service business (McDonald's, Pizza Hut) and the motel business (Homestead).

The fact that most consumers cannot tell the difference between contractual and corporate VMNs shows how successfully the contractual organisations compete with corporate chains.

Administered VMN
A vertical marketing network that coordinates successive stages of production and distribution, not through common ownership or contractual ties but through the size and power of one of the parties.

Administered VMN An **administered VMN** coordinates successive stages of production and distribution—not through common ownership or contractual ties but through the size and power of one of the parties. Manufacturers of a top brand can obtain strong trade cooperation and support from resellers. Thus, Arnott's, Panasonic, Unilever and Simplot can command unusual cooperation from resellers regarding displays, shelf space, promotions and price policies. And large retailers such as Aldi, Coles Myer and Woolworths can exert strong influence on manufacturers that supply the product they sell.

Horizontal marketing networks

Horizontal marketing networks A channel arrangement in which two or more companies at one level join together to follow a new marketing opportunity.

Another channel development is **horizontal marketing networks**, in which two or more companies at one level join together to follow a new marketing opportunity. By working together, companies can combine their capital, production capabilities or marketing resources to accomplish more than any one company working alone. Companies might join forces with competitors or non-competitors.[17] They might work with each other on a temporary or permanent basis, or they might create a separate company.[18]

It is claimed that the development of such strategic alliances will be important if Australian products are to gain distribution in some overseas markets. By working together companies can gain impact, scale and flexibility that would not be achieved if each acted by itself.

Hence when Australian bands performed in Los Angeles under the banner 'Wizards of Oz' they potentially reached more booking agents than they could individually. Qantas works with the domestic tourist industry to offer tour packages and promotional activities, such as visits by travel agents and writers, to expand the overall market of visitors to this country. In Victoria's Goulburn Valley, the fruit canners have at different times joined forces to market their product overseas under a single brand name in order to achieve greater impact and wider distribution. Such symbiotic marketing arrangements have increased dramatically in recent years and the end is nowhere in sight.

Hybrid marketing channel networks

Hybrid marketing channel networks
Multichannel distribution systems in which a single firm sets up two or more marketing channels to reach one or more marketing segments.

Multichannels (See hybrid marketing channels)

In the past many companies used a single channel to sell to a single market or market segment. Today, with the proliferation of customer segments and channel possibilities, more and more companies have adopted **hybrid marketing channel networks**, or **multichannel networks**, that involve multichannel distribution. Hybrid marketing channels occur when a single firm sets up two or more marketing channels to reach one or more customer segments. IBM is an example of a company that uses such hybrid marketing channels effectively. After selling 'big iron' for many years through its own salesforce, its market fragmented with the advent of the microcomputer. As a result, IBM added 18 new channels in less than 10 years.[19]

Inghams sells dressed chicken portions to KFC as well as to myriad independent takeaway food shops, and also sells chicken products to every part of the food services industry, including McDonald's and KFC. Hungry Jack's (Burger King in the USA and Asia) owns a burger meat patty production unit in Queensland and sells patties to other sectors of the food services industry as well as in branded consumer packs.

The marketer using such multichannels gains sales with each new channel but also risks offending existing channels. Existing channels can cry 'unfair competition' and threaten to drop the marketer unless it limits the competition or repays them in some way, perhaps by offering them exclusive models or special allowances.

In some cases, the marketer's channels are all under its own ownership and control. For example, at one time Coles Myer operated department stores (Myer and Grace Bros), mass-merchandising stores (Coles Supermarkets, Bi-Lo, Target and Kmart) and specialty stores (Megamart and Liquorland). Each store offered different product assortments to different market segments; in such cases there may be no conflict with outside channels, but the marketer might face internal conflict over how much financial support each channel deserves. Today, Myer has been sold and Coles Ltd no longer operates department stores.

Increasingly, the Internet figures in such hybrid marketing networks. In Chapter 15 we illustrate this point further when we examine the emerging online activities of major retailers like Coles Supermarkets and Woolworths-Safeway. They are only a few among the many online marketers we might examine such as booksellers, music retailers, toys retailers, retailers of flowers and all manner of consumer goods that are either restructuring their marketing channels to deal more directly with customers (**disintermediation**), or restructuring their entire business so as to move from a physically bound business to an online business (**reintermediation**). Digital technologies, particularly the Internet, are opening up opportunities for some existing channel members and new entrants while presenting threats to many other marketing channel members.

Channel design decisions

We now look at several channel decision problems facing manufacturers. In designing marketing channels, manufacturers struggle between what is ideal and what is practical. A new firm usually starts by selling in a limited market area. Because it has limited capital, it typically uses only a few existing intermediaries in each market—a few manufacturers' sales agents, a few wholesalers, some existing retailers, a few trucking companies and a few warehouses. Deciding on the best channels might not be a problem: the problem might be to convince one or a few good intermediaries to handle the line.

If the new firm is successful, it might branch out to new markets. Again, the manufacturer will tend to work through the existing intermediaries, although this strategy might mean using different types of marketing channels in different areas. In smaller markets the firm might sell directly to retailers; in larger markets it might sell through distributors. In one part of the country it might grant exclusive franchises because the merchants normally work this way; in another it might sell through all outlets willing to handle the merchandise. The manufacturer's channel network thus evolves to meet local opportunities and conditions.

Designing a channel network calls for analysing consumer service needs, setting the channel objectives and constraints, identifying the major channel alternatives and evaluating them.

Disintermediation
Removing a marketing channel, as when a consumer invests directly in the money market rather than investing via their bank—often a myth perpetuated by those who are pro-technology in the case of the effects of online businesses such as Amazon.com.

Reintermediation
Disintermediation is mostly a myth, and most often marketing channels are altered by disruptive technologies—such as how the Internet has enabled banks to act as online share brokers, and how online auctions and reverse auctions have enabled broadly dispersed buyers and sellers to transact without the need for traditional intermediaries.

Analysing consumer service needs

Customer value delivery networks
Marketing channels in which each channel member adds value for the customer.

Like most marketing decisions, designing a channel begins with the customer. Marketing channels can be thought of as **customer value delivery networks** in which each channel member adds value for the customer. As noted earlier, the success of one company depends not just on its own actions, but on how well its entire channel competes with the channels of other companies.

Designing marketing channels starts with finding out what values consumers in various target segments want from the channel.[20] Do consumers want to buy from nearby locations or are they willing to travel to more distant centralised locations? Would they rather buy over the phone or through the mail? Do they want immediate delivery or are they willing to wait? Do consumers value breadth of assortment or do they prefer specialisation? Do consumers want many add-on services (delivery, credit, repairs, installation) or will they obtain these elsewhere? The more decentralised the channel, the faster the delivery, the greater the assortment provided and the more add-on services supplied, the greater the channel's service level.

Setting channel objectives and constraints

Channel objectives should be stated in terms of the desired service level of target consumers. Usually, a company can identify several segments wanting different levels of channel service. The company should decide which segments to serve and the best channels to use in each case. In each segment the company wants to minimise the total channel cost of delivering the desired service level.

The company's channel objectives are also influenced by the nature of its products, company policies, intermediaries, competitors and the environment. Product characteristics greatly affect channel design. For example, perishable products require more direct marketing to avoid delays and too much handling. Bulky products, such as building materials or soft drinks, require channels that minimise shipping distance and amount of handling.

Company characteristics also play an important role. For example, the company's size and financial situation determine which marketing functions it can handle itself and which it gives to intermediaries. And a company marketing strategy based on speedy customer delivery affects the functions that the company wants its intermediaries to perform, the number of its outlets and the choice of its transportation methods.

Intermediaries' characteristics influence channel design. The company must find intermediaries who are willing and able to perform the needed tasks. In general, intermediaries differ in their abilities to handle promotion, customer contact, storage and credit. For example, a manufacturer's representatives who are hired by several different firms can contact customers at a low cost per customer because several clients share the total cost. But the selling effort behind the product is less intense than if the company's own salesforce did the selling.

When designing its channels, a company needs to consider competitors' channels. It may want to compete in or near the same outlets that carry competitors' products. Thus, food companies want their brands to be displayed next to competing brands—KFC wants to locate near McDonald's. In other industries, producers may avoid the channels used by competitors. Avon decided not to compete with other cosmetics makers for scarce positions in retail stores and instead created a profitable direct and online selling operation to offices and homes. However, this is not to say that it will never use traditional channels or a combination of channels in the future.

Finally, environmental factors such as economic conditions and legal constraints affect channel design decisions. For example, in a depressed economy producers want to distribute their goods in the most economical way, using shorter channels and dropping unneeded services that add to the final price of the goods. Legal regulations prevent channel arrangements that 'may tend to substantially lessen competition or tend to create a monopoly'.

Identifying the major alternatives

When the company has defined its channel objectives, it should next identify its major channel alternatives in terms of types of intermediaries, number of intermediaries and the responsibilities of each channel member.

Types of intermediaries

A firm should identify the types of intermediaries available to carry on its channel work. For example, suppose a manufacturer of test equipment has developed an electronic device that detects poor mechanical connections in any machine with moving parts. Company executives think that this product would have a market in all industries where electric, combustion or steam engines are made or used. This market includes such industries as aviation, car, railway, food canning, construction and oil. The company's current salesforce is small, and the problem is how best to reach these different industries. The following channel alternatives might emerge from management discussion:

- *Company salesforce.* Expand the company's direct salesforce. Assign salespeople to territories and have them contact all prospects in the area, or develop separate company salesforces for different industries.
- *Manufacturer's agency.* Hire manufacturer's agencies—independent firms whose salesforces handle related products from many companies—in different regions or industries to sell the new test equipment.
- *Industrial distributors.* Find distributors in the different regions or industries who will buy and carry the new line. Give them exclusive distribution, good margins, product training and promotional support.

Sometimes, a company must develop a channel other than the one it prefers because of the difficulty or cost of using the preferred channel. Still, the decision sometimes turns out extremely well. For example, Tooheys Blue Label beer initially succeeded in penetrating the Victorian market, which was 'owned' by Foster's Brewery, not by competing head-to-head in hotel draught beer sales, but by tackling the packaged beer market. This involved a wider range of retail outlets, some of which were seeking a strong competitor and alternative to Foster's.

Number of marketing intermediaries

Companies must also determine the number of intermediaries to use at each level. Three strategies are available.

Intensive distribution Producers of fast-moving consumer goods and common raw materials typically seek **intensive distribution**—stocking their product in as many outlets as possible. These goods must be available where and when consumers want them. For example, toothpaste, chocolate bars and similar items are sold in millions of outlets to provide maximum brand exposure and consumer convenience.

Exclusive distribution By contrast, some producers deliberately limit the number of intermediaries handling their products. The extreme form of this practice is **exclusive distribution**, whereby a limited number of dealers are given the exclusive right to distribute the company's products in their territories. Exclusive distribution is often found in the distribution of new cars and some brands of women's clothing. By limiting distribution, the manufacturer hopes for stronger distributor selling support and more control over intermediaries' prices, promotion, credit and services. Exclusive distribution often enhances the product's image and allows higher mark-ups.

Selective distribution Between intensive and exclusive distribution lies **selective distribution**—the use of more than one but fewer than all the intermediaries who are willing to carry a company's

Intensive distribution
Stocking the product in as many outlets as possible.

Exclusive distribution
Giving a limited number of dealers the exclusive right to distribute the company's products in their territories.

Selective distribution
The use of more than one but fewer than all the intermediaries who are willing to carry the company's products.

products. The company does not have to spread its efforts over many outlets, including many marginal ones. It can develop a good working relationship with selected intermediaries and expect a better than average selling effort. Selective distribution lets the producer gain good market coverage with more control and less cost than intensive distribution. We find television, furniture and small appliance brands are often distributed selectively.

Responsibilities of channel members

The producer and intermediaries need to agree on the terms and responsibilities of each channel member. They should agree on price policies, conditions of sale, territorial rights and specific services to be performed by each party. Working backwards from the end-consumer price, the producer should establish a recommended retail price and a fair set of discounts for intermediaries. It must define each intermediary's territory and be careful of the location of any new resellers it decides to accept. Mutual services and duties need to be carefully spelled out, especially in franchise and exclusive distribution channels. For example, McDonald's provides franchisees with promotional support, a record-keeping system, training and general management assistance. In turn, franchisees must meet company standards for physical facilities, cooperate with new promotion programs, provide requested information and buy specified food products.

Evaluating the major channel alternatives

Suppose a company has identified several channel alternatives and wants to select the one that will best satisfy its long-run objectives. The firm must evaluate each alternative against economic, control and adaptive criteria.

Economic criteria

Each channel alternative will produce a different level of sales and costs. The first step is to determine the sales levels that would be produced by a company salesforce compared with a sales agency. Most marketing managers believe that a company salesforce will sell more. Company salespeople sell only the company's products and are better trained to handle them. They sell more aggressively because their future depends on the company. And they are more successful because customers prefer to deal directly with the company.

On the other hand, the sales agency could possibly sell more than a company salesforce. First, the sales agency may have more salespeople than the company can initially afford. Second, the agency salesforce may be just as aggressive as a direct salesforce, depending on how much commission the line offers in relation to other lines carried. Third, some customers prefer dealing with agents who represent several manufacturers rather than with salespeople from one company. Fourth, the agency has many existing contacts, whereas a company salesforce would have to build them from scratch.

The next step is to estimate the costs of selling different volumes through each channel. The costs are shown in Figure 14.10. The fixed costs of using a sales agency are lower than those of setting up a company sales office. But costs rise faster through a sales agency because sales agents get a larger commission than company salespeople. There is one sales level (S_B) at which selling costs are the same for the two channels. The company would prefer to use the sales agency at any sales volume below S_B, and the company sales branch at any volume higher than S_B. In general, sales agents tend to be used by smaller firms, or by larger firms in smaller territories where the sales volume is too low to warrant a company salesforce.

Control criteria

Next, evaluation must be broadened to consider control issues with the two channels. Using a sales agency poses more of a control problem. A sales agency is an independent business firm interested

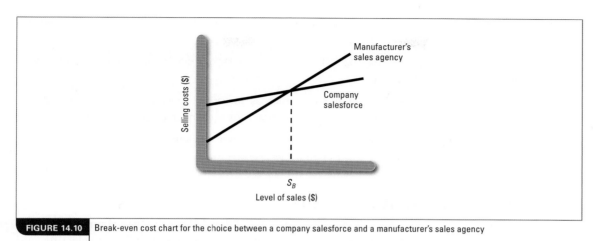

FIGURE 14.10 Break-even cost chart for the choice between a company salesforce and a manufacturer's sales agency

in maximising its profits. The agent may concentrate on the customers who buy the largest volume of goods from its entire mix of client companies rather than those most interested in a particular company's goods. And the agency's salesforce might not master the technical details of the company's products or handle its promotion materials effectively.

Adaptive criteria

Each channel involves some long-term commitment and loss of flexibility. A company using a sales agency may have to offer a five-year contract. During this period, other means of selling, such as a company salesforce, may become more effective, but the company cannot drop the sales agency. To be worthy of consideration, a channel involving a long commitment should be greatly superior on economic or control grounds.

Designing international marketing channels

International marketers face many additional complexities in designing their channels. Each country has its own unique distribution network that has evolved over time and changes very slowly. These channel systems can vary widely from country to country. Thus, global marketers must usually adapt their channel strategies to the existing structures within each country. In some markets, the distribution system is complex and hard to penetrate, consisting of many layers and large numbers of intermediaries. When one considers the organisation of marketing channels in Japan and what it takes to build a relationship with Japanese firms, it is perhaps no wonder that many Western firms have had great difficulty breaking into the closely knit, tradition-bound Japanese distribution network.

At the other extreme, distribution systems in developing countries may be scattered and inefficient, or lacking altogether. For example, China and India are large markets, each containing hundreds of millions of people. In reality, however, these markets are much smaller than the population numbers suggest. Because of inadequate distribution systems in both countries, most companies can profitably access only a small portion of the population located in each country's most affluent cities.[21]

Nevertheless, these accessible markets in China and India are often larger than the combined markets of Australia and New Zealand, depending on the product in question. Thus, international marketers face a wide range of channel alternatives. Designing efficient and effective channel systems between and within various country markets poses a difficult challenge.

Channel management decisions

Once the company has reviewed its channel alternatives and decided on the best channel design, it must implement and manage the chosen channel. Channel management calls for selecting and motivating individual intermediaries and evaluating their performance over time.

Selecting channel members

Producers vary in their ability to attract qualified intermediaries. Some producers have no difficulty signing up intermediaries, particularly where well-recognised brand names are involved. In some cases, the promise of exclusive or selective distribution for a desirable product will draw enough applicants.

At the other extreme are producers who have to work hard to line up enough qualified intermediaries. Small food producers often cannot afford the money necessary to get grocery stores to carry their products. For this reason they often supply the food services sector—airlines, armed forces, educational institutions and the like—for quite some time until they can afford to 'go retail'.

When selecting intermediaries, the company should determine which characteristics distinguish the better intermediaries. It will want to evaluate the intermediaries' business experience, other lines carried, growth and profit record, profitability, degree of cooperation and reputation. If the intermediaries are sales agents, the company will want to evaluate the number and character of other lines carried, and the size and quality of the salesforce. If the intermediary is a retail store that wants exclusive or selective distribution, the company will want to evaluate the store's customers, location and future growth potential.

Motivating channel members

Once selected, intermediaries must be continuously motivated to do their best. The company must sell not only through the intermediaries, but to them. Most producers see the problem as finding ways to gain the cooperation of intermediaries. They use the carrot-and-stick approach. They offer such positive motivators as higher margins, special deals, premiums, cooperative advertising allowances, display allowances and sales contests. At times they will use negative motivators, such as threatening to reduce margins, to slow down delivery or to end the relationship altogether. A producer using this approach has usually not done a good job of studying the needs, problems, strengths and weaknesses of its distributors.

More advanced companies try to forge long-term partnerships with their distributors. This involves building a planned, professionally managed, vertical marketing network that meets the needs of both the manufacturer and the distributors.[22] The manufacturer sets up a section in the marketing area called key account management whose job it is to identify the distributors' needs and build programs to help each distributor market the company's product. This department and the distributors jointly plan the merchandising goals, inventory levels, merchandising strategies, sales training and advertising and promotion plans. The aim is to convince distributors that they can make their money by being part of an advanced VMN.

Category management was introduced by retailers in an endeavour to coordinate the efforts of many departments within their organisations. Category managers are responsible for product categories such as 'oral hygiene products'. This category includes pre-rinses, gargles, toothpastes, toothbrushes and dental flosses. Where producers do not use such a title, the **key account manager** is the supplier's equivalent of the retailer's category manager.

Evaluating channel members

The producer must regularly check intermediaries' performance against such standards as sales quotas, average inventory levels, customer delivery time, treatment of damaged and lost goods, cooperation in company promotion and training programs, and services to the customer. The company should recognise and reward intermediaries who are performing well. Intermediaries who are performing poorly should be helped or, as a last resort, replaced. A company may periodically 'requalify' its intermediaries and prune the weaker ones.[23]

Manufacturers need to be sensitive to their dealers. Those who treat their dealers lightly risk not only losing their support but also risk causing legal problems.

Efficient customer response (ECR)

The marketing channels we have outlined rely on channel members fulfilling the roles described. Retail buyers and wholesalers have made the decisions on which merchandise to buy and sell in various selling periods. They have also decided when to take stock into inventory. Marketing organisations offer all manner of 'trade' deals to have these intermediaries take stock early and/or in larger volumes than sales might suggest they need. This can lead to high inventory levels in the wrong part of the channel at the wrong time. High inventory costs coupled with stockouts at store level suggested that a more efficient method was needed.

Efficient customer response (ECR) programs have developed whereby greater efficiencies have been introduced into conversion operations, distributing and stocking inventory, while at the same time promoting added value for the customer. In such a program, retail buyers and wholesalers give up some of their authority and suppliers analyse retail sales and inventory information and finally make the decision as to when to produce and distribute finished goods to the intermediaries. EDI and extranets are used as tools whereby intermediaries may review scheduled shipments from suppliers. Cutting trade promotions, reducing inventory levels, reducing the number of people needed and increasing shipment sizes all serve to reduce logistics costs under ECR programs.

Category management
A management approach introduced by retailers and increasingly adopted by the marketing organisations in an endeavour to coordinate the efforts of many departments.

Key account manager
A sales manager who manages the interaction with a major customer.

SELF-CHECK QUESTIONS

15 In Australia, there is a concentration of ownership in the retail sector. How might this impact on the relationships between the marketer of consumer goods and the retailing intermediary?

16 How might a service provider such as Qantas or Singapore Airlines motivate intermediaries in the travel industry?

17 What part does information flow play in consumer goods marketing? Is this flow different in the services sector? If so, describe the differences.

SUMMARY

Just as the marketing concept is receiving increased recognition, so more marketing organisations are paying attention to *marketing logistics network management*. At the heart of the concept of the marketing logistics networks is the integration of a number of aspects of *logistics management*. Logistics is an area of potentially high cost savings and improved customer satisfaction. Marketing logistics network management involves coordinating the activities of the entire chain to deliver maximum value to customers. No logistics system can both maximise customer service and minimise distribution costs. Instead, the goal of integrated logistics management is to provide a targeted level of service at the least cost. The major marketing logistics networks functions include effective and efficient *conversion operations*, *order processing*, *warehousing*, *inventory management* and *transportation*.

The marketing logistics networks concept recognises that improved logistics requires teamwork—in the form of close working relationships across functional areas inside the company, and across various organisations in the supply chain. Organisations can achieve logistics harmony between functions by creating cross-functional logistics teams, integrative supply manager positions and senior-level logistics executives with cross-functional authority. Channel partnerships at the downstream or customer end of such networks can take the form of cross-company teams, shared projects and information-sharing systems. Through such partnerships, many companies have switched from anticipatory-based distribution systems to customer-triggered response-based distribution systems.

Distribution channel decisions are among the most complex and challenging decisions facing the firm. Each channel network creates a different level of sales and costs. Once a distribution channel has been chosen, the firm must usually stick with it for a long time. The chosen channel strongly affects, and is affected by, the other elements in the marketing mix.

Each firm needs to identify alternative ways to reach its market. Available means vary from direct selling to using one, two, three or more intermediary channel levels. Marketing channels face continuous and sometimes dramatic change. Three of the most important trends are the growth of *vertical*, *horizontal* and *hybrid marketing networks*. These trends affect channel cooperation, conflict and competition.

Channel design begins with assessing customer channel-service needs and company channel objectives and constraints. The company then identifies the major channel alternatives in terms of the types of intermediaries, the number of intermediaries and the channel responsibilities of each. Each channel alternative must be evaluated according to economic, control and adaptive criteria. Channel management calls for selecting qualified intermediaries and motivating them. Individual channel members must be evaluated regularly.

MARKETING ISSUE

Among the aims of a recent research study was the objective of unearthing the link between marketing logistics competency and organisational performance—both financial (e.g. sales revenue, profit and cash flow) and non-financial (e.g. perceived brand quality). Employing structural equation modelling, the study found that there was no statistically significant relationship between the two. That is, logistics management competency could not explain any of the variance in organisational performance in the sample of Australian and New Zealand organisations who responded in the study.

In providing likely explanations, the researchers indicated that in the main senior managers responded, and they should be able to report accurately how their organisations use marketing logistics management. However, we wonder whether or not the researchers were correct in stating that perhaps there is a lack of integration of marketing logistics management within many organisations such that to uncover the true competence in use of marketing logistics, rather than employ a survey of a single respondent within each organisation, the researchers might have been advised to employ a number of managers across various functional areas such as marketing, operations and the like.

Conduct a small number of personal interviews within organisations with which you are familiar. Is there a single person responsible for marketing logistics management within these organisations, or is the role fragmented? What do you suggest might be the ideal structure in this regard? Might it vary by industry?

Source: Stewart Adam and David Bednall, 'The Influence of Marketing Logistics Networks on Organisational Performance in Australia and New Zealand', Multimedia CD-ROM. In G. Troilo (ed.), *EMAC 2005*, Proceedings of the 34th European Marketing Academy Conference, Milan, Italy, available from <www.emac2005.org>, accessed 10 January 2006.

KEY TERMS

administered VMN	554	exclusive distribution	557	marketing logistics network management	530
category management	561	franchise organisation	553	multichannels	554
channel conflict	549	horizontal marketing networks	554	order processing	539
channel level	547			physical distribution	528
containerisation	545	hybrid marketing channel networks	554	reintermediation	555
contractual VMN	553	intensive distribution	557	retailer co-operatives	553
conversion operations	538	intermodal transportation methods	542	selective distribution	557
corporate VMN	552			services marketing logistics	531
cross-docking	530	inventory (sometimes referred to as stocks)	541	vertical marketing network (VMN)	552
customer value delivery networks	556	key account manager	561	wholesaler-sponsored voluntary chains	553
direct marketing channel	547	logistics	530		
disintermediation	555	marketing channels	545		
distribution centre	541	marketing logistics networks	528		

DISCUSSING THE ISSUES

1 What are the differences, if any, between the marketing logistics networks decisions that might be faced by a marketer of short-shelf-life products, such as fresh chicken, a marketer of long-shelf-life products, such as laundry detergent, and a marketer of consumer durables such as refrigerators and washing machines?

2 Consider Figure 14.4 and prepare an argument as to whether or not the five so-called logistics trade-offs presented in this figure are in fact must-do's. What organisations are needed to conduct the flow of products, ownership, payment, information and promotion from the manufacturer to the customer? Are these organisations considered to be part of the distribution channel?

3 Why has franchising been such a fast-growing form of retail organisation? Are there any negatives associated with buying and developing a franchised business?

4 Wholesalers are said to perform a number of market functions. However, if they hold inventory, are they slowing down the distributive process and adding unnecessarily to costs? Are wholesalers simply dinosaurs whose time has come and gone?

5 Describe the flows in the marketing channels involved in the following purchase situations:

(a) consumers buying airline tickets to a holiday destination

(b) consumers deciding on and buying a home extension

(c) consumers buying hand-held computers for personal use.

6 Which distribution strategies—intensive, selective or exclusive—are used for the following products and why?

(a) Piaget watches

(b) Lexus cars

(c) Dell microcomputers

(d) Snickers chocolate bars

REFERENCES

1. See Toll Group, <toll.com.au>, accessed 7 January 2006; Victoria Racing Club, <www.vrc.net.au>, accessed 7 January 2006; Robyn Stubbs, 'Ladies First as VRC Punts $1M', *The Australian Financial Review*, 6 November 2002, p. 6; Stewart Oldfield and Katrina Nicholas, 'Bookies Lose a Bundle in Record Spree', *The Australian Financial Review*, 6 November 2002, p. 6; Ben Woodhead, 'New TAB Terminals May Throw Punters', *The Australian Financial Review*, 5 November 2002, p. 32; Katrina Nicholas, 'More Turn to a Bet with the Net', *The Australian Financial Review*, 5 November 2002, p. 32; Ben Woodhead, 'TABs Put Their Money on Technology in Cup Betting', *The Australian Financial* Review, 4 November 2002, p. 10; and Stewart Adam, 'OnetoOne eMarketing Strategy Alignment: Five Internet Case Studies', refereed paper, Academy of Marketing 2001 (2001: A Marketing Odyssey), Cardiff University, UK, 2–4 July 2001, pp. 1–20 (Multimedia CD-ROM).
2. Ronald Henkoff, 'Delivering the Goods', *Fortune*, 28 November 1994, pp. 64–78.
3. Joan Bergman, 'Strategic Partnering Makes Substantial Progress', *Retail Asia*, September/October 1995, pp. 41–42.
4. 'Managing Logistics in the 1990s', *Logistics Perspective*, July 1990, pp. 1–6.
5. Shlomo Maital, 'The Last Frontier of Cost Reduction', *Across the Board*, February 1994, p. 51.
6. Francis J. Quinn, 'Logistics' New Customer Focus', *Business Week*, 10 March 1997, p. 68; and Gail DeGeorge, 'Ryder Sees the Logic of Logistics', *Business Week*, 5 August 1996, p. 56.
7. See Louis Stern, Adel I. El-Ansary and Anne T. Coughlan, *Marketing Channels*, 5th edn, Upper Saddle River, NJ, Prentice Hall, 1996, p. 160; Patrick Byrne, 'A New Roadmap for Contract Logistics', *Transportation and Logistics*, April 1993, pp. 58–62; Ronald Henkoff, 'Delivering the Goods', *Fortune*, 18 November 1994, pp. 64–77; and Scott Wooley, 'Replacing Inventory with Information', *Forbes*, 24 March 1997, pp. 54–58.
8. For a discussion on the nature of group technology and its benefits see Danny Samson, *Manufacturing and Operation Strategy*, Sydney, Prentice Hall Australia, 1996, pp. 52–53.
9. 'Linking with Vendors for Just-In-Time Service', *Chain Store Age Executive*, June 1993, pp. 22A–24A.
10. For a readable guide to the aim of reducing inventories and stockless production, see Robert W. Hall, *Zero Inventories*, Homewood, Illinois, Dow Jones-Irwin, 1983.
11. For an explanation of inventory carrying costs see Core Logistics Consulting at <http://www.corelogistics.com.au/Inventory_Management_Consultants_Australia.html>, accessed 6 January 2006.
12. Bureau of Industry Economics, *International Performance Indicators: Overview*, Research Report No. 53, Canberra, ACT, Australian Government Publishing Service, 1994, pp. 35–41.
13. Louis W. Stern, Adel I. El-Ansary and Anne T. Coughlan, *Marketing Channels*, 5th edn, Upper Saddle River, NJ, Prentice Hall, 1996, p. 3.
14. Simon Lloyd, 'House-brand Showdown', *Business Review Weekly*, 21 September 2005, <www.brw.com.au/fearticle.aspx?relId=14763>, accessed 7 January 2006.
15. See IndustrySearch at <www.industrysearch.com.au/news/viewrecord.asp?ID=16350&SearchField=>, and Sigma media release at <www.amcal.com.au/PDF/Press/Max%20Capalaba%20opening%20press%20release.pdf>, accessed 7 January 2006.
16. See Carol Steinberg, 'Millionaire Franchisees', *Success*, March 1995, pp. 65–69; Meg Whittemore, 'New Directions in Franchising', *Nation's Business*, January 1995, pp. 45–52; *The Franchising Handbook*, Spring 1995 (1020 N. Broadway, Suite 111, Milwaukee, WI 53202); Norman D. Axelrad and Robert E. Weigand, 'Franchising—A Marriage of System Members', in Sidney Levy, George Frerichs and Howard Gordon (eds), *Marketing Managers Handbook*, 3rd edn, Chicago, Dartnell, 1994, pp. 919–934; Richard C. Hoffman and John F. Preble, 'Franchising into the Twenty-First Century', *Business Horizons*, November–December 1993, pp. 35–43; Lawrence S. Welch, 'Developments in International Franchising', *Journal of Global Marketing*, vol. 6, nos. 1–2, 1992, pp. 81–96; and Rollie Tillman, 'Rise of the Conglomerchant', *Harvard Business Review*, November–December 1971, pp. 44–51.
17. This has been called 'symbiotic marketing'. For more reading see Lee Adler, 'Symbiotic Marketing', *Harvard Business Review*, November–December 1966, pp. 59–71; P. 'Rajan' Varadarajan and Daniel Rajaratnam, 'Symbiotic Marketing Revisited', *Journal of Marketing*, January 1986, pp. 7–17; and Gary Hamel, Yves L. Doz and C. D. Prahalad, 'Collaborate with Your Competitors and Win', *Harvard Business Review*, January–February 1989, pp. 133–139.
18. See Allan J. Magrath, 'Collaborative Marketing Comes of Age Again', *Sales & Marketing Management*, September 1991, pp. 61–64; and Lois Therrien, 'Cafe au Lait, à Croissant and Trix', *Business Week*, 24 August 1992, pp. 50–51.
19. See Rowland T. Moriarity and Ursala Moran, 'Managing Hybrid Marketing Systems', *Harvard Business Review*, November–December 1990, pp. 146–155; and also see Frank V. Cespedes and E. Raymond Corey, 'Managing Multiple Channels', *Business Horizons*, July–August 1990, pp. 67–77.

20. See Louis W. Stern and Frederick D. Sturdivant, 'Customer-Driven Distribution Systems', *Harvard Business Review*, July–August 1987, p. 35.
21. See Philip Cateora, *International Marketing*, 7th edn, Homewood, IL, Irwin, 1990, pp. 570–571; and for a technical discussion of how service-oriented firms choose to enter international markets, see M. Krishna Erramilli, 'Service Firms' International Entry-Mode Approach: A Modified Transaction–Cost Analysis Approach', *Journal of Marketing*, July 1993, pp. 19–38.
22. See James A. Narus and James C. Anderson, 'Turn Your Industrial Distributors into Partners', *Harvard Business Review*, March–April 1986, pp. 66–71; and Marty Jacknis and Steve Kratz, 'The Channel Empowerment Solution', *Sales & Marketing Management*, March 1993, pp. 44–49.
23. See Katherine M. Hafner, 'Computer Retailers: Things have gone from Worse to Bad', *Business Week*, 8 June 1987, p. 104.

PHOTO/AD CREDITS

CASE STUDY
Assessing a franchise opportunity

Time for a change

Bill and Ann Miller had been clerical employees of large organisations all their lives. Neither really enjoyed their jobs, they were a means to an end. However, they wanted to fulfil their ambition of running their own business, being their own boss and creating an asset that could be sold later to help fund their retirement. They were in their early fifties and felt that now was the time to act before it was too late.

As neither had real commercial experience they felt that taking up a franchise was the sensible way to go as they would be given systematic guidance and training by the franchising firm. They had attended various seminars on 'starting your own business' run by the state government, among others. They were aware of the many pitfalls in running a small business but felt that with Bill's experience with dealing with numbers and regulations, Ann's capacity for detail and their preparedness for hard work they could make a go of it.

Franchising in Australia

In Australia, franchises generate at least $80 billion a year which is about 12% of GDP. About 25% of all retail expenditure goes through a franchise.

Richard Evans, CEO of the Franchise Council of Australia, said: 'Many people look into franchising after being made redundant, or after they have taken early retirement but soon find they relish the challenge. Franchises provide a layer of protection for people wanting to buy into a small business, in that the systems are already established and, if followed, should lead to few problems.' Stephen Giles, a partner in a firm that advises on businesses and franchising says: 'franchising is a good option for people who are interested in buying a business. Many have worked for others, possibly in management positions but may not have run their own

business. One of the great virtues of franchising is that you are in business for yourself, but not by yourself.' Franchises provide a layer of protection for people wanting to buy into a small business in that the systems and a brand name are usually already established. There are at least 800 franchisor companies in Australia from which to choose.

From a franchisor's point of view, franchising allows them to expand the availability of their products or service more rapidly than if they did it themselves and they do not have to provide the capital for setting up new outlets—the franchisee provides that.

There are a range of established ways of gaining the funds to buy into a franchise. Maquarie Research Equities found that after five years in business 70% of small-to-medium size enterprises in Australia had left the market. In contrast, just 12% of franchises had suffered the same fate. Banks are aware of this when they appraise loan applications by people wishing to start a business. Increasingly, though, they are assessing applications on a case by case basis as they see that some franchises are more risky than others and some franchisees as more potentially able to run a franchise than others.

A franchisor is chosen

Bill and Ann realised that they would have to find a business that would match their capabilities and their ability to acquire other skills. They realised that some franchisors might be looking for franchisees who had skills and experience they did not possess. This limited them, they felt, to retailing where essentially they would run a shop. They believed that they had outgoing personalities and could deal with people in a friendly, purposeful way. Neither had had experience in selling but felt that they could learn this and would be motivated as it would be their livelihood that depended on their being able to

sell. They also felt that if they chose the right franchise the products should be in demand and somewhat sell themselves.

After much time exploring the range of franchises that were on offer, Bill and Ann contacted an organisation that ran retail outlets supplying fresh, ready-to-cook meat products which put them in touch with the person who held the Master Franchise for the state. This person had acquired the right to appoint new franchisees in the state. During a subsequent meeting Bill and Ann were given a pamphlet from the franchisor titled 'Profit from our Success'. It had short sections with headings as follows: Excellent cash flow and ROI; Complete training—no experience necessary; A proven business system that is structured for franchising; Existing and proposed locations for sale throughout Australia; Estimated costs and income provided per location. The leaflet also went on to say that the franchisor carefully chose shop locations that would provide a realistic return on investment. The franchisor had just over 100 franchised outlets around Australia at the time. It had recently won an award from the Franchisor's Association of Australia and NZ for excellence in retail management.

The Master Franchisor said they could franchise a shop in a new shopping centre that was being developed in an inner suburb of the city. The terms included:

1 payment for all the necessary plant and equipment required ($100 000)

2 payment for the fitout of the shop ($88 000)

3 payment for lost goodwill in the event that the business failed.

Other terms included paying both the franchisor and the state Master Franchisor a percentage of revenue or profits of the outlet.

Assessing the franchise

Bill and Ann were provided with what were said to be the operating reports of three particular franchised shops, which were not named, but in another state:

Year total	Shop 1	Shop 2	Shop 3
Gross sales (GS)	490 000	624 900	794 200
Gross profit (GP)	220 800	280 500	383 100
GP—% of GS	45	44.8	48

They were told that they would be trained, and offered initial support, by the Master Franchisor at no cost to themselves. They were also given other material that alerted them to the following:

There could be no guarantee of success; the gross sales or profitability of the franchise were subject to factors like:
- ◉ their personal commitment to the business
- ◉ their compliance with the franchisor's systems
- ◉ their pricing policies
- ◉ the training they gave to their staff
- ◉ the gross profit they expected
- ◉ their willingness to use marketing and promotion
- ◉ the location of the store
- ◉ the location of the catchment area in which their shop was located
- ◉ other retailers close to theirs and the nature of their businesses
- ◉ neighbouring and competing shopping centres
- ◉ the management of their shopping centre
- ◉ the prevailing business conditions and economic climate in the state
- ◉ consumer tastes.

This gave Bill and Ann some food for thought. One of the things that concerned them was the fact that they would be in a new shopping centre whose success was unknown at the moment. It was in a relatively poor area of the city that was, nevertheless, being upgraded. It was only about 10 minutes from the CBD by car and had other suburban shopping centres not far away. It was on one of the routes to the airport but they felt that this was not necessarily an advantage.

The Millers sought a loan from their bank to gain the finance for acquiring the franchise. As part of the process the bank contacted the Master

CASE STUDY

Franchisor who said that from his experience he forecast that sales through the proposed outlet in the new shopping centre would be $10 000 per week. This had also been suggested as the expected sales to the Millers in talks with other representatives of the franchisor. The bank said that it was prepared to lend up to $200 000 to purchase the franchised shop. The moment of decision had arrived.

Some further data

By this time, the new shopping centre had opened. It was very early days and estimates of likely numbers of people visiting a week, 'foot traffic', were unreliable. There was a major food retailer located at one end of the centre; other tenants were a newsagency that was also a State Lotteries agency, a post office, a fruit and vegetable shop and a bakery. Their prospective store was near one of the entrances on the route to the supermarket, which also sold various meat products.

Bill and Ann were also able to gain information from the Master Franchisor about the performance of the existing franchises in Adelaide. Each of these was located in a shopping centre. They were also able to track down a publication called *The Shopping Centre Directory*, which gives facts and figures on all the major shopping centres in Australia. From the Australian Bureau of Statistics they were able to obtain the sociodemographics of the areas in which each of these shopping centres was located. From this information (in the Appendix) they believed that they could make an independent assessment of the likely sales of the shop that had been offered to them and so decide whether to take the plunge.

Sources: G. Bryant, 'Investing in Brand Names', *The Australian*, 26 November 2003; M. Fenton-Jones, 'Fresh Approach to Franchise Funding', *The Australian Financial Review*, 3 February 2004.

QUESTIONS

1. What other information do you think Bill and Ann should obtain before making the decision?

2. In what way would you use this information?

3. What quantitative analysis can you do to assist in making the decision?

4. What other, perhaps qualitative, factors do you feel should be taken into account?

5. Do you think Bill and Ann should take up the franchise offer?

Appendix

There were 12 existing franchised stores in metropolitan Adelaide mostly in shopping centres that were located in suburbs of differing socioeconomic level. Two of the franchises were not in shopping centres and have been excluded from the table below, which gives some of the key statistics.

All of these figures, except the socioeconomic grading, were taken from the Shopping Centre Directory for the year prior to Bill and Ann's decision. The weekly turnover and operating profit were supplied by the franchisor.

The socioeconomic grading of the location of the new shopping centre would be 1. It was smaller than any of those in the table above at a GLA of around 8500 and with some 250 car parking spaces.

Weekly turnover ($)	Weekly operating profit ($)	No. of majors	GLA	Socio-economic level	No. of shops	Size of catch	MAT	No. of car parks	Traffic per year	Food hall seats
8 500	1120	5	35 425	1	107	192	121	2490	7	0
9 925	1710	1	12 250	3	83	43	57	622	2.5	0
12 320	1880	3	22 266	2	49	135	86	1380	3.64	0
10 780	1970	4	39 380	2	96	133	142	2840	6.02	0
9 442	1250	5	68 380	1	130	155	206	3830	8.9	421
19 491	3526	2	14 000	3	53	63	68	816	3.69	140
11 051	1430	5	20 000	1	70	50	96	1270	3.5	280
10 084	1490	4	76 670	2	204	227	300	4100	10.2	600
14 620	1980	5	66 180	2	172	270	247	3600	8.4	500
20 410	3680	4	49 580	3	141	110	190	3570	5.8	470

Explanation of terms:

No. of majors	=	number of major retailers, like Myer or David Jones, in a centre
GLA	=	a measure of retail floor area in the centre, in sq. metres
Socioeconomic level	=	a grading of the socioeconomic make-up of the centre's catchment area into low (1), medium (2) and high (3), based upon indices of ABS data on: average income, % employed, % of households on 'low income', % with a car, % owner occupier, etc. The franchisor also classified areas where their shops were in terms like 'low class area' and the classification derived in the table above matches theirs
No. of shops	=	total number of retail outlets in the centre
Size of catch.	=	the estimated population size in the centre's catchment area
MAT	=	a measure of the retail turnover in the centre per year
Traffic per year	=	an estimate of the number of people who visit the centre a year (this would be equivalent to 'foot traffic')
Food hall seats	=	the number of places at tables in the centre's food hall, if it has one

CHAPTER 15

Retailing and wholesaling

Australian Retailers Association:
www.ara.com.au

Franchise Council of Australia:
www.franchise.org.au

National Retail Association:
www.nationalretailassociation.com.au

New Zealand Retailers Association:
www.retail.org.nz

Retail Wire: www.retailwire.com

Retailing is a challenging business these days. The list of high-profile failures in recent years is long: in Australia alone, Harris Scarfe in Adelaide, Gowings in Sydney and Daimaru in Melbourne and the Gold Coast have failed and disappeared in recent years. And Australia isn't unique in losing well-known department stores: US chain Winn-Dixie stores filed for bankruptcy in March 2005, blaming competition from Wal-Mart.[1] It was one of a string of mergers and failures in US department stores in 2005; department store giant Sears has been purchased by Kmart, Macy's and Strawbridge's have merged and luxury retailer Neiman Marcus has been purchased by private equity holders. Most recently, department store giant Myer, which boasted the 'largest department store in the southern hemisphere' is discussing selling off its stores across Australia after years of poor performance.[2] It would be easy to blame the problems of traditional department stores like Myer and Sears on the discount chains and specialist 'category killers', but many of those are also experiencing problems.[3] For example, Toys 'R' Us, perhaps the best known of the specialist discounting category killers, was bought out by private equity investors in 2005 after losing sales to other discounters such as Wal-Mart and Target.

There is no shortage of explanations put forward by various analysts for the problems of long-term retailers: an increase in the number of discounters, a loss in sales to online retailers, growing consumer preference for smaller specialist stores and the difficulties for department stores in covering the costs of large retail spaces. For today's time-pressed shopper, there is often little reason to find their way to the fifth or sixth floor of a large department store in a retail complex when a host of smaller retailers are located more conveniently, close to ground level. It's also difficult for a large department store to compete in every category; for example, department store Myer admits that it has been carrying fewer large-ticket items such as whitegoods and furniture because competitors like Harvey Norman and Ikea attract more shoppers. This can then mean the beginning of a vicious cycle; a smaller product range offers less choice to customers and makes them more likely to shop at competitors which offer a wider choice (and often lower prices). And if a department store like Myer decides to close its whitegoods or furniture departments, what will it do with the space, since the store is often locked into long-term leasing arrangements?

Specialty stores like Ikea can offer a much wider range of items in a particular area than traditional department stores.

There are, however, examples of very successful department stores; at the same time that its major competitor Myer was suffering falling profits and discussing selling off its stores, David Jones posted record profits in 2005 of approximately $70 million, a huge turnaround for the chain after a $25.5 million loss in 2002–03.[4] David Jones has achieved this turnaround with a radical overhaul of its stock, decreasing the emphasis on house brands, ditching well-known fashion brands like Country Road and positioning itself around aspirational brands like Collette Dinnigan and upcoming trendy brands like Sass and Bide. It's a strategy which has worked for successful department stores like Saks Fifth Avenue in the USA and Selfridges in Britain, and which has reinforced David Jones's position as the top department store in Australia. David Jones's positioning around brands has left Myer competing with other chains such as the mid-range Target (also owned by Myer's parent, Coles-Myer) and with the growing discount chains like DFO, which operates factory outlets for major brands.

So while the story of David Jones shows that department stores can still be successful, the traditional department store offering a full range of products is likely to continue to be challenged by newer, more specialised operators in each of its departments. It's always going to be hard for a department store to compete in furniture against Ikea, in electrical appliances against Harvey Norman or in hardware against Bunnings. However, even being a specialist doesn't guarantee success, as the problems of Toys 'R' Us show. The rise and fall of department stores illustrate a fundamental lesson of marketing; unless an operator provides more value than its competitors it won't succeed. Department stores used to offer convenience and the security of a trusted name, but that benefit seems to be outweighed for many consumers today by the lower prices and wider ranges offered by the specialists like Ikea or discount stores like Wal-Mart. We haven't seen the last of the department stores yet, but if they don't continue to offer value for customers and for shareholders we soon will.

After reading this chapter you should be able to:

1. Discuss traditional and online store retailing, and the different ways to classify stores: by degree of service provided, breadth and depth of the product line, relative price levels, control of outlets and type of store cluster.

2. Outline the key retailer marketing decisions: target market and positioning, product, price, promotion and place.

3. Compare the different types of wholesalers, including full-service and limited-service merchant wholesalers, brokers and agents, and manufacturers' sales branches.

4. Explain the wholesaler marketing decisions of target market and positioning and marketing mix decisions, and describe trends in wholesaling.

In this chapter we examine the nature of retailing and wholesaling. In the first section we look at the nature of retailing and its importance, the major types of store and non-store retailers, the decisions retailers make and the future of retailing. In the second section, we discuss the same topics for wholesalers. We introduce the topic of online retailing, which is discussed further in Chapter 18.

Retailing

Retailing All activities involved in selling goods or services directly to final consumers for their personal, non-business use.

Retailers Businesses whose sales come primarily from retailing.

What is retailing? We all know that David Jones and Kmart are retailers, but so are Avon representatives, the local Westin Hotel, a bank, a doctor seeing patients and Amazon.com. We define **retailing** as all the activities involved in selling goods or services directly to final consumers for their personal, non-business use. Many institutions—financial institutions, manufacturers, wholesalers, **retailers**—do retailing. But most retailing is done by retailers—businesses whose sales come primarily from retailing. And although most retailing is done in retail stores, in recent years non-store retailing—selling by direct and online means such as direct mail, telephone, fax, door-to-door sales, vending machines, on the Internet or by SMS—has grown considerably.

Retail stores come in all shapes and sizes, and new retail types keep emerging. They can be classified by one or more of several characteristics: amount of service, product line sold, relative prices, control of outlets and type of store cluster, which now includes whether they have a physical presence, an online presence or both. These classifications and the corresponding retailer types are shown in Table 15.1.

Amount of service

Different products need different amounts of service, and customer service preferences vary. We discuss three levels of service—self-service, limited service and full service—and the types of retailers that use them.

Self-service retailers
Retailers that provide few or no services to shoppers; shoppers perform their own locate–compare–select process.

Self-service retailers grew rapidly in Australia during the 1950s, having started in the USA during the Depression of the 1930s. Today, self-service is the basis of all discount operations and is typically used by sellers of convenience goods (e.g. supermarkets) and nationally branded, fast-moving shopping goods (such as those found in Kmart or Big W).

Limited-service retailers Retailers that provide only a limited number of services to shoppers.

Limited-service retailers, such as the hardware chains, provide limited sales assistance because they carry more shopping goods about which customers need information. They also offer additional

TABLE 15.1 Different ways to classify retail outlets

Amount of service	Product line sold	Relative price emphasis	Control of outlets	Type of cluster
Self-service (including electronic dispensing machines and online)	Specialty store	Discount store	Corporate chain	Central business district
Limited service	Department store	Off-price retailers	Voluntary chain and retailer co-operative	Regional shopping centre
Full service	Supermarket	Catalogue showrooms	Franchise organisation	Community shopping centre
	Convenience store		Merchandising conglomerate	Highway strips
	Mass merchant, superstore and hypermarket			
	Service business			
	Street vendor			

services, such as merchandise return, that are not usually offered by low-service stores. Their increased operating costs result in higher prices.

Full-service retailers, such as specialty stores and first-class department stores, are distinguished by the fact that salespeople assist customers in every phase of the shopping process. Full-service stores usually carry more specialty goods and slower-moving items such as cameras, jewellery and fashions, which benefit from active selling by a salesperson. They provide more liberal return policies, various credit plans and often extras such as lounges and restaurants. More services means higher operating costs, which are passed along to customers as higher prices. Online retailers may also be distinguished on the basis of the service they provide. The purely transaction-based e-commerce online company is a far cry from one that allows customer personalisation and sends its customers information on new offers and products carried.

Product line sold

Retailers can also be classified by the length and breadth of their product assortments. Among the most important types are the specialty store, the department store, the supermarket, the convenience store and the superstore.

Specialty stores and combination stores

A **specialty store** carries a narrow product line with a deep assortment within that line. Examples include stores selling sporting goods, furniture, books and electronics. Specialty stores can be further classified by the narrowness of their product lines. A clothing store is a single-line store, a men's clothing store is a limited-line store and a men's custom shirt store is a fine-line specialty store.

Specialty stores are flourishing for several reasons. The increasing use of strategic market segmentation, market targeting and product specialisation has resulted in a greater need for stores that focus on specific products and segments. And because of changing consumer lifestyles and the increasing number of two-income households, many consumers have higher incomes but less time to spend shopping. They are attracted to specialty stores that provide high-quality products, convenient locations, good hours, excellent service and ease of access.

Combination stores sell a combination of products normally associated with specialty stores such as pharmaceutical products, grocery products and general merchandise. Although smaller in number, they are a growing store type.

Department stores

A **department store** carries a wide variety of product lines—typically clothing, home furnishings and household goods. Each line is operated as a separate department, which may be managed by specialist buyers or merchandisers, or this function may be performed centrally. Most countries have their own well-known national department stores (such as Myer and David Jones in Australia) though some department store chains, such as the British Marks & Spencer, have successfully expanded into Asia.

The first department store, Bon Marché, opened in Paris in 1838 and department stores grew rapidly during the first half of the twentieth century.[5] But after World War II they began to lose ground to other types of retailers,

Full-service retailers
Retailers that provide a full range of services to shoppers.

Specialty store A retail store that carries a narrow product line with a deep assortment within that line.

Combination store
Combined grocery and general merchandise stores.

Department store
A retail organisation that carries a wide variety of product lines—typically clothing, home furnishings and household goods; each line is operated as a separate department, which may be managed by specialist buyers or merchandisers or this function may be performed centrally.

Selected Sanity stores that carry a 'Fast Tracks' kiosk can offer a larger range of product selections. The Fast Tracks kiosks allow the customer to download single tracks, whole albums or even personalised compilation CDs.

including discount stores, specialty store chains and 'off-price' retailers. The heavy traffic, poor parking and growth of alternatives to central city retailing, where many department stores had made their biggest investments, made downtown shopping less appealing. As a result, most department stores around the world are struggling, and many have closed or merged with others; Bon Marché, Mark Foys, Georges, Anthony Hordern and John Martin have disappeared, and the share of retail dollars spent at department stores has decreased.[6]

Most department stores have opened stores in suburban shopping centres such as Chadstone and Westfield Parramatta, while others have remodelled their stores or set up 'boutiques' within them that compete with specialty stores. Since the 1960s many large department stores have been joining rather than fighting the competition by diversifying into discount and specialty stores. The Coles group's outlets, for example, include 2500 stores Australia wide, operating under a range of brand names including more than 2600 Coles Supermarkets and Bi-Lo (grocery), Liquorland, Theo's and Vintage Cellars (liquor), Kmart and Target (apparel and houseware chains), Megamart (durables), Officeworks (officeware) and Coles Express (fuel and convenience stores).[7]

Supermarkets

Supermarkets Large, low-cost, low-margin, high-volume, self-service stores that carry a wide variety of food, laundry and household products.

Supermarkets are large, low-cost, low-margin, high-volume, self-service stores that carry a wide variety of food, laundry and household products.

The first supermarkets introduced the concepts of self-service, customer turnstiles and checkout counters. Supermarket growth took off in the mid-1960s in Australia. The growing availability of home refrigerators and greater car ownership reduced the need for small neighbourhood stores. Stores selling grocery, meat, produce and household goods in a single location allowed one-stop shopping and lured consumers from greater distances, giving supermarkets the volume needed to offset their lower margins. A large supermarket can have sales of more than $60 million a year, twice the sales of the average department store.[8]

However, most supermarkets today are facing slow sales growth because of slower population growth and an increase in competition from convenience stores, discount food stores and regional centres, which offer a range of specialty food stores. They are also being influenced by the trend towards out-of-home eating. Thus, supermarkets are looking for new ways to build their sales. Most chains now operate fewer but larger stores. They practise 'scrambled merchandising', carrying many non-food items—beauty aids, houseware, toys, appliances, DVDs, sporting goods and garden supplies—attempting to find high-margin lines to improve profits.

Supermarkets are also improving their facilities and services to attract more customers. Typical improvements are better locations, improved décor, longer trading hours, EFTPOS, home delivery, specialised services such as banking and even car and truck fuel. Although consumers have always expected supermarkets to offer good prices, convenient locations and speedy checkout, today's more affluent and sophisticated food buyer wants more. Many supermarkets, therefore, are 'moving upscale' with the market, providing enhanced fresh fruit and vegetable departments, 'from-scratch' bakeries, gourmet deli counters and seafood departments. At the same time, other supermarkets, like the German company Aldi, are competing with a limited range of products, basic service and a high proportion of lower-priced generic brands. Finally, to attract more customers, large supermarket chains are more likely to customise their stores for individual neighbourhoods. Thus a Woolworths store in Double Bay in Sydney's eastern suburbs, or Elsternwick in Melbourne's inner eastern suburbs, is more likely to carry kosher foods and delicacies such as smoked eel than a store in Melbourne's or Sydney's outer suburbs. They are tailoring store size, product assortments, prices and promotions to the economic and ethnic needs of local markets. The advent of electronic scanning at the checkout and quick-response retail systems has made this practice more cost effective.

Convenience stores

Convenience stores (C-stores) are small stores that carry a limited line of high-turnover convenience goods. Examples include 7-Eleven, NightOwl and Food Plus. These stores are located near residential areas and remain open for long hours, seven days a week. Convenience stores must charge high prices to make up for higher operating costs and lower sales volume. But they satisfy an important consumer need, and Canada's Alimentation Couche-Tard, owners of the Circle K chain of convenience stores, was the fastest growing retailer in the world in 2005 (see Table 15.2A overleaf). Consumers use C-stores for 'fill-in' purchases during off-peak hours or when time is short, and they are willing to pay for the convenience. The number of convenience stores has increased in recent years, growing by up

Convenience stores are growing rapidly worldwide, catering to consumers who value their convenient location, even at the cost of slightly higher prices.

to 18% per year in some markets.[9] Their clientele is biased towards young people who are out at night and want a range of products, including petrol and snacks. C-stores are constantly revamping their offerings in an attempt to remain strongly differentiated from other types of food stores, while adapting to today's fast-paced consumer lifestyles. Because of their location, many service station sites operated by Shell and BP contain C-stores and many 7-Eleven stores sell fuel through their franchised network of service stations, C-stores and truckstops, maximising the opportunity for impulse sales to customers buying fuel. Franchising, discussed later in this chapter, has been a stimulant to the growth of C-stores, such as the NightOwl franchise group in Queensland.

Mass merchants, superstores and hypermarkets

These types of stores are all larger than the largest supermarkets. **Mass merchants** such as Bunnings Warehouse, Home Hardware, Mitre 10 and Retravision carry a large assortment of home and home improvement merchandise. Bunnings Warehouse, for instance, carries over 40 000 products compared with some 12 000 lines carried by a supermarket. Bunnings Warehouse pioneered the 'shed' concept in Australian hardware and home improvement retailing, and is the fourth fastest growing retailer in the world (see Table 15.2B overleaf). Another British mass-merchant chain of do-it-yourself outlets, FOCUS Wickes, was the second fastest growing retailer in the world in 2005.[10]

Superstores and **hypermarkets** combine supermarket, discount and warehouse retailing. 'Category killers' are a particular type of superstore, providing a very deep assortment in a particular category (e.g. Officeworks).

A typical superstore or hypermarket might have 50 or more checkout counters. They carry more than routinely purchased goods, also selling furniture, appliances, clothing and many other things. The hypermarket operates like a warehouse. Products in wire 'baskets' are stacked high on metal racks; forklifts move through aisles during selling hours to restock shelves. The store gives discounts to customers who carry their own heavy appliances and furniture out of the store. Superstores and hypermarkets such as those operated by Carrefour and Wal-Mart have grown quickly in Europe, the USA and Asia, and Wal-Mart and Carrefour are now the two largest retailers in the world (see Table 15.2 overleaf). Their size has meant that they have been able to achieve further cost savings by investing heavily in the use of new technology, as discussed in Marketing Highlight 15.1. However, they have not been successful in some of their new locations; when Wal-Mart expanded into Germany, German shoppers responded unfavourably to a range of Wal-Mart practices, including using workers to pack bags for shoppers (standard practice in the USA) and to what were perceived to be insincere smiles at the check-out.[11] Carrefour's model was also unsuccessful in Japan, and the company closed its Japanese stores.

Convenience store (C-store) A small store, located near a residential area, open long hours seven days a week, and carrying a limited line of high-turnover convenience goods.

Mass merchant A type of store carrying a large assortment of merchandise such as in hardware (Bunnings Warehouse) or electrical goods and furniture (Harvey Norman) or personal care and healthcare (Priceline).

Superstore A store almost twice the size of a regular supermarket carrying a large assortment of routinely purchased food and non-food items, and offering such services as dry cleaning, photo developing, cheque cashing, bill paying, car care and pet care.

Hypermarkets Huge stores that combine supermarket, discount and warehouse retailing; in addition to food, they carry furniture, appliances, clothing and many other items.

TABLE 15.2A Top 10 global retailers

DT Rank 04	Country of origin	Name of company	Formats	2003 group sales* (US$m)	2003 retail sales (US$m)
1	US	Wal-Mart	Discount, Hypermarket, Supermarket, Superstore, Warehouse	258 681	256 329
2	France	Carrefour	Cash & Carry, Convenience, Discount, Hypermarket, Specialty, Supermarket	79 796	79 796
3	US	Home Depot	DIY	64 816	64 816
4	Germany	Metro	Cash & Carry, Department, DIY, Food Service, Hypermarket, Specialty, Superstore	60 674	60 503
5	US	Kroger	Convenience, Discount, Specialty, Supercentre, Supermarket, Warehouse	53 791	53 791
6	UK	Tesco	Convenience, Department, Hypermarket, Supermarket, Superstore	51 535	51 535
7	US	Target	Department, Discount, Supercentre	48 163	46 781
8	Netherlands	Ahold	Cash & Carry, Convenience, Discount, Drug, Hypermarket, Specialty, Supermarket	63 473	44 584
9	US	Costco	Warehouse	42 546	41 693
10	Germany	Aldi Einkauf	Discount, Supermarket	40 060e	40 060e

* = includes non-retail e = estimate

Source: Deloitte 2005 Global Powers of Retailing, January 2005 available at <www.deloitte.com>, p. G13.

TABLE 15.2B Ten fastest growing retailers, 1998–2003

Growth rank	Sales rank	Country of origin	Name of company	Formats	2003 retail sales (US$m)	5 year retail sales CAGR % (Local currency)
1	131	Canada	Couche-Tard	Convenience, Food Service	4377	55.4%
2	214	UK	FOCUS Wickes	DIY	2682e	54.2%
3	116	US	Amazon.com	E-commerce	5264	53.9%
4	211	Australia	Wesfarmers/Bunnings	DIY	2741e	40.6%
5	142	US	Asbury Automotive	Auto	4000e	33.9%
6	94	Hong Kong SAR	Hutchison Whampoa/ AS Watson	Drug, Specialty, Supermarket	6631e	31.9%
7	73	Japan	Yamada Denki	Specialty	8330	31.1%
8	222	Japan	Fast Retailing/Uniqlo	Specialty	2538	30.2%
9	106	US	Sonic Automotive	Auto	5939	29.9%
10	213	Japan	Daiso-sangyo	Discount	2683	29.9%

e = estimate CAGR = Compound Annual Growth Rate

Source: Deloitte 2005 Global Powers of Retailing, January 2005 available at <www.deloitte.com>, p. G11.

A variety of other retailers have adopted the low-cost superstore concept. New Zealand's Warehouse chain is the country's largest retailer, and plans to expand into hypermarkets, offering supermarket products and general merchandise based on Wal-Mart's model.[12] However, superstores and hypermarkets have not been a strong feature of Australian retailing, apart from limited examples such as the Pick 'n Pay hypermarket at Aspley in Queensland, now owned by the Coles Group. Their growth has been constrained by the generally 'overshopped' nature of the Australian market and the absence of large concentrations of population. Superstores have also been less successful in Asian countries, where car ownership tends to be lower, and where high property costs make the typical sprawling superstore design less efficient. This has led to some changes in the design of superstores, with a vertical, 19 story warehouse-style shopping centre being developed in Hong Kong.[13]

Relative prices

Retailers can also be classified according to their prices. Most retailers charge regular prices and offer normal quality goods and customer service. Some offer higher-quality goods and service at higher prices. The retailers that feature low prices are discount stores and 'off-price' retailers.

Discount stores

A **discount store** sells standard merchandise at lower prices by accepting lower margins and selling higher volume. The use of occasional discounts or specials does not make a discount store. A true discount store regularly sells its merchandise at lower prices, offering mostly national brands, not inferior goods. Early discount stores cut expenses by operating in warehouse-like facilities in low-rent but heavily travelled districts. They slashed prices, advertised widely and carried a reasonable width and depth of products. The most common examples specialised in selling refrigerators and other major electrical appliances (whitegoods), smaller appliances including sound systems and television sets (brown goods) and furniture.

In recent years, facing intense competition from other discounters and department stores, many discount retailers have 'traded up'. They have improved their décor, added new lines and services and opened suburban branches, which has led to higher costs and prices. And as some department stores have cut their prices to compete with discounters, the distinction between many discount and department stores has become blurred. As one retail analyst put it, 'it is hard to be a credible discounter when everyone's doing it. It's no longer a unique selling point.' As a result, several major discount chains have closed or been sold because they lost their price advantage, most recently the Sydney Gowings chain and the 450-store Crazy Clark's, Go-Lo, Warehouse, Chickenfeed chain.[14] Discount stores have been growing rapidly in European grocery retailing, however, typified by chains like German Aldi and Spanish Dia. In Germany, hard discounters account for around 40% of retail sales, and while other countries lag behind this figure, discount retailers are growing, with Dia showing growth of over 150% over five years.[15]

Off-price retailers

When the major discount stores traded up, a new wave of off-price retailers moved in to fill the low-price, high-volume gap. Ordinary discounters buy at regular wholesale prices and accept lower margins to keep prices down. **Off-price retailers**, on the other hand, buy at less than regular wholesale prices and charge consumers less than retail. They tend to carry a changing and unstable collection of higher-quality merchandise, often leftover goods, overruns and irregulars obtained at reduced prices from manufacturers or other retailers. Off-price retailers have made the biggest inroads in clothing, accessories and footwear.

Discount store
A retail institution that sells standard merchandise at lower prices by accepting lower margins and selling at higher volume.

Off-price retailers
Retailers that buy at less than regular wholesale prices and sell at less than retail, usually carrying a changing and unstable collection of higher-quality merchandise, often leftover goods, overruns and irregulars obtained from manufacturers at reduced prices. They include factory outlets, independents and warehouse clubs.

15.1

Tiny transmitters in every product—great technology or technological overkill?

Envision a world in which every product contains a tiny transmitter, loaded with information. Imagine a time when we could track every item electronically—anywhere in the world, at any time, automatically. Producers could track the precise flow of goods up and down the supply chain, ensuring timely deliveries and lowering inventory and distribution costs. Retailers could track real-time merchandise movements in their stores, helping them manage inventories, keep shelves full and automatically reorder goods.

And picture the futuristic new world that such technology would create for consumers: as you stroll through the aisles of your supermarket, you pluck a six-pack of your favourite beverage from the shelf. Shelf sensors detect your selection and beam an ad to the screen on your shopping cart, offering special deals on salty snacks that might go well with your beverage. When you reach the shampoo section, electronic readers scan your cart and note that you haven't made the usual monthly purchase of your favourite brand. 'Did you forget the shampoo?' asks the screen. As your shopping cart fills, scanners detect that you might be buying for a dinner party; the screen suggests a wine that complements the meal you've planned. After shopping, you leave the store. Exit scanners automatically total up your purchases and charge them to your credit card. At home, readers track what goes into and out of your pantry, automatically updating your shopping list when stocks run low. To plan your Sunday dinner, you scan the chicken you just purchased. An embedded transmitter chip yields serving instructions and recipes for several accompanying dishes. You put the chicken into your 'smart oven', which follows instructions coded on the chip and cooks the chicken to perfection. Is this great technology, or what?

Seems far-fetched? Not really. In fact, it might soon become a reality with the backing of such marketing heavyweights as Wal-Mart, Home Depot, Target, Procter & Gamble, Coca-Cola, IBM, Gillette and even the US Department of Defense.

This futuristic technology is exploding onto today's marketing scene, boosted by the rapid development of tiny, affordable radiofrequency identification (RFID) transmitters—or smart chips—that can be embedded in all of the products you buy. The transmitters are so small that several would fit on the head of a pin. Yet they can be packed with coded information that can be read and rewritten at any point in the supply chain.

RFID technology (also called Auto-ID) provides producers and retailers with amazing new ways to track inventories, trends and sales. They can use embedded chips to follow products—everything from ice-cream and cat food to tyres, insulation and jet engines—step by step from factories, to warehouses, to retail shelves, to recycling centres.

The smart chips make today's barcode systems seem badly outmoded. Whereas barcodes must be visible to be read, embedded RFID chips can be read in any location. Barcodes identify only a product's manufacturer. In contrast, the chips can identify each individual product item and can carry codes that reveal an almost endless supply of information. Thus, beyond identifying an item as a litre of Dairy Farmers skim milk, an embedded smart chip can identify that specific litre of milk—its manufacture date, expiration date, location in the supply chain and a storehouse of other product-specific information.

Although it may seem futuristic, Auto-ID technology is already in use. Every time drivers breeze through an automated toll booth they're using an RFID chip. Exxon are using RFID chips to allow drivers to pay for petrol by flashing a card, and Gillette recently launched two RFID pilot projects. The first project uses embedded transmitters to track products from the factory to grocery store shelves. Gillette hopes that the technology will improve service to its retail customers while at the same time reducing its inventories by up to 25%. In the second project, Gillette has installed readers on shelves in selected Wal-Mart and Tesco stores. It claims that retailers lose more than $30 billion a year in sales because shelves aren't fully stocked. The shelf readers track Gillette's razors as they come and go, and prompt store staff to restock when quantities dwindle. Other large manufacturers are also developing their RFID plans; Procter & Gamble (P&G) plans to have the chips on products in broad distribution as soon as 2008. By 2010, P&G will be able to link shopper loyalty card information with data about the products they buy.

Since they can be used to track stock movements very accurately, RFIDs are also valuable in decreasing stock losses. Rick Tysdal, chief operating officer of lock maker Hampton products, says his company is already seeing savings as RFID tags prevent the loss of supplies of locks and security devices. 'The transparency in the supply chain saves a ton of labour costs in dealing with the back and forth of deductions,' he says. 'And it saves us money because we get paid more.'

Even smaller retailers are putting smart chips to work. Fashion retailer Prada recently installed the chips in its store in New York. Based on scans of items in customers' hands, video screens show personalised product demonstrations and designer sketches. In dressing rooms, readers identify each item of clothing a customer tries on and offer additional size, colour and design information through interactive touch screens.

Not everyone is a fan of RFID, however; Wal-Mart required an initial 100 suppliers to be RFID-capable by the end of 2004, and is extending its trials of RFID, requiring more suppliers to install the system. This is causing concern among some suppliers, many of whom see the costs of RFID as being borne by them as a condition of supply to large retailers, without allowing them to capture any benefits. While Australian companies like Coles, Amcor and frozen food manufacturer Patties Foods are trialling RFID projects, Australian suppliers to Woolworths breathed a sigh of relief in 2005 when Woolworths announced that it had put RFID implementation

on the backburner, saying it has more important projects to work on.

There's also resistance from consumer groups, which worry about invasion of consumers' privacy. If companies can link products to specific consumers and track consumer buying and usage, they fear marketers will gain access to too much personal information. Says one analyst, 'backers of the technology appear torn between the urge to hype its huge potential and fear that consumers will get spooked'.

To counter these concerns, Auto-ID technology proponents point out that the transmitters have limited range, most under 6 metres. So reading chips inside consumers' homes or tracking them on the move would be nearly impossible. The Auto-ID industry is also working to address consumer privacy concerns. Among other things, it is drafting a privacy policy that includes giving customers the option of permanently disabling the chips at the checkout. And according to an RFID consultant, the basic mission is not to spy on consumers. It's to serve them better. 'It's not Orwellian. That is absolutely, positively not the vision of Auto-ID,' she says. 'The vision is for . . . brand manufacturers and retailers to be able to have right-time, right-promotion, real-time eye-to-eye [contact] with the consumer.'

In coming years, as smart chips appear on more and more products, RFID technology will no doubt bring significant benefits to both marketers and the customers they serve. 'The idea of someone using tiny radio transmitters to influence consumer purchase behaviour was once only the stuff of paranoid delusions,' says the analyst. 'But in the not-so-distant future, it could become the basis of a new generation of marketing.'

Sources: Jack Neff, 'A Chip over Your Shoulder?' *Advertising Age*, 22 April 2002, p. 4; 'Business: The Best Thing since the Bar-Code: The IT Revolution', *The Economist*, 8 February 2003, pp. 57–58; 'Gillette, Michelin Begin RFID Pilots', *Frontline Solutions*, March 2003, p. 8; 'RFID Benefits Apparent', *Chain Store Age*, March 2003, p. 63; Faith Keenan, 'If Supermarket Shelves Could Talk', *Business Week*, 31 March 2003, pp. 66–67; Jack Neff, 'P&G Products to Wear Wire', *Advertising Age*, 15 December 2004, pp. 1, 32; Greg Lindsey, 'Prada's High-Tech Misstep', *Business 2.0*, March 2004, pp. 72–75; Kevin Higgins, 'Brave New RFID World', *Food Engineering*, January 2004, p. 81; Robert Spiegel, 'RFID Report', *Supply Chain Management Review*, April 2004, pp. 17–18, and information accessed online at <www.autoidlabs.org>,

July 2004; Kelly Mills, 'Woolies in No Hurry on RFID', *The Australian*, 19 July 2005, p. 33; Kelly Mills, 'Patties Tries Slice of RFID Pie', *The Australian*, 30 August 2005, p. 29; Michelle Phillips, 'Retail Chips are down for Individual Privacy', *The West Australian*, 26 October 2005, p. 26; Dan Roberts and Jonathan Birchall, 'Suppliers yet to be Convinced on System', *Financial Times*, 18 July 2005, p. 14; Dan Roberts and Jonathan Birchall, 'RFID Tag Roll-out Hits Resistance', *Financial Times*, 18 July 2005, p. 14; Ben Woodhead, 'Customers Snub Amcor's Tag Plan', *The Australian Financial Review*, 2 December 2005, p. 21.

Questions

1 Take-up of RIFID technology has been much faster in the USA than in the Pacific Rim countries. What do you think might be the reasons behind this?

2 As a consumer, how do you think you would react to the knowledge that all your purchases are tagged? What might be the implications for retailers?

Factory outlets Off-price retailing operations that are owned and operated by manufacturers and that normally carry the manufacturer's surplus, discontinued or irregular goods.

Independent off-price retailers Off-price retailers that are either owned and run by entrepreneurs or are divisions of larger retail corporations.

Warehouse clubs (or wholesale clubs) Off-price retailers that sell a limited selection of brand name grocery items, appliances, clothing and a hodgepodge of other goods at deep discounts to members who pay annual membership fees.

Chain stores Two or more outlets that are commonly owned and controlled, employ central buying and merchandising and sell similar lines of merchandise.

The three main types of off-price retailers are factory outlets, independents and warehouse clubs. **Factory outlets** are owned and operated by manufacturers and normally carry the manufacturer's surplus, discontinued or irregular goods. Such outlets sometimes group together in factory outlet malls, such as the ones operated by the DFO (Discount Factory Outlets) group, where dozens of outlet stores offer prices as low as 50% below retail on a wide range of items.[16]

Independent off-price retailers are owned and run by entrepreneurs or are divisions of larger retail corporations. These retailers have only a limited presence in the Pacific region. The Coles Group tried to establish a presence in this market with its 'Look Alive' outlets, but the venture was not successful and was closed.

Warehouse clubs (or wholesale clubs) sell a limited selection of brand-name grocery items, appliances, clothing and assorted other goods at deep discounts to members who pay an annual membership fee. These wholesale clubs operate in huge, low-overhead, warehouse-like facilities and offer few frills. Often, stores are draughty in the winter and stuffy in the summer. Customers are usually required to buy in bulk rather than select individual packs, and must wrestle furniture, heavy appliances and other large items into the checkout line. Such clubs make no home deliveries and often don't accept credit cards. But they do offer rock-bottom prices—typically 20–40% below supermarket and discount store prices. Warehouse clubs are a very minor part of retailing in Australia and Southeast Asia. In the USA, although these clubs account for around 4% of retail sales, they have been experiencing strong growth in recent years, in the face of overall sluggish retail growth. The largest warehouse club is Costco, which is experiencing growth of around 15% per year.[17]

Control of outlets

Although there are many more independently owned retail stores than any other form of ownership in Australia and New Zealand, a feature of these countries is the dominance of all retailing turnover by a limited number of firms. This has implications for suppliers, which have to gain distribution with key retailers if they are to gain market coverage. This has been responsible for some product failures, when a brand has lost retail shelf space in a key chain such as Woolworths, or where a company develops a product that might cannibalise a retailer-brand-dominated category, and cannot gain shelf space. Between them, Coles and Woolworths account for 78% of the packaged goods market in Australia, in contrast with Britain, where the four largest chains control only 56% of the market, and so failure to sell through Coles or Woolworths means that a manufacturer is locked out of most of the market.[18]

Corporate chains

The chain store is one of the most important retail developments. **Chain stores** are two or more outlets that are commonly owned and controlled, employ central buying and merchandising and sell similar lines of merchandise. Corporate chains appear in all types of retailing but they are strongest in department stores, consumer electronics and hardware stores, grocery stores, liquor stores, chemists, shoe stores and clothing stores. **Corporate chains** gain many advantages over independents. Their size allows them to buy in large quantities at lower prices. They can afford to hire corporate-level specialists to deal with such areas as pricing, promotion, merchandising, inventory control and sales forecasting. Moreover, chains gain promotional economies because their advertising costs are spread over many stores and a large sales volume.

Corporate chain See chain stores.

Voluntary chains and retailer co-operatives

The great success of corporate chains caused many independents to band together in one of two forms of contractual associations. One is the **voluntary chain**—a wholesaler-sponsored group of independent retailers that engages in group buying and common merchandising, such as Metcash, Australia's largest grocery wholesaler. The other form of contractual association is the **retailer co-operative**—a group of independent retailers that band together to set up a jointly owned central wholesale operation and conduct joint merchandising and promotion efforts. Examples in Australasia include Amcal Chemists (with 560 member chemists) and Mitre 10 in hardware. These organisations give independents the buying and promotion economies they need to meet the prices of corporate chains.

Voluntary chain A wholesaler-sponsored group of independent retailers that engages in group buying and common merchandising.

Retailer co-operative A contractual association of independent retailers who engage in group buying and merchandising.

Franchise organisations

A **franchise** is a contractual association between a manufacturer, wholesaler or service organisation (the franchisor) and independent businesspeople (franchisees) who buy the right to own and operate one or more units in the franchise system. The main difference between a franchise and other contractual systems (voluntary chains and retail co-operatives) is that franchise systems are normally based on some unique product or service, on a method of doing business or on the trade name, goodwill or patent that the franchisor has developed. Franchising has been prominent in fast foods, motels, petrol stations, video stores, health and fitness centres, car rentals, hairdressing, real estate, travel agencies and dozens of other product and service areas. Franchising is one of the fastest growing forms of retailing, commanding 35% of all retail sales in the USA. One of the best-known and most successful franchisers, McDonald's, now has more than 30000 stores in 119 countries, serving more than 50 million customers a day.[19] More than 70% of McDonald's restaurants worldwide are owned and operated by franchisees. Gaining fast is Subway Sandwiches and Salads, one of the fastest-growing franchises, with nearly 25000 outlets in 83 countries.[20]

Franchise A contractual association between a manufacturer, wholesaler or service organisation (a franchisor) and independent businesspeople (franchisees) who buy the right to own and operate one or more units in the franchise system.

A franchisor will typically charge a franchisee an initial fee, a royalty on sales, lease fees for equipment and a share of the profits. McDonald's franchisees might invest as much as $600000 to $1 million in initial startup costs for a franchise. Then McDonald's charges a percentage service fee and a rental charge on the franchisee's sales.

In Australia the franchise sector has grown at 15% per annum and it is now claimed that Australia is the most franchised country in the world: the Franchisors Association says that Australia has nearly twice as many franchised companies as the USA on a per capita basis, with around 850 franchise chains employing more than 500000 people, and representing around 12% of Australia's GDP. However, slowing retailing spending and high rents are putting many franchise chains and their franchisees under pressure, and the failure of franchise chains such as juice bars Nrgize and Juice Station emphasises that franchise operations face all the risks of larger retail stores.[21]

Franchising has been growing strongly over the past ten years.

Shopping centres in the central business district often offer clusters of high quality shops at the base of office blocks catering to both office workers, tourists and locals, like Sydney's MLC Centre.

Merchandising conglomerates

Merchandising conglomerates are companies that combine several different retailing forms under central ownership and share some distribution and management functions. The Harvey Norman group is one example, having diversified out of franchising electrical goods and furniture departments into computers and sporting goods, through its part ownership of Rebel Sport. Diversified retailing, which provides superior management systems and economies that benefit all the separate retail operations, is likely to increase even further in the future.

Type of store cluster

Most stores today cluster together to increase their customer pulling power and to give consumers the convenience of one-stop shopping. The main types of store clusters are the central business district and the shopping centre.

Central business districts

Central business districts (CBDs) were the main form of retail cluster until the late 1950s. Every large city and town had a CBD with department stores, specialty stores, banks and movie theatres. However, when people began to move to the suburbs these CBDs, with their traffic and parking problems, began to lose business. Merchants opened branches in suburban shopping centres, and the decline of the CBDs continued. In recent years many city councils have joined with merchants to try to revive central business shopping areas by building malls and providing additional parking, and generally beautifying High Street shopping areas. Some CBDs have made a comeback—others remain in a slow and possibly irreversible decline.

Shopping centres

A **shopping centre** is a group of retail businesses planned, developed, owned and managed as a unit, usually positioned around a transport hub, and also providing car parking. A *regional shopping centre*, the largest and most dramatic shopping centre, can be like a small town. Shopping centres are large and getting larger; Chadstone Shopping Centre in Victoria boasts over 14 million visitors each year. Such shopping centres house 300 or more retailers and service organisations that include fashion stores, dry cleaning, photo developing, eateries, post offices, photo finishing, banking and cinemas. Shoppers are increasingly using shopping centres as leisure and social destinations.[22] In the USA the latest trend is for lifestyle centres to fill shopping malls, bringing together gyms, spas, beauty salons, food outlets and apparel stores.[23]

A *community shopping centre* contains between 15 and 40 retail stores. It normally contains a variety of retail outlets, often including a supermarket, specialty stores, professional offices and sometimes a bank. Most shopping centres are community shopping centres, often in the form of *strip shopping centres*. A **strip shopping centre** is usually built along an arterial road, and the larger centres also encompass side roads and other major roads where these intersect with the shopping street. Unlike other forms of shopping centres, they are not centrally owned or managed.

In Australia and New Zealand strip shopping centres have been a major component in the retail distribution line-up. Some of these strips faltered from the 1950s because of lack of car parking—

Merchandising conglomerates
Companies that combine several different retailing forms under central ownership and that share some distribution and management functions.

Shopping centre
A group of retail businesses planned, developed, owned and managed as a unit.

Strip shopping centre
A group of retail businesses located along an arterial road.

convenience had been their major asset. These strips often found a new life as low-rent specialist centres offering products such as antiques, repairs or fashion clothing. The growth in regional shopping centres in the 1990s has placed further pressure on those strips that have remained viable.

Shopping strips along highways have not experienced the same pressure as neighbourhood strips. This is because they offer high-visibility parking and low rents. They have been favoured by furniture stores, car sales outlets and, in more recent times, electrical retailers and home furnishing chains such as Freedom Furniture stores.

SELF-CHECK QUESTIONS

1   Retail stores can be classified by five main characteristics: amount of service, product line, relative prices, control of outlets and type of cluster. Select a retailer in your area. Classify the retailer on the basis of the characteristics mentioned.

2   Think about the retailer classification you have just completed. How could this form of classification assist the retailer? How could it assist the supplier?

Retailer marketing decisions

Retailers are continually searching for new marketing strategies to attract and hold customers. In the past they attracted customers with unique products, more or better services than competitors or credit cards. Today, national brand manufacturers, responding to the growth of discount retailing, are selling their branded goods through discount outlets, as well as through higher service channels.[24] Thus, stores offer similar assortments—national brands are not only found in department stores but also in mass merchandise and off-price discount stores. As a result, stores are looking more and more alike; they have become 'commoditised'. In any city a shopper can find many stores but few assortments. This is as true of traditional retailers as it is of online retailers.

Service differentiation among retailers has also been eroded. Many department stores have trimmed their services whereas discounters have increased theirs. Customers have become smarter and more price sensitive. They see no reason to pay more for identical brands, especially when service differences are shrinking. And because credit cards are now widely accepted, consumers no longer need credit from a particular store.

Retailers face major marketing decisions about their target markets, product assortment and services, price, promotion and placement. They are increasingly concerned with the process of service delivery (customer service), as well as ensuring that their people are up to the task. We discuss some of these decisions in the next section.

Target market and positioning decisions

Retailers must first define their target markets and then decide how they will position themselves in these markets. Should the store focus on upscale, mid-scale or downscale shoppers? Do target shoppers want variety, depth of assortment, convenience or low prices? Until they define and profile their markets, retailers cannot make consistent decisions about product assortment, services, pricing, advertising, store décor or any of the other decisions that must support their positions.

Too many retailers have failed to define their target markets and positions clearly. They have tried to have 'something for everyone' and in doing so often end up satisfying no market well. Every retail outlet must define its major target markets in order to design effective marketing strategies.

For example, some observers have argued that the combination store Kmart in Australia positioned itself too closely to the Target chain in the early 2000s. As a consequence, Target has been profitable while Kmart has experienced difficulties.

Retailers undertake periodic marketing research to check that they are satisfying target customers with their assortment, décor and location. Consider a store that wants to attract wealthy consumers, but whose store image is shown by the solid red line in Figure 15.1. This store does not currently appeal to its target market—it must change its target market or redesign itself as a 'classier' store. Suppose the store then upgrades its products, services and salespeople, and raises its prices. Some time later, a second customer survey might reveal the image shown by the dotted red line in Figure 15.1. The store has established a position that matches its target market choice.

Product assortment and services decisions

Retailers must decide on three major product variables: product assortment, services mix and store atmosphere.

The retailer's product assortment must match target shoppers' expectations. The retailer must determine both the product assortment's width and its depth. Another product assortment element is the quality of the goods: the customer is interested in not only the range of choice but also the quality of the products available.

However, no matter what the store's product assortment and quality level, there will always be competitors with similar assortments and quality. Therefore, the retailer must search for other ways to differentiate itself from similar competitors. It can use any of several product differentiation strategies. First, it can offer merchandise that no other competitor carries—its own private brands or national brands which it holds exclusively. Thus, various supermarket chains have established their own brands that are available exclusively through their outlets. Second, the retailer can feature blockbuster merchandising events, such as the famous Christmas window displays each year at Myer's Melbourne flagship store in Bourke Street.

Or the retailer can offer surprise merchandise, as when Dimmeys in Melbourne offers surprise assortments of seconds, overstocks and sales. Finally, the retailer can differentiate itself by offering a highly targeted product assortment—Just Jeans carries a range of jeans and casual wear and Giordano is renowned for its T-shirts and other casual wear.

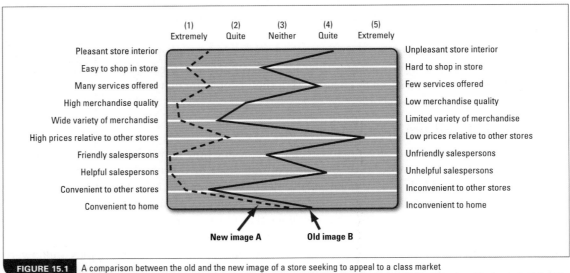

FIGURE 15.1 | A comparison between the old and the new image of a store seeking to appeal to a class market
Source: Adapted from David W. Cravens, Gerald E. Hills and Robert B. Woodruff, *Marketing Decision Making: Concepts and Strategy*, Irwin, 1976, p. 234. Reproduced with the permission of the McGraw-Hill Companies.

Retailers must also decide on a services mix to offer customers. The old corner grocery stores offered home delivery, credit and conversation—services that today's supermarkets largely neglect. The services mix is one of the key tools of non-price competition for setting one store apart from another. Table 15.3 lists some of the major services that full-service retailers can offer.

Because a substantial number of purchases are made on impulse, store atmosphere is also critical for the retailer. The store should have an atmosphere that suits the target market and encourages customers to buy. Retail specialist Paco Underhill studies the effect of the retail environment on consumer behaviour, and describes how small factors such as narrow aisles in the store can have a major effect on sales. Underhill calls this the 'butt-brush' factor—the discomfort felt by shoppers as they are trying to browse if people are walking behind them in a narrow aisle. The solution? Making aisles wider so customers feel more comfortable and will spend more time browsing, or if this isn't possible (since wider aisles require more space to display the same amount of merchandise) placing items which customers tend to browse over before buying (such as jewellery and accessories) at the end of aisles, or at the back of the store, where there is typically more space.[25]

Price decisions

A retailer's price policy is a crucial positioning factor and must be decided in relation to its target market, its product and service assortment and its competition. Ideally, all retailers would like to achieve high mark-ups *and* high volume, but the two seldom go together. Most retailers seek either high mark-ups on lower volume (most specialty stores) or low mark-ups on higher volume (mass merchandisers and discount stores).

Retailers must also pay attention to pricing tactics. Most retailers will put low prices on some items to serve as 'traffic builders' or 'loss leaders'. On some occasions they run storewide sales; on others they plan mark-downs on slower-moving merchandise. For example, some retailers expect to sell 50% of a fashion product at the normal mark-up, 25% at a 40% mark-up and the remaining 25% at cost.

Promotion decisions

Retailers use the normal promotion tools—advertising, public relations, personal selling and sales promotion, as well as direct and online marketing tools—to reach consumers. Retailers advertise in newspapers and magazines and on radio and television, often by way of co-operative advertising with their suppliers. Advertising might be supported by circulars and direct mail. Personal selling

TABLE 15.3 Typical retail services		
Primary services	**Supplementary services**	
Alterations	Baby strollers	Packaging and gift wrapping
Complaint handling	Bill payment	Personal shopping
Convenient store hours	Bridal registry	Product locator
Credit	Cheque cashing	Restaurants or snack bars
Delivery	Children's playrooms	Shopping consultants
Fitting rooms	Demonstrations	Shopping information
Installation and assembly	Layby	Shows, displays and exhibits
Merchandise returns and adjustments	Lost and found	Special ordering
Parking		Wheelchairs
Service and repair		
Telephone ordering		
Toilets		

requires careful training of salespeople in how to greet customers, meet their needs and handle their complaints. Sales promotions might include in-store demonstrations, displays, contests and visiting celebrities. Public relations activities such as press conferences and speeches, store openings, special events, newsletters, magazines and public service activities are always available to retailers.

Place decisions

Retailers, particularly fast-food chains, often state that the keys to marketing success are location, location and location. While this is an overstatement, a retailer's location is, nevertheless, the key to attracting customers. And the costs of building or leasing facilities have a major impact on the retailer's profits. Thus, site location decisions are among the most important the retailer makes. Large retailers usually employ specialists who select locations by using advanced methods. Data such as demographic details on surrounding residents, global positioning software to map the position of competitors, traffic flow studies and competitive intelligence on the performance of competitors are combined to create models which predict sales for various locations, allowing the retailer to select the site with the highest chance of profitability.[26]

SELF-CHECK QUESTIONS

3 Should a marketing organisation discuss its marketing strategy with its retailing intermediaries? When, and what form might this communication take?

4 Should retailers discuss their marketing strategies with their suppliers? If so, when, and what form might this communication take?

5 Might the marketing mix employed by retailers differ from the mix used by supplier organisations? How might this differ?

The future of retailing

Consulting firm Deloitte has identified what it considers to be the top 10 issues facing retailers:[27]

- *Changes in the global economy.* Strong growth in Asia and inflationary pressure in the USA, which has been one of the main drivers of the global economy, will mean that retail sales growth opportunities will increasingly come from outside the USA, and that manufacturing industries will increasingly switch to China and India. In turn, this is likely to drive increased growth in these economies, with flow-on effects for nearby countries.

- *The challenge in locating, understanding and serving the customers who are most likely to purchase.* An understanding of changing demographic patterns and accurate segmentation and targeting of the most valuable customers will become increasingly important. Ageing populations will also create challenges for retailers in maintaining their workforce as older workers retire and are replaced with a smaller pool of generations X and Y who seem to place less emphasis on careers.

- *Increased use of the Internet.* The Internet competes strongly with bricks and mortar stores, placing pressure on retailers to differentiate themselves and develop an emotional connection with their customers. The Internet creates a multi-channel experience for shoppers, allowing them to choose how to collect information on products, order, buy and return products. The impact of the Internet on retail stores is discussed further in Marketing Highlight 15.2.

- *Increased emphasis on risk management.* High-profile accounting irregularities, and the resulting corporate scrutiny by both governments and consumers, are placing pressure on retailers to improve their risk management, and to place more attention on ethics, good corporate governance and reliable reporting. Organisations are increasingly realising that strong ethics, good governance and reliable financial reporting benefit the company in the long run.

▸ *Strengthened supply chain links.* Collaboration between suppliers and retailers have dramatically reduced the time it takes for products to be available on shelves, using technology such as RFIDs (radio frequency identification tags). This has been critical in the emergence of fast-growing chains like Zara (owned by the Inditex group) and its competitor Mango, Europe's most profitable fashion chains, based on a formula of 'fast fashion' or rapidly changing stock lines, a method copied by the Australian chain of 'Cotton on' stores.[28] Marketing Highlight 15.3 discusses how the largest retailers are working with their suppliers to lower prices by increasing the efficiency of the supply channel.

▸ *Rapid industry change.* The rapid pace of change in retail creates pressure for retailers to keep up with developments, and also creates dangers for retailers who fall behind. Some of these changes include huge technological developments (such as RFIDs) and the growth in fast fashion discussed above. Other changes include 'channel blurring' where the same products can be purchased in numerous outlets, the growth of China as a manufacturer of choice and, most recently, the growth of 'pop-up stores' or temporary stores which are set up temporarily to cope with periods of high seasonal demand. Rapid development is likely to continue in lower-cost, faster and more secure payment systems; for example, US Piggly Wiggly supermarket chain now offers customer payment using fingerprint recognition, so the customer doesn't have to carry cash, instead using direct debit from their bank account, at lower cost than conventional debit systems.[29]

▸ *The need to differentiate.* In a retail environment coping with the rapid and radical changes discussed above, the Deloitte's report argues that the basis of retail success is no longer location or price, but is instead by offering value and emotional connections with consumers. Successful differentiation requires effective branding through listening to customers, and creating a compelling, consistent experience. Some of the most loyal customers in retail are companies that cater to the luxury and 'masstige' markets, providing prestige for the masses, as consumers trade up, paying a premium for luxury items.

▸ *Providing a preferred consumer experience.* In a highly competitive market, retailers need to become customer focused, or customer-centric. This requires attention to every step of the product delivery process: product availability through a responsive supply chain, customer segmentation, data mining to detect new trends, relationship management and friendly helpful service, all combined to provide a preferred customer experience, in order to create long-term loyal customers.

▸ *Strategic execution.* Successful retailers are incorporating strategic business plans into their operational goals. Once these plans have been developed, the retailer needs to ensure that they have the right actions in place to achieve their goals, that results are being measured accurately and that performance is being reviewed and managed on an ongoing basis.

▸ *A need to go global.* As their home markets become saturated, retailers will increasingly look to emerging markets for growth opportunities. The 250 largest global retailers sell in 5.5 countries each on average, up from 4.5 five years earlier. European retailers, with initial out-of-country experience within Europe, have led this global trend, and are now among the most common international brands in Asia. China provides an attractive growing market, as do central Europe and the Persian Gulf. This drive for expansion by global retailers provides both an opportunity and a challenge for local retailers, to anticipate and respond to increasing competition, and to maintain their own positions in their home markets.

Online retailing—big, and growing, but there's still a lot of hype

Internet retailing (or etailing) is huge, and it's growing fast, much faster than total retailing sales. Christmas 2005 was a record year for online retailing, with sales of $18.1 billion in November and December in the USA alone, according to the research firm ComScore Networks. That's an increase of 25% on 2004 figures, while total retail sales only increased 6.3%. It's a similar picture in the UK, where 2005 online Christmas sales rose by almost 50% over the previous year's sales, contrasting sharply with an increase of just 2.6% in total retail sales. In the UK, online shopping has increased by 2000% in the past five years according to one estimate. This is the sort of growth that is encouraging predictions that online retailing will soon dominate traditional retailing. 'Within a decade most things will be bought online,' says Dan Wagner, an entrepreneur who runs online shops for the likes of the BBC and Mothercare. He's not the first to predict it: Faith Popcorn, a well-known US trend watcher, made the brave forecast in 2002 on her website that 'by 2010, 90% of consumer goods will be home-delivered'.

So will we soon see the end of retail stores as we know them? It's unlikely, because looking a little more deeply at the enthusiastic stories of huge growth reveals another story, which suggests that, while it's certainly growing, online retailing still

Despite its late entry into online sales, Wal-Mart's online site has captured a large share of online sales, providing a strong challenge to other online retailers.

represents only a very small percentage of total retail sales. Most reports about online commerce come from the USA, which is the world's largest online market, but when travel, auctions and tickets are excluded, even in the USA, e-commerce represented only 2.3% of total US retail sales in the last quarter for which US Department of Commerce figures are available. That's a similar figure to the UK, where online sales represent around 2% of retail spending.

In Australia and other large Pacific economies like Singapore and Hong Kong, online retailing has had even less of an impact. All three countries are characterised by highly urbanised populations, in contrast to the USA. With most of the population in these countries living close to shopping centres, ordering online and waiting for delivery is much less attractive, and the statistics reflect this; Australian pre-Christmas online spending in November 2005 added up to just $235 million, or just over 1% of the monthly retail spending of $17 224 million. A Myer spokesman said that Australian online sales are '. . . not a very substantial figure. We looked at online shopping, but we don't think it's for us just yet. We are mainly in the apparel business and the apparel market isn't really there yet.'

So e-commerce is certainly big, and is having a profound impact on some categories of retailers such as travel agents, since one of the largest categories of online sales is travel. Airlines like Qantas have seen an opportunity to cut their costs, by selling directly to the customer and cutting agent commissions, with the result that more and more customers are booking directly with the airlines online.

Apart from travel, while online retailing is certainly pulling in large amounts of money, it's still a small percentage of total retailing sales, and experts expect that the high recent growth in sales will slow. The growth in total sales and enthusiastic predictions for etailing also disguise some worrying signs for existing operators. Many of the major players have faced substantial setup costs, but margins are generally low online, as operators strive to keep customers away from lower-cost entrants. The most famous of the pure play etailers, Amazon, only started making profits in 2003, after a string of losses as high as $1.4 billion in 2000. Despite recently having shipped 1.5 million in pre-orders of the latest Harry Potter book in 2005, Amazon's Chief Financial Officer, Thomas Szkutak, said that the store 'did little more than break even on the book'. And while Amazon is now making profits, they don't appear to be increasing; in February 2006 the company announced its fourth consecutive quarter of decreased profits relative to the same quarter one year earlier.[30]

The recent growth of Wal-Mart online presents a new and powerful competitor for online retailers. For Christmas 2005, Wal-Mart was the third most popular shopping site, despite very limited promotion of the site by Wal-Mart. The powerful 'clicks and mortar' competitors like Wal-Mart and Borders are particularly dangerous for the pure play Internet operators, because they offer a powerful brand name with high visibility and implied security, and also offer convenient in-store locations for exchange of items. The other huge worry for etailers is the increasing cost of advertising online, with sharp rises in online ad costs. The home pages of popular sites like Yahoo, AOL and MSN are sold out months in advance, and the top sites have increased their rates sharply, with AOL increasing its rates by 20% in the September 2005 quarter. MSN charges between several hundred thousand dollars and $US1 million for a prime 24-hour spot on its home page, up from $US25 000 to $US50 000 a year earlier. In comparison, a 30-second spot on the number two ranked show in the USA, *Desperate Housewives*, costs only $US574 504. At these rates, advertising online is becoming much more expensive, and threatens the already narrow margins of many operators.

The increasing competition for the etail dollar and rising advertising costs suggest that there will be repetitions of the high-profile online collapses, like US and Hong Kong online grocers Webvan and adMart and retailers boo.com and eToys. There's no doubt that lots of customers love online shopping. But don't expect it to dominate in-store any time soon. And that prediction that 90% of sales will be home delivered by 2010? It disappeared from Faith Popcorn's website around 2003, and the site doesn't make any predictions now. More conservative predictions suggest that etailing will only reach about 6% of retail sales by 2009. Richard Hyman, chairman of Verdict, a UK market research agency, is sceptical about the Internet ever controlling more than 20% of retail sales. He says: 'Without a significant unforeseen enhancement to technology— so you can touch and feel something—I can't see it. It is mostly women that shop regularly and most are not shopping to buy anything specific. It is a pleasurable activity which may or may not result in them making a purchase, and you can't do that on the internet. That's a major disadvantage.'

Whatever the level of online sales, given the high level of competition, low margins and rising advertising costs, we can probably expect to see some more etailers added to the pile of dot.com business failures.

Sources: Australian Bureau of Statistics, *Retail Trade, Australia*, Catalogue no. 8501.0, 9 January 2006; ACNielsen, 'Global Consumer Attitudes towards Online Shopping', October 2005, available at ACNielsen.com; Sean Aylmer, 'Advertising Rates Skyrocket on the Top Websites', *The Australian Financial Review*, 18 November, 2005, p. 59; Michael Barbaro, 'Internet Sales Show Big Gains over Holidays', *The New York Times*, 30 December 2005, p. 1; Jonathan, Birchall, 'Much More in Store at Walmart.com', *Financial Times*, 7 June 2005, p. 8; Suzan Burton, 'Where Are All the Shoppers? E-tailing Lessons for the Asia Pacific', *Quarterly Journal of Electronic Commerce*, vol. 3, no. 4, 2002, pp. 331–342; Sarah Butler, 'Internet Stores Expect a Merry Christmas as Online Sales Soar', *The Times*, 16 November 2005, p. 7; Roger Collis, 'Travel Agents Losing out to Airline Sites', *International Herald Tribune*, 3 June 2005, p. 9; Drew DeSilver, 'Amazon Blows Past Street's Predictions', *The Seattle Times*, 27 July 2005, p. E1; Julia Finch, 'Dixons Tells Web Shoppers to be Wary: Warning of Rise in Small Online Firms Going Bust: Christmas Goods May Never Arrive, says Clare', *The Guardian*, 24 November 2005, p. 25; 'Happy e-birthdays—Internet Businesses', *The Economist*, 23 July 2005; Simon Hayes, 'Online Shopping Flopping', *The Australian*, 20 December 2005, p. 21; Allister Heath and Richard Orange, 'Sales Provide Happy New Year for retailers', *The Business*, 8 January 2006; Mylene Mangalindan, 'Web Retail Sales Seen Rising 22% in US this Year', *The Asian Wall Street Journal*, 25 May 2005, p. M8; Rod Myer, 'Web Forces Travel Agents to Work Smarter', *The Australian Financial Review*, 29 December 2005, p. 28; Maija Palmer, 'Online Shopping Sparkles for Retailers', *Financial Times*, 20 January 2006, p. 3; US Census Bureau News, Quarterly Retail E-Commerce Sales, 3rd Quarter 2005, CB05-161, available at <www.commerce.gov>.

Questions

1 Which retailers do you think are most threatened by the rise in online buying? Why? Which seem to face the lowest threat?

2 Is there a difference between an online auction house such as eBay and an online retailer such as Amazon.com? If so, how are they different?

3 When do you shop online? When don't you? Ask a few others the same questions. What do the answers suggest are the challenges for traditional retailers and etailers?

15.2

SELF-CHECK QUESTIONS

6 It might be argued that a major issue in retailing management is channel blurring: an increasing overlap between the positions occupied by department stores, discounters and supermarkets. Do you agree with this proposition? In any event, select examples to illustrate your position.

7 The level of customer service is a major marketing tool used by retailers, and this level of service is ultimately reflected in other marketing mix decisions such as product assortment and pricing. Do you agree with this proposition? Select examples to argue a case for or against this proposition.

Wholesaling

Wholesaling All activities involved in selling goods and services to those buying for resale or business use.

Wholesalers Firms engaged primarily in wholesaling activity.

Wholesaling includes all activities involved in selling goods and services to those buying for resale or business use. A retail bakery acts like a wholesaler when it sells pastry to the local hotel. However, we call **wholesalers** those firms engaged primarily in wholesaling activity. Wholesaling is a huge industry, with revenue in the 2006 financial year estimated to be $330 billion in Australia, or nearly 13% of the country's total, and employing around 450 000 people.[31] Wholesalers differ from retailers in several ways. First, because they deal mostly with business customers rather than final consumers, wholesalers pay less attention to promotion, atmosphere and location. Second, wholesalers usually cover larger trade areas and have larger transactions than retailers. Third, wholesalers face different legal regulations.

Wholesalers buy mostly from producers and sell mostly to retailers, industrial consumers and other wholesalers. But why are wholesalers used at all? For example, why would a producer use wholesalers rather than selling directly to retailers or consumers? Quite simply, wholesalers are often better at performing one or more of the following channel functions:

- *Selling and promoting.* Wholesalers' salesforces help manufacturers reach many small customers at a low cost. The wholesaler has more contacts and the buyer often trusts the wholesaler more than they trust the distant manufacturer.
- *Buying and assortment building.* Wholesalers can select items and build assortments needed by their customers, thereby saving the consumers much work.
- *Bulk breaking.* Wholesalers save their customers money by buying in carload lots and breaking bulk (breaking large lots into small quantities).

- *Warehousing*. Wholesalers hold inventories, thereby reducing the inventory costs and risks of suppliers and customers.
- *Transportation*. Wholesalers can provide quicker delivery to buyers because they are closer than the producers.
- *Financing*. Wholesalers finance their customers by giving credit, and they finance their suppliers by ordering early and paying bills on time.
- *Risk bearing*. Wholesalers absorb risk by taking title and bearing the cost of theft, damage, spoilage and obsolescence.
- *Market information*. Wholesalers give information to suppliers and customers about competitors, new products and price developments.
- *Management services and advice*. Wholesalers often help retailers to train their salespeople, improve store layouts and displays and set up accounting and inventory control systems.

SELF-CHECK QUESTIONS

8   What functions do wholesalers perform for grocery manufacturers?

9   What margins might such wholesalers expect?

Types of wholesalers

Wholesalers fall into three major groups (see Table 15.4): merchant wholesalers, brokers and agents and manufacturers' sales branches and offices.

Merchant wholesalers

Merchant wholesalers are independently owned businesses that take title to the merchandise they handle. They are the largest single group of wholesalers. Merchant wholesalers include two broad types: full-service wholesalers and limited-service wholesalers.

Merchant wholesaler
An independently owned business that takes title to the merchandise it handles.

Full-service wholesalers

Full-service wholesalers provide a full set of services, such as carrying stock, using a salesforce, offering credit, making deliveries and providing management assistance. They are either wholesale merchants or industrial distributors.

Full-service wholesalers
Wholesalers that provide a full set of services, such as carrying stock, using a salesforce, offering credit, making deliveries and providing management assistance.

TABLE 15.4 Classification of wholesalers

Merchant wholesalers	Brokers and agents	Manufacturers' sales branches and offices

Full-service wholesalers
    Wholesale merchants
    Industrial distributors
Limited-service wholesalers
    Cash-and-carry wholesalers
    Truck wholesalers
    Drop shippers
    Rack jobbers
    Producers' co-operatives
    Mail order wholesalers
	Brokers
	Agents
		Sales branches and offices
		Purchasing offices

Customer value by improving the supply chain

US retailer Wal-Mart is the largest retailer in the world, and with annual sales exceeding $165 billion, it is also the USA's largest private employer. You don't get that big without being good at what you do, and retailers the world over study Wal-Mart to examine what they can learn to improve their own operations. A large part of Wal-Mart's recent success is that its massive size gives it the ability to push its suppliers for lower prices, but Wal-Mart was keeping a tight rein on expenses long before its huge size gave it significant advantages in bargaining with suppliers. The company is also renowned for investment in technology to develop advanced information systems, which allow daily stock replenishment and low inventory costs, while ensuring that stock is always available or, at worst, rapidly restocked. A critical part of Wal-Mart's strategy involves focusing on adding value at every level of its supply chain, to allow it to provide lower prices to its customers, while maintaining profitable margins for Wal-Mart.

Wal-Mart's practices have given it the lowest cost structure in the industry. Its operating expenses amount to only 16% of sales, compared with 23% at Kmart. Thus, Wal-Mart can charge lower prices but still reap higher profits, allowing it to offer better service, such as its famous 'greeter' who greets customers at the door. Its processes create a 'productivity loop'; Wal-Mart's lower prices and better service attract more shoppers, producing more sales, making the company more efficient and enabling it to lower prices even more.

Wal-Mart has been used as a model by many other retailers; Australian retail giant Woolworths

Woolworths has used supply chain restructure to lower costs, and deliver record profits to the company.

has drawn on the Wal-Mart strategy and has been investing heavily to improve the efficiency of its supply chain in its widely discussed 'Project Refresh'. The project, involving a complete overhaul of the Woolworths' supply chain, was launched in 1999 and had delivered $3.2 billion in cumulative savings by 2005, with the company expecting to save a further $4.5 billion from 2005 to 2008, in a supply chain revolution. The savings allow Woolworths to provide lower prices to customers, shaving its profit margins, but increasing its profits by obtaining more sales at lower prices.

Woolworths has been reluctant to reveal details of its Project Refresh innovations (and took one former employee to court to prevent him from using information in a new job with a competitor) but is known to have focused on more efficient transport management, in-store goods handling, distribution centres and information technology. This has involved around 40 technology projects, each with budgets of between $1 million and $200 million, following the lead of Wal-Mart and Tesco in Britain, which have both invested heavily in technology to drive down distribution costs and increase customer retention. Specific projects include the introduction of an automated stock checking and replenishment system known as 'AutoStockR', which has enabled the company to reduce the amount of stock held in warehouses, while ensuring that the stores don't run out of stock. The company has also constructed new distribution centres, using new smaller-sized pallets which run on castor wheels for easier loading and unloading. The new roller-based pallets can be rolled directly into the store, where staff unload the stock onto shelving, reducing double handling between the distribution centre and the store shelf, with an estimated 30% saving in labour cost.

And like Wal-Mart, Woolworths is using its savings and higher profits to expand in other markets. The company has spent $2.5 billion to acquire 150 New Zealand supermarkets and Australian stores from its rival Foodland Associated. Woolworths states that it will use its learnings from Project Refresh to cut costs, improve margins and grow its market share in New Zealand.

So has the massive investment been worth it? Woolworths say they have exceeded their savings target for the early stages of the project, and the company's earnings grew 14% in 2005 (far ahead of rival chain Coles), putting pressure on its competitors to improve their own supply chain efficiency. Project Refresh shows that effective investment can provide returns to customers and to shareholders. It also shows that good marketing strategy involves thinking about the whole value chain—suppliers, internal customers and working on what can add value to all the stakeholders involved in the process.

Sources: Lorrie Grant, 'An Unstoppable Marketing Force: Wal-Mart Aims for Domination of the Retail Industry Worldwide', *USA Today*, 6 November 1998, p. B1; Mathew Charles, 'Woolies' Sales Growth Beating Coles Myer's', *The Advertiser*, 23 August 2005, p. 34; Kelly Mills, 'Woolies in No Hurry on RFID', *The Australian*, 19 July 2005, p. 33; Richard Gluyas, 'Criterion', *The Australian*, 1 March 2005, p. 25; David James, 'Costs and Value', *Business Review Weekly*, 14 July 2005, p. 67; Simon Lloyd, 'The Powerful Price Premium', *Business Review Weekly*, 8 December 2005, pp. 78–79; Kelly Mills, 'Woolies Saving on Chain Revamp', *The Australian*, 1 March 2005, p. 30; Ben Woodhead, 'Retailers Spend $1bn to Woo Customers', *The Australian Financial Review*, 25 October 2005, p. 1; Ben Woodhead, 'Reams of Smart Data with Somewhere to go', *The Australian Financial Review*, 10 February 2005, p. 18.

Questions

1 Marketing is often concerned with provision of goods to end-customers, and leaves efficiency in the supply chain to the logistics department. Is this a problem, or a natural division of work?

2 Woolworths could use the savings from its supply chain efficiency to provide higher returns to shareholders, rather than providing cost savings to customers. What might be the advantages and disadvantages of this strategy?

3 Wal-Mart has been very successful in the USA, but has failed to replicate its success in other markets such as Germany, where customers reacted badly to being confronted by Wal-Mart's traditional 'greeter' at the door. Do you think customers in different countries want different things from their retail stores? If so, do you think a company like Wal-Mart would be better to try and alter its model in Germany, or try to change the preferences of German buyers?

15.3

Wholesale merchants sell mostly to retailers and provide a full range of services. They vary in the width of their product line. Some carry several lines of goods to meet the needs of both general merchandise retailers and single-line retailers. Others carry one or two lines of goods in a greater depth of assortment. Examples are hardware wholesalers, pharmaceutical wholesalers and clothing wholesalers. Some specialty wholesalers carry only part of a line in great depth. Examples are health food, seafood and car parts wholesalers. They offer customers deeper choice and greater product knowledge.

Industrial distributors are merchant wholesalers who sell to producers rather than to retailers. They provide inventory, credit, delivery and other services. They may carry a broad range of merchandise, a general line or a specialty line. Business-to-business distributors may concentrate on such lines as maintenance and operating supplies, original equipment goods (such as ball bearings and motors) or equipment (such as power tools and forklift trucks).

Limited-service wholesalers

Limited-service wholesalers offer fewer services to their suppliers and customers. There are several types of limited-service wholesalers.

⦿ *Cash-and-carry wholesalers* carry a limited line of fast-moving goods, sell to small retailers for cash and normally do not deliver. A small fish store retailer, for example, normally drives at dawn to a cash-and-carry fish wholesaler and buys several crates of fish, pays on the spot,

Limited-service wholesalers Wholesalers that offer only limited services to their suppliers and customers.

drives the merchandise back to the store and unloads it. Small retailers use the services of Metcash Trading's IGA and A. G. Campbell's Wholesale Cash and Carry to overcome their scale disadvantages.

- ◉ *Truck wholesalers* (also called cash-van operators) perform a selling and delivery function. They carry a limited line of goods (such as snack foods) that they sell for cash as they make their rounds of supermarkets, small grocery stores, hospitals, restaurants, factory cafeterias and hotels.

- ◉ *Drop shippers* operate in bulk industries such as coal, timber and heavy equipment. They do not carry inventory or handle the product. Once an order is received, they find a producer who ships the goods directly to the customer. The drop shipper takes title and risk from the time the order is accepted to the time it is delivered to the customer. Because drop shippers do not carry inventory, their costs are lower and they can pass on some savings to customers.

- ◉ *Rack jobbers* serve grocery and pharmaceutical retailers, mostly in the area of non-food items. These retailers do not want to order and maintain displays of hundreds of non-food items. Rack jobbers send delivery trucks to stores, and the delivery person sets up racks of toys, paperbacks, hardware items, health and beauty aids or other items. They price the goods, keep them fresh and keep inventory records. Rack jobbers sell on consignment; they retain title to the goods and bill the retailers only for the goods sold to consumers. Thus, they provide such services as delivery, shelving, inventory and financing. They do little promotion because they carry many branded items that are already highly advertised.

- ◉ *Producers' co-operatives*, owned by farmer members, assemble farm produce to sell in local markets. Their profits are divided among members at the end of the year. They often try to improve product quality and promote a co-op brand name, such as the world's biggest wholesaler of bananas, Chiquita Bananas.

- ◉ *Mail order wholesalers* send catalogues to retail, industrial and institutional customers offering jewellery, cosmetics, special foods and other small items. Their main customers are businesses in small outlying areas. They have no salesforces to call on customers. The orders are filled and sent by mail, truck or other means.

Brokers and agents

Brokers and agents differ from merchant wholesalers in two ways: they do not take title to goods and they perform only a few functions. Their main function is to aid in buying and selling, and for these services they earn a commission on the selling price. Like merchant wholesalers, they generally specialise by product line or customer type.

Brokers

Broker A wholesaler who does not take title to goods and whose function is to bring buyers and sellers together and assist in negotiation.

A **broker** brings buyers and sellers together and assists in negotiation. Brokers are paid by the parties hiring them. They do not carry inventory, get involved in financing or assume risk. The most familiar examples are food brokers, real estate brokers, insurance brokers and security brokers.

Agents

Agent A wholesaler who represents buyers or sellers on a more permanent basis, performs only a few functions and does not take title to goods.

Agents represent buyers or sellers on a more permanent basis. There are several types.

- ◉ *Manufacturers' agents* (also called manufacturers' representatives) are the most numerous type of agent wholesaler. They represent two or more manufacturers of related lines. They have a formal agreement with each manufacturer covering prices, territories, order-handling procedures, delivery and warranties and commission rates. They know each manufacturer's product line and use their wide contacts to sell the products. Manufacturers' agents are used in such lines as apparel, furniture and electrical goods. Most manufacturers' agents are small businesses, with only a few employees who are skilled salespeople. They are hired by small producers who cannot afford to maintain their own field salesforces and by large producers who want to open new territories or sell in areas that cannot support a full-time salesperson.

● *Selling agents* contract to sell a producer's entire output—the manufacturer is either not interested in doing the selling or feels unqualified. The selling agent serves as a sales department and has much influence over prices, terms and conditions of sale. The selling agent normally has no territory limits. Selling agents are found in such product areas as textiles, industrial machinery and equipment, coal and coke, chemicals and metals.

● *Purchasing agents* generally have a long-term relationship with buyers. They make purchases for buyers and often receive, inspect, warehouse and ship goods to the buyers. One type consists of resident buyers in major apparel markets, purchasing specialists who look for apparel lines that can be carried by small retailers located in small cities. They know a great deal about their product lines, provide helpful market information to clients, and can obtain the best goods and prices available.

● *Commission merchants* (or houses) are agents that take physical possession of products and negotiate sales. They are not normally used on a long-term basis. They are used most often in agricultural marketing by farmers who do not want to sell their own output and who do not belong to co-operatives. Typically, the commission merchant will take a truckload of farm products to a central market, sell it for the best price, deduct a commission and expenses and pay the balance to the farmer.

Manufacturers' sales branches and offices

The third major type of wholesaling is that done in **manufacturers' sales branches and offices** by sellers or buyers themselves, rather than through independent wholesalers. Manufacturers often set up their own sales branches and offices to improve inventory control, selling and promotion. Sales branches carry inventory and are found in such industries as timber and car equipment and parts. Some large retailers set up purchasing offices in major market centres elsewhere in the world. These purchasing offices perform a role similar to that of brokers or agents but are part of the buyer's organisation.

Manufacturers' sales branches and offices
Wholesaling by sellers or buyers themselves rather than through independent wholesalers.

SELF-CHECK QUESTIONS

10 Would you agree with the proposition that grocery wholesalers will decline in prominence as the trading hours for large chain stores are extended? Why do you hold your particular view?

11 Would the above statement be more accurate for full-service retailers than for limited-service retailers?

12 Why might a food manufacturer use an agent? Under what circumstances might a broker be used rather than an agent?

Wholesaler marketing decisions

Wholesalers have experienced mounting competitive pressures in recent years. They have faced new sources of competition, more demanding customers, new technologies and more direct buying programs by large industrial, institutional and retail buyers. As a result, they have had to improve their strategic decisions on target markets, product assortments and services, price, promotion and place.

Target market and positioning decisions

Wholesalers, like retailers, must define their target markets—they cannot serve everyone. They can choose a target group by size of customer (only large retailers), type of customer (convenience food stores only), need for service (customers who need credit) or other factors. Within the target group, they can identify the more profitable customers, design stronger offers and build better relationships with these customers. They can propose automatic reordering systems, set up management training and advisory systems or even sponsor a voluntary chain. They can discourage less profitable customers by requiring larger orders or adding service charges to smaller ones.

Marketing mix decisions

Like retailers, wholesalers must decide on product assortment and services, as well as the other marketing mix elements we are now familiar with—prices, promotion and place.

Product assortment and services decisions

The wholesaler's 'product' is its assortment. Wholesalers are under great pressure to carry a full line and stock enough for immediate delivery. But this practice can damage profits. Wholesalers today are cutting down on the number of lines they carry, choosing to carry only the more profitable ones. Wholesalers are also rethinking which services count most in building strong customer relationships and which should be dropped or charged for. The key is to find the mix of services most valued by their target customers.

Price decisions

Wholesalers usually mark up the cost of goods by a standard percentage—say, 20%. Expenses may account for 17% of the gross margin, leaving a profit margin of 3%. In grocery wholesaling, the average profit margin is often less than 2%. Wholesalers are trying new pricing approaches. They might cut their margin on some lines in order to win important new customers. They might ask suppliers for special price breaks when they can use these to achieve an increase in the supplier's sales.

Promotion decisions

Most wholesalers are not promotion minded. Their use of trade advertising, sales promotion, personal selling and public relations is largely scattered and unplanned. Many are behind the times in personal selling. They still see selling as a single salesperson talking to a single customer instead of a team effort to sell, build and service major accounts. And wholesalers also need to adopt some of the non-personal promotion techniques used by retailers. They need to develop an overall promotion strategy and to make greater use of supplier promotion materials and programs.

Place decisions

Wholesalers typically locate in low-rent areas and have tended to invest little money in their buildings, equipment and systems. As a result, their materials-handling and order-processing systems are often out of date. In recent years, however, large and progressive wholesalers are reacting to rising costs by investing in automated warehouses and online ordering systems. Progressive wholesalers are adapting their services to the needs of target customers and finding cost-reducing methods of doing business. Orders are fed from the retailer's system directly into the wholesaler's computer, and the items are picked up by mechanical devices and automatically taken to a shipping platform where they are assembled. Many wholesalers are making increasing use of technology, such as RFIDs for tracking and inventory control, and using computer modelling for better demand management. For example, convenience store chain 7-11 has entered into a $200 million contract with wholesaler

Metcash, and is using technology to record sales and automatically reorder stock, rather than relying on franchisees to identify the gaps on their shelves.[32]

SELF-CHECK QUESTIONS

13 Might wholesalers employ a different marketing mix to their suppliers? If so, describe such differences.

14 Explain the meaning of the statement: A wholesaler's product is its assortment.

Trends in wholesaling

Wholesaling has been one of Australia's growing sectors. It's the sixth fastest growing of the industry sectors, and this growth is expected to continue to increase over the next five years.[33] However, the wholesaling industry also faces considerable challenges. The industry remains vulnerable to one of the most enduring trends of the last decade—fierce resistance to price increases and the winnowing out of suppliers who are not adding value based on cost and quality. Progressive wholesalers constantly watch for better ways to meet the changing needs of their suppliers and target customers. They recognise that, in the long run, their only reason for existence comes from adding value by increasing the efficiency and effectiveness of the entire marketing channel. To achieve this goal, they must constantly improve their services and reduce their costs.

Wholesalers will continue to increase the services they provide to retailers—retail pricing, co-operative advertising, marketing and management information reports, accounting services, online transactions and others. Rising costs, on the one hand, and the demand for increased services, on the other hand, will put the squeeze on wholesaler profits. Wholesalers who do not find efficient ways to deliver value to their customers will be squeezed out by more efficient competitors. However, the increased use of computerised, automated and web-based systems will help wholesalers to contain the costs of ordering, shipping and inventory holding, boosting their productivity.

Finally, facing slow growth in their domestic markets and the development of global retailers, many of the large wholesalers are now going global. For example, Australian wholesaler Metcash competes in the Southeast Asian region with local partners in a number of countries such as Indonesia and The Philippines. These large international operations will put pressure on smaller, less efficient wholesalers, and are likely to lead to increasing consolidation in the wholesaling business.

SELF-CHECK QUESTIONS

15 It might be argued that, although wholesalers must manage their marketing mix like other marketing organisations, they are primarily concerned with profitable selling and efficient physical distribution. Do you agree?

16 The level of customer service is a major marketing tool used by wholesalers and this level of service is ultimately reflected in other marketing mix decisions such as product assortment and pricing. Do you agree with this proposition? Select examples to argue a case for or against.

SUMMARY

Retailing and *wholesaling* consist of many organisations bringing goods and services from the point of production to the point of use. Retailing includes all activities involved in selling goods or services directly to final consumers for their personal, non-business use. Retailers can be classified as *store retailers* and *non-store retailers*. Store retailers can be further classified by the amount of service they provide (*self-service, limited service* or *full service*); product line sold (*specialty stores, department stores, supermarkets, convenience stores, superstores, hypermarkets* and *service businesses*); relative prices (*discount stores, off-price retailers* and *catalogue showrooms*); control of outlets (*corporate chains, voluntary chains* and *retailer co-operatives, franchise organisations* and *merchandising conglomerates*); and type of store cluster (*central business districts* and *shopping centres*).

Despite strong growth in online retailing, most goods and services are still sold through 'bricks and mortar' stores, apart from some specific categories, such as travel purchases, where a shift in consumer purchases to the Internet has put strong pressure on travel agents.

Each retailer must make decisions about its target markets, product assortment and services, price, promotion and place. Retailers need to choose target markets carefully and position themselves strongly.

Wholesaling includes all the activities involved in selling goods or services to those who are buying for the purpose of resale or for business use. Wholesalers perform many functions, including selling and promoting, buying and assortment building, bulk breaking, warehousing, transporting, financing, risk bearing, supplying market information and providing management services and advice. Wholesalers fall into three groups. Merchant wholesalers take possession of the goods. They include *full-service wholesalers* (*wholesale merchants, industrial distributors*) and *limited-service wholesalers* (*cash-and-carry wholesalers, truck wholesalers, drop shippers, rack jobbers, producers' co-operatives* and *mail order wholesalers*). *Agents* and *brokers* do not take possession of the goods but are paid a commission for aiding buying and selling.

Manufacturers' *sales branches* and *offices* are wholesaling operations conducted by non-wholesalers to bypass the wholesalers. Progressive wholesalers are adapting their services to the needs of target customers and are seeking cost-reducing methods of doing business.

MARKETING ISSUE

Australia and Hong Kong both suffer from a particular retail problem: a very high concentration of supermarket sales by two players (in Australia, Coles and Woolworths, in Hong Kong, Park 'n Shop and Welcome). In both countries, around 70% of supermarket sales are made through the two market leaders, and if a major food retailer loses shelf space in these outlets it can cripple profits. The problem is exacerbated by the move by supermarkets to expand the space allocated to their home brands.

Manufacturers can sometimes make up for lost shelf space by winning contracts to manufacture home brands, but the profits on producing private label products are typically far less than on producing branded goods. In addition, since the contracts to produce private labels are subject to competing bids, the ongoing uncertainty in such a bid can create additional problems. For example, in 2005 Australian manufacturer Greens Foods issued a profit warning after losing the contract to manufacture peanut butter under licence to the Dick Smith brand.

1   Discuss possible strategies for a food manufacturer selling its products through supermarkets which control a high percentage of category sales.

2   What are the advantages and disadvantages of each strategy?

KEY TERMS

agent	594	independent off-price retailers	580	self-service retailers	572
broker	594	limited-service retailers	572	shopping centre	582
chain stores	580	limited-service wholesalers	593	specialty store	573
combination store	573	manufacturers' sales branches and offices	595	strip shopping centre	582
convenience store	575	mass merchant	575	supermarkets	574
corporate chain	581	merchandising conglomerates	582	superstore	575
department store	573	merchant wholesaler	591	voluntary chain	581
discount store	577	off-price retailers	577	warehouse clubs (wholesale clubs)	580
factory outlets	580	retailers	572	wholesalers	590
franchise	581	retailer co-operatives	581	wholesaling	590
full-service retailers	573	retailing	572		
full-service wholesalers	591				
hypermarkets	575				

DISCUSSING THE ISSUES

1 In deciding where to shop, many consumers are coming to value quality of service more than such factors as price or convenience. Some prefer to shop online for this reason. If this trend continues, what impact might it have on full-service retailers? Would such a continuing trend have the same impact on department stores as it would on supermarkets? Why?

2 Are wholesalers 'dinosaurs'? In answering this question, consider the functions performed by such intermediaries.

3 If businesses are today seeking to produce to order using just-in-time techniques, why do they utilise wholesalers and retailers who serve to distance the marketing organisation from its customers, and add to costs by holding finished goods inventory?

4 Do you think that the distinction between large retailers and large wholesalers is becoming more and more blurred? How does this manifest itself? How might consumers be affected if such a blurring is occurring in certain industry sectors?

REFERENCES

1. Florence Chong, 'Wal-Mart Driving Dixie Down', *The Australian*, 3 March 2005, p. 42.
2. Simon Evans, 'Melbourne Store Would Be Sold', *The Australian Financial Review*, 23 September 2005, p. 58.
3. Wendy Tanaka, 'Neiman Marcus Latest of Many Retailers to Merge, but Each for Own Reasons', *The Philadelphia Inquirer*, 3 May 2005.
4. Sue Mitchell, 'Retail Goliath Turns its Fortunes Around', *The Australian Financial Review*, 8 September 2005, p. 17; Simon Lloyd, 'Big Plans in Store', *Business Review Weekly*, 23 June 2005, p. 36.
5. Anonymous, 'Department Store Decline', *Business Review Weekly*, 1 September 2005, pp. 30–31.
6. Ibid.
7. <www.colesgroup.com>, Accessed 13 September 2006.
8. Anonymous, 'Department Store Decline', *Business Review Weekly*, 1 September 2005, pp. 30–31.
9. David Turner, 'Why Selling to Little People is no longer Child's Play', *Financial Times*, 6 June 2005, p. 14.
10. Deloitte, 'Global Powers of Retailing', <www.deloitte.com/dtt/cda/doc/content/US_CB_GlobalPowers2005.pdf>, accessed 13 January 2006.
11. Jonathan Birchall, 'The Cultural Maelstrom of International Retailing', *Financial Times*, 4 June 2005, p. 7.
12. Tina Morrison, 'Wholesale Changes at Retail Chain', *International Herald Tribune*, 15 July 2005, p. B3.
13. Joshua Fellman, 'HK to Get MegaBox Mall', *The Australian Financial Review*, 20 October 2005, p. 65.
14. Kirsty Needham, 'Everything Must Go . . . Including Us', *The Sydney Morning Herald*, 25 November 2005, p. 5; Sue Mitchell and Henry Byrne, 'Gowings Pays Price for Overreaching', *The Australian Financial Review*, 9 November 2005, p. 8.
15. Jeremy Grant, 'Feelings Soften Towards Hard Discounters', *Financial Times*, 29 August 2005, p. 17.
16. Damien Lynch, 'Factory Outlets Suit SMEs', *The Australian Financial Review*, 17 May 2005, p. 50.

17. John Helyar, Ann Harrington and Sol Price, 'The Only Company Wal-Mart Fears', *Fortune*, 24 November 2003, pp. 158–166; and also Tiffany Meyers, 'Marketers Learn Luxury Isn't Simply for the Very Wealthy', *Advertising Age*, 13 September 2004, pp. S2, S10.

18. David James, 'Coles' Brave New World', *Business Review Weekly*, 7 April 2005, p. 66.

19. <www.mcdonalds.com/corp/about.html>, accessed 13 January 2006.

20. See David Stires, 'Fallen Arches', *Fortune*, 29 April 2002, pp. 74–76; Anne Field, 'Your Ticket to a New Career', *Business Week*, 12 May 2003, pp. 100–101; information accessed online at <www.subway.com>, January 2006; and information accessed online at <www.mcdonalds.com/corp.html>, January 2006.

21. Jacqui Walker, 'The Franchise Crack-Up', *Business Review Weekly*, 4 August 2005, p. 36.

22. For a discussion of the social importance of shopping malls, and the implications for retailers, see Paco Underhill, *Call of the Mall*, New York, Simon & Schuster, 2004.

23. Carolyn Cummins, 'Landlords Brace for Lower Rents', *The Sydney Morning Herald*, 16 July 2005, p. 62.

24. Jeremy Grant, 'Feelings Soften Towards Hard Discounters', *Financial Times*, 29 August 2005, p. 17.

25. Paco Underhill, *Why We Buy: The Science of Shopping*, New York, Simon & Schuster, 2000.

26. Kath Walters, 'Position Perfect', *Business Review Weekly*, 18 August 2005, p. 26.

27. Deloitte, Global Powers of Retailing, 2005, <www.deloitte.com/dtt/cda/doc/content/US_CB_GlobalPowers2005.pdf>, accessed 13 January 2006.

28. Jacqui Walker, 'The Smart Shops', *Business Review Weekly*, 6 October 2005, pp. 28–37.

29. Jonathan Birchall, 'US Supermarket Encourages Shoppers to Keep in Touch', *Financial Times*, 13 July 2005, p. 14.

30. Randall Stross, 'Life of Amazon not an Open Book', *The Sydney Morning Herald*, 13 February 2006, p. 21.

31. 'A Wholesale Lot of Difference', *Business Review Weekly*, 8 September 2005, p. 32–33.

32. Julia May, 'Under Siege', *Business Review Weekly*, 11 August 2005, p. 57.

33. 'A Wholesale Lot of Difference', *Business Review Weekly*, 8 September 2005, p. 32–33.

PHOTO/AD CREDITS

571. Courtesy of IKEA Stores; **573.** Courtesy of Sanity; **582.** © Authorised by Katrin Neubauer, Marketing Manager MLC Centre, Sydney, Design by There Visual Communication Design.

CASE STUDY

Evolution of camera stores at the beginning of the third millennium

Introduction

This case study examines facts and changes in consumer purchase behaviour in the drastically shifting analogue and digital cameras retail market observed in the last few years. First, the evolution of sales of analogue and digital cameras is reviewed. Second, a series of statistics is unveiled describing the demographic profile of camera purchasers by type of store. Third, the purchaser of cameras to shopper ratio is examined followed by the trends observed in the market for prints regarding the proportion of units produced for both analogue and digital technologies. Last, the proportion of digital prints is examined in terms of methods used between online, retail and home.

Evolving technology

In recent years the rapid evolution of photographic equipment technology has had a significant impact on consumer demand. As shown in Figure 1, the trend observed in terms of sales by camera type had reached an important turning point by the start of the new millennium; from 81.4% of camera market sales in 1995, analogue cameras now occupy only 18.2% of the total sales in the USA.

A reverse phenomenon has been observed for digital cameras where in 2000 the total number sold accounted for only 19.7% of the market while in 2005 sales reached 82% of market share. In marketing terms, this trend is not an evolution, it is a revolution! The impact for manufacturers is without precedent in this sector since the introduction of the Polaroid instant picture system in 1957, although the Polaroid never had the mega impact digital technology has had in the last few years.

Demographic profiles of consumers by type of store

Figure 2 (overleaf) shows the demographic breakdown (i.e. household income, head of household age and head of household education)

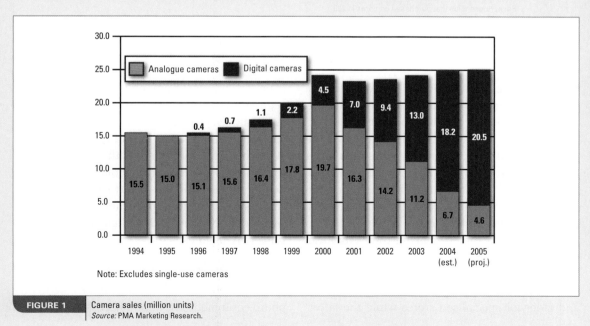

FIGURE 1 Camera sales (million units)
Source: PMA Marketing Research.

Note: Excludes single-use cameras

Jean Boisvert, Assistant Professor of Marketing, American University of Sharjah, United Arab Emirates

	Camera stores	Electronics and video stores	Discount stores	Other mass retailers
Household income				
Under $15 000	7%	4%	17%	18%
$15 000–$28 999	11%	12%	24%	14%
$30 000–$49 999	18%	24%	27%	21%
$50 000–$74 999	27%	32%	21%	25%
$75 000 and over	38%	29%	12%	23%
Total	100%	100%	100%	100%
Head of household age				
Under age 25	1%	5%	6%	2%
Age 25–34	10%	25%	18%	10%
Age 35–44	18%	29%	30%	28%
Age 45–54	26%	24%	23%	29%
Age 55–64	24%	12%	13%	18%
Age 65–74	14%	4%	9%	12%
Age 75 and over	8%	1%	2%	2%
Total	100%	100%	100%	100%
Head of household education				
Some high school or less	0%	0%	4%	7%
Graduate high school	12%	19%	30%	25%
Some college—no degree	23%	21%	27%	26%
Associate's degree	20%	10%	12%	14%
Bachelor's degree	27%	32%	20%	23%
Post-graduate degree	18%	18%	6%	6%
Total	100%	100%	100%	100%

Note: Discount stores include discount stores and combination/hypermarkets. Other mass retailers include supermarkets, catalogue showrooms, chemists, wholesale clubs and department stores.
Base: Households that purchased cameras in 2001.

FIGURE 2   Distribution of camera sales across demographic groups (by outlet type)
Source: 2002 PMA Camera/Camcorder, Digital Imaging Survey.

for each of the four categories. The data shows that specialised camera stores appear to attract a different type of customer than other stores. For example, in terms of income, 38% of customers patronising specialised shops earn $75 000 and over, while discount stores attract only 12% of the same income category. In contrast, electronic/video stores and mass retailers attract similar income profiles.

Moreover, customers making their purchase at specialised camera stores are generally older than the clientele of other types of retail shop; specifically, more than 22% of the buyers are 65 and older for specialised stores while the latter

is underrepresented among the 25–44 years age segment as compared to other type of camera retail outlets. Furthermore, in terms of education, specialised camera stores and electronics/video stores have similar profiles with 45% and 50% of their customers respectively holding a university degree. These statistics contrast with those of the discount stores and other mass retailers where only 26% and 29% of their customers hold university degrees.

Purchaser to shopper ratio

When camera shoppers go to a retail shop to buy photo equipment, they don't necessarily actually

CASE STUDY

purchase from that store. Figure 3 reveals that the purchaser to shopper ratio varies considerably by type of outlet reaching a proportion of 66% for specialised shops from a low of 16% for warehouse clubs.

In contrast, for discount stores, mail-order catalogues and hypermarkets, approximately 50% of shoppers end up purchasing a camera which puts those outlets between specialised stores and warehouse clubs in converting shoppers to purchasers.

Digital prints

The digital technology and instant pictures being seen on most digital cameras' rear screen have had an impact on the prints people make from their files as compared to traditional prints from film. While the sales of digital cameras currently account for approximately 82%, digital prints made from digital files grabbed only 30% (7.7 billion divided by 25.9 billion) of the volume in 2005, despite the growth shown in Figure 4 (overleaf).

In terms of method used for digital prints, Figure 5 shows that in 2000 when only 7.9% of homes had a digital camera, 90% of these were printing their pictures at home. Consumers were using their own printers at home 90% of the time despite a small 7.9% of home penetration. This habit drastically changed when the percentage of home penetration of digital cameras increased significantly to 52% by 2005. During that period, digital home prints went from 90% in 2000 down to 52% in 2005. During the same period, the use of retail outlets for digital prints went from a mere 6% in 2000 up to 40% in 2005. Online services offering digital prints have remained stable at around 8% of the market between 2001 and 2005.

Conclusion

In the photographic equipment sector, digital technology has created drastic changes in consumer habits forcing manufacturers and retailers to adapt their strategies and tactics at a very fast pace in recent years. However, once the transition from analogue to digital is over, certain trends will emerge; for instance, the need for information will make retailers know their customers better than ever before, which should contribute to better targeting of consumers in the future. Competition between camera

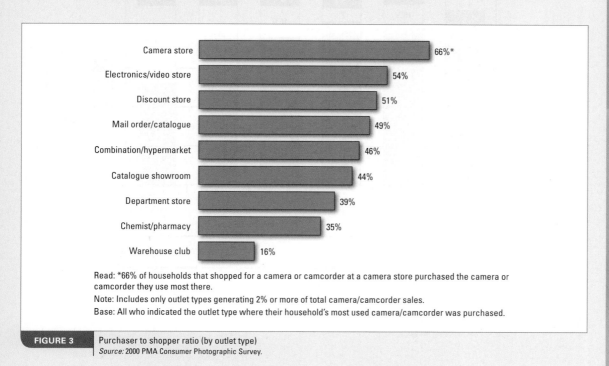

Read: *66% of households that shopped for a camera or camcorder at a camera store purchased the camera or camcorder they use most there.

Note: Includes only outlet types generating 2% or more of total camera/camcorder sales.

Base: All who indicated the outlet type where their household's most used camera/camcorder was purchased.

FIGURE 3 Purchaser to shopper ratio (by outlet type)
Source: 2000 PMA Consumer Photographic Survey.

CASE
STUDY

manufacturers will continue, but the fight to capture an ongoing share of consumers' prints will be one of the major challenges for retailers.

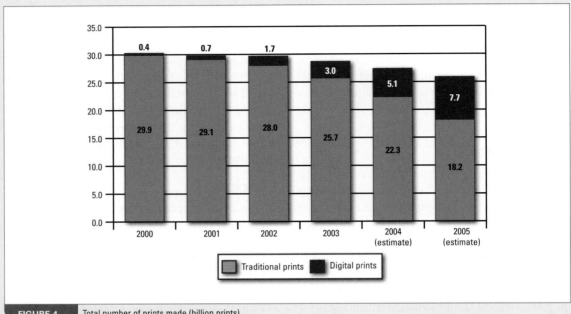

FIGURE 4 **FIGURE 4**   Total number of prints made (billion prints)
Source: PMA Marketing Research.

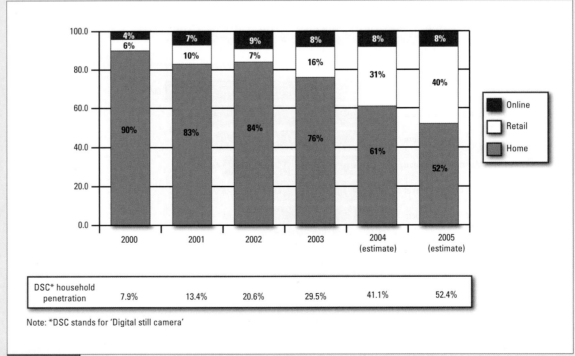

FIGURE 5   Digital prints by method (% of total prints)
Source: PMA Marketing Research.

QUESTIONS

1 The remarkable reverse phenomenon shown in Figure 1 regarding the sales of digital versus analogue cameras has forced retailers to make major decisions in terms of retail management. Identify the areas where retail managers must concentrate their efforts in order to adapt to the changes and stay competitive.

2 Based on Figure 2, how would you describe the difference between specialised camera stores and electronics/video shops in terms of customer approach by retail employees?

3 In terms of purchaser to shopper ratio, we saw in Figure 3 that department stores and warehouse clubs have a 39% and 16% ratio respectively. What can both types of retailers do to increase their ratio?

4 In view of the fast-growing digital print market, retailers must respond to customers who want fast, easy to obtain prints. What can retailers do to meet customers' expectations?

5 Figure 5 shows that the online method used for digital printing does not seem to be taking off, remaining at around 8% of the total market for the last five years. (a) How would you explain this phenomenon? (b) What could be done to increase consumer use of this option?

CASE STUDY

CHAPTER 16

Marketing communications

Absolut Cut: www.absolutcut.com

Advertising Principles:
www.advertisingprinciples.com

Advertising Standards Bureau:
www.advertisingstandardsbureau.com.au

Direct Marketing Australia:
www.directmarketingaustralia.com

Office of the Privacy Commissioner:
www.privacy.gov.au

Salmat: www.salmat.com.au

Word of mouth Marketing Association:
www.womma.org

Advertising is everywhere. It's been said that the average person is exposed to 3000 to 10 000 advertising messages each day. We don't even notice most of them, but companies continue to spend large amounts of money hoping that their particular message will be noticed by potential buyers, and will ultimately influence people's behaviour—whether the message is aiming to get you to buy a product or to behave in a particular way (such as to stop smoking, or vote for a political party). The influence of advertising is typically subtle, and many people don't even realise when they are influenced by advertising. For example, if you see an advertisement for McDonald's, and buy McDonald's two hours later, do you even know if the advertisement influenced you to buy McDonald's? With careful measurement of sales figures with and without advertising, McDonald's is likely to have a better idea of whether advertising influences its customers to buy more often, or buy more, than they know themselves.

So advertising is likely to continue to be important in communicating with consumers, even though many consumers claim that they aren't influenced by advertising. However, there is no doubt that with much more advertising around it's harder for marketers to get consumers to notice *their* advertisements and influence customers' and potential customers' behaviour. So the challenge for marketers is to get what's called 'cut-through': to get a particular message noticed by consumers in the clutter of advertisements and marketing messages. This is leading marketers to try to achieve more targeted communications, and to use more forms of communications: personalised direct mail, targeted at people who are shown by data mining techniques to be most likely to buy; Internet advertising, targeting people who are searching for a particular product, so they are presented with advertising which is relevant; 'advertorial' or favourable content in newspapers, magazines, TV and radio, to influence buyers' attitudes; and 'buzz' or 'viral' marketing, to encourage consumers to pass on favourable messages.

An extreme example of an attempt to communicate with consumers without traditional advertising is the recent launch in Australia of Absolut Cut, a ready to drink version of Absolut vodka. New alcoholic drinks are typically launched with an average of $3 million in media advertising, but instead liquor distributor Maxxium used a range of marketing tools, including point-of-sale material, events, photographic exhibitions and public relations. They took out short-term leases on two bars in Sydney and Melbourne, hired bands to perform at the bars and served free Absolut Cut—and then the bars closed down and weren't used again. This short-term blitz was backed up with a six-month photographic exhibition, which invited artists to submit photos representing their view of the city in which they lived, and the public were invited to join in and upload their work onto a website. Public relations was used to promote the initiatives, and to create interest in the brand. It's too early to see what the effect will be on long-term sales, but similar initiatives in the UK resulted in 21 000 website visitors in one month, staying an average of 16 minutes each.

Absolut used a range of marketing tools to promote its new ready to drink vodka.

While the launch of Absolut Cut without any spending on traditional media is still unusual for a major brand, marketing communications are now much more than advertising. Think about a typical TV show; Initiative, a media-buying firm, estimates that there are 27 different avenues for marketers to reach the audience of the show, including promotional emails, web broadcasts, product placement and games or trivia contests. Marketing communications now need to do more than develop an ad and get it noticed; they need to present relevant messages which engage the customer, and which lead to a favourable response.[1]

After reading this chapter you should be able to:

1. Describe integrated marketing communication (IMC) and classify IMC media, tools and technologies.

2. Outline the steps in developing integrated marketing communication, including identifying a target audience and determining the response sought.

3. Describe the communication process, beginning with selecting a message, selecting the media, selecting a message source and collecting feedback.

4. Define the ways of setting an integrated marketing communication budget: affordable, percentage-of-sales, competitive parity and objective-and-task methods.

5. Explain integrated marketing communication media, tools and technologies—advertising, public relations, direct and online marketing, sales promotion and personal selling—and the factors involved when setting the integrated marketing communication program: type of product and market, push versus pull strategies, buyer-readiness states and product life-cycle stage.

6. Describe the nature of media advertising, including the major decisions involved: advertising budgeting, setting strategy, creative execution, media selection and evaluation in terms of communication and sales outcomes.

7. Define public relations and outline the more common forms of this IMC tool.

8. Explain the need for socially responsible marketing communication and how this is achieved.

Modern marketing calls for more than developing a good product, pricing it attractively, making potential customers aware of the product and making it available to target customers. More than ever, marketing organisations must integrate their various communications so that they interact with customers and potential customers in a coordinated and strategic manner. They must also gain synergy from the media they use and the approaches these media allow. This approach is termed integrated marketing communications (IMC).

Integrated marketing communications

Integrated marketing communications (IMC) entails coordinating the organisation's promotional efforts using communication elements such as advertising, public relations, personal selling, sales promotion, and direct and online marketing. For most organisations, the main decision is not whether to spend money on marketing communications, but how much to spend on each promotional element. An organisation's integrated marketing communications program consists of a specific blend of the above-mentioned elements that will most effectively meet such objectives as to *inform*, *persuade* and *remind* consumers, *reinforce* their attitudes and perceptions and influence them to *behave* in a particular way.

The need for integrated marketing communications

The shift from mass marketing to targeted marketing, and the corresponding use of a larger, richer mix of communication channels and promotion tools, poses a problem for marketers. Customers don't distinguish between message sources the way marketers do. In the consumer's mind, advertising messages from different media and different promotional approaches all become part of a single message about the company. Conflicting messages from these different sources can result in confused company images and brand positions.

All too often, companies fail to integrate their various communications channels. The result can be a hodgepodge of communications to consumers: mass-media advertisements say one thing, while a price promotion sends a different signal and a product label creates still another message; company sales literature says something altogether different and the company's website seems to be out of synch with everything else.

The problem is that these communications often come from different company sources. Advertising messages are planned and implemented by the advertising department or advertising agency. Personal selling communications are developed by sales management. Other functional specialists are responsible for public relations, sales promotion, **direct marketing**, websites and other forms of marketing communications.

Recently, such functional separation has been a major problem for companies and their Internet communications. Many companies first organised their new web and other digital communications operations into separate groups or divisions, isolating them from mainstream marketing activities. However, whereas some companies have compartmentalised the new communications tools, customers won't. According to one IMC expert:[2]

> The truth is, most [consumers] won't compartmentalize their use of the new systems. They won't say, 'Hey, I'm going off to do a bit of Web surfing. Burn my TV, throw out all my radios, cancel all my magazine subscriptions and, by the way, take out my telephone and don't deliver any mail anymore.' It's not that kind of world for consumers, and it shouldn't be that kind of world for marketers either.

Integrated marketing communications (IMC) The concept under which a company carefully integrates and coordinates its many communications channels to deliver a clear, consistent and compelling message about the organisation and its products.

Direct marketing An interactive system of marketing which uses one or more advertising media to effect a measurable response and/or transaction at any location.

Thus, if treated as a special case, the Internet—or any other marketing communication tool—can be a disintegrating force in marketing communications. Instead, all the communication tools must be carefully integrated into the broader marketing communications mix. Today, the best bet is to wed the emotional pitch and impact of traditional brand marketing with the interactivity and real service offered online. For example, print and television ads can build consumer preference for a brand, but can also point viewers to the company's website, to provide further information about the product.

IMC builds brand identity and strong customer relationships by tying together all of the company's messages and images. Brand messages and positioning are coordinated across all communication activities and media. IMC means that the company's advertising and personal selling communications have the same message, look and feel as its website. And its public relations materials say the same thing as its direct mail campaign.[3] IMC calls for recognising all contact points where the customer may encounter the company, its products and its brands. Each *brand contact* will deliver a message, whether good, bad or indifferent. The company must strive to deliver a consistent and positive message with each contact.

Classifying IMC media, tools and technologies

To aid our examination of IMC, a classification of the available media, tools and technologies according to communication categories is presented in Table 16.1. **Mass communication** involves the use of mass media such as free-to-air television, radio, newspaper and magazines, as well as other media such as cinema and outdoor. We focus on two of these elements in particular in this chapter—the major mass communication element of advertising and the more targeted element, public relations.

We begin with an overview of the mass communication category and the question: what is advertising? **Advertising** is any paid form of non-personal presentation and promotion of ideas, goods or services by an identified sponsor, often meeting long-term objectives related to brand image. Advertising may be mass communication—free-to-air television (FTA-TV), newspapers and

Mass communication
The use of mass media such as free-to-air television, radio, newspapers and magazines, as well as other media, such as cinema and outdoor.

Advertising Any paid form of non-personal presentation and promotion of ideas, goods or services by an identified sponsor.

TABLE 16.1 A classification of integrated marketing communications media, tools and technology

Integrated marketing communications category	Media, tools and technologies
Mass communication	Advertising via FTA-TV; radio; newspapers; magazines; outdoor; cinema; co-operative advertising; motion pictures. With or without sales promotion incentives.
Targeted communication	Pay-TV (satellite, cable and narrowcast microwave TV with no back-channel); home shopping (FTA-TV or Pay-TV); public relations; door-to-door selling; catalogues; telephone directories (Yellow Pages); events (Formula One championship); sponsorships; mobile and static trade exhibitions; automatic vending machines. With or without sales promotion incentives.
In-store communication	Retail counter selling; merchandising; location-TV and radio (narrowcast or closed); aisle displays; electronic aisle messaging; point-of-purchase media (e.g. trolley advertising); packaging. With or without sales promotion incentives.
One-to-one communication	Database marketing in all its forms: direct mail; interactive TV; telemarketing (telephone or fax); telesales; electronic dispensing and kiosks; direct selling (home and office); online value transformation. With or without sales promotion incentives.

Source: Adapted from the concept of 'seamless' integrated communication, Martin Williams, *Interactive Marketing*, Sydney, Prentice Hall Australia, 1994, p. xiv; see also Philip Kotler, *Kotler on Marketing: How to Create, Win, and Dominate Markets*, New York, The Free Press, 1999, p. 107; Don Peppers and Martha Rogers, 'One-to-one Media in the Interactive Future', in Edward Forrest and Richard Mizerski, eds, *Interactive Marketing*, Lincolnwood, Illinois, NTC Business Books, 1995, pp. 113–34.

magazines, radio, cinema, outdoor advertising and advertising within films (e.g. a reported $35 million was paid by Ford to have James Bond drive an Aston Martin in the latest Bond film, rather than the BMW he had driven in previous films). The mass communication category also includes co-operative advertising, exemplified by supermarket advertisements for a range of products. While the advertising may be organised by and appear under the heading of the retailer, it is typically paid for by the manufacturers of the brands advertised. Advertising can also be targeted (e.g. Pay-TV advertising or online advertising linked to a particular site or Internet search). Newspaper and television advertising are the most important media for advertising, as shown in Tables 16.2A and 16.2B.

Targeted communication enables marketing organisations to tailor their messages to suit various market segments. This category, in common with mass communication, largely sees customers self-select the message or product involved, even though the marketer's communication is targeted. A number of media tools and technologies enable such targeted communication:

> *Pay-TV*, which now includes satellite, fibre-optic cable and narrowcast microwave TV broadcasts
> *home shopping* programs on FTA-TV and shopping channels on Pay-TV
> *public relations* campaigns such as that targeting shareholders of BHP Billiton prior to an annual general meeting. The aim is to build good relations with the marketing organisation's various publics by obtaining favourable publicity, building up or reinforcing a good corporate image, and handling or heading off unfavourable rumours, stories and events
> *door-to-door selling*, by such companies as Amway into homes and offices
> *catalogues*, ranging from those distributed by letterbox drops by Scouts and Guides to direct mail catalogues by companies such as Salmat based on demographic profiling
> *telephone directories* such as Yellow Pages Online
> *events* such as the Olympics and Formula One car racing
> *sponsorships*, ranging from sponsorship of one person in a fun run to naming rights sponsorship such as the Telstra Sydney–Hobart yacht race
> *trade exhibitions*, whether mobile or static, target hard-to-reach decision makers such as chefs and information technology professionals
> *online search* advertising, which presents advertising which is relevant to a particular web page, or which is targeted to a particular search on a search engine such as Google.

In-store communication involves the use of media, tools and technologies at store level and includes:

> *retail counter* selling of items such as cosmetics to specific market segments
> *merchandising*, or ranging items in such a way as to ensure they are easily found in store (e.g. by grouping like items in a category such as 'oral hygiene')
> *location-TV and radio* (narrowcast or closed)—for example, when a hardware store sets up a 'do-it-yourself' video showing how to install an automatic garden watering system
> *aisle displays*, for example promotional gondola ends in supermarkets
> *electronic aisle messaging*, where messages relating to stock in particular aisles are directed at shoppers entering the aisle
> *point-of-purchase media* such as conventional and electronic trolley advertising
> *packaging*, which performs the dual role of protecting contents and advertising the product at point of sale.

One-to-one communication involves the use of integrated database marketing in the forms listed overleaf. Database marketing offers the advantage of tracking an individual customer's buying pattern and calculating the value of the customer to the firm over the lifetime of the relationship.

Targeted communication
Marketing organisations tailor their messages to suit various market segments.

In-store communication
The use of media, tools and technology at store level.

One-to-one communication
The use of integrated database marketing to track an individual customer's buying pattern.

TABLE 16.2A Advertising spending in Australia in local currency at current prices ($A million)

	Total	Newspapers	Magazines	TV	Radio	Cinema	Outdoor/ Transport	Internet
1993	4 933	2 016	410	1 761	456	25	265	0
1994	5 414	2 301	497	1 870	477	31	238	0
1995	5 915	2 560	532	2 022	510	37	254	0
1996	5 954	2 481	574	2 084	525	41	249	0
1997	6 568	2 746	733	2 248	540	47	254	0
1998	7 061	3 011	766	2 400	557	53	274	0
1999	7 372	3 074	796	2 454	644	58	311	35
2000	8 054	3 359	837	2 746	684	69	276	83
2001	7 666	3 131	773	2 671	695	64	271	61
2002	7 813	2 991	789	2 845	702	58	261	167
2003	8 544	3 252	822	3 134	737	66	297	236
2004	9 655	3 637	895	3 507	827	74	327	388
2005	10 403	3 843	948	3 707	876	78	350	601
2006*	11 120	3 998	1 003	3 890	920	82	375	852
2007*	11 915	4 186	1 060	4 081	966	86	401	1 135

* estimate

TABLE 16.2B Advertising spending in the Asia-Pacific region at current prices ($US million)

	Total	Newspapers	Magazines	TV	Radio	Cinema	Outdoor/ Others	Internet
1993	49 461	16 100	4 074	19 651	2 880	38	6 717	0
1994	52 723	17 342	4 336	21 180	2 928	45	6 892	0
1995	57 031	18 759	4 702	23 205	3 153	49	7 163	0
1996	60 799	19 274	5 109	25 685	3 279	52	7 385	15
1997	65 106	21 177	5 615	27 318	3 351	70	7 521	55
1998	62 633	19 865	5 412	26 990	3 214	78	6 967	105
1999	64 552	20 880	5 532	27 723	3 217	79	6 799	323
2000	71 347	23 306	6 005	30 645	3 453	94	7 067	777
2001	69 871	22 552	5 781	30 046	3 438	90	7 081	883
2002	70 263	22 042	5 765	30 701	3 462	90	7 087	1 116
2003	74 043	23 263	5 954	32 409	3 566	105	7 177	1 569
2004	80 116	25 281	6 113	34 708	3 773	127	7 706	2 408
2005	84 554	26 532	6 464	36 016	3 942	147	8 004	3 449
2006*	89 996	28 236	6 787	38 047	4 150	163	8 358	4 255
2007*	97 395	30 316	7 427	41 164	4 407	180	8 806	5 095

* estimate

Source: Zenithoptimedia, Advertising expenditure forecasts, October 2005.

We present a detailed examination of direct marketing in Chapter 18. One-to-one communication types include:

- *Direct mail*, usually with the objective of stimulating interaction with a potential or existing customer, and often used to stimulate a sale in response to a particular offer.
- *Interactive TV*, involving techniques that engage FTA-TV and Pay-TV viewers: for example, by voting to evict a contestant from a reality TV show, or by ordering a product.
- *Telemarketing* (telephone, fax or online), which may be inbound or outbound to an interaction centre (or call centre); however, it usually involves a response by the consumer to a marketing communication aimed at them personally.
- *Telesales*, which usually involve business-to-business organisations which telephone retail stores for their orders once or twice a week.
- *Electronic dispensing and kiosks* such as ATMs, which now sell or provide information on a wide range of products and services. Because they rely on interaction with a known customer from the organisation's database, they perform a one-to-one communication and fulfilment function.
- *Direct selling* (home and office) or personal selling, which involves one-to-one marketing communication by the marketer's salesforce for the purpose of making sales and building customer relationships. We examine direct selling more fully in Chapter 17.
- *Individualised online communications*, which are one-to-one interactions between consumers and marketing organisations using private networks, the Internet, intranets (internal to the company) and extranets (internal markets that suppliers and customers may access, but not the general public). The communication may be from a retailer such as Dymocks emailing individuals about new books that might suit their previously established reading tastes. Alternatively, the communication between a manufacturer and retailer could depend on electronic stock monitoring, used by companies such as Pacific Brands (owners of Bonds, Berlei and Holeproof). The manufacturer monitors stock levels, and can restock using a just-in-time system, so the retailer maintains stock without needing to keep high levels of inventory. Both parties win, by ensuring stock levels don't run low and sales aren't lost.

Sales promotion
Short-term incentives to encourage purchase of a product or service.

Regardless of which communication category marketers use, they may all involve use of sales promotion at different points in time. **Sales promotion** involves the use of short-term incentives to encourage purchase of a product or service. We examine sales promotion further in Chapter 17.

It is evident that marketing managers face many decisions about which media, tools and technologies they might best use as part of their IMC program. The marketer needs to manage and respond to a complex marketing communications system (see Figure 16.1). Marketing organisations communicate with intermediaries, consumers and various publics. In turn, intermediaries communicate with their own consumers and publics. Consumers communicate with each other and other publics by word-of-mouth, and the effect of this word-of-mouth is often more powerful than the planned communications from marketing organisations. As Figure 16.1 indicates, each group provides feedback to every other group.

SELF-CHECK QUESTIONS

1 List three mass communication media, tools or technologies.
2 List three direct marketing techniques.
3 Why might sponsorship be described as targeted communication?

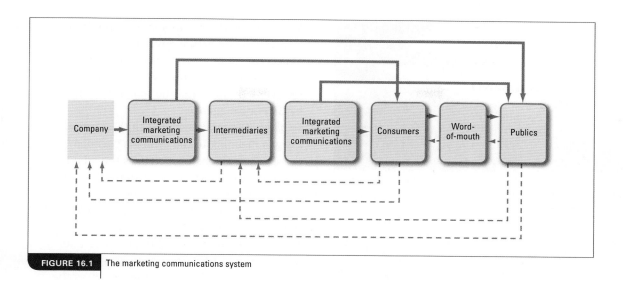

FIGURE 16.1   The marketing communications system

Having gained a clear picture of the various marketing communication elements available to marketing management, we next turn our attention to gaining an understanding of how communication works.

The communication process

Communication involves the nine elements shown in Figure 16.2. Two of these elements are the parties in a communication—sender and receiver. Another two are the major communication tools—message and media. Four are major components of communication—encoding, decoding, response and feedback. The last element is noise in the system. These elements are defined below and applied to a Telstra BigPond magazine advertisement.

⊚ *Sender*. The party sending the message to another party—BigPond.
⊚ *Encoding*. The process of putting thought into symbolic form—BigPond's advertising agency assembles words and illustrations into an advertisement that will convey the intended message.

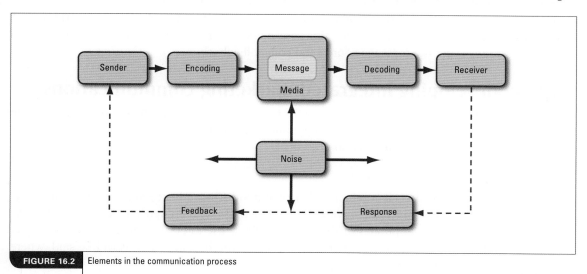

FIGURE 16.2   Elements in the communication process

The marketer develops a message which is interpreted by the consumer.

- *Message*. The set of symbols that the sender transmits—the actual advertisement.
- *Media*. The communication channels through which the message moves from sender to receiver—in this case, the magazines chosen by BigPond's agency.
- *Decoding*. The process by which the receiver assigns meaning to the symbols encoded by the sender—a consumer notices the ad and interprets the words and illustrations it contains.
- *Receiver*. The party receiving the message sent by another party—the consumer who looks at the advertisement.
- *Response*. The reactions of the receiver after being exposed to the message—any of hundreds of possible responses, such as the consumer likes BigPond's service better, is more likely to turn to BigPond next time their contract is due for renewal, or does nothing.
- *Feedback*. That part of the receiver's response communicated back to the sender—Telstra's research shows that consumers like and remember the ad, sales may increase or consumers may write or phone BigPond praising or criticising the ad or BigPond's cable or ADSL products.
- *Noise*. The unplanned static or distortion during the communication process that results in the receiver getting a different message from the one the sender sent—for example, the consumer might not even notice the ad, or if they do may only glance at it briefly, since it is competing with other ads (and with the content of the magazine) for the consumer's attention.

This model shows the key factors in good communication. Senders need to know what audiences they want to reach and what responses they want. They must be good at encoding messages, taking into account how the target audience is likely to decode them. They must send the message through media that reach target audiences. And they must develop feedback channels so that they can assess the audience's response to the message.

Thus, the marketing communicator must make the following decisions: identify the target audience; determine the response sought; choose a message; choose the media through which to send the message; select the message source and collect feedback.

Steps in developing integrated marketing communications

We now examine the steps in developing an effective integrated communications program. The marketer must start by deciding who is the target audience, and what is the response that they are seeking to achieve with the communication.

Identifying the target audience

The marketer must start with a clear target audience in mind. The audience may be potential buyers or current users, those who make the buying decision or those who influence it. The audience may be individuals, groups, special publics or the general public. The target audience will heavily affect the communicator's decisions on what will be said, how it will be said, when it will be said, where it will be said and who will say it.

Determining the response sought

Once the target audience has been defined, the marketing communicator must decide what response is sought. Of course, in most cases the desired final response is purchase. But purchase is sometimes the result of a long process of consumer decision making. The marketer needs to know where the target audience now stands and to what state it needs to be moved. For example, an advertising burst for a new car may start the consumer down the path to a purchase by causing that consumer to open a special savings account with CitiBank. It may be many more months, however, before the car is actually purchased.

The target audience may be in any of six **buyer-readiness states**—awareness, knowledge, liking, preference, conviction or purchase—which are shown in Figure 16.3.[4]

Awareness

First, the communicator must be able to gauge the target audience's awareness of the product or organisation. The audience may be totally unaware of it, know only its name or know one or a few things about it. If most of the target audience is unaware, the communicator tries to build awareness—perhaps starting with simple name recognition. This process can begin with simple messages repeating the name. Even then, building brand awareness can take time.

Knowledge

The target audience might be aware of the company or product but know little else. The effective communicator therefore needs to learn how many people in its target audience have little, some or much knowledge about the product or organisation. It might then decide to select product knowledge as its first communication objective.

Liking

If target audience members know the product, how do they feel about it? Liking can be measured using market research—for example, asking consumers to indicate their attitude on a scale ranging from 'Dislike very strongly', 'Dislike somewhat', 'Indifferent', 'Like somewhat' to 'Like very strongly'. If the audience dislikes the organisation or its products, the communicator must learn why and then develop a marketing communications campaign to create favourable feelings.

Preference

The target audience might like the product but not prefer it to others. This can be measured by asking a sample of consumers how they would rate the product or service compared to its competitors. If competing products are preferred, the communicator must try to build consumer preference. The communicator can promote the product's quality, value, performance and other features, and check on the campaign's success by measuring the audience's preferences again after the campaign.

Buyer-readiness states
The stages consumers normally pass through on their way to purchase, including awareness, knowledge, liking, preference, conviction or purchase.

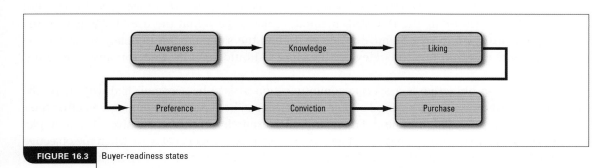

FIGURE 16.3 Buyer-readiness states

Conviction

A target audience might prefer the product but not have a strong intention to buy it. For example, some potential customers may prefer the organisation or its brands but not yet be sure. The communicator's job is to build the conviction that taking the next step and buying the brand is the right thing to do.

Purchase

Finally, some members of the target audience might have conviction but not quite get around to making the purchase. They might wait for more information or plan to act later. The communicator must lead these consumers to take the final step. Actions might include offering the product at a low price, offering a premium or letting consumers try it on a limited basis.

Of course, marketing communications alone cannot create positive feelings and conviction about a product. The product itself must provide superior value for the customer. In fact, outstanding marketing communications can actually speed the demise of a poor product. The more quickly potential buyers learn about a poor product, the more quickly they become aware of its faults. Thus, effective marketing communication relies on good product design, so that customers are satisfied with the product and willing to rebuy it.

SELF-CHECK QUESTIONS

4   Consider Figure 16.2, 'Elements in the communication process'. Why are response and feedback not considered to be the same thing?

5   To what extent can marketing communications alone create consumer conviction about a product?

Major decisions in communications

Having determined the target audience and the response sought, marketing management must make five important decisions. These decisions are the specific objectives setting, budget, message decisions, media decisions and campaign evaluation (see Figure 16.4). Deciding the budget is so important that we will address it separately later in the chapter, after reviewing the other four factors.

Setting objectives

The first step in developing a marketing communication is to set specific objectives. These objectives should be based on past decisions about the target market, positioning and marketing mix. Colley lists 52 possible advertising objectives in his well-known book *Defining Advertising Goals for Measured Advertising Results*, describing the DAGMAR method.[5] Colley argues that the use of DAGMAR turns advertising objectives into specific measurable goals, and the same process of determining specific objectives and determining the relevant measures should be followed for any marketing communication.

Advertising objective
A specific communication task to be accomplished with a specific target audience during a specific period of time.

Informative advertising
Advertising used to inform consumers about a new product or feature and to build primary demand.

An **advertising objective** is a specific communication task to be accomplished with a specific target audience during a specific period of time. Objectives can be classified by purpose: whether their aim is to inform, persuade or remind. Figure 16.5 lists examples of these objectives. For example, **informative advertising** is used heavily when introducing a new product category when the objective is to build primary demand. Thus, producers of digital versatile disc players (DVD) first informed

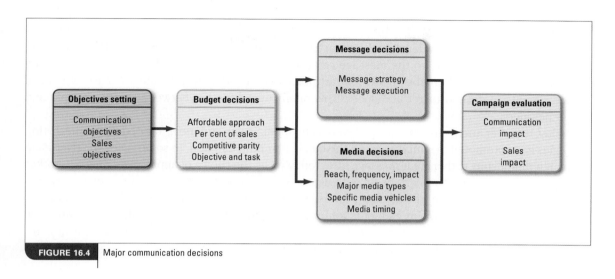

FIGURE 16.4 | Major communication decisions

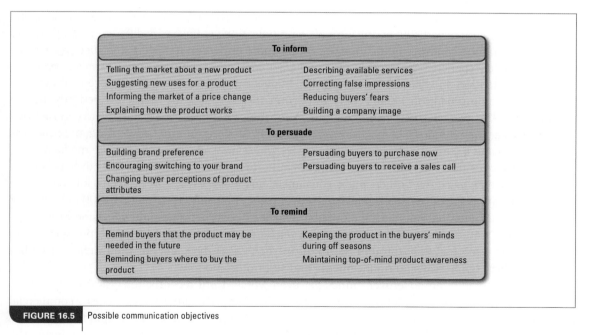

FIGURE 16.5 | Possible communication objectives

consumers of the sound and convenience benefits of DVDs. **Persuasive advertising** becomes more important as competition increases and a company's objective is to build selective demand. For example, once DVD players have become established and accepted, marketers of high-end brands then try to persuade consumers that their brand offers the best value for money.

Some persuasive advertising has become **comparison advertising**, which compares one brand directly or indirectly with one or more other brands. For example, rental car company Avis positions itself against market leaders Hertz by claiming: 'We're number two, so we try harder'.

Reminder advertising is important for mature products—it keeps consumers thinking about the product. Expensive Coca-Cola ads on television are designed to remind people about Coca-Cola, not to inform or persuade them.

Persuasive advertising Advertising used to build selective demand for a brand by persuading consumers that it offers the best quality for their money.

Comparison advertising Advertising that compares one brand directly or indirectly with one or more other brands.

Reminder advertising Advertising used to keep consumers thinking about a product.

Message and media decisions

In the past, most marketers developed messages and media plans independently. Media planning was often seen as secondary to the message creation process. The creative department first created good advertisements; then the media department selected the best media for carrying these advertisements to desired target audiences. This often caused friction between creative people and media planners.

Today, however, media fragmentation, ever-rising media costs and more focused target marketing strategies have promoted the importance of the media planning function. In some cases an advertising campaign might start with a great message idea, followed by the choice of appropriate media. In other cases, however, a campaign might begin with a good media opportunity, followed by advertisements designed to take advantage of that opportunity. Increasingly, companies are realising the benefits of planning these two important elements jointly. Messages and media should blend harmoniously to create an effective overall communications campaign. This realisation has resulted in greater cooperation between the creative and media functions.

Creating the message

A large budget does not guarantee a successful communications campaign. Two marketers can spend the same amount on advertising or any form of communication yet have very different results. Studies have shown that the creativity of the message can be more important to advertising success than the number of dollars spent. No matter how big the budget, marketing communications can succeed only if they gain attention and communicate well. The budget must be invested in effective messages.

Effective communication is especially important in today's costly and cluttered advertising environment. The average city-dwelling Australian consumer has five FTA-TV stations to choose from, plus newspapers and hundreds of magazines. Add cable-TV stations, Internet advertising, the countless radio stations and a continual barrage of catalogues, direct mail ads and out-of-home media and we soon see that consumers are bombarded with ads at home, at work and at all points in between.

All this advertising clutter bothers many consumers, and it also causes big problems for advertisers. Take the situation facing network television advertisers. Typically, they pay $10 000–$20 000 for 30 seconds of advertising time during a popular five-city, network, prime-time television program— even more if it's an especially popular program such as *60 Minutes* (around $20 000 per spot) or an event such as a football final (around $30 000). In such cases their ads are sandwiched in with a clutter of other commercials, announcements and station promotions.

But wait—if you're an advertiser, things get even worse! Until recently, television viewers were pretty much a captive audience for advertisers. Those who changed channels during boring commercial breaks usually found only more of the same on the other channels. With the growth in Pay-TV, VCRs, DVDs and the Web, today's viewers have many more options. They can mute the sound during the ad breaks or they can avoid ads by watching commercial-free videotapes and DVDs. They can 'zap' commercials by pushing the fast-forward button during programs that were recorded 'off air'.

Thus, just to gain and hold attention, today's communications must be better planned, more imaginative, more entertaining and more rewarding to consumers. Effective message design will therefore play an increasingly important role in communication success. Marketing Highlight 16.1 shows how marketers are responding to this advertising clutter by attempting to find new channels and new ways to get their message across.

Designing the message

Having defined the desired audience response, the communicator turns to developing an effective message. Ideally, the message should get *attention*, hold *interest*, arouse *desire* and obtain *action* (a framework known as the *AIDA model).* In practice, few messages take the consumer all the way from awareness to purchase, but the AIDA framework suggests the desirable qualities of a good message.

In putting the message together, the marketing communicator must decide what to say (*message content*) and how to say it (*message structure and format*).

Message content The communicator has to work out an appeal or theme that will produce the desired response. Any appeal should have three characteristics. First, it should be meaningful, pointing out benefits that make the product more desirable or interesting to consumers. Second, an appeal must be believable—consumers must believe that the product or service will deliver the promised benefits. However, the most meaningful and believable benefits may not be the best ones to feature. Appeals should also be distinctive—they should tell how the product is better than the competing brands. For example, the most meaningful benefit of owning a wristwatch is that it keeps accurate time, yet few watch ads feature this benefit. Instead, based on the distinctive benefits they offer, wristwatch advertisers might select any of a number of communication themes.

There are three types of appeals: rational, emotional and moral. **Rational appeals** relate to the audience's self-interest. They show that the product will produce the desired benefits. Examples are messages showing a product's quality, economy, value or performance. Thus, in its ads Mercedes offers automobiles that are 'engineered like no other car in the world', stressing engineering design, performance and safety.

Emotional appeals attempt to stir up either negative or positive emotions that can motivate purchase. Communicators may use positive emotional appeals such as love, pride, joy and humour. For example, advocates for humorous messages claim that they attract more attention and create more liking and belief in the sponsor. In a recent survey, Americans picked humour as their favourite ad approach, with 85% saying they like ads with humorous themes.[6]

Properly used, humour can capture attention, make people feel good and give a brand personality. Anheuser-Busch has used humour effectively for years, helping consumers relate to its brands. However, advertisers must be careful when using humour. Used poorly, it can detract from comprehension, overshadow the product or even irritate consumers.

Communicators can also use negative emotional appeals, such as fear, guilt and shame that get people to do things they should (brush their teeth, buy new tyres) or to stop them doing things they shouldn't (smoke, drink too much, eat unhealthy foods).

Moral appeals are directed to the audience's sense of what is 'right' and 'proper'. They are often used to urge people to support social causes such as a cleaner environment, better race relations, equal rights for women and aid to the disadvantaged.

Message structure The communicator must also decide how to handle three message structure issues. The first is whether to draw a conclusion or leave it to the audience. Recent research suggests that in many cases, rather than drawing a conclusion, the advertiser is better off asking questions and letting consumers come to their own conclusions.[7] The second message structure issue is whether to present the strongest arguments first or last. Presenting them first gets strong attention but may lead to an anticlimactic ending. The third message structure issue is whether to present a one-sided argument (mentioning only the product's strengths) or a two-sided argument (touting the product's strengths while also admitting its shortcomings). Usually, a one-sided argument is more effective in sales presentations—except when audiences are highly educated or likely to hear opposing claims, or when the communicator has a negative association to overcome. In this spirit, Listerine ran the message 'The taste you hate twice a day'. In this case, a two-sided message was used to enhance the advertiser's credibility and make buyers more resistant to competitor attacks.

Rational appeals
Message appeals that relate to the audience's self-interest and show that the product will produce the desired benefits; examples include appeals of product quality, economy, value or performance.

Emotional appeals
Message appeals that attempt to stir negative or positive emotions that can motivate purchase; examples include fear, guilt, shame, love, humour and joy appeals.

Moral appeals Message appeals that are directed to the audience's sense of what is right and proper.

Marketers seek alternative media

As consumers, we're used to ads on television, in magazines and newspapers, on the radio and along the roadways. But these days, no matter where you go or what you do, you will probably run into some new form of marketing communication.

Advertisements on shopping trolleys, ads on shopping bags and even advertising decals on supermarket floors urge you to buy a particular product. A bus rolls by, fully wrapped in advertising for a brand of soft drink. You escape to the Bledisloe Cup rugby match, and watch a streaker running across the field, wearing only Vodafone branding. You decide to watch the cricket at home on TV. Adam Gilchrist hits a six, and the cameras pan to five men dressed like Merv Hughes, holding up placards which spell out the number six and a sponsor's name.

You pay to see a movie at your local movie theatre, and the movie is full of not-so-subtle promotional plugs for Pepsi, BMW, Ray-Ban sunglasses or any of a dozen other products. You stop off for something to eat at the local shopping centre, to find the sandwich shop is prominently promoting sandwiches bundled with Mt Franklin mineral water. You buy your sandwich and water and sit down to eat, to find that the table you eat at has two pages from *New Idea* magazine under the plastic table top for you to read as you eat, while an overhead TV constantly booms out advertisements. You wander into the latest bookstore, and find that they are promoting the latest offering from best-selling author Fay Weldon, titled *The Bulgari Connection*. You may not even know what Bulgari is, but if you pick up the book you'll rapidly discover that it's a luxury jewellery company which also makes perfume. And the next time you see Bulgari perfume in a store you might just try the tester . . .

You catch a taxi home, and notice a TV screen in the back of the seat in front of you playing ads. You head home and turn on the TV to find the characters on your favourite reality TV program talking about ordering pizza from Pizza Hut, eating M&Ms, drinking Pepsi Max and lounging around on what is identified as Freedom Furniture. You switch to a travel show, and see glowing reviews of holiday destinations and see them listed as sponsors at the end of the program. You decide to play the latest video game and find that your action character is jumping into a Jeep on the way to the skateboarding park. You decide to email a friend, and click on their home page as an easy link to email them. You've got used to advertisements on your friend's web page, but today there is some news: your friend's web page tells how they are getting the insurance, fuel and registration costs for their car paid in return for having the car wrapped in a vinyl coating advertising a new brand of vodka. But of course, most consumers think that they aren't influenced by advertising . . .

These days, you're likely to find ads—well, anywhere. One agency even rents space on the foreheads of college students for temporary advertising tattoos. Consumers, especially younger ones, are spending less time watching TV, and if they do are often recording the shows and fast forwarding the ads. In response, advertisers are seeking new outlets to place their advertisements, to ensure that their brand is noticed by the consumer. Faced with a proliferation of alternative advertising venues, the advertising industry is creating new names, with some arguing that a new term 'ambient advertising' needs to be used in addition to the traditional term of 'outdoor advertising' because lots of the new advertising vehicles aren't actually outside. Others use the term 'out-of-home advertising' to cover all non-TV and radio advertising.

The proliferation of advertising irritates many consumers, who resent it all as intrusive and manipulative. But for many marketers, alternative venues for advertising can save money and provide a way to reach selected consumers where they live, shop, work and play. 'We like to call it the captive pause, where consumers really have nothing else to do but either look at the person in front of them or look at some engaging content as well as 15-second commercials,' says an executive of an alternative-media firm.

The average person waits in line for about 30 minutes a day, and many spend even more time on public transport. So companies like American Express, Snapple and Calvin Klein are testing new technologies to reach captive consumers. Riders on Manhattan's and Hong Kong's subway systems now see a series of light boxes placed in the dark tunnels that create a moving commercial as the train passes by. Hong Kong buses have television screens playing advertisements as tired commuters make their way home. The ads are unpopular with many commuters but bring money to the bus company and so are likely to stay.

These days a marketer can advertise almost anywhere. However, the challenge remains one of deciding what is the most effective way to communicate with consumers. The smartest marketers are still the ones who are rigorously testing new methods of communicating with customers, to work out if that ad on the table really results in more sales of *New Idea*, and even if it does if it's a more effective

method of selling magazines than running an ad on television.

Sources: Wayne Friedman, 'EagleEye Marketers Find Right Spot', *Advertising Age*, 22 January 2001, pp. S2–S3; Stephanie Mehta, 'Ads Invade Video Games', *Fortune*, 26 May 2003, p. 46; Brian Hindo, 'Getting a Head', *Business Week*, 12 January 2004, p. 14; Sam Jaffe, 'Easy Riders', *American Demographics*, March 2004, pp. 20–23; Julian Lee, 'The Car in Front is a Volvo Ad: Marketers Have Designs on Your Motor', *The Sydney Morning Herald*, 4 February 2006, p. 1; Nick Moore, 'Beware of Ambient Ambush', *B&T Weekly*, vol. 54, no. 2516, 29 April 2005, p. 23; Camille Alarcon, 'Need to Split Ambient and Outdoor', *B&T Weekly*, vol. 54, no. 2515, 29 April 2005, p. 4; Paul McBeth, 'Products in Programs', *B&T Weekly*, vol. 54, no. 2458, 6 February 2004, pp. 9, 22; Anonymous, 'Making a Million Dot Com', *The Sydney Morning Herald*, 31 December 2005, p. 3.

Questions

1 Many consumers claim that they aren't influenced by advertising. Do you think this is true? What might be a way of testing this claim?

2 How can the effectiveness of out-of-home advertising be measured?

3 What products do you think might be most effectively promoted using out-of home-advertising? Which do you think will be least effective? Why?

16.1

The advertiser must also choose a tone for the ad. Memorable and attention-getting words must be found. For example, in Table 16.3 the themes on the left would have had much less impact without the creative phrasing on the right.

Message format The marketing communicator also needs a strong *format* for the message. In a print ad, the communicator has to decide on the headline, copy, illustration and colour. To attract attention, marketers can use novelty and contrast; eye-catching pictures and headlines; distinctive formats; message size and position; and colour, shape and movement. A small change in the way a message is designed can lead to a big difference in its effect. An illustration is the first thing the reader notices, and that illustration must be strong enough to draw attention. Then the headline must effectively entice the right people to read the copy. The copy—the main block of text in the ad—must be simple but strong and convincing. Moreover, these three elements must also work effectively together. Even

TABLE 16.3 Message theme and creative copy	
Message theme	**Creative copy**
7-Up is not a cola.	'The un-cola'
A BMW is a well-engineered car.	'The ultimate driving machine'
Shop by turning the pages of your telephone directory.	'Let your fingers do the walking'
We don't rent as many cars, so we have to do more for our customers.	'We try harder'

then, a truly outstanding ad will be noted by less than 50% of the exposed audience; about 30% of the exposed audience will recall the main point of the headline; about 25% will remember the advertiser's name; and less than 10% will have read most of the body copy. Less-than-outstanding ads, unfortunately, will not achieve even these results.

Selecting media

The marketer must next choose the *channel of communication*. There are two broad types of communication channels—*personal* and *non-personal*.

Personal communication channels In **personal communication channels**, two or more people communicate directly with each other. They might communicate face to face, over the telephone, through the mail or online, by email, instant messaging or in a chat room. Personal communication channels are effective because they allow for personal addressing and feedback.

Some personal communication channels are controlled directly by the company. For example, company salespeople contact buyers in the target market. But other personal communications about the product may reach buyers through channels not directly controlled by the company. These might include independent experts—consumer advocates, consumer buying guides and others—making statements to target buyers. Or they might be neighbours, friends, family members and associates talking to target buyers. This last channel, known as **word-of-mouth influence**, has considerable effect in many product areas.

Personal influence carries great weight for products that are expensive, risky or highly visible. For example, buyers of automobiles and major appliances often go beyond mass-media sources to seek the opinions of knowledgeable people.

Companies can take steps to put personal communication channels to work for them. For example, they can create marketing programs that will generate favourable word-of-mouth communications about their brands. This is often done by targeting *opinion leaders*—people whose opinions are sought by others—by supplying potential influencers with the product on attractive terms or by educating them so they can inform others. **Buzz marketing** involves cultivating opinion leaders and getting them to spread information about a product or service to others in their communities (see Marketing Highlight 16.2).

Non-personal communication channels **Non-personal communication channels** are media that carry messages without personal contact or feedback. They include major media, atmospheres and events. *Major media* include print media (newspapers, magazines, direct mail), broadcast media (radio, television), display media (billboards, signs, posters) and online media (email, websites). *Atmospheres* are designed environments that create or reinforce the buyer's leanings toward buying a product. Thus, lawyers' offices and banks are designed to communicate confidence and other qualities that might be valued by their clients. *Events* are staged occurrences that communicate messages to target audiences. For example, public relations departments arrange press conferences, grand openings, shows and exhibits, public tours and other events.

Non-personal communication affects buyers directly. In addition, using mass media often affects buyers indirectly by causing more personal communication. Communications first flow from television, magazines and other mass media to opinion leaders and then from these opinion leaders to others. Thus, opinion leaders step between the mass media and their audiences and carry messages to people who are less exposed to media. This suggests that mass communicators should aim their messages directly at opinion leaders, letting them carry the message to others.

When using non-personal communication channels, the four major steps in media selection are:

Personal communication channels Channels through which two or more people communicate directly with each other, including face to face, person to audience, over the telephone or through the mail.

Word-of-mouth influence Personal communication about a product between target buyers and neighbours, friends, family members and associates.

Buzz marketing Cultivating opinion leaders and getting them to spread information about a product or service to others in their communities.

Non-personal communication channels Media that carry messages without personal contact or feedback, including media, atmospheres and events.

1   deciding on reach, frequency and impact
2   selecting major media types
3   selecting specific media vehicles
4   deciding on media timing.

Deciding on reach, frequency and impact To select media, the marketer must determine the reach and frequency necessary to achieve their objectives. **Reach** is a measure of the percentage of people in the target market who are exposed to an ad campaign during a given period of time. For example, an advertiser might try to reach 70% of the target market during the first three months. **Frequency** is a measure of how many times the average person in the target market is exposed to the message. For example, an advertiser might want an average exposure frequency of three. The marketer must also decide on **media impact**—the qualitative value of a message exposure through a given medium. For example, the Internet is very good at allowing the consumer to obtain lots of information about a product. In contrast, for products with low awareness, messages on television may have more impact than the Internet because television can raise awareness more rapidly than the Internet.

Suppose the advertiser's product might appeal to a market of one million consumers. The goal is to reach 700 000 consumers (70% of 1 000 000). If the marketer wants the average consumer to receive three exposures, 2 100 000 exposures (700 000 × 3) must be bought. If the advertiser wants exposures of 1.5 impact (assuming 1.0 impact is the average), a rated number of exposures of 3 150 000 (2 100 000 × 1.5) must be bought. If 1000 exposures with this impact cost $10, the advertising budget will have to be $31 500 (3150 × $10). In general, the more reach, frequency and impact the advertiser seeks, the higher the advertising budget will have to be.

Selecting major media types The media planner has to know the reach, frequency and impact of each of the major media types. The major advertising media along with their relative advantages and limitations are summarised in Table 16.4. The major media types are television, newspapers, magazines, radio, Internet and outdoor/cinema.

Reach The percentage of people in the target market exposed to an ad campaign during a given period.

Frequency The number of times the average person in the target market is exposed to an advertising message during a given period.

Media impact The qualitative value of a message exposure through a given medium.

TABLE 16.4 Profiles of major media types

Medium	Advantages	Limitation
Newspapers	Flexibility; timeliness; good local market coverage; broad acceptance; high believability.	Short life; poor reproduction quality; small 'pass-along' audience.
Television	Combines sight, sound and motion; appealing to the senses; high attention; high reach.	High absolute cost; high clutter; fleeting exposure; less audience selectivity.
Radio	Mass use; high geographic and demographic selectivity; low cost.	Audience presentation only; lower attention than television; non-standardised rate structures; fleeting exposure.
Magazines	High geographic and demographic selectivity; credibility and prestige; high-quality reproduction; long life; good 'pass-along' readership.	Long ad purchase lead times; some waste circulation; no guarantee of position.
Outdoor/ cinema	Flexibility; high repeat exposure; low cost; low competition.	No audience selectivity; creative limitations.
Online	High selectivity; immediacy; interactive capabilities; easy to measure number of exposures.	Demographically skewed audience; audience controls exposure; less effective at conveying emotional messages.

Buzz marketing—a powerful new way to spread the word

Buzz marketing is all the rage. Rather than relying on traditional methods of promotion, buzz marketing involves getting consumers themselves to spread information about a product or service to others in their communities. 'In a successful buzz-marketing campaign, each carefully cultivated recipient of the brand message becomes a powerful carrier, spreading the word to yet more carriers, much as a virus rampages through a given population,' says one expert. Buzz marketing is also known as *viral marketing*, reflecting the marketer's hope that consumers will be so interested in the message that they will pass it on to their friends, who will pass it on to their friends, just as a virus is spread from one person to another. It also goes by other names— 'stealth', 'whisper' or 'under-the-radar' marketing— reflecting the marketer's typical aim of starting consumers talking about a product without realising they are responding to a marketing campaign.

Why the new trend? For starters, buzz/viral marketing is typically much cheaper than conventional advertising. It's a great way to extend brand exposure without blowing out the marketing budget. Buzz marketing's increasing popularity can also be attributed to the growing ranks of sceptical consumers—such as teens and twenty-somethings—who are notoriously disdainful of mass-media advertising. Instead of the usual ad pitches, buzz marketing tries to spread the word through grassroots opinion leaders.

Perhaps the single most important reason that marketers are employing buzz marketing is that it works. Consider the following examples.

- *Lee jeans.* Jeans manufacturer VF Jeanswear wanted to re-energise the image of its stodgy Lee jeans brand among younger target consumers— mostly young males aged 17 to 22. So VF came up with one of the most freewheeling and influential buzz-marketing campaigns to date. The campaign played on target consumers' weakness for video games and computers. First, VF developed a list of 200 000 'influential' guys from a list of web surfers. It then sent them a trio of grainy video clips that were hilarious in their apparent stupidity. The videos appeared to be ultra-low-budget flicks meant to draw visitors to the web game sites of amateur film makers, such as open-shirted Curry, a 23-year-old race car driver. To the young web surfers who received them, the clips seemed like delicious examples of the oddball digital debris that litters the Web. So not many of the recipients who forwarded the flicks to their friends would have guessed that they were actually helping a marketing campaign orchestrated by Lee.

  According to VF research, the 'stupid little films' were so intriguing that, on average, recipients forwarded them to an average of six friends. Despite virtually no advertising, around 100 000 visitors stormed the fictional film makers' websites the week they went live, crashing the server. The marketing connection only became clear a few months later, after a TV and radio ad blitz finally revealed the three characters to be fictional antagonists developed as part of an online computer game. And that was a key to the program: to play the game at an advanced level, participants had to snag the product identification numbers—the 'secret code'—off Lee items, which of course required a visit to a store. Ultimately, the effort drove thousands of kids aged 17 to 22 into the stores and helped propel Lee sales upward by 20%.

- *Burger King.* Burger King's subservient chicken (www.subservientchicken.com) is probably one of the best known viral successes, even in Australasian markets where Burger King is a relatively minor brand. Visit the website and you see the Burger King logo, with the words 'Contacting the Chicken' underneath it. Then the screen dissolves to a living room, where the subservient chicken—someone in a giant chicken suit and a garter belt—awaits your bidding. The room has the look of one of those web-cam sites, complete with tacky furniture and bare walls that make it somehow seedy and suggestive. Type in commands, and the chicken does exactly what you ask. It will flap its wings, roll over or jump up and down. In other words, you can have your way with the chicken. Get it? Have it your way! The site promotes Burger King's new TenderCrisp chicken and ties the new product into Burger King's successful 'Have It Your Way' marketing campaign.

'As viral marketing goes, subservientchicken.com is a colossal success,' says an advertising expert. 'There is great overlap between Web habitués and Burger King's core audience.' If nothing else, the site gets consumers to interact with the brand. And it gets them buzzing about Burger King's edgy new positioning. Hit the 'tell a friend' button, and the site presents you with a pre-written email to send to a friend promoting the site. According to the chain, the site received more than 46 million hits in the week following its launch. By now it's probably received a billion hits.

⦿ *Carlton Draught Big Ad.* The most recent high-profile viral ad campaign in Australia is the pre-launch on the Internet of a television ad for a beer (www.bigad.com.au). The ad, a parody of large budget ads, features thousands of people forming the shape of a man drinking a glass of beer. It was originally sent to 4000 Fosters employees, and by the time it was launched on

Burger King's fun site, The Subservient Chicken, created huge buzz, as consumers passed the link on to friends. Most attempted viral campaigns aren't this successful.

television had already been seen by hundreds of thousands, with the company reporting that the ad had been downloaded by 220 000 people in just 24 hours after its release. Sales of the beer grew by 30% following the launch of the ad.

The essence of buzz marketing is that consumers decide whether they will pass the message on. Marketers are particularly interested in whether the most influential consumers will see and pass on the message. So in an effort to make sure these influential people are targeted, big companies are putting extraordinary efforts into identifying and targeting those who they think will be most influential in creating a buzz around a new product. For example, Procter & Gamble uses a huge stealth teenage salesforce, having recruited around 280 000 strong teenagers—roughly 1% of the US teen population—as part of an arm of Procter & Gamble called Tremor. Their mission is to help companies spread the word about their brands among teens, who are maddeningly difficult to reach and influence through advertising. The Tremor individuals deliver endorsements in school cafeterias, at sleepovers, by SMS and by email—and they do it for free. Initially focused only on P&G brands, Tremor's forces are now being tapped to talk up just about any brand, from Sony, Coca-Cola and Kraft to Toyota and Valvoline motor oil. One member of Tremor, Gina Lavagna, tells how she received a $2 minidisc for Sony's Net MD and six $10-off coupons, and rushed four of her friends to a mall near her home to show them the digital music player, which sells for $US99 and up. 'I've probably told 20 people about it,' she says, adding, 'At least 10 are extremely interested in getting one.' Her parents got her one for Christmas.

Tremor recruits teens with a wide social circle and the gift of the gab. (Tremorites have an average 170 names on their list of friends; a typical teen has 30.) While P&G screens the kids it taps, it doesn't coach them beyond encouraging them to feel free to talk to friends. The kids, natural talkers, do the work without pay, except by coupons, product samples and the thrill of being something of an 'insider'. 'It's cool to know about stuff before other people,' says one Tremorite.

More than just talk, such buzz can give a real lift to a brand's sales. CoverGirl sent groups of Tremor girls in three cities a booklet of make-up tips in a thin round tin with some $1-off coupons. Nothing fancy, but CoverGirl wanted to see if it would give its lipstick, mascara and foundation a boost. It did. Purchases rose 10% among teens in the targeted cities. P&G's buzz marketing effort has been so successful that the packaged-goods giant is now building a new network of equal or greater size, one that will focus on mothers—a much bigger and more affluent target than teens. Says P&G's marketing chief: 'The possibilities are almost limitless'.

But how long will consumers co-operate in buzz marketing, without becoming jaded when they realise they are helping companies to sell their products? Consumers won't pass on a message unless it is interesting to them and their friends, or unless there is some benefit to them. One of the reasons Carlton's Big Ad campaign worked is undoubtedly that all the extras in the shoot (the company won't say how many, but even with digital enhancement there were clearly a lot of them) sent the ad on to their friends and family. Most viral campaigns don't get that big starting boost. All the big advertising agencies are developing digital marketing arms, and more and more companies are trying to develop viral marketing campaigns. It's likely that it's going to get harder to get consumers to pay attention to, and pass on, viral marketing campaigns.

Sources: Excerpts adapted from Gerry Khermouch and Jeff Green, 'Buzz Marketing', *Business Week*, 30 July 2001, pp. 50–56; Melanie Wells, 'Nabbing Teens', *Forbes*, 2 February 2004, pp. 85–88; Bob Garfield, 'War & Peace and Subservient Chicken', 26 April 2004, accessed at <www.adage.com>; and Gregg Cebrzynski, 'Burger King Says It's OK to Have Your Way with the Chicken', *Nation's Restaurant News*, 10 May 2004, p. 16. See also Simon Canning, 'Business Big Shot', *The Australian*, 23 July 2005, p. 34; Richard Cooke, 'Young, Wired and Bombarded by Ads', *The Sydney Morning Herald*, 23 November 2005, p. 4; Julian Lee, 'Very Big Ad Shows Why We Still Call Carlton a Beer', *The Sydney Morning Herald*, 28 July 2005, p. 29; Lia Timson, 'Think Big', *The Sydney Morning Herald*, 24 September 2005, p. 3; Paul McIntyre, 'Viral Ads Catch on in Ad Land', *The Sydney Morning Herald*, 25 June 2005, p. 4.

Questions

1 Are all products equally suited to buzz/viral marketing campaigns? Can they be applied in both business-to-business and business-to-consumer marketing?

2 Do you think that buzz marketing is a substitute for, or an addition to, traditional mass market communication? Why or why not?

3 Do you think buzz marketing will continue to be as successful as more companies adopt it, and as more consumers become aware they are contributing to a marketing campaign?

Media planners consider many factors when making their media choices. The *media habits* of target consumers will affect media choice—for example, television and the Internet are the best media for reaching teenagers. So will the *nature of the product*—products which need to convey detailed information might be best advertised in magazines or online. Different *types of messages* may require different media. A message announcing a major sale tomorrow will require radio or newspapers; a message with a lot of technical data might require magazines, direct mailings or an online ad and website. Cost is also a major factor in media choice. Television is very expensive; newspaper advertising costs much less. The media planner looks at both the total cost of using a medium and at the cost per 1000 exposures—the cost of reaching 1000 people by using the medium.

Ideas about media impact and cost must be re-examined regularly. For a long time, television and magazines dominated in the media mixes of national advertisers, with other media often being neglected. In recent years, however, the costs and clutter of these media have gone up, audiences have dropped and marketers are adopting strategies targeting narrower segments. As a result, television and magazine advertising revenues have levelled off or declined. Advertisers are turning increasingly to alternative media, ranging from direct mail and outdoor advertising to catalogues, in-store media and the Web.

Given these and other media characteristics, the media planner must decide how much of each media type to buy. For example, in launching a new biscuit, a company might decide to spend $1 million on daytime network television, $500 000 on women's magazines and $250 000 on daily newspapers in five major markets.

Selecting specific media vehicles The media planner must now choose the best **media vehicle**—specific media within each general media type. For example, television vehicles include programs popular with younger audiences such as *Big Brother*, programs watched more by older audiences, such as the early evening news, or programs targeted at a specific demographic, such as *Business Sunday*. Magazines might include *Business Review Weekly* (to target managers), *New Idea* (to target women) and *Dolly* for the teenage market. If advertising is placed in magazines, the media planner must look up circulation figures and the costs of different ad sizes, colour options, ad positions and frequencies for various specific magazines. The planner then evaluates each magazine on such factors as credibility, status, reproduction quality, editorial focus and advertising submission deadlines. Knowing this, the media planner can then decide which vehicles give the best reach, frequency and impact for the money in reaching the targeted audience.

Media planners also compute the cost per 1000 persons reached by a vehicle. If a full-page, four-colour advertisement in *New Idea* costs $15 000 and *New Idea*'s readership is two million people, the cost of reaching 1000 people is about $8. The same advertisement in *Family Circle* may cost only $10 000 but reach only 910 000, at a cost per 1000 people of about $11. The media planner would rank each magazine by cost per 1000 and favour those magazines with the lower cost per 1000 for reaching target consumers.

The media planner must also consider the costs of producing ads for different media. Whereas newspaper ads may cost very little to produce, flashy television ads may cost millions. On average, advertisers must pay in excess of $50 000 to produce a single 30-second television commercial. Some major commercials can be much more expensive. For example, the budget to make the second series of Qantas ads featuring the Australian Children's Choir in 2004 was reported to be over $10 million. On top of this, of course, the advertiser must pay for the advertising time. In 2005, an Australian advertiser could expect to pay more than $26 000 for a spot in a Sunday night movie which might reach approximately one and a quarter million people. In contrast, a national regional spot would cost around $8000 and reach about 700 000. At the other end of the scale, a late-night spot in one regional market might cost only a few hundred dollars.[8]

Thus, the media planner must balance media cost measures against several media impact factors. First, costs should be balanced against the media vehicle's audience quality. For a baby wipes advertisement, *New Idea* magazine would have a high exposure value and *Business Review Weekly* would have a low exposure value. Second, the media planner should consider audience attention. Readers of *Vogue*, for example, typically pay

Media vehicles Specific media within each general media type, such as specific magazines, television shows or radio programs.

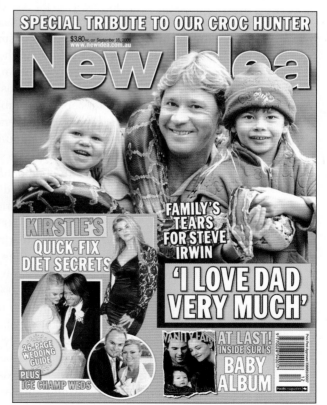

Magazines allow targeted advertising to people who are most likely to be interested in the product or service.

more attention to ads than do readers of *The Bulletin*. Third, the planner should assess the vehicle's editorial quality—*The Australian* and *The Australian Financial Review* are more believable and prestigious than a local community paper.

Deciding on media timing The advertiser must also decide how to schedule the advertising over the course of a year. Suppose sales of a product peak in December and drop in March. The company can vary its advertising to follow the seasonal pattern, to oppose the seasonal pattern or to be the same all year. Most companies do some seasonal advertising. Some do only seasonal advertising; for example, greeting card marketers tend to advertise cards only before major holidays or events.

Continuity Scheduling ads evenly within a given period.

Pulsing Scheduling ads unevenly in bursts during a time period.

Finally, the advertiser has to choose the pattern of the ads. **Continuity scheduling** means scheduling ads evenly within a given period. **Pulsing** means scheduling ads unevenly during a given time period. Thus, 52 ads could either be scheduled at one per week during the year or pulsed in several bursts. Those who favour pulsing feel that the audience will learn the message more completely and that money can be saved. However, some media planners believe that, although pulsing achieves minimal awareness, it sacrifices depth of advertising communication.[9]

Collecting feedback

After sending the message the communicator must research both the communication effect and the sales effect on the target audience. Measuring the *communication* effects of an ad—**copy testing**—tells whether the ad is communicating well. Copy testing can be done before or after an ad is printed or broadcast. Before the ad is placed, the advertiser can show it to consumers, ask how they like it and measure message recall or attitude changes resulting from it. After the ad is run, the advertiser can measure how the ad affected consumer recall or product awareness, knowledge and preference.

Copy testing Measuring the communication effect of an advertisement before or after it is printed or broadcast.

Recall testing involves asking the target audience members whether they remember the message, how many times they saw it, what points they recall, how they felt about the message and their past and present attitudes towards the product and the company. By comparing before and after results, the marketer can then establish how the communication affected consumer recall or product awareness, knowledge and preference.

Feedback on marketing communications may suggest changes in the promotions program or in the product offer itself. Figure 16.6 shows an example of feedback measurement. For example, Virgin Blue uses newspapers and billboards to inform consumers about the airline, its routes and its fares. Suppose feedback research showed that 80% of all fliers in an area recalled seeing the airline's ads and were aware of its flights and prices. Suppose that research showed that 60% of these aware fliers had flown Virgin Blue, but only 20% of those who had tried it were satisfied. These results suggest that although promotion is creating *awareness*, the airline isn't giving consumers the *satisfaction* they expect. Therefore, Virgin Blue needs to improve its service while staying with the successful communications program. In contrast, suppose the research showed that only 40% of consumers were aware of the airline, only 30% of those aware had tried it, but 80% of those who had tried it returned. In this case, Virgin Blue needs to strengthen its promotion program to take advantage of its power to create customer satisfaction.

A marketer is usually primarily interested in measuring the behavioural effect of a message—how many people bought a product, talked to others about it or visited a store. The *sales effects* of advertising are often harder to measure than the communication effects. Sales are affected by many factors besides advertising—such as product features, price and availability. One way to measure the sales effect of advertising is to compare past sales with past advertising expenditures. Another way is through experiments. In Western Australia, DuPont was one of the first companies to use advertising

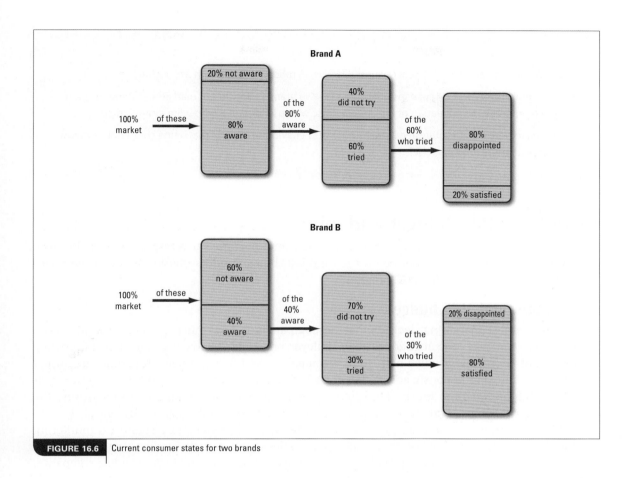

FIGURE 16.6   Current consumer states for two brands

experiments. DuPont's paint department divided 56 sales territories into high, average and low market-share territories. In one-third of the group DuPont spent the normal amount for advertising; in another third the company spent two and a half times the normal amount; and in the remaining third it allotted four times the normal amount. At the end of the experiment, DuPont estimated how many extra sales had been created by higher levels of advertising expenditure. It found that higher advertising spending increased sales at a diminishing rate and that the sales increase was weaker in its high-market-share territories.[10] More complex experiments could be designed to include other variables, such as difference in the ads or media used.

Marketing psychologist Max Sutherland, former chairman and creative director of NFO MarketMind, pioneered a research technique using continuous tracking of advertising to test the effect of different types of advertising on consumer awareness. One conclusion that he has reached from his studies is that many advertisers present too many executions of a television advertisement on air at the same time, with resulting confusion in the message conveyed to the viewer. Another conclusion is that with low-involvement products advertisers should stay with the same message over a long period of time if the product is to be captured in the audience's collective memory.[11]

Setting the IMC budget and mix

We have looked at the steps in planning and sending communications to a target audience. But how does a marketing organisation decide on the total IMC budget and its division between the major promotional tools to create the IMC program?

Setting the total IMC budget

One of the hardest marketing decisions facing companies is how much to spend on IMC. Lord Leverhulme, founder of consumer goods giant Unilever, once said: 'I know that half of my advertising is wasted, but I don't know which half'. John Wanamaker, the US department store magnate, would repeat this saying, and famously added: 'I spent $2 million for advertising, and I don't know if that is half enough or twice too much'. Marketers are putting increasing emphasis on measuring the impact of their IMC, but many still struggle with how much to spend on each element of the IMC mix. Different industries and companies vary widely in how much they spend on marketing communications. Spending on IMC may be 20–30% of sales in the cosmetics industry and only 5–10% in the industrial machinery industry. Within a given industry, both low- and high-spending companies can be found.

How do companies determine their IMC budget? Four common methods used to set the total budget for advertising are the affordable method, the percentage-of-sales method, the competitive-parity method and the objective-and-task method.[12]

Affordable method

Affordable method
Setting the communications budget at what management thinks the company can afford.

Some companies use the **affordable method**: they set the IMC budget at what they think the company can afford. Small businesses often use this method, reasoning that the company cannot spend more on communications than it can afford. They begin with total revenues, deduct operating expenses and capital outlays, and then devote some portion of the remaining funds to the IMC element in question.

Unfortunately, this method of setting budgets completely ignores the effect of marketing communications on sales volume. It leads to an uncertain annual IMC budget, which makes long-range market planning difficult. Although the affordable method can result in overspending on marketing communication, it more often results in underspending.

Percentage-of-sales method

Percentage-of-sales method Setting the communications budget at a certain percentage of current or forecasted sales or as a percentage of the sales price.

Many companies use the **percentage-of-sales method**, setting their IMC budget at a certain percentage of current or forecasted sales. Or they budget a percentage of the sales price. For example, car companies often budget a fixed percentage for IMC based on the planned car price. Oil companies set the budget at some fraction of a cent for each litre of petrol and oil sold under their labels.

A number of advantages are claimed for the percentage-of-sales method. First, using this method means that IMC spending is likely to vary with what the company can 'afford'. It also helps management to think about the relationship between marketing communications spending, selling price and profit per unit. Finally, it supposedly creates competitive stability because competing firms tend to spend about the same percentage of their sales on IMC.

However, in spite of these claimed advantages, the percentage-of-sales method has little to justify it. It wrongly views sales as the cause of IMC rather than as the intended result—a form of inverted logic. The budget is based on availability of funds rather than on opportunities. It may prevent the increased spending sometimes needed to turn around falling sales. Because the budget varies with year-to-year sales, long-range planning is difficult. Finally, the method does not provide any basis for nominating a specific percentage, except what has been done in the past or what competitors are doing.

Competitive-parity method

Other companies use the **competitive-parity method**, setting their IMC budgets to match competitors' outlays. They watch competitors' advertising or get industry IMC spending estimates from publications or trade associations, or undertake an analysis of competitive websites and then base their budgets on the industry average, or on an estimate of what their competitors are spending.

Two arguments support this method. First, competitors' budgets represent the collective wisdom of the industry. Second, spending what competitors spend helps prevent promotion wars. Unfortunately, neither argument is valid. There are no grounds for believing that the competition has a better idea of what a company should be spending on IMC than the company itself does. Companies differ greatly, and each has its own special IMC needs. Furthermore, no evidence indicates that budgets based on competitive parity prevent promotion wars.

Competitive-parity method Setting the communications budget to match competitors' outlays.

Objective-and-task method

The most logical IMC budget-setting method is the **objective-and-task method**. Using it, marketers develop their marketing communications budgets by:

- ⊚ defining specific objectives
- ⊚ determining the tasks that must be performed to achieve these objectives
- ⊚ estimating the costs of performing these tasks.

The sum of these costs is the proposed marketing communications budget. The objective-and-task method makes management spell out their assumptions about the relationship between dollars spent and IMC results. But it is also the most difficult method to use. It is often hard to work out which specific tasks will achieve specific objectives. For example, suppose Mitsubishi wants 95% awareness for its new 380 range among its target market during the six-month introductory period in Australasia. What specific messages and media schedules would Mitsubishi need in order to attain this objective? How much would these messages and media schedules cost? Mitsubishi's local management must consider such questions even though they are hard to answer. With the objective-and-task method, the company sets its IMC budget based on what it wants to accomplish with promotion.

Objective-and-task method Developing the communications budget by (1) defining specific objectives; (2) determining the tasks that must be performed to achieve these objectives; and (3) estimating the costs of performing these tasks. The sum of these costs is the proposed communications budget.

Other product-specific factors

The communications budget for each product also depends on other product-specific factors. Here we describe some specific factors that should be considered when setting the communications budget.

- ⊚ *Stage in the product life cycle.* New products typically need larger communications budgets to build awareness and to gain consumer trial. Mature brands usually require lower budgets as a ratio to sales.

- ⦿ *Market share*. Low-market-share brands usually need more spending as a percentage of sales than high-share brands. Building market or taking share from competitors requires larger spending than simply maintaining current share.
- ⦿ *Competition and clutter*. In a market with many competitors and high advertising spending, a brand must generally advertise more heavily to be heard above the noise in the market.
- ⦿ *Advertising frequency*. When many repetitions are needed to put across the brand's message to consumers, the advertising budget must be larger.
- ⦿ *Product differentiation*. A brand that closely resembles other brands in its product class (cigarettes, beer, soft drinks) requires heavy advertising to set it apart. When the product differs greatly from its competitors, advertising can be used to point out the differences to consumers.[13]

Setting the communications budget is no easy task. How does a company know if it is spending the right amount? Some critics charge that large consumer-packaged-goods firms tend to spend too much on advertising, and industrial companies generally underspend on advertising.[14] They claim that the large consumer companies use image advertising extensively without really knowing its effects. They overspend as a form of 'insurance' against not spending enough. On the other hand, industrial advertisers often rely too heavily on their salesforces to bring in orders. They underestimate the power of company and product image in pre-selling to industrial customers. Thus, they do not spend enough on advertising to build customer awareness and knowledge.

How much impact does advertising really have on consumer buying and brand loyalty? An American research study analysing household purchases of frequently bought consumer products came up with the following surprising conclusion:

> Advertising appears effective in increasing the volume purchased by loyal buyers but less effective in winning new buyers. For loyal buyers, high levels of exposure per week may be unproductive because of a levelling off of ad effectiveness . . . Advertising appears unlikely to have some cumulative effect that leads to loyalty . . . Features, displays and especially price have a stronger impact on response than does advertising.[15]

These findings did not sit well with the advertising community, and several people attacked the study's data and methodology. They claimed that the study measured mostly short-run sales effects. Thus, it favoured pricing and sales promotion activities that tend to have more immediate impact. Most advertising, on the other hand, takes many months or even years to build strong brand positions and consumer loyalty. These long-run effects are difficult to measure. This debate underscores the fact that the subject of measuring the results of advertising spending remains poorly understood.

Setting the IMC mix

The concept of integrated marketing communications suggests that the company must blend the promotion tools carefully into a coordinated *promotion mix*. But how does the company determine what mix of promotion tools it will use? Companies within the same industry differ greatly in the design of their promotion mixes. For example, Avon spends most of its promotion funds on personal selling and direct marketing, whereas Clinique spends heavily on consumer advertising. Hewlett-Packard relies on advertising and promotion to retailers, whereas Dell Computer uses only direct marketing. Designing the IMC mix is even more complex when one tool must be used to promote another. Thus, when KFC decides to run a sales promotion in its fast-food outlets, it has to run ads to inform the public. When Nestlé uses a consumer advertising/sales promotion campaign to back a new chocolate bar, it has to set aside money to promote this campaign to the resellers (wholesalers and retailers) to win their support. We now look at factors that influence the marketer's choice of communication tools.

The nature of each IMC tool

Each IMC tool has unique characteristics and costs. Marketers must understand these characteristics in order to select their tools correctly.

Advertising Because of the many forms and uses of advertising, generalising about the effects of advertising is difficult.[16] However, advertising has several general effects. Advertising can reach masses of geographically dispersed buyers at a low cost per exposure, and it enables the seller to repeat a message many times. For example, television advertising can reach huge audiences. An estimated 143 million Americans tuned in to at least part of the most recent Super Bowl, more than 43 million people watched at least part of the last Academy Awards broadcast, and 51 million fans tuned in to watch the final episode of *Friends*. 'If you want to get to the mass audience,' says a media services executive, 'broadcast TV is where you have to be.' He adds, 'For anybody introducing anything who has to lasso audience in a hurry—a new product, a new campaign, a new movie—the networks are still the biggest show in town.'[17]

Beyond its reach, large-scale advertising says something positive about the seller's size, popularity and success. Because of advertising's public nature, consumers tend to view advertised products as more legitimate. Advertising is also very expressive—it allows the company to dramatise its products through the artful use of visuals, print, sound and colour. On the one hand, advertising can be used to build up a long-term image for a product (such as Coca-Cola ads). On the other hand, advertising can trigger quick sales (as when department stores advertise their sales).

Public relations Public relations offers several advantages. One is believability—news stories, features and events seem more real and believable to readers than ads. Public relations can reach many prospects who avoid salespeople and advertisements; the message gets to the buyers as 'news' rather than as a sales-directed communication. Because of the growing use of public relations, we discuss it separately later in this chapter.

Direct marketing Although there are many forms of direct marketing—telephone marketing, direct mail, online marketing and others—they all share four distinctive characteristics. Direct marketing is *non-public*: the message is normally directed to a specific person. Direct marketing is *immediate* and *customised*: messages can be prepared very quickly and can be tailored to appeal to specific consumers. Finally, direct marketing is *interactive*: it allows a dialogue between the marketing team and the consumer, and messages can be altered depending on the consumer's response. Thus, direct marketing is well suited to highly targeted marketing efforts and to building one-to-one customer relationships. However, companies must be careful in the use of customer data for direct marketing; since the recent extension of strict privacy laws in Australia, all companies with a turnover over $3 million a year (and also some small businesses) are limited in how they can use customer data, and use of any customer data must comply with Section 3 of the Privacy Act. This section sets out 10 principles in handling customer data, and ensures, among other controls, that confidential data, or data collected for another purpose, can't be used for marketing purposes,

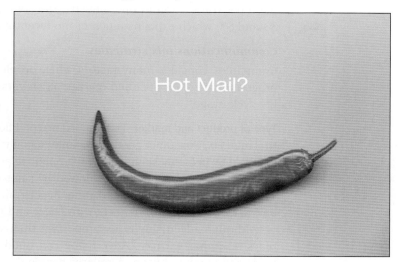

Direct Marketing Australia has used attention grabbing promotions, such as sending fresh chillies through the mail, to draw attention to its mailouts.

except under certain conditions.[18] Despite limitations on data use imposed by the privacy principles, direct marketing—both by mail and email—has grown enormously in the past 10 years, and we discuss this increasingly popular promotional tool in greater detail in Chapter 18.

Sales promotion Sales promotion, discussed further in Chapter 17, includes a wide assortment of tools—coupons, contests, cents-off deals, premiums and others. Sales promotion attracts consumer attention and provides an incentive for the consumer to buy the product by providing discounts or additions that give additional value to consumers. Sales promotions invite and reward quick response. Advertising says 'buy our product'. Sales promotion says 'buy it now'.

Companies use sales promotion tools to create a stronger and quicker response by adding urgency and changing consumers' perceived value-for-money equation. It can be used to dramatise product offers, to create product trial and to boost sagging sales. Sales promotion effects are usually short-lived, however, and may not be effective in building long-run brand preference. Even worse, if the product is regularly on promotion, buyers who would have paid full price may stock pile by buying additional stock whenever the product is on promotion, with the result that total sales may not increase and profits will fall because the product is bought at a discount.

Personal selling **Personal selling** is the most effective tool at certain stages of the buying process, particularly in building up buyers' preferences, convictions and actions. Compared with advertising, personal selling has several unique qualities. It involves personal interaction between two or more people, so each person can observe the other's needs and characteristics and make quick adjustments. Personal selling also lets all kinds of relationships spring up, ranging from a matter-of-fact selling relationship to a deep personal friendship. The effective salesperson keeps the customer's interests at heart in order to build a long-run relationship. Finally, with personal selling the buyer usually feels a greater need to listen and respond, even if the response is a polite 'no, thank you'.

These unique qualities come at a cost. A salesforce requires a longer-term commitment than advertising—advertising can be turned on and off, but salesforce size is harder to change. Moreover, personal selling is the company's most expensive IMC tool, costing some industrial companies an average of over $400 per sales call.[19] Australian and New Zealand firms spend up to three times as much on personal selling as they do on advertising. However, personal selling is also conducted via call centres, or interaction centres as they are coming to be called. Where a salesperson might cost $400 per transaction in one industry, the comparison costs for a call centre might range between $3 and $7, which explains much of the recent growth in telemarketing.[20]

Communications mix strategies

Companies consider many factors when developing their integrated marketing communications program: type of product and market, 'push versus pull' strategy, buyer-readiness state and product life-cycle stage.

Type of product and market The importance of different IMC tools varies between consumer and industrial markets. Consumer goods companies usually spend the most on advertising, then sales promotion, followed by personal selling and then public relations. Business-to-business marketers usually spend the most on personal selling, followed by sales promotion, advertising and public relations. These expenditures include direct marketing. In general, personal selling is used more heavily with expensive and risky goods and in markets with fewer and larger sellers.

Although advertising is less important than sales calls in business-to-business marketing, it still plays an important role. Advertising can build product awareness and knowledge, develop sales leads and reassure buyers. Similarly, personal selling can add greatly to consumer goods marketing efforts. Well-trained consumer goods salespeople can sign up more dealers to carry a particular

Personal selling
Oral presentation in a conversation with one or more prospective purchasers for the purpose of making sales.

brand, convince them to give the brand more shelf space and urge them to use special displays and promotions.

Push versus pull strategy The marketing communications mix is heavily affected by whether the company chooses a push or pull strategy. The two strategies are contrasted in Figure 16.7. A **push strategy** involves 'pushing' the product through marketing (distribution) intermediaries to final consumers. The manufacturer directs its marketing activities (primarily personal selling and trade promotion) at intermediaries to induce them to order and carry the product and to promote it to final consumers. Using a **pull strategy**, the manufacturer directs its marketing activities (primarily advertising, consumer promotion and direct marketing) towards final consumers to induce them to buy the product. If the strategy is effective, consumers will then demand the product from marketing intermediaries such as retailers and dealers, who will then demand it from producers. They may also approach the marketer directly. Thus, under a pull strategy, consumer demand 'pulls' the product through the channels.

Some small industrial goods marketers use only push strategies; some direct and online marketing companies use only pull strategies. Most large companies use a combination of both. For example, Colgate-Palmolive uses mass-media advertising to pull its products, and a large salesforce and trade promotions to push its products through the channels. In recent years, consumer goods companies have been decreasing the pull portions of their IMC mixes in favour of more push, partly as they realise that in-store promotions, close to the point of purchase, are most effective in influencing consumer choice, but also partly as a response to powerful retailers demanding higher fees for listing, placing and promoting products.

Online, web server technology permits banner advertisements to be 'pushed' to users who are searching on key words at a portal site such as Google. While the user searches for a city or town, banner ads for Travel.com or City.org appear. In contrast, a marketing organisation that uses META tags to help consumers searching for a product find their website quickly is employing an online pull strategy (see Chapter 18).

Buyer-readiness state Marketing communication tools vary in their effects at the different stages of buyer readiness discussed earlier in the chapter. Advertising, along with public relations, plays the major role in the awareness and knowledge stages, being more important than that played by 'cold calls' from salespeople. Customer liking, preference and conviction are affected more by personal

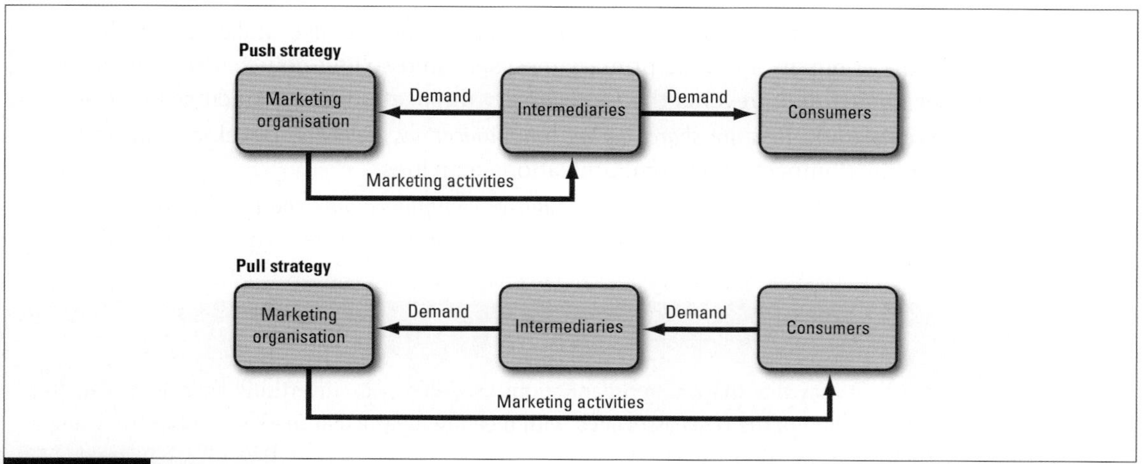

Push strategy
A promotion strategy that calls for using the salesforce and trade promotion to push the product through channels; the producer promotes the product to wholesalers, the wholesalers promote to retailers and the retailers promote to consumers.

Pull strategy
A promotion strategy that calls for spending a lot on advertising and consumer promotion to build up consumer demand; if successful, consumers will ask their retailers for the product, the retailers will ask the wholesalers and the wholesalers will ask the producers.

FIGURE 16.7 Push versus pull strategy

selling, closely followed by advertising. Finally, closing the sale is done mostly with direct marketing, sales calls (personal and call centre) and sales promotion. Clearly, personal selling, given its high costs, should focus on the later stages of the customer buying process.

Product life-cycle stage The effects of different marketing communication tools also vary with stages of the product life cycle. In the introduction stage, advertising, direct marketing, online marketing and public relations are good for producing high awareness, and sales promotion is useful in promoting early trial. Personal selling must be used to get the trade to carry the product. In the growth stage, advertising, direct and online marketing and public relations continue to be powerful, whereas sales promotion can be reduced because fewer incentives are needed. In the mature stage, sales promotion again becomes important relative to advertising. Buyers know the brands, and advertising is needed only to remind them of the product. In the decline stage, advertising is kept at a reminder level, public relations is dropped and salespeople give the product only a little attention. Sales promotion, however, might continue to be strong.

Integrating the promotion mix

Having set the promotions budget and mix, the company must now take steps to see that all of the promotion mix elements are smoothly integrated. Here is a checklist for integrating the firm's marketing communications.[21]

1 *Analyse trends—internal and external—that can affect the company's ability to do business.* Look for areas where communications can help the most. Determine the strengths and weaknesses of each communications function. Develop a combination of promotional tactics based on these strengths and weaknesses.

2 *Audit the pockets of communications spending throughout the organisation.* Itemise the communications budgets and tasks and consolidate these into a single budgeting process. Reassess all communications expenditures by product, promotional tool, stage of the life cycle and observed effect.

3 *Identify all contact points for the company and its brands.* Work to ensure that communications at each point are consistent with the overall communications strategy and that communications efforts are occurring when, where and how *customers* want them.

4 *Team up in communications planning.* Engage all communications functions in joint planning. Include customers, suppliers and other stakeholders at every stage of communications planning.

5 *Create compatible themes, tones and quality across all communications media.* Make sure each element carries the company's unique primary messages and selling points. This consistency achieves greater impact and prevents the unnecessary duplication of work across functions.

6 *Create performance measures that are shared by all communications elements.* Develop systems to evaluate the combined impact of all communications activities.

7 *Appoint a director responsible for the company's persuasive communications efforts.* This move encourages efficiency by centralising planning and creating shared performance measures.

SELF-CHECK QUESTIONS

9 Would it be accurate to say that marketing organisations use full-service advertising agencies because of their better understanding of the costs associated with meeting a particular marketing objective using a specific communication campaign (task)?

10 Would personal selling to an individual supermarket such as Coles in Australia or Carrefour (the French supermarket chain with outlets throughout Asia) be considered to have a more direct effect on sales of Pepsi than communicating with young consumers via cinema advertising?

Trends in advertising spending

Earlier we defined advertising as any paid form of non-personal presentation and promotion of ideas, goods or services by an identified sponsor, often meeting long-term 'indirect' objectives related to brand image. Table 16.5 shows spending on advertising for the Asia–Pacific region. Figure 16.8 shows the trends in advertising across different media from 1995 to 2005 in Australia.

In 2005 in Australia the retail sector was the largest spending sector, with a total advertising spend of $1.8 billion, followed by motor vehicles with $864 million and then entertainment and leisure with $698.[22] Advertising as a percentage of sales is low in the car industry and high in food, pharmaceuticals, toiletries, cosmetics and confectionery. However, the expenditure on advertising over a period of time in any single country changes with the change in economic conditions and

TABLE 16.5 Advertising expenditure in $US million at current prices. All years based on $US1= $A								
	Total	Newspapers	Magazines	TV	Radio	Cinema	Outdoor/ Transport	Internet
Australia	7 653	2 827	697	2 727	644	57	257	442
Hong Kong	2 486	949	327	955	90	0	148	17
New Zealand	1 391	541	159	454	176	9	35	17
Singapore	1 182	460	56	473	114	7	71	n/a
Malaysia	1 252	759	47	371	47	5	23	n/a
Asia–Pacific total	84 554	26 532	6 464	36 016	3 942	147	8 004	3 449

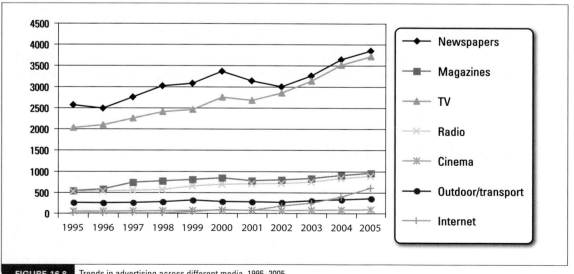

FIGURE 16.8 Trends in advertising across different media, 1995–2005
Source: Zenithoptimedia, Advertising expenditure forecasts, October 2005.

consumer confidence. Internet advertising has created an important and rapidly growing new channel for advertising. To date, it is still relatively small compared to television and newspaper spending, but it is growing faster than any other form of advertising. The Internet also presents problems for advertisers; in one study, 12% of large marketers complained about the limited reach, advertising clutter and insufficient audience targeting and tracking systems for Internet communications.[23]

Most commentators also predict that newspaper and FTA TV advertising will grow more slowly than other media. Anne Parsons, the chief executive of MediaCom, has suggested that big marketers are steadily moving money away from FTA TV and newspapers. 'Clients consistently want to talk about other media,' she says. 'Newpapers and free-to-air TV will be used for 'need-to-do' advertising by marketers in categories such as retail, financial services and automotive. The more interesting advertising will be done in other sectors, particularly online.'[24] The world's biggest advertiser is Procter & Gamble, with a global budget of $3 billion in 2004. A decade ago, 90% of P&G's advertising budget was spent on television; now, for some of its products, only around a quarter of its budget is spent on TV. This change is a response to increasing fragmentation of media, making consumers more difficult and more expensive to reach. As a result, consumer products companies like P&G are spending more of their communications budgets on so-called 'below-the-line' forms of promotion, such as in-store promotions, posters, coupons and sponsorship.[25]

Another big change in advertising is in who is spending; until recently, advertising was primarily used by private enterprises. However, one of the most recent trends is for governments to spend large amounts of money on advertising. In 2003 and 2004, the last years for which full figures are available, the Australian government was the third largest spender on advertising, after Coles Myer and Nestlé.[26] In the last quarter of 2005, the Australian government was the largest spender on advertising as the government attempted to sell the advantages of its industrial relations spending in one of the biggest ever advertising campaigns in Australia.[27] Government spending tends to be very cyclical; governments spend much more before elections and policy changes, so this period was atypical, but government spending on advertising is likely to remain high.

SELF-CHECK QUESTIONS

11 Why do retailers, whether grocery or department stores, spend so much on media advertising?

12 Google doesn't spend anything on mass-media advertising. Does this suggest that other organisations are overspending? Or would Google be even more successful if it used media advertising?

13 Why do you think Anne Parsons suggests that marketers in categories such as retail, financial services and automotive will continue to use television more than other companies? What do you think she means by 'need-to-do' advertising?

International advertising decisions

International advertisers face many complexities not encountered by domestic advertisers. The most basic issue concerns the degree to which global advertising should be adapted to the unique characteristics of the markets of various countries. Some large advertisers have attempted to support their global brands with highly standardised worldwide advertising. Standardisation produces many benefits—lower advertising costs, greater coordination of global advertising efforts and a more consistent worldwide company or product image. However, standardisation also has drawbacks. Most importantly, it ignores the fact that the markets of different countries differ greatly in their cultures, demographics and economic conditions. Thus, most international advertisers attempt to develop global advertising strategies that bring efficiency and consistency to their worldwide advertising efforts. Then they adapt their advertising programs to make them more responsive to consumer needs and expectations within local markets.

Companies vary in the degree to which they adapt their advertising to local markets. For example, Kellogg's Frosted Flakes commercials were almost identical worldwide, with only minor adjustments for local cultural differences.[28] The advertising used a tennis theme that had worldwide appeal and featured teenage actors with generic good looks—neither too Northern European nor too Latin American. Of course, Kellogg translated the commercials into different languages. In the English version, for example, Tony the lion growled 'They're Gr-r-reat!', whereas in the German version it was '*Gr-r-rossartig!*'. Other adaptations were more subtle. In the American ad, after winning the match, Tony leapt over the net in celebration. In other versions, he simply 'high fived' his young partner. The reason: Europeans do not jump over the net after winning at tennis.

In contrast, Parker Pen Company changes its advertising substantially from country to country.

> Print ads in Germany simply show the Parker Pen held in a hand that is writing a headline—
> 'This is how you write with precision'. In the United Kingdom, where it is the brand leader,
> [ads emphasise] the exotic processes used to make pens, such as gently polishing the gold nibs
> with walnut chips . . . In the United States, the ad campaign's theme is status and image. The
> headlines are . . . 'Here's how you tell who's boss' and 'There are times when it has to be Parker'.
> The company considers the different themes necessary because of different product images
> and . . . customer motives in each market.[29]

Global advertisers face several additional problems. For instance, advertising media costs and availability differ considerably from country to country. Some countries have too few media to handle all the advertising offered to them. Other countries are peppered with so many media that an advertiser cannot gain national coverage at a reasonable cost. Media prices are often negotiated and may vary greatly. For example, one study found that the cost of reaching 1000 consumers in 11 different European countries ranged from $1.58 in Belgium to $5.91 in Italy. For women's magazines, the advertising cost per page ranged from $2.51 per 1000 circulation in Denmark to $10.87 in Germany.[30]

Countries also differ in the extent to which they regulate advertising practices. Many countries have extensive systems of laws restricting how much a company can spend on advertising, the media used, the nature of advertising claims and other aspects of the advertising program. Such restrictions often require that advertisers adapt their campaigns from country to country. Consider the following examples:

> When General Mills Toy Group's European subsidiary launched a product of G.I. Joe-type war toys
> and soldiers, it had to develop two television commercials, a general version for most European
> countries and another for countries that bar advertisements for products with military or violent
> themes. As a result, in the version running in Germany, Holland and Belgium, jeeps replaced the toy
> tanks, and guns were removed from the hands of toy soldiers.[31]
>
> A 30-second Kellogg commercial produced for British TV would require [several] alterations to
> be acceptable [elsewhere] in Europe: reference to iron and vitamins would have to be deleted in
> the Netherlands. A child wearing a Kellogg's T-shirt would be edited out in France, where children
> are forbidden from endorsing products on TV. In Germany, the line 'Kellogg makes cornflakes the
> best they've ever been' would be cut because of rules against making competitive claims. After
> alterations, the 30-second commercial would be [only] about five seconds long.[32]

Thus, although advertisers may develop global strategies to guide their overall advertising efforts, specific advertising programs must usually be adapted to meet local cultures and customs, media characteristics and advertising regulations.

Public relations

Public relations Building good relations with the company's various publics by obtaining favourable publicity, building up a good 'corporate image' and handling or heading off unfavourable rumours, stories and events. Major PR tools include press relations, product publicity, corporate communications, lobbying and counselling.

Publicity Activities to promote a company or its products by planting news about it in media not paid for by the sponsor.

Another major mass communication tool is **public relations**—building good relations with the company's various publics by obtaining favourable publicity, building up a good 'corporate image', and handling or heading off unfavourable rumours, stories and events. Public relations is used to promote products, people, places, ideas, activities, organisations and even nations.

The earlier name for marketing public relations was **publicity**, which was seen simply as activities to promote a company or its products by planting news about it in media not paid for by the sponsor. Public relations (PR) is a much broader concept that includes publicity and many other activities. For example, Krispy Kreme opened its first store in Australia in 2003. Krispy Kreme dropped boxes of doughnuts accompanied by a press release to key media outlets and community organisations in the local area. In total, more than 30 000 doughnuts were given away in a three-month period, resulting in over 1000 media mentions around Australia.[33] This combination of sampling and PR resulted in an unprecedented level of publicity for a company which at the time had only one outlet in Australia. Most companies can't obtain this level of publicity for a new product, but PR is a strategy which can be used by any organisation.

PR departments use many different tools:

- *Press relations.* Placing newsworthy information into the news media to attract attention to a person, product or service.
- *Product publicity.* Publicising specific products.
- *Corporate communication.* Creating internal and external communication to promote understanding of the company or institution.
- *Lobbying.* Dealing with legislators and government officials to promote or defeat legislation and regulation.
- *Counselling.* Advising management about public issues and company positions and image.[34]

PR can have a strong impact on public awareness at a much lower cost than advertising. The company does not pay for the space or time in the media. Instead, it pays for staff to develop and circulate information and manage events. If the company develops an interesting story, it could be picked up by several different media, having the same effect as advertising that would cost millions of dollars, as Marketing Highlight 16.3 illustrates. And it would have more credibility than advertising. PR results can sometimes be spectacular, as discussed above in the case of Krispy Kreme's launch in Australia, backed only by PR and sampling.

Despite its potential strengths, PR is sometimes described as a marketing stepchild because of its limited and scattered use. The PR department is usually located at a company's headquarters. Its staff can be so busy dealing with various publics—stockholders, employees, legislators, government officials—that PR programs in support of product marketing objectives may be ignored. And marketing managers and PR practitioners do not always talk the same language. Many PR practitioners see their job as simply communicating, and are less concerned with measuring the impact of their

Krispy Kreme successfully launched their brand in Australia using sampling and public relations.

efforts. Marketing managers, on the other hand, tend to be much more interested in how advertising and PR affect sales and profits.

However, this situation is changing. Many companies now want their PR departments to manage all their activities with a view to marketing the company and improving the bottom line. Some companies are setting up special units called marketing public relations to support company and product promotion and image making directly. Many companies hire marketing PR firms to handle their PR programs or to assist the company PR team. In one survey of American marketing managers, three-quarters reported that their companies used marketing PR. They found it particularly effective in building brand awareness and knowledge for both new and established products. In several cases, it proved more cost effective than advertising.[35]

Major public relations tools

PR professionals use several tools. One of the major tools is news. PR professionals find or create favourable news about the company and its products or people. Sometimes news stories occur naturally, and sometimes the PR person can suggest events or activities that would create news. Speeches can also create product and company publicity. Marketing Highlight 16.3 discusses how Boeing and Airbus used a range of communication strategies, including PR, in an attempt to convince Qantas to buy their planes.

Increasingly, company executives must field questions from the media or give talks at trade associations or sales meetings, and these events can build or hurt the company's image. Another common PR tool is special events, ranging from news conferences, press tours, grand openings and fireworks displays to laser shows, hot-air balloon releases, multimedia presentations and star-studded spectaculars that will reach and interest target publics.

PR people also prepare written materials to reach and influence their target markets. These materials include annual reports, brochures, articles and company newsletters and magazines. Audiovisual materials such as films, slide-and-sound programs and video and audio cassettes are increasingly being used as communication tools. Corporate identity materials can also help to create a corporate identity that the public immediately recognises. Logos, stationery, brochures, signs, business forms, business cards, buildings, uniforms and company cars and trucks all become marketing tools when they are attractive, distinctive and memorable.

Do you want to buy a plane?

How many businesses get to make a $24 billion sale? Just what would you do to try and influence customers if you had the chance of winning a sale that big? Qantas found out, when Boeing and Airbus pulled out all stops to try to win Australia's largest capital expenditure in 2005, a $24 billion purchase of new planes and options to upgrade Qantas's fleet.

Qantas's purchase is an extreme case of a high-involvement business purchase—the choice of plane is critical for an airline, because fuel costs (which vary between planes) now make up around 22% of the cost of a plane ticket. And of course the price is huge, at around $265 million for each plane. So the airline will go to extreme lengths to make the right decision, and sales negotiations can take months, or even years—Qantas had a dedicated team of five people working on the decision for six months. The team sometimes worked round the clock, modelling every flight that each plane would make over its projected life with the airline, to allow Qantas to compare the competing offers from Boeing and Airbus on fuel and maintenance costs.

Both manufacturers were trying to sell Qantas their latest fuel-efficient offerings—Airbus was pushing the Airbus 350 and Boeing the 777 'Worldliner' and 787 'Dreamliner' to replace Qantas's ageing B767s. The airline was keen to place all its orders with one manufacturer, to allow it to obtain the greatest leverage in negotiating a price. The total order, to be delivered over 10 years, added up to the largest aeroplane order in what had been a good year for both manufacturers. So what sort of marketing would you expect from the rival aeroplane makers? Heavy use of sales teams, of course, and repeated visits from Boeing and Airbus senior executives to meet with Qantas's senior executives, to pitch the benefits of their respective planes.

Large business sales don't usually involve mass-media campaigns, but $24 billion is a very large potential sale. So in addition to the traditional tools of business selling, Boeing and Airbus both used advertising heavily, taking out multiple full-page colour ads for their planes in newspapers like *The Australian Financial Review*, and magazines like *Fortune* and *The Economist*. Both companies used billboards around Qantas's headquarters at Sydney airport, with Airbus alone using four billboards proclaiming the fuel burn, payload and seating configuration advantages of the company's yet to be built A350 plane. Airbus's regional vice-president, Rod Mahoney, said that the 'messages are targeted at people in the (aviation) industry, and of the people who drive around the airport, a lot of them work for Qantas'. That might be a subtle way of suggesting that the billboards were targeted at the Qantas CEO, Geoff Dixon, and the Qantas board, who would make the decision about which planes to buy—after all, why advertise to members of the public? Advertising to members of the public only makes sense if they will have any input into the airline's decision, but Boeing's head of communications in the Asia–Pacific admitted that Boeing was trying to raise its brand recognition in Australia, spending $700 000 on advertising in 2005 in Australia alone. 'We really want people to be saying to Qantas or Air New Zealand, "Put me on the two o'clock 777 instead of the two o'clock brand x".'

Robert Pollack, Boeing's Vice President Brand and Market Positioning, also says that selling a new plane is up to passengers. Pollack, who comes from a background selling mobile phones, says that 'One of the first things that we looked at was how other industries marketed products. Consumers don't buy aeroplanes but they fly in aeroplanes. So if there is a perception that one aeroplane is better than another it can be a very effective way to sell it to the airlines. The concept we try to take out is Boeing makes a better aeroplane and as a result your flight will be better.'

So marketing wasn't restricted to repeated visits by sales teams and high-level executives, corporate visits and advertising. Both airlines used public relations heavily, with briefings for aviation writers

Airbus used public relations push (with direct selling) and pull strategies (advertising to users) in its bid to win Qantas's business.

by test pilots, and stories fed to the media about their respective successes. Airbus flew its new A380, the world's largest plane, to Australia on one of its first long-haul test flights, guaranteeing blanket media coverage. Boeing filled its new long-range 777 plane with executives and carefully chosen journalists, and broke the record for a non-stop flight by a commercial airliner, flying 21 596 kilometres without refuelling, from Hong Kong to London, eastbound, generating lots of publicity.

In the end, Boeing won the deal, after competing offers which Qantas's chief financial officer, Peter Gregg, said were 'within a bee's knee of each other'. Boeing will supply Qantas with up to 115 of its 787 Dreamliners, and will also provide Qantas's low-cost subsidiary, Jetstar, with an international fleet of 787s. (But don't expect to fly on them any time soon—none of the planes will be available to Qantas before 2008.)

So did the Boeing and Airbus communications blitz sway Qantas's decision? Not at all, according to Peter Gregg. 'In fact, I wanted to put up my own billboard at the airport with a pencil and a sharpener and a line 'Boeing and Airbus, sharpen your pencils'. And it seems they did; Qantas says that it got a substantial discount on its purchase. Qantas's CEO, Geoff Dixon, said that Boeing won the deal on price and fuel efficiency. He also said that the ease of reconfiguring the 787 was a strong selling point, after Qantas had previously faced more costs than expected in reconfiguring the Airbus jets when switching them between domestic and international routes.

Even if Qantas said that all that advertising and public relations made no difference, it didn't dampen Boeing's enthusiasm for advertising. The day after the deal, full-page, co-branded ads again ran in *The Australian Financial Review*, trumpeting the advantages of the new planes for Qantas and Jetstar. But after a $24 billion order, Boeing could afford to pay for a few more ads, couldn't it?

Sources: Simon Canning, 'Ultimate Big Ticket Item on Sale', *The Australian*, 21 July 2005, p. 17; Steve Creedy, 'Lord of the Flyers', *The Australian*, 17 December 2005, pp. 29, 32; Kevin Done, 'Airlines Adopt a Slimming Regime', *Financial Times*, 29 July 2005, p. 19; Dominic Gates, 'Boeing Snares Coveted Qantas 787 Deal', *The Seattle Times*, 14 December 2005, p. A1; James Hall, 'Boeing and Airbus Jostle for Qantas Order', *The Australian Financial Review*, 5 December 2005, p. 14; James Hall, 'Qantas Backs Boeing with $24bn Deal', *The Australian Financial Review*, 15 December 2005, pp. 1, 18; Tansy Harcourt, 'Airbus Flies in A380 with Eye on Qantas Order', *The Australian Financial Review*, 31 October 2005, p. 14; Scott Rochfort, 'Wake Up, Geoff—Airbus is Talking', *The Sydney Morning Herald*, 27 October 2005, p. 25; Andrea Rothman, 'Boeing's Big Jets Fly Past Rival', *The Australian Financial Review*, 22 November 2005, p. 15.

Questions

1 Qantas's spokesperson says that the advertising and PR campaign made no difference. Would he know? Would he say if it did?

2 Would you expect public opinion to be important in the choice of a plane? Why or why not?

3 Is it possible to measure the outcomes from PR? If so, how?

16.3

Companies can also improve public goodwill by contributing money and time to community service activities. For example, McDonald's Corporation receives substantial favourable publicity from sponsoring accommodation for sick children and their families through the Ronald McDonald House Charities. Even though McDonald's is only one of a number of corporate sponsors, the name of the charity (based on McDonald's support for the first house of the charity in the USA in 1974) means that McDonald's is indelibly linked with the benefits provided by the charity.[36]

SELF-CHECK QUESTIONS

17 What value might be added to a promotional campaign for a new food product by publicising its benefits to cookery editors of women's magazines?

18 What outcomes might there be for a university by offering lecturers to talk at community-interest-group gatherings at no charge to these community bodies?

19 In early 2006 Telstra announced that it was ending its five-year sponsorship of the Australian Museum of Contemporary Arts and also its sponsorship of Bangarra Dance Theatre. If Telstra received some benefit from these sponsorships, what might be the effect of stopping sponsorship? What might be the role of public relations in increasing the benefits of sponsorships, and managing withdrawal from these sorts of arrangements?

Legal issues for marketing communications

The arrival of the Information Age has been a two-edged sword. On the one hand, marketers are able to target consumers better and in the process maintain efficiencies in spending marketing communication dollars. On the other hand, there is greater opportunity to intrude on the consumer, and a growing body of legal and ethical issues now regulates what marketers can and can't do in their marketing communications. Companies must avoid misleading and deceptive practices with their communications, and with their other actions. They must comply with privacy laws in the collection and use of personal data, as covered briefly in this chapter, and in more detail in Chapter 21. In some countries, such as Singapore, the use of comparative advertising isn't allowed, while it is common in Australia and the USA. The marketer needs to know the legislation relevant to their communications programs, and make sure they comply with those laws.

SUMMARY

This chapter examines a number of integrated marketing communications media, tools and technologies: advertising, public relations, direct and online marketing, sales promotion and personal selling. These elements fall into a number of integrated marketing communication classifications: *mass communication* (e.g. advertising and public relations); *targeted communication* (e.g. home shopping via Pay-TV); *in-store communication* (e.g. gondola-end theme banners); and *one-to-one communication* (e.g. direct mail, kiosks and website banner ads).

In preparing marketing communications, the communicator has to understand the nine elements of any communication process: *sender, receiver, encoding, decoding, message, media, response, feedback* and *noise*. Deciding on the integrated marketing communications requires decisions on five key issues: the *objectives*, the *budget*, the *message*, the *media* and, finally, *evaluation of results*. The communicator's first task is to identify the target audience and its characteristics. Next, the communicator has to define the response sought, whether it is *awareness, knowledge, liking, preference, conviction* or *purchase*. Then a message is constructed with an effective content, structure and format. Media must be selected, both for personal and non-personal communication. The message must be delivered by a credible *source*—someone who is an expert and who is trustworthy and likeable. Finally, the communicator must collect *feedback* by watching how much of the market becomes aware, tries the product and is satisfied in the process.

Messages must be designed, evaluated and executed effectively. The *media decision* calls for defining reach, frequency and impact goals; selecting major media types; selecting media vehicles; and scheduling the media. Message and media decisions must be closely coordinated for maximum campaign effectiveness.

The marketing organisation has to decide how much to spend on marketing communications. Factors that determine the communications budget include the product's life-cycle stage, its market share, the competition and amount of clutter, desired advertising frequency and product differentiation. The four main approaches are to spend what the organisation can afford (*affordable method*), to use a percentage of sales (*percentage-of-sales method*), to base IMC on competitors' spending (*competitive-parity*) *method* or to base it on an analysis and costing of the communication objectives and tasks (*objective-and-task method*).

Then the budget must be divided between the major tools to create the *integrated marketing communications program*. Marketing organisations are guided by the characteristics of each IMC tool, the type of product/market, the desirability of a push or a pull strategy, the buyer's readiness state and the product life-cycle stage.

Advertising is the use of paid media by a seller to inform, persuade or remind about its products or organisation. It is a strong element in any IMC program.

International advertising decisions involve additional complexities. A global strategy will usually need to be adapted to local customs and advertising regulations.

Public relations aims to gain favourable publicity and create a favourable image. It is the least used of the major IMC tools, although it has great potential for building awareness and preference. Public relations involves setting PR objectives, selecting PR messages and vehicles, implementing the PR plan and evaluating PR results.

MARKETING ISSUE

The year 2005 was a bad year for the advertising revenue of Australian television stations. The years 2003 and 2004 saw double-digit rates in advertising revenue, but revenue dropped substantially in 2005, with media analysts predicting a growth in revenue of only 3% to 4% in 2006, compared with a consumer price index in 2005 of 2.8%. The decrease in advertising spending is partly due to a shift in advertising to online channels, but also due to lower TV advertising by FMCG companies, which are facing pressure from the powerful retailers to develop in-store promotions at the point of sale.

The only bright spot for the TV networks is increasing amounts being spent on television advertising by the Australian federal government, with reports that in early October 2005 each of the three TV networks received an order for an additional $400 000 worth of ads to be run the following night. As part of its campaign to sell its changes to industrial relations policy to Australian voters, the Federal government allocated $55 million to TV, print and direct mail promotions, and in October the government bought 11 000 TV spots in capital cities. When added to its spending on outdoor, print advertising and direct mail, that amounted to an estimated spending of $22 million in advertising in one month by the government. That's about twice what a car manufacturer would spend on a major product launch. While not a typical month, this high rate of government spending on advertising is part of an ongoing trend; the largest ever advertising campaign in Australia was a $211 million campaign over four years selling the new goods and services tax, and every year the federal government is listed as one of the top spenders on advertising in Australia.

So is this flood of taxpayer-funded advertising effective?

It seems that the $55 million industrial relations campaign made very little difference, if any, to the public's attitude to the legislation. Polls showed that the public's strong opposition to the government's industrial relations changes barely shifted after the advertising blitz, and the popularity of the Prime Minister, John Howard, fell sharply while the advertising was on air. Moreover, the intensity of the advertising was probably counterproductive, according to Professor of Marketing John Roberts; people who disagreed with the policy were likely to have their views reinforced by the endless advertising, while others became habituated by the deluge and ignored the ads. 'It's hard to believe they have done any research on this,' he said. 'There is this naïve belief you get sometimes in management that if a campaign is not working properly you simply open the spigot a bit more, but it doesn't work that way.'

What's the lesson here? Well-planned advertising can be very effective, but it's very hard to change negative attitudes to a product (or a policy) with advertising. And if your (hopefully well-researched) ad campaign isn't working, it's probably better to stop throwing good money away on a bad campaign.[37]

1 What might be appropriate measures for the government's campaign? What could they do if research says that the campaign isn't working?

2 Can you think of an example where advertising has changed your mind about a product, service or policy? If so, how? If not, why not?

3 As governments spend more money on marketing, more and more marketing jobs will be created to communicate political messages to voters. Is this different from commercial marketing? If so, how?

KEY TERMS

DISCUSSING THE ISSUES

1 What do you think is the most effective communication method for long-term brand building? Why?

2 According to advertising expert Stewart Henderson Britt, good advertising objectives explain in detail the intended audience, the advertising message, the desired effects and the criteria for determining effectiveness (e.g. not just 'increase awareness' but 'increase awareness 20%'). Why should these components be part of the advertising objectives? What are some effects, or tasks, an advertiser might want a campaign to achieve?

3 Should media scheduling vary by product category and brand? Why or why not?

4 What is the significance of the fact that advertising expenditure fell after 11 September 2001 even more rapidly than it had already been falling throughout 2001? Might it mean that forecast sales lead to advertising expenditure levels?

5 Is public relations something companies only turn to when their ship has spewed oil into a penguin rookery, or by government when rivers in a developing country are so polluted (by a company or a lax government) that they can no longer support the people who once depended on them for their existence? Or is public relations mainly used when media budgets are to be cut? Explain your answers.

6 What ethical issues are raised by marketing communications?

REFERENCES

1. 'Absolut Cut, *Ad News*, 1 July 2005, p. 15; 'Absolut Makes a Cut into Pre-mix Drinks', *B & T Weekly*, 20 April 2005; Julian Lee, 'Word-of-Mouth Campaign a Cut above the Rest', *The Sydney Morning Herald*, 28 April, 2005 p. 29; John, MacPherson, 'Tapping the Emotions', *The Age*, 26 February 2005, p. 5; Emma Rigby, 'Campaign of the Month', *Revolution*, 28 February 2005, p. 73; Neil Shoe-bridge, 'Take it to the Streets', *Business Review Weekly*, 16 June 2005, p. 96; Gary Silverman, 'Advertisers Try to Keep Tabs on Fickle Viewers', *Financial Times*, 21 July 2005, p. 29; Brian Steinberg, 'TV Networks Find New Ways to Attract Ads', *The Asian Wall Street Journal*, 28 June 2005, pp. A8–A9.

2. Don E. Schultz, 'New Media, Old Problem: Keep Marcom Integrated', *Marketing News*, 29 March 1999, p. 11. Also see Michael McLaren, 'Key to Tech Marketing is Integrated Message', *B to B*, 10 February 2003, p. 16; and Claire Atkinson, 'Integration Still a Pipe Dream for Many', *Advertising Age*, 10 March 2003, pp. 1, 47.

3. For more on integrated marketing communications see Don E. Schultz, Stanley I. Tannenbaum and Robert F. Lauterborn, *Integrated Marketing Communications*, Chicago, IL, NTC, 1992; Don E. Schultz and Philip J. Kitchen, *Communication Globally: An Integrated Marketing Approach*, New York, McGraw-Hill, 2000; Prasad A. Naik and Kalyan Raman, 'Understanding the Impact of Synergy in

Multimedia Communications', *Journal of Marketing Research*, November 2003, pp. 375–388; and Don E. Schultz and Heidi Schultz, *IMC: The Next Generation*, New York, McGraw-Hill, 2004.

4. See Robert J. Lavidge and George A. Steiner, 'A Model of Predictive Measurements of Advertising Effectiveness', *Journal of Marketing*, vol. 25, no. 6, 1961, pp. 59–62.

5. See Russell H. Colley, *Defining Advertising Goals for Measured Advertising Results*, New York, Association of National Advertisers, 1961.

6. Carolyn Setlow, 'Humorous, Feel-Good Advertising Hits Home with Consumers', *DSN Retailing Today*, 22 April 2002, p. 14.

7. See <www.advertisingprinciples.com> for an excellent resource on the evidence on the effects of advertising.

8. 'Easy Marketing Tips for Busy People', available from <www.nrma.com.au/pub/nrma/business/index.shtml>, accessed 6 November, 2005.

9. For a discussion of the effect of different media schedules and how they can be determined by ad tracking see Max Sutherland and Alice K. Sylvester, *Advertising and the Mind of the Consumer: What Works, What Doesn't, and Why*, 2nd edn, London, Allen & Unwin, 2000.

10. See Robert D. Buzzell, 'E. I. DuPont de Nemours & Co: Measurement of Effects of Advertising', in *Mathematical Models and Marketing Management*, Boston, Division of Research, Graduate School of Business Administration, Harvard University, 1964, pp. 157–179.

11. See Max Sutherland and Alice K. Sylvester, op. cit.

12. For a more comprehensive discussion on setting promotion budgets see J. Thomas Russell and W. Ronald Lane, *Kleppner's Advertising Procedure*, 14th edn, Englewood Cliffs, NJ, Prentice Hall, 1999, pp. 148–152.

13. See Donald E. Schultz, Dennis Martin and William P. Brown, *Strategic Advertising Campaigns*, Chicago, Crain Books, 1984, pp. 192–197.

14. For a good discussion see David A. Aaker and James Carman, 'Are You Overspending?', *Journal of Advertising Research*, August/September 1982, pp. 57–70.

15. Gerard J. Tellis, 'Advertising Exposure, Loyalty, and Brand Purchase: A Two-Stage Model of Choice', *Journal of Marketing Research*, May 1988, pp. 134–135. For counterpoints see Magid M. Abraham and Leonard M. Lodish, 'Getting the Most out of Advertising and Promotion', *Harvard Business Review*, May–June 1990, pp. 50–60.

16. One of the best resources for the effectiveness of advertising was still in press at the time of writing: J. Scott Armstrong, *Persuasive Advertising: An Evidence-Based Approach for Developing Advertisements*, forthcoming from Palgrave Macmillan. Also see <www.advertising principles.com>, an excellent resource on the effects of advertising.

17. 'Super Bowl XXXVIII Drives CBS to its Most Watched and Highest Rated Week in Adults', 3 February 2004, accessed online at <www.viacom.com>; Brian Steinberg, 'Advertising: Newest TV Spinoffs: "Situ-mercials"', *Wall Street Journal*, 2 March 2004, p. B11, and '"Friends" End Draws 51 Million Viewers', CNN.com, 7 May 2004.

18. See <www.privacy.gov.au> for more information on privacy legislation, and for the specific requirements for organisations of different sizes.

19. See 'Median Costs per Call by Industry', *Sales & Marketing Management*, 28 June 1993, p. 65.

20. Rochelle Burbury, 'Boom Pushes Call Centres to $86Bn Mark', *The Weekend Australian Financial Review*, 1–2 May 1999, p. 7.

21. Based on Matthew P. Gonring, 'Putting Integrated Marketing Communications to Work Today', *Public Relations Quarterly*, Fall 1994, pp. 45–48.

22. Camille Alarcon, 'Demand Still Hot for Media; Slowing Economy and Rising Petrol Prices Haven't Been Enough to Dampen Media Spending in the Past Financial Year', *B & T Weekly*, 9 September 2005, p. 11.

23. Neville Shoebridge, 'Net Bosses Blinded by the Light', *The Australian Financial Review*, 12 September 2005, pp. 1, 55.

24. Neville Shoebridge, 'Business Scales Back Ad Spend', *The Australian Financial Review*, 14 November 2005, pp. 1, 50.

25. The Rise of the Superbrands', *The Economist*, 5 February 2005, pp. 60–62.

26. Camille Alarcon, 'Demand Still Hot For Media; Slowing Economy and Rising Petrol Prices Haven't Been Enough to Dampen Media Spending in the Past Financial Year', *B & T Weekly*, 9 September 2005, pp. 11–12.

27. Nick O'Malley, 'Hey Big Spender: Canberra Becomes No. 1 Advertiser', *The Sydney Morning Herald*, 24 November 2005, p. 4.

28. Michael Lev, 'Advertisers Seek Global Messages', *New York Times*, 18 November 1991, p. D9.

29. Philip R. Cateora, *International Marketing*, 7th edn, Homewood, IL, Irwin, 1990, p. 462.

30. Ibid., p. 475.

31. Michael R. Czinkota and Ilkka A. Ronkainen, *International Marketing*, 2nd edn, Chicago, Dryden, 1990, p. 615.

32. Cateora, op. cit., pp. 466–467.

33. Simon Canning, 'Tried and Tasted Strategy', *The Australian*, 25 March 2004; Maria Ligerakis, 'Hole in One', *Professional Marketing*, February 2004, pp. 10–13.

34. Adapted from Scott M. Cutlip, Allen H. Center and Glen M. Brown, *Effective Public Relations*, 7th edn, Englewood Cliffs, NJ, Prentice Hall, 1994, pp. 8–21.

35. Tom Duncan, *A Study of How Manufacturers and Service Companies Perceive and Use Marketing Public Relations*, Muncie, Indiana, Ball State University, December 1985; Neville Shoebridge, 'PR: Not So Good at Handling its Own Story Either', *The Australian Financial Review*, 21 November 2005, p. 47.

36. <www.rmhc.org.au>, accessed 6 November 2005.

37. Nick O'Malley, 'Hey Big Spender: Canberra Becomes No. 1 Advertiser', *The Sydney Morning Herald*, 24 November 2005, p. 4; Neville Shoebridge, 'Networks Losing Ad-Talks Muscle, *The Australian Financial Review*, 31 October 2005, p. 47; Neville Shoebridge, 'Summer Season Brings Ad Rate Rises, *The Australian Financial Review*, 31 October 2005, p. 47.

PHOTO/AD CREDITS

CASE STUDY

Government advertising: benefiting society or political parties?

Andrew Hughes, Australian National University

Introduction

Governments in Australia at all levels are increasing their spending on all forms of advertising. According to the Department of Prime Minister and Cabinet (PM&C) since the 1996/97 financial year expenditure on government advertising has totalled $929 million (Finance and Public Administration References Committee 2005, p. 13).

In 2003–2004 prices, the total expenditure on government advertising through the federal government's Central Advertising System for the period 1996–97 to 2003–04 was $1.014 billion (Finance and Public Administration References Committee 2005, p. 13).

With election year 'spikes' in spending (Finance and Public Administration References Committee 2005, p. 31) noted by many researchers, the question many people ask is whether any of this advertising is effective. Are these ads really informing or reminding people about a program that may be of benefit to them or is it merely done for political purposes, that is, to promote specific party policy objectives and to persuade people to vote for one particular party over another?

Before these questions can be answered there needs to be a brief examination of theory on advertising effectiveness.

Advertising effectiveness

Advertising effectiveness is defined by the world's leading marketing organisation, the American Marketing Association (AMA) as being:

An evaluation of the extent to which a specific advertisement or advertising campaign meets the objectives specified by the client. There is a wide variety of approaches to evaluation, including inquiry tests, recall tests, and market tests. The measurement approaches include recall of ads and advertising themes, attitudes toward the advertising, persuasiveness, and impact on actual sales levels (<www.marketingpower.com>, viewed 20 January 2006).

It therefore can be seen that measuring advertising effectiveness can be a complex process, but at the centre is the need to meet the objectives for the organisation. These may be in relation to the advertising itself, the overall campaign, and even corporate and strategic objectives.

However, advertising has many forms and therefore each type used in a campaign should have its own objective. According to the AMA an advertising objective is:

A statement prepared by the advertiser (often in association with an advertising agency) to set forth specific goals to be accomplished and the time period in which they are to be accomplished. Objectives can be stated in such terms as products to be sold, the amount of trial purchases, the amount of repeat purchases, audience members reached, the frequency with which audience members are reached, and percentages of the audience made aware of the advertising or the product (<www.marketingpower.com>, viewed 20 January 2006).

When it comes to determining advertising objectives, an organisation should always try to ensure that they can be turned into specific measurable goals, a technique favoured by Colley, whose book *Defining Advertising Goals for Measured Advertising Results (DAGMAR)* sets out 52 possible advertising objectives and ways to measure them effectively.

In summary, then, the effectiveness of any advertising can be measured by how well it meets the objectives of the organisation, be these

CASE
STUDY

increased sales, awareness or votes! So going back to the issue of government advertising, can we now measure how effective it has been and therefore whether or not it has been a waste of taxpayers' money or a wise investment that has helped society?

Case study—Defence Force recruitment advertising

It should be noted that while a large amount of money is spent on government advertising, some of it is for largely uncontroversial purposes, such as recruiting for the Australian Defence Force (ADF). According to a research note prepared by the Federal Parliamentary Library, from the period 1991 to 2004 the federal government has spent $166.8 million on Defence Force recruitment (Finance and Public Administration References Committee 2005, p. 26). The overall objective for the Defence Force recruiting campaign was stated in the 2000 Department of Defence White Paper—to have a permanent total Defence Force size of 54 000 by the year 2010.

In the 2004/05 financial year, the Defence Personnel Executive, the section of the Department of Defence that handles recruitment advertising, spent over $17 million on recruitment advertising, which although large is still a dramatic decrease from the $42.1 million spent in the 2000/01 financial year (Department of Defence Annual Report 2005).

So applying the theory explained above, has the campaign been successful? Certainly awareness levels of the Defence Force are high, particularly of the wide range of occupations available with the Defence Forces. Although figures are unavailable on the actual reach and frequency effectiveness of the Defence Force campaign, it could be safely assumed that it has been successful here as the targeted audience of people aged 18–35 are exposed to many ADF recruiting ads in different media types, from bus shelters and cinemas, to TV and the Internet.

However, the objective of the campaign is not about increased awareness of the Defence Force but about increasing its size to 54 000 personnel by 2010. According to a recent report (Bishop 2005) the ADF will fail to meet this target and has for the past six years failed to meet their yearly recruiting target by 20%. Advertising can't solely be to blame for this occurring, as there have also been high-profile inquiries into bullying of recruits and the ADF is also competing for the same target market as large corporations which offer better pay and conditions. But could the advertising have been more effective in achieving its objective by perhaps showing how the ADF was a better product for prospective applicants than large corporations or showing what recruits did in training, rather than using the more formal, conservative ads favoured by the ADF?

Can you do it better?

Once the initial recruitment figures showed that the campaign wasn't working, the ADF could have found out why their advertising was not meeting their objectives and asked if their objectives were realistic. But what else could they have done? Time to put yourself into the ADF's marketing manager shoes and answer the following questions.

Sources: American Marketing Association <www.marketingpower. com>, accessed 20 January 2006; Department of Defence, 2005, *Annual Report*, Commonwealth of Australia, Canberra; R. Colley, *Defining Advertising Goals for Measured Advertising Results*, Association of National Advertisers, New York, 1961; Sen. M. Bishop (2005) 'Second reading debate: Defence Legislation Amendment Bill (No. 1) 2005', Senate, *Debates*, 6 September 2005; Senate Finance and Public Administration Reference Committee, 2005, 'Government Advertising and Accountability', Commonwealth of Australia, Canberra.

QUESTIONS

1. Once the initial figures came through that the campaign was not working, what should have been the first measure of effectiveness that the ADF might have used to ascertain if their advertising was effective?

2. How would you redesign the ADF ads to improve their effectiveness? In particular, what things would you do to make the ads more appealing to women?

3. Government advertising also includes campaigns such as road safety, healthy diets and industrial relations changes. Taking one of these campaigns as an example, how does the ADF campaign compare with it and what lessons could the ADF learn from it?

CASE STUDY

CHAPTER 17

Managing sales promotion and selling

Boeing: www.boeing.com

Flight Centre: www.flightcentre.com

Pepto Bismal: www.pg.com

O nce an organisation has designed a product to respond to customer desires, it needs to decide on other components of the marketing mix. For example, the organisation needs to decide how it can best make customers aware of the product, and the best way to sell the product. For some products, these decisions are relatively straightforward; if you are selling fast-moving consumer goods, it's critical to obtain wide distribution so customers can find the product where they normally shop. The biggest challenge then may be how to make consumers aware of the new product. Should the marketer offer free trials in-store for a new food product, or perhaps have some form of sales promotion, such as a discount or competition to encourage trial?

For many products, however, the selling process is more complex, and the role and structure of the salesforce are much more important in making a sale. This is particularly true of financial services (such as home loans or insurance products), complex electronic products or situations where there are a large number of competing products (such as airflights or holiday packages). In these sorts of circumstances the buyer may not feel confident enough to decide between competing products, and an expert salesperson can play a critical role in influencing the purchase decision. The organisation then needs to decide how it will best sell its product (through its own sales staff or through a third party?) and how best to encourage staff to sell one product rather than another.

Whether an organisation is using its own selling staff or selling through a third party, commissions are commonly used to encourage sales staff to make more sales. Yet commissions alone can result in salesperson activity that is incompatible with the long-term interests of the organisation, and can encourage the stereotypical behaviour of the pushy salesperson, encouraging salespeople to push products that aren't suitable for the customer, resulting in long-term customer dissatisfaction. The insurance industry found this out years ago, when sales of life insurance were typically rewarded by a one-off commission to the sales agent. Many dissatisfied customers didn't renew their life insurance policies, meaning that the insurance company didn't even recoup the cost of the commission, and also suffered damage to its reputation as a result of its salesforce activity.

Salespeople play an important role in creating value for customers and building customer relationships.

In an attempt to ensure that sales staff's activity is consistent with the long-term interests of the company, many organisations have changed to reward systems which are more consistent with the long-term interests of the organisation. For example, mobile phone sellers are often rewarded with a 'trailing' commission system, where they receive an ongoing commission based on the value of each customer. Car companies will typically reward salespeople partly on sales volume, but also on the customer's satisfaction, as measured by post-purchase surveys. These value- and satisfaction-based reward systems have the advantage that the salesperson is rewarded for producing more profitable and more satisfied customers and research shows that providing customer-satisfaction-based incentives does encourage sales staff to be more customer oriented.[1]

But commissions and other incentives to sales staff (whether sales based or satisfaction based) also add to costs, and these costs either need to be passed on to customers or absorbed by the organisation in lower margins. So deciding how much commission or incentive to provide to the sales staff is not an easy decision. Telstra and Qantas, Australia's largest phone company and airline respectively, have recently made decisions to cut the commission they pay their external sales channels—third-party mobile phone retailers for Telstra, and travel agents for Qantas. The action has followed strong price competition in both industries, and runs a risk that agents will recommend competitors. The news also sent shock waves through both industries, with shares in Flight Centre, Australia's largest travel agency, dropping 12% on the news of Qantas's new commission structure, reflecting the importance of commissions for travel agencies.[2] Both Qantas and Telstra are large, and have significant sales channels themselves which they hope will pick up some of the business which has formerly gone through agents (with commissions), so the savings in commission may more than compensate for any lost sales. The risk appears to be higher for Telstra, however, which is said to obtain about half of its new contracted customers and about 80% of its lower-revenue, prepaid customers from third-party dealers.[3] Their new strategies will be a test of whether the old commission structure added value, and both companies are likely to be watching the results nervously.

After reading this chapter you should be able to:

1. Describe sales promotion tools and techniques that may be used to create immediacy, close sales and reward loyal customers.

2. Discuss the role of a company's salespeople in creating value for customers and building customer relationships.

3. Identify the six major salesforce management steps.

4. Explain how companies design salesforce strategy and structure.

5. Explain how companies recruit, select and train salespeople.

6. Describe how companies compensate and supervise salespeople, and how they evaluate salesforce effectiveness.

7. Discuss the personal selling process, distinguishing between transaction-oriented marketing and relationship marketing.

Many marketing organisations use a salesforce to maintain relationships with their customers and to develop dialogue with potential customers. Robert Louis Stevenson once noted that 'everyone lives by selling something'. Salesforces are found in non-profit as well as for-profit organisations, and often trade under department names other than sales or marketing departments. Universities employ international divisions and agents to sell their courses to potential students, often far from the university's home country. Churches use membership committees to attract new members. Government bodies such as the Australian government's Austrade conduct seminars on potential export markets in order to encourage exporters to enter new markets. Hospitals and museums use fundraisers to contact donors and raise money. In this chapter we examine the role of personal selling in the organisation, salesforce management decisions and basic principles of personal selling.

Salespeople are not the only means that companies use to close sales, maintain relationships and reward loyalty. If marketing organisations use mass communication to help consumers form a preference for a brand of toothpaste, they are also likely to use sales promotions. If marketing organisations have their salespeople target individual business customers to buy consumables and industrial products, or use direct and online techniques, they are also likely to use sales promotions. We begin this chapter with a detailed examination of the types of sales promotion tools and their use, before turning to a discussion of personal selling and sales management.

Sales promotion

Sales promotion
Short-term incentives to encourage purchase of a product or service.

'Sales promotion' has different meanings in different contexts, because sales promotions take many forms depending on the objectives to be met, the type of market and product and the budget available. However all **sales promotions** are tools used to prompt an immediate sale, whether in-store or through direct channels. The term covers a range of incentives used with mass-marketed consumer goods that are promoted via media advertising as well as by direct marketing. Sales promotions are also used in business-to-business marketing.

In the UK, sales promotion is regarded as any controlled activity conducted through the media. In the USA it is any out-of-the-ordinary consumer or trade offer or aid of limited duration that speeds up a sale. The definition from the Council of Sales Promotion Agencies tries to overcome an image of short-term effectiveness:

> [Sales promotion is] the act of influencing customer/consumer perception and behaviour to build market share and sales which reinforce brand image.

The main tools of sales promotion include:
- samples
- redeemable coupons
- cash-back offers
- cents-off deals or price packs
- premium offers
- advertising specialties
- patronage rewards
- point-of-purchase (POP) promotions
- contests and games of chance and skill.

Each of these tools is designed to give immediacy and to encourage purchase of a product or service by changing the perceived value-for-money equation. We see these tools everywhere. All too often, however, they are used to overcome a problem such as faltering sales in a poor selling period rather than as proactive selling tools. And if used too often they can simply be a waste of money if they do not deliver a short- or long-term increase in profits. If products are frequently on promotion, consumers will alter their buying habits; they may stock up when a product is on sale (e.g. for fast-moving consumer goods) or delay purchases until the product is on sale (e.g. with new seasons' fashion lines). If promotions result in this sort of behaviour, they may appear to be successful (because sales will increase during the period of promotion) but the promotion will actually be decreasing profits for the marketing organisation.

Rapid growth of sales promotions

Sales promotion tools are used by most organisations, including manufacturers, distributors, retailers and not-for-profit institutions. They are targeted towards final buyers (*consumer promotions*), retailers and wholesalers (*trade promotions*), business customers (*business promotions*) and members of the salesforce (*salesforce promotions*). Today, in the average US consumer packaged-goods company, sales promotion accounts for around 76% of all marketing expenditures.[4]

Several factors have contributed to the rapid growth of sales promotion, particularly in consumer markets. First, inside the company, product managers face greater pressures to increase their current sales, and promotion is viewed as an effective short-run sales tool. Second, externally, the company faces more competition and competing brands are less differentiated. Increasingly, competitors are using sales promotion to help differentiate their offers. Third, advertising efficiency has declined because of rising costs, media clutter and legal restraints. Finally, consumers have become more deal oriented, and ever-larger retailers are demanding more deals from manufacturers. Marketing Highlight 17.1 discusses the issues underlying this increasing use of promotions.

The growing use of sales promotion has resulted in *promotion clutter*, similar to advertising clutter. Consumers are increasingly tuning out promotions, weakening their ability to trigger immediate purchase. Manufacturers are now searching for ways to rise above the clutter, such as offering larger coupon values or creating more dramatic point-of-purchase displays.

Purpose of sales promotion

Sales promotion tools vary in their specific objectives. The goal may be to increase usage, like the Sun-Herald adhesive note promotion, which encourages occasional buyers to subscribe. Or the goal may be to get trial: when McDonalds launched its Deli Choices sandwich range, it promoted the range by attaching adhesive notes to the front page of major newspapers, offering a free Deli Choice roll. Similarly free samples distributed in a store are often used to generate immediate sales. Sellers use sales promotions like these to attract new triers, to reward brand-loyal customers and thereby retain them, to reduce the time between purchases, and even to turn light users into medium or heavy users. The aim might also be to regain past purchasers who have ceased buying. New triers of a product category fall into one of three groups:

1 non-users
2 loyal users of another brand
3 brand switchers.

Research shows that only a small percentage of consumers are 100% brand loyal, and that most consumers switch between different brands.[5] These brand switchers can often be induced to buy another brand through sales promotions. This is often because brand switchers are not fully satisfied with any one single brand, and a sales promotion presents a different value-for-money perception, thereby tipping the scales in favour of the promoted brand. However, the brand switcher is unlikely to become brand loyal because of a sales promotion alone. When coupled with image advertising there is a greater likelihood of long-term adoption, but no guarantee of this. Where there are already great differences between brands, there is a greater likelihood of the switch to a promoted brand becoming a permanent change. Where most brands are seen as similar in taste, performance or perceptual value, then brand switching is likely to continue.

Many marketers think of sales promotions as having the effect of breaking down brand loyalty, in contrast to advertising which is thought of as a means of building up brand loyalty. Because of this, a great deal of thought needs to go into splitting the budget between the two. Product managers will often determine what they need to spend on trade promotions first, followed by sales promotions,

Adhesive notes are an increasingly popular sales promotion tool.

and then spend whatever is left on mass media, targeted media or one-to-one media. The danger in doing this is that the price- or deal-promoted brand is lowered in value in consumers' eyes. In other words, it represents value only when promoted in some way. Thus, the exact opposite effect to the desired result may occur. No one knows the exact parameters, but the risk appears to increase greatly if a company puts a well-known leading brand on promotion more than 30% of the time.[6] If consumers buy extra products during a promotion, but do not use the product any faster (such as detergent or toothpaste) promotions can result in a temporary increase in sales (at lower margins) followed by a fall in sales, with an overall loss of margin. So the effect of promotion depends in part on the product; some products, such as bathroom tissue, coffee, detergents and paper towels, tend to be stored or 'stockpiled' by consumers, who don't use the product any faster.[7] In contrast, other products, such as bacon, salted snacks, soft drinks and yogurt, tend to be used faster if the consumer has more in their cupboards, so promotion can increase total sales more easily.[8]

Most analysts believe that sales promotion activities do not build long-term consumer preference and loyalty, unlike advertising. Instead, sales promotion usually produces short-term sales that cannot be maintained. Those companies with low market share find sales promotions advantageous because they cannot match the media spending by market leaders. Nor can they gain and keep valuable shelf space unless they buy their way in with trade promotion coupled with the excitement of a few sales promotions. Thus, price competition is often used for small or emerging brands seeking to enlarge their share. Promotion can be very effective for a new product, by encouraging consumers to try the product, but is usually less effective for a market leader whose growth lies in expanding the entire product category.[9]

As discussed in Marketing Highlight 17.1, powerful supermarket chains can put pressure on their suppliers to use promotion as a way of increasing supermarket profits and attracting customers. The result is that many packaged-goods companies believe they are forced into using more sales promotions than they would really like to. Companies such as Kellogg, Kraft and Procter & Gamble have blamed the heavy use of sales promotion for decreasing brand loyalty, increasing consumer price sensitivity, emphasising short-run marketing planning and eroding brand-quality image.

Other marketers, however, dispute this.[10] They argue that the heavy use of sales promotion is a symptom of these problems, not a cause. They point to more basic causes, such as slower population growth, more educated consumers, industry overcapacity, the decreasing effectiveness of advertising, the increase in retailer power and the focus by companies on short-run profits.

These marketers assert that sales promotions provide many important benefits to manufacturers as well as to consumers. Sales promotions let manufacturers adjust to short-term changes in supply and demand and to differences in customer segments. They let manufacturers charge a higher trade price to test 'how high is high'. Sales promotions encourage consumers to try new products instead of staying with their current choices. They lead to more varied retail formats. Finally, sales promotions lead to greater consumer awareness of prices, and consumers themselves enjoy some satisfaction from seeing themselves as smart shoppers when they take advantage of special offers.

Sales promotions are often used in conjunction with 'theme' or 'image' advertising. The addition of sales promotion razzamatazz to a media campaign can rejuvenate a tired series of advertisements, and give them more pulling power. Also, it should not be forgotten that sales promotions can develop the relationship between key account managers and buyers at retail level, and be motivating for both external and internal salespeople. In summary, successful use of sales promotions relies on using them correctly—starting with setting objectives, selecting the right tools, developing the best program, pre-testing where necessary before implementing the promotion, and completing the process with an evaluation of the effectiveness of the promotion.

Changing push and pull in the supermarkets

Consumer packaged-goods companies such as Kraft, Procter & Gamble, Kellogg and Gillette grew into giants by using mostly pull promotion strategies. They used massive doses of advertising to differentiate their products, gain market share and build brand equity and customer loyalty. But during the past few decades, companies around the world have become more 'pushy', de-emphasising advertising and putting more of their marketing budgets into trade and consumer sales promotions. Trade promotions (trade allowances, displays, co-operative advertising, slotting fees, discounts and premiums like buy-one-get-one-free offers) constitute the largest expense for manufacturers, after the cost of manufacturing the product, and promotions now account for around 48% of total marketing spending by fast-moving consumer goods (FMCG) manufacturers. In contrast, mass-media advertising spending now comprises only about 25% of FMCG marketing spend, down from about 40% 20 years ago.

Why have these companies shifted so heavily toward push strategies? One reason is that mass-media campaigns have become more expensive and less effective in recent years. Television advertising costs have risen while audiences have fallen off, making TV advertising less cost effective. And in these days of brand extensions and me-too products, companies sometimes have trouble finding meaningful product differences to feature in advertising. So they have differentiated their products through price reductions, premium offers, coupons and other push techniques.

But a large factor speeding the shift from pull to push has been the growing strength of retailers. Retail giants now have the power to demand and get what they want—and what they want is more push. Mass-media advertising dollars go to the TV stations, newspapers and magazines, but push promotion benefits the retailers directly. Consumer promotions give retailers an immediate sales boost, and cash from trade allowances and other trade promotions contributes significantly to retailer profits, since the margins on grocery items are very low. Thus, producers must often use push just to obtain good shelf space and other support from important retailers.

The problem is particularly acute in Australian supermarkets, where Coles and Woolworths control over 78% of the packaged grocery market and, with their related companies, also control around 30% of all retail spending, making Australia one of the most concentrated retail markets in the world. In contrast, in Britain the top four supermarket chains together control only 56% of the market. This means that Coles and Woolworths can ask for increased promotional spending by their suppliers, because, as one retail specialist puts it, 'If I am in packaged food and I don't get to deal with Coles and Woolworths, I am out of business'.

However, many marketers are concerned that the increased use of push will lead to fierce price competition and a never-ending spiral of price slashing and deal making. If used improperly, push promotion can mortgage a brand's future for short-term gains. Sales promotion buys short-run reseller support and consumer sales, but advertising builds long-run brand equity and consumer preference. By robbing the media advertising budget to pay for more sales promotion, companies might win the battle for short-run earnings but lose the war for long-run brand equity, consumer loyalty and market share. In fact, some analysts blame the shift away from advertising dollars for a recent two-decade-long drop in the percentage of consumers who buy only well-known brands.

Of special concern is the overuse of price promotions. The regular use of price as a selling tool can destroy brand equity by encouraging consumers to seek value through price rather than through the benefits of the brand. Many marketers are too quick to drive short-term sales by reducing prices rather than building long-term brand equity through advertising. In fact, studies show that almost 60% of consumers now go to the store to make a purchase without a specific brand in mind. Once they get to the store, shoppers are often more swayed by special prices, sales and premium offers than by branding.

In cases where price is a key part of the brand's positioning, featuring price makes sense. But for brands where price does not underlie value, 'price promotions are really desperate acts by brands that have their backs against the wall,' says one marketing executive. 'Generally speaking, it is better to stick to your guns with price and invest in advertising to drive sales.'

Jack Trout, a well-known marketing consultant, cautions that some categories tend to self-destruct by always being on sale. Discount pricing has become routine for a surprising number of companies. Even Coca-Cola and Pepsi, two of the world's most popular brands, engage in regular price wars that ultimately tarnish their brand equity. Trout offers several 'Commandments of Discounting', such as 'Thou shalt not offer discounts because everyone else does', 'Thou shalt be creative with your discounting', 'Thou shalt put time limits on the deal', and 'Thou shalt stop discounting as soon as you can'.

Many consumer companies know that it's not a question of sales promotion versus advertising, or of push versus pull. Success lies in finding the best mix of the two: consistent advertising to build long-run brand value and consumer preference, and sales promotion to create short-run trade support and consumer excitement. The company needs to blend both push and pull elements into an integrated promotion program that will meet immediate consumer and retailer needs as well as long-run strategic needs.

However, with moves by Coles to lift sales of home brands in its stores to 30% of all goods sold (up from the current levels of 10–12%, which are low by world standards) Australian manufacturers are reporting increasing pressure from retailers to do even more in-store promotional activity. The heavy promotion expenses for companies which sell in Australian supermarkets aren't likely to change any time soon.

Sources: 2005 Trade Spending Survey, Wilton, CT, Cannondale Associates, 2005; Jack Trout, 'Prices: Simple Guidelines to Get Them Right', *Journal of Business Strategy*, November–December 1998, pp. 13–16; Tim Ambler, 'Kicking Price Promotion Habit is like Getting off Heroin—Hard', *Marketing*, 27 May 1999, p. 24; Alan Mitchell, 'When Push Comes to Shove, It's All About Pull', *Marketing Week*, 9 January 2003, pp. 26–27; 'Promotions and Incentives: Offers You Can't Refuse', *Marketing Week*, 15 April 2004, p. 31; E. Craig Stacey, 'Abandon TV at Your Own Risk', *Advertising Age*, 7 June 2004, p. 32; Simon Evans, 'Coles Bows to Suppliers' Pressure', *The Australian Financial Review*, 2 August, 2005 p. 15; John Hennessy, 'Trade Dollars not Very Loyal', *Retail Wire*, 21 March 2005, <www.retailwire.com>, accessed 3 January 2006; Brad Howarth, 'Stuck in the Middle', *Business Review Weekly*, 2 June 2005, p. 58; David James, 'Coles' Brave New World', *Business Review Weekly*, 7 April 2005, p. 66; Neil Shoebridge, 'Coles Lifts Incentives for House Brands', *The Australian Financial Review*, 5 September 2005, p. 54; David Wellman, 'Changing Expectations: Suppliers and Retailers Remain Unhappy with Trade Promotion Spending and Results. Both Sides, However, Believe Change is Coming', *Frozen Food Age*, 1 May 2005, p. 33.

Questions

1 What are the advantages of trade promotion? What are the disadvantages?

2 What strategies could be used by manufacturers to counter the market power of Coles and Woolworths?

3 Do you think that the Internet has the potential to be an alternative to in-store promotion? Why or why not?

17.1

Setting sales promotion objectives

Sales promotion objectives are as varied as the methods used. Sellers may use consumer promotions to increase short-term sales or to help build long-term market share. The objective may be one of the following:

- to entice consumers to try a new product or brand
- to lure consumers away from competitors' products or brands
- to get consumers to 'load up' on a mature product
- to hold and reward loyal customers.

In general terms, sales promotions should be consumer franchise-building promotions—they should promote the product's positioning and include a selling message along with the deal. Loyalty programs such as retailer stamps (e.g. buy 10 coffees and get one free) and airline frequent-flyer programs do help to build and maintain customer relationships. However, the objective should be to build *long-run* consumer demand rather than to prompt temporary brand switching, or reward customers by giving them something that they would have paid for. If properly designed, every sales promotion tool has consumer franchise-building potential, even where a price cut is included.[11]

Selecting sales promotion tools

Many tools can be used to accomplish sales promotion objectives. The marketing planner should consider the type of market, the sales promotion objectives, the competition and the costs and effectiveness of each tool.

Consumer promotion tools

The main consumer promotion tools include samples, redeemable coupons, cash-back offers, cents-off deals, premium offers, advertising specialties, patronage rewards, point-of-purchase displays and demonstrations, as well as contests, sweepstakes and games.

Samples are offers of a trial amount of a product, such as a miniature tube of toothpaste distributed as a letterbox drop, or a sachet of perfume stitched into a magazine such as *Dolly*. Some samples are free, while others carry a small price to help cover costs. Sampling is often used to introduce new consumer and industrial goods. It is a very effective but expensive way to create awareness of and trial of a new product.

Redeemable coupons are used extensively in the USA, where consumers clip some five billion of them in a year and, with an average face value of 70 cents, save some $US3.5 billion ($A6.3 billion) per year.[12] Coupons have much lower usage in Australia and Southeast Asia, because the powerful supermarket chains have resisted their use. As a result, coupons in these countries will sometimes be redeemed by direct mail, as a cash-back offer, but unless the offer is very good cash-back offers tend to have much lower take-up rates than coupons.

Cash-back offers (or rebates) usually involve the consumer sending in labels—in South Australia a letter suffices because of the local state consumer protection laws—that the manufacturer exchanges for money. The marketer may refund all or part of the purchase price in exchange for this 'proof of purchase'. The more 'qualifiers' one puts on such a scheme, the lower the redemption rate. Qualifiers in this instance refer to requirements such as sending a stamped, self-addressed envelope. If the cash-back offer is for $2 and it costs the consumer a dollar in postage to reclaim the cash, then many consumers won't bother to take up the offer.

Cents-off deals or **price packs** are the most common form of promotion at store level in Australia and Southeast Asia. Such promotions are usually offered for a one-week period, and are financed by the marketer, even though it may appear to consumers that the retailer is offering the promotion. These sorts of promotions are attractive to retailers, because sales managers, key account managers and every salesperson in the field knows that price cuts are usually the quickest way to lift sales and meet a sales budget. Some offers do not involve a direct cut in price but may involve 'two for one' deals. That is, for the price of a single pack, the buyer gets two packs—or perhaps even a related product such as a toothbrush bundled with toothpaste for the price of the toothpaste.

Premium offers are goods offered at a greatly reduced price as an incentive to buy a product. Such an offer may be promoted on the outside of the pack, or the pack itself may contain a bonus, such as a commemorative mug or reusable glass, thus forming the offer. In all instances in which a manufacturer organises such an offer in Australia, it is taken up by mail or phone. If a retailer

Samples Free or discounted goods provided at store level or through the media, such as inserts designed to facilitate product trial.

Redeemable coupons Coupons carried on-pack or in other media that when forwarded to a marketer or an appointed agent will be redeemed for a product or service, or even a discount on the next purchase.

Cash-back offers Cash discounts usually received by forwarding 'proof of purchase' where state legislation permits.

Cents-off deals Temporary price discounts, usually offered at retail level; however, they are also offered by direct marketers.

Price packs Reduced prices that are marked by the producer directly on the label or package.

Premium offers Goods offered free of charge or at a reduced price as an incentive to buy a product.

organises such an offer, then it is usually honoured at store level. A self-liquidating offer is another type of offer in which a product or service is sold below its normal price. A marketer of canned Indian curries might, for instance, offer a rice steamer at half the usual retail price. In such cases, a mailing house is usually used to receive the coupon or proof of purchase and to dispatch the premium.

Advertising specialties take the form of pens, key rings and other novelty items that are given out freely to consumers either in-store or at special events, such as sporting events. Many sales managers favour this type of incentive for use with industrial buyers where their company policy permits the acceptance of such gifts. In one US study, 63% of all consumers surveyed were either carrying or wearing an advertising specialty item. More than three-quarters of those who had an item could recall the advertiser's name or message before showing the item to the interviewer.[13]

Advertising specialties Useful articles imprinted with an advertiser's name, given as gifts to consumers.

Patronage rewards are cash, merchandise or service rewards offered to consumers who make continual use of a company's product or service. They are akin to 'volume rebates' offered by suppliers to industrial companies purchasing a certain volume each year or month. The most common are the 'loyalty' or 'frequent buyer' cards offered by many coffee shops and sandwich bars, where a buyer is rewarded with a free item after purchasing a number of items. As with any loyalty scheme, such rewards are only effective if they increase sales more than the cost of the loyalty scheme. A loyalty scheme which gives away products to customers who would have bought them at full price will decrease revenues, unless the scheme attracts substantial extra sales, so any loyalty scheme should be carefully considered.

Patronage rewards Cash, merchandise or service rewards offered to consumers who make continual use of a company's product or service, for example frequent-flyer plans.

Trading stamps such as the Green Shield Stamps offered by retailers in the UK and occasionally by Asian retailers are another form of patronage rewards. Stamps are issued at the checkout depending on the total value of the purchases made, and can later be redeemed on goods that range from saucepans to new motor vehicles. Trading stamps might have offered some temporary advantage to the first retailer to offer them, but the stamps are easily copied by other retailers, and then result in increased costs for every retailer, without resulting in extra sales.[14]

Point-of-purchase (POP) promotions can take a number of forms. They may include theme promotions by companies, such as one by Birdseye involving fishing nets and imitation fish hanging over the frozen food cabinet, paid for by the manufacturer and organised with the retail buyers. For a fee approaching $5000 per large store per week, theme displays can be set up to provide additional merchandising space, usually to coincide with a cents-off or other type of sales promotion. Alternatively, promotions may consist of using prominent in-store positions, such as gondola ends. POP promotions may also include wobblers and danglers (advertising signs which hang off shelves) or small posters. However, this form of promotion is often resisted by retailers as it can create clutter and mess. It is always wise to ask the retail buyer before committing funds to fancy POP display material that might never be used.

Point-of-purchase (POP) promotions Offers ranging from theme promotions in-store to specially arranged selling areas.

Contests and games of chance and skill give consumers a chance to win something either through skill or the 'luck of the draw'. A contest that asks the consumer to write in and 'say why you like Vegemite best of all in 20 words or less' is considered a game of skill. So too is the contest that asks the consumer to fill in the missing letter in a word such as 'Ve_emite'. These kinds of contests are sometimes linked to secondary prizes through a random draw of a number or name. Under these circumstances, the contest becomes a game of chance. Where a game of chance is involved, the relevant government department responsible for gaming and lotteries needs to vet the conditions of entry and allocate an approval number. This number must be featured on every contest form or advertisement, whether in the main media or on-pack. There are also requirements as to publication of the rules of entry as well as the publication of prize winners. Once again, the greater the number of conditions of entry the lower the response rate. Many marketers achieving a response rate of 3–5% feel they have achieved a reasonable result. While it does not sound a very large proportion of

Contests and games of chance and skill Promotional events that give consumers the chance to win something of value by luck or by the use of skill.

acceptances, a promotion can create some excitement at store level, and when coupled with media advertising and/or publicity the desired result often shows up in the sales response. The truth is that many people buy the product because they intend to take up the offer, but forget when they get home after shopping and are surrounded by hungry children, spouses and animals.

Trade promotion tools

More promotional funds are directed to wholesalers and retailers than to consumers. These funds take the form of trade promotions organised by sales and key account managers and their retail counterparts, the buyer. Such moneys are spent in an endeavour to gain distribution, good merchandising space and co-operative advertising, and to gain sales in cents-off promotions.

Many sales promotions aimed at consumers are accompanied by trade promotions, whereby the various department managers at store level can win prizes for the best merchandising display or the highest sales levels during a promotion.

Manufacturers also pay various allowances to retailers for such activities as advertising, displays and physical distribution. In some cases, the manufacturer may offer free goods to wholesalers and retailers who buy a certain quantity or who carry and merchandise a certain flavour or size in a range of products. In some industries, 'push money'—cash or incentives—is paid to dealers or their salesforce to 'push' the manufacturer's goods. Marketing Highlight 17.2 discusses how promotion and the salesforce are used by coffee suppliers to try to win long-term contracts from cafés.

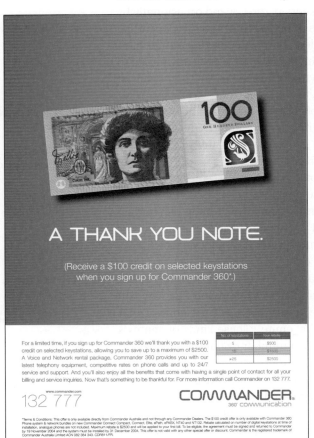

Promotions can be used to achieve additional sales, for example by offering a discount on related products after a sale.

Business-to-business promotion tools

Industrial marketers also use promotions to gain awareness for new products, or to increase penetration of a particular industry by increasing business leads for their salesforce. They use many of the already mentioned sales promotion tools, adapting them to suit their own situations, but here we concentrate on conventions, trade shows and sales contests.

Conventions and trade shows are used by vendors to gain such benefits as finding new sales leads, contacting customers, introducing new products, meeting new customers, selling more to existing customers and educating customers with publications and audiovisual presentations. For example, at PC exhibitions, companies such as Microsoft, Compaq and others ranging from hardware marketers to software firms and retailers talk directly with business and home computer users, displaying all manner of electronic communications hardware and software. By showing the latest technology as well as existing products, the potential buyers come to the seller more readily.

The food services industry is another example where similar approaches are taken to reach the catering industry. Chefs usually work different hours from manufacturers' salespeople, and an exhibition showing the latest products can be invaluable in attracting these normally inaccessible customers. About 85% of attendees make a final purchase decision about one or more of the products displayed and, based on US experience, the cost per person reached is lower than an industrial sales call. Trade shows require several decisions, including which trade shows to participate in, how much to spend on each trade show, how to build dramatic exhibits that attract attention and how to follow up sales leads effectively.[15]

A sales contest organised by businesses marketing to other businesses is often used in an attempt to give incentive to a firm's salesforce, a distributor's salesforce or a dealer network to increase their sales performance during a specified period. The good performers might be rewarded by trips, cash prizes or gifts. For example, Masport, the New Zealand manufacturer of lawnmowers and other lines, offers such incentives to its dealers in Australia. High-performing dealers—known as VIP dealers—may find themselves invited to attractive destinations such as Hawaii to attend an all-expenses-paid sales convention. Sales contests work best when tied to precise, measurable and achievable sales objectives, such as finding a specified number of new accounts or reviving a specified number of old accounts, or increasing profitability or cash flow from existing dealers. However, territories and selling conditions should be similar enough for all employees to believe they have an equal opportunity to win. Otherwise, employees who do not think the contest's goals are reasonable or equitable will not take up the challenge, and may even become demotivated and less inclined to push the product.[16]

Developing sales promotion programs

A number of decisions must be made in order to decide the sales promotion program. First, the marketer must decide on the *size of the incentive*. A certain minimum incentive is necessary if the promotion is to succeed; a larger incentive will produce more sales response, but will cost more. The marketer also must set *conditions for participation*. Incentives might be offered to everyone or only to select groups. For example, a premium might be offered only to those who turn in a proof of purchase; in this case South Australia would be excluded. A contest might be offered only in New South Wales and Victoria. It might be made by the national radio station JJJ-FM to people under 25 years in those states, to win tickets to a concert or some other desirable prize.

The marketer must then decide how to *promote and distribute the promotion* program itself. A $2 cash-back offer on a pack of Nestlé Lean Cuisine in return for two labels could be promoted by direct mail, or in a television commercial or women's magazine advertisement. It could also be done by bundling together two packs as a separate promotional pack with $2 off the normal retail price. Increasingly, marketers are blending several media into a total campaign concept. The *length of the promotion* is also important. If the sales promotion period is too short, many prospects (who may not be buying during that time) will miss it. If the promotion runs too long, the deal will lose some of its 'act now' force. If it is too short in relation to the stockturns of the product, many consumers may miss it. If it runs for too long, it will lose its 'immediacy' impact. For example, fresh chicken has stockturns of 100 plus per annum, and so a sales promotion for one or two weeks might be appropriate. Singapore Airlines, with a lower frequency of usage, might run its sales promotion for two months.

Evaluation is also very important. Yet many companies fail to evaluate their sales promotion programs, and others evaluate them only superficially. The most common evaluation method is to compare sales before, during and after a promotion. Suppose a company has a 6% market share before the promotion, which jumps to 10% during the promotion, falls to 5% right after and rises to 7% later on. The promotion seems to have attracted new triers and stimulated more buying by current customers. But after the promotion, sales fell, probably as consumers used up their inventories. The long-run rise to 7% means that either the company gained some new users, or existing users started buying more often. If the brand's share had returned to the old level, then the promotion may have changed only the *timing* of demand rather than the *total* demand.

Consumer research would also show the kinds of people who responded to the promotion and what they did after it ended. *Surveys* can provide information on how many consumers recall the promotion, what they thought of it, how many took advantage of it and how it affected their buying.

The battle for your daily coffee fix

Coffee consumption is increasing all over the world and, as discussed in Marketing Highlight 7.2 on pages 250–1, this is leading to strong competition as the global brands like Starbucks, Gloria Jeans and McCafé battle it out with each other and with the smaller chains and independent coffee stores. This competition between the chains is highly visible to consumers, as new stores regularly open and others close as the competition becomes too strong or the costs become too high; it's been estimated that one in ten cafés fails within 12 months of opening. But there is another battle going on, and it's one which is far less visible to most consumers—the battle to get a particular brand of coffee into a particular coffee shop, and into your cup of coffee. It's a battle which is being fought, overwhelmingly, with personal selling and promotion.

In almost every country, people are drinking more coffee, especially out of home. In Australia, out of home coffee consumption is growing by about 15% per year. Despite the high visibility of the chains, the majority of Australia's estimated 5000 coffee outlets are independents, creating around $1.1 billion in coffee sales per year. But for coffee shops and suppliers, it's a highly competitive market, said to be one of the most saturated coffee markets in the world, where even major players like Starbucks have

Personal selling is particularly important in B2B with salespeople or 'key account managers' selling products ranging from coffee to aeroplanes.

failed to make their targets. Most consumers are loyal to the outlet, not to the brand of coffee, and so apart from a small percentage of consumers who will choose their outlet on the basis of the coffee served, the coffee you drink will depend on the brand that the outlet buys. The cost of the coffee is a relatively small component of the price of a cup of coffee— generally less than 10%—but supplying coffee beans to cafés and restaurants is still a large market. The biggest of the chains, like Gloria Jeans, roast and supply their own factory, but for the coffee suppliers supplying coffee to other largely independent outlets is big business.

There are two major groups involved. On the one side there are the suppliers: the big coffee brands, like Vittoria and Lavazza, which are mostly long-term coffee suppliers. They have now been joined by a powerful new entrant, with Coca-Cola Amatil recently buying the Grinders coffee brand. On the other side are the coffee shops and restaurants, mostly small businesses, trying to keep their costs down, but also trying to ensure that their customers will be happy with the taste of the coffee they purchase. Both sides are trying to get the best deal, and the coffee companies are investing large amounts in sales and promotions to win more business from the independents.

The first part of the selling process is the sales-force, who try to meet with the busy coffee shop and restaurant owners to gain interest in *their* brand of coffee. As any salesperson knows, it's often hard to get a small business owner to take time to speak to a sales representative, because successful small business owners are usually busy. Good salespeople are persistent, however, and work at establishing a relationship with a buyer or potential buyer. 'Every week I get at least two new reps trying to sell me their blend—even though they know we've signed a contract with Nestlé,' says one barista. 'It doesn't make any difference, they still keep coming in.' 'One day I had three sales reps from the same company in here,' says another. 'They were all in those shiny suits looking like used car salesmen saying "we'll give you this, we'll give you that". Three of them, mind you. But what they really wanted was our site and exposure for their brand.'

Good salespeople also choose the targets for their attention carefully; there's no point in spending a lot of time on a small buyer whose business won't ever repay a large cost to win them over. 'All the big players can get aggressive, but they're pretty choosy as well,' says the barista, as he serves a long line of business types. 'If you're doing 20 or 30 kilos [a week in coffee beans] no one wants to know you, but if you're doing, say, 40 or 50 kilos they'll offer you a scheme.'

What sort of scheme? Well, that's where promotion comes in; large coffee companies are offering attractive packages to sign cafés up to a three-year contract; standard packages include a free espresso machine (with 24-hour servicing), a professional electric grinder, barista training, staff uniforms, aprons, printed menus, unlimited cups and saucers, umbrellas, windbreaks and, of course, endless supplies of discounted coffee beans. The total value of such a package could be more than $40 000. Some companies have even been reported to offer overseas holidays or cash payments of up to $20 000 to win over busy cafés, though such offers have been criticised as 'bad ethics, bad for business' by the food services marketing manager at Lavazza.

The upfront incentives come at a cost, however; one coffee shop which changed coffee brands mid-contract (after claiming that customers complained about the coffee) is being sued by one of the large coffee companies for breaking their contract. The big coffee companies aren't interested in providing large incentives up front without being able to lock cafés into contracts, and will signal that very clearly by threatening legal action against those who break their supply contracts.

Competition in the coffee market is only likely to increase with Coca-Cola Amatil's (CCA) recent purchase of the Grinders brand, and with rumours that Pepsi will enter the coffee market. Competitors fear that CCA's huge salesforce will be able to bundle services and products—such as fridges and bottled water—offered to café owners, undercutting the independent coffee chains. For café owners, it's good news, as the coffee suppliers try to win their business. For consumers, the message is that if you care about the brand of coffee you drink, find a café that serves your favourite brand, and hope they don't get offered a better deal by a rival supplier.

Sources: Mark Chipperfield, 'Coffee Wars', *The Sydney Morning Herald* (The Sydney Magazine), 22 September 2005, p. 72; Neil Shoebridge, 'The Coffee Smells Good', *The Australian Financial Review*, 7 February 2005, p. 48; Neil Shoebridge, 'Starbucks to Continue with Daily Grind', *The Australian Financial Review*, 18 April 2005, p. 50.

Questions

1 Most consumers would say that taste is an important part of their decision to buy coffee from a particular outlet. Why then does the highlight suggest that selling and promotion are such a strong part of the café owner's decision process?

2 How important do you think that branded merchandise such as windbreaks, cups and umbrellas are for coffee companies?

3 Why do you think Lavazza's marketing manager might describe upfront payments as 'bad ethics, bad for business'?

17.2

Sales promotions can also be evaluated through *experiments* that vary factors such as incentive value, length and distribution method.

Clearly, sales promotion plays an important role in the total promotion mix. To use it well, the marketer must define the sales promotion objectives, select the best tools, design the sales promotion program, implement the program and evaluate the results. Moreover, sales promotion must be coordinated carefully with other promotion mix elements within the integrated marketing communications program.

SELF-CHECK QUESTIONS

1 Provide examples of recent sales promotion incentives that you, or others around you, have been exposed to.

2 Which of the sales promotion techniques you were exposed to caused you to respond? In what ways did you respond?

3 If consumers do not respond to a sales promotion, such as an on-pack cash-back coupon, does this mean the sales promotion was a failure? Why or why not? What do you think is the best method of evaluating this type of promotion?

The role of personal selling

There are many types of personal selling jobs, and the role of personal selling can vary greatly from one industry to another and from one company to another. In this section we look at the nature of personal selling positions and at the role the salesforce plays in modern marketing organisations.

The nature of personal selling

People who do selling in organisations go by many names: *salespeople, sales representatives, key account managers, sales consultants, sales engineers, agents, district managers* and *account development reps* to name just a few. Personal selling has been undertaken for as long as people have traded their produce and the output from their personal endeavour, but today personal selling brings with it new challenges and a greater dependence on collaborative tools and technologies. Modern salespeople are a far cry from the many unfortunate stereotypes epitomised by the 'tell 'em anything, but make a sale' used-car salespeople of yesteryear. Today, most **salespeople** are well-educated, well-trained professionals who work to build and maintain long-term relationships with customers. They build these relationships by listening to their customers, assessing customer needs and organising the company's efforts to solve customer problems and satisfy customer needs. For example, consider Boeing, the aerospace giant that dominates the worldwide commercial aircraft market with a 55% market share:

Salespeople Salespeople are involved in two-way personal communication with customers with whom they build long-term relationships.

Boeing's success in the commercial aeroplane industry is largely due to the solid, long-term relationships fostered by staff at all levels.

Selling high-tech aircraft at $100 million or more a copy is complex and challenging. A single big sale can easily run into billions of dollars. Boeing salespeople head up an extensive team of company specialists—sales and service technicians, financial analysts, planners, engineers—all dedicated to finding ways to satisfy airline customer needs. The selling process is nerve-rackingly slow—it can take 2 or 3 years from the first sales presentation to the day the sale is announced. After getting the order, salespeople then must stay in almost constant touch to keep track of the account's equipment needs and to make certain the customer stays satisfied. Success depends on building solid, long-term relationships with customers, based on performance and trust. 'When you buy an airplane, it is like getting married,' says the head of Boeing's commercial airplane division. 'It is a long-term relationship.'[17]

The role of the salesforce

Personal selling is the interpersonal arm of the promotion mix. Advertising consists of one-way non-personal communication with target consumer groups. In contrast, personal selling involves two-way personal communication between salespeople and individual customers—whether face to face, by telephone, video conference or other means. This means that personal selling can be more effective than advertising in complex selling situations. Salespeople can probe customers to learn more about their problems. They can adjust the marketing offer to fit the special needs of each customer and negotiate terms of sale. They can build long-term personal relationships with key decision makers.

Some firms have no salespeople at all—for example, direct marketing companies that sell solely through mail-order catalogues or companies that sell through manufacturers' reps, sales agents or brokers. In most firms, however, the salesforce plays a major role. In companies that sell business products, such as IBM or DuPont, the company's salespeople work directly with customers. For many customers, salespeople may be the only contact. To these customers, the salesforce *is* the company. In consumer product companies such as Lever-Rexona or Nike which sell through intermediaries, final consumers rarely meet salespeople or even know about them. However, the salesforce plays an important behind-the-scenes role. It works with wholesalers and retailers to gain their support and to help them be more effective in selling the company's products.

The salesforce also serves as a critical link between a company and its customers. In many cases, salespeople serve both masters—the seller and the buyer. First, they represent the company to customers. They find and develop new customers and communicate information about the company's offerings. They sell products by approaching customers, presenting their products, answering objections, negotiating prices and terms, and closing sales. In addition, salespeople provide services to customers, carry out market research and intelligence work, and fill out sales call reports.

At the same time, salespeople represent customers to the company, acting inside the firm as 'champions' of customers' interests. Salespeople relay customer concerns about company products and actions back to those who can handle them. They learn about customer needs, and work with others in the company to develop greater customer value. Thus, the salesperson often acts as an 'account manager' who manages the relationship between the seller and the buyer.

As companies move towards a stronger market orientation, their salesforces are becoming more market focused and customer oriented. The old view was that salespeople should worry about sales and the company should worry about profit. However, the current view holds that salespeople should be concerned with more than just producing sales—they must also know how to produce customer satisfaction and company profit. They should be able to look at sales data, measure market potential, gather market intelligence and develop marketing strategies and plans. They should know how to orchestrate the company's efforts towards delivering customer value and company profit. A market-oriented rather than a sales-oriented salesforce will be more effective in the long run. Beyond winning new customers and making sales, it will help the company to create long-term, profitable relationships with customers.

Many organisations use a combination of their own salesforce and selling through independent agents or brokers who are typically paid on commission. For example, over the past 10 years, most of the large banks have started selling their home mortgages through brokers, as well as through their own salesforce. Several banks are now looking at expanding the use of these brokers to include the sales of other financial products.[18]

Managing the salesforce

Salesforce management The analysis, planning, implementation and control of salesforce activities. It includes setting salesforce strategy; and recruiting, selecting, training, supervising and evaluating the firm's salespeople.

We define **salesforce management** as the analysis, planning, implementation and control of salesforce activities. It includes setting salesforce objectives, designing salesforce strategy and recruiting, selecting, training, supervising and evaluating the firm's salespeople. The major salesforce management decisions are shown in Figure 17.1 and are discussed in the following subsections.

Designing salesforce strategy and structure

Marketing managers face a number of salesforce strategy and design questions. How should salespeople and their tasks be structured? How big should the salesforce be? Should salespeople sell alone or work in teams with other people in the company, or even alliance partners? Should they sell in the field or by telephone? These issues are addressed in the following pages.

Salesforce structure

Salesforce strategy influences the structure of the salesforce. The salesforce structure decision is simple if the company sells one product line to one industry with customers in many locations. In that case the company would use a territorial salesforce structure. If the company sells many products to many types of customers, it might need a product salesforce structure or a customer salesforce structure.

Territorial salesforce structure A salesforce organisation that assigns each salesperson to an exclusive geographical territory in which that salesperson carries the company's full line.

Territorial salesforce structure In the **territorial salesforce structure**, each salesperson is assigned an exclusive territory in which to sell the company's full line. This salesforce structure is the simplest sales organisation and has many advantages. It clearly defines the salesperson's job, and because only one salesperson works the territory they get all the credit or blame for territory sales. The territorial structure also increases the salesperson's desire to build local business ties that, in turn,

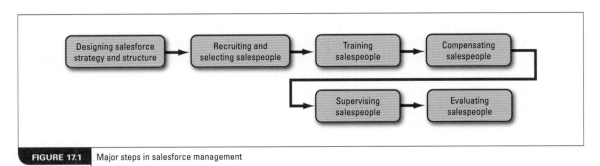

FIGURE 17.1 Major steps in salesforce management

improve the salesperson's selling effectiveness. Finally, because each salesperson travels within a small geographical area, travel expenses are relatively small.

A **territorial sales organisation** is often supported by many levels of sales-management positions. Starting at the bottom of the organisation, sales merchandisers report to sales representatives, who report to retail supervisors, who report to directors of retail sales operations, who report to one of a number of regional sales managers. Regional sales managers, in turn, report to one of a number of general sales managers, who report to a vice-president and general sales manager.[19]

Territorial sales organisation The simplest sales organisation, offering advantages such as effective selling in a defined geographical area.

Product salesforce structure Salespeople must know their products—especially when the products are numerous, unrelated and complex. This need, together with the trend towards product management, has led many companies to the **product salesforce structure**, in which the salesforce sells along product lines. For example, the packaging company Visy uses different salesforces for its industrial carton business and its colour-printed retail packs, because different skills and product knowledge are important in each case. For retail packs, design, choice of colour, short production runs and intricate shapes and sizes are all factors that determine which company will secure the business. For industrial cartons, carton quality, speed of delivery and price are important factors as the production runs are often very long.

Product salesforce structure A salesforce organisation under which salespeople specialise in selling only a portion of the company's products or lines.

The product structure, however, can lead to problems if many of the company's products are bought by the same customers. For example, pharmaceutical company Wyeth has several salesforce teams communicating the technical details and trial outcomes of different products to the same doctors. To avoid several salespeople calling on the same client at any one time, their visits are coordinated electronically. The extra costs of maintaining separate field teams needs to be compared with the benefits of better product knowledge and attention to individual products achieved by a specialised salesforce.

Customer salesforce structures Companies often use a **customer salesforce structure** in which they organise the salesforce along customer or industry lines. Separate salesforces may be set up for different industries, for serving current customers versus finding new ones, and for major versus regular accounts. Xerox, for example, classifies its customers into major groups, each served by a different salesforce. The top group consists of large national accounts with multiple and scattered locations; these customers are handled by national account managers. Next are major accounts that, although not national in scope, may have several locations within a region; these are handled by one of Xerox's major account managers. The third customer group consists of standard commercial accounts, which are served by account representatives. All other customers are handled by marketing representatives.

Customer salesforce structure A salesforce organisation under which salespeople specialise in selling only to certain customers or industries.

The biggest advantage of customer specialisation is that each salesforce can know more about specific customer needs. It can also reduce total salesforce costs. At one time a pump manufacturer used highly trained sales engineers to sell to all its customers—to manufacturers who needed highly technical assistance and to wholesalers who did not. Later, the company split its salesforce and used lower-paid, less technical salespeople to deal with the wholesalers. This change reduced salesforce costs without reducing customer service.

The major disadvantage of a customer structure arises when customers are scattered across the country. Such geographical disbursement means a great deal of travel by each of the company's salesforces.

Complex salesforce structures When a company sells a wide variety of products to many types of customers over a broad geographical area, it often combines several types of salesforce structures. Salespeople can be specialised by territory and product, by territory and market, by product and market or by territory, product and market. A salesperson might then report to one or more line and staff managers.

Salesforce size

Once the company has set its strategy and structure, it is ready to consider salesforce size. Salespeople constitute one of the company's most productive—and most expensive—assets. Therefore, increasing their number will increase both sales and costs.

Workload approach
An approach to setting salesforce size in which the company groups accounts into different-sized classes and then determines how many salespeople are needed to call on them the desired number of times.

Many companies use some form of **workload approach** to set salesforce size. Under this approach, a company groups accounts into different-sized classes and then determines how many salespeople are needed to call on them the desired number of times. The company might think as follows: suppose we have 100 Type A accounts and 200 Type B accounts. Type A accounts require 36 calls a year and Type B accounts 12 calls a year. In this case, the salesforce's workload—the number of calls it must make per year—is 6000 calls [(100 × 36) + (200 × 12) = 3600 + 2400 = 6000)]. Suppose our average salesperson can make 1000 calls a year. The company thus needs six salespeople (6000/1000).[20]

Facing tremendous pressure to cut costs, many companies are shrinking their salesforces because the sales department is one of the costliest to maintain. Consider the case of Coca-Cola Amatil Ltd (CCA), the Australian franchisee for Coca-Cola and a range of snack-food products. CCA used to maintain an army of reps to call on small milkbar (corner store) accounts. The milkbar reps would often make up to 30 sales calls per day, giving them just enough time to take an order and maybe show one new product. When CCA looked at the costs of putting these reps in front of milkbar customers—salary, car, phone, office support and so forth—it saw a good deal of wasted time and money. Now CCA contacts these small accounts through its new telemarketing department, and the field reps make few milkbar calls and concentrate their efforts on larger accounts. Each milkbar has a day of the week when it will be contacted or when it can phone in. This move has resulted in a much lower cost per order and made small accounts financially feasible.

Other salesforce strategy and structure issues

Sales management must also decide who will be involved in the selling effort and how various sales and sales-support people will work together.

Outside salesforce (or field salesforce) Outside salespeople who travel to call on customers.

Outside and inside salesforces The company may have an **outside salesforce (or field salesforce)**, an inside salesforce, or both.

To reduce time demands on their outside salesforces, many companies have increased the size of their inside salesforces. Inside salespeople include technical support people, sales assistants and telesales operators. Technical support people provide technical information and answers to customers' questions. Sales assistants provide clerical backup for outside salespeople. They call ahead and confirm appointments, conduct credit checks, follow up on deliveries and answer customers' questions when outside salespeople cannot be reached. Telemarketers use the phone to find new leads and to qualify prospects for the field salesforce, or to sell and service accounts directly, while telesales people ring customers such as retailers on a routine basis.

Inside salesforce
Salespeople who conduct business from their offices via telephone or visits from prospective buyers.

The **inside salesforce** frees outside salespeople to spend more time selling to major accounts and finding major new prospects. Depending on the complexity of the product and customer, a telemarketer can make from 20 to 33 decision-maker contacts a day, compared with the average of four that an outside salesperson can see. And for many types of products and selling situations, telemarketing can be as effective as a personal call, but much less expensive. For example, whereas a typical personal sales call can cost well over $200, a routine industrial telemarketing call costs only about $5 and a complex call about $20.[21] Telemarketing can be used successfully by both large and small companies:

DuPont uses experienced former field salespeople as telemarketing reps to help sell the company's complex chemical products. Housed in DuPont's state-of-the-art Corporate Tele-marketing Centre, the telemarketers handle technical questions from customers, smooth out product and distribution problems, and alert field sales reps to hot prospects. The teamwork pays off—80 per cent of the leads passed on to the field force are converted into sales. Notes one DuPont telemarketer: 'I'm more effective on the phone. [When you're in the field], if some guy's not in his office, you lose an hour. On the phone, you lose 15 seconds . . . Through my phone calls, I'm in the field as much as the rep is.' There are other advantages, quips the rep. 'Customers can't throw things at you . . . and you don't have to outrun dogs.'[22]

Even small and medium enterprises (SMEs) can use telemarketing to save money and still lavish attention on buyers. Under the old system, in one SME sales engineers spent one-third of their time on the road, training distributor salespeople and accompanying them on calls. They could make about four contacts a day. Now, each of five sales engineers on the firm's telemarketing team calls about 30 prospects a day, following up on leads generated by ads and direct mail. Because it takes about five calls to close a sale, the sales engineers update a prospect's computer file after each contact, noting the degree of commitment, requirements, next call date and personal comments. 'If anyone mentions he's going on a fishing trip, our sales engineer enters that in the computer and uses it to personalise the next phone call,' says the managing director, noting that this is just one way to build good relations. Another is that the first mailing to a prospect includes the sales engineer's business card with his picture on it. Of course, it takes more than friendliness to sell $15000 machine tools (special orders may run to $200000) over the phone, but the telemarketing approach is working well. When this SME's customers were asked, 'Do you see the sales engineer often enough?' the response was overwhelmingly positive, despite their only contact being over the phone.[23]

Team selling The days when a single salesperson handled a large and important customer are vanishing rapidly. Today, as products become more complex, and as customers grow larger and more demanding, one person simply cannot handle all of a large customer's needs. Instead, most companies now use **team selling** to service large, complex accounts. Sales teams might include people from sales, marketing, engineering, finance, technical support and even upper management. For example, Procter & Gamble assigns teams consisting of salespeople, marketing managers, technical service people and logistics and information-systems specialists to work closely with large retail customers such as Kmart and Target. In such team-selling situations, salespeople help to coordinate a whole-company effort to build profitable relationships with important customers.[24]

> **Team selling** Using teams of people from sales, marketing, engineering, finance, technical support and even upper management to service large, complex accounts.

Yet companies recognise that just asking their people for teamwork does not produce it. They must revise their compensation and recognition systems to give credit for work on shared accounts, and they must set up better goals and measures for salesforce performance. They must emphasise the importance of teamwork in their training programs while at the same time honouring the importance of individual initiative.

Having set the strategy, structure and size of the salesforce, the company now must set up systems for recruiting and selecting, training, compensating, supervising and evaluating salespeople.

Recruiting and selecting salespeople

The basis of successful salesforce operation is the selection of good salespeople. The performance levels of an average and a top salesperson can be quite different. In a typical salesforce, the top 30% of the salespeople might bring in 60% of the sales. Careful salesperson selection can thus greatly increase overall salesforce performance. For example, one study found that more optimistic salespeople were more successful in selling than less optimistic individuals, with the top half, ranked on optimism, selling 20% more, and also being less likely to quit.[25]

Beyond the differences in sales performance, poor selection results in costly turnover. One US study found an average annual salesforce turnover rate for all industries of 27%, and in some industries it can be over 50% in the first year.[26] The costs of high turnover can be considerable. When a salesperson quits, the cost of finding and training a new salesperson—plus the cost of lost sales—can run as high as $50 000. And a salesforce with many new people is less productive.[27]

What makes a good salesperson?

What sets great salespeople apart from all the rest? In an effort to profile top sales performers, Gallup Management Consulting Group, a division of the well-known Gallup polling organisation, has interviewed as many as half a million salespeople. Its research suggests that the best salespeople possess four key talents: intrinsic motivation, disciplined work style, the ability to close a sale and, perhaps most important, the ability to build relationships with customers.[28]

Super salespeople are motivated from within. 'Different things drive different people—pride, happiness, money, you name it,' says one expert. 'But all great salespeople have one thing in common: an unrelenting drive to excel.' Some salespeople are driven by money, a hunger for recognition or the satisfaction of competing and winning. Others are driven by the desire to provide service and to build relationships. The best salespeople possess some of each of these motivations. 'A competitor with a strong sense of service will probably bring in a lot of business while doing a great job of taking care of customers,' observes the managing director of the Gallup Management Consulting Group. 'Who could ask for anything more?'

Whatever their motivations, salespeople must also have a disciplined work style. If salespeople aren't organised and focused, and if they don't work hard, they can't meet the ever-increasing demands customers make these days. Great salespeople are tenacious about laying out detailed, organised plans, then following through in a timely, disciplined way. One sales trainer comments: 'Some people say it's all technique or luck. But luck happens to the best salespeople when they get up early, work late, stay up till two in the morning working on a proposal, or keep making calls when everyone is leaving at the end of the day.'

Other skills mean little if a salesperson can't close the sale. So what makes for a great closer? For one thing, it takes unyielding persistence. 'Great closers are like great athletes,' says one sales trainer. 'They're not afraid to fail, and they don't give up until they close.' Great closers also have a high level of self-confidence and believe they are doing the right thing.

Effective recruitment selection and training are essential in creating successful salespeople.

Perhaps most important in today's relationship-marketing environment, top salespeople are customer problem solvers and relationship builders. They have an instinctive understanding of their customers' needs. Talk to sales executives and they'll describe top performers in these terms: empathetic, patient, caring, responsive, good listeners, honest. Top performers can put themselves on the buyer's side of the desk and see the world through their customers' eyes. They don't want just to be liked, they want to add value for their customers.

Recruitment and selection procedures

When recruiting, companies should analyse the sales job itself and the characteristics of its most successful salespeople to identify the traits needed by a successful salesperson in their industry. Then, it must recruit the right salespeople. The human resources department looks for applicants by getting names from current salespeople, using employment agencies, placing classified ads, searching the Web and working through university placement services. Another source is to attract top salespeople from other companies. Proven salespeople need less training and can be immediately productive.

Recruitment will usually attract many applicants, from which the company must select the best. The selection procedure can vary from a single informal interview to lengthy testing and interviewing. Many companies give formal tests to sales applicants. Tests typically measure sales aptitude, analytical and organisational skills, personality traits and other characteristics. Test results count heavily in such companies as IBM, Prudential, Procter & Gamble and Gillette. Gillette claims that tests have reduced turnover by 42% and that test scores have correlated well with the later performance of new salespeople. But test scores provide only one piece of information in a set that includes personal characteristics, references, past employment history and interviewer reactions.[29]

Training salespeople

New salespeople may spend anywhere from a few weeks or months to a year or more in training. In addition, most companies provide continuing sales training via seminars, sales meetings and the Web throughout the salesperson's career. In all, US companies spend more than $7 billion annually on training salespeople. Although training can be expensive, it can also yield dramatic returns. For example, one study found that sales training conducted by a major telecommunications firm paid for itself in 16 days and resulted in a six-month return on investment of 812%. Similarly, Nabisco analysed the return on its two-day Professional Selling Program, which teaches sales reps how to plan for and make professional presentations. Although it cost about $1000 to put each sales rep through the program, the training resulted in additional sales of more than $122 000 per rep and yielded almost $21 000 of additional profit per rep.[30]

Training programs have several goals. Salespeople need to know and identify with the company and its products, so most training programs begin by describing the company's objectives, organisation, financial structure, facilities and chief products and markets. They also need to know about customers and competitors. So the training program teaches them about competitors' strategies and about different types of customers and their needs, buying motives and buying habits. Finally, because salespeople must know how to sell effectively, they are also trained in the basics of the selling process.

Today, many companies are adding web-based training to their sales training programs, as discussed in Marketing Highlight 17.3. The industry for online training is expected to more than triple to $23.7 billion by 2006.[31] Such training may range from simple text-based product information to Internet-based sales exercises that build sales skills to sophisticated simulations that re-create the dynamics of real-life sales calls. Networking equipment and software maker Cisco Systems has learned that using the Internet to train salespeople offers many advantages:

Keeping a large sales force up to speed on hundreds of complex, fast-changing products can be a daunting task. Under the old training process, newly hired Cisco salespeople travelled to a central location for several 5-day training sessions each year. 'We used to fly people in and put them through a week of death-by-PowerPoint,' says a Cisco training executive. This approach involved huge program-development and travel costs. Perhaps worse, it cost salespeople precious lost-opportunity time spent away from their customers. To address these issues, Cisco launched

MARKETING HIGHLIGHT

17.3

Point, click and sell—welcome to the web-based salesforce

There are few rules at Fisher Scientific International's sales training sessions. The chemical company's salespeople are allowed to show up for workshops in their pyjamas. And no one flinches if they stroll in at midnight for their first class, take a dozen breaks to call clients or invite the family cat to sleep in their lap while they take an exam. Sound unorthodox? It would be if Fisher's salespeople were trained in a regular classroom. But for the past few years the company has been using the Internet to teach the majority of its salespeople in the privacy of their homes, cars, hotel rooms or wherever else they bring their laptops.

To get updates on Fisher's pricing or refresh themselves on one of the company's highly technical products, all salespeople have to do is log on to the website and select from the lengthy index. Any time of the day or night, they can get information on a new product, take an exam or post messages for product experts—all without ever entering a corporate classroom. Welcome to the world of the web-based salesforce.

In the past few years, sales organisations around the world have begun saving money and time by using a host of new web approaches to train reps, hold sales meetings and even conduct live sales presentations. Fisher Scientific's reps can dial up the website at their leisure, and whereas newer reps might spend hours online going through each session in order, more seasoned sellers might just log on for a quick refresher on a specific product before a sales call. 'It allows them to manage their time better, because they're only getting training when they need it, in the doses they need it in,' comments John Pavlik, director of the company's training department. If salespeople are spending less time on training, Pavlik says, they're able to spend more time on what they do best: selling.

Training is only one of the ways sales organisations are using the Internet. Many companies are using the Web to make sales presentations and service accounts. For example, computer and com-

munications equipment maker NEC Corporation has adopted web-based selling as an essential marketing tool.

After launching a new line of servers on 11 September 2001, NEC had to rethink its sales approach. Following the terrorist attacks on 11 September 2001, the company began looking for ways to cut down on salesforce travel. According to Dick Csaplar, marketing manager for the new server line, NEC's old sales approach—travelling to customer sites to pitch NEC products—became unworkable literally overnight. Instead, NEC adopted a new web-based sales approach. While the initial goal was to keep people off aeroplanes, web selling has now grown into an intrinsic part of NEC's sales efforts. Web selling reduces travel time and costs. Whereas the average daily cost of salesperson travel is $663, an hour-long web conference costs just $60. More importantly, web selling lets sales reps meet with more prospective customers than ever before, creating a more efficient and effective sales organisation. Csaplar estimates that he's doing 10 customer web conferences a week, during which he and his sales team show prospects product features and benefits. Customers love it because they get a clear understanding of NEC's technology without having to host the NEC team onsite. And Csaplar was pleased to find that web-based selling is an effective way to interact with customers and to build customer relationships. 'By the time we're done

Internet selling support: sales organisations around the world are now using a host of new web approaches to train reps, hold sales meetings and even conduct live sales presentations.

with the Webcast, the customer understands the technology, the pricing, and the competition, and we understand the customer's business and needs,' he says. Without webcasts, 'we'd be lost on how to communicate with the customer without spending a lot of money,' says Csaplar. 'I don't see us ever going back to the heavy travel thing.'

The Internet can also be a handy way to hold sales strategy meetings. Consider Cisco Systems, which provides networking solutions for the Internet. Sales meetings used to take an enormous bite out of Cisco's travel budget. Now the company saves about $1 million per month by conducting many of those sessions on the Web using PlaceWare web conferencing software. Whenever Cisco introduces a new product, it holds a web meeting to update salespeople, in groups of 100 or more, on the product's marketing and sales strategy.

Usually led by the product manager or a vice-president of sales, the meetings typically begin with a 10-minute slide presentation that spells out the planned strategy. Then, salespeople spend the next 50 or so minutes asking questions via teleconference. The meeting's leader can direct attendees' browsers to competitors' websites or ask them to vote on certain issues by using the software's instant polling feature. 'Our salespeople are actually meeting more online then they ever were face-to-face,' comments Mike Mitchell, Cisco's distance learning manager, adding that some salespeople who used to meet with other reps and managers only a few times a quarter are meeting online nearly every day. 'That's very empowering for the sales force, because they're able to make suggestions at every step of the way about where we're going with our sales and marketing strategies.'

Thus, web-based technologies can produce big organisational benefits for salesforces. They help conserve salespeople's valuable time, save travel dollars and give salespeople a new vehicle for selling and servicing accounts. But the technologies also have some drawbacks. For starters, they're not cheap. Setting up a web-based system can cost up to several hundred thousand dollars. And such systems can intimidate low-tech salespeople or clients. 'You must have a culture that is comfortable using computers,' says one marketing communications manager. 'As simple as it is, if your salespeople or clients aren't comfortable using the Web, you're wasting your money.' Also, web tools are susceptible to server crashes and other network difficulties, not a happy event when you're in the middle of an important sales meeting or presentation.

For these reasons, some high-tech experts recommend that sales executives use web technologies for training, sales meetings and preliminary client sales presentations, but resort to old-fashioned, face-to-face meetings when the time draws near to close the deal. 'When push comes to shove, if you've got an account worth closing, you're still going to get on that plane and see the client in person,' says sales consultant Sloane. 'Your client is going to want to look you in the eye before buying anything from you, and that's still one thing you just can't do online.'

Sources: Portions adapted from Melinda Ligos, 'Point, Click, and Sell', *Sales and Marketing Management*, May 1999, pp. 51–55; and Tom Kontzer, 'Web Conferencing Embraced', *Information Week*, 26 May 2003, pp. 68–70. Also see Julia Chang, 'No Instructor Required', *Sales and Marketing Management*, May 2003, p. 26; Nicole Ridgeway, 'A Safer Place to Meet', *Forbes*, 28 April 2003, p. 97; Andy Cohen, 'Virtual Sales Meetings on the Rise', *Sales and Marketing Management*, August 2003, p. 12; and Daniel Tynan, 'Next Best Thing to Being There', *Sales and Marketing Management*, April 2004, p. 22.

Questions

1 What do you think are the advantages of web-based selling? When might it be least useful?

2 What are the disadvantages of web-based selling? When might it be less useful?

17.3

its Field E-Learning Connection—an internal learning portal through which Cisco's salespeople around the world can plan, track, develop, and measure their skills and knowledge. The site links salespeople to tens of thousands of Web-based learning aids. Learning involves the blending of audio and video, live broadcasts of classes, and straight content. Content can be turned into an MP3 file, viewed on-screen, downloaded to the computer, even printed out in magazine form. Under the new system, Cisco can conduct a single training session that reaches up to 3000 people at once, worldwide, by broadcasting it over the company's global intranet. Live events can then be archived as video-on-demand modules for viewers who missed the live broadcast. The system also provides electronic access to Cisco experts or 'e-mentors,' who can respond via e-mail or phone, or meet learners in a virtual lab, connect to their screens, and walk them through exercises. The Field E-Learning Connection has improved training by giving Cisco salespeople anywhere, anytime access to a vast system of training resources. At the same time, it has cut field training costs by 40 percent to 60 percent while boosting salesperson 'face time' with customers by 40 percent.[32]

Compensating salespeople

To attract good salespeople a company must have an appealing compensation plan. Compensation is made up of several elements—a fixed amount, a variable amount, expenses and fringe benefits. The fixed amount, usually a salary, gives the salesperson some stable income. The variable amount, which might be commissions or bonuses based on sales performance, rewards the salesperson for greater effort and success. Expense allowances, which repay salespeople for job-related expenses, let salespeople undertake needed and desirable selling efforts. Fringe benefits, such as paid vacations, sickness or accident benefits, pensions and life insurance, make it easier to attract and retain good salespeople.

Management must decide what *mix* of these compensation elements makes the most sense for each sales job. Different combinations of fixed and variable compensation give rise to four basic types of compensation plans—straight salary, straight commission, salary plus bonus and salary plus commission. One study of salesforce compensation plans showed that 70% of all companies surveyed use a combination of base salary and incentives. The average plan consisted of about 60% salary and 40% incentive pay.[33]

The salesforce compensation plan can both motivate salespeople and direct their activities. Compensation should direct the salesforce toward activities that are consistent with the organisation's marketing objectives. Table 17.1 illustrates how a company's compensation plan should reflect its

TABLE 17.1 The relationship between overall marketing strategy and salesforce compensation

	Strategic goal		
	To gain market share rapidly	**To solidify market leadership**	**To maximise profitability**
Ideal salesperson	• An independent self-starter	• A competitive problem solver	• A team player • A relationship manager
Sales focus	• Deal making • Sustained high effort	• Consultative selling	• Account penetration
Compensation role	• To capture accounts • To reward high performance	• To reward new and existing account sales	• To manage the product mix • To encourage team selling • To reward account management

Source: Sam T. Johnson, *Compensation and Benefits Review*, pp. 53–60. Copyright © 1992 by Sage Publications. Reprinted by permission of Sage Publications.

overall marketing strategy. For example, if the strategy is to grow rapidly and gain market share, the compensation plan might include a larger commission component coupled with a new-account bonus to encourage high sales performance and new-account development. In contrast, if the goal is to maximise current account profitability, the compensation plan might contain a larger base-salary component with additional incentives for current account sales or customer satisfaction.

More and more companies are moving away from high commission plans that may drive salespeople to make short-term grabs for business. They worry that a salesperson who is pushing too hard to close a deal may ruin the customer relationship. One salesforce expert notes: 'The last thing you want is to have someone ruin a customer relationship because they're pushing too hard to close a deal'. Instead, companies are designing compensation plans which reward salespeople for building customer relationships and growing the long-term value of each customer.[34]

Supervising salespeople

New salespeople need more than a territory, compensation and training—they need *supervision*. Through supervision, the company *directs* and *motivates* the salesforce to do a better job.

Companies vary in how closely they supervise their salespeople. Many help their salespeople in identifying customer targets and setting call norms. Some may also specify how much time the salesforce should spend prospecting for new accounts and set other time-management priorities. One tool is the *annual call plan* that shows which customers and prospects to call on in which months and which activities to carry out. Activities include taking part in trade shows, attending sales meetings and carrying out marketing research. Another tool is *time-and-duty analysis*. In addition to time spent selling, the salesperson spends time travelling, waiting, eating, taking breaks and doing administrative chores.

Companies often specify how much time their salesforce should spend prospecting for new accounts. For example, a company might want its salespeople to spend 25% of their time prospecting and to stop calling on a prospect after three unsuccessful calls. Companies set up prospecting standards for several reasons. If left alone, many salespeople will spend most of their time with current customers, who are better known quantities. Moreover, whereas a prospect might never deliver any business, salespeople can depend on current accounts for some business. Therefore, unless salespeople are rewarded for opening new accounts, they might avoid new-account development.

Figure 17.2 shows how salespeople spend their time. On average, actual face-to-face selling time accounts for less than 30% of total working time! If selling time could be raised from 30% to 40%, this would be approximately a 33% increase in the time spent selling. Companies are always looking for ways to save time—using phones instead of travelling, simplifying record-keeping forms, finding better call and routing plans and supplying more and better customer information.

Many firms have adopted *salesforce automation systems*, computerised salesforce operations for more efficient order-entry transactions, improved customer service and better salesperson decision-making support. Salespeople use laptops, hand-held computing devices and web technologies, coupled with customer-contact software and customer relationship management (CRM) software, to profile customers and prospects, analyse and forecast sales, manage account relationships, schedule sales calls, make presentations, enter orders, check inventories and order status, prepare sales and expense reports, process correspondence and carry out many other activities. Salesforce automation not only lowers salesforce costs and improves productivity, it also improves the quality of sales management decisions. For example, pharmaceutical representatives use hand-held computers to log their call reports with management, download emails and updated product information and plan their next day's activities, all without coming in to the office.

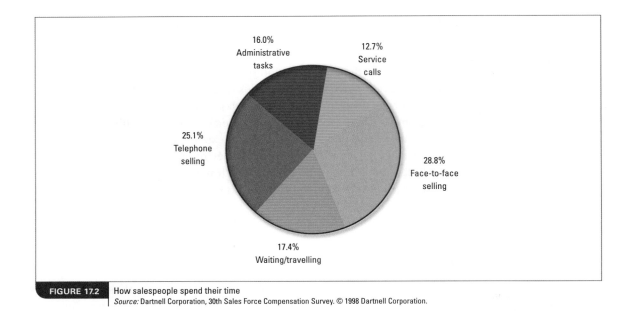

How salespeople spend their time
Source: Dartnell Corporation, 30th Sales Force Compensation Survey. © 1998 Dartnell Corporation.

Motivating salespeople

Some salespeople will do their best without any special urging from management. But selling often involves frustration. Salespeople usually work alone and often travel away from home. They may face aggressive, competing salespeople and difficult customers. They sometimes lack the authority to do what is needed to win a sale and may therefore lose large orders they have worked hard to obtain. So salespeople often need special encouragement to work at their best level. Management can boost salesforce morale and performance through its organisational climate, sales quotas and positive incentives. There's good reason for management to try to ensure that sales staff are motivated and happy with their job: research shows that if the salespeople are satisfied with their job, then customers will be more satisfied.[35]

Organisational climate Organisational climate describes the feeling that salespeople have about their opportunities, value and rewards for a good performance. Some companies treat salespeople as if they are not very important, and performance and turnover suffer accordingly. Other companies treat their salespeople as critical employees and allow virtually unlimited opportunity for income and promotion. Not surprisingly, a company's attitude towards its salespeople affects their behaviour. If they are held in low esteem, there is high turnover and poor performance. If they are held in high esteem, there is less turnover and higher performance.

Treatment from the salesperson's immediate superior is especially important. A good sales manager keeps in touch with the salesforce through emails and phone calls, visits in the field and evaluation sessions in the home office. At different times, the sales manager acts as the salesperson's boss, companion, coach and confessor.

Sales quotas Many companies set **sales quotas** for their salespeople—standards stating the amount they should sell and how sales should be divided among the company's products. Compensation is often related to how well salespeople meet their quotas.

Sales quotas are set when the annual marketing plan is developed. The company first decides on a sales forecast that is reasonably achievable. Based on this forecast, management plan production, workforce size and financial needs. The company then sets sales quotas for its regions and territories.

Sales quotas Standards set for salespeople stating the amount they should sell and how sales should be divided among the company's products.

Generally, sales quotas are set higher than the sales forecast to encourage sales managers and salespeople to their best effort. If they fail to make quotas, the company may still make its sales forecast.

Positive incentives Companies also use several incentives to increase salesforce effort. Sales meetings provide social occasions, breaks from routine, chances to meet and talk with senior management and opportunities to air feelings and identify with a larger group. Companies also sponsor sales contests to spur the salesforce on to make a greater than normal selling effort.[36] Other incentives include honours, merchandise and cash awards, trips and profit-sharing plans.

Evaluating salespeople

We have thus far described how management communicates what salespeople should be doing and how it motivates them to do it. This process requires good feedback. And good feedback means getting regular information about salespeople to evaluate their performance.

Management gets information about its salespeople in several ways. The most important source is *sales reports*, including weekly or monthly work plans and longer-term territory marketing plans. Salespeople also write up their completed activities on *call reports* and turn in *expense reports* for which they are partly or wholly repaid. Additional information comes from personal observation, customer surveys and talks with other salespeople.

Using various salesforce reports and other information, sales management evaluates members of the salesforce. It evaluates salespeople on their ability to 'plan their work and work their plan'. Formal evaluation forces management to develop and communicate clear standards for judging performance. It also provides salespeople with constructive feedback and motivates them to perform well.

SELF-CHECK QUESTIONS

7 Take a position on the following statement: 'All good salespeople are outgoing, aggressive and energetic.' Support your argument with examples.

8 Why is motivation of particular significance in the management of salespeople?

The personal selling process

We now turn from designing and managing a salesforce to the actual personal selling process. The **selling process** consists of several steps that the salesperson must master. These steps focus on the goal of getting new customers and obtaining orders from them. However, most salespeople spend much of their time maintaining existing accounts and building long-term customer *relationships*. We discuss the relationship aspect of the personal selling process in a later section.

Selling process The steps that the salesperson follows when selling, including prospecting and qualifying, preapproach, approach, presentation and demonstration, handling objections, closing and follow-up.

Steps in the selling process

As shown in Figure 17.3, the selling process consists of seven steps: prospecting and qualifying, preapproach, approach, presentation and demonstration, handling objections, closing, and follow-up.

Prospecting and qualifying

The first step in the selling process is **prospecting**—identifying qualified potential customers. Approaching the right potential customers is crucial to selling success. As one expert puts it: 'If the sales force starts chasing anyone who is breathing and seems to have a budget, you risk accumulating a roster of expensive-to-serve, hard-to-satisfy customers who never respond to whatever value

Prospecting The step in the selling process in which the salesperson identifies qualified potential customers.

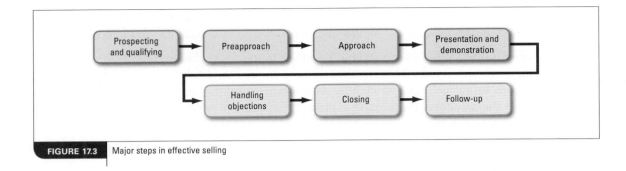

FIGURE 17.3 Major steps in effective selling

proposition you have.' He continues, 'The solution to this isn't rocket science. [You must] train salespeople to actively scout the right prospects. If necessary, create an incentive program to reward proper scouting.' Another expert concludes: 'Increasing your prospecting effectiveness is the fastest single way to boost your sales.'[37]

The salesperson must often approach many prospects to get just a few sales. Although the company supplies some leads, salespeople need skill in finding their own. They can ask current customers for referrals. They can cultivate referral sources, such as suppliers, dealers, non-competing salespeople and bankers. They can search for prospects in directories or on the Web and track down leads using the telephone and direct mail. Or they can drop in unannounced on various offices (a practice known as 'cold calling').

Salespeople also need to know how to *qualify* leads—that is, how to identify the good ones and screen out the poor ones. Prospects can be qualified by looking at their financial ability, volume of business, special needs, location and possibilities for growth.

Preapproach

Before calling on a prospect, the salesperson should learn as much as possible about the organisation (what it needs, who is involved in the buying) and its buyers (their characteristics and buying styles). This step is known as the **preapproach**. The salesperson can consult standard industry and online sources, acquaintances and others to learn about the company. The salesperson should set *call objectives*, which may be to qualify the prospect, to gather information or to make an immediate sale. Another task is to decide on the best approach, which might be a personal visit, a phone call or a letter. The best timing should be considered carefully because many prospects are busiest at certain times. Finally, the salesperson should give thought to an overall sales strategy for the account.

Preapproach The step in the selling process in which the salesperson learns as much as possible about a prospective customer before making a sales call.

Approach

During the **approach** step, the salesperson should know how to meet and greet the buyer and get the relationship off to a good start. This step involves the salesperson's appearance, opening lines and the follow-up remarks. The opening lines should be positive to build goodwill from the beginning of the relationship. This opening might be followed by some key questions to learn more about the customer's needs or by showing a display or sample to attract the buyer's attention and curiosity. As in all stages of the selling process, listening to the customer is crucial.

Approach The step in the selling process in which the salesperson meets and greets the buyer to get the relationship off to a good start.

Presentation and demonstration

During the **presentation** step of the selling process, the salesperson tells the product 'story' to the buyer, presenting customer benefits and showing how the product solves the customer's problems. The problem-solver salesperson fits better with today's marketing concept than does a hard-sell salesperson or the glad-handing extrovert. Buyers today want solutions, not smiles; results, not

Presentation The step in the selling process in which the salesperson tells the product 'story' to the buyer, showing how the product will make or save money.

razzle-dazzle. They want salespeople who listen to their concerns, understand their needs and respond with the right products and services.

This *need-satisfaction approach* calls for good listening and problem-solving skills. 'I think of myself more as a . . . well, psychologist,' notes one experienced salesperson. 'I listen to customers. I listen to their wishes and needs and problems, and I try to figure out a solution. If you're not a good listener, you're not going to get the order.' Another salesperson suggests, 'It's no longer enough to have a good relationship with a client. You have to understand their problems. You have to feel their pain.' One sales manager suggests that salespeople need to put themselves in their customers' shoes: 'Make yourself a customer and see first-hand how it feels,' he says.[38]

The qualities that buyers *dislike most* in salespeople include being pushy, late, deceitful and unprepared or disorganised. The qualities they *value most* include empathy, good listening, honesty, dependability, thoroughness and follow-through. Great salespeople know how to sell, but more importantly they know how to listen and to build strong customer relationships.

Today, advanced presentation technologies allow for full multimedia presentations to only one or a few people. CDs and DVDs, online presentation technologies and hand-held and laptop computers with presentation software have replaced the flip chart. An example from Credant Technologies shows what is possible:[39]

> Until 6 months ago, Credant Technologies, a firm that sells security software programs for handhelds, used standard presentation equipment—laptops and LCD projectors—to showcase its products to potential clients. That's no longer the case. Each member of the company's sales team is now equipped with Presenter-to-Go, a credit card-sized device that slips into handheld PDAs or pocket PCs to make them compatible with projectors. The $200 device reads PowerPoint, Microsoft Word, and Excel files, as well as Web pages, allowing salespeople to create presentations on computers, then transfer them to a PDA. It also lets reps add notes to presentations instantaneously by transmitting handwriting on their pocket PC to the screen. And it includes a wireless remote control, so sales reps can move freely throughout the presentation room, unattached to their laptop or projector-advancing button. When Credant Regional Account Executive Tom Gore met recently with an important prospect, he wowed buying executives with a feature that enabled him to type some of their comments into his PDA. Within seconds, their comments appeared on screen. 'It makes each presentation more personal and interactive,' Gore says.

Handling objections

Customers almost always have objections during the presentation or when asked to place an order. The problem can be logical or psychological. And objections are often unspoken. In handling objections, the salesperson should use a positive approach, seek out hidden objections, ask the buyer to clarify any objections, take objections as opportunities to provide more information and turn the objections into reasons for buying. Every salesperson needs training in the skills of **handling objections**.

Closing

After handling the prospect's objections, the salesperson now tries to close the sale. Some salespeople do not get around to **closing** or do not handle it well. They may lack confidence, feel guilty about asking for the order or not recognise the right moment to close the sale. Salespeople should know how to recognise closing signals from the buyer, including physical actions, comments and questions. For example, the customer might sit forward and nod approvingly or ask about prices and credit terms. Salespeople can use one of several closing techniques. They can ask for the order, review

Handling objections
The step in the selling process in which the salesperson seeks out, clarifies and overcomes customer objections to buying.

Closing The step in the selling process in which the salesperson asks the customer for an order.

points of agreement, offer to help write up the order, ask whether the buyer wants this model or that one or note that the buyer will lose out if the order is not placed now. The salesperson may offer the buyer special reasons to close, such as a lower price or an extra quantity at no charge.

Follow-up

Follow-up The last step in the selling process in which the salesperson follows up after the sale to ensure customer satisfaction and repeat business.

The last step in the selling process—**follow-up**—is necessary if the salesperson wants to ensure customer satisfaction and repeat business. Right after closing, the salesperson should complete any details on delivery time, purchase terms and other matters. The salesperson should then schedule a follow-up call when the initial order is received, to make sure there is proper installation, instruction, and servicing. This visit would reveal any problems, assure the buyer of the salesperson's interest and reduce any buyer concerns that might have arisen since the sale.

Personal selling and customer relationship management

Relationship marketing The process of creating, maintaining and enhancing strong, value-laden relationships with customers and other stakeholders.

The principles of personal selling as just described are transaction oriented—their aim is to help salespeople close a specific sale with a customer. But in many cases the company is not seeking simply a sale: it has targeted a major customer that it would like to win and serve. The salesforce plays an important role in building and managing profitable customer relationships. 'My company is selling something intangible,' says one salesperson. 'What we are really selling is "Hey, when the time comes, we'll be there." It all comes down to trust.'[40]

The company would like to show the customer that it has the capabilities to serve the customer's needs in a superior way over the long haul, in a mutually profitable relationship. In order to achieve this, most companies are trying to move away from transaction marketing, with its emphasis on making a sale. Instead, they are practising **relationship marketing**, which emphasises building and maintaining profitable long-term relationships with customers by creating superior customer value and satisfaction. Recognition of the importance of relationship marketing has increased rapidly in the past few years. Companies are realising that when operating in maturing markets and facing stiffer competition, it costs a lot more to wrest new customers from competitors than to keep current customers.

Today's customers are large and often global. They prefer suppliers who can sell and deliver a coordinated set of products and services to many locations, who can quickly solve problems that arise in their different parts of the nation or world, and who can work closely with customer teams to improve products and processes. For these customers, the sale is only the beginning of the relationship.

Relationship marketing is based on the premise that important accounts need focused and continuous attention. Studies have shown that the best salespeople are not only those who are highly motivated and good closers, they are also customer-problem solvers and relationship builders. Good salespeople working with key customers do more than call when they think a customer might be ready to place an order. They also study the account and understand its problems. They call or visit frequently, work with the customer to help solve the customer's problems and improve its business, and take an interest in customers as people.

SELF-CHECK QUESTIONS

9 List and describe the steps in the selling process.

10 Why is qualifying leads highlighted as a step in the selling process?

11 Comment on this statement: 'Many salespeople fail spectacularly because they do not know when and how to close a sale.'

SUMMARY

Sales promotions are often used by mass marketers in conjunction with advertising as an incentive to create immediacy or to change a value-for-money perception, but the real strengths of sales promotions come to the fore when they are used as a direct marketing tactical weapon, even in business-to-business dealings. The incentives cover a range of items: samples, redeemable coupons, cash-back offers, cents-off deals, premium offers, advertising specialties, patronage rewards, point-of-purchase promotions, as well as contests and games of chance and skill. Sales promotion calls for setting sales objectives; selecting tools; developing, pretesting and implementing the sales promotion program; and, as with all forms of direct marketing, evaluating results.

Most companies use salespeople, and many companies assign them a key role in the marketing mix. The high cost of the salesforce calls for an effective sales management process consisting of six steps: *designing salesforce strategy and structure, recruiting and selecting, training, compensating, supervising* and *evaluating salespeople.*

As an element of the marketing mix, the salesforce is very effective in achieving certain marketing objectives and carrying out such activities as *prospecting, communicating, selling and servicing,* and *information gathering.* A market-oriented salesforce needs skills in marketing analysis and planning in addition to the traditional selling skills.

In *designing a salesforce,* sales management must address such issues as what type of *salesforce structure* will work best (territorial, product or customer structured), how large the salesforce should be, who will be involved in the selling effort and how its various sales and sales-support people will work together (inside or outside salesforces, and team selling).

To hold down the high costs of hiring the wrong people, salespeople must be recruited and selected carefully. *Training* programs familiarise new salespeople not only with the art of selling, but with the company's history, its products and policies and the characteristics of its market and competitors. The salesforce *compensation* system helps to reward, motivate and direct salespeople. All salespeople need supervision, and many need continuous encouragement because they must make many decisions and face many frustrations. Periodically, the company must *evaluate* their performance to help them do a better job.

The art of selling involves a seven-step process: *prospecting and qualifying, preapproach, approach, presentation and demonstration, handling objections, closing* and *follow-up.* These steps help marketers close a specific sale. However, a seller's dealings with customers should be guided by the larger concept of *relationship marketing.* The company's salesforce should help to orchestrate a whole-company effort to develop profitable long-term relationships with key customers based on superior customer value and satisfaction.

MARKETING ISSUE

Salespeople have long suffered from a poor reputation, and there is no sign that it's getting better. While most salespeople are highly professional, a small proportion of unprofessional salespeople who indulge in unprofessional techniques (e.g. pushy or unethical selling) have resulted in a poor image of salespeople, and a reluctance by many people to go into sales. In addition, it's not a career for everyone; how would you cope with a job where most potential customers saw you as an interruption to their time, and over 90% of people that you manage to talk to aren't interested in your offer?

Yet salespeople have a critical role in many organisations; for example, in pharmaceutical companies, drug representatives call on doctors, provide information about new drugs and provide samples that doctors can give to their patients to try. These drug representatives are a critical part of the sales team, although they don't go by the name of salespeople. And experience as a drug representative is seen as so important that in some companies all new employees in management must work as a drug representative for some period.

However, salespeople have never had a strong reputation, and increased use of telephone sales, particularly companies calling individuals at home, has reinforced this negative public attitude to salespeople. In 2005, the NSW government Office of Fair Trading reported a 50% increase in complaints about telemarketing.[41] Largely as a result of this negative consumer reaction, there are moves to limit the use of telephone sales. For example, the Australian government is following the lead of the US government,

and introducing 'do not call' legislation which will allow people to opt out of telephone sales calls. The legislation is being resisted by many organisations, who believe it will limit their ability to contact potential customers. Following the introduction of do not call legislation in the USA, 100 million phone numbers were listed by consumers.[42] So there is likely to be ongoing tension between organisations which rely on their salesforces and customers who often resent telephone sales as an unwelcome intrusion on their time. And the salespeople? They get caught in the middle!

1 Is it a problem for organisations if members of the public don't trust salespeople?

2 Can marketers do anything to counter the bad reputation of salespeople?

3 What, if anything, can an organisation do to improve the attraction of sales for new employees?

KEY TERMS

DISCUSSING THE ISSUES

1 Sometimes, salespeople blame the marketing function for not meeting a sales forecast—'the reason we didn't reach budget was the lousy ad campaign!'. And, sometimes, marketing people will blame the salesforce for a drop in market share—'the only thing our sales team can do well is cut the price, and even that didn't save us from losing market share this year. They don't seem to appreciate that we make the bullets for them to fire!' What do such views indicate? What are your views on the matter?

2 Why would sales departments and their retailing clients in some industries not favour sales promotions, whereas marketing departments do?

3 Do salespeople always have to be confident and outgoing? Are optimism and extraversion necessary personality traits for an effective sales career? Are these views stereotypical and not representative of the situation? Illustrate your answer with examples.

4 Why do so many salesforce compensation plans combine base salary with bonuses or commissions? What are the advantages and disadvantages of using bonuses as incentives rather than commissions?

5 The surest way to become a salesforce manager is to be an outstanding salesperson. What are the advantages and disadvantages of promoting top salespeople to management positions? Why might an outstanding salesperson refuse to be promoted?

6 What kinds of companies would find it worthwhile to have an internal salesforce? What major factors determine whether selling through an intermediary might be more effective?

REFERENCES

1. Scott Widmier, 'The Effects of Incentives and Personality on Salesperson's Customer Orientation', *Industrial Marketing Management*, vol. 31, no. 7, 2002, pp. 609–615.
2. Tansy Harcourt, 'Qantas Cuts Commissions to Agents', *The Australian Financial Review*, 6 December 2005, p. 13.
3. Michael Sainsbury, 'Telstra to Cut Dealer Commissions', *The Australian*, 15 January 2005, p. 27.
4. *2002 Trade Promotion Spending & Merchandising Industry Study*, Wilton, CT, Cannondale Associates, 2002, p. 13; and *Trade Promotion Spending & Merchandising 2003 Industry Study*, Wilton, CT, Cannondale Associates, 2003, p. 7. Also see 'Promotions and Incentives: Offers You Can't Refuse', *Marketing Week*, 15 April 2004, p. 31; and E. Craig Stacey, 'Abandon TV at Your Own Risk', *Advertising Age*, 7 June 2004, p. 32.
5. A. S. C. Ehrenberg, M. D. Uncles and G. J. Goodhardt, 'Understanding Brand Performance Measures: Using Dirichlet Benchmarks', *Journal of Business Research*, vol. 57, 2004, pp. 1307–1325.
6. For a good summary of the research on whether promotion erodes consumer preference and loyalty for leading brands see Robert C. Blattberg and Scott A. Neslin, *Sales Promotion: Concepts, Methods and Strategies*, Englewood Cliffs, NJ, Prentice Hall, 1990, pp. 471–475.
7. David R. Bell, Jeongwen Chiang and V. Padmanabhan, 'The Decomposition of Promotional Response: An Empirical Generalization', *Marketing Science*, vol. 18, no. 4, 1999, pp. 504–526.
8. David R. Bell, Ganesh Iyer and V. Padmanabhan, 'Price Competition under Stockpiling and Flexible Consumption', *Journal of Marketing Research*, vol. 39, no. 3, 2005, pp. 292–303.
9. See Kent F. Mitchel, 'Advertising/Promotion Budgets: How Did We Get Here, and What Do We Do Now?', *Journal of Consumer Marketing*, Fall 1985, pp. 405–407.
10. See Paul W. Farris and John A. Quelch, 'In Defense of Price Promotion', *Sloan Management Review*, Fall 1987.
11. See Roger Strang, Robert M. Prentice and Alden G. Clayton, *The Relationship between Advertising and Promotion in Brand Strategy*, Cambridge, MA, Marketing Science Institute, 1975, Chapter 5; and P. Rajan Varadarajan, 'Cooperative Sales Promotion: An Idea Whose Time Has Come', *Journal of Consumer Marketing*, Winter 1986, pp. 15–33.
12. 'DSN Charts: Coupons', *Discount Store News*, 3 May 1999, p. 52.
13. 'Power to the Key Ring and T-Shirt', *Sales and Marketing Management*, December 1989, p. 14; and Chad Kaydo, 'Your Logo Here', *Sales and Marketing Management*, April 1998, pp. 65–70.
14. See 'Coupons', *Progressive Grocer 1987 Nielsen Review*, September 1987, pp. 16–18; Alison Fahey, 'Red Letter Cut from Coupon War', *Advertising Age*, 3 April 1989, p. 38; and Scott Hume, 'Coupons Go In-Store', *Advertising Age*, 21 May 1990, p. 45.
15. See Richard Szathmary, 'Trade Shows', *Sales and Marketing Management*, May 1992, pp. 83–84; Srinath Gopalakrishna, Gary L. Lilien, Jerome D. Williams, and Ian Sequeira, 'Do Trade Shows Pay Off?', *Journal of Marketing*, July 1995, pp. 75–83; Barbara Axelson, 'Trade Shows Gain Larger Share of Marketing Budgets: Computers Help Make Manufacturing Top Category', *Advertising Age's Business Marketing*, May 1999, p. S14; Peter Jenkins, 'Making the Most of Trade Shows', *Nation's Business*, June 1999, p. 8; Thomas V. Bonoma, 'Get More out of Your Trade Shows', *Harvard Business Review*, January–February 1983, pp. 75–83; and Johnathan M. Cox, Ian K. Sequeira and Alissa Eckstein, '1988 Trade Show Trends: Shows Grow in Size; Audience Quality Remains High', *Business Marketing*, June 1989, pp. 57–60.
16. For more on sales contests see C. Robert Patty and Robert Hite, *Managing Salespeople*, 3rd edn, Englewood Cliffs, NJ, Prentice Hall, 1988, pp. 313–327.
17. Quote from Laurence Zuckerman, 'Selling Airplanes with a Smile', *New York Times*, 17 February 2002, p. 3.2. Also see Bill Kelley, 'How to Sell Airplanes, Boeing-Style', *Sales and Marketing Management*, 9 December 1985, pp. 32–34; J. Lynn Lunsford, 'Boeing Beats out Airbus to Sell Virgin Blue $3 Billion in Jets', *Wall Street Journal*, 16 January 2003, p. B6; and Joann Muller, '7 Digital 7', *Forbes*, 21 June 2004, p. 117.
18. Joyce Moullakis, 'NAB Looks to Widen its Sales Options', *The Australian Financial Review*, 7 December 2005, p. 46.
19. See Rayna Skolnik, 'Campbell Stirs up its Salesforce', *Sales and Marketing Management*, April 1986, pp. 56–58.
20. For more on this and other methods for determining salesforce size see Mark W. Johnson and Greg W. Marshall, *Churchill/Ford/Walker's Sales Force Management*, New York, McGraw-Hall/Irwin, 2003, pp. 142–147; and Douglas J. Dalrymple, William L. Cron and Thomas E. DeCarlo, *Sales Management*, 8th edn, New York, John Wiley & Sons, 2004, pp. 112–116.
21. See Rudy Oetting and Geri Gantman, 'Dial "M" for Maximize', *Sales and Marketing Management*, June 1991, pp. 100–106; and 'Median Costs per Call by Industry', *Sales and Marketing Management*, 28 June 1993, p. 65.

22. See Martin Everett, 'Selling by Telephone', *Sales and Marketing Management*, December 1993, pp. 75–79.

23. See 'A Phone is Better than a Face', *Sales and Marketing Management*, October 1987, p. 29; Aimee L. Stern, 'Telemarketing Polishes its Image', *Sales and Marketing Management*, June 1991, pp. 107–110; and Richard L. Bencin, 'Telefocus: Telemarketing Gets Synergized', *Sales and Marketing Management*, February 1992, pp. 49–57.

24. See Frank V. Cespedes, Stephen X. Doyle and Robert J. Freedman, 'Teamwork for Today's Selling', *Harvard Business Review*, March–April 1989, pp. 44–54, 58; and Joseph Conlin, 'Teaming Up', *Sales and Marketing Management*, October 1993, pp. 98–104.

25. See Martin E. P. Seligman, *Learned Optimism*, Sydney, Random House, 1992, Chapter 6.

26. Martin E. P. Seligman, *Learned Optimism*, Sydney, Random House, 1992, p. 102. See Chapter 6 of this book for a discussion of the effect of optimism on salesforce turnover and effectiveness.

27. See George H. Lucas Jr, A. Parasuraman, Robert A. Davis and Ben M. Enis, 'An Empirical Study of Salesforce Turnover', *Journal of Marketing*, July 1987, pp. 34–59; Lynn G. Coleman, 'Sales Force Turnover has Managers Wondering Why', *Marketing News*, 4 December 1989, p. 6; and Thomas R. Wotruba and Pradeep K. Tyagi, 'Met Expectations and Turnover in Direct Selling', *Journal of Marketing*, July 1991, pp. 24–35.

28. Quotes and other information in this section on super salespeople are from Geoffrey Brewer, 'Mind Reading: What Drives Top Salespeople to Greatness?', *Sales and Marketing Management*, May 1994, pp. 82–88; Andy Cohen, 'The Traits of Great Sales Forces', *Sales and Marketing Management*, October 2000, pp. 67–72; Julia Chang, 'Born to Sell?', *Sales and Marketing Management*, July 2003, pp. 34–38; and Henry Canaday, 'Recruiting the Right Staff', *Selling Power*, April 2004, pp. 94–96.

29. See 'To Test or Not to Test', *Sales and Marketing Management*, May 1994, p. 86.

30. Robert Klein, 'Nabisco Sales Soar after Sales Training', *Marketing News*, 6 January 1997, p. 23; and Geoffrey James, 'The Return of Sales Training', *Selling Power*, May 2004, pp. 86–91.

31. Julia Chang, 'No Instructor Required', *Sales and Marketing Management*, May 2003, p. 26.

32. See 'SMM's Best of Sales and Marketing: Best Trained Sales Force—Cisco Systems', *Sales and Marketing Management*, September 2001, pp. 28–29; and 'E-Learning: Field Training—How Cisco Spends Less Time in the Classroom and More Time with Customers', accessed at <http://business.cisco.com/prod/tree.taf%3Fpublic_view_true&kbns_1&asset_id_86360.html>, August 2003.

33. Christen P. Heide. 'All Levels of Sales Reps Post Impressive Earnings', press release, <www.dartnell.com>, 5 May 1997; and Dartnell's 30th Sales Force Compensation Survey, Dartnell Coporation, August 1998.

34. Geoffrey Brewer, 'Brain Power', *Sales and Marketing Management*, May 1997, pp. 39–48; Don Peppers and Martha Rogers, 'The Money Trap', *Sales and Marketing Management*, May 1997, pp. 58–60; Michele Marchetti, 'No Commissions? Are You Crazy?', *Sales and Marketing Management*, May 1998, p. 83; and Don Peppers and Martha Rogers, 'The Price of Customer Service', *Sales and Marketing Management*, April 1999, pp. 20–21.

35. Christian Homburg and Ruth M. Stock, 'The Link between Salespeople's Job Satisfaction and Customer Satisfaction in a Business-to-Business Context', *Journal of the Academy of Marketing Science*, vol. 32, no. 2, 2004, pp. 144–158.

36. For a discussion of the design and effects of sales contests, see William H. Murphy, Peter A. Dacin and Neil M. Ford, 'Sales Contest Effectiveness', *Journal of the Academy of Marketing Science*, vol. 32, no. 2, 2004, pp. 127–143.

37. Quotes from Bob Donath, 'Delivering Value Starts with Proper Prospecting', *Marketing News*, 10 November 1997, p. 5; and Bill Brooks, 'Power-Packed Prospecting Pointers', *Agency Sales*, March 2004, p. 37.

38. Quotes from David Stamps, 'Training for a New Sales Game', *Training*, July 1997, pp. 46–52; Erin Stout, 'Throwing the Right Pitch', *Sales and Marketing Management*, April 2001, pp. 61–63; Andy Cohen, 'Customers Know Best', *Sales and Marketing Management*, January 2003, p. 10; and William F. Kendy, 'How to be a Good Listener', *Selling Power*, April 2004, pp. 41–44.

39. Adapted from Betsy Cummings, 'On the Cutting Edge', *Sales and Marketing Management*, 3 June 2003, pp. 39–43.

40. Renée Houston Zemanski, 'Well Connected', *Selling Power*, March 2003, pp. 32–34.

41. Rachel Lebihan, 'Don't Call Me, I Won't Call You', *The Australian Financial Review*, 7 October 2005, p. 13.

42. Ibid.

PHOTO/AD CREDITS

CASE STUDY

Australian pizza wars: sales promotion—is that the answer?

Bill Proud, Queensland University of Technology

Introduction

In Australia what started out as a locally owned family-operated industry has developed into a highly competitive fast-food franchise business. Over the past 15 to 20 years, the aggressive marketing activities of the leading pizza chains contributed to the increased consumption of the product and at the same time made it difficult for new companies to enter the marketplace. There have been many attempts at entry into the marketplace but it has now rationalised out to four major operators—Domino's, Pizza Hut, Eagle Boys and Pizza Haven—and a number of other smaller operators.

Over the last couple of years all of the operators in the marketplace have faced a number of marketing and communication challenges and each has handled these challenges differently. Pizza Hut, one of the longest established operators in the market, decided to recruit a new director of marketing recently, and has given her the challenge of resurrecting Pizza Hut's market share and competing with the three other aggressive operators—Domino's, Eagle Boys and Pizza Haven.

At a senior level in Pizza Hut there had been disagreement between managers over the marketing and advertising strategy that would help develop the company to its full potential. Should they continue the price war or should they now develop new sales, promotional and advertising initiatives?

Australian pizza market

The total Australian pizza market, comprising quick service restaurant (QSR) outlets, small chains and independents, was valued at $1.4 billion. The Australian QSR pizza market was estimated at $663 million in 2004, equating to approximately 47% of the Australian pizza market and approximately 7% of the Australian fast-food market. Since 2004, the market has continued to grow at a rate of approximately 1% a year.

The Australian pizza market has been affected by an increasing move away from dine-in restaurants to takeaway outlets. The average number of times the average Australian dines out fell from 1.8 times a week in 2000 to 1.6 times a week in 2002.

Pizza is one of Australia's top five most popular meal solutions. The pizza market is fiercely competitive and a price war commenced 11 years ago with Pizza Hut starting two-for-one deals and Pizza Haven following, forcing small pizzerias to become more production oriented. A two-pizza, garlic bread and soda offer that cost $19.90 in 1995 sells for $19.95 today. When accounting for the rise in the Australian Consumer Price Index, that same deal should have brought in $26.38 in 2004. Operators fear that such a trend is not sustainable in the long term, as the combination of the price war and high operating costs results in very low margins.

Promotions encouraging volume purchases are popular as they absorb the cost differential. While the first pizza might cost $9, all subsequent pizzas are $1 to $2 cheaper.

The competition has forced operators to manage their businesses smarter, faster and more cost effectively. Furthermore, the operators strive to differentiate themselves not only on the basis of price but also on marketing, service and operations.

Demand for heated delivery bag systems has also soared in the past few years, but as pizza prices decreased operators placed a carryout-only mandate on bargain deals, to which consumers adapted.

To speed pickup and improve quality, holding cabinets have been installed in some of Domino's units, while Eagle Boys has taken that concept a step further by introducing a 'two-minute instant pizza system' which allows customers to choose from a limited menu of four pizzas, pay for their orders and leave in two minutes—or it's free.

Delivery versus pick up

Between 50% and 80% of Australian pizza customers pick the pizza up themselves, as the carryout pizzas sold at chains typically cost $2 less than delivered pizzas. However, delivery wasn't always second to carryout. In 1993, the year Australia's pizza price war began, delivery accounted for 85% of Pizza Hut's sales. Current pricing is set according to takeaway price, consequently increasing consumer preference for takeout.

However, a very gradual shift back to delivery is already underway in Australia. The current carryout–delivery mix at Domino's stores is 55–45, and expected to further equalise with time.

Competitors

Although Pizza Hut ruled Australia in the 1970s and 1980s, and Domino's was successful when it arrived in 1983, the foreign chains have not learned quickly enough to adapt products, services and operating practices to the Australian culture. Consequently, Australian businesses such as Pizza Haven (1984) and Eagle Boys (1987) arrived on the scene, both posing stiff competition.

Domino's Pizza Australia New Zealand Limited ('Domino's Pizza') is Australia's largest pizza chain in terms of both network store numbers and network sales. Pizza Hut, owned by YUM! Brands Inc., a US-based company with a market capitalisation of approximately $14.9 billion in 2005, holds approximately 37% of the pizza market. Eagle Boys, a privately owned pizza chain based in Brisbane, with core focus on regional Queensland and New South Wales, owns approximately 12% of the national market.

Pizza Haven is a privately owned pizza chain with approximately 103 stores, which operate predominantly in the southern states of Australia, and commands an 11% share.

The pizza market can be viewed in terms of three purchasing channels: pickup, home delivery and dine-in, with the first two being the key growth areas.

Marketing promotional activities

The pizza market is characterised by the following marketing and promotional activities:
- Expansion into new geographic markets
- Pushing sales from existing stores
- Innovation in product and menus
- Innovation in eating occasions
- Sales promotion opportunities.

There are many who believe that the pizza market has reached saturation due to changing consumer eating habits. Australia is also awash with fast-food stores, takeaway stores and restaurants, leaving little room for overall growth in the market.

The obvious strategy is for operators to try to steal market share from each other. At the same time Australians are becoming more health conscious and want a better choice of fresher, lower-fat foods from their fast-food providers.

The growth in numbers of fast-food chain outlets in recent times has been at the expense of independent operators who have simply been driven out of business.

In a saturated market, growth opportunities come from:
- pushing out the competition and taking their share
- branching out with new ventures that appeal to different non-traditional consumer segments.

In response to these challenges, the pizza operators are looking at a number of alternatives.

Product and promotion initiatives

Pizza Hut has been undertaking the same promotion initiatives as the other three major operators, heavily promoting the product through television and through flyers in the letterbox. Local store marketing efforts represent additional activities and include print advertising such as newspaper inserts and direct mail. Most of the major pizza operators use flyers and direct mail on a weekly basis. These include a variety of limited time offers including new product promotions, value promotions and partnership promotions. This enables the pizza operators to target different consumer groups that have different preferences and requirements.

Most companies run their campaigns throughout the year incorporating offers for each consumer segment. Pizza Hut has now decided that they will experiment with SMS ordering and online ordering.

Skybay innovation

In September 2004 BraveSky, Visa, Telstra and the NAB launched Skybay, a new service that sends consumers retail offers by SMS. It is free to sign up to receive special value offers from retailers, including Pizza Hut. Skybay offers Pizza Hut a sustainable and cost-effective use of the mobile channel for direct marketing and advertising purposes, while maintaining a relationship with the consumer based on high value and trust.

Promotions via Skybay are not executed in isolation. Pizza Hut adopts integrated campaigns linking all promotional elements. This innovation has now been adopted by Domino's and the market is starting to move in relation to SMS ordering. This, combined with 'limited time' offers centred on new products or major marketing campaigns, can be as simple as a 'buy one get one free' deal or reduced prices on specific days, such as Tuesdays.

In summary it appears that Pizza Hut is leading the market in the SMS ordering area but Domino's is following closely. Will SMS be the solution to the problem of Pizza Hut's marketing strategy or will the market still be driven primarily by price?

QUESTIONS

1. As a pizza operator, if you were charged with the responsibility of engendering customer loyalty and building brand equity, would the SMS service enhance your ability to market to customers?

2. Is the SMS sales promotion methodology a long-term tool or a short-term promotion effort?

3. Looking at the facts presented in the case, would you continue with a strong price promotion strategy or move towards sales promotion and other marketing initiatives?

4. Which do you believe is the stronger driver of sales in the pizza market—product innovation or promotion innovation?

5. Design a short-term sales promotion strategy to drive market share for the number two pizza operator in the market.

CASE STUDY

CHAPTER 18

Direct and online marketing

Mass-media audiences have continued to fragment with the proliferation of new media and as a result it has become more expensive to communicate with smaller audiences in these media. New media include digital television and radio and TCP/IP technologies—the underlying technology for the operation of the Internet—which is blurring the boundaries between telecommunications, media and home entertainment. Mobile phones also feature in this scenario, particularly as their video capabilities increase. Intel's alliance with Apple Corporation and Intel's move into home entertainment products and their new positioning statement—'Leap ahead'—are further proof of the convergence in telephony, media and TCP/IP (Internet) technologies.

For these and other more positive reasons, more organisations have turned to direct and online marketing as their competitive strategic stance. They know that because direct and online marketing is all about maintaining a dialogue with end-customers and others in their marketing logistics network—and mostly synchronously—they believe they will gain a competitive edge. By staying connected with customers, suppliers and alliance partners, competitors can be prevented from engaging in meaningful communications with these same customers and suppliers.

One company that knows this very well is Microsoft Corporation. Although it does communicate en masse with consumers and potential consumers alike—via free-to-air television (FTA-TV), press and magazine advertising, public relations programs and trade exhibitions—it also uses direct and online marketing tools and technologies to meet its objectives. As might be expected, Microsoft is at the forefront in its use of direct marketing tools such as narrowcast television, as well as online TCP/IP (transmission control protocol/Internet protocol) technologies such as email, instant messaging and the Web and has more recently focused its attention on gaming with the XBox 360 and operating systems for smartphones and pocket PCs. Microsoft does commercial battle on many fronts, and its competitive strategy relies on one-to-one communication and knowledge of individual customer requirements.

Marketing organisations like Microsoft genuinely want to stay engaged with customers and have moved away from the so-called 'leaky bucket' approach with its high acquisition costs and continual customer

Intel®Viiv™—a leap into home entertainment.

seepage—often before the company has reached a break-even point in servicing these customers. When customers are unknown to the marketing organisation, as is likely to be the case when intermediaries are involved, then marketing organisations can find themselves in financial difficulties quite suddenly. Companies like eBay have relatively low customer acquisition costs to begin with, and over time this becomes lower as totally satisfied customers become advocates and helpdesks rolled into one, and as the company adds value-adding products for its customers such as Skype VoIP (voice over Internet protocol).

An IDC study highlighted the extent to which email is a dominant collaborative tool, and also used exercises to ascertain which of a number of tools could best enhance collaboration. The situation facing many companies, particularly those engaged in business-to-business activities, which wish to stay connected in a meaningful way is that they are increasingly turning to collaborative tools to do so with their customers. This enables some to co-develop new products in as short a time as possible. And when we consider the fact that more than 50 million business users use consumer IM (instant messaging) services and even more use VoIP services like Skype, despite many an IT department's discouragement, we can see that people continue proactively to seek out and use new collaborative tools. If the new tools provide incremental value over existing tools—just as email provided value over phone and fax—then their adoption is fast and widespread. It is also clear that organisations which harness this aspect of human nature are leaders in the use of direct and online marketing.[1]

After reading this chapter you should be able to:

1 Explain the nature of direct and online marketing.

2 Discuss the benefits of direct and online marketing to both marketing organisations and their customers and identify the reasons for the rapid growth in this area of integrated marketing communication.

3 Discuss the various direct marketing techniques and their application.

4 Explain how direct and online marketing campaigns are developed, pre-tested, implemented and evaluated.

5 Discuss the public policy and ethical issues facing direct and online marketers.

Creating awareness, gaining share of mind, building a positive brand image and positioning mass-produced and mass-marketed products and brands is the job of media advertising. Public relations assists in this task. In many instances, these tasks are a prerequisite to making sales. This is the case whether the sales are to be made through channels that include wholesaling and retailing intermediaries, or through a more direct channel such as the home or office party plans used by Avon and Nutrimetics. Buyers order products at these home or office functions, or unseen, directly from a catalogue or online via a transacting website. Other buyers place their orders via telephone in response to a television commercial asking viewers to call a 1300 or 1-800 number. Figure 18.1 shows the range of approaches that might be used singly or in tandem to interact with customers. It must be remembered that customers determine the way they would prefer to be communicated with and fulfilled. (Note that, while the Net is a public network, intranet websites are accessed by company employees only, and extranet websites are accessed by both employees and known customers.)

Advertising and public relations set the scene. Sales promotion provides value-adding incentives to buy. Trade promotion ensures that the product is displayed advantageously in stores, with co-operative advertising support, often at promotional prices. There is, however, another element in competitive marketing strategy. This element aims to create an immediate sale, or to open a dialogue and develop an ongoing relationship with potential customers that will bring about a sale or a series of transactions sooner rather than later. In this chapter, we examine this approach—direct and online marketing. It integrates marketing communication techniques, using traditional and new media, with traditional and electronic fulfilment approaches and sophisticated customer relationship management techniques.

Various terms are used to describe the separate parts of this approach to marketing: one-to-one marketing (OnetoOne), direct marketing or direct-order marketing, e-marketing, interactive marketing. Regardless of the term used, the Information Age allows many marketers—and often the products themselves—to communicate with customers in real-time and to obtain a measured response for a measured input of expenditure. Moreover, this interactivity in marketing communications permits both parties to learn from the exchange.[2] In addition, the marketer can often fulfil a customer's order immediately, or synchronously, as when MusicMatch Jukebox software is delivered over the Net after payment is made. One-to-one consumer-to-consumer marketing is also evident when one of us buys software from an individual eBay vendor and, after payment is made through PayPal, the vendor provides a link to the software for 48 hours. Seen this way, online marketing is both a form of OnetoOne communication and also a step beyond marketing communication, because online fulfilment may also be possible, or at the very least initiated through an online order-processing system. Fulfilment may entail delivery of the product, or information about delivery, or even how to install the product or overcome a problem. This concept was first raised in Chapter 14 and is discussed further in this chapter.

Another feature of a direct and online marketer is 'accessible memory'.[3] That is, marketing organisations use a database to accumulate what they learn from customers. Companies such as Microsoft and Red Hat, the Linux distributor, learn which hardware–software combinations exhibit problems and, more importantly, they record the solutions to such problems. This is often referred to as a company's **knowledgebase**. The companies also gather other salient points about their customers. The companies learn of their customers' computer hardware setup when requested, and also which benefits they would like to see built into the next version of a piece of software. This information can then be distributed electronically to all frontline people involved in customer service.

In this chapter we first turn our attention to the broader aspects of direct marketing before looking more closely at online marketing communication, fulfilment tools and technologies, customer relationship management (CRM) and database management. In short, we examine OnetoOne communication as well as aspects of fulfilment using newer digital technologies such as the Net, intranets and extranets.

Knowledgebase
Database of frequently asked questions or solutions to problems maintained by a company to assist customers.

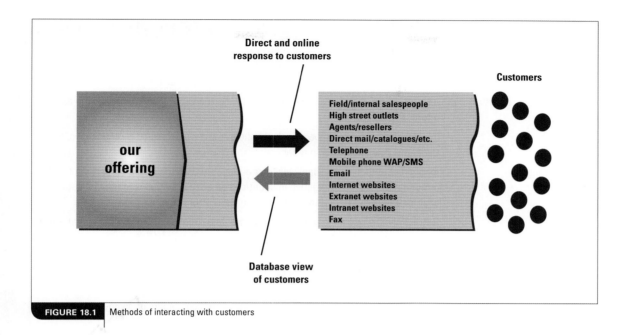

Customers

Field/internal salespeople
High street outlets
Agents/resellers
Direct mail/catalogues/etc.
Telephone
Mobile phone WAP/SMS
Email
Internet websites
Extranet websites
Intranet websites
Fax

Direct and online
response to customers

our
offering

Database view
of customers

FIGURE 18.1 Methods of interacting with customers

What is direct marketing?

Direct marketing is sometimes a single approach taken by organisations to market their products and services, but it is best viewed as part of an integrated direct marketing campaign, as illustrated by Microsoft's promotional activities. The Australian Direct Marketing Association endorses the following definition:

> **Direct marketing** is an interactive system of marketing which uses one or more advertising media to effect a measurable response and/or transaction at any location.[4]

This definition highlights the fact that any media can be used. Importantly, a measured response is sought from a measured input of expenditure. This response may take many forms, only one of which is the placement of an order, or what we think of as a commercial transaction. And the response or transaction can take place in any one of a number of ways—by telephone, post, email, electronic dispensing machine, a personal visit to an office or to the home, return small text message (SMS) or submitting an online 'form' at a website. A response or transaction may entail paying an energy bill at a kiosk, or placing an order by telephone in response to receipt of a communication directed to the receiver by name, by direct mail or email, or delivered en masse via a television commercial.

Direct marketing, with its historical roots in direct mail activities, now includes the promotional and fulfilment activities shown in Table 18.1 overleaf. There is some confusion as to just what can be considered direct marketing. Are we simply talking about one-to-one (hereafter referred to as OnetoOne) communications between a marketing organisation and its recorded customer base? Or are we talking about a Channel One marketing channel with no intermediaries such as retailers standing between the seller and the buyer? Are we simply talking about marketing communications that result in a transaction? Usually direct marketing refers to those activities that embrace 'targeted media' (such as Home Shopping via FTA-TV) but which permit interaction, and also OnetoOne media (such as direct mail or even FTA-TV with perhaps a telephone line backchannel) that enable

Direct marketing
An interactive system of marketing which uses one or more advertising media to effect a measurable response and/or transaction at any location.

TABLE 18.1 Forms of direct and online marketing

Direct print and reproduction	Making a tailored offer using printed or reproduced materials such as a mailing, a printed catalogue or CD-ROM version delivered to a list or database. Synchronous if the customer responds in real-time when the offer is received.
Direct-response television and radio	Interactive marketing, using FTA-TV, Pay-TV, narrowcast TV and radio, as well as interactive TV and radio. In some cases, there will be a back-channel for order placement; in other cases, the telephone or mail is used to order.
Telemarketing	Inbound or outbound personal selling or automated voice response unit selling to a list or database. May be interactive in situations where a donation is made or a vote is cast, or where orders are taken immediately the offer is made.
Telesales	Outbound calls, usually order-taking with prompts, from a known and stable database of customers; usually involves calls to middlemen.
Electronic dispensing and kiosks	A range of technologies used in receiving orders and payments as well as delivering products and services; now includes the use of 'smart' card technologies and digital cash, to a known database of customers or to potential customers.
Direct selling	Personal selling into the home or office to potential customers or a known clientele (database).
Electronic shopping (also referred to as e-commerce/ e-business). See 'What is online marketing?'	Recording responses, including taking orders, from inbound electronic signals or messages, in response to communications via any number of media: FTA-TV, broadband interactive TV, Pay-TV, narrowcast TV, the Internet (email, secure transaction websites, and fax), quick response direct marketing where same-day or fast-track fulfilment is involved, e.g. gifts ordered from Wishlist.com.au.
Direct and online database marketing (see the section on this topic later in the chapter)	The development and maintenance of electronic databases to interact with past, present and/or potential customers and others in the marketing channel, on a one-to-one basis, often in real-time, and where the databases are used to maintain value-laden relationships and to generate a measurable response and/or transactions through the integrated use of electronic network tools and technologies.[5]

interaction between buyers and sellers (see Marketing Highlight 18.1). In each case, the aim is to add to or maintain the currency of the marketer's database, to maintain a relationship with the consumer, to take an order or receive a payment or some other piece of salient information. The key point is that there is interactivity.

When an order is taken, the aim is to fulfil it without the use of intermediaries such as retailers. Then the question arises: is a retailer with an operation such as Australia's Myer Direct a direct marketer? The answer is that any marketing organisation using Myer Direct to communicate with customers and fulfil their orders is not employing direct marketing. Myer Direct, on the other hand, is a direct marketing organisation in its own right.

Do note at this point that only some of the direct marketing activities listed in Table 18.1 are capable of fulfilling the buyer in real-time. When using the term real-time, we are referring to such situations as when a household buys mountain water or carbonated beverages from a route salesperson, or telephones a 1-800 number to register its answer (and biographical details) to an FTA-TV quiz, or pays its energy bill at a kiosk within a supermarket, or a member downloads cash into a smart card at a public telephone booth or at home over the Net. These examples include transactions such as transferring money between bank accounts, paying 'anyone' including paying bills, not just the exchange of products or services for cash or credit as when buying an airline ticket.

By examining Table 18.1 in more detail we can appreciate the commonly used direct marketing terms and their meanings. In Table 18.2 we show the phenomenal growth in expenditure in direct marketing, and where it is worthwhile to examine the notes concerning what has been and not been included. We follow this table in examining direct and online marketing tools and technologies in detail in the rest of the chapter.

The major differences between mass marketing and OnetoOne marketing are set out in Table 18.3 where it should be noted that interactivity is designed to retain individual known customers who are profitable, rather than the mass marketer's aim of maintaining or increasing market share which may or may not be profitable.

SELF-CHECK QUESTIONS

1   Using the media categories mentioned in Table 18.1, where would you place the following: TV Shopping Network, Asia Business News Channel, FTA-TV channels such as NBC (USA), TV One (NZ) or Network 10 (Australia)?

2   Provide examples of marketing organisations that use each of the types of direct marketing mentioned in Table 18.1.

3   Indicate which of the examples given in Question 2 were 'single shot' direct mail and which were examples of integrated database marketing.

TABLE 18.2 Direct expenditure in Australia 2000–2004 ($A billions)

2000	2001	2002	2003	2004
8122.4	8077.9	8715.5	9408.4	11 122.8

Notes: From 2004, the formula for Telemarketing changed from cost to the company of running Telemarketing Call Centres to the cost of calls, thereby conforming to international practice. The category 'Stuffers'—promotional pieces put in with accounts—depends in the business-to-business section on the number of companies in Australia as supplied by ABS, which in 2004 turned to Australian Taxation Office figures, thereby sourcing an additional 956 337 companies. For Magazines there was a substantial increase in rates in 2004. Internet usage by business grew substantially in 2004 raising both the cost component and advertising expenditure. At the suggestion of ADMA Research Committee, Exibitions were excluded, as were Shopping Dockets because of uncertain small figures. A revision of Internet costs following receipt of better information led to a large reduction in that category, resulting in a reduction total to $11 122 800 000.

Source: Commercial Economic Advisory Service of Australia (CEASA), Sydney.

TABLE 18.3 Mass marketing versus one-to-one marketing

Mass marketing	One-to-one marketing
Average customer	Individual customer
Customer anonymity	Customer profile
Standard product	Customised market offering
Mass production	Customised production
Mass distribution	Individualised distribution
Mass advertising	Individualised message
Mass promotion	Individualised incentives
One-way message	Two-way message
Economies of scale	Economies of scope
Share of market	Share of customer
All customers	Profitable customers
Customer attraction	Customer retention

Source: The above figure is excerpted from the book *Enterprise One to One: Tools for Competing in the Interactive Age*, by Don Peppers and Martha Rogers PhD, <www.marketing1to1.com>, New York, Doubleday, 1997.

Contextual marketing—breaking through the fear of spam and worse

To shield customers from competitors' marketing communication and to overcome the fear of spam and the anti-social actions of hackers, it is now more necessary than ever to harness the power of positive word-of-mouth from loyal customers. After all, the communications we trust most are from those who figure prominently in our lives. Sometimes this word-of-mouth is action based rather than mere words alone.

The most brand-loyal customers must surely be those who tattoo their preferred brand name on their body as Harley-Davidson riders and many UK soccer 'loyalists' do. This personal graffiti is a form of action-based communication which cannot be erased by time alone. It makes wearing a brand-emblazoned T-shirt very passé indeed. However, due to the Internet (Net) and its graphical face the World Wide Web (Web), another form of brand loyalty is in evidence today, and the pass-it-on power of contextual marketing needs to be harnessed if online brand loyals are to assist marketers to meet their sales and profit objectives.

Evidence of extreme brand loyalty.

As online marketing takes hold—now that people in Australasia have joined others in the USA, Northern Europe, Korea and Japan who use this marketing channel for many of their purchases—word-of-mouth takes on a new dimension. The initial killer application—killer app.—in online marketing was email. Email changed the way we communicate and the speed at which we communicate, and has allowed us to span far greater distances than before. The terms reach, richness and affiliation apply when we think of email. They also apply in commercial use of the Web. Reach refers to the wide number of people involved, while richness refers to the depth of the content. Affiliation is akin to the notion of customer intimacy brought into marketing management vernacular by Treacy and Wiersema. Marketers cleverly turned to email and instant messaging to spread their message and, more importantly, to have their customers spread the message for them. Contextual marketing, as the approach has come to be called, also involves interactive websites, mobile phone short and multimedia messaging services (SMS/MMS) and Net-connected wireless application protocol (WAP) mobile phones.

Contextual marketing relies on richness of content for its pass-it-on power—often something funny, like a spoof of a new advertisement converted to an MPEG movie or Windows AVI file that runs a short movie clip when received. Most importantly, the theme of the website or the email should be related to the product. For example, nearly all major movies are promoted on the Web today, for the simple reason that this is the appropriate context in which to display such visual and aural delights. The website promoting *Planet of the Apes* made use of a treasure hunt to entice patrons to become involved. The movie *Swordfish*, relying as it did on a hacker trying to crack computer passwords and steal a large amount of money, offered $US100 000 to anyone who could crack 10 passwords. The Spielberg movie *AI* (Artificial Intelligence) made use of a web-based computer game and Blogging (web logs).

As these examples illustrate, direct and online marketing increasingly requires marketing organisations to exceed customer expectations about the products supplied, and to provide contextual experiences that cause customers to promote the brand to their friends—friend-to-friend (f2f)—in real-time. The issue for these marketing organisations is not simply to provide memorable experiences on 3D graphically enriched commercial websites—referred to by some as 'flow'—where the challenge of using a computer exceeds the users' ability. Regardless of whether those they are dealing with are described as visitors, patrons or guests, the marketing organisation must ultimately convert them to known subscribers who regularly interact online.

This then is the interactive world of direct and online marketing—one that involves the use of database information in marketing communication and in fulfilment, in using traditional and online marketing channels, and in customer relationship management. Additionally, direct and online marketing is able to harness developments in data mining, and in Net technologies such as Groove Networks, that enable relationship enhancement at deeper levels.

Sources: See Kim B. Sheehan and Caitlin Doherty, 'Re-Weaving the Web: Integrating Print and Online Communications', *Journal of Interactive Marketing*, vol. 15, no. 2, 2001, pp. 47–59; Philip Evans and Thomas S. Wurster, 'Getting Real about Virtual Commerce', *Harvard Business Review*, vol. 77, no. 6, 1999,

pp. 84–94; J. Aldred, 'Word-of-Mouth Infects the Web', *Internet World*, May/June 2000, pp. 30–32; Pierre Berthon, M. B. Holbrook and J. M. Hulbert, 'Beyond Market Orientation: A Conceptualization of Market Evolution', *Journal of Interactive Marketing*, vol. 14, no. 3, 2000, pp. 5–14; Thomas P. Novak, Donna L. Hoffman and Y.-F. Yung, 'Measuring the Customer Experience in Online Environments: A Structural Modeling Approach', *Journal of Marketing Science*, vol. 19, no. 1, 2000, pp. 22–42; Donna L. Hoffman and Thomas P. Novak, 'Marketing in Hypermedia Computer-Mediated Environments: Conceptual Foundations', *Journal of Marketing*, vol. 60, no. 3, 1996, pp. 50–68; Thomas O. Jones and W. Earl Sasser, 'Why Satisfied Customers Defect', *Harvard Business Review*, November–December 1995, pp. 88–89; Frederick E. Reichheld and Phil Schefter, 'e-Loyalty: Your Secret Weapon on the Web', *Harvard Business Review*, July–August 2000, pp. 105–113; J. Slaton, 'Pass It On', *TheStandard.com*, 18 September 2000; M. Treacy and F. Wiersema, 'Customer Intimacy and other Value Disciplines', *Harvard Business Review*, January–Febuary 1993, pp. 84–93. More interactive examples were to be found on the trail provided by the game producers at <www.cloudmakers.org/trail/#7.05>. Also see cases on partner relationship management at <www.groove.net/solutions/scenarios/partners.html> for examples of the developments occurring in direct and online marketing. Also visit the websites for Apple Corporation, <www.apple.com>; Dreamworks SKG, <www.dreamworks.com>; Groove Networks, <www.groove.net>; Lucas Film, <www.lucasfilm.com>; Yahoo! Groups, <www.yahoo.com>; Warner Bros, <www.warnerbros.com>.

Questions

1 Why is contextual marketing considered to be important?

2 Evans and Wurster coined the terms reach, richness and affiliation when discussing online marketing. Explain their meaning and relevance.

3 Why does the database seem to be so important in harnessing the power of contextual marketing?

18.1

What is online marketing?

Most people think of the **Internet (Net)** and its graphical face—the **World Wide Web (Web)**—when this question is asked. However, the Net is a 'cluster of related IT innovations' and only one aspect—albeit an increasingly important one—of online marketing.[6] We see online marketing as an extension to direct marketing, and define it thus: **online marketing** entails interaction with known customers and others in the marketing channel, on a one-to-one basis, often in real-time, to maintain value-laden relationships and to generate a measurable response and/or transactions using electronic network tools and technologies.

Today, we tend to think of a number of electronic network tools and technologies, such as private wide area networks (WANs) in business-to-business activity, as well as the interconnectivity between businesses and consumers, and between consumers themselves, afforded by mobile phones and particularly short/multimedia messaging services (SMS/MMS), and the slowly developing wireless application protocol (WAP) mobile commerce (m-commerce) which relies on 3G mobile phone networks.

Internet (Net) The world's largest public computer network which connects many other computers and computer networks.

World Wide Web (Web) The graphical face of the Internet.

Online marketing Interaction with known customers and others in the marketing channel, on a one-to-one basis, often in real-time, to maintain value-laden relationships and to generate a measurable response and/or transactions using electronic network tools and technologies.

Interconnected microprocessors have penetrated our world to such an extent that they are involved in all manner of devices, from 'fly-by-wire' jetliners to appliances at work and at home.[7] What is more, Intel and others are enabling household appliances such as LG's air conditioners and refrigerators to interconnect and the brands involved are being positioned on this attribute in marketing communication. We live in an increasingly wired world where the exchange of 'bits' rather than 'atoms' makes up a large part of the economy.[8] And in this wired world, consumers are more knowledgeable and increasingly selective about whom they will accept communication from, no matter the means employed and regardless of content.[9] They are also turning more readily to peer-to-peer communication as Marketing Highlight 18.2 illustrates.

Marketing organisations around the world have changed, both in form and value, as a result of three entwined factors: digitisation, globalisation and deregulation.[10] Digital information systems have enabled new ways of doing business to the point where the vast majority of all non-cash transactions in Australia and New Zealand are electronic, although this may not necessarily involve the Internet.[11] Globalisation as a process continues unabated and has brought benefits to countries like Australia and New Zealand, but arguably can have negative effects in others in terms of both economic and cultural consequences. Deregulation has been a two-edged sword in industries such as energy and transportation in Victoria. Consumer prices have increased, and the private sector that thought it would benefit from a mixture of privatisation and deregulation has not done so. Banking is largely a matter of electronic transactions, and deregulation in Australia in the early 1980s led to soaring debt. A four pillars government policy (i.e. four main banks), fee increases, cost cutting through headcount reduction and branch closures over the two decades that followed led to profit growth. At the same time, consumer attitudes towards banks plummeted, which has led to banks re-establishing some store-front operations.

Marketing organisations have turned to the Net either to grow their revenue base (e.g. intercountry transactions) or for productivity reasons (e.g. disintermediation).[12] These tend to embrace such prompts to use the Web as the following: wanting to gain a global presence; establishing and maintaining a competitive edge; shortening or eradicating components of marketing logistics networks (disintermediation) or revamping them (reintermediation); making cost savings; and gaining a research advantage.[13] As the banking sector has shown, providing incentives for migrating customers to the Web works to the banks' advantage: the cost of a customer transaction is less than 10 cents using the Net compared with 70 cents for a telephone banking transaction, $1.10 for an automatic teller transaction (ATM) and up to $1.70 for a transaction conducted in a High Street outlet.

It was originally envisaged that businesses would use the Web mainly for consumer marketing (B2C, in the vernacular of the online marketer). However, use of the Web in business-to-business/ government marketing (B2B and B2G) has so far outstripped its use in consumer marketing. One reason for this may be the fact that early use of the Net took a broadcast medium approach and largely failed, with clickthroughs on banner ads failing to exceed the 2% level.[14] There is, however, a mere exposure effect and researchers have continued to study such aspects of online marketing communication as 'attitude toward the site' and how this is related to brand attitude and purchase intention.[15] There are other roles for the Web, and its use in consumer marketing has grown. The USA remains the clear leader in consumer use of the Web for online purchases, accounting for $A166 billion B2C sales in 2003 compared with Australian online transactions at $A16 billion.[16] Japan seems to be less enthusiastic about Web-based commerce. This is partly due to Net access costs, partly to the competing physical world express delivery system, Takkuhaiban, and partly to a preoccupation with mobile telephone use (DoCoMo iMode), as well as the reluctance of Japanese consumers to use anything other than cash, thus explaining why it came last in per capita spending on holiday shopping in 2004.[17] Broadband Internet penetration is higher in Korea than in any other country, given that over 90% of households have access to low-cost ADSL. Koreans are heavy users of the Web for shopping, which may reflect the fact that most households have broadband access to the Net and the fact that Koreans have adopted personal avatars which they buy items for on the Web. Koreans are heavy mobile phone users with usage slightly higher than Australians.[18]

It is instructive to put use of the Net and Web in Australasia in context by comparing and contrasting household use of various media. Whereas nearly all households use the telephone and view FTA-TV, only one-third of households view Pay-TV. Internet penetration stands at some 53% in Oceania/Australia.[19] Net usage in Australasia is lower than the 68% usage in North America and, as already indicated, the adoption level of the Net for transactions is much lower in Australia.[20]

Due to interactivity in real-time, online marketing fits more closely with direct response marketing than with the mass-marketing paradigm of old. This view will become clearer as we examine the nature of online marketing strategy in the following sections. While many see online marketing as a means of many communicating to many, and many to one, we see its major role in terms of one-to-one interactive communication.[21] We next turn our attention to this strategic use of online marketing.

Online OnetoOne marketing strategy

Marketing organisations using the Net do so in the knowledge that the medium permits interactive communication, as well as being useful for business processes such as order taking and processing. Most importantly, it facilitates customer relationship management (CRM). However, usage of the Net by Australian and New Zealand businesses differs from that in countries like the UK, even though there are only minor cultural differences between the three countries.[22] Where the culture is different, particularly in regard to the role of guanxi (connections) and trust in collective societies such as those in Southeast Asia, there are arguably more barriers to rapid adoption of the Net in marketing strategy.[23] UK marketing organisations have readily adopted the Net for their competitive marketing strategy and have been willing to provide a reason for consumers to shop via this medium.[24] So far, Australasian marketing organisations seem to have been less willing to interact online on a OnetoOne basis than those in the UK, and this applies to large, medium and small businesses.[25]

Regardless of this apparent anomaly, there are sound reasons for strategic use of the Web, particularly where customers have varying requirements of the companies they deal with and where customers represent different value to the companies. To identify the degree to which direct response techniques in general, and the Web in particular, might be used in competitive marketing strategy, questions need to be asked of customers. Based on the answers to these questions concerning their needs and value to the organisation (X and Y axes), businesses may find themselves in one of four quadrants in a OnetoOne differentiation strategy matrix, as illustrated in Figure 18.2 on page 702. Depending on how differentiated customers' needs are, and how differentiated the customer valuations are to the business, a firm can establish its position in terms of the most appropriate strategy to adopt, from mass marketing (Quadrant I) through to OnetoOne marketing (Quadrant IV).[26]

Marketing organisations in Quadrant I are best suited to using a mass-marketing approach, including mass-media advertising, to position their brands in consumers' minds and to ensure they have

Volkswagon adopts a niche strategy with its EOS model.

Being online means being digital

Nicholas Negroponte, director of MIT's Media Lab, IT adviser to world leaders and author of the bestseller *Being Digital*, points out that, due to the 'combined forces of convenience, imperative and deregulation', all manner of media have become 'digitally driven'. It is true that once a newspaper article is typed into a word processor its form is bits rather than atoms and it can be transmitted and reproduced in many ways—some the intellectual property holder never dreamt of. This technological feat applies to photographs, film, video, voice, data—virtually anything except the human holding the digital camera or composing the words captured in a digital device. The fictional USS *Enterprise* crews of *Star Trek* fame, *Dr Who* and author Douglas Adams's equally fictional characters in *The Hitch-Hikers' Guide to the Galaxy* are thus far the exception to the rule in terms of animate objects becoming bits and then being reconstructed again . . . and again . . . and again.

What do bits and atoms have to do with marketing, you ask? Everything! Well, just about everything, to be more precise. The fact is that businesses everywhere have taken on a new form. The marketplace for many firms has become the 'marketspace'. This is true not just in their partnering with suppliers, but in their formation of the digital, global equivalent of

the Japanese *keiretsu*, or network alliances, sometimes with their arch-rivals. It has even spawned new types of businesses, where those who own popular website domain names like MensBowTies.com—and where there is no trading business—earn click-through income from third parties such as Formalwear hire companies which do trade. But nowhere is the paradigm shift to be seen more clearly than in the field of marketing communications.

A potted history of communications is very telling in this regard. Humanity developed language around 10 000 BC. Advertisements first appeared in about 3000 BC, with the first textbooks appearing in Egypt in 2800 BC. Then came the Chinese printing press in AD 2 and the German Gutenberg Press very much later in AD 1455. We experienced 200 years of 'industrial revolution' from about 1750 to the present wherein all manner of communications devices were developed, ranging from the first typewriter (1798) to the first telephone (1877), the first computer (ENIAC, 1946) and on to what Fred Schneider of Andersen Consulting (now Accenture) terms the 'All-in-One' device.

Schneider's 'All-in-One' device is a devilishly simple concept that consumer electronics companies such as Intel, LG.Philips and Sony are turning into reality with willing help from technology titan Microsoft Corporation—with software, smartphones and the Xbox 360 games console—and other companies like Sling Media that allows TV to be streamed to Internet-connected devices. WebTV came, went and is experiencing a second coming when beamed through such devices as the Pocket PC and smartphone. Streaming video-on-demand, music-on-demand, as well as voice- and data-on-demand are set to push ownership of new products such as iPods and Zen Nomad music and TV players even higher. We can see why telephone companies (telcos) such as Australia's Telstra and SingTel's Optus wanted to be in Pay-TV and why media *keiretsus* like News Corp's News Ltd want to be involved in telephony, and have turned to the Internet. It is why Microsoft joined with the NBC to form MSNBC. It is why Bill

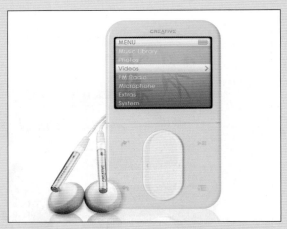

Creative ZEN Vision: MP3 player—chosen by many for its good looks and functionality.

Gates wanted to put communication satellites into orbit together with Motorola in the Iridium satellite system. It is why, in 1999, the Packers folded a number of assets into ecorp including Australia's number one local portal site, NineMSN—itself an alliance between PBL's Nine Network, Microsoft Corporation and Telstra. It is also why Telstra bundles Pay-TV with its telephone services.

Projections have been made that, while Australia's Pay-TV might bring revenues of $2.5 billion per year and video-on-demand may be worth $1.3 billion, the real action is in local and long-distance telephony where the market value is seen to be $24 billion—the same figure projected for home shopping in Australia through interactive broadband services. The sleeper may yet be home gambling and betting which is predicted to be worth $12 billion a year with the Packers once again featuring prominently in Australia and Asia. Interactive broadband services already enable punters to bet on a horse or play an online 'slot machine'. In fact, such future broadband services might allow you to sell property over the cable, download the cash to a 'smart' card reader in your all-in-one television, then proceed to gamble the proceeds—all from the one connection.

But when is this new interactive online service going to appear in lounge rooms across the Asia–Pacific region? When are happy home-makers going to be able to play along with games show contestants, or pose their own question to a hapless president or prime minister on an interactive Ricky Lake Show, or maybe press a single button linked by infrared controls to their interactive TV and so order their new car straight from the virtual assembly line? And when will students no longer need to go to school or university but will mix their course work and MTV on the same wall-size interactive TV screen from their beds?

The plain truth is that affordable bandwidth will be the missing link for a major section of the region and a major part of the world's population for quite some time. The copper wires that carry our voice and data so far, and so slowly, are not up to the task of carrying interactive, full-motion video, even with the help of Digital Signal Line (DSL) compression technology touted by the telcos.

So don't sell your High Street or Jurong West video-hire shop just yet! As this rollout of fibre-optic cable proceeds, the somewhat fanciful scenario described above will become a reality. However, it will be a case of infrastructure development for some time to come.

Once the infrastructure is in place, being an online marketer will indeed mean being digital. Such a marketspace will then see a global market accessible to even the smallest online firm that seeks to fill the gaps in the market.

Sources: Quoted sections from Nicholas Negroponte, *Being Digital*, London, Hodder & Stoughton, 1995, p. 13; Fred Schneider, 'Virtual Retailing', *Andersen Consulting*, vol. 11, no. 1, July 1994; Market Projections by the Broadband Services Expert Group (BSEG), 1995; Anonymous, 'Planned Use of the W3 for Selling from the Yankee Group, *Business Week*, reprinted in the *The Australian Financial Review*, 19 June 1995, p. 19; and Caryn Meller, 'Pay-TV Pays Up', <www.mcs.mq.edu.au/minm/Collier_NowlandStory.html>; the term 'marketspace' was coined by J. Rayport and J. Sviokla, 'Managing in Marketspace', *Harvard Business Review*, vol. 72, no 6, 1994, pp. 141–150.

Questions

1 Do you have Pay-TV connected? List the features you believe 'you could not live without' and those that are not 'value for money'.

2 What is the (forecast) proportional revenue breakdown for such services as telephony, home shopping, video-on-demand, home gambling and Pay-TV in your country or region? Does this differ markedly from the figures put forward for Australia in this highlight?

3 How might Microsoft integrate its software and Pay-TV ambitions?

18.2

merchandising space in traditional retail outlets. Those in Quadrant II may find niche marketing the most appropriate strategy to adopt—as Volkswagen does with its EOS cabriolet model (pictured) in a global market that includes Australasia. The marketers that fall into Quadrant III do so because, while the needs of customers remain quite similar, it is mainly business travellers (in the case of airlines)

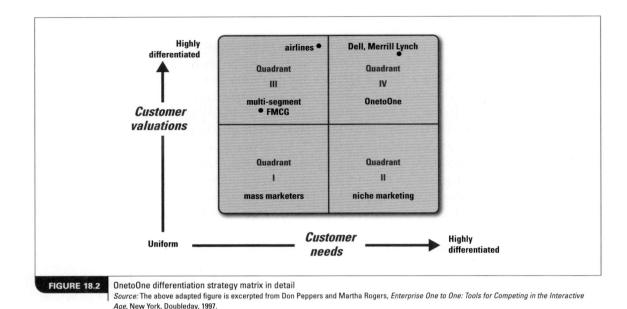

FIGURE 18.2 OnetoOne differentiation strategy matrix in detail
Source: The above adapted figure is excerpted from Don Peppers and Martha Rogers, *Enterprise One to One: Tools for Competing in the Interactive Age,* New York, Doubleday, 1997.

who account for the bulk of the airlines' customers, revenue and profits. In a similar fashion, FMCG manufacturers have large segments of customers who all want the same product (e.g. dishwashing liquid). However, it is their supermarket customers who account for the bulk of their sales. Companies like Cisco (with the largest online sales revenue in the world), Dell Computers, Merrill Lynch and J. B. Were stockbrokers fall into Quadrant IV. These marketing organisations have customers with a wide range of requirements, and some customers are worth much more than others. In Dell's case, customers range from those making a single purchase, not to be repeated for three years, to a large business that buys thousands of computers and peripherals each year. Their customers' needs also vary widely in that home users have fairly similar requirements, while business uses are varied—the configuration of computers may vary almost on a one-by-one basis within the same client company, not to mention between companies and industries.

There are two further questions: How capable is the business of identifying and interacting with individual customers? And how capable is the business of tailoring its behaviour to the needs of small customer groups or individual customers?[27] Figure 18.3 illustrates how a marketing organisation might seek to realign its marketing strategy in the face of competitive positioning and how customers are positioned. In Figure 18.3, the customers have highly differentiated needs and different customers represent different valuations to the business. Moreover, competitors A and B are more able to meet customers' requirements, albeit for different reasons. The company must realign its marketing strategy. To do so, it must be able to take advantage of the situation, and be capable of customising its offer and of interacting on a OnetoOne basis with customers. The firm would be wise to realign by adopting an online OnetoOne marketing strategy that incorporates use of the Web in interactive marketing communication—as an online marketing channel or to supplement traditional marketing channels—and to enhance relationships.

A marketing organisation that finds its customers have highly differentiated needs and offer great variety in their returns to the organisation (e.g. share-of-wallet in the financial services sector) might well consider an online OnetoOne marketing strategy, particularly if its competitors are already further advanced in their adoption of this strategy. Full use of the Net and Web involves such strategic knowledge. Businesses using Groove Networks technology to enhance both synchronous

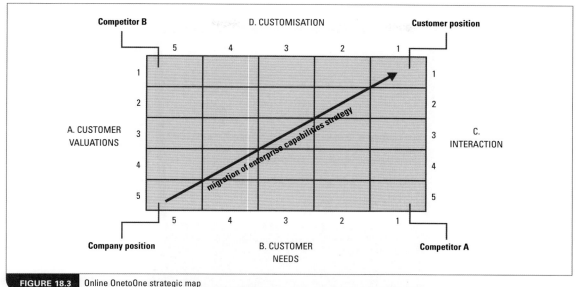

FIGURE 18.3 Online OnetoOne strategic map

Source: Stewart Adam, 'OnetoOne eMarketing Strategy Alignment: Five Internet Case Studies', refereed paper, *Academy of Marketing 2001,* 2001: A Marketing Odyssey, Cardiff University, United Kingdom, 2–4 July 2001, p. 5, (multimedia CD-ROM), based on Don Peppers and Martha Rogers, *Enterprise One to One,* New York, Doubleday, 1999, p. 72; and Don Peppers, Martha Rogers and Bob Dorf, *The OnetoOne Fieldbook,* New York, Doubleday, 1999, p.168.

and asynchronous communication have adopted a legal peer-to-peer online marketing strategy (see Marketing Highlight 18.3), and as the earlier discussion on Groove Networks illustrated are indicative of businesses suited to employing an online OnetoOne marketing strategy. Not all marketing organisations benefit from using the Web as a direct response tool, but many that are not using the Web might well benefit greatly from its adoption—provided they integrate customer interface Web technology with back-office business processes and enterprise processes generally. In other words, it is not enough simply to mount a 'vanity' website that remains locked into a one-way mass-marketing communication paradigm, completely overlooking the fact that customers today are learning customers more so than ever before, and that the use of the Web coupled with database technology means that businesses have become **learning organisations**.[28]

Arguably, commentaries to the effect that small and micro-sized marketing organisations are able to gain access to world markets using the Net, as extolled by government, are examples of wishful thinking.[29] Rather, it appears that most marketing organisations are communicating and maintaining relationships, mostly in support of offline sales, in local markets.[30] The explanation of this feature of Australasian use of the Net lies in the fact that large US-based online businesses such as eBay. com and Amazon.com gained early-mover advantage and much attendant publicity around the world, and they dominate categories such as auctions and online book retailing, even in their new host countries—remembering that the likes of eBay are global organisations as the buyer and seller can log into any country with a single authentication. As evidence of this, Amazon's 2003 global sales totalled some $A6.5 billion or nearly half of the total of all online sales in Australia in 2003.[31] Local online marketing organisations tend to dominate in categories such as classified advertising and groceries, for the obvious reason that buyer–seller proximity is required. Content analysis of the Sensis-owned Trading Post's website at <www.tradingpost.com.au> (pictured overleaf) illustrates this point. Furthermore, content analysis of Australasian websites shows a remarkable absence of the features required for transactions by international buyers (e.g. an online currency converter), or for customer relationship management purposes (e.g. multilingual communications choice at

Learning organisation
A learning organisation is defined by its ability to innovate, adopt and change in line with its changing environment.

Trading Post makes it easy to buy and sell.

websites) with other than local markets.[32] While widespread use of the Net to its full potential is yet to emerge—due partly to the more realistic valuations being placed on new and existing businesses that employ Net technologies by world capital markets—more sophisticated online OnetoOne marketing continues to develop in Australasia in the three areas of marketing already mentioned: marketing communication, marketing channel and CRM. We examine these marketing roles for the Net further in the next section.

From marketing communication to transacting and relationship management

Do marketing organisations move in a linear fashion from using the Net in marketing communication through to transacting online with known customers, and then to maintaining the customer relationships that have developed on a OnetoOne basis? While intuitively appealing, the answer to this seems to be 'No'. We can see the integration of direct and online marketing in Figure 18.4. Most marketing organisations begin by communicating their offer by using television as an acquisition medium (e.g. SMS your first and last name now to this number) or direct mail to a now known subscriber base—or another approach from Cell C1. Those that began business on the Net may use their customer knowledge to generate a self-perpetuating f2f campaign involving email (or another online approach from Cell C2), or even a combination of offline and online approaches.

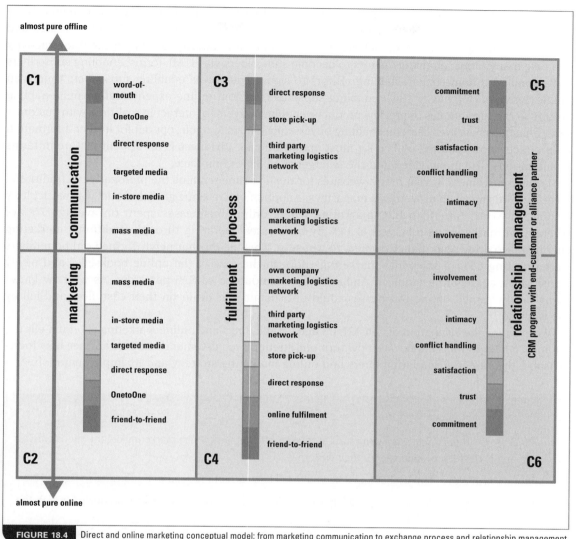

almost pure offline

C1

communication
- word-of-mouth
- OnetoOne
- direct response
- targeted media
- in-store media
- mass media

C3

process
- direct response
- store pick-up
- third party marketing logistics network
- own company marketing logistics network

C5

management
- commitment
- trust
- satisfaction
- conflict handling
- intimacy
- involvement

C2

marketing
- mass media
- in-store media
- targeted media
- direct response
- OnetoOne
- friend-to-friend

C4

fulfilment
- own company marketing logistics network
- third party marketing logistics network
- store pick-up
- direct response
- online fulfilment
- friend-to-friend

C6

relationship
CRM program with end-customer or alliance partner
- involvement
- intimacy
- conflict handling
- satisfaction
- trust
- commitment

almost pure online

FIGURE 18.4 Direct and online marketing conceptual model: from marketing communication to exchange process and relationship management
Source: Adapted from Stewart Adam, 'A Model of Web Use in Direct and Online Marketing Strategy', *Electronic Markets: The International Journal of Electronic Commerce and Business Media*, vol. 12, no. 4, 2002, p. 267, <www.tandf.co.uk/journals/routledge/10196781.html>.

The marketing organisation that adopts a marketing communication approach from Cell C1 in Figure 18.4 may proceed to fulfil customer requirements using one or more traditional offline methods from Cell C3, such as its own marketing logistics network (MLN) or the services of a third party, and may seek to maintain customer intimacy and handle conflict resolution using traditional methods such as the telephone and through the company's own outlets, from Cell C5. Many different permutations are possible. For example, an airline may communicate with frequent-flyer subscribers using direct mail to announce special holiday packages (C1). The airline may direct its customers to the company website as the only means of taking up the special discounted package holidays (C4). On the website, subscribers could be asked to opt for receiving marketing communication on future package deals, and even to email information on the current package to their friends (f2f) directly from the website (C6). This last step meets privacy and anti-spam legislation requirements and enables the company to build consumer trust (see Chapter 21 for more on this legislation).

Even if a marketing organisation uses sophisticated Web design features, the task remains one of reaching the target market with reasons why the company or brand website should be visited and revisited. Such sophistication in website design includes interactivity and vividness.[33] Interactivity can take many forms: enabling visitors to become subscribers via HTML forms; enabling subscribers to personalise a home page; enabling visitors to sign a guestbook; enabling subscribers to join an online community (chat or IRC); enabling subscribers to join online experiential events; enabling visitors to take up samples or preview products; enabling buyers to interact in real-time with customer service/installers via Web camera; enabling buyers/subscribers to opt in/opt out for further information on products (now required by law for most organisations). Vividness is an evident feature in terms of animations, streaming video and the emergence of 3D e-commerce.

Getting customers to visit brand websites for the first time remains the prerogative of traditional media advertising, such as women's magazines. Adoption of a revenue growth model was particularly evident in North American B2C marketing where online businesses spent on average 75% of revenue on marketing effort—versus 13% by businesses operating through traditional marketing channels—to draw potential customers to websites. This meant that newly formed online retailers were directing 68% of sales into marketing effort; in the case of the online bookseller and newly transformed aggregating landlord Amazon.com it amounted to $25 per order. As we now know, many newly formed online businesses could not sustain this drain on their cash flow and fell by the wayside.[34]

We examine the evaluation of Cells C1, C3 and C5 and direct and online marketing effort in Cells C2, C4 and C6 later in this chapter. We now turn our attention to customer databases and see how indispensable they are in formulating direct and online marketing strategy and its implementation.[35]

SELF-CHECK QUESTIONS

4   What are the three online marketing roles ascribed to the Net, and which marketing organisations employ to varying degrees to value-add for their customers?

5   Provide examples of brands that might be said to fall into each of the quadrants indicated in Figure 18.2.

6   Does it matter from a marketing strategy viewpoint the path(s) taken for various products through the cells shown in Figure 18.4?

Direct and online database use

Databases lie at the heart of modern marketing science and practice, particularly when marketing organisations adopt a direct and online strategy. Marketing scientists turn to databases when searching for published studies concerning the many facets examined in textbooks, presented at conferences such as the Australian and New Zealand Marketing Academy (see the archive database at <anzmac.org>) and in published refereed journals such as the *Australasian Marketing Journal* (see the archive database at <anzmac.org/amj>). Marketing practitioners use databases to record customer information including invoicing and deliver-to addresses, demographic information and historical transaction data that enable monitoring of the lifetime value of the customer to the company. These databases may previously have been referred to as secondary data by more traditional marketers engaged in marketing research activities, but they are no longer simply a by-product of the organisation's accounting system. We begin by examining the nature of database marketing.

What is direct and online database marketing?

The term database appears many times throughout this discussion on direct and online marketing. A suitable definition of direct and online database marketing is:

Direct and online database marketing entails development and maintenance of electronic databases to interact with past, present and/or potential customers and others in the marketing channel, on a one-to-one basis, often in real-time, and where the databases are used to maintain value-laden relationships and to generate a measurable response and/or transactions through the integrated use of electronic network tools and technologies.

Direct and online database marketing
Entails development and maintenance of electronic databases to interact with past, present and/or potential customers and others in the marketing channel, on a one-to-one basis, often in real-time, and where the databases are used to maintain value-laden relationships and to generate a measurable response and/or transactions through the integrated use of electronic network tools and technologies.

Lists Direct and online marketing entails hiring lists containing names of qualified potential customers.

When using database technology, the intention is to engage in OnetoOne dialogue and elicit a desired, measurable response in target groups and individuals. Note that a list and a database are not the same thing. A **list** is simply names, addresses and contact numbers, and can be hired for direct mailing purposes or developed from internal sources such as a list of company CEOs in a particular region or country. Those prospects who, on being contacted, interact or agree to interact with the marketing organisation become part of its database.

Databases may take one of three forms: hierarchical, network or relational. Hierarchical databases have been in use the longest; they permit access to customer transaction data using account numbers, but may not allow the easy extraction of data (data mining) relevant to market segmentation and the tailoring of offers. Network databases are similar to hierarchical databases, but with multiple access points to the data held. This makes them more flexible in use, but they are more expensive to maintain and more complex to use. Relational databases are now more commonly used in marketing—the data are entered via the Web and accessed by marketing management via company intranets/extranets. Data are stored in two-dimensional tables of rows and columns, where each row represents the attribute data for each entity (customer), and columns represent the same attribute (first name, last name, address and so on) for all records. The tables are linked together by common keys such as account numbers, and can be easily reconfigured. Most importantly, they are easily accessed and manipulated so as to link a single record in one table with another record in a second table, or to link many records in one table with many in a second table, or to link each record in a table with many in another table and on and on in a daisy chain fashion. Large firms tend to use third-party software such as SAP and Oracle, while small and medium enterprises are likely to be using open-source My SQL or PostgreSQL on a Linux machine (see <RedHat.com> for an example of a Linux distribution), or Microsoft Access or FoxPro on a PC or Mac.

A database contains attribute information in columns that may relate to individuals or organisations, set out under the fields grouped under customer data, item data and invoice data as in Figure 18.5 overleaf. The fields shown in Figure 18.5 are a guideline only. The complexity of the databases used and whether or not they are linked to external databases depend on the nature of the product, service and industry. Most importantly, such relational databases should enable easy monitoring of the aggregated dollar purchases

Harris Technology employ database technology to present its products online and to monitor customer lifetime value.
Source: <www.harristechnology.com/home/hts>

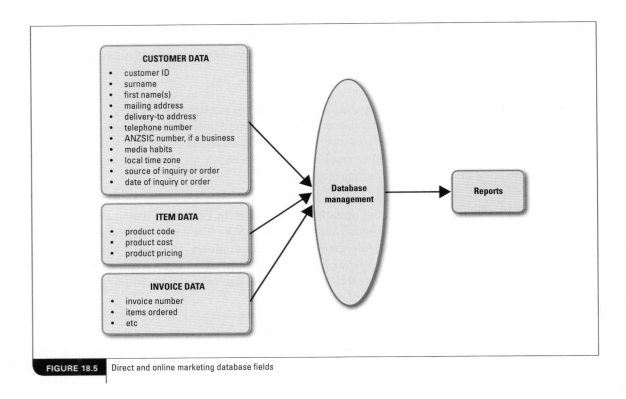

FIGURE 18.5 Direct and online marketing database fields

Privacy guidelines
Countries such as Australia
have extended privacy
legislation to include
most profit and non-profit
organisations.

and profitability of individual customers, so that their customer lifetime value to the business can be monitored.[36] It should be noted that **privacy guidelines** indicate that companies must disclose the purposes for which they are gathering customer information, and must be prepared and able to show individuals the information they hold on them.[37]

How are direct and online marketing databases used?

While business-to-business marketers are heavy users of direct and online marketing databases, consumer products marketers also use these databases. This is particularly true of service organisations such as airlines, financial services organisations and hotels. FMCG marketers and their retailing intermediaries increasingly use customer databases for purposes such as customer retention programs. One study found that almost two-thirds of all large consumer products companies are currently using or building such databases—for example, the Omomatic club uses a database to target its marketing effort.[38] Palace Cinemas maintains a database of club members who receive discounted tickets to all movies, with the proviso that 'no free list' movies are excluded. It uses the database to send birthday greetings and a free ticket gift to its database members just before their birthdays. American Express uses its database to tailor offers of different value to its various cardholders (blue, green, gold, platinum and black), given that the holders of each class of card represent a different value to the company. It is capable of linking cardholder spending with postcode data. If a new restaurant opens in a particular postcode zone, Amex can offer a special discount to those within walking distance or those who eat out a lot.

Marketing organisations use their databases in a number of ways: identifying prospects; deciding which customers should receive a particular offer; deepening customer loyalty; reactivating customers; and data mining. We examine each in turn.

◉ *Identifying prospects*. Many companies generate sales leads by advertising their products or offers. Ads generally have a response feature, such as a business reply card or toll-free phone number. The database is built from these responses. The company sorts through the database to identify the best prospects, then reaches them by mail, phone or personal call in an attempt to convert them to customers.

◉ *Deciding which customers should receive a particular offer*. Companies identify the profile of an ideal customer for an offer. Then they search their databases for individuals most closely resembling the ideal type. By tracking individual responses, the company can improve its targeting precision over time. Following a sale, it can set up an automatic sequence of activities: one week later, send a thankyou note; five weeks later send a new offer; ten weeks later (if customer has not responded), phone the customer and offer a special discount. As Marketing Highlight 18.3 illustrates, there can be abuses in this area of marketing.

◉ *Deepening customer loyalty*. Companies can build customers' interest and enthusiasm by remembering their preferences and sending appropriate information, gifts or other materials. For example, Mars (Uncle Bens), a market leader in pet food as well as chocolate confectionery, maintains an exhaustive pet database. In Germany, the company has collected the names of virtually every family that owns a cat. It obtained these names by offering the public a free booklet entitled 'How to take Care of your Cat'. People who requested the booklet filled out a questionnaire, providing their cat's name, age, birthday and other information. Mars then sends a birthday card to each cat in Germany each year, along with a new cat food sample and money-saving coupons for Mars brands. The result is a lasting relationship with the cat's owner.

◉ *Reactivating customer purchases*. The database can help a company to make attractive offers of product replacements, upgrades or complementary products just when customers might be ready to act. In the USA, General Electric maintains a customer database containing each customer's demographic and psychographic characteristics along with an appliance purchase history. Using this database, GE marketers assess how long customers have owned their current appliances and which past customers might be ready to purchase again. They can determine which customers need a new GE video recorder, compact disc player, stereo receiver or something else to go with other recently purchased electronics products. Or they can identify the best past GE purchasers and send them gift certificates or other promotions to apply against their next GE purchase. A rich customer database allows GE to build profitable new business by locating good prospects, anticipating customer needs, cross-selling products and services and rewarding loyal customers.

◉ *Data mining*. Companies maintain many databases in what today are large data warehouses. **Data mining** entails checking databases for patterns and trends that are hypothesised to exist, or in order to find new connections between data items. Modern software enables open-ended queries that involve systematic searches for relationships and patterns within and between databases. Four types of relationships might be searched for: *associations*—for example the association between sales of two product categories; *classes*—for example if males aged 25–39 buy beer and disposable nappies, examination of gender (as a class) might mean that the connection between data in different fields can be more easily made; *clusters*—for example the examination of demographics and supermarket location would be undertaken because this is a logical relationship and mining this data cluster would identify market segments among other things; *sequences*—for example in anticipation of finding patterns and trends, a supermarket might predict the incidence of cooked chicken being purchased based on purchases of snack foods.[39]

Data mining Data mining entails checking databases for patterns and trends that are hypothesised to exist, or in order to find new connections between data items.

Databases are repositories for any type of data a computer can store—text, numerical data, images and sounds—and they can all be mined. There are several new analytical tools; however, their explanation is beyond our scope. Suffice it to say that the main techniques involve such familiar statistical techniques as regression, correlation and factor analysis in addition to more elementary visual presentation and analysis of data. It should not be forgotten that marketing organisations use their customer databases in order to maintain customer intimacy, at times to cross-sell related products and ultimately to ensure a repeat purchase of the same brand of the major product. At all times these organisations are intent on ensuring they are marketing to the most profitable customers rather than to all customers, many of whom they can neither satisfy nor make money from.

Figure 18.6 is a graphical depiction of an attempt by a rugby league sporting magazine to gain new subscribers as well as have existing customers renew their subscriptions. The company is using interactive Pay-TV to communicate with potential and existing subscribers. Existing subscribers might be made a 'relationship offer' of a free subscription to a movie channel, for one week, if they take up a two-year subscription to the magazine 'on the spot' using the infrared selector provided with their interactive-TV set. Potential subscribers might be approached with a different offer via interactive Pay-TV to subscribe for a trial period at no cost, once again on the proviso that they act immediately. As the trial period comes to a close, the marketing organisation would make a further subscription offer to those who had not renewed, as well as approach those who trialled the magazine to take up a subscription. Those who did not renew or subscribe on the first offer might receive a second approach via direct selling.

We know that integrated direct and online marketing is big business and that, while direct mail has been the most popular medium worldwide, online techniques can be expected to become as popular. The key to success in direct and online marketing is quite often the use of a mailing list in the first instance, or possibly a database developed from use of such a list. While many firms build up their own databases, others simply hire a privacy-guidelines-compliant list compiled by other firms (see <Listbank.com.au> for an example). In Australia, the 'List of Lists' is a compendium of more than 1000 lists that sets out the availability of lists compiled by others.

We turn to an example at this point. Roman cites a Citicorp campaign used to market home equity loans. Instead of using only direct mail plus a toll-free number, Citicorp used direct mail plus coupon plus toll-free number plus outbound telemarketing plus print advertising. Although the second campaign cost more, it resulted in a 15% increase in the number of new accounts compared with direct mail alone. Roman concluded:

> When a mailing piece which might generate a 2 per cent response on its own is supplemented by a toll-free [1-800 or 1300] number ordering channel, we regularly see response rise by 50–125 per cent. A skilfully integrated outbound telemarketing effort can add another 500 per cent lift in response. Suddenly our 2 per cent response has grown to 13 per cent or more by adding interactive marketing channels to a 'business as usual' mailing. The dollars and cents involved in adding media to the integrated media mix is normally marginal on a cost-per-order basis because of the high level of responses generated . . . Adding media to a marketing program will raise total response . . . because different people are inclined to respond to different stimuli.[40]

Maximarketing Rapp and Collins's maximarketing model details seven steps for effective integrated database marketing.

Rapp and Collins call the direct marketing approach illustrated in Figures 18.5 and 18.6 maximarketing. The approach suggests that direct and online databases should be developed, maintained and data mined.[41] **Maximarketing** consists of a set of steps designed to reach the prospect, make the sale and develop the relationship. We can see from the discussion so far that integrated database marketing goes far beyond the use of one-shot direct marketing tools and technologies.

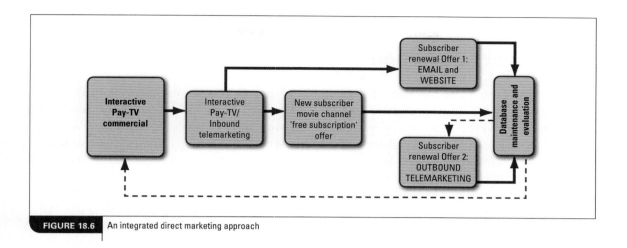

FIGURE 18.6   An integrated direct marketing approach

Direct and online marketing tools and techniques

So far, we have discussed direct and online marketing in broad terms. We now examine each of the available direct and online marketing tools and techniques in detail, before turning to their evaluation in the last section of this chapter.

Direct print and reproduction

Direct print and reproduction marketing involves mail-outs of letters, product lists, samples and paper-based and digital catalogues to a list or known database of customers, or to a targeted group that the marketer wishes to convert to a database entry. A catalogue may be sent to a database of rural dwellers who have asked to receive a retailer's catalogue, or with whom the retailer already has a relationship. The term direct print and reproduction marketing does not refer to the broadly aimed mailing to all post office box holders at one or all post offices that ends up in waste bins outside the post office—the ubiquitous 'scattergram'. Direct print and reproduction marketing uses a combination of mailing to those the company wishes to add as customers and to those who have already responded to previous offers.

Direct mail

Companies such as Direct Response Australia provide **direct mail** services using their database management and printing systems. Such companies sort the mail and speedily deliver bundles batched by postcode to various post offices. They earn a substantial discount from Australia Post for this service. The services of these companies are used to deliver all manner of materials, ranging

Direct print and reproduction marketing
The use of printed materials such as direct mail and catalogues to convey offers to consumers, whether targeted to the recipient by name, or to the business or householder by a broader targeting method.

Direct mail Printed materials sent by mail and conveying offers to consumers, whether targeted to the recipient by name, or to the business or householder by a broader targeting method.

Peer-to-peer addiction

Time was that when using the Internet (Net) to collect data marketing researchers wanted to know how technically savvy the respondents were. To find this out, they asked respondents to inform them of the frequency of their usage of such Internet tools as WHOIS, FINGER, emails with attachments and so on. They also asked how long respondents had been using the Net and Web. Today, they would not bother with such information. Why? One reason is that Net use has become ubiquitous. Another is because they are interested in the interactivity enabled by many other tools and technologies that have also become ubiquitous in their use in the Western world and which people use almost on a daily basis.

The BBC recently changed the name of its seven-year-old television show *Click Online* to *Click*. This points to the fact that being online no longer has the significance that it once had. We are interconnected by many more devices and networks than the Internet, and we 'click' these devices to connect with others via voice, text and multimedia excerpts. In short, connectivity has become woven into the fabric of our existence and it is often hard to distinguish which particular medium is in use. Nowhere is this truer than our use of devices that were once simple mobile phones.

Mobile phone users moved from seeking phone functionality to seeking a fashion accessory or in some cases to show their individuality. This is part of the reason that Nokia became such a popular brand of mobile phone the world over. Today, phone users are more likely to fall into one of three camps—those who own a micro mobile phone they can put in their shirt pocket or small clutch bag, those who use an 'always on' device like a Blackberry or a smartphone and, lastly, those who use a convergent device—a pocket PC or PDA—that is a multi-band mobile phone and a pocket PC rolled into one. Pocket PCs come in many forms, with many familiar brands produced under contract in Taiwan by HTC (taiwanhightech. ecnext.com/coms2/companydesc_125)—the world's largest producer of personal digital assistants (PDAs).

HTC usually contract manufactures many brands of the one class of device—producing none under its own name. For example, Himalaya is a class of pocket PC that has been marketed in various parts of the world as O2 XDA II, T-Mobile MDA II, Qtek 2020, iMate Phone Edition.

The pocket PC is different from the smartphone in that where the smartphone is either on or off—and is mostly left on—the pocket PC can be in one of seven states: Suspended, Resuming, Unattended, ScreenOff, UserIdle, BacklightOff, or On. This is because the pocket PC has both a computer 'engine' and a telephone 'engine'. The pocket PC is never quite off unless the battery is removed for an extended period. However, persistent storage has arrived, so even removal of a battery does not mean software or data loss.

Adopters of the small footprint mobile phone clearly seek the convenience that a micro device offers. The 'always on' Blackberry and smartphone users are mostly business users often found working in the financial services sector. Pocket PC users want a mobile phone, but also value such multiple functions as still and video camera, customisable polyphonic ring tones, Microsoft office suite of software and remote control capabilities using Bluetooth, among other features.

The many telcos marketing mobile phone plans will bundle one of the three devices mentioned, depending of course on how much users are prepared to pay each month. Users are more likely to buy the more expensive devices outright from the likes of Harris Technology (HT.com.au) or Organiser World (OW.com.au) rather than take on an expensive mobile phone contract with a telco. However, it has to be said that telcos have done such a good job marketing mobile phones that there is almost universal adoption of these devices—some users having multiple devices for work and personal use, and some having one device but using multiple SIM (subscriber identity module) cards for one reason or another.

However, from another viewpoint, the telcos have

done a bad thing in pandering to our desire to be 'wired'. In short, they have helped create a social monster. On the one hand, there are younger people who sleep with their mobile phones under their pillows, and if one in their social group is an insomniac then the rest are soon awake and texting each other from under the bedclothes. If poor sleeping habits are not bad enough, then consider the unrealistic debt levels some youngsters, or their families, hold thanks to mobile phone usage. What started out as a device to keep them safe and somewhat traceable when out on their own has turned into a device that devours money, and even creates user health problems from the amount of texting that is undertaken.

Blackberry users have become the butt of jokes concerning their addiction to their devices, particularly to email—epitomised by their use in the syndicated UK comic strip *Alex* and published daily in the likes of *The Australian Financial Review*. Firms have even found it necessary to run programs to wean their Blackberry users off their devices so that they take a break from work and so devote some attention to their families on weekends and vacations.

Pocket PC users are often geeks who love to fiddle with the pocket PC or mobile phone engines, or both. Their interconnectedness came into focus in late 2005 when many decided to upgrade their devices to Windows Mobile 5. Of course, many were already connected in the endeavour to undertake earlier upgrades to Windows 2003 SE. This is not software that can be purchased over the counter at the nearest computer shop, but rather has to be obtained—leaked, some suggest—from Microsoft, then 'built' by the users of particular devices to take account of various features such as Bluetooth, WiFi, still and video cameras and of course whether the phone is tri-band, quad-band and more. These users are known to each other by their aliases, for example Toenailed. These interconnected users behave very much like those involved in Linux open source projects. The group relies on an inner core of very technically savvy individuals who receive praise as more and more breakthroughs are made, and various problems are overcome.

Of course, not all pocket PC users are geeks who

are connected to the various Web-based development forums that have largely replaced the News Groups that can still be found on the Net. Many who are not geeks have benefited from the work of the development forums. When they have had a problem they have found little support from the marketing organisations behind their devices and have had to turn to the Web-based development forums for answers in the form of patches and software updates—not all of which might be considered to be legal in that they may breach intellectual property laws.

Where mobile phone development heads in the future is anyone's guess. About the only thing that Sony's Play Stations and Microsoft's Xbox devices do not do is make telephone calls, though they do make use of the Web. Certainly in the case of music and video, Apple has shown that mobility is the 'killer app'. with its iTunes devices and online sales. And soon, video and streaming television will experience the same mobility. One thing that is sure though is that as technological convergence continues, users will pay more for their addictions—peer-to-peer and otherwise.

Sources: See Mike Calligaro, 'Power to the System', Windows Mobile Team Blog, <blogs.msdn.com/windowsmobile/archive/category/10500.aspx>, 10 August 2005, accessed 10 January 2006; and Sumner Lemon, 'Taiwan's HTC to put Blackberry on Windows Devices', *InfoWorld*, IDG News Services, 16 March 2005, <infoworld.com/article/05/03/16/HNblackberrywindows_1.html>, accessed 11 January 2006.

Questions

1 Consider the three classes of mobile phone discussed and, employing your experiences, advise the bases upon which the market for each of the devices mentioned might be segmented.

2 Should telcos be permitted to capitalise on the seeming addiction of many in the community to their mobile phones? Is this an ethical issue, or simply the result of one societal group who is using their mobile phones to excess? Analyse the academic literature, and then interview classmates, friends and relatives and try to establish if there is a general need to be connected with others that might explain the high usage of mobile phones.

18.3

from direct marketing offers to the prospectus for a new share issue, or even notice of a company's annual general meeting. Direct mail also reflects the Information Age in that all manner of videotapes, audiotapes and CDs join digital items such as computer diskettes and CD-ROMs to be used as mailing pieces. Many of the digital items are interactive, allowing potential consumers to complete details on themselves and enabling configuration of the preferred product before an online registration or order is made. Thus, even direct mail can be seen to be synchronous in nature (receive and send a reply instantaneously).

Catalogues

Catalogue A printed listing of products, often featuring high-quality reproduction of the items on sale.

The use of **catalogues** harks back to the days when many consumers were unable to visit retail outlets because of the distances involved. Today, the development of economical and fast colour printing and distribution techniques has seen a resurgence in their use. There are at least four perceptions that must be held by consumers for catalogues to be a successful direct marketing tool—unique product offerings, an air of authority by the seller, value for money offerings and a guarantee of satisfaction.

There are full-line merchandise catalogues such as those mailed twice a year to country-based customers or others on request by department stores. Retail catalogues from stores such as David Jones and Myer are perhaps the most familiar catalogues to Australians. Hardly a week goes by when one retailer or another is not mailing or undertaking a geographically targeted letterbox drop of minor catalogues. Kmart, Big W, Target and Ikea are perhaps the most prolific distributors to homes. There are also business-to-business catalogues. Second-hand food-processing equipment marketers mail catalogues on a monthly basis to engineers and plant managers in the food industry in order to make their sales, as do such companies as Debden Diaries.

Specialty consumer catalogues also abound. Electronic retailers and wholesalers such as Dick Smith Electronics, Harvey Norman, International Software Warehouse, Jaycar and Radio Parts Group compete by way of catalogues. Because of the large numbers of small components, consumers are encouraged to order by part numbers. International Software Warehouse runs a direct mail business with sales generated from its catalogues and website. A firm with physical outlets might run a Microsoft-products-only catalogue as an insert in magazines like *Australian & New Zealand PC User*, in which readers are directed to write to or phone the Sydney and Melbourne retail outlets or to buy by mail. The direct marketer might go further by directing readers to ask for the firm's free issue of their main catalogue, comprising 80–100 pages of succinct descriptions of over 400 software products, in return for posting their business card or sending it by fax.

Catalogue development, like so many aspects of promotion, is a specialist function carried out by graphic designers working for large retailers or their agencies. Like theme advertising, there is the need to develop a cover story or theme, body copy and colour photography in most instances, and to avoid clutter. A major benefit is that sales results can be attributed to individual catalogues as well as to individual positions in the catalogue. There is usually a lag of two to three weeks when phone or mail order sales are to be made. However, a catalogue for a '15% off' sale by Target or Myer can bring almost instantaneous results.

Direct response television, radio and print marketing

Direct response television, radio and print marketing Use of mass-promotion media combined with a direct response offer, usually involving telemarketing.

Direct marketers often put television and radio commercials to air that persuasively describe a product and then give a toll-free number for viewers to call and place an order. We have all seen and heard the commercial that goes like this: 'Our telephone operators are standing by right now . . . order now and received absolutely free . . . don't send any money . . . we'll bill you!' Similar creative styles are often employed in the print media. **Direct response television, radio and print marketing** is often used to build a database as well as to make immediate sales. At one time or another, nearly all the tools of direct marketing are employed. Often companies employ sales promotion coupled with telemarketing techniques, which we examine next.

One form of Pay-TV is already flourishing—'narrowcast TV'—and attracting many advertising dollars. Doctor's TV Network, for instance, has been narrowcast into surgery waiting rooms and some hospitals since 1990. One weakness to be overcome with this type of broadcasting is that it is not possible to identify viewers with the same accuracy as database marketing, with which it can be coupled. Marrying narrowcast television and interactive television technology solves this issue.

Telemarketing

There is little that is routine in **telemarketing**, and this is the feature that distinguishes it from telesales. Viewers are either invited to call an 1-800, 0055 or 1300 number and place their order or seek information—inbound telemarketing—or human telephone operators or computers with voice recognition capabilities 'cold call', seeking an order or perhaps a donation to an organisation such as CARE Australia or the Red Cross—outbound telemarketing. The same techniques are used to enable FTA-TV or Pay-TV viewers to enter a contest and thus identify themselves and become part of a database. Such a contest may involve nominating the 'catch of the day' in baseball or cricket, or identifying a particular holiday destination at the end of a television show on fishing or travel destinations.

Telemarketing covers a broad range of activities, with differing objectives. At one end of the continuum it is employed to generate new sales leads and build the database. At the other end lies full account management. In between the two are many other means of employing telemarketing.

Marketers seeking subscription renewals to magazines and clubs often employ telemarketing. So, too, do insurance companies seeking to ensure that policy holders do not default on their second or later payment. They also use telemarketing to handle complaints.

A major use of telemarketing relates to customer service. Motor vehicle manufacturers make regular follow-up calls to ensure that dealer service and car performance and satisfaction are all at a level that might ultimately result in a repeat purchase of the brand. In most cases this information is quantified and reported internally and to the dealer network. Such methods can also be used to ascertain whether products are failing to perform, through defect levels or reduced life.

Whether telemarketing is employed with the mass media or with consumer markets or in business-to-business marketing, the attraction once again is the ability to measure the response in relation to input costs. Those starting out with a telemarketing campaign often use kits supplied by telecommunications companies, which include a number of publications advising on lists and even a video on the use of telemarketing.

Not all marketers are enamoured of direct marketing, and with telemarketing in particular. Direct mail is seen as an intrusion, while telemarketing is regarded as a tool that requires careful monitoring. One outcome in Australia has been the introduction of 'calling number display' or 'caller ID' technology. This allows people to see a caller's number before privacy is invaded. However, telcos charge customers for this service. As telemarketing is adopted on the scale seen in the USA, but where households do not have the same historical experience of direct response marketing, many households simply use a telephone answering machine or an integrated fax machine to block the efforts of marketers.

However, as with businesses—which found that most of their inbound communication arrives via facsimile machines and, more lately, via electronic mail and other online services including SMS/MMS—many telemarketers have adopted fax, email and mobile phone marketing provided people have opted to receive such commercial electronic messages. Using the Net to communicate

Telemarketing The use of telephone operators in a variety of ways to attract new customers, to contact existing customers to ascertain satisfaction levels, or to take orders.

with potential buyers is frowned on by some Net aficionados. More than one company has found it necessary to close its electronic mail site because of heavy retaliatory mailings after a promotion using email. Despite this, predictions are for continued growth in electronic shopping via this medium. The advent of VoIP and broadband adoption will see greater use of interactive technologies, although, as already mentioned, spam, viruses and worms are having a negative effect.

Telesales

Telesales Routine order taking by telephone operators.

Telesales are used by marketing firms of all persuasions, not just by direct marketers. The method usually involves a permanent part-time bank of telephone operators who routinely call customers to take their orders. The only differentiating feature between this method and telemarketing is that in telesales the calls are routinely made to regular customers such as retailers. Not all direct marketers would agree with this differentiation between telemarketing and telesales.

On average, a field salesperson can make five or six calls a day, depending on the industry—some 30 calls per week—whereas a telesales operator can make 30–40 a day. In other words, five field salespeople are needed for every telesales operator. As a result, the economics of telesales in such companies far outweighs those of a field force.

Telesales operators are usually set up with a computer workstation linked to a minicomputer. They are therefore able to see on one screen the sales for this time last week, last month and last year. Items on a cents-off promotion can be made to flash or give some other cue. Even the weather, which impacts on fast-food sales, can be displayed. The telesales operator is thus in a better position than the retailer's personnel to know what should be ordered, and can prompt them for more orders.

Electronic dispensing and kiosks

Electronic dispensing machines Machines that dispense products (food) and services (cash), usually by inserting cash, transaction or stored-value card.

Not all **electronic dispensing machines** are as user friendly as the familiar Coca-Cola vending machine. However, vending machines have progressed beyond the stage where buyers simply insert a coin and press a button to select the product or service of their choice—they can now be instructed to provide a can of Coke via mobile phone. Perhaps not surprisingly, vending machines are purported to have existed in Egypt in 215 BC, where sacrificial water could be purchased from coin-operated devices.

This method of direct selling took off after World War II. The variety and convenience of impulse lines sold through these machines is staggering—cigarettes, hot and cold carbonated and non-carbonated beverages, chocolates and sweets, newspapers and magazines, snacks such as packets of potato chips as well as hot chips, hosiery, cosmetics, toothbrushes, toothpaste, condoms, paperback novels, T-shirts, insurance policies, pizza, and audio and video cassettes. Automatic vending machines are found everywhere: in factories, offices, lobbies, retail stores, service stations, airports and banks, as well as in bus and train terminals.

EFTPOS (electronic funds transfer at point of sale) Retailer cash registers electronically linked to bank accounts; consumers may pay directly using a 'cash card' or a credit card, and funds may also be credited to an account if goods are returned.

Electronic dispensing machines (EDMs) and card-reading telephones that dispense and receive cash are popular today, as are **EFTPOS** machines used by retailers. They are now found in banks, casinos, licensed clubs and hotels, in fact anywhere there are high pedestrian densities. One 'smart card' system, the Mondex system, developed by NatWest Bank and British Telecom, is a system that allows telephones and all manner of devices to conduct transactions involving chip-to-chip cash transactions, and even permits such transactions over the Net.

However, the expensive equipment and the labour required to service dispensing machines make them a costly channel and, in the case of physical goods, prices are often 15–20% higher than those in retail stores. Likewise, banks apply a charge when more than, say, 15 transactions per month are put through automatic teller machines (ATMs). Customers must also put up with irritating machine breakdowns, out-of-stock items and, for vending machines, the fact that the merchandise cannot be easily returned.

Kiosks are something of an innovation in the arsenal of direct marketing weaponry. Kiosks often do not dispense anything, but simply allow orders to be placed or payments made. An energy supplier such as Tasmania's Hydroelectric Corporation (HEC) might install manned or unmanned electronic kiosks in shopping plazas or even in a large supermarket for customer convenience in paying bills; they also handle customer service inquiries and even sign up new customers. Banks are setting up kiosks for the same reason. They can be closer to their existing customer base and thus cross-sell all manner of superannuation and other financial products—even loans. Today, postal services kiosks allow us to buy a range of products from stamps to prepaid envelopes, postal cartons, postcards and aerograms.

> **Kiosks** Electronically networked mini-offices, staffed or unstaffed, and capable of dispensing information, products and services as well as capable of receiving payments by instalment or in full.

Direct selling

Door-to-door retailing as practised by Tupperware, Nutrimetics, Avon, Aussie Home Loans and the like is encompassed by the direct marketing category of **direct selling**.

The advantages of door-to-door selling are consumer convenience and personal attention. However, the costs of hiring, training, paying and motivating salespeople are high. This results in high prices. Although some door-to-door companies are still thriving, the incidence of double-income households in which both parties are working has caused many companies to sell into offices or to adopt telemarketing or some other combination of direct marketing. It is not uncommon for today's Avon lady to drop the catalogue in the letterbox and phone later to take the order.

> **Direct selling** Selling directly to consumers or to businesses rather than using a reseller, such as a retailer or agent.

Electronic shopping

Many forms of **electronic shopping** were evident in the latter half of the 1990s. The earliest such services were electronic bulletin boards accessed by microcomputers. Interactive cable television, the Net and the more recent convergence of the two technologies are the most recent methods of online shopping.

The Information Age has also entered the retailing arena in ways other than mere scanning and checkout technology. The humble shopping trolley's static advertisement is giving way to a flat television screen. The screen is activated by an infrared sensor to advise on specials and the like as the customer enters a particular aisle. The extra costs will be amortised somewhat by the fact that the trolley can record the route taken in-store by a shopper, and this can later be linked to actual purchases.

> **Electronic shopping** Purchasing via an electronic bulletin board or facilities such as Telstra's Discovery, or (in the future) via interactive cable television.

SELF-CHECK QUESTIONS

10 It is evident that technology is a driver for direct and online marketing. List and describe the main technologies involved in bringing interactivity to direct and online marketing.

11 Does synchronous marketing differ from interactive marketing? If so, in what ways?

12 Is interactivity important to the direct marketing of all products and services? Illustrate your answer with examples.

Evaluating direct and online marketing results

As with all marketing effort, the evaluation of outcomes in relation to input dollars is vital. The most common assessment is to compare sales before, during and after a sales promotion or other direct and online marketing program or campaign. However, the profitability of such offers and the return on investment are even more important.

Suppose a grocery marketer has a 6% market share before a sales promotion starts; this jumps to 10% during the promotion, falls to 5% immediately the offer concludes and then rises to 7% some weeks later. The promotion seems to have attracted new triers and more buying from existing customers. After customers used up their stock of product bought on promotion, their purchases were reflected in the 7% post-promotion market share. This indicates that the company has gained some new users. If the market share returns to the old 6% level, then all that has happened is that sales have been brought forward during the promotion and now total demand has gone back to the old level.

Omnibus consumer research, or research using consumer panels, will show the kinds of people who respond to sales promotions if used with mass-media advertising alone, and what they did after the promotion ended. Aided and unaided recall tests can also be used to establish the level of excitement created by a mass-media sales promotion, and this can be linked with who took up the offer and why, and how it affected their later buying patterns. Such sales promotions can also be evaluated through experiments by way of controlled store tests. By varying the incentive value, qualifiers, the duration and communication method, optimal sales promotion methods can be determined over time. If sales promotions are used in database marketing, there is the opportunity for more detailed analysis.

Evaluating direct marketing

Direct and online marketing organisations are usually interested in a number of measures of performance, both for individual programs and integrated campaigns. They set up their programs so as to allow later monitoring of such factors as:

- sales lead generation
- database generation
- fulfilment response
- product inquiries
- sales response
- profitability
- return on the investment made in programs and campaigns
- lifetime customer value

In nearly every case, monitoring and reporting is easily permitted by the computer technology used. Only the term fulfilment requires an explanation at this point. Simply taking an order for a single product on a once-off basis is rarely profitable for any firm. Order processing and delivery is thought of in terms of **fulfilment response** by direct marketers. Just as mass marketers using middlemen to reach the end-consumer must think of customer service levels to ensure repeat sales, so too must direct marketers think in terms of delivery response times and accuracy of delivery, among other things. Similar but different logistics issues are involved for each type of marketer. As all marketers know, totally satisfied customers are more likely to repeat the buying experience and promote the brand to others.[42]

Fulfilment response
Direct and online marketers think in terms of delivery response times and accuracy of delivery, among other things, when responding to meet product orders.

Evaluating online marketing

Separate discussion of the evaluation of online marketing is warranted, and it is to this aspect that we next direct your attention. We examine the evaluation of the three major aspects of online marketing: online marketing communication, online marketing channel performance and online CRM. We also discuss the evaluation of marketing databases.

Online marketing communication

Just as marketing organisations using mass media are concerned with target audience rating points (TARPs), which are a reflection of audience reach and frequency, so those organisations using the Net/Web in integrated marketing communication seek to measure both effectiveness (did they reach the target market) and efficiency (how cost effectively did they reach the target market). The only sure way to track individual behaviour at a website, thereby building a truer picture of website usage and measuring return on Web investment, is to allow subscriber-only access to the site. This approach works well in the case of extranet usage by business-to-business (B2B) and business-to-government (B2G) subscribers (customers and vendors).

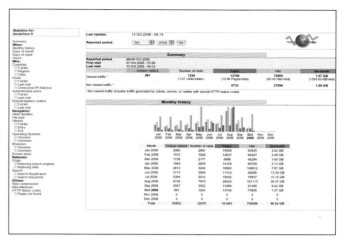

AWStats graphically presents Webserver log file information.
Source: AWStats, <http://ns3744.ovh.net/awstats/awstats.pl?config=destailleur.fr>.

However, it would be unrealistic for every corporate website to expect home users to subscribe to their particular site. Marketing organisations tend to use one or more of three categories of measurement to ascertain the return on their online marketing investment: web-centric measures, audience-centric measures and network-centric measures.

Web-centric measures Evaluating the success of websites in marketing communication began with the use of web-centric measures such as analysis of **hits** and computer log files (web server software such as Webtrends, <www.webtrends.com>. AWStats (pictured) logs the IP address of each visitor, as well as setting out the time the user visited the website, the particular pages visited, the time the process was completed and the size of objects sent to the visitor), and analysis of **page impressions** (page impression indicates one person viewing one page) or **page views**.[43]

Audience-centric measures Audience-centric measures are now favoured by many organisations. Third-party research company Nielsen//NetRatings (www.neilsennetratings.com.au) provides such measures using web user panels, and by other means. A quasi-solution to this is the use of **cookies** (text file IP identifiers for each host site stored on the user's computer).[44] Cookies are easily generated by META tags used in the HTML header on the index page on the host site.[45] Cookies are not a sure-fire measure of an audience for many reasons including the fact that Web users are likely to be removing cookies along with pernicious spyware via such software as NoAdWare (see <NoAdWare.net>).

Network-centric measures Many enlightened marketing organisations use the services of Hitwise.com, either to ascertain their performance in their own right, to understand better how they compare to specific competitors or to an industry, or to assist with the planning and reporting on a variety of customer acquisition campaigns such as search engine marketing, affiliate marketing and online advertising. Hitwise has become the most sophisticated online competitive intelligence service in Australasia, the UK and the USA. While analysis of a site's **log files** provides information on how that individual site is performing, and extrapolations from panel data give some inkling of how people use the Web, it takes an analysis of network traffic using aggregate data from Net service providers (ISPs) to gain the most complete information about online performance. Hitwise subscribers monitor their website's relative performance within one of 160+ categories in terms of how the top-level domain name (e.g. corporate site) and nominated lower level domains (e.g. brands) are performing relative to others in the nominated, or customised, category. The measures provided include the market share of user visits, page views and average session duration. Hitwise also provides information

Hits The record of the number of files requested by guests to a particular web page. The more links and graphics there are on a web page, the more hits will be recorded. The visitor is not, however, identified.

Page impressions The number of web pages viewed by a single visitor to a site.

Page views A measure of the number of pages a visitor views at a particular website. However, many sites have many pages at a number of levels (taking a television approach to website design), while others are composed of a few long 'scrolling' files (taking a magazine approach to website design).

Cookies Short identifier pieces of text which are deposited on a visitor's computer by a website. On each subsequent visit, the website software records the cookie response and thus measures repeat guest visits.

Log files All host servers maintain a record of the IP address of the guest's computer and of every file sent out. This is termed a log file.

Clickstream The path followed by website visitors.

on referring sites and next site visited (**clickstream** analysis), which enables organisations to determine whether referring site payments provide a return on investment, and whether customers were satisfied or continued to search other sites in the same category. In addition, Hitwise Search Intelligence gives marketers an indication of which search terms have been successful in driving traffic to competitive websites, which assists in the development of search marketing campaigns.

Because of the arrangements that Hitwise has in place with associated ISPs and other data providers, it is able to interpret such user information as gender and age and use this demographic information in the analysis of the other data captured. Hitwise monitors more than two million Australians and reports on how they interact with over 500 000 websites. Monitoring over 30% of the active Internet population on a daily basis, Hitwise also provides organisations with insights about their immediate competitors.[46]

Online marketing channel performance

The Web is an online marketing channel, or it may be used to supplement traditional marketing channels. We saw in Chapter 14 that marketing channels are not solely concerned with physical distribution but also with flows such as information and payment. For the publisher Penguin Books, online retailer Amazon.com is a one-member (Channel 2) marketing channel. An alternative one-member channel involves using Angus & Robertson bookstores. The difference between the two is simply that Amazon.com does not have a physical presence at the retail level, whereas Angus & Robertson has both a physical presence and an online means of customer fulfilment. Dymocks is similarly structured. Service organisations such as Federal Express and Australia Post also use the Net as a means of customer fulfilment based on the information they provide. A FedEx customer can track a client's parcel over the Net, and Commonwealth Bank business and home users can track their savings or cheque account status using the Net.

Extranet An online service provided to key customers using a secure information-based or transacting website on the public Internet.

As we saw in Chapters 14 and 15, marketing channel members as well as their upstream and downstream suppliers and customers are connected by bidirectional flows of information, legal title to goods and services and payments (or debt). Channel members are self-serving in the sense that they seek a profit from the value they add for other channel members. Their only reason for existence is value transformation for their customers. The Net, more particularly the use of an **extranet**, plays a coordination role, particularly between those involved in conversion operations, whether in manufacturing or the services sector, and suppliers. Additional coordination costs arise when outsourcing conversion and other operations. Increasingly, the coordination of value-adding tasks within organisations and between alliance partners involves the Net in its **intranet** and extranet guise.[47]

Intranet A secure web service for employees only or in the case of a university for staff and registered students only.

Online marketing channels are judged in the same way that more traditional direct marketing is judged—fulfilment response, in terms of product inquiries, sales response and profitability.

CRM and customer lifetime value

One major attraction of database marketing, indeed of all forms of direct and online marketing, is that it is possible to calculate in advance what response rate will be required (say, 15%) to break even, as well as other needed response rates such as average purchase levels. Many firms have developed methods of analysis for existing direct marketers and undertake feasibility studies for companies interested in the mathematics of direct marketing. There are many factors to be taken into account, as Table 18.4 shows. The model in Table 18.4 is a spreadsheet approach to calculating the **customer lifetime value** for individuals whose details are recorded in a database and who are approached over time with a number of offers to renew their subscription to the rugby league sporting magazine referred to earlier in Figure 18.6. The lifetime value model, adapted here from Jackson and

Customer lifetime value The amount by which revenues from a given customer over time exceed the company's costs of attracting, selling and servicing that customer.

TABLE 18.4 Hypothetical lifetime value model

	Year 1	Year 2	Year 3	Year 4	Year 5
New customers	1000				
Repeat customers		645	401	261	173
Retention rate		64.50%	62.10%	65.20%	66.40%
Revenue					
Price @	$22	$23	$24	$25	$26
Price incentive @	$5				
Free gift @	$5				
Net price @	$12	$23	$24	$25	$26
Total customer revenue	$12 000	$14 835	$9 613	$6 529	$4 509
Discount rate	1.00	1.20	1.44	1.73	2.07
Total customer revenue (NPV)	$12 000	$12 363	$6 676	$3 774	$2 178
Advertising space revenue @	$20	$21	$22	$23	$24
Total ad revenue	$12 000	$14 835	$9 613	$6 529	$4 509
Discount rate	1.10	1.31	1.58	1.89	2.27
Total ad revenue (NPV)	$10 909	$11 324	$6 084	$3 454	$1 986
Total revenue (NPV)	$22 909	$23 687	$12 760	$7 228	$4 164
Expenses					
Direct cost	65.00%	65.00%	65.00%	65.00%	65.00%
Total direct cost	$14 891	$15 397	$8 294	$4 698	$2 707
Discount rate	1.10	1.31	1.58	1.89	2.27
Total direct cost (NPV)	$13 537	$11 753	$5 249	$2 486	$1 192
Renewal Effort 1					
Target customers	1000	645	401	261	173
Renewal rate	55.00%	52.00%	52.00%	52.00%	52.00%
Customer renewals	550	335	208	136	90
Renewal Effort 2					
Target customers	440	310	155	95	75
Renewal rate	16.00%	17.00%	18.00%	19.00%	20.00%
Customer renewals	70	53	28	18	15
Renewal Effort 3					
Target customers	370	250	152	85	75
Renewal rate	6.00%	7.00%	8.00%	9.00%	10.00%
Customer renewals	22	18	12	8	8
Total customer renewals	643	406	248	162	113
Total mailing quantity	1810	1205	708	441	323
Renewal cost/'000	$250	$250	$250	$250	$250
Total renewal cost	$250	$89	$84	$88	$92
Discount rate	1.20	1.44	1.73	2.07	2.49
Total renewal cost (NPV)	$208	$62	$49	$42	$37
Relationship marketing effort					
Target customers	1000	645	401	261	173
Marketing cost/'000	$500	$500	$500	$500	$500
Total marketing cost	$500	$326	$205	$133	$88
Discount rate	1.10	1.31	1.58	1.89	2.27
Total marketing cost (NPV)	$455	$249	$130	$70	$39
Total expenses (NPV)	$14 200	$12 064	$5 428	$2 599	$1 268
Contribution (NPV)	$8 709	$11 623	$7 332	$4 630	$2 896
Initial investment	$7 000				
Total lifetime value	$1 709	$13 332	$20 665	$25 294	$28 191
Individual lifetime value	$1.71	$8.10	$10.10	$10.97	$11.37

Source: Adapted from the lifetime value models developed by Rob Jackson and Paul Wang, *Strategic Database Marketing*, Lincolnwood, Ill, NTC Business Books, 1996, pp. 188–201.

Wang's buildup models, illustrates a number of important aspects of integrated database marketing as well as providing a method of assessing database performance. They make the important point that it is 'more valuable to a business to achieve qualified customers upfront and focus on retaining them than it is to constantly search out new customers'.[48]

Table 18.4 shows the revenue from customer subscriptions to the magazine and also from space advertising. It further shows the direct costs (cost of goods sold) and the effects of three efforts to persuade the customer base to renew their subscriptions over time. That is, as one renewal effort succeeds with some customers, those who did not respond to one mailing are approached again. Finally, in this scenario, the direct marketer turns to a relationship marketing device—in this instance, an expensive mailing of a discounted wine offer to those customers who renewed their annual subscription before the three renewal mailings were sent. This offer can be varied each year, and might involve cross-subscriptions to, or free issues of, other company magazines. In this way, the loyal customers who receive this additional offer have the relationship strengthened. It should also be remembered that not all customers are of equal value, and that the marketer's attention should be focused on the best customers over time. Quite often this entails seeking to activate former customers.

The ultimate aim of database marketing is to be able to open dialogue with the target accounts that make up the database, and over a period of time build a profile of the accounts on the basis of their geodemographics, psychographics and lifestyles, attitudes and purchase behaviour. Although this is also the aim of all marketing, it should be obvious that mass marketing using television and print media alone does not provide as accurate a focus on consumers as marketers would like. 'Dear Householder' is often the only way one can address an FTA-TV and radio commercial or a magazine advertisement, in the hope that the message will be received by self-selecting members of the audience. In using databases the aim is to be able not only to address the communication 'Dear Ms Fraser', but also to go on to direct a sequence of offers that are related to her individual needs and lifestyle. That is, it is possible to manage the relationship with customers. And, lastly, it is then possible to compare the 'lifetime value' of Ms Fraser as a customer with other customers.

Regardless of whether a business list, a household list or a specialised list (such as new parents) is used, there is a need to ensure that the list is up to date. There is no greater waste than to send a $100-per-unit mailing to senior executives, only to find later that 25% of mailings were not seen because the database was not current. Usually, business mail is not returned to the sender in such instances—it is put in the wastepaper basket! Another issue relates to lists that duplicate names and addresses. No matter how personal the mailing from American Express offering free issue of a Gold Card, it looks bad from the recipient's viewpoint if they already have a Gold Card. The exclusivity of the Gold Card is demeaned in such an instance, and any other offers contained in the mailing are ignored. Specialist firms can purge or 'clean' lists of duplicates held on mainframes and they also try to ensure that the current mailing address is being used. Also, relational database programs for the personal computer, such as Microsoft Access, are capable of purging databases of duplicates.

Like many other marketing tools, database marketing requires a special investment. Marketing organisations must invest in computer hardware, database and data-mining software, analytical programs, communication links and skilled personnel.[49] The database interface must be user friendly and available to all marketing groups, including those in product and brand management, new-product development, marketing communications and trade promotion, direct marketing, telesales, field sales, order fulfilment and customer service.

As many more marketing organisations move into direct and online database marketing, the very nature of marketing is changing. While mass marketing and traditional retailing will continue long into the future, more and more customers in Australasia will benefit from this OnetoOne approach.

Evaluating database performance

Profitable use of a database requires customer relationship management and keeping track of sales, so as to be able to predict future sales levels more accurately. Mail order giants in the USA have identified the three criteria to use: recency of purchase, frequency of purchase and monetary value of purchase.

One way to use these criteria is to award points to each criterion and thereby build up a score for each record or account in the database. The idea is to get away from merely talking about such things as 'average purchases' and to talk meaningfully about individual accounts. If such a system is maintained, it is possible to approach only those with high scores—and therefore a high probability of purchasing from the next catalogue mailing or round of telemarketing.

Here, we work through an example and build up points for a small number of accounts to see how this rating system works. First, taking recency of purchase, we might award points on the following basis:

- 24 points—purchase made in current quarter
- 12 points—purchase made in last 6 months
- 6 points—purchase made in last 9 months
- 3 points—purchase made in last 12 months

Looking next to frequency of purchase, we might say that this equates to number of purchases × 5 points. Then we would award points based on the monetary value of purchases. These points could be based on 10% of the dollar value of the purchases, with a ceiling of nine points to remove any distortion from overly large purchases. Thus, it is possible for a computer system that is maintaining a relational database to maintain these records and then to report weekly, monthly or on an as-needed basis, as shown in Table 18.5.

Clearly, there is still some arbitrariness in the initial allocation of points to such criteria as recency of purchase. Over time, though, the marketer can do 'what-if' analyses in an endeavour to become more accurate in predicting purchase behaviour by account.

Break-even and profitability are determined by the relationship between contribution to selling cost, overhead and profit associated with an average order; the selling cost per thousand or per advertisement; and the response rate.

TABLE 18.5 Sample computer analysis of database accounts by recency, frequency and monetary value, July 2004

Account number	Month	Recency points	No. of purchases	Frequency points	Dollar purchases	Monetary points	Total points	Cumulative total points
25209	4	6	2	10	39.95	3.22	19.22	39.00
25101	10	24	1	5	59.95	6.00	35.00	77.00
25252	1	3	3	15	69.00	6.90	24.90	67.00

Note: June = 1, July = 12

Source: Adapted from *Successful Direct Marketing Methods*, 4th edn, Bob Stone, NTC Business Books, 1988. Reproduced with the permission of the McGraw-Hill Companies.

Privacy

Cross-referencing data
A privacy issue arises where an individual's personal information such as health status, work attendance levels and other information is interconnected and used without permission.

A major direct and online marketing issue in most countries is the matter of privacy. There is the issue of **cross-referencing of data** on an individual concerning matters such as health status, work attendance levels and their relationships. The issue of cross-referencing data on individuals is a matter that concerns the Privacy Commission in Australia. For instance, a bad credit rating obtained as a teenager may trouble a person for years unless some action is taken to have their name removed by the initiating bank or agency. This information, as well as other personal information, can be obtained in many instances from the company or government agency concerned—often legally and sometimes illegally.

A greater amount of public information is available in the USA on its citizens than is available in Australia at present; however, the concerns are the same in both countries, and in Europe. In the USA, the equivalent of local governments freely make available not just land title information but also information about mortgages, including the principal and the mortgagee.

Unwanted post mail and email

The receipt of mailings by post and email by those who do not want to receive them is another privacy concern.

Spam (spamming)
Sending unsolicited email usually to large numbers of people with a view to making a sale.

One solution to the problem of unwanted post mail is to ask people which product categories—if any—they would like to receive information about. This is the approach taken by many marketers in their online marketing communications, often due to requirements in the country hosting the website. (See Chapter 21 for Australian requirements.) In Australia, a National Principles and Guide for the Fair Handling of Personal Information has been released.[50] **Spamming** threatens the Net's usefulness in online marketing research that uses email, as well as threatening to clog the IP system as more and more Net servers are withdrawn because of attacks by the unscrupulous. The European Society for Opinion and Marketing Research (ESOMAR) has gone so far as to publish guidelines for Net research for its 96 member countries.[51]

SUMMARY

Advertising and publicity are mass-promotion tools concerned with building awareness, positive attitudes and brand image, and they have an 'indirect' impact on sales. Direct and online marketing tools, however, give a measured response for a measured dollar input. Many, but not all, of these responses involve commercial transactions or sales. The tools discussed in this chapter are designed to open and maintain a dialogue with individual customers and lead to a sale, or other planned response, in as short a time as possible. In particular, direct and online marketing aims to manage customer relationships so as to ensure a stream of exchanges, and to monitor the lifetime value of individual customers.

Direct mail and catalogue marketing is a 'one-shot', orchestrated program of mailing letters, product lists, samples and catalogues to households, whether identified by name and address or more broadly. *Direct response television and radio marketing* aims as much to build a database for future use as to gain immediate sales. Often such offers use telemarketing by asking consumers to ring a 1-800, 0055 or 1300 number. *Telemarketing* is used by consumer goods marketers as well as business-to-business marketers, not only because of cost savings per customer contact but also because it is fast and flexible. Marketers requiring an immediate sales response use this method and so do customer service sections of companies doing follow-up. While telemarketing is used in a variety of situations, the *telesales* method covers routine calls by vendors in a set customer base, usually retailers or other businesses.

The Information Age is well and truly upon marketers and their customers. *Electronic dispensing machines* and *kiosks* range from high-technology snack food and beverage vending machines to technologies that dispense cash, and include EFTPOS machines used by retailers and 'smart card' technology. Kiosks enable marketing organisations to locate close to customers and facilitate relationship maintenance. Electronic dispensing now involves the Net; companies use this medium to make offers, receive orders and fulfil the customer's requirements in real-time.

Although *direct selling* is declining as a means of selling, many firms still rely almost exclusively on selling door to door or through organised party and office plans.

There are several different forms of electronic shopping, the most promising of which are interactive Pay-TV and use of the Web. *Online marketing* is mainly the domain of business-to-business marketers. Online marketing embraces online sales transactions and payment systems (e-commerce) as well as relationship development, maintenance and enhancement (e-business).

With the use of *databases* in *direct and online marketing*, the emphasis is on identifying the customer on the basis of geodemographic, psychographic and mediagraphic profiles and then maintaining a record of purchases made by product category over time. This enables tailor-made offers to be made and increases the ability to predict the likely response rate to a planned expenditure level on a direct marketing offer. Wherever possible, direct and online marketing programs should be pre-tested and an evaluation of outcomes undertaken. The notion of 'lifetime value of customers' means that customer databases are valuable assets. Like all assets, they require expenditure on maintenance to ensure their usefulness over time.

Privacy issues arise in this area as a result of the ever-increasing possibilities of *data cross-referencing*. Concerns also exist about the means used to build the database and the possibilities of database abuse, particularly in online marketing where *spamming* threatens many commercial uses of the Net. Privacy guidelines are now in place (see Chapter 21).

MARKETING ISSUE

Direct and online marketing relies on database use to track customer profiles and purchases. Direct and online marketing can become more intrusive than the interruptions to television programs that commercial breaks involve. While the Australian *Spam Act, 2003* requires that those who receive commercial electronic messages 'opt in' to receive such messages, in practice many of us forget what messages we have agreed to receive and from whom. It can often get to the point that when confronted by an email or phone call from an organisation that we do know well, we simply vent our spleen. It is only natural that people receiving an early-evening phone call experiencing the tell-tale clicks and hisses of telephone exchanges in a distant land will say things like 'What is the weather like in Mumbai?' or 'Whatever you are selling, I already have one!' or 'What do you mean that I have won a free Thai holiday for two and you cannot tell me how I've won it?'

While the Australian Direct Marketing Association (ADMA) has an industry code of practice, and there is legislation concerning privacy and spam, the plain fact is that there is a large issue facing direct and online marketers that needs to be resolved. Can you think of solutions to this problem that do not necessarily require government intervention?

KEY TERMS

catalogue	714	direct selling	717	learning organisation	703
clickstream	720	EFTPOS (electronic funds transfer at point of sale)	716	lists	707
cookies	719			log files	719
cross-referencing data	724	electronic dispensing machines	716	maximarketing	710
customer lifetime value	720	electronic shopping	717	online marketing	697
data mining	709	extranet	720	page impressions	719
direct and online database marketing	707	fulfilment response	718	page views	719
direct mail	711	hits	719	privacy guidelines	708
direct marketing	693	Internet (Net)	697	spam (spamming)	724
direct print and reproduction marketing	711	intranet	720	telemarketing	715
		kiosks	717	telesales	716
direct response television, radio and print marketing	714	knowledgebase	692	World Wide Web (Web)	697

DISCUSSING THE ISSUES

1 Is it the case that e-commerce is really a term used in lieu of direct and online marketing? Or is it that the term e-commerce refers to the least difficult aspect of using the Net—transacting online—while direct and online marketing is a more encompassing term? What are your views?

2 Consider this proposition put forward by an MBA student: if all companies used direct and online marketing databases, there would be no need for traditional marketing research. Put forward your own argument for or against this proposition.

3 Might there be situations where the use of site-centric measures would provide enough information to evaluate online marketing expenditure?

4 Consider the information made available in Figure 18.7. Assuming that each of the files shown in Figure 18.7 is an individual online questionnaire for different clients, why might the firm want to monitor hits?

Top 30 of 86 total URLs				
#	Hits		KBytes		URL
1	1196	3.78%	198060	72.02%	/mfc/mfc.html
2	823	2.60%	486	0.18%	/mfc/mfc_success.html
3	254	0.80%	1160	0.42%	/afl/survey.html
4	189	0.60%	7665	2.79%	/dunetmr/dunetmr.html
5	175	0.55%	6986	2.51%	/netmr/netmr.html
6	165	0.52%	262	0.10%	/marketing_style.css
7	164	0.52%	1657	0.60%	/animate.js
8	139	0.44%	116	0.04%	/cgi-bin/bformmail.pl
9	136	0.43%	6489	2.36%	/wvsurvey/wvsurvey.html
10	115	0.36%	91	0.03%	/wvsurvey/wvsuccess.html

FIGURE 18.7 Monthly 'hits' reported for a marketing research Web server

5 In this chapter it is stated that Australian and New Zealand companies use the Web differently from their UK counterparts. Why might this still be the case?

6 Do you agree with the proposition that use of the Web for marketing is more closely aligned to direct marketing than to mass marketing? Argue for or against this proposition.

REFERENCES

1. See John Markoff, 'New Chips Come from Core of Intel's Strategy', *The Australian Financial Review*, 3 January 2006, p. 12; and Frederick F. Reichheld and Phil Schefter, 'e-Loyalty: Your Secret Weapon on the Web', *Harvard Business Review*, vol. 78, no. 4, 2000, pp. 105–113.

2. For a discussion on the many meanings applied to the concept of a 'learning organisation' see Don Tapscott, *The Digital Economy*, New York, McGraw-Hill, 1996, pp. 202–203.

3. See George Day and Rashi Glazer, 'Harnessing the Marketing Information Revolution: Toward the Market-driven Learning Organisation', in Robert C. Blattberg, Rashi Glazer and John D. C. Little (eds), *The Marketing Information Revolution*, Boston, MA, Harvard Business School Press, 1994, pp. 272–276; and Robert C. Blattberg and John Deighton, 'Interactive Marketing: Exploiting the Age of Addressability', *Sloan Management Review*, vol. 33, no. 1, 1991, pp. 5–14. Also see Microsoft's Knowledge Base interface at <www. microsoft.com/kb/>.

4. Bob Stone, *Successful Direct Marketing Methods*, 4th edn, Lincolnwood, Illinois, NTC Business Books, 1988, p. 3.

5. This definition incorporates notions of database marketing from a definition by K. B. DeTienne and J. A. Thompson, 'Database Marketing and Organizational Learning Theory: Toward a Research Agenda', *Journal of Consumer Marketing*, vol. 13, no. 5, 1996, pp. 12–34.

6. Quotation from M. B. Prescott and C. Van Slyke, 'Understanding the Internet as an Innovation', *Industrial Management and Data Systems*, vol. 97 no. 3, 1997, pp. 119–124.

7. Don Tapscott, op. cit (note 2).

8. See Nicholas Negroponte, *Being Digital*, London, Hodder & Stoughton, 1995.

9. See Australian Privacy Commissioner, reported at <www.privacy.gov.au>, accessed 30 May 2003.

10. See Larry Downes and Chunka Mui, *Unleashing the Killer App.: Digital Strategies for Market Dominance*, Boston, MA, Harvard Business School Press, 1998.

11. Department of Industry, Science and Technology (DIST), Stats. Electronic Commerce in Australia (98/050), Canberra, 1998.

12. Ward Hanson, *Principles of Internet Marketing*, Cincinnati, Ohio, South-Western College Publishing; for a discussion on disintermediation and reintermediation from various perspectives see Efraim Turban, David King, Jae Lee, Merrill Warkentin and H. Michael Chung, *Electronic Commerce: A Managerial Perspective*, Upper Saddle River, NJ, Prentice Hall, 2002, p. 295; Jagdish N. Sheth, Abdolreza Eshghi and Balaju C. Krishnan, *Internet Marketing*, Fort Worth, Texas, Harcourt College Publishers, 2001, pp. 79–81; and Stewart Adam and Eugene Clark, *eMarketing@Internet*, 2nd edn, Sydney, Pearson Education Australia (Multimedia CD-ROM), 2001, Chapter 10.

13. Hooim Im Ng, Ying Jie Pan and T. D. Wilson, 'Business Use of the World Wide Web: A Report on Further Investigations', *International Journal of Information Management*, vol. 18, no. 5, 1998, pp. 291–314.

14. Charles Hofacker and Jamie Murphy, 'World Wide Web Banner Advertisement Copy Testing', *European Journal of Marketing*, vol. 32, no. 7/8, 1998, pp. 703–712.

15. Gordon C. Bruner II and Anand Kumar, 'Web Commercials and Advertising Hierarchy of Effects', *Journal of Advertising Research*, vol. 40, no. 1, 2, 2000, pp. 35–44.

16. e-Commerce Statistics, available at <jhemans.powerup.com.au/Internet_Statistics/ecommerce_e-commerce_statistics.htmIbid>, accessed 5 January 2006.

17. National Retail Federation statistics, available at <shop.org/learn/stats_hol2004_spending.asp>, accessed 5 January 2006; ITC, *Broadband Korea: Internet Case Study*, March 2003, available at <itu.int/ITU-D/ict/cs/korea/material/CS_KOR.pdf>, accessed 4 January 2006; Paul Budde Communication, 'Broadband Access among Internet Households 2001', reprinted in Helen Meredith, 'DSL, We Export What We Cannot Have', *The Australian Financial Review*, 24 May 2001, p. 46.

18. 'Internet Usage Statistics—The Big Picture', available at <internetworldstats.com/stats.htm>, accessed 4 January 2006.

19. Michael Heraghty, 'US Internet Usage Reaching Saturation Point', <www.vision.com/press_and_news/vision_news/1999/nov_11_1999.html>, accessed 24 December 2001. Also see the Computer Industry Almanac at <www.c-i-a.com>; and Michelle Beeby, 'The Devil is in the e-Tail', *The Australian Financial Review*, 19 January 2000, p. 21.

20. See Donna R. Hoffman and Thomas P. Novak, 'Marketing in Hypermedia-computer-mediated Environments: Conceptual Foundations, *Journal of Marketing*, vol. 60, no. 3, 1996, pp. 50–68.

21. Stewart Adam, Rajendra Mulye and Kenneth R. Deans, 'The Evolution of Relationships in e-Marketing', in Jagdish N. Sheth, Atul Parvatiyar and G. Shainesh (eds), *Customer Relationship Management: Emerging Concepts, Tools and Applications*, New Delhi, Tata McGraw-Hill, 2001, pp. 135–142.

22. Stewart Adam, Rajendra Mulye, Kenneth R. Deans and Dayananda Palihawadana, 'e-Marketing in Perspective: A Three Country Comparison of Business Use of the Internet', *Marketing Intelligence and Planning*, vol. 20, no. 4, 2002, pp. 243–251.

23. Brian Corbitt and Theersak Thanasankit, 'The Challenge of Trust and "Guanxi" in Asian e-Commerce', in M. Singh, M. Teo and T. Teo (eds), *e-Commerce Diffusion: Strategies and Challenges*, Melbourne, Heidelberg Press, 2001, pp. 141–158. Also see Michael Backman and Charlotte Butler, *Big in Asia: 25 Strategies for Business Success*, Basingstoke, UK, Palgrave Macmillan, Houndmills, 2002.

24. Adam, Mulye, Deans and Palihawadana, 2002, op. cit. (note 22).

25. Simpson Poon and Paula M. C. Swatman, 'A Longitudinal Study of Expectations in Small Business Internet Commerce', *International Journal of Electronic Commerce*, vol. 3, no. 3, 1999, pp. 21–33.

26. Don Peppers, Martha Rogers and Bob Dorf, *The OnetoOne Fieldbook*, New York, Doubleday, 1999.

27. Stewart Adam, 'OnetoOne eMarketing Strategy Alignment: Five Internet Case Studies', refereed paper, Academy of Marketing 2001 (2001: A Marketing Odyssey), Cardiff University, UK, 2–4 July 2001, pp. 1–20 (Multimedia CD-ROM).

28. The term 'vanity' website was coined by Cisco Systems' T. Walsh, 'Has Australia Missed the Information Boat?' *The Australian Financial Review*, 12 January 2001, p. 44.

29. The Australian government's National Office for the Information Economy website and publications take this approach. See NOIE, 'e-Commerce beyond 2000', Canberra, Commonwealth Department of Communications, Information Technology and the Arts, 2000, <www.noie.gov.au>.

30. Stewart Adam and K. R. Deans, 2000, 'Online Business in Australia and New Zealand: Crossing a Chasm', in (Eds, A. Ellis and A. Treloar), Proceedings of AUSWEB2K: The Sixth Australian World Wide Web Conference, (19–24), Cairns, Australia: Southern Cross University. Available at <http://ausweb.scu.edu.au/aw2k/papers/adam/index.html>, accessed 11 May 2006.

31. e-Commerce Statistics, op. cit (note 16).

32. Stewart Adam, 'The Role of the Web in Marketing and Organisational Performance', unpublished doctoral thesis, Deakin University, Melbourne, 2004.

33. Philip Evans and Thomas S. Wurster, 'Getting Real about Virtual Commerce', *Harvard Business Review*, vol. 77, 1999, pp. 84–94.

34. Mary Beth Grover, 'Electronic Retailing's Big Earnings Remain Elusive', *BRW Reprint from Forbes Magazine*, 9 April 1999, pp. 88–91.

35. Much of the commentary in this section is drawn from Stewart Adam, 'A Model of Web Use in Direct and Online Marketing Strategy', *Electronic Markets: The International Journal of Electronic Commerce and Business Media*, vol. 12, no. 4, 2002, pp. 262–269. See <www.electronicmarkets.org>.

36. For a good summary on developing a customer database see Bob Stone, 1988, op. cit., Chapter 2 (note 4). For more on the use of databases in direct and online marketing see Merlin Stone, Derek Davies and Alison Bond, *Direct Hit: Direct Marketing with a Winning Edge*, London, FT Pitman Publishing, 1995, Chapter 9; and Alan Tapp, *Principles of Direct and Database Marketing*, 2nd edn, London, FT Prentice Hall, 2000, Chapters 3 and 4.

37. See Australian Privacy Commissioner's website, <www.privacy.gov.au>, accessed 1 November 2001; and the Ten Privacy Principles summarised from Olga Ganopolsky, 'Privacy Rules OK!', *Communiqué*, September 2001, pp. 12–15, <www.cmq.com.au>.

38. *18th Annual Survey of Promotional Practices*, Naperville, IL, Carol Wright Promotions, Inc., 1996, p. 36.

39. See Dan Ziffer, 'All That Glitters', *Communiqué*, vol. 12.01, December 2001, pp. 10–16; Joe Schwartz, 'Databases Deliver the Goods', *American Demographics*, September 1989, pp. 23–25; Gary Levin, 'Database Draws Fevered Interest', *Advertising Age*, 8 June 1992, p. 31; Jonathan Berry, 'A Potent New Tool for Selling: Database Marketing', *Business Week*, 5 September 1994, pp. 56–62; and Richard Cross and Janet Smith, 'Customer Bonding and the Customer Core', *Direct Marketing Magazine*, February 1995, p. 28.

40. Ernan Roman, *Integrated Direct Marketing*, New York, McGraw-Hill, 1989, p. 3.

41. See Stan Rapp and Thomas L. Collins, *The New Maxi-Marketing*, New York, McGraw-Hill, 1996.

42. Thomas O. Jones and W. Earl Sasser, 'Why Satisfied Customers Defect', *Harvard Business Review*, November–December 1995, pp. 88–98.

43. Stewart Adam and Eugene Clark, *eMarketing@Internet*, 2nd edn, Sydney, Pearson Education Australia (Multimedia CD-ROM), 2001, pp. 107–108, provide the following definitions: hits represent the record of number of files requested by guests to a web page. This figure can be manipulated in a number of ways, not the least of which includes placing large numbers of blank graphics (.jpg or .gif) files in a page. A page view or page impression relates to a page viewed by a single guest, thus making it a somewhat more reliable metric. This measure may also be manipulated for a total site or give a misreading because a website with more television-type web pages and usually with more hyperlinks on the page will have higher page views recorded than one with a few long magazine-type scrolling screens.

44. See Dave Chaffey, Richard Mayer, Kevin Johnston and Fiona Ellis-Chadwick, *Internet Marketing*, Harlow, UK, Pearson Education, 2000, pp. 306–307; and Stewart Adam and Eugene Clark, 2001, pp. 30–32 (note 12).

45. See Scott Clark, 'Back to Basics: META tags', 1999, <www.webdeveloper.com/html/html_metatags.html>, accessed 26 December 2001.

46. Personal communication, Tessa Court, Marketing Vice-President, Hitwise Market Intelligence, 10 January 2006.

47. See Charles Steinfeld, Robert Kraut and Alice Plummer, 'The Impact of Interorganizational Networks on Buyer–Seller Relationships', *Journal of Computer-Mediated Communication*, vol. 1, no. 3, 1997, at <www.209.130.1.169/jcmc/vol1/issue3/steinfld.html>.

48. Rob Jackson and Paul Wang, *Strategic Database Marketing*, Lincolnwood, IL, NTC Business Books, 1996, p. 188.

49. See such software as Cognos Scenario, <www.cognos.com>; Oracle, <www.oracle.com>; SAP, <www.sap.com>; SPSS, <www.spss.com>; SQL Server 2000, <www.microsoft.com/Australia/sql/default.asp>; Enterprise Miner, <www.sas.com>.

50. See the website for the Australian Direct Marketing Association for updates on policies and legislation affecting the direct and online industry at <www.adma.com.au>.

51. See the European Society for Opinion and Marketing Research (ESOMAR) guidelines for Internet research at <www.esomar.nl>.

PHOTO/AD CREDITS

Jeffrey Lim, University of Sydney

CASE STUDY

If music be the food of love, log on

Trends come and go but one that is likely to stay and even grow is instant access to music, especially in digital music downloads. The Internet revolution has not only increased consumers' accessibility and convenience in music listening, but has inevitably enabled and empowered them to source and share music with one another. Like many other products, the Internet Age has transformed music from being a physical product (cassettes, CDs, DVDs, etc.) to a digital product (i.e. downloading of a digital music file or MP3 file from the Net). Consumers today have a choice to experience music through a variety of ways, notably by attending a live concert, listening to the radio and pre-recorded music or simply going online. Such a trend is hurting CD sales, as portable devices such as iPods are already replacing CDs and cassettes.

Nevertheless, the shift from the traditional means of purchasing music (e.g. stepping into a retail store to browse, listen and purchase music CD/DVDs) to downloading music via an online music provider is one global trend that has taken the global music industry by storm. Moreover, the much debated (viewed as unauthorised) music file swapping via peer-to-peer networks has caused much concern among record companies. Clearly, online music providers and record companies regard peer-to-peer networks as having taken away potential revenues from them as well as stealing royalties from the artists. Traditional retailers are also feeling the pressure from online music providers and peer-to-peer networks, as more consumers turn to digital music. Figure 1 illustrates typical routes a consumer could utilise to acquire music online and the issues associated with them.

The digital music landscape

The digitisation of music has ushered the music industry worldwide into a new era in terms of marketing, distribution and revenue generation. Advancing technologies and changing consumer preferences are impacting on CD sales at the local and international levels. Record companies have to rethink their traditional CD-sales-dependent business model to maintain their profitability. According to the Australian Record Industry Association (ARIA), in the first half of 2005 only 22.7 million units of recorded music sales (CDs, music DVDs, records and cassettes) were made, a drop of 7.54% compared to the same period in 2004, representing a wholesale value of $209 million, a drop of 11.82% (*ARIA News*, 2005). However, this 'physical' downturn is seemingly superseded by the accelerated growth in popularity of digital music downloads. According to the International Federation of the Phonographic Industry (IFPI), digital music sales totalled $US790 million in the first half of 2005, compared with $US220 million for the same period in 2004 (*IFPI News*, 2005).

A study by ARIA (2003) found that Internet file sharing and CD burning does have a negative impact on recorded music sales in the Australian market. The sharp rise in illegal copying and distribution of music via the Net is seen as the main contributor to this downturn. According to the report, about 3.4 million Australians have illegally downloaded music via peer-to-peer networks, the largest age segment being those under 25 years old. Only about one-third

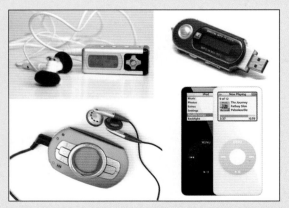

No shortage of MP3 players in the market catering for different consumer needs.

CASE
STUDY

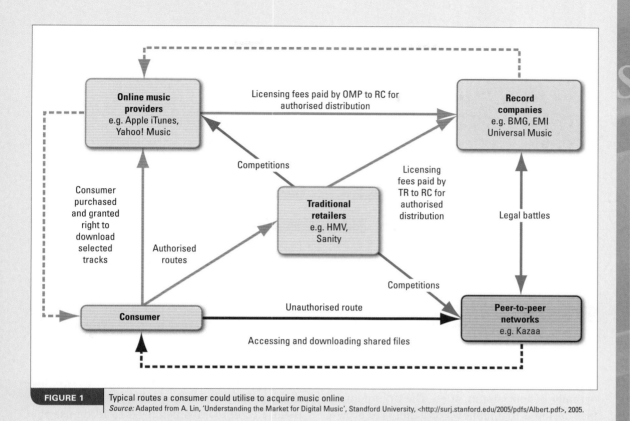

Typical routes a consumer could utilise to acquire music online
Source: Adapted from A. Lin, 'Understanding the Market for Digital Music', Standford University, <http://surj.stanford.edu/2005/pdfs/Albert.pdf>, 2005.

of those surveyed under 25 years agreed that burning music and downloading music from the Net without permission constitute stealing, compared to about half of the general population who attributed these acts to stealing. Of those who have file shared, more than 50% indicated that they would not purchase music they have downloaded, representing a 12% decrease overall in CD purchasing behaviour (see Figure 2 overleaf).

The Recording Industry Association of America (RIAA), with member companies distributing more than 80% of the pre-recorded music in the USA, reported that the number of CDs shipped had dropped from 940 million to 760 million during the period 2000 to 2004 (RIAA, 2004). This decline in recorded music sales, similar to the Australian market, is judged to be caused by file-sharing activities rampant in the online environment.

The Net has clearly created an 'added' incentive for instant music access and downloads, with more consumers increasingly feeling comfortable in doing so. The ARIA Chief Executive, Stephen Peach, reiterated this concern with this comment:

> Ultimately the consumer is the loser. With copying rampant there is diminishing motive to invest in music production or risk supporting the new talent. File-sharing and CD burning contributes to the slow but steady weakening of the local and international music industry (ARIA, 2003).

Digital music downloads: a crisis or revival?

While it seems quite clear that the online environment has contributed to the decline of music sales in stores, mainly due to file sharing, a recent study conducted by Oberholzerand and Stumpf (2004) has indicated otherwise. They not only found that the effect on album sales of file

CASE STUDY

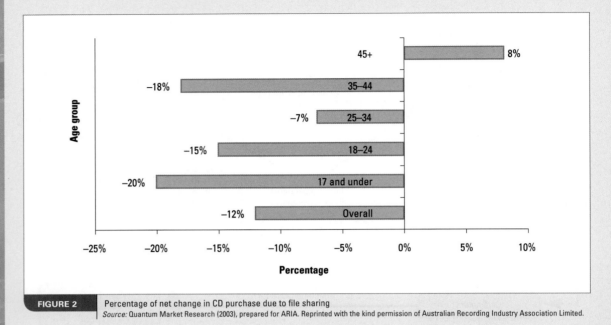

sharing is negligible but that file sharing could actually benefit album sales. The argument for file sharing is that it allows consumers to browse from each others' files and discuss music in online chat rooms, a learning experience which ultimately enhances new sales. The availability of file sharing thus has both positive and negative effects: decreasing people's willingness to pay for music due to 'free' downloads and inducing people legally to acquire music more via online music providers to share with others in the online community. In other words, total music consumption actually increases through the help of cyberspace. There are also others that see the Net as a window of opportunity rather than a crisis to the music industry. EMI Chairman Eric Nicoli commented:

> We've moved on from the days when the main impact of digital technology was to harm our industry by facilitating rampant online and physical theft. The day is surely within our sights when digital growth outstrips physical decline and we can all compete for share of a growing pie (Reuters, 2006).

Whether or not one sees the Net as reviving the music industry is perhaps not the main issue. Record companies need to recognise the changing times they are facing and the changing consumer preference for accessing music instantly online. Just as the Sony Walkman changed the way we listen to music, so the 'iPodisation' of music could be viewed as replacing the stacks of cumbersome CDs lying around at home. Does it make more sense to be seen carrying thousands of your favourite tracks in a mini device while on the move or holding even a stack of 10 CD albums (all of which are not your favourite tracks) in one hand and a Discman in the other? Record companies must realise that 'they would no longer be in sole control of formats and distribution' and the Net is definitely an avenue where consumers are empowered to choose what they prefer (Eliezer, 2005).

However, one universal problem all players in the music industry do agree on and are hoping to be able to respond assertively but positively to is the illegal file-sharing behaviour among the online community. ARIA's legal action against Kazza in 2004 for copyright infringement which resulted in its closure in Australia in 2005 is

TABLE 1 Top 10 online music sites

Site	Audience, 000	Reach, %
AOL Music	12 188	9.69
Yahoo! Music	11 334	9.01
iTunes	4 847	3.85
MSN Music	2 690	2.14
MTV Networks Music	2 528	2.01
BeMusic	1 578	1.25
A-Z Lyrics Universe	1 160	0.92
Universal Music	1 114	0.89
Sony Music	960	0.76
eBay Musical Instruments	923	0.73

Source: Nielsen/NetRatings NewView, The Center for Media Research, <www.mediapost.com/research/index.cfm?loc=1>.

just one of the many legal victories the record industry is expecting. The 20 000 lawsuits against individuals across 17 countries who illegally operate music file-sharing networks and the increase in the number of legitimate online music providers (see Table 1) from 50 in 2003 to 335 in 2005 (Reuters, 2006) are seen by the record industry as promising signs that consumer attitudes are changing. According to IFPI, more are turning to subscription-fee-based services which enable them to download music legally, helping the music industry to achieve a triple increase in global revenues to $US1.1 billion in 2005 (IFPI, 2006).

Conclusion

The advent of the Internet has definitely transformed the way products are marketed and consumed. Industry players cannot ignore the changing times and consumer trends they are facing. Record companies must realise that consumers are becoming more demanding and have been empowered by technology to choose. To survive and remain profitable, they need to harness the power of the Internet to their advantage. Traditional business models will be

challenged and new online business models (e.g. Apple iTunes) put in place as an alternative. Technological solutions (e.g. CD copy control) and regulations may be enforced to curb file sharing and CD burning (although they may not stop it completely). Education, with the hope of changing consumer attitudes over time, is currently seen as an appealing alternative to get consumers to adopt legal download behaviour. The 'Download Legally' education campaign launched in 2005 is clearly one of the many steps the music industry will take in its 'drive to help people enjoy music and film on the internet safely, legally and responsibly' (IFPI News, 2006).

Sources: Australian Recording Industry Association, 'ARIA Half Year Results', 12 September 2005, <www.aria.com.au/pages/news-halfyearsales2005.htm>, accessed 30 January 2006; Australian Recording Industry Association, 'Impact of Internet Music File Sharing and CD Burning', 16 July 2003, <www.aria.com.au/pages/news-and-press-releases-file-sharing-cd-burning.htm>, accessed 23 January 2006; C. Eliezer, 'The Times, They Are a'Changing', *Business Review Weekly—The Innovation Issue*, June/July 2005, pp. 62–66; International Federation of the Phonographic Industry, 'Digital Music Report', 2006, <www.ifpi.org/site-content/library/digital-music-report-2006.pdf>, accessed 25 January 2006; International Federation of the Phonographic Industry News, 'Recording Industry "Download Legally" Education Campaign Reaches out to Midem', 21 January 2006, <www.ifpi.org/site-content/press/20060121.html>, accessed 30 January 2006; International Federation of the Phonographic Industry News, 'Digital Sales Triple to 6% of Industry Retail Revenues as Global Music Market Falls 1.9%', 3 October 2005, <www.ifpi.org/site-content/press/20051003.html>, accessed 25 January 2006; A. Lin, 'Understanding the Market for Digital Music', Stanford University, 2005, <http://surj.stanford.edu/2005/pdfs/Albert.pdf>, accessed 30 January 2006; F. Oberholzer and K. Stumpf, 'The Effect of File Sharing on Record Sales: An Empirical Analysis', <www.unc.edu/~cigar/papers/FileSharing_March2004.pdf>, accessed 30 January 2006; *PC Magazine*, <www.pcmag.com/>, accessed 27 January 2006; Quantum Market Research, 'Understanding CD Burning and Internet File Sharing and Its Impact on the Australian Music Industry', 2003, <www.aria.com.au/pages/documents/AriaIllegalMusicResearchReport_Summary.pdf>, accessed 23 January 2006, prepared for ARIA; Recording Industry Association of America, 'Yearend Report on Market Report on U.S. Recorded Music Shipment', 2004 <www.riaa.com/news/newsletter/pdf/2004yearEndStats.pdf>, accessed 20 January 2006; Reuters, 'Digital Music Sales Tripled in 2005', from *ZDNet News*, 2006, <http://news.zdnet.com/2100-1035_22-6028755.html>, accessed 24 January 2006; Reuters, 'EMI Chairman Sees Net Reviving Music Industry', from *ZDNet News*, 2006, <http://news.adnet.com/2100-9595_22-6030115.html>, accessed 21 January 2006; The Center for Media Research, 'Top Online Music Sites', <www.centerformediaresearch.com/cfmr_brief.cfm?fnl=050624>, accessed 19 January 2006.

CASE STUDY

QUESTIONS

1. If you were the Marketing Manager of a traditional music retailer such as HMV or Sanity, how would you capitalise on this trend towards digital music?

2. What other opportunities and threats does the Internet create in other industries?

3. What is the future of digital music?

4. Identify/suggest some key initiatives the music industry can pursue to curb unauthorised music file sharing.

5. Determine, through your own research, whether there are any changes to the digital music landscape.

CHAPTER 19

Sustainable competitive advantage

Bell Canada: www.bell.ca

Casella Wines:
www.casellawine.com.au

Kodak: wwwau.kodak.com

Procter & Gamble: www.pg.com

Telstra: www.telstra.com.au

Bell Canada and Telstra have several things in common. Each is the traditional incumbent telephone company of its country; both are used to dominating markets— in earlier times as a matter of right through a legislated monopoly and in more recent times through the sheer weight of inertia and access to the entire customer base in their respective countries (see introduction to Chapter 7). But they also have another thing in common. Both companies experienced a flattening off in revenue and decline in earnings in 2005 and are facing major technological and competitive shifts that are shaking these businesses to their foundations and forcing them to develop market-based competitive strategies. The solution for successful growth requires a marketing transformation by both companies—a transformation that requires strategic market focus and development of a new sustainable competitive advantage.

On 15 November 2005 Telstra's new chief executive of four months, Sol Trujillo, unveiled Telstra's growth strategy to be fuelled by the vision:

To give the customer a powerful, seamless user experience across all devices and all platforms in a 1 Click, 1 Touch, 1 Button, 1 Screen way—whether that customer is an individual, small business, large business or government agency.

It was announced that the overarching themes by which revenue growth of 2–2.5% per annum and earnings growth (before interest and tax) of 3–5% per annum will be achieved are:

Increasing revenue by providing new integrated services targeted to business and consumer segments that have different needs and value services differently, with a seamless one click, one touch or one screen approach.

Cutting costs through simplifying processes and systems and reducing duplication and complexity of existing networks by operating under a one factory approach which will lead to new efficiencies.

Under its new CEO, Sol Trujillo, Telstra starts its reinvention.

In early 2006 Telstra was putting in place a number of initiatives including:

- Implementing a simple straightforward process that puts the customer at the centre of the business.
- Reorganising marketing around market managers who will have full accountability for market performance and profitability around customer segments.
- Establishing a clear focus to win the market through intimate knowledge of markets and customers.
- Making a $10 billion investment in a new digital network.

Trujillo stated that strategic marketing is the first key pillar in the process and its goal is to transform Telstra into one of the best customer-driven marketing organisations in the global telecommunications industry. A starting point involved detailed market segmentation studies conducted in the consumer and SME markets in early 2006 followed by the development of a segment-based marketing structure to be operational from May 2006.

Its first half 2005/06 financial year results announced in February 2006 showed a 10.3% fall in net profit to $2.14 billion with revenue from its core phone network plunging much faster than expected and market share loss in the highly competitive mobiles market. Growth in its Internet and IP solutions business (42%), mobiles (4.6%), Sensis (advertising and directories business 6.3%) and Pay TV (29%) has not been enough to offset the decline in its fixed-line business. In its Internet and IP solutions business, wholesale revenue (coming from wholesale broadband sales to third-party marketers) has grown much faster than retail, putting at risk the company's direct relationship with its end-customers.

Telstra faces a major challenge around its ability to develop and implement competitive strategies in the rapid growth markets in which it already operates and in new emerging markets that will be open to new, nimble competitors.[1]

After reading this chapter you should be able to:

1 Discuss competitor analysis, emphasising the determination of competitors' objectives and strategies, strengths and weaknesses, and reactions—and assess whether to attack or avoid particular competitors.

2 Define generic competitive strategies and the value disciplines of market leaders and the strategy of value innovation.

3 Determine when a company needs to move towards, or adopt, one-to-one marketing strategies.

4 Explain the fundamentals of competitive strategies based on competitive positions in the market for market leaders, market challengers, market followers and market nichers.

5 Illustrate the need for balance in customer and competitor orientation, and contrast the differences between competitor-centred, customer-centred and market-centred orientations.

Competitive advantage An advantage over competitors gained by offering consumers greater value, either through lower prices or by providing more benefits that justify higher prices.

Today, understanding customers is not enough. Under the marketing concept, companies gain **competitive advantage** by designing offers that satisfy target consumer needs *better than competitors' offers*. They might deliver more customer value by offering consumers lower prices for similar products and services, or by providing more benefits that justify higher prices. Thus, marketing strategies must consider not only the needs of target consumers but also the strategies of competitors. The first step is **competitor analysis**, the process of identifying and assessing key competitors. The second step is developing **competitive marketing strategies** that position the company strongly against competitors and give it the greatest possible competitive advantage.

Competitor analysis The process of identifying major competitors; assessing their objectives, strategies, strengths and weaknesses and reaction patterns; and selecting which competitors to attack or avoid.

Competitive marketing strategies Defined by the marketing actions taken to move an organisation from its current competitive position to a desired future competitive position. An organisation's competitive position is defined by its position in the market relative to competitors as seen by the relevant target market.

Competitor analysis

To plan effective competitive marketing strategies the company needs to find out all it can about its competitors. It must constantly compare its products, prices, channels and promotion with those of close competitors. In this way the company can find areas of potential competitive advantage and disadvantage. And it can launch more effective marketing campaigns against its competitors and prepare stronger defences against competitors' actions.[2]

But what do companies need to know about their competitors? They need to know: Who are our competitors? What are their objectives? What are their strategies? What are their strengths and weaknesses? What are their reaction patterns? Figure 19.1 shows the major steps in analysing competitors.

Identifying the company's competitors

Normally, it would seem a simple task for a company to identify its competitors. Coca-Cola knows that Pepsi is its major competitor; and Virgin Blue knows that it competes with Qantas. At the narrowest level, a company can define its competitors as other companies offering a similar product or service to the same customers at similar prices. Thus, Holden might see Ford as a major competitor, but not Mercedes or Hyundai.

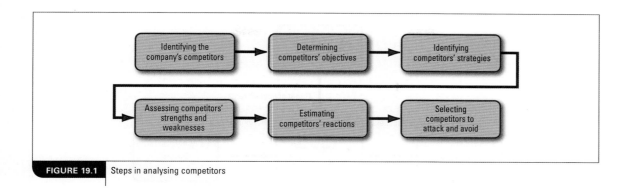

FIGURE 19.1 Steps in analysing competitors

But companies actually face a much wider range of competitors. The company might define competitors as all firms making the same product or class of products. Thus, Holden would see itself as competing against all other car makers. Even more broadly, competitors might include all companies making products that supply the same service. Here Holden would see itself competing against not only other car makers, but also companies that make trucks, motorcycles or even bicycles. Finally, and still more broadly, competitors might include all companies that compete for the same consumer dollars. Here Holden would see itself competing with companies that sell major consumer durables, new homes or overseas holidays. A further dimension of competition has emerged through Internet trading—eBay and other online auction companies have entered the second-hand car market and are only a step away from providing competitive price information on new car alternatives for consumers and fleet buyers. This kind of 'infomediary' is changing the structure of competition and enabling the entry of new competitors.

Companies must avoid 'competitor myopia'. A company is more likely to be 'buried' by its latent competitors than its current ones. For example, Kodak, in its film business, has been worrying about the growing competition from Fuji, the Japanese film maker. But Kodak faces a much greater threat to its film processing and supplies business from digital technology. These digital cameras sold by Canon and Sony, and now mobile phones sold by Motorola and Nokia, take video and still pictures that can be displayed on a television set or downloaded onto a computer, shared instantly across the Internet with family and friends, turned into hard copy and later erased. What greater threat is there to a film business than a filmless camera?

Companies can identify their competitors from the *industry* point of view. They might see themselves as being in the cosmetic industry, the pharmaceutical industry, the telecommunication industry or the beverage industry. A company must understand the competitive patterns in its industry if it hopes to be an effective 'player' in that industry. Michael Porter suggests that five major forces drive industry competition. These are shown in Figure 19.2 overleaf. He proposes that the structure of the industry itself, its suppliers and its buyers have a major influence on the evolution of the industry and its profit potential. The threat of substitutes and new entrants also influences the appropriate strategies to be adopted. These parties exert differing levels of power and act as forces which shape the evolution of the industry, control the competitive balance and influence the profit potential.

It is important to note that industry structure is not static. Major or minor changes may be occurring at any point in time. Some industries may be undergoing structural change or convergence with other industries. Hence, definition of the relevant 'industry' is important for structural analysis purposes. From an airline's perspective, is the relevant industry 'transportation' or 'leisure air travel' or is it 'tourist holidays'? The latter implies that the industry includes accommodation as well as travel. Since much of the competition revolves around holiday packages in this market through

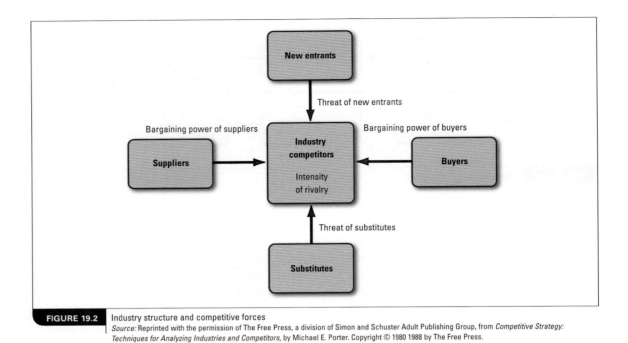

FIGURE 19.2 Industry structure and competitive forces

Source: Reprinted with the permission of The Free Press, a division of Simon and Schuster Adult Publishing Group, from *Competitive Strategy: Techniques for Analyzing Industries and Competitors*, by Michael E. Porter. Copyright © 1980 1988 by The Free Press.

alliances or networks of airlines, hotels, coaches and resorts, the 'tourist holidays' definition may be more appropriate.

Porter has reinterpreted this model in the light of the Internet's influences on industry structure. The following observations are made in relation to each competitive force which can have both positive and negative impacts on a competitor's position:

- *New entrants:* Reduced barriers to entry because of less need for salesforce. Access to distribution channels and physical assets.
- *Substitutes:* Additional new substitution threats and potential market expansion from e-tailers offering a wide range of products and services.
- *Suppliers:* The Internet provides a channel for suppliers to end-users as well as enabling procurement processes that can standardise products and reduce differentiation.
- *Buyers:* Improves bargaining power through wider choice and reduces switching costs.
- *Rivalry of competitors:* Migrates competition to price by reducing differences between competitors as well as widening the geographic market by increasing the number of competitors.[3]

In any industry, a small number of factors will be relevant. Analysis of industry structure using this model provides an assessment of the strength of competitive position of industry competitors as a group and this in turn reflects on the individual industry competitor. It is useful also to assess the sustainability of a firm's competitive advantage including those of pure dot com businesses.

The implication is that the firm should influence the balance of forces through strategic moves, thereby strengthening the firm's position. Alternatively, the strategist might reposition the firm so that its capabilities provide the best defence against the array of competitive forces. A further approach is to anticipate shifts in the factors underlying the forces and respond to them, thus exploiting change by choosing a strategy appropriate to the new competitive balance before competitors recognise it.

Companies can also identify competitors from a *market* point of view. Here they define competitors as companies that are trying to satisfy the same customer need or serve the same customer group.

From an industry point of view, Coca-Cola might see its competition as Pepsi, Schweppes and other soft drink manufacturers. From a market point of view, however, the customer really wants 'thirst quenching'. This need can be satisfied by iced tea, fruit juice, bottled water and many other fluids. Similarly, BHP Billiton's steel division might define its competitors as other makers of steel for housing construction. But from a market point of view, competitors would include all firms making construction materials for housing. In general, the market concept of competition opens the company's eyes to a broader set of actual and potential competitors. This leads to better long-run market planning.

The key to identifying competitors is to link industry and market analysis by mapping out *product/ market segments.* In the car industry this would involve identifying of all the main market segments and determining which competing products are sold in which segments. In this way we might find that Holden competes with Ford and Toyota with most of its segment entries. Clearly, each product/ market segment would pose different competitive problems and opportunities.

Determining competitors' objectives

Having identified the main competitors, marketing management now ask: What does each competitor seek in the marketplace? What drives each competitor's behaviour?

The marketer might at first assume that all competitors will want to maximise their profits and will choose their actions accordingly. But companies differ in the emphasis they put on short-term versus long-term profits. And some competitors might be oriented toward 'satisficing' rather than 'maximising' profits. They have target profit goals and are satisfied in achieving them, even if more profits could have been produced by other strategies.

Thus, marketers must look beyond competitors' profit goals. Each competitor has a mix of objectives, each of differing importance. The company wants to know the relative importance that a competitor places on current profitability, market share growth, cash flow, technological leadership, service leadership and other goals. Knowing a competitor's mix of objectives reveals whether the competitor is satisfied with its current situation and how it might react to different competitive actions. For example, a company that pursues low-cost leadership will react much more strongly to a competitor's cost-reducing manufacturing breakthrough than to the same competitor's advertising increase.

A company must also monitor its competitors' objectives for various product/market segments. If the company finds that a competitor has discovered a new segment, this might be an opportunity. If it finds that competitors plan new moves into segments now served by the company, it will be forewarned and, hopefully, forearmed. As customers move from buying products from showrooms and retailers to online purchasing, market segmentation is further categorised by the buying behaviour via the Internet channel.

Identifying competitors' strategies

The more that one firm's strategy resembles another firm's strategy, the more the two firms compete. In most industries the competitors can be sorted into groups that pursue different strategies. A **strategic group** is a group of firms in an industry following the same or a similar strategy in a given target market. For example, in the major appliance industry, Hoover, Email, Westinghouse and Philips all belong to the same strategic group. Each produces a full line of medium-priced appliances supported by good service. Miele and AEG, on the other hand, belong to a different strategic group. They produce a narrow line of very high quality appliances, offer a high level of service and charge a premium price.

Strategic group A group of firms in an industry following the same or a similar strategy.

Some important insights emerge from strategic group identification. If a company enters one of the groups, the members of that group become its key competitors. Thus, if a company enters the first group against Hoover, Email and Philips, it can succeed only if it develops some strategic advantages over these large competitors.

Although competition is most intense within a strategic group, there is also rivalry between groups. First, some of the strategic groups may appeal to overlapping customer segments. For example, no matter what their strategy, all major appliance manufacturers will go after the apartment and home builders' segment. Second, customers might not see much difference in the offers of different groups—they might see little difference in quality between Email and Miele. Finally, members of one strategic group might expand into new strategy segments. Thus, Philips might decide to offer a premium-quality, premium-priced line of appliances to compete with Miele.

The company needs to look at all the dimensions that identify strategic groups within the industry. It needs to know each competitor's product quality, features and mix; customer services; pricing policy; distribution coverage; salesforce strategy; and advertising and sales promotion programs. And it must study the details of each competitor's R&D, manufacturing, purchasing, financial and other strategies.

To understand a competitor's strategies the firm needs to engage in the gathering of competitive intelligence. There are three sources—individuals within its own company, third parties and competitors. Third-party sources include advertising agencies, bankers, consultants, customers, distributors, equipment manufacturers, financial analysts, government, suppliers and trade associations.[4]

Competitors also reveal elements of their strategies through press releases and their actions in the marketplace. Marketing Highlight 19.1 describes how one company uses information from competitors to develop and implement its strategy.

Assessing competitors' strengths and weaknesses

Marketers need to assess carefully each competitor's strengths and weaknesses in order to answer the critical question: what *can* our competitors do? As a first step, companies can gather data on each competitor's goals, strategies and performance over the last few years. Admittedly, some of this information will be hard to obtain. For example, business products companies find it hard to estimate competitors' market shares because they do not have the same syndicated data services that are available to consumer packaged-goods companies.

Companies normally learn about their competitors' strengths and weaknesses through secondary data, personal experience and hearsay. They can also conduct primary marketing research with customers, suppliers and dealers. In the late 1990s, a growing number of companies turned to benchmarking, comparing the company's products and processes with those of competitors or leading firms in other industries to find ways to improve quality and performance. Benchmarking has become a powerful tool for increasing a company's competitiveness.[5]

Estimating competitors' reactions

Next, the company wants to know: what *will* our competitors do? A competitor's objectives, strategies and strengths and weaknesses go a long way towards explaining its likely actions, as well as its likely reactions to company moves such as price cuts, promotion increases or new product introductions. In addition, each competitor has a certain philosophy of doing business, a certain internal culture and guiding beliefs. Marketing managers need a deep understanding of a given competitor's mentality if they want to anticipate how the competitor will act or react.[6]

Each competitor reacts differently. Some do not react quickly or strongly to a competitor's move. They may feel their customers are loyal; they may be slow in noticing the move; they may lack the funds to react. Some competitors react only to certain types of moves and not to others. They might always respond strongly to price cuts in order to signal that these will never succeed. But they might not respond at all to advertising increases, believing these to be less threatening. Other competitors react swiftly and strongly to any action. Thus, Colgate does not let a new toothpaste come easily into the market. Many firms avoid direct competition with Colgate and look for easier prey, knowing that Colgate will react fiercely if challenged. Finally, some competitors show no predictable reaction pattern. They might or might not react on a given occasion, and there is no way to foresee what they will do based on their economics, history or anything else.

In some industries, competitors live in relative harmony; in others, they fight constantly. Knowing how major competitors react gives the company clues on how best to attack competitors or how best to defend the company's current positions.[7]

Selecting competitors to attack or avoid

A company has already largely selected its major competitors through prior decisions on customer targets, distribution channels and marketing mix strategy. These decisions define the strategic group to which the company belongs. Management must now decide which competitors to compete against most vigorously. The company can focus on one of several classes of competitors.

Strong or weak competitors

Most companies prefer to aim their shots at their weak competitors. This requires fewer resources and less time. But in the process the firm may gain little. The argument could be made that the firm should also compete with strong competitors in order to sharpen its abilities. Furthermore, even strong competitors have some weaknesses, and succeeding against them often provides greater returns.

A useful tool for assessing competitor strengths and weaknesses is **customer value analysis**. The aim of customer value analysis is to determine the benefits that target customers value and how customers rate the relative value of various competitors' offers. In conducting a customer value analysis, the company first identifies the major attributes that customers value and the importance customers place on these attributes. Next, it assesses the company's and competitors' performance on the valued attributes. The key to gaining competitive advantage is to take each customer segment and examine how the company's offer compares with that of its major competitor. If the company's offer exceeds the competitor's offer on all important attributes, the company can charge a higher price and earn higher profits, or it can charge the same price and gain more market share. But if the company is seen as performing at a lower level than its major competitor on some important attributes, it must invest in strengthening those attributes or finding other important attributes where it can build a lead on the competitor.

Customer value analysis Analysis conducted to determine what benefits target customers value and how they rate the relative value of various competitors' offers.

Close or distant competitors

Most companies will compete with competitors who resemble them most. Thus, Toyota competes more against Ford than against Jaguar. At the same time, the company may want to avoid trying to 'destroy' a close competitor. For example, APD snack food (now CCA Snackfoods) moved aggressively against Arnott's in the Australian snack-food market with great success. However, the conquest turned out to be a questionable victory. Due to continuing losses, Arnott's sold its snack-food business to Frito-Lay. As a result, CCA Snackfoods which became part of Coca-Cola Amatil faced a much larger competitor—and it suffered the consequences. Frito-Lay was able to penetrate the Australian market with some of its well-known American brands of chips and take market share from CCA. In 1998 CCA Snackfoods was sold to Frito-Lay.

'Well-behaved' or 'disruptive' competitors

A company really needs and benefits from competitors. The existence of competitors results in several strategic benefits. Competitors may help increase total demand. They may share the costs of market

Competitive intelligence—to have it is not enough: use it!

What follows is a factual account of the use and non-use of competitive intelligence by a successful Australian company that has become a world player in its industry. For competitive sensitivity reasons the company remains un-named!

The situation

This large multinational company has manufacturing and marketing operations in Australasia, Asia and North America. Each business unit, seven in total, operates in highly competitive markets with varying degrees of success.

Some key issues faced by this company were:

1   Four business units were losing market share in markets they were well positioned to lead. They were operating in mature markets where competitors and the multinational company were well established. The product in these markets had become a commodity.

2   One business unit was losing market share in a growth market in which it was well positioned. A considerable investment in building local manufacturing capability had been made over the preceding three-year period. Although competition was intense, competitors' products were inferior in most cases and so the 'loss of market share' was difficult to comprehend.

3   The two remaining business units were relatively new and were able to leapfrog their well-entrenched competitors in key market segments, even though they were not as well known in the marketplace. The two units that were succeeding in outperforming their competitors operated in the same market but in different segments of that market. They were succeeding in being 'first to market' in key target segments and beating their competitors to market with new products by up to a full three months.

An issue with all seven business units was that their management viewed their own markets as very different from each other and believed that whatever they were doing 'right' or 'wrong' to achieve their business objectives was not relevant to the other business units within the company.

An external consulting organisation was engaged to understand how the two business units least expected by Head Office to lead their market were achieving this and to understand what was happening (or not happening) in the other five business units. The approach employed by the consulting organisation was to perform a 'marketing audit' of each unit and conduct a comparative analysis to make recommendations.

Key findings

All seven business units used exactly the same business and marketing planning, reporting and segmentation processes. However, each business unit implemented elements of their ongoing planning and reporting process very differently—especially in the area of gathering and interpreting competitive intelligence.

1. The mature business and markets case—an inactive approach

These four businesses had developed a sense of general complacency and comfort in their marketing capability as a result of five continuous years of market leadership. The salesforce had little knowledge of competitive strengths and weaknesses and also of their competitors' marketing strategies. The sales group had moved close to adopting an 'order-taking' approach as opposed to one capable of positioning the strengths of the business units. This resulted in an inability to move beyond 'discounting' as the key strategy to win competitive business.

The majority of competitive intelligence gathering over the preceding two years had moved towards the historical measurement of market share reporting of revenue and unit sales. Very little market information about competitive activity was gathered, although it was a 'task' of the office secretary occasionally to read local newspapers to look for any major announcements from competitors. When they did find announcements, they were cut out of the newspaper and circulated around the office. These were never discussed within the business or considered in marketing strategy development as a part of marketing planning.

The focus on competitors in the two most recent annual business and marketing plans preceding the recent decline in market share had consisted of documenting competitors' weaknesses and those competitors' relative failure to 'eat into' the leadership position held by the four business units in their respective mature markets. There was very little proactive competitive strategy.

2. The emerging business and markets case— a narrow approach

This business unit was less complacent than the other four units operating in mature markets. A difference was that it was actively gathering competitive intelligence from press releases and marketing activities of competitors within its emerging marketplace. Another difference was that the salesforce was provided with training on positioning products against competitors' and regular quarterly updates about competitor activities were distributed.

One issue facing this business was that its major competitor was 'proving' their new products in other emerging markets and then launching them into the business unit's marketplace having 'proved' the products from both a manufacturing and a marketing perspective.

However, this business unit was not aware of this because it was only gathering intelligence about its competitors from within its own marketplace. As a result, its overall market share was eroding due to its competitors' ability to launch new and improved products quickly and effectively without this business being aware of their market testing in other emerging markets.

3. The new businesses—a proactive approach

These two businesses were operating in highly competitive markets. They were smaller than their two well-resourced major multinational competitors and

were not expected to outperform them in key target segments as quickly as they had.

The major factor differentiating these two businesses from the other business units in the company as well as their competition was their focus on gathering competitive intelligence from all over the world—not just in their own market—and analysing this intelligence on a fortnightly basis.

Each marketing manager was tasked with clipping any press releases from competitors on a fortnightly basis. In addition, all members of the salesforce were given incentives and the tools to gather competitive intelligence and encouraged to pass information directly to the marketing team through their line managers on a weekly basis. Then, fortnightly without fail, all marketing managers were committed to spending one full hour together reviewing their competitive intelligence and evaluating this against a checklist of their competitive strategies.

The outcome of this was that over the past 24 months they had determined that a major competitor was launching a product in different countries in Europe and announcing this launch in the local press of those countries. Within six months, the new product would be launched into one geographical sector of the market, then six weeks later the product would roll out across the remaining market sectors in a standard way.

The two new businesses, upon evaluating this, then altered their competitive strategy to ensure they launched a competitive product (if the market was wanting it) within three months of the European launch into the same geographical segments as their competitor—in most cases beating the competition to market by three months. They also established processes to monitor and track the performance of their competitors' products in the European market to learn from their success or failure. In addition, the salesforce was fed with competitive market intelligence that it could use to position their products proactively against their major competitors.

Source: Paige Carlyle, Consulting Partner, Interstrat, June 2005.

Questions

1 What lessons can be learned from this story?

2 What role can the salesforce play in competitive intelligence?

3 Where does the real advantage come from collecting press releases as a source of competitive intelligence?

and product development and help to legitimise new technologies. They may serve less attractive segments or lead to more product differentiation.

However, a company might not view all its competitors as beneficial. An industry often contains 'well-behaved' competitors and 'disruptive' competitors.[8] Well-behaved competitors play by the rules of the industry. They favour a stable and healthy industry, set reasonable prices in relation to costs, motivate others to lower costs or improve differentiation, and accept reasonable levels of market share and profits. Disruptive competitors, on the other hand, break the rules. They try to buy share rather than earn it, take large risks and, in general, shake up the industry. For example, Kellogg's finds Goodman Fielder (Uncle Tobys) to be a well-behaved competitor because it plays by the rules and adopts marketing strategies designed to grow the market. But both see Sanitarium as a disruptive competitor because of actions it took during 1998–1999 which disrupted the Australian market. By attacking Kellogg's head on, claiming in advertisements that 'Kellogg's Nutri-Grain brand contains more sugar than chocolate cake and ice-cream', Sanitarium made customers look at all cereal products in a negative way. As a result of Sanitarium's campaign, there was a significant decline in the cereal market with retailers devoting less shelf space to breakfast cereals in their stores. In 2006 again sluggish sales in the $910 million breakfast cereal market has signalled a new round of competitive strategies. Sales of breakfast cereal rose 2.5% in 2005 over 2004, but sales at Sanitarium, which has a health food focus, grew 9.6%. Kellogg's, with 42.8% share, has lost share to its smaller rivals while Uncle Tobys and Sanitarium hold share of about 18%.[9]

A company might be smart to support well-behaved competitors, aiming its attacks at disruptive competitors. Thus, some analysts claim that Kellogg's Corn Flakes promotional discounts were intentionally designed to target head-on Sanitarium's Weet-Bix to signal its intentions to bring any current or future competitors into line.

The implication is that 'well-behaved' companies would like to shape an industry that consists of only

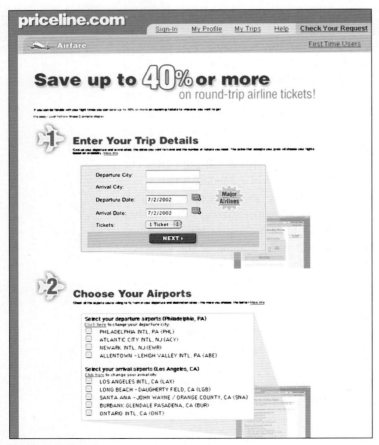

Priceline's strategies challenge competitors.

Source: <www.priceline.com>.

well-behaved competitors. Through careful licensing, selective retaliation and coalitions, they can shape the industry so that the competitors behave rationally and harmoniously, follow the rules, try to earn share rather than buy it and differentiate to compete less directly. Poorly behaving competitors are often driven by short-term strategies (marketing myopia) and will damage their own profitability in the long run.

Again, the rapid growth in electronic business, and the integral part of the Internet, is taking this managed stability out of online competitors' hands and giving greater choice and control to customers. You can bid for a seat on a flight by logging onto <www.priceline.com> or by visiting <www.ebay.com> auctions and specifying how much you are prepared to pay. This opens up a whole new set of competitive challenges.

Designing a competitive intelligence system

We have described the main types of information that companies need about their competitors. This information must be collected, interpreted, distributed and used. The cost in money and time of gathering competitive intelligence is high, and the company must design its competitive intelligence system in a cost-effective way.

The competitive intelligence system first identifies the vital types of competitive information and the best sources of this information. Then, the system continuously collects information from the field (salesforce, channels, suppliers, market research firms, trade associations) and from published data (government publications, speeches, articles). Next, the system checks the information for validity and reliability, interprets it and organises it in an appropriate way. Finally, it sends key information to relevant decision makers and responds to inquiries from managers about competitors.

With this system, company managers will receive timely information about competitors in the form of phone calls, bulletins, newsletters and reports. In addition, managers can connect with the system when they need an interpretation of a competitor's sudden move, when they want to know a competitor's weaknesses and strengths, or when they need to know how a competitor will respond to a planned company move.

Smaller companies that cannot afford to set up formal competitive intelligence offices can assign specific executives to watch specific competitors. Thus, a manager who used to work for a competitor might follow that competitor closely; they would be the 'in-house expert' on that competitor. Any manager needing to know the thinking of a given competitor could contact the assigned in-house expert.[10]

SELF-CHECK QUESTIONS

1   Outline the types of analysis to be undertaken to understand a firm's competitors.

2   Describe 'well-behaved' and 'disruptive' competitors in an industry you know. Give examples of the actions of these competitors which support your classification of them.

3   How is the Internet affecting the structure and nature of competition?

Competitive strategies

Having identified and evaluated its major competitors, the company must now design broad competitive marketing strategies that will best position its offer against competitors' offers and give the company the strongest possible competitive advantage. But what broad marketing strategies might the company use? Which ones are best for a particular company, or for the company's different divisions and products?

No one strategy is best for all companies. Each company must determine what makes the most sense given its position in the industry and its objectives, opportunities and resources. Even within a company, different strategies may be required for different businesses or products. Toshiba uses one marketing strategy for its leading brands in stable consumer markets *and* a different marketing strategy for its new high-tech computer products for the commercial market. We now look at broad competitive marketing strategies that companies can use.

Basic competitive strategies

More than a decade ago Michael Porter suggested four basic competitive positioning strategies that companies can follow—three winning strategies and one losing one.[11] The three winning strategies include:

- *Overall cost leadership.* Here the company works hard to achieve the lowest costs of production and distribution so that it can price lower than its competitors and win a large market share. The Warehouse in New Zealand and Franklins in Australia are leading retail practitioners of this strategy.
- *Differentiation.* Here the company concentrates on creating a highly differentiated product line and marketing program so that it comes across as the class leader in the industry. Most customers would prefer to own this brand if its price is not too high. Hewlett-Packard and BOC follow this strategy in printers and LPG gas respectively.
- *Focus.* Here the company focuses its effort on serving a few market segments well rather than going after the whole market. The insurance group APIA (Australian Pensioners Insurance Agency), a part of the Promina Group, focuses only on the 'over 55' pensioner sector of the market, and within that it dominates the Australian market segment.[12]

Companies that pursue a clear strategy—one of the above—are likely to perform well. The firm that carries out that strategy best will make the most profits. But firms that do not pursue a clear strategy—*middle-of-the-roaders*—do the worst. Myer department stores encountered difficult times over the last decade because they did not stand out as the lowest in cost, highest in perceived differentiation or best in serving some market segment. Middle-of-the-roaders try to be good on all strategic counts, but can end up being not very good at anything. A new classification of competitive marketing strategies was developed by Michael Treacy and Fred Wiersema.[13] They suggest that companies gain leadership positions by delivering superior value to their customers. Companies can pursue any of three strategies—called **value disciplines**—for delivering superior customer value. These are:

- *Operational excellence.* The company provides superior value by leading its industry in price and convenience. It works to reduce costs and to create a lean and efficient value delivery system. It serves customers who want reliable, good-quality products or services, but who want them cheaply and easily. Examples include Kmart and Dell Computer.
- *Customer intimacy.* The company provides superior value by precisely segmenting its markets and then tailoring its products or services to match exactly the needs of targeted customers. It builds detailed customer databases for segmenting and targeting, and empowers its marketing people to respond quickly to customer needs. It serves customers who are willing to pay a premium to get precisely what they want, and it will do almost anything to build long-term customer loyalty and to capture customer lifetime value. Examples are IBM Global Services and Omega Watches.
- *Product leadership.* The company provides superior value by offering a continuous stream of leading-edge products or services that make their own and competing products obsolete. It is

Value disciplines
A value discipline underlines the operating model a company chooses to deliver the value proposition it offers to its market. It chooses one of three possible value disciplines: best total cost, best product or best total solution. Once selected, the value discipline shapes the company's plans and decisions, operating structure, culture and management processes, all designed to deliver superior customer value according to that discipline.

open to new ideas, relentlessly pursues new solutions, and works to reduce cycle times so that it can get new products to market quickly. It serves customers who want state-of-the-art products and services, regardless of the costs in terms of price or inconvenience. Examples include Intel, Sony and Nestlé.

Some companies successfully pursue more than one value discipline at the same time. For example, Federal Express excels at both operational excellence and customer intimacy. However, such companies are rare—few firms can be the best at more than one of these disciplines. By trying to be *good at all* the value disciplines, a company usually ends up being *best at none.*

Treacy and Wiersema have found that leading companies focus on and excel at a single value discipline, while meeting industry standards on the other two. They design their entire value delivery system to single-mindedly support the chosen discipline. For example, Target knows that customer intimacy and product leadership are important. Compared with other discounters, it offers very good customer service *and* an excellent product assortment. But it offers less customer service and less depth in its product assortment than specialty and department stores that pursue customer intimacy or product leadership strategies. Instead, it focuses obsessively on operational excellence—on reducing costs and streamlining its order-to-delivery process in order to make it convenient for customers to buy just the right products at the lowest prices.

Classifying competitive strategies as value disciplines is appealing. It defines marketing strategy in terms of the single-minded pursuit of delivering value to customers. It recognises that management must align every aspect of the company with the chosen value discipline—from its culture, to its organisation structure, to its operating and management systems and processes.

Competitive advantage from philanthropy

A small number of companies have started to use philanthropy to achieve both social and economic objectives. This is based on the assumption that both social and economic advantage do not necessarily conflict and that they should form part of a competitive strategy. Most companies today that give to what they see as worthy causes do so as good corporate citizens and hope to increase brand awareness and gain goodwill from alignment with a cause. However, companies like Cisco Systems have done this in a way that also achieves competitive advantage. Through the Cisco Networking Academy it has invested in an educational program to train computer network administrators to alleviate a potential constraint on its growth and at the same time give appealing job opportunities to high school and university graduates. DreamWorks SKG, the movie production company, has each of its six divisions working with the Los Angeles Community College district and local high schools to create specialised curriculums that combine classroom instruction with internships and mentoring with particular focus on low-income students. Even though very few will join DreamWorks, it will gain from a strengthening of the entertainment cluster it depends upon.

The company that initiates corporate philanthropy usually will get a disproportionate benefit from the superior reputation and relationships it creates in a particular area. For example, Exxon Mobil's program to fight malaria in African countries to improve public health gains directly by having healthier workers and contractors as well as by building strong relationships with local governments. This advances its objective of being the preferred resource-development partner in those countries and regions.[14]

One-to-one marketing strategies

In their book, *Enterprise One to One: Tools for Competing in the Interactive Age*, Peppers and Rogers talk about how customers have different needs in relation to a firm, and how they represent different values to a firm. Depending on how differentiable a firm's customer base is, the natural competitive strategy of a firm might be mass marketing, niche or target marketing, or something else. By mapping the customer base according to how differentiable it is, the enterprise can begin to make plans for 'migrating' towards doing business as a one-to-one enterprise.[15]

Peppers and Rogers pose two questions to help a firm to map its position on a customer differentiation matrix. This was discussed in Chapter 18 and shown in Figure 18.2. The first question is: *how different are your customers in terms of their value to the business?* The second question is: *how different are your customers in terms of what they need from your business?* Are their needs all about the same, or is each customer quite different? If the business falls into Quadrant IV (see Figure 18.2), which includes customers of high value to the business and those who also have highly differentiated requirements, then one-to-one marketing strategies are appropriate. The firm may already be actively engaged in implementing a number of initiatives designed to create long-lasting relationships with those kinds of customers. This requires a comprehensive customer database that tracks individual transactions and communication with an increasing number of customers through cost-efficient interactive mechanisms such as electronic data interchange (EDI) or the World Wide Web. In addition, the offer needs to be mass customised.

If a company wants to adopt a one-to-one approach as the focus of its competitive marketing strategy—whether to lead, challenge or follow—it needs to make a hard-nosed assessment of the market needs and its capability to deliver as well as the relative positions of its closest competitors. Figure 19.3 shows a strategy-mapping process to assist the business in assessing the position of customers in terms of needs and valuations and the position of the firm in terms of production flexibility and communication. In Figure 19.3 the customer position is 1–1, reflecting the need for one-to-one marketing strategies. But the firm's position at 5–5 reflects a mass-production and mass-marketing strategy. In this example, the firm has a long way to go to align to market conditions.

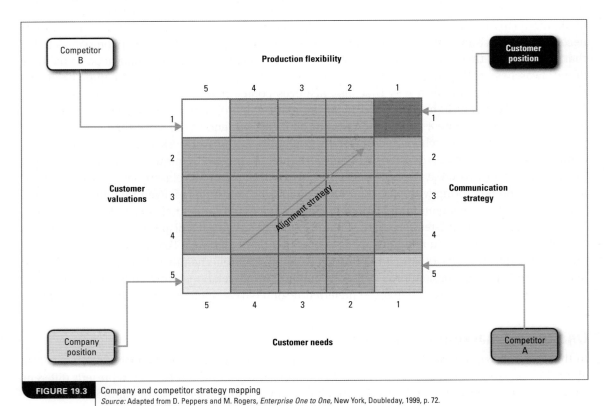

FIGURE 19.3   Company and competitor strategy mapping
Source: Adapted from D. Peppers and M. Rogers, *Enterprise One to One*, New York, Doubleday, 1999, p. 72.

Competitor A is positioned as having a high level of production flexibility but operating a mass-communication approach, while competitor B has little production flexibility but is communicating in a highly individual, interactive and personal manner. Both competitors need some realignment but are placed in a better position than the 5–5 company to address the market.[16]

However, competing on a one-to-one customer basis has other dimensions which require consideration, namely the strength of the customer relationship and the intensity of competitive rivalry between firms competing for the same customers. In a business-to-business marketing environment these customers are often referred to as 'named accounts'—large enterprises that through their existing or potential value to the business command individual attention. If the customer relationship is strong and the competitive rivalry is low, the firm should compete on the basis of spreading its offerings across the departments of the customer organisation, achieving a greater share of the customer's budget. This is worth a very substantial investment and should be very profitable. If the customer relationship is weak and rivalry is intense then competition needs to be around innovation. If both the customer relationship and rivalry are strong, there is a strong case for collaboration with competitors to share the available business. If both are weak, where no one company has a commanding share of the customer's business, as occurs often in the early stages of a new innovative solution (such as mobile printing discussed in the opening of Chapter 10), the challenge is to grow share of the customer from competitors to the company. This is where relationship marketing, discussed in Chapters 2 and 18, plays a major role.[17]

As discussed in Chapter 18, online marketing can play an important role in implementing one-to-one marketing strategies,[18] but all of the marketing needs to be in alignment—product development speed and flexibility, file selling, direct marketing and delivery as well as after-sales service—in order to achieve an effective one-to-one strategy.

SELF-CHECK QUESTIONS

4   Give examples of companies that seem to fit Porter's framework of cost leadership, differentiation and focus.

5   Give examples that seem to fit Treacy and Wiersema's framework of operational excellence, customer intimacy and product leadership.

6   Can these two frameworks be reconciled or combined? If so, how?

7   Under what circumstances should a firm implement one-to-one marketing strategies?

The age of revolution

Many industries today are facing revolutionary transformation through technological convergence, market changes and the appearance of unexpected new competitors from outside the traditional industry. The microcomputer has transformed the computer industry from a vertically integrated mainframe-oriented structure to a specialised industry where each player has a specific role in the value chain from components suppliers to computer manufacturers and software producers to dealers to end-users. The Internet has changed the telecommunications industry from one dominated by telecommunication equipment suppliers like Ericsson and telcos like Telstra to new infrastructure suppliers like Cisco and new communications and trading companies like AOL Time Warner and eBay. In the international airline industry, economic and security uncertainties accompanied by strategic group alliances held together by loyalty programs and co-share arrangements have restructured the way in which players can survive. The dot-com bubble, cut short by economic downturn and the failure of many pure online companies to yield a profit, showed the possibility for future revolution in information-based businesses such as music, entertainment, financial services and education. The way in which brokerage companies now operate is testament to the potential for revolution. Radical innovation which produces new ways of creating and delivering value involves new products, technologies, processes and marketing.[19]

How can an industry leader—the one with most to lose—deal with radical innovation or industry revolution? D'Aveni suggests five different counter-revolutionary strategies depending upon the stage of progress of the revolution.

1   *Containment strategies* designed to lock in customers, raise switching costs, load up distribution channels and launch blocking brands can be successful if the revolution is seen early. Microsoft has done this with its Windows software making the switching costs very high. Sony has been able to stave off Microsoft in the video game industry with the Sony PlayStation range, which has a much larger library of games than the technologically more advanced Microsoft Xbox range.

2   *Shaping strategies* to encompass the new technology or business model are required when a revolutionary change cannot be contained. The incumbent will try to modify the new value proposition, technology or business model so it no longer threatens the old one. For example, the big three US car makers created a joint venture to develop new electric technologies for environmentally cleaner cars and ensured that none of them would gain access to breakthroughs before the other two. Also they were able to direct research to hybrid technologies which would not replace the internal combustion engine but would enhance it.

3   *Absorption strategies* designed to bring the revolution inside the existing business or look for ways of acquiring the revolutionary companies are used when a revolution is likely to succeed. In the soft drink industry, New Age beverages like Snapple and Gatorade made revolutionary inroads against Coca-Cola, PepsiCo and Cadbury Schweppes, which reacted by creating polarised groups of suppliers, bottlers and distributors which made it impossible for the new beverages to get retail and restaurant distribution. Later PepsiCo acquired Gatorade, Cadbury Schweppes took over Snapple and Coca-Cola bought Mad River.

4   *Neutralisation strategies* meet a revolution head on and terminate it. Microsoft's Internet Explorer was bundled in with other software and provided free which put an end to Netscape Navigator's dominance as an Internet browser. Sometimes legal action is used as was the case with the Recording Industry Association of America, which succeeded in the courts in shutting down MP3 revolutionary Napster—the music swapping website—in July 2001. Microsoft seems to be continually in court defending its new product developments from other software company challenges.

5   *Annulment strategies* involve the market leader in sidestepping the threat by shifting the basis of competition and making the attack irrelevant. IBM sidestepped revolutionary threats in the computer hardware business by becoming one of the largest information technology and Internet consulting companies in the world competing with firms like Accenture. Later it became an outsourcer and competed with firms like EDS. It avoided the hardware threats by developing its competencies in software and services and through its repositioning as an e-business solutions company.[20]

These competitive strategies strike at the heart of businesses facing revolutionary disruption in their industries and are designed to enable industry leaders to remain in market leadership positions. They involve much more than marketing strategies alone and require the entire organisation and its resources, capabilities and people to get behind the strategy which is required for survival.

Value innovation

In so many markets competition is fierce and companies compete for market share in what Kim and Mauborgne describe as a 'red ocean' or bloodbath of competitive activity—contesting the same marketspace with fiercely competitive matching strategies in a hyper-competitive environment. Their book, *Blue Ocean Strategy*, provides a methodology for analysing, creating and capturing new market opportunities. The book uses the 'blue ocean' analogy to describe uncontested and typically undefined market opportunities and describes the markets most companies compete in as 'red oceans' due to the fierce competitive rivalry that exists in most markets today.[21]

The authors studied 150 strategic moves spanning 100+ years across more than 30 industries and found that the most successful strategies were built around the concept they call **value innovation**, which involves creating significant leaps in value for both the company and its customers in a manner which makes rivals obsolete. In generic startegy terms this means being able to achieve both significant differential advantage as well as substantial cost advantage through innovation in value to customers and value to the business.

In order for a company to create a blue ocean strategy the authors suggest six principles outlined in Table 19.1.

The US wine market and Casella Wines provide the basis for one example used by the authors to explain the blue ocean strategy process. The USA is the third largest consumer of wine worldwide and is an intensely competitive market with local wines from California, Oregon, Washington and New York competing with European, Australian and South American wines. With all of this competition the number of wines available to the consumer has exploded; however, the demand levels have remained fairly stagnant resulting in much consolidation at the producer and retailer levels of the value chain. Conventional wisdom would suggest this industry is hardly attractive, so how do the incumbents make the right strategic moves to break out of this increasingly unattractive set of market conditions? The authors suggest first detailing the bases of competition on a strategy canvas. In this example, pricing, packaging, advertising, ageing of wine, prestige, complexity of wine taste and range of wine varieties make up the key bases of competition. When current offerings are mapped against these bases, two value lines emerge, a budget wine line-up and a premium wine line-up. The budget wines are low priced and offer low levels of benefits, while the premium wines are more expensive and follow a classic differentiation strategy. These competitive groupings mean that it is very difficult to set a company on a strong profitable growth track as it will not work to benchmark competitors and try to out-compete them by offering a little more for a little less. The authors suggest that market research is not the answer either as their research suggested that customers can barely imagine how to create an uncontested marketspace and usually suggest they want more for less based on the most common industry offers.

In order for a company to make a strategic shift in these circumstances it must change its focus from competitors to alternatives and from customers to non-customers of the existing industry. Marketing Highlight 19.2 describes how Casella implemented value innovation in the US wine market.

Value innovation
This involves creating significant leaps in value for both the company and its customers in a manner which makes rivals obsolete and creates an uncontested marketspace.

TABLE 19.1 Principles for creating a blue ocean strategy	
Formulation principles	**Execution principles**
Reconstruct market boundaries	Overcome key organisational hurdles
Focus on the big picture, not the numbers	Build execution into the strategy
Reach beyond existing demand	
Get the strategic sequence right	

Source: Adapted from Figure 1-4 in Kim and Mauborgne, *Blue Ocean Strategy*, Boston, Harvard Business School Press, 2005, p. 21.

Casella finds a blue ocean in the 'red' US wine market

In the US wine industry, conventional strategic thinking resulted in companies overdelivering on prestige and quality of wine at a price point. This meant that costs were increased as wine makers increased the complexity of their wines (ageing them for longer, using better oak storage, etc.) in order to win awards and pursue increased levels of prestige.

Casella Wines, an Australian winery, redefined the problem of the wine industry by looking across alternatives and specifically defining a new problem statement: how to make a fun non-traditional wine that is easy to drink for everyone. Casella looked at the alternatives of beer, spirits and ready-to-drink cocktails which made up three times the sales of wine and found that Americans saw wine as a turnoff relative to these alternatives. American consumers saw the industry as intimidating and pretentious and the complexity of the wine's taste created flavour challenges for the average consumer even through it was a key basis for competition.

With this key insight Casella Wines was ready to redraw the strategic profile of the US wine industry. In order to achieve this they turned to what Kim and Mauborgne describe as a four-actions framework:

1   Which of the factors that the industry takes for granted should be eliminated?
2   Which factors should be reduced well below the industry's standard?
3   Which factors should be raised above the industry standard?
4   Which factors should be created that the industry has never offered?

By using this framework Casella Wines created a wine [yellow tail] whose strategic profile broke away from the competition and created a 'blue ocean'. Casella did not position wine in the traditional way, rather they positioned it as a social drink accessible to everyone, beer drinkers, cocktail drinkers and other non-wine drinkers. Within two years [yellow tail] became the number one imported wine in the USA and by 2003 it was the number one red wine, even outstripping Californian labels.

[yellow tail] is positioned as a social drink accessible to everyone.

Casella Wines applied all four actions—eliminate, reduce, raise and create—to unlock uncontested marketspace in the US wine market.

By looking at the alternatives to wine Casella Wines created three new factors in the US wine industry—easy drinking, easy to select, and fun and adventure—as well as eliminating or reducing everything else. The [yellow tail] brand reduced the range by producing just a red and a white wine initially. They also reduced the prestige of the wine by leveraging the Australian cultural characteristics of laid-back, fun and adventurous. By providing this additional value, Casella was able to raise its pricing above the budget wines to more than double a jug of wine.

Through the [yellow tail] brand Casella Wines was able to deliver additional value to its customers and at the same time reduce its costs to deliver that value. Also, Casella has been unaffected by competitors and has been able to grow the US wine market. This value innovation is the essence of blue ocean strategy.

Source: W. Chan Kim and R. Mauborgne, *Blue Ocean Strategy: How to Create Uncontested Market Space and Make the Competition Irrelevant*, Boston, Harvard Business School Press, 2005.

Questions

1 What lessons can be learned from Casella's marketing strategy?

2 How could Casella grow its position further in the US wine market?

3 In what other industries do you see value innovation in the form of blue ocean strategies?

19.2

Competitive positions

Not all industries are facing the revolutionary impacts seen in the technology sectors of computers and communications. Many are much more stable and exhibit slower changes in market trends and industry restructure. Firms competing in a given target market will, at any point in time, differ in their objectives and resources. Some firms will be large, others small. Some will have many resources, others will be strapped for funds. Some will be old and established, others new and fresh. Some will strive for rapid market-share growth, others for long-term profits. And the firms will occupy different competitive positions in the target market.

We will adopt a classification of competitive strategies based on the role each firm plays in the target market—that of leading, challenging, following or niching. Suppose that an industry contains the firms shown in Figure 19.4 overleaf. Forty per cent of the market is in the hands of the **market leader**, the firm with the largest market share. Another 30% is in the hands of a **market challenger**, a runner-up that is fighting hard to increase its market share. Another 20% is in the hands of a **market follower**, another runner-up that wants to hold its share without rocking the boat. The remaining 10% is in the hands of **market nichers**, firms that serve small segments not being pursued by other firms.

We now look at specific marketing strategies that are available to market leaders, challengers, followers and nichers. You should remember, however, that these classifications often do not apply to a whole company, but only to its position in a specific industry. Large and diversified companies such as Fletcher Challenge, CSR or Unilever might be leaders in some markets and nichers in others. For example, Unilever leads in many segments, such as dishwashing and laundry detergents, but it challenges Cussons in the hand soaps market. Such companies often use different strategies for different business units or products, depending on the competitive situation of each.[22]

Market-leader strategies

Most industries contain an acknowledged market leader, the firm with the largest market share. It usually leads the other firms in price changes, new product introductions, distribution coverage and promotion spending. The leader may or may not be admired or respected, but other firms concede its dominance. The leader is a focal point for competitors, a company to challenge, imitate or avoid. Some of the best-known market leaders are Nokia (mobile phones) Toyota (cars), Woolworths

Market leader The firm with the largest market share in an industry; it usually leads other firms in price changes, new product introductions, distribution coverage and promotion spending.

Market challenger A runner-up firm in an industry that is fighting hard to increase its market share.

Market follower A runner-up firm in an industry that wants to hold its share without rocking the boat.

Market nicher A firm in an industry that serves small segments that the other firms overlook or ignore.

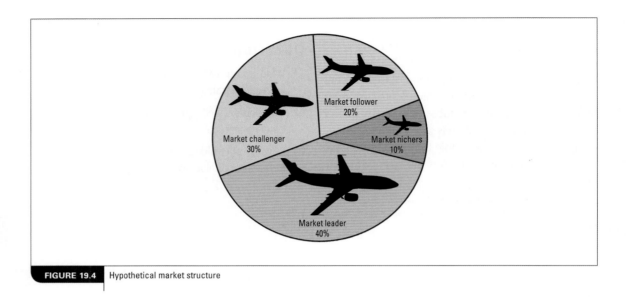

FIGURE 19.4 | Hypothetical market structure

(supermarkets), Hewlett-Packard (printers), Disney (entertainment) Cadbury Schweppes (chocolate confectionery), Billabong (surf and beachwear), Coca-Cola (soft drinks), Symantec (anti-virus software), McDonald's (fast food), Gillette (razors and blades) and Oracle (enterprise software systems).

A leading firm's life is not easy. It must maintain a constant watch. Other firms keep challenging its strengths or probing for its weaknesses. The market leader can easily miss a turn in the market and plunge into second or third place. A product innovation may come along and hurt the leader (as when Cussons Imperial Leather soap beat Colgate's and Unilever's leading brands). Or the leading firm might grow fat and slow, losing against new and faster rivals. (Xerox's share of the world copier market fell from more than 80% to less than 35% in just five years when Japanese producers challenged with cheaper and more reliable copiers.)

Leading firms want to remain number one. This calls for action on three fronts. First, the firm must find ways to expand total demand. Second, the firm must protect its current market share through good defensive and offensive actions. Third, the firm can try to expand its market share further, even if market size remains constant (see Marketing Highlight 19.3).

Expanding the total market

The leading firm normally gains the most when the total market expands. If we do more picture taking, Kodak stands to gain the most because it sells more than 75% of the country's film. If Kodak can persuade us to take pictures using traditional film, or take pictures on more occasions, or take more pictures on each occasion, it will benefit greatly. Similarly if Telstra can convince its mobile phone users to call more often or communicate via various means such as SMS and transfer of photo images it also stands to benefit greatly. In general, the market leader should look for new users, new uses and more usage of its products.

New users Every product class can attract buyers who are still unaware of the product, or who are resisting it because of its price or its lack of certain features. A seller can usually find new users in many places. For example, Revlon might find new perfume users in its current markets by persuading women who do not use perfume to try it. Or it might find users in new demographic segments by, say, producing cologne for men. Or it might expand into new geographical segments, perhaps by selling its perfume in other countries.

Johnson & Johnson's Baby Shampoo provides a classic example of developing new users. When the baby boom had passed and the birthrate had slowed down, the company grew concerned about future sales growth. But Johnson & Johnson's marketers noticed that other family members sometimes used the baby shampoo for their own hair. Management developed an advertising campaign aimed at adults. In a short time Johnson & Johnson's Baby Shampoo became a leading brand in the total shampoo market.

New uses The marketer can expand markets by discovering and promoting new uses for the product. DuPont's nylon provides a classic example of new-use expansion. Every time nylon became a mature product, some new use was discovered. Nylon was first used as a fibre for parachutes; then for women's stockings; later as a major material in shirts and blouses; and still later in car tyres, upholstery and carpeting.

More usage A third market-expansion strategy is to persuade people to use the product more often or to use more on each occasion. Campbell advertises that 'Soup is Good Food' to encourage people to eat soup more often. And it runs ads containing new recipes in *Better Homes and Gardens* and other home magazines to remind buyers that 'soup makes good food'.

Some years ago the Michelin Tyre Company found a creative way to increase usage on each occasion. It wanted French car owners to drive more kilometres per year, resulting in more tyre replacement. Michelin began rating French restaurants on a three-star system. It reported that many of the best restaurants were in the south of France, leading many Parisians to take weekend drives south. Michelin also published guidebooks with maps and sights along the way to entice further travel.

Protecting market share

While trying to expand total market size, the leading firm must also constantly protect its current business against competitor attacks. Coca-Cola must constantly guard against Pepsi; Gillette against Bic; Kodak against Fuji; McDonald's against Hungry Jack's and KFC; Holden against Ford.

What can the market leader do to protect its position? First, it must prevent or fix weaknesses that provide opportunities for competitors. It needs to keep its costs down and its prices in line with the value the customers see in the brand. The leader should 'plug holes' so that competitors do not jump in. But the best defence is a good offence, and the best response is *continuous innovation*. The leader refuses to be content with the way things are and leads the industry in new products, customer services, distribution effectiveness and cost cutting. It keeps increasing its competitive effectiveness and value to customers. It takes the offensive, sets the pace and exploits competitors' weaknesses.

Increased competition in recent years has sparked management's interest in models of military warfare. Leader companies have been advised to protect their market positions with competitive strategies patterned on successful military defence strategies. Six defence strategies that a market leader can use are shown in Figure 19.5 overleaf.

Position defence The most basic defence is a position defence in which a company builds fortifications around its current position. But simply defending one's current position or products rarely works. Even such lasting brands as Coca-Cola and Panadol cannot be relied upon to supply all future growth and profitability for their companies. These brands must be improved and adapted to changing conditions, and new brands must be developed. Coca-Cola today, in spite of producing more than a third of America's soft drinks, is aggressively extending its beverage lines and has diversified into desalinisation equipment and plastics. John West canned seafood continuously expands its range to protect its position against its rivals.

Blue Banner follows a hot new strategy

Blue Banner produces one product—pickled onions. Since its inception more than 40 years ago this Tasmanian company has manufactured locally grown 'picklers' packaged in 525 gram bottles and large 2.2 kilogram catering jars. It has grown from its home state where it continues to hold a market leadership position of more than 85% market share to other parts of Australia where it has achieved up to 15% of the pickled onion market in several states. It has always held a premium-price position over competing brands in all its state markets and has maintained a consistent strategy based on high product quality and unique taste created from the special 'crunchy' qualities of Tasmanian onions and the 'home made' tasting quality of its secret recipe and curing process. To protect its competitive advantage Blue Banner has followed a long-standing strategy of buying the entire Tasmanian crop of pickler onions and not compromising the uniqueness that comes from its high-cost manufacturing process. The brand has an image of freshness and quality through its association with its Tasmanian heritage.

The Blue Banner business has been consistently profitable over the years and has achieved modest sales growth in line with the capacity limitations of its Hobart plant. The market for pickled onions has been flat over the last 10 years and it appears that there is limited opportunity for growth of this business. In recent years management has been exploring new growth opportunities. As well as researching export markets it introduced a line extension to its product range—Blue Banner chilli—available in 525 gram, 250 gram tall and 250 gram 'gourmet' round jars. This 'hot' flavoured version of its classic spicy recipe has achieved steady sales growth, but also seems to have cannabilised, in part, its core product sales. One of the issues being considered by the marketing group at Blue Banner is how to carve out new market segments that will provide significant future growth for the business.

Source: Interview with Ben Wignall, ex-owner and consultant to current owners of Blue Banner Pickled Onions, by Linden Brown, December 2005. For product information see <www.bluebanner.com.au>.

Blue Banner leverages its Tasmanian heritage.

Questions

1 Blue Banner has built a competitive advantage around its product quality and brand image which are in part related to its niche positioning as a small Tasmanian one-product company. What can it do to enhance and strengthen its brand image?

2 How could Blue Banner gain significant increases in its market share from its existing pickled onion business and compete effectively against the big Australian players in the market?

3 What do you believe is the most promising path for future growth of Blue Banner—export markets, line extensions like 'chilli' in the Australian market, new products like pickled cabbage or gherkins?

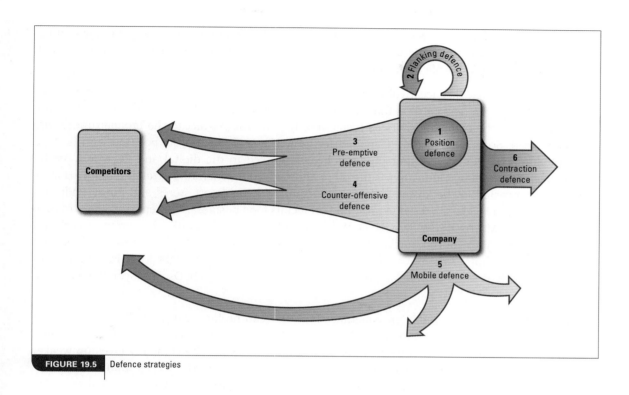

FIGURE 19.5 Defence strategies

Flanking defence When guarding its overall position, the market leader should watch its weaker flanks closely. Smart competitors will normally attack the company's weaknesses. Thus, the Japanese successfully entered the small-car market because car makers left a gaping hole in that submarket. Using a flanking defence, the company carefully checks its flanks and protects the more vulnerable areas. Coles Myer launched its Megamart stores in 2003 to protect the home appliances part of its business being attacked by discounters such as Bing Lee, Good Guys and Retravision Stores. However, these strategies do not always work and Coles Myer sold six of the stores to Harvey Norman in late 2005 and announced it would close the other three after reporting a loss from this business of $35.8 million in the previous financial year.[23]

Pre-emptive defence The leader can launch an aggressive pre-emptive defence, striking competitors before they can move against the company. A pre-emptive defence assumes that an ounce of prevention is worth a pound of cure. Thus, when threatened in 1993 by the impending entry of Toys 'R' Us into the Australian market, Coles Myer launched a new chain of stores, World 4 Kids, before the US company's entry. In 1999 a pre-emptive move by Dymocks into online book trading was made to blunt the entry of US company Borders. While these moves may delay or reduce the impact of a new entrant, it will rarely be enough to win the 'war' that may follow. For instance, by early 2006, Borders had 16 locations across four states and a formidable online bookstore teamed with Amazon.com.

Counter-offensive defence When a market leader is attacked, despite its flanking or pre-emptive efforts, it can launch a counter-offensive defence. When Fuji attacked Kodak in the film market, Kodak counter-attacked by dramatically increasing its promotion and introducing several innovative new film products. Sometimes companies hold off for a while before countering. Mercedes-Benz developed its 'A' class models when Japanese car makers targeted its C class models. Speedo entered the beach swimwear market with specially created swimwear designs to counter-attack Seafolly. This may seem a dangerous game of 'wait and see', but there are often good reasons for not barrelling in. By waiting, the company can understand the competitor's offence more fully and perhaps find a gap through which a successful counter-offensive can be launched.

Mobile defence A mobile defence involves more than aggressively defending a current market position. The leader stretches to new markets that can serve as future bases for defence and offence. Through *market broadening*, the company shifts its focus from the current product to the broader underlying consumer need. Sony entered the PC market for growth and defence of its position with its Vaio range of Notebook PCs as its other products became linked to the digital and PC world. *Market diversification* into unrelated industries is the other alternative for generating 'strategic depth'. Harvey Norman has invested in the leisure industry by acquiring Rebel Sport stores and Burns Philp has acquired Goodman Fielders in order to grow and protect its food business.[24] When Australian tobacco companies Philip Morris and W. D. & H. O. Wills (part of Coca-Cola Amatil) faced growing curbs on cigarette smoking, they moved quickly into new consumer products industries. Amatil moved into soft drinks and Philip Morris moved into the wine industry and also bought Kraft Foods and now owns brands such as Kraft, Jacobs, Maxwell House, Milka, Nabisco, Oreo, Oscar Mayer, Philadelphia, Post and Tang.[25]

Contraction defence Large companies sometimes find they can no longer defend all positions. Their resources are spread too thinly and competitors are nibbling away on several fronts. The best action then appears to be a contraction defence (or strategic withdrawal). The company gives up weaker positions and concentrates its resources on stronger ones. During the 1970s many companies diversified wildly and spread themselves too thinly. In the slow-growth 1980s and recession-bound early 1990s, many pruned their portfolios to concentrate resources on products and businesses in their core industries. These companies now serve fewer markets but serve them much better. For example, Gateway computers withdrew in 2002 from the European and Australasian markets to concentrate on its American business.[26]

Expanding market share

Market leaders can also grow by increasing their market share. In many markets, small market-share increases result in very large sales increases. For example, in large markets such as financial services, telecommunications and food retailing, a 1% increase in market share translates into millions of dollars profit. No wonder normal competition turns into marketing warfare in such markets.

Many studies have found that profitability rises with increasing market share.[27] Businesses with very large relative market shares averaged substantially higher returns on investment. Because of these findings many companies have sought expanded market shares to improve profitability. Colgate-Palmolive, for example, declared that it wanted to be at least number one or two in each of its markets, or else it would get out. Colgate thus shed its disposable nappy business because it could not achieve the number one or two position.

Other studies have found that many industries contain one or a few highly profitable large firms, several profitable and more focused firms, and a large number of medium-sized firms with poorer profit performance.

The large firms . . . tend to address the entire market, achieving cost advantages and high market share by realising economies of scale. The small competitors reap high profits by focusing on some narrower segment of the business and by developing specialised approaches to production, marketing and distribution for that segment. Ironically, the medium-sized competitors . . . often show the poorest profit performance. Trapped in a strategic 'No Man's Land', they are too large to reap the benefits of more focused competition, yet too small to benefit from the economies of scale that their larger competitors enjoy.[28]

Thus, it appears that profitability increases as a business gains share relative to competitors in its *served market*. For example, Mercedes holds only a small share of the total car market, but it earns high profits because it is a high-share company in its luxury car segment. And it has achieved this high share in its served market because it does other things right, such as producing high quality, giving good service and holding down its costs.

Companies must not think, however, that gaining increased market share automatically improves profitability. Much depends on their strategies for gaining increased share. Many high-share companies endure low profitability, and many low-share companies enjoy high profitability. The cost of buying higher market share may far exceed the returns. Higher shares tend to produce higher profits only when unit costs fall with increased market share or when the company offers a superior quality product and charges a premium price that more than covers the cost of offering higher quality.

The mindsets of today's market leaders

A study by Wiersema of the mindsets of some of the new market leaders like Cisco, eBay, Nokia, Dell and Yahoo, which have been able to carve out sustainable competitive leadership positions in the last 10 years, and the older leaders like General Electric, Wal-Mart, Mercedes-Benz and Intel suggests they have been able to elevate the concept of customer focus to new heights which has enabled them to capture and keep customers over an extended time period. There are four mindsets that these leaders have in common:

1 They create a larger than life presence and stay out front in the customers' mind.
2 They seek out customers who stretch their capabilities.
3 They make sure that customers realise the full value of their offers and innovative solutions.
4 They act boldly and take the initiative even though this involves risks and they gain the respect and support of their customers.[29]

Market-challenger strategies

Firms that are second, third or lower in an industry are sometimes quite large, such as Ford, Coles Supermarkets and Optus. These runner-up firms can adopt one of two competitive strategies. They can attack the leader and other competitors in an aggressive bid for more market share (market challengers). Or they can play along with competitors and not rock the boat (market followers). We now focus on competitive strategies for market challengers.

Defining the strategic objective and competitor

A market challenger must first define its strategic objective. Most market challengers seek to increase their profitability by increasing their market share. But the strategic objective chosen depends on the competitor. In most cases the company can choose which competitors to challenge.

The challenger can attack the market leader, a high-risk but potentially high-gain strategy which makes good sense if the leader is not serving the market well. To succeed with such an attack, a company must have some sustainable competitive advantage over the leader—a cost advantage leading to lower prices or the ability to provide better value at a premium price. In the construction equipment industry, Komatsu successfully challenged Caterpillar by offering the same quality at much lower prices. Audi is challenging BMW's 3 series sedan and coupe with its A3 sedan and sport models positioned on equal performance at a better price in the medium-sized European car segment. And Kimberly Clark grabbed a big share of the toilet tissue market with Kleenex by offering a softer and more absorbent product than the one offered by market leader Sorbent. When attacking the leader a challenger must also find a way to minimise the leader's response. Otherwise its gains may be short lived.[30]

The challenger can avoid the leader and instead attack firms its own size, or smaller local and regional firms. Many of these firms are underfinanced and will not be serving their customers well. Several of the major beer companies grew to their present size not by attacking large competitors but by absorbing small local or regional competitors.

Thus, the challenger's strategic objective depends on which competitor it chooses to attack. If the company goes after the market leader, its objective may be to wrest a certain market share. Bic knows that it can't topple Gillette in the razor market—it simply wants a larger share. Or the challenger's goal might be to take over market leadership. Dell entered the personal computer market late, as a challenger, but quickly became the market leader in the 'computer savvy' business. If the company goes after a small local company, its objective may be to put that company out of business. The important point remains: the company must choose its opponents carefully and have a clearly defined and attainable objective.

Choosing an attack strategy

How can the market challenger best attack the chosen competitor and achieve its strategic objectives? Five possible attack strategies are shown in Figure 19.6.

Frontal attack In a full frontal attack, the challenger matches the competitor's product, advertising, price and distribution efforts. It attacks the competitor's strengths rather than its weaknesses. The outcome depends on who has the greater strength and endurance. Even great size and strength may not be enough to successfully challenge a firmly entrenched and resourceful competitor.

Unilever is the world's largest packaged goods company. It has twice the worldwide sales of Procter & Gamble (P&G) and five times the sales of Colgate-Palmolive. In Australia Unilever is a small player in the dental hygiene market which is dominated by Colgate. However, when Unilever

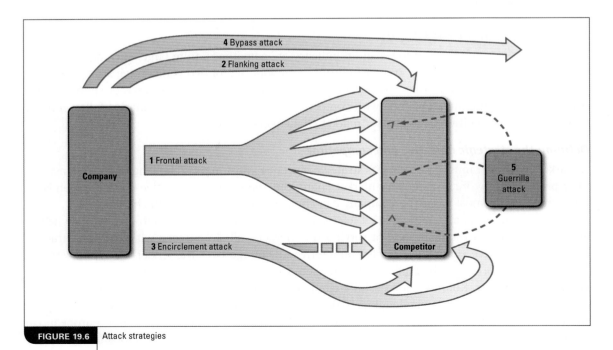

FIGURE 19.6 Attack strategies

launches a toothpaste brand worldwide it attacks Colgate head-on, with only limited success in the Australian market. Conversely, Unilever leads the clothes-washing market against Colgate which, in turn, attacks Unilever head-on with new and existing brands. P&G is a late entrant in the Australian market but with acquisitions and aggressive growth strategies it has claimed a large share of the hair-care market with Pantene Pro-V, Pert 2-in-1 and Vidal Sassoon. When these giants clash they usually adopt frontal attacks to claim a substantial share of the market.

If the market challenger has fewer resources than the competitor, a frontal attack makes little sense. Arnott's learned this the hard way when it launched frontal attacks on the leader in the crisps snack market. It then sold its snack-food business to concentrate on its core biscuit market.

Flanking attack Rather than attacking head on, the challenger can launch a flanking attack. The competitor often concentrates its resources to protect its strongest positions, but it usually has some weaker flanks. By attacking these weak spots the challenger can concentrate its strength against the competitor's weakness. Flank attacks make good sense when the company has fewer resources than the competitor. Cadbury Schweppes flanked Coca-Cola when it created its flavoured mineral waters with 'schweppervescence'. Its Sunburst orange drink also flanked Coca-Cola's Fanta brand at a time when the market leader was focusing on Lion Nathan's challenge with Pepsi.

Another flanking strategy is to find gaps that are not being filled by the industry's products, fill them and develop them into strong segments. In 1990 Plumrose Australia and QUF Industries had a stranglehold on the yoghurt dairy dessert market. Allowrie Farmers recognised an unserved consumer segment for cottage cheese, sour cream and fruit desserts and launched the Fruche dairy dessert. This segment has grown to become a large part of the market. Fruche is now synonymous with cottage cheese and fruit desserts, and Plumrose Australia and QUF Industries have had a difficult time establishing rival brands. RedBull recognised the consumer need for energy drinks and entered the night club segment with little or no challenge from competing brands.

Encirclement attack An encirclement attack involves attacking from all directions, so that the competitor must protect its front, sides and rear at the same time. The encirclement strategy makes sense when the challenger has superior resources and believes that it can quickly break the competitor's hold on the market. An example is Seiko's attack on the watch market. For several years Seiko has been gaining distribution in every major watch outlet and overwhelming competitors with its variety of constantly changing models. In Australia and New Zealand it offers over 100 models, but its marketing clout is backed by the 2300 models it makes and sells worldwide.

Bypass attack A bypass attack is an indirect strategy. The challenger bypasses the competitor and targets easier markets. The bypass can involve diversifying into unrelated products, moving into new geographical markets or leapfrogging into new technologies to replace existing products. Technological leapfrogging is a bypass strategy used often in high-technology industries. Instead of copying the competitor's product and mounting a costly frontal attack, the challenger patiently develops the next technology. When satisfied with its superiority, it launches an attack where it has an advantage. Thus, Minolta toppled Canon from the lead in the 35 millimetre SLR camera market when it introduced its technologically advanced auto-focusing Maxxum camera. Canon's market share dropped towards 20% while Minolta's zoomed past 30%. It took Canon three years to introduce a matching technology.[31] Microsoft bypassed Palm Pilot, the market leader, by introducing its Windows-based operating system integrated into PDAs and licensed it to Compaq, Toshiba and HP. It took three years for Palm to respond.[32]

Guerrilla attack A guerrilla attack is another option available to market challengers, especially the smaller or poorly financed challenger. The challenger makes small, periodic attacks to harass and demoralise the competitor, hoping eventually to establish permanent footholds. It might use selective price cuts, executive raids, intense promotional outbursts or assorted legal actions. Normally, guerrilla actions are taken by smaller firms against larger ones. But continuous guerrilla campaigns can be expensive and they must eventually be followed by a stronger attack if the challenger wishes to 'beat' the competitor. Thus, guerrilla campaigns are not necessarily cheap.

Market-follower strategies

Not all runner-up companies will challenge the market leader. The effort to draw away the leader's customers is never taken lightly by the leader. If the challenger's lure is lower prices, improved service or additional product features, the leader can quickly match these to diffuse the attack. The leader probably has more staying power in an all-out battle. A hard fight might leave both firms weakened, so the challenger must think twice before attacking. In fact, many firms prefer to follow rather than attack the leader.

A follower can gain many advantages. The market leader often bears the huge expenses involved in developing new products and markets, expanding distribution channels and informing and educating the market. The reward for all this work and risk is normally market leadership. The market follower, on the other hand, can learn from the leader's experience and copy or improve on the leader's products and marketing programs, usually at a much lower investment. Although the follower will probably not overtake the leader, it can often be as profitable.[33]

In some industries—such as oil, fertilisers and chemicals—opportunities for differentiation are low, service quality is often comparable and price sensitivity runs high. Price wars can erupt at any time. Companies in these industries avoid short-run grabs for market share because that strategy only provokes retaliation. Most firms decide against stealing each other's customers. Instead they present similar offers to buyers, usually by copying the leader. Market share shows a high stability.

This is not to say that market followers are without strategies. A market follower must know how to hold current customers and win a fair share of new consumers. Each follower tries to bring distinctive advantages to its target market—location, services, financing. The follower is a major target of attack by challengers. Therefore the market follower must keep its manufacturing costs low and its product quality and services high. It must also enter new markets as they open up. Following is not the same as being passive or existing as a carbon copy of the leader. The follower must define a growth path, but one that does not create competitive retaliation.

The market-follower firms fall into one of three broad types. The *cloner* closely copies the leader's products, distribution, advertising and other marketing moves. The cloner originates nothing—it simply attempts to live off the market leader's investments. The *imitator* copies some things from the leader but maintains some differentiation in terms of packaging, advertising, pricing and other factors. The leader doesn't mind the imitator as long as the imitator does not attack aggressively. The imitator may even help the leader avoid the charges of monopoly. Finally, the *adaptor* builds on the leader's products and marketing programs, often improving them. The adaptor may choose to sell to different markets to avoid direct confrontation with the leader. But often the adaptor grows into a future challenger, as many Japanese firms have done after adapting and improving products developed elsewhere.

In the financial services industry insurance companies are quick to follow an innovator's moves. Companies such as Legal and General, Sun Alliance and Mercantile Mutual follow the lead of the larger and more aggressive firms.

Market-nicher strategies

Almost every industry includes firms that specialise in serving market niches. Instead of pursuing the whole market, or even large segments of the market, these firms target segments within segments, or niches. This is particularly true of smaller firms because of their limited resources. But smaller divisions of larger firms might also pursue niching strategies. Toyota's move to enter the premium-priced luxury car segment with Lexus, with a specialised focus, could be considered a niche strategy as its mainstream business was focused on high volume and competitively priced models. As it has progressed and its market share of this segment has grown, this market has started to become a higher volume business for the company.

The main point about niching is that firms with low shares of the total market can be highly profitable through smart niching. A study of highly successful mid-sized companies found that, in almost all cases, these companies niched within a larger market rather than going after the whole market.[34] An example is Parker, which niches in the high-price pen and pencil market. It makes high-quality, well-designed writing instruments. By concentrating on the high-price niche, Parker has enjoyed good sales growth and profit. The study also identified other features shared by the successful smaller companies—offering high value, charging a premium price and strong corporate cultures and vision.

Why is niching profitable? The main reason is that the market nicher ends up knowing the target customer group so well that it meets its needs better than other firms that sell casually to this niche. As a result, the nicher can charge a substantial mark-up over costs because of the added value. Where the mass marketer achieves *high volume*, the nicher achieves *high margins*.

Nichers try to find one or more market niches that are safe and profitable. An ideal market niche is big enough to be profitable and has growth potential. It is one that the firm can serve effectively. Perhaps most importantly, the niche is of little interest to major competitors. And the firm can build the skills and customer goodwill to defend itself against an attacking major competitor as the niche grows and becomes more attractive.

The key idea in nichemanship is specialisation. The firm must specialise along market, customer, product or marketing mix lines. Here are several specialist roles open to a market nicher:

- *End-use specialist.* The firm specialises in serving one type of end-use customer. For example, a law firm can specialise in the criminal, civil or business law markets.
- *Vertical-level specialist.* The firm specialises at some level of the production–distribution cycle. For example, a copper firm may concentrate on producing raw copper, copper components or finished copper products.
- *Customer size specialist.* The firm concentrates on selling to small, medium or large customers. Many nichers specialise in serving small customers who are neglected by the majors.
- *Specific customer specialist.* The firm limits its selling to one or a few major customers. Many firms sell their entire output to a single company such as Kmart, BHP or Telstra.
- *Geographical specialist.* The firm sells only in a certain locality, region or area of the world.

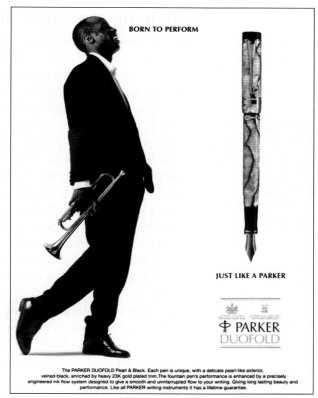

BORN TO PERFORM

JUST LIKE A PARKER

PARKER
DUOFOLD

The PARKER DUOFOLD Pearl & Black. Each pen is unique, with a delicate pearl-like exterior, veined black, enriched by heavy 23K gold plated trim. The fountain pen's performance is enhanced by a precisely engineered ink flow system designed to give a smooth and uninterrupted flow to your writing. Giving long lasting beauty and performance. Like all PARKER writing instruments it has a lifetime guarantee.

Market-niche strategies: Parker niches in the well-designed, high-price pen and pencil market.

⊚ *Product or feature specialist.* The firm specialises in producing a certain product, product line or product feature. Within the laboratory equipment industry are firms that produce only microscopes or, even more narrowly, only lenses for microscopes.

⊚ *Quality–price specialist.* The firm operates at the low or high end of the market. For example, Hewlett-Packard specialises in the high-quality, high-price end of the hand calculator market.

⊚ *Service specialist.* The firm offers one or more services not available from other firms. An example is a bank that takes loan requests over the phone and hand-delivers the money to the customer.

Niching carries a major risk in that the market niche may dry up or be attacked. That is why many companies practise *multiple niching.* By developing two or more niches, the company increases its chances of survival. Even some large firms prefer a multiple-niche strategy rather than serving the total market. One large law firm has developed a national reputation in the three areas of mergers and acquisitions, bankruptcies and prospectus development, and does little else.[35]

SELF-CHECK QUESTIONS

8 List the strategic issues facing a market leader.

9 Outline the advantages and disadvantages of a market-follower strategy.

10 Give examples of different types of market-niche strategies.

Balancing customer and competitor orientations

We have stressed the importance of a company watching its competitors closely. Whether a company is a market leader, a challenger, a follower or a nicher, it must find the competitive marketing strategy that positions it most effectively against its competitors. And it must continually adapt its strategies to the fast-changing competitive environment.

The question now arises: can the company spend too much time and energy tracking competitors, damaging its customer orientation? The answer is yes! A company can become so competitor centred that it loses its even more important customer focus. A **competitor-centred company** is one whose moves are based mainly on competitors' actions and reactions. The company spends most of its time tracking competitors' moves and market shares and trying to find strategies to counter them.

This mode of strategy planning has some pluses and some minuses. On the positive side, the company develops a fighter orientation. It trains its marketers to be on constant alert, watching for weaknesses in their own position and watching for competitors' weaknesses. On the negative side, the company becomes too reactive. Rather than carrying out its own consistent customer-oriented strategy, it bases its moves on competitors' moves. As a result, it does not move in a planned direction towards a goal. It does not know where it will end up because so much depends on what the competitors do.

A **customer-centred company**, in contrast, focuses more on customer developments in designing its strategies. Clearly, the customer-centred company is in a better position to identify new opportunities and set a strategy that makes long-run sense. By watching customer needs evolve, it can decide what customer groups and what emerging needs are the most important to serve, given its resources and objectives.

In practice, today's companies must be **market-centred companies**, watching both their customers and their competitors. They must not let competitor watching blind them to customer

Competitor-centred company A company whose moves are mainly based on competitors' actions and reactions; it spends most of its time tracking competitors' moves and market shares and trying to find strategies to counter them.

Customer-centred company A company that focuses on customer developments in designing its marketing strategies.

Market-centred company A company that pays balanced attention to both customers and competitors in designing its marketing strategies.

focusing. Figure 19.7 shows that companies have moved through four orientations. In the first stage, they were product oriented, paying little attention to either customers or competitors. In the second stage, they became customer oriented and started to pay attention to customers. In the third stage, when they began to pay attention to competitors, they became competitor oriented. Today, companies need to be market oriented, paying balanced attention to both customers and competitors.[36]

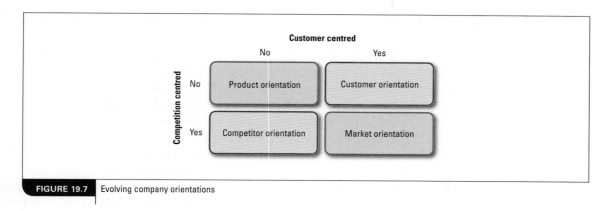

FIGURE 19.7   Evolving company orientations

SUMMARY

In order to prepare an effective marketing strategy, a company must consider its competitors as well as its customers. It must continuously analyse competitors and develop *competitive marketing strategies* that effectively position it against competitors and give it the strongest possible *competitive advantage*.

Competitor analysis first involves identifying the company's major competitors, using both an industry *and* a market-based analysis. The company then gathers information on competitors' objectives, strategies, strengths and weaknesses and reaction patterns. With this information in hand, it can select competitors to attack or avoid. Competitive intelligence must be collected, interpreted and distributed continuously. Company marketing managers should be able to obtain full and reliable information about any competitor affecting their decisions. The rapidly growing area of online trade is spawning new competitors and changing the competitive structure of industries. It also poses challenges for information collection on competitors.

Which *competitive marketing strategy* makes the most sense depends on the company's industry position and its objectives, opportunities and resources. In today's highly competitive 'red ocean' markets where companies aggressively compete for market share, it is becoming increasingly important to incorporate value innovation into strategy—a process that incorporates both differentiation and cost advantages by defining uncontested marketspaces and the delivery models to address them. The company's competitive marketing strategy also depends on whether it is a market leader, challenger, follower or nicher. Information technology is creating opportunities for powerful new strategies based on the philosophy of one-to-one marketing. This emphasises share-of-mind and brand loyalty through relationship-focused strategies more than market share. Firms basing their marketing strategies on one-to-one relationships and delivery of unique-to-the-customer solutions need to understand their capabilities to adopt this strategy profitably.

A *market leader* faces three challenges: expanding the total market, protecting market share and expanding market share. The market leader is interested in finding ways to expand the total market because it will benefit most from any increased sales. To *expand market size*, the leader looks for *new users* of the product, *new uses* and *more usage*. To protect its existing market share, the market leader has several defences: *position defence, flanking defence, pre-emptive defence, counter-offensive defence, mobile defence* and *contraction defence*. The most sophisticated leaders cover themselves by doing everything right, leaving no openings for competitive attack. Leaders can also try to increase their market shares. This makes sense if profitability increases at higher market-share levels.

A *market challenger* is a firm that aggressively tries to expand its market share by attacking the leader, other runner-up firms or smaller firms in the industry. The challenger can choose from a variety of attack strategies, including a *frontal attack, flanking attack, encirclement attack, bypass attack* and *guerrilla attack*.

A *market follower* is a runner-up firm that chooses not to rock the boat, usually out of fear that it stands to lose more than it might gain. The follower is not without a strategy, however, and seeks to use its particular skills to gain market growth. Some followers enjoy a higher rate of return than the leaders in their industry.

A *market nicher* is a smaller firm that serves some part of the market that is not likely to attract the larger firms. Market nichers often become specialists in some end-use, customer size, specific customer, geographic area or service.

A competitive orientation is important in today's markets, but companies should not overdo their focus on competitors. Companies are more likely to be hurt by emerging consumer needs and new competitors than by existing competitors. Companies that balance consumer and competitor considerations are practising a true market orientation.

In many mature industries today companies are setting up strategy groups to explore new, emerging or uncontested markets. We have seen the spectacular success of Apple's iPod which has created a new market. How would you go about doing this in the retailing industry or the finance industry—both industries that appear to be oversupplied and aggressively contested? Use the value innovation process outlined earlier in the chapter to map out a 'blue ocean' marketspace in one of these industries.

KEY TERMS

competitive advantage	738	customer-centred company	766	market leader	755
competitive marketing strategies	738	customer value analysis	743	market nicher	755
competitor analysis	738	market-centred company	766	strategic group	741
competitor-centred company	766	market challenger	755	value disciplines	748
		market follower	755	value innovation	753

DISCUSSING THE ISSUES

1. Industry structure has been affected by online communication and delivery of value. How has structure been affected in the financial services industry?

2. What different strategic groups can you identify in the international airlines industry? Which groups compete with which other groups?

3. There is a growing capability for companies to pursue one-to-one marketing strategies. Under what conditions is this most appropriate?

4. Some market leaders are facing up to revolutionary strategies which are striking at the heart of their viability. Provide an example of where this is happening and what counter strategies the market leader is adopting.

5. How could Nokia expand the total market for mobile communications? Discuss the role marketing strategy would play in getting new users, communicating new uses or increasing usage of mobile communications.

6. The goal of the marketing concept is to satisfy customer wants and needs. What is the goal of a competitor-centred strategy? Discuss whether the marketing concept and the competitor-centred strategy are in conflict.

REFERENCES

1. Michael Sainsbury and Michael West, 'Bourse Rebuffs Telstra Revolution', *The Australian*, 16 November 2005, p. 23; Michael Sainsbury and Steve Lewis, 'Telstra to Slash Jobs for Digital', *The Australian*, 16 November 2005, p. 1; 'Telstra's Strategy for Growth' Letter to Shareholders from Sol Trujillo, 28 November 2005; Tony Boyd, 'Telstra Woes Put Pressure on Share Sale', *The Australian Financial Review*, 10 February 2006, p. 1; Tony Boyd, 'Profit Delayed after Surge in Customers', *The Australian Financial Review*, 10 February 2006, p. 68. Transcript of Telstra podcast with Telstra CEO, Sol Trujillo. Subject: Telstra Strategic Review, 14 November 2005 (www.telstra.com)

2. David Aaker outlines a series of questions to provide structure for competitive analysis in *Strategic Market Management*, 6th edn, New York, Wiley, 2001.

3. Michael E. Porter, 'Strategy and the Internet', *Harvard Business Review*, March 2001, pp. 63–78.

4. For a detailed account of competitive intelligence approaches see Ian H. Gordon, *Competitor Targeting: Winning the Battle for Market and Customer Share*, Ontario, John Wiley & Sons, 2002, Chapter 5.

5. For an application of competitive benchmarking see Roger J. Best, *Market-Based Management*, 4th edn, New Jersey, Prentice Hall, 2006, Chaper 11.

6. David Aaker, *Developing Business Strategies*, 6th edn, New York, Wiley, 2001; S. Venkataraman, Ming-Jer Chen and Ian C. MacMillan, 'Anticipating Reactions: Factors that Shape Competitor Responses', in George S. Day and David J. Reibstein, *Wharton on Dynamic Competitive Strategy*, New York, John Wiley, 1997.

7. Richard D'Aveni, 'The Empire Strikes Back: Counterrevolutionary Strategies for Industry Leaders', *Harvard Business Review*, vol. 80, no. 11, November 2002, p. 66. See also Linden Brown, *Competitive Marketing Strategy*, Melbourne, Nelson, 1990, pp. 113, 115 (a more detailed description of this example and the method of competitive positioning research is found on pp. 111–115 and 174–177). For a good discussion of the underlying rules of competitive interaction and reaction see Gloria P. Thomas and Gary F. Soldow, 'A Rules-Based Approach to Competitive Interaction', *Journal of Marketing*, April 1988, pp. 63–74. Also see Walter D. Brandt Jr, 'Profiling Rival Decision Makers', *Journal of Business Strategy*, January/February 1991, pp. 8–11.

8. See Michael E. Porter, *Competitive Advantage*, New York, The Free Press, 1985, Chapter 6.

9. Neil Shoebridge, 'Big Breakfast Brands Sagging', *The Australian Financial Review*, 20 February 2006, p. 42; Neil Shoebridge, 'Crunch Time for Kellogg', *Business Review Weekly*, 30 March 1998, pp. 50–54.

10. For more discussion, see Leonard M. Fuld, *Monitoring the Competition*, New York, John Wiley & Sons, 1988; Howard Schlossberg, 'Competitive Intelligence Pros Seek Formal Role in Marketing', *Marketing News*, 5 March 1990, pp. 2, 28; Michele Galen, 'These Guys Aren't Spooks, They're "Competitive Analysts"', *Business Week*, 14 October 1991, p. 97; and Norton Paley, 'Choose Competitors Carefully', *Sales & Marketing Management*, June 1994, pp. 57–58.

11. Michael Song, 'Competitive Forces and Strategic Choice Decisions: An Experimental Investigation in the United States and Japan', *Strategic Management Journal*, vol. 23, no. 10, October 2002, p. 969; Terry Robinson, 'Differentiation Through Service: A Perspective from the Commodity Chemicals Sector', *The Service Industries Journal*, vol. 22, no. 3, July 2002, p. 149. Also see Michael E. Porter, *Competitive Advantage* (note 8); Pankaj Ghemawat, 'Sustainable Advantage', *Harvard Business Review*, September–October 1986, pp. 53–58; Michael E. Porter, 'From Competitive Advantage to Corporate Strategy', *Harvard Business Review*, May–June 1987, pp. 43–59; and George S. Day and Robin Wensley, 'Assessing Competitive Advantage: A Framework for Diagnosing Competitive Superiority', *Journal of Marketing*, April 1988, pp. 1–20.

12. See <www.promina.com.au/dirp/promina/promina.nsf/content/home>.

13. Michael Treacy and Fred Wiersema, 'Customer Intimacy and Other Value Disciplines', *Harvard Business Review*, January–February 1993, pp. 84–93; Michael Treacy and Fred Wiersema, 'How Market Leaders Keep Their Edge', *Fortune*, 6 February 1995, pp. 88–98; Richard D'Aveni, 'The Empire Strikes Back: Counterrevolutionary Strategies for Industry Leaders', *Harvard Business Review*, vol. 80, no. 11, November 2002, p. 66.

14. Michael E. Porter and Mark R. Kramer, 'The Competitive Advantage of Corporate Philanthropy', *Harvard Business Review*, December 2002, pp. 57–68.

15. Don Peppers and Martha Rogers, *Enterprise One to One: Tools for Competing in the Interactive Age*, New York, Doubleday, 1997, Chapter 3; Don Peppers, 'Is Your Company Ready for One-to-One Marketing?', *Harvard Business Review*, vol. 77, no. 1, January–February 1999, p. 151; J. Patrick O'Halloran, 'Marketing Is Not a One-Night Stand', *The Journal of Business Strategy*, vol. 22, no. 5, September/October 2001, p. 31.

16. Don Peppers, Martha Rogers and Bob Dorf, *The One to One Fieldbook*, Oxford, Capstone Publishing, 1999, pp. 165–168; Behram Hansotia, 'Incremental Value Modeling', *Journal of Interactive Marketing*, vol. 16, no. 3, Summer 2002, p. 35.

17. For a description of different competitive strategies related to strengthening relationships and lessening the intensity of competition when competing for individual customers see Ian H. Gordon, *Competitor Targeting: Winning the Battle for Market and Customer Share*, Ontario, John Wiley & Sons, 2002, Chapter 6.

18. See more on Internet marketing strategies in Rafi Mohammed, Robert J. Fisher, Bernard J. Jaworski and Aileen M. Cahill, *Internet Marketing: Building Advantage in the Networked Economy*, New York, McGraw-Hill/Irwin/marketspaceU, 2002, Chapter 5.

19. For a comprehensive review of the innovative enterprise see the special edition of the *Harvard Business Review*, August 2002, entitled 'The Innovative Enterprise: Turning Ideas into Profit'. Also see Gary Hamel, *Leading the Revolution*, Boston, Harvard Business School Press, 2000, Chapter 1.

20. Richard D'Aveni, 'The Empire Strikes Back: Counterrevolutionary Strategies for Industry Leaders', *Harvard Business Review*, November 2002, pp. 67–74.

21. Kim W. Chan and R. Mauborgne, *Blue Ocean Strategy: How to Create Uncontested Market Space and Make the Competition Irrelevant*, Boston, Harvard Business School Press, 2005.

22. Anonymous, 'Laundry Needs: Activity in the Market Heats Up', *Retail World*, vol. 55, no. 15, 5–16 August 2002, p. 29; Jane Bainbridge, 'Imperial Leather Targets Women with Dream Sequence Ad', *Marketing*, 19 December 2002, p. 19.

23. Anonymous, 'Harvey Norman Buys Megamart Stores', *The New Zealand Herald*, 10 November 2005, <www.nzherald.co.nz/organisation/story.cfm?o_id=41&ObjectID=10354413>, accessed 20 December 2005.

24. Sue Mitchell, 'Burrows on Goodman Board', *The Australian Financial Review*, 19 March 2003, at <http://afr.com/companies/2003/03/19/FFXBFQAPEDD.html>.

25. Altria corporate website, <www.altria.com/about_altria/01_04_our_companies_brands.asp>, accessed 21 March 2003; Suzanne Kapner, 'South African Breweries Near a Deal to Buy Miller', *New York Times*, Late Edition (East Coast), 30 May 2002, p. C.1.

26. Ian Fried, 'Gateway Makes Plans to Exit Britain, Ireland', *CNET News.com*, 8 August 2001 at <http://80-global.umi.com.ezproxy.lib.uts.edu.au/pqdweb?Did=000000078979412&Fmt=3&Deli=1&Mtd=1&Idx=5&Sid=6&RQT=309>, accessed 17 March 2003.

27. Raj Sethuraman, 'The Asymmetric Share Effect: An Empirical Generalization on Cross-price Effects', *JMR, Journal of Marketing Research*, vol. 39, no. 3, August 2002, p. 379; Joel E. Urbany, 'Are Your Prices Too Low?', *Harvard Business Review*, vol. 79, no. 9, October 2001, p. 26; see also Robert D. Buzzell, Bradley T. Gale and Ralph G. M. Sultan, 'Market Share—the Key to Profitability', *Harvard Business Review*, January–February 1975, pp. 97–106; and Ben Branch, 'The Laws of the Marketplace and ROI Dynamics', *Financial Management*, Summer 1980, pp. 58–65. Others suggest that the relationship between market share and profits has been exaggerated. See Carolyn Y. Woo and Arnold C. Cooper, 'Market-Share Leadership—Not Always So Good', *Harvard Business Review*, January–February 1984, pp. 2–4; and Robert Jacobson and David A. Aaker, 'Is Market Share All It's Cracked Up to Be?', *Journal of Marketing*, Fall 1985, pp. 11–22.

28. John D. C. Roach, 'From Strategic Planning to Strategic Performance: Closing the Achievement Gap', *Outlook*, Spring 1981, p. 21. Michael Porter makes the same point in *Competitive Strategy* (note 8). For a treatise on strategies for conquering markets see Jack Trout, *Trout on Strategy: Capturing Mindshare, Conquering Markets*, New York, McGraw-Hill, 2004.

29. Fred Wiersema, *The New Market Leaders: Who's Winning and How in the Battle for Customers*, New York, The Free Press, 2001, pp. 63–64.
30. See Michael E. Porter, 'How to Attack the Industry Leader', *Fortune*, 19 April 1985, pp. 153–166; Brian Leavy, 'Attacking Industry Leaders—Undermining Their Virtuous Cycles', *Irish Marketing Review*, vol. 9, 1996, p. 48.
31. See Otis Port, 'Canon Finally Challenges Minolta's Mighty Maxxum', *Fortune*, 2 March 1987, pp. 89–90.
32. Bradley Johnson, 'Palm Can Stay ahead of Rivals by Keeping Firm Grip on its Brand', *Advertising Age*, Midwest region edition, vol. 72, no. 47, 19 November 2001, p. 16; Palm corporate website, <www.palmsource.com>, accessed 20 March 2003; Business Brief— Palm Inc., 'Spinoff of Software Unit to Proceed after IRS Ruling', *Wall Street Journal*, Eastern edition, 7 January 2003, p. 1.
33. See Daniel W. Haines, Rajan Chandran and Arvind Parkhe, 'Winning by Being First to Market . . . Or Last?', *Journal of Consumer Marketing*, Winter 1989, pp. 63–69; William T. Robinson, 'Product Development Strategies for Established Market Pioneers, Early Followers, and Late Entrants', *Strategic Management Journal*, vol. 23, no. 9, September 2002, p. 855.
34. Donald K. Clifford and Richard E. Cavanagh, *The Winning Performance: How America's High- and Mid-size Growth Companies Succeed*, New York, Bantam Books, 1985.
35. Philip Kotler, *Marketing Management: The Millennium Edition*, Englewood Cliffs, NJ, Prentice Hall, 2000, Chapter 8.
36. See Kenichi Ohmae, 'Getting Back to Strategy', *Harvard Business Review*, November–December 1988, pp. 149–156; Charles H. Noble, 'Market Orientation and Alternative Strategic Orientations: A Longitudinal Assessment of Performance Implications', *Journal of Marketing*, vol. 66, no. 4, October 2002, p. 25.

PHOTO/AD CREDITS

Joe Williams, Flinders University

CASE STUDY
How the mighty (Reds) are fallen

Competitive advantage is the basis of success for professional sports clubs just as much as it is for McDonald's, Channel 9 or the Commonwealth Bank of Australia. For large football clubs in the English Premier League (EPL) the search for sustainable competitive advantage (SCA) is becoming even more intense. This case examines the search for SCA by one such club. Liverpool Football Club (the Reds) has won more league championships and European Cups than any other English club (see Table 1). Formed in 1892 Liverpool ruled the roost in the seventies and eighties, but has not won the major competition—the English league—since 1990. Liverpool's strengths have been a loyal and vociferous fan base, history of winning, excellent manager and player selection, a worldwide market for club merchandise and a playing style focused on attack.

The major players in the EPL are Chelsea, Manchester United, Arsenal and Liverpool. See Table 2 for recent turnover estimates.

Chelsea has only recently joined the ranks of 'major player' and was considered an 'also ran' outfit until Russian oil oligarch Roman Abramovitch bought the club in 2002. He has since invested over $500 000 000 in new players. Chelsea's Stamford Bridge ground does not need to be filled for Chelsea to survive. Abramovitch's money makes up any gaps between receipts and expenditure. This income certainty is the key competitive advantage for Chelsea over all other English clubs.

Other sources of income for Premier League clubs include:

- Net transfer payments for players (income from players sold minus income from players bought)
- Broadcasting rights—especially Pay TV and pay per view TV
- Sponsorships
- Merchandise sales (club kits, memorabilia, clothing, etc.)
- Prize money (for on-field performances)
- Fees to access premium content from club websites.

'Success' can be gauged in any of these ways: winning major trophies (or getting close), snaring lucrative sponsorships or financial investments, selling lots of club merchandise. Ultimately

TABLE 2 Total turnover (2005) estimates

Clubs	Turnover ($m)
Arsenal	324
Everton	141
Chelsea	358
Manchester United	397
Liverpool	214

TABLE 1 Major trophies won by English clubs (at February 2006)

Club	League Championship[1]	European Cup[2]	Other Europe[3]	FA Cup	League Cup
Liverpool	18	5	3	6	7
Manchester United	15	2	1	11	1
Arsenal	13	0	2	10	2
Everton	9	0	1	5	0
Chelsea	2	0	2	3	3

1. Covers the 'League Championship' 1888–1992 and the Premier League 1992–2005.
2. Covers the European Cup and the European Champions' League.
3. Covers the UEFA Cup, Cup Winners Cup in various guises.

success depends on 'on-field' performance. For some clubs, mere survival or finishing in a better position than last season is success. For others, consolidating Premier League status is success.

Liverpool's mission statement is: 'This club exists to win trophies'. Most fans would change that to: 'This club exists to win Premier League and Champions' League trophies'. Less prestigious trophies are nice to win but they hardly cut the ice for a club ahead of all others in major trophy wins.

The Liverpool story

Since 1990 the club has been relatively unsuccessful. Relative, that is, to its traditional major competitors and to its new major competitor, Chelsea. Even in the 'barren' spell from 1990 to 2005 the Reds won the FA Cup twice, League Cup three times, UEFA Cup once and the biggest competition in club football, the European Champions League, once (see Table 3). For the vast majority of clubs in the EPL such a haul is the stuff of dreams.

But not for Liverpool. The crown has slipped. The league title is still a dream. When Arsenal and Manchester United were swapping league titles on a regular basis from 1993 Liverpool struggled to finish in the top four.

We can answer the question 'what went wrong at Liverpool' in resource terms. One clear change involves the choice of manager. In the 1990s and beyond Liverpool's managers have not matched the calibre of the three managers from the glory days—Shankly, Paisley and Dalglish. On the other hand, Manchester United has had Sir Alec Ferguson at the helm for more than

20 years and Arsenal has had Arsene Wegner in charge for nine years. They have both been very successful. Chelsea for the past two highly successful seasons has had Jose Mourinho who has bought a very strong team.

Access to funds to buy and retain the best players is critical. These funds are used to entice other clubs to sell their best players and to attract and retain players by paying higher wages. Liverpool could not compete with United or Chelsea in access to funds.

The funds issue pervades all aspects of the resource base. In that context football clubs are less like businesses. The SCA of business innovation is less obvious in football. A new, successful on-field formation or tactic is not patentable and is relatively easily copied. Embracing new technology such as streaming of live games to fans all over the world is, however, now feasible once current television contracts are completed. This innovation is open to all clubs, but the more successful ones take larger shares of the available fees.

Nevertheless, football clubs are similar to other businesses in marketing terms such as market leader (Chelsea), challengers (Liverpool, Manchester United, Arsenal) and followers (most other clubs capable of making the top of the table). The 'niche' category in marketing applies to businesses focused on a small product or market segment. This has no parallel in the EPL in terms of the hunt for trophies.

Chelsea's league dominance is now nearly total. Chelsea won the league title in a canter in 2005, beating Liverpool by 37 points, and, as at the time of writing, look set to continue this

TABLE 3 Liverpool's trophy haul 1964–2005					
Decade	League title	European Cup	UEFA Cup	FA Cup	League Cup
1960s	2	0	0	1	0
1970s	4	2	2	1	0
1980s	6	2*	0*	2	4
1990s	1	0*	0*	1	1
2000–end 2005	0	1	1	1	2

* Liverpool were banned from all European competitions 1986–1992.

CASE STUDY

rouble-fed superiority. A new Chelsea ground and attached mall, hotel and entertainment complex—'Chelsea Village'—will produce profits to supplement Chelsea's attempts to globalise its brand into lucrative merchandising markets and sponsorship deals. The dominance on the pitch is set to continue off it.

It's not only Liverpool having to compete with such a behemoth; it's the other highly successful clubs who also face a spell in the relative doldrums. Manchester United was bought by the Glazer family from America in mid-2005. The club is now saddled with huge debt and a period of consolidation is needed there. Arsenal's ageing and depleted squad needs an overhaul and transfer kitties have been raided to help pay for the new stadium at Ashburton Grove. The $250 000 000 sponsorship deal from the Emirates airline will cushion that blow somewhat.

But will the fans continue to support an Arsenal bereft of its winning touch? Is the only way to success based on on-pitch performance? Is the sponsorship deal likely to produce new trophies?

Liverpool's 2005 European Champions League success has rekindled dreams of EPL glory. Further investment is needed, not least for new players and a bigger ground. Is it enough? Is it the right strategy?

The options open to Liverpool include:

- Finding a cashed-up investor who won't mind waiting for a return on funds deployed.
- Relying on a youth policy to unearth the footballing gems of the 2010–2015 seasons.
- Running the club to make financial profits by increasing ticket prices, selling expensive stars and increasing brand exposure.
- Focusing on teamwork and team spirit, committed players, better tactics.
- Accepting that the glory days (in league terms at least) are over and that the most that can be expected is top four finish and the odd cup win.

- Searching for and then developing new sustainable competitive advantages, especially new players.
- Hoping that Chelsea's SCAs will prove to be transitory and that Mr Abramovitch will sell up or zip up his cheque book.
- Hoping the authorities will cap salaries, squad size or change nationality requirements and so level the playing field somewhat.

In the short term, Liverpool will have to rely on its current resources and trust in teamwork, team spirit and commitment to win trophies. This then attracts better players, more investment, more merchandise sales and more television exposure. These all make the club stronger and better equipped to counter Chelsea's overwhelming advantages.

When all this is said and done, we should remember that Liverpool's plight is as nothing compared with other stalwarts of the English game. Near neighbours Everton used to be the leading light in English football. Indeed, at one stage the club was known as the Millionaire's Club. Unfortunately for Everton, millionaires can't compete effectively with billionaires. Everton nowadays flirts dangerously with relegation but at least it has relatively recent glory days to remember.

Not so the likes of Middlesbrough, Newcastle, Sunderland, Charlton or Portsmouth and many other clubs which still attract healthy support. Success for most EPL clubs is measured by retaining Premier League status and having one of those 'good runs' in domestic or UEFA Cups.

SCA is relative in terms of market type, era and extraneous influences. Liverpool's new glory days could be just around a corner, but reaching that corner, let alone turning it, will require a strategic approach to competitive advantage.

The search for—and the use of—sustainable competitive advantages is never ending. Ask Liverpool Football Club.

QUESTIONS

1. Compare Liverpool Football Club with a significant manufacturing business regarding its:
   - ⊛ resource development and allocation
   - ⊛ mission/vision
   - ⊛ expectations of the fans
   - ⊛ expectations of its owner

   What similarities and differences do you see?

2. How can Liverpool Football Club redevelop a winning set of sustainable competitive advantages? Why won't other clubs be able to prevent such success?

3. Do any professional sports clubs in Australia have SCAs similar to those enjoyed by Chelsea in the English Premier League? Or those enjoyed by Manchester United? If not, what SCAs are available to your favourite professional sports club?

4. Is it wise to put all of a club's eggs into one basket? In other words, should Liverpool Football Club aim to rebuild its lost dominance by sinking increased funds into its Youth Academy? Or into one or two world-class stars? Or into a 60 000 seater stadium? Develop your answer by dismissing (or supporting) each of these options.

5. Is the history of a professional sports club any real guide to its future prospects? Compare your answer with one you would give involving a manufacturing business.

6. Who is in the market for what Liverpool Football Club offers? How can that market be satisfied? What makes this market different from, say, the market for Coca-Cola? Answer in terms of resources, expectations and SCAs.

CASE STUDY

PART 4

EXTENDING MARKETING MANAGEMENT

CHAPTER 20

Tapping into markets across the globe

Atlassian: www.atlassian.com

Ballistic Media:
www.ballisticpublishing.com

GroundProbe:
www.groundprobe.com

Y ou don't have to be BHP Billiton, CSR or Fosters to tap into markets around the world. Many of the new small businesses being founded in Australia and New Zealand today have overseas expansion as part of their plan of fulfilling a long-term aim—to dominate a global niche. An example of this is an Adelaide media and publishing house, Ballistic Media, which publishes material for the digital arts industry. It used the vehicle of the Computer Graphics Society website which had been formed by one of the owners in 2000 to create an online forum for digital artists to share ideas and post their work. It became clear that artists wanted to publish their work and recruiters wanted to see it. So Ballistic Media was formed in 2003 and a book of digital art was printed and sold via its website. Books are printed in China, stored in Singapore and the USA and shipped direct to customers. In 2004–05 the company achieved revenue of $1.45 million—95% from overseas and all business obtained direct from its website.

Few new companies can rely solely on a website to build business in markets across the globe. WebIT Technologies with revenue of $2.21 million in 2004–05 claims that it succeeded overseas by landing one big multinational client. Atlassian Software Systems launched its business into the overseas market using the web to reach potential customers. Before setting up an office in New York and later relocating to San Francisco in early 2005, Atlassian had sold its licensed software to more than 1000 customers in more than 30 countries via the web. Their success in using the web to build overseas business was directly related to having an international .com site, pricing in US dollars, and providing free licenses for open source projects and non-profit organisations which generated awareness and usage. By focusing on providing excellent service through personalised, quick and accurate responses to web enquiries; relatively low prices enabling small teams within large companies to get access without getting budget approval; and transparency of bugs identified by users with suggested fixes, the company generated positive word-of-mouth which fuelled its growth. Atlassian has shown how to successfully build an overseas business with careful use of limited resources.

Another 'born global' company, GroundProbe, started in 2001 from research conducted at the

Using innovation and expertise Atlassian and GroundProbe are tapping into global markets.

University of Queensland on a project using radar to monitor the movement of mine walls and warn of possible rock falls. In this case significant funding was raised to enable it to construct a detection unit and a mining company signed a long-term contract to use it. By the end of 2005 GroundProbe had built 26 units which were leased out to mining companies around the world and had strategically located offices in four countries.

These companies represent a small sample of Australian and New Zealand companies doing business across the globe—and indicate that there are many different ways to do it.[1]

After reading this chapter you should be able to:

1 Describe the context of globalisation and trends in globalism.

2 Outline the key elements of deciding whether to go international, which markets to enter and how to enter the market—through exporting, joint venturing or direct investment.

3 Describe the role of alliances and the forces that have created the 'virtual' organisation.

4 Explain the primary issue of deciding on the global marketing program, whether to use a standardised or adapted marketing mix, or some combination of the two.

5 Outline the basic competitive strategy profiles for international markets and illustrate alliances that have been formed by market leaders, challengers, followers and specialists.

6 Explain the impact of the Internet as a vehicle for new businesses to be 'born global'.

I n this chapter we explore many of the different entry modes and competitive strategies that are used successfully to tap into overseas markets.

Global marketing in the twenty-first century

At the start of the twenty-first century the world is becoming more and more globally linked in terms of migration of production, technology, capital, people, information and business. Some businesses have been operating globally for many years. Coca-Cola, IBM and Nestlé are examples. However, the pace of business globalisation is now increasing at an exponential rate. As we saw from the chapter opening, much smaller companies are achieving global reach in a short period of time. The pace of globalisation has been accelerated by the rapid growth of corporate intranets, extranet connections with suppliers and customers and the World Wide Web. Now Internet startups, or 'upstarts' as some people refer to them, like Neuromonics and CyGenics in the health and biotechnology sector have become global from day one.[2]

As markets and companies become global they face a variety of competitive situations. One organisation might need to adopt a variety of strategies sometimes simultaneously across a range of different markets, and certainly over time as its competitive position changes. Strategies will include greenfields development, alliances in some markets, acquisition in others and a variety of offensive and defensive moves in both new and existing markets. They will include electronic business initiatives as well as physical marketplace activities. Strategy becomes increasingly complex and multidimensional, a mosaic of different strategies in different markets—a kind of 'global chess', but tied together by an overall global mentality and strategy.

Many companies have been carrying on international activities for decades. Ericsson, Coca-Cola, IBM, Kodak, Nestlé, Shell, Bayer, American Express, Sony and others are familiar to most consumers around the world. But today global competition is intensifying. Foreign firms are expanding aggressively into new international markets, and home markets are no longer as rich in opportunity. Domestic companies that never thought about foreign competitors suddenly find these competitors in their own backyards. The firm that stays at home to play it safe might not only lose its chance to enter other markets but also risks losing its home market.

In Australia and New Zealand, names such as Toyota, Ikea, McDonald's, BMW and Google have become household words. Other products and services that appear to be insiders are produced or owned by foreign companies: Bantam books, Streets ice-cream, Holden cars, Speedo swimwear, Arnott's biscuits, Kiwi shoe polish, Lipton tea and Carnation milk, to name just a few. The Asian region has attracted huge foreign investments in basic industries such as steel, petroleum, building materials and chemicals. Australia and New Zealand are big tourist destinations and have attracted foreign investment in real estate, resulting in American-owned cattle stations and timber plantations, Japanese real estate in Queensland resorts and city hotels run by French corporations like the Accor Group. Few Australasian industries are now safe from foreign competition.

Although some companies would like to stem the tide of foreign imports through protectionism, this response would be only a temporary solution. In the long run, it would raise the cost of living and protect inefficient domestic firms. The answer is that more Australasian firms must learn how to enter foreign markets and increase their global competitiveness. Many companies have been successful at international marketing: Fletcher Challenge, Qantas, CSR, Cochlear and Orica and dozens of other Australasian firms have made the world their market. But there are too few like them. Every government runs an export promotion program, trying to persuade its local companies to export. The government in Australia provides incentives and tax breaks for companies that develop new export markets. Many countries go even further and subsidise local companies by granting preferential land and energy costs—some even supply cash outright so that local companies can charge lower prices than their foreign competitors.[3]

The longer companies delay taking steps toward internationalising, the more they risk being shut out of growing markets in Western Europe, Eastern Europe, the Pacific Rim and elsewhere. Domestic businesses that thought they were safe now find companies from neighbouring countries invading their home markets. All companies contemplating global marketing will have to consider some basic questions: What market position should we try to establish in our country, in our economic region and globally? Who will our global competitors be, and what are their strategies and resources? Where should we produce or source our products? What strategic alliances should we form with other firms around the world?

Ironically, although the need for companies to go abroad is greater today than in the past, so are the risks. Companies that go global confront several major problems. First, high debt, inflation and unemployment in many countries have resulted in highly unstable governments and currencies, which limits trade and exposes Australasian firms to many risks. Second, governments are placing more regulations on foreign firms, such as requiring joint ownership with domestic partners, mandating the hiring of nationals and limiting profits that can be taken from the country. Third, foreign governments often impose high tariffs or trade barriers in order to protect their own industries. Finally, corruption is a continuing problem—officials in several countries often award business not to the best bidder but to the highest briber. The Australian Wheat Board fiasco revealed in 2006 in relation to its dealings with Iraq several years earlier is testimony to the hazards and difficulties of operating in some overseas markets.

You might conclude that companies are doomed whether they stay at home or go abroad. But companies selling in global industries have no choice but to internationalise their operations. A **global industry** is one in which the competitive positions of companies in given local or national markets are affected by their overall global positions. Therefore, a **global firm** is one that, by operating in more than one country, gains R&D, production, marketing and financial advantages that are not available to purely domestic competitors. The global company sees the world as one market. It minimises the importance of national boundaries and raises capital, sources materials and components and manufactures and markets its goods wherever it can do the best job. For example, Ford's 'world truck' sports a cab made in Europe and a chassis built in North America. It is assembled in Brazil and imported to Asia for sale. Nike's Air Max shoes comprise more than 50 components sourced from the USA, Taiwan, South Korea, Japan and Indonesia. They are designed by Nike's US and Taiwan operations and marketed worldwide. Thus, global firms gain advantages by planning, operating and coordinating their activities on a worldwide basis.

Because firms around the world are globalising at a rapid rate, domestic firms in global industries must act quickly before the window closes on them. This does not mean that small and medium-size firms must operate in a dozen countries to succeed. These firms can practise global nichemanship. But the world is becoming smaller, and every company operating in a global industry—whether large or small—must assess and establish its place in world markets.

As shown in Figure 20.1 (overleaf), a company faces six major decisions in international marketing. Each decision is discussed in this chapter.

Global industry An industry in which the competitive positions of companies in given local or national markets are affected by their overall global positions.

Global firm A firm that, by operating in more than one country, gains R&D, production, marketing and financial advantages that are not available to purely domestic competitors.

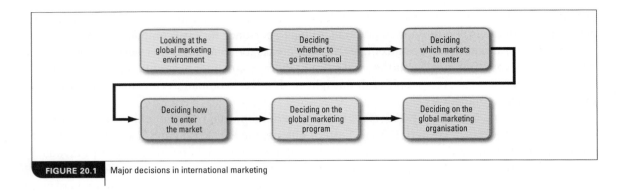

FIGURE 20.1 | Major decisions in international marketing

Looking at the global marketing environment

In this section we will review the concept of globalisation and globalism trends which provide a context for understanding the global marketing environment, the key elements of which are the economic, cultural, political-legal and social marketing environment, which were discussed in Chapter 5.

What is globalisation?

Globalisation The process by which firms operate on a global basis, organising their structure, capabilities, resources and people in such a way as to address the world as one market.

Globalisation is the process by which firms operate on a global basis, organising their structure, capabilities, resources and people in such a way as to address the world as one market. The objective in its purest sense is to serve the global market by maximising the capabilities and advantages that individual countries have to offer—manufacturing productivity, R&D capability, market access, attractive interest rates and marketing experience. Strategic decisions are not taken from any particular country's perspective, there is no nationality bias in senior management and it involves ongoing global searches for technology, people and alliance partners from which global competitive advantage can be achieved. In practice, this is not absolute but a matter of degree. For instance, Nestlé operations around the world are influenced by the founding culture emanating from Switzerland, as are those of Hewlett-Packard flowing from Silicon Valley, and Nokia originating from Finland.

Globalism trends

Many forces are coming together at this point in history and triggering the globalisation of industries, companies and individuals. Trade blocs are forming which are consolidating market regions such as the European Union, North America and Japan and the regions of Asia–Pacific, southern Africa and Latin America. Global communications and media are bringing information, services, cultures and brands to all corners of the world. Industries such as finance, computers, telecommunications and media have become global. The slowdown of the US economy and the demise of many of the fledging dot coms in 2000 and 2001 have reverberated around the world.

A growing number of companies around the world are looking at their business in a global context. For some this means considering the company's markets and operations together within an integrated framework. For others it means standardising products and marketing programs and rationalising R&D

and production to create global economies of scale with tactical product, service and marketing done on a country-by-country basis. For a growing number of firms it means *transformation* from domestic or multinational players to a single global entity operating seamlessly anywhere in the world. BHP Billiton, the Australian-headquartered minerals and resources group, and Fletcher Challenge, the diversified New Zealand-based resources and building products company, are both undergoing this transformation. For Australian companies the road to globalisation has been a rocky one. For instance, Australian financial institutions have struggled to extend their reach into the key financial markets of North America and Europe. The National Australia Bank (NAB), like other banks, has expanded internationally. But its American banking interests were sold in 2000 and a multi-billion dollar write-down was incurred from its investment there. The AMP, one of the Australian icons of the insurance industry prior to 2000, expanded into the UK market. Its lack of success there and troubles at home have had huge impacts on its market value, which has fallen from a high of $20 per share in the first few days of its public float in 1998 (changing from a mutual society to a public corporation) to around $8.50 per share in February 2006. The June 2001 merger with South African-based Billiton has firmly established BHP's global position—it is the world's biggest coal producer, third biggest aluminium producer, third biggest iron ore miner and it has a profitable position in both oil and gas. However, for BHP to become global in the resources industry it has had to, in part, leave behind its roots and increase its foreign ownership levels to around 60%.

Nokia has already become a global company. Its mobile products division operates as a world business. New products are rolled out worldwide in months rather than years. Manufacturing has been consolidated into fewer plants and operations have been standardised so production can be moved from place to place rapidly. Human resource policies are standardised to facilitate personal transfers.

Global advertising is consolidated through fewer agencies that design world campaigns and adaptation to local markets.[4] The massive global advertising, promotion and publicity campaign by Microsoft to launch Windows 95 (and then Windows 2000 and XP) simultaneously around the world illustrates the speed of market penetration that can be achieved in multiple markets.[5] Even more spectacular has been the global launch of successive models of iPod from Apple in 2005 and the global launch of new Harry Potter books through bookshops opening at midnight with the fanfare of people dressed as the book's characters to create excitement.

A global strategy means that a company competes on the basis of its entire combination of competencies, infrastructure and products in all its markets, rather than on a country-by-country basis. To do this effectively requires integration of activities and communication between managers in different countries. Implementing the company's global strategy requires less bureaucracy, flatter organisational structures, effective and quick communication and a clear understanding in each market area of the corporate vision. Orica, the Australian-based chemicals and explosives group, is an example of a successful company that is progressively becoming global in its operations—see Marketing Highlight 20.1.

Deciding whether to go international

Not all companies need to venture into foreign markets to survive. Many companies are local businesses, like restaurants and plumbers, which are protected from international competition and need to market well only in the local marketplace.

However, companies that operate in global industries where their strategic positions in specific markets are strongly affected by their overall global positions must think and act globally. Thus, car firms must organise globally if they are to gain purchasing, manufacturing, financial and marketing advantages. Firms in a global industry must compete on a worldwide basis if they are to succeed.

MARKETING

20.1

HIGHLIGHT

Orica uses acquisitions to become a major global marketer

Orica achieves domestic and international growth profitably.

Consider the planning undertaken by Orica. This Australian-based chemicals and explosives group has been transformed over the 2002–2006 period from an ailing, underperforming (largely domestic) company with unhappy shareholders to a global player. It began with a cost-cutting and culture-change drive to be performance and customer focused—with reward based on achievement. Underpinning the customer-focused culture has been the development of market-based plans that included export markets in the Pacific area as well as domestic markets. This is nowhere more evident than in the ChlorAlkali Division which manufactures and markets chemicals for water purification, swimming pools and manufacturing processes. ChlorAlkali undertook a rigorous marketing planning process to segment its market, develop product and service offerings of perceived value and position these differently to specific customer segments and assess the export potential of its products in near neighbour countries. Supported by targeted promotion and selling effort this has achieved remarkable success—revenue and profit growth has been substantial over this period. This kind of success has enabled Orica to embark on a growth strategy based around growing existing businesses and 'bolt-on' acquisitions which provide a ready fit to the business. In 2003 this began with the acquisition of chemical trading

company Fernz, which has increased the revenue of Orica's trading company Chemnet by 50%. Also the merger of Orica's Incitec (agricultural fertilisers) with farmer-owned Pivot added substantial growth and strength to that business.

On 19 September 2005 the company announced that it had signed an agreement to acquire from the Macquarie consortium (an Australian investment bank and partners) the businesses of Dyno Nobel in Europe, the Middle East, Africa, Asia and Latin America.

While it will take some time to implement fully, the impending acquisition consolidates Orica as a leading global supplier of explosives, initiating systems and blasting services to the mining, construction and quarrying industries and builds substantially on its Australian base of operations. Prior to this major acquisition it was operating as a supplier of explosives and blasting services in more than 40 countries.

Orica announced a net profit after tax and before significant items for the year ended 30 September 2005 of $335 million, a 3% increase over the previous year with sales revenue up 11% over 2004—showing a profitable transition to a global marketer.

Sources: Interview with David Morgan, General Manager, Chemnet, Orica, February 2006 by Linden Brown; Michael Bachelard, 'Orica Revived by Broom at the Top', *The Australian*, 1 April 2003, p. 22. See also company announcements at <www.orica.com.au/BUSINESS/COR/orica/COR00254. NSF/Page/News>, accessed 10 February 2006.

Questions

1 How has Orica changed from an ailing company in 2002 to a significant global player in 2006?

2 What are some of the underlying success factors in its transformation?

3 What options does it have for future growth globally?

20.1

Any of several factors might draw a company into the international arena. Global competitors might attack the company's domestic market by offering better products or lower prices. The company might want to counterattack these competitors in their home markets to tie up their resources. Or the company might discover foreign markets that present higher profit opportunities than the domestic market. The company's domestic market might be shrinking or the company might need an enlarged customer base in order to achieve economies of scale. Or it might want to reduce its dependence on any one market in order to reduce its risk. Finally, the company's customers might be expanding abroad and require international servicing.

Before going abroad, the company must weigh up several risks and answer many questions about its ability to operate globally. Can the company learn to understand the preferences and buyer behaviour of consumers in other countries? Can it offer competitively attractive products? Will it be able to adapt to other countries' business cultures and to deal effectively with foreign nationals? Do the company's managers have the necessary international experience? Have management considered the impact of foreign regulations and political environments?

Because of the risks and difficulties of entering foreign markets, most companies do not act until some situation or event thrusts them into the international arena. Someone—a domestic exporter, a foreign importer, a foreign government—might ask the company to sell abroad. Or the company is saddled with overcapacity and must find additional markets for its goods.

Many factors can motivate firms to move toward internationalisation and it is important to understand them from a strategy perspective. In fact, most of these motivations could emerge directly from further analysis of gaps or issues associated with generating generic competitive positions discussed in Chapter 19 and later in this chapter. The extended analysis might reveal both proactive and reactive motivations for internationalisation.[6]

Some, or a combination of, internationalisation motivations have to be internalised and promoted by individuals within the firm or associated with it. These individuals may become change agents driving the firm toward internationalisation.[7] Representative internal change agents include enlightened management or a significant internal event, while external change agents may include demand, export agents and distributors, customers or competitors. Czinkota and Ronkainen have developed a framework for categorising firms into stages of internationalisation, and this is outlined in Table 20.1 (overleaf). The framework covers a spectrum ranging from totally domestically oriented firms to firms that have had experience in many different international markets.

Internationalisation is gradual and is usually a sequenced one-market-at-a-time approach. The later stages of internationalisation strongly reflect a multinational marketing strategy.

TABLE 20.1 Six stages of internationalisation

Stage 1: The completely uninterested firm

Profile:

- small
- no exporting or plans to export
- will not fill unsolicited export orders

Stage 2: The partially interested firm

Profile:

- small
- small number of export orders
- exploring export opportunities but uncertain about future exports

Stage 3: The exploring firm

Profile:

- small to medium
- small number of export orders
- exports going to closely proximate markets, e.g. Asia
- management committed to the desirability of exports
- actively seeking export assistance
- past export profits are typically below expectations

Stage 4: The experimental exporter

Profile:

- small to medium
- small number of export orders
- exports going to closely proximate markets, e.g. Asia
- management committed to exports
- actively seeking export assistance
- export is based on product and technological advantage and profit expectations

Stage 5: The experienced small exporter

Profile:

- small to medium
- significant number of export orders
- exports going to closely proximate markets, e.g. Asia
- may go global if it has substantial experience
- management totally committed to exports
- actively seeking export assistance
- export is based on product and technological advantage, managerial urge and profit expectations

Stage 6: The experienced large exporter

Profile:

- medium to large
- export orders half of total orders
- exports going global
- substantial experience exporting into new markets
- management totally committed to exports
- management structure 'institutionalises' exports
- generally able to fund export drive without assistance
- export is based on product and technological advantage, managerial urge, market expansion and profit expectations.

Source: M. R. Czinkota & I. A. Ronkainen, *International Marketing: International Edition*, 4th edn, Fort Worth, Dryden Press, 1995.

Deciding which markets to enter

Before going overseas, the company should try to define its international *marketing objectives and policies.* First, it should decide what *volume* of foreign sales it wants. Most companies start small when they go abroad. Some plan to stay small, seeing foreign sales as a small part of their business. Other companies have bigger plans, seeing foreign business as equal to or even more important than their domestic business. Still others, as noted in the chapter opening, gear themselves to be global from the start.

Second, the company must choose *how many* countries it wants to market in. Generally, it makes better sense to operate in fewer countries with deeper penetration in each.

Third, the company must decide on the *types* of countries to enter. A country's attractiveness depends on the product, geographical factors, income and population, political climate and other factors. The seller may prefer certain country groups or parts of the world.

After listing possible international markets, the company must screen and rank them. Possible factors include market size, market growth, cost of doing business, competitive advantage, legal and tax requirements and risk level. The goal is to determine the potential of each market, using indicators such as demographic and geographical characteristics; economic, technological and sociocultural factors; and national goals and plans. Then the marketer must decide which markets offer the greatest long-run return on investment.

Selecting an overseas market can impact on the other activities of the Australian firm. This is because the outcome may influence the profitability of the firm in its domestic as well as in its other overseas markets. Not only will this impact on overall profits but it might also impact on other areas such as its global reputation. This is illustrated in situations like the impact on Union Carbide following the Bhopal calamity, the security of a firm's intellectual property (in some countries intellectual piracy is common) and the physical risk to its personnel in countries like Laos and the Philippines.

Underpinning the selection of markets to enter should be a strategic orientation that treats market entry selection as part of the firm's overall strategy linked to both its resource base and a distinctive competence, on the one hand, and its position in relation to competitors on the other.

In isolating the markets that offer the greatest potential, it is necessary to take both the situation of the firm and the circumstances of the overseas market(s) into account. In doing so, the characteristics of the individual markets as well as the extent to which one overseas market is integrated with another need to be considered. Where there is an integrated group of overseas markets, entering one may facilitate subsequent or simultaneous entry into others.

In addition to balancing the firm's strategic orientation with the characteristics of the overseas market(s), market entry decisions should also take into account:

- *The structure of the global industry of which the firm is a part*—consideration of the structure of the industry recognises that in whatever it does the firm is part of a network and the strengths deriving from this network can affect the decision as to which market to enter.

⊚ *The strategy of current or potential global competitors*—the inclusion of competitor strategy recognises that markets are dynamic and the fact of entering an overseas market is likely in many instances to provoke a competitive reaction, either from firms in that market or from firms in other countries.

Selection of overseas markets involves comparison. This can be difficult because the quality of data varies from country to country. Although the expansion of global databases and international online services has helped comparison, difficulties remain due to differences between countries in both recency and rigour of data collection. These limitations make a structured approach to overseas market selection desirable.

There are a number of different approaches to market selection and these have different implications for small and medium as opposed to large firms. The first category of approaches focuses on whether to enter overseas markets on an incremental basis, which entails moving from one to another only after establishing a presence in the first, or whether to enter a number of overseas markets simultaneously and, on the basis of experience, decide in which markets to concentrate. The advantages of incremental entry are that it enables the firm to gain experience at a measured pace, requires the commitment of fewer resources and involves less risk in terms of exposure. However, this approach does involve greater competitive risk as competitors may leapfrog into other markets. For instance, seeing what an Australian firm is doing in Thailand, competitors may move immediately into Malaysia, Indonesia and the Philippines, which were potential target markets for the firm following its establishing a presence in Thailand. The incremental approach, however, may preclude achieving economies of scale and result in a *haphazard* approach to entering overseas markets. The simultaneous entry approach does enable the firm to acquire overseas experience rapidly, facilitates achieving economies of scale in overseas activities and is likely to prevent pre-emption by competitors in other markets. Offsetting these advantages is the fact that it is a resource-intensive strategy and one that entails higher operating risk.

The second category of approaches to overseas market entry focuses on whether a concentrated as opposed to diversified approach should be adopted. If a firm decides to concentrate its resources in a limited number of markets, it is likely to have a more focused effort, encounter reduced operating risks and have the costs and benefit from economies of scale in exploiting information and acquiring experience. On the other hand, it will have all its 'eggs in one basket' and if something happens to the selected markets, such as the events leading to the breakup of communist regimes in the former Centrally Planned Economies in 1989–1991, the firm is in an exposed position. In addition, this approach leaves the firm largely ignorant about potential in the rest of the world. A diversified strategy spreads both risk exposure and broadens knowledge of potential in a variety of markets, as well as offering greater strategic flexibility. It can, however, result in the firm spreading itself too thinly, may affect its ability to be competitive as economies of scale prove elusive and may require greater management resources at the headquarters location.

SELF-CHECK QUESTIONS

6 What should a company consider when deciding on which markets to enter?

7 What are the typical stages of internationalisation through which firms progress?

Screening for market selection

Analysing the attractiveness of individual markets

The purpose of screening is to enable the firm to arrive at a portfolio of attractive overseas markets. One approach is to develop two separate matrices designed to help evaluate export market attractiveness and the firm's competitiveness.

The first matrix, which relates to the overseas market, involves rating the characteristics of the market, the competitive conditions, the financial and economic conditions and the legislative and sociopolitical conditions for the category of products/services to be offered by the Australian firm. In this matrix the exporter would expand the assessment criteria under each of the headings of market characteristics, competitive conditions, economic conditions and legislative/sociopolitical conditions and give each factor a rating on a scale of 1–5, where 1 is very unattractive and 5 is very attractive. The exporter may also want to give different weightings to the factors. By adding up the scores given for each factor the exporter will establish a total score for one particular export market. When this is repeated for other export markets, the exporter can compare the scores for each market. The market showing the highest score would be the most attractive export market.

The second matrix, which relates to the Australian firm, involves rating management characteristics, marketing characteristics, technology attributes and production-related competencies in terms of potential competitiveness in the overseas market.

As a result of the ratings of individual characteristics on both export market attractiveness and firm's competitiveness, an overall assessment of both aspects is arrived at from which the suitability of entering the overseas market can be determined. Countries that rated high for the firm on both export market attractiveness and competitiveness would constitute a portfolio of attractive markets for the firm to consider entering. Austrade has developed an 'export capability tool' which prospective exporters can complete online to self-assess their capabilities for exporting. This can be found at <www.austrade. gov.au/australia/layout/0,,0_S2-1_2zh-2_-3_-4_-5_-6_-7_,00.html> (accessed 14 February 2006).

A major Australian brewer and wine producer such as Fosters, in evaluating overseas markets to enter, might undertake the above exercise and arrive at the following five markets—California, Western Canada, the UK, Denmark and Singapore. First, this selection may be based on its capacity to supply, its ability to fund increments to current production, its willingness to modify the product and the suitability of such markets for a standard marketing approach. Second, selection would be influenced by characteristics of the overseas markets such as level of wine consumption, a willingness to try an imported product and the relative absence of tariff and non-tariff barriers.

A screening approach

The matrix approach, which involves an analysis of each country, is time consuming and may be beyond the management resources of many small and medium-sized Australian firms. In these circumstances, an alternative approach might involve commencing the selection procedure by considering all markets in the world and then by screening markets in relation to a succession of criteria. Unsuitable markets are progressively eliminated from consideration. The result of this process is likely to be a small group or cluster of markets which offers the greatest potential. As the selection procedure moves from stage to stage, a greater degree of analysis is likely to be required. As a consequence, most effort is put into studying those markets that are likely to offer the most promise in relation to the characteristics of the firm and the opportunities of the market.

The approach to progressive screening described below and shown in Figure 20.2 (overleaf) is a modified version of that developed by Toyne and Walters (1993). This was first developed by Fletcher and Brown.[8] It is made up of five stages.

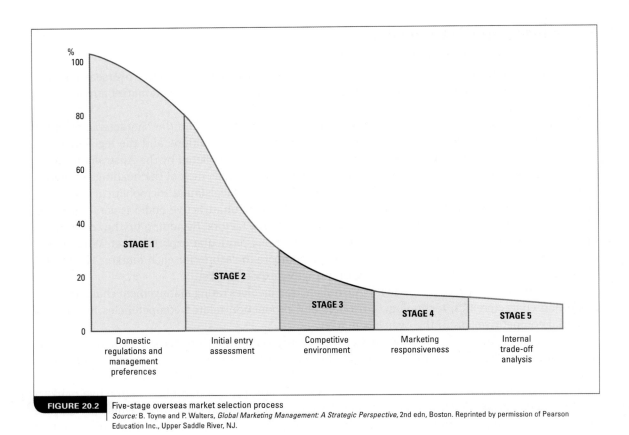

FIGURE 20.2 Five-stage overseas market selection process
Source: B. Toyne and P. Walters, *Global Marketing Management: A Strategic Perspective*, 2nd edn, Boston. Reprinted by permission of Pearson Education Inc., Upper Saddle River, NJ.

Stage 1 This involves answering the following questions relating to domestic considerations.

Question 1. Which overseas markets are of no interest to the firm regardless of their apparent potential?

This issue, while often irrational, does impact on market selection. It is often due to the prejudice or preference of the senior executives. For example, an unhappy holiday experience in India may result in a refusal by the CEO to contemplate exporting to that country.

Question 2. Which remaining overseas markets should be excluded because of regulations initiated by or involving support of the Australian government?

These regulations may be political, such as embargos on 'rogue' states, defence related (export of defence equipment allowed to friendly countries only) or have economic/protectionist motives (restrictions on the export of merino sheep).

At the conclusion of this portion of the analysis, it is likely that possibly 20% of world markets can be excluded from further consideration.

Stage 2 This involves answering the following questions relating to macroenvironmental factors in overseas markets and an initial assessment of general prospects. The second step, described as 'initial entry assessment', screens out economically unattractive markets.

Question 3. Which remaining overseas markets have the least attractive political and social environments?

This question can be assessed by considering the political and economic environment, the domestic economic conditions and the external economic relations of the country. At this stage of the analysis, economic considerations could also be included such as the ease with which profits can be repatriated, freedom to convert local currency and the volatility of the exchange rate.

Question 4. Which remaining overseas markets are least attractive because of their nature and potential size?

There are a number of simple ways of estimating likely demand sufficient for a screening activity. These involve assessing not only current demand but also likely demand in the future as well as untapped or unfilled demand which may exist in a particular market. Some of the more common techniques are as follows:

- *Demand pattern analysis*—by analysing local production, inventory and patterns of international trade for a product in an overseas country, it is possible to estimate consumption trends and market opportunities.
- *International product life cycle*—by comparing the stage of the life cycle for the product in the overseas market compared to the stage in Australia, and by reflecting on what happened in Australia between that earlier stage and the present one, it is possible to predict what may happen to the product in an overseas market as the product moves along the life-cycle curve.
- *Income elasticity measurements*—this is the relationship between change in demand for a product divided by the change in income. This measure can be used for predicting change in likely quantity demanded for a particular product category.
- *Proxy and multiple factor indices*—when information about the product in the overseas market is unavailable, it is possible to estimate likely demand using demand patterns for another product or service that is correlated with demand for the firm's own product/service. For example, electrification of villages will be associated with demand for refrigerators. A multiple factor index involves two or more proxy variables believed to correlate with demand for the product.

This second step may indicate that demand for the product/service does not exist in a further 50% of world markets.

Stage 3 By this stage, only about 30% of world markets remain. In this stage and the next, the more expensive and time-consuming elements of evaluation are applied to the remaining limited number of countries offering potential. During this phase, it is important to answer the following questions relating to the likely competitive environment in the overseas market.

Question 5. Which remaining overseas markets have substantial entry barriers to products from Australia to protect domestic industry or conform to trade relations arrangements with other countries?

These barriers may relate to entry, exit and the marketplace. Entry barriers can be both tariff and non-tariff-like quotas, quarantine or standards. Such barriers also include aspects that impinge on the form of overseas market entry such as regulations relating to local content and ownership. Exit barriers may relate to repatriation of profits, dividends and capital, taxation issues and technology transfer. Marketplace barriers can include access to skilled personnel, availability of warehouse space, transportation, allocation of critical inputs such as power and water and control over prices.

These barriers may take different forms all of which would serve to rule out markets from further consideration. This is reflected in the composition of the markets in Japan and China. In the former, the main barrier is the complex and multilayered distribution system which underpins a major sector of business activity and generates significant employment. In China, by contrast, the tariff and non-tariff barriers are a continuing legacy of the previous regime, designed to create a climate for the development of indigenous industry. Although in both countries the barriers are being lowered, they still continue to operate as a substantial impediment to Australian firms wishing to enter these markets.[9]

Question 6. Which remaining overseas markets should be avoided because competitors (both domestic and foreign) are already well entrenched in them?

This will require some knowledge as to whether the competitors are local, Australian or foreign and how they will react to entry into their markets. With each competitor or potential competitor, knowledge as to relative strengths and weaknesses in relation to the firm's operation helps establish whether a market should be excluded because of potential competitive reaction. There are a number of competitive strategies which might influence selection of markets. These include entering a market so as to pre-empt the entry of others, entering a market in which there are already competitors and confronting them, and entering a market where large competitors do not exist. The latter strategy might be designed both to build up share of market and gain experience for attacking more competitive markets in other countries at a latter stage.

Stage 4 This stage involves answering the following questions relating to the degree to which markets are unlikely to respond to, or prohibit, certain market activities.

Question 7. Which remaining overseas markets are not large enough to justify the marketing effort that will be necessary to gain a satisfactory market share?

This requires an assessment as to what share of the total market in the country the firm can reasonably expect to obtain, given domestic and other foreign competition and affordability of the product. In cases where this demand is not sufficient to justify risk or costs of entry, the market should be excluded from further consideration.

Question 8. Which remaining overseas markets are unlikely to respond to those marketing activities which are considered necessary to establish the product/service in the marketplace effectively?

It will need to be determined whether the market allows or prevents the firm achieving its objectives. These may be couched in terms of product such as achievement of brand identity and product-line extension, and in terms of pricing such as ability to achieve acceptable levels of return on investment and match changes in competitors' pricing. The market will also need to be assessed in terms of whether the firm will be able to achieve its objectives in promotion such as securing media coverage, optimising salesforce effectiveness and attaining advertising objectives as well as its objectives in distribution such as achievement of coverage, building up appropriate inventory levels and ability to modify the channel when this becomes necessary.

Question 9. Which remaining overseas markets prohibit the form of presence that the firm considers optimal and can afford when entering a new overseas market?

The answers to previous questions and the firm's preferred way of operating overseas may yield an indication as to which form of market presence would be most appropriate for each market. It is necessary to establish whether the desired form is permissible as some may not be allowed, and whether those forms which are allowed are likely to be profitable. If the company always operates overseas via licensing its technology and the government limits the size of allowable licensing fee, then the attractiveness of the market may be questionable. Before the reforms of the Indian economy in 1993, the Indian government restricted royalty payments to 3% maximum, taxable at 50% yielding 1.5% net. Most Australian firms found this figure unattractive.

Question 10. Which remaining overseas markets are unattractive because of costs and problems of reaching them from Australia?

Answering this question involves ensuring that reasonable logistics links exist both between Australia and the overseas market and within the overseas market. The impact of the cost of logistics on both ability to compete and on demand also need to be considered. Also relevant in selecting a market is whether these links are reliable and timely. This means that delivery can be relied upon, that the time taken for goods to reach the destination does not adversely impact on ability to compete and that the goods arrive in an acceptable condition.

Stage 5 The final stage involves eliminating markets because of internal trade-offs. At this stage, it is likely that less than 10% of markets remain for consideration. It may be useful to create a weighting system that reflects the goals of the firm and perceived importance to the firm of circumstances in the overseas market. This weighting could then be applied to answers to the final two questions below. Appraising the remaining countries in relation to these final questions is likely to result in only a few markets being contemplated for entry.

Question 11. Which remaining overseas markets are no longer attractive because of the extent to which resources need to be committed and changes made to existing company resources?

Some of the remaining markets may require more resources than others. A trade-off is likely to be necessary—first, between markets which require more resources and those which require fewer in terms of anticipated pay off, and, second, between specific overseas markets and alternative use of resources necessary for entry in the Australian market.

Question 12. Do any of the markets still under consideration fail to meet the company's objectives or match its competitive advantages?

This last question recognises that market attractiveness does not exist independently of a firm's competitive strategy. The process by which the remaining markets have been arrived at should mean that the answer is 'no'. However, it is useful to pose a check question of this type at the conclusion of the screening process.

   With the several remaining markets having promise, no final decision should be made until these markets have been visited by a responsible executive to see whether the impressions of potential are justified. It is only then that they should be ranked in order of attractiveness.

Deciding how to enter the market

Having identified promising overseas markets, the next issue to be addressed is the mode of entry that is most appropriate for the market(s) selected. Although this is treated as a separate decision to market selection it is often directly related, because of a preference by the firm for a specific mode of entry. Modes of entry can be divided into those that aim to sell the product and those that aim to transfer know-how to the host country. They also vary in the level of risk associated with each of those entries (see Figure 20.3 overleaf).

Export-based entry

These entry forms are driven by a desire to sell either product/service or technology overseas with the minimum commitment of resources.

Indirect exporting

This refers to the use of agencies in the home country to get the product into the foreign market. Indirect export can be subdivided into export agents who receive a commission for **exporting** goods produced by firms, and export merchants who buy the goods from the manufacturer and subsequently export them. In addition, firms can export using specific agencies established to market overseas

Exporting Entering a foreign market by exporting products and selling them through international marketing middlemen (indirect exporting) or through the company's own department, branch or sales representatives or agents (direct exporting).

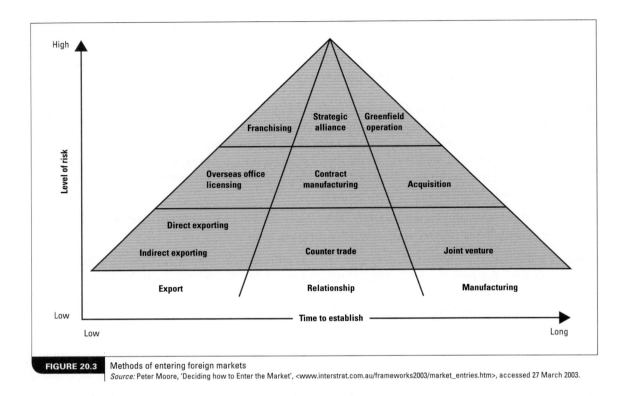

FIGURE 20.3 Methods of entering foreign markets

Source: Peter Moore, 'Deciding how to Enter the Market', <www.interstrat.com.au/frameworks2003/market_entries.htm>, accessed 27 March 2003.

products in their category. This is often referred to as cooperative exporting. Cooperative exporting has long been a feature of the export of agricultural products from Australia and not only takes the form of cooperative associations but also of statutory corporations set up by state or federal governments which involve government, trading and grower representatives. Examples are the Australian Meat and Livestock Corporation, the Australian Wheat Board and the Australian Dairy Corporation. To varying degrees these bodies set conditions and influence or control the export of the product category. Another form of indirect exporting is that of piggybacking whereby an inexperienced exporter uses the facilities of an experienced exporter to enter and market products into an overseas market. This can be initiated by government as happens when a government trade promotion agency initiates a 'foster firm' scheme for inexperienced exporters. It can also be encouraged by the private sector as happens when an industry group such as the Australian Business Chamber or the Metal Trades Export Group of Australia encourages those members which are successful in international business to seek opportunities overseas for newer and smaller members.

One example of indirect exporting is BHP Steel which for many years exported its steel products through Australian export agents such as Brown and Dureau and Gollin and Co.

Direct exporting

In this case the firm itself contacts the buyers overseas and either sells direct to the end-user or arranges for firms in the target market to act as agents and/or distributors for its products. The firm establishes its own export sales organisation which becomes responsible for all marketing activities in respect of overseas sales. This group identifies potential markets and segments and is involved in export documentation, shipment and planning both strategy and marketing activities in the overseas market. While direct export entails greater commitment of resources, it enables the firm to exercise greater control over the conditions under which its products are sold. For many small and medium-sized firms, direct exporting is the dominant form of foreign market involvement. Another variant that is becoming increasingly important, especially with the advent of the Internet, is direct marketing. This is proving to be a very useful entry mode for small firms and firms initially entering a new overseas market.

Typical Australian examples are to be found among exporters of saddles to Mexico and the USA by Southern Cross Saddlery, educational computer software to the UK, Spain, the USA and Canada by eWord Technologies and exporters of gluten/wheat-free snack bars to the UK, Italy, Canada and Hong Kong by LEDA Nutrition. These examples and other stories of successful small exporters can be found at the Austrade website, <www.austrade.gov.au/australia/layout/0,,0_S2-1_CLNTXID0027-2_-3_PWB1469368-4_-5_-6_-7_,00.html> (accessed 20 February 2006).

Establishing a sales office in the overseas market

Whereas direct exporting involves appointing a non-employee in the overseas market to represent your firm and set up a network of distributors, establishing a sales office in the overseas market represents a further commitment of resources beyond that entailed in the usual form of direct exporting. Establishing a sales office in the overseas market also enables a greater measure of control over what happens to the product in that market. The office not only controls the selling of the product or service but also its promotional program. This refinement also enables the firm to set up and control its own distribution channels.

When Barbecues Galore of Australia first entered the US market they established a sales office in Los Angeles. This served as the base for expansion horizontally into other areas of the USA and vertically into specialty retailing.

Licensing

Licensing enables a firm to earn overseas income from its technical innovations, its brand, its corporate image or its other proprietary assets without engaging in either manufacturing or marketing overseas. It usually involves an 'upfront' payment for the transfer of know-how and a royalty linked to volume produced and sold in the overseas market. Although there is a minimal commitment of resources involved, this form of market entry provides limited return especially in cases where the licensee does not fully develop the potential that the market has to offer. A further disadvantage is that licensing agreements are usually for a fixed term during the course of which the firm is prevented from entering the market directly. In addition, there is a risk that licensing might lead to 'cloning a competitor' should the licensee export to other markets in competition with the licensor or continue to manufacture the product after the expiration of the licensing period. However, with an increasing number of countries accepting the new WTO regime on intellectual property protection, this risk is less than was formerly the case. A final problem occurs when the licensee produces substandard products under the company's brand and the firm's global image suffers as a result.

Licensing A method of entering a foreign market in which the company enters into an agreement with a licensee in the foreign market, offering the right to use a manufacturing process, trademark, patent, trade secret or other item of value for a fee or royalty.

Franchising

Whereas international licensing usually applies to products, in the services industry the variant of international franchising is becoming increasingly common, especially in the global expansion of hotel and fast-food chains. The franchisor gives the franchisee the right to undertake business in a specified manner under the franchisor's name in return for a royalty payment that usually takes the form of a fee or a percentage of sales. Many of the advantages and disadvantages that apply to licensing apply to franchising. In particular, one of the problems of international expansion in both the retail and hospitality sectors is the cost of purchasing or renting sites and this responsibility is usually that of the franchisee. Franchising is also important where contact with customers and well-managed operation of the business are critical to success. The franchisor can lay down guidelines for this interface and management to ensure a uniform projection and include in the franchising agreement penalties or threat of abrogation of contract for non-compliance. Successful franchising involves the establishment of performance standards and mechanisms for monitoring and control. Because of this, franchising can often be more resource intensive than licensing.

Australian firms have achieved considerable success using this mode of growth. Cartridge World, based in Adelaide, recycles and refills print cartridges and is well established with franchises in the USA and has appointed franchisees in the massive potential markets of India and China. Kip McGrath Education Centres has a franchise of 500 education centres, tutoring children in 15 countries. The biggest markets for exports by Australian franchisors are New Zealand and Britain, but many are looking to Asia for expansion opportunities, particularly China.[10]

Manufacturing-based entry

Often referred to as direct foreign investment (DFI), this can take a number of forms that vary from limited equity involvement to total ownership of the overseas operation.

Joint venturing

Joint venturing Entering foreign markets by joining with foreign companies to produce or market a product or service.

The most common form of manufacturing-based entry into overseas markets for Australian firms is that of **joint venturing**. This is because Asia is the target of many such firms and the governments of many Asian countries have foreign investment laws that mandate some local equity in any investment in their country. Joint ventures are a means of the firm limiting its equity exposure in an overseas market and can provide a vehicle for entering markets where the economic systems and marketing environments are so different that it is necessary to have a local partner in order to be successful. Where the object of the joint venture is the building of a major infrastructure project, a number of foreign firms might be involved in a consortium together with local interests from either or both the public and the private sectors. Egis Consulting Australia (formerly CMPS&F) was involved with the government in water supply projects in Indonesia and Signet Engineering of Western Australia with private sector interests in a gold-processing plant in Chile. When the manufacture of products is involved, the more common form of joint venture is that between an Australian and a local firm. The Australian firm brings to the joint venture technology and production expertise while the local partner provides access to the distribution network as well as familiarity with the local marketing environment. This is what happened when Kirby Refrigeration formed a joint venture with the Simakulthorn Company in Thailand in the 1980s for the manufacture of refrigeration compressors. Selecting the 'right' joint venture partner is often a problem—one Kirby Refrigeration addressed by locating a partner which was also a family company in Thailand with a similar set of values. As a mode of entry, joint ventures reduce the capital and other resource commitment required, involve a spreading of risk and result in access to contacts and expertise in penetration of the local market. The main disadvantages are the risk of conflict between the Australian firm and its joint venture partner, problems of communication and management when different cultures are involved and the fact that the Australian firm has only partial control. Because of this, joint ventures are likely to have a limited lifespan unless the partners can develop an agreed corporate mission and agree on a common strategy and mode of governance.

Acquiring

This involves entering an overseas market by acquiring an existing company. It is an entry technique often employed by multinational firms that are cash rich. For small and medium firms, this technique is often beyond their resources. Acquiring an existing operation enables rapid entry into the overseas market in that it usually provides an established distribution channel and existing customer base. It is a desirable strategy in cases where the industry is highly competitive or where there are substantial entry barriers for a new entrant. Such a move requires considerable research lest the equipment is outdated, the assets of the company are overvalued, labour laws inhibit change and increased productivity or the intellectual assets of the firm cannot be protected. Many of Australia's larger corporations like ANZ, Telstra, Pacific Dunlop, CSR and BHP Billiton have adopted this approach. Cochlear is an outstanding example of a company that has become a global leader through a combination of internal development and acquisition—see Marketing Highlight 20.2.

Greenfield operation

This occurs where a firm decides to build its own manufacturing plant in an overseas country using its own funds. This is an attractive entry option when there are no suitable firms to acquire or the firm needs to establish its own operation because of technology or logistics considerations. It enables firms to utilise the latest production technologies while at the same time selecting the most attractive locations in terms of labour costs, local taxes, land prices and transportation. Firms wishing to rationalise their operations on a global basis are more likely to find this the most attractive entry option despite the costs in terms of capital and management. A typical Australian example is the decision by the Ansell Division of Pacific Dunlop to establish a factory in Thailand to produce rubber gloves and balloons.

Relationship-based entry

These forms of entry are more reliant on the creation of relationships than those discussed previously. They occur where a considerable degree of cooperation is necessary in order to achieve success. This is because the level of resource commitment by the Australian or New Zealand firm is usually modest and both parties to the transaction have a mutual stake in the outcome.

Contract manufacturing

In **contract manufacturing** the firm contracts the production to a local manufacturer but retains control over the marketing of the product. It is a strategy suitable in circumstances where the overseas market does not justify establishing a manufacturing operation and where there are high barriers to imports. It requires little investment and is a relatively quick way of entering an overseas market. Because brand name and company reputation are involved, it does require the exercise of quality control by the Australian firm so that the contract manufacturer meets the Australian firm's quality and delivery standards. Contract manufacture can also include cooperative manufacture. This is becoming an increasingly common feature of global business. It entails either various parts being produced in different countries, for example the Airbus aircraft, or different functions being carried out in different countries. For example, Fujitsu and NEC now conduct R&D in one country, component manufacture in another, assembly in a third and servicing in a fourth.

Contract manufacturing Joint venturing to enter a foreign market by contracting with manufacturers in the foreign market to produce the product.

Strategic alliances

Although sometimes this term is used in a broader context, as a market entry strategy **strategic alliances** refer to collaborations between firms in various countries to exchange or share some value-creating activities. Strategic alliances are partnerships between firms. The strategic alliance partners contractually pool, exchange or integrate business resources for mutual gain. They remain separate businesses and aim to learn and acquire from each other technologies, products, skills and knowledge that would not otherwise be available to them or their competitors. The inexorable move to alliances has been expressed this way: 'Globalisation mandates alliances, makes them absolutely essential to strategy. Uncomfortable, perhaps—but that's the way it is. Like it or not, the simultaneous developments that go under the name of globalisation make alliances—entente—necessary.'[11]

Strategic alliances An agreement between two organisations to work together to achieve joint objectives. It may take the form of a contractual agreement, an equity sharing joint venture or an agreement to work together on specific projects.

Cochlear—an ear for the market

With the exception of a few very large Australian firms the opportunities for Australian companies to globalise and adopt global strategies is confined to focusing on narrow niche products and markets— businesses that are highly specialised in their expertise and activities. This has been achieved with some success by high-technology Australian firms in the biotechnology area.

The Australian star in this sector is Sydney-based Cochlear, which is set to dominate world markets in its specialised area. Cochlear Ltd (owned by Pacific Dunlop) has gained US regulatory approval for its most advanced ear implant system—the Nucleus 24 system—an implant in the cochlea, which is a shell-shaped part of the inner ear. Cochlear now has the opportunity to sell implants to over 200 000 severely hearing impaired Americans—100 times the total number of Nucleus 24 implants sold worldwide to June 1998. The hearing-aid manufacturer has had its system approved by most other countries for 12 months. Cochlear's implant had an estimated 70% share of the global market in 1998. By 2001, there were 31 500 Cochlear Nucleus implants worldwide and a sales revenue of $144 million and profit of $20 million in 2000. By mid-2002 Cochlear had 60–65% of global sales, Advanced Bionics (a US company) had 30%, which included nearly half of the North American market, and Med-El (an

Australian firm) had 5–10% with its main focus on Europe. Total worldwide market sales in 2001–2002 were around $400 million. Cochlear's sales were $256 million for 2001–2002 with an after-tax profit of just over $40 million.

In July 2002 the US Food and Drug Administration (FDA) reported a possible link between hearing implants and meningitis. In response Cochlear and Med-El indicated that the incidence of meningitis among users of their devices was no higher than in the general population. Cochlear also said that it had no reports of meningitis since its latest model, the Nucleus 24 Contour, was released in 2000. However, Advanced Bionics conceded that its product—the Clarion C11—might leave recipients exposed to a greater risk and withdrew it from the market. This has opened a wider window into the US market for Cochlear until Advanced Bionics can correct the situation.

Cochlear's vision of being the global leader in innovative implantable hearing solutions has become a reality. Global market share of Cochlear implants is estimated at 70%. In 2005 the drivers of sales growth included increasing unit sales (up 16.1% to 10 802 units for the year), benefits from the distributor businesses in the Netherlands, Belgium, France and Japan that were acquired during the year and the acquisition of Entific Medical Systems in March 2005 (contributing $14.8 million of sales from March to June 2005). Europe (37% growth) was the star growth performer followed by the USA, then Asia.

Cochlear implant unit sales grew 11.9% in the first half of 2004–05 but accelerated to 20.0% in the second half, helped by the release of its next-generation Nucleus Freedom cochlear implant system. This system provides the best hearing performance ever available. This effort has resulted in Nucleus Freedom offering the next step in cochlear implant technology and is a platform for future innovations. In anticipation of the Nucleus Freedom launch, detailed market research was conducted in

Cochlear is a successful global company.

multiple markets. This helped identify key messages that would resonate with candidates and provided a basis for fact-based marketing decisions. During the year, marketing resources were rebalanced between corporate marketing and regional marketing and the focus between recipients and professionals (rather than solely healthcare professionals) was also rebalanced. Net profit after tax grew by 48.3% over the previous year to $54.5 million in 2005.

Cochlear is a textbook case of globalisation for a technology company.

Sources: Donald D. Hensrud, 'Can You Hear Me Now?', *Fortune*, vol. 147, issue 5, 17 March 2003, p. 142; Beth Quinlivan, 'Cochlear's Chance', *Business Review Weekly*, 8–14 August 2002, p. 38; Nina Field, 'US Approval is Music to Cochlears', *The Australian Financial Review*, 29 June 1998, p. 25; Melanie Warner, 'Cool Companies 1998', *Fortune*, 6 July 1998, pp. 45-61; <www.cochlear.com/Corporate/Investor/AnnualReport2005/ed04_president/pres01_report.htm> (annual report for year ending June 2005).

Questions

1 Why is it that most Australian companies that have globalised are operating in specialised niche markets?

2 How has Cochlear been able to maintain a lead in the hearing implant market?

3 What are the most important factors for further globalisation success?

20.2

The firms involved might be competitors in the Australian market which see collaboration as being necessary in order to enter and compete in an overseas market. Alternatively, the alliance may be between a group of firms whose activities complement each other. These strategic alliances can involve joint R&D, shared manufacturing as is common in the automotive industry, the use of common distribution channels or any other activities in the value chain. In distribution alliances, the members both agree to use an existing distribution network. The airline network Star Alliance formed between Air New Zealand, United Airlines, SAS, Air Canada, Lufthansa, Singapore Airlines and Thai International is an example of such an alliance as this involves pooling of route information, common access to frequent-flyer programs and sharing of passenger traffic on certain routes using code share flights.

Strategic alliances have become a preferred business strategy because of the opportunities of e-business and the globalisation of industries and organisations. The main advantage to a firm is the ability it acquires to operate beyond its own capabilities. The factors driving the increased prevalence of strategic alliances include:

- moving into new markets
- filling knowledge gaps
- pooling to gain operational economies
- building complementary resource capabilities
- speeding up new product introduction (time-based competition)
- value creation through electronic business.

Strategic alliances are now viewed as a more effective diversification strategy than the traditional conglomerate approach. Human relationships between alliance members are a major influence on the development and maintenance of strategic alliances, especially for senior management.

Implementation and management of strategic alliances

The implementation of strategic alliances can be difficult and time consuming, particularly with cross-cultural alliances. The failure rate is high. Most strategic alliances do not seem to live up to initial management expectations over time. One study suggests that 7 out of 10 joint ventures fail to meet either partner's management expectations.[12] The challenges and obstacles to strategic alliances may be summarised as:[13]

- autonomy (of alliance members)
- forward momentum
- focus on the external environment
- politicking (internal agendas that go against alliance development)
- change and innovation (commitment)
- learning (desire and commitment to learn about each other)
- people (having the best people committed to the alliance)
- 'black box' (fear of giving up something)
- culture.

Studies on the matching of partners has led to the following observations about the success of strategic alliances:[14]

- Ventures tend to be more successful where partners are homogeneous.
- Ventures are less successful where neither partner is related to its venture.
- Ventures last longer between partners of similar cultures, asset sizes and venturing experience levels.

High levels of management energy are required to maintain and develop alliances with a substantial number of members. This is a special problem for management of the alliance founder or driving company. The management of MIPS Inc. expended very high levels of management energy to form and maintain the Advanced Computing Environment (ACE), which proposed the MIPS R4000 RISC computer chip for standard use in the consortium. Despite the high level of management energy expended, the ACE consortium foundered and MIPS Inc. was eventually taken over by Silicon Graphics Inc.[15]

In relation to the management of people in a virtual organisation, seven elements of trust are critical success factors:[16]

1   Don't place blind trust in everyone.
2   Trust needs boundaries.
3   Trust demands learning.
4   Trust requires toughness especially when wrong matches are made.
5   Trust includes component parts which must bond to the goals of the whole virtual organisation.
6   Trust still requires 'touch' or physical face-to-face contact throughout the virtual organisation, although this may not be in the conventional workplace environment.
7   Trust requires a multiplicity of strong leaders in the virtual organisation.

These elements of trust point towards a complex set of human behaviours that may make or break the formation and development of strategic alliances.

Countertrade

This involves the linking of an import and an export transaction in a conditional manner. It includes barter, counterpurchase, buyback, offsets and debt exchange, all of which can result in a firm entering an overseas market. In **countertrade** there is a mutually dependent relationship between buyer and seller.

Countertrade
International trade involving the direct or indirect exchange of goods for other goods instead of cash. Forms include barter, compensation (buyback) and counterpurchase.

Australian examples include a barter deal between Hancock Mining and Romania involving Australian coal and Romanian machinery; a counterpurchase deal between Elders Countertrade and the Trading Corporation of Bangladesh involving the exchange of nominated goods over a fixed term; a buyback deal involving Bulk Materials Coal Handling and Coalimex of Vietnam for the rehabilitation of a coal washery; and an offsets arrangement between the Royal Australian Air Force and McDonnell Douglas for the supply of F/A-18 aircraft.

Deciding on the global marketing program

Companies that operate in one or more foreign markets must decide how much, if at all, to adapt their marketing mixes to local conditions. At one extreme are companies that use a **standardised marketing mix** worldwide. Standardisation of the product, advertising, distribution channels and other elements of the marketing mix promises the lowest costs because no major changes have been introduced. This thinking is behind the idea that Coca-Cola should taste the same around the world and that Ford should produce a 'world car' that suits the needs of most consumers in most countries.

At the other extreme is an **adapted marketing mix**. The producer adjusts the marketing mix elements to each target market, bearing more costs but hoping for a larger market share and return. Nestlé, for example, varies its product line and its advertising in different countries. Many possibilities exist between the extremes of standardisation and complete adaptation. For example, Coca-Cola sells the same beverage worldwide and in most markets it uses television spots showing a thousand children singing the praises of Coke. For different local markets, however, it edits the commercials to include close-ups of children from those markets. The question of whether to adapt or standardise the marketing mix has been much debated in recent years, although this is of less interest in Australia and New Zealand given the absence of world brands.

International corporations face a major strategy trade-off between standardising and localising their global operations and marketing. The argument for standardising is that it saves costs and allows the promotion of one central brand or corporate image worldwide. The argument for localising is that every market is different and victory will go to the competitor which best adapts the offer to the local market. Clearly, the answer is 'It all depends'. Bartlett and Ghoshal proposed the circumstances under which each approach works best. In their *Managing Across Borders*, they describe a number of forces that favour *global integration* (e.g. capital-intensive production, homogeneous demand and so on) over *national responsiveness* (e.g. local standards and barriers, strong local preferences).[17] They go on to distinguish three organisational strategies:

1 A *global strategy* treats the world as a single market. This strategy is warranted when the forces for global integration are strong and the forces for national responsiveness are weak. This characterises consumer electronics, for example, where most buyers around the world will accept a fairly standardised pocket radio, CD player or television. Bartlett and Ghoshal go on to point out that Matsushita has performed better than GE and Philips in the consumer electronics market because Matsushita operates in a more globally coordinated and standardised way.

2 A *multinational strategy* treats the world as a portfolio of national opportunities. This strategy is warranted when the forces favouring national responsiveness are strong and the forces favouring global integration are weak. This characterises the branded packaged goods business

Standardised marketing mix An international marketing strategy for using basically the same product, advertising, distribution channels and other elements of the marketing mix in all the company's international markets.

Adapted marketing mix An international marketing strategy for adjusting the marketing mix elements to each international target market, bearing more costs but hoping for a larger market share and return.

with its food products, cleaning products and so on. Bartlett and Ghoshal cite Unilever as a better performer than Kao and P&G because Unilever grants more autonomy in decision making to its local branches.

3 A *'glocal' strategy* standardises certain core elements and localises other elements. This strategy makes sense for an industry such as telecommunications where each nation requires some adaptation of its equipment but the providing company can also standardise some of the core components. Bartlett and Ghoshal cite Ericsson as balancing these considerations better than NEC (which is too globally oriented) or ITT (which is too locally oriented).

The message, then, is that international companies must review whether they have organised their international operations and marketing programs appropriately, given the characteristics of the global industry and global market in which they operate. Interestingly, in a recent survey senior executives of corporations with worldwide operations agreed with several of Bartlett and Ghoshal's views. This provides some tentative empirical support for their typology of international business organisations.

One of the most successful 'glocal' companies is ABB, formed by a merger between the Swedish company ASEA and the Swiss company Brown Boveri. ABB's products are industrial and include power transformers, electrical installations, instrumentation, auto components, air conditioning equipment and railroad equipment. With $US25 billion in sales and 240 000 employees, ABB is headed by Percy Barnevik, one of Europe's most dynamic CEOs. The company's motto is 'ABB is a global company local everywhere'. Barnevik established English as the company's official language (all ABB managers must be conversant in English) and all financial results must be reported in American dollars. ABB is organised with the aim of reconciling three contradictions: to be global and local; to be big and small; and to be radically decentralised with centralised reporting and control. ABB has only 100 staff at its headquarters, compared with the 3000 that populate Siemens' headquarters. The company's many product lines are organised into eight business segments, 50 business areas, 1200 companies and 4500 profit centres, with the average employee belonging to a profit centre of around 50 employees.

Managers are regularly rotated between countries and mixed-nationality teams are encouraged. Depending on the type of business, some are treated as superlocal businesses with lots of autonomy and others as superglobal businesses with major central control. Barnevik uses a proprietary software system called Abacus which allows him to review performance data each month in each of the 4500 profit centres. When the system flags exceptional or deficient performances, he contacts the appropriate managers, business area managers and local company presidents. He wants his managers to be locally knowledgeable but also attuned to global considerations in making their decisions.[18]

In 2003 the company developed another alliance with Intel, Microsoft and Accenture to be able to provide ABB's capability on a local as well as a global scale. This alliance partnership thus combines ABB's automation and power products with the robust software, computing and networking skills of Microsoft and Intel and Accenture's program management and integration expertise. Now ABB can support its local customers with its global capabilities.[19]

Global or multinational?

One of the most vigorous debates in international marketing is the preference for *multinational* or *global* marketing. For the strategist, this debate raises many key questions, including:

- Which approach provides a better picture for developing a future competitive position—an aggregation of several national and industry competitive position models, or a model that starts with an overall global competitive position?
- Which elements of the marketing mix or aspects of the value chain can be effectively standardised or modified to service global customer sets?

- Which external or environmental variables (such as economic, political, legal and cultural variables) require analyses that go beyond a global perspective to a regional or national level?
- What is the impact of global telecommunications, media and computing on the development of effective international competitive marketing strategies?
- How does a multinational firm convert to a global company?
- Is true globalisation ever really possible—or even desirable?

Although the issue has been vigorously debated, there is increasing recognition that a global strategy can possess sufficient flexibility to have a standardised business strategy and yet still market and deliver products adapted for many different markets. A global marketing planning matrix accommodating both standardisation and adaptation is presented in Table 20.2.[20]

TABLE 20.2 Global planning matrix		Adaptation		Standardisation	
		Full	**Partial**	**Full**	**Partial**
Business function	Research and development				
	Finance and accounting				
	Manufacturing				
	Procurement				
	Marketing				
Products	Low cultural grounding				
	High economies or efficiencies				
	Low cultural grounding				
	Low economies or efficiencies				
	High cultural grounding				
	High economies or efficiencies				
	High cultural grounding				
	Low economies or efficiencies				
Marketing mix elements	Product design				
	Brand name				
	Product positioning				
	Packaging				
	Advertising theme				
	Pricing				
	Advertising copy				
	Distribution				
	Sales promotion				
	Customer service				
Countries	Country A				
Region 1	Country B				
Region 2	Country C				
	Country D				
	Country E				

Product

Five strategies allow for adapting product and promotion to a foreign market (see Figure 20.4). We discuss the three product strategies here and then look at the two promotion strategies.[21]

Straight product extension means marketing a product in a foreign market without any change. Top management tell their marketing people: 'Take the product as is and find customers for it'. The first step, however, should be to find out whether foreign consumers use that product and what form they prefer.

Communication adaptation involves modifying the message so it fits with different cultural environments. One Australian company launched a swimming-pool cover in southern California with the advertising benefits that it kept leaves out of the pool and extended the swimming season—both powerful advantages in Australia. What they overlooked, however, was the absence of a leaves problem in southern California because of the semi-arid conditions, and the fact that the climate already ensured that pool water stayed warm.

Product adaptation involves changing the product to meet local conditions or wants. McDonald's serves beer in Germany and coconut, mango and tropical mint shakes in Hong Kong. Australian and New Zealand firms are accustomed to catering for small market segments and this strategy of tailoring to local needs is something that they can often be more responsive to than larger-scale producers.

Dual adaptation occurs when both product and promotion adaptation are undertaken to tailor the offer to local needs and cultural differences. James Hardie does this in the building supplies industry.

Product invention consists of creating something new for the foreign market. This strategy can take two forms. It might mean reintroducing earlier product forms that happen to be well adapted to the needs of a given country. For example, the National Cash Register Company reintroduced its crank-operated cash register at half the price of a modern cash register and sold large numbers in Asia, Latin America and Spain. On the other hand, a company might create a new product to meet a need in another country. For example, an enormous need exists in less developed countries for low-cost, high-protein foods. Companies are researching the nutrition needs of these countries, creating new foods and developing advertising campaigns to gain product trial and acceptance. Product invention can be costly, but the payoffs are worthwhile.

Promotion

Companies can adopt the same promotion strategy they used in the home market or adapt their communications for each local market.

Straight product extension Marketing a product in the foreign market without any change.

Communication adaptation A global communication strategy of fully adapting advertising messages to local markets.

Product adaptation Adapting a product to meet local conditions or wants in foreign markets.

Product invention Creating new products or services for foreign markets.

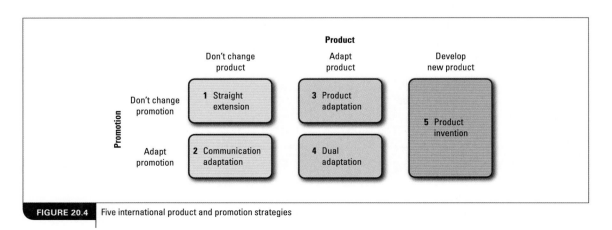

FIGURE 20.4   Five international product and promotion strategies

Consider the message. Some global companies use a standardised advertising theme around the world, changing the copy in minor ways to adjust for language differences. Sometimes colours are changed to avoid taboos in other countries. Purple is associated with death in most of Latin America, white is a mourning colour in Japan and green is associated with jungle sickness in Malaysia. Even names are sometimes changed. In Sweden, Helene Curtis changed the name of Every Night Shampoo to Every Day because Swedes usually wash their hair in the morning. Kellogg's also had to rename Bran Buds cereal in Sweden, where the name roughly translates as 'burned farmer'.

Other companies fully adapt their communications to local markets. A bicycle company might use a pleasure theme in a developed country and a reliability theme in a developing country.

Media also need to be adapted internationally because media availability varies from country to country. Television advertising time is very limited in Europe, ranging from four hours a day in France to none in Scandinavian countries. Advertisers must buy time months in advance, and they have little control over air times. Magazines also vary in effectiveness. For example, they are a major medium in Italy and a minor one in Austria. Newspapers are national in the UK but only local in Spain.

Price

Companies also face many problems in setting their international prices. For example, how might Coca-Cola set its prices globally? It could set a uniform price all around the world. But this amount would be too high a price in poor countries and not high enough in rich ones. Coca-Cola could charge what consumers in each country would bear. But this strategy ignores differences in the actual cost from country to country. Finally, the company could use a standard mark-up of its costs everywhere. But this approach might price Coca-Cola out of the market in some countries where costs are high.

Regardless of how companies go about pricing their products, their foreign prices will probably be higher than their domestic prices. A Gucci handbag selling for $100 in Italy might sell for $300 in Australia. Why? Gucci must add the cost of transportation, tariffs, importer margin, wholesaler margin and retailer margin to its factory price. Depending on these added costs, the product might have to sell for two to five times as much in another country to make the same profit.

Another problem involves setting a *transfer price* for goods the company ships to its foreign subsidiaries. Consider the following example:

> The Swiss pharmaceutical company Hoffman-LaRoche charged its Italian subsidiary only $22 a kilogram for librium in order to make high profits in Italy, where the corporate taxes were low. It charged its British subsidiary $925 per kilogram for the same librium in order to keep the profits at home instead of in Britain, where corporate taxes were high. The British government sued Hoffman-LaRoche for back taxes and won.

If the company charges too high a price to a foreign subsidiary, it ends up paying higher tariff duties, although it might pay lower income taxes in that country. If the company charges too low a price to its subsidiary, it can be charged with *dumping*. Dumping occurs when a company either charges less than its costs or less than it charges in its home market. Thus, Harley-Davidson accused Honda and Kawasaki of dumping motorcycles on the US market. The US International Trade Commission agreed and responded with a special five-year tariff on Japanese heavy motorcycles, starting at 45% and gradually dropping to 10%. Similarly, Canada has been accused of dumping soft wood onto the US market resulting in the collapse of the local lumber industry.[22] In Australia there have been criticisms that our anti-dumping laws are constructed in favour of the importer and that, by the time the case is proven, the local manufacturer or supplier may have been forced out of business.

Last but not least, many global companies face a *grey market* problem. For example, Minolta sold its cameras to Hong Kong distributors for less than it charged German distributors because of lower transportation costs and tariffs. Minolta cameras ended up selling at retail for $195 in Hong Kong and $290 in Germany. Some Hong Kong wholesalers noticed this price difference and shipped Minolta cameras to German dealers for less than the dealers were paying their German distributor. The German distributor couldn't sell its stock and complained to Minolta. Thus, a company often finds some enterprising distributors buying more than they can sell in their own country and shipping goods to another country to take advantage of price differences. International companies try to prevent grey markets by raising their prices to lower-cost distributors, dropping those who cheat or altering the product for different countries.

Distribution channels

Whole-channel view
Designing international channels that take into account all the necessary links in distributing the seller's products to final buyers, including the seller's headquarters organisation, channels between nations and channels within nations.

The international company must take a **whole-channel view** of the problem of distributing products to final consumers. Figure 20.5 shows the three major links between the seller and the final buyer. The first link, the seller's headquarters organisation, supervises the channels and is part of the channel itself. The second link, channels between nations, moves the products to the borders of the foreign nations. The third link, channels within nations, moves the products from their foreign entry point to the final consumers. Some Australian suppliers may think their job is done once the product leaves their hands, but they would do well to pay more attention to its handling within foreign countries. Apart from ensuring an efficient distribution system, it may also provide opportunities for forward integration by which the supplier can capture some of the value added in the distribution chain.

Within-country channels of distribution vary greatly from nation to nation. First are the large differences in the *numbers and types of intermediaries* serving each foreign market. For example, an Australian company marketing in China must operate through a frustrating maze of state-controlled wholesalers and retailers. Chinese distributors often carry competitors' products and frequently refuse to share even basic sales and marketing information with their suppliers. Hustling for sales is an alien concept to Chinese distributors, who are used to selling all they can obtain. Working with or getting around this system sometimes requires substantial time and investment.[23] Another difference lies in the *size and character of retail units* abroad. Whereas large-scale retail chains dominate the Australian scene, most foreign retailing is done by many small independent retailers. In India, millions of retailers operate tiny shops or sell in open markets. Their mark-ups are high, but the real price is lowered through price haggling. Supermarkets could offer lower prices, but they are difficult to build and open because of many economic and cultural barriers. Incomes are low, and people prefer to shop daily for small amounts rather than weekly for large amounts. They lack storage and refrigeration to keep food for several days. Packaging is not well developed because it would add too much to the cost. These factors have kept large-scale retailing from spreading rapidly in developing countries.

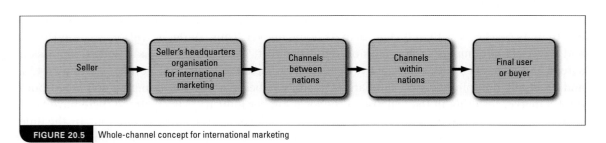

FIGURE 20.5 Whole-channel concept for international marketing

SELF-CHECK QUESTIONS

12 Compare and contrast global, multinational and 'glocal' strategies.

13 What are the advantages and disadvantages of a standardised strategy worldwide?

14 What factors should be taken into account by firms considering a standardised marketing mix versus an adapted marketing mix?

15 What aspects of each element of the marketing mix need to be considered in the global marketing program?

Deciding on the marketing organisation

Companies manage their international marketing activities in at least three different ways. Most companies first organise an *export department*, then create an *international division* and finally become a *global organisation*.

Export department

A firm normally gets into international marketing by simply shipping out its goods. If its international sales expand, the company organises an export department with a sales manager and a few assistants. As sales increase, the export department can then expand to include various marketing services so that it can go after business actively. If the firm moves into joint ventures or direct investment, the export department will no longer be adequate.

International division

Many companies get involved in several international markets and ventures. A company might export to one country, license to another, have a joint venture in a third and own a subsidiary in a fourth. Sooner or later it will create an international division or subsidiary to handle all its international activity.

International divisions are organised in a variety of ways. The international division's corporate staff consists of marketing, manufacturing, research, finance, planning and personnel specialists. They plan for and provide services to various operating units. Operating units may be organised in one of three ways. They may be *geographical organisations*, with country managers who are responsible for salespeople, sales branches, distributors and licensees in their respective countries. Or the operating units may be *world product groups*, each responsible for worldwide sales of different product groups. Finally, operating units may be *international subsidiaries*, each responsible for its own sales and profits.

Global organisation

In Australia a handful of firms have passed beyond the international division stage and have become truly global organisations. They stopped thinking of themselves as national marketers who sell abroad and started thinking of themselves as global marketers. The top corporate management and staff plan worldwide manufacturing facilities, marketing policies, financial flows and logistical systems.

The global operating units report directly to the chief executive or executive committee of the organisation, not to the head of an international division. Executives are trained in worldwide operations, not just domestic or international. The company recruits management from many countries, buys components and supplies where they cost the least, and invests where the expected returns are greatest.

A good example is Oroton, based in Sydney. It designs, sources and manufactures leather and jewellery products from a large number of countries around the world and markets its products worldwide. Oroton has retail outlets in Australia, New Zealand and several other countries as a means of targeting its distribution to consumers and managing its high-quality image. It is at pains not to identify itself as an Australian company, but to position itself as a global firm.

Major companies must go more global in the twenty-first century if they hope to compete. As foreign companies successfully invade the domestic market, Australian companies must move more aggressively into foreign markets. They will have to change from companies that treat their foreign operations as secondary to companies viewing the entire world as a single, borderless market.[24]

An alternative structure—the virtual organisation

The processes of organisational change and developments in technology are converging to produce new types of business organisations. The new information infrastructure has provided a foundation for a new form of organisation—the '**virtual corporation**', which does not exist in the bricks and mortar sense. Using information technology, its purpose is to link people, assets and ideas to enable an opportunistic network of organisations to join quickly to exploit fast-changing opportunities.[25] The characteristics of the virtual organisation are shown in Figure 20.6.

Virtual corporation
An organisation electronically linked with other organisations to create a product or service without an obvious physical 'shop front'. An example is the 'library without walls' from which information is obtained electronically.

The most important characteristic of a virtual organisation is that it is created to meet a specific opportunity in a defined time period.[26] Communication and the pursuit of common objectives form the basis of the relationships between firms and individuals who will increasingly be electronically connected through the new infrastructure.[27]

The cross-border nature of e-business means that vast pools of commercial knowledge are rapidly washing around the world through the electronic infrastructure, challenging businesses in all industries to view the accumulation of knowledge and the conversion of it to commercially profitable

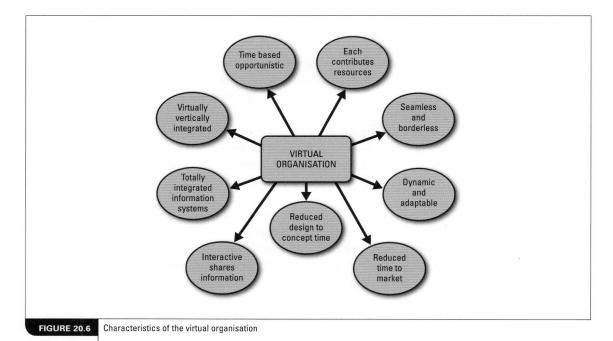

FIGURE 20.6 Characteristics of the virtual organisation

outcomes as a cornerstone of strategy formulation. The scope of electronic business is transforming individuals, businesses and industries as it affects industry structure, virtual/alliance structure and marketing strategy.

The combination of strategic alliances and e-business leads to the theme of the virtual organisation discussed earlier in this chapter. Goldman, Nagel and Preiss from the Agile Manufacturing Enterprise Forum (AMEF) at the Lehigh University's Iacocca Institute have proposed a model of a virtual organisation made of many strategic alliances linked through a powerful information infrastructure.

The key feature of the virtual organisation structure is *agility*:

> For a company, to be agile is to be capable of operating profitably in a competitive environment of continually, and unpredictably, changing customer opportunities. For an individual, to be agile is to be capable of contributing to the bottom line of a company that is constantly reorganising its human and technological resources in response to unpredictably changing customer opportunities.[28]

Individuals, teams, businesses (in strategic alliances) and even industries (especially within converged industry structures) are all reconfigurable in this model. Goldman, Nagel and Preiss have renamed the virtual corporation the **agile corporation** in their model.

Agile corporation
An organisation that is constantly able to reorganise its structure and its human, technological and financial resources in response to continuously changing market opportunities. This kind of organisation maintains the highest level of flexibility in order to be able to respond to unpredictable changes in its environment.

SELF-CHECK QUESTION

16 What are the benefits and drawbacks of adopting a global strategy approach to business?

Basic competitive strategy profiles[29]

Most of the basic competitive strategy profiles introduced in Chapter 19 apply here in a global context. Also, the *built to last* characteristics proposed by Collins and Porras[30] and introduced in Chapter 3 should be considered, along with the research findings of Treacy and Wiersema[31] on *market leaders* noted in Chapter 19.

While a particular market may be the focus of attention, if the context is global the Australian or New Zealand firm will usually need to consider alliances with firms in the same or related industries to put together an appropriate penetration strategy. In an alliance network, the firm must consider the overall strategy of the group of which it is a part. The basis of competitive advantage and market coverage needs to be looked at from the alliance network's viewpoint as well as from the individual firm's standpoint.[32] In this section we review the basic strategies of firms in different competitive positions and also illustrate examples of alliances that are often part of the strategy involved.

Global leader strategy

A global leader is an innovator in technologies, products and markets with high global share and wide country market coverage.

Microsoft, Ericsson, Coca-Cola and Intel are clear global leaders in their respective markets. They adopt aggressive global strategies designed to be ahead of their competitors in new expanding markets. Intel and Ericsson lead in their respective technologies. Microsoft, through a range of alliances with computer makers, dominates the operating systems and application software for PCs. Coca-Cola's focus on brand management, worldwide coverage and intensive distribution and advertising makes it the leading and most profitable soft drink company in the world.

If the intent is rapidly to achieve leadership in the new market, the firm needs to develop a network of alliances that can rapidly deliver innovative products and services with appropriate support and resource leverage. The alliance network must be planned with foresight to include additional or different alliance players as the market evolves and as competition responds to the new entrant. The strategy should contain the following elements:

- ⊙ focus on mainstream markets
- ⊙ resource leverage for rapid penetration entry
- ⊙ market positioning to take the high and middle end of the market
- ⊙ integration of alliance partners into a seamless organisation to deliver the offer.

In Australia, Qantas has formed a range of alliance relationships through its OneWorld membership to deliver worldwide passenger travel. A simplified picture of Qantas's alliance network is shown in Figure 20.7.

Global challenger strategies

Strategy 1

A global challenger mounts a frontal or encirclement attack on the leader in all markets with increasing country market coverage and high global share but less than the leader.

Pepsi's challenge to Coca-Cola in many of its major markets is a major threat. Nokia, of Finland, is a growing threat to Ericsson's worldwide communications business.

Strategy 2

A global challenger can flank or bypass a world leader with increasing country market coverage and high global share but less than the leader.

Burger King's challenge to McDonald's and Mobil Oil's to Shell involve strategies to map out new geographic markets in which the leaders are weak.

To be a major threat it is necessary to design a challenger alliance network with sufficient resource leverage to have a major impact on the market. Market entry may be narrowly focused on key market

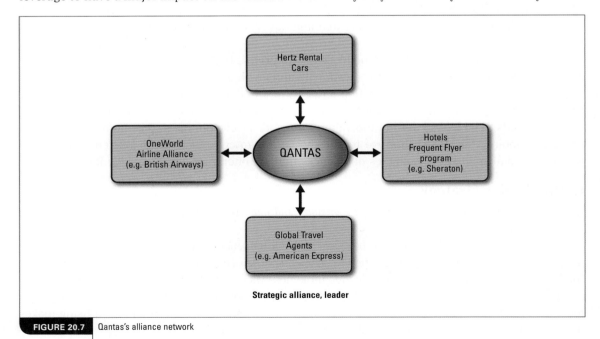

FIGURE 20.7   Qantas's alliance network

segments or focused on broader market coverage. The specific strategy will be determined in part by the strength of incumbent competitors. The principles discussed in Chapter 19 on challenger strategies apply. Optus has adopted alliance networks to challenge Telstra and future competitors in the Australian communications industry, as seen in Figure 20.8.

Global follower strategy

A global follower engages in rapid imitation of leader or challenger with moderate country market coverage and emphasis on price-sensitive markets. The result is overall moderate share with high shares in selected country markets.

Korean companies Hyundai and Daewoo are following their Japanese counterparts, Toyota and Nissan, into an increasing number of Asian markets.

As discussed in Chapter 19, followers usually rely for their success on speed of implementation and lower costs. Here the alliance network requires the following elements:

- alliance configuration of small units
- communication lines and relationships enabling rapid decision making and implementation
- low-cost structures
- well-organised competitive intelligence system providing early information on competition developments and initiatives
- competencies in imitating and improving products, services, delivery processes and customer communications.

The alliance network of Singapore Airlines, which is competing with Qantas in the Australasian airline travel markets, is shown in part in Figure 20.9 overleaf.

Global nicher strategies

Strategy 1

A global nicher engages in rapid penetration of narrow market segments by selective targeting of country markets and small share of overall market.

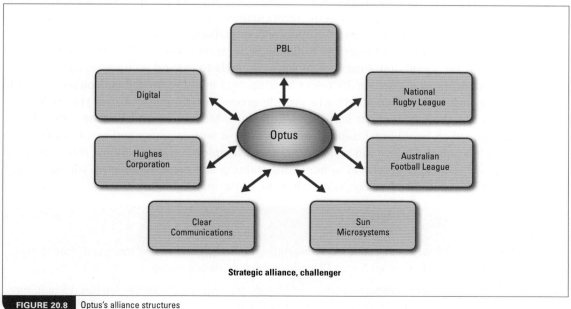

Strategic alliance, challenger

FIGURE 20.8 Optus's alliance structures

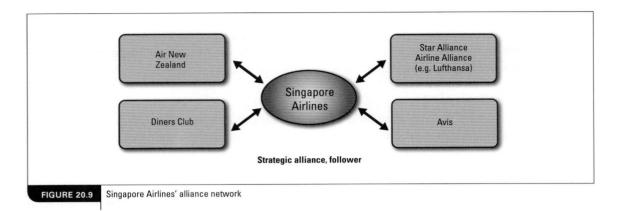

FIGURE 20.9 Singapore Airlines' alliance network

Examples include BMW, Toshiba (laptops), ASKO (dishwashers), Vodafone and Ikea (furniture). However, it is possible in the growing 'marketspace' of electronic markets for niche competitors to go global from day one.

Sausage Software, a Melbourne-based company, started business in 1995 by offering its HotDog Web Editor—a program that makes it easy to publish information on the World Wide Web—for sale entirely on the Internet. Almost all business comes from exports to the USA, Canada and Europe to organisations such as Microsoft, IBM, Coca-Cola, NASA and the US Navy. Customers can download its programs and pay electronically. After many ups and downs, Sausage Software developed to become a leading Australian Internet-based software company and was purchased by Telstra in 1999.[33]

Strategy 2

In this strategy there is infiltration or slow penetration of selected narrow markets with focus on selected country markets and low share of the overall market.

The South African supermarket store group Aldi and the American confectionery company Hershey have adopted this strategy in overseas markets.

The alliance network for new market entry should be composed of partners that specialise in various parts of the value chain relevant to the target market—product or service supply, specialised distribution, specialised customer communication and specialised support services.

Australian furniture removalist Overseas Shipping Services has developed an alliance network of specialists around the world and a network of sales channels to expand its international removals business. This network as it exists in 2006 was built up over many years and is depicted in part in Figure 20.10. Its extensive channel networks provide access to customers all over the world even though it only has three of its own branches—in Sydney, Melbourne and Brisbane. Its alliance partners are Australian-based organisations which provide it with business and services that allow it to provide a full range of relocation services. Another example of an international niche specialist adopting a global strategy is Interstrat, a marketing training and consultancy firm, whose strategy for penetration of a specialised market is described in Marketing Highlight 20.3.

SELF-CHECK QUESTIONS

17 Explain the key alliance strategies and marketing strategies for market leaders, followers and niche specialists. (You might need to refer to Chapter 19 for the relevant marketing strategies.)

18 Outline an example of challenger strategies in an industry with which you are familiar. Identify the alliance relationship and the leader that is being challenged.

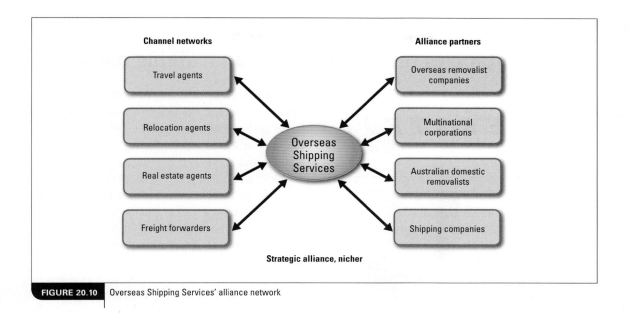

Channel networks

Alliance partners

Travel agents

Relocation agents

Real estate agents

Freight forwarders

Overseas Shipping Services

Overseas removalist companies

Multinational corporations

Australian domestic removalists

Shipping companies

Strategic alliance, nicher

FIGURE 20.10 Overseas Shipping Services' alliance network

Global collaborator strategy

A global collaborator is an innovator in research and development of technologies, products and markets, and sets standards which it shares with other firms. This shows small or moderate country market shares but high shares when all strategic 'standards users' are included.

For example, Hewlett-Packard sells many of its competitors' products to provide its customers with tailored solutions in its 'network systems' division. Sony provides Trinitron screens to PC vendors as well as using them in its own products. Now Apple has licensed its operating system to other computer makers as a strategy for expanding the 'Macintosh' system markets and encouraging more extensive software development. Other companies generating sales and share growth through collaboration are Philips and Canon.

Internet startups: born global

As we discussed in the chapter opening there are an increasing number of Australasian companies that are 'born global' from day one. Whittle Programming of Melbourne can claim to be a 'born global' company. Because of the specialised nature of its product (a computer software program for the design of open pit mines to maximise extraction) and the necessary size of the customer's operation to support the purchase, the Australian market was too small to support Whittle's activities. From the outset, the product was designed to be sold globally and the company's first sale was to a mining firm in Spain. Currently, Whittle has licensed the software to over 200 companies, half of which are outside Australia (see <www.whittle.com.au/>, accessed 20 Febuary 2006).

BomWeb is another 'born global' company, a small Australian startup which has released a new operating system designed for electronic procurement over the Internet. It aims at providing organisations with seamless technology for reverse auctions where the buyer names the price and specifications and the supplier decides whether to accept the bid. According to the company's website, it now services the following industries—electricity and energy, retail, chemicals, agrochemicals, food manufacturing, construction, metals and banking (see <www.bomweb.com.au/consulting.asp>, accessed 20 February 2006).

MARKETING HIGHLIGHT

20.3

Interstrat tackles the North American training market

Interstrat develops marketing software in Poland for the US market.

Interstrat is an example of a niche specialist which has successfully moved its operations and customer base from Australia to North America. Interstrat began operations in Sydney in 1988 offering marketing skills workshops to Australian companies. It was established to bridge the marketing knowledge and capability gaps among Australian and multinational organisations and offered a wide range of services. During the nineties it expanded its reach to Asia–Pacific, conducting marketing training programs for global companies operating in China, Japan, Singapore and the Philippines. In 2000 it obtained its first global contract with a large US-based global corporation by first providing programs in its Asia–Pacific region followed by programs in North America. This required a highly customised approach in one specialist area of marketing skills development which was used as a base for developing other highly customised and specialised offerings. Its unique blend of online and offline delivery supported by proprietary software tools for on-the-job use by marketers in applied marketing decision making has enabled it to add to its customer base. The use of alliance partners, client referrals and test sites have been key elements of its marketing strategy to establish credibility and add new clients at a rate consistent with its ability to deliver. Its strategy of narrowing its service range and specialising in a specific niche—of marketing skill areas and specific industries—enabled it to establish a viable competitive position in a specialised field in a very large potential market for its services.

By early 2006 Interstrat's infiltration strategy was providing steady growth in sales and profitability from large North American-based corporations and it had established a network of marketing professionals as alliance partners based in the major cities of the USA.

Sources: Interview with Peter Moore, Product Development Manager, Interstrat, by Linden Brown, February 2006; also see Interstrat website, <www.interstrat.net>.

Questions

1 How has Interstrat been able to gain credibility and acceptance in the North American market?

2 How important is the niche approach to the success of Interstrat's growth?

3 How could Interstrat move from being a niche player in the North American market to becoming a major company in this service area?

Another successful company is a web designer, Glass Onion, which has tapped into the growing role that the Internet plays in communicating, transacting and promoting. The success of this operation can be seen from its global client list which includes AMP, Nestlé and Hewlett-Packard (see <www.glassonion.com.au/?flashver=3>, accessed 20 February 2006).[34]

SELF-CHECK QUESTIONS

19 Outline different forms of organisation for international marketing.

20 Illustrate each of the basic competitive strategy profiles using global companies as examples.

SUMMARY

Companies today can no longer afford to pay attention only to their domestic market, no matter how large it is. Many industries are global industries, and those firms that operate globally achieve lower costs and higher brand awareness. At the same time, *global marketing* is risky because of variable exchange rates, unstable governments, protectionist tariffs and trade barriers and several other factors in the global marketing environment. Given the potential gains and risks of international marketing, companies need a systematic way to make their international marketing decisions.

As a first step, a company must understand the *global marketing environment*. It must assess each foreign market's *economic, political–legal and cultural characteristics.* Second, the company must decide whether it wants to go abroad and consider the potential risks and benefits. Third, the company must decide the volume of international sales it wants, how many countries it wants to market in, and which specific markets it wants to enter. This decision calls for weighing the probable rate of return on investment against the level of risk. Fourth, the company must decide how to enter each chosen market—whether through *exporting, joint venturing* or *acquisition.* Many companies start as exporters, move to joint ventures and finally make a direct investment in foreign markets. An important form that is adopted by many companies today includes alliances. SMEs particularly need to develop networks of *strategic* alliances which provide access to technologies, new products and new markets. These alliance arrangements encompass a variety of *strategies* and *relationships.* In response, new organisations are being created to take advantage of those opportunities—'*virtual' organisations* which involve linkages and alliances by companies in pursuit of common objectives and markets.

Companies must decide how much their products, promotion, price and channels should be adapted for each foreign market. The company must also develop an effective organisation for international marketing. Most firms start with an *export department* and graduate to an *international division. A* few become *global organisations,* with worldwide marketing planned and managed by the top officers of the company. Global organisations view the entire world as a single borderless market. Finally, global players must adopt a basic competitive strategy.

The explosion of Internet infrastructure and related potential for online marketing and business is transforming industries, companies and work habits. Many of the steps noted above are being bypassed or modified by Internet startups which are 'born global'. With potential instant access to global markets and the use of technology to enable mass customisation a new breed of global competition is growing rapidly.

MARKETING ISSUE

You are an international marketing manager of an import/export company based in Hong Kong. You trade globally in top-brand merchandise, sourcing products from global manufacturers and selling to retail chains in the USA, Europe, Japan, Southeast Asia and Australia. You are aware of a ruling by the European Court of Justice in Luxembourg in July 1998 outlawing the distribution of upmarket brands to discount chains in Europe without the prior agreement of manufacturers. You are also aware that your main competitor disregards this ruling and sells at a discount in the so-called 'grey' market from its Asian base.

Large British and European discount chains have approached you, being outside the EU, to supply top-brand products to them at a discount without the agreement of manufacturers.

These potential deals would launch your business into the big league and also ensure lucrative business in the USA. Despite its illegality the size of these deals is tempting. What would you do?

KEY TERMS

adapted marketing mix	801	global firm	781	product invention	804
agile corporation	809	global industry	781	standardised marketing mix	801
communication adaptation	804	globalisation	782	straight product extension	804
contract manufacturing	797	joint venturing	796	strategic alliances	797
countertrade	800	licensing	795	virtual corporation	808
exporting	793	product adaptation	804	whole-channel view	806

DISCUSSING THE ISSUES

1 What is the philosophy behind a global strategy? What are the advantages and disadvantages?

2 With all the inhibitors facing companies that 'go global', why are so many companies choosing to expand internationally? What are the advantages of expanding beyond the domestic market?

3 How valid is the step-by-step internationalisation process when some new businesses gain immediate global access through the Internet?

4 Some companies are 'born global'. What are the advantages and disadvantages of operating in a global market in a new business?

5 Consider an industry in which there are a number of niche players and in which alliances seem to be important to success. Describe which alliances are most important for at least one of the niche players and indicate why.

6 How has the Internet assisted Australian-based SMEs to enter overseas markets? Give examples.

REFERENCES

1. Kristen Le Mesurier, 'Global Ambition', *Business Review Weekly*, 16 February–8 March 2006, pp. 58–59; Amanda Gome, 'Mine of its Own', *Business Review Weekly*, 16 February–8 March 2006, p. 41.
2. See Amanda Gome, 'Take-off', *Business Review Weekly*, 16 February–8 March 2006, pp. 31–38.
3. Peter O'Byrne, 'Australia: Doubling SME Exporters', *International Trade Forum*, no. 2, 2002, p. 12.
4. Rob Gray, 'The Borderless World', *Campaign*, 25 October 2002, p. SS8; Kanya Sirisagul, 'Global Advertising Practices: A Comparative Study', *Journal of Global Marketing*, vol. 14, no. 3, 2000, p. 77; Jae H. Pae, 'Global Advertising Strategy: The Moderating Role of Brand Familiarity and Execution Style', *International Marketing Review*, vol. 19, no. 2/3, 2002, p. 176. For more detailed analysis see Greg Myers, 'Ad Worlds: Brands, Media, Audiences', in *Globalisation in Advertising*, Edward Arnold Publishing, 1998, Chapter 4; Rosabeth Moss Kanter, 'Afterword: What Thinking Globally Really Means', in P. Barnevik and R. Moss Kanter (eds), *Global Strategies: Insights from the World's Leading Thinkers*, Boston, MA, Harvard Business School Press, 1994.
5. Ara C. Trembly, 'Aimed at Today's "Road Warrior", Mobile Devices Make Their Debut', *National Underwriter*, Life & health/financial services edition, vol. 107, no. 1, 6 January 2003, p. 21; Eryn Brown, 'Just Another Product Launch', *Fortune*, vol. 144, no. 9, 12 November 2001, p. 102.
6. Ian Fillis, 'Barriers to Internationalisation: An Investigation of the Craft Microenterprise', *European Journal of Marketing*, vol. 36, no. 7/8, 2002, p. 912; Jeryl Whitelock, Viewpoint: 'Theories of Internationalisation and Their Impact on Market Entry', *International Marketing Review*, vol. 19, no. 4/5, 2002, p. 342.
7. M. R. Czinkota and I. A. Ronkainen, *International Marketing: International Edition*, 4th edn, Fort Worth, Dryden Press, 1995, p. 215; Jan Kees Looise, 'Employee Participation in Multinational Enterprises: The Effects of Globalisation on Dutch Works Councils', *Employee Relations*, vol. 24, no. 1/2, 2002, p. 29.
8. Richard Fletcher and Linden Brown, *International Marketing*, 3rd edn, Sydney, Prentice Hall, 2005, Chapter 7.
9. Ian Young, 'Trade Barriers Start to Fall Following WTO Entry', *Chemical Week*, vol. 164, no. 34, 2002, p. 27.
10. See Jacqui Walker, 'Franchises', *Business Review Weekly*, 19–25 January 2006, pp. 32–39; Nicholas Way, 'Fill It Up', *Business Review Weekly*, 19–25 January 2006, pp. 58–59; Jacqui Walker, 'Business Lessons', *Business Review Weekly*, 19–25 January 2006, pp. 54–57.
11. Henry Chesbrough and David Teece, 'Organizing for Innovation: When is Virtual Virtuous?', *Harvard Business Review*, 1 August 2002, at <http://harvardbusinessonline.hbsp.harvard.edu/relay.jhtml?name=itemdetail&id=1210> (originally published in H. W. Chesbrough and D. J. Teece, 'When Is Virtual Virtuous? Organizing for Innovation', *Harvard Business Review*, January–February 1996, pp. 65–73); Kenichi Ohmae, in F. Kodama, 'Technology Fusion and the New R&D', *Harvard Business Review*, July–August 1993, p. 70. Ohmae is a leading business thinker on globalisation; see, for instance, K. Ohmae, *The Borderless World: Power and Strategy in the Interlinked Economy*, London, William Collins, 1990.
12. E. R. Stafford, 'Using Co-operative Strategies to make Alliances Work', *Long Range Planning*, June 1994, Figure 1 and p. 64 referring to independent McKinsey & Co plus Coopers & Lybrand reports.
13. P. Lorange, J. Roos and P. S. Bronn, 'Building Successful Strategic Alliances', *Long Range Planning*, December 1992, p. 15.

14. Gary Hamel, Yves Doz and C. K. Prahlad, 'Collaborate with Your Competitors and Win', in *Harvard Business Review on Strategic Alliances*, Harvard Business School Publishing, 6 January 2003, at <http://harvardbusinessonline.hbsp.harvard.edu/b01/en/common/item_detail.jhtml?id=1334>; K. R. Harrigan, 'Strategic Alliances and Partner Asymmetrics', Strategy Research Centre, Graduate School of Business, Columbia University, New York, Paper Number 54, pp. 30–31.

15. B. Gomes-Cassares, 'Group versus Group: How Alliance Networks Compete', *Harvard Business Review*, July–August 1994, pp. 65–70.

16. C. Handy, 'Trust and the Virtual Organization', *Harvard Business Review*, May–June 1995, pp. 44–48.

17. See Iris Berdrow, 'International Joint Ventures: Creating Value through Successful Knowledge Management', *Journal of World Business*, vol. 38, no. 1, February 2003, p. 15; Christopher A. Bartlett and Sumantra Ghoshal, *Managing Across Borders*, Cambridge, MA, Harvard Business School Press, 1989; Siew Meng Leong and Chin Tiong Tan, 'Managing Across Borders: An Empirical Test of the Bartlett and Ghoshal (1989) Organizational Typology', *Journal of International Business Studies*, 3rd Quarter 1993, pp. 449–464.

18. William Taylor, 'The Logic of Global Business: An Interview with ABB's Percy Barnevik', *Harvard Business Review*, March–April 1991, pp. 91–105. See also Adrian Slywotzky and David Morrison, *The Profit Zone*, New York, Times Business, 1997, pp. 235–251. Also see the 2005 financial success of BHP Billiton reported by Yvonne Ball, 'Miners Leave Investors Spoilt for Choice', *The Weekend Australian Financial Review*, 18–19 February 2006, p. 12.

19. ABB press release, at <www.abb.com/global/abbzh/abbzh251.nsf!OpenDatabase&db=/global/abbzh/abbzh250.nsf&v=553E&e=us&url=/global/seitp/seitp202.nsf/viewUNID/99A2D9D61FFBE79BC1256CDA00598ED8!OpenDocument>, accessed 24 March 2003.

20. J. A. Quelch and E. J. Hoff, 'Customizing Global Marketing', *Harvard Business Review*, May–June 1986; also in Barnevik and Moss Kanter, op. cit., p. 181 (note 6) (adapted).

21. See Warren J. Keegan, *Global Marketing Management*, 5th edn, Englewood Cliffs, NJ, Prentice Hall, 1995, pp. 489–494.

22. See George Yip, 'Global Strategy . . . in a World of Nations?', *Sloan Management Review*, Fall 1989, pp. 29–41; Tim Grogan, 'U.S. Moves to Settle Lumber Rift', *Engineering News-Record*, vol. 250, no. 3, 27 January 2003, p. 10. For another example of dumping allegations see Tim Grogan, 'STEEL: Casualties Are Beginning to Mount', *Engineering News-Record*, vol. 246, no. 25, 25 June 2001, p. 84.

23. See John Byrne and Kathleen Kerwin, 'Borderless Management', *Business Week*, 23 May 1994, pp. 24–26; Leslie Chang and Peter Wonacott, 'Cracking China's Market—Adapting to Chinese Customs, Cultural Changes, Companies from U.S., Europe Find Profit', *Wall Street Journal*, Eastern edition, 9 January 2003, p. B.1,M; Asher Bolande, 'Scaling Up', *Far Eastern Economic Review*, vol. 165, no. 50, 19 December 2002, p. 46.

24. See Kenichi Ohmae, *The End of the Nation State*, London, Harper Collins, 1995.

25. W. H. Davidow and M. S. Malone, *The Virtual Corporation*, New York, HarperCollins, 1992.

26. EIPs: 'The Secret of Agile Corporations', vol 5, no. 2, at <www.syntelinc.com/ezine/02/05/EIP.jsp>, accessed 18 March 2003; K. Priess, S. L. Goldman and R. N. Nagel, *Cooperate to Compete: Building Agile Business Relationships*, New York, Van Nostrand Reinhold, 1996, pp. 158–161.

27. Davidow and Malone, op. cit (note 25).

28. S. L. Goldman, R. N. Nagel and K. Preiss, *Agile Competitors and Virtual Organisations: Strategies for Enriching the Customer*, New York, Van Nostrand Reinhold, 1995, pp. 3–4.

29. This section draws heavily on Linden Brown, *Competitive Marketing*, Melbourne, Nelson, 1997, Chapter 15.

30. J. C. Collins and J. I. Porras, *Built to Last: Successful Habits of Visionary Companies*, New York, Harper Business, 1994.

31. M. Treacy and F. Wiersema, *The Discipline of Market Leaders*, Reading, Addison Wesley, 1995, pp. 31–41.

32. Linden Brown and Hugh Pattinson, 'Information Technology and Telecommunications: Impacts on Strategic Alliance Formation and Management', *Management Decision*, vol. 33, no. 4, 1995, pp. 41–52

33. Andy Boze, 'HotDog Professional 6.2', *Information Technology and Libraries*, vol. 20, no. 1, March 2001, p. 51; Malcolm Surry, 'Cyber Scramble Down Under', *Asian Business*, vol. 35, no. 8, August 1999, p. 46.

34. Judy Hartcher, 'Big Moves from Small Business', *Australian CPA*, vol. 72, no. 10, November 2002, p. 42, company website, <www.bomweb.com/displaypage.asp?PID=6>, accessed 23 March 2003; Gayle Bryant, 'Web's New Role', *Business Review Weekly*, 5–11 December 2002, pp. 72–73.

PHOTO/AD CREDITS

779. GroundProbe Pty Ltd.

Dr Wayne MacArthur, Massey University

CASE STUDY

Creating an export market using a business cluster: the TENZ case

New Zealand exporters have always suffered from size, or more importantly, lack of size. Ninety-six per cent of New Zealand companies are categorised as small to medium businesses (SMEs) with the number of employees being 20 or less. Coupled with a small but highly deregulated local market of 4 000 000 people, many companies need to explore export opportunities if they are ever to achieve any economies of scale. However, as SMEs, many lack the resources of finance and skilled marketing people to make any headway on their own in the global marketplace.

Take the following into consideration. A company needs to find an export market. Generally, an SME with small staffing levels will not have a dedicated marketing manager, and may not even have a sales manager, with these two positions being filled by the founder and owner of the company. In the case of New Zealand, many of the SMEs are involved in niche manufacturing or the supply of services to small niche markets. In both cases the CEO (founder) will be experienced in either area, but in the majority of cases will not have any marketing experience or knowledge, and limited sales experience. Therefore the difficulties encountered in (1) finding an export market, (2) conducting relevant and appropriate market research, (3) visiting the market of a different culture and language and (4) conducting negotiations to provide both business and security for both parties are nearly insurmountable.

If these barriers weren't sufficient to deter an unsophisticated SME from exploring the export markets, then consider the costs associated with export development when most SMEs suffer from restricted capital and financial resources. The greatest failing of any SME when entering the export market is underestimating the true costs involved, and overestimating their chances of success within a particular timeframe.

Realising these difficulties, in the mid-1990s Tradenz (New Zealand government's export agency—now called Trade & Enterprise) sponsored an initiative to assist New Zealand's telecommunication equipment manufacturers which, for the most part, fell squarely into the definition of SMEs. Headed by a senior Tradenz manager, and partially funded by Tradenz, an organisation very similar to a business cluster was formed under the heading of Telecommunication Export of New Zealand (TENZ).

Membership was limited only to CEOs of those New Zealand companies involved in the manufacture of telecommunication products, or companies involved in the supply of telecommunication service, and those consulting in the area. Companies paid an annual fee based upon the number of employees, which gave them access to assistance from Tradenz, and attendance at monthly meeting of the CEOs.

The monthly meetings would cover export opportunities discovered by Tradenz and by the members themselves, from forays into the marketplace. While there was slight competition, most companies had sufficient differentiation within their product range not to compete directly with other members.

An early initiative was a Trade Mission to the southern cone countries of Latin America (Chile, Argentina, Peru and Brazil). Led by the then head of Tradenz, Rick Christie, with regional marketing expertise provided by Wayne MacArthur, representatives from approximately 16 member companies spent three weeks in the region.

The TENZ cluster, with the support of the New Zealand government through Tradenz, regional embassies and trade offices, was able to achieve a number of notable successes normally unavailable to individual exporters. Tradenz was able to organise access to leading political and business leaders in the telecommunications sectors of all countries. The embassies provided their facilities for functions to develop relationships, which is the key to export success.

After the three-week period, a number of companies had returned to New Zealand with signed export orders totalling in excess of $NZ5 000 000, with many other companies returning with requests for quotations, identifiable projects and the groundwork established for long-term relationships.

Digi-Tech Ltd, a New Zealand manufacturer, had reached its market potential in New Zealand and had developed a limited export market to Australia and Singapore. These two export markets would be considered two of the easiest for New Zealand exporters because of English being the common language and the close similarities in the business culture and legal systems.

Based on this success it had been trying to establish an export market in Argentina and Brazil, but because of a locally manufactured product they faced local protectionism in the form of import duties of 24% of the FOB value.

By belonging to TENZ and participating in the trade mission, they were able to meet a local Argentinian company which was manufacturing a similar but non-competitive product. After a short period of time, they were able to establish a joint venture to manufacture 60% of the product in Argentina. This resulted in major benefits for both companies.

First, Digi-Tech paid a much lower rate of duty (approximately 4%) for the raw product they shipped to Argentina, thereby making the finished product much more price competitive in the Argentinian market. Second, under the free trade agreement, MERCOSUR—the finished product—was also exported from Argentina to the much larger market in Brazil, duty free. And third, as the finished product was also going to be exported to other markets in Latin America, the Argentinian joint venture partner was able to access government export grants and credits only available to local exporters.

So Digi-Tech Ltd benefited from duty-free access to both Argentina and Brazil, and also by being considered a 'locally made' product they had preferential access to government tenders. The Argentinian partner benefited from having a sophisticated product to add to its range and enjoying tax benefits from the subsequent exports.

Some flow-on effects of the cluster were also evident; Digi-Tech engineers were visiting an overseas market to install some equipment for the National Security Service of the country. While on-site, they were able to diagnose a problem in the installation of equipment, provided by two other New Zealand companies, and rectify it, saving considerable cost (and some embarrassment) to the two other companies. The longer-term benefit of this action was to establish the reputation of New Zealand telecommunication companies as being reliable and supportive.

TENZ provided the necessary resources of market knowledge, contacts and relationships, and the relative cultural expertise to assist Digi-Tech greatly. Digi-Tech were able to grow their business through their association with TENZ and eventually use the knowledge gained to be far more effective in their future export development.

While the success of such a cluster as TENZ was easily recognisable, it failed to build on the early framework it had established. While most member companies continued to support TENZ, they also conducted their own export development outside the frameworks and kept this information to themselves.

So while the basis behind TENZ had great merit, and some successes were evident, for a number of reasons the cluster failed to gain major momentum. After some years, the sharing of marketplace intelligence declined, membership declined and Tradenz quietly withdrew their support, and today TENZ no longer exists.

QUESTIONS

1. What are three major problems encountered in business clusters?

2. What are three major benefits of belonging to a business cluster?

3. How would you determine an equitable structure for funding the cluster?

4. What would you have done to ensure the long-term success of TENZ?

5. Is a business cluster a good idea?

CHAPTER 21

Responsible marketing

What is a 'responsible' marketing organisation? A search of the *Oxford English Dictionary* indicates that a responsible organisation is 'accountable' . . . but to whom or to what is left unstated, and it is we who must fill in the gaps with regard to responsibility in general and marketing responsibility in particular. A global Google search on 'responsible marketing' brings up the use of such words by organisations like PhillipMorrisUSA, <http://www.philipmorrisusa.com/en/responsible_marketing/default.asp> and Foster Group Limited's Alcohol in the Community Policy incorporating Responsible Marketing Guidelines, <http://www.fosters.com.au/about/docs/Fosters_Community_Responsible_Marketing.pdf>. Arguably, these organisations have a vested interest in using this term, and their commentary does not help our quest.

We do know that responsible marketing organisations aim to meet social needs which include those of employees and customers. The triple bottom line paradigm that many organisations espouse is aimed at ensuring that organisations keep a weather eye on their social and environmental bottom line, in addition to the more traditional financial bottom line. Whether this is merely rhetoric depends largely on how faithfully management follow such guidelines, just as good governance depends on how ethically managers behave. Assigning a dollar value to environmental and social outcomes can be controversial and, as with statistics in general, can be made to argue many different points.

In the wired world we now inhabit, organisations have many new incentives to act as good 'corporate citizens' (to use another popular term in the triple bottom line vernacular). Crikey.com.au is one website that very early in the piece allowed us to peek behind the corporate veil, particularly in light of the boardroom decisions by some that might not be considered to be good corporate citizens. Crikey has now extended its activities to include exposés of the many levels of government in Australia. The site is highly entertaining, if nothing else. Arguably, this corporate watchdog site relies on organisational whistleblowers for some of its juiciest information. In a similar vein, Notgoodenough.org.au sets out to enable customers to gripe about poor purchases and alerts organisations (for a fee) to the negative word-of-mouth about the company or brand that is gaththering pace on electronic networks.

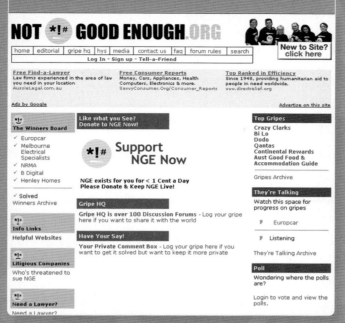

Blogs now exist for many topics, allowing people to interact on their favourite topics.

Into the increasingly publicity savvy digital world have come two new entrants which seem to have captured the hearts and minds of many, particularly those who want to spread negative publicity concerning recalcitrant organisations. Wikis and Blogs have entered the picture, particularly for younger Generation Y sceptics. Wiki is Hawaiian for 'quick', and Wiki sites like Corpknowpedia.org live up to their name by allowing information to spread very quickly indeed. As one wit noted, 'bad news can travel around the world in the time it takes good news to cross the street', and Wiki sites enable news to spread like a viral contagion simply by allowing one commentator after another to add their views to a theme. Blogs—weblogs—are similar but different. Blogs are more like an electronic diary, and take various forms. One form might enable people to communicate love for their pets. Another might take the form of a doctoral undertaking, as was Dr Simon Pockley's 'The Flight of Ducks'. A more prominent form of blogging involves bringing the scurrilous internal and external activities of companies to the attention of society in general, and often to the attention of the media.

Sony BMG is one company that has suffered at the hands of a blogger. It might also be argued that the company suffered more at the hands of its decision making, and that the computer wizard Mark Russinovich merely communicated this information to the world at large. Sony had quietly introduced a digital rights management system (DRM) onto music CDs that employed hidden files which could not be uninstalled, and if removed might bring a computer to a stop. One argument was that in trying to deal with illegal breaches of copy protection, Sony BMG had itself acted illegally. Why this information travelled so quickly is largely due to the fact that the BBC and television programs such as *USA Today* picked up on the Blog storyline and took the message to a wider audience.

The 'blogosphere' has taken a hold of the imaginations of many, but as yet organisations have been slow to set up their own 'official' Blogs. When you think about it, an official Blog site for employees might act as a safety valve, just as an official site for customers enables a community to communicate with each other and in many cases this allows misconceptions and other issues to be quickly aired and deactivated. Some act as an unofficial, and inexpensive, helpdesk. Universities have long used Blackboard and WebCT software to enable students to air their gripes and in the process other students are often able to sort out the difficulties being experienced, or to take the heat out of a debate. eBay allows buyers and sellers to remain anonymous and communicate with each other and for each to rate the other in a public display of trust. Yahoo! groups is used for open communication by many companies as it enables interaction by like-minded individuals. The aim in each case is for the organisation to illustrate that it is responsible, regardless of the differences in how this strategy is implemented.[1]

After reading this chapter you should be able to:

1. Discuss social criticisms of marketing's impact on individual consumers.

2. Identify and define criticisms of marketing's impact on society as a whole.

3. Outline citizen and public actions to regulate marketing—consumerism, environmentalism and regulation—and the way they affect marketing strategies.

4. Explain responsible marketing and how ethical behaviour involves implementing various enlightened marketing philosophies.

5. List and define the key principles for public policy towards marketing.

6. Discuss the need for legal compliance programs in marketing and the issues involved in implementing them.

This chapter discusses the need for responsible marketing, and in the process examines social and ethical issues that arise in the science and practice of marketing. Additionally, we examine marketing law from the viewpoint of the corporate commitment that is necessary if legal compliance programs are to be implemented and maintained. We examine the social and ethical issues by way of answers to the following questions: What are the most frequently raised social issues in marketing? What steps have private and corporate citizens taken to remedy marketing ills? What steps have legislators and government agencies taken to remedy marketing ills? What steps have responsible organisations taken to ensure they remain socially responsive and ethical in their marketing? How can marketing organisations introduce effective legal compliance programs? We examine how marketing management affects these issues and how marketing itself is affected by each of these issues.

Social and ethical issues in marketing

A variety of social and ethical issues arise from marketing practice and emerge as areas of attention for marketing scientists. These matters generate considerable criticism of marketing practice, some of which is justified but much of which is not.[2] The underlying concern is whether certain marketing practices hurt individual consumers, society as a whole or other business firms (see Marketing Highlight 21.1, for example).

Marketing's impact on individual consumers

Consumers have many concerns about how well marketing systems serve their interests. Studies usually show that consumers hold mixed or even slightly unfavourable attitudes toward marketing practices.[3] One consumer survey found that consumers are worried about high prices, poor-quality and dangerous products, misleading advertising claims and several other marketing-related problems (see Figure 21.1). Consumer advocates, government agencies and other critics have accused marketing of harming consumers through high prices, deceptive practices, high-pressure selling, shoddy or unsafe products, planned obsolescence and poor service to disadvantaged consumers.

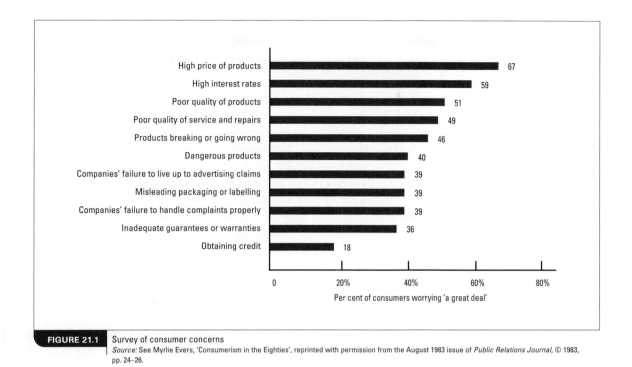

FIGURE 21.1 Survey of consumer concerns

Source: See Myrlie Evers, 'Consumerism in the Eighties', reprinted with permission from the August 1983 issue of *Public Relations Journal,* © 1983, pp. 24–26.

High prices

Many critics charge that marketing systems cause prices to be higher than they would be under more 'sensible' systems. They point to three factors—*high costs of distribution, high advertising and promotion costs* and *excessive gross profit margins.*

High costs of distribution A longstanding charge is that greedy intermediaries mark up prices beyond the value of their services. Critics claim that there are too many intermediaries or that they are inefficient and poorly run, that they provide unnecessary or duplicate services, and that they practise poor management and planning. As a result, distribution costs too much, and consumers pay for these excessive costs in the form of higher prices.

Large retailers would argue differently, citing their growth in market share and removal of the less efficient smaller store from the marketplace as evidence of their increasing efficiency. They would also argue that their gross margins are small—1.5% profit on sales—and that competition keeps prices low. And after all, if the retailer did not distribute products, manufacturers would have to do so, and they would be much less efficient.

High advertising and promotion costs Modern marketing is also accused of pushing up prices to cover the costs of heavy advertising and sales promotion. For example, a dozen tablets of a heavily promoted brand of aspirin sell for the same price as 100 tablets of less promoted brands. Differentiated products—cosmetics, detergents, toiletries—include promotion and packaging costs that may amount to 40% or more of the manufacturer's price to the retailer. Critics charge that much of the packaging and promotion adds only psychological value to the product rather than functional value. Retailers use additional promotion—advertising, displays and sales promotions—that adds several cents more to retail prices. Even though most of these monies are paid by the manufacturer, they in turn are reflected in the prices we pay.

MARKETING HIGHLIGHT 21.1

Does more fun in marketing mean questionable ethics?

Many marketing practitioners, even a few marketing scientists, argue that marketing campaigns should be fun. Viewers and readers should enjoy the pizzazz created by vendors selling their wares. However, some sellers go beyond what the audience expects— not by totally satisfying them, but rather by trying to catch their attention in novel ways. As more than one advertising agency supremo has put it: 'It doesn't matter what you say . . . It's how you say it!' Another more sceptical adman went further and stated: 'if you really have nothing to say . . . sing it!'.

Those of you who are avid Internet users will have noticed that one cannot help but trip over pornography on the Web, and how the purveyors of porn are very adept at using technology to present pop-up after pop-up promising more and more risqué delights. No matter how many times one closes the web browser to try and escape their electronic clutches, another window appears in its place. Or perhaps your Internet service provider is lax and allows email from the junk-mail jockeys to flood into your life, thereby ignoring Australia's *Spam Act 2003* and leaving themselves open to litigation. If you have not experienced this first hand, then you have read or listened to the complaints and cries concerning the descent of humanity into moral turpitude. And, of course, it is all the fault of marketing and advertising practitioners out for a quick degrading buck—or so writers of letters to the editor and those voicing their opinions on call-back radio would have it.

Post-modern marketing evangelist Stephen Brown makes some very telling points about the origins of marketing practice (if not the science itself), which he lays at the dirty feet of the many marketing shysters who have appeared throughout economic history. In an examination of present-day marketing, he points to a 'typology of tastelessness' and elaborates on the 4Cs of malodorous marketing, of which pornography dressed up as fashion is but one titivating example. Perhaps these blatant attempts at using pornography to sell are examples of unethical behaviour by advertising and marketing practitioners, and perhaps they are a reaction to the fact that those who have grown up with television programs like *Survivor* and *Big Brother* are blasé about porn?

Leaving porn to one side, it must also be noted that there are many other suggestions put forward by earnest marketing consultants and writers which are not quite so visibly unethical, or morally disturbing, but which nevertheless raise the ire of consumer protection agencies. Selling under the guise of conducting marketing research is one practice that not only flies in the face of codes of practice by marketing research associations (e.g. ESOMAR, Marketing Research Societies in Australia and New Zealand), and direct marketing associations such as the Australian Direct Marketing Association (ADMA), but can be illegal under most circumstances. Breaching people's privacy is another.

Other issues may arise such as a failure by company employees to act responsibly. When companies decide to allow pricing decisions to be made too far out in the field, or down the line there have been cases of collusion between competitors. We might reasonably expect companies to be actively engaged in legal compliance programs and thereby ensure that all employees understand the various activities that they must not engage in as they are tantamount to anti-competitive behaviour.

Big Brother—does it desensitise its audience to pornography and unethical behaviour?

The fact is that many companies do not run such programs, or, if they do, run them in a half-hearted fashion, or let employee education slip in times of economic downturn. In such circumstances, salespeople can unwittingly find themselves in pricing discussions with their counterparts from other companies. They should know what to do to terminate such a discussion effectively. Moreover, the company leaves itself exposed to heavier fines because it has not sought to protect itself.

No wonder then that marketing organisations find their company and brand names dishonourably mentioned in the news media, their corporate reputations in tatters and their market value destroyed. Marketing practitioners know that ignorance under the law is no defence. They also need to know more about what is considered ethical behaviour and legal compliance, and then act responsibly.

Sources: For more on post-modernist marketing see Stephen Brown, 'Torment Your Customers (They'll Love It)', *Harvard Business Review*, October 2001, pp. 82–88, reprinted as Stephen Brown, 'Treat 'em Mean', *Business Review Weekly*, 10–16 January 2002, pp. 64–67, which draw from Stephen Brown, *Marketing—The Retro Revolution*, London, Sage Publications, 2001; and also see the following professional marketing websites: The World Association of Opinion and Marketing Research Professionals (ESOMAR), <www.esomar. org>; Social and Marketing Research Society of Australia (SMRSA), <www. mrsa.com.au>; Marketing Research Society of New Zealand, <www.mrsnz. org.nz> and the Australian Direct Marketing Association (ADMA), <www. adma.com.au>.

Questions

1 Does marketing management need to inject more fun into its activities?

2 Does more fun in marketing necessarily lead to ethically questionable activities?

3 Can organisations be held responsible for the questionable activities of their employees?

21.1

Marketers answer these charges in several ways. First, consumers *want* more than the merely functional qualities of products. They also want psychological benefits—they want to feel wealthy, beautiful or special. Consumers can usually buy functional versions of products at lower prices but often are willing to pay more for products that also provide desired psychological benefits. A brand can be the means by which consumers have a relationship with a product category. Second, branding gives buyers confidence. A brand name implies a certain quality, and consumers are willing to pay for well-known brands even if they cost a little more. Third, heavy advertising is needed to inform millions of potential buyers of the merits of a brand. If consumers want to know what is available on the market, they must expect manufacturers to spend large sums of money on advertising or gaining a highly prized place in the Google search rankings. Fourth, heavy advertising and promotion might be necessary for a firm to match competitors' efforts. Finally, heavy sales promotion is needed from time to time because goods are produced ahead of demand in a mass-production economy despite every effort to apply just-in-time processes. Usually, special incentives must be offered in order to synchronise the making and selling of products and thus ensure minimal inventories and holding costs. While finished goods inventories are not involved in the case of services, there is still the need to synchronise demand with service availability as is the case when consumers are prompted to contact a call centre, either to place an order or to report a service delivery issue.

Excessive middlemen gross profit margins Critics also argue that some companies take excessive gross profit margins—the difference between their buying and selling prices expressed as a percentage of their selling price. They point to the pharmaceutical industry, where a pill costing 5 cents to make might cost the consumer between 40 and 90 cents to buy. They point to the pricing tactics of funeral homes that prey on the emotions of bereaved relatives and to the high charges for Pay-TV, Internet services and car repairs.

Marketers respond that most businesses try to deal fairly with consumers because they want repeat business. Most consumer abuses are unintentional. When shady marketers do take advantage of consumers, they should be reported via an inexpensive method such as the small claims courts tribunals to state agencies such as the Office of Fair Trading, or to federal agencies such as the Australian Competition and Consumer Commission (ACCC). Marketers also respond that consumers often do not understand the reason for high gross margins. For example, pharmaceutical marketing organisations might well argue that their gross margins need to cover the costs of purchasing, promoting and distributing existing medicines plus the high research and development costs of finding and developing new medicines, or paying licence fees where another company has done the development and owns the intellectual property in the drug or equipment.

Deceptive practices

Marketers are sometimes accused of deceptive practices that lead consumers to believe they will get more value than they actually do. Deceptive practices fall into three major groups: deceptive pricing, deceptive promotion and deceptive packaging. *Deceptive pricing* includes practices such as falsely advertising 'factory' or 'wholesale' prices or a large price reduction from a bogus high retail list price. *Deceptive promotion* includes practices such as overstating the product's features or performance, luring the customer to the store for a bargain that is out of stock, or running rigged contests. *Deceptive packaging* includes exaggerating package contents through subtle design, not filling the package to the top, using misleading labelling, describing size in misleading terms or misleading consumers as to the country of origin of the product.

Deceptive practices have led to legislation and other consumer-protection reforms. In Australia, the *Trade Practices Act 1974* gave federal legislators the power to regulate 'unfair or deceptive acts or practices'. The Trade Practices Act is administered by the ACCC, which publishes several guidelines listing deceptive practices. It is often a tough problem to define what is 'deceptive'. The Trade Practices Act has been modified a number of times, and has been extended to the states of Australia through the Fair Trading Acts.

Marketers argue that most companies avoid deceptive practices because such practices harm their business in the long run. They may state that they know that if consumers do not get what they expect they will switch to more reliable products. They may argue that, in any event, consumers usually protect themselves from deception.[4]

High-pressure selling

Salespeople are sometimes accused of high-pressure selling that persuades people to buy goods they had not thought of buying. It is often said that encyclopaedias, insurance, real estate, cars and jewellery are *sold*, not *bought*. Salespeople are trained to deliver smooth, well-rehearsed presentations to entice purchase. They sell hard because sales contests promise big prizes to those who sell the most. This latter aspect varies by country. For example, Australian sales representatives in the pharmaceutical industry are paid higher salaries as a proportion of their total remuneration than their North American counterparts. However, the North American salesperson receives higher commissions and higher total remuneration. This even extends to bonuses for high achievement in sales training programs. Arguably, this produces higher pressure to sell—both on the salesperson and in turn by the salesperson.

Marketers know that buyers can often be talked into buying unwanted or unneeded things. Laws require door-to-door salespeople to announce that they are selling a product. Buyers also have a 'cooling-off period' in which they can cancel a contract after rethinking it. In addition, consumers can complain to state and federal consumer protection agencies if they feel that undue selling pressure has been applied, or pursue a variety of other legal remedies, for example in small claims courts or tribunals.

Unsafe products

Another criticism is that products lack the quality they should have. One complaint is that many products are not made well or that services are not performed well. Such complaints have been lodged against goods manufacturers and services ranging from home appliances, motor cars and clothing to home and car repair services, and including utilities such as telecommunications and energy.

A second complaint is that many products deliver little benefit. For example, some consumers are surprised to learn that many of the 'healthy' foods being marketed today, ranging from cholesterol-free salad dressings and low-fat frozen dinners to high-fibre bran cereals, may have little nutritional value. In fact, some of these products may even be harmful.[5]

A third complaint concerns product safety. Product safety has been a problem for several reasons, including manufacturer indifference, increased production complexity, poorly trained labour and poor quality control. However, most manufacturers *want* to produce quality goods. Companies selling poor-quality or unsafe products risk damaging conflicts with consumer groups and regulators, and in the end disillusion shareholders and rating agencies—the former reducing access to capital, and the latter increasing the cost of servicing loans. Moreover, unsafe products can result in product liability suits and large awards for damages. More fundamentally, consumers who are unhappy with a firm's products will avoid future purchases and, because of Internet access, can easily talk other consumers into doing the same. Today's marketers know that customer-driven quality results in customer satisfaction, which in turn creates profitable customer relationships.

Planned obsolescence

A further criticism is that some producers follow a program of planned obsolescence, causing their products to become obsolete before they should actually need replacement. For example, critics contend that some producers continually change consumer concepts of acceptable styles to encourage more and earlier buying. An obvious example is the constantly changing clothing fashions. Other producers are accused of holding back attractive functional features, then introducing them later to make older models obsolete. Critics claim that this occurs in the consumer electronics and computer industries. Still other producers are accused of using materials and components that will break, wear, rust or rot sooner than they should.

Marketers respond that consumers *like* style changes; they get tired of the old goods and want a new look in fashion or a new design in cars. Companies frequently withhold new features when they are not fully tested, when they add more cost to the product than consumers are willing to pay, and for other good reasons. But they do so at the risk of a competitor introducing the new feature and stealing the market. Moreover, companies often put in new materials to lower their costs and prices. They do not design their products to break down earlier, because they do

People buying special interest magazines rarely complain because their interests are usually met.

not want to lose customers to other brands. Instead, they implement total quality programs to ensure that products will consistently meet or exceed customer expectations. Thus, much of so-called planned obsolescence is the working of the competitive and technological forces in a free society—forces that lead to ever-improving goods and services.

Marketing's impact on society as a whole

The marketing system has been accused of adding to several 'evils' in society at large. Advertising has been a special target—so much so that the American Association of Advertising Agencies launched a campaign to defend advertising against what it felt to be common but untrue criticisms. From time to time such campaigns have been embarked on by counterpart organisations in other countries. The Federation of Commercial Television Stations (FACTS) in Australia has undertaken a similar promotional campaign.

False wants and too much materialism

Social commentators have charged that the marketing system urges too much interest in material possessions. People are judged by what they *own* rather than by who they *are*. To be considered successful, people must own a large home, two cars and the latest consumer electronics. This drive for wealth and possessions hit new highs in the 1980s, when phrases such as 'greed is good' and 'shop till you drop' seemed to characterise the times. The movie *Rosalie Goes Shopping* illustrated—in a somewhat exaggerated way—how family life can become dominated by a never-ending desire to buy (and on credit).[6] In the 1990s, although many social scientists have noted a reaction against the opulence and waste of the 1980s and a return to more basic values and social commitment, our infatuation with material things continues. For example, when asked in a recent poll what they value most in their lives, subjects listed enjoyable work (86%), happy children (84%), a good marriage (69%) and contributions to society (66%). However, when asked what most symbolises success, 85% said money and the things it will buy.[7] Since the terrorist activities in the USA in 2001, and the Bali bombings in 2002 and 2005, safety needs would no doubt rank more highly than in previous years.

Analogies may be drawn between how households have run down savings to 'keep up with the Joneses' and take up new technologies in the 1990s and similar behaviour in the 1920s immediately prior to the Great Depression.[8] In Australia this meant 'between 1992 and 2001, the ratio of gross household debt to household discretionary income rose from 90% to 148%'.[9] Another alarming indicator in this regard is the inequality in the distribution of wealth such that in the USA 1% of households hold 39% of the nation's wealth, and thereby receive as much after-tax income as the combined incomes of the lowest earning 100 million households.[10] The situation is little different in the UK and in Australia and New Zealand.

Too few social goods

Business has been accused of overselling private goods at the expense of public goods. As private goods increase, they require more public services that are usually not forthcoming. For example, an increase in car ownership (private good) requires more highways, traffic control, parking spaces and police services (public goods). The overselling of private goods results in 'social costs'. For cars and trucks, the social costs include traffic congestion, air pollution and deaths and injuries from motor vehicle accidents. One option is to make consumers pay the social costs. For example, in countries such as France, the UK, Norway, Singapore and some parts of the USA varying tolls apply, with premiums being charged where drivers travel in underused car pool lanes, and drivers have to pay tolls to use central business district roads.[11]

The idea is that if the costs of driving are high enough, consumers will travel at non-peak times or use public transport.

Cultural pollution

Critics accuse the marketing system of creating cultural pollution. Our senses are being assaulted constantly by advertising. Commercials interrupt serious programs; pages of ads obscure printed matter; billboards mar beautiful scenery; Java and Flash generated hypermedia advertisements (banner ads and interstititals) mar the educational qualities of the Internet (WWW). These interruptions pollute people's minds with messages of materialism, sex, power or status. Although most people do not find advertising overly annoying (some even think it is the best part of television programming), some critics call for sweeping changes.

Marketers answer the charges of 'commercial noise' with these arguments. First, they hope that their ads reach primarily the target audience. But because of mass communication channels, some ads are bound to reach people who have no interest in the product and are therefore bored or annoyed. People who buy magazines addressed to their interests—such as *Vogue* or *Fortune*—rarely complain about the ads because the magazines advertise products of interest. Second, ads make much of television and radio free-to-air media and keep down the costs of magazines and newspapers. Many people think commercials are a small price to pay for these benefits.

Too much political power

Another criticism is that business wields too much political power. 'Oil', 'tobacco', 'car' and 'pharmaceutical' interest groups lobby politicians to support an industry's interests against the public interest. Advertisers are accused of holding too much power over the mass media, limiting their freedom to report independently and objectively. One critic has asked: 'How can *Life* . . . and *Reader's Digest* afford to tell the truth about the scandalously low nutritional value of most packaged foods . . . when these magazines are being subsidised by such advertisers as Kellogg's, Nabisco and others? . . . The answer is *they cannot and do not.*'[12]

All industries promote and protect their interests. They have a right to representation in government and the mass media, although their influence can become too great. Fortunately, many powerful business interests once thought to be untouchable have been tamed in the public interest. Moreover, because the media receive advertising revenues from many different advertisers, it is easier to resist the influence of one or a few of them. Too much business power tends to result in counter-forces that check and offset these powerful interests.

Marketing's impact on other businesses

Critics also charge that an organisation's marketing practices can harm other companies and reduce competition. Three major problems are involved: acquisition of competitors, marketing practices that create barriers to entry, and unfair competitive marketing practices.

Critics claim that firms are harmed and competition reduced when companies expand by acquiring competitors rather than by developing their own new products. In the food industry alone during the past decade, R. J. Reynolds acquired Nabisco brands; Philip Morris bought General Foods and Kraft; Procter & Gamble gobbled up Richardson-Vicks, Noxell and parts of Revlon; Nestlé absorbed Carnation globally and in Australia took most of the food industry assets held by Pacific Dunlop; and Unilever acquired Brooke Bond. These and other large acquisitions in other industries have caused concern that vigorous young competitors will be absorbed and competition will be reduced.

Acquisition is a complex subject. Acquisitions can sometimes be good for society. The acquiring marketing organisation might gain economies of scale that lead to lower costs, lower prices and greater

Private public partnerships (PPPs) in energy have not always led to the promised returns.

international competitiveness. A well-managed marketing organisation might take over a poorly managed marketing organisation and improve its efficiency. An industry that was not very competitive might become more competitive after the acquisition. But acquisitions can also be harmful, and are therefore closely regulated by the government.

Critics have also charged that marketing practices bar new companies from entering an industry. Large marketing companies can use patents and heavy promotion spending, and can tie up suppliers or dealers to keep out or drive out competitors. People concerned with anti-monopoly regulation recognise that some barriers are the natural result of the economic advantages of doing business on a large scale. Other barriers could be challenged by existing and new laws. For example, some critics have proposed a progressive tax on advertising spending to reduce the role of selling costs as a major barrier to entry.

Yet other critics have attacked decisions to create greater competition in such areas as energy production and distribution, where public utilities have tended to dominate the scene. In the mid-1990s the Australian state of Victoria was one of the first governments to pass public debt to the private sector when it created six distribution firms and two power generation companies from what had previously been a large public utility. North American energy providers such as Entergy were notable investors in newly privatised Australian 'retailers' such as CitiPower until the promised returns from such private public partnerships (PPPs) failed to materialise. Such PPPs have occurred in energy, communications, mass transit, housing, water resources and in education and health services in countries as diverse as Australia, New Zealand, Thailand and the UK. Critics of privatisation claim that such moves did not lead to lower energy prices for consumers in Britain, or lower energy costs in Victoria, or lower road user costs in Sydney, and that the opposite effect is often quite likely. The passing of time and the later withdrawal of many of the early investors from these areas due to a lack of profitability seem to show that the initial lower prices are not sustainable. For example, lower prices offered by private operators in public transport may lead to government subsidisation and a burden on all taxpayers, and not just the users.[13]

Finally, some firms have in fact used unfair competitive marketing practices with the intention of hurting or destroying other firms. They might set their prices below costs, threaten to cut off business with suppliers or discourage the buying of a competitor's products. Various laws work to prevent such predatory competition. It is difficult, however, to prove that the intent or action was really predatory. For example, Virgin Blue has often accused Qantas of uncompetitive activity by making an abundance of seats available on new routes taken up by Virgin Blue. Such accusations raise the question as to whether or not the market leader—with some 80% of the domestic Australian market immediately after the demise of Ansett—was engaging in unfair competition or merely providing healthy competition as a result of its more efficient marketing systems.

SELF-CHECK QUESTIONS

1   'Too many commercials for household products such as dishwashing liquids show happy women in gleaming new kitchens and bathrooms, caring for other members of the household unit.' Discuss this statement. Is it correct? If so, is it false and misleading to promote in this manner? What other issues are involved?

2   If cigarettes are such a harmful product, why are bans limited to their advertising, rather than their use? Is it simply a case of powerful industry groups winning over health experts when lobbying politicians?

Private and public actions to regulate marketing

Because some people view business as the cause of many economic and social ills, grassroots movements have arisen from time to time to keep business in line. The two major movements have been *consumerism* and *environmentalism.*

Consumerism

Business firms have been the target of organised consumer movements since the 1960s. Consumers have become better educated, products have become more complex and hazardous, and marketing organisations have raised consumers' expectations as they seek to gain sustainable competitive advantage. In the USA, Ralph Nader forced many issues, and other well-known writers have accused big business of wasteful and unethical practices. Since then, many consumer groups have been organised, politicians lobbied and consumer laws passed. The consumer movement has spread internationally and has become very strong in Europe.[14]

But what is the consumer movement? **Consumerism** is an organised movement of citizens and government agencies to improve the rights and power of buyers in relation to sellers. Traditional sellers' rights include:

Consumerism An organised movement of consumers whose aim is to improve the rights and power of buyers in relation to sellers.

- The right to introduce any product in any size and style, provided it is not hazardous to personal health or safety; or, if it is, to include proper warnings and controls.
- The right to charge any price for the product, provided no discrimination exists between similar kinds of buyers.
- The right to spend any amount to promote the product, provided it is not defined as unfair competition.
- The right to use any product message, provided it is not misleading or dishonest in content or execution.
- The right to use any buying incentive schemes, provided they are not unfair or misleading.

Traditional buyers' rights include:

- The right not to buy a product that is offered for sale.
- The right to expect the product to be safe.
- The right to expect the product to perform as claimed.

Comparing these rights, many believe that the balance of power lies on the sellers' side. True, the buyer can refuse to buy. But critics feel that the buyer has too little information, education and protection to make wise decisions when facing sophisticated sellers. Consumer advocates call for the following additional consumer rights:

- The right to be well informed about important aspects of the product.
- The right to be protected against questionable products and marketing practices.
- The right to influence products and marketing practices in ways that will improve the 'quality of life'.

Each proposed right has led to more specific proposals by consumerists. The right to be informed includes the right to know the true interest on a loan (consumer credit code), the true cost per unit of a brand (unit pricing), the ingredients in a product (ingredient labelling), the nutrition in foods (nutritional labelling), product freshness (use-by dating) and the true benefits of a product (truth in advertising). Proposals related to consumer protection include strengthening consumer rights in cases of business fraud, requiring greater product safety and giving more power to government agencies to establish and enforce minimum standards of commercial conduct. Proposals relating to quality of life include controlling the ingredients that go into certain products (detergents have become more eco-friendly) and packaging (soft drink and fast-food containers have become recyclable and less of an environmental irritant), reducing the level of advertising 'noise', putting consumer representatives on marketing organisation boards to protect consumer interests and giving consumers more forms of legal redress.

Consumers have not only the *right* but also the *responsibility* to protect themselves instead of leaving this function to someone else. Consumers who believe they got a bad deal have several remedies available, including writing to the marketing organisation president or to the media, contacting federal, state or local agencies and going to small claims tribunals.

Environmentalism

While consumerists consider whether the marketing system is efficiently serving consumer wants, needs and demands, environmentalists are concerned with marketing's effects on the environment and with the costs of serving consumers. They are concerned with damage to the ecosystem caused by strip mining, forest depletion, acid rain, loss of the atmosphere's ozone layer, toxic wastes and litter. They are also concerned about the loss of recreational areas and about the increase in health problems caused by bad air, polluted water and chemically treated food. These concerns are the basis for **environmentalism**—an organised movement of concerned citizens, businesses and government agencies seeking to protect and improve people's living environment.

Environmentalists are not necessarily against marketing and consumption; they simply want people and organisations to operate with more care for the environment and thus achieve 'sustainable development'. The marketing system's goal should not be to maximise consumption, consumer choice or consumer satisfaction, but rather to maximise quality of life. Moreover, 'quality of life' means not only the quantity and quality of consumer goods and services, but also the quality of the environment. Environmentalists want environmental costs included in both producer and consumer decision making.

Environmentalism has hit some industries hard. Steel companies and public utilities have had to invest billions of dollars in pollution control equipment and costlier fuels. The motor vehicle industry has had to introduce expensive emission controls in cars. The packaging industry has had to find ways to reduce litter. The petroleum industry has had to create unleaded petrol and reduced-lead petrol for older cars. Industries often resent environmental regulations, especially when they are imposed too rapidly to allow companies to make proper adjustments. These companies have absorbed large costs and have passed them on to buyers.

Thus, marketers' lives have become more complicated. Marketers must monitor the ecological properties of their products and packaging. They must raise prices to cover environmental costs, knowing that the product will be harder to sell. Yet environmental issues have become so important in our society that there is no turning back to the time when few managers worried about the effects of product and marketing decisions on environmental quality. The 1990s might be thought of as the 'Earth Decade', in which protection of the natural environment became the major issue facing people around the world. Companies have responded with 'green marketing'—developing ecologically safer products, recyclable and biodegradable packaging, better pollution controls and more energy-efficient operations (see Marketing Highlight 21.2).

Environmentalism creates some special challenges for global marketers. As international trade barriers come down and global markets expand, environmental issues are having an ever greater impact on international trade. Countries in North America, Western Europe, the Pacific Rim and other regions have developed stringent environmental standards. In the USA, for example, more than two dozen major pieces of environmental legislation have been enacted since 1970, and recent events suggest that more regulation is on the way. A side accord to the North America Free Trade Agreement

Environmentalism
An organised movement of concerned citizens, businesses and government seeking to protect and improve people's living environment.

(NAFTA) set up a commission for resolving environmental matters. And the European Union's Eco-Management and Audit Regulation provides guidelines for environmental self-regulation.[15]

However, environmental policies still vary widely from country to country, and uniform worldwide standards are not expected for another 15 years or more.[16] Although countries such as Australia, Denmark, Germany, Japan, New Zealand and the USA have developed environmental policies and high public expectations, countries such as China, India, Brazil and Russia are in only the early stages of developing such policies. The Kyoto accord is one environmental policy which by early 2006 was still not agreed to by the USA and Australia; however, European countries endorse the move to reduce the levels of 'greenhouse gases'. The accord was agreed in Kyoto, Japan, in 1997, and 'targets carbon-rich gases—mainly the by-product of burning oil, gas and coal—that some scientists believe could catastrophically change weather patterns'.[17] The accord 'commits 38 industrialised countries to an overall cut of 5.2% of these "greenhouse gases" by 2010, compared with their 1990 levels'.[18] Thus it seems that environmental factors that motivate consumers in one country might have no impact on consumers in another. For example, PVC soft drink bottles cannot be used in Switzerland or Germany. However, they are preferred in France, which has an extensive recycling process for them. Thus, international companies are finding it difficult to develop standard environmental practices that work around the world. Instead, they are creating general policies, and then translating these policies into tailored programs that meet local regulations and expectations.

Public actions to regulate marketing

Community concerns about marketing practices usually lead to public attention and legislative proposals. New pieces of legislation will be proposed and debated—many will be defeated, others will be modified and a few will become workable laws.

Some of the laws that affect marketing were listed in Chapter 5. The task is to translate these laws into a *language* that marketing executives understand as they make decisions about competitive relations, products, price, promotion and channels of distribution. Figure 21.2 (overleaf) illustrates the major legal issues facing marketing management. We examine the matter of legal compliance programs later in this chapter.

SELF-CHECK QUESTIONS

3 Consider the rights of buyers and sellers outlined in this section. Do you believe that the balance of power lies with sellers or buyers? Why?

4 If you believe there to be an imbalance in the power of sellers and buyers, should market forces redress the imbalance or should government intercede?

Towards responsible marketing

At first, many companies opposed consumerism and environmentalism. They thought that the criticisms were either unfair or unimportant. Today, most companies have grown to accept the new consumer rights, at least in principle. They might oppose certain pieces of legislation as inappropriate ways to solve certain consumer problems in their industry, but by and large they recognise the consumer's right to information and protection. Many of these companies have responded positively to consumerism and environmentalism in order to serve consumer needs better. After all, management of these organisations live in the same environmental space as those who buy their products.

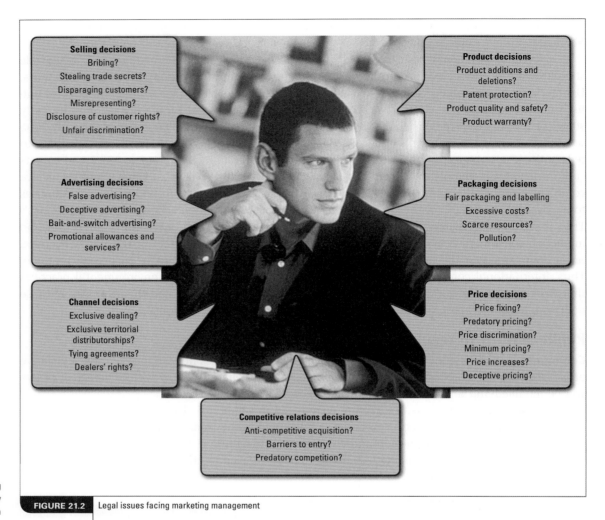

FIGURE 21.2 | Legal issues facing marketing management

Enlightened marketing
A marketing philosophy holding that an organisation's marketing should support the best long-run performance of the marketing system; its six principles include consumer-oriented marketing, principle of innovativeness, principle of adding value, sense of mission, maintaining social responsibility and employing marketing metrics.

Consumer-oriented marketing A principle of enlightened marketing that holds that the organisation should view and organise its marketing activities from the consumer's point of view.

Enlightened marketing

The philosophy of **enlightened marketing** holds that a marketing organisation's marketing should support the best long-run performance of the marketing system. Enlightened marketing consists of six principles: *remaining market-oriented, continuing innovativeness, adding value, having a sense of mission, maintaining social responsibility* and *employing marketing metrics.*

Remaining market oriented

Remaining market-oriented means that the marketing organisation continually views and organises its marketing activities from the consumer's point of view (**consumer-oriented marketing**), all the while taking competitors' strategies into account, and remaining focused on long-term profitability, or surpluses in the case of not-for-profit organisations. It should work hard to sense, serve and satisfy the needs of a defined group of customers, in recognition of the fact that it cannot be all things to all people.[19]

Continuing innovativeness

The **principle of innovativeness** requires that the marketing organisation continuously seeks real product and marketing improvements, as opposed to mere cosmetic changes. The marketing organisation that overlooks new and better ways to do things will eventually lose customers to another marketing organisation that has found a better way.

Adding value

According to the **principle of adding value**, the marketing organisation should put most of its resources into value-building marketing investments. Many things marketers do—one-shot sales promotions, minor packaging changes, advertising puffery—might raise sales in the short run but add less value than would actual improvements in the product's attributes (e.g. quality) and meeting changing customer requirements. Enlightened marketing calls for building long-run consumer loyalty by continually improving the value consumers receive from the organisation's marketing offer.

Sense of mission

Having a **sense of mission** means that the marketing organisation should define its mission in broad *social* terms rather than narrow *marketing* or *financial* terms. When a marketing organisation defines a social mission, employees feel better about their work and have a clearer sense of direction. For example, defined in narrow marketing terms, Johnson & Johnson's mission might be 'to sell Band-Aids, and baby oil' or 'to sell shaving requisites' (the latter since it acquired Gillette). But the marketing organisation states its mission more broadly:

> We believe that our first responsibility is to the doctors, nurses and patients, to mothers and all others who use our goods and services. In meeting their needs everything we do must be of high quality. We must constantly strive to reduce our costs in order to maintain reasonable prices. Customers' orders must be serviced promptly and accurately. Our suppliers and distributors must have an opportunity to make a fair profit. We are responsible to our employees, the men and women who work for us throughout the world. Everyone must be considered as an individual. We must respect their dignity and recognise their merit . . . We are responsible to the communities in which we live and work and to the world community as well. We must be good citizens—support good works and charities and bear our fair share of taxes. We must encourage civic improvements and better health and education. We must maintain in good order the property we are privileged to use, protecting the environment and natural resources.[20]

Many companies have embraced the newer notion of a Statement of Values for the organisation. Consider the Statement of Values for Dun & Bradstreet International in Figure 21.3 overleaf.

Reshaping the basic task of selling consumer products into the larger mission of serving the interests of consumers, employees, suppliers and others in the 'world community' helps to give a sense of purpose to Johnson & Johnson and D&B employees.

Principle of innovativeness
A principle of enlightened marketing that requires that an organisation seek real product and marketing improvements.

Principle of adding value A principle of enlightened marketing that holds that an organisation should put most of its resources into value-building marketing investments.

Sense of mission
A principle of enlightened marketing that holds that an organisation should define its mission in broad social terms rather than narrow financial terms.

'The D&B management team is committed to making D&B a successful organisation and great place to work. There are many opportunites for development and I have held four different roles in four different divisions throughout my time here.' Kate O'Keeffe, Consultant—Organisational Development

---

VALUES STATEMENT

All our activities and decisions must be based on, and guided by, these values:

Treat all people with respect and dignity; value differences

Pursue an unrelenting quest for quality; use speed and simplicity to achieve goals

Conduct ourselves with the highest level of integrity and business ethics

Place the interests of customers first; our success depends on their success

Commit to teamwork; seek out and utilize the ideas and skills of all associates

Reach for the highest standards of performance; show a passion for winning

By behaving in accordance with these values, we will provide outstanding service to our Customers, maintain a leadership position in our business, improve satisfaction for our associates and provide superior value to our shareholders.

FIGURE 21.3 Dun & Bradstreet International's statement of values

---

Maintaining social responsibility

Maintaining social responsibility
A principle of enlightened marketing that holds that an organisation should make marketing decisions by considering consumers' wants, the organisation's requirements, consumers' long-run interests and society's long-run interests.

Following the principle of **maintaining social responsibility**, an enlightened marketing organisation makes marketing decisions by considering consumers' wants and interests, the marketing organisation's requirements and society's long-run interests. The marketing organisation is aware that neglecting consumer and societal long-run interests is a disservice to consumers and society. Alert companies view societal problems as opportunities while at the same time wanting to be good corporate citizens.

A socially responsible marketer wants to design products that are not only pleasing but also beneficial. The difference is shown in Figure 21.4. Products may be classified according to their degree of immediate consumer satisfaction and long-run consumer benefit. **Deficient products**, such as bad-tasting, ineffective or harmful medicine, have neither immediate appeal nor long-run benefits. **Pleasing products** give high immediate satisfaction but might hurt consumers in the long term. Examples include some arthritis drugs which reduce the symptoms but raise blood pressure, and cigarettes. **Salutary products** have low appeal but benefit consumers in the long run. Seat belts and air bags in motor vehicles are salutary products. **Desirable products** give both high immediate satisfaction and high long-run benefits. A desirable product with immediate satisfaction and long-run benefit would be a tasty and nutritious breakfast food.

The challenge posed by pleasing products is that they sell very well but may end up hurting the consumer. The product opportunity, therefore, is to add long-run benefits without reducing the product's pleasing qualities. The challenge posed by salutary products is to add some pleasing qualities so that they will become more desirable in the consumers' minds. For example, synthetic fats and fat substitutes promise to improve the appeal of more healthful low-calorie and low-fat foods.

Deficient products
Products that have neither immediate appeal nor long-run benefits.

Pleasing products
Products that give high immediate satisfaction but may hurt consumers in the long run.

Salutary products
Products that have low appeal but benefit consumers in the long run.

Desirable products
Products that give both high immediate satisfaction and high long-run benefits.

Employing marketing metrics

The enlightened marketing organisation seeks to measure the financial and non-financial returns it gains from expenditure on marketing effort. Marketing management have tended to stress non-financial measures such as brand attitude when reporting to top management and their governing

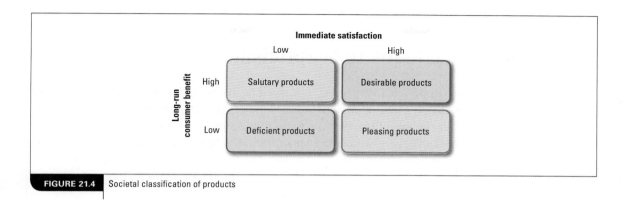

Immediate satisfaction

		Low	High
Long-run consumer benefit	High	Salutary products	Desirable products
	Low	Deficient products	Pleasing products

FIGURE 21.4 Societal classification of products

bodies. In some situations financial measures such as market share are alluded to. However, most industries are not in a position to assess market share accurately. And when they can, it is not as meaningful a measure as one might think.

Mostly, marketing management have made less effort to make the connection between marketing expenditure and financial outcomes such as profit and cash flow, thereby reducing the faith that senior managers and directors with financial backgrounds have in the efficacy of marketing. In Australia, the AMI (Australian Marketing Insititute) is working with academia, by matching an Australian Research Council grant of $265 000, to establish appropriate marketing metrics. It has long been recognised by management that such 'generic' measures are often less important than the specific measures used in particular industries.[21] For example, the poultry industry produces short-shelf-life products with 100+ stockturns each year, and thus depends on effective cash flow management. Retail market share is not fully measured by ACNielsen as other FMCG products might be. Market share is a less important measure of the effectivess of marketing effort in this industry both because the sales by company are tied to particular retailers, and because the larger proportion of sales is made through the foodservice sector (which is measured infrequently). Nor are brand awareness and brand attitude effective non-financial measures, as both private and retail labels are involved. A more appropriate measure is the effectivess of the marketing effort at an industry level for such a commodity. One such measure is consumer attitudes toward white meat over red meat at an industry level rather than at a brand or company level.

Marketing ethics

Conscientious marketing management faces many moral dilemmas. The best thing to do is often unclear. Because not all managers have fine moral sensitivity, companies need to develop corporate *marketing ethics policies*—broad guidelines that everyone in the organisation must follow. These policies should cover distributor relations, advertising standards, customer service, pricing, product development and general ethical standards.

The finest guidelines cannot resolve all the difficult ethical situations the marketer faces. If marketers choose immediate sales-producing actions in all these cases, their marketing behaviour might well be described as immoral or even amoral. If they refuse to go along with *any* of the actions, they might be ineffective as marketing managers and unhappy because of the constant moral tension. Managers need a set of principles that will help them figure out the moral importance of each situation and decide how far they can go in good conscience.

But *what* principle should guide companies and marketing managers on issues of ethics and social responsibility? One philosophy is that such issues are decided by the free market and legal system.

Poor governance leads to scepticism

When halfway across the Indian Ocean in 1969, your humble scribe heard a news report of the implosion that saw an end to the mining bubble of the 1960s in Australia. The star of the bubble was a mining stock—the nickel company Poseidon—whose share price had risen spectacularly from $1 to $280, before plummeting back to the depths from which it should never have risen. Like the liner in the movie of the same name, Poseidon finally sank to financial obscurity, but not before it took with it the finances of the many investors scrambling after easy returns.

Many serious mining companies like Rio Tinto and Western Mining did make money for their investors during the 1960s, and their canny management served their investors, and themselves, well. But Poseidon's share price rose on an assay based on fiction rather than fact, and also based on short supply due to a soon to end mining strike in Canada. Naturally it fell when reality finally took hold.

Investors seem to make money and lose money in regular cycles. It also seems that with regular monotony managers try to convince investors that their company is making the requisite return on investment, even when it is not. This is surely the case with companies like retailer Harris Scarfe, insurer HIH, mobile telco One.Tel and miner Sons of Gwalia, which are more recent failures. While HIH made corporate history for being a spectacular failure, there have been many others in the more than 30-year gap between Poseidon and HIH. Many of these failures were like the grand failure of Enron in the USA in that poor management or greedy management (or both) saw to it that the reported profits pleased investors even when reality later showed otherwise. To do this requires the duplicity of senior management, and a lack of separation of the actions of accountants and auditors in accounting firms. In short, there are governance issues involved in the companies and their advisers.

Perhaps it is little wonder then that some organisations are unethical in their dealings with customers. Those who spruiked the returns to be made

by investing in CBD apartments come to mind. So do those who entice a buyer to buy a car on eBay and to pay the seller in advance, only never to deliver the car. And so too does the unscrupulous seller of a West Highland White Terrier at top price on the Web who, in the end, delivers a white cross-breed of unknown origins.

What then is one to think? Are all sellers unscrupulous? Are all companies rip-off merchants? Thankfully, while the popular press feeds on such gross behaviour and readers thrive on such titivation, there are successful businesses with a history of treating employees firmly but with fairness, and who deal honestly with customers, government, suppliers and other stakeholders. An examination of the businesses and ventures with which Dick Smith and his long-time business partner Ike Bain have been associated soon puts a different light on the place of honesty, trust and commitment in business dealings, and how relationships in marketing start with those at the top.

From paying off creditors after suffering inventory theft in his early years Dick Smith joined forces with Ike Bain in creating two enterprises. First, when Dick was 28 years old and Ike 20, came the successful Dick Smith Electronics chain in Australia and New Zealand (DSE)—which was ultimately sold to Woolworths Ltd in two tranches in the early 1980s. Next came Australian Geographic which they built from a mainly news-stand delivered magazine to a subscription-only magazine with over 200 000 members and retail outlets throughout Australia—which was later sold to publishers John Fairfax and Sons for $41 million. Other ventures such as chartering and filling Jumbo jets with people who wanted to visit the South Pole and receive their commemorative medallion—despite the advice of Qantas—are noteworthy for the way they were promoted and the way people entrusted their money to Dick Smith knowing they would receive value in return. Dick Smith Foods was also a notable venture which saw Dick Smith put his money into the fight to arrest the sale of every iconic Australian fast-moving consumer goods brand to overseas interests.

Many things are notable about the way Dick (the Electronic Dick as he was called in some ads and on their truck in Australia, or Dickhead as the company logo was referred to internally) built and maintained relationships in business. For one, Dick Smith turned every encounter into fun and an opportunity to spread the word. For another, he had empathy with those around him and was honest in his relationships—telling an employee to pay import duty when customs were unaware it was due is such an example. The adage 'what goes around, comes around' must have been coined with Dick and Ike in mind, for the honest way they dealt with a potential US partner when introducing DSE to California. When talks broke down and DSE had to go it alone with a retail outlet in the same strip as the US entrepreneur, he freely volunteered to give them—yes, give—a complete listing of his catalogue customers in California.

While businesses form relationships with businesses and those at the top, consumers also form relationships with brands in the case of high-involvement products such as those sold by DSE and Australian Geographic. In the case of DSE, Dick Smith is the brand—or more correctly, a line drawing of his highly recognisably geek-like head is the logo. However, even today DSE deals with a target market which values dealing with salespeople who are knowledgeable about the kits, resistors, capacitors and computers they sell, and will go to any lengths to provide good service. Australian Geographic reeks of quality, and the stores are knowledge bases of Australian heritage and science, as much as they are retailing Australiana to locals and overseas visitors. In short, Dick and Ike ensured the business was transparent to all around them, including customers, thus engendering trust.

Dick Smith is not the only businessperson to present his honesty and trust to all around him. It is clear, however, that he believes passionately in the ventures he takes on, and that he has always surrounded himself with those who are capable and who hold similar values. Most importantly, these cherished values are constantly communicated to all involved in the business, and reported widely so that they regularly reach the ears of business customers and consumers alike.

Sources: The positive commentary is based on Ike Bain, *The Dick Smith Way*. Sydney, McGraw-Hill, 2003. The negative commentary is based on Trevor Sykes, 'The Great, the Cowboys and the Criminals', *The Australian Financial Review*, Perspective, 10–11 December 2005, pp. 20–21; Adam Shand, 'The Fatal Weakness of Ray Williams', *The Australian Financial Review*, Perspective, 18–19 January 2003, pp. 21 and 23; and Stewart Adam, Media commentary 'Online Buyer Beware', *A Current Affair*, Nine Network, 13 July 2005.

Have Dick around to make it a real Australia Day

Most Aussies want to buy food that is not only grown here by Australian farmers, but is sold by an Australian owned business so that the profits stay here creating wealth for our children's future. With so much of the labelling misleading there is one way you can guarantee Australian made and owned - that is, with Dick Smith Foods.

www.dicksmithfoods.com.au

Dick Smith has iconic status in Australia because of his business dealings.

Questions

1 Do you agree with the proposition that governance issues in business have led to a conundrum with regard to creating and maintaining trust, commitment and overall satisfaction among customers? Justify your answer.

2 Might there be a difference between business and consumer markets in terms of the importance of relationships in marketing?

3 Discuss the ways in which Dick Smith and Ike Bain have employed internal marketing in adding value and overcoming scepticism.

21.2

Under this principle, companies and their managers are not responsible for making moral judgments. Companies can in good conscience do whatever the system allows.

A second philosophy puts responsibility not in the system, but in the hands of individual companies and managers. This more enlightened philosophy suggests that a marketing organisation should have a 'social conscience'. Companies and managers should apply high standards of ethics and morality when making corporate decisions, regardless of 'what the system allows'. History provides an endless list of examples of marketing organisation actions that were legal and allowed but were highly irresponsible.

Each marketing organisation and marketing manager must work out a philosophy of socially responsible and ethical behaviour. Under the societal marketing concept, each manager must look beyond what is legal and allowed and develop standards based on personal integrity, corporate conscience and long-run consumer welfare. A clear and responsible philosophy will help the marketing manager deal with the many knotty questions posed by marketing and other human activities.

As with environmentalism, the issue of ethics provides special challenges for international marketers. Business standards and practices vary a great deal from one country to the next. For example, bribes and kickbacks are illegal for most Western firms but they are standard business practice in many South American and Middle Eastern countries. The question arises as to whether a marketing organisation must lower its ethical standards to compete effectively in countries with lower standards. In one study on this matter, two researchers posed this question to chief executives of large international companies and got a unanimous response: No.[22] For the sake of all the marketing organisation's stakeholders—customers, suppliers, employees, shareholders and the public—it is important to make a commitment to a common set of shared standards worldwide. The reference to 'stakeholders' is an oft-repeated one, but commentators have expressed some scepticism about the notion:

> Compared with the traditional nostrum of maximising revenue and being ultimately responsible to the shareholders, the 'stakeholder thesis' of unifying the interests of suppliers, consumers and staff promises a wider spread of benefit. It suggests decentralisation and a broader distribution of responsibility for the company's activities.
>
> There are disquieting overtones here. What say do the shareholders or customers have in the type of environmentalism or ethics that are embraced? Precious little. As Mr Wheeler (Body Shop) says of the Body Shop campaigns, 'Anita (Roddick) generally chooses them. But the shareholders don't complain.'[23]

Many industrial and professional associations have suggested codes of ethics, and many companies are now adopting their own codes. For example, the Australian Marketing Institute, an association of marketing practitioners and scientists, developed the code of professional conduct shown in Figure 21.5. Companies are also developing programs to teach managers about important ethics issues and help them find the proper responses. According to a survey of Fortune 1000 companies, over 40% of these companies are holding ethics workshops and seminars and one-third have set up ethics committees. Further, more than 200 major US companies have appointed high-level ethics officers to champion ethical issues and to help resolve ethics problems and concerns facing employees. These ethics specialists often employ hotlines through which employees can ask questions about proper ethical behaviour or report questionable practices. At one company in the USA, Raytheon, the ethics officer receives about 100 calls each month. Most involve minor issues, but about 10% point out serious ethical problems that must be addressed by top management.[24]

1. Members shall conduct their professional activities with respect for the public interest.

2. Members shall at all times act with integrity in dealing with clients or employers, past and present, with their fellow members and with the general public.

3. Members shall not intentionally disseminate false or misleading information, whether written, spoken or implied, or conceal any relevant fact. They have a duty to maintain truth, accuracy and good taste in advertising, sales promotion and all other aspects of marketing.

4. Members shall not represent conflicting or competing interests except with the express consent of those concerned given only after full disclosure of the facts to all interested parties.

5. Members, in performing services for a client or employer, shall not accept fees, commissions or any other valuable consideration in connection with those services from any one other than their client or employer except with the consent (express or implied) of both.

6. Members shall refrain from knowingly associating with any enterprise which uses improper or illegal methods in obtaining business.

7. Members shall not intentionally injure the professional reputation or practice of another member.

8. If a member has evidence that another member has been guilty of unethical practices it shall be their duty to inform the Institute.

9. Members have a responsibility to continue the acquisition of professional skills in marketing and to encourage the development of these skills in those who are desirous of entry into, or continuing in, the profession of marketing management.

10. Members shall help to improve the body of knowledge of the profession by exchanging information and experience with fellow members and by applying their special skill and training for the benefit of others.

11. Members shall refrain from using their relationship with the Institute in such manner as to state or imply an official accreditation or approval beyond the scope of membership of the Institute and its aims, rules and policies.

12. The use of the Institute's distinguishing letters must be confined to Institute activities, or the statement of name and business address on a card, letterhead and published articles.

13. Members shall cooperate with fellow members in upholding and enforcing this Code.

FIGURE 21.5 Australian Marketing Institute Code of Professional Conduct

Many companies have developed innovative ways to educate employees about ethics:

Citicorp (Citibank) has developed an ethics board game, which teams of employees use to solve hypothetical quandaries. General Electric employees can tap into specially designed software on their personal computers to get answers to ethical questions. At Texas Instruments, employees are treated to a weekly column on ethics over an electronic news service. One popular feature: a kind of Dear Abby mailbag, answers provided by the marketing organisation's ethics officer, . . . that deals with the troublesome issues employees face most often.[25]

Still, written codes and ethics programs do not ensure ethical behaviour. Ethics and social responsibility require a total corporate commitment. They must be a component of the overall corporate culture. According to David R. Whitman, Chairman of the Board of Whirlpool Corporation, 'In the final analysis, "ethical behaviour" must be an integral part of the organisation, a way of life that is deeply ingrained in the collective corporate body . . . In any business enterprise, ethical behaviour must be a tradition, a way of conducting one's affairs that is passed from generation to generation of employees at all levels of the organisation. It is the responsibility of management, starting at the very top, to both set the example by personal conduct and create an environment that not only encourages and rewards ethical behaviour, but which also makes anything less totally unacceptable.'[26]

The future holds many challenges and opportunities for marketing managers in the twenty-first century. Technological advances in solar energy, personal computers, interactive television, modern medicine and new forms of transportation, recreation and communication provide abundant marketing opportunities. However, forces in the socioeconomic, cultural and natural environments increase the limits under which marketing can be carried out. Companies that are able to create new values in a socially responsible way will have a world to conquer.

SELF-CHECK QUESTIONS

5 What would you do in this situation? You are a key account executive with a major grocery company. You are under your sales budget for the month. You believe that an expensive gift sent to the wife of a major retail buyer would be enough to induce an increased order for the month. Such a gift would be against the policies of both your employer and the retail chain in question. The policies of both companies state that gifts may not be given or received by company employees.

6 If Internet service providers adopt an industry code banning the transmission of pornography on the Internet, would this ensure that users no longer view such material on the Net? Why or why not?

Towards a public policy for marketing practice

Several principles that might guide the formulation of public policy towards marketing practices are examined next. These principles reflect assumptions underlying much of modern marketing theory and practice.

- *The principle of consumer and producer freedom.* As much as possible, marketing decisions should be made by consumers and producers under relative freedom. Marketing freedom is important if a marketing system is to deliver a high standard of living. People can achieve satisfaction in their own terms rather than in terms defined by someone else. This leads to greater fulfilment through a closer matching of products to desires. Freedom for producers and consumers is the cornerstone of a dynamic marketing system. But more principles are needed to implement this freedom and prevent abuses.

- *The principle of curbing potential harm.* As much as possible, transactions freely entered into by producers and consumers are their private business. The political system curbs producer or consumer freedom only to prevent transactions that harm or threaten to harm the producer, consumer or third parties. Transactional harm is a widely recognised ground for government intervention. The major issue is whether there is sufficient actual or potential harm to justify the intervention.

- *The principle of meeting basic needs.* The marketing system should serve disadvantaged consumers as well as affluent ones. In a free-enterprise system, producers make goods for markets that are willing and able to buy. Certain groups who lack purchasing power might go without needed goods and services, causing harm to their physical or psychological wellbeing. While preserving the principle of producer and consumer freedom, the marketing system should support economic and political actions to solve this problem. It should strive to meet the basic needs of all people, and all people should share to some extent in the standard of living it creates.

◉ *The principle of economic efficiency.* The marketing system strives to supply goods and services efficiently and at low prices. The extent to which a society's needs and wants can be satisfied depends on how efficiently its scarce resources are used. Free economies rely on active competition and informed buyers to make a market efficient. To make profits, competitors must watch their costs carefully while developing products, prices and marketing programs that serve buyer needs. Buyers get the most satisfaction by finding out about different competing products, prices and qualities and choosing carefully. The presence of active competition and well-informed buyers keeps quality high and prices low.

◉ *The principle of innovation.* The marketing system encourages authentic innovation to bring down production and distribution costs and to develop new products to meet changing consumer needs. Much innovation is really imitation of other brands, with a slight difference to provide a selling point. The consumer may face 10 very similar brands in a product class. But an effective marketing system encourages real product innovation and differentiation to meet the wants of different market segments.

◉ *The principle of consumer education and information.* An effective marketing system invests heavily in consumer education and information to increase long-run consumer satisfaction and welfare. The principle of economic efficiency requires this investment, especially in cases where products are confusing because of their numbers and conflicting claims. Ideally, companies will provide enough information about their products. But consumer groups and the government can also give out information and ratings. Students in public schools can take courses in consumer education to learn better buying skills.

◉ *The principle of consumer protection.* Consumer education and information cannot do the whole job of protecting consumers. The marketing system must also provide consumer protection. Modern products are so complex that even trained consumers cannot evaluate them with confidence. Consumers do not know whether a mobile phone gives off cancer-causing radiation, whether a new motor vehicle has safety flaws or whether a new pharmaceutical product has dangerous side effects. A government agency has to review and judge the safety levels of various foods, drugs, toys, appliances, fabrics, cars and housing. Consumers might fail to understand the environmental consequences of buying certain products, so consumer protection also covers production and marketing activities that might harm the environment. Finally, consumer protection prevents deceptive practices and high-pressure selling techniques where consumers would be defenceless.

These seven principles are based on the assumption that marketing's goal is not to maximise marketing organisation profits or total consumption or consumer choice, but rather to maximise life quality. Life quality means meeting basic needs, having available many good products and enjoying the natural and cultural environment. Properly managed, the marketing system can help to create and deliver a higher quality of life to people around the world.

SELF-CHECK QUESTIONS

7   Consider the situation where a small, recently established firm wishes to position its new product close to that of a major established firm. Is this a breach of the 'principle of innovation'?

8   The Australian government of the early 1990s encouraged the introduction of two sets of fibre-optic cable infrastructure, at $4 billion each, as part of the introduction of competition in the converging telecommunications and Pay-TV industry. Is such a government policy in keeping with the 'principle of economic efficiency'?

Towards legal compliance in marketing

Codes of ethics and ethical standards are important. However, it is important for marketers to realise that these codes and standards operate within the shadow of the law. Almost every decision made in marketing has some legal significance. Whether hiring salespeople, commissioning advertising materials, introducing a new product, designing labels or putting warnings on packages, there are legal ramifications. Some of these are obvious, while some are not. The impact of the law of torts and product liability, together with product standards, is more obvious than the impact of intellectual property law, for example. The latter will be of even greater concern as marketers embrace new interactive media such as the World Wide Web (WWW) which will make it easier to develop promotional claims 'on-the-fly' and perhaps more easily make an unintended breach of the law.

Intellectual property is also the concern of developers of 'content' in all manner of existing and future software products ranging from paper-based books to CD-ROM titles to the D-I-Y publisher on the WWW.[27] This aspect of the law also impacts on hardware manufacturers as has been seen in notable US cases involving the silicon chip maker Intel and its competitors.

By being proactive in allocating resources to ensure that defects are eliminated and by involving employees at all levels—noting that fewer levels exist now than in the past—firms have developed a quality culture, and have gone on to use all manner of tools and techniques to improve production and delivery systems. They have also been able to alleviate people problems such as poor attitudes to work and workmanship.

We suggest that, in like manner, marketing organisations need to be proactive in allocating resources to develop a culture within the organisation that ensures that the people involved in marketing are educated in legal matters affecting their sphere of influence, thus adopting the role of self-regulators (see Marketing Highlight 21.2 for both positive and negative examples). For example, a regional sales manager having a drink with counterparts from other firms at the end of the day would make a point of leaving the group if the discussion turned to pricing issues or any other matter that could be construed as a possible uncompetitive practice in breach of the Trade Practices Act by their respective companies.

Involvement of senior management

Such a culture can only be fostered by top management commitment and implemented by way of continuing education. A senior manager should be placed in charge of such a program, probably at a level reporting to the CEO. The Group Managing Director of Shell International—Mark Moody-Stuart—reportedly sees himself as 'Ethics Director' and says that part of his job entails deciding what is acceptable and what is not.[28] This is not to say that the task of implementing a legal compliance program would be undertaken on a day-to-day basis by the Group Managing Director of Shell International. However, such a program would require his commitment in the first instance. Small and medium-sized businesses (SMEs) must be even more concerned about legal compliance because a major lawsuit could mean the death of the business. SMEs may not be able to afford a compliance officer, but they will have to ensure that managers have sufficient legal literacy and work closely with legal advisers to ensure that legal compliance needs are met.

Putting a compliance program in place: Australian Standard AS 3806-1998

Released by Standards Australia on 5 February 1998 and drawing together comments from courts, opinions of legal practitioners and best practice, this Australian Standard provides a guide to business in designing a compliance program or assessing whether their existing compliance programs are adequate. The AS 3806 standard establishes requirements for:

- positive commitment to compliance at board and CEO level communicated to staff
- positive promotion of compliance by all managers
- continuous monitoring and improvement of all compliance procedures
- the integration of all compliance procedures into the organisation's day-to-day operating procedures, systems and documents
- adequate numbers of senior staff with high status and sufficient 'clout' to take responsibility for compliance
- ongoing education and training of all staff.

While Australian standards are not binding law, the ACCC has made it clear that it will regard AS 3806 as the 'benchmark' for compliance programs. The standard is generic and can be used to assist both public and private organisations with developing, implementing and maintaining effective compliance systems in any form of legal, industry or in-house regulatory arrangements.

Legal education

The need to educate and train members of the marketing organisation cannot be overstated. The courts have commented adversely where firms have avoided their responsibilities in this regard. In *TPC v ICI Australia Operations Pty Ltd* (1992) ATPR 41-185, Justice Lockhart noted: 'There is no evidence that [the three executives directly involved] received any compliance training before, during or since the commission of the offences'.

The courts have also pointed out that where a compliance program exists it must be updated. In effect, we are referring to risk management here, since such compliance programs are designed to ensure that employees know when to seek legal advice, thus reducing the likelihood of expensive litigation, both in terms of fees and fines, and the loss of the good standing of the marketing organisation in the broader community.

Coverage of a legal compliance program

The following commentary concerning legal compliance in marketing has been adapted from a coverage suggested by Eugene Clark.[29] It is not intended to be all-encompassing but seeks only to give marketers a few examples of some of the key areas that should be part of a legal compliance program. Marketers who do not have at least a basic understanding of such issues may be living dangerously and putting both themselves and their organisation at serious risk.

Competition law

Most developed countries have made provision in their legislation for the prohibition of various forms of anti-competitive conduct. Examples of such activities include contracts, arrangements or understandings that substantially lessen competition, price fixing among competitors, the misuse of market power, resale price maintenance, and mergers and acquisitions or exclusive dealing arrangements which have a substantially lessening effect on competition within a particular marketplace. The major source of Australian competition law is found in Part IV of the Trade Practices Act and case decisions interpreting this legislation.[30]

Contract and consumer law

Laws governing the sale of goods and services deal with the matter differently in different countries, although the intent of the legislation is much the same. In Australia, the laws governing the sale of goods and services is covered by a three-tiered scheme including common law (reported decisions of courts), state legislation (such as the Sale of Goods Act and Fair Trading Act in each state) and Commonwealth legislation (most notably the Trade Practices Act).

Some of the more important developments in this area include:

- ◉ *unconscionability*—new guidelines covering consumer as well as business-to-business activities that are deemed unconscionable (Trade Practices Act, section IVA)
- ◉ *estoppel*—covering the importance of, and legal liability arising from, precontractual negotiations. The aim is to ensure that businesspeople act in good faith and honour the legitimate expectations of those with whom they deal
- ◉ *consumer protection*—enhanced remedies for enforcement of consumer laws; increased financial penalties for offences against consumer protection legislation; 'post-sale' protection for subsequent owners of goods
- ◉ *complaints handling*—more assistance to help companies identify weaknesses in their present schemes and remedy them; for example, access to justice reports, Standards Australia, Australian Standard: Complaints handling AS 4269-1995
- ◉ *tendering, outsourcing and partnering legal reforms governing tendering and outsourcing*
- ◉ *electronic commerce*—reforms to cover electronic contracting; electronic funds transfer (EFT and EFTPOS); use of smart-card technology; privacy; Internet (and digital derivatives) commerce; and cybercrime such as hacking and identity theft.

Standards

There continues to be a proliferation of standards at a global and national level, within regions and at local level within nation states. The movement to standardise legal requirements between countries (e.g. WTO) and trading partners also continues (e.g. Australia and New Zealand Closer Economic Relations Agreement).

Product liability

All marketing organisations know of the importance of quality control, yet somehow this does not always translate into error-free design, error-free manufacture, durable finished goods and accurate labelling. Class actions seem endemic in the USA and are now more likely in Australia (e.g. asbestos cases) and New Zealand. This is because legislation was introduced in Australia during 1992 which liberalised the ability of plaintiffs to engage in representative or class actions.[31]

Marketing communication

Marketing communication takes many forms, all of which can be the subject of misinterpretation by consumers or customers. Salespeople might stretch the truth due to a lack of product knowledge as a result of inadequate training. Marketing organisations need to consider the promotional tools used pre-transaction, at the point at which transactions occur and post-transaction. Where mistakes are discovered post-transaction, companies must move swiftly to remedy such errors. An example of this occurred in the case of *David Golf & Engineering Pty Ltd v Austgolf Corporation Ltd* in which Austgolf produced a brochure showing that its golf bag tags were cheaper than those of its competitor, David Golf & Engineering.[32] However, the competitor's prices were overstated and out of date. In response to its competitor's complaint, Austgolf wrote to all golf clubs and anyone who had placed an order and informed them that the prices in the brochure were inaccurate. Because of such prompt action, Austgolf successfully resisted an order for corrective advertising. This result can be contrasted with a US case wherein Listerine was ordered to spend $US10 million in advertising proclaiming that its mouthwash did not prevent colds or sore throats.[33]

It is likely that continuing legal attention will be paid to such areas as cigarette advertising at sporting and cultural events, environmental advertising surrounding such products as 'organically grown' foodstuffs, country-of-origin food labelling, entitlement to use the Olympic symbol, and privacy issues surrounding advertising on the WWW.

One of the most important codes is the Australian Direct Marketing Association Code of Practice produced and administered by the Australian Direct Marketing Association (ADMA).[34] The code binds all ADMA members, their employees, agents and subcontractors. Specific provisions of the code deal with marketing claims, unfair conduct, availability of goods or services, cancellation and refunds, payment, unordered goods or services and responding to complaints. The code also covers fair conduct relevant to telemarketing as well as electronic commerce.[35] Part E of the code deals with fair conduct in relation to data protection. The code also incorporates a complaints procedure. In the event of a breach of the code, the Code Authority can employ a number of sanctions, including:

- requiring a formal apology for breach
- requiring corrective advertising or the withdrawal of offending advertisements or statements
- requiring correction or deletion of relevant records and personal information
- recommending refund or replacement of goods or services where appropriate
- requiring the member to take specified remedial action to correct the breach and avoid recurrence
- seeking a written undertaking from the member that the breach will not be repeated
- recommending to the CEO that membership be revoked.

Where a member demonstrates wilful non-compliance with the code, the Code Authority can recommend that the member be publicly expelled from the Association.

The ADMA Code Authority issues an annual report found at <www.adma.com.au/consumer/codeAuthority.htm>.

Sales and after-sales finance

In this area, the first question marketing organisations must answer is whether or not credit will be extended to consumers and customers, and then what the nature of these credit facilities will be. It is sometimes said that second-hand car buyers do not buy cars, they buy finance. By this it is meant that car dealers differentiate their offerings from each other by way of the financial terms offered to the buyer, many of whom are low-income earners. The details of any credit policy must be spelt out: basic trading terms, settlement terms, rebate policy, collection procedures and use of credit referencing, among others.

Again, this is an area where employee education and training is vital. Usually, employees involved in credit negotiations in Australia will need to know such aspects of the law as the Consumer Credit Code, contract law, bills of sale, privacy legislation (see Marketing Highlight 21.3), commercial law, small claims procedures, bankruptcy provisions and, if a corporation, the Trade Practices Act.

Franchising

One of the most popular vehicles for starting a new business or expanding an existing one is franchising. Franchising is an area where specialised legal knowledge is required, because of the exclusive rights and obligations granted under a franchise agreement. Such rights might relate to exclusive distribution rights in a particular geographic area or the obligation to run a business in a particular manner and to pay management or other fees to the franchisor. Franchise agreements associated with image fast-food chains extend right down to allowing the franchisor to decide who the business may be sold to and under what circumstances the agreement might or might not be renewed.

The present Franchising Code of Conduct came into effect in 1998 and is now one of the mandatory codes under Part IVB of the Trade Practices Act. It applies to all franchise agreements formed after 1 July 1998. The code requires a comprehensive set of disclosures and provides a dispute resolution procedure for franchise disputes. The major aim of the code is to assist franchisees in making an informed decision prior to signing a franchising agreement. The code is enforced by the ACCC.

MARKETING HIGHLIGHT 21.3

So what if you have zero privacy?

If you saw the movie *2001: A Space Odyssey* you may remember the scene where the two astronauts step into the 'cone of silence' to prevent the paranoid shipboard computer—HAL—from hearing their conversation. When all is said and done, our lives are not that much different—many of us are just as concerned about being overheard or snooped on by business, government and even friends and colleagues. We cannot function without someone wanting to extract a piece of information from us or about us whether we like it or not. Try to open a new bank account without the exact number of identifiers required, such as a driver's licence and/or passport. Try visiting a bulk-billing medical centre without your Medicare card. Even your family pet probably carries a small identifying computer chip—a personal pet tracking system—that enables your pet to be caught if on the loose, and you to be fined if it is found where it shouldn't be or does what it shouldn't do.

Researchers in Japan have gone a step further and mounted a miniature camera and 'electronic steering' on cockroaches, supposedly to sniff out people trapped in fallen buildings. And if you drive an upmarket car, geostationary orbiting satellites are probably tracking it. Moreover, you can be tracked from cell to cell via your mobile phone. Judging by the granting of a recent US patent to track humans—allowing activation by the implantee, or remote activation—it may not be long before many of us are wearing an in-body GPS (global positioning system) and our lives are totally 'wired'. Fanciful? Think again! After all, this is the Information Age.

Our lives are heading further and further in the direction of total transparency, as business gets set to make money by 'plugging us in', and then by selling us privacy systems. If you are not concerned, then perhaps the systems that are supposed to be protecting us may make you so. First, there is Carnivore, the 'black-box packet-sniffer' that is used to filter email traffic passing through your ISP. Next there is Echelon, which is a network of satellites and listening posts in Australia, Canada, the UK and New Zealand, run by the US National Security Agency. Echelon is supposedly able to snoop on email and that, on its own, is a good enough reason for encrypting our email.

Some years ago, Australians said no to a plastic identification card—the Australia card—designed to act as a personal identifier. However, the reality is that we leave so many tracks from so many facets of our lives that the card may be the least of our privacy concerns. Clearly, some see privacy as a non-issue. Scott McNealy, when CEO of Sun Microsystems, said 'You have zero privacy anyway . . . Get over it!' Others see many issues involved, particularly respondents to the Australian Privacy Commissioner's July 2001 study.

Approximately two in five respondents (42%) said they had refused to deal with an organisation because of concerns over the use and protection of their personal information. These people were more likely to belong to the 40–49 years age group—with 50% of this age group refusing to deal with a business due to privacy concerns—and to be living in a capital city (47% in capital cities, 40% in regional areas and 32% in rural locations).

The Australian Privacy Commissioner's office is responsible for overseeing such matters in Australia.

With effect from 21 December 2001, the Australian Privacy Act was extended to include most profit and non-profit organisations. On the Privacy Commissioner's website we read: 'The purpose of the Office of the Federal Privacy Commissioner (OFPC) is to promote an Australian culture that respects privacy. Our Strategic Plan 2000 identifies four key result areas in the lead-up to the commencement of the *Privacy Amendment (Private Sector) Act 2000*'. Ten privacy principles are put forward to meet these goals. They are summarised here:

● *Collection.* It is desirable to collect information directly from individuals by lawful and fair means, and use it only for the organisation's activities.

⊛ *Use and disclosure.* Use and disclose information only for the purpose for which the information was first collected.

⊛ *Data quality.* Keep the information current and accurate.

⊛ *Data security.* Keep the information secure.

⊛ *Openness.* The information must be available to those who ask for it.

⊛ *Access and accuracy.* In most instances, people must be allowed to see information held that concerns them.

⊛ *Identifiers.* An identifier, such as a Medicare number, cannot be adopted by another organisation.

⊛ *Anonymity.* Individuals must be allowed to remain anonymous while transacting.

⊛ *Transborder data flows.* Information about individuals can only be forwarded to a foreign country in special circumstances.

⊛ *Sensitive information.* Sensitive, personal, information (e.g. religious beliefs or criminal record) must be given a higher level of protection and collected only with the individual's consent.

Sources: See Australian Privacy Commissioner's website at <www.privacy. gov.au>, accessed 30 May 2003; the 10 Privacy Principles summarised from Olga Ganopolsky, 'Privacy Rules OK!', *Communiqué,* September 2001, pp. 12–15, <www.cmq.com.au>; Scott McNealy's quotation reprinted in Toby Lester, 'The Reinvention of Privacy', *The Atlantic Hotline,* <www.the atlantic.com/hotline/>, accessed 1 November 2001; Sean Nicholls, 'America's New War (on Privacy)', *The Age e)Mag,* November 2001, p. 35. For more on Echelon, see the European Commission Final Report at <www. cryptome.org/echelon-ep-fin.htm>, and Echelon Watch at <www.aclu.org/ echelonwatch/>, accessed 3 November 2001. For more on Carnivore see <www.epic.org/privacy/carnivore/>, accessed 3 November 2001.

Questions

1 What is your position on the issue of privacy? Do you agree with Scott McNealy, CEO of Sun Microsystems, that no matter what, you will never have privacy, OR, that privacy is a human right?

2 Why do the Australian Privacy Commissioner's survey results show a difference in the results recorded for different age groups and between city and rural dwellers?

3 Do the companies you deal with in the online environment enunciate privacy guidelines such as the ten summarised in the highlight? If not, why not?

21.3

In addition to the code, many other laws apply to franchising, including the consumer protection provisions of the Trade Practices Act, contract law and tort laws, such as passing off.

Intellectual property

Starting with the birth of a company and continuing throughout the business's life cycle, there is a need to protect such aspects as the business name, the trading name and trademarks, as well as Internet domain names. Other aspects of intellectual property also need to be protected, such as designs, new ideas and new ways of doing or making things, and patents are taken out for this purpose. As well, protection is needed for products such as computer software and genetic engineering, and secret formulas as in the case of Coca-Cola. In 1994 and 1995 Australia substantially reformed its trademarks law and significantly expanded the nature of what constitutes a mark to include anything that distinguishes one's product or service. Such distinguishing marks as visual devices, sounds, smells and three-dimensional shapes are included as long as they can be represented in writing. Thus, Chanel may be able to protect its aroma, Harley-Davidson the sound of its motorcycle and Coca-Cola the distinctive shape of its bottle via trademarks.

However, it is not just a matter of protecting one's own interests. There should also be an ethos in all businesses that employees do not infringe the rights of others.

Intellectual property protection is a specialised area requiring input from a number of professionals, starting with accountants and lawyers. Training in this area of legal compliance is needed on a national basis as well as at the corporation level.

The major areas covered by intellectual property laws include the following:

- *Copyright* protects individual ideas as expressed in various permanent forms such as original literary, dramatic, musical or artistic works; sound recordings, films, and broadcasts.[36] A website featuring the opening of the Olympic Games may, for example, involve several elements of copyright. The opening score for the Olympic Anthem is a musical work. The lyrics constitute a literary work and the broadcast of the event is itself protected. Likewise photographs of sports persons and sports events are copyright protected as artistic works. Works of architecture such as the Sydney Olympics sports stadium also enjoy copyright protection and may not be copied without authorisation.

- *Design* refers to the overall appearance of the product resulting from one or more visual features of the product. A good example of the marketability of design is seen in products such as the iMac or the iPod.[37]

- *Trademarks* can be any sign capable of being represented graphically which is capable of distinguishing goods or services. A trademark may consist of words, including personal names, designs, letters, numerals or the shape of goods or their packaging. Even sounds (the Harley sound) or smells (e.g. scented yarn) and distinctive combinations of colours may be capable of trademark protection. The Australian Football League has registered the sound of a football siren for football and associated services. Marks such as 'Mercedes' can be worth billions of dollars.[38] Owners of trademarks therefore are aggressive in protecting their turf. For example, at one point in time, Lion Nathan, the owners of XXXX brewer Castlemaine Perkins and the cheeky cartoon character in XXXX ads threatened to sue Brisbane rock band Six Foot Hick. The band had produced a T-shirt with the words 'Don't F..k with Queensland' on it. The design on the shirt featured a cartoon character resembling Mr Fourex but with his face replaced by a caricature of former premier Joe Bjelke-Peterson with shotgun in hand. Lawyers for the brewer demanded that all the T-shirts be destroyed and that the image be removed from the rock group's website.[39]

- *Patent* protection is given to an invention of a device, substance, method or process that is considered useful.[40] A new drug, a new method of doing electronic business, a new tool, a new engine are all examples of possible patents. Standard patents can take a long time to process and be very expensive. For this reason, Australia recently developed the 'innovation patent' process designed to protect smaller inventions (e.g. a gadget). The filing procedures and level of inventiveness required of an innovation patent are less.[41]

- *The Circuit Layouts Act* protects the owners of computer-chip circuitry. This protection lasts for 20 years. Such layout design is especially important in computer game simulations.[42]

- *Confidential information (e.g. trade secrets).* Some intellectual property can only be protected by keeping it confidential. For example, Coke's secret formula, a secret recipe or a hot new marketing concept, may be given legal protection as long as it is kept in commercial confidence. Employees, for example, who access such trade secrets on a confidential basis have a legal duty to keep the information confidential and to use it only for the purposes agreed upon. In *Fraser v Thames Television Ltd* [1984] QB 44, three rock stars successfully sued for the breach of confidentiality of their idea for a television series to be called Rock Follies.

- *Trade Practices Act.* The TPA also often comes into play in intellectual property marketing cases. For example, to use without permission Ian Thorpe's image and likeness to sell your swimming pools would be a breach of the TPA because you would be giving the impression that there was a connection or relationship between you and Ian Thorpe which you do not have. The same conduct may also violate other laws such as that of the tort of 'passing off'.

There are many other legal developments that the marketer should be aware of, but this brief account should at least give you the basic idea. Importantly, legal compliance is not a once-off affair. A legal compliance program must be constantly reviewed, audited and updated to keep abreast of important changes in the legal and ethical environment of business.

International agreements At the Uruguay Round of GATT there was agreement on Trade-Related Intellectual Property Rights (TRIPS). This agreement provides a single multilateral framework of principles, rules and disciplines dealing with a broad range of intellectual property including trademarks, patents, copyright, integrated circuits, geographical indications, plant variety rights and confidential information. Among the principles are those of non-discrimination and transparency. Among the reforms are the extension of patent terms to 20 years; the acceptance of detailed enforcement provisions relating to right-holders' powers, court procedures and enforcement; protection of circuits; and the adoption of a disputes framework administered by the World Trade Organisation.

Copyright reforms A brief look at the Australian amendments to the *Copyright Act 1968* provides some insight into the areas covered by such legislation. Performers' rights over unauthorised recordings have been extended from 20 to 50 years. Customs has been given greater powers to intercept unauthorised imports of copyright materials, including diskettes, tapes and semiconductor chips. Copyright owners of computer programs and sound recordings are granted exclusive right to authorise the rental of these works. Furthermore, Australia has adopted the notion of moral rights which means copyright owners are now able to take action where their works are treated in a derogatory manner, and they will gain the right to be named as the author of a work.

Protection of computer chips Legislation has been adopted in a number of countries to protect the layout of computer integrated circuits. A circuit layout is similar to a layout plan used by architects and engineers and shows the location of the elements, switches and interconnections which comprise an integrated circuit. The representation must be in a material form which can include the storage of the layout in computer form. The legislation protects what are termed 'EL rights' to the creator of an 'eligible layout'. The circuit itself or its packaging is usually labelled to give notice of the creator's EL rights. The designer of the circuit layout is given automatic protection without the need for registration. Protection under such legislation extends for a minimum of 10 years and a maximum of 20 years in Australia.

Digital copyright The digital copyright amendments were passed in September 2000 and came into effect in March 2001. The amendments require both owners and users of copyright to think carefully about how text, illustrations, photographs and other material are consumed when published in the form of bits and bytes.

Major features of the *Copyright Amendment (Digital Agenda) Act 2000* are that it:

- Adopts a new technology-neutral right of communication (applying to works such as books, plays, software, sound recordings and film equally). This public communication right replaces the previous broadcast and diffusion rights and is aimed at helping copyright owners to enforce their own rights. This right will apply to future technologies as well, for example Web-TV, without the need to amend the Copyright Act. The definition of broadcasting is retained in respect of broadcasts as a copyright subject matter, with the definition expanded to include wireless and cable transmission. The amendments also make it clear that the owner of copyright in broadcasts is the broadcaster and not service providers such as telecommunications carriers. It is also clear that the broadcasting licensee is the one responsible for obtaining licences for the broadcast of underlying copyright material contained in the broadcast.

- Empowers licence holders, as well as copyright owners, to monitor and prosecute infringers. Retained are the existing compulsory statutory licences and Copyright Tribunal jurisdiction in relation to the broadcasting of works and other subject matter.
- Extends existing fair use exceptions to an online environment so that one may reproduce up to 10% of the whole of a work. Neither is copyright infringed by browsing, that is, the making of a temporary reproduction or copy of the subject matter as part of the technical process of making or receiving a communication. Also excluded are certain caching practices.
- Makes illegal the abuse of commercial copyright protection measures, including program locks and encryption of broadcasts, by circumvention devices.
- Makes illegal the intentional tampering with rights management information electronically attached to copyright material.
- Makes carriers and ISPs liable for the transmission of infringing material where the carrier or ISP had control over the contents. For example, if an ISP provides access to a small business that provides music on hold to its subscribers, then the ISP is not liable because it did not control the content. However, if an ISP provides a music on-hold service to its customers without permission of the copyright holders, then the ISP would be liable because it directly controls the content. Carriers are only liable if they authorised the infringing actions. The Act gives greater guidance here, indicating that whether conduct has been authorised will depend upon the extent of the person's power to prevent the doing of the act concerned, the nature of any relationship between the person and the person who did the act concerned and whether the person took any reasonable steps to prevent or avoid the doing of an act, including whether the person complied with any relevant industry codes or practice.

Moral rights As of 21 December 2000 amendments to the Copyright Act have introduced moral rights into the Australian intellectual property regime. Authors thus now enjoy the following three moral rights:

1 To be identified with their works, that is, the right of attribution. This would include reproduction, publication and performance in public, transmission or adaptation.

2 Not to have authorship falsely attributed, that is, the right against false attribution. This could include the insertion of a person's name in/on a work or the authorisation of the insertion in a way that falsely implies that the person is the author of the work or that the work is an adaptation of the work of that person. It can also include dealing commercially with a work altered by a person other than the author, as being the unaltered work of the author.

3 Not to have their works subjected to derogatory treatment, that is, the right of integrity. This right also precludes (in relation to artistic works) the destruction of the work or an exhibition in public of the work in a manner that is prejudicial to the author's honour or reputation. To prove an infringement it must be shown that the act was a derogatory treatment; that the distortion or alteration was material; and that the action was prejudicial to the author's honour and reputation. An action will not be derogatory if the treatment was reasonable.[43]

Moral rights belong to the individual who created the work and cannot be assigned or transferred to another person. For example, a painting may have the copyright owned by the person who commissioned the painting, yet the moral rights are owned by the painter as the creator of the work.

Moral rights last for the duration of the copyright protection of the work, that is, for 70 years after the author's death (except for the right of integrity in relation to films). Where the author or creator of a work dies, the moral rights can be exercised by the author's legal personal representative.

There is no breach of the right of integrity if the action taken was reasonable in the circumstances. Whether an action was reasonable will depend upon:

- the nature of the work
- the purpose for which the work is used
- the manner in which the work is used
- the context in which the work is used
- any relevant practice in the industry
- any practice contained in a voluntary code of practice in the industry
- whether the work was made in the course of employment or as an independent contractor
- whether the treatment was required by law or necessary to avoid a breach of the law.

Joint authorship Where there is more than one author, the moral rights belong to each of the authors. A consent given by one of the joint authors does not affect the moral rights of the other.[44]

An author or creator can consent to acts or omissions that would ordinarily be an infringement of their moral rights. Such consent must be in writing. Thus an employer may want to amend the provisions of their standard employment contract to ensure that the employee consents to acts or omissions that have already occurred or may occur in the future in relation to the moral rights of employees who are creators or authors of works. Thus, a consent may allow an employer not to acknowledge the employee as the author of a work; publish the work and distribute it without acknowledgment or make substantial changes to or materially alter the work without the employee's consent. A consent will be invalid if given under duress or as a result of misleading or deceptive conduct made by the employer.[45]

Under the *Copyright Amendment (Moral Rights) Act 2000* (Cwlth) a court is able to award a wide range of remedies for a breach of a creator's moral rights. These include:

- damages
- injunction
- declaration that a moral right has been infringed
- order of a public apology by the infringer
- an order that a false attribution or derogatory treatment of the work be removed or reversed.

Innovative patent Australia has amended its patent laws, replacing the seldom used petty patents with an innovation patent. The logic of the innovation patent stems from the fact that standard patents last for 20 years, but can take a year or more to acquire, including numerous responses to the patent office inquiries. This makes standard patents unsuitable for smaller inventions. The innovation patents will provide protection for eight years only. They are designed to give businesses protection in relation to more minor applications.[46]

Gene Technology Act 2000

The *Gene Technology Act 2000* (Cwlth) regulates the 'dealings' with genetically modified organisms. 'Dealings' include research, manufacturing, production, commercial release and importing. The Act establishes a scheme for the assessment of risks to human health and the environment associated with various opportunities for public input.

Transport law

A sale is not finalised until the goods are delivered. This is a major strategic area of marketing warranting the employment of specialised personnel. They need to keep abreast of legislation covering rail, road and sea transport. They also need to be fully conversant with bills of lading and other relevant documentation.

International marketing law

A number of matters concerning international marketing law require examination.

Sale of goods Sales contracts made in the global marketplace need special attention. This is because they transcend different legal systems and because different currencies are involved. International marketers need to be knowledgeable about the convention governing Contracts for the International Sale of Goods, because the terms of this convention will apply unless the exporter's contract states otherwise. The 'documentary' nature of international trade cannot be overstated.

Product liability Exporters and importers need to be aware of their potential liability for damage to persons and property caused by defective goods. What would an Australian exporter of rolled steel do in the event of defects being discovered during the customer's manufacturing process in Taiwan? Shipping the steel back for rectification would not be an affordable solution. Thus careful attention must be paid to quality management, packaging and labelling, contingency plans for product recalls, customer complaints and adequate insurance protection.

International standards Marketers can expect greater pressure for their organisations to seek national and international accreditation if they wish to continue their supply arrangements. Increasingly, we will witness alliances of small and emerging businesses seeking accreditation and gaining access to export markets via electronic methods of promotion and fulfilment. The arduous process of gaining accreditation requires input from experienced people as processes require blueprinting and small teams of personnel scrutinise the methods in use.

International distribution Gaining business in many parts of the world requires local knowledge. Agency arrangements, distributorships, licensing arrangements and joint venture formation are a few of the more common legal strategies that international marketers can employ to ensure their goods and services reach customers and consumers in overseas markets. Most importantly, mechanisms for payment from such intermediaries need to be thought through and agreed by way of contract.

Export transactions International marketers should seek specialised advice on how best to structure an export operation so as to minimise the tax liability, particularly to avoid paying double taxation.

International finance and trade settlements Expert advice is available to international marketers in a startup situation from a range of bodies such as Austrade.[47] A sale is not finalised until the goods and services are paid for. If prepayment cannot be arranged, then letters of credit or bills of exchange should be considered. Where exporters have to operate under an open account arrangement, the creditworthiness of customers must be given a high priority. Where the sales transaction is conducted in another currency, the exporter should consider a forward exchange contract, or similar mechanism, as a safeguard against currency fluctuations. The idea is to reduce risk in the areas of credit, transfer and exchange.

Transport Reliability is the keyword when it comes to distributing goods over long distances to international markets. Marketers need to be knowledgeable about the laws, conventions and customs governing international transport—particularly the legal nature and significance of the documentation employed. Once again, education and training are needed.

International customs, anti-dumping and competition law Export marketers must ensure that they comply with customs laws as well as anti-dumping and competition laws.

Export incentives and assistance As already indicated, many sources of assistance—both financial and information based—are available to the international marketer from public and commercial sources.

Dispute resolution in international trade International marketers should be aware of the various sources of assistance available to resolve disputes, especially in relation to arbitration. The Institute of Arbitrators Australia (IAA) and the Australian Centre for International Commercial Arbitration (ACICA) are such sources in Australia. Contracts for the sale of goods and/or services should contain provisions that deal with dispute resolution. Wherever possible, alternative dispute resolution should be used so that the business relationship continues and the parties resolve the dispute as quickly, inexpensively and harmoniously as possible.

There are many other developments that the international marketer should be aware of, particularly in the areas of electronic commerce, credit and payment.

SELF-CHECK QUESTIONS

9 Place yourself in the role of a regional sales manager on a visit to a major client in another city. You accidentally meet the managers of two competitors over pre-dinner drinks at the motel you are patronising. Is it possible to avoid discussing business matters? Should you have dinner with the other managers? Discuss the situation in general.

10 Provide examples of products whose smell, sound and shape you might wish to protect. Say why you wish to protect these products.

11 The Commissioner of the US Federal Trade Commission pointed to the case 'where a Panamanian company sent out [bogus] invoices for entries in an international telefax directory. The invoices were mailed from the Czech Republic using a Swiss correspondence address on the invoice. Criminal proceedings brought in Switzerland against the company had to be abandoned because it was not possible to prove that a criminal act had been performed on Swiss soil.[48] Comment on this case in the light of the Internet being used for such schemes in the future.

SUMMARY

A marketing system should sense, serve and satisfy consumer needs and improve the quality of consumers' lives. In working to meet consumer needs, marketers might take some actions that are not to everyone's liking or benefit. Marketing managers should be aware of the main *criticisms of marketing*.

Marketing's *impact on individual consumer welfare* has been criticised for its high prices, deceptive practices, high-pressure selling, shoddy or unsafe products, planned obsolescence and poor service to disadvantaged consumers. Marketing's *impact on society* has been criticised for creating false wants and too much materialism, too few social goods, cultural pollution and too much political power. Critics have also questioned marketing's *impact on other businesses*—for harming competitors and reducing competition through acquisitions, practices that create barriers to entry and unfair competitive marketing practices.

Concerns about the marketing system have led to *citizen-action movements. Consumerism* is an organised social movement intended to strengthen the rights and power of consumers relative to sellers. Alert marketers view it as an opportunity to serve consumers better by providing more consumer information, education and protection.

Environmentalism is an organised social movement seeking to minimise the harm done to the environment and quality of life by marketing practices. It calls for curbing consumer wants when their satisfaction would be at too much environmental cost. Citizen action has led to the passage of many laws to protect consumers in the area of product safety, truth in packaging, truth in lending and truth in advertising.

Many companies originally opposed these social movements and laws, but most of them now recognise a need for positive consumer information, education and protection. Some companies have followed a policy of *enlightened marketing* based on the six principles of *remaining market-oriented, continuing innovativeness, adding value, having a sense of mission, maintaining social responsibility* and *employing marketing metrics*.

Increasingly, companies are responding to the need to provide marketing organisation policies and guidelines to help their managers deal with questions of *marketing ethics*.

It is suggested that marketing organisations should adopt a *legal compliance* program in an endeavour to prevent legal problems. Such a program will uncover any business practices that might expose the company to criticism or legal action. On a broader scale, such a program enables an organisation to meet the claims it makes to being an ethical marketer in its mission statement or its statement of values.

It is perhaps appropriate that the last word on the subject of legal compliance in marketing in the Information Age—and the science and practice of marketing—should go to Nicholas Negroponte, the world-renowned information technology expert:

> I think the law is an early-warning system telling us 'this is a big one'. National law has no place in cyberlaw. Where is cyberspace [marketspace]? If you don't like banking laws in [your country], set up your machine on the Grand Cayman Islands. Don't like copyright laws in [your country]? Set up your machine in China. Cyberlaw is global law, which is not going to be easy to handle, since we seemingly cannot even agree on world trade of automobile body parts.[49]

How often do we come across a product such as a digital camera range that offers different models at different price points? Let us consider a hypothetical range—Brand X— with various picture quality, here described in terms of the megapixels on offer (4 megapixels, 5 megapixels and 6 megapixels), also offering a single 3× zoom capability— where dividing the longer focal length on offer (105 mm) by the shorter length offered (35 mm) we can ascertain that each camera in this range has a 3× zoom lens. In this example, the 4 Mp camera is offered to consumers at $299, the 5 Mp camera at $450 and the 6 Mp camera at $599.

Let us consider further that there is no cost differential from the manufacturer of the cameras without the CCD, or image sensor, and that each costs $50. Let us further assume that the company marketing Brand X has the CCD manufactured under licence and the costs are $40, $50 and

$60 for each of the three sensors. Let us further hypothesise that the following ex-marketer and retail prices apply:

	Brand X ex-marketer price	Retail gross margin (approx.)	Retail selling price
4 megapixels	$135	55%	$299
5 megapixels	$160	64%	$450
6 megapixels	$187	69%	$599

Examine the marketer's mark-up and the retailers' gross margin, and take into account the costs involved. Are there any legal issues? Are there any ethical issues? Perhaps this is just how market forces work, and how companies respond? What are your views?

KEY TERMS

DISCUSSING THE ISSUES

1. Sales meetings with competitors? One often hears of salespeople meeting in their favourite after-work bar or restaurant for some relaxation. They are like-minded people, and have often worked together in earlier times. Sometimes, key account managers and more senior sales managers keep up these practices after they are promoted. Do you see any issues involved with such practices?

2. Does marketing create barriers to entry or does it reduce them? How can a small manufacturer of household cleaning products use advertising to compete with Lever & Kitchen?

3. John Bloaggsus put his dinner suit into a dry cleaning store—QwikClean—on his way to work in the morning as he was attending a company function that night. He planned to change at work and go directly to the function. He chose QwikClean because it advertised on the shop window in large sign writing '24-hour dry cleaning'. John worked until 6.30 pm and then walked to the shop to pick up his suit. You guessed it . . . the dry cleaners had shut at 6.00 pm. John missed his company function and was told the next day by his managing director that he could kiss his promotion goodbye. John went to see his solicitor in an attempt to prosecute the dry cleaners for false advertising. What advice do you think the solicitor will give John? Why?

4 Big Coating Works (BCW) Pty Ltd put in a tender to the prime contractor (lead builder) of a police station that had won the state government tender. Along the way, it discovered that the government architects had specified the lowest cost concrete walls for the cells, leading to a very rough and pitted concrete finish, but that BCW were expected to provide the highest standard of finish. This meant that much of the filling would be at their cost. Believing this unreasonable, they ended up in dispute with the builder and the government over what they regarded as an unconscionable contract. What are your views?

5 If you had the power to change our marketing system in any way feasible, decide what improvements you would make. What improvements would you make as a consumer or entry-level marketing practitioner?

6 Society is becoming more litigious. Once, it required a lone consumer to take on the task of succeeding at law before anyone else would take on a company that had for instance produced a poor product such as silicon breast implants. Today class actions of the kind depicted in the movie *Erin Brockovich* are much more likely, even in Australia and New Zealand. Do such class actions benefit all concerned?

REFERENCES

1. Kath Walters, 'Blogging Power', *Business Review Weekly*, 15–21 December 2005, pp. 78–79; Anonymous, 'Russinovich Joins Class Action Legal Team', <www.pcdoctor-guide.com/wordpress/?p=1787>, accessed 4 January 2006; Crikey.com.au, accessed 4 January 2006; Notgoodenough.org.au, accessed 4 January 2006.
2. See Steven H. Star, 'Marketing and its Discontents', *Harvard Business Review*, November–December 1989, pp. 148–154.
3. See John F. Gaski and Michael Etzel, 'The Index of Consumer Sentiment toward Marketing', *Journal of Marketing*, July 1986, pp. 71–81; Faye Rice, 'How to Deal with Tougher Customers', *Fortune*, 3 December 1990, pp. 38–48; and Richard W. Pollay and Banwari Mittal, 'Here's the Beef: Factors, Determinants, and Segments in Consumer Criticism of Advertising', *Journal of Marketing*, July 1993, pp. 99–114.
4. See Theodore Levitt, 'The Morality (?) of Advertising', *Harvard Business Review*, July–August 1970, pp. 84–92.
5. See Anonymous, 'Choice Cuts—Caffeine Tea', *Choice*, May 1995, p. 4; and also see Australian Consumers' Association, 'From Gas Heater to Flamethrower', *Choice*, July 1992, pp. 16–19. For a discussion on the law of tort based on the legal ramifications of *Donoghue v Stevenson*, see Eugene Clark, George Cho and Arthur Hoyle (eds), *Marketers and the Law*, Sydney, LawBook Company, 2000, pp. 162–165.
6. The award winning German film *Rosalie Goes Shopping*, directed by Bernd Heinl, premiered at the Cannes Film Festival in 1990. The film stars Marianne Sagebrecht as Rosalie, who is married to a former Vietnam pilot turned crop duster, and a hapless immigrant victim of American consumer society. She beats the system into submission by becoming variously a computer hacker and con woman as she discovers that if she owes the bank $US100 000 the bank wants its money, but if she owes the bank $US1 000 000, the bank is a pawn in her hands.
7. See Anne B. Fisher, 'A Brewing Revolt against the Rich', *Fortune*, 17 December 1990, pp. 89–94; and Norval D. Glenn, 'What Does Family Mean?', *American Demographics*, June 1992, pp. 30–37.
8. Peter Brain, 'We All Fall Down', *The Australian Financial Review*, 2 November 2001, pp. 3, 7; also see Peter Brain, *Beyond Meltdown: The Global Battle for Economic Growth*, Scribe Publications, 1999.
9. Ibid., Brain 1999, p. 2.
10. Ibid.
11. See Kimn Clark, 'Real-World-O-Nomics: How to Make Traffic Jams a Thing of the Past', *Fortune*, 31 March 1997, p. 34.
12. Op. cit. See Anne B. Fisher, 'A Brewing Revolt Against the Rich,' *Fortune*, 17 December 1990, pp. 89–94; and Norval D. Glenn, 'What Does Family Mean?', *American Demographics*, June 1992, pp. 30–37.
13. See Nicole Lindsay, 'Victorian Tram Lines May Merge', *The Australian Financial Review*, 18 October 2002, p. 6.
14. For more details see Paul N. Bloom and Stephen A. Greyser, 'The Maturing of Consumerism', *Harvard Business Review*, November–December 1981, pp. 130–139; Robert J. Samualson, 'The Aging of Ralph Nader', *Newsweek*, 16 December 1985, p. 57; and Douglas A. Harbrecht, 'The Second Coming of Ralph Nader', *Business Week*, 6 March 1989, p. 28.
15. Noble Robinson, Ralph Earle III and Ronald A. N. McLean, 'Transnational Corporations and Global Environmental Policy', *Prizm*, First Quarter, 1994, pp. 51–63.
16. Ibid., p. 56.
17. BBC News, 'Europe Backs Kyoto Accord', <http://news.bbc.co.uk/hi/english/world/europe/newsid_1252000/1252556.stm>, 31 March 2001, accessed 1 April and 4 November 2001.
18. Ibid.
19. Paul D. Ellis, 'Market Orientation and Marketing Practice in a Developing Economy', *European Journal of Marketing*, vol. 39, no. 5/6, 2005, pp. 629–645; John C. Narver and Stanley F. Slater, 'The Effect of a Market Orientation on Business Profitability', *Journal of Marketing*, vol. 54, 1990, pp. 20–35.
20. Quoted from 'Our Credo', Johnson & Johnson, New Brunswick, New Jersey. Reprinted with permission.
21. Neil Shoebridge, 'Marketers' Measure', *Business Review Weekly*, 1–7 December 2005, p. 63.

22. John F. Magee and P. Ranganath Nayak, *Prizm*, First Quarter, 1994, pp. 65–77.

23. Anne McElvoy, 'Ethics and Business: The New Morality Maze', *The Australian Financial Review*, 24 January 1996, p. 14.

24. John A. Byrne, 'Businesses Are Signing Up for Ethics 101', *Business Week*, 15 February 1988, pp. 56–57.

25. Kenneth Labich, 'The New Crisis in Business Management', *Fortune*, 20 April 1992, pp. 167–176, here p. 176.

26. From 'Ethics as a Practical Matter', a message from David R. Whitman, Chairman of the Board of Whirlpool Corporation, as reprinted in Ricky E. Griffin and Ronald J. Ebert, *Business*, Englewood Cliffs, NJ, Prentice Hall, 1989, pp. 578–579. For more on marketing ethics, see Lynn Sharp Paine, 'Managing for Organizational Integrity', *Harvard Business Review*, March–April 1994, pp. 106–117.

27. Eugene Clark, 'The New Law and Order: Reforms Heat Up', *Professional Marketing*, April 1996, pp. 38–40.

28. Anne McElvoy, 1996, op. cit., p. 14.

29. See Eugene Clark's books co-authored with John Livermore: *Australian Marketing Law*, Sydney, The Law Book Company, 1994; and *Marketers and the Law*, Sydney, The Law Book Company, 2000 (with George Cho and Arthur Hoyle).

30. Australian Trade Practices Report, 41-207 (1993).

31. See N. Francey, 'High Court Clears the Way for Class Actions', *Australian Lawyer*, vol. 27, May 1995, on *Carnie v Esanda Finance Corporation Ltd*, in which the High Court took a broad view of such legislation and thus cleared the way for more representative actions to be utilised at state as well as federal levels. Note also that recent changes have been made to the unconscionable conduct provisions found in Part IVA of the Trade Practices Act. These changes empower the ACCC to bring a representative action on behalf of small businesses that are victims of unconscionable conduct at the hand of larger businesses.

32. Australian Trade Practices Report, 41-207 (1993).

33. See J. Huby, 'Corrective Advertising: Punishment or Promotion', *Australian Professional Marketing*, June 1993, p. 46. See generally, ACCC website, <www.accc.gov.au>.

34. See the Australian Direct Marketing Association Code of Practice at <www.adma.com.au>. See also the Commonwealth Government's Model Code: Building Consumer Sovereignty in Electronic Commerce—A Best Practice Model for Business, found at: <www.treasury.gov.au/ecommerce>. Compare what is happening in the UK where the Office of Fair Trading is providing assistance to marketers regarding Distance Selling Guidelines: <www.oft.gov.uk>.

35. The e-commerce guidelines are based on the OECD Guidelines for Consumer Protection in Electronic Commerce. See generally <www.oecd.org/EN/home/>.

36. *Copyright Amendment 1968* (Cth), *Copyright Act, Copyright Act (Digital Agenda) Act 2000* (Cth).

37. *Design Act 2003* (Cth).

38. *Trademarks Act 1995* (Cth).

39. Kevin Mead, 'Band Feels a Lawsuit Coming on as Fourex Joke Falls Flat', *The Weekend Australian*, 11–12 December 2004, p. 9.

40. *Patents Act 1990* (Cth).

41. See IP Australia website, available at <www.ipasutralia.gov.au>.

42. *Circuits Layout Act 1989* (Cth).

43. Section 195AS of the *Copyright Amendment (Moral Rights) Act 2000* (Cth).

44. *Copyright Amendment (Moral Rights) Act 2000* (Cth), sections 195AZ, 5AZ(5), 195ZK(5) and 195AZI(5).

45. *Copyright Amendment (Moral Rights) Act 2000* (Cth), sections 195AWB(1) and (2).

46. See IP Australia website, available at <www.ipaustralia.gov.au>.

47. See <austrade.gov.au>.

48. See Prepared Remarks of Roscoe B. Starek III, Commissioner, US Federal Trade Commission, on the topic 'Consumer Protection in the Age of Borderless Markets and the Information Revolution', at <www.webcom.com/~lewrose/speech/starek.html>.

49. Nicholas Negroponte, *Being Digital*, London, Hodder & Stoughton, 1995. See generally, Eugene Clark, George Cho and Arthur Hoyle (eds), *E-business: Law and Management for the 21st Century*, Canberra, Info-sys Law International Publications.

PHOTO/AD CREDITS

Jan Charbonneau, Massey University and Andrew Hercus, Christchurch College of Education

CASE STUDY
The marketing maul: Lions and All Blacks vs ambush marketers

Imagine the scene: June 2005, Test 1 of the long anticipated match-up between the British and Irish Lions (Lions) and New Zealand's iconic All Blacks at Christchurch's Jade Stadium. Circling the field are signs for official sponsors such as DHL and Adidas. Fans are cheering and television cameras from around the world are pointing towards the players as they stream onto the field from an entrance covered with signage for Paul Kelly Motors. An official sponsor of the Lions Tour? The Lions? The All Blacks? No, a sponsor of Jade Stadium—which paid no official sponsor fee for all this local, national and international publicity. Nor did other Jade Stadium sponsors such as Ricoh or DB Draught. What's the harm you might well ask? Imagine that you are competitors Canon or Steinlager which paid to be official sponsors. You might well question whether it was money well spent or if you got your money's worth.

Sponsorship is big business. In 2004, an estimated $US28 billion was spent worldwide on sponsorship, up from $US26 billion in 2003, $US24 billion in 2002 and dramatically up from the US$4 billion spent in 1987 (Researchandmarkets. com 2005; IEG 2002; Meenaghan 1994). Major sporting events like the Olympics, Commonwealth Games, various sports' World Cups or the 2005 Lions Tour of New Zealand rely heavily on the financial contributions of sponsors. For example, approximately 40% of the cost of running the Olympics is contributed by sponsors. The sum of $US550 million was contributed for Sydney 2000 (SOCOG 2002) and €693 million for Athens 2004 by worldwide sponsors like Coke and McDonald's alone (IOC 2004), not considering the contributions of lower-tier sponsors and official suppliers such as Adidas.

For this kind of money, sponsors expect results! And results they usually get! Olympic sponsors, for example, gain the rights to use one of the most recognised symbols in the world—the multicoloured interlocking rings—in their promotional campaigns. According to International Olympic Committee (IOC) research, Olympic sponsors are the most respected of sporting sponsors. This respect translates at the consumer level into an increased likelihood of purchasing sponsors' products (IOC 1997). Besides results, sponsors also expect exclusivity (being the only official sponsor for a product/ service category)—intending that they, not their competitors, benefit from association with the sponsored event. Enter the ambushers!

Ambush marketing refers to any actions organisations, often competitors, take to associate themselves with a sponsored event— without paying the fees required to be an official sponsor. Ambushers seek to create consumer confusion as to who is the official sponsor, capturing whatever marketplace goodwill and media attention official sponsorship offers, hoping to enhance corporate and brand image through implied endorsement by the sponsored event and generate sales in the long term. Given the exclusive nature of sponsorship agreements, ambushers also hope to defuse any potential benefits accruing to official sponsors, thereby reducing any potential competitive advantage to be gained by the sponsorship. As Brewer (1993, p. 68) noted, 'The reasons [for ambushing] are obvious. Sponsorships cost a fortune. And the field has become so cluttered that consumers often can't sort out who supports what anyway. Ambushers figure they can identify themselves with an event without having to shell out the exorbitant fees'.

In most countries the unauthorised use of registered trademarks, logos or slogans or misleading the public by falsely naming a company as an official sponsor amounts to an infringement of intellectual property laws or trade

practices legislation. However, most ambush marketing campaigns do not blatantly infringe existing legislation, staying well within the letter of the law. Rather, ambush marketing campaigns creatively and ingeniously associate their names with the event, avoiding actual infringement. A classic example was American Express's slogan 'If you're travelling to Lillehammer, you will need a passport but you don't need a visa', creatively (and legally) ambushing Visa, an official sponsor of the 1994 Winter Olympics.

Given the increasingly creative nature of ambushers, traditional forms of protection in trademark, copyright, competition, trade practices and advertising legislation are often ineffective, requiring the enactment of ambush-specific laws. For example, the UK enacted the Olympic Symbols Etc. (Protection) Act 1995 to protect the British Olympic Committee from unauthorised use of Olympic symbols and protected words such as 'Olympian'. Prior to the Cricket World Cup in 2003, South Africa enacted legislation making ambush marketing a criminal offence. For Sydney 2000, the Australian government enacted and amended ambush-specific legislation—the *Sydney 2000 Games (Indicia and Images) Protection Act 1996* and the *Olympic Insignia Protection Act 1987*—to supplement existing intellectual property rights. The UK has already enacted tough legislation to protect against ambush marketing at the 2012 Summer Games in London. The legislation confers 'exclusive rights (on the London Organising Committee and its licensees) . . . to the use of any visual or verbal representation (of any kind) likely to create in the public mind an association between the London Olympics and goods or services', making any infringements unlawful (www.marketinglaw.co.uk).

Whether there is specific-event anti-ambushing laws or protection is available through a country's existing intellectual property or business practices legislation, controlling ambush marketing requires vigilance, persistence and constant pursuit of alleged infringements—not just during events but in lead-up and wind-down periods.

Both the Lions and All Blacks organisations have Intellectual Property Divisions charged with protecting their brands. In New Zealand during the Lions Tour, both the Lions and All Blacks closely monitored apparel sales and black market tickets, using private investigators to ferret out counterfeit team jerseys. Corporate promotional activities were monitored with both organisations pursuing companies using tickets as contest prizes, contrary to ticketing regulations. Cease and desist letters were used extensively to combat unauthorised use of All Blacks and Lions' trademarks (images, athlete photos, etc.) as these could imply an association with the tour. This monitoring extended even to pursuing non-sponsors placing congratulatory messages in local newspapers.

In the UK, the Lions actively pursued Gillette for running an advertising campaign featuring prominent Lions' players Robinson and O'Driscoll in an effort to protect official sponsor SureMen (Gillette's competitor). After a long legal battle, the ads were finally withdrawn. The Lions closed down many unofficial websites and limited the range of activities that contractually could be undertaken by Lions players acting as 'rugby ambassadors' for non-official sponsors.

Venues presented their own particular challenges to the All Blacks, Lions and their official sponsors. The Olympics requires that all venues used are 'clean', having only authorised signage from official sponsors. According to Andrew Hercus, who investigated ambush marketing at the beach volleyball Athens 2004 competition, the 'clean stadia' policy and aggressive monitoring of all officials, athletes, visitors and volunteers resulted in a low incidence of the traditional competitor ambushes occurring in venues at previous Olympics.

Many major sporting events, both national and international, however, do not have the luxury of either purpose-built venues or bidding city requirements for clean stadia. These events use pre-existing venues, used by a range of other teams and sports, often with pre-existing sponsorship arrangements. For the 2005 Lions Tour, existing facilities in Christchurch, Auckland

CASE STUDY

CASE
STUDY

and Wellington were used. Jade Stadium, the Christchurch venue, for example, has its own corporate sponsors as does the local Super 14 team, Canterbury Crusaders—each with their own contractual arrangements relative to signage and on-site facilities. As a further complication, the New Zealand Rugby Football Union (NZRU) governs many entities including the All Blacks, Super 14 and the National Provincial Championship. Each of these entities has their own sponsorship agreements, often with competing companies. For example, sports apparel retailer Champions of the World was licensed by the NZRU as an official supplier of Lions Tour merchandise, even though competitor Rebel Sports have the naming rights for the New Zealand section of the Super 14 competition.

As part of their sponsorship packages, official sponsors of the All Blacks, Lions and Lions Tour only have the rights to control signage 1.2 metres above the field of play. 'Official sponsor' signage had to compete in a signage-cluttered Jade Stadium (see photo) for the attention of the 1.26 million television viewers across New Zealand and the millions worldwide. If any of the 42 000 in attendance wanted a beer, their only choice was DB Draught, which has an exclusive vending agreement with Jade Stadium (competitors Guinness and Steinlager are official sponsors of the Lions and All Blacks respectively). As part of their sponsorship packages, official sponsors were provided with rights of first refusal to purchase in-stadium video opportunities, taken up by some like Guinness. Remaining time was then sold to companies like Vodafone, competitor of official sponsor New Zealand Telecom.

Given the cluttered stadium and promotional efforts undertaken by a range of non-official sponsors, were Christchurch consumers confused? Remember that consumer confusion is the aim of ambush marketers. Research was conducted by the authors in mid-2005 in Christchurch to determine recognition levels for official sponsors. Over 400 rugby fans and the general public were exposed to showcards with official Lions, All Blacks and Tour sponsors, major competitors and Jade Stadium sponsors.

Official All Blacks sponsors Adidas, Steinlager and Ford fared well with both rugby fans and the general public, with Adidas achieving over 80% recognition. Both Adidas and Ford promoted their official sponsor status extensively with television advertising and integrated promotional campaigns. However, official All Blacks sponsor Telecom was recognised as such by only one-third of respondents—despite extensive television advertising, inserts in phone bills and significant

DB Draught and Ricoh—official Jade Stadium sponsors get free publicity during 2005 Lions Tour.
© Andrew Hercus, 2005. Used with permission.

Jade Stadium sponsor, Paul Kelly Motors.
© Andrew Hercus, 2005. Used with permission.

on-site promotions such as a WW II-style bunker reinforcing their war-related ad campaign theme 'Unite for Victory'. Both rugby fans and the general public were confused as to whether Mastercard or Visa was the official sponsor. Mastercard, as the official All Blacks sponsor, did not widely promote its official sponsor status.

Official Lions sponsors Zurich and Guinness achieved good recognition; however so did Vodafone—a non-sponsor! Official Lions Tour sponsor DHL was recognised by just over half of the rugby fans and one-third of the general public as an official tour sponsor—a somewhat disappointing result considering the tour was named and promoted as the DHL New Zealand Lions Series 2005. Powerade, an official All Blacks and Lions sponsor, achieved very low recognition scores—comparable to those received by McDonald's. While McDonald's is a well-known sport sponsor (e.g. Olympics), the company had no connection with the Lions, All Blacks or the tour other than limited pre-existing signage at Jade Stadium.

For the Lions Tour, official sponsors signed on with full knowledge of terms and conditions—for example, signage protection only to 1.2 metres and the use of existing facilities with existing sponsors (at various levels). As such, was it reasonable for official sponsors to expect high levels of exclusivity and general public recognition of their official sponsorship status? Was it money well spent? For some the answer

Official tour sponsor DHL and 'non-sponsor' McDonald's.
© Andrew Hercus, 2005. Used with permission.

was 'yes', for others . . . While more exclusivity can be guaranteed for events such as the Olympics or the 2011 Rugby World Cup where 'clean stadia' will be enforced, it comes at a much higher cost.

Sources: Anonymous, 'Maximizing the Value of Sponsorship', 2005, *ResearchandMarkets.com*; Anonomous, '"Crack-down on Olympic Profiteering" Raises Fears', <www.marketinglaw.co.uk>; G. Brewer, 'Be Like Nike?', *Sales and Marketing Management*, September 1993, pp. 67–74; A. Hercus, 'Minimizing the Impact of Ambush Marketing on Beach Volleyball as an Olympic Discipline', *SMAANZ Conference Proceeding*, 2005; IEG Sponsorship Report 2002; IOC, 'Olympic Rings', *Marketing Matters*, vol. 11, 1997, pp. 5–7; IOC, *Olympic Marketing Fact File*, 2004, IOC Marketing Department; T. Meenaghan, 'Point of View: Ambush Marketing: Immoral or Imaginative Practice?', *Journal of Advertising Research*, vol. 34, no. 3, 1994, pp. 77–88; SOCOG, *Auditor-General's Report to Parliament*. Interviews include Stuart Robertson, Product Manager, New Zealand Rugby Football Union (All Blacks), July/August 2005, and Jon Davis, Commercial Manager, British and Irish Lions/Six Nations Properties (Lions), September 2005.

QUESTIONS

1. Why might a company sponsor a major event? Why might their competitors engage in ambush marketing?

2. Some would suggest that ambush marketing is an illegal or at least unethical practice. Others say it's just good marketing. Discuss the legal and ethical issues pertaining to ambush marketing. Make reference to specific legislation in your home country.

3. How might technology such as the Internet and camera-enabled mobile phones change the scope of ambush marketing?

4. Would ambush marketing be considered to be 'responsible' marketing? Is engaging in ambush marketing consistent with efforts to create a corporate image of social responsibility?

5. What measures might a company or event manager use to protect against or counter ambush marketing?

CASE STUDY

Answers to self-check questions

CHAPTER ONE

1. Consumer goods marketing involves physical products and intermediaries such as retailers, while non-profit marketing quite often involves services such as health care and means direct involvement by the marketing organisation with the end-user.

2. See the linking of these terms in Figure 1-2 and their definitions in the section 'What is marketing?'

3. Additionally, the marketing organisation seeks to meet its own objectives such as making a profit or a surplus.

4. While basic needs will remain unchanged, consumers will want to experience products and demand brands that meet their individual requirements. Also, they are more likely to want their requirements met quickly as their perception of timeliness is changed through use of online marketing channels. Businesses will continue to experience metamorphosis as they increasingly become part of online network alliances dedicated to exceeding customer expectations in terms of supplying business inputs, providing service delivery and achieving higher customer retention levels and profits.

5. Marketing management is the analysis, planning, implementation and control of programs designed to create, build and maintain beneficial exchanges with target buyers for the purpose of achieving organisational objectives.

6. In developed countries both might be regarded as examples of latent demand.

7. Public transport is one such example of irregular demand that might be considered.

8. One might consider this an example of the selling concept in action, rather than the marketing concept.

9. Not necessarily. It might be a natural preoccupation of the industry in its early stages of development—for example, optic fibre cable installation comes before Pay-TV. However, if there is a low adoption rate, perhaps consumer needs, wants and demands have not been considered.

10. As the CEO at J&J put it: 'It's plain good business sense' for marketing organisations to adopt a stance that takes society's interests into account when making marketing decisions.

11. One approach would be to fund social service media advertising designed to make youthful drinkers more aware of the dangers of drinking and driving. Another might be to sponsor rehabilitation where people succumb to alcohol addiction. Yet another might be to make less of an association in media advertising between drinking alcoholic beverages and sporting prowess, and in other ways reduce perceptions that alcohol is a social lubricant.

12. Smaller firms are also involved as they, too, find themselves competing with both large and small marketing organisations from abroad.

13. Just as there are financially rich and poor nations and societal groups, there are information rich and information poor. The two are related in that it costs a great deal to gain the infrastructure necessary to access such things as digital information.

14. Globalisation means, among other things, that 'best practice' is judged by customers now experiencing a broader range of competing marketers who have already learned that maintaining relationships means providing customer service over an extended period of time. Customer retention is of paramount importance.

15. Information is increasingly the key to sustainable competitive advantage. Such information takes many forms. On one hand, intellectual property is increasingly becoming the main asset of firms such as News Corporation and Fairfax as they seek to position themselves in customers' minds. Knowledge of individual customer's requirements is increasingly the key to keeping such customers loyal in the long run. These, and many other business activities in the information age, are only made possible by increasingly powerful information technology infrastructure and innovation in the way such technologies are used.

CHAPTER TWO

1. It's hard to draw any meaningful conclusions from a comparison of companies in different companies. It would be much more useful if Jane can compare satisfaction data with a company in the same industry and/or track what's happening over time.

2. It is appropriate for a private hospital to lift satisfaction levels as described. However, the meaning of service levels must be established. This term has different meanings in different industry settings and to different customers. Do the patrons mean that the hospital provides food and beverages on time, or of a high quality, or do they mean that the hospital is clean? It must be established which factors are important for the product in question and then appropriate monitoring can take place.

3. Relationships between buyers and sellers are important in nearly all marketing situations. Even the purchase of an impulse line requires trust that the brand has been applied to product that is 'fit for purpose'. There is thus a relationship, albeit different from the relationship between a sales engineer and a Caterpillar buyer spending $1 000 000.

4. Customer lifetime value is critical, because the longer the customer stays with an organisation, the more likely they are to repay costs to acquire them. Sometimes customers only buy once (e.g. a wedding dress) but they may still provide business by recommending others.

5. Training cannot overcome poor human resources selection. Training is very important and can ensure that good service is provided in most situations.

6. This ensures that managers never lose sight of the customer and ensures that they understand employee needs as well.

7. Among other outcomes this ensures that employees see the experience and qualifications they each hold. Employees are thus more likely to take responsibility for their own self-development, and employers are able to assign people to—or employees assign themselves to—appropriate projects.

8. In many cases, processes are invisible to customers, such as the process airlines use to allocate seats or prepare meals. Discussion here will centre on visible processes such as customer service level provided by a voice response telephone system, or an order processing system that ensured speedy delivery.

9. While McDonald's QSCV—quality, service,

cleanliness and value—might not be unique, it does form the basis of a system that involves crew focusing on customer satisfaction.

10. Process is more than simply a mechanistic approach to gaining competitive advantage. It must pervade all areas or departments within the organisation, even those that have little or no direct customer contact.

11. As Beckham (1992) puts it: 'we have to think of ourselves as customer satisfiers—customer advocates focused on whole processes'.

12. Marketing must deliver quality marketing (high standards) in such activities as marketing research, sales training, advertising, customer service and others.

13. Internal marketing is important for all organisations, but even more important in service organisations, where employees have a critical role in the customer's experience.

CHAPTER THREE

1. Corporate strategy focuses on developing overall mission and vision, corporate financial objectives, corporate resources and the portfolio of business. Business strategy encompasses business definition and objectives and resource allocation across its portfolio of products and markets. It also includes competitive strategy and development of competitive advantage. Marketing strategy (as an example of functional strategy) centres on marketing objectives, positioning, and targeting of the marketing mix to each product/market and market segment.

2. Customer value is the value that is delivered by the business to its customers. Business value is reflected by profit which is the value taken out of the market and delivered to shareholders.

3. A mission statement should be market-oriented, realistic, specific and related to the particular market environment. It should also include reference to core competencies and be motivational for company employees. Check the annual reports of BHP, NAB, Telecom NZ, Telstra and Qantas to compare and evaluate missions against the criteria noted above.

4. An example of a business specific objective is: To increase profit from the current base of $10 million to $12 million to $15 million over the next two years. A marketing objective is: To increase unaided brand awareness from current level 20% to 25% by the end of the next year.

5. The BCG model relates investment and divestment strategies and portfolio position to two variables: market growth rate and relative market share. It is a simple generic conceptual model to assist an evaluation of the portfolio mix. In contrast, the GE model is more complex and allows tailoring by companies enabling them to use relevant variables to depict industry attractiveness and business strength.

6. Advantages of portfolio models: useful to depict current and future positions and mix of businesses as a basis for strategic analysis and planning; enable managers to work logically through the strategic process. Disadvantages: difficult and time-consuming to implement; tend to focus on current situation and existing business; can be too constraining—'thinking only inside the box'.

7. Alternative expansion strategies are:
   (a) Market penetration: example, Pepsi strategy to increase market share of the existing youth cola segment at the expense of Coke.
   (b) Market development: example, ICI has expanded its fertiliser business by extending its Incitec crop care division beyond its traditional Queensland/New South Wales market to other Australian state markets.
   (c) Products development: example, OzEmail has introduced a low-price international phone call service via the Internet to its existing customers.
   (d) Diversification: example, Coles Myer launched a new chain, 'Officeworks', targeted to business customers and consumers to service small business and home office.

8. The impact of the Internet is transforming companies resulting from new Internet competitors, cost reduction from the new distribution channels to market and the creation of new kinds of customer value from information. All these impact the long-term competitive position of the company and should be accounted for in strategic planning.

9. Gap analysis is a planning tool to identify the likely gap in outcomes between objectives and continuation of the existing strategy. The profit gap can be reduced by:
   (a) growth initiatives (as described in 7)
   (b) cost/volume/margin improvement opportunities as shown in Figure 3-12.

10. Marketing strategy focuses on customer value creation and maintenance. Its thrust is to develop a profitable market position through creating satisfied customers. It does this by the effective delivery of value through products and services to identified target market segments.

11. Marketing's role is to lead and coordinate the process of customer value creation at the company, product and market level. It provides the philosophy of market focus and alignment of company offers to meet current and future customers' needs. Marketing should guide other departments in terms of how they contribute to customer value and what is required by those departments to enhance competitive advantage and position.

12. Marketing's rationale to other departments to reduce conflicts is the common goal of customer value creation as the means of achieving business objectives. All departments, by their actions, contribute to or reduce customer value.

13. Refer to Figure 3-15 for the factors.

Target consumers	End-users
Demographic/economic	Population profile, economic drivers like GNP, inflation, unemployment, interest rates
Technological/natural	Product and information technology trends, 'green' movement, conservation of resources
Political/Legal	Deregulation trends, employment wage standards
Social/Cultural	Trends in cultural values and lifestyles

Target consumers	End-users
Competitors	Direct and indirect
Suppliers	Key resources and capability providers
Marketing channels	Distributors and dealers
Publics	Investors, unions, general public
Marketing management	Involves analysis, planning, implementation and control of the marketing process
Marketing mix	The product, price, promotion and place represent the offer by the company to the target consumers

14. The additional elements in the extended marketing mix can be illustrated with reference to an airline.

Additional elements in the extended marketing mix	
Process	Ticket purchasing, checking baggage, seating on board, baggage retrieval, claims for late baggage
People	Telephone sales/reservations, check-in staff, on-board cabin crew, pilot announcements, airport baggage staff
Physical evidence	Staff uniforms, signage, airplanes, frequent flier lounges

15. The extended marketing mix of an airline service promoted and distributed via the Internet is:
Process: Online ticket purchase, authorisation and delivery (via print own ticket), insurance claims for lost baggage online. (Other processes like check-in baggage and seating remain physical.)
People: People become virtual (video) or replaced with online cost and itinerary information, booking enquiries, seat availability, payment with integrated Internet/call centre help. Other people factors remain.
Physical existence: Supplemented by website graphics, video and branding.

CHAPTER FOUR
1. The marketing process involves:
- analysing marketing opportunities
- selecting target markets
- designing marketing strategies
- planning marketing programs
- implementing marketing activities
- controlling marketing effort.

2. The four organisational levels are: corporate, divisional, business unit and product.
3. The strategic marketing plan develops and documents broad marketing objectives and strategies. The tactical marketing plan outlines specific actions detailing the marketing mix programs.
4. While the terms are sometimes used interchangeably, the business plan incorporates all functional plans including financial, production, human resource and R&D plans as well as a marketing plan which focuses on products and markets.
5. The major sections in a marketing plan are laid out and described in Table 4-1.
6. The current market situation provides an analysis of market profiles, segments and trends, competition,

channel structure, product offers and relevant elements of the macro-environment.
7. **S** Strengths—those specific internal strengths that provide differential capabilities in relation to main competitors;
W Weaknesses—those specific company weaknesses that represent a disadvantage in serving markets relative to competitors;
O Opportunities—those market and environmental trends that can be specifically targeted by the company to achieve growth and profitability;
T Threats—those external factors, such as competitors, that can negatively impact the company's ability to achieve its objectives.
8.

Objective 1 Strategy	Increase awareness of Hugo Boss Fragrances Conduct a worldwide advertising campaign targeting retailers and the consumer to promote awareness of the Hugo Boss brand and product range.
Objective 2 Strategy	Increase market share of Hugo Boss Fragrances Create differentiated point of sale stands and retailer incentives to feature the product range.

9. Continual market scanning is required of daily load factors, sales, pricing and seasonal influences on travellers. Periodic examination of the market by Qantas would include distribution trends (i.e. travel agents versus direct sales versus Internet channels) and changing customer value preferences in line with value perception of Qantas's offerings.
10. Qantas should monitor the impact of new rivals (such as Impulse and Virgin) in its domestic and international markets, as well as the perceived relative value offered by competitors on its main routes. It should also monitor the development of competitive networks in the form of competing airline alliances such as the Star Alliance network.
11. An important macro-environmental aspect to be monitored by Qantas is the substitution between travel and other forms of communication such as tele- and video-conferencing. At the same time, Internet-based communication is creating new relationships, and presents opportunities for Qantas to promote travel to meet newly acquired friends or business partners.
12. Marketing implementation turns marketing plans into actions. For example, an advertising plan is converted into timing of advertising spots, money to be spent, people responsible to make it happen. This is doing the part of marketing involving day-to-day activities.
13. Successful implementation of marketing requires:
(i) an action program to pull people and activities together;
(ii) simple, flexible organisation that enables quick response;
(iii) decision and reward systems that support effective action;
(iv) human resources planning that has the skilled and motivated people available at the right time; and

(v) company culture that acts as a glue to tie people together through common values, beliefs and goals.

14. The functional marketing organisation has different marketing activities headed by a functional specialist. This contrasts with a geographical organisation in which sales and marketing people are responsible for different countries or regions. Further specialisation has occurred in many companies that have a product management organisation in which a person takes full responsibility for management of a particular product. For companies that sell a small number of products to many markets, a market management organisation has evolved in which market managers take responsibility for sales and profits in particular market segments.

15. Marketing control involves the evaluation of results against plans and the taking of corrective action to ensure objectives are achieved.

16. Operating control relates to the annual plan in terms of checking performance against budgets and taking corrective action.

17. Strategic control evaluates how well the firm's strategies are matched with market opportunities and looks for necessary re-alignment requirements.

18. The marketing audit lies at the foundation of the strategic marketing process because of its comprehensive examination of the external and internal (firm) environment as the basis for improving a company marketing performance. It is a major tool of strategic control.

CHAPTER FIVE

1. No. Some products are more likely to be scrutinised by the government (e.g. financial products), while others will be more scrutinised by other publics (e.g. development projects), which may cause media interest and citizen action. Each organisation needs to consider the implications for different publics, and decide on their marketing program accordingly.

2. Marketing research firms are service agencies, as are media placement agencies and sales agents.

3. Yes, they should, as internal publics include those such as the internal sales-force who are an important part of any marketing strategy.

4. The population of most countries is comprised of peoples from different countries who have different cultural backgrounds that impact.

5. Demographers and marketers differentiate between Generation X and Y according to their year of birth. On this basis, there are clearly different groups. However not everyone within one group will behave in a similar manner to others within the group; some Gen Xers may be more like Gen Yers and vice versa. People towards the top of the age range of Generation X may be more similar to the baby boomers than to Generation Y. So while marketers talk about these groups to describe consumers, there are not hard and fast boundaries between the groups.

6. Membership of associational groups such as Greenpeace entail adopting values which then impact on needs, wants and demands, as well as the type of information seeking done and the manner in which it is sought.

CHAPTER SIX

1. Although information from internal records can be gathered quickly, it is often incomplete, having been gained for purposes other than the task at hand.

2. Salespeople, in particular, are important sources of information from the marketing environment. They are but one source of marketing intelligence.

3. Though it may be legal, the practice could result in criticism of the company and unfavourable media attention. Most companies (like P&G) will have ethical standards which preclude activities which may be legal, but which may be seen by some as unethical.

4. Different people will be more likely to respond to different survey methods. All the techniques have advantages and disadvantages, as outlined in the chapter. Which method is best depends on the specific circumstances, and what the marketer is trying to learn. Often, a combination of methods will be used, at different stages of the research process.

5. The marketing research process consists of these four steps:
   (i) defining the problem and research objectives,
   (ii) developing the research plan
   (iii) implementing the research plan
   (iv) interpreting and reporting the findings.

6. Some marketing research firms now offer single-source data systems that electronically monitor both consumers' purchases and their exposure to various marketing efforts in an attempt to evaluate the link between the two more effectively.

7. Managers of SMEs can carry out marketing research by way of observation, informal focus groups and experiments, thus reducing some of the costs that larger firms might not find so prohibitive.

CHAPTER SEVEN

1. A major implicaton is that marketers need to understand how marketing stimuli are changed into responses inside the consumer's mind and the impact of both so-called 'controllable' and 'non-controllable' factors.

2. No, each factor won't be important in every buying decision. For example, if people have bought the product before, their decision to rebuy (or not rebuy) will be influenced most by their prior experience, and less by the marketer's actions at the time of repurchase. In contrast, if the consumer has never bought the product before, the marketer's actions can be critical in influencing demand for the product, and in influencing the consumer to pay a particular price.

3. Behavioural science is increasingly showing that both learning and genetics are important in our behaviour. If behaviour is influenced by genetics, it is difficult, or perhaps impossible to change, but the marketer still needs to identify how different groups will tend to behave (e.g. what products people might be genetically programmed to prefer) and what marketing influences will cause people to respond in the behaviour which the marketer is trying to encourage.

4. Personality refers to the unique psychological characteristics that lead to relatively consistent and lasting responses to one's own environment. Self-concept is a related concept. Both have an influence on consumers' chosen lifestyle.

5. For discussion purposes, select from: Psychological, personal, cultural, social, past experiences, marketing programs and environmental influences. These impact on consumer lifestyle.

6. Lifestyle is a person's pattern of living as expressed in his or her psychographics. Discussion should centre on the major AIO dimensions—activities (work, hobbies, shopping, sports, social events), interests (food, fashion, family, recreation) and opinions (about themselves, social issues, business, products).

7. Low involvement products tend to be those where the consumer sees little risk in the purchase, and as a result, they will tend to buy with limited or no information seeking. In contrast, high involvement products involve more (financial or social) risk for the consumer, so purchase will tend to involve greater information seeking and greater use of reference groups.

8. Complex buying behaviour (to increase the chance of making the best choice) and/or dissonance-reducing buying behaviour.

9. This statement is not true. Habitual buying behaviour occurs under conditions of low consumer involvement and little significant brand difference.

10. A pure impulse purchase or an habitual purchase.

11. Information search for complex products entails a wider search, with information sought from commercial and experiential sources rather than personal sources.

12. One implication is that for practical, ethical and legal reasons marketers should take care in stating that a product is 'new' or 'improved'. As a result, the consumer is more likely to see and be influenced by advertising for these products (where post-purchase dissonance is most likely to occur).

13. The makers of such toilets added the digital sound of running water to their product to mask the sounds of nature, and thus preserve modesty.

14. The marketer might use animation involving a cuddly animal using the inner sole.

CHAPTER EIGHT

1. Business markets are characterised by fewer, larger buyers, close supplier–customer relationships, professional purchasing and demand ultimately derived from the demand for customer goods and services.

2. Marketing organisations need to get very close to their customers in order to understand the buying influences and to be able to tailor solutions more closely to individual customer needs.

3. Business buyer behaviour is directly affected by economic, technical and user groups within the organisation as well as strategic issues of the company to do with its ability to compete.

4. The differences between business and consumer buyer behaviour relate to complexity and size of purchase, different degrees of economical involvement and accountability by buyers.

5. Institutions tend to have low budgets, captive clients and are price sensitive.

6. This is driven by accountability to governments for wise use of tax-payers' money and the need to be seen as fair.

CHAPTER NINE

1. The qualified available market for Internet service providers are those who may be interested for educational reasons, have incomes over $57 000, own a computer with a modem and who know how to use the IT in question.

2. We need to know if we are seeking to have those who already buy, buy more or more often. We need to retain existing customers, but usually only if they are profitable, or can become profitable.

3. *Market potential* is defined by the number of existing and potential customers for a defined set of products/ services that satisfy the core customer need.

   Untapped opportunity is defined by the number of potential customers that are not buying due to factors such as lack of awareness, lack of availability, lack of ability to use, lack of product attractiveness and affordability (as depicted in Figure 9.3).

4. When discussing sales forecasting it is necessary to specify where, when, under what economic conditions and with how much marketing support sales will be made.

5. *Market demand* for a product or service is the total volume that would be bought by a defined consumer group in a defined geographical area during a defined time period in a defined marketing environment under a defined level and mix of industry marketing effort. The upper limit to market demand is called *market potential*.

6. A legal monopolist, such as Telstra prior to competition, might possibly have had the entire market demand to itself. It may indeed have reached the upper market demand limit in a particular time frame.

7. Rather than use a light beer, substitute a food product such as Nestlé Yogurt.

8. Distribution methods differ between consumer and industrial products. Consumer products' end-users tend to be geographically dispersed, while industrial customers tend be geographically concentrated by industry type.

9. Such a scheme might also be used in sales territory management. Also, such schemes might be used to establish competitor numbers and sizes by turnover or labour force.

10. By collating industry statistics and promulgating these among member companies.

11. Business customers are very likely to comply with requests for intentions to purchase. Such intentions are only as accurate as their forecast of economic activity—usually derived from consumer confidence levels in the case of the construction industry.

12. Salespeople might underestimate where a bonus is paid for exceeding a budget. They might overestimate where they are anxious to prove the worth of their account list or territory.

13. Many industrial marketing organisations employ zero-based budgeting whereby they start from zero and build-up a forecast of sales on a customer-by-customer basis. This is because the customer is closer to the end-consumer than they are and has a better picture of demand. Demand for the industrial marketer is derived from the demand for consumer goods and services.

CHAPTER TEN

1. Market segmentation involves dividing a market for a product or service into distinct groups of buyers with different needs. The purpose of segmentation is to enable marketers to design marketing strategies targeted to specific segments.

2. Segmentation bases for a bank could be:
   - age (consumer life-cycle stage);
   - gender (targeting women); and
   - lifestyle.

3. Bases of segmentation of the Philippines market for CSR building materials could be:
   - geographic (town versus rural);
   - intermediaries (timber/building suppliers, builders);
   - sector (institutions, government, commercial, consumer); and
   - consumer income levels.

4. Requirements for effective segmentation of Singapore Airlines' business market include ability to identify, access and measure the revenue of business customers according to travel frequency, company, personal preferences and responsiveness to the outline's marketing efforts.

5. Similar general requirements as in answer 4 are relevant to the segmentation of the Chinese market for marketing education. This should also include an assessment of the profitability (and ability to pay) of different segments and any differential responses to marketing effort. An important segmentation challenge here is to identify and reach this market.

6. Development of detailed customer profile databases and technology enabling faster response and tailoring to individual needs is providing the opportunity for targeting segments of one customer. This is occurring with computers and with many information-based products like investment management services.

7. Segment evaluation and selection is based on a process of measuring segment sizes, growth rates, potential profitability, existing and future competition, and relating company strengths and resources to relevant segments. The most attractive segments combined with a good company alignment will lead to selection of segments for priority targeting.

8. The computer market exhibits a range of marketing strategies. Unbranded clone products are marketed using an undifferentiated strategy with the primary appeal of low price. Major corporations like HP and Sony target several segments using a differentiated strategy. Apple targets mainly education and desktop publishing markets using a concentrated marketing strategy.

9. Market positioning is defined by the attributes and characteristics of a product or service held in consumers' minds relative to competing products.

10. Different positioning strategies for the market for Pay-TV could represent the following forms:

Positioning strategies for the Pay-TV market	
Product attributes	The range of entertainment, quality of movies etc.
Benefit	Convenience and choice
Usage occasions	24-hour availability of news, movies, sport
Users	People who are up-to-date with latest information and entertainment
Against a competitor	Direct comparison of Optus Vision with Foxtel
Product class	e.g. position against video hire

11. Selection of competitive advantage to communicate depends on a firm's ability to make its offer unique and to deliver the communicated advantage. The advantage needs to be highly valued by target buyers, distinctive, superior, not easily copied by competitors, affordable to customers, profitable to the firm and capable of communication to the market.

CHAPTER ELEVEN

1. One significant feature of this placement is the need for such marketers to rely on the extended marketing mix: product, price, placement, promotion, people and processes. Physical evidence is often also included in the extended marketing mix for services.

2. The extended marketing mix is involved in that the hotel is measuring service quality and conducting such measurement at various points in the *process*. It is also gaining feedback on its *people*.

3. One feature is that demand for industrial products is derived from demand for consumer goods and services.

4. The household buyer plans the purchase of multi-packs of corn chips which are later consumed on impulse by other members of the household.

5. Unsought products are goods and services that the consumer either does not know about or knows about but does not think of buying. Credit card adoption is a recent phenomenon.

6. That they are intangible in nature, customised to suit the buyer, delivered on demand and bought for the benefits they provide.

7. That services are different from physical goods because of their intangibility, the higher involvement and personal nature of many services, the variability of many service encounters, the fact that they are consumed as and when they are bought, and that once consumed cannot be repeated.

8. No inconsistency is indicated. Pine II and Gilmore are referring to experiential benefits, whereas the nature of services discussed in Question 7 relates to attributes.

9. Each not-for-profit organisation is likely to have different measures of its effectiveness, but measures might include donations, number of volunteers, or the incidence of some other desired behaviour (e.g. the change in the number of people undergoing cancer checks).

10. Funding for political marketing may come from different sources, including donations to the party and government funding allocated to the party, which

will generally be a factor of the number of votes received by the party. The major course of funding is government funding, which is financed by taxes. The target of the marketing will vary depending on the campaign, but taxpayers, or groups of taxpayers, are usually the targets of faulty marketing.

11. This is certainly one perspective. It is akin to saying that consumers experience services and that they likewise vote and contribute to social causes because of what they experience.

12. Marketers attempt to build into products attributes that meet the needs (provide the benefits sought) of consumers. Those wanting the benefits of mobile telephony (without the penalties of weight) seek small products that have such attributes as light-weight batteries with long life.

13. Because a brand is vital for consumers to identify the products or services of one seller or group of sellers and to differentiate them from those of competitors.

14. Comparing such packages as milk in bottles and milk in cartons we see that the printed carton has enabled branding and differentiation between products such as plain milk, flavoured milk and other milk products with reduced fat or calcium-enriched for different market segments.

15. When General Motors-Holden's introduced a low-priced car (Barina) and a more highly priced luxury car (Statesman) in addition to its family car (Commodore), it stretched its product line upward and downward.

16. (i) A product manager might add new products to use up excess manufacturing capacity.
    (ii) The salesforce and distributors might want a more complete product line to satisfy customers.
    (iii) A product manager may wish to add items to the product line to increase sales and profits.

17. Breadth, length, depth and consistency.

18. They have the same meaning.

19. Maxwell House adapts its product packaging for Japan, and adapts flavour and sweetness for other countries. Red on packaging indicates a fire sale in Japan.

20. Chevrolet's name change for the Nova car in Puerto Rica is often cited. Nova means 'no go' in Spanish. Muslims do not use alcohol, so even hair shampoos use lime juice instead of alcohol as a cleaning agent.

CHAPTER TWELVE

1. Competition and technology make existing products obsolete and compel firms to introduce new ones to survive. Also, variations in market attitudes, needs and preferences occur and create opportunities for companies to gain competitive advantage from new products.

2. Marketing factors and internal product development factors are the main sources of new products. Refer to Table 12-2.

3. The eight major steps are summarised in Figure 12-4.

4. The main disadvantages of test marketing are exposure of the new product to competitors and the delay in full-scale launch which may be pre-empted by a competitor. These disadvantages can be minimised if reliable simulated test marketing can be conducted.

5. The main advantage of the Internet is speed to market, rapid response (or non-response) by customers, tailoring the test to specific consumers and enabling rapid correction and retesting of modified products. The disadvantages lie in potential widespread exposure of faulty products, poor quality of feedback or non-response of consumers providing insufficient information for guiding improvement.

6. How 'new' a product is, is determined by prospective buyers not by new features or technologies.

7. It is important to identify the addressable potential market as being the most likely proportion of the population to adopt the new product. It is easy to overstate potential market size with consequences for profitability.

8. There are many similarities between the traditional life-cycle concept and the technology adoption cycle. Both are based on the same premise of the adoption–diffusion process. Two major differences are the highlighting of the 'chasm' phase and the 'bowling alley' stage in the technology cycle. These stages seek to explain the circumstances surrounding lack of acceptance (the chasm) and early niche-based adoption (the bowling alley). The latter is similar to the early growth phase in the traditional product-life-cycle concept. The traditional PLC concept also describes variations to the classical model such as fads, fashion and pyramided life cycles.

9. Lead users are often the prime developers or instigators of new products. Their role is in assisting development, evaluation and testing of new products and leading the adoption and diffusion process.

10. The chasm is the phase in the cycle beyond the early market but prior to acceptance by the mainstream market. To move out of the chasm, a company needs to identify specific 'opinion leader' customers and negotiate deals to have them use the product and become a reference site or referee. The product needs to be tailored as much as possible to meet their specific needs. The strategy then is to extend the product application to similar customers and/or modify the product for related applications for a different customer segment. This leads the company towards bowling alley strategies targeting niche markets.

11. A summary of relevant strategies for the pioneer at each stage of the life cycle is as follows:

Strategies for the pioneer at each stage of the life cycle	
Introduction	Product concept positioning and market development activities such as promotion and use of opinion leaders
Growth	Brand building and development of distribution channels, product range and market segment targeting
Maturity	Consolidation of distribution, competitive pricing and brand consolidation using reminder advertising
Decline	Cost reduction, rationalisation of product range and harvesting profit from the product

12. Yes. The brand represents an identity that can exist well beyond the product's life as the brand

encompasses successive technology versions. For example, today's Apple Macintosh is very different from the first one introduced.

CHAPTER THIRTEEN

1. Price should be related to, and consistent with, all the other elements of the marketing mix because it is a part of the overall offer to consumers. When price is changed, consumer perceptions change—not only in terms of the price, but also in relation to other elements of the mix.

2. Organisational considerations and costs often dominate the price-setting process. Marketing objectives and strategies are often set without due regard for customer perceptions of price and value. If price is set mainly on the basis of these internal factors, the price position established may not be the most appropriate one for a company. For example, if cost plus a mark-up is used to determine the selling price, it is quite possible that price may be either too high or too low in relation to the customers' perceptions of value.

3. Target costing is used for the purpose of developing a product or service to be sold at a price level acceptable to customers and profitable for the business. It implies that the firm starts with customers and the value they see in particular offers and the prices they are prepared to pay for those offers. The firm is using a market-driven approach to setting price and then organising product development in such a way as to meet cost and profit targets.

4. External factors should dominate pricing decisions when there is competition, when consumers have a clear perception of price and value, and when market needs are changing. Internal factors should be the main drivers when the firm needs to rationalise its product range, when it has few competitors and when there is a need to gain profitability from margin improvements and cost efficiencies.

5. In the car industry the luxury segment of the market is price inelastic—small reductions or increases in price have very little impact on demand. The budget end of the market for cars like Hyundai and Daewoo are price elastic—relatively small price changes have relatively large demand shifts.

6. Large national banks like the Commonwealth and Westpac have high fixed costs due to their large branch networks. When price changes result in volume fluctuations, there is a large impact on their profits because most costs are fixed. Banks like Citibank with low fixed costs are not affected nearly so much in profit by changes in business levels because a larger proportion of their costs vary with business activity.

7. The challenge with 'commodities' is to create customer-perceived value through non-product factors like service, information, personal relationships and more responsiveness to customer requirements.

8. A market skimming strategy by Foxtel would enable it to target its offer to specific 'high need' segments at a high profit margin and manage a careful penetration of the market while at the same time gearing up its capacity to service demand in a controlled manner. The disadvantage of this strategy would be a rapid penetration entry by Optus Vision which would enable it to dominate the market ahead of Foxtel.

9. Price penetration strategies are being adopted by Internet share brokers like e*trade and price bidders like Priceline. Both of these are very successful in penetrating new markets, but many 'price' competitors have not succeeded.

10. Service mix options for Country Link's travel market include:
    - train–bus travel links;
    - 14-day, one, three and six-month passes;
    - day tripper links with Sydney trains, buses and ferries; and
    - city–country travel packages.

11. Dell could use segmented pricing for different customer types such as business customers and consumers. Promotional pricing and geographical pricing are also relevant. A range of standard packages reflecting different product combinations and service support could be introduced as value pricing packages. Discounts could be offered for volume buying and early payment.

12. BMW's pricing strategy in support of its 3-series has been designed to widen its market and attract new customers who aspire to BMW by skimming its price strategy on its 5- and 7-series models. It, like Mercedes-Benz, has introduced penetration pricing at the bottom of its range in the luxury market.

13. The implications of Aussie Home Loans' low mortgage rates are as follows:
    - For customers—lower costs and access to home ownership for many more people.
    - For competitors—price competition forcing their offers to be more price competitive.
    - For Aussie Home Loans—the need for very careful control of its overhead costs and its margins.

14. In the current oligopolistic international market a business class air fare cut by Qantas would most likely be matched by Singapore Airlines.

CHAPTER FOURTEEN

1. The focus is on marketing logistics networks as marketing management face a broader task of co-ordinating the activities of many entities in bringing their products to market. Physical distribution is only one of the many activities involved.

2. The broader focus also takes in demand chain management (nee supply chain management), and this means that costs such as transport costs can be reduced by the greater efficiencies enabled by including both inbound and outbound logistics management within the focus of marketing management.

3. Such flows include: information; physical goods, title to the goods; payment or credit.

4. Customer service, or service quality, is an aspect of marketing concerning all types of marketing organisations.

5. Marketing logistics network decisions: cycle-time reduction; conversion operations location; make or buy or vertically integrate or network (purchasing); manufacturing and operations process decisions such

as product scheduling (lot sizes and costs), order processing and costs, warehouse numbers and costs, inventory levels and costs, and transport costs.

6. Many services, such as legal services, are outsourced from manufacturing organisations. In this sense, both need to be vibrant to succeed.

7. See Figure 14-4. Note that the extended marketing mix includes people and processes and that services marketers also include physical evidence.

8. This is possibly true, but other factors come in to play such as the nature of many service sector jobs of being casual or short-term.

9. In Australia, manufacturing is not seen to be as glamorous an occupation as, for example, working in the telecommunications industry, even though the latter does not employ relatively high numbers of people. This is true in many developed countries.

10. Country Road sells through its own stores, through Myer and also via Myer Direct. Microsoft has its own direct operations and uses original equipment manufacturers (OEMs) and retailers.

11. This is not always true. A marketer with a factory outlet must be careful not to undercut its retailers' prices lest it lose its wider distribution.

12. For example, compare Nestlé's marketing channels with those employed by Qantas. It is wise to consider the flows involved in the comparison.

13. They each allow smaller stores to compete with high-volume chains in terms of buy and sell prices.

14. There are *manufacturer-sponsored retailer franchise systems* (Ford dealers); *manufacturer-sponsored wholesaler franchise systems* (e.g. licensed Coke bottlers); *service-firm-sponsored retailer franchise systems* (Avis, McDonald's). While franchises bring a systems approach to what would otherwise be a small business, a downside is that often the franchisee cannot sell the business to whoever they choose.

15. It might mean that the retail sector could use undue force in its dealings with suppliers (other than those transnational companies with multiple high-profile brands) and thus achieve unreasonably low buy prices for manufacturer-branded products as well as housebrands and generic products.

16. Apart from providing favourable margins, Qantas might provide incentives such as travel and accommodation to agents who achieve certain sales targets. It might also provide particular packages to large retailers such as Thomas Cook or Jetset.

17. Both sectors rely on marketing information flowing back from the retailer to the supplier. Where Qantas is linked to its agents directly, manufacturers in Australia still rely on third parties such as AC Nielsen.

CHAPTER FIFTEEN

1. There will be many answers to this question, but a typical supermarket would be classified by low service, a long and wide product line (though note that the chapter discusses how product length is gradually decreasing, as the supermarkets offer fewer alternatives) low relative prices, high control of outlets, and is usually positioned in a shopping centre.

2. This sort of information will assist the retailer in identifying what it is currently offering to customers, and possibly in helping to identify where there might be room for variation in the store to increase sales to customers (e.g. by offering a wider range of gourmet foods in one store, and more bulk discounts in others). This sort of information might also assist the supplier by helping to show what products are likely to be most attractive to the supermarket's customers, and thus to the retailer's management. For example some food offerings will only be attractive to supermarkets that offer higher levels of service (e.g. a delicatessen department).

3. This should be undertaken at a number of management levels: senior, middle and at the functional key account level. Senior and middle level might invite senior- and middle-level management to a 'think-tank' or 'conference' while key account management might invite the retail controllers and/or category managers to plant inspections and the like.

4. This should also be undertaken at a number of management levels: senior, middle and category manager level. Communication forms might be similar to those indicated in question 1.

5. Retailers use the same marketing mix elements but different emphases may be involved. Grocery retailers, and 'shed' hardware stores tend to place more emphasis on price. Supplying marketers tend to rely more on product innovation and main media advertising.

6. This is particularly true of the situation in Australia between Kmart and Target.

7. This is often the case. Compare Coles' Bi-Lo with Coles Supermarkets.

8. Wholesalers perform many functions for supplier marketers such as these: selling and promoting; buying and assortment building; bulk breaking; warehousing; transportation; financing; risk bearing; market information; management services and advice.

9. A wholesaler might expect to receive 3% margin on cost for selling activities and profit and another 7% on cost for distributing and selling—a total of 10% on cost.

10. This was the situation in New South Wales where Woolworths' growth has been at the expense of smaller stores once trading hours were extended. However, Woolworths went on to become a wholesaler in its own right in 1997 and thus compete with Davids.

11. Both types are affected.

12. An agent is empowered to change prices whereas a broker cannot. Agents and brokers represent a variable cost, rather than a fixed cost to the manufacturer or importer. This may appeal to the smaller or startup manufacturer or where a new and complex market such as Japan is being entered for the first time.

13. Wholesalers tend to use product assortment, personal selling and placement as key marketing mix elements in their marketing strategy. Grocery marketers tend to rely on product innovation and promotion.

14. Wholesalers perform a function of aggregating the products from many suppliers. Their positioning is often based on the number of products they carry, as are their costs.

15. This is true for wholesalers. They may be called distributors in such as the grocery industry, but even so, they may have a selling function to perform.

16. This is true. For example, Sigma acts as a pharmaceutical wholesaler and maintains electronic links and manages inventories for independent pharmacies—to the advantage of each party.

CHAPTER SIXTEEN

1. See Table 16-2.

2. Direct mail, direct email and SMS.

3. Sponsorship such as Formula 1 racing sponsorship is targeted towards those interested in motor vehicles. Most sponsors of this event are targeting this segment, even marketers of social causes such as 'If you drink and drive . . .'

4. The target audience may be in any of six buyer-readiness states: awareness, knowledge, liking, preference, conviction or purchase. A response might be a purchase, or it may be an intention to purchase. Getting feedback involves asking the target audience whether they remember the message, how many times they saw it, what points they recall, how they felt about the message, and their past and present attitudes towards the product and company. Feedback also entails measuring sales levels.

5. Marketing communications *alone* will only rarely result in conviction. This is possible where there are clear and important differences between alternatives, and these differences are effectively conveyed to a consumer by communications. More commonly, marketing communications will combine with other marketing elements (e.g. personal selling, product quality) to result in conviction. Most importantly, product performance must live up to the expectations created by the communications.

6. An emotional appeal is likely to be most effective for luxury products, and/or for products which the consumer doesn't evaluate in depth (e.g. impulse purchases). A rational appeal is likely to be most effective when the consumer does evaluate in depth (e.g. computers). A moral appeal might be effective where the behaviour or its consequences are visible to others (e.g. not littering, not drinking and driving).

7. Advertisers must know where consumers lie on this continuum. Those unaware of a category need would not necessarily respond to advertising aimed at increasing brand awareness. Those who are satisfied with a competitor's brand might not readily respond to advertising aimed at stimulating category need. There are of course many other examples of such misdirected promotion.

8. Sometimes the interval between the communication and the purchase decision can be long (e.g. cars, post-graduate study, holidays). Under these circumstances, other measures (e.g awareness, attitude) will provide an earlier measure of the effect of marketing communication.

9. This is one reason. Another might be that many less sophisticated marketing organisations do not have marketing departments that can carry out such tasks.

10. It is not so much a question of one having more effect than the other. Both are important. However, selling to supermarkets has an 'indirect' effect whereas advertising acts directly on the consumer.

11. On one hand they must promote themselves against their competition, while they must also advertise manufacturers' specials (often to reward loyal customers), as well as promote their own generic and house brand products.

12. Google has benefited from substantial public relations (PR) exposure, because of the novelty of its offerings, and because its services are free, it is often recommended to others, thus benefiting from favourable word of mouth (WOM) promotion. Most other organisations can't get as much PR or favourable PR, so need to use more advertising. Perhaps Google could have become better known faster using advertising, but PR and WOM have been very effective in increasing awareness and promotion.

13. Television is very effective at creating awareness by a mass audience. So for mass market products trying to create awareness fast, it is likely to remain an attractive communication channel. 'Need-to-do advertising' isn't a standard term, but marketers of mass market offerings must create high levels of awareness, so mass market channels (like TV and newspapers) are an obvious choice.

14. The media planner is aiming to inform as wide an audience as possible in the initial stages of the media campaign.

15. A memorable advertisement has greater impact and will reside in the memory longer than one that remains virtually unnoticed. Whether such an advertisement has a greater impact in causing potential consumers to buy is another matter. Both aspects require testing.

16. One argument for pulsing concerns the fact that there are off-seasons for both sports. Another concerns the fact that some major play-offs are worth heavier promotion than where weak teams are involved.

17. Unpaid testimonials by 'neutral' but significant others, such as cookery editors, often have greater credibility than advertising by identifiable sponsors.

18. Not only might the community be favourably disposed to making bequests and donations to the university, but potential students may make the university their first preference or select a particular course based on such talks.

19. The effect of stopping any sponsorship will depend on the aims of the sponsorship, and whether these have been achieved. For example, the aim of the sponsorship may have been to create awareness, and after a certain period, ongoing sponsorship may not be worthwhile, because awareness may have achieved high levels. There can be a public backlash if a organisation stops sponsorship of an event which is seen to provide public benefits as Westpac bank found out when it suggested that it would stop sponsoring a rescue helicopter. Under these circumstances, PR can be important in conveying to the public why the sponsorship is being stopped, and/or explaining what public benefit will be provided in its place.

CHAPTER SEVENTEEN

1. Examples should fall into one of the following categories: samples; redeemable coupons; cash-back offers; cents-off deals or price packs; premium offers;

advertising specialities; patronage rewards; point-of-purchase (POP) promotions; contests and games of chance and skill.

2. Some may prompt trial of a new product; some may induce multiple purchases; some may induce usage in a new way; and some may bring forward a purchase, from among other examples.

3. Sales might increase due to excitement at point of purchase, whereas the cash-back offer is not taken up. This is a sign of success.

4. Sales positions differ by industry type and company. They range from least to highest difficulty: from those who merely *deliver* a product, to being an inside *order taker*, or one who *builds goodwill* or *educates buyers* (called 'missionary' selling); or positions where the major emphasis is on *technical knowledge*; and lastly to the *creative selling* of tangible products and intangibles such as advertising ideas. The last is the most difficult.

5. All marketing organisations have a salesforce, even if it is a cyber-salesforce such as a vending machine or Super-ATM where technology is employed.

6. Because in selling intangibles, there is no direct evidence for the prospective buyer to assess. For example, an advertising executive selling a client on an idea must impart a vision to the client, as well as convince the client to part with a lot of money in the hope that future sales revenue and profits will stem from such a campaign.

7. It is necessary to argue whether *all* need to be outgoing (not necessarily), *and* aggressive (definitely not) *and* energetic (depends on one's definition of energetic—although being a self-starter is important).

8. Salespeople need to be able to recover from the many rebuffs (negative responses) they receive. They need to be able to see a sales goal and want to achieve it (motivated to achieve). It is for this reason that it could be said that not everyone is suited to being a salesperson.

9. See Figure 17-3 for the steps in the selling process.

10. Salespeople need to know how to identify the good prospects on the basis of such factors as ability to pay, volume of business, special needs, location and growth potential.

11. Timing means a lot when deciding when and if to close a sale. Saying: 'How will you be paying—cash or charge?' is but one cue as to whether a retail customer is ready to decide. Sometimes closure is attempted too early and sometimes the opportunity is missed altogether.

CHAPTER EIGHTEEN

1. TV Shopping Network—targeted media; Asia Business News Channel—targeted media; Network 10—mass media.

2. Instructors should guide students in selecting a different marketing organisation for each of the categories described in Table 18-1.

3. Separate those that use integrated database marketing from the likes of a retailer distributing brochures via a letterbox drop (a 'scattergram').

4. Marketing communication; marketing channel; and relationship management.

5. Quadrant 1—Public transit companies; Quadrant 2—Peugeot and Citroën; Quadrant 3—Lever

and Kitchen with brands such as Omomatic; and Quadrant 4—Dell Computers or Merrill Lynch.

6. It may well matter, for at this stage marketing scientists have yet to unequivocally state from their research which paths lead to the highest performance, whether measured by short-term indicators such as revenue and profit, or longer term measures such as those suggested in a balanced scorecard approach.

7. A list may be a panel of people who have agreed to be regularly interviewed about their telephone usage or their TV viewing habits. We might email such a list of people with an invitation to buy a product. Those who do go into a database of customers and are monitored over time as to their purchases.

8. Exercise equipment might be one such example.

9. Organisations such as the Red Cross need to be able to classify their donors by blood group. At different times various blood groups are in short supply. It is more efficient (speed) and effective (results in relation to costs) to communicate with those with the blood type needed rather than the market at large.

10. Most technologies relate to telecommunications and the merging with information technology such as multimedia personal computers that are now used in kiosks and dispensing machines; publishing and direct-response broadcasting; online shopping; and in database management.

11. Interactivity implies that the consumer can place an order, or seek further information via such tools as the World Wide Web. Examples of synchronous marketing are as follows: if the order is placed and the item is received immediately, or with a short lag, such as in receiving a software upgrade over the World Wide Web; or subscribing to a video channel via telephone, fax or Web-TV and shortly afterwards being able to see 'pay-per-view' movies over cable.

12. Marketers must manage consumer expectations, including fulfilment time lags. Interactivity is important because marketers need to know what customers want, not simply tell them what is on offer.

13. Instructors should assist students to differentiate between short, medium and long-term performance indicators, and how some indicators such as brand identity are missing.

14. Students should be guided in thinking on this matter by instructors providing examples where their own privacy has been invaded.

CHAPTER NINETEEN

1. The steps and areas of analysis are shown in Figure 19-1. The industry analysis model in Figure 19-2 also provides a useful strategic approach to competitive analysis.

2. In the oil industry, petrol suppliers Shell, Mobil and BP would regard each other as 'well behaved' competitors. They compete on price tactically, but employ mainly service, range and advertising strategies to build market share. The cut-price retail operators like Bogas and Solo would be regarded as disruptive competitors.

3. Industries are being restructured with new virtual companies providing Internet-based products and services such as wineplanet—a virtual wine shop. Some established companies like HP are bypassing

traditional distribution channels while other new companies like Amazon.com are competing across different product categories—books, music, gifts, toys. The Internet has changed the nature of competition mainly through increased speed of new products to market and faster customer service response.

4.

Cost leadership	Franklins
Differentiation	Colgate Palmolive
Focus	Lactos Cheese

5.

Operational excellence	Target (retail)
Customer intimacy	Accenture (Management Consultants)
Product leadership	Hewlett-Packard (printers)

6. Yes, they can be reconciled as follows:
- Cost leadership and operational excellence are similar and are geared to target price-sensitive markets.
- Customer intimacy and product leadership are two focal points of a differentiation strategy.

7. It is suitable when there is a high diversity of individual customer needs and also diversity of value to the business, and it has the capability to deliver.

8. Market leader issues include market growth, cannibalisation, share leadership defence and competition from substitutes.
- (a) Attack the market leader—an example is Canon's attack on HP printers.
- (b) Attack smaller competitors—an example is NAB attacking St. George Bank in the home lending market.

9. Market follower strategy:
- Advantages—lower cost, lower risk, less investment in market and technology.
- Disadvantages—harder to obtain a viable market position, usually will need to compete on price and therefore maintain lower costs.

10. Some examples are as follows:

Market follower strategy	
End-use specialists	Consultant engineers who specialise in regional shopping centres
Customer size specialists	Citibank targets 'high worth' individuals
Specific customer specialists	Orica sells its specialised chemicals to a few large customers

CHAPTER TWENTY

1. The move towards globalisation is linked to technological advancement, which has allowed the migration of production, technology, capital, people, information and business across nations. This movement has both increased and changed domestic competition with all the new global players. As a consequence the opportunities in domestic markets have decreased, and this has prompted internationalisation in firms.

2. The major risk of ignoring these global changes is the risk of losing the home market to global competitors, or not being aware of the global opportunities and missing the chance to enter new markets, such as European markets and those in the Pacific Rim.

3. The main forces in the global marketing environment include global competition, brands, advertising, customers, technologies, communications and the globalisation of an increasing number of industries from finance to motor cars to fast food. Change motivators include profit opportunity, competitive pressures, managerial desire and excess capacity.

GATT is a major influence on the facilitation of world trade. The world economy and regional and country politics are also major influences. Trade blocs have created regions such as EC and ASEAN which are moving towards single market blocs providing trading advantages for bloc members.

4. An example of a proactive Australian company is Poppy lipsticks and make-up. It has taken advantage of its unique products and benefited from economies of scale in America and some European countries. An example of a reactive company is the American funds management company called Massachusetts Financial Services; it has expanded from the American business due to market saturation, taking advantage of changes in the superannuation laws in Australia which have given them an opportunity to compete here.

5. It has compressed the stages in terms of time, enabling Internet exporters like Boots Online to export rapidly to a variety of countries by taking orders from their website and shipping direct to end-customers. This bypasses intermediaries and potentially speeds up fulfilment of orders.

6. It should consider marketing objectives, sales volume targets from offshore business, the number of countries to enter and the types of countries to consider, using criteria to determine the attractiveness of individual countries. Its attitude to risk will play a decisive role in setting objectives and formulating strategies.

7. There are six stages in the typical internationalisation progress: Stage 1: The completely uninterested firm; Stage 2: The partially interested firm; Stage 3: The exploring firm; Stage 4: The experimental exporter; Stage 5: The experienced small exporter; and Stage 6: The experienced large exporter.

8. Challenges to alliance partners relate to the creation of compatibility in terms of cultures and venture experience levels as well as a strong desire and commitment by the people in the partnership for it to succeed.

9. Ventures tend to be successful where partners are fairly homogeneous, trust is developed and a major effort is made by people to work together with common, well understood and agreed goals.

10. The pros and cons of each strategy revolve around the amount of commitment, risk, control and profit potential. Each strategy should also be considered as part of a strategy sequence—exporting leading to joint ventures or direct investment, which in turn leads to progressive commitment to an increasing number of markets over time.

11. The most enduring joint ventures are those where each partner has a clear and relatively equal contribution to make towards the success of the venture, the sizes and cultures of the partners are similar, and clear sustainable goals are established and achieved over time. Success also relies on continual communication and understanding of all key levels of the organisation (and between parent companies if applicable).

12. A global strategy treats the world as a single market in which standardised offerings are made, and marketing strategies are driven from the centre and are similar in all country markets. A multinational strategy treats the world as a portfolio of national opportunities in which there is some autonomy in decision-making in local branches. A global strategy standardises certain core elements and localises others. There may be some standardisation of product but with localisation of promotion, distribution, pricing and service.

13. The main advantages of a standardised strategy worldwide are economies of scale and resource usage, as well as clear focus on direction and positioning of the business and its products. The main disadvantages lie in less tailoring to specific needs of each market, less flexibility and responsiveness to both local market needs and competition.

14. Factors to be considered are: desired future competitive position, customer needs (global and local customers), level of industry globalisation, target legal/political commonalities and differences, cultural similarities, and differences with respect to promotion and positioning.

15. Elements such as product quality, range, depth and aspects of required technical support need to be considered. Also, price in terms of terms of trade, financing arrangements, discount structure and price position together with distribution channels and members are important.

16. The major benefits from a global strategy are: cost reduction through economies of scale and reduced duplication; improved quality through more competition; enhanced customer preference such as the availability of use of a product across nations; and competitive leverage through more places of competition. The major drawbacks are that all global activities incur much higher costs than those of domestic firms.

17. Examples of alliance linkages are shown in Figures 20.7–10. Leader strategies strive to create the dominant alliance group. Challengers develop an alliance partner network to match leader strengths. Followers are usually looking for a low-cost network. Specialists are trying to strengthen their focus through alliances.

18. Westpac is challenging NAB and ANZ for business with high-worth clients. It has sought an alliance with the Bank of Melbourne to strengthen its business in the Victorian market. The end result of this alliance is likely to be a takeover by Westpac.

19. The main forms include an export department, an international division and a global organisation. There are many variations on the last two factors. The global organisation becomes particularly complex when marketing managers may be reporting to a country manager and a regional manager as well as divisional managers at regional and global levels.

20. Basic competitive strategy profiles:

Basic competitive strategy profiles	
Global leader	Mercedes-Benz
Global challenger	BMW
Global niche	Porsche

CHAPTER TWENTY-ONE

1. It might be argued that sophisticated consumers can see that such advertising does not always mirror reality. However, the less well educated, and cultures at an earlier stage of development, may come to feel alienated as they believe they have missed out.

2. This is a question with political overtones. It might be argued that government is as addicted to the tax revenue from cigarettes as the smokers are to tobacco.

3. Critics feel that the buyer has too little information, education or protection to make wise decisions when facing sophisticated sellers.

4. The answer to this question depends on your political stance, and whether you believe in interventionist government or not.

5. Company policy decrees that this activity is not tolerated. So too does the retailer's policy. Giving a gift under such circumstances is risking dismissal. Risk aversion comes into the picture, given these policies.

6. The answer to this question largely depends on your view of people's desire to conform and their moral fibre. It is unlikely that all users would comply.

7. It depends on the degree of innovation, not how closely a product is positioned to a competitive offering in the likes of advertising. Innovation is in the eyes of the consumer. It also depends on where the ideas for the innovation came from.

8. Many critics of this action by the then Australian government would argue that developing two fibre-optic cables is not in keeping with this principle.

9. It is wisest not to put yourself in such a situation due to the possible legal implications.

10. Smell—perfume; sound—rock group or music company; shape—computer keyboard such as Microsoft's Natural keyboard.

11. More and more the issue will become: Where was the crime committed? It will take some time for the law to catch up with the events made possible by such technology as the Internet and satellite television.

Actual product A product's parts, styling, features, brand name, packaging and other attributes that combine to deliver core product benefits.

Adapted marketing mix An international marketing strategy for adjusting the marketing-mix elements to each international target market, bearing more costs but hoping for a larger market share and return.

Administered VMN A vertical marketing network that coordinates successive stages of production and distribution, not through common ownership or contractual ties but through the size and power of one of the parties.

Adoption process The mental process through which an individual passes from first learning about an innovation to final adoption.

Advertising Any paid form of non-personal presentation and promotion of ideas, goods or services by an identified sponsor.

Advertising objective A specific communication task to be accomplished with a specific target audience during a specific period of time.

Advertising specialties Useful articles imprinted with an advertiser's name, given as gifts to consumers.

Affordable method Setting the communications budget at what management thinks the company can afford.

Age and life-cycle segmentation Dividing a market into different age and life-cycle groups.

Agent A wholesaler who represents buyers or sellers on a more permanent basis, performs only a few functions and does not take title to goods.

Agile corporation An organisation that is constantly able to reorganise its structure and its human, technological and financial resources in response to continuously changing market opportunities. This kind of organisation maintains the highest level of flexibility in order to be able to respond to unpredictable changes in its environment.

Allowance Promotional money paid by manufacturers to retailers in return for an agreement to feature the manufacturer's products in some way.

Alternative evaluation The stage of the buyer decision process in which the consumer uses information to evaluate alternative brands in the choice set.

Approach The step in the selling process in which the salesperson meets and greets

the buyer to get the relationship off to a good start.

Aspirational groups Groups to which an individual wishes to belong.

Attitude A person's relatively consistent evaluations, feelings and tendencies towards an object or an idea.

Augmented product Additional consumer services and benefits built around the core and actual products.

Australian and New Zealand Standard Industrial Classification (ANZSIC) System of classifying industry into 19 major groups and 86 subdivisions.

Baby boom The major increase in the annual birthrate following World War II and lasting until the early 1960s. The 'baby boomers', now moving into middle age, are a prime target for marketers.

Basing-point pricing A geographical pricing strategy in which the seller designates a city as a basing point and charges all customers the freight cost from that city to the customer location, regardless of the city from which the goods are actually shipped.

Behavioural segmentation Dividing a market into groups based on consumers' knowledge of, attitude towards, uses for and responses to a product.

Belief A descriptive thought or conviction that a person holds about something.

Benchmarking Comparison of a company's performance and processes with its competitors and with best-practice companies, using specific measures such as scrap levels, power costs, process waste, order-processing cycle times and productivity measures.

Benefit segmentation Dividing the market into groups according to the different benefits that consumers seek from the product.

Brand A name, term, sign, symbol or design, or a combination of these, intended to identify the goods or services of one seller or group of sellers and to differentiate them from those of competitors.

Brand equity The value of a brand, based on the extent to which it has high brand loyalty, name awareness, perceived quality, strong brand associations and other assets such as patents, trademarks and channel relationships.

Brand extension A new or modified product launched under an already successful brand name.

Brand image The set of beliefs consumers hold about a particular brand.

Brand personality The specific mix of human traits that are attributed to a particular brand.

Brand repositioning Because of competitive action, or due to implementation of a new strategy, a marketer might need to change both the product and its image to meet customer expectations with its brand(s) better.

Brand strategy Entails decisions on brand positioning, brand name, brand sponsorship and brand development (see Figure 11.7).

Break-even pricing (target profit pricing) Setting price to break even on the costs of making and marketing a product, or to make the desired profit.

Broker A wholesaler who does not take title to goods and whose function is to bring buyers and sellers together and assist in negotiation.

Business analysis A review of the sales, costs and profit projections for a new product to find out whether these factors satisfy the company's objectives.

Business buying process The decision-making process by which business buyers establish the need for purchased products and services and identify, evaluate and choose between alternative brands and suppliers.

Business market All the organisations that buy goods and services to use in the production of other products and services or for the purpose of reselling or renting them to others at a profit.

Business portfolio The collection of businesses and products that make up the company.

Buyer The person who makes an actual purchase.

Buyer-readiness states The stages consumers normally pass through on their way to purchase, including awareness, knowledge, liking, preference, conviction or purchase.

Buying centre All the individuals and units that participate in the organisational buying decision process.

Buzz marketing Cultivating opinion leaders and getting them to spread information about a product or service to others in their communities.

By-product pricing Setting a price for by-products in order to make the main product's price more competitive.

Capital items Industrial goods and services that enter the finished product partly, including installations and accessory equipment.

Captive product pricing The pricing of products that must be used along with a main product, such as blades for a razor and film for cameras.

Cash-back offers Cash discounts usually received by forwarding 'proof of purchase' where state legislation permits.

Cash cows Low-growth, high-share businesses or products—established and successful units that generate cash, which the company uses to pay its bills and support other business units that need investment.

Cash discount A price reduction to buyers who pay their bills promptly.

Catalogue A printed listing of products, often featuring high-quality reproduction of the items on sale.

Category management A management approach introduced by retailers and increasingly adopted by the marketing organisations in an endeavour to coordinate the efforts of many departments.

Causal research Marketing research to test hypotheses about cause and effect relationships.

Cause marketing Marketing an idea or social cause, such as nuclear-free living, not drinking alcohol and driving, or catching public-transport to and from work.

Cents-off deals Temporary price discounts, usually offered at retail level; however, they are also offered by direct marketers.

Chain stores Two or more outlets that are commonly owned and controlled, employ central buying and merchandising and sell similar lines of merchandise.

Channel conflict Disagreement among marketing channel members on goals and roles—on who should do what and for what rewards.

Channel level A layer of middlemen that performs some work in bringing the product and its ownership closer to the final buyer.

Clickstream The path followed by website visitors.

Closing The step in the selling process in which the salesperson asks the customer for an order.

Co-branding The practice of using the established brand names of two different companies on the same product.

Cognitive dissonance Buyer discomfort caused by post-purchase conflict.

Combination store Combined grocery and general mechandise stores.

Commercialisation Introducing a new product into the market.

Communication adaptation A global communication strategy of fully adapting advertising messages to local markets.

Comparison advertising Advertising that compares one brand directly or indirectly with one or more other brands.

Competitive advantage An advantage over competitors gained by offering consumers greater value, either through lower prices or by providing more benefits that justify higher prices.

Competitive marketing strategies Defined by the marketing actions taken to move an organisation from its current competitive position to a desired future competitive position. An organisation's competitive position is defined by its position in the market relative to competitors as seen by the relevant target market.

Competitive-parity method Setting the promotions budget to match competitors' outlays.

Competitor analysis The process of identifying major competitors; assessing their objectives, strategies, strengths and weaknesses and reaction patterns; and selecting which competitors to attack or avoid.

Competitor-centred company A company whose moves are mainly based on competitors' actions and reactions; it spends most of its time tracking competitors' moves and market shares and trying to find strategies to counter them.

Complex buying behaviour Consumer buying behaviour in situations characterised by high consumer involvement in a purchase and significant perceived differences among brands.

Concentrated marketing A market-coverage strategy in which a company goes after a large share of one or a few submarkets.

Concept testing Testing new product concepts with a group of target consumers to find out if the concepts have strong consumer appeal.

Consumer market All the individuals and households who buy or acquire goods and services for personal consumption.

Consumer products Products bought by final consumers for personal consumption.

Consumer-oriented marketing A principle of enlightened marketing that holds that the organisation should view and organise its marketing activities from the consumer's point of view.

Consumerism An organised movement of consumers whose aim is to improve the rights and power of buyers in relation to sellers.

Containerisation Putting goods in boxes or trailers that are easy to transfer between two transportation modes. They are used in 'multimode' systems commonly referred to as piggyback, fishyback, trainship and airtruck.

Contests and games of chance and skill Promotional events that give consumers the chance to win something of value by luck or by the use of skill.

Continuity scheduling Scheduling ads evenly within a given period.

Contract manufacturing Joint venturing to enter a foreign market by contracting with manufacturers in the foreign market to produce the product.

Contractual VMN A vertical marketing network in which independent firms at different levels of production and distribution join together through contracts to obtain more economies or sales impact than they could achieve alone.

Convenience products Consumer goods and services that the customer usually buys frequently, immediately and with the minimum of comparison and buying effort.

Convenience store A small store, located near a residential area, open long hours seven days a week, and carrying a limited line of high-turnover convenience goods.

Conversion operations Includes services production and physical product manufacturing operations.

Cookies Short identifier pieces of text which are deposited on a visitor's computer by a website. On each subsequent visit, the website software records the cookie response and thus measures repeat guest visits.

Copy testing Measuring the communication effect of an advertisement before or after it is printed or broadcast.

Core product The problem-solving services or core benefits that consumers are really buying when they obtain a product.

Corporate chain See chain stores.

Corporate VMN A vertical marketing network that combines successive stages of production and distribution under single ownership—channel leadership is established through common ownership.

Cost-plus pricing Adding a standard mark-up to the cost of the product.

Countertrade International trade involving the direct or indirect exchange of goods for other goods instead of cash. Forms include barter, compensation (buyback) and counter-purchase.

Cross-docking Picking shipments received from suppliers then reloading onto transport without any storage in a warehouse.

Cross-referencing data A privacy issue arises where an individual's personal information such as health status, work attendance levels and other information is interconnected and used without permission.

Cultural environment Institutions and other forces that affect society's basic values, perceptions, preferences and behaviours.

Culture The set of basic values, perceptions, wants and behaviours learned by a member of society from family and other important institutions.

Customer-centred company A company that focuses on customer developments in designing its marketing strategies.

Customer lifetime value The amount by which revenues from a given customer over time exceed the company's costs of attracting, selling to and servicing that customer.

Customer relationship management The overall process of building and maintaining profitable customer relationships by delivering superior customer value and satisfaction.

Customer salesforce structure A salesforce organisation under which salespeople specialise in selling only to certain customers or industries.

Customer satisfaction The extent to which a product's perceived performance matches a buyer's expectations. If the product's performance falls short of expectations, the buyer is dissatisfied. If performance matches or exceeds expectations, the buyer is satisfied or delighted.

Customer value The difference between the values the customer gains from owning and using a product and the costs of obtaining the product.

Customer value analysis Analysis conducted to determine what benefits target customers value and how they rate the relative value of various competitors' offers.

Customer value delivery networks Marketing channels in which each channel member adds value for the customer.

Data mining Data mining entails checking databases for patterns and trends that are hypothesised to exist, or in order to find new connections between data items.

Decider The person who ultimately makes a buying decision or any part of it—whether to buy, what to buy, how to buy or where to buy.

Decline stage The product life-cycle stage at which a product's sales decline.

Deficient products Products that have neither immediate appeal nor long-run benefits.

Demand curve A curve that shows the number of units the market will buy in a given time period, at different prices that might be charged.

Demands Human wants that are backed by buying power.

Demarketing Marketing in which the task is to temporarily or permanently reduce demand.

Demographic segmentation Dividing the market into groups based on demographic variables such as age, sex, family size, family life cycle, income, occupation, education, religion and nationality.

Demography The study of human populations in terms of size, density, location, age, sex, race, occupation and other statistics.

Department store A retail organisation that carries a wide variety of product lines—typically clothing, home furnishings and household goods; each line is operated as a separate department, which may be managed by specialist buyers or merchandisers or this function may be performed centrally.

Derived demand Organisational demand that ultimately comes from (derives from) the demand for consumer goods.

Descriptive research Marketing research to describe marketing problems, situations or markets better—such as the market potential for a product or the demographics and attitudes of consumers.

Desirable products Products that give both high immediate satisfaction and high long-run benefits.

Differentiated marketing A market-coverage strategy in which a company decides to target several market segments and designs separate offers for each.

Direct and online database marketing Entails development and maintenance of electronic databases to interact with past, present and/or potential customers and others in the marketing channel, on a one-to-one basis, often in real-time, and where the databases are used to maintain value-laden relationships and to generate a measurable response and/or transactions through the integrated use of electronic network tools and technologies.

Direct mail Printed materials sent by mail and conveying offers to consumers, whether targeted to the recipient by name, or to the business or householder by a broader targeting method.

Direct marketing An interactive system of marketing which uses one or more advertising media to effect a measurable response and/or transaction at any location.

Direct marketing channel A marketing channel that has no intermediary levels.

Direct print and reproduction marketing The use of printed materials such as direct mail and catalogues to convey offers to consumers, whether targeted to the recipient by name, or to the business or householder by a broader targeting method.

Direct-response television, radio and print marketing Use of mass-promotion media combined with a direct response offer, usually involving telemarketing.

Direct selling Selling directly to consumers or to businesses rather than using a reseller, such as a retailer or agent.

Discount store A retail institution that sells standard merchandise at lower prices by accepting lower margins and selling at higher volume.

Disintermediation Removing a marketing channel, as when a consumer invests directly in the money market rather than investing via their bank—often a myth perpetuated by those who are pro-technology in the case of the effects of online businesses such as Amazon.com.

Dissonance-reducing buying behaviour Consumer buying behaviour in situations characterised by high involvement but few perceived differences among brands.

Distributed marketing information systems Internal and external information can be obtained, analysed and reported on over digital networks, even around the world.

Distribution centre A large and highly automated warehouse designed to receive goods from various plants and suppliers, take orders, fill them efficiently and deliver goods to customers as quickly as possible.

Diversification A strategy for promoting company growth by starting up or acquiring businesses outside the company's current products and markets.

Dogs Low-growth, low-share businesses or products that may generate enough cash to maintain themselves but do not promise to be a large source of cash.

Economic environment Factors that affect consumer buying power and spending patterns.

Economic value added A measure of operating profit (before interest and after tax) less cost of all capital employed to produce the profit. This can be thought of as economic profit which is added to the value of the business as a result of operations. The term EVA (short for economic value added) is a registered trademark of Stern Stewart & Co.

EFTPOS (electronic funds transfer at point of sale) Retailer cash registers electronically linked to bank accounts; consumers may pay directly using a 'cash card' or a credit card, and funds may also be credited to an account if goods are returned.

Electronic dispensing machines Machines that dispense products (food) and services (cash), usually by inserting cash, transaction or stored-value card.

Electronic shopping Purchasing via an electronic bulletin board or facilities such as Telstra's Discovery, or (in the future) via interactive cable television.

Embargo A ban on the import of a certain imports.

Emotional appeals Message appeals that attempt to stir negative or positive emotions that can motivate purchase; examples include fear, guilt, shame, love, humour and joy appeals.

Engel's laws Differences noted more than a century ago by Ernst Engel regarding family spending patterns in response to increased income; categories studied included food, housing, transportation, health care and other goods and services.

Enlightened marketing A marketing philosophy holding that an organisation's marketing should support the best long-run performance of the marketing system; its six principles include consumer-oriented marketing, principle of innovativeness, principle of adding value, sense of mission, maintaining social responsibility and employing marketing metrics.

Environmentalism An organised movement of concerned citizens, businesses and government seeking to protect and improve people's living environment.

Event marketing Combines elements of marketing physical products with those of services, particularly the experiential aspects of sporting, entertainment and other staged events delivered over a period of time.

Exchange The act of obtaining a desired object from someone by offering something in return.

Exclusive distribution Giving a limited number of dealers the exclusive right to distribute the company's products in their territories.

Executive summary The opening section of the marketing plan that presents a short summary of the main goals and recommendations to be presented in the plan.

Experience curve (learning curve) The drop in the average per-unit production cost that comes with accumulated production experience.

Experiences marketing Adding value for customers buying products and services through customer participation and connection by managing the environmental aspects of the relationship.

Experimental research The gathering of primary data by selecting matched groups of subjects, giving them different treatments, controlling unrelated factors and checking for differences in group responses.

Exploratory research Marketing research to gather preliminary information that will help to define problems better and suggest hypotheses.

Exporting Entering a foreign market by exporting products and selling them through international marketing middlemen (indirect exporting) or through the company's own department, branch, or sales representatives or agents (direct exporting).

Extranet An online service provided to key customers using a secure information-based or transacting website on the public Internet.

Factory outlets Off-price retailing operations that are owned and operated by manufacturers and that normally carry the manufacturer's surplus, discontinued or irregular goods.

Fads Fashions that enter quickly, are adopted with great zeal, peak early and decline fast.

Fashion A currently accepted or popular style in a given field.

Fast-moving consumer goods (FMCG) Products such as weekly grocery items which are consumed in a single use or on a few usage occasions.

Financial intermediaries Banks, credit companies, insurance companies and other businesses that help finance transactions or insure against the risks associated with the buying and selling of goods.

Fixed costs Costs that do not vary with production or sales level.

FOB-origin pricing A geographical pricing strategy in which goods are placed free on board a carrier, and the customer pays the freight from the factory to the destination.

Focus group A group of six to ten people brought together for a few hours with a trained interviewer to talk about a product, service or organisation. The interviewer 'focuses' the group discussion on important issues.

Follow-up The last step in the selling process in which the salesperson follows up after the sale to ensure customer satisfaction and repeat business.

Forecasting The art of estimating future demand by anticipating what buyers are likely to do under a given set of conditions.

Franchise A contractual association between a manufacturer, wholesaler or service organisation (a franchisor) and independent businesspeople (franchisees) who buy the right to own and operate one or more units in the franchise system.

Franchise organisation A contractual vertical marketing network in which a channel member called a franchisor links several stages in the production–distribution process.

Freight-absorption pricing A geographical pricing strategy in which the company absorbs all or part of the actual freight charges in order to get the business.

Frequency The number of times the average person in the target market is exposed to an advertising message during a given period.

Fulfilment response Direct and online marketers think in terms of delivery response times and accuracy of delivery, among other things, when responding to meet product orders.

Full-service retailers Retailers that provide a full range of services to shoppers.

Full-service wholesalers Wholesalers that provide a full set of services, such as carrying stock, using a sales force, offering credit, making deliveries and providing management assistance.

Functional discount (or trade discount) A price reduction offered by the seller to trade channel members who perform certain functions, such as selling, storing and record keeping.

Gatekeeper The person in the organisation's buying centre who controls the flow of information to others.

Gender segmentation Dividing a market into different groups based on sex.

General need description The stage in the industrial buying process in which the company describes the general characteristics and quantity of a needed item.

Generation Y The people born between 1965 and 1976 in the 'birth dearth' following the baby boom.

Generation X The children of the baby boomers, born between 1977 and 1994.

Geographic segmentation Dividing a market into different geographical units such as nations, regions, states, municipalities, cities or neighbourhoods.

Global firm A firm that, by operating in more-than one country, gains R&D, production, marketing and financial advantages that are not available to purely domestic competitors.

Global industry An industry in which the competitive positions of companies in given local or national markets are affected by their overall global positions.

Globalisation The process by which firms operate on a global basis, organising their structure, capabilities, resources and people in such a way as to address the world as one market.

Going-rate pricing Setting price based largely on following competitors' prices rather than on company costs or demand.

Government market Governmental units—federal, state and local—that purchase or rent goods and services for carrying out the main functions of government.

Growth-share matrix A portfolio-planning method that evaluates a company's strategic business units in terms of their market growth rate and relative market share. SBUs are classified as stars, cash cows, question marks or dogs.

Growth stage The product life-cycle stage at which a product's sales start climbing quickly.

Habitual buying behaviour Consumer buying behaviour in situations characterised by low consumer involvement and few significant perceived brand differences.

Handling objections The step in the selling process in which the salesperson seeks out, clarifies and overcomes customer objections to buying.

Hits The record of the number of files requested by guests to a particular web page. The more links and graphics there are on a web page, the more hits will be recorded. The visitor is not, however, identified.

Horizontal marketing networks A channel arrangement in which two or more companies at one level join together to follow a new marketing opportunity.

Hybrid marketing channel networks Multichannel distribution systems in which a single firm sets up two or more marketing channels to reach one or more marketing segments.

Hypermarkets Huge stores that combine supermarket, discount and warehouse retailing; in addition to food, they carry furniture, appliances, clothing and many other items.

Idea generation The systematic search for new product ideas.

Idea screening Screening new product ideas in order to spot good ideas and drop poor ones as soon as possible.

Income segmentation Dividing a market into different income groups.

Independent off-price retailers Off-price retailers that are either owned and run by entrepreneurs or are divisions of larger retail corporations.

Industrial market All the individuals and organisations acquiring goods and services that enter into the production of other products and services that are sold, rented or supplied to others.

Industrial products Goods bought by individuals and organisations for further processing or for use in conducting a business.

Industry A group of firms that offer a product or class of products that are close substitutes for each other; the set of all sellers of a product.

Influencer A person whose view or advice carries some weight in making a final buying decision.

Information search The stage of the buyer decision process in which the consumer is aroused to search for more information; the consumer may simply have heightened attention or may go into active information search.

Informative advertising Advertising used to inform consumers about a new product or feature and to build primary demand.

Inside salesforce Salespeople who conduct business from their offices via telephone or visits from prospective buyers.

Institutional market Schools, hospitals, nursing homes, prisons and other institutions that provide goods and services to people in their care.

In-store communication The use of media, tools and technology at store level.

Integrated marketing communications (IMC) The concept under which a company carefully integrates and coordinates its many communications channels to deliver a clear, consistent and compelling message about the organisation and its products.

Intensive distribution Stocking the product in as many outlets as possible.

Intermarket segmentation Forming segments of consumers who have similar needs and buying behaviour even though they are located in different countries.

Intermodal transportation methods Method of transportation whereby two (or more) modes of transport are used, for example piggybacking truck trailers on rail cars.

Internal marketing One part of a marketing organisation marketing its capabilities to another part of the organisation.

Internal records Information gathered from sources within the company to evaluate marketing performance and to detect marketing problems and opportunities.

Internal transportation methods Method of transportation whereby two (or more) modes of transport are used, for example piggybacking truck trailers on rail cars.

International Standard Industrial Classification (ISIC) International classification system for industry types.

Internet (Net) The world's largest public computer network which connects many other computers and computer networks.

Intranet A secure Web service for employees only or in the case of a university for staff and registered students only.

Introduction stage The product life-cycle stage when the new product is first distributed and made available for purchase.

Inventory (sometimes referred to as stocks) There are three kinds of inventory: raw materials or input supplies to a conversion process; work-in-process and finished goods.

Involvement The importance of the product for the consumer. High-involvement products are typical of important, risky, infrequently purchased goods. Low involvement products are typically frequently purchased, low-cost, low-risk purchases.

Joint venturing Entering foreign markets by joining with foreign companies to produce or market a product or service.

Key account manager A sales manager who manages the interaction with a major customer.

Kiosks Electronically networked mini-offices, staffed or unstaffed, and capable of dispensing information, products and services as well as capable of receiving payments by instalment or in full.

Knowledgebase Database of frequently asked questions or solutions to problems maintained by a company to assist customers.

Labels May range from simple tags attached to products to complex graphics that are part of the package.

Leading indicators Factors that change in the same direction but in advance of company sales.

Learning Changes in an individual's behaviour arising from experience.

Learning organisation A learning organisation is defined by its ability to innovate, adopt and change in line with its changing environment.

Licensing A method of entering a foreign market in which the company enters into an agreement with a licensee in the foreign market, offering the right to use a manufacturing process, trademark, patent, trade secret or other item of value for a fee or royalty.

Lifestyle A person's pattern of living as expressed in his or her activities, interests and opinions.

Limited-service retailers Retailers that provide only a limited number of services to shoppers.

Limited-service wholesalers Wholesalers that offer only limited services to their suppliers and customers.

Line extension Using a successful brand name to introduce additional items in a given product category under the same brand name, such as new flavours, forms, colours, added ingredients or package sizes.

Lists Direct and online marketing entails hiring lists containing names of qualified potential customers.

Log files All host servers maintain a record of the IP address of the guest's computer and of every file sent out. This is termed a log file.

Logistics The process of planning, implementing and controlling the efficient, cost-effective flow and storage of material, in-process inventory, finished goods and related information from point of origin to point of consumption for the purpose of conforming to customer requirements.

Macroenvironment The larger societal forces that affect the whole micro-environment—demographic, economic, natural, technological, political and cultural forces.

Maintaining social responsibility A principle of enlightened marketing that holds that an organisation should make marketing decisions by considering consumer's wants, the organisation's requirements, consumers' long-run interests and society's long-run interests.

Manufacturers' brand (or national brand) A brand created and owned by the producer of a product or service.

Manufacturers' sales branches and offices Wholesaling by sellers or buyers themselves rather than through independent wholesalers.

Market The set of all actual and potential buyers of a product.

Market-buildup method A forecasting method that calls for identifying all the potential buyers in each market and estimating their potential purchases.

Market-centred company A company that pays balanced attention to both customers and competitors in designing its marketing strategies.

Market challenger A runner-up firm in an industry that is fighting hard to increase its market share.

Market demand The total volume of a product or service that would be bought by a defined consumer group in a defined geographic area in a defined time period in a defined marketing environment under a defined level and mix of industry marketing effort.

Market development A strategy for promoting company growth by identifying and developing new market segments for current company products.

Market-factor index method A forecasting method that identifies market factors that correlate with market potential and combines them into a weighted index.

Market follower A runner-up firm in an industry that wants to hold its share without rocking the boat.

Market leader The firm with the largest market share in an industry; it usually leads other firms in price changes, new product introductions, distribution coverage and promotion spending.

Market nicher A firm in an industry that serves small segments that the other firms overlook or ignore.

Market orientation A situation in which a business has a strong customer focus and competitor orientation supported by effective interfunctional coordination that enables the business to deliver profitable customer value over time.

Market penetration A strategy for promoting company growth by increasing sales of current products to current market segments without changing the product in any way.

Market-penetration pricing Setting a low price for a new product in order to attract a large number of buyers and a large market share.

Market positioning Arranging for a product to occupy a clear, distinctive and desirable place relative to competing products in the minds of target consumers; formulating competitive positioning for a product and creating a detailed marketing mix.

Market potential The upper limit of market demand.

Market segment A group of consumers who respond in a similar way to a given set of marketing stimuli.

Market segmentation Dividing a market into direct groups of buyers who might require separate products or marketing mixes; the process of classifying customers into groups with different needs, characteristics or behaviour.

Market-skimming pricing Setting a high price for a new product to skim maximum revenue from the segments willing to pay the high price; the company makes fewer but more profitable sales.

Market targeting Evaluating each market segment's attractiveness and selecting one or more segments to enter.

Marketing An organisational function and a set of processes for creating, communicating, and delivering value to customers and for managing customer relationships in ways that benefit the organisation and its stakeholders.

Marketing audit A comprehensive, systematic, independent and periodic examination of a company's environment, objectives, strategies and activities to determine problem areas and opportunities and to recommend a plan of action to improve the company's marketing performance.

Marketing channels A set of interdependent organisations involved in the process of making a product or service available to users.

Marketing concept The marketing management philosophy which holds that achieving organisational goals depends on determining the needs and wants of target markets and delivering the desired satisfactions more effectively and efficiently than competitors.

Marketing control The process of measuring and evaluating the results of marketing strategies and plans, and taking corrective action to ensure that marketing objectives are attained.

Marketing environment The actors and forces outside marketing that affect marketing management's ability to develop and maintain successful transactions with its target customers.

Marketing implementation The process that turns marketing strategies and plans into marketing actions in order to accomplish strategic marketing objectives.

Marketing information system (MIS) People, equipment and procedures to gather, sort, analyse, evaluate and distribute needed, timely and accurate information to marketing decision makers.

Marketing intelligence Systematic collection and analysis of publicly available information about competitors and developments in the marketplace.

Marketing intermediaries Firms that help the organisation to promote, sell and distribute its goods to final buyers; they include resellers, physical distribution firms, marketing services agencies and financial intermediaries.

Marketing logistics networks System of efficiently and effectively making and getting products and services to end-users.

Marketing logistics network management Managing the network of players providing customer fulfilment ranging from providers of inputs (raw materials, components and capital equipment) and extending to conversion operations, and including marketing channel intermediaries and those involved in physical movement of product.

Marketing management The analysis, planning, implementation and control of programs designed to create, build and maintain beneficial exchanges with target buyers for the purpose of achieving organisational objectives.

Marketing mix The set of controllable marketing variables that the company blends to produce the response it wants in the target market.

Marketing process The process of (i) analysing marketing opportunities; (ii) selecting target markets; (iii) developing the marketing mix; and (iv) managing the marketing effort.

Marketing research The function that links the consumer, customer and public to the marketer through information—information used to identify and define marketing opportunities and problems; to generate, refine and evaluate marketing actions; to monitor marketing performance; and to improve understanding of the marketing process.

Marketing services agencies Marketing research companies, advertising agencies, media firms, marketing consulting agencies and other service providers that help the organisation target and promote its products to the right markets.

Marketing strategy The marketing logic by which the business unit hopes to achieve its marketing objectives. Marketing strategy consists of specific strategies for target markets, marketing mix and marketing expenditure level.

Marketing strategy development Designing an initial marketing strategy for a new product based on the product concept.

Mass communication The use of mass media such as free-to-air television, radio, newspapers and magazines, as well as other media, such as cinema and outdoor.

Mass merchant A type of store carrying a large assortment of merchandise such as in hardware (Bunnings Warehouse) or electrical goods and furniture (Harvey Norman) or personal and healthcare (Priceline).

Materials and parts Industrial goods that enter the manufacturer's product completely, including raw materials and manufactured materials and parts.

Maturity stage The stage in the product life cycle in which sales growth slows or levels off.

Maximarketing Rapp and Collins's maximarketing model details seven steps for effective integrated database marketing.

Media impact The qualitative value of a media exposure through a given medium.

Media vehicles Specific media within each general media type, such as specific magazines, television shows or radio programs.

Membership groups Groups that have a direct influence on a person's behaviour and to which a person belongs.

Merchandising conglomerates Companies that combine several different retailing forms under central ownership and that share some distribution and management functions.

Merchant wholesaler An independently owned business that takes title to the merchandise it handles.

Microenvironment The forces close to the organisation that affect its ability to serve its customers—the organisation, marketing channel firms, customer markets, competitors and publics.

Micromarketing A form of target marketing in which companies tailor their marketing programs to the needs and wants of narrowly defined geographic, demographic, psychographic or behaviour, or benefit, segments.

Mission statement A statement of the organisation's purpose—what it wants to accomplish in the larger environment.

Modified rebuy An industrial buying situation in which the buyer wants to modify product specifications, prices, terms or suppliers.

Monopolistic competition A market in which many buyers and sellers trade over a range of prices rather than a single market price.

Moral appeals Message appeals that are directed to the audience's sense of what is right and proper.

Motive (or drive) A need that is sufficiently pressing to direct the person to seek satisfaction of the need.

Multibranding A strategy under which a seller develops two or more brands in the same product category.

Multichannels (See hybrid marketing channel networks.)

Natural environment Natural resources which are needed as inputs by marketers or which are affected by marketing activities.

Needs States of felt deprivation.

New product A good, service or idea that is perceived by some potential customers as new.

New-product development The development of original products, product improvements, product modifications and new brands through the company's own R&D efforts.

New task An industrial buying situation in which the buyer purchases a product or service for the first time.

Non-personal communication channels Media that carry messages without personal contact or feedback, including media, atmospheres and events.

Non-profit marketing Involves activities by organisations not motivated by profit which ultimately lead to a donation, bequest or some other contribution.

Objective-and-task method Developing the promotions budget by (1) defining specific objectives; (2) determining the tasks that must be performed to achieve these objectives; and (3) estimating the costs of performing these tasks. The sum of these costs is the proposed promotions budget.

Observational research The gathering of primary data by observing relevant people, actions and situations.

Occasion segmentation Dividing the market into groups according to occasions when buyers get the idea, make a purchase or use a product.

Off-price retailers Retailers that buy at less than regular wholesale prices and sell at less than retail, usually carrying a changing and unstable collection of higher-quality merchandise, often leftover goods, overruns and irregulars

obtained from manufacturers at reduced prices. They include factory outlets, independents and warehouse clubs.

Oligopolistic competition A market in which there are a few sellers who are highly sensitive to each other's pricing and marketing strategies.

One-to-one communication The use of integrated database marketing to track an individual customer's buying pattern.

Online (Internet) marketing research Collecting primary data through Internet surveys and online focus groups.

Online marketing Interaction with known customers and others in the marketing channel, on a one-to-one basis, often in real-time, to maintain value-laden relationships and to generate a measurable response and/or transactions using electronic network tools and technologies.

Opinion leaders People who exert influence on others' opinions and buying behaviour.

Optional product/service pricing The pricing of optional or accessory products along with a main product.

Order processing All of the activities involved in receiving, processing and fulfilling sales-order information.

Order-routine specification The stage of the industrial buying process in which the buyer writes the final order with the chosen supplier(s), listing the technical specifications, quantity needed, expected time of delivery, return policies, warranties and so on.

Outside salesforce (or field salesforce) Outside salespeople who travel to call on customers.

Packaging The activities of designing and producing the container or wrapper for a product.

Page impressions The number of web pages viewed by a single visitor to a site.

Page views A measure of the number of pages a visitor views at a particular website. However, many sites have many pages at a number of levels (taking a television approach to website design), while others are composed of a few long 'scrolling' files (taking a magazine approach to website design).

Patronage rewards Cash, merchandise or service rewards offered to consumers who make continual use of a company's product or service, for example frequent-flyer plans.

Percentage-of-sales method Setting the communications budget at a certain

percentage of current or forecasted sales or as a percentage of the sales price.

Perception The process by which people select, organise and interpret information to form a meaningful picture of the world.

Performance review The stage of the industrial buying process in which the buyer rates its satisfaction with suppliers, deciding whether to continue, modify or drop the relationship.

Permission marketing A process of converting strangers into friends and friends into customers.

Personal communication channels Channels through which two or more people communicate directly with each other, including face to face, person to audience, over the telephone or through the mail.

Personal selling Oral presentation in a conversation with one or more prospective purchasers for the purpose of making sales.

Personality A person's distinguishing psychological characteristics that lead to relatively consistent and lasting responses to his or her own environment.

Persuasive advertising Advertising used to build selective demand for a brand by persuading consumers that it offers the best quality for their money.

Physical distribution The tasks involved in planning, implementing and controlling the physical flow of materials and final goods from points of origin to points of use to meet the needs of customers at a profit.

Physical distribution firms Warehouse, transportation and other firms that help the organisation stock and move goods from their points of origin to their destinations.

Pleasing products Products that give high immediate satisfaction but may hurt consumers in the long run.

Point-of-purchase (POP) promotions Offers ranging from theme promotions in-store to specially arranged selling areas.

Political environment Laws, government agencies and pressure groups that influence and limit various organisations and individuals in a given society.

Political marketing Politicians market themselves, as well as political ideologies and their political parties.

Portfolio analysis A tool by which management identify and evaluate the various businesses that make up the company.

Post-purchase behaviour The stage of the buyer decision process in which consumers take further action after the purchase, based on their satisfaction or dissatisfaction.

Preapproach The step in the selling process in which the salesperson learns as much as possible about a prospective customer before making a sales call.

Premium offers Goods offered free of charge or at a reduced price as an incentive to buy a product.

Presentation The step in the selling process in which the salesperson tells the product 'story' to the buyer, showing how the product will make or save money.

Price The amount of money charged for a product or service, or the sum of the values consumers exchange for the benefits of having or using the product or service.

Price elasticity A measure of the sensitivity of demand to changes in price.

Price packs Reduced prices that are marked by the producer directly on the label or package.

Primary data Information collected for the current research purpose.

Primary demand The level of total demand for all brands of a given product or service, for example the total demand for motorcycles.

Principle of adding value A principle of enlightened marketing that holds that an organisation should put most of its resources into value-building marketing investments.

Principle of innovativeness A principle of enlightened marketing that requires that an organisation seek real product and marketing improvements.

Privacy guidelines Countries such as Australia have extended privacy legislation to include most profit and non-profit organisations.

Private brand (or house brand) A brand created and owned by a reseller of a product or service.

Problem recognition The first stage of the buyer decision process in which the consumer recognises a problem or need.

Procurement managers and officers Business managers responsible for buying company supplies, raw materials and capital items, directly from suppliers in most instances.

Product Anything that can be offered to a market for attention, acquisition, use or consumption that might satisfy a want or need. It includes physical objects, services, persons, places, organisations and ideas.

Product adaptation Adapting a product to meet local conditions or wants in foreign markets.

Product-bundle pricing Combining several products and offering the bundle at a reduced price.

Product category A grouping of products, often at retail level, which may be substituted for each other or which in some way supplement each other.

Product concept The idea that consumers favour products that offer the most quality, performance and features and that the organisation should therefore devote its energy to making continuous product improvements; a detailed version of the new product idea stated in meaningful consumer terms.

Product design The process of designing a product's style and function: creating a product that is attractive; easy, safe and inexpensive to use and service; and simple and economical to produce and distribute.

Product development A strategy for promoting company growth by offering modified or new products to current market segments; developing the product concept into a physical product in order to ensure that the product idea can be turned into a workable product.

Product idea An idea for a possible product that the company can see itself offering to the market.

Product image The way consumers perceive an actual or potential product.

Product invention Creating new products or services for foreign markets.

Product life cycle (PLC) The course of a product's sales and profits during its lifetime. It involves five distinct stages: product development, introduction, growth, maturity and decline.

Product line A group of products that are closely related because they function in a similar manner, are sold to the same customer groups, are marketed through the same types of outlets or fall within given price ranges.

Product-line pricing Setting the price steps between various products in a product line based on cost differences between the products, customer evaluations of different features and competitors' prices.

Product/market expansion grid A portfolio planning tool for identifying company growth opportunities through market penetration, market development, product development or diversification.

Product mix (or product assortment) The set of all product lines and items that a particular seller offers for sale to buyers.

Product position The way the product is defined by consumers on important attributes—the place the product occupies in consumers' minds relative to competing products.

Product quality The ability of a product to perform its functions; it includes the product's overall durability, reliability, precision, ease of operation and repair, and other valued attributes.

Product salesforce structure A salesforce organisation under which salespeople specialise in selling only a portion of the company's products or lines.

Product specifications The stage of the industrial buying process in which the buying organisation decides on and specifies the best technical product characteristics for a needed item.

Production concept The philosophy that consumers favour products that are available and highly affordable and that management should therefore focus on improving production and distribution efficiency.

Promotional allowance A payment or price reduction to reward dealers for participating in advertising and sales support programs.

Promotional pricing Temporarily pricing products below the list price, and sometimes even below cost, to increase short-run sales.

Proposal solicitation The stage of the industrial buying process in which the buyer invites qualified suppliers to submit proposals.

Prospect theory A theory that describes how people make decisions when the outcome is uncertain.

Prospecting The step in the selling process in which the salesperson identifies qualified potential customers.

Psychographic segmentation Dividing a market into different groups based on social class, lifestyle or personality characteristics.

Psychographics The technique of measuring lifestyles and developing lifestyle classifications; it involves measuring the major AIO dimensions (activities, interests, opinions).

Psychological pricing A pricing approach that considers the psychology of prices and not simply the economics—the price is used to say something about the product.

Public Any group that has an actual or potential interest in, or impact on, an organisation's ability to achieve its objectives.

Public relations Building good relations with the company's various publics by obtaining favourable publicity, building up a good 'corporate image' and handling or heading off unfavourable rumours, stories and events. Major PR tools include press relations, product publicity, corporate communications, lobbying and counselling.

Publicity Activities to promote a company or its products by planting news about it in media not paid for by the sponsor.

Pull strategy A promotion strategy that calls for spending a lot on advertising and consumer promotion to build up consumer demand; if successful, consumers will ask their retailers for the product, the retailers will ask the wholesalers and the wholesalers will ask the producers.

Pulsing Scheduling ads unevenly in bursts during a time period.

Purchase decision The stage of the buyer decision process in which the consumer actually buys the product.

Pure competition A market in which many buyers and sellers trade in a uniform commodity—no single buyer or seller has much effect on the going market price.

Pure monopoly A market in which there is a single seller—it may be a government monopoly, a private, regulated monopoly or a private non-regulated monopoly.

Push strategy A promotion strategy that calls for using the salesforce and trade promotion to push the product through channels; the producer promotes the product to wholesalers, the wholesalers promote to retailers and the retailers promote to consumers.

Quality The totality of features and characteristics of a product or service that bear on its ability to satisfy stated or implied needs.

Quantity discount A price reduction to buyers who buy large volumes.

Question marks Low-share business units in high-growth markets that require a lot of cash to hold their share or build into stars.

Rational appeals Message appeals that relate to the audience's self-interest and show that the product will produce the desired benefits; examples include appeals of product quality, economy, value or performance.

Reach The percentage of people in the target market exposed to an ad campaign during a given period.

Redeemable coupons Coupons carried on-pack or in other media that when forwarded to a marketer or an appointed agent will be redeemed for a product or service, or even a discount on the next purchase.

Reference groups Groups that have direct (face-to-face) or indirect influence on a person's attitudes or behaviour.

Reference prices Prices that buyers carry in their minds and refer to when they look at a given product.

Reintermediation Disintermediation is mostly a myth, and most often marketing channels are altered by disruptive technologies—such as how the Internet has enabled banks to act as online share brokers, and how online auctions and reverse auctions have enabled broadly dispersed buyers and sellers to transact without the need for traditional intermediaries.

Relationship marketing The process of creating, maintaining and enhancing strong, value-laden relationships with customers and other stakeholders.

Reminder advertising Advertising used to keep consumers thinking about a product.

Reseller market All the individuals and organisations that acquire goods for the purpose of reselling or renting them to others at a profit.

Resellers Distribution channel firms that help the organisation find customers or make sales to them.

Retailer co-operatives A contractual association of independent retailers who engage in group buying and merchandising.

Retailers Businesses whose sales come primarily from retailing.

Retailing All activities involved in selling goods or services directly to final consumers for their personal, non-business use.

Return on marketing investment (ROMI or marketing ROI) The net return from a marketing investment divided by the costs of the marketing investment.

Salesforce management The analysis, planning, implementation and control of salesforce activities. It includes setting salesforce strategy; and recruiting, selecting, training, supervising and evaluating the firm's salespeople.

Salespeople Salespeople are involved in two-way personal communication with customers with whom they build long-term relationships.

Sales promotion Short-term incentives to encourage purchase of a product or service.

Sales quotas Standards set for salespeople stating the amount they should sell and how sales should be divided among the company's products.

Salutary products Products that have low appeal but benefit consumers in the long run.

Sample A segment of the population selected for marketing research to represent the population as a whole.

Samples Free or discounted goods provided at store level or through the media, such as inserts designed to facilitate product trial.

Sampling error Error in the results of a survey which occurs if the sample is not representative of the group being investigated.

Sealed-bid pricing Setting price based on how the firm thinks competitors will price rather than on its own costs or demand—used when a company bids for jobs.

Seasonal discount A price reduction to buyers who buy merchandise or services out-of-season.

Secondary data Information that already exists somewhere, having been collected for another purpose.

Segmented pricing Selling a product or service at two or more prices, where the difference in prices is not based on differences in costs.

Selective demand The demand for a given brand of a product or service, for example the demand for a Honda motorcycle.

Selective distribution The use of more than one but fewer than all the intermediaries who are willing to carry the company's products.

Self-service retailers Retailers that provide few or no services to shoppers; shoppers perform their own locate–compare–select process.

Selling concept The idea that consumers will not buy enough of the organisation's products unless the organisation undertakes a large-scale selling and promotion effort.

Selling process The steps that the salesperson follows when selling, including prospecting and qualifying, preapproach, approach, presentation and demonstration, handling objections, closing and follow-up.

Sense of mission A principle of enlightened marketing that holds that an organisation should define its mission in broad social terms rather than narrow financial terms.

Sequential product development A new product development approach in which one company department works individually to complete its stage of the process before passing the new product along to the next department and stage.

Service blueprinting All the stages involved in providing service to a customer.

Service delivery When customers and representatives of an organisation interact with one another. Such interactions play a large part in determining whether or not the customer is satisfied and remains loyal to the marketer, particularly in service and experiential encounters.

Service inseparability Services that cannot be separated from their providers, whether the providers are people or machines.

Service intangibility Almost pure services, such as a haircut, may be distinguished from almost pure physical products, such as coffee, in that there is no physical element.

Service perishability Almost pure services, such as a rock concert, may be distinguished from almost pure physical products, such as coffee, in that there is no stored physical inventory. Once the concert is over, there is only the memory of it.

Service variability Almost pure services, such as a restaurant or cruise line experience, involve interaction between a patron/guest and customer service personnel. There is the potential for service variability in what have been termed 'moments of truth'.

Services Any activity or benefit that one party can offer to another that is essentially intangible and does not result in the ownership of anything.

Services marketing logistics Coordinating non-material activities necessary to provide a service in a cost-efficient way and to provide the service quality expected.

Shopping centre A group of retail businesses planned, developed, owned and managed as a unit.

Shopping products Consumer goods and services that the customer, in the process of selection and purpose,

characteristically compares on such bases as suitability, quality, price and style.

Simultaneous product development An approach to developing new products in which various company departments work closely together, overlapping the steps in the product development process to save time and increase effectiveness.

Single-source data systems Electronic monitoring systems that link consumers' exposure to television advertising and promotion (measured using television meters) with what they buy in stores (measured using checkout scanners).

Social classes Relatively permanent and ordered divisions in a society whose members share similar values, interests and behaviours.

Societal marketing concept The idea that the organisation should determine the needs, wants and interests of target markets and deliver the desired satisfactions more effectively and efficiently than competitors in a way that maintains or improves the consumer's and society's well-being.

Spam (spamming) Sending unsolicited email usually to large numbers of people with a view to making a sale.

Specialty products Consumer goods and services with unique characteristics or brand identification for which a significant group of buyers is willing to make a special purchase effort.

Specialty store A retail store that carries a narrow product line with a deep assortment within that line.

Standardised marketing mix An international marketing strategy for using basically the same product, advertising, distribution channels and other elements of the marketing mix in all the company's international markets.

Stars High-growth, high-share businesses or products that often require heavy investment to finance their rapid growth.

Statistical demand analysis A set of statistical procedures used to discover the most important factors affecting sales and their relative influence; the most commonly analysed factors are prices, income, population and promotion.

Straight product extension Marketing a product in the foreign market without any change.

Straight rebuy An industrial buying situation in which the buyer routinely reorders something without modification.

Strategic alliances An agreement between two organisations to work

together to achieve joint objectives. It may take the form of a contractual agreement, an equity sharing joint venture or an agreement to work together on specific projects.

Strategic business unit (SBU) A unit of the company that has a separate mission and separate objectives and that can be planned independently of other company businesses. An SBU can be a company division, a product line within a division or sometimes a single product or brand.

Strategic group A group of firms in an industry following the same or a similar strategy.

Strategic planning The process of developing and maintaining a strategic fit between the organisation's goals and capabilities and its changing marketing opportunities. It relies on developing a clear company mission, supporting objectives, a sound business portfolio and coordinated functional strategies.

Strip shopping centre A group of retail businesses located along an arterial road.

Style A basic and distinctive mode of expression.

Subculture A group of people with shared value systems based on common life experiences and situations.

Supermarkets Large, low-cost, low-margin, high-volume, self-service stores that carry a wide variety of food, laundry and household products.

Superstore A store almost twice the size of a regular supermarket carrying a large assortment of routinely purchased food and non-food items, and offering such services as dry cleaning, photo developing, cheque cashing, bill paying, car care and pet care.

Supplier search The stage of the industrial buying process in which the buyer tries to find the best vendors.

Supplier selection The stage of the industrial buying process in which the buyer reviews proposals and selects a supplier or suppliers.

Suppliers Firms and individuals that provide the resources needed by the company and its competitors to produce goods and services.

Supplies and services Industrial goods and services that do not enter the finished product at all.

Survey research The gathering of primary data by asking people questions about their knowledge, attitudes, preferences and buying behaviour.

Systems buying Buying a packaged solution to a problem, which avoids making all the separate decisions involved in buying each item or service separately.

Target market A set of buyers sharing common needs or characteristics that the company decides to serve.

Targeted communication Marketing organisations tailor their messages to suit various market segments.

Tariff A tax, levied by a government against certain imported products, that is designed either to raise revenue or protect domestic firms.

Team selling Using teams of people from sales, marketing, engineering, finance, technical support and even upper management to service large, complex accounts.

Technological environment Forces that affect new technologies, creating new product and market opportunities.

Telemarketing The use of telephone operators in a variety of ways to attract new customers, to contact existing customers to ascertain satisfaction levels, or to take orders.

Telesales Routine order taking by telephone operators.

Territorial salesforce structure A salesforce organisation that assigns each salesperson to an exclusive geographical territory in which that salesperson carries the company's full line.

Territorial sales organisation The simplest sales organisation, offering advantages such as effective selling in a defined geographical area.

Test marketing The stage of new product development in which the product and marketing program is introduced into more realistic market settings.

Time-series analysis Breaking down past sales of a product or service into its trend, cycle, season and erratic components, and then recombining these components to produce a sales forecast.

Total cost ownership TCO includes all costs associated with purchasing and using a product over its life.

Total costs The sum of the fixed and variable costs for any given level of production.

Total customer cost The total of all the monetary, time, energy and psychic costs associated with a marketing offer.

Total customer value The total of all of the products, services, personnel and image values that a buyer receives from a marketing offer.

Total quality management (TQM) A recognised system (set in place by the management of a firm) that empowers employees to accept or reject their own output to agreed standards, based on the premise that each work group is a customer of the preceding group, and that continual advancement should be made towards zero defects. Under such a system, statistical process controls allow observation of deviation from agreed standards, and immediate rectification of the process or the product.

Trade-in allowance A price reduction given for turning in an old item when buying a new one.

Transaction A trade between two parties that involves at least two things of value, agreed-upon conditions, a time of agreement and a place of agreement.

Two-part pricing A strategy for pricing services in which price is broken into a fixed fee plus a variable usage rate.

Undifferentiated marketing A market-coverage strategy in which a company might decide to ignore market segment differences and go after the whole market with one market offer.

Uniform delivered pricing A geographical pricing strategy in which the company charges the same price plus freight to all customers regardless of their location.

Unsought products Consumer goods and services that the consumer either does not know about or knows about but does not normally think of buying.

User The person who consumes or uses a product or service.

Utility The satisfaction or pleasure that an individual derives from the consumption of a good or service.

Value adding Refers to actions taken by an individual organisation or groups of organisations to create additional value to be delivered to customers.

Value analysis An approach to cost reduction in which components are studied carefully to determine if they can be redesigned, standardised or made by less costly methods of production.

Value-based pricing Setting price based on buyers' perceptions of value rather than on the seller's cost.

Value chain The activities performed to deliver a product to a customer.

Value constellation This refers to a situation where value is created from a wide variety of synchronous and interactive sources in the electronic environment.

Value disciplines A value discipline underlines the operating model a company chooses to deliver the value proposition it offers to its market. It chooses one of three possible value disciplines: best total cost, best product or best total solution. Once selected, the value discipline shapes the company's plans and decisions, operating structure, culture and management processes, all designed to deliver superior customer value according to that discipline.

Value innovation This involves creating significant leaps in value for both the company and its customers in a manner which makes rivals obsolete and creates an uncontested marketspace.

Value pricing Offering just the right combination of quality and good service at a fair price.

Variable costs Costs that vary directly with the level of production.

Variety-seeking buying behaviour Consumer buying behaviour in situations characterised by low consumer involvement but significant perceived brand differences.

Vertical marketing network (VMN) A distribution channel structure in which producers, wholesalers and retailers act as a unified network—either one channel member owns the others, has contracts with them, or wields so much power that they all cooperate.

Virtual corporation A virtual corporation is an organisation electronically linked with other organisations to create a product or service without an obvious physical 'shop front'. An example is the 'library without walls' from which information is obtained electronically.

Voluntary chain A wholesaler-sponsored group of independent retailers that engages in group buying and common merchandising.

Wants The form taken by human needs as they are shaped by culture and individual personality.

Warehouse clubs (or wholesale clubs) Off-price retailers that sell a limited selection of brand name grocery items, appliances, clothing and a hodgepodge of other goods at deep discounts to members who pay annual membership fees.

Whole-channel view Designing international channels that take into account all the necessary links in distributing the seller's products to final buyers, including the seller's headquarters organisation, channels between nations and channels within nations.

Wholesaler-sponsored voluntary chains Contractual vertical marketing networks in which wholesalers organise voluntary chains of independent retailers to help them compete with large corporate chain organisations.

Wholesalers Firms engaged primarily in wholesaling activity.

Wholesaling All activities involved in selling goods and services to those buying for resale or business use.

Word-of-mouth influence Personal communication about a product between target buyers and neighbours, friends, family members and associates.

Workload approach An approach to setting salesforce size in which the company groups accounts into different-sized classes and then determines how many salespeople are needed to call on them the desired number of times.

World Wide Web (Web) The graphical face of the Internet.

Zone pricing A geographical pricing strategy in which the company sets up two or more zones—all customers within a zone pay the same total price, and this price is higher in the more distant zones.

Page numbers in bold indicate a definition of the term.